CORNERSTONE
B I B L I C A L
COMMENTARY

# CORNERSTONE
## BIBLICAL
## COMMENTARY

### Isaiah
**Larry L. Walker**

### Jeremiah & Lamentations
**Elmer A. Martens**

GENERAL EDITOR:
**Philip W. Comfort**

*with the entire text of the*
NEW LIVING TRANSLATION

TYNDALE HOUSE PUBLISHERS, INC.  WHEATON, ILLINOIS

Cornerstone Biblical Commentary, Volume 8

Visit Tyndale's exciting Web site at www.tyndale.com

Tyndale's quill logo is a trademark of Tyndale House Publishers, Inc.

Designed by Luke Daab and Timothy R. Botts

**Library of Congress Cataloging-in-Publication Data**

Martens, E. A.
    Isaiah-Lamentations / Elmer A. Martens, Larry L. Walker.
        p. c.m. — (NLT biblical commentary ; v. 8)
    Includes bibliographical references.
    ISBN-10: 0-8423-3434-3 (hc)
    ISBN-13: 978-0-8423-3434-1 (hc)
        1. Bible. O.T. Isaiah—Commentaries.    2. Bible. O.T. Jeremiah—Commentaries.
    3. Bible. O.T. Lamentations—Commentaries.    I. Walker, Larry L.    II. Title.
    III. Series
        BS1515.53.M37 2005
        224′.1077—dc22                                                        2005003415

Printed in Thailand

10   09   08   07   06   05
  9    8    7    6    5    4    3    2    1

# CONTENTS

## CONTRIBUTORS TO **VOLUME 8**

**Isaiah: Larry L. Walker**
*BD, Northern Baptist Seminary;*
*MA, Wheaton College Graduate School;*
*PhD, Dropsie College for Hebrew and Cognate Learning.*

**Jeremiah & Lamentations: Elmer A. Martens**
*PhD, Claremont Graduate School;*
*Professor Emeritus of Old Testament and President Emeritus,*
*Mennonite Brethren Biblical Seminary, Fresno, CA.*

# GENERAL EDITOR'S PREFACE

The *Cornerstone Biblical Commentary* is based on the second edition of the New Living Translation (2004). Nearly 100 scholars from various church backgrounds and from several countries (United States, Canada, England, and Australia) participated in the creation of the NLT. Many of these same scholars are contributors to this commentary series. All the commentators, whether participants in the NLT or not, believe that the Bible is God's inspired word and have a desire to make God's word clear and accessible to his people.

This Bible commentary is the natural extension of our vision for the New Living Translation, which we believe is both exegetically accurate and idiomatically powerful. The NLT attempts to communicate God's inspired word in a lucid English translation of the original languages so that English readers can understand and appreciate the thought of the original writers. In the same way, the *Cornerstone Biblical Commentary* aims at helping teachers, pastors, students, and lay people understand every thought contained in the Bible. As such, the commentary focuses first on the words of Scripture, then on the theological truths of Scripture—inasmuch as the words express the truths.

The commentary itself has been structured in such a way as to help readers get at the meaning of Scripture, passage by passage, through the entire Bible. Each Bible book is prefaced by a substantial book introduction that gives general historical background important for understanding. Then the reader is taken through the Bible text, passage by passage, starting with the New Living Translation text printed in full. This is followed by a section called "Notes," wherein the commentator helps the reader understand the Hebrew or Greek behind the English of the NLT, interacts with other scholars on important interpretive issues, and points the reader to significant textual and contextual matters. The "Notes" are followed by the "Commentary," wherein each scholar presents a lucid interpretation of the passage, giving special attention to context and major theological themes.

The commentators represent a wide spectrum of theological positions within the evangelical community. We believe this is good because it reflects the rich variety in Christ's church. All the commentators uphold the authority of God's word and believe it is essential to heed the old adage: "Wholly apply yourself to the Scriptures and apply them wholly to you." May this commentary help you know the truths of Scripture, and may this knowledge help you "grow in your knowledge of God and Jesus our Lord" (2 Pet 1:2, NLT).

PHILIP W. COMFORT
GENERAL EDITOR

# ABBREVIATIONS

## GENERAL ABBREVIATIONS

| | | | | | |
|---|---|---|---|---|---|
| *b.* | Babylonian Gemara | Gr. | Greek | no. | number |
| *bar.* | baraita | Heb. | Hebrew | NT | New Testament |
| c. | *circa,* around, approximately | ibid. | *ibidem,* in the same place | OL | Old Latin |
| | | | | OS | Old Syriac |
| cf. | *confer,* compare | i.e. | *id est,* the same | OT | Old Testament |
| ch, chs | chapter, chapters | in loc. | *in loco,* in the place cited | p., pp. | page, pages |
| contra | in contrast to | | | pl. | plural |
| DSS | Dead Sea Scrolls | lit. | literally | Q | Quelle ("Sayings" |
| ed. | edition, editor | LXX | Septuagint | | as Gospel source) |
| e.g. | *exempli gratia,* for example | 𝔐 | Majority Text | rev. | revision |
| | | *m.* | Mishnah | sg. | singular |
| ET | English translation | masc. | masculine | *t.* | Tosefta |
| et al. | *et alli,* and others | mg | margin | v., vv. | verse, verses |
| fem. | feminine | MS | manuscript | vid. | *videur,* it seems |
| ff | following (verses, pages) | MSS | manuscripts | viz. | *videlicet,* namely |
| | | MT | Masoretic Text | vol. | volume |
| fl. | flourished | n.d. | no date | *y.* | Jerusalem Gemara |
| | | neut. | neuter | | |

## ABBREVIATIONS FOR BIBLE TRANSLATIONS

| | | | | | |
|---|---|---|---|---|---|
| ASV | American Standard Version | NCV | New Century Version | NKJV | New King James Version |
| CEV | Contemporary English Version | NEB | New English Bible | NRSV | New Revised Standard Version |
| ESV | English Standard Version | NIV | New International Version | NLT | New Living Translation |
| GW | God's Word | NIrV | New International Reader's Version | REB | Revised English Bible |
| HCSB | Holman Christian Standard Bible | NJB | New Jerusalem Bible | RSV | Revised Standard Version |
| JB | Jerusalem Bible | NJPS | The New Jewish Publication Society Translation (*Tanakh*) | TEV | Today's English Version |
| KJV | King James Version | | | | |
| NAB | New American Bible | | | TLB | The Living Bible |
| NASB | New American Standard Bible | | | | |

## ABBREVIATIONS FOR DICTIONARIES, LEXICONS, COLLECTIONS OF TEXTS, ORIGINAL LANGUAGE EDITIONS

ABD *Anchor Bible Dictionary* (6 vols., Freedman) [1992]

ANEP *The Ancient Near East in Pictures* (Pritchard) [1965]

ANET *Ancient Near Eastern Texts Relating to the Old Testament* (Pritchard) [1969]

ANF *Ante-Nicene Fathers*

BAGD *Greek-English Lexicon of the New Testament and Other Early Christian Literature,* 2nd ed. (Bauer, Arndt, Gingrich, Danker) [1979]

BDAG *Greek-English Lexicon of the New Testament and Other Early Christian Literature,* 3rd ed. (Bauer, Danker, Arndt, Gingrich) [2000]

BDB *A Hebrew and English Lexicon of the Old Testament* (Brown, Driver, Briggs) [1907]

BDF *A Greek Grammar of the New Testament and Other Early Christian Literature* (Blass, Debrunner, Funk) [1961]

BHS *Biblia Hebraica Stuttgartensia* (Elliger and Rudolph) [1983]

CAD *Assyrian Dictionary of the Oriental Institute of the University of Chicago* [1956]

COS *The Context of Scripture* (3 volumes, Hallo and Younger) [1997–2002]

DBI *Dictionary of Biblical Imagery* (Ryken, Wilhoit, Longman) [1998]

DBT *Dictionary of Biblical Theology* (2nd edition, Leon-Dufour) [1972]

DCH *Dictionary of Classical Hebrew* (5 volumes, D. Clines) [2000]

DJD *Discoveries in the Judean Desert* [1955–]

DJG *Dictionary of Jesus and the Gospels* (Green, McKnight, Marshall) [1992]

DOTP Dictionary of the Old Testament: Pentateuch. (T. Alexander, D.W. Baker) [2003]

DPL *Dictionary of Paul and His Letters* (Hawthorne, Martin, Reid) [1993]

EDNT *Exegetical Dictionary of the New Testament* (3 vols., H. Balz, G. Schneider. ET) [1990–1993]

HALOT *The Hebrew and Aramaic Lexicon of the Old Testament* (L. Koehler, W. Baumgartner, J. Stamm; trans. M. Richardson) [1994–1999]

IBD *Illustrated Bible Dictionary* (3 vols., Douglas, Wiseman) [1980]

IDB *The Interpreter's Dictionary of the Bible* (4 vols., Buttrick) [1962]

ISBE *International Standard Bible Encyclopedia* (4 vols., Bromiley) [1979–1988]

KBL *Lexicon in Veteris Testamenti libros* (Koehler, Baumgartner) [1958]

LCL Loeb Classical Library

L&N *Greek-English Lexicon of the New Testament: Based on Semantic Domains* (Louw and Nida) [1989]

LSJ *A Greek-English Lexicon* (9th edition, Liddell, Scott, Jones) [1996]

MM *The Vocabulary of the Greek New Testament* (Moulton and Milligan) [1930; 1997]

NA$^{26}$ *Novum Testamentum Graece* (26th edition, Nestle-Aland) [1979]

NA$^{27}$ *Novum Testamentum Graece* (27th edition, Nestle-Aland) [1993]

NBD *New Bible Dictionary* (2nd edition, Douglas, Hillyer) [1982]

NIDB *New International Dictionary of the Bible* (Douglas, Tenney) [1987]

NIDBA *New International Dictionary of Biblical Archaeology* (Blaiklock and Harrison) [1983]

NIDNTT *New International Dictionary of New Testament Theology* (4 vols., C. Brown) [1975–1985]

NIDOTTE *New International Dictionary of Old Testament Theology and Exegesis* (5 vols., W. A. VanGemeren) [1997]

PGM *Papyri Graecae magicae: Die griechischen Zauberpapyri.* (Preisendanz) [1928]

PG *Patrologia Graecae* (J. P. Migne) [1857–1886]

TBD *Tyndale Bible Dictionary* (Elwell, Comfort) [2001]

TDNT *Theological Dictionary of the New Testament* (10 vols., Kittel, Friedrich; trans. Bromiley) [1964–1976]

TDOT *Theological Dictionary of the Old Testament* (8 vols., Botterweck, Ringgren; trans. Willis, Bromiley, Green) [1974–]

TLOT *Theological Lexicon of the Old Testament* (3 vols., E. Jenni) [1997]

TWOT *Theological Wordbook of the Old Testament* (2 vols., Harris, Archer) [1980]

UBS$^3$ *United Bible Societies' Greek New Testament* (third edition, Metzger et al) [1975]

UBS$^4$ *United Bible Societies' Greek New Testament* (fourth corrected edition, Metzger et al) [1993]

WH *The New Testament in the Original Greek* (Westcott and Hort) [1882]

## ABBREVIATIONS FOR BOOKS OF THE BIBLE

### Old Testament

| | | | | | |
|---|---|---|---|---|---|
| Gen | Genesis | 1 Sam | 1 Samuel | Esth | Esther |
| Exod | Exodus | 2 Sam | 2 Samuel | Ps, Pss | Psalm, Psalms |
| Lev | Leviticus | 1 Kgs | 1 Kings | Prov | Proverbs |
| Num | Numbers | 2 Kgs | 2 Kings | Eccl | Ecclesiastes |
| Deut | Deuteronomy | 1 Chr | 1 Chronicles | Song | Song of Songs |
| Josh | Joshua | 2 Chr | 2 Chronicles | Isa | Isaiah |
| Judg | Judges | Ezra | Ezra | Jer | Jeremiah |
| Ruth | Ruth | Neh | Nehemiah | Lam | Lamentations |

| | | | | | |
|---|---|---|---|---|---|
| Ezek | Ezekiel | Obad | Obadiah | Zeph | Zephaniah |
| Dan | Daniel | Jonah | Jonah | Hag | Haggai |
| Hos | Hosea | Mic | Micah | Zech | Zechariah |
| Joel | Joel | Nah | Nahum | Mal | Malachi |
| Amos | Amos | Hab | Habakkuk | | |

## New Testament

| | | | | | |
|---|---|---|---|---|---|
| Matt | Matthew | Eph | Ephesians | Heb | Hebrews |
| Mark | Mark | Phil | Philippians | Jas | James |
| Luke | Luke | Col | Colossians | 1 Pet | 1 Peter |
| John | John | 1 Thess | 1 Thessalonians | 2 Pet | 2 Peter |
| Acts | Acts | 2 Thess | 2 Thessalonians | 1 John | 1 John |
| Rom | Romans | 1 Tim | 1 Timothy | 2 John | 2 John |
| 1 Cor | 1 Corinthians | 2 Tim | 2 Timothy | 3 John | 3 John |
| 2 Cor | 2 Corinthians | Titus | Titus | Jude | Jude |
| Gal | Galatians | Phlm | Philemon | Rev | Revelation |

## Deuterocanonical

| | | | | | |
|---|---|---|---|---|---|
| Bar | Baruch | 1–2 Esdr | 1–2 Esdras | Pr Man | Prayer of Manasseh |
| Add Dan | Additions to Daniel | Add Esth | Additions to Esther | Ps 151 | Psalm 151 |
| Pr Azar | Prayer of Azariah | Ep Jer | Epistle of Jeremiah | Sir | Sirach |
| Bel | Bel and the Dragon | Jdt | Judith | Tob | Tobit |
| Sg Three | Song of the Three Children | 1–2 Macc | 1–2 Maccabees | Wis | Wisdom of Solomon |
| | | 3–4 Macc | 3–4 Maccabees | | |
| Sus | Susanna | | | | |

# MANUSCRIPTS AND LITERATURE FROM QUMRAN

Initial numerals followed by "Q" indicate particular caves at Qumran. For example, the notation 4Q267 indicates text 267 from cave 4 at Qumran. Further, 1QS 4:9-10 indicates column 4, lines 9-10 of the *Rule of the Community*; and 4Q166 1 ii 2 indicates fragment 1, column ii, line 2 of text 166 from cave 4. More examples of common abbreviations are listed below.

| | | | | | |
|---|---|---|---|---|---|
| CD | Cairo Geniza copy of the *Damascus Document* | 1QIsa[b] | Isaiah copy [b] | 4QLam[a] | Lamentations |
| | | 1QM | *War Scroll* | 11QPs[a] | Psalms |
| 1QH | *Thanksgiving Hymns* | 1QpHab | *Pesher Habakkuk* | 11QTemple[a,b] | *Temple Scroll* |
| 1QIsa[a] | Isaiah copy [a] | 1QS | *Rule of the Community* | 11QtgJob | *Targum of Job* |

# IMPORTANT NEW TESTAMENT MANUSCRIPTS

(all dates given are AD; ordinal numbers refer to centuries)

### Significant Papyri (𝔓 = Papyrus)

𝔓1 Matt 1; early 3rd
𝔓4+𝔓64+𝔓67 Matt 3, 5, 26; Luke 1-6; late 2nd
𝔓5 John 1, 16, 20; early 3rd
𝔓13 Heb 2-5, 10-12; early 3rd
𝔓15+𝔓16 (probably part of same codex) 1 Cor 7-8, Phil 3-4; late 3rd

𝔓20 James 2-3; 3rd
𝔓22 John 15-16; mid 3rd
𝔓23 James 1; c. 200
𝔓27 Rom 8-9; 3rd
𝔓30 1 Thess 4-5; 2 Thess 1; early 3rd
𝔓32 Titus 1-2; late 2nd
𝔓37 Matt 26; late 3rd

𝔓39 John 8; first half of 3rd
𝔓40 Rom 1-4, 6, 9; 3rd
𝔓45 Gospels and Acts; early 3rd
𝔓46 Paul's Major Epistles (less Pastorals); late 2nd
𝔓47 Rev 9-17; 3rd

𝔓49+𝔓65 Eph 4-5; 1 Thess
    1-2; 3rd
𝔓52 John 18; c. 125
𝔓53 Matt 26, Acts 9-10;
    middle 3rd
𝔓66 John; late 2nd
𝔓70 Matt 2-3, 11-12, 24; 3rd
𝔓72 1-2 Peter, Jude; c. 300

𝔓74 Acts, General Epistles; 7th
𝔓75 Luke and John; c. 200
𝔓77+𝔓103 (probably part of
    same codex) Matt 13-14,
    23; late 2nd
𝔓87 Phlm; late 2nd
𝔓90 John 18-19; late 2nd
𝔓91 Acts 2-3; 3rd

𝔓92 Eph 1, 2 Thess 1; c. 300
𝔓98 Rev 1:13-20; late 2nd
𝔓100 James 3-5; c. 300
𝔓101 Matt 3-4; 3rd
𝔓104 Matt 21; 2nd
𝔓106 John 1; 3rd
𝔓115 Rev 2-3, 5-6, 8-15; 3rd

## Significant Uncials

א (Sinaiticus) most of NT; 4th
A (Alexandrinus) most of NT;
    5th
B (Vaticanus) most of NT; 4th
C (Ephraemi Rescriptus) most
    of NT with many lacunae;
    5th
D (Bezae) Gospels, Acts; 5th
D (Claromontanus), Paul's
    Epistles; 6th (different MS
    than Bezae)
E (Laudianus 35) Acts; 6th
F (Augensis) Paul's Epistles; 9th
G (Boernerianus) Paul's
    Epistles; 9th

H (Coislinianus) Paul's
    Epistles; 6th
I (Freerianus or Washington)
    Paul's Epistles; 5th
L (Regius) Gospels; 8th
Q (Guelferbytanus B) Luke,
    John; 5th
P (Porphyrianus) Acts—
    Revelation; 9th
T (Borgianus) Luke, John; 5th
W (Washingtonianus or the
    Freer Gospels) Gospels; 5th
Z (Dublinensis) Matthew; 6th
037 (Δ; Sangallensis) Gospels;
    9th

038 (Θ; Koridethi) Gospels;
    9th
040 (Ξ; Zacynthius) Luke; 6th
043 (Φ; Beratinus) Matt,
    Mark; 6th
044 (Ψ; Athous Laurae)
    Gospels, Acts, Paul's
    Epistles; 9th
048 Acts, Paul's Epistles,
    General Epistles; 5th
0171 Matt 10, Luke 22;
    c. 300
0189 Acts 5; c. 200

## Significant Minuscules

1 Gospels, Acts, Paul's
    Epistles; 12th
33 All NT except Rev; 9th
81 Acts, Paul's Epistles,
    General Epistles; 1044
565 Gospels; 9th
700 Gospels; 11th

1424 (or Family 1424—a
    group of 29 manuscripts
    sharing nearly the same
    text) most of NT; 9th-10th
1739 Acts, Paul's Epistles; 10th
2053 Rev; 13th
2344 Rev; 11th

f¹ (a family of manuscripts
    including 1, 118, 131, 209)
    Gospels; 12th-14th
f¹³ (a family of manuscripts
    including 13, 69, 124, 174,
    230, 346, 543, 788, 826,
    828, 983, 1689, 1709—
    known as the Ferrar group)
    Gospels; 11th-15th

## Significant Ancient Versions

### SYRIAC (SYR)
syrᶜ (Syriac Curetonian)
    Gospels; 5th
syrˢ (Syriac Sinaiticus)
    Gospels; 4th
syrʰ (Syriac Harklensis) Entire
    NT; 616

### OLD LATIN (IT)
itᵃ (Vercellenis) Gospels; 4th
itᵇ (Veronensis) Gospels; 5th
itᵈ (Cantabrigiensis—the Latin
    text of Bezae) Gospels, Acts,
    3 John; 5th
itᵉ (Palantinus) Gospels; 5th
itᵏ (Bobiensis) Matthew, Mark;
    c. 400

### COPTIC (COP)
copᵇᵒ (Boharic—north Egypt)
copᶠᵃʸ (Fayyumic—central Egypt)
copˢᵃ (Sahidic—southern Egypt)

#### OTHER VERSIONS
arm (Armenian)
eth (Ethiopic)
geo (Georgian)

# TRANSLITERATION AND NUMBERING SYSTEM

*Note:* For words and roots from non-biblical languages (e.g., Arabic, Ugaritic), only approximate transliterations are given.

## HEBREW/ARAMAIC

### Consonants

| | | | | | | |
|---|---|---|---|---|---|---|
| א | *aleph* | = ' | מ, ם | *mem* | = *m* |
| ב, בּ | *beth* | = *b* | נ, ן | *nun* | = *n* |
| ג, גּ | *gimel* | = *g* | ס | *samekh* | = *s* |
| ד, דּ | *daleth* | = *d* | ע | *ayin* | = ' |
| ה | *he* | = *h* | פ, פּ, ף | *pe* | = *p* |
| ו | *waw* | = *w* | צ, ץ | *tsadhe* | = *ts* |
| ז | *zayin* | = *z* | ק | *qoph* | = *q* |
| ח | *heth* | = *kh* | ר | *resh* | = *r* |
| ט | *teth* | = *t* | שׁ | *shin* | = *sh* |
| י | *yodh* | = *y* | שׂ | *sin* | = *s* |
| כ, כּ, ך | *kaph* | = *k* | ת, תּ | *taw* | = *t, th* (spirant) |
| ל | *lamedh* | = *l* | | | |

### Vowels

| | | | | | | |
|---|---|---|---|---|---|---|
| ַ | *patakh* | = *a* | ָ | *qamets khatuf* | = *o* |
| חַ | *furtive patakh* | = *a* | | *holem* | = *o* |
| ָ | *qamets* | = *a* | וֹ | *full holem* | = *o* |
| הָ | *final qamets he* | = *ah* | | *short qibbuts* | = *u* |
| ֶ | *segol* | = *e* | | *long qibbuts* | = *u* |
| ֵ | *tsere* | = *e* | וּ | *shureq* | = *u* |
| ֵי | *tsere yod* | = *e* | | *khatef patakh* | = *a* |
| ִ | *short hireq* | = *i* | | *khatef qamets* | = *o* |
| ִ | *long hireq* | = *i* | | *vocalic shewa* | = *e* |
| ִי | *hireq yod* | = *i* | | *patakh yodh* | = *a* |

## Greek

| | | | | | | |
|---|---|---|---|---|---|---|
| α | *alpha* | = *a* | ε | *epsilon* | = *e* |
| β | *beta* | = *b* | ζ | *zeta* | = *z* |
| γ | *gamma* | = *g, n (before* γ, κ, ξ, χ) | η | *eta* | = *ē* |
| δ | *delta* | = *d* | θ | *theta* | = *th* |
| | | | ι | *iota* | = *i* |

| κ | kappa | = k | | τ | tau | = t |
|---|---|---|---|---|---|---|
| λ | lamda | = l | | υ | upsilon | = u |
| μ | mu | = m | | φ | phi | = ph |
| ν | nu | = n | | χ | chi | = ch |
| ξ | ksi | = x | | ψ | psi | = ps |
| ο | omicron | = o | | ὠ | omega | = ō |
| π | pi | = p | | ‘ | rough | = h (with |
| ρ | rho | = r (ῥ = rh) | | | breathing | vowel or |
| σ, ς | sigma | = s | | | mark | diphthong) |

## THE TYNDALE-STRONG'S NUMBERING SYSTEM

The Cornerstone Biblical Commentary series uses a word-study numbering system to give both newer and more advanced Bible students alike quicker, more convenient access to helpful original-language tools (e.g., concordances, lexicons, and theological dictionaries). Those who are unfamiliar with the ancient Hebrew, Aramaic, and Greek alphabets can quickly find information on a given word by looking up the appropriate index number. Advanced students will find the system helpful because it allows them to quickly find the lexical form of obscure conjugations and inflections.

There are two main numbering systems used for biblical words today. The one familiar to most people is the Strong's numbering system (made popular by the *Strong's Exhaustive Concordance to the Bible*). Although the original Strong's system is still quite useful, the most up-to-date research has shed new light on the biblical languages and allows for more precision than is found in the original Strong's system. The Cornerstone Biblical Commentary series, therefore, features a newly revised version of the Strong's system, the Tyndale-Strong's numbering system. The Tyndale-Strong's system brings together the familiarity of the Strong's system and the best of modern scholarship. In most cases, the original Strong's numbers are preserved. In places where new research dictates, new or related numbers have been added.[1]

The second major numbering system today is the Goodrick-Kohlenberger system used in a number of study tools published by Zondervan. In order to give students broad access to a number of helpful tools, the Commentary provides index numbers for the Zondervan system as well.

The different index systems are designated as follows:

TG  Tyndale-Strong's Greek number          ZH  Zondervan Hebrew number
ZG  Zondervan Greek number                  TA  Tyndale-Strong's Aramaic number
TH  Tyndale-Strong's Hebrew number          ZA  Zondervan Aramaic number

So in the example, "love" *agapē* [TG26, ZG27], the first number is the one to use with Greek tools keyed to the Tyndale-Strong's system, and the second applies to tools that use the Zondervan system.

1 Generally, one may simply use the original four-digit Strong's number to identify words in tools using Strong's system. If a Tyndale-Strong's number is followed by capital a letter (e.g., TG1692A), it generally indicates an added subdivision of meaning for the given term. Whenever a Tyndale-Strong's number has a number following a decimal point (e.g., TG2013.1), it reflects an instance where new research has yielded a separate, new classification of use for a biblical word. Forthcoming tools from Tyndale House Publishers will include these entries, which were not part of the original Strong's system.

# *Isaiah*

LARRY L. WALKER

# INTRODUCTION TO
# *Isaiah*

THIS BEAUTIFUL AND ELOQUENT BOOK is so filled with messianic passages that it has been called the Gospel according to Isaiah. In this magnificent prophetic writing the message is presented in such an attractive and striking manner that its superior style is without dispute. Its attention-getting imagery captivates the reader and vividly communicates Isaiah's message in an unforgettable way. Isaiah's influence on later literature and culture is profound. The New Testament writers quote Isaiah more than any of the other prophets, and many of these quotations are of strategic significance for properly understanding the overall message of Scripture.

The book of Isaiah has also been remarkably influential on art, music, political theory, missions, and evangelism over a long period of time. Many who are not otherwise familiar with Scripture recognize phrases and concepts from this great book. Likewise, throughout church history those who have studied Scripture have been continuously drawn to Isaiah by the majesty and appeal of its prophetic writing.

## AUTHORSHIP

The authorship of the book of Isaiah has been much discussed in modern times. The traditional view of both Jews and Christians is that the prophet Isaiah of eighth century BC Jerusalem is the author of the sixty-six chapters attributed to him. However, this view has been challenged by modern criticism, which finds at least two, and possibly three or more authors for these chapters. Those advocating two authors (a widespread view) claim that the traditional Isaiah of Jerusalem wrote chapters 1–39 and that "Deutero-Isaiah," most likely living in Babylon, wrote chapters 40–66. Those suggesting at least three authors usually divide "Deutero-Isaiah" into two parts and call the third section (chs 56–66) "Trito-Isaiah." Some also suggest that additional sections within the book have other authors.

The traditional view of the unity of Isaiah and its single authorship is based on internal biblical evidence. In 2 Chronicles 32:32 reference is made to *The Vision of the Prophet Isaiah Son of Amoz*, which is included in *The Book of the Kings of Judah and Israel*. Some believe it possible that both Zephaniah and Jeremiah are dependent upon sections of Isaiah 40–66 (Young 1958:44-48).

Isaiah's authorship of the later, disputed chapters of his book was a tradition accepted by the New Testament writers as they quoted and used this material. Examples of this are found in Matthew (3:3), Mark (1:2), Luke (3:4-6), John (12:38), and Paul (Rom 10:16-21). Within the New Testament, such personalities as John the Baptist (John 1:28), the Ethiopian eunuch (Acts 8:28-34), and the elders of Nazareth (Luke 4:16-20) attribute these disputed chapters to a prophet named Isaiah. It seems unlikely that they would ever think about this material in the way that modern scholars present it.

Serious theological and ethical problems arise if the New Testament evidence is ignored or denied. Some suggest that the New Testament authors were ignorant of the truth concerning the authorship of Isaiah, but for those who accept the New Testament as inspired and reliable, it is not enough to say that New Testament writers were unlearned and naive men. Furthermore, that would not apply to Paul, who was "brought up and educated under Gamaliel" and "at his feet learned to follow . . . Jewish laws and customs very carefully" (Acts 22:3). Paul would have been aware of any Jewish tradition of a "Deutero-Isaiah," and if there had been composite authorship of this outstanding book, careful Jewish tradition would surely have preserved this information as it did in other cases of composite authorship (e.g., Psalms and Proverbs).

An even greater problem is created by those who suggest that the New Testament writers knew better but were simply accommodating themselves to commonly accepted (but erroneous) ideas of their time. This raises not only ethical questions, but also the question of which other statements in the New Testament might only be reflections of what their authors believed about God, angels, demons, and the life to come. Either case—ignorance of the truth or deliberate accommodation of error—creates more problems than it solves.

In addition to the New Testament witness concerning Isaiah's authorship, other lines of evidence support the traditional understanding of the text. For example, it can be shown that the last chapters of Isaiah reflect the Canaanite background of Jerusalem rather than the alleged Babylonian setting of Deutero-Isaiah. The imagery used and the natural references to the terrain and topography are all in keeping with the tradition that Judah is the setting for these chapters, rather than with the theory of a Deutero-Isaiah living in Babylon. The landscape and the climate of Canaan provide the alleged Deutero-Isaiah with the majority of his metaphors, which are based on mountains, forests, snow, land made fertile by rain (not by the overflow of rivers or by irrigation), and drought, and make frequent mention of Lebanon, the sea, and the islands. Such references are very natural in a message originating from Canaan, whereas they would be highly unusual and contrived for a resident of Babylonia.

When "Deutero-Isaiah" portrays an idolater, he shows him taking his hatchet and going into the forest to cut down a tree, a very natural act in ancient Canaan, but not in Babylonia, where virtually the only tree was the palm tree, which was not very suitable for making idols.

When the chapters refer to the circumstances of the exiles (e.g., 42:22; 51:14), they bear no relation to what we know of the actual experience of those who were transported to Babylon (cf. Jer 29; Ezekiel). The prophet was not offering an eyewitness report but using conventional stereotypes. Smart (1965:20) observes,

"When we search for evidence of the prophet's residence in Babylon, we are surprised how hard it is to find any that is convincing."

Although obvious differences of style and even vocabulary can be detected throughout the sixty-six chapters, stylistic similarities running throughout the material can also be identified, such as Isaiah's famous title for God, the "Holy One of Israel," which is found equally distributed throughout the two major parts of the book.

**Isaiah of Jerusalem.** Isaiah of Jerusalem had one of the longest ministries of any prophet. According to the opening words of his book, his life overlapped with the reigns of four Judahite kings: Uzziah (792–740 BC), Jotham (750–732), Ahaz (735–715), and Hezekiah (715–686). This means that the length of his service could have exceeded half a century, from around the time of King Uzziah's death (probably in 740 BC; 6:1) to the accession of the Assyrian ruler Esarhaddon in 681 BC (37:38).

Isaiah's name means "the LORD saves." His father Amoz "according to Jewish tradition, was a brother of Amaziah, the father of King Uzziah of Judah. If the tradition is correct, Isaiah was a nephew of King Amaziah and a cousin of King Uzziah" (Youngblood 1993:10-11). Isaiah apparently had access to King Ahaz, King Hezekiah, members of the royal court, and the priests (see 7:3; 8:2; 22:15-25; 38:1).

Isaiah was married and his wife was called a "prophetess" (cf. the Heb. of 8:3). He had at least two sons, one named Shear-jashub (7:3) and another Maher-shalal-hash-baz (8:1, 3), whose names were "signs and symbols in Israel from the LORD Almighty" (8:18).

Judging by his writing, Isaiah was cultured and educated; there is universal agreement as to the excellent literary character of his book. He is generally acknowledged as the greatest of the Hebrew writers, and has been called the evangelist of the Old Testament, the Prince of the Prophets, and the St. Paul of the Old Testament.

Isaiah also left us a record of the "events of Uzziah's reign, from beginning to end" (2 Chr 26:22) and a record of "the events of Hezekiah's reign and his acts of devotion" (2 Chr 32:32). Isaiah also refers to those following him who would pass on his work to future generations (Isa 8:16). Jewish and Christian traditions agree that Isaiah's life ended when he was put in a hollow log and sawed in two by the evil Judahite king Manasseh (cf. Heb 11:37).

## DATE AND OCCASION OF WRITING

During Isaiah's childhood, when Israel was ruled by King Jeroboam and Judah by King Uzziah, the nation enjoyed a period of freedom and prosperity. Throughout this period, Egypt was weak and Assyria was occupied with problems elsewhere. Before Uzziah's death in the middle of the eighth century, Jotham seems to have been regent for some years. Several years before his own death in 731 BC, he apparently put his son Ahaz on the throne. Neither Uzziah nor Jotham removed the idolatrous high places.

Most prophets address one historical setting—their own! One of the unique features of Isaiah's book (and one that has contributed to the theory of multiple authors) is that it addresses at least three different historical settings. The first period is the era of the prophet himself (c. 739–701 BC), the second is the time of the Exile (605–539 BC), and the third speaks of the return from Babylon (after 539 BC). Other periods are referred to in passing or are involved in the book's message, such as the distant messianic era.

**The Assyrian Period.** This earliest period covers the time of Assyria's emergence as a world power to its final destruction by the Medo-Babylonian coalition in 609 BC. For a period of about seventy-five years (823–745 BC), Assyria's neighbors (including Israel and Judah) enjoyed a period of relief from invasion, but the complacency of God's covenant people ended after the accession of the great Assyrian king Tiglath-pileser III (745–727 BC). This signaled the end of Assyrian weakness and the beginning of their expansionist policies.

As the southern kingdom of Judah witnessed the Assyrian threat facing Israel, her northern neighbor, she was faced with a decision about being pro-Assyrian or anti-Assyrian. Judah thought that if it allied with Assyria soon enough (and not merely when it had to), Assyria might later favor or at least accommodate Judah as a faithful ally.

When Ahaz ascended the throne of Judah in 735 BC, a new pro-Assyrian policy was apparently adopted that explains why Pekah king of Israel and Rezin king of Aram attacked Judah in 735 BC (2 Kgs 16:5; 2 Chr 28:5-15). Ahaz and his court were sufficiently intimidated by the Aramean-Israelite threat (7:2) that they sent to Tiglath-pileser III for help (2 Kgs 16:7-9). These events provided the background for Isaiah's early public ministry. He preached that Judah should be more concerned about being pro-God because he saw Judah turning away from the Lord of their covenant and getting caught up in power politics (Isa 1:21-23; 2:12-17). Isaiah saw with prophetic clarity that Assyria was no friend to Judah. The enemy would quickly accept all that Judah gave voluntarily and then seize the rest by force (Isa 8:5-8). Nevertheless, Ahaz pursued this foolish course and eventually, after Tiglath-pileser III had deposed Pekah and destroyed Damascus (732 BC), Ahaz went to Damascus and appeared before the Assyrian king and was impressed with what he saw there (2 Kgs 16:10-16; cf. 2 Chr 28:20-21). The irony of all this was that the respite Ahaz gained by this treaty would have been his in any case (Isa 7:14-16). Tiglath-pileser III died in 727 BC, to the pleasure of the subject nations who hoped that they could then be free of the Assyrian yoke (cf. Isa 14). A number of insurrections immediately broke out.

Although the next Assyrian king, Shalmaneser V (727–722 BC), was not the great king that his father Tiglath-pileser III had been, he continued a similar approach in matters of state and by 724 BC had secured his empire in the east well enough that he could turn to the west, where he laid siege to the Phoenician city of Tyre and then to the Israelite city of Samaria. According to Assyrian records, over 20,000 Israelites were deported at this time and settled in the northern parts of the Assyrian Empire (ANET 284-285). Sometime during the siege, Shalmaneser V died and was succeeded by Sargon II (722–705 BC). Although Shalmaneser V is mentioned at the beginning of 2 Kgs 17:3-7, the end of the text says only that "the king of Assyria took the city" (cf. 2 Kgs 18:9-10). However, Sargon II claimed to have conquered it, so some believe that Sargon II may have been the general in charge of the siege, or that the actual fall of the city came so shortly before his accession that Sargon II could claim it for himself (Tadmor 1958:37-39).

The death of Shalmaneser V was followed by widespread revolts, including that of Babylon. His successor, Sargon II, was occupied with particularly severe troubles in the north; thus, Babylon and other territories enjoyed a brief respite. With Hezekiah's ascent to the throne came a change in Judah's foreign policy; although Ahaz had been pro-Assyrian, Hezekiah was firmly anti-Assyrian. Exactly as Isaiah had foretold, Assyria clearly did not intend to cease her conquests in the area north of Judah. Meanwhile, Egypt observed this approaching Assyrian threat and was only too eager to encourage the people of Judah and their neighbors in their anti-Assyrian stance. Judah shifted from dependence upon Assyria to dependence upon Egypt, but Isaiah equally denounced both tactics (Isa 29–31).

Revolts broke out during the time of the next Assyrian king, Sennacherib (705–681 BC), son of Sargon II. Merodach-baladan once again emerged, for example. Possibly it was about this time that the Babylonian envoys visited Hezekiah (Isa 39:1). Unfortunately, Hezekiah fell for their ploy on that occasion and ultimately became the moving force in a new coalition. Some see the hand of Egypt behind this policy, promising help and support, but Isaiah was opposed to the entire arrangement. Egypt was of no help and Assyria could be left to God, so all this political maneuvering was a useless affront to God that could only result in disaster (Isa 22:5-14; 29:15-16; 30:1-18). Isaiah was correct in his predictions, for the next Assyrian monarch, Sennacherib (705–681 BC), defeated Babylon in the first years of his campaigns, again secured his eastern border, and eventually stood at the gates of Jerusalem. The fate Isaiah had predicted years before had finally come to pass as the Assyrian flood reached Judah's neck. The horrors of Assyrian warfare are depicted on pictorial representations found in Sennacherib's palace (Russell 1991).

When the Assyrians arrived at the gates of Jerusalem, they were only stopped by the Lord himself. Hezekiah paid Sennacherib tribute and eventually the Assyrian ruler returned home, boasting that he had penned Hezekiah "like a bird in a cage." Apart from the significant burden of the tribute, however, he left what appears to have been the chief city of the confederacy intact and one of the main instigators of that rebellion still secure on his throne. This behavior was not at all consistent with Assyrian policy or with Sennacherib's behavior on this campaign. If any city should have been destroyed or any king deposed, it was Jerusalem and Hezekiah. The biblical account of a judgment from God that decimated the Assyrian army and forced its hasty departure explains the outcome well. For Sennacherib to mention such a defeat would have been totally out of keeping with his position as king of Assyria and inconsistent with the style of the royal annals.

**The Babylonian Period.** Although chapters 1–39 are largely tied to local historic events, the situation is different with chapters 40–66. Chapters 40–55 seem to be offering hope to a people in exile, and chapters 56–66 appear to address a people who had returned from exile and faced both old and new problems. Such apparent differences lie behind the Deutero- and Trito-Isaiah theories.

A coalition of Babylon and Medo-Persia toppled what was left of the Assyrian empire in 609 BC. Since God's covenant people were convinced that they were especially favored, the prophet could not fully bring them to face their peril. Therefore, the Babylonian destruction of Jerusalem in 586 BC was a traumatic experience. Babylon continued the Assyrian policy of deportation in which the leadership of a conquered nation was exiled to some distant land where they would be less inclined to rebel. Some Judahites (citizens of the southern kingdom of Judah) had been deported already (598 BC; 2 Kgs 24:8-17) prior to the fall of Jerusalem in 586 BC, when the policy was carried out again with more severity (2 Kgs 25:8-21). The deported Judahites eventually found themselves in Babylonia during its bright but brief interlude of political ascendancy.

As a result of this disaster and defeat, some believed that their God had abandoned them. Therefore, they were in grave danger of succumbing to attractive and seductive Babylonian religious ideas and losing their identity as the Lord's covenant people. Chapters 40–55 addressed this situation, reminding the people that their Lord had not abandoned them but had chosen to demonstrate through them his superiority over the Babylonian deities. This superiority would be seen in God's ability to destroy the idols of the pagans, to redeem his people from their sins, and to bring them back to their homeland.

**The Persian Period.** The third and final historical period in the background of Isaiah's book is that of the Persians. It was then that the Jews returned from the Babylonian exile to Jerusalem. Cyrus II (the Great; 559–530 BC), grandson of Cyrus I, came to the throne around 559 BC and is usually credited with founding the Persian (Achaemenid) Empire. In 547 BC, he marched through Assyria, and in 539 BC his Persian forces entered the city of Babylon while Daniel the prophet was there (Dan 1:21; 6:28; 10:1).

Apparently, the Persians reasoned that people were more disposed to obey a conqueror they liked than one they hated, so Cyrus completely reversed the previous exile policy of the earlier Mesopotamian rulers and granted exiles the right to return home. He even provided imperial funds for the rebuilding of national shrines (Ezra 1:1-4; ANET 316). In this respect, he gave considerable impetus to the syncretistic trends that were already at work in the religions of the Near East and would only accelerate in centuries to come. Wiseman (NBD 258) notes that "Cyrus I was a contemporary of Ashurbanipal of Assyria (c. 668 BC) and therefore possibly even known to Isaiah who foresaw the restoration of the Jerusalem Temple through this new power which would free Jews from exile (Isa 44:28). Cyrus would be God's 'Messiah,' an anointed deliverer and an instrument of God's plan (Isa 45:1)."

The promise that they could return home proved entirely trustworthy. This return from exile was brought about by a man specifically named in advance by the miracle of predictive prophecy, the Persian emperor, Cyrus. Finally, in 539 BC, the time had come for the Medo-Persians to complete the conquest that they had begun seventy-five years earlier when they had needed Babylon's help. They needed that help no longer, and in the dramatic fashion described in Daniel 5, they swept into Babylon and ended the brief Neo-Babylonian Empire.

In keeping with a policy also applied to other subject people groups, Cyrus granted the Jews permission to return home. We have a Hebrew copy of this edict in Ezra 1:1-4 and an Aramaic memorandum of the same in Ezra 6:3-5 (cf. 2 Chr 36:22-23). Cyrus's own inscriptions agree with the Old Testament view of him as a sympathetic ruler. In his first year, he issued a decree (in the Cyrus Cylinder) by which he "gathered together all the inhabitants [who were exiles] and returned them to their homes" (ANET 316). In the same decree, he restored deities to their renovated temples. The Jews had no images to take back, but they did restore their Temple and its fittings upon their return to Jerusalem (Ezra 6:3). Although this policy does have parallels, it should be noted that not all Persian kings adopted it. According to Josephus (*Antiquities* 11.1-18), Cyrus was inspired to allow the Jewish exiles to return after he had read Isaiah's prophecy. Isaiah wrote about this historical period, describing the return of the Jews from Babylonia to their homeland as the second exodus.

Throughout his ministry, Isaiah delivered messages of both warning and comfort, and these messages alternate and recur throughout his book. He wrote to call the Lord's covenant people, and especially those from Judah, to repent of their rebellion and hypocrisy and to turn in faith to the Lord of their fathers. Assyrian invaders were the immediate threat to Jerusalem and Judah. Isaiah warned his audience to turn to God and not to any human political alliance (Aram, Egypt, or Israel) for salvation from the disaster facing them. The Assyrian menace was very real, and the outrageous sinful behavior of the rebellious people of Judah was also very real. Isaiah captured this moment of truth.

## AUDIENCE

Isaiah was called to preach to a sinful people that were rebellious, obstinate, and disobedient. His audience mocked him and resisted his message even as the power of Assyria increased from Tiglath-pileser to Shalmaneser to Sargon to Sennacherib, who finally appeared at the gates of Jerusalem.

With personal pathos and eloquent language, Isaiah pleaded with his recalcitrant countrymen to repent and turn from their sinful ways. The prophet stretched the very limits of the Hebrew language in his graphic and vivid imagery. With a great variety of literary images, he described the nation's sinful condition before the "Holy One of Israel." In striking language, he depicted the horrors of Assyrian warfare and the resultant suffering of the people and destruction of their lands. Even the prophet's family was involved in communicating God's warning—his sons had symbolic names. But just as one son bore the ominous name Maher-shalal-hash-baz ("Swift to plunder and quick to carry away," 8:1), so also the other son bore a name of hope, Shear-jashub ("a remnant will return," 7:3). Although Isaiah (and his sons) had to bear the bad news of judgment ("plunder," "carry away"), he was also privileged to bear the good news ("a remnant will return") of hope for the future restoration of God's people.

Some of the most glowing words of comfort and hope to be found anywhere are found in the prophecies of Isaiah. Especially in the last chapters of his book, Isaiah wrote to comfort those who had lost all hope, especially in the Exile. Although the prophets primarily preached to people of their own time and place, they did at times communicate a message for those removed from them in space (cf. the oracles against the foreign nations, chs 13–23) or far removed in time (e.g., the many promises of the Messiah and his ministry).

## CANONICITY AND TEXTUAL HISTORY

Unlike some Old Testament books, the canonicity of Isaiah has never been a matter of dispute, and the Hebrew text of Isaiah is well preserved. The major ancient witnesses to the text are the Septuagint, the Targum, the Latin versions, the Peshitta, and the scrolls from Qumran (1QIsa$^a$, 1QIsa$^b$).

The newest critical edition of the Masoretic Text (MT) is based on the Aleppo Codex prepared by Aaron ben Asher in the early tenth century and now published in facsimile as *The Aleppo Codex* (Goshen-Gottstein 1976). The first critical edition of a book of the Old Testament text based on this MS is *The Book of Isaiah*, in the Hebrew University Bible project (Goshen-Gottstein 1965). That the Hebrew text of Isaiah has been generally well preserved may reflect the high esteem in which it has been held. Very few changes have been effected in the new translations since the discovery and publication of the Isaiah Dead Sea Scrolls.

The discovery of two manuscripts of Isaiah (1QIsa$^a$ and 1QIsa$^b$) at Qumran was an event of major textual importance. These two manuscripts preceded the traditional Hebrew text by a millennium and one of them (1QIsa$^a$) is complete, which is not the case with any other Old Testament book found at Qumran. There are few significant variations between 1QIsa$^a$ and the MT. According to one recent calculation, there are twenty-one Dead Sea Scroll manuscripts (some of which are fragments) of Isaiah from Qumran. This is quite impressive (cf. Tov 1997:491). Cave 4 alone yielded eighteen manuscripts, of which two are substantial. The majority of variations from the MT are in spelling and do not affect translation or meaning.

Variants between the Greek of the Septuagint and the Hebrew of the MT are often suspect because they appear most often to be attempts to smooth out or to interpret difficult passages in the MT. At one time, it was thought that such variants in the Greek originated from the Septuagint translators themselves, but now the evidence from Qumran suggests that these translators were closely following a Hebrew original of a somewhat different text type from the MT, now called Alexandrian (Cross 1975).

In addition to the Septuagint, the other ancient Greek versions are the more literal one of Aquila that is dated to the second century AD, the more idiomatic one of Symmachus that is dated to about the second or third century AD, and that of

Theodotion (about midway between the other two), who apparently lived at the end of the second century AD (Tov 1992:143-148).

According to Grelot (1992) and Chilton (1985), the Targums are basically early Aramaic paraphrases of the Hebrew text. They are the translations of Jews living in Palestine and Babylonia from a century before Christ to the eighth or ninth century after him. Because they paraphrased the text, these free translations into Aramaic reflect the interpretation of the Hebrew text by these early Jewish interpreters and translators. The Targum on Isaiah by Jonathan ben Uzziel is usually dated from about the time of Christ.

## LITERARY STYLE

Isaiah's superb literary style is acknowledged by all, and the use of numerous figures of speech and graphic imagery enables the prophet to present his important message vividly. I have discussed the outstanding style of Isaiah's language in more detail elsewhere (Walker 1991:104-108).

Scholars have often commented on Isaiah's penchant for punning. One scholar devotes twenty pages to puns or paronomasia in chapters 1–39 alone (Schoekel 1963:86-106), and another specifically discusses more than twenty puns in chapters 1–39 (Glueck 1970:50-78). Isaiah made superb use of the poetic style of his age, the chief characteristic of which was parallelism. Isaiah's book also contains beautiful examples of such literary features as chiasm and inclusio.

Isaiah used vivid imagery and a variety of symbols to communicate spiritual truth to the people in a graphic and vivid manner. VanGemeren (1990:252) says, "Much of the book's brilliance derives from imagery." He gives examples from war (63:1-6), social life (3:1-17), and rural life (5:1-7).

Rather than using simple literal language when describing judgment, the prophet graphically announced, "Your people will be burned—like thornbushes cut down and tossed in a fire" (33:12). Of those who attempted to escape God's holy wrath poured out in judgment, he said that "Those who flee in terror will fall into a trap, and those who escape the trap will be caught in a snare" (24:18). There is striking anthropomorphic judgment language in 11:4, where God destroys the wicked with the "breath from his mouth."

Some of the most graphic language in Isaiah describes the Lord as a victorious warrior. "I have been treading the winepress alone; no one was there to help me. In my anger I have trampled my enemies as if they were grapes. In my fury I have trampled my foes. Their blood has stained my clothes. . . . I crushed the nations in my anger and made them stagger and fall to the ground" (63:3, 6). In his desire to communicate his message, the prophet did not hesitate to use terminology borrowed from Canaanite religion for depicting the Lord's absolute conquest: "In that day the LORD will take his terrible, swift sword and punish Leviathan, the swiftly moving serpent, the coiling, writhing serpent. He will kill the dragon of the sea" (27:1).

Obviously, the imagery Isaiah chose was familiar to those who heard the prophet speak. His audience had the background experience to appreciate the meanings of the donkey and the ox (1:3), the "canopy of cloud during the day and smoke and flaming fire at night" (4:5), "not a sandal strap broken" (5:27), the "battle flag on the mountain" (18:3), "a shelter from the heat" (25:4), the "tender green shoot, like a root in dry ground" (53:2), the lamb led to slaughter or silent before the shearers (53:7), and the clay and the potter (64:8).

Like other prophets, Isaiah made excellent use of animal imagery. He spoke of locusts, as Joel did (33:4; cf. Joel 1:2–2:11). Another example is found in Isaiah 10:14, "I have robbed their nests of riches and gathered up kingdoms as a farmer gathers eggs. No one can even flap a wing against me or utter a peep of protest" (cf. Deut 32:11-15). Such imagery is also used in 11:6-9 to illustrate the tranquility and concord that true righteousness brings. The salvation that changes inner nature and brings peace is presented as harmony among kinds of animals that are normally at odds.

## MAJOR THEMES

Themes and theological concerns are not always easy to separate, and some overlap among them is expected. The following are some of the more noteworthy themes that may be treated on their own.

**Servant of the Lord.** The important theme of the servant is found in four passages (42:1-9; 49:1-13; 50:4-11; 52:13–53:12). The importance of this subject is reflected in its Christocentric use in the early preaching of the church. In two early chapters of Acts, Jesus is called "servant" four times (Acts 3:13, 26; 4:27, 30). In his early preaching, Peter made bold use of this theme as he addressed the Jerusalem crowd (Acts 3:13-15), and he again reflected this theme in his epistle (1 Pet 2:20-25). Paul stressed Christ's servanthood in the famous passage in Philippians 2:5-11. Reference to the suffering servant is also found in Hebrews 9:28, which makes use of Isaiah 53:12.

**Idolatry.** The subject of idolatry receives particular attention by the prophet. With biting sarcasm, Isaiah lashed out against the folly of worshiping something that originated from mere humans. With ridicule the prophet describes those who bow down to what they themselves made. The worker makes an idol for himself and then worships this work of his own hands! Modern humans still foolishly worship that which is produced by their own imaginations.

**Creation.** Related to the theme of idolatry is the theme of the Creator and his creation. More than any other prophet, Isaiah referred to God as Creator. In contrast to the idol makers who created their own lifeless gods and then worshiped them, God created the entire universe, including the idol makers who were meant to worship him. He alone is the one true God, the Creator of all, without peer. Isaiah maintains a sharp distinction between the Creator and his creatures. God is high and lifted up (6:1); the Holy One fills the whole earth with his glory (6:3). In contrast, all the peoples and nations of the earth are but a "drop in the bucket" (cf. 14:22-23; 40:15, 21-23; 47:1-4). The Creator is the eternal "I AM" before whom the homemade idols are nothing (2:6-22; 43:8-13). Idols cannot explain the past or determine—or even predict—the future (Isa 41:22-23; 43:8-9; 44:6-8; 45:20-23); they are merely the reflections of their creators, fallen humans with all their limitations and perverted ways.

The contrast between God and the people is more than that between the infinite and the finite. God is thrice-holy and morally perfect while the people were unholy and immoral. Isaiah's response to his vision of God was "I am a sinful man" (6:5). This meant more than that he was ceremonially unclean, as the words "filthy lips" testify. The people were sinful in their conversations and lifestyle.

**The Messiah.** The book of Isaiah is especially rich in references—direct and indirect—to the Messiah. Commentators have referred to the book as the "Fifth Gospel" (Sawyer 1996) or the "Gospel of Isaiah" (MacRae 1977). The book contains references to the Messiah's birth (7:14; cf. 8:8, 10), his life and ministry (9:1-7; 35:5-6; 53:2-3), his empowering by the Holy Spirit (11:2; 42:1; 61:1), his suffering and death (50:5-6; 53:3-5, 7-10), and his resurrection and glorious ultimate victory (53:11-12). The New Testament often refers to these messianic passages in Isaiah.

**Holiness.** Another major theme in Isaiah is that of God's holiness. Isaiah's vision of the Lord in chapter 6 especially focuses on the Lord's holiness, and Isaiah's favorite title for the Lord is "the Holy One of Israel." Isaiah refers to the divine Spirit more than any other prophet and notes the work of the Spirit in the ministry of the Messiah. The impeccable holiness of the Lord is contrasted with defiled and erring humans who stray like wandering sheep and whose righteousness is like filthy rags (64:6).

**Zion.** The earliest use of this term referred to the original, small, local site of Mount Zion in the Jerusalem area, but in ever-larger circles, the term came to be used of Jerusalem in general, to the greater Jerusalem area, to the people of Jerusalem, to the people of God at that time, and eventually to the people of God at any place and time. In Isaiah, the term is especially used of the presence of God among his people. Isaiah uses the term about forty-eight times, more frequently than any other prophet or book in the Bible (the Psalms use the term about thirty-eight times).

**Theological Concerns.** All the basic theological concerns are represented in Isaiah. Three core theological issues—God, sin, and salvation—are fundamental to a theological framework, and Isaiah covers them all. Basic questions include, Who is God? What is his nature? What is mankind? What is the relationship of human creatures to their Creator? What is sin and its bearing on all this? What is salvation and who is the Savior? These fundamental issues are all encountered repeatedly in Isaiah. Sin is a grievous evil against a holy God, and its proper treatment is a gracious work of the divine redeemer. How the Lord's justice, grace, and mercy work together for the removal of sin and the forgiveness of the sinner is an unfathomable mystery for humans, but Isaiah presents these basic truths in vivid and moving language.

**God.** The Lord is presented as the thrice-holy God in stark contrast to rebellious and sinful humans, especially the Judahites of Isaiah's time. Isaiah's favorite title for the

Lord is "the Holy One of Israel." The Lord is God, Creator, and Redeemer; it is he who created, sustains, and governs the universe in the natural and moral spheres. The Lord is sovereign in history and rules over all the nations; they are accountable to him as the ultimate Judge of all (chs 13–23). Isaiah makes it clear that the mighty kingdom of Assyria was merely the rod of God's anger, in his hand to punish his sinful and rebellious covenant people.

**Sin.** Isaiah's encounter with the thrice-holy God left him with a burning sense of sin (6:1-7). Isaiah was to be the mouthpiece for God, but his lips were unclean, as were those of the people. Compared to their perfect God, the people were deeply imperfect. Compared to the Holy One of Israel, they were defiled and polluted. Their own righteousness could only be compared to "filthy rags" (64:6). Their sins had left them estranged from God and facing judgment. The terribly high cost of sin is made very clear in the book of Isaiah as sinners face judgment from the Holy One of Israel.

Unclean in their sin, the people manifested their inner corruption in their outward rebellion. Isaiah marked out pride and rebellion for special condemnation (cf. 2:6-22; 7:1-9). The most amazing feature of this prideful rebellion was its sheer stupidity (1:2-3). When the people exalted themselves, the result was arrogance and exploitation of others. Pride and arrogance are marks of stupidity or folly, leading sinful people to view the world upside down, imagining themselves in the place of God. Those who are wise in their own eyes are stupid in God's eyes (cf. 5:21). In 1:2-3, obtuse and rebellious people are compared to dumb animals. For Isaiah, it was obvious that mortals must look to something beyond themselves and the works of their own hands. Who among us can escape death, the thief of all mortals (cf. ch 14)? On a national level, what earthly nation can forever dominate its neighbors (cf. chs 13–23)? Which human leaders in all their pompous power can be depended upon to never fail their people (chs 7, 21, 28–30)?

Like other eighth-century prophets, Isaiah was concerned about social sins (1:16-17; 5:7-8; 26:5-6; 58:6-12); he targeted many of the same ones cataloged in the preaching of Amos, and called for the same righteousness and justice to be manifested in society. These social sins included oppressive treatment of widows and orphans (1:17, 21-23; 3:14), theft (1:21), lying and dishonesty (59:4, 14), violence (59:6), murder (1:21; 59:3), bribery and perversion of justice (1:23; 3:9; 5:23; 10:1-2; 29:21), expropriation of land belonging to the poor (5:8-10), drunkenness (5:11-17, 22; 28:1-14), and inordinate concern with the accumulation of wealth and status (3:16–4:1; 9:9-12; 22:15-19; 32:9-14).

In addition to the costly effects of sin on the social environment, Isaiah revealed its costs to the natural environment—the land with its cities, houses, and fields would be ravaged (6:11) by the Assyrians and Babylonians. Isaiah and the other prophets knew that the earth is the Lord's (6:3) and is not a god in itself. It is part of God's creation graciously put under our stewardship to be used but not abused; if we harm it, we will not enjoy its fertility and bounty. This environmental damage to the land and the people living off of it is a solemn truth also noted elsewhere (cf. Deut 27–28).

**Judgment.** The consistent rebellion and sin against the Holy One of Israel by his own covenant people could only result in judgment. God's hatred for all that corrupts his people is personal and passionate (9:12, 17, 21; 10:4), and his response to sin is either judgment or forgiveness and redemption. The theme of judgment appears throughout Isaiah and assumes many forms. It may come as natural disaster (24:4-5), military defeat (5:26-30), disease (1:5-6), or in other guises. The hand of God is the ultimate source of judgment (43:27-28). The horrific judgments of God through the Assyrians and Babylonians were intended to get the people's attention and persuade them to repent. God reacted to his people with a passion against sin but also with a compassion that desired for them to turn to him and be saved. It is obvious in Isaiah that the means of salvation can only be through God's activity—the Creator must become the Redeemer.

**Salvation.** Sin must be dealt with in order to accomplish the salvation of God's people, who can ultimately be accounted righteous only when another bears their iniquities. This substitutionary atonement ultimately makes possible God's announcement of pardon and redemption. The price of atonement was paid by none other than the ideal king, the Messiah, who suffered for his people (42:1-9; 49:5-6; 50:4-9; 52:13–53:12) in order to redeem them (9:2-7).

**Repentance.** To benefit from the salvation offered by the Lord, God's people must repent, renounce their sin, and be faithfully obedient in response to God's promises. As long as proud sinners insist on their own exaltation, they have no hope (1:11, 17; 5:15). Isaiah directs them to abandon trust in themselves, to repent, and to commit their way to God in order to enjoy his resources and benefits (12:2; 26:2-6; 30:15; 55:6-9; 57:15). As sin results in the degradation and devaluation of the sinner, so redemption renews significance and worth.

Isaiah, as his name reflects, is a prophet of "the LORD who saves." A Holy God offended by sin will either judge his people or extend his forgiveness and salvation. The theology of Zion and the promised remnant guaranteed God's presence as much for cleansing judgment as for protection and salvation.

## OUTLINE

The book of Isaiah may conveniently be divided into three major parts. The first division (chs 1–35) contains judgments against God's covenant people and against the foreign nations. The second division (chs 36–39) covers primarily historical material. The third and final division (chs 40–66) is mostly words of consolation for the exiled people of God.

The first section, on the judgments of God, contains many indictments against the people of Judah; it also contains a long series of prophecies against foreign nations. The historical narrative of the second section is primarily related to King Hezekiah and the Assyrian siege of Jerusalem. This was a critical period in the life of Israel and, except for 38:9-20, has parallel material in 2 Kings 18:13–20:19. The third section emphasizes comfort and restoration, and can be divided into three parts of nine chapters each (40–48; 49–57; 58–66). The first two parts each conclude with the statement, "There is no peace for the wicked" (48:22; 57:21). The first part focuses on the deliverance of God's people through the instrumentality of Cyrus, the second on the theme of the Suffering Servant and the glory of Zion. The third and concluding part summarizes the future blessed condition of the true Israel in contrast with the miserable condition and doom of the apostates.

I. The Judgments of God (1:1–35:10)
   A. Coming Judgments and the Deliverance of Zion (1:1–6:13)
      1. The condition of God's people (1:1-31)
      2. The future kingdom and its introductory judgments (2:1-4:6)
      3. The vineyard and its fruits (5:1-30)
      4. Isaiah's commission (6:1-13)
   B. The Sign of Immanuel (7:1–12:6)
      1. Immanuel's birth (7:1-17)
      2. The Assyrian crisis (7:18-8:22)
      3. The Davidic kingdom and king (9:1-7)
      4. God's anger against Israel (9:8-10:4)
      5. Judgment on Assyria (10:5-34)
      6. The Branch from Jesse's roots (11:1-16)
      7. The Song of Redemption (12:1-6)
   C. Judgments on the Nations (13:1–23:18)
      1. Babylon and Assyria (13:1-14:27)
      2. Philistia (14:28-32)
      3. Moab (15:1-16:14)
      4. Damascus (Aram) (17:1-14)
      5. Cush (18:1-7)
      6. Egypt (19:1-25)
      7. Egypt and Cush (20:1-6)
      8. Desert by the Sea (Babylon) (21:1-10)
      9. Dumah (Edom) (21:11-12)
     10. Arabia (21:13-17)
     11. The Valley of Vision (Jerusalem) (22:1-25)
     12. Tyre (23:1-18)
   D. The Isaiah Apocalypse (24:1–27:13)
      1. Desolation of the earth and the world city (24:1-23)
      2. Praise for victory (25:1-5)
      3. Feast of the nations and the overthrow of Moab (25:6-12)
      4. Song of praise (26:1-21)
      5. Overthrow of world power and the prosperity of Zion (27:1-13)

COMMENTARY ON

# Isaiah

◆ **I. The Judgments of God (1:1–35:10)**
   **A. Coming Judgments and the Deliverance of Zion (1:1–6:13)**
      **1. The condition of God's people (1:1–31)**

These are the visions that Isaiah son of Amoz saw concerning Judah and Jerusalem. He saw these visions during the years when Uzziah, Jotham, Ahaz, and Hezekiah were kings of Judah.*

<sup>2</sup>Listen, O heavens! Pay attention, earth!
   This is what the LORD says:
"The children I raised and cared for
   have rebelled against me.
<sup>3</sup>Even an ox knows its owner,
   and a donkey recognizes its master's
      care—
but Israel doesn't know its master.
   My people don't recognize my care
      for them."
<sup>4</sup>Oh, what a sinful nation they are—
   loaded down with a burden of guilt.
They are evil people,
   corrupt children who have rejected
      the LORD.
They have despised the Holy One
      of Israel
   and turned their backs on him.

<sup>5</sup>Why do you continue to invite
      punishment?
   Must you rebel forever?
Your head is injured,
   and your heart is sick.
<sup>6</sup>You are battered from head to foot—
   covered with bruises, welts, and
      infected wounds—
without any soothing ointments
   or bandages.

<sup>7</sup>Your country lies in ruins,
   and your towns are burned.
Foreigners plunder your fields before
      your eyes
   and destroy everything they see.
<sup>8</sup>Beautiful Jerusalem* stands abandoned
   like a watchman's shelter in a
      vineyard,
like a lean-to in a cucumber field after
      the harvest,
   like a helpless city under siege.
<sup>9</sup>If the LORD of Heaven's Armies
   had not spared a few of us,*
we would have been wiped out like
      Sodom,
   destroyed like Gomorrah.

<sup>10</sup>Listen to the LORD, you leaders of
      "Sodom."
   Listen to the law of our God, people
      of "Gomorrah."
<sup>11</sup>"What makes you think I want all your
      sacrifices?"
   says the LORD.
"I am sick of your burnt offerings
      of rams
   and the fat of fattened cattle.
I get no pleasure from the blood
   of bulls and lambs and goats.
<sup>12</sup>When you come to worship me,
   who asked you to parade through
      my courts with all your
      ceremony?
<sup>13</sup>Stop bringing me your meaningless
      gifts;

the incense of your offerings
  disgusts me!
As for your celebrations of the new
    moon and the Sabbath
  and your special days for fasting—
  they are all sinful and false.
    I want no more of your pious
      meetings.
¹⁴ I hate your new moon celebrations
    and your annual festivals.
  They are a burden to me. I cannot
    stand them!
¹⁵ When you lift up your hands in prayer,
    I will not look.
  Though you offer many prayers,
    I will not listen,
  for your hands are covered with the
    blood of innocent victims.
¹⁶ Wash yourselves and be clean!
  Get your sins out of my sight.
  Give up your evil ways.
¹⁷ Learn to do good.
  Seek justice.
  Help the oppressed.
  Defend the cause of orphans.
  Fight for the rights of widows.

¹⁸ "Come now, let's settle this,"
    says the LORD.
  "Though your sins are like scarlet,
    I will make them as white as snow.
  Though they are red like crimson,
    I will make them as white as wool.
¹⁹ If you will only obey me,
    you will have plenty to eat.
²⁰ But if you turn away and refuse to
    listen,
  you will be devoured by the sword
    of your enemies.
  I, the LORD, have spoken!"

²¹ See how Jerusalem, once so faithful,
    has become a prostitute.
  Once the home of justice and
    righteousness,
  she is now filled with murderers.
²² Once like pure silver,
    you have become like worthless slag.
  Once so pure,

you are now like watered-down wine.
²³ Your leaders are rebels,
    the companions of thieves.
  All of them love bribes
    and demand payoffs,
  but they refuse to defend the cause
    of orphans
  or fight for the rights of widows.

²⁴ Therefore, the Lord, the LORD of
      Heaven's Armies,
    the Mighty One of Israel, says,
  "I will take revenge on my enemies
    and pay back my foes!
²⁵ I will raise my fist against you.
    I will melt you down and skim off
      your slag.
  I will remove all your impurities.
²⁶ Then I will give you good judges again
    and wise counselors like you used
      to have.
  Then Jerusalem will again be called
    the Home of Justice
    and the Faithful City."

²⁷ Zion will be restored by justice;
    those who repent will be revived
      by righteousness.
²⁸ But rebels and sinners will be
    completely destroyed,
  and those who desert the LORD
    will be consumed.

²⁹ You will be ashamed of your idol
      worship
    in groves of sacred oaks.
  You will blush because you worshiped
    in gardens dedicated to idols.
³⁰ You will be like a great tree with
      withered leaves,
    like a garden without water.
³¹ The strongest among you will
      disappear like straw;
    their evil deeds will be the spark
      that sets it on fire.
  They and their evil works will burn
      up together,
    and no one will be able to put out
      the fire.

---

1:1 These kings reigned from 792 to 686 BC.   1:8 Hebrew *The daughter of Zion.*   1:9 Greek version reads *a few of our children.* Compare Rom 9:29.

## NOTES

**1:1 *visions*.** The Hebrew *khazon* [TH2377, ZH2606] is singular. Goldingay (1998) points out that elsewhere the term is used only of a single vision, and he suggests that it applies here only to the first chapter. Further, he suggests that 2:1, rather than introducing the next chapter, is a colophon to the opening chapter.

**1:2 *Listen, O heavens*.** The entire universe is called as witness to God's indictment of his people (cf. Deut 30:19; 31:28; 32:1).

**1:3 *Even an ox knows its owner, and a donkey recognizes its master's care*.** In vivid and striking language, the rebellious and obtuse people of Judah are compared to animals.

**but *Israel doesn't know its master*.** God's people did not spiritually recognize or acknowledge their Master (cf. Hos 2:10; 4:1). Even the instincts of such creatures as oxen or donkeys exceed those of the spiritually obtuse Judahites.

**1:4 *sinful nation*.** The contrast with God's holiness highlights the sick condition of the people.

**children.** The concept of the covenant people as God's children is also found in Deut 30:9; 32:5; Hos 2:1; 1 Chr 29:10 and elsewhere. Israel calls God "Father" in Isa 63:16 and 64:7. In Jer 31:8 and Mal 1:6 God calls himself the Father of Israel.

**rejected the LORD.** "Rejected" translates the Heb. *'azab* [TH5800, ZH6440]. This customary word for "divorce" is used twenty-five times in Isaiah.

**the Holy One of Israel.** Isaiah's preferred name for God occurs twenty-six times in his book and only six times elsewhere in the OT.

**1:8 *Jerusalem*.** The literal "daughter of Zion" (so NLT mg) personifies the city of Jerusalem and her inhabitants.

**1:9** This verse is quoted by Paul in Rom 9:29, where it is linked with Isa 10:22-23.

**the LORD of Heaven's Armies.** Heb. *yhwh tseba'oth*. Traditionally, "the LORD of hosts" (KJV, NRSV, NASB, ESV, cf. NJPS, REB) but with variations in new versions: "the LORD Almighty" (NIV, TEV); "the LORD All-Powerful (NCV, CEV); "the LORD of Armies" (GW). This Heb. term for armies or hosts is used of both earthly and heavenly forces. It is often translated in the LXX by *pantokratōr* "Almighty," a word found in the NT in Rev 1:8; 4:8; 11:17 and elsewhere.

**1:10 *Sodom . . . Gomorrah*.** The covenant people of God would have been deeply offended at being compared with these perverted Gentile cities. Isaiah's mention of the two infamous cities no doubt reminded his hearers of the reference to them in Deut 29:23. Sodom is mentioned again in Isa 3:9 and in Ezek 16:46, 48-49, 55-56.

**1:11 *fattened cattle*.** Refers to cattle developed by special feeding for special use.

**1:13 *new moon*.** The reference is to the New Moon festivals that were celebrated on the first day of each month with special sacrifices.

**1:14 *annual festivals*.** These celebrations included the Passover, the Festival of Weeks, and the Feast of Tabernacles.

**1:15 *I will not look*.** The same imagery of God lit. "hiding his eyes" is also found in 8:17 and 59:2. Hypocritical worship is repulsive to God.

**blood of innocent victims.** This could refer to the sin of murder (cf. 1:21) or even to the mistreatment of widows and orphans (1:17) that resulted in their loss of life.

**1:17 *orphans*.** Lit., "fatherless" (*yatom* [TH3490, ZH3846]). This reflects the family structure of ancient Near Eastern society. Orphans, along with ***widows***, were among the weak and exploited elements of society.

**1:18 *scarlet . . . crimson*.** This refers to blood shed by the hands of murderers. Scarlet and crimson are two shades of deep red, symbolic of sin that leads to bloodshed and death. Apparently sin is never described as black in the Bible.

***white as snow . . . wool*.** These symbolize cleanliness, purity, and innocence (cf. Rev 1:14).

**1:24 *the Lord, the LORD of Heaven's Armies, the Mighty One of Israel*.** This stacking of names stresses God's authority and introduces the verdict of judgment.

**1:25 *remove all your impurities*.** This imagery of purifying fire is also found in 4:4 and 48:10, as well as in Zech 13:9; Mal 3:3; 1 Pet 1:7. The smelting process was designed to purify.

**1:29 *groves of sacred oaks*.** This refers to sites where pagan sacrifices were offered and sexual immorality took place (cf. 65:3; 66:17).

C O M M E N T A R Y

The opening chapters of Isaiah describe the condition of the Judahites (1:1-31). Among other indictments, they are called a fruitless vineyard (5:1-30). Nonetheless, hopeful words about the coming kingdom are also included (2:1-4:6). The section closes with an account of the prophet's commission (6:1-13).

The opening words identify Isaiah as the son of Amoz (not Amos) and as the recipient of visions concerning the city of Jerusalem and the surrounding areas. These visions also include references to other nations that shared history with Judah. The Hebrew word for "visions" used here also introduces the prophecies of Obadiah, Micah, and Nahum. The opening verses also place Isaiah historically by identifying the kings of Judah who were his contemporaries: Uzziah (792–740 BC), Jotham (750–732 BC), Ahaz (735–715 BC), and Hezekiah (715–686 BC). The historical background has already been discussed in the Introduction.

The introduction is immediately followed by a message to a nation that is rebelling against its Lord. These opening words are in the form of a lawsuit against God's people and, in a very general way, are a preview of chapters 1–39. The people are said to be even more obtuse than animals, since other creatures know better than to ignore the hand that feeds them (1:3). The people of Judah are described as evil, corrupt, and "loaded down with a burden of guilt" (1:4). Isaiah's message repeatedly focuses on the sin of rebellion as the root of the nation's illness and problems, and their condition is vividly described in terms of a sick body covered from head to foot with "bruises, welts, and infected wounds—without any soothing ointments or bandages" (1:6). As a result of their attitude and conduct, the nation is plundered and lies in ruins; it is vividly compared to an abandoned "watchman's shelter" after the harvest is finished (1:8).

In 1:10, the wicked people are compared to the sinners of ancient Sodom and Gomorrah and admonished to "listen to the law of our God," a law that is both moral and ceremonial. The rebels had maintained their ceremonial observances in various external practices but had disobeyed the more basic moral laws. Instead of their offered incense being an aroma pleasing to the Lord as originally intended, it had become disgusting and repulsive to him (1:13). Eventually the Lord, the Holy One of Israel, said of their religious practices, "I want no more of your pious meetings. I hate your new moon celebrations and your annual festivals. They are a burden to me. I cannot stand them!" (1:13-14). God further warned the people that the sin they accommodated in their lives would affect their prayers and therefore said, "When you lift up your hands in prayer I will not look" (1:15).

In addition to observing the law, the people were to "Seek justice. Help the oppressed. Defend the cause of orphans. Fight for the rights of widows" (1:17). The Lord's people were instructed to help each other at a time long before governmental social agencies existed to address such needs. The good news for these sinful people was forgiveness—the Lord promised that "though your sins are like scarlet," they could become "as white as snow" (1:18) on the condition that they would "only obey me" (1:19). On the other hand, if they turned away and refused to listen, they would be destroyed by their enemies (1:20). The prophets often depicted Jerusalem as a prostitute in pitiful condition (1:21). Jerusalem had been unfaithful to her covenant Lord and had gone after other lovers. In another graphic image, Jerusalem's former "pure silver" had now become "worthless slag," and her former purity had deteriorated into "watered-down wine" (1:22). The city's leaders had associated with thieves taking bribes, but had refused to come to the aid of orphans and widows (1:23).

The spiritual and moral condition of the people could only provoke the wrath and judgment of the Holy One of Israel. "The Lord, the LORD of the Heavenly Armies, the Mighty One of Israel" would give vent to his holy wrath and pour out his fury on them, calling them his "enemies" and "foes" (1:24). God starkly said, "I will raise my fist against you" (1:25). However, the Lord would never totally destroy his people; a remnant would always remain. This remnant motif appears repeatedly in Isaiah, especially in chapters 1–12 and 28–29, but it began in Genesis with Noah and Lot (Graham 1976:217ff). The purpose of this judgment on God's covenant people was to melt them down, skim off their slag, and remove their impurities (1:25).

◆       ## 2. The future kingdom and its introductory judgments (2:1–4:6)

This is a vision that Isaiah son of Amoz saw concerning Judah and Jerusalem:

2 In the last days, the mountain of the
    LORD's house
  will be the highest of all—
    the most important place on earth.
  It will be raised above the other hills,
    and people from all over the world
    will stream there to worship.
3 People from many nations will come
    and say,
  "Come, let us go up to the mountain
    of the LORD,
    to the house of Jacob's God.

There he will teach us his ways,
  and we will walk in his paths."
For the LORD's teaching will go out
  from Zion;
  his word will go out from Jerusalem.
4 The LORD will mediate between nations
  and will settle international
  disputes.
They will hammer their swords into
  plowshares
  and their spears into pruning hooks.
Nation will no longer fight against
  nation,
  nor train for war anymore.

⁵Come, descendants of Jacob,
let us walk in the light of the LORD!
⁶For the LORD has rejected his people,
the descendants of Jacob,
because they have filled their land
with practices from the East
and with sorcerers, as the
Philistines do.
They have made alliances with
pagans.
⁷Israel is full of silver and gold;
there is no end to its treasures.
Their land is full of warhorses;
there is no end to its chariots.
⁸Their land is full of idols;
the people worship things they
have made
with their own hands.
⁹So now they will be humbled,
and all will be brought low—
do not forgive them.
¹⁰Crawl into caves in the rocks.
Hide in the dust
from the terror of the LORD
and the glory of his majesty.
¹¹Human pride will be brought down,
and human arrogance will be
humbled.
Only the LORD will be exalted
on that day of judgment.

¹²For the LORD of Heaven's Armies
has a day of reckoning.
He will punish the proud and
mighty
and bring down everything that
is exalted.
¹³He will cut down the tall cedars
of Lebanon
and all the mighty oaks of Bashan.
¹⁴He will level all the high mountains
and all the lofty hills.
¹⁵He will break down every high tower
and every fortified wall.
¹⁶He will destroy all the great trading
ships*
and every magnificent vessel.
¹⁷Human pride will be humbled,
and human arrogance will be
brought down.

Only the LORD will be exalted
on that day of judgment.

¹⁸Idols will completely disappear.
¹⁹When the LORD rises to shake the earth,
his enemies will crawl into holes
in the ground.
They will hide in caves in the rocks
from the terror of the LORD
and the glory of his majesty.
²⁰On that day of judgment they will
abandon the gold and silver idols
they made for themselves to worship.
They will leave their gods to the
rodents and bats,
²¹    while they crawl away into caverns
and hide among the jagged rocks in
the cliffs.
They will try to escape the terror
of the LORD
and the glory of his majesty
as he rises to shake the earth.
²²Don't put your trust in mere humans.
They are as frail as breath.
What good are they?

## CHAPTER 3
¹The Lord, the LORD of Heaven's Armies,
will take away from Jerusalem and
Judah
everything they depend on:
every bit of bread
and every drop of water,
²all their heroes and soldiers,
judges and prophets,
fortune-tellers and elders,
³army officers and high officials,
advisers, skilled craftsmen, and
astrologers.

⁴I will make boys their leaders,
and toddlers their rulers.
⁵People will oppress each other—
man against man,
neighbor against neighbor.
Young people will insult their elders,
and vulgar people will sneer at the
honorable.

⁶In those days a man will say to his
brother,

"Since you have a coat, you be our
leader!
Take charge of this heap of ruins!"
⁷But he will reply,
"No! I can't help.
I don't have any extra food or clothes.
Don't put me in charge!"

⁸For Jerusalem will stumble,
and Judah will fall,
because they speak out against the
LORD and refuse to obey him.
They provoke him to his face.
⁹The very look on their faces gives
them away.
They display their sin like the people
of Sodom
and don't even try to hide it.
They are doomed!
They have brought destruction upon
themselves.

¹⁰Tell the godly that all will be well
for them.
They will enjoy the rich reward they
have earned!
¹¹But the wicked are doomed,
for they will get exactly what they
deserve.

¹²Childish leaders oppress my people,
and women rule over them.
O my people, your leaders mislead you;
they send you down the wrong
road.

¹³The LORD takes his place in court
and presents his case against his
people!
¹⁴The LORD comes forward to pronounce
judgment
on the elders and rulers of his
people:
"You have ruined Israel, my vineyard.
Your houses are filled with things
stolen from the poor.
¹⁵How dare you crush my people,
grinding the faces of the poor into
the dust?"
demands the Lord, the LORD of
Heaven's Armies.

¹⁶The LORD says, "Beautiful Zion*
is haughty:
craning her elegant neck,
flirting with her eyes,
walking with dainty steps,
tinkling her ankle bracelets.
¹⁷So the Lord will send scabs on her
head;
the LORD will make beautiful Zion
bald."

¹⁸On that day of judgment
the Lord will strip away everything
that makes her beautiful:
ornaments, headbands, crescent
necklaces,
¹⁹    earrings, bracelets, and veils;
²⁰scarves, ankle bracelets, sashes,
perfumes, and charms;
²¹rings, jewels,
²²    party clothes, gowns, capes, and
purses;
²³mirrors, fine linen garments,
head ornaments, and shawls.

²⁴Instead of smelling of sweet perfume,
she will stink.
She will wear a rope for a sash,
and her elegant hair will fall out.
She will wear rough burlap instead
of rich robes.
Shame will replace her beauty.*
²⁵The men of the city will be killed with
the sword,
and her warriors will die in battle.
²⁶The gates of Zion will weep and mourn.
The city will be like a ravaged
woman,
huddled on the ground.

## CHAPTER 4

In that day so few men will be left that
seven women will fight for each man, saying, "Let us all marry you! We will provide
our own food and clothing. Only let us
take your name so we won't be mocked as
old maids."

²But in that day, the branch* of the
LORD
will be beautiful and glorious;

the fruit of the land will be the pride
    and glory
of all who survive in Israel.
³All who remain in Zion
    will be a holy people—
those who survive the destruction
    of Jerusalem
and are recorded among the
    living.
⁴The Lord will wash the filth from
    beautiful Zion*
and cleanse Jerusalem of its
    bloodstains

with the hot breath of fiery
    judgment.
⁵Then the LORD will provide shade for
    Mount Zion
and all who assemble there.
He will provide a canopy of cloud
    during the day
and smoke and flaming fire
    at night,
covering the glorious land.
⁶It will be a shelter from daytime heat
and a hiding place from storms and
    rain.

**2:16** Hebrew *every ship of Tarshish.*   **3:16** Or *The women of Zion* (with corresponding changes to plural forms through verse 24); Hebrew reads *The daughters of Zion;* also in 3:17.   **3:24** As in Dead Sea Scrolls; Masoretic Text reads *robes / because instead of beauty.*   **4:2** Or *the Branch.*   **4:4** Or *from the women of Zion;* Hebrew reads *from the daughters of Zion.*

## NOTES

**2:2** *mountain of the LORD's house.* This phrase refers to the reign of the Lord. The term "mountain" can represent a kingdom or kingship, as in Jer 51:25 where the kingdom of Babylon is thus referred to (cf. DBI 572-574). References to Mount Zion are common in Isaiah (cf. 11:9; 27:13; 56:7; 57:13; 65:25; 66:20), and God will ultimately elevate Zion as the spiritual center of the world. Mountains and mountain imagery pervade the history of revelation. For example, the law was given at Mount Sinai, and at the Mount of Transfiguration, God again gave a blinding revelation reminiscent of Sinai (Peter responded by calling it the holy mountain; 2 Pet 1:16-18). Also there was the Sermon on the Mount (Matt 5:1ff); the Mount Olivet discourse (Matt 24); and the Ascension. Christ built his church as a city on a hill, to give light to the world (Matt 5:14; cf. Isa 60:3).

*the most important place on earth.* Lit., "the mountain of the LORD's temple will be established as chief among the mountains." In the OT world, mountains were often viewed as the dwelling places of the gods. Israel's God (Yahweh) had his residence on Mount Zion (Jerusalem), and his domain would eventually prevail over all other mountains.

**2:4** *swords into plowshares.* The language of war weapons being turned into farm implements (i.e., instruments that benefit people) reflects the nature of this kingdom of peace.

**2:6** *East.* The reference is probably to Aram and Mesopotamia.

*made alliances with pagans.* Lit., "clasp hands with pagans." The wicked people were not only influenced by their pagan neighbors, but even made deals with them.

**2:10** *caves in the rocks.* The limestone terrain of the Palestinian landscape is filled with crevices in which people often sought refuge (cf. 2:19; Judg 6:2; 1 Sam 13:6).

**2:11** *day of judgment.* The Heb. expression occurs several times in Jer 2-4. Here it refers to the "day of reckoning" of the next verse. The expression itself is neutral and its meaning depends on its context.

**2:16** *all the great trading ships.* The Heb. is lit. "every ship of Tarshish" (so the NLT margin) and probably refers to a class of notable large ships, perhaps because of their connection with the place of Tarshish.

**2:18** *Idols.* Isaiah repeatedly condemned and ridiculed idolatry (30:22; 31:7; 40:19-20; 44:9-20).

**2:22 Don't put your trust in mere humans.** Lit., "cease from man." The reference includes man-made idols and the system of idolatry. Humans have a tendency to idolize their own ideas and products. Isaiah refers to humans as "frail as breath," and asks, "What good are they?"

**3:1 The Lord, the Lord of Heaven's Armies.** This introduces the glorious God who acts in judgment, in contrast to the immediately preceding (2:22) "mere humans."

**3:2-3** The leaders of society will be removed by the enemy, a common military tactic (cf. 2 Kgs 24:14; 25:18-21). These leaders represent the various authorities in their society— governmental, military, and religious.

**fortune-tellers . . . astrologers.** Although actually useless and in fact misleading, these individuals were valued by spiritually blind and rebellious Judahites and are therefore listed here with other leaders of society.

**army officers.** Lit., "captain of fifty," a basic military unit (cf. 2 Kgs 1:9).

**3:4 boys.** Heb. na'ar, which is not a precise indicator of age. Instead of mature leaders, the condemned people will be ruled by immature and even childish leaders. This was probably fulfilled when a series of young kings followed Hezekiah; the oldest were in their twenties and others were even younger. Some take the terms adverbially, as "childishly" or "arbitrarily," referring to the nature of the rule and not to the age of the rulers. The versions struggle for the best word in this context: "mere lads" (NASB), "boys" (NIV, NRSV, GW, NJPS), "youths" (REB), "young boys" (NCV), "children" (CEV), and "immature boys" (TEV).

**toddlers their rulers.** "Toddlers" translates Heb. ta'alulim. The Heb. has been variously understood, but it surely is a parallel to the preceding line. Some versions have "infants shall rule over them" (ESV), and "babes shall govern them" (NJPS), but the word could be related to the root 'll which in the hithpael stem means "to act capriciously" (cf. Num 22:29; Exod 10:2; 1 Sam 6:6; Judg 19:25). Some of the modern versions have "govern as fancy takes them" (NEB); "govern as the whim takes them" (REB); "the fickle shall govern them" (NAB).

**3:5 Young people will insult their elders.** "Young people" translates Heb. na'ar, the same word translated "boys" in the preceding verse. This behavior is totally alien to the teaching of Scripture, which links fear of God (Lev 19:32) with respect for old age.

**3:8 refuse to obey him.** Their rebellion against God was deliberate, not out of ignorance.

**3:9 brought destruction.** The Heb. word ra'ah, translated "destruction," means "evil," whether moral or natural. The moral evil of the people brought natural evil (destruction) upon them.

**3:10-11** The difficulties encountered in translating some of this passage may reflect its archaic nature, according to Holladay (1968).

**3:10 rich reward they have earned!** This accords with the law of the harvest: "as one sows so shall one reap."

**3:12 women rule over them.** Throughout the world of the Bible, male leadership was the norm; women rulers usually represented an abnormal and even dangerous situation.

**3:13 in court . . . presents his case.** Elements of a lawsuit in Isaiah and elsewhere in the OT have been noted by several scholars, such as Marshall (1962) and Huffmon (1959).

**3:16 Beautiful Zion.** As the NLT margin indicates, the Heb. is lit. "daughters of Zion," which here designates the women of the city.

**dainty steps.** The Heb. tapop [TH2952, ZH3262] may be related to tap [TH2945, ZH3251] (child) and refer to short childlike steps. It could also be onomatopoetic, like the English "tap."

**3:17 *make beautiful Zion bald.*** This translates a phrase that includes the words translated in the KJV as "discover their secret parts." The meaning of the Heb. *poth* [TH6596, ZH7327] is uncertain but is usually understood in the light of Akkadian *putu* (forehead, front). Some think it refers to exposure of the private parts (RSV, NRSV), but it probably refers to the shaven head, a worldwide sign of female humiliation. The versions have "make bare their foreheads" (REB); "lay their foreheads bare" (NJB); "bare their heads" (NAB). In any case, the women are disgraced.

**3:18-23** Full discussions of all this jewelry and finery worn by the women can be found in Compstonk (1926/27) and Platt (1979).

**3:24 *instead.*** This word is repeated for effect in the Heb. (*takhath* [TH8478A, ZH9393]) five times in this verse.

**4:1 *seven women will fight for each man.*** This reflects the great disproportion between male and female in a population decimated by war. Compare the desperation of the daughters of Lot, which caused them to act in such a shameful manner (Gen 19:32).

**4:2 *in that day.*** The meaning of this phrase is determined by context. Here it refers to the messianic age when the "Branch of the LORD will be beautiful and glorious."

***branch.*** Heb. *tsemakh* [TH6780, ZH7542]. Sometimes used as a messianic title (cf. Baldwin 1964). The NLT mg offers "Branch" (capitalized) in the messianic sense as a viable alternate rendering. The Targum substitutes "Messiah" here for "branch" (Levey 1974:24). See 11:1, where the term is parallel with the "shoot" from Jesse, and 53:2, where "shoot" is used of the Messiah.

**4:5 *Zion.*** In specific geographical terms, Zion was only a small (though important) part of Jerusalem; here, as frequently throughout the book, Isaiah uses "Zion" as a metaphor.

***cloud . . . smoke and flaming fire.*** This verse and the next use language that reflects the Exodus experience (Exod 13:21-22; 14:21-22; 40:34). Isaiah also refers to the Exodus elsewhere (11:15-16; 31:5; 51:10).

COMMENTARY

Chapter 2 opens with a description of the Lord's future reign. It is described as taking place in the "last days" (2:2) of the indeterminate future. Here it refers to the time when the "mountain of the LORD's house" (2:2) would become the center of worldwide attention for those who wanted to worship him, and for those who wanted to learn the Lord's ways and "walk in his paths" (2:3). The Lord's truth will go out from Jerusalem (2:3), "the LORD will mediate between nations," and all wars will stop (2:4) as God's people "walk in the light of the LORD!" (2:5). This opening paragraph moves from the old Jerusalem of the past to the glorious Zion of the future and from an era when the Canaanites worshiped their gods on the high places to a time when one holy mountain would dominate the scene.

Beginning with 2:6, the scene changes abruptly as the Lord condemns his people because "they have filled their land with practices from the East and with sorcerers." Jerusalem was "once the home of justice and righteousness" (1:21), but it had become full of pagan alliances and divination (2:6). Although his covenant people enjoyed a land of wealth and prosperity (2:7), they also bowed before idols and worshiped the work of their hands (2:8). The Lord could no longer ignore their sins and therefore had to humble them and bring them low (2:9).

Isaiah 2:10-18 gives a graphic description of coming judgment, as the people desperately attempt to escape, seeking refuge in the rocky caves from "the terror of the LORD and the glory of his majesty" (2:10). However, this was all wasted effort; judgment would fall on all, including the great trees of Lebanon and Bashan and the high mountains and hills (2:14). Great and small sailing vessels will be destroyed in this judgment from God (2:13-16). All human pride will be "brought down," and "only the LORD will be exalted on that day of judgment" (2:17; cf. 2:11). Even the idols in which they put their trust "will completely disappear" (2:18).

Isaiah 2:19-22 continues the graphic description of sinners fleeing the holy wrath of God as it is poured out upon the land. The misled and disillusioned people will then abandon their idols to the moles and bats as they "crawl away into caverns" and try to "hide among the jagged rocks in the cliffs" (2:21). This verse forms an inclusio with 2:10 (the two verses frame this passage); both verses describe the frantic attempt of the wicked, who try to escape "the terror of the LORD and the glory of his majesty." The concluding verse of this chapter warns against the humanism behind idolatry. Not only are the idols nothing, but the human sinners that made them are only "as frail as breath" (2:22) and of no help to anyone. Only the Holy One of Israel, the Almighty Creator of the universe, deserves worship.

Chapter 3 continues the description of judgment as the Lord cuts the people off from "everything they depend on" (3:1). The nation's leaders are especially singled out for removal, and in their place boys and toddlers (probably youth, but possibly childish or immature adults) will rule over them (3:4; cf. 3:12). Women as well as children are mentioned as oppressing the people. The negative reference to women (3:12) probably reflects the general fact that the women of that time normally ruled only if their husbands (the rulers) had been killed or died a natural death. This pathetic condition reflects the social disorder brought about by God's judgment.

The Lord is described in 3:13 as sitting in court as a great prosecuting attorney presenting his case against his people. The first to be condemned are the leaders (3:14), who were especially responsible for having ruined the Lord's vineyard. They had taken advantage of the poor and extorted gain from the unprotected. God's holy wrath was provoked, as reflected in the sharp words, "How dare you crush my people?" (3:15). God is again identified by the stacked titles "the Lord, the LORD of Heaven's Armies" (3:15).

Chapter 3 closes with a unique indictment against "Beautiful Zion," who pranced arrogantly about (3:16). Her dress and accessories further accentuate her gaudy appearance. They will disappear as the Lord substitutes ropes for sashes and sackcloth for rich robes. Their perfumed bodies will stink and their well-set hair will fall out. With their artificial finery gone, shame will replace beauty (3:24). Finally, the men and warriors will perish, leaving the women desolate in a society in which women were very dependent on men (3:25). The concluding verse describes the utterly defeated condition brought about by God's judgment through the Assyrians. The city is depicted as "a ravaged woman, huddled on the ground" (3:26). Chapter 4 begins with a concluding verse on the judgment described in chapter 3 and properly belongs to that passage.

Isaiah 4:2 initiates a shift in 4:2-6 to a description of a future time of restoration and relief. This is comparable to the similar shift from judgment to redemption between chapter 1 (and including 2:1) to 2:2-5. Israel (called here the "branch of the LORD") will become lush and beautiful, and the people will become "a holy people" (4:2-3). Jerusalem's filth and bloodstains will be washed away by the "hot breath of fiery judgment" (4:4).

Elsewhere, "branch of the LORD" is a messianic title indicating the royal and priestly roles of the Messiah (cf. the NLT footnotes at Jer 23:5 and 33:15 and the text at Zech 3:8; 6:12). The English versions disagree as to whether or not the reference here is messianic and should therefore be capitalized. The NIV has "Branch," and the NIV Study Bible has this note: "A messianic title related to the 'shoot' and 'branch' (11:1; 53:2) descended from David, but some believe that here 'branch' refers to Judah." Grogan (1986:44-45) gives a helpful summary of differing views on the issue.

In vivid imagery, Jerusalem is described as shaded by "a canopy of cloud during the day and smoke and flaming fire at night" (4:5) that will protect them from heat, storms, and rain. The allusions here are to the time of the Exodus, when Israel was guided through the desert by a pillar of cloud by day and a pillar of fire by night (Exod 13:20-22; 14:19-20). During that time in the wilderness, the fiery cloud covered the tabernacle like a protective shield (Num 9:15-18). During Isaiah's time, the people were still, in a sense, on their pilgrimage. Their final rest would be in the new Zion.

◆     ## 3. The vineyard and its fruits (5:1-30)

Now I will sing for the one I love
  a song about his vineyard:
My beloved had a vineyard
  on a rich and fertile hill.
2 He plowed the land, cleared its stones,
  and planted it with the best vines.
In the middle he built a watchtower
  and carved a winepress in the
    nearby rocks.
Then he waited for a harvest of sweet
    grapes,
but the grapes that grew were
    bitter.

3 Now, you people of Jerusalem and
    Judah,
you judge between me and my
    vineyard.
4 What more could I have done for
  my vineyard
that I have not already done?
When I expected sweet grapes,

why did my vineyard give me bitter
  grapes?

5 Now let me tell you
  what I will do to my vineyard:
I will tear down its hedges
  and let it be destroyed.
I will break down its walls
  and let the animals trample it.
6 I will make it a wild place
  where the vines are not pruned and
    the ground is not hoed,
a place overgrown with briers and
    thorns.
I will command the clouds
  to drop no rain on it.

7 The nation of Israel is the vineyard of
  the LORD of Heaven's Armies.
The people of Judah are his pleasant
    garden.
He expected a crop of justice,
  but instead he found oppression.

He expected to find righteousness,
    but instead he heard cries of
        violence.

⁸What sorrow for you who buy up
    house after house and field after
        field,
    until everyone is evicted and you
        live alone in the land.
⁹But I have heard the LORD of Heaven's
    Armies
    swear a solemn oath:
"Many houses will stand deserted;
    even beautiful mansions will be
        empty.
¹⁰Ten acres* of vineyard will not produce
    even six gallons* of wine.
    Ten baskets of seed will yield only
        one basket* of grain."

¹¹What sorrow for those who get up
    early in the morning
    looking for a drink of alcohol
and spend long evenings drinking
        wine
    to make themselves flaming drunk.
¹²They furnish wine and lovely music
    at their grand parties—
    lyre and harp, tambourine and
        flute—
but they never think about the LORD
    or notice what he is doing.

¹³So my people will go into exile far away
    because they do not know me.
    Those who are great and honored will
        starve,
    and the common people will die
        of thirst.
¹⁴The grave* is licking its lips in
        anticipation,
    opening its mouth wide.
    The great and the lowly
    and all the drunken mob will be
        swallowed up.
¹⁵Humanity will be destroyed, and
    people brought down;
    even the arrogant will lower their
        eyes in humiliation.
¹⁶But the LORD of Heaven's Armies will
    be exalted by his justice.

The holiness of God will be
    displayed by his righteousness.
¹⁷In that day lambs will find good
        pastures,
    and fattened sheep and young
        goats* will feed among the ruins.

¹⁸What sorrow for those who drag their
        sins behind them
    with ropes made of lies,
    who drag wickedness behind them
        like a cart!
¹⁹They even mock God and say,
    "Hurry up and do something!
    We want to see what you can do.
    Let the Holy One of Israel carry out
        his plan,
    for we want to know what it is."

²⁰What sorrow for those who say
    that evil is good and good is evil,
    that dark is light and light is dark,
    that bitter is sweet and sweet is
        bitter.
²¹What sorrow for those who are wise
    in their own eyes
    and think themselves so clever.
²²What sorrow for those who are heroes
    at drinking wine
    and boast about all the alcohol they
        can hold.
²³They take bribes to let the wicked
        go free,
    and they punish the innocent.

²⁴Therefore, just as fire licks up
        stubble
    and dry grass shrivels in the flame,
    so their roots will rot
    and their flowers wither.
    For they have rejected the law of the
        LORD of Heaven's Armies;
    they have despised the word of the
        Holy One of Israel.
²⁵That is why the LORD's anger burns
    against his people,
    and why he has raised his fist to
        crush them.
    The mountains tremble,
    and the corpses of his people litter
        the streets like garbage.

But even then the LORD's anger is not
    satisfied.
His fist is still poised to strike!

²⁶ He will send a signal to distant nations
    far away
and whistle to those at the ends of
    the earth.
They will come racing toward
    Jerusalem.
²⁷ They will not get tired or stumble.
    They will not stop for rest or sleep.
Not a belt will be loose,
    not a sandal strap broken.
²⁸ Their arrows will be sharp
    and their bows ready for battle.
Sparks will fly from their horses'
    hooves,

and the wheels of their chariots
    will spin like a whirlwind.
²⁹ They will roar like lions,
    like the strongest of lions.
Growling, they will pounce on their
    victims and carry them off,
and no one will be there to rescue
    them.
³⁰ They will roar over their victims on
    that day of destruction
like the roaring of the sea.
If someone looks across the
    land,
only darkness and distress will
    be seen;
even the light will be darkened
    by clouds.

5:10a Hebrew *A ten yoke,* that is, the area of land plowed by ten teams of oxen in one day.   5:10b Hebrew *a bath* [21 liters].   5:10c Hebrew *A homer* [5 bushels or 182 liters] *of seed will yield only an ephah* [20 quarts or 22 liters].   5:14 Hebrew *Sheol.*   5:17 As in Greek version; Hebrew reads *and strangers.*

## NOTES

**5:1** *I will sing for the one I love.* The language here is similar to that found in the Song of Songs (cf. Song 6:3; 8:11, 12).

**5:2** *watchtower.* migdal [TH4026, ZH4463]) refers to something more substantial than the "shelter" (*sukkah* [TH5521, ZH6109]) of 1:8.

*carved a winepress.* This refers to a container cut out of rock to catch grape juice flowing from a winepress. For helpful information on the cultural background of this passage and for the terminology of viticulture, see Walsh (1998).

*bitter.* This translates a Heb. word derived from the verb "to stink."

**5:6** *briers and thorns.* The same pair of Heb. terms is used again in 7:23-25; 9:18; 10:17; 27:4; 32:13. This alliterated pair (*shamir* [TH8068, ZH9031] and *shayith* [TH7898, ZH8885]) is found only in Isaiah.

**5:7** *vineyard.* For additional examples of Israel being referred to as a vineyard, see 3:14; Ps 80:8-18; Jer 2:21; 12:10; Ezek 15:6-8; Hos 10:1.

*justice . . . oppression . . . righteousness . . . violence.* In the Heb., there is a wordplay involving the similar sounding words for "justice" (*mishpat* [TH4941, ZH5477]) and "oppression" (*mispakh* [TH4939, ZH5384]), and for "righteousness" (*tsedaqah* [TH6666, ZH7407]) and "violence" (*tse'aqah* [TH6818, ZH7591]).

**5:8** *What sorrow.* Heb. *hoy,* a word traditionally translated "woe" (cf. 5:11, 14, 18, 20, 21, 22). These verses pinpoint in concise but vivid language the various features of a corrupt society. For the use of this term in other prophets, see Clifford (1966) and Williams (1967).

**5:10** *Ten acres . . . six gallons . . . one basket.* These expressions attempt to give modern equivalents to the Heb. measures. The NLT footnote gives the Heb. terminology. Ten acres of vineyard should normally produce several thousands of gallons of wine. The condemned land was able to produce only a miniscule fraction of what it should have yielded.

**5:12 *wine and lovely music.*** For the combination of these at feasts, see Amos 6:5-6.

**5:14 *The grave.*** Heb. *she'ol* [TH7585, ZH8619], a term that refers to the place of the dead, which means it can refer to the "grave" (in this world) where the dead are last placed, or the "realm of the dead" (in the next world) where they live on. The city with all its pomp descended into Sheol (cf. Ps 9:17; Prov 27:20).

***licking its lips in anticipation.*** More lit., "Sheol makes large her soul," or as the KJV has it, "hell hath enlarged herself." The Heb. *nepesh* [TH5315, ZH5883] is the word for "soul" but also has a broad semantic range, as we have learned from Ugaritic usage. It means "soul, breath" but also the throat, the place from which the breath emanates, and sometimes it signifies "appetite." The NLT captures the basic idea in this context. Other versions have "Sheol has enlarged its throat" (NASB), "the grave enlarges its appetite" (NIV), and, "the world of the dead is hungry for them" (TEV).

**5:17 *young goats.*** This reading follows the LXX instead of the Heb. "strangers," as the NLT margin explains. Modern translations differ in how they handle the Heb. of this verse.

**5:19 *Hurry. . . . We want to see.*** The Heb. here is the same as for Maher and Hash in the name Maher-Shalal-Hash-Baz. It is possible that when Isaiah named his son (8:3), he was responding to this language of mockery used by the sarcastic sinners of Judah.

**5:20 *say that evil is good and good is evil.*** Sin causes moral confusion—the inability to discern good from evil. Rejecting God's standards leads to dependence on personal standards, which merely reflect the sinner's values. Note the switching of labels and the word games in modern culture concerning such moral issues as fornication, adultery, and homosexuality, and even with such life-and-death issues as abortion, infanticide, and euthanasia.

**5:24 *fire licks up stubble and dry grass.*** The Heb. multiplies the sibilants here: *qash leshon 'esh wakhashash.* This may be intended to reflect crackling sparks and sputtering flames, something we would expect from Isaiah.

**5:25 *his fist.*** This is found twice in this verse. The Heb. lit. says, "his hand is stretched out against." This language is used again in 9:12, 17, 21; 10:4.

***The mountains tremble.*** When God manifests himself, even the mountains tremble at his presence (cf. 64:3; Jer 4:24-26).

**5:26 *send a signal.*** Lit., "lift up a banner," a practice used as a signal for gathering troops (13:2) or summoning nations (11:10, 12; 49:22; 62:10). Assyria and Babylon both invaded Judah; they were instruments of God's judgment on the rebellious people.

***far away . . . those at the ends of the earth.*** Here the reference is probably to Assyria and Babylon. Both invaded Israel and Judah and took many of the people captive.

## COMMENTARY

This chapter contains the famous "Song about the LORD'S Vineyard," in which a vineyard disappoints its owner. This vivid song contains the parable itself (5:1-6), its interpretation (5:7), and a concluding application (5:8-30). The application contains several "sorrows" that address the bad fruit of the vineyard, the specific sins of the wayward people. The imagery used here is anticipated by 3:14, where the vineyard is a metaphor for Judah. The first seven verses of chapter 5 are preparatory to the remainder of the chapter, which identifies the worthless grapes.

Although the owner had carefully prepared the soil and faithfully tended the vineyard, it produced only bitter grapes (5:2). The people of Judah and Jerusalem were called to witness and judge this situation (5:3). In view of all that he had invested in the vineyard, the disappointed owner now declared a judgment of destruction on it (5:4-6). The identity of the owner is unknown until the statement, "I will command the clouds to drop no rain on it" (5:6), and 5:7 makes it clear that this passage refers to the Lord and his people. The judgment removed God's protection from the vineyard and withheld rain from it (5:6). The Lord of the vineyard had expected his people to produce a crop of justice and righteousness, but instead they had produced only oppression and violence (5:7). God's standards for social justice are repeatedly raised in the book of Isaiah, and the covenant people's disregard and violation of them are repeatedly condemned. For a study of the influence of this passage on the parable of the tenants in the NT (Mark 12:1-12; Matt 21:33-46), see the study by Weren (1998), who traces the patterns and connections between them.

The rest of the chapter pertains to Judah's guilt and judgment as it describes the vineyard's bitter fruit. The features of the corrupt society are noted in concise and vivid language. Destruction is declared against the greedy (5:8-10) and self-indulgent who give no thought to the Lord (5:11-13), the arrogant and haughty (5:14-17), those who mock and taunt the Holy One of Israel (5:18-19), those who pervert language to their own advantage (5:20), the self-deceived (5:21), those who abuse alcohol, and those who promote injustice (5:22-23). This catalog describes the social, moral, and spiritual sinfulness of the people. Blinded by their many sins, the people of Judah were spiraling downward, oblivious to the judgment awaiting them. In their mockery, they used Isaiah's special name for God, "The Holy One of Israel" (5:19). They also played word games, just as people today pervert language when they switch the labels on what is good and what is bad (5:20). The Holy One of Israel is the one who decides right and wrong, not blind and rebellious sinners.

The remainder of the chapter vividly describes the judgment God would pour out on his people as he gave expression to his holy wrath against sin. They would be consumed like straw, and their roots and flowers would wither away because they had rejected the "law of the LORD of Heaven's Armies" and had "despised the word of the Holy One of Israel" (5:24). The Lord's "fist" is mentioned twice; it is poised to strike and crush them, leaving "the corpses of his people [to] litter the streets like garbage" (5:25). When God summons the waiting and poised enemy to race in for the kill (5:26-27), the enemies "will roar like lions" and eagerly "pounce on their victims" (5:29). The defeated people will have no one to help them, and they will be carried off into captivity (5:29). Darkness and sorrow descend as the clouds blot out the light. God's earlier presence among his people was as a cloud of protection by day and a fiery cloud of light by night (cf. Exod 13:21-22; 14:21-22), but now his presence will be in the cloud of judgment that blots out the light.

◆     ## 4. Isaiah's commission (6:1-13)

It was in the year King Uzziah died* that I saw the Lord. He was sitting on a lofty throne, and the train of his robe filled the Temple. ²Attending him were mighty seraphim, each having six wings. With two wings they covered their faces, with two they covered their feet, and with two they flew. ³They were calling out to each other,

"Holy, holy, holy is the LORD of
    Heaven's Armies!
The whole earth is filled with
    his glory!"

⁴Their voices shook the Temple to its foundations, and the entire building was filled with smoke. ⁵Then I said, "It's all over! I am doomed, for I am a sinful man. I have filthy lips, and I live among a people with filthy lips. Yet I have seen the King, the LORD of Heaven's Armies."

⁶Then one of the seraphim flew to me with a burning coal he had taken from the altar with a pair of tongs. ⁷He touched my lips with it and said, "See, this coal has touched your lips. Now your guilt is removed, and your sins are forgiven."

⁸Then I heard the Lord asking, "Whom should I send as a messenger to this people? Who will go for us?"

I said, "Here I am. Send me."

⁹And he said, "Yes, go, and say to this people,

'Listen carefully, but do not
    understand.
Watch closely, but learn nothing.'
¹⁰Harden the hearts of these people.
    Plug their ears and shut their eyes.
That way, they will not see with their
    eyes,
nor hear with their ears,
nor understand with their hearts
    and turn to me for healing.'"*

¹¹Then I said, "Lord, how long will this go on?"

And he replied,

"Until their towns are empty,
    their houses are deserted,
    and the whole country is a
        wasteland;
¹²until the LORD has sent everyone away,
    and the entire land of Israel lies
        deserted.
¹³If even a tenth—a remnant—survive,
    it will be invaded again and burned.
But as a terebinth or oak tree leaves
    a stump when it is cut down,
    so Israel's stump will be a holy seed."

6:1 King Uzziah died in 740 BC.   6:9-10 Greek version reads *And he said, "Go and say to this people, / 'When you hear what I say, you will not understand. / When you see what I do, you will not comprehend.' / For the hearts of these people are hardened, / and their ears cannot hear, and they have closed their eyes— / so their eyes cannot see, / and their ears cannot hear, / and their hearts cannot understand, / and they cannot turn to me and let me heal them."* Compare Matt 13:14-15; Mark 4:12; Luke 8:10; Acts 28:26-27.

NOTES

**6:1** *the year King Uzziah died.* After a long reign of fifty-two years, the king died in 740 BC.

*sitting on a lofty throne.* More lit., the Heb. has "sitting on a throne, high and exalted." "High" (*ram*) and "exalted" (*nissa'*) are the same two Heb. words used of God in 57:15 and of the suffering servant in 52:13.

*train of his robe.* Like the "Son of Man" in Rev 1:13, he was wearing a long flowing garment. In the ancient Near East, such dress was worn by dignitaries and royalty.

**6:2** *seraphim.* This is the plural of "seraph," a Heb. term meaning "burning" or "glowing" that probably corresponds to the "living beings" of Rev 4:6-9 that also had six wings. Miscall (1993:34) suggests some wordplay here (not at all unusual for Isaiah) and notes that "seraph" (*sarap* [TH8314, ZH8597]) is very similar to another Heb. root, *tsarap* [TH6884, ZH7671], meaning "purge" in 1:25. He also notes the use of *sarap* [TH8313, ZH8596] in 1:7, as well as the use of both roots in 6:6. Although the seraphim are not mentioned elsewhere, see the description of the cherubim in Ezek 1:1-28; 10:1-22; Rev 4:8.

**6:3** *Holy, holy, holy.* The Heb. triple usage is for emphasis (cf. the triple use of the Heb. for "Temple of the Lord" in Jer 7:4, where the NLT translates the Heb. as "repeated"). This is the only place a threefold use of a single word is found in the Heb. Bible (cf. its echo in Rev 4:8). However, even a twofold use of a word can express a superlative or indicate totality (the DSS copy of Isaiah, 1QIsaª, only has the word twice).

**6:4** *shook . . . smoke.* The scene at Mount Sinai has several parallels, such as smoke (Exod 20:18), trembling of the ground (Exod 19:18), and loud sounds (Exod 19:18-19). The Heb. word for "shake" (*nua'* [TH5128, ZH5675]) is used in the next chapter (7:2) for the shaking of the heart of king Ahaz.

**6:5** *filthy lips.* The Heb. says "man of unclean lips," which implies a man with a sinful heart (cf. Mark 7:20-23). For some ancient Near Eastern background on this, see Hurowitz (1989).

**6:6** *burning coal he had taken from the altar.* Coals of fire were taken inside the Most Holy Place on the Day of Atonement, when sacrifice was made to atone for sin (Lev 16:12).

**6:7** *touched my lips.* Similar language is used in the commissioning of Jeremiah (Jer 1:9).

**6:8** *for us.* This plural pronoun refers to the triune Godhead or to the divine council. The form is the regular Heb. plural, which has been understood in various ways. Sometimes it is called a plural of majesty.

**6:9-10** This OT passage is frequently quoted in the NT. It is quoted by Jesus in Matt 13:14-15; Mark 4:12; Luke 8:10; by John in John 12:40; and by Paul in Acts 28:26-27. Paul alludes to Isa 6:9-10 in Rom 11:7-10, 25. Israel's deafness and blindness are also mentioned in 29:9; 42:18; 43:8.

**6:9** *this people.* Note this distinction; they are no longer "my people" (cf. 3:12; 5:13) or "his people" (5:25).

*Listen carefully.* The Heb. imperatives mean "Listen carefully" (*shim'u* [TH8085, ZH9048]) but "do not understand," and "watch closely" (*re'u* [TH7200, ZH8011]) but "learn nothing." Both are followed by infinitive absolutes that usually indicate continuous action in this position (when they follow their cognate finite verbal forms). The negatives "not understand" and "learn nothing" are qal imperfects with imperative force, as the prohibitive particle *'al* [TH408, ZH440] indicates. Apparently, the verbs are meant to convey sarcasm and underscore the total refusal of the people to listen to the prophet's message. The entire subject of obduracy is complex and variously understood, but see Chi (1974) and Chisholm (1996). Modern English versions use a variety of translations to render the meaning of the Heb. syntax: "Be ever hearing, but never understanding" (NIV); "Keep listening, but do not comprehend" (NRSV); "However hard you listen, you will never understand" (REB); "Listen carefully, but you shall not understand!" (NAB); "Listen and listen, but never understand!" (NJB); "Hear, indeed, but do not understand" (NJPS).

**6:10** This verse contains a literary feature known as a chiasm, a common literary device in the OT. It consists of an abc/cba inversion of terms: hearts . . . ears . . . eyes/eyes . . . ears . . . hearts.

*Harden the hearts of these people.* The Heb. lit. says, "Make the heart of this people fat," which means to make them obtuse and unresponsive. Other versions have "render the hearts of this people insensitive" (NASB), "make the heart of this people calloused" (NIV), "make the mind of this people dull" (NRSV, TEV), "make these people close-minded" (GW), and "make the minds of these people dumb" (NCV).

*Plug their ears.* The Heb. lit. says, "Make their ears heavy" and should be understood in a sense parallel to the "fat" hearts of the previous line. Other versions render "their ears dull" (NASB, NIV) and "stop their ears" (NRSV).

**6:12 sent . . . away.** The Heb. *rakhaq* [TH7368, ZH8178] means "be far away." For this usage in contrast to "near," see 13:5-6; 33:13; 57:19.

*deserted.* The Heb. *'azab* [TH5800, ZH6440] is one of a number of verbs meaning "abandon, reject, despise." If the people reject and abandon the Lord (in favor of evil and idols), he will do the same to Israel.

**6:13 stump.** Heb. *matsebeth* [TH4678, ZH5169] (cf. HALOT 1:621); a rare word found twice in this verse and nowhere else in Isaiah. This is an important figure, used also in 11:1. Here it signifies the remnant of Israel.

COMMENTARY

In chapters 6 and following, unlike the earlier chapters (1-5), the prophet speaks of kings and of the great hopes that the people had in them and in their promises. Isaiah does not present a positive or hopeful picture of human kings and their rule. This section opens with the death of yet one more human king, after which the prophet sees the Lord of Heaven's Armies enthroned (cf. 33:22; 41:21).

Chapter 6 appropriately takes a central position within chapters 1-12, for it relates both to what precedes and what follows it. Chapters 1-5 are general in character, treating matters of judgment and salvation in broad strokes without linking them to specific historical events, but chapters 7-12 reveal just how the Lord's judgment will be poured out on God's people in specific events. For example, the hardening predicted in 6:10 is reflected in Ahaz's response to Isaiah in chapter 7. Isaiah's encounter with the Holy One of Israel had great influence on the prophet and his message. This experience of the prophet, in which he was both cleansed and called, probably refers to his commissioning at the time when King Uzziah died. However, the words "call" and "commission" are not found in the text. Concerning the view that chapters 1-5 were preached before the experience recorded in chapter 6 (the year Uzziah died), it should be noted that Isaiah's ministry is said to have included the time of Uzziah's reign (1:1), a view supported by Milgrom (1964).

**The Scene in Heaven.** The awesome opening scene depicts the Holy Lord of Heaven's Armies, seated on a lofty throne surrounded by seraphim that praise and worship him (6:1-4). The overall impression conveyed by this vision is the glory and majesty of the exalted Lord. The throne emphasizes God as the sovereign ruler that deserves worship. In 6:1, 8, and 11, God is called *'adonay* [TH136, ZH151], "Ruler" or "Lord" (lit., "my lords"). Niehaus (1995:251) has noted several parallels between this theophany and the one at Sinai. The angels chant praise to the Lord, whose glory (6:3; cf. Exod 24:16; 1 Kgs 8:11) fills the whole earth. The Temple was filled with a cloud of smoke (6:4, cf. Exod 40:34-35; 1 Kgs 8:10) and the "shaking" phenomenon occurred (6:4). This language also resembles Amos 9:1, where Amos sees the Lord standing in judgment above the altar at Samaria, commanding him to strike the tops of the pillars so that a shaking results. This is appropriate language for this theophany because "all of God's judgment intrusions into history foreshadow his eschatological return, when he will remove 'what can be shaken— that is, created things—so that what cannot be shaken may remain' " (Niehaus 1995:251; cf. Heb 12:27). For the long flowing robe, note the similar language used of the clothing of the "Son of Man" in Revelation 1:13. Kings and other important officials customarily wore long robes as a sign of their authority.

The creatures surrounding the throne are briefly described as each having six wings: "with two wings they covered their faces, with two they covered their feet, with two they flew" (6:2). They joined in singing praise to the threefold Holy One whose glory fills the earth. The seraphim around the throne are not mentioned elsewhere in the Old Testament, although they bear some resemblance to the cherubim Ezekiel saw in his vision (Ezek 1:1-28; 10:1-22; cf. Rev 4:8). The traditional interpretation of the seraphim relates them to the Hebrew word for "burning," so some think these creatures are so-called because they burn with the love of God. Other interpretations suggest that their swiftness is like a rapidly spreading fire, or that they glow brightly like a blazing fire. Joines (1967) and others also note that the Hebrew can apparently be used of a "darting, venomous (or burning) serpent" in 14:29 and 30:6 (cf. also Num 21:6). Wildberger (1991:264) compares the Hebrew word with the Egyptian word *sfr* (fabulous winged creature) and the later Egyptian (Demotic) *serref* (griffin). The closest help for identifying Isaiah's description may come from Tell Halaf with the discovery of the depiction of a guardian angel that has three pairs of wings, but otherwise the body of a human being (ANEP #655). The seraphim probably represent celestial beings, and in this context are perhaps related in some way to God's holiness.

Even these angelic creatures dare not look at the thrice-holy Lord, so they use two of their six wings to cover their faces. Motyer (1993:76) comments, "their task was to receive what the Lord would say, not to pry into what he is like" (cf. Deut 29:29). If that is true for such heavenly beings, it applies all the more to humans (cf. Exod 33:20; Judg 13:22).

**Isaiah's Call.** In response to such an overwhelming vision of "the LORD of Heaven's Armies" (6:3), Isaiah confessed, "It's all over! I am doomed, for I am a sinful man." He said that he had filthy lips and was living among a people with filthy lips (6:5). The word "doomed" may reflect the earlier event at Mount Sinai, when people were warned to keep their distance from that awesome revelation of God on pain of death (Exod 19:21; cf. Exod 33:20). Perhaps Isaiah specifically mentioned his lips and the lips of the people among whom he lived because they were not using their gift of speech as the seraphs did to exalt and praise "the King, the LORD of Heaven's Armies" (6:5). The purification of Isaiah's lips represents the cleansing of his inner person. In commenting on another passage from Isaiah (Isa 29:13), Jesus said, "These people honor me with their lips, but their hearts are far from me" (Matt 15:8).

One of the seraphim took a burning coal from the altar and touched Isaiah's lips with it, removing his guilt and sins (6:6-7). In a number of places, the Old

Testament speaks of the purifying and cleansing effects of fire, so this may be another possible explanation for the presence of the "burning" seraphim in this passage. Perhaps "lips" are mentioned in 6:7 because Isaiah was to become a mouthpiece for the Lord. The Lord, the Almighty Triune One, requested a messenger who was willing to go ("for us") to his people. Isaiah made a positive response to this invitation.

Isaiah was, therefore, in a position to hear and respond to the voice of the Lord when he spoke for the first time in 6:8. Isaiah lit. hears the voice of "my lords" speaking from the throne of the threefold holy one (this name of God occurs three times in this chapter—6:1, 8, 11).

Isaiah's assigned message was to be one of judgment, described more in terms of effect than of content (6:9-13). Webb (1996:61) observes that "sentence has been passed on the nation in heaven; Isaiah's preaching will put it into effect on the earth." Isaiah is warned (6:9-10) that the rebellious people will continue their resistance, resulting in ever-increasing spiritual obtuseness, and finally in the inability to respond or even to understand. This limitation would be part of God's judgment against them. Since they had chosen indifference and rebellion, they would now experience the inevitable judgment due to them. The prophet's preaching was intended to bring about a negative response. McLaughlin (1994) studies this motif in other passages (29:9-10; 44:18; 63:17), including what he calls its reversal in some passages (32:3-4a; 42:6-7); he concludes that the motif has to do with the Lord's hardening the hearts of his covenant people, more than the hearts of Pharaoh and other non-Israelites.

Jesus quoted this passage in the parable of the sower (Matt 13:14-15; Mark 4:12; Luke 8:10) and John reported the people's failure to respond (John 12:38-41). Paul also quoted from this passage on more than one occasion (Act 28:27; Rom 11:8) to rest blame on obdurate hearers (Acts 28:6-27; cf. Rom 11:7-10, 25; cf. Chi 1974). Evans (1989:137-145, 148-162) helpfully summarizes the later treatments of the subject by the rabbis and church fathers and summarizes obduracy in Isaiah as "a condition, brought on variously by arrogance, immorality, idolatry, injustice, and false prophecy, that renders God's people incapable of discerning God's will. . . . It is also understood to be a condition that God brings about himself, as part of his judgment upon his wayward people" (Evans 1989:46). The subject of "obduracy" in Scripture is not easy to grasp and B. S. Childs, in an excursus on the hardening of Pharaoh, concludes with the understatement that "efforts to illuminate the concept of hardness . . . have been less than satisfactory" (1974:170). Calvin, in his commentary on Isaiah, wrote of Isaiah 6:10:

> True, this prediction was not the cause of their unbelief, but the Lord
> foretold it, because he foresaw that they would be such as they are here
> described. . . . If you inquire into the first cause, we must come to the pre-
> destination of God. But as that purpose is hidden from us, we must not too
> eagerly search into it; for the everlasting scheme of the divine purpose is
> beyond our reach.

By means of an effective chiastic (abc/cba) arrangement (hearts, ears, eyes/eyes, ears, hearts), the Lord revealed how he would "harden the hearts" of the people, "plug their ears," and "shut their eyes" (6:10-11). Just as the Lord hardened Pharaoh's heart when he refused to listen to God's message spoken through Moses (Exod 4:21; 7:14), so the Israelites would eventually find themselves unable to repent. Israel's blind and deaf condition is mentioned several more times in the book (29:9; 42:18; 43:8). Any response to the true message from God is ultimately one of acceptance or rejection, and those who persist in rejection harden their hearts more and more. God allowed this to happen as part of his judgment on them (Hollenbach 1983).

When asked, "How long will this go on?" (6:11), the Lord replied that it would go on until their empty towns had been overrun by the invaders, the people had been forced out of their homes, and their unproductive fields had been trampled underfoot. Isaiah was to continue preaching this message until the people had been carried off captive into a foreign land, far removed from their beloved homeland. The prophet himself had predicted this in 1:7-8, as had Moses earlier (Lev 26; Deut 28).

However, this chapter closes with the good news that from a remaining "stump," "a holy seed" would grow again (6:13). The "holy seed" refers to the few that were faithful in Israel (1 Kgs 19:18), the remnant that would survive God's judgment (4:3; 10:20-23; 11:11, 16; 46:3). Later in the book (11:1), this small remnant group is again compared to a mere stump and in 53:2 the same imagery is used in a messianic sense. This remnant consisted of a tenth of the people, who were perhaps called "holy" because the tithe (tenth) was considered holy to the Lord. The small remnant, the stock or stump, was probably what Paul had in view in Romans 11:5.

This chapter not only gives us an awesome view of God but also a picture of his servant Isaiah, who had a profound experience of God's grace and was willing to be sent and spent in the service of the Holy One of Israel (6:8).

◆    ## B. The Sign of Immanuel (7:1-12:6)
### 1. Immanuel's birth (7:1-17)

When Ahaz, son of Jotham and grandson of Uzziah, was king of Judah, King Rezin of Syria* and Pekah son of Remaliah, the king of Israel, set out to attack Jerusalem. However, they were unable to carry out their plan.

²The news had come to the royal court of Judah: "Syria is allied with Israel* against us!" So the hearts of the king and his people trembled with fear, like trees shaking in a storm.

³Then the LORD said to Isaiah, "Take your son Shear-jashub* and go out to meet King Ahaz. You will find him at the end of the aqueduct that feeds water into the upper pool, near the road leading to the field where cloth is washed.* ⁴Tell him to stop worrying. Tell him he doesn't need to fear the fierce anger of those two burned-out embers, King Rezin of Syria and Pekah son of Remaliah. ⁵Yes, the kings of Syria and Israel are plotting against him, saying, ⁶'We will attack Judah and capture it for ourselves. Then we will install the son of Tabeel as Judah's king.' ⁷But this is what the Sovereign LORD says:

"This invasion will never happen;
it will never take place;
⁸for Syria is no stronger than its
capital, Damascus,
and Damascus is no stronger than
its king, Rezin.
As for Israel, within sixty-five years
it will be crushed and completely
destroyed.
⁹Israel is no stronger than its capital,
Samaria,
and Samaria is no stronger than its
king, Pekah son of Remaliah.
Unless your faith is firm,
I cannot make you stand firm."

¹⁰Later, the LORD sent this message to King Ahaz: ¹¹"Ask the LORD your God for a sign of confirmation, Ahaz. Make it as difficult as you want—as high as heaven or as deep as the place of the dead.*"

¹²But the king refused. "No," he said, "I will not test the LORD like that."

¹³Then Isaiah said, "Listen well, you royal family of David! Isn't it enough to exhaust human patience? Must you exhaust the patience of my God as well? ¹⁴All right then, the Lord himself will give you the sign. Look! The virgin* will conceive a child! She will give birth to a son and will call him Immanuel (which means 'God is with us'). ¹⁵By the time this child is old enough to choose what is right and reject what is wrong, he will be eating yogurt* and honey. ¹⁶For before the child is that old, the lands of the two kings you fear so much will both be deserted.

¹⁷"Then the LORD will bring things on you, your nation, and your family unlike anything since Israel broke away from Judah. He will bring the king of Assyria upon you!"

7:1 Hebrew *Aram;* also in 7:2, 4, 5, 8.   7:2 Hebrew *Ephraim,* referring to the northern kingdom of Israel; also in 7:5, 8, 9, 17.   7:3a *Shear-jashub* means "A remnant will return."   7:3b Or *bleached.*   7:11 Hebrew *as deep as Sheol.*   7:14 Or *young woman.*   7:15 Or *curds;* also in 7:22.

# NOTES

**7:2 *royal court of Judah.*** Lit., "house of David." This is a reference to Ahaz, who belonged to David's dynasty (cf. 2 Sam 7:8-11).

***Israel.*** As the NLT margin indicates, the Heb. is "Ephraim," used for the northern kingdom of Israel. The same is true in 7:5, 8, 9, 17.

***shaking.*** The Heb. is *nua'* [TH5128, ZH5675]. The same word is used in 6:4, where the heavenly voices shook the foundations of the Temple.

**7:3 *Shear-jashub.*** As the NLT margin indicates, the name means "a remnant will return." Isaiah gave each of his sons symbolic names.

***aqueduct that feeds water into the upper pool.*** The exact location of this site is uncertain but it is probably at a junction where the watercourse connects with the pool. It is possible that Ahaz was out checking the city's water supply at the time.

***field where cloth is washed.*** Clothes were cleaned and bleached at that time by trampling on them in a solution of soap or bleach (cf. Mal 3:2; Mark 9:3).

**7:4 *burned-out embers.*** Variously translated as "stubs of smoldering firebrands" (NASB), "smoldering stumps of firebrands" (NRSV), and "smoldering stubs of firewood" (NIV). This refers to Damascus, capital of Aram, and to the northern kingdom of Israel. Both were crushed by the Assyrians.

**7:6 *son of Tabeel.*** This Aramaic name is probably from the Aramean region known as "land of Tob," east of the Jordan River (cf. Judg 11:3). The name could mean "God is good" (cf. the name Tabrimmon, which means "Rimmon is good" in 1 Kgs 15:18).

**7:8 *within sixty-five years.*** The Assyrian king Esarhaddon, and shortly after him, Ashurbanipal, had settled foreigners in Israel by 670 BC. The intermarriage of these with the local inhabitants resulted in the group later called Samaritans (cf. 2 Kgs 17:24-34).

**7:9 Unless your faith is firm, I cannot make you stand firm.** The end of this verse contains a wordplay in the Heb. that could be translated, "If you do not stand firm (*'aman* [TH539, ZH586]) in your faith, you will not stand (*'aman*) at all." The versions have tried in various ways to translate this: "have firm faith or you will fail to stand firm" (REB); "if your faith is not enduring, you will not endure" (TEV); "if you don't remain faithful, you won't remain standing" (GW).

**7:11 sign.** The Heb. *'ot* [TH226, ZH253] is often used of a miraculous sign. Here the sign is described as without limits: **as high as heaven or as deep as the place of the dead [Sheol]**.

**7:14 virgin.** This translates the much discussed Heb. term, *'almah* [TH5959, ZH6625]. As the NLT mg indicates, the Heb. word could also be understood as "young woman." The more specific term in Heb. for "virgin" is *bethulah* [TH1330, ZH1435], which is used to express the concept of virginity in Deut 22:14-20. This Isaiah reference is not to a virgin birth in its immediate historical setting, as the entire context makes clear. There has only been one virgin birth in history. On the other hand, no one can prove that the Heb. *'almah* cannot mean "virgin." By avoiding the technical term for "virgin," Isaiah provided a term useful for the immediate context and also one that Matthew could use as a reference to the virgin birth of Jesus. Perhaps the closest English term to match *'almah* is "young maiden," which could refer to a virgin but not demand that meaning. I agree with Oswalt (1986:210) who observes, "But if Isaiah wanted to stress the virginity of the mother here, why did he not use *bethulah*, which has no implication beyond virginity, whereas *'almah* does. The conclusion to which we are driven is that while the prophet did not want to stress the virginity, neither did he want to leave it aside as he could have done by using *'ishah* [TH802, ZH851] or some other term for 'woman.'"

The range of possible meanings for *'almah* has been a challenge for translators faced with the choice of the right word to represent it accurately. The long-lasting and highly influential Latin translation (Vulgate) translates this word as *virgo* (virgin) only here and in Gen 24:43; in all its other occurrences, it is translated with Latin words meaning "girl" or "youth" (the Latin does regularly use *virgo* for the Heb. *bethulah*). The LXX translates *'almah* as *parthenos*, which always means "virgin." Also following the LXX, Matthew has *parthenos* [TG3933, ZG4221] (Matt 1:23).

The rendering of the KJV's "virgin" is repeated in the NKJV, NIV, NASB, ESV, and NAB. The ASV (1901) added to its margin the possible translation "maiden." In 1952, the RSV reversed that decision and put "virgin" in the margin and "young woman" in the text. Most modern versions, facing a hard choice, have used "young woman" (RSV, NRSV, NEB, REB, NJB, TEV, NJPS), usually with a footnote. TLB used "virgin" in the text accompanied by a long footnote. The NCV has "maiden" in the text, and the TEV has "young woman"; both add footnotes. The CEV uses "virgin" in the text. All of this reflects the frustration of interpreters and translators in dealing with this word in this context.

**Immanuel.** The name is found again in 8:8, and in 8:10 it is translated "God is with us." Some think it is an alternate name for Maher-shalal-hash-baz (8:3). The name is ultimately realized in Jesus, who as the incarnate Son of God was "God with us."

**7:15 yogurt and honey.** The precise meaning of the Heb. word translated "yogurt" is uncertain (cf. NLT mg), but it surely is a dairy product. These two items probably represent the simple diet of peasants living off the land. Normal farming would have been devastated by the Assyrian invasion.

## COMMENTARY

The setting here is in the time of King Ahaz of Judah (in his first or second year), King Rezin of Aram, and King Pekah of Israel (7:1). During this time, Jerusalem withstood an attack led by the kings Rezin and Pekah, who were in alliance against

Judah. The background (cf. 2 Kgs 16; 2 Chr 28) of that ominous event is described in the following verses.

One day King Ahaz was in the area of the "upper pool," probably evaluating the city's water supply in case of a prolonged siege (7:3). Isaiah and his son Shear-jashub were sent to encourage the king. The name Shear-jashub (meaning "a remnant will return") can be understood as a threat that God's judgment would fall on the people leaving only a remnant, or as a promise that by God's grace there would be a surviving remnant. This name provided a good summary and reminder of Isaiah's two-pronged message. Ridderbos (1985:83) suggests that the name is also appropriate in this setting where Ahaz is "offered a choice between ruin and salvation."

In order to bolster the king's faith, the Lord promised to show him a sign (7:10-16), but Ahaz was not interested in any sign because he did not want to hear any message from God. His mind was already made up, and he would appeal to Assyria for help. He claimed that he did not want to test the Lord, but this was obviously only pretense. This attitude of the king was sharply denounced by Isaiah who spoke of "my God" instead of "your God," as he promised the king a sign whether he wanted it or not (7:13).

The virgin or young woman (see note on 7:14) is not identified, and speculation has included a variety of candidates, including Isaiah's wife, some unnamed girl known to Isaiah or Ahaz, or even any mother in general. Grogan (1986:62-63) lists ten basic issues that must be addressed and solved before a satisfactory understanding of this difficult passage can be achieved. He correctly observes that an adequate interpretation must do full justice to Isaiah's language in its context as well as to Matthew's application of the prophecy (Matt 1:23).

As a sign, the prophet predicted that a child would be born with the meaningful name Immanuel, lit., "God with us" (7:14). Before this child would be able to distinguish between right and wrong, the two enemies of Ahaz would be destroyed by Assyria (7:16). However, because Ahaz refused to trust God, Assyria would invade Judah and cause great damage (7:17). The name "Immanuel" was a rebuke to Ahaz because if God was indeed with them, why should they have feared the Assyrians? In Numbers 14:9, the expression "the LORD is with us" was meant to reduce Israel's fear of the Canaanites. Although the name as used in Isaiah was undoubtedly intended as a good word for the people, God can obviously "be with" people in various ways—positive or negative. This name, like that of Shear-jashub, is capable of bearing either good or bad news. Most, but not all, commentators agree that 7:14-16 is concerned with the same child, since there is no change of reference within these verses. Ridderbos (1985:85-86) is undoubtedly correct when he says, "there is much to be said for letting go of the directly messianic conception of the text and for understanding it in an indirect messianic sense. . . . Even though the final fulfillment of this text takes place through the birth of Christ, its initial meaning may lie in another fact, in which it found provisional fulfillment (cf. Matt 2:15 with Hos 11:1; Matt 2:18 with Jer 31:15)." Although Jesus never bore the name Immanuel, the term describes who he was.

◆     2. The Assyrian crisis (7:18–8:22)

18In that day the Lord will whistle for the army of southern Egypt and for the army of Assyria. They will swarm around you like flies and bees. 19They will come in vast hordes and settle in the fertile areas and also in the desolate valleys, caves, and thorny places. 20In that day the Lord will hire a "razor" from beyond the Euphrates River*—the king of Assyria—and use it to shave off everything: your land, your crops, and your people.*

21In that day a farmer will be fortunate to have a cow and two sheep or goats left. 22Nevertheless, there will be enough milk for everyone because so few people will be left in the land. They will eat their fill of yogurt and honey. 23In that day the lush vineyards, now worth 1,000 pieces of silver,* will become patches of briers and thorns. 24The entire land will become a vast expanse of briers and thorns, a hunting ground overrun by wildlife. 25No one will go to the fertile hillsides where the gardens once grew, for briers and thorns will cover them. Cattle, sheep, and goats will graze there.

## CHAPTER 8

Then the LORD said to me, "Make a large signboard and clearly write this name on it: Maher-shalal-hash-baz.*" 2I asked Uriah the priest and Zechariah son of Jeberekiah, both known as honest men, to witness my doing this.

3Then I slept with my wife, and she became pregnant and gave birth to a son. And the LORD said, "Call him Maher-shalal-hash-baz. 4For before this child is old enough to say 'Papa' or 'Mama,' the king of Assyria will carry away both the abundance of Damascus and the riches of Samaria."

5Then the LORD spoke to me again and said, 6"My care for the people of Judah is like the gently flowing waters of Shiloah, but they have rejected it. They are rejoicing over what will happen to* King Rezin and King Pekah.* 7Therefore, the Lord will overwhelm them with a mighty flood from the Euphrates River*—the king of Assyria and all his glory. This flood will overflow all its channels 8and sweep into Judah until it is chin deep. It will spread its wings, submerging your land from one end to the other, O Immanuel.

9"Huddle together, you nations, and
     be terrified.
Listen, all you distant lands.
Prepare for battle, but you will be
     crushed!
Yes, prepare for battle, but you will
     be crushed!
10Call your councils of war, but they will
     be worthless.
Develop your strategies, but they
     will not succeed.
For God is with us!*"

11The LORD has given me a strong warning not to think like everyone else does. He said,

12"Don't call everything a conspiracy,
     like they do,
and don't live in dread of what
     frightens them.
13Make the LORD of Heaven's Armies
     holy in your life.
He is the one you should fear.
He is the one who should make you
     tremble.
14   He will keep you safe.
But to Israel and Judah
     he will be a stone that makes people
     stumble,
     a rock that makes them fall.
And for the people of Jerusalem
     he will be a trap and a snare.
15Many will stumble and fall,
     never to rise again.
They will be snared and captured."

16Preserve the teaching of God;
     entrust his instructions to those
     who follow me.

[17]I will wait for the LORD,
     who has turned away from the
        descendants of Jacob.
   I will put my hope in him.

[18]I and the children the LORD has given
me serve as signs and warnings to Israel
from the LORD of Heaven's Armies who
dwells in his Temple on Mount Zion.

[19]Someone may say to you, "Let's ask
the mediums and those who consult the
spirits of the dead. With their whisperings and mutterings, they will tell us what
to do." But shouldn't people ask God for
guidance? Should the living seek guidance from the dead?

[20]Look to God's instructions and teachings! People who contradict his word are
completely in the dark. [21]They will go
from one place to another, weary and
hungry. And because they are hungry,
they will rage and curse their king and
their God. They will look up to heaven
[22]and down at the earth, but wherever
they look, there will be trouble and anguish and dark despair. They will be
thrown out into the darkness.

**7:20a** Hebrew *the river.* **7:20b** Hebrew *shave off the head, the hair of the legs, and the beard.* **7:23** Hebrew
*1,000 shekels of silver,* about 25 pounds or 11.4 kilograms in weight. **8:1** *Maher-shalal-hash-baz* means
"Swift to plunder and quick to carry away." **8:6a** Or *They are rejoicing because of.* **8:6b** Hebrew *and the son
of Remaliah.* **8:7** Hebrew *the river.* **8:10** Hebrew *Immanuel!*

## NOTES

**7:18** *flies.* The reference is possibly to the Tsetse fly of Egypt, an appropriate figure for
the Egyptian army.

**bees.** This is an appropriate image for Assyria, the land of bees. The Amorite enemy that
chased the Israelites (Deut 1:44) was described as a swarm of bees (cf. Ps 118:12).

**7:20** *hire a "razor."* Shaving in ancient Near Eastern culture was considered shameful
or repugnant (cf. 2 Sam 10:4-5; Isa 50:6; cf. 3:17). Contempt for those who were bald or
shaved is seen in 2 Kgs 2:23. However, shaving was also done at times of cleansing. The
leper who was to be cleansed was to shave his head, his beard, his eyebrows, and all his
hair (Lev 14:9). The Nazirite, defiled by a death near him, was to shave his head (Num
6:9). The Levites, for their purification from contact with the dead, were to shave thoroughly (Num 8:7).

**shave off everything.** As the NLT mg explains, the Heb. refers to shaving of the body
parts—head, legs, and face. More lit. the Heb. reads "shave your head and the hair of your
legs, and to take off your beards also" (NIV). This is a picture of complete humiliation.
Oswalt (1986:217) mentions the practice during WW II of shaving the heads of women
guilty of consorting with Germans. The badge of respect in that culture was the beard and
its loss was a great insult. Since *regel* ("feet" or "legs"; [TH7272, ZH8079]) can function as a
euphemism for private parts (cf. the Heb. of 1 Sam 24:3-4), shaving of pubic hair may also
be involved here.

**7:23** *briers and thorns.* This is the fulfillment of 5:5-6.

**8:1** *signboard and clearly write.* Writing from this period and much earlier has been
found on a variety of surfaces, including clay, wood, pottery, and metal. The word for
"signboard" (*gillayon* [TH1549, ZH1663]) is also found in 3:23, where it is translated "mirrors." Other versions have "tablet" (NASB, NRSV), "large scroll" (NIV, NCV), "large piece
of writing material" (TEV), and "large writing tablet" (REB, GW). The CEV simply says
"something to write on."

**Maher-shalal-hash-baz.** The name means "Swift to plunder and quick to carry away,"
as the NLT mg indicates.

**8:2** *Uriah the priest.* According to 2 Kgs 16:10-11, he served under King Ahaz.

**8:3** *wife.* The Heb. *nebi'ah* [TH5031, ZH5567] (prophetess) is probably used because she was married to a prophet. There is no record of her prophesying, and we are not certain of exactly how the term functions here. Known prophetesses in the Bible are Miriam, sister of Moses and Aaron, who was apparently unmarried (Exod 15:20); Deborah, wife of Lappidoth (Judg 4:4); Huldah, wife of Shallum (2 Kgs 22:14); Noadiah (Neh 6:14); Anna (Luke 2:36); and Philip's daughters (Acts 21:9).

**8:4** *old enough to say 'Papa' or 'Mama.'* That was probably about two years old (cf. 7:16).

**8:6** *gently flowing waters of Shiloah.* The reference is probably to the waters that flow from the Gihon spring (2 Chr 32:30) and eventually to the Pool of Siloam (cf. John 9:6). Here the imagery appropriately pictures the gentle but life-sustaining power of God.

*Shiloah.* Heb. *shiloakh* [TH7975, ZH8942] plus the definite article. Oswalt (1986:225) says "an apparently ineffectual little stream." The root idea can mean "to be at ease" and has cognates in other Semitic languages (NIDOTTE 4:117). Oswalt and others doubt this refers to the famous Siloam sites connected with the famous tunnel that dates from the time of Hezekiah.

*King Rezin and King Pekah.* Both kings died in 732 BC (cf. 2 Kgs 16:9).

**8:7** *Euphrates River.* As the NLT mg indicates, the Heb. has only "river," but there is no question but that this refers to the famous river of Assyria. Great rivers often represented invading armies (cf. 28:17-19). Here it stands in contrast to the gentle waters of Shiloah.

**8:8** *chin deep.* More lit., "reaching up to the neck" (NIV). Other versions have "shoulder high" (TEV), and "rising to Judah's throat" (TEV). Only Jerusalem escaped the Assyrian invasion into Judah.

*submerging your land from one end to the other, O Immanuel.* The Heb. is quite full here, reading something like, "overflow and go over . . . reaching to the neck . . . stretching of wings filling the breadth of your land . . . Immanuel." The reference is undoubtedly to the invading Assyrian army in 701 BC, which overwhelmed all the cities of Judah except Jerusalem.

**8:9** *Huddle together.* Heb. *ro'u* (here taken as a form of *r'h,* "associate with" [TH7462B, ZH8287]). The challenge seems to be to the Assyrians (cf. also NRSV, REB, NAB, NJB). The Heb., however, is ambiguous because the form here, (*ro'u*) could come from *ra'a'* [TH7489B, ZH8318] meaning "to break," which doesn't seem to fit here, or from a homograph meaning "to be wicked" [TH7489A, ZH8317], which doesn't seem to fit well either. The NIV has "raise the war cry," taking it from the root *rua'* [TH7321, ZH8131].

**8:10** *God is with us.* Lit., "Immanuel" (cf. NLT mg).

**8:11** *a strong warning.* Lit., "with his strong hand upon me." This expression is used elsewhere of a prophet's understanding of God's presence and support (cf. Ezek 1:3; 37:1).

**8:14** *Israel and Judah.* Lit., "both houses of Israel."

**8:17** *turned away.* Lit., "hiding his face."

*I will put my hope in him.* This verse and part of 8:18 are partially quoted in Heb 2:13 in the context of the Messiah's trust in God.

**8:18** *serve as signs.* The names of Isaiah, Shear-jashub, and Maher-shalal-hash-baz all carry a meaning significant in their context. Isaiah means "the LORD saves," Shear-jashub means "a remnant will return," and Maher-shalal-hash-baz means "swift is the plunder; speedy is the prey." The children's names should have been constant reminders to the people that the invaders were indeed swiftly coming for the spoils of war, but that ultimately after the loss of land and nationhood, a remnant would return from the exile. The prophet's name, meaning "the LORD saves," should have been a sign of hope.

**8:19** *mediums and those who consult the spirits of the dead.* During times of crisis, the people often turned to such sources (e.g., King Saul, when he went to the medium to contact the spirit of Samuel; see 1 Sam 28:8-11).

*whisperings and mutterings.* The two verbs involved are *tsapap* [TH6850, ZH7627] (found only in Isaiah; cf. 10:14; 29:4; 38:14) and *haga* [TH1897, ZH2047]. Used here in a pejorative sense they probably refer to the inarticulate (moaning, squeaking, chirping) and false communication of the mediums and spiritists in contrast to the clear word of the Lord.

**8:21** *rage and curse their king and their God.* Elsewhere, severe punishment is promised to those who curse God or a ruler (cf. Exod 22:28; Lev 24:15-16).

COMMENTARY

King Ahaz failed to recognize that his real enemy was Assyria (cf. 7:17, 20). The terminology of 7:18-25 reflects that used in chapter 5 (cf. "whistle," 7:18 with 5:26). The swarms of flies and bees (7:18) would make escape impossible, and the people would be humiliated as they were shaved (7:20) by the Assyrians. The loss of the beard in that culture was considered an especially great insult. Verses 20-21 apparently describes a return to the simple life of the nomads as the invasion brings an end to the people's normal agricultural life (notice the mention of both "yogurt" and "honey" in 7:15). The dismal state of affairs is graphically described in the remaining verses of this chapter.

Chapter 8 opens with the Lord's instructions to Isaiah to make a public notice, a "large signboard," with the name Maher-shalal-hash-baz written on it. This was to be witnessed by two honest men, Uriah the priest and Zechariah son of Jeberekiah (8:1-2). After this, Isaiah and his wife had a boy named Maher-shalal-hash-baz who would witness—within his first couple of years—the fall of Aram and the northern kingdom of Israel.

The Lord reminded Isaiah that the rebellious people had rejected his care for them, care that was like "the gently flowing waters of Shiloah" (8:6). He again warned Isaiah of the impending judgment because the people had spurned his warnings and were instead only rejoicing over what would happen to the two kings, Rezin and Pekah, rather than considering their own condition (8:5-6). The Lord would overwhelm them with a "mighty flood from the Euphrates River" as the Assyrian army would "submerge the land from one end to the other" (8:8). We know from Assyrian records that all of Judah except Jerusalem was destroyed.

The concluding section of this passage encourages the people to trust the Lord and "not to think like everyone else does" (8:11ff). The people were admonished to "Make the LORD of Heaven's Armies holy in your life" (8:13), for they had been too concerned about mere humans and their plans. They were reminded that the Lord "is the one you should fear" and "the one who should make you tremble" (8:13; cf. 1 Pet 3:14-15). The reference to the "stone" and the "rock" is cited in Romans 9:33 (cf. Isa 28:16; 1 Pet 2:8).

As a record of all that God had predicted, Isaiah was to write down this prophecy and entrust it to his disciples, who were to pass it down through future generations (8:16). Isaiah gave clear and open witness to what God had predicted, and explained to the people that the names of his children were signs and reminders, though the people preferred to turn to those involved in the occult for answers (8:19). The Lord challenged the people to consider what the occult sources had said as compared to what he had warned, and to note that "people who contradict his word are completely in the dark" (8:20). Rejection of God's word leads to spiritual darkness.

◆      ## 3. The Davidic kingdom and king (9:1-7)

*Nevertheless, that time of darkness and despair will not go on forever. The land of Zebulun and Naphtali will be humbled, but there will be a time in the future when Galilee of the Gentiles, which lies along the road that runs between the Jordan and the sea, will be filled with glory.

2*The people who walk in darkness
    will see a great light.
For those who live in a land of deep
        darkness,*
    a light will shine.
3You will enlarge the nation of Israel,
    and its people will rejoice.
They will rejoice before you
    as people rejoice at the harvest
    and like warriors dividing the
        plunder.
4For you will break the yoke of their
        slavery
    and lift the heavy burden from their
        shoulders.
You will break the oppressor's rod,

just as you did when you destroyed
    the army of Midian.
5The boots of the warrior
    and the uniforms bloodstained
        by war
will all be burned.
    They will be fuel for the fire.

6For a child is born to us,
    a son is given to us.
The government will rest on his
        shoulders.
    And he will be called:
Wonderful Counselor,* Mighty God,
    Everlasting Father, Prince of Peace.
7His government and its peace
    will never end.
He will rule with fairness and justice
    from the throne of his ancestor
        David
    for all eternity.
The passionate commitment of the
    LORD of Heaven's Armies
    will make this happen!

9:1 Verse 9:1 is numbered 8:23 in Hebrew text.   9:2a Verses 9:2-21 are numbered 9:1-20 in Hebrew text. 9:2b Greek version reads *a land where death casts its shadow.* Compare Matt 4:16.   9:6 Or *Wonderful, Counselor.*

NOTES
9:1 [8:23] *The land of Zebulun and Naphtali.* These northern tribal allotments suffered greatly during the Assyrian invasions of Tiglath-pileser III in 734 and 732 BC (cf. 2 Kgs 15:29). When the armies from the east invaded Israel from the north, these were the areas they first encountered.

9:2 [1] *will see a great light.* This light of the messianic age is also described in Matt 4:12-16 (cf. John 8:12; 9:4). Malachi 4:2 speaks of the "sun" of righteousness, and elsewhere Isaiah speaks of a "light" for the Gentiles (42:6; 49:6).

9:4 [3] *break the yoke of their slavery and lift the heavy burden.* Isaiah predicted that God would break the bondage imposed by the Assyrian army (cf. 10:26-27). This may refer to the event recorded in 37:36-39.

*Midian.* The reference is to Gideon's defeat of Midian, recorded in Judg 7:22-25.

**9:6 [5]** *a child is born to us, a son is given to us.* This messianic promise, whether the exact wording is intentional or just a result of poetic parallelism, is theologically precise because the eternal Son was not born (i.e., did not have his beginning) that first Christmas, although a human child appeared at that time. Levey (1974:45) notes that Targum Jonathan supplies explicit reference to "Messiah" here.

*The government will rest on his shoulders.* The Messiah claimed that all authority had been conferred on him (Matt 28:18).

*Wonderful Counselor.* Some scholars and translators find five names in this passage by distinguishing "Wonderful" from "Counselor" (NASB), but most find only four (NRSV, NIV, REB, NJB, NLT, ESV). The Heb. *pele'* [TH6382, ZH7099] can function as a substantive, or as an adjective derived from its construct use in Heb. ("marvel of a counselor"; cf. Holladay 1971:291). It seems best to see these titles as all matching in translated form. Isaiah does not mean that the child will actually bear these names, but that they are descriptive of who he is.

*Mighty.* The Heb. *gibbor* [TH1368, ZH1475] is used elsewhere of those who are valiant in battle (cf. Ps 24:8).

**9:7 [6]** *His government and its peace will never end.* The kingdoms of this world come and go with the passing of history, but this greater messianic kingdom continues in the kingdom of the greater son of David.

### COMMENTARY

The prophecies of judgment in chapters 7 and 8 were fulfilled when the Assyrians invaded the areas of Zebulun and Naphtali. The Assyrian king Tiglath-pileser brought suffering and great loss in his invasions of 734 and 732 BC. This was a period of great darkness and gloom for the people after the prophecies spoken to Ahaz and to the people. The Assyrian invasions brought hunger and deprivations, but this physical suffering was intensified by the spiritual darkness in which they lived as they vainly turned to gods of wood and stone.

This chapter opens with one of the most striking messianic prophecies of the Old Testament. Although the northern tribal areas of Zebulun and Naphtali would be invaded and humbled, there would be a distant future time when those areas would be filled with the glorious presence of the Messiah. The people who once lived in darkness would see a great light and rejoice as at harvest time (9:1-3; cf. Matt 4:15-16). A time was coming when peace would prevail and battle gear ("boots of the warrior . . . uniforms") would no longer be needed (9:4-5).

The reason given is that "a child is born" and "a son is given." This is a precise theological description of the eternal son of God who was indeed given (not born), and of the human child who was actually born (9:6). Four names are given, and unlike the name "Immanuel," these names would not ordinarily be given to Hebrew boys. Each of the names consists of two elements, one of which focuses on the son's divine nature. "Wonderful Counselor" is lit. "a Wonder of a Counselor." Counselors were important in the royal courts at that time and the office of counselor was well known to the people (cf. the example of Ahithophel, the famous counselor in David's court; see 2 Sam 16:23). The title "Mighty God" emphasizes the Son's deity and strength. The title "Everlasting Father" emphasizes the eternal nature of the Son who is one with the Father. The literal Hebrew, "father of eternity," has been understood in different ways, especially since "father" has a great range of meaning. The Hebrew expression could mean "possessor" or "originator" of eternity (cf. Gen 4:20-21). Of course, the relationships within the Trinity are a great mystery and are expressed in language beyond that of everyday use. For example, what kind of a "son" is just as old as his father and older than his mother? The beautiful title "Prince of Peace" reflects the nature of his rule, which will bring a cessation of warfare and a "wholeness" to society, an idea included in the Hebrew word translated "peace." He would be a ruler from the line of David. His ever-expanding government of peace would never end and would be characterized by fairness and justice, guaranteed by the "passionate commitment of the LORD of Heaven's Armies" (9:7).

Although Isaiah 9:6-7 is not quoted in the New Testament, the names find meaning and fulfillment in the Messiah. "Wonderful Counselor" is revealed in the wonders performed by the Messiah and in his wise counsel (cf. Col 2:3). It should be noted that the Hebrew word translated "counselor" includes more than counseling in the modern sense of the word. In Hebrew, it also connotes planning and deciding (HALOT 1:421). "Mighty God" identifies the child with the Godhead, and "Everlasting Father" places the child outside the created order (cf. John 1:1; Col 1:16-17). The "Prince of Peace" conquers not by a sword but by the message of peace (Eph 2:17).

◆     ### 4. God's anger against Israel (9:8–10:4)

⁸The Lord has spoken out against Jacob;
his judgment has fallen upon Israel.
⁹And the people of Israel* and Samaria,
who spoke with such pride and
arrogance,
will soon know it.
¹⁰They said, "We will replace the broken
bricks of our ruins with finished
stone,
and replant the felled sycamore-fig
trees with cedars."

¹¹But the LORD will bring Rezin's
enemies against Israel
and stir up all their foes.
¹²The Syrians* from the east and the
Philistines from the west
will bare their fangs and devour
Israel.
But even then the LORD's anger will
not be satisfied.
His fist is still poised to strike.

¹³For after all this punishment, the
people will still not repent.
They will not seek the LORD of
Heaven's Armies.
¹⁴Therefore, in a single day the LORD
will destroy both the head and
the tail,
the noble palm branch and the
lowly reed.
¹⁵The leaders of Israel are the head,
and the lying prophets are the tail.
¹⁶For the leaders of the people have
misled them.
They have led them down the path
of destruction.
¹⁷That is why the Lord takes no pleasure
in the young men
and shows no mercy even to the
widows and orphans.
For they are all wicked hypocrites,
and they all speak foolishness.

But even then the LORD's anger will
   not be satisfied.
His fist is still poised to strike.

18 This wickedness is like a brushfire.
   It burns not only briers and thorns
but also sets the forests ablaze.
   Its burning sends up clouds of
      smoke.
19 The land will be blackened
   by the fury of the LORD of Heaven's
      Armies.
The people will be fuel for the fire,
   and no one will spare even his own
      brother.
20 They will attack their neighbor on
      the right
   but will still be hungry.
They will devour their neighbor
      on the left
   but will not be satisfied.
In the end they will even eat their
   own children.*
21 Manasseh will feed on Ephraim,
   Ephraim will feed on Manasseh,

and both will devour Judah.
   But even then the LORD's anger will
      not be satisfied.
His fist is still poised to strike.

## CHAPTER 10

1 What sorrow awaits the unjust
      judges
   and those who issue unfair laws.
2 They deprive the poor of justice
   and deny the rights of the needy
      among my people.
They prey on widows
   and take advantage of orphans.
3 What will you do when I punish you,
   when I send disaster upon you from
      a distant land?
To whom will you turn for help?
   Where will your treasures be safe?
4 You will stumble along as prisoners
   or lie among the dead.
But even then the LORD's anger will
      not be satisfied.
His fist is still poised to strike.

9:9 Hebrew *of Ephraim*, referring to the northern kingdom of Israel.   9:12 Hebrew *Arameans*.   9:20 Or *eat their own arms*.

NOTES

9:9 [8] *Israel.* Lit., "Ephraim"; this tribe name was frequently used in reference to the northern kingdom.

9:10 [9] *broken bricks . . . finished stone.* Bricks were made of baked clay and crumbled easily, in contrast to the hard stone that was cut or dressed and more durable.

*sycamore-fig trees with cedars.* The famous cedars of Lebanon were the most prized wood in that part of the world (cf. 1 Kgs 7:2-3), in contrast to the common sycamore-fig trees.

9:12 [11] *will bare their fangs.* Lit., "devour with open mouth."

*fist is still poised to strike.* Lit., "hand is still upraised."

9:20 [19] *eat their own children.* The Heb. reads, "eat their own arms" (cf. NLT mg). Modern versions have "eats the flesh of his own arm" (NASB), "devoured the flesh of their own kindred" (NRSV, NJPS), and "feed on the flesh of his own offspring" (NIV).

COMMENTARY

The sharp break between 9:7 and 9:8 resembles the break between 2:2-4 and 2:5-7. Isaiah often used this striking switch from anger to consolation and back again. This whole section is organized around a refrain ("the LORD's anger will not be satisfied") that first appeared in 5:25 (where the NLT uses the present tense) and emphasizes God's anger (9:12, 17, 21; 10:4).

Despite the Lord's concern, God's covenant people bragged that they could take care of themselves. Although their land might lie in ruins from judgment, they "will replace the broken bricks" and "replant the felled" trees (9:10). Earlier in the same century, Amos had predicted that the people of Samaria would not get to live in their beautiful houses of cut stone. In response to the unrepentant and brazen attitude of his rebellious people, the Lord warns that he will bring in surrounding enemies who "will bare their fangs and devour" them, but even then "the LORD's anger will not be satisfied" (9:12). "His fist is still poised to strike" because "after all this punishment, the people will still not repent" and turn to the Lord Almighty (9:12).

In response to their rebellion and idolatry, the "LORD of Heaven's Armies" will completely destroy the entire nation. The expression "both the head and the tail" (9:14) uses opposites to express totality (cf. a similar use of such language in 3:1-3, which is also directed against the leaders). Shockingly, the Lord would not even have mercy on the "widows and orphans" in this situation because "they are all wicked hypocrites" (9:17), caught up in the rampant evil so pervasive throughout the community of God's covenant people. This society was spiritually dead, dry as tinder ready for the fire that consumes all in its path in burning judgment against the people (cf. 5:25). The wicked people had become "fuel for the fire" (9:19).

This gruesome picture includes a scene of family strife and civil war, as the people even attacked and devoured their neighbors, "on the right" and "on the left" (9:20). The chapter concludes with a terrifying picture of the Lord, whose "fist is still poised to strike" (9:21). The mention of Manasseh's battle with Ephraim (9:21) may allude to the war between Jephthah and the Ephraimites during the period of the Judges, when 42,000 Ephraimites died in the struggle between the descendants of the two sons of Joseph. The warfare between the north and the south had continued intermittently since the division of the kingdom (cf. 1 Kgs 14:30); by Isaiah's time, those various northern tribes had joined forces to invade Judah (cf. 7:1; Wolf 1985:100).

The final paragraph (10:1-4) of this section describes the judgment on those who exploited the weaker ("poor" and "needy") people in society, which at that time were especially the widows and the fatherless. This is a frequent theme in Isaiah (cf. 1:17; 5:23). In the time of judgment, they would end up either stumbling along as captives (10:4) or be with the dead. Either way, they faced a dismal future when none of their ill-gotten wealth would be of help to them.

◆  ## 5. Judgment on Assyria (10:5-34)

⁵ "What sorrow awaits Assyria, the rod
    of my anger.
  I use it as a club to express my
    anger.
⁶ I am sending Assyria against a godless
    nation,
  against a people with whom I am
    angry.

Assyria will plunder them,
    trampling them like dirt beneath
    its feet.
⁷ But the king of Assyria will not
    understand that he is my tool;
    his mind does not work that way.
  His plan is simply to destroy,
    to cut down nation after nation.

8 He will say,
  'Each of my princes will soon be
    a king.
9 We destroyed Calno just as we did
    Carchemish.
  Hamath fell before us as Arpad did.
  And we destroyed Samaria just as
    we did Damascus.
10 Yes, we have finished off many
    a kingdom
  whose gods were greater than those
    in Jerusalem and Samaria.
11 So we will defeat Jerusalem and her
    gods,
  just as we destroyed Samaria with
    hers.'"

12 After the Lord has used the king of
Assyria to accomplish his purposes on
Mount Zion and in Jerusalem, he will turn
against the king of Assyria and punish
him—for he is proud and arrogant. 13 He
boasts,

  "By my own powerful arm I have
    done this.
  With my own shrewd wisdom
    I planned it.
  I have broken down the defenses
    of nations
    and carried off their treasures.
  I have knocked down their kings
    like a bull.
14 I have robbed their nests of riches
    and gathered up kingdoms as a
      farmer gathers eggs.
  No one can even flap a wing against me
    or utter a peep of protest."

15 But can the ax boast greater power
    than the person who uses it?
  Is the saw greater than the person
    who saws?
  Can a rod strike unless a hand moves it?
  Can a wooden cane walk by itself?
16 Therefore, the Lord, the LORD of
    Heaven's Armies,
  will send a plague among Assyria's
    proud troops,
    and a flaming fire will consume its
      glory.

17 The LORD, the Light of Israel, will be
    a fire;
  the Holy One will be a flame.
  He will devour the thorns and briers
    with fire,
    burning up the enemy in a single
      night.
18 The LORD will consume Assyria's glory
    like a fire consumes a forest in
      a fruitful land;
    it will waste away like sick people
      in a plague.
19 Of all that glorious forest, only a few
    trees will survive—
    so few that a child could count
      them!

20 In that day the remnant left in Israel,
    the survivors in the house of Jacob,
  will no longer depend on allies
    who seek to destroy them.
  But they will faithfully trust the LORD,
    the Holy One of Israel.
21 A remnant will return;*
    yes, the remnant of Jacob will
      return to the Mighty God.
22 But though the people of Israel are
    as numerous
    as the sand of the seashore,
  only a remnant of them will return.
  The LORD has rightly decided to
    destroy his people.
23 Yes, the Lord, the LORD of Heaven's
    Armies,
  has already decided to destroy the
    entire land.*

24 So this is what the Lord, the LORD of
Heaven's Armies, says: "O my people in
Zion, do not be afraid of the Assyrians
when they oppress you with rod and club
as the Egyptians did long ago. 25 In a little
while my anger against you will end, and
then my anger will rise up to destroy
them." 26 The LORD of Heaven's Armies will
lash them with his whip, as he did when
Gideon triumphed over the Midianites at
the rock of Oreb, or when the LORD's staff
was raised to drown the Egyptian army in
the sea.

²⁷ In that day the LORD will end the
    bondage of his people.
He will break the yoke of slavery
    and lift it from their shoulders.*

²⁸ Look, the Assyrians are now at Aiath.
They are passing through Migron
    and are storing their equipment at
    Micmash.
²⁹ They are crossing the pass
    and are camping at Geba.
Fear strikes the town of Ramah.
All the people of Gibeah, the
    hometown of Saul,
    are running for their lives.
³⁰ Scream in terror,
    you people of Gallim!
Shout out a warning to Laishah.
Oh, poor Anathoth!

³¹ There go the people of Madmenah,
    all fleeing.
The citizens of Gebim are trying
    to hide.
³² The enemy stops at Nob for the rest
    of that day.
He shakes his fist at beautiful
    Mount Zion, the mountain of
    Jerusalem.

³³ But look! The Lord, the LORD of
    Heaven's Armies,
will chop down the mighty tree
    of Assyria with great power!
He will cut down the proud.
    That lofty tree will be brought down.
³⁴ He will cut down the forest trees with
    an ax.
Lebanon will fall to the Mighty One.*

10:21 Hebrew *Shear-jashub;* see 7:3; 8:18.   10:22-23 Greek version reads *only a remnant of them will be saved. / For he will carry out his sentence quickly and with finality and righteousness; / for God will carry out his sentence upon all the world with finality.* Compare Rom 9:27-28.   10:27 As in Greek version; Hebrew reads *The yoke will be broken, / for you have grown so fat.*   10:34 Or *with an ax / as even the mighty trees of Lebanon fall.*

## NOTES

**10:9 *Calno.*** This was a region in northern Aram (cf. Amos 6:2).

***Carchemish.*** This large city was located on the Euphrates River near Calno. It was an ancient city-state that had treaties with the surrounding areas as early as the second millennium BC.

***Hamath.*** This city was located on the Orontes River along a major trade route.

***Arpad.*** This ancient Aramean city was near Hamath and south of Calno. It was annexed by Tiglath-pileser III after a two-year siege in 740 BC. It rebelled with Hamath and other cities in 720 but was reconquered by Sargon II (NBD 86).

**10:10 *Samaria.*** Samaria fell to Shalmaneser V and Sargon II in 722 BC.

**10:13-14 *I . . . I . . . I.*** The repetition of the personal pronoun reflects the arrogance and the boastful attitude of the king.

**10:15 *ax . . . saw . . . rod . . . cane.*** Several penetrating questions emphasize the fact that Assyria did not act independently of the sovereign God.

**10:17 *will be a fire.*** Cf. Isa 30:33; 31:9 and see Deut 4:24, where the Lord is described as a burning fire.

**10:20 *that day.*** For connection with the messianic age, see 11:10-11; 12:1, 4.

**10:21 *remnant.*** Heb. *she'ar.* The remnant that survives will no longer depend on Assyria as Ahaz had (2 Chr 28:16, 20); instead, they will "faithfully trust the LORD." This remnant will fulfill the promise expressed in the name of Isaiah's son Shear-jashub ("a remnant will return," 7:3). Paul quoted this passage in Rom 9:27 and applied it to the believing remnant in Israel.

**10:25 *In a little while.*** Although the Assyrian incursions (from Tiglath-pileser III through Sennacherib) lasted for about three decades, they amounted to a very short time within the history of Israel.

**10:27 lift it from their shoulders.** This renders the LXX; the NLT mg gives the reading of the Heb.: "for you have grown so fat," which is the reading adopted for the text by the NIV. "Fat" is often used in Heb. to refer to growth or prosperity.

**10:28 Aiath.** This is possibly Ai, southeast of Bethel.

*Migron.* Migron may be south of Micmash.

*Micmash.* Michmash was located about seven miles north of Jerusalem.

**10:29 Geba.** Geba was about seven miles from Jerusalem.

*Ramah.* Ramah was about five miles from Jerusalem.

*Gibeah.* Gibeah was about three miles north of Jerusalem.

**10:30 Gallim . . . Laishah.** These were probably close to the last-mentioned sites.

*Anathoth.* Anathoth was about five miles northwest of Jerusalem.

**10:31 Madmenah . . . Gebim.** These are uncertain sites. Madmenah may be just north of Mount Scopus.

**10:32 Nob.** Nob was probably in the area of Mount Scopus, next to Jerusalem. Wildberger (1991:454) has a very helpful topographical map of the possible Assyrian line of march. For more on the Assyrian itinerary, see Christensen (1976).

**COMMENTARY**

Webb (1996:71) suggests a chiastic outline of this passage, which reflects the general flow of thought:

A. Proud Assyria will be judged (10:5-19)

    B. Don't rely on Assyria; instead, identify with the remnant who rely on the Lord (10:20-27)

A'. Proud Assyria will be judged (10:28-34)

God used Assyria to express his anger "against a godless nation" (10:5-6), but the king of Assyria did not grasp the fact that he was only a tool in the hands of a sovereign God because "his mind does not work that way" (10:7). He bragged that "each of my princes will soon be a king" (10:8) as he listed his victories over cities on his way into Samaria and Judah (10:10), and he boasted that "by my own powerful arm I have done this" (10:13). But he was reminded of the sayings, "can the ax boast greater power than the person who uses it?" and "can a rod strike unless a hand moves it?" (10:15). After this striking imagery, the section closes with the statement that "the LORD will consume Assyria's glory" (10:18).

The next section (10:20-27) describes the "survivors in the house of Jacob" who will "faithfully trust the LORD" (10:20). This is the "remnant of Jacob" that will return to the "Mighty God" (10:21). The remnant that escapes and survives will no longer lean on Assyria. Paul quoted from this passage in Rom 9:27 and applied it to the believing remnant of his time.

The people were admonished by "the LORD of Heaven's Armies" that they should "not be afraid of the Assyrians" who oppressed them as the "Egyptians did long ago" (10:24), for the day was coming when "the LORD will end the bondage of his people" (10:27). The same God that delivered his people in the times of Moses and Gideon would do it again (10:26).

The third section (10:28-34) in this passage picks up the itinerary (see notes above) of the invading Assyrians as they approached Jerusalem. However, the "Lord, the LORD of Heaven's Armies, will chop down this mighty tree of Assyria" (10:33). Most of Sennacherib's army was destroyed by the Angel of the Lord in 701 BC (cf. 37:36).

### ◆ 6. The Branch from Jesse's roots (11:1-16)

Out of the stump of David's family*
  will grow a shoot—
yes, a new Branch bearing fruit from
  the old root.
2 And the Spirit of the LORD will rest
  on him—
the Spirit of wisdom and
  understanding,
the Spirit of counsel and might,
  the Spirit of knowledge and the fear
  of the LORD.
3 He will delight in obeying the LORD.
  He will not judge by appearance
  nor make a decision based on
  hearsay.
4 He will give justice to the poor
  and make fair decisions for the
  exploited.
The earth will shake at the force of his
  word,
  and one breath from his mouth will
  destroy the wicked.
5 He will wear righteousness like a belt
  and truth like an undergarment.

6 In that day the wolf and the lamb will
  live together;
the leopard will lie down with the
  baby goat.
The calf and the yearling will be safe
  with the lion,
  and a little child will lead them all.
7 The cow will graze near the bear.
  The cub and the calf will lie down
  together.
The lion will eat hay like a cow.
8 The baby will play safely near the hole
  of a cobra.
Yes, a little child will put its hand in
  a nest of deadly snakes without
  harm.

9 Nothing will hurt or destroy in all my
  holy mountain,
for as the waters fill the sea,
  so the earth will be filled with
  people who know the LORD.

10 In that day the heir to David's throne*
  will be a banner of salvation to all
  the world.
The nations will rally to him,
  and the land where he lives will be
  a glorious place.*
11 In that day the Lord will reach out his
  hand a second time
  to bring back the remnant of his
  people—
those who remain in Assyria and
  northern Egypt;
  in southern Egypt, Ethiopia,* and
  Elam;
  in Babylonia,* Hamath, and all the
  distant coastlands.
12 He will raise a flag among the nations
  and assemble the exiles of Israel.
He will gather the scattered people
  of Judah
  from the ends of the earth.

13 Then at last the jealousy between
  Israel* and Judah will end.
They will not be rivals anymore.
14 They will join forces to swoop down
  on Philistia to the west.
Together they will attack and
  plunder the nations to the east.
They will occupy the lands of Edom
  and Moab,
  and Ammon will obey them.
15 The LORD will make a dry path through
  the gulf of the Red Sea.*
He will wave his hand over the
  Euphrates River,*

sending a mighty wind to divide it into
seven streams
so it can easily be crossed on foot.
16 He will make a highway for the
remnant of his people,

the remnant coming from
Assyria,
just as he did for Israel long ago
when they returned from
Egypt.

11:1 Hebrew *the stump of the line of Jesse.* Jesse was King David's father.   11:10a Hebrew *the root of Jesse.*
11:10b Greek version reads *In that day the heir to David's throne* [literally *the root of Jesse*] *will come, / and
he will rule over the Gentiles. / They will place their hopes on him.* Compare Rom 15:12.   11:11a Hebrew *in
Pathros, Cush.*   11:11b Hebrew *in Shinar.*   11:13 Hebrew *Ephraim,* referring to the northern kingdom of Israel.
11:15a Hebrew *will destroy the tongue of the sea of Egypt.*   11:15b Hebrew *the river.*

## NOTES

**11:1 *stump.*** The messianic Branch will appear as a shoot from the stump of David. The
terms for "shoot" (*khoter* [TH2415, ZH2643]), "Branch" (*netser* [TH5342, ZH5916]), and "root"
(*shoresh* [TH8328, ZH9247]) are all messianic terminology in Isaiah (cf. 4:2 and 53:2). The
Targum Jonathan makes an explicit reference to the Messiah here, which is used in the
Midrash as a point of discussion concerning the time of the Messiah's ministry (Levey
1974:49).

***David's family.*** As the NLT mg indicates, the Heb. does not mention David, but only the
"stump of Jesse." However, the context makes it clear that the reference is to the royal family of David.

***Branch.*** Heb. *netser;* the Heb. name for Nazareth is *natsar* or *natserath,* and the term *notsri*
is a Talmudic and modern Heb. term identifying a follower of Jesus of Nazareth.

**11:2 *Spirit.*** Isaiah referred to the Holy Spirit more than any other prophet did (cf. 30:1;
32:15; 34:16; 40:13; 42:1; 44:3; 48:16; 59:21; 61:1). The word is not capitalized in many
modern versions (NASB, NRSV, REB, NJB) or in the KJV, but it is capitalized in the NLT,
NCV, NAB, GW, CEV, and NIV. There are no capital letters in Heb., and translators must
decide whether this is a reference to deity or not.

**11:4 *earth . . . wicked.*** Such parallelism could possibly be between "earthly-minded" and
"wicked," and this is the translation used by Leupold (1971 2:220); however, it is uncertain
if such an abstract concept as "earthly-minded" was a perspective represented in the language in this way.

***force of his word.*** Lit., "rod of his mouth." This may be compared to the "sword of his
mouth" in Rev 1:16; 2:16; 19:15.

***breath from his mouth.*** Lit., "breath of his lips" (cf. 2 Thess 2:8).

**11:5 *wear righteousness like a belt and truth like an undergarment.*** Righteousness and
truth were such an integral part of the Messiah's ministry that they are described as items of
his clothing. Righteousness and truth are often found together in Isaiah and elsewhere. The
use of the belt for tightening up loose garments is frequently mentioned in connection
with preparation for action such as running or fighting (cf. 5:27).

**11:9 *my holy mountain.*** See comments on 2:2-4 (cf. Zech 8:3; Heb 12:18-28).

**11:10 *In that day.*** See 10:20, 27.

***heir to.*** Lit., "root of" (cf. NLT mg).

***David's throne.*** As in 11:1, the Heb. does not say "David's throne," but only "root of Jesse"
(cf. Rom 15:12; Rev 5:5; 22:16).

**11:11 *second time.*** This probably refers to the return from exile, since the first time was the
deliverance from Egypt.

***remnant.*** See 1:9; 10:20-22.

*southern Egypt, Ethiopia.* As the NLT mg indicates, the Heb. reads "Pathros, Cush," which are two areas (Lower and Upper) of Egypt, but note that Upper Egypt refers to the South and Lower Egypt refers to the North. (Because the Nile runs from south to north, the south is upriver, hence "upper.") Ethiopia is the modern name for ancient Cush.

*Elam.* This land is northeast of the lower Tigris Valley.

*Babylonia.* The Heb. has Shinar (cf. NLT mg), an ancient name for Babylonia.

*Hamath.* The site was in Aram on the Orontes River.

*distant coastlands.* The Heb. for "coasts of the sea," *'iyye hayyam,* [TH339/3220, ZH362/3542] is an expression found only here and in 24:15. It designates the most distant areas, including islands (cf. 41:1, 5; 42:4; Gen 10:5).

**11:12 *raise a flag among the nations.*** This metaphor refers to a "banner" (NIV) or "ensign" (Heb. *nes* [TH5251, ZH5812]) set up as a rallying point for Israel and Judah. The strife that existed between them would be abolished, and the fighting would cease. In 11:10 this banner or sign is identified as the Messiah, whose offer of salvation is presented in the imagery of Israel's return and restoration from exile, an event already predicted in 5:13 and 6:12. Oswalt suggests that this verse is simply saying in poetry what the preceding verses state in prose, and notes the chiastic arrangement of the verse, "where the first and fourth phrases are parallel, as are the second and third" (1986:288).

*ends of the earth.* Lit., "from the four wings of the earth."

**11:13 *Israel.*** The Heb. reads "Ephraim" (so the NLT mg), representing the northern kingdom.

*jealousy between Israel and Judah.* Before the exile, Ephraim/Israel and Judah were often fighting each other (cf. 9:21).

**11:14 *nations to the east.*** In this context, the reference is probably to the Midianites (cf. 9:4).

**11:15 *Red Sea.*** Lit., "sea of Egypt" (cf. NLT mg).

*Euphrates River.* The Heb. simply says, "the river," which is clearly a reference to the Euphrates. Here, the Euphrates River represents the Assyrian-Babylonian empires.

**11:16 *make a highway.*** Similar language is also found in 57:14; 62:10. The concept of a highway as an easy route home for the returnees is found several times in Isaiah (35:8; 40:3-4; 42:16; 49:11).

*from Egypt.* Isaiah refers frequently to the Exodus (4:5; 10:26-27; 35:8-10; 43:16-17; 50:2; 63:11, 12).

## COMMENTARY

The preceding chapter ended with the world powers depicted as felled trees lying on the ground, but chapter 11 opens with a description of a new "shoot" and a "new Branch" that will sprout from the root of Jesse. In contrast to the trees cut down in the preceding chapter, this chapter opens with a picture of new growth from the house of David. The prophet described the elevation of the house of David in a king who so greatly surpassed the ordinary human limits that, like the miracle child of 9:6, he could be none other than the Messiah. This messianic son is called after the name of Jesse rather than of David, probably because of the lost splendor of David's house at that time in history. The new ruler of David would sprout from an insignificant beginning, branch out, and become the most powerful ruler the world had ever witnessed, in contrast to the mere human kingdom of Assyria.

This Messiah (anointed one) is empowered by the "Spirit of the LORD," who is described as the "Spirit of wisdom and understanding, of counsel and might, and of knowledge and fear of the Lord" (11:2). The words "counsel and might" appear in the titles of 9:6. In the Old Testament, the Spirit often falls on the leaders of the people, such as Moses and the elders (Num 11:25), the judges (Jdg 3:10; 6:34), the kings (1 Sam 11:6; 16:13), and the prophets (1 Sam 10:10; 2 Sam 23:2; 1 Kgs 22:24; Hos 9:7; Mic 3:8). These people were thus enabled to be instruments through whom God carried on his work. In the messianic era, the Spirit would be given in generous measure to all of the people of God (32:15; Joel 2:28ff). The Spirit would "rest" on the Messiah, coming down on him never to leave again. This one Spirit is revealed from various angles according to the gifts he communicates, six of which are mentioned by pairs, indicating the fullness of the Spirit received by the Messiah (cf. Rev 5:6). The gifts listed seem especially designed to help him in his royal office.

The character of the Messiah's reign is described in 11:3-5. In contrast to the situation in Isaiah's day, under the Messiah's influence, decisions will be fair and just, and not based on appearance or hearsay (11:3). The Messiah will "wear righteousness like a belt and truth like an undergarment" (11:5).

Using illustrations from the animal world, Isaiah presents a scene of peace and security (11:6-8). The absence of hostility between animals normally in conflict reflects a change of nature and a return to a paradise in which sin and its effects are absent. The animals are grouped in pairs that link a wild animal with a domesticated one. In this scene, even infants and children, who often suffer the most in a sin-cursed world, are safe. A similar description appears in 65:20-25 in the picture of the new heaven and new earth. In 11:9, the lesson is applied in the transition from animals to humans. The whole world will know the Lord and his standards.

In 11:10 the "heir to David's throne" is presented as a banner for the nations (cf. Paul's use in Rom 15:12). Whereas in 5:26 there was a "signal to distant nations" to come racing against Jerusalem, now the invitation is to participate in the Messiah's glorious reign (cf. 2:2-4). In 11:12, a "flag" is mentioned in a similar way.

In 11:15-16, the prophet again speaks of the return of the dispersed, especially those from Egypt and Assyria (cf. 11:11). This return will be accompanied by the same kinds of miracles as took place during the Exodus under Moses. The miraculous return of the Jews from Babylonia was a glorious work of God (Ps 126). Already in the Old Testament, Judah's returnees are viewed as representing the twelve tribes (Ezra 6:17; 8:35).

◆     ## 7. The Song of Redemption (12:1-6)

In that day you will sing:
  "I will praise you, O LORD!
You were angry with me, but not
    any more.
  Now you comfort me.
2 See, God has come to save me.

I will trust in him and not be afraid.
The LORD GOD is my strength and my
    song;
  he has given me victory."
3 With joy you will drink deeply
    from the fountain of salvation!

⁴In that wonderful day you will sing:
"Thank the LORD! Praise his name!
Tell the nations what he has done.
Let them know how mighty he is!
⁵Sing to the LORD, for he has done
wonderful things.

Make known his praise around the
world.
⁶Let all the people of Jerusalem* shout
his praise with joy!
For great is the Holy One of Israel
who lives among you."

12:6 Hebrew *Zion.*

NOTES

**12:1** *In that day.* See 10:20, 27. This probably refers to the time of deliverance described in 11:1–12:6. When such deliverance is experienced, the redeemed sing in praise (as after the Exodus).

**12:2** *LORD GOD.* This translates two forms of the personal name of God: "Yah" (*yah*) and "Yahweh" (*yhwh*). The NIV translates it, "The LORD, the LORD." The KJV has "LORD JEHO-VAH." Other versions have "Yah the LORD" (NJPS) and "LORD GOD" (ESV) for this unusual Heb. combination.

*is my strength and my song.* Surely Isaiah is echoing the language found in Exod 15:2.

**12:3** *fountain of salvation.* Lit., "wells of salvation"; this is probably a reference to God's provision for the Israelites during the desert wanderings (cf. Exod 15:25, 27).

**12:6** *Jerusalem.* The Heb. reads "Zion" (so NLT mg).

*shout his praise.* The Heb. has two verbs: "shout aloud" (*tsahal* [TH6670A, ZH7412]) and "sing for joy" (*ranan* [TH7442, ZH8264]). They are used again in 54:1, where Zion rejoices over the restoration of her people.

*Holy One of Israel.* Isaiah uses this title for God frequently (cf. 1:4; 6:1).

COMMENTARY

Chapters 1–12 conclude with this passage in chapter 12 containing two short songs (vv. 1-2; 3-6) of praise from the redeemed people, thanking God for his past deliverance and for his promises of future blessing. When God again delivers his people as during the Exodus, the songs of Israel's youth will be renewed and the people will sing as in the old days (cf. Hos 2:15). Therefore, this passage ends with these words of praise from the redeemed people. Both songs echo the Psalms and the Song of Moses (Exod 15).

The first song (12:1-2) praises the Lord for relief after a time of wrath ("You were angry with me, but not any more," 12:1). In 12:2, the Lord is praised as the One "I will trust in . . . and not be afraid" for "he has given me victory." He has provided Israel's salvation, so they need have no fear (cf. Exod 15:2; Ps 27:1; 118:14).

The second song develops the theme of joy and announces God's greatness to all the world, since the celebration of such good news cannot be contained. The prophet addresses the redeemed who with joy "drink deeply from the fountain of salvation!" (12:3; cf. John 7:37). In public witness, they "thank the LORD!" and "praise his name!" (12:4). They let his deeds on behalf of his people be made known among the nations, so that they also may join in honoring him. Webb (1996:79) notes, "only as the nations hear of the LORD's glorious deeds will they be able to recognize at last that he alone is God, and come to Zion to learn of his ways" (cf. 2:3).

Let the Lord's people rejoice, for "great is the Holy One of Israel" (12:6) who lives among them, and this is the greatest blessing of all (cf. Joel 2:27; Ezek 48:35; Rev 21:3). Thus, this chapter ends with a reference to the name so dear to Isaiah ("Holy One of Israel"), and forms a fitting conclusion to the prophecies of chapters 7–12.

◆   ## C. Judgments on the Nations (13:1–23:18)
### 1. Babylon and Assyria (13:1–14:27)

Isaiah son of Amoz received this message concerning the destruction of Babylon:

2 "Raise a signal flag on a bare hilltop.
Call up an army against Babylon.
Wave your hand to encourage them
as they march into the palaces of
the high and mighty.
3 I, the LORD, have dedicated these
soldiers for this task.
Yes, I have called mighty warriors
to express my anger,
and they will rejoice when I am
exalted."

4 Hear the noise on the mountains!
Listen, as the vast armies march!
It is the noise and shouting of many
nations.
The LORD of Heaven's Armies has
called this army together.
5 They come from distant countries,
from beyond the farthest horizons.
They are the LORD's weapons to carry
out his anger.
With them he will destroy the whole
land.

6 Scream in terror, for the day of the
LORD has arrived—
the time for the Almighty to
destroy.
7 Every arm is paralyzed with fear.
Every heart melts,
8    and people are terrified.
Pangs of anguish grip them,
like those of a woman in labor.
They look helplessly at one another,
their faces aflame with fear.

9 For see, the day of the LORD is coming—
the terrible day of his fury and
fierce anger.
The land will be made desolate,
and all the sinners destroyed with it.
10 The heavens will be black above them;
the stars will give no light.
The sun will be dark when it rises,
and the moon will provide no light.

11 "I, the LORD, will punish the world for
its evil
and the wicked for their sin.
I will crush the arrogance of the proud
and humble the pride of the mighty.
12 I will make people scarcer than gold—
more rare than the fine gold of
Ophir.
13 For I will shake the heavens.
The earth will move from its place
when the LORD of Heaven's Armies
displays his wrath
in the day of his fierce anger."

14 Everyone in Babylon will run about like
a hunted gazelle,
like sheep without a shepherd.
They will try to find their own people
and flee to their own land.
15 Anyone who is captured will be cut
down—
run through with a sword.
16 Their little children will be dashed
to death before their eyes.
Their homes will be sacked, and
their wives will be raped.

17 "Look, I will stir up the Medes against
Babylon.
They cannot be tempted by silver
or bribed with gold.
18 The attacking armies will shoot down
the young men with arrows.
They will have no mercy on helpless
babies

and will show no compassion for
children."

¹⁹ Babylon, the most glorious of
kingdoms,
the flower of Chaldean pride,
will be devastated like Sodom and
Gomorrah
when God destroyed them.
²⁰ Babylon will never be inhabited again.
It will remain empty for generation
after generation.
Nomads will refuse to camp there,
and shepherds will not bed down
their sheep.
²¹ Desert animals will move into the
ruined city,
and the houses will be haunted
by howling creatures.
Owls will live among the ruins,
and wild goats will go there to
dance.
²² Hyenas will howl in its fortresses,
and jackals will make dens in its
luxurious palaces.
Babylon's days are numbered;
its time of destruction will soon
arrive.

## CHAPTER 14

But the LORD will have mercy on the descendants of Jacob. He will choose Israel
as his special people once again. He will
bring them back to settle once again in
their own land. And people from many
different nations will come and join them
there and unite with the people of Israel.*
²The nations of the world will help the
LORD's people to return, and those who
come to live in their land will serve them.
Those who captured Israel will themselves
be captured, and Israel will rule over its
enemies.
³In that wonderful day when the LORD
gives his people rest from sorrow and
fear, from slavery and chains, ⁴you will
taunt the king of Babylon. You will say,

"The mighty man has been destroyed.
Yes, your insolence* is ended.

⁵ For the LORD has crushed your wicked
power
and broken your evil rule.
⁶ You struck the people with endless
blows of rage
and held the nations in your angry
grip
with unrelenting tyranny.
⁷ But finally the earth is at rest and
quiet.
Now it can sing again!
⁸ Even the trees of the forest—
the cypress trees and the cedars
of Lebanon—
sing out this joyous song:
'Since you have been cut down,
no one will come now to cut us
down!'

⁹ "In the place of the dead* there is
excitement
over your arrival.
The spirits of world leaders and
mighty kings long dead
stand up to see you.
¹⁰ With one voice they all cry out,
'Now you are as weak as we are!
¹¹ Your might and power were buried
with you.*
The sound of the harp in your palace
has ceased.
Now maggots are your sheet,
and worms your blanket.'

¹² "How you are fallen from heaven,
O shining star, son of the morning!
You have been thrown down to the
earth,
you who destroyed the nations
of the world.
¹³ For you said to yourself,
'I will ascend to heaven and set my
throne above God's stars.
I will preside on the mountain of the
gods
far away in the north.*
¹⁴ I will climb to the highest heavens
and be like the Most High.'
¹⁵ Instead, you will be brought down to
the place of the dead,

down to its lowest depths.
<sup>16</sup>Everyone there will stare at you and
ask,
'Can this be the one who shook the
earth
and made the kingdoms of the
world tremble?
<sup>17</sup>Is this the one who destroyed the world
and made it into a wasteland?
Is this the king who demolished the
world's greatest cities
and had no mercy on his prisoners?'
<sup>18</sup>"The kings of the nations lie in stately
glory,
each in his own tomb,
<sup>19</sup>but you will be thrown out of your
grave
like a worthless branch.
Like a corpse trampled underfoot,
you will be dumped into a mass
grave
with those killed in battle.
You will descend to the pit.
<sup>20</sup>   You will not be given a proper
burial,
for you have destroyed your nation
and slaughtered your people.
The descendants of such an evil
person
will never again receive honor.
<sup>21</sup>Kill this man's children!
Let them die because of their
father's sins!
They must not rise and conquer the
earth,
filling the world with their cities."

<sup>22</sup>This is what the LORD of Heaven's
Armies says:
"I, myself, have risen against
Babylon!
I will destroy its children and its
children's children,"
says the LORD.
<sup>23</sup>"I will make Babylon a desolate place
of owls,
filled with swamps and marshes.
I will sweep the land with the broom
of destruction.
I, the LORD of Heaven's Armies, have
spoken!"

<sup>24</sup>The LORD of Heaven's Armies has sworn
this oath:

"It will all happen as I have
planned.
It will be as I have decided.
<sup>25</sup>I will break the Assyrians when they
are in Israel;
I will trample them on my
mountains.
My people will no longer be their
slaves
nor bow down under their heavy
loads.
<sup>26</sup>I have a plan for the whole earth,
a hand of judgment upon all the
nations.
<sup>27</sup>The LORD of Heaven's Armies has
spoken—
who can change his plans?
When his hand is raised,
who can stop him?"

14:1 Hebrew *the house of Jacob.* The names "Jacob" and "Israel" are often interchanged throughout the Old Testament, referring sometimes to the individual patriarch and sometimes to the nation.   14:4 As in Dead Sea Scrolls; the meaning of the Masoretic Text is uncertain.   14:9 Hebrew *Sheol;* also in 14:15.   14:11 Hebrew *were brought down to Sheol.*   14:13 Or *on the heights of Zaphon.*

## NOTES

**13:1** *message concerning the destruction.* This translates the Hebrew word for "oracle" (*massa'* [TH4853A, ZH5363]), a term that often refers to a message of doom.

**13:1** *Babylon.* Babylon became a great kingdom that was ultimately conquered by the Persian King Cyrus in 539 BC. During the time of Isaiah, Babylon was still part of the Assyrian Empire (cf. 14:24-27). In Scripture, it often represents the world powers arrayed against God's kingdom (cf. 1 Pet 5:13); its final destruction is proclaimed in Rev 14:8; 16:19; 17-18.

**13:2 *signal flag.*** Heb. *nes*; this is similar to the one raised in 5:26 and 11:12 that summoned the Assyrians.

**13:3 *dedicated these soldiers.*** This refers to those set apart to carry out God's will. For example, cf. 10:5, where the Lord calls Assyria "the whip of my anger."

**13:4 *on the mountains.*** This is appropriate language for invaders from Media and Persia, which are mountainous countries. Babylon, a flat site by contrast, was conquered by Cyrus the Persian in 539 BC.

***armies march . . . Heaven's Armies.*** The Heb. involves a wordplay involving the word for "vast armies" (*tsaba'* [TH6635, ZH7372]) and the word for "Heaven's Armies" (*tseba'ot*).

**13:5 *distant countries.*** To the Hebrews, Persia was a far distant country.

**LORD's *weapons.*** Assyria was the weapon in God's hand during Isaiah's day, and later, Babylon would be God's weapon (cf. 10:5).

**13:6 *day of the LORD.*** See 2:11, 17, 20.

***Almighty to destroy.*** The Heb. engages in wordplay on "Almighty" (*shadday* [TH7706, ZH8724]) and "destroy" (*shod* [TH7701, ZH8719]).

**13:7 *Every arm is paralyzed with fear.*** More lit., "hands go limp," an expression referring to a lack of courage and resolve (cf. Jer 6:24). Translators vary in their attempt to communicate their understanding of this expression: "hands will be feeble" (NRSV, ESV), "courage will melt away" (NCV), and "hands will hang limp" (TEV, REB).

**13:8 *like those of a woman in labor.*** This imagery represents intense suffering from judgment and warfare (cf. 26:17; Jer 4:31; 6:24).

**13:10 *heavens will be black.*** Such cosmic darkness is used elsewhere to picture "the day of the LORD" (cf. Jer 4:24-28; Ezek 30:3, 18; Joel 2:10; Rev 6:12-13). Jesus used similar language to describe the destruction of Jerusalem (Matt 24:29).

**13:12 *gold of Ophir.*** The exact location of Ophir is uncertain, but Solomon imported large quantities of gold from there (cf. 1 Kgs 9:28; 10:11).

**13:13 *shake the heavens. The earth will move.*** Such phenomena often accompanied the awesome presence of the Lord (cf. Exod 19:16).

**13:16 *children will be dashed to death.*** An invading enemy would often do this to eliminate future warriors and even future populations (cf. Ps 137:8-9; Hos 10:14; Nah 3:10).

***wives will be raped.*** This was part of the suffering experienced by women during warfare. With their husbands killed, they became easy prey for the enemy.

**13:17 *the Medes.*** The Medes lived in the area of what is now northwestern Iran. They joined with the Persians to conquer Babylon in 539 BC.

**13:18 *babies.*** Lit., "fruit of the womb."

**13:19 *Babylon, the most glorious of kingdoms.*** The famous hanging gardens of Nebuchadnezzar were one of the seven wonders of the ancient world. The city of Babylon was renowned for its beautiful temples and palaces (Dan 4:29-30).

**13:20 *Babylon will never be inhabited again.*** The site was completely deserted by the seventh century AD, never to experience its former glory again. Even roaming nomads were superstitious about camping in the area.

**13:21 *wild goats.*** The Heb. term (*sa'ir* [TH8163A, ZH8538]) is associated with demons in Lev 17:7; 2 Chr 11:15. In Rev 18:2, fallen Babylon becomes a home for demons. The NRSV renders the term as "goat-demons" here.

**14:8 *trees of the forest . . . sing out.*** Isaiah repeatedly personified nature and was especially fond of using the imagery of trees.

**14:9 leaders.** The Heb. *'attudim* [TH6260, ZH6966] is "male goats," a term used for leaders of the flock. In Zech 10:3, the term is parallel to "shepherds." Many languages use animal names to denote various classes of society or kinds of people. Animal names have also been closely associated with political parties and lodges.

**14:11 sound of the harp.** Dan 3:5 lists the musical instruments used in Babylon, and Amos 6:5-6 associates music with luxury and complacency.

*maggots . . . worms.* These are associated with decomposition in the grave and with Gehenna (hell), as described by Jesus (Mark 9:48).

**14:12 shining star, son of the morning.** The Heb. word (*helel* [TH1966, ZH2122]) translated "shining star" in the NLT is the word translated in the Latin Vulgate as "Lucifer" (light-bearer). This term then became a name for Satan and subsequently had significant influence on western thinking about Satan, who is known as the "angel of light" (2 Cor 11:14). The KJV translated this phrase as "Lucifer, son of the morning." For a very readable account of this tradition in its literary and cultural context, see Youngblood (1998). The modern versions give a variety of translations: "bright morning star" (REB), "Day Star" (NRSV, NJB, ESV), "star of the morning" (NASB), "morning star" (NAB), and "Shining One" (NJPS).

**14:13 far away in the north.** The reference is to Mount Zaphon (cf. NLT mg), also called Casius, which is located about twenty-five miles northeast of the ancient site of Ugarit in Syria. It was the residence of Hadad, or Baal, of the Canaanite pantheon. The site played a significant role in the Ugaritic/Canaanite mythological tradition.

**14:14 Most High.** This is contrasted with "lowest depths" (Sheol) in the next verse.

**14:18 tomb.** The Heb. is *bayith* [TH1004, ZH1074] (house). The extravagant houses built by grandiose tyrants are nothing more than mausoleums for the dead.

**14:19 branch.** The Heb. is *netser* [TH5342, ZH5916]. Contrast this worthless branch with the messianic Branch.

*dumped . . . with those killed in battle.* The Heb. reads "covered with the slain" in contrast to lying in state in royal clothing.

**14:23 owls.** The uncertainty of the meaning of the Heb. *qippod* [TH7090, ZH7887] is reflected in the various versions: "owls" (NIV), "bittern" (KJV, NJPS), "hedgehog" (NRSV, NJB, ESV), "bustard" (REB), and "hoot owls" (NAB).

**14:27 hand is raised.** Lit., "hand stretched out." God's hand was stretched out against Egypt at the Red Sea episode (cf. Exod 15:12).

C O M M E N T A R Y

Following the first twelve chapters that focused on Jerusalem and Judah, the next section (13:1–23:18) comprises a distinct unit within the book of Isaiah and mostly concerns the nations surrounding God's people. Although Isaiah's primary concern was with the people of Judah and Jerusalem, his prophetic message was also international in scope, like passages in Jeremiah (40–51), Ezekiel (25–32), Amos (1–2), and Zephaniah (2:4-15). The oracle against Babylon (13:1–14:23) leads the list and is picked up again in 21:1-10. During the time of Isaiah, Babylon was still part of the Assyrian Empire (14:25). Although modern translations often treat 14:24–27 (concerning Assyria) as separate from the preceding material addressing Babylon's king (14:1-23), it should be remembered that Babylon succeeded Assyria, and the two are closely related in many ways.

The name "Babylon" is found often in Isaiah and has provoked much discussion in relation to the question of authorship, since Babylon was not the major power in Isaiah's time. Like the name "Zion," Babylon has numerous connotations and can be used to refer to any empire or system opposed to God. Babylon's significance in the history of Israel may account for this additional oracle against it. Babylon is depicted as a great power to arise in the future and is described as the "most glorious of kingdoms" (13:19). Assyria, though dominant then, would witness the fall of its capital city, Nineveh, to Babylon in 612 BC. Next, the Medes arose as God's instrument in the destruction of Babylon's power (13:17). Nebuchadnezzar was the last powerful king of Babylon; he ruled until 562 BC, making Babylon one of the world's most beautiful cities and his gardens there one of the seven wonders of the ancient world. The eventual capture and downfall of Babylon took place during the reign of Belshazzar in 539 BC, when Cyrus captured the city. Although he did not destroy the city, he brought the empire to an end. Babylon continued to be a city of some importance, but it began to decline slowly, and by the time of the death of Alexander the Great, who had planned to rebuild it, the decline became more rapid. Later, it disappeared from the scene of world history and vanished until archaeologists unearthed its ruins in the 19th century. For a good overview of Babylon, see Yamauchi (Harrison 1985:32-48).

The last section (14:1-23) of this passage consists of a taunt for Babylon's king, which Payne (1986:732) calls a "parody of a lament." The opening verses of chapter 14 link the description of Babylon's fall in chapter 13 with the taunt song that constitutes most of chapter 14.

**The Oracle against Babylon.**    The oracle begins with the summoning of an army against Babylon (13:1-5; the Medes and the Persians are the ones being assembled). The Lord commanded the armies of Israel and the angelic hosts of heaven, and here he also stood in full control of the armies of Cyrus. Assyria was a weapon of God's anger (cf. 10:5), and the Medes and Persians were also weapons of the Lord (13:5).

The destruction of Babylon is described in terms of "the day of the LORD" (13:6, 9), and this vivid description contains elements found elsewhere. The darkening of the sun and moon and the shaking of heaven and earth are also mentioned in Joel 2:10 and in Revelation 6:12-14. Isaiah had already introduced similar language earlier (5:30). Darkness and earthquakes often accompany a theophany, such as God's descent on Mount Sinai in Exodus 19:16-18. But the language of 13:10 can also refer to more than physical darkness. These statements about the heavenly bodies ("stars . . . sun . . . moon") no longer functioning may figuratively describe the total turn around of the political structure of the Near East, since Genesis 1:14-16 speaks of the sun, moon, and stars assigned "to govern" the world. Such collapsing-universe terminology can be understood to describe the arrival of a new order. The same would be true of the heavens trembling and the earth shaking, figures of speech suggesting all-encompassing destruction. Amos described the Fall of Samaria with such language as the sun going down at noon (Amos 8:9), and Ezekiel used similar language to describe the fall of Egypt (Ezek 32:7-8). Similar imagery is found in Joel 2:10, Revelation 6:12-14, and Isaiah 34:3. All this may be poetic, not literal, meaning the "lights" went out for these pagan nations. In 14:17-22, Isaiah focuses specifically on the destruction of Babylon. The Medes are mentioned because they, along with the Persians, captured Babylon in 539 BC. Although the Persians under King Cyrus were known for humane treatment of their enemies, the Medes were infamous for their cruelty as they raped women and dashed little children to death (13:16). Isaiah described the Chaldean pride (13:19) and glory with the same words that he had used to describe the branch of the Lord in 4:2; however, Babylon would become desolate like Sodom and Gomorrah (cf. 1:9). Her beautiful sites would be turned over to desert animals (13:21), and even the "nomads will refuse to camp there" (13:20). The place that once heard the music of merriment would echo only the sounds of the night creatures. The "wild goats" (13:21) are sometimes associated with demons in goat form called satyrs (see note; cf. Lev 17:7; 2 Chr 11:15).

When the Persian king Cyrus conquered Babylon, he did not level the site, and the walls were not destroyed until after an uprising was put down by Darius Hystaspis in 518 BC. The plan of Alexander the Great to make Babylon the capital of his world empire was never realized due to his early death, and by the last century before Christ, Strabo called the site a wilderness. By the time of the Muslim conquest in the seventh century AD, the site was desolate and deserted.

Since Babylon had captured the people of Judah, her collapse would signal their release. At this point, Isaiah inserted the joyful theme of God's compassion toward his people and their return home. All of this is greatly elaborated in chapters 40–66.

Chapter 14 contains a link between the description of Babylon's fall in chapter 13 and the taunt song against its king in 14:4-23. God's special love for his people, here called "the descendants of Jacob" (14:1), includes, but is not limited to, the people of Judah deported to Babylon. God will bring about the restoration of his people so that even strangers will desire to join them, so in a sense, Israel would eventually rule over, or at least assimilate, their own former captors (14:1-2). Nations that once dominated God's people will serve them and join in worshiping their God (cf. 11:10-12). All this is Old Testament language and imagery for the extension of God's reign over all nations, and of their service within it. Already in Esther 8:17, we read of outsiders joining God's covenant people out of fear; Acts 2:9-11 records the mixed group at Pentecost, and Acts 17:4, 17 mention Gentiles within the synagogues of Thessalonica and Athens. Impressed by the God of the Jews, Gentiles would often join them, but all this was only a harbinger of things to come in the messianic era.

The joy that accompanied the destruction of Babylon was as great as that experienced during the Exodus (14:4-8). The "king of Babylon" (14:4) probably does not refer to a specific ruler but to a representative line of rulers or to a kind of ruler. The whole world of the ancient Near East rejoiced at the fall of the harsh tyrant who had "struck the people with endless blows of rage" (14:6) in the same way that Assyria had done earlier (cf. 10:4); Babylon's weapon would also be broken by the Lord (cf.

9:4). The joy expressed by the nations is paralleled by the trees' singing out, "Since you have been cut down, no one will come now to cut us down" (14:8). Isaiah repeatedly personified nature and was especially fond of using the imagery of trees. Since good lumber was lacking in the alluvial plains of Mesopotamia, the kings of both Assyria and Babylon imported lumber from the famous trees of Lebanon for use in their extensive building projects.

Babylon's fall into Sheol, "the place of the dead" (14:9), is described in 14:9-15. Isaiah presents a graphic picture of the destiny of the king of Babylon (cf. 30:33) as his arrival in Sheol stirred up a commotion in the realm of the dead. Deceased earlier rulers seem stunned at the sight of the ultimate fate of the great king of former fame (14:10-11). The former status of the king is sharply contrasted with his humiliation in Sheol, as his former gorgeous robes were replaced by a covering of maggots and worms, and "the sound of the harp in your palace has ceased" (14:11). The end of the palace music means the end of pleasure and merriment (cf. Amos 6:5-6).

Much of the language in this passage is hyperbolic, and 14:12-14 seem to exaggerate conditions, since neither the Assyrian nor the Babylonian rulers claimed deity. The expression, "mountain of the gods far away in the north" (14:13) refers to Mount Zaphon (also called Mount Casius) to the north of Canaan. This was the religious equivalent of Mount Olympus among the Greeks and the residence of the Canaanite gods led by Baal or El. The language of challenge and self-promotion, especially with the old translation of "Lucifer" from the Latin in 14:12, has led some to see in this passage a reference to Satan (cf. Luke 10:18). The idea that the devil was called Lucifer before his fall was a very widespread idea in the past and shows up in literature affected by the Latin Bible and the KJV. However, the translation "Lucifer" is untenable and is no longer found in new versions. In the Luke passage, Jesus seems to be referring to an event of his own time, when the power of his kingdom was advancing against the powers of the kingdom of darkness. Although Satan is not the immediate referent in Isaiah, the rest of Scripture makes it clear that he is the evil being behind evil kings and behind the evil world city represented by Babylon. Thomas (1991:126) says, "Despite the fact that Satan is not referred to specifically in 14:12, his shadow lies behind this passage." The identification of the king of Tyre in Ezekiel 28 presents similar problems of interpretation to those found in Isaiah 14. Another example of addressing Satan through another person would be when Jesus spoke to Peter and said, "Get away from me Satan!" (Matt 16:23).

The next section shifts back to the earthly scene, where people were staring in astonishment at the corpse of the Babylonian king. The despot was merely "dumped into a mass grave" (14:19); his body was treated like a "worthless branch" to be discarded (14:18-19), in contrast to the glorious "Branch" from Jesse's root (cf. 11:1). This former world ruler was not even given a proper burial (14:20), in contrast to all the pomp that such world rulers expected. What a contrast to the "stump of David's family" (11:1) that would bear much fruit! This wretched dictator ended with neither tombstone nor offspring.

The Lord was determined to crush Babylon (14:22-23). Three times (in the Hebrew), the expression "declares the Lord" shows God's absolute opposition to Babylon. Its very site would be swept clean with the "broom of destruction" (14:23), and all the descendants of the king would be cut off without honor. This was partially fulfilled through Sennacherib's destruction of Babylon in 689 BC, but ultimately by the Medes and Persians in 539 BC. In contrast to Babylon, who will not have children or "children's children" left (14:22), Israel will always survive through a remnant (cf. 10:20-22; 11:11, 16).

Assyria was the major power of Isaiah's time (14:24-27), although references to God's judgment on Assyria are found elsewhere (e.g., 10:5-34). In this passage, the verses summarize the prophecy against Babylon. Also, Assyria preceded Babylon as a world ruler from Mesopotamia, so Isaiah repeated the announcement of Assyria's downfall to reinforce his predictions regarding Babylon. Earlier (cf. 8:10), God had promised to frustrate the plans of nations opposed to Judah, and in this passage the nations learn that God's designs cannot be frustrated. Twice earlier (9:4; 10:27), Isaiah referred to removing the burdensome yoke from Israel's shoulders. However, before Assyria's end, the Lord would use her as an instrument to punish other nations, several of which are listed in the following messages of doom.

◆     ## 2. Philistia (14:28-32)

28This message came to me the year King
Ahaz died:*

29 Do not rejoice, you Philistines,
   that the rod that struck you is
      broken—
   that the king who attacked you
      is dead.
For from that snake a more poisonous
      snake will be born,
   a fiery serpent to destroy you!
30 I will feed the poor in my pasture;
   the needy will lie down in peace.
But as for you, I will wipe you out with
      famine

and destroy the few who remain.
31 Wail at the gates! Weep in the
      cities!
   Melt with fear, you Philistines!
A powerful army comes like smoke
      from the north.
   Each soldier rushes forward eager
      to fight.

32What should we tell the Philistine
messengers? Tell them,

   "The LORD has built Jerusalem*;
      its walls will give refuge to his
      oppressed people."

14:28 King Ahaz died in 715 BC.   14:32 Hebrew *Zion.*

NOTES

14:28 *message.* The Hebrew is "oracle" (*massa'* [IH4853A, ZH5363]), as at 13:1.

*the year King Ahaz died.* This was probably 715 BC, but the chronology is not certain.

14:29 *Philistines.* Since the Philistines lived in the coastal area along the main route from Egypt to Mesopotamia, they were especially vulnerable to enemy attacks. Philistia was never a kingdom but was a society centered around five major cities.

*the rod that struck you.* If this is a reference to Sargon II and the remaining words refer to the progression of Assyrian kings, the sequence would be Sargon II, Sennacherib,

Esarhaddon, and Ashurbanipal, each of whom marched through Philistia and Canaan, but this is highly speculative.

*from that snake.* The Heb. has the strange expression, "from the root of that snake." In Egypt a snake was often used as the symbol of a ruler; it was often embroidered on their robes and represented on their headdresses.

*fiery serpent.* Heb. *sarap me'opep* [TH8314/5774, ZH8597/6414]. This probably refers to a darting, venomous snake. The KJV translates "fiery flying serpent" (cf. "flying serpent" in REB, NAB). Perhaps its darting action gave rise to the idea of flying, an idea reflected in some translations: Other versions, like the KJV, have the combination of "flying fiery serpent" (NRSV, GW). The idea of "flying fiery dragon" is found in the CEV, while the TEV simply has "flying dragon," and the NCV has "quick, dangerous snake."

**14:31 *Wail . . . Weep.*** Note the similar response from other nations under God's judgment (13:6; 15:2; 16:7; 23:1).

*comes like smoke from the north.* The various invading armies from the east always entered into Philistia and Canaan from the north. The "smoke" probably refers to the dust they stirred up.

**14:32 *built Jerusalem.*** Lit., "established Zion" (cf. NLT mg).

## COMMENTARY

After pronouncing judgment on the world powers of Babylon and Assyria, Isaiah turned to Israel's immediate neighbors, beginning with Philistia. Perhaps the Philistines were considered first among the neighbors because they lived within Palestine itself; in fact, Palestine gets its name from Philistia. Probably no other Canaanite group touched and affected the history of Israel as did the Philistines. They seem to have been Israel's perennial enemy.

The Philistines (or their immediate predecessors) were already present in the days of Abraham (Gen 21:32, 34), of Isaac (Gen 26), of Moses (Exod 13:17), and of Joshua. During the days of the Judges, the Philistines oppressed Israel under both Shamgar (Judg 3:31) and Samson (Judg 13–14). King Saul fought with them and they killed his son Jonathan (1 Sam 31). David finally subdued them, but they continued to appear sporadically after that time as a problem to the Israelites. Motyer (1993:147) gives a good summary of the Philistine historical background during the time of Isaiah. See also Tadmor (1966).

The prophets often referred to the Philistines as being under God's judgment, and pronouncements against the land of Philistia were common (Amos 1:6-8; Zeph 2:4-7; Jer 15:15-17; 47; Ezek 25:15-17; Zech 9:5-7). For more on the Philistines in general, see Howard (Hoerth 1994:231-250) and Kitchen (Wiseman 1973:53-78).

**The Oracle against Philistia.** This oracle against Philistia is the only one that Isaiah dated precisely ("the year King Ahaz died"). Suggested dates for this event range from 727 BC to 715 BC. It is possible that the occasion for this message was the Philistine revolt against Assyria, while King Sargon II (cf. 20:1) was preoccupied with serious revolts elsewhere. Tiglath-pileser III had died in 727 BC.

The interpretation of 14:29 varies greatly. Some suppose that the reference is to some sequence of Assyrian rulers who invaded the area: Tiglath-pileser III, Shalmaneser V, Sargon II, and Sennacherib. Others suggest a sequence of powers, for example, Assyria, Babylon, and a couple of others. Some have even suggested a messianic reference here, with the "rod that struck you" being the house of David, since no other king was so consistently victorious over the Philistines (cf. 1 Sam 17:50; 18:25-30; 19:8; 23:1-5; 2 Sam 5:17-25; 8:1). Targum Jonathan translates, "for the Messiah shall come forth from the descendants of Jesse, and his deeds among you shall be like those of the flying serpent" (Levey 1974:55).

The description of the Assyrian army in 14:31 is a more compact version of the one given in 5:26-29. The call to "weep" (14:31) is often associated with messages of doom (13:6; 15:2; 16:7; 23:1). Verse 32 implies that the Assyrian invasion that would destroy the Philistines would be unsuccessful against Judah. The reference in 14:32 is to Zion, not Jerusalem, (cf. NLT mg) and seems to look forward to the time mentioned in 2:2-4. Other references in these judgment oracles to Zion's exaltation include 14:1-2; 16:5; 18:7; 19:17.

◆     ## 3. Moab (15:1-16:14)

This message came to me concerning Moab:

In one night the town of Ar will be leveled,
and the city of Kir will be destroyed.
2 Your people will go to their temple in Dibon to mourn.
They will go to their sacred shrines to weep.
They will wail for the fate of Nebo and Medeba,
shaving their heads in sorrow and cutting off their beards.
3 They will wear burlap as they wander the streets.
From every home and public square will come the sound of wailing.
4 The people of Heshbon and Elealeh will cry out;
their voices will be heard as far away as Jahaz!
The bravest warriors of Moab will cry out in utter terror.
They will be helpless with fear.

5 My heart weeps for Moab.
Its people flee to Zoar and Eglath-shelishiyah.
Weeping, they climb the road to Luhith.
Their cries of distress can be heard all along the road to Horonaim.

6 Even the waters of Nimrim are dried up!
The grassy banks are scorched.
The tender plants are gone;
nothing green remains.
7 The people grab their possessions and carry them across the Ravine of Willows.
8 A cry of distress echoes through the land of Moab
from one end to the other—
from Eglaim to Beer-elim.
9 The stream near Dibon* runs red with blood,
but I am still not finished with Dibon!
Lions will hunt down the survivors—
both those who try to escape and those who remain behind.

## CHAPTER 16
1 Send lambs from Sela as tribute to the ruler of the land.
Send them through the desert to the mountain of beautiful Zion.
2 The women of Moab are left like homeless birds
at the shallow crossings of the Arnon River.
3 "Help us," they cry.
"Defend us against our enemies.
Protect us from their relentless attack.

Do not betray us now that we have
escaped.
⁴Let our refugees stay among you.
Hide them from our enemies until
the terror is past."

When oppression and destruction
have ended
and enemy raiders have
disappeared,
⁵then God will establish one of David's
descendants as king.
He will rule with mercy and truth.
He will always do what is just
and be eager to do what is right.

⁶We have heard about proud Moab—
about its pride and arrogance and
rage.
But all that boasting has
disappeared.
⁷The entire land of Moab weeps.
Yes, everyone in Moab mourns
for the cakes of raisins from Kir-
hareseth.
They are all gone now.
⁸The farms of Heshbon are abandoned;
the vineyards at Sibmah are
deserted.
The rulers of the nations have broken
down Moab—
that beautiful grapevine.
Its tendrils spread north as far as the
town of Jazer
and trailed eastward into the
wilderness.

Its shoots reached so far west
that they crossed over the Dead Sea.*

⁹So now I weep for Jazer and the
vineyards of Sibmah;
my tears will flow for Heshbon and
Elealeh.
There are no more shouts of joy
over your summer fruits and
harvest.
¹⁰Gone now is the gladness,
gone the joy of harvest.
There will be no singing in the
vineyards,
no more happy shouts,
no treading of grapes in the
winepresses.
I have ended all their harvest joys.
¹¹My heart's cry for Moab is like a
lament on a harp.
I am filled with anguish for
Kir-hareseth.*
¹²The people of Moab will worship
at their pagan shrines,
but it will do them no good.
They will cry to the gods in their
temples,
but no one will be able to save
them.

¹³The LORD has already said these things
about Moab in the past. ¹⁴But now the
LORD says, "Within three years, counting
each day,* the glory of Moab will be
ended. From its great population, only a
few of its people will be left alive."

15:9 As in Dead Sea Scrolls, some Greek manuscripts, and Latin Vulgate; Masoretic Text reads *Dimon;* also in
15:9b. 16:8 Hebrew *the sea.* 16:11 Hebrew *Kir-heres,* a variant spelling of Kir-hareseth. 16:14 Hebrew
*Within three years, as a servant bound by contract would count them.*

NOTES

**15:1 Ar.** The location of this site is unknown. Gerald Mattingly suggests the site as Khirbet
el-Bahi (ABD 1:321).

**Kir.** If this refers to Kir Hareseth, it is about fifteen miles south of the Arnon River and may
have been the capital of Moab at this time.

**15:2 Dibon.** Dibon was located about four miles north of the Arnon River.

**sacred shrines.** Heb. *bamoth* [ᵀᴴ1116, ᶻᴴ1195]. These were "high places," built on the heights
for pagan Canaanite worship.

**Nebo.** This was probably near Mount Nebo, north of the Arnon River.

*Medeba.* Medeba was a few miles southeast of Nebo and about six miles south of Heshbon.

*shaving their heads . . . cutting off their beards.* These were typical signs of mourning in ancient Near Eastern culture.

**15:3 *burlap.*** The Heb. *saq* [TH8242, ZH8566] refers to coarse dark cloth made from goat's hair and worn by mourners. It is usually translated "sackcloth."

*home.* The Heb. says "roofs," which were flat in that culture and were used for many outdoor activities.

**15:4 *Heshbon.*** Heshbon was located about eighteen miles east of the northern part of the Dead Sea.

*Elealeh.* Elealeh was about a mile north of Heshbon, with which it is always associated.

*Jahaz.* It was possibly just north of the Arnon River and about twenty miles from Heshbon. The entry for Jahaz in ABD (3:612) lists six possible sites.

**15:5 *Zoar.*** Probably it was somewhere near the southern end of the Dead Sea. Lot fled there from Sodom (Gen 14:2; 19:23, 30).

*Eglath-shelishiyah.* This appears to be a place name, though the site is unknown. Though not suitable here, the words could be translated and understood more lit.: "a three-year-old heifer" (cf. 1 Sam 1:24).

*Luhith . . . Horonaim.* The locations of these sites are unknown (cf. Jer 48:5).

**15:6 *Nimrim.*** Some identify this site with the Wadi en-Numeirah, ten miles from the southern end of the Dead Sea.

**15:7 *Ravine of Willows.*** Possibly this was the border between Moab and Edom.

**15:8 *Eglaim.*** Eglaim was probably near the northern border of Moab.

*Beer-elim.* Beer-elim was probably close to the southern border of Moab.

**15:9 *Dibon.*** As the NLT mg indicates, this is not what the Masoretic (traditional Heb.) Text reads. The MT reads "Dimon," probably because that is what the Heb. for "blood" (*dam* [TH1818, ZH1947]) sounds like. This is probably another example of Isaiah's penchant for wordplay.

*Lions.* This could refer to actual lions, or it could refer to the Assyrians (cf. 5:29; Jer 50:17). Animal names were sometimes used as titles of leaders among nomadic tribes. See the references in 2 Sam 23:20 and 1 Chr 11:22 to the "Ariels" of Moab, which in context suggest a warrior or an elite fighter; the NLT translates the term there as "champions."

**16:1 *Sela.*** Sela was the capital of Edom, located south of the Dead Sea. It was very inaccessible and naturally fortified. The name means "cliff."

*mountain of beautiful Zion.* More lit., "mount of the daughter of Zion."

**16:2 *Arnon.*** This indicates that the women were fleeing south, away from the northern invader.

**16:5 *David's descendants.*** Lit., "tent [house] of David." See 7:2; 9:7; Amos 9:11.

*just . . . right.* The Heb. terms for "justice" and "righteousness" are frequent in Isaiah, though they are sometimes obscured by English translations (cf. 9:7; 11:4; 28:6; 32:16; 33:5; 42:1, 3-4; 51:5).

**16:6 *proud Moab.*** Although small, Moab manifested as much pride as Babylon did.

**16:7 *cakes of raisins.*** Heb. *'ashishe* [TH0808, ZH0861], the plural construct of a word found only here and defined by HALOT 1:95 as "man" (cf. NIV). It is translated "foundations" in the NKJV and "prosperous farmers" in the REB, but most versions link it to the Heb. cognate *'ashishah* [TH0809, ZH0862] and translate it here as "raisin cakes" (HCSB, NASB, NRSV,

NJPS, ESV, NCV). If the English expression "raisin cakes" is understood as implying the presence of bread, it would be anachronistic since as far as we know raisins were not mixed into breads in the ancient Near East.

Another Hebrew word (*tsimmuqim* [TH6778, ZH7540]) found in 1 Sam 25:18; 30:12; 2 Sam 16:1; and 1 Chon. 12:40 [12:41] seems to refer to a similar item. It is described in HALOT 2:1033 as a "cake of dried grapes" and translated in 1 Sam 25:18 as "clusters of raisins" (KJV) or "cakes of pressed raisins" (NAB) "bunches of raisins" (TEV, GW, REB), and "handfuls of raisins" (CEV). Also notice the description of the figs in this same verse.

**16:8 Sibmah.** Sibmah was perhaps three miles west of the larger city, Heshbon (cf. Jer 48:32), and was possibly its suburb.

**Jazer.** Jazer was about fifteen miles north of the Dead Sea.

**Dead Sea.** The Heb. only has "sea" here, a designation that sometimes refers to the Mediterranean (cf. Ps 80). Here the reference is probably to the Dead Sea.

**16:10 no treading of grapes.** Instead, the enemy will tread the people.

**16:11 heart's cry.** The Heb. has *me'ay* [TH4578, ZH5055] (my bowels), an unusually strong anthropomorphism, especially if the subject is the Lord. The KJV has "my bowels shall sound like an harp."

**16:14 Within three years.** This time period is also designated in 20:3 and 37:30.

*counting each day.* The point seems to be a definite period of time, not a day less for the employer and not a day more for the employee.

## COMMENTARY

Although the oracles against Philistia and Edom are relatively brief, the oracle against Moab covers two chapters and is exceeded in length only by those against Egypt and Babylon. Other prophecies against Moab are found in Isaiah 11:14; 25:10; Jeremiah 4:8; Ezekiel 25:8-11; Amos 2:1-3; and Zephaniah 2:8-11.

The nation was located east of the Jordan River and the Dead Sea, and like the Philistines, the Moabites had been enemies of Israel for centuries, despite the fact that Moab and Israel both descended from Terah, the father of Abraham (Gen 11:27). King Balak of Moab had hired Balaam to seduce the Israelites into idolatry when they were about to enter the Promised Land (Num 25), and King Eglon had oppressed Israel for eighteen years during the time of the Judges. Under Saul and David, Israel had established control over Moab, although this was contested during the period of the divided kingdom. Generally, when the Moabites were not under Israel's authority, they made raids across the river into Israel (2 Kgs 13:20). They worshiped the deity Chemosh (1 Kgs 11:33) at their "shrines" (15:2; see also 16:12), which were built on hilltops and were traditionally known as "high places."

**The Oracle against Moab.** The oracle predicts the destruction and ruin of the land of Moab, and identifies many of its cities by name. This passage vividly describes the weeping and wailing that would be found in Moab after the coming invasion brought about by God. Isaiah mentions about fifteen cities that would be involved in the general lament (described in the Hebrew with a variety of words for weeping and wailing). Most of these cities were originally part of Israelite territory when

Moses and Joshua defeated Sihon, king of the Amorites. All of the cities north of the Arnon River once belonged to the tribe of Reuben, but throughout the years, the Moabites had pushed the Israelites out of these regions. Isaiah personified several cities as he vividly portrayed the plight of the devastated country.

"Shaving their heads" and "cutting off their beards" (15:2) reflect the customs of mourners then, as the sound of wailing covered the entire land (15:4, 8). Even Isaiah's heart wept for Moab (15:5). The "lions" (15:9) could refer to a ravaging army (cf. 5:29), or it could refer to literal lions and wild animals running freely over the landscape (cf. 13:21).

According to 16:1, the fugitives from Moab would learn about possible refuge in Judah and "send lambs . . . to the mountain of beautiful Zion." In the past, people from Judah had found refuge in Moab (Ruth 1:1), but now the reverse would take place. Now Moab must pay tribute to Jerusalem instead of to Samaria, capital of the northern kingdom, as they did in the past when Mesha of Moab paid 100,000 lambs a year to Ahab (2 Kgs 3:4). Notice, however, that the payment this time was not to Jerusalem, but to "the mountain of beautiful Zion" (16:1). Also notice the mention of "one of David's descendants" who will rule "with mercy and truth" and "will always do what is just" (16:5). Although the good King Hezekiah may have fulfilled this in part, the final reference seems to find fulfillment in Jesus the Messiah (cf. Acts 15:16), who will always do what is just and right. The distinct messianic overtones seem obvious, especially when compared to 9:6 and Amos 9:11. Targum Jonathan renders the first part of 16:1 as, "They shall send tribute to the mighty Messiah of Israel" (Levey 1974:56). Moab is representative of the nations that will come to the mountain of God to learn his ways (cf. 2:1-4).

The "pride and arrogance and rage" of Moab are noted, with the observation that "all that boasting has disappeared" (16:6) as the "entire land of Moab weeps" (16:7). The solution to Moab's situation could have been found in submission to the God of Israel, but according to 16:6, pride was a hindrance to that solution. Like Assyria and Babylon, Moab was extremely proud despite its relative insignificance.

In the mourning scene of 16:7-12, the focus is on the destruction of the vineyards that were once so plentiful. This was the end of the fruit of the vine in wine, grapes, and raisins. This passage contains a chiastic or introverted parallelism of the place names Kir-hareseth, Heshbon, Sibmah, and Jazer. Each is mentioned, once in 16:7-8 and a second time in 16:9-11. In 16:12, Moab's need to submit to the God of Israel is pointed out, for when the Moabites prayed at the shrine of their gods, they were wasting their time by praying to idols that could not answer.

The concluding verses (16:13-14) of this chapter give an additional word from the Lord concerning Moab. A precise date is added to the fulfillment of the judgment. This three-year interval compares with the three-year signs mentioned in 20:3 and 37:40, and probably provides grounds for confidence in even longer-range prophecies (cf. 14:24-27). Soon the country would be humbled, with barely a remnant surviving.

◆     ## 4. Damascus (Aram) (17:1-14)

This message came to me concerning Damascus:

"Look, the city of Damascus will
disappear!
It will become a heap of ruins.
²The towns of Aroer will be deserted.
Flocks will graze in the streets and
lie down undisturbed,
with no one to chase them away.
³The fortified towns of Israel* will also
be destroyed,
and the royal power of Damascus
will end.
All that remains of Syria*
will share the fate of Israel's
departed glory,"
declares the LORD of Heaven's
Armies.

⁴"In that day Israel's* glory will grow
dim;
its robust body will waste away.
⁵The whole land will look like a
grainfield
after the harvesters have gathered
the grain.
It will be desolate,
like the fields in the valley of
Rephaim after the harvest.
⁶Only a few of its people will be left,
like stray olives left on a tree after
the harvest.
Only two or three remain in the
highest branches,
four or five scattered here and there
on the limbs,"
declares the LORD, the God of Israel.

⁷Then at last the people will look to
their Creator
and turn their eyes to the Holy One
of Israel.
⁸They will no longer look to their idols
for help
or worship what their own hands
have made.

They will never again bow down to
their Asherah poles
or worship at the pagan shrines
they have built.
⁹Their largest cities will be like a
deserted forest,
like the land the Hivites and
Amorites abandoned*
when the Israelites came here so long
ago.
It will be utterly desolate.
¹⁰Why? Because you have turned from
the God who can save you.
You have forgotten the Rock who
can hide you.
So you may plant the finest grapevines
and import the most expensive
seedlings.
¹¹They may sprout on the day you set
them out;
yes, they may blossom on the very
morning you plant them,
but you will never pick any grapes
from them.
Your only harvest will be a load of
grief and unrelieved pain.

¹²Listen! The armies of many nations
roar like the roaring of the sea.
Hear the thunder of the mighty forces
as they rush forward like thundering
waves.
¹³But though they thunder like breakers
on a beach,
God will silence them, and they will
run away.
They will flee like chaff scattered by
the wind,
like a tumbleweed whirling before
a storm.
¹⁴In the evening Israel waits in terror,
but by dawn its enemies are dead.
This is the just reward of those who
plunder us,
a fitting end for those who
destroy us.

17:3a Hebrew *of Ephraim*, referring to the northern kingdom of Israel.   17:3b Hebrew *Aram*.   17:4 Hebrew
*Jacob's*. See note on 14:1.   17:9 As in Greek version; Hebrew reads *like places of the wood and the highest
bough*.

NOTES

**17:1 Damascus.** Damascus (along with Jericho) is one of the oldest continuously inhabited cities in the world. It is mentioned in connection with Abraham (Gen 14:15; 15:2).

**the city . . . will disappear!** The former glory of Damascus (representing Aram) will collapse into ruins. The Heb. word for "city" used here is *me'ir* [TH5892, ZH6551], lit., "from a city," and the similar sounding Heb. word "heap of ruins" (*me'i* [TH4596, ZH5075]) involves another of Isaiah's typical wordplays. Livingston gives a good overview of the city of Damascus (in Harrison 1985:96-106), and Malamat has a good summary of the Arameans (Wiseman 1973:134-155). Other prophecies concerning Damascus are found in Amos 1:3-5; Jer 49:23-27; Zech 9:1.

**17:2 Aroer.** This is the name of at least three known sites, one in southern Judah, about twelve miles southeast of Beersheba (1 Sam 30:28), and two in Transjordan—one on the rim of the Arnon Gorge (Deut 2:36; Josh 12:2) and the other to the north, east of Rabbah in Ammon (Josh 13:25; Judg 11:26). Surely one of the latter two sites is intended here because this was the area partly depopulated by Tiglath-pileser III. The Aroer located about fourteen miles east of the Dead Sea on the Arnon River marked the southern boundary of Aram's sphere of control (cf. 2 Kgs 10:32-33) and fits the context nicely. This Aroer, located in the Arnon Gorge, was taken by Hazael, the king of Aram, and became the southwest extremity of that nation (2 Kgs 10:32-33). It was apparently regained by Moab, for Jeremiah includes Aroer in his prophecy against Moab (Jer 48:19). This is probably the site of Isaiah's reference.

**towns of Aroer.** The Heb. involves wordplay on "towns of" (*'arey* [TH5892, ZH6551]) and "Aroer" (*'aro'er* [TH6177, ZH6876]).

**17:3 Israel.** The northern kingdom of Israel (here called Ephraim in the Heb.; cf. the NLT mg) had presumptuously allied itself with Damascus/Aram (cf. 7:2) against the Assyrian threat. Isaiah again (cf. 8:4) stated that Aram and Israel would be defeated by the Assyrians.

**Syria.** Heb. *Aram* (cf. the NLT mg). Syria did not exist until intertestamental times.

**17:4 Israel.** As the NLT mg indicates, the Heb. has *Jacob*.

**17:5 valley of Rephaim.** This refers to a small fertile area west of Jerusalem (cf. Josh 15:8).

**17:8 idols.** The Heb. has "altars" (*mizbekhoth* [TH4196, ZH4640]), probably used for Baal worship (cf. 1 Kgs 16:32).

**Asherah poles.** These were carved wooden images used in Canaanite Baal worship.

**pagan shrines.** The Heb. *khammanim* [TH2553, ZH2802] were incense altars often associated with "high places" (Lev 26:30) and with Baal worship (2 Chr 34:4).

**17:10 the Rock.** See 26:4; 30:29; 44:8; Deut 32:4, 15, 18.

**17:12 roaring of the sea.** This depicts Assyria, which is called a "mighty flood" in 8:7.

**17:13 chaff . . . tumbleweed.** See the similar description of the enemy in 29:5; 41:15-16; Ps 83:13.

COMMENTARY

Damascus was the capital of ancient Aram (as it is today of Syria). The city is located on a fertile plain east of snow-capped Mount Hermon, on the edge of the Arabian Desert, about 135 miles northeast of Jerusalem. This location on caravan routes from north to south and east to west put it in conflict with competing powers, especially Israel and Judah.

From the time of King David on, the Arameans of Damascus were often at war with Israel (1 Kgs 22:31; 2 Kgs 6:8), and this conflict intensified during the reigns of

Omri and Ahab. During the time of King Ahaz of Judah, the Arameans allied themselves with the northern kingdom of Israel and attacked Jerusalem (cf. 7:1-2).

**The Oracle about Damascus and Israel.** The first paragraph describes the desolate
condition of Damascus and Israel as a result of judgment. Damascus, the capital of
Aram, "will disappear" and "become a heap of ruins" (17:1). What would be left in
Aram is compared to "Israel's departed glory" (17:3). The disappearance of "royal
power" (17:3) from Damascus probably refers to 732 BC, when Tiglath-pileser III
captured it and made it an Assyrian province. At that time, many Israelite cities were
also captured (cf. 9:1).

In 17:4 (note the break in the NLT format), the prophet shifts from Damascus
to Israel, a change prepared for by the end of 17:3. Verses 4-6 continue the vivid
description of the former glory of Israel that "will grow dim" (17:4), and comparison is made with the desolation of the abandoned grain fields of Rephaim (17:5)
after the harvest. The scarcity of people left is illustrated with the vivid imagery of
only a few "stray olives" (17:6) left on the tree after it had been stripped. This pictures the dreadful situation that should waken the people to their need of God
their Creator, the Holy One of Israel, and turn them away from their idolatrous
practices (17:7-8).

The next passage (17:9-11) continues the description of their deserted and desolate landscape, a terrible situation resulting from their turning away from the Rock
that was able to hide them and the God who could save them (17:9-10). Even
though they toiled at planting the best vineyards, their only harvest would be "a
load of grief and unrelieved pain" (17:11).

◆    ### 5. Cush (18:1-7)

Listen, Ethiopia*—land of fluttering
    sails*
    that lies at the headwaters of the
    Nile,
<sup>2</sup> that sends ambassadors
    in swift boats down the river.

Go, swift messengers!
Take a message to a tall, smooth-
    skinned people,
    who are feared far and wide
for their conquests and destruction,
    and whose land is divided by
    rivers.

<sup>3</sup> All you people of the world,
    everyone who lives on the
    earth—
when I raise my battle flag on the
    mountain, look!

When I blow the ram's horn,
    listen!
<sup>4</sup> For the LORD has told me this:
"I will watch quietly from my dwelling
    place—
as quietly as the heat rises on
    a summer day,
or as the morning dew forms during
    the harvest."
<sup>5</sup> Even before you begin your
    attack,
while your plans are ripening
    like grapes,
the LORD will cut off your new growth
    with pruning shears.
He will snip off and discard your
    spreading branches.
<sup>6</sup> Your mighty army will be left dead in
    the fields

for the mountain vultures and wild
    animals.
The vultures will tear at the corpses
    all summer.
The wild animals will gnaw at the
    bones all winter.

⁷ At that time the LORD of Heaven's
    Armies will receive gifts

from this land divided by rivers,
from this tall, smooth-skinned
    people,
who are feared far and wide for
    their conquests and destruction.
They will bring the gifts to Jerusalem,*
    where the LORD of Heaven's Armies
    dwells.

18:1a Hebrew *Cush.*  18:1b Or *land of many locusts;* Hebrew reads *land of whirring wings.*  18:7 Hebrew *to Mount Zion.*

NOTES

**18:1** *Listen.* The Heb. *hoy* [TH1945, ZH2098], instead of the customary *massa'* [TH4853A, ZH5363], is used in these oracles.

*Ethiopia.* Heb. *kush.* Ethiopia is an anachronism here. Cush is the ancient name of that general area. Hayes (1996:280) summarizes, "This was a black, African civilization on African soil, known and respected throughout the ancient world."

*fluttering sails.* More lit., this means something like "whirring wings" (*tsiltsal* [cf. "act of whirring," TH6767A, ZH7527]). This is sometimes understood as a reference to the area where the humming and whirring sounds of tsetse flies, locusts, and other insects are heard, but it is also sometimes understood as a reference to the land of whirring wings, in the sense that numerous troops were ready to swarm against the enemy like locusts or crickets (cf. 7:18). The view represented in the NLT understands "whirring wings/fluttering sails" as a reference to a kind of light papyrus or reed boat that was especially suitable for river transportation in the lands of Cush and Egypt, but not intended for large bodies of water. Other modern translations express their different interpretations of the Heb.: "sailing ships" (REB), "buzzing insects" (NAB), "whirring locust" (NJB), "whirring wings" (NIV), and "fluttering sails" (ESV). The KJV has "shadowing with wings."

**18:2** *river.* This translates the Heb. word (*yam*) for "sea," but the "Nile" (18:1; lit. "rivers of Cush," probably the White Nile and Blue Nile) is probably the reference in this context. Several translations translate "Nile" here (TEV, REB, NRSV, CEV).

*smooth-skinned.* The precise meaning of the Heb. *morat* [TH4803, ZH5307] is unclear. The versions render "scattered and peeled" (KJV), "powerful and treading down" (NKJV), "smooth" (NASB, NRSV), "smooth-skinned" (REB), and "bronzed" (NAB, NJB).

**18:7** *bring the gifts to Jerusalem.* The Psalmist describes the time when Egypt would "come with gifts of precious metals," and "Ethiopia bow in submission to God" (Ps 68:31).

COMMENTARY

After addressing the countries to the north (Babylon, Assyria, and Aram) and countries adjacent to Israel (Philistia and Moab), Isaiah turned southward to address Cush and Egypt. This passage is a transitional unit and lacks the customary introductory particle, which is a marker in these oracles (see note on 18:1).

In chapter 18, Isaiah addresses Cush (later called Ethiopia). This brief oracle provides a transition to the following chapters (19–20) involving Egypt and Cush. Although far from Jerusalem, Cush was still part of God's creation and was accountable to him, especially as they might relate to God's covenant people. For more on the general culture of the Cushites, see Hayes (1996).

Kitchen (NBD 256) identifies Cush as the area "south of Egypt" (i.e. Nubia or northern Sudan, the Ethiopia of classical writers, not modern Abyssinia). The rulers of Cush (from the upper or southern Nile area) invaded Egypt and controlled it from about the middle of the eighth century BC to the middle of the seventh century BC, a rule that ended when the Assyrian kings Esarhaddon and Ashurbanipal invaded Egypt.

**The Oracle against Cush.** The opening words of this message briefly describe these tall people as known for their fast boats and smooth-skinned complexions (18:2). The somewhat elaborate description of the people from Cush suggests that they were a novelty and called for a bit of detailed information. They were also feared because their conquests resulted in widespread destruction.

The Lord warned that the whole world should take note when he raised the battle flag and blew the ram's horn (18:3). The Lord was watching quietly from his dwelling place and would rise to the occasion and snip off their spreading branches with pruning shears (18:5). Verse 6 gives a grisly description of the corpses lying exposed to animals and birds of prey that "tear at the corpses" and "gnaw at the bones."

In conclusion, 18:7 mentions that "the LORD of Heaven's Armies" will receive gifts from this land. In 16:1, the Moabites were asked to send tribute to Jerusalem (Zion) as gifts. According to 2 Chronicles 32:23, gifts were brought to Hezekiah after Sennacherib's death.

◆     ## 6. Egypt (19:1-25)

This message came to me concerning Egypt:

Look! The LORD is advancing against Egypt,
   riding on a swift cloud.
The idols of Egypt tremble.
   The hearts of the Egyptians melt with fear.

2 "I will make Egyptian fight against Egyptian—
brother against brother,
neighbor against neighbor,
city against city,
   province against province.
3 The Egyptians will lose heart,
   and I will confuse their plans.
They will plead with their idols for wisdom
   and call on spirits, mediums, and those who consult the spirits of the dead.

4 I will hand Egypt over
   to a hard, cruel master.
A fierce king will rule them,"
   says the Lord, the LORD of Heaven's Armies.

5 The waters of the Nile will fail to rise and flood the fields.
   The riverbed will be parched and dry.
6 The canals of the Nile will dry up,
   and the streams of Egypt will stink with rotting reeds and rushes.
7 All the greenery along the riverbank
   and all the crops along the river will dry up and blow away.
8 The fishermen will lament for lack of work.
   Those who cast hooks into the Nile will groan,

and those who use nets will lose
heart.
⁹There will be no flax for the
harvesters,
no thread for the weavers.
¹⁰They will be in despair,
and all the workers will be sick
at heart.

¹¹What fools are the officials of Zoan!
Their best counsel to the king of
Egypt is stupid and wrong.
Will they still boast to Pharaoh of
their wisdom?
Will they dare brag about all their
wise ancestors?
¹²Where are your wise counselors,
Pharaoh?
Let them tell you what God plans,
what the LORD of Heaven's Armies
is going to do to Egypt.
¹³The officials of Zoan are fools,
and the officials of Memphis* are
deluded.
The leaders of the people
have led Egypt astray.
¹⁴The LORD has sent a spirit of
foolishness on them,
so all their suggestions are wrong.
They cause Egypt to stagger
like a drunk in his vomit.
¹⁵There is nothing Egypt can do.
All are helpless—
the head and the tail,
the noble palm branch and the
lowly reed.
¹⁶In that day the Egyptians will be as
weak as women. They will cower in fear

beneath the upraised fist of the LORD of
Heaven's Armies. ¹⁷Just to speak the name
of Israel will terrify them, for the LORD
of Heaven's Armies has laid out his plans
against them.

¹⁸In that day five of Egypt's cities will
follow the LORD of Heaven's Armies. They
will even begin to speak Hebrew, the language of Canaan. One of these cities will
be Heliopolis, the City of the Sun.*

¹⁹In that day there will be an altar to the
LORD in the heart of Egypt, and there will
be a monument to the LORD at its border.
²⁰It will be a sign and a witness that the
LORD of Heaven's Armies is worshiped in
the land of Egypt. When the people cry to
the LORD for help against those who oppress them, he will send them a savior
who will rescue them. ²¹The LORD will
make himself known to the Egyptians.
Yes, they will know the LORD and will give
their sacrifices and offerings to him. They
will make a vow to the LORD and will keep
it. ²²The LORD will strike Egypt, and then
he will bring healing. For the Egyptians
will turn to the LORD, and he will listen to
their pleas and heal them.

²³In that day Egypt and Assyria will be
connected by a highway. The Egyptians
and Assyrians will move freely between
their lands, and they will both worship
God. ²⁴And Israel will be their ally. The
three will be together, and Israel will be
a blessing to them. ²⁵For the LORD of
Heaven's Armies will say, "Blessed be
Egypt, my people. Blessed be Assyria, the
land I have made. Blessed be Israel, my
special possession!"

19:13 Hebrew *Noph*.    19:18 Or *will be the City of Destruction.*

NOTES

19:1 *riding on a swift cloud.* This is a metaphor of the victorious Lord heading for Egypt by
riding on a cloud. Similar imagery is also found in Ps 68:4, and Ps 104:3 refers to the clouds
as God's chariot; Joel 2:2 describes the "day of the Lord" as a "day of clouds and blackness"
(cf. Zeph 1:15). The prophet Ezekiel (Ezek 30:3), in his judgment oracle against Egypt,
describes the day of the LORD as "a day of clouds and gloom, a day of despair for the nations."
Imagery found in the ancient Canaanite texts (Ugaritic) describe Baal in similar language. This
kind of imagery is also found in the NT, which speaks of those who will "see the Son of Man
arrive on the clouds of heaven with power and great glory" (Matt 24:30; cf. Matt 26:64).

**19:2 *Egyptian fight against Egyptian.*** Civil strife and discord are known to have prevailed in Egypt before the Cushite dynasty took over, which happened close to Isaiah's time. The Libyan dynasty clashed with the Cushites and with the Saites of Dynasty 24. We also know from history that Piankhi, a Nubian prince, raided Egypt in about 728 BC; his successor, Shabako, also invaded that land, successfully uniting Ethiopia and Egypt under Nubian rule (715–664 BC). Thereafter, Psammetichus I, a prince of Sais in the Delta, arose to gain control of all Egypt. All of this involved the internal strife described by Isaiah.

**19:3 *confuse their plans.*** Cf. Ps 33:10.

**19:5 *Nile.*** The Heb. has "sea" (*yam* [TH3220, ZH3542]), which stands for the Nile here, as in 18:2.

**19:6 *Nile.*** The Heb. has "river" (*nahar* [TH5104A, ZH5643]), which refers to the Nile.

**19:8 *fishermen.*** In Num 11:5, reference is made to the Israelites' memory of the fish they enjoyed in Egypt.

**19:11 *fools.*** The description of the counselors of Zoan as "fools" is striking in view of the proverbial fame of Egypt's wisdom (cf. 1 Kgs 4:30; Acts 7:22).

**19:13 *Zoan.*** Located in the northeast section of the Delta, Zoan was once the capital of the nation. Its earliest history is obscure, but it became prominent as a capital of the pharaohs. At a later period, it was used occasionally by Nubian rulers as a royal residence.

**19:13 *Memphis.*** This translates the Heb. for "Noph," as stated in the NLT mg. The officials of Zoan and the leaders of Memphis are paired to represent the leadership of the doomed nation. Zoan and Memphis were also the current and ancient capitals of Egypt. Memphis lies at the southern tip of the Delta, about fourteen miles south of Cairo. By giving two termini, one north and one south, the prophet in effect indicated that throughout the length and breadth of the land there was not a wise man who could cope with the existing emergency.

**19:15 *the head and the tail, the noble palm branch and the lowly reed.*** The two pairs of opposites used here also occur in 9:14 and represent the totality of the population, both the leaders and the common laborers.

**19:16 *In that day.*** Note the six-fold repetition of this phrase (19:16, 18, 19, 21, 23, 24).

**19:18 *Hebrew, the language of Canaan.*** The Heb. says only "the language of Canaan," which is assumed to be Heb. here.

***Heliopolis, the City of the Sun.*** Since the Heb. for "destruction" is so similar to the Heb. for "sun," the expression is sometimes translated "City of Destruction" (NIV, NCV, NASB, ESV). Some would say that later Jewish scribes parodied the name by exchanging the Heb. word for "sun" (*kheres* [TH2775A, ZH3064]) with the almost identical Heb. word for "destruction" (*heres* [TH2041A, ZH2239]). Only one stroke in the first letter distinguishes the two words. A number of versions and ancient texts, including the Dead Sea Scrolls, have the reading "City of the Sun" (*'ir kheres* [TH2775B, ZH6557], i.e., Heliopolis, a center for the worship of the sun god Ra that was destroyed by Nebuchadnezzar; Jer 43:12-13).

**19:19 *In that day.*** This is probably the same referent as in 2:2-4; 11:10; 46:2; 49:6. Then not only Egypt but also other Gentiles will enjoy God's favor.

***altar . . . monument.*** The references to an "altar" (*mizbeakh* [TH4196, ZH4640]) and "monument" (*matsebah* [TH4676, ZH5167]) are another example of Isaiah's penchant for wordplay.

**19:23 *highway.*** The Heb. word *mesillah* [TH4546, ZH5019] is a common figure in the book that indicates the removal of barriers. This imagery is very appropriate in view of Israel's hilly terrain (cf. 11:16; 33:8; 35:8; 40:3; 49:11; 62:10).

**19:25 Blessed be Egypt, my people. Blessed be Assyria.** This is a striking use of blessing language that at one time was reserved only for Israel (cf. Deut 7:6; 1 Pet 2:9).

COMMENTARY

This chapter contains an oracle about Egypt and, in essence, carries on through the next chapter with reference there to Ethiopia (Cush). For parallel passages to this oracle against Egypt, see Jeremiah 46 and Ezekiel 29-32.

The Bible references to specific times in Egypt's history cover a span of approximately 2,000 years—from Abraham's visit (Gen 12:10-13:1), when Egypt was already ancient, to the conversion of the Ethiopian eunuch (Acts 8:26-40). From the days of the patriarchs, when the sons of Jacob found refuge from famine within her borders, Egypt had a profound effect on the nation of Israel. But Joseph's farsighted wisdom was soon forgotten by the Egyptians, and the Israelites were severely oppressed during the time of their 400-year tenure in Egypt.

Under Solomon, relations between the two countries were friendly, but his son Rehoboam experienced losses under Pharaoh Shishak, who belonged to a new dynasty. The expansionist policies of Assyria during the eighth century BC caused some Israelites to favor an alliance with Egypt as a safeguard, an attitude especially manifested during the time of Hezekiah. In chapter 19, and later in chapters 30 and 31, Isaiah warned against making any such alliances.

Webb (1996:94) suggests a twofold division for this passage; 19:1-15 depicts the Lord bringing judgment on Egypt, and 19:16-25 points to her final repentance and gathering into the kingdom of God. The passage carries the typical two great themes of prophetic preaching, judgment and salvation.

**The Oracle about Egypt.** The opening verse describes the Lord as "riding on a swift cloud" (19:1), using a metaphor also found in Psalms 68:4 and 104:3, a sight that makes the Egyptians "melt with fear" (19:1). The language of "advancing against Egypt" (19:1) does not deny God's omnipresence, but focuses the reader's attention on that one place that he will judge, demonstrating his power over their gods. Earlier, at the time of the plagues and the Exodus of Israel, God's presence had been felt in Egypt, and it had been a disaster for the country and its gods.

The next section (19:2-4) describes infighting among the Egyptians: "brother against brother . . . city against city" (19:2). The Lord "will confuse their plans" although they call on "their idols . . . spirits, mediums, and those who consult the spirits of the dead" (19:3). Egypt was famous for its wisdom, but the greater wisdom of the Lord frustrated their attempts to save themselves. Three times the Lord declares that he will judge the Egyptians: "I will make Egyptian fight against Egyptian" (19:2), "I will confuse their plans" (19:3), and "I will hand Egypt over to a hard, cruel master" (19:4).

In 19:5-10, the description of judgment continues with a vivid picture of drought, as the canals of the Nile and the streams of Egypt dried up (19:6). Even the "riverbed will be parched and dry" (19:5), with the result that the fishermen "lament for lack of work" (19:8). Since the Nile was Egypt's lifeline, the drought would bring loss of income for all those employed in water-related work. "There will be no flax for the harvesters, no thread for the weavers" (19:9).

The next section continues to expose the folly of the leaders of Egypt (famed internationally for their "wisdom"), whose counselors are described as "fools" and whose counsel is "stupid and wrong" (19:11). The Egyptian leaders "have led Egypt astray" (19:13). Their counsel is wrong because "the LORD has sent a spirit of foolishness on them" (19:14). In the eyes of the Lord, the traditional wise ones of Egypt were only fools and there was "nothing Egypt can do" (19:15).

Eventually, they will all "cower in fear beneath the upraised fist of the LORD of Heaven's Armies" (19:16). The "upraised fist" of the Lord is very strong language in itself, but here it is used with the title of God often used by Isaiah in judgment scenes (cf. 14:26-27). In fact, "just to speak the name of Israel" would strike deep terror in their hearts (19:17).

In 19:18, five Egyptian cities are mentioned that will someday speak Hebrew (see note). The cities are not identified and the use of five could be intended to convey a small or representative number (cf. 17:6; 30:17) in contrast to the vast number of Egyptian villages. Some believe the number could refer to occupied Jewish settlements (cf. such sites as Elephantine or Leontopolis). Since many Jews did live in Egypt in later times, it is possible that at the time of Isaiah, a beginning of these settlements could be observed (cf. the cities of Jer 44:1 where Jews settled). Watts (1985:259) surveys and summarizes information on the surprisingly large number of Israelite and Jewish migrations and settlements in Egypt from patriarchal times through the Hellenistic period. Kissane (1941:211) suggests that possibly the use of "five" could allude to the idea of the five cities overthrown in Joshua's first major campaign, seen as an earnest of the coming total conquest (Josh 10:22-43).

"The language of Canaan" (see note on 19:18) is an expression that has also evoked much speculation. Since Hebrew evolved out of Canaanite, Hebrew is usually understood as the referent. However, it must next be determined whether this kind of terminology then refers symbolically to Egypt's allegiance to the Lord (religious use) or whether it signifies only the presence of Jews in Egypt (ethnic use). Of course, the two uses do overlap. The former interpretation would refer to the religious language of faith and trust in the God of Israel. This would be a symbolic reference to Egypt's allegiance to the Lord (cf. 19:21-22, 25). Another possibility is that 19:18 refers to members of the covenant community that moved to Egypt and spread the worship of the true God there. After the Babylonian invasion and the murder of Gedaliah, a number of Jews did flee to Egypt and were allowed to reside there (Jer 43:7; 44:1). However, the fugitives from Judah in Jeremiah 44:17-19 appear more interested in the Queen of Heaven than in the Lord. Yet another interpretation understands the expression "language of Canaan" not to refer to the Hebrew language or to the ethnic presence of Jews in Egypt, but to the language of "the merchant people" (cf. 23:11; Hos 12:7; Ezek 17:4). This understanding of the phrase has in view Jews or Egyptians who swore by the Lord but retained the language of Canaan, the idolatrous merchant people. This would be a mongrel speech, the expression of a mixed or impure religion, in contrast to the pure language that is associated with conversion to God in Zephaniah 3:9.

The significance of "Heliopolis, the City of the Sun" (19:18) adds to the problem of interpretation. Isaiah may have played on the word for "sun," just as he used "Dimon" to represent "Dibon" in 15:9. Heliopolis was an important center for the worship of the sun god Ra, but that worship would be destroyed when Israel's God took action. Jeremiah 43:13 seems to offer support for this explanation.

The text then goes on to say that at that time "there will be an altar to the LORD in the heart of Egypt" (19:19). Other than the altars erected by Noah (the first person to build an altar to the Lord) and by Moses (at Rephidim and Sinai), there is no biblical record of an altar being erected to the Lord outside of the land of Israel. In addition to the "altar" in the heart of Egypt, there is also to be a "monument" located at the border (19:19). It was legitimate to set up monuments (KJV, "pillars") as memorials but not as religious symbols (cf. Deut 16:22). Such a monument could be a memorial of the Lord's promise to Abraham (cf. Gen 12:3; 22:18), which included a promised deliverer, a savior. Most commentators also mention the situation in Joshua 22:26-27, when an altar was built near the Jordan River by the Transjordanian tribes.

This chapter ends with a reference to the time when "the LORD will make himself known to the Egyptians" who will then give their "sacrifices and offerings to him" (19:21). At that time, the Lord will "listen to their pleas and heal them" (19:22). The description of Egypt's participation in the worship of the Lord resembles the descriptions in 18:7 and 60:7 (cf. Zeph 3:10). Zechariah 14:16-19 presents a similar picture, although there the Egyptians seem less eager to serve God. Offerings from foreigners are also mentioned in 56:7; 60:7 (cf. Zech 14:16-19).

The allegiance of foreign powers to the God of Israel reaches a climax in these verses (19:23-25) when Assyria joins Egypt and Israel in worshiping the Lord. These ancient enemies are pictured as standing at a connecting highway through Israel, a road of equal access. In 11:16, Isaiah had spoken about a highway from Egypt and Assyria that would make possible the return of Israel from captivity. But the highway in 19:23-25 was for the former captors—the Assyrians and the Egyptians! For centuries, Egyptians and Assyrians had fought each other, but in the future they will be linked in a bond of friendship sealed by their common allegiance to the Lord (cf. 25:3). The new highway linking former enemies would signal a new peace and harmony, not only in social and commercial matters, but in spiritual reality; they will worship together. Egyptians and Assyrians, once enemies, will become brothers and sisters in the Lord and "will both worship God" (19:23). In addition, Israel will be a third party in this new order, not third in rank, but one of three united in spirit before God, forming a spiritual body and a blessing. This finds its reality in God's new people, the new humanity, where Jews and Gentiles are made one by virtue of their faith in Christ (Eph 2:14).

◆       7. Egypt and Cush (20:1-6)

In the year when King Sargon of Assyria sent his commander in chief to capture the Philistine city of Ashdod,* ²the LORD told Isaiah son of Amoz, "Take off the burlap you have been wearing, and remove your sandals." Isaiah did as he was told and walked around naked and barefoot.

³Then the LORD said, "My servant Isaiah has been walking around naked and barefoot for the last three years. This is a sign—a symbol of the terrible troubles I will bring upon Egypt and Ethiopia.* ⁴For the king of Assyria will take away the Egyptians and Ethiopians* as prisoners. He will make them walk naked and barefoot, both young and old, their buttocks bared, to the shame of Egypt. ⁵Then the Philistines will be thrown into panic, for they counted on the power of Ethiopia and boasted of their allies in Egypt! ⁶They will say, 'If this can happen to Egypt, what chance do we have? We were counting on Egypt to protect us from the king of Assyria.'"

20:1 Ashdod was captured by Assyria in 711 BC.   20:3 Hebrew *Cush;* also in 20:5.   20:4 Hebrew *Cushites.*

NOTES

20:1 *Sargon.* This is the only reference to Sargon II (721–705 BC) in the Bible.

*Ashdod.* This was the chief and northernmost of the five great Philistine cities; it was located about thirty-three miles west of Jerusalem and two or three miles from the coast.

20:2 *burlap.* Traditionally called "sackcloth," this was a kind of clothing worn by mourners (cf. 15:3); it is possible that prophets also wore it (2 Kgs 1:8; Zech 13:4; Matt 3:4).

*Isaiah . . . walked around naked and barefoot.* This seems to be the only symbolical act recorded in Isaiah. "Naked" (*'arom* [TH6174, ZH6873]) does not necessarily mean absolute absence of any covering (although it does in Job 1:21). It can simply indicate stripped (as in the NIV here) of most normal clothing. "Barefoot" (*yakhep* [TH3182, ZH3504]) is only found five times in the OT and three of them are in this chapter.

20:4 *buttocks bared.* The Heb. is "buttocks" (*shet* [TH8351, ZH9268]) "bared" (*khasap* [TH2834, ZH3103]) and virtually all the translations carry this same idea (KJV, NASB, NCV, NIV, NJB, NRSV, ESV, NAB, REB, TEV, GW, NJPS). See 2 Sam 10:4 for a parallel of this practice, which was intended to bring about great shame in that culture.

20:6 *They will say.* The Heb. has the fuller, "the people who live on this coast will say," possibly referring to the coastal nations of Phoenicia, Philistia, and Judah.

COMMENTARY

This chapter's oracle addressing both Egypt and Cush is also an epilogue to chapters 18–19, just as 16:13-14 is to 15:1–16:12. The prediction given in 19:23-25 was a long way from being fulfilled in Isaiah's day, and 20:1-6 portrays the hatred between the Assyrians and the Egyptians in his time. Isaiah had already declared the destiny of Cush (ch 18), and Egypt (ch 19), and now he presents a summary of this general theme.

    The general background was the revolt of Philistia against Assyria (713–711 BC; cf. 14:28-31). In 715 BC, Egypt was overcome by Shabako, ruler of Cush, who united Egypt and Cush under a Cushite suzerainty that prevailed until 664 BC. This general period seems to be what the prophet was discussing in chapter 20. Isaiah 20:1 is the only place in the Bible where the name of Sargon II appears, and his very existence was at one time doubted by some. As successor of Shalmaneser V, he ascended to the Assyrian throne in either 722 or 721 BC, ruling until 705 BC. Although mentioned only here in the Scriptures, Sargon played an important role in the history of Israel and Judah.

By 711 BC, Sargon II of Assyria had sent troops to quell the revolt at the Philistine city of Ashdod where the uprising had started. With Ashdod in ruins, the revolt was ended. King Yamani of Ashdod fled to Egypt, but facing the wrath of Assyria under Sargon II, the Egyptians handed him over to the Assyrians (Webb 1996:97).

Although Judah may have sympathized with this revolt, Isaiah made it very clear that the rebels could expect no help from Egypt. By symbolic action and by preaching, the prophet warned of the dangers of trusting Egypt. Having vainly turned to Egypt and Cush they, like the Philistines, would not know where to turn next ("what chance do we have?" 20:6). Unless they turned to the Lord, there would be no help.

**The Oracle against Egypt and Cush.** To communicate his message, Isaiah was to "take off the burlap" he was wearing and also to remove his sandals and walk around "naked and barefoot" (20:2), looking like a captive of Assyria. Possibly he was completely naked because that was the disgrace normally suffered by captives, who without clothing or sandals had no protection from the blazing sun or the stones that dug into their feet over the endless miles. However, it is also possible that the prophet was not "stark naked" but kept on a very short tunic or breechcloth when going about his public work (see note on 20:2). The point seems to be that his attire was viewed as unnatural and noteworthy. Also we need not imagine that Isaiah walked around this way for the entire "three years" (20:3) anymore than we need to assume that Ezekiel lay on his side for 390 days without getting up (Ezek 4:9). Perhaps part of each day was used for such purposes. Other prophets were asked to go through equally difficult experiences as signs to Israel. Hosea endured a trying marriage, and Ezekiel's wife died as an illustration for the nation (Ezek 24:16-24).

◆     ## 8. Desert by the Sea (Babylon) (21:1-10)

This message came to me concerning Babylon—the desert by the sea*:

Disaster is roaring down on you from the desert,
like a whirlwind sweeping in from the Negev.
²I see a terrifying vision:
I see the betrayer betraying,
the destroyer destroying.
Go ahead, you Elamites and Medes,
attack and lay siege.
I will make an end
to all the groaning Babylon
caused.

³My stomach aches and burns with pain.
Sharp pangs of anguish are upon me,
like those of a woman in labor.
I grow faint when I hear what God is planning;
I am too afraid to look.
⁴My mind reels and my heart races.
I longed for evening to come,
but now I am terrified of the dark.
⁵Look! They are preparing a great feast.
They are spreading rugs for people to sit on.
Everyone is eating and drinking.

But quick! Grab your shields and
prepare for battle.
You are being attacked!

⁶Meanwhile, the Lord said to me,
"Put a watchman on the city wall.
Let him shout out what he sees.
⁷He should look for chariots
drawn by pairs of horses,
and for riders on donkeys and camels.
Let the watchman be fully alert."

⁸Then the watchman* called out,
"Day after day I have stood on the
watchtower, my lord.

Night after night I have remained at
my post.
⁹Now at last—look!
Here comes a man in a chariot
with a pair of horses!"
Then the watchman said,
"Babylon is fallen, fallen!
All the idols of Babylon
lie broken on the ground!"
¹⁰O my people, threshed and winnowed,
I have told you everything the LORD
of Heaven's Armies has said,
everything the God of Israel has
told me.

**21:1** Hebrew *concerning the desert by the sea.*    **21:8** As in Dead Sea Scrolls and Syriac version; Masoretic Text reads *a lion.*

## NOTES

**21:1 *Babylon.*** The Heb. has only "concerning the desert by the sea" (cf. NLT mg), which is commonly understood to refer to Babylonia. Other symbolic names used by Isaiah include his refererence to Cush as "the land of whirring wings" (18:1), Edom as "Dumah" (21:11), which is Hebrew for "silence [of death]" (cf. Ps 94:17; 115:17), Jerusalem as "Ariel," which means either "hearth" or "lion of God" (29:1), and Egypt as "Rahab" which means "stormy arrogance" (30:7). Although Babylon was in the middle of a desert and not a coastal town, the site was near the two main rivers of that area. Also Jer 51:13 addresses Babylon as a "city rich with water."

**21:2 *Elamites.*** Elam was located in what today is southern Iran. The Medes lived in Media, located in today's northwest Iran.

**21:5 *eating and drinking.*** According to Dan 5, Belshazzar held a feast the very night that Babylon was captured.

**21:7 *camels.*** Camels were used in warfare, as shown in Judg 6:5.

**21:8 *watchman.*** As the NLT mg indicates, the Heb. of the MT is the word for "lion." The LXX translators apparently read it as a personal name (Uriah), and some have suggested that the reference is about shouting out or roaring like a lion.

**21:9 *Babylon is fallen.*** This line is used in Rev 14:8 and 18:2.

## COMMENTARY

This is the first of two oracles that do not use a direct name for the nation involved. Most commentators understand it to refer to Babylon or Babylonia, which is mostly desert but does border on the sea known today as the Persian Gulf. The attack from Elam and Media (21:2), which border Babylonia, also implies this identification, and 21:9 seems to confirm this view. The cryptic "Desert by the Sea" may be a derogatory title. Payne (1986:734) suggests, "the name Babylon is withheld till verse 9, so that the oracle seems particularly obscure to modern readers; it was probably intended to be cryptic even to the prophet's first hearers, no doubt in order to compel their careful attention."

Chapter 21 comprises three burdens dealing respectively with Babylonia, Edom, and Arabia. These will be followed by a fourth, on Jerusalem (ch 22).

**Oracle against Babylon.** Babylon's fall is described and the invading Elamites and Medes are compared to "a whirlwind sweeping in from the Negev" (21:1-4). The Elamites were a perpetual enemy of Assyria and Babylon, and later they were part of the Persian army that conquered Babylon. At the collapse of Babylon, the groaning of the many nations she enslaved would come to an end. The graphic and gruesome scene brings the prophetic response, "My stomach aches and burns with pain. Sharp pangs of horror are upon me, like the pangs of a woman in labor" (21:3).

The prophet and the watchman are described in 21:5-9, concluding with the watchman's emphatic words, "Babylon is fallen, fallen! All the idols of Babylon lie broken on the ground!" (21:9).

◆     ## 9. Dumah (Edom) (21:11-12)

¹¹This message came to me concerning Edom*:

Someone from Edom* keeps calling to me,
"Watchman, how much longer until morning?
When will the night be over?"
¹²The watchman replies,
"Morning is coming, but night will soon return.
If you wish to ask again, then come back and ask."

21:11a Hebrew *Dumah*, which means "silence" or "stillness." It is a wordplay on the word *Edom*.
21:11b Hebrew *Seir*, another name for Edom.

### NOTES

**21:11 *Edom*.** The Hebrew behind the first word translated "Edom" is *dumah* [TH1746, ZH1873], a word meaning "silence" (cf. NLT mg). It is a wordplay on the similar Hebrew word for Edom, the land south of the Dead Sea.

***When will the night be over?*** The Heb. phrase *mah millel* is variously translated in modern English versions: "what of the night" (NRSV, NJPS), "what is left of the night" (NIV, REB), "how much longer the night" (NAB), "what time of night" (NJB, ESV), "how far gone is the night" (NASB), "how much of the night is left" (NCV), and "how soon will the night be over" (TEV).

### COMMENTARY

The title of this oracle undoubtedly reflects Isaiah's frequent use of wordplay (see note on 21:11). "Edom" (21:11a) translates the Hebrew for "Dumah" (as the NLT mg indicates). "Seir" is also another name for Edom (see 21:11b; it is mentioned only in the NLT footnote). Seir was sometimes used to designate the land of the Edomites (cf. Obad 17) and seems to have been to Edom what Zion was to Israel (cf. Obad 8, 17).

The people of Edom were descendants of Esau, and like the Moabites, were also constant enemies of Israel from the time of the Exodus. They lived south of the Dead Sea, and whenever a weakness was perceived in Judah, the Edomites were quick to move in for the plunder. Kenneth Hoglund provides a good overview of Edom (Hoerth 1994:335-347).

**The Oracle about Edom.** This brief message concerning Edom surprisingly covers only two verses. They are limited to the one theme of the watchman, and his role is enigmatic. It seems that the call to the watchman concerns a question of how much longer the night of suffering will last before the hope of morning appears. The watchman replies that although "morning is coming, . . . night will soon return." Motyer (1999:149) thinks the text is saying that "true dawn is in the undated future and in the meantime darkness predominates."

◆        **10. Arabia (21:13-17)**

¹³This message came to me concerning Arabia:

> O caravans from Dedan,
>     hide in the deserts of Arabia.
> ¹⁴O people of Tema,
>     bring water to these thirsty people,
>     food to these weary refugees.
> ¹⁵They have fled from the sword,

> from the drawn sword,
> from the bent bow
>     and the terrors of battle.

¹⁶The Lord said to me, "Within a year, counting each day,* all the glory of Kedar will come to an end. ¹⁷Only a few of its courageous archers will survive. I, the LORD, the God of Israel, have spoken!"

**21:16** Hebrew *Within a year, as a servant bound by contract would count it.* Some ancient manuscripts read *Within three years,* as in 16:14.

#### NOTES

**21:13 Arabia.** The term means "desert" or "steppe" and is the name given to the peninsula lying east of Palestine and the Red Sea. It is the largest peninsula in the world, covering an area of almost one million square miles, but only a small part of Arabia is in view here.

**Dedan.** The Dedanites were descendants of Abraham and Keturah (Gen 25:1-3); they were a trading tribe of the Arabs. Their merchant activities are mentioned in Ezek 28:20; 38:13 (Jer 21:13-17 should be compared with Jer 49:28-33).

**21:16 Kedar.** In a restricted sense, Kedar is the name for an Ishmaelite tribe of nomads that roamed as far as the Elamite (Persian) Gulf. In this passage, it is probably a comprehensive term for all of the northern Arabian tribes. Kedar is named about a dozen times in the OT and was known for its flocks (60:7; Ezek 27:21).

#### COMMENTARY

The oracle against Arabia is not surprising here since Edom often worked in close conjunction with the Arabians, the descendants of Ishmael, especially the Dedanites (cf. Ezek 25:13). Arabians are mentioned only a few times in the Old Testament. The queen of Sheba who came to Jerusalem to visit Solomon was an Arabian. During the reign of Jehoram (in Elisha's time), a raiding party from Arabia carried off his wives and sons (2 Chr 21:16-17), leaving only Ahaziah, the youngest (2 Chr 22:1).

**The Oracle against Arabia.** The concluding verses of this chapter (21:13-17) concern Arabia. In a chapter containing oracles about the desert (cf. the Heb. of 21:1), some reference to the Arabs is not surprising. It is difficult to ascertain how much of this area was intended in Isaiah's prophecy, but he was probably referring to the immediate western and central area and the northern section.

By Hezekiah's day, Arabians served as mercenaries in the defense of Jerusalem against Sennacherib's invasion. But Isaiah warned that the day would come when caravans (the Arabians were famous traders) would have to leave the main trade roads for fear of their lives (21:13).

The weapons used by the Arabs were ineffective against the superior weapons of the Assyrians and, later, of the Babylonians (21:15). Eventually, the Lord would tell Nebuchadnezzar and his army to attack Kedar and blot out the warriors from the East (Jer 49:28), which he did (Jer 49:28-29; cf. Jer 2:10).

◆     **11. The Valley of Vision (Jerusalem) (22:1-25)**

This message came to me concerning Jerusalem—the Valley of Vision*:

What is happening?
    Why is everyone running to the
        rooftops?
²The whole city is in a terrible
        uproar.
    What do I see in this reveling city?
Bodies are lying everywhere,
    killed not in battle but by famine
        and disease.
³All your leaders have fled.
    They surrendered without
        resistance.
The people tried to slip away,
    but they were captured, too.
⁴That's why I said, "Leave me alone
        to weep;
    do not try to comfort me.
Let me cry for my people
    as I watch them being destroyed."

⁵Oh, what a day of crushing defeat!
    What a day of confusion and terror
brought by the Lord, the LORD of
        Heaven's Armies,
    upon the Valley of Vision!
The walls of Jerusalem have been
        broken,
    and cries of death echo from the
        mountainsides.
⁶Elamites are the archers,
    with their chariots and charioteers.
    The men of Kir hold up the shields.
⁷Chariots fill your beautiful valleys,
    and charioteers storm your gates.

⁸Judah's defenses have been stripped
        away.
    You run to the armory* for your
        weapons.
⁹You inspect the breaks in the walls of
        Jerusalem.*
    You store up water in the lower
        pool.
¹⁰You survey the houses and tear some
        down
    for stone to strengthen the walls.
¹¹Between the city walls, you build a
        reservoir
    for water from the old pool.
But you never ask for help from the
        One who did all this.
    You never considered the One who
        planned this long ago.

¹²At that time the Lord, the LORD of
        Heaven's Armies,
    called you to weep and mourn.
He told you to shave your heads in
        sorrow for your sins
    and to wear clothes of burlap to
        show your remorse.
¹³But instead, you dance and play;
    you slaughter cattle and kill sheep.
    You feast on meat and drink wine.
You say, "Let's feast and drink,
    for tomorrow we die!"

¹⁴The LORD of Heaven's Armies has revealed this to me: "Till the day you die, you will never be forgiven for this sin." That is the judgment of the Lord, the LORD of Heaven's Armies.

¹⁵This is what the Lord, the LORD of Heaven's Armies, said to me: "Confront Shebna, the palace administrator, and give him this message:

¹⁶"Who do you think you are,
   and what are you doing here,
building a beautiful tomb for
   yourself—
a monument high up in the rock?
¹⁷For the LORD is about to hurl you
   away, mighty man.
He is going to grab you,
¹⁸crumple you into a ball,
   and toss you away into a distant,
      barren land.
There you will die,
   and your glorious chariots will be
      broken and useless.
You are a disgrace to your master!

¹⁹"Yes, I will drive you out of office," says the LORD. "I will pull you down from your high position. ²⁰And then I will call my servant Eliakim son of Hilkiah to replace you. ²¹I will dress him in your royal robes and will give him your title and your authority. And he will be a father to the people of Jerusalem and Judah. ²²I will give him the key to the house of David— the highest position in the royal court. When he opens doors, no one will be able to close them; when he closes doors, no one will be able to open them. ²³He will bring honor to his family name, for I will drive him firmly in place like a nail in the wall. ²⁴They will give him great responsibility, and he will bring honor to even the lowliest members of his family.*"

²⁵But the LORD of Heaven's Armies also says: "The time will come when I will pull out the nail that seemed so firm. It will come out and fall to the ground. Everything it supports will fall with it. I, the LORD, have spoken!"

22:1 Hebrew *concerning the Valley of Vision.* 22:8 Hebrew *to the House of the Forest;* see 1 Kgs 7:2-5. 22:9 Hebrew *the city of David.* 22:24 Hebrew *They will hang on him all the glory of his father's house: its offspring and offshoots, all its lesser vessels, from the bowls to all the jars.*

## NOTES

**22:1** *message.* This is a translation of the Hebrew word *massa'* [TH4853A, ZH5363] (oracle), which has been the heading for several recent chapters (13; 15; 17; 19).

*Jerusalem.* Lit., "Valley of Vision" (cf. NLT mg).

*rooftops.* Perhaps a better translation is "housetop" (KJV, NASB, NRSV, NAB, NJB, ESV). The tops of the houses were flat and various activities took place there.

**22:6** *Kir.* This is not to be confused with Kir of Moab (15:1). This Kir has not been identified with certainty and could even be another name for Media (cf. 21:2).

**22:9-11** *lower pool . . . old pool.* There is still discussion about the identity and relationship of these pools. An "upper pool" is mentioned in 7:3; 36:2. Hezekiah made a pool and a tunnel as a precaution against Sennacherib's invasion (2 Kgs 20:20). If the "Upper Pool" and the "Old Pool" are the same, the reference could be to the Gihon spring and pool.

**22:12** *shave your heads.* See Jer 16:6; Ezek 27:31.

**22:15-16** *Shebna . . . monument.* The discovery of what is possibly the very lintel of Shebna's tomb contains an inscription in archaic Heb. that is the third longest of its kind (Avigad 1953).

**22:18** *crumple you into a ball, and toss you away.* The Heb. is cryptic here involving the same root (*tsnp* [TH6801A, ZH7571] "to wind, wrap") in three words in sequence: *tsanop yitsnapeka tsenepa.* Lit., something like "winding up he will wind you a winding." The root is found in the word for "turban" (a wrapping) in Lev 16:4; Isa 3:23; 62:3; Zech 3:5; Job 29:14. The point seems to be the definite preparation for Shebna's rejection and ejection from the land. The translations must then translate this language in context: "roll you tightly [to be cast]" (NASB); "whirl you round and round and throw you" (NRSV, ESV); "roll you up tightly and throw you" (REB); "he will roll you up tightly . . . and throw you" (NIV).

**22:20 Eliakim son of Hilkiah.** See 36:3, 11, 22; 37:2.

**22:22 key.** Heb. *mapteakh*, from the root meaning "to open" has cognates in Akkadian and Arabic and can refer to a "badge of office" (NIDOTTE, 2:1059). The language here appears to be reflected in Rev 3:7, which also refers to "the key of David" where it is used of Christ as a symbol of his authority as the Davidic Messiah.

*key to the house of David.* This refers to the authority delegated to him by the king, who belonged to David's dynasty and perhaps controlled entrance into the royal palace. Although similar language is used of Christ (Rev 3:7), the reference in Isaiah is probably not intended to be directly messianic. In a sense, the role of Eliakim here pictures Christ because they both have authority to bind or loose, but the authority of Christ is absolute (cf. Matt 16:19).

**22:23 nail.** This Heb. word (*yathed* [TH3489, ZH3845]) is commonly used of a tent peg or stake (Judg 4:21; 5:26; cf. Isa 54:2).

C O M M E N T A R Y

The three kingdoms described in chapter 21 were Babylon, Edom, and Arabia, and now these are followed by a fourth, Jerusalem. The feature linking this chapter with the preceding oracles against foreign peoples is probably the background common to so many of the oracles—that is, the threat posed by Assyria, which was to be God's instrument of punishment in the ancient Near East during this period.

The reason for the choice of the name "valley of vision" is uncertain. Jerusalem does have two major valleys around it: the Kidron Valley east of Jerusalem, and the Hinnom Valley to the southwest. These join the Tyropean Valley at the foot of the hill on which the City of David stood. Since Jerusalem was repeatedly referred to as "exalted Mount Zion," perhaps this reference to the city as a valley is derogatory—Jerusalem was now a valley from which nothing could be seen.

The prophecy falls into two parts. In the first, the city of Jerusalem comes under the wrath of God (22:1-14); the second deals with an individual ruler (22:15-25).

**The Oracle about Jerusalem.** In the opening paragraph (22:1-4), the prophet witnesses a chaotic condition with "everyone running to the rooftops" (22:1) and "bodies . . . lying everywhere" (22:2). Those who tried to "slip away" were "captured, too" (22:3). The prophet wept as he watched the people being destroyed (22:4). The passage continues with a vivid description of the horrific conditions and explains that the "the Lord, the LORD of Heaven's Armies" has brought this dreadful situation upon the "Valley of Vision" (22:5). Apparently, with prophetic insight, Isaiah was witnessing the conditions resulting from the fall of Jerusalem to the Babylonians in 586 BC. The Elamites and the "men of Kir" (22:6) were probably mercenaries in the Babylonian army (Kidner 1994:646), but Oswalt (1986:410) thinks such references are "being used in a more figurative sense in line with the references in 21:2." At any rate, the people made desperate attempts to make repairs and fix things, for example, by tearing down their houses "for stone to strengthen the walls" (22:10). However, the people "never ask for help from the

One who did all this," the very One "who planned this long ago" (22:11). This message closes (22:12-14) with the incredible attitude of this perishing people: "Let's feast and drink, for tomorrow we die!" (22:13), a verse quoted by Paul in 1 Corinthians 15:32.

The latter half of this chapter (22:15-25) concerns the prideful condition of a certain "palace administrator" (22:15) named Shebna who built a "beautiful tomb" (22:16) for himself. Although this prophecy against Shebna is Isaiah's only prophecy against an individual, it is against a historical character who seems to represent the carnal attitude of the age regarding luxury, greed, and desire for personal glory. He appears again with Eliakim (22:20; 36:3; 37:2). The reference to "glorious chariots" (22:18) also reflects the wealth and social standing of Shebna, for the possession of chariots seemed to be a privilege reserved in former times for kings (cf. 2 Sam 15:1; 1 Kgs 1:5) and those in high office (cf. Gen 41:43). Perhaps Shebna's flashy manner of driving about the area in elaborate chariots could be compared to a contemporary man who is more interested in driving a showy car than in doing his work. The fact that he is called "a disgrace to your master" (22:18) may reflect some negative personal data omitted from the text. Historically, Shebna's demotion is apparent in Isaiah 36:3 and 37:2, where he is spoken of as second to Eliakim.

The Lord's response to him was, "I will drive you out of office . . . [and] pull you down from your high position" (22:19) and "replace you" with "my servant Eliakim son of Hilkiah" who would be a "father to the people of Jerusalem and Judah" (22:20). Eliakim stands in contrast to Shebna, over whom he may have been promoted, judging from their appearance together in 36:3. At any rate, to him would be given "the key to the house of David," defined as "the highest position in the royal court" (22:22). This statement probably reflects the practice, still followed in some areas of the Middle East, of the owner of an important key (sizeable at that time) publicly wearing it on his shoulder for all to see. Eliakim could be a picture of the greater son of David (cf. Rev 3:7, where the imagery of the "key of David" is used in a messianic sense). The authority to "open doors" and to "shut doors" belonged to the second in command to the king. This is probably the background of the commission to Peter (Matt 16:19). Several other honors and privileges are then listed as going with this position (22:22-24).

The chapter concludes with the prediction that the Lord would remove "the nail that seemed so firm . . . [and] everything it supports will fall with it" (22:25). "The time will come" translates the often-used Hebrew expression, "in that day" and refers to the time when the "LORD of Heaven's Armies" will come in judgment and "pull out the nail that seemed so firm" (22:25). Just as one peg could not bear the weight of an unlimited number of bowls and jars, so Eliakim, like Shebna, would someday collapse under the load placed on him and fall from power. It could also mean that since Eliakim was the nail fastened in a sure place, his descendants—not Eliakim himself—would be the ones to fall. In either case, Eliakim's effectiveness was only temporary.

## ◆   12. Tyre (23:1-18)

This message came to me concerning Tyre:

Weep, O ships of Tarshish,
    for the harbor and houses of Tyre
    are gone!
The rumors you heard in Cyprus*
    are all true.
2 Mourn in silence, you people of the
    coast
    and you merchants of Sidon.
Your traders crossed the sea,
3    sailing over deep waters.
They brought you grain from Egypt*
    and harvests from along the Nile.
You were the marketplace of the
    world.

4 But now you are put to shame, city of
    Sidon,
    for Tyre, the fortress of the sea, says,
"Now I am childless;
    I have no sons or daughters."
5 When Egypt hears the news about Tyre,
    there will be great sorrow.
6 Send word now to Tarshish!
    Wail, you people who live in distant
    lands!
7 Is this silent ruin all that is left of
    your once joyous city?
    What a long history was yours!
    Think of all the colonists you sent to
    distant places.

8 Who has brought this disaster on Tyre,
    that great creator of kingdoms?
Her traders were all princes,
    her merchants were nobles.
9 The LORD of Heaven's Armies has
    done it
    to destroy your pride
    and bring low all earth's nobility.
10 Come, people of Tarshish,
    sweep over the land like the
    flooding Nile,
    for Tyre is defenseless.*
11 The LORD held out his hand over the sea
    and shook the kingdoms of the earth.
He has spoken out against Phoenicia,*
    ordering that her fortresses be
    destroyed.
12 He says, "Never again will you rejoice,
    O daughter of Sidon, for you have
    been crushed.
Even if you flee to Cyprus,
    you will find no rest."

13 Look at the land of Babylonia*—
    the people of that land are gone!
The Assyrians have handed Babylon
    over
    to the wild animals of the desert.
They have built siege ramps against
    its walls,
    torn down its palaces,
    and turned it to a heap of rubble.

14 Wail, O ships of Tarshish,
    for your harbor is destroyed!

15 For seventy years, the length of a
king's life, Tyre will be forgotten. But then
the city will come back to life as in the
song about the prostitute:

16 Take a harp and walk the streets,
    you forgotten harlot.
Make sweet melody and sing your songs
    so you will be remembered again.

17 Yes, after seventy years the LORD will
revive Tyre. But she will be no different
than she was before. She will again be a
prostitute to all kingdoms around the
world. 18 But in the end her profits will be
given to the LORD. Her wealth will not be
hoarded but will provide good food and
fine clothing for the LORD's priests.

23:1 Hebrew *Kittim;* also in 23:12.   23:3 Hebrew *from Shihor,* a branch of the Nile River.   23:10 The meaning
of the Hebrew in this verse is uncertain.   23:11 Hebrew *Canaan.*   23:13 Or *Chaldea.*

NOTES

23:1 *Cyprus.* This translates the Hebrew *kittim* [TH3794, ZH4183]. Cyprus was an island that
had close ties with Tyre (Ezek 27:6), and was situated about 150 miles northwest of it.

*ships of Tarshish.* The precise location of Tarshish is still debated. Traditionally, it has been linked with Tartessos in Spain. The expression "ships of Tarshish" may refer to a kind of ship used for any long distance trip, like the term "China Clipper," without necessarily denoting a specific destination. The phrase is also found in 2:16 where the NLT translates "trading ships" in parallel with "magnificent vessel." The NIV does the same thing in these two passages.

**23:2 Sidon.** Sidon was the ancient sister city of Tyre; the two were already paired in the ancient Keret Epic from Ugarit. They were also mentioned together in ancient Hittite incantations and in the Amarna correspondence in the middle of the second millennium BC.

**23:3 Egypt.** As the NLT mg indicates, "Egypt" translates Heb. *shikhor* [TH7883, ZH8865], which is a synonym for the Nile (Josh 13:3). In Jer 2:18, Egypt and Shihor are counterparts to Assyria and the Euphrates.

**23:7 colonists you sent to distant lands.** Her colonies were her strength and glory (Watson 1976).

**23:11 Phoenicia.** As the NLT mg indicates, "Phoenicia" translates the Heb. word for "Canaan," but this word can also refer to the "merchants" of Canaan as in 23:8.

**23:13 Babylonia.** As the NLT mg indicates, "Babylonia" translates the Heb. for "Chaldea." The precise meaning of this word is debated and modern translations are divided over the choice between Chaldea (found in the NRSV, REB, NAB, NJB, NJPS, and ESV) and Babylonia (found in the NIV, NCV, TEV, GW, and CEV).

**23:15 seventy years.** This seems to be a round figure (e.g., "the length of a king's life"), used to indicate the length of Judah's captivity (Jer 25:11; 29:10). Some commentators observe that the seventy years could cover the period from the campaign of Sennacherib (701 BC) to the eventual decline of Assyria (c. 630 BC), a time that would allow Tyre to regain its strength.

## COMMENTARY

This chapter concludes the prophecies against the surrounding pagan nations (chs 13–23), beginning with Babylon (ch 13) and ending here with Tyre. Jerusalem (ch 22) is the exception, and it was probably put there for a purpose. Babylon and Tyre (Phoenicia) especially represented pride and the attempt to live apart from God. In Revelation 17 and 18, both nations may be indicated. Although not mentioned by name, Tyre may be "the great prostitute, who sits on many waters." Revelation 17:1 seems to echo Isaiah 23:17 in saying, "she will again be a prostitute to all kingdoms around the world."

Tyre was a very old city (founded before 2000 BC) and was considered the chief city of Phoenicia. It was located twenty-five miles south of Sidon and thirty-five miles north of Mount Carmel. The main city was on the mainland, with a fortress located on an island a short distance offshore. Because Phoenicia consisted of only a narrow strip of arable land, the people turned to the sea for commerce and eventually became one of the great maritime powers of the ancient world. The country was about 140 miles in length and was at no point more than fifteen miles wide; it was wedged between the mountains and the sea. The Phoenicians founded colonies as far away as Africa (Carthage) and Spain (Tarshish), and they have been credited with visiting India, Britain, and even the west coast of Africa.

As early as the time of Solomon, commercial contacts between Phoenicia and

Israel were taking place. King Hiram of Tyre supplied cedar and craftsmen for the temple (1 Kgs 5:8-9) and sailors for Solomon's commercial fleet (1 Kgs 9:27), but by Isaiah's time, Tyre's strength had waned. Assyria threatened but never conquered Tyre, although Luli, King of Tyre, was forced to flee to Cyprus in 701 BC (the year when Sennacherib besieged Hezekiah's Jerusalem). Where Sennacherib failed, his successor Esarhaddon succeeded. Throughout the century that followed, Tyre (like Judah) looked to Egypt for help against Assyrian aggression, until Assyria's decline finally set in.

Tyre regained her independence for a short period until the rise of the Babylonians. A thirteen-year siege under Nebuchadnezzar brought Phoenicia to an end in 572 BC. An attempt to regain some power during the time of Alexander the Great resulted in the total destruction of both Tyre and Sidon in 332 BC.

The successful maritime commerce of the Phoenicians of Tyre led to a greed and arrogance that were strongly denounced by Isaiah. Tyre, the symbol of world trade and commerce, is compared to a harlot who sells her soul and honor for sensual pleasures and the material riches of the world (23:15-17). Other prophets also had something to say about Tyre (Ezek 26-27; Amos 1:9-10). Craigie has written a good overview of the history and culture of Tyre and Sidon (Harrison 1985:266-274).

**The Oracle against Tyre.** The first three verses of this message describe the maritime nature of this small nation, famous for its ships, harbor, and related commercial interests. The great wealth of Phoenicia was directly based on its extensive seafaring enterprises, but 23:4ff reveal the coming judgment on Tyre (and Phoenicia). Even Egypt (23:5) and Tarshish (23:6), with which Tyre carried on trade, would be involved, and Tyre would reflect in sorrow on her earlier colonizing of "distant places" (23:7).

It is clear in 23:8-12 that the Lord was behind this judgment on the arrogant merchants. It is declared that, "The LORD of Heaven's Armies has done it to destroy your pride" (23:9), and "the LORD . . . held out his hand over the sea and shook the kingdoms of the earth" (23:11). Isaiah 23:13 parenthetically looks at Babylonia, which was handed over to the "wild animals" through the instrumentality of the Assyrians. The Babylonians (Chaldeans) may have been introduced here because they are the ones that eventually conquered Tyre, but some believe that the term refers to the Assyrians because they came from Chaldea. The Assyrian king Sennacherib did destroy the city of Babylon in 689 BC and prevented the Babylonians from emerging for another sixty-five years.

The final paragraph of this chapter reveals that "after seventy years the LORD will revive Tyre" (23:17). Although she will be restored and revived, "in the end her profits will be given to the LORD" (23:18). She will return again and "be a prostitute to all kingdoms around the world" (23:17). The meaning of this passage is difficult because there is no evidence that Tyre used her profits to help Israel after the people returned from captivity, except that Tyre was there to provide materials for the construction of the temple at the time of the return, according to Ezra 3:7. At any rate, although Tyre will be allowed to make profits, they will be given to the Lord and not hoarded (cf. 60:5-7, 11-12). Psalm 72:10 refers to the time when the kings of Tarshish will bring tribute to the Lord.

There seems to be no evidence that the prophecy applies to any event in the New Testament (although in Acts 21:3-4 we read about the local believers found in Tyre and it should perhaps be noted that by c. AD 200 Tyre had become the seat of a Christian bishopric).

## D. The Isaiah Apocalypse (24:1–27:13)
### 1. Desolation of the earth and the world city (24:1-23)

Look! The LORD is about to destroy the earth
and make it a vast wasteland.
He devastates the surface of the earth
and scatters the people.
2 Priests and laypeople,
servants and masters,
maids and mistresses,
buyers and sellers,
lenders and borrowers,
bankers and debtors—none will be spared.
3 The earth will be completely emptied
and looted.
The LORD has spoken!

4 The earth mourns and dries up,
and the crops waste away and wither.
Even the greatest people on earth waste away.
5 The earth suffers for the sins of its people,
for they have twisted God's instructions,
violated his laws,
and broken his everlasting covenant.
6 Therefore, a curse consumes the earth.
Its people must pay the price for their sin.
They are destroyed by fire,
and only a few are left alive.
7 The grapevines waste away,
and there is no new wine.
All the merrymakers sigh and mourn.
8 The cheerful sound of tambourines is stilled;

the happy cries of celebration are heard no more.
The melodious chords of the harp are silent.
9 Gone are the joys of wine and song;
alcoholic drink turns bitter in the mouth.
10 The city writhes in chaos;
every home is locked to keep out intruders.
11 Mobs gather in the streets, crying out for wine.
Joy has turned to gloom.
Gladness has been banished from the land.
12 The city is left in ruins,
its gates battered down.
13 Throughout the earth the story is the same—
only a remnant is left,
like the stray olives left on the tree
or the few grapes left on the vine after harvest.

14 But all who are left shout and sing for joy.
Those in the west praise the LORD's majesty.
15 In eastern lands, give glory to the LORD.
In the lands beyond the sea, praise the name of the LORD, the God of Israel.
16 We hear songs of praise from the ends of the earth,
songs that give glory to the Righteous One!

But my heart is heavy with grief.
  Weep for me, for I wither away.
Deceit still prevails,
  and treachery is everywhere.
17 Terror and traps and snares will be
    your lot,
  you people of the earth.
18 Those who flee in terror will fall
    into a trap,
  and those who escape the trap will
    be caught in a snare.

Destruction falls like rain from the
    heavens;
  the foundations of the earth
    shake.
19 The earth has broken up.
  It has utterly collapsed;
  it is violently shaken.
20 The earth staggers like a drunk.
  It trembles like a tent in a
    storm.

It falls and will not rise again,
  for the guilt of its rebellion is very
    heavy.

21 In that day the LORD will punish the
    gods in the heavens
  and the proud rulers of the nations
    on earth.
22 They will be rounded up and put in
    prison.
  They will be shut up in prison
  and will finally be punished.
23 Then the glory of the moon will
    wane,
  and the brightness of the sun
    will fade,
  for the LORD of Heaven's Armies will
    rule on Mount Zion.
  He will rule in great glory in
    Jerusalem,
  in the sight of all the leaders of
    his people.

## NOTES

**24:1** *about to destroy.* Translates the Heb. participle *boqeq* from the root *bqq* meaning "to lay waste," with the only Semitic cognates being in Arabic and Syriac (NIDOTTE 1:705). This unusual verb is used three times in this ch (twice in v. 2), and found elsewhere only twice in Jeremiah and twice in Nahum.

**make . . . vast wasteland.** Translates the Heb. root *blq*, "to devastate," a verb found only here and in Nah 2:10. The combination of *boqeq* and *boleqah* in this verse provides another example of alliteration and assonance typical of Isaiah.

**devastates.** The Heb. verb is *'wh* in the piel stem. The root meaning is "warp, pervert, bend, ruin" and it is found only one other time (21:3) in this book.

**24:4** *earth . . . dries up . . . crops . . . wither.* Similar language is used of Moab in 15:6 and 16:8.

**24:5** *everlasting covenant.* Heb. *berit 'olam*, the same words found in Gen 9:16.

**24:6** *a curse consumes the earth.* The Heb. here, *'alah 'akhelah 'erets*, is alliterative, and even the first word of the next sentence begins with an aleph.

**24:10** *chaos.* The Heb. word *tohu* is used by Isaiah here and in 29:21; 34:11; 40:17, 23; 41:29; 44:9; 45:18; 49:4 (cf. 45:19). Its only other occurrence in the prophetic writings is in Jer 4:23. The term recalls the *tohu wabohu* of Gen 1:2 ("formless" [TH8414, ZH9332] and "empty" [TH922, ZH983]), and both words are also found in Isa 34:11.

**24:14** *all who are left.* Although not specifically in the Heb., this is contextually valid. The Heb. simply has "they."

**24:16** *Deceit still prevails, and treachery is everywhere.* More lit. the Heb. reads "Woe to me! Woe to me! Alas for me! The treacherous deal treacherously, and the treacherous deal very treacherously" (NASB). The Heb. shows both alliteration and assonance, *razi li razi li* *'oy li, bogedim bagadu ubeged bogedim bagadu.* Forms of the verb *bagad* [TH898, ZH953] (be treacherous, unfaithful) are found over a dozen times in chs 21–48.

**24:17** *Terror and traps and snares.* Again, the Heb. behind these words shows another example of Isaiah's penchant for wordplay: *pakhad wapakhat wapakh.*

**24:18** *Destruction falls like rain from the heavens.* The Heb. *'arubbot mimmarom niptakhu* is more lit. "the windows from on high are open" (KJV). The Heb. word (*'arubbot*) translated "windows" is distinctive and is the same word used in the account of the deluge during the time of Noah (Gen 7:2; 8:11). The versions render this as "windows of heaven are opened" (NRSV, ESV), "windows above are opened" (NASB), "windows of heaven above are opened" (REB), "torrents of rain will fall from the sky" (TEV), "the floodgates in the sky will be opened" (GW), and "sluices are opened on high" (NJPS).

**24:22** *punished.* The Heb. verb is *paqad* [TH6485, ZH7212], which means "to visit," either in blessing or in punishment. The context here certainly indicates the latter.

**24:23** *moon . . . sun.* For similar usages of "sun and moon," see 60:19-20; Rev 21:23; 22:5.

*the LORD of Heaven's Armies will rule on Mount Zion.* See 2:2-4.

### COMMENTARY

Following the judgments on the nations (chs 13–23), the next section of the book of Isaiah (chs 24–27) addresses the entire world. These chapters are closely related to the previous ones, but go beyond them in concern about the consummation of all things. As chapters 13–23 depict the futures of individual nations, chapters 24–27 picture the general future of all nations. The overall flow of the prophet's vision of God's purposes, therefore, is from the prophet's own people (chs 1–12), to the surrounding countries (chs 13–23), to the entire world.

These chapters are often called the Apocalypse of Isaiah and carry the general theme of "the day of the LORD," an idea repeated throughout the section. Some describe these chapters as a finale in which a number of preceding themes echo and blend together into one concluding harmony.

Through the centuries interpreters have applied these chapters to a wide variety of historical circumstances—from the days of the Assyrian invasion to the time of Messiah's victory. Luther applied these chapters to the Roman invasion, but Calvin regarded the material as a summary of the preceding prophecies against both Israel and the foreign nations. Alexander lists some of the many historical references given to this material by a variety of interpreters (Alexander 1992:408).

Chapters 24–27 reveal that all that is hostile to God will eventually be brought down, and future blessings will be bestowed on God's people. Such themes comfort and reassure God's people in times of hardship and duress. Similar apocalyptic literature is also found in the books of Daniel and Revelation and in the closing chapters of Zechariah, each of which describes the nature of the end times.

**The Coming Desolation.** Chapter 24 begins and ends with a scene of destruction and desolation, which includes all classes of people—"none will be spared" (24:2). The earth "will be completely emptied and looted" (24:3), as the rain ceases and the crops wither because of the drought. God's wrath has been provoked because the sinful people have "twisted God's instructions, violated his laws, and broken his everlasting covenant" (24:5). These strong words probably refer back to the covenant of Gen 9:8-17, and Motyer (1999:163) thinks that the background of this judgment scene is the story of the great deluge of Noah's time (Gen 6-9). Note the references to "rain" (or floodgates; see note on 24:18; cf. Gen 7:11), the "everlasting/eternal covenant" (24:5; cf. Gen 9:16); and the "curse" (24:6; cf. Gen 5:29; 8:21).

In contrast to the future singing described in 24:14ff, the music (24:7-8) ceases and all becomes silent with the loss of the vineyard and wine. "Gone are the joys of wine and song" (24:9) that characterized Judah (cf. 5:11-13). As "the city writhes in chaos" (24:10), doors are locked for protection from looters, but the city gates have been "battered down" (24:12). The city is not identified, but several suggestions are noted and summarized by Millar (1976:15-21). Throughout the earth, only a remnant survives (24:13), but "all who are left will shout and sing for joy" (24:14).

The scene then changes abruptly to a picture of shouting and singing for joy (24:14). This unidentified remnant ("all who are left") in the west, as well as those in the east, will "give glory to the LORD" and "praise the name of the LORD, the God of Israel" (24:15). Their songs of praise can be heard from the ends of the earth and their "songs . . . give glory to the Righteous One" (24:16). With another sudden shift, the action returns to a heart that is heavy with grief, as the scene reveals that "treachery is everywhere" (24:16) and "terror and traps and snares" await the people of the earth (24:17). The graphic cosmic language of the last part of 24:18 echoes the language of the great deluge of Noah's time, with its reference to the destructive rain and the shaking of the foundations of the earth. The whole earthly order again proves unstable under God's judgment (24:19). Everything has broken up and collapsed (24:19). "The earth staggers like a drunk"; it "falls and will not rise again" because "the guilt of its rebellion is very heavy" (24:20). The reference to the drunken man may be a subtle reference to Noah.

The chapter closes with a paragraph announcing that the "LORD will punish the gods in the heavens and the proud rulers of the nations on earth" (24:21). Rebels in both places will be "rounded up and put in prison" (24:22; cf. 2 Pet 2:4; Jude 6; Rev 20:1-3), and Isaiah 14 pictures the great king of Babylon descending into the realm of Sheol. In the natural world, the sun and the moon were created to rule the day and the night, but compared to the glorious reign of the Lord at Mount Zion, their brightness will wane and fade as the Lord of Heaven's Armies rules on Zion (24:23; cf. Rev 21:22-27). Some in Isaiah's audience actually worshiped these heavenly bodies, so they needed to be reminded that the objects of their adoration and worship would pass away. "Both the heavenly and the earthly representatives of a nation would be held responsible for offences committed under their rule" (Caird 1980:179).

◆     ## 2. Praise for victory (25:1-5)

O LORD, I will honor and praise your
   name,
   for you are my God.
You do such wonderful
   things!
You planned them long ago,
   and now you have accomplished
   them.
2 You turn mighty cities into heaps
   of ruins.
   Cities with strong walls are
   turned to rubble.
Beautiful palaces in distant lands
   disappear
   and will never be rebuilt.
3 Therefore, strong nations will
   declare your glory;
   ruthless nations will fear you.

4 But you are a tower of refuge to the
   poor, O LORD,
   a tower of refuge to the needy
   in distress.
You are a refuge from the storm
   and a shelter from the heat.
For the oppressive acts of ruthless
   people
   are like a storm beating against
   a wall,
5   or like the relentless heat of the
   desert.
But you silence the roar of foreign
   nations.
As the shade of a cloud cools
   relentless heat,
   so the boastful songs of ruthless
   people are stilled.

### NOTES

25:1 *wonderful . . . planned.* The Heb. words are *pele'* [TH6382, ZH7099] and *'etsot* (from the root *y'ts* [TH3289, ZH3619]); both are found in the name of the messianic child mentioned in 9:6.

25:3 *ruthless.* Heb. *'arats* [TH6206, ZH6907] (to dread, shake in terror). Used three times in consecutive verses (25:3, 4, 5), this word focuses on the plight of the exploited.

25:4 *poor . . . needy.* These stand in contrast to the strong and ruthless nations of the preceding verse.

*a tower of refuge . . . a shelter.* For similar language concerning God's protection, see 4:5-6.

### COMMENTARY

Webb (1996:108) suggests that this chapter celebrates the triumph of God with feasting and praise and that the banquet in 25:6-8 is the centerpiece with two songs of praise framing it, one personal (25:1-5) and one communal (25:9-12). This chapter expresses praise and thanksgiving for victory, and it continues the description of Mount Zion and the New Jerusalem begun in 24:23.

The opening words are reminiscent of language found in the Psalms (cf. Ps 118:28), with which the prophet was surely familiar. "For you are my God" (25:1) is a very personal expression of faith and confidence. The prophet ascribes praise to the Lord for his marvelous acts of judgment; he is the one who can "turn mighty cities into heaps of ruins." Even "cities with strong walls are turned to rubble," and beautiful palaces disappear, never to be rebuilt (25:2). Grogan (1986:158) suggests that these references to the city of destruction in chapters 24-27 "do not have any particular city in view but are general designations of society organized apart from any reference to God, a concept not unlike 'the world' as it so often appears in a depreciatory sense in the NT." The reference must be to the proud world powers that had terrorized and oppressed the covenant people but that now must submit to the God of Israel.

By contrast, Isaiah praised the Lord for being a refuge and shelter from the weather extremes of storm and heat (25:4). Under his reign, a reversal of fortunes will occur as the poor and the needy are rescued. The idea that those who depend on God are helped and those who depend on themselves are judged is found throughout Scripture (e.g., 1 Sam 2:1-10; Jas 5:1-6).

◆     ## 3. Feast of the nations and the overthrow of Moab (25:6-12)

6 In Jerusalem,* the LORD of Heaven's
    Armies
will spread a wonderful feast
for all the people of the world.
It will be a delicious banquet
with clear, well-aged wine and
    choice meat.
7 There he will remove the cloud of
    gloom,
the shadow of death that hangs
    over the earth.
8 He will swallow up death forever!*
The Sovereign LORD will wipe away
    all tears.
He will remove forever all insults and
    mockery
against his land and people.
The LORD has spoken!

9 In that day the people will proclaim,
    "This is our God!

We trusted in him, and he
    saved us!
This is the LORD, in whom we trusted.
Let us rejoice in the salvation he
    brings!"
10 For the LORD's hand of blessing will
    rest on Jerusalem.
But Moab will be crushed.
It will be like straw trampled down
    and left to rot.
11 God will push down Moab's people
as a swimmer pushes down water
    with his hands.
He will end their pride
    and all their evil works.
12 The high walls of Moab will be
    demolished.
They will be brought down to the
    ground,
down into the dust.

25:6 Hebrew *On this mountain;* also in 25:10.   25:8 Greek version reads *Death is swallowed up in victory.*
Compare 1 Cor 15:54.

### NOTES
**25:6 Jerusalem.** Although the NLT has "Jerusalem" in the translation, the footnote indicates that the Heb. lit. reads "on this mountain," an expression that also occurs in 25:7, 10.

**25:6 LORD of Heaven's Armies.** This Heb. title is traditionally rendered as "LORD of hosts" (KJV).

**25:7 cloud of gloom.** The Heb. is *pene hallot* [TH3875, ZH4287], lit. "face of the covering" (KJV). It is usually understood as referring to something like a shroud (cf. the parallelism in the NIV translation, "the shroud that enfolds . . . the sheet that covers all nations"). This ties in with "swallow up death forever" in the next verse. However, others suggest that the reference is to a veil of spiritual blindness (2 Cor 3:15) or a covering as a sign of grief (2 Sam 15:30). Other versions have "shroud" (NRSV), "the veil shrouding" (REB), "veil of grief covering" (GW), "burial clothes" (CEV), "covering" (ESV), and "shroud . . . over the faces" (NJPS). Whatever it is, the Lord will remove it.

**25:10** *hand of blessing.* The Heb. has only "hand"; the NLT contextually supplies "of blessing."

*Jerusalem.* As the NLT mg indicates, the Heb. is "on this mountain."

*like straw trampled down and left to rot.* The Heb., *mathben bemo madmenah* [TH4087, ZH4523], is lit., "as straw is trampled down in the manure." The Heb. is very graphic and probably refers to a manure pile or waste pit (cf. "dunghill," KJV). *madmenah* also makes a wordplay on the Moabite place name, "Madmen" (Jer 48:2); this is typical of Isaiah's literary style.

COMMENTARY

Following the outline for the chapter noted in the previous section (25:1-5), we find here the communal song of praise. The Lord is king in Zion (24:23), and he prepares a banquet there for all peoples. This kingdom is not limited to Israel, but includes the redeemed humanity from all nations. At this time, a veil or shroud will be removed (25:7). This is probably not a veil of spiritual blindness (cf. 2 Cor 3:15), but the covering worn by suffering humanity during their time of grief (cf. 2 Sam 15:30). At Zion, the Lord will wipe away all tears and remove death forever.

The Lord will prepare a wonderful feast for "all the people of the world" (25:6). The phrase "in Jerusalem" translates the Hebrew for "on this mountain," which refers back to Zion (24:23; cf. 46:13). The salvation of the poor and needy is especially highlighted with the vivid description of a rich feast.

The "wonderful feast" and the "delicious banquet" (25:6) introduce a strong positive note with their implied celebration. The adjectives define the high quality of provision—"wonderful feast . . . delicious banquet . . . well-aged wine . . . choice meat" (25:6). It is a celebration "for all the people of the world" (25:6). Grogan (1986:159) notes that "the Gentile prodigals find that the fatted calf is killed for them on their return to the Lord." Webb (1996:108) uses the pun (English only) that "the host is the LORD of Hosts."

"There" (25:7) refers to "the mountain of the LORD" (cf. the Heb.), and the "cloud of gloom" probably refers to a shroud (cf. the Heb. and the note on 25:7). The next line has the parallel "shadow of death." This victory celebration includes victory over death, the ultimate enemy (25:8). During the time of this messianic banquet at Zion, the Lord will "remove the cloud of gloom" and "the shadow of death," and he will also "swallow up death forever" (25:7-8). In Canaanite religion, the god "Death" was known as the great "swallower" of his victims, but here the Lord swallows Death (25:8). This reference to God's swallowing up of death and his wiping away all tears is aptly quoted by Paul in 1 Corinthians 15:54 (cf. Rev 7:17; 21:4), in his great passage on the resurrection. The end result of the Lord's action is the removal of all "insults and mockery against his land and people" (25:8). The final defeat of death means ultimate salvation for God's people.

God's people continued to praise him, proclaiming, "This is our God. We trusted in him, and he saved us" (25:9)—an excellent summary of the experience of faith and salvation. These verses call for rejoicing, because "the LORD's hand of blessing will rest on Jerusalem" (25:10). By contrast, "Moab will be crushed . . . and left to rot" (25:10). Grogan (1986:161) says of this verse that "in a powerful anthropomorphic figure, the prophet pictures the Lord's hand resting in blessing on Mount Zion and his feet trampling on Moab in judgment." Moab's high walls "will be demolished . . . brought down to the ground, down into the dust" (25:12). Perhaps "Moab" is used here because in Hebrew the word sounds similar to the word for "enemy" and because Moab (like Babylon) can be used generically to represent the enemies of God and his people (cf. the similar use of Edom in 34:1-17). Elsewhere, Moab is a picture of pride (cf. 25:11c; 16:6).

◆      4. Song of praise (26:1-21)

In that day, everyone in the land of Judah will sing this song:

Our city is strong!
    We are surrounded by the walls
        of God's salvation.
²Open the gates to all who are
        righteous;
    allow the faithful to enter.
³You will keep in perfect peace
    all who trust in you,
    all whose thoughts are fixed
        on you!
⁴Trust in the LORD always,
    for the LORD GOD is the eternal Rock.
⁵He humbles the proud
    and brings down the arrogant city.
    He brings it down to the dust.
⁶The poor and oppressed trample it
        underfoot,
    and the needy walk all over it.

⁷But for those who are righteous,
    the way is not steep and rough.
    You are a God who does what is right,
    and you smooth out the path ahead
        of them.
⁸LORD, we show our trust in you by
        obeying your laws;
    our heart's desire is to glorify your
        name.
⁹All night long I search for you;
    in the morning I earnestly seek for
        God.
    For only when you come to judge the
        earth
    will people learn what is right.
¹⁰Your kindness to the wicked
    does not make them do good.

Although others do right, the wicked
        keep doing wrong
    and take no notice of the LORD's
        majesty.
¹¹O LORD, they pay no attention to your
        upraised fist.
    Show them your eagerness to
        defend your people.
    Then they will be ashamed.
    Let your fire consume your
        enemies.

¹²LORD, you will grant us peace;
    all we have accomplished is really
        from you.
¹³O LORD our God, others have ruled us,
    but you alone are the one we
        worship.
¹⁴Those we served before are dead and
        gone.
    Their departed spirits will never
        return!
    You attacked them and destroyed
        them,
    and they are long forgotten.
¹⁵O LORD, you have made our nation
        great;
    yes, you have made us great.
    You have extended our borders,
    and we give you the glory!

¹⁶LORD, in distress we searched for you.
    We prayed beneath the burden of
        your discipline.
¹⁷Just as a pregnant woman
    writhes and cries out in pain as she
        gives birth,
    so were we in your presence, LORD.
¹⁸We, too, writhe in agony,

but nothing comes of our suffering.
We have not given salvation to the
    earth,
nor brought life into the world.
¹⁹ But those who die in the LORD will live;
    their bodies will rise again!
Those who sleep in the earth
    will rise up and sing for joy!
For your life-giving light will fall
    like dew
on your people in the place of the
    dead!

²⁰ Go home, my people,
    and lock your doors!
Hide yourselves for a little while
    until the LORD's anger has passed.
²¹ Look! The LORD is coming from
    heaven
to punish the people of the earth
    for their sins.
The earth will no longer hide those
    who have been killed.
They will be brought out for all
    to see.

## NOTES

**26:1** *In that day.* This phrase is repeated throughout these chapters (cf. 24:21; 25:9; 27:1).

*walls.* The Heb. has an additional term, *khel* [TH2426, ZH2658] (ramparts), which the NLT omits (cf. KJV's "walls and bulwarks"). *khel* (only here in Isaiah) probably refers to sloping fortifications of earth or stone (HALOT 1:312; cf. 2 Sam 20:15).

**26:3** *perfect peace.* The Heb. is lit. "peace, peace." Repetition is used in Heb. for emphasis (cf. 6:3).

*thoughts.* This translates the Heb. *yetser* [TH3336, ZH3671], which refers to a frame of mind or a mind-set; today we would call it a "worldview." The KJV has "mind."

**26:4** *LORD GOD.* The Heb. is *yah yhwh* [TH3050/3068, ZH3363/3378] and is treated in a variety of ways in the versions: "LORD Jehovah" (KJV), "the LORD, the LORD" (NIV, GW), LORD GOD (NRSV, ESV), "GOD the LORD" (NASB), and "Yah the LORD" (NJPS).

**26:7** *You are a God who does what is right.* The Heb. has simply the one word *yashar* [TH3477A, ZH3838] (upright). The term is not used elsewhere as a divine title, but of God's word (Ps 33:4), his judgments (Ps 119:37), and his ways (Deut 32:4). A Book of Jashar is referred to in Josh 10:13 and 2 Sam 1:18.

*smooth out the path.* The picture of preparing someone's path ahead of them is found elsewhere in Isaiah (cf. 40:3-4; 42:16; 45:13).

**26:8** *show our trust.* The Heb. uses the verb *qawah* [TH6960, ZH7747], which basically means "to hope," and here refers to confidence in the Lord. The title of the national anthem of Israel, Hatikvah, "The Hope," is etymologically related to this verb.

**26:11** *upraised fist.* The Heb. is more lit. translated, "upraised hand," a graphic image of power (cf. 9:12, 17, 21).

**26:13** *others have ruled us.* The reference is probably to such foreign powers as Egypt and Assyria.

**26:14** *dead.* Heb. *metim* [TH4191, ZH4637], but the Heb. also has a parallel term, "departed spirits" (*repa'im* [TH7496, ZH8327]), which is omitted in the NLT (cf. 14:9-10).

**26:18** *nothing comes of our suffering.* The Heb. has the graphic expression, "gave birth to wind" which is retained with slight variations in the NIV, NASB, NRSV, NCV, NJPS, and ESV.

**26:19** *their bodies will rise again!* The larger context of this is more lit. "Thy dead *men* shall live, *together with* my dead body shall they arise" (KJV). The Heb. here translated "bodies" is *nebelah* [TH5038, ZH5577], which is the word for "corpse" (NASB, NRSV, GW, NJPS). For more on the different interpretations of this verse see Motyer (1993:218-220). Many scholars have not recognized a belief in the resurrection and next life as part of the

OT worldview, and this is probably due primarily to two factors: 1) the assumption of evolving theology in Israel which did not include such advanced thinking until after the Exile and 2) the conceptual nature of the language and imagery used to express the OT worldview. The latter is especially to be noted and is being better understood, among other things, by the light of the Ugaritic texts and the language in them (Smick 1968). Some of the Heb. terms are now accepted as having extended semantic fields not recognized before. The OT texts and culture cannot be separated from the larger surrounding ancient Near Eastern world and its ideas about resurrection and the afterlife. The bibliography on the subject is quite extensive, but a very helpful survey of this material is available in the doctoral dissertation of Archie England (England 1994). A belief in the next life where a body was located and had to have its needs met was not limited to the Egyptians with their well-known preparation of mummies for this next existence but was also widely held, in various forms, among other cultures of the ancient Near East.

Probably the two least contested OT passages concerning the resurrection are Dan 12:2 and Isa 26:19 but now more are being considered. In one article, Ridenhour (1976) conceded seven more passages (1 Kgs 17:17-24; 2 Kgs 4:18-37; 13:20-21; Hos 6:1-3; Ezek 37:1-14; Job 19:25-27; and Isa 53:10-11).

A better understanding of this subject in the OT is important, for it is a subject that provides a background for the apostolic proclamation of a resurrection as linked to the Messiah. The apostolic message was not preached in a conceptual vacuum in this regard. England asks, "How could the first-century believers have understood Christ's resurrection if the Old Testament theoretically provided them with such an inadequate message for understanding the resurrection concept?" (England 1994:3-4).

*dew.* Used elsewhere to depict new life and fruitfulness (cf. 2 Sam 1:21; Hos 14:5), the dew here penetrates the earth to Sheol, the abode of the dead, and gives them life.

### COMMENTARY

This opening song of the redeemed (here identified as "everyone in the land of Judah") is a direct response to the closing verses of chapter 25. In several respects, this chapter parallels the preceding chapter and reinforces its message; it is also an especially good example of comfort provided during difficult days by a look at the future. As the chapter opens, the unnamed city of the redeemed is strong and "surrounded by the walls of God's salvation" (26:1), in contrast to the "arrogant city" (26:5) that will be destroyed (cf. 24:12-13; 25:2). Moab will be trampled (25:10), but this city is safe. While the walls of the "arrogant city" are brought "down to the dust" (26:5), the "LORD GOD is the eternal Rock" (26:4).

No particular city is named, probably because the prophet was continuing to reveal a general plan concerning the ages. There is a reference in 25:2 to the walls that turned to rubble, but in 26:1 we read of the superior "walls of God's salvation." God's people thank and praise him (26:7-15) in contrast to the wicked, who pay no attention when God threatens with his "upraised fist" (26:11). Their waiting in trust and obedience (see note on 26:8) is not only for God's overthrow of evil and the destruction of the wicked, but for the appearance of God himself. During this wait, there is perplexity because God's "kindness to the wicked does not make them do good" (26:10). Certain people do not respond to kindness, and the longer God delays his judgment, the worse they become. This kindness on the part of God (26:10) may refer to God's general blessings, resulting in good harvests and prosperity.

Praise continues for the Lord who made the nation great and extended its borders (26:15).

Distress and delight, suffering and security are combined in 26:16-19. First, words of lament reveal the distress and suffering they experienced under the discipline of the Lord (26:16-18). The statement that they had "not given salvation to the earth, nor brought life into the world" (26:18) may refer to their failure to witness to those outside their community. Finally, there are words of assurance and hope for the future: "those who die in the LORD will live; their bodies will rise again!" (26:19). The NLT rendering makes it clear that such words refer to the resurrection of the body (cf. Dan 12:2) and link this passage with 25:8. This profound truth is simply and directly stated. Although this passage and Daniel 12:2 are the two Old Testament passages most often cited on the concept of the resurrection in the Old Testament, other passages could also be mentioned (1 Kgs 17:17-24; 2 Kgs 4:18-37; 13:20-21; Ezek 37:1-14; Job 19:25-27; Isa 53:10-11). Though scholars have debated the presence of resurrection language in 26:14-21, the language and the context suggest that Isaiah and his audience understood the concept. Much confusion has resulted from the misunderstanding of various terms related to immortality and resurrection (restore, revive, resuscitate, etc.). Using the resurrection language in Daniel as a basis for assigning a late date to it is confused reasoning. In the ancient Near East, bodily existence in the next life seems largely to have been assumed (see England 1994).

The closing paragraph (26:20-21) of this chapter promises hope for God's people amid the anger of the Lord unleashed against their enemies. The people are told, "Hide yourselves for a little while until the LORD's anger has passed" (26:20; cf. Exod 12:22-23). That holy wrath of God will be unleashed on their enemies, not on them. The Lord "is coming from heaven to punish the people of the earth for their sins" (26:21).

◆     5. Overthrow of world power and the prosperity of Zion (27:1-13)

In that day the LORD will take his terrible, swift sword and punish Leviathan,* the swiftly moving serpent, the coiling, writhing serpent. He will kill the dragon of the sea.

2 "In that day,
  sing about the fruitful vineyard.
3 I, the LORD, will watch over it,
  watering it carefully.
Day and night I will watch so no one
  can harm it.
4    My anger will be gone.
If I find briers and thorns growing,
  I will attack them;

I will burn them up—
5   unless they turn to me for help.
Let them make peace with me;
  yes, let them make peace with me."
6 The time is coming when Jacob's
  descendants will take root.
Israel will bud and blossom
  and fill the whole earth with fruit!

7 Has the LORD struck Israel
  as he struck her enemies?
Has he punished her
  as he punished them?
8 No, but he exiled Israel to call her
  to account.

She was exiled from her land
as though blown away in a storm
from the east.
⁹The LORD did this to purge Israel's*
wickedness,
to take away all her sin.
As a result, all the pagan altars will be
crushed to dust.
No Asherah pole or pagan shrine
will be left standing.
¹⁰The fortified towns will be silent and
empty,
the houses abandoned, the streets
overgrown with weeds.
Calves will graze there,
chewing on twigs and branches.
¹¹The people are like the dead branches
of a tree,

broken off and used for kindling
beneath the cooking pots.
Israel is a foolish and stupid
nation,
for its people have turned away
from God.
Therefore, the one who made them
will show them no pity or mercy.

¹²Yet the time will come when the LORD
will gather them together like handpicked
grain. One by one he will gather them—
from the Euphrates River* in the east to
the Brook of Egypt in the west. ¹³In that
day the great trumpet will sound. Many
who were dying in exile in Assyria and
Egypt will return to Jerusalem to worship
the LORD on his holy mountain.

27:1 The identification of Leviathan is disputed, ranging from an earthly creature to a mythical sea monster in
ancient literature.  27:9 Hebrew *Jacob's*. See note on 14:1.  27:12 Hebrew *the river.*

## NOTES

**27:1 *Leviathan*.** Passages in Ugaritic literature speak of Leviathan, the "fleeing serpent"
(*btn brkh*) or "the tortuous serpent" (*btn 'qltn*), and the adjectives used to describe him
are identical to those used in this verse (*bariakh* [TH1281, ZH1371] and *'aqallathon* [TH6129,
ZH6825]). The Hebrew uses three different terms here, which some have equated with the
three nations involved with Israel at that time: Assyria, Babylon, and Egypt. However,
Leviathan or Lotan (the vocalization is uncertain) probably represents the heathen
nations in general. "Dragon of the sea" repeatedly refers to Egypt (cf. 51:9; Ps 74:13).
In Rev 13:1, the beast from the sea represents evil power. For a helpful overview of
the use of this language in the unfolding revelation in the OT, see Day (1998).

**27:2 *vineyard*.** Vineyard imagery is also found in Jer 12:10-17; 1 Kgs 21:1-24; Mark
12:1-12; John 15:1-8.

**27:6 *take root*.** See 11:1, 10. For bud and blossom, see 4:2.

**27:8 *a storm from the east*.** The prophet uses this term to represent judgment (cf. 4:4;
41:16). The east wind, the sirocco, was a dry wind from the desert dreaded by the Israelites
because it blew the hot desert sand before it (Gen 41:6; Job 27:21-22; Jer 18:17) and was
destructive (cf. Jer 4:11; Ezek 19:12). However, it was not as harsh as the four winds that
scattered Elam (Jer 49:36), or the destructive wind against Babylon (Jer 51:1).

**27:9 *Israel's wickedness*.** "Israel" here translates the Heb. "Jacob," as the NLT mg indicates.

***crushed to dust*.** See Exod 34:13. After the captivity, idolatry never reappeared among
the people. They were corrupted by other influences, but they never again yielded to the
worship of idols.

***Asherah pole*.** God's judgment is described as destroying the pagan altars; the prediction
was that there wouldn't be an "Asherah pole or incense altar" left standing (cf. 17:8).
Asherah poles represented a goddess worshiped by the Canaanites; they were forbidden by
the Lord (Deut 16:21).

**27:12 Euphrates River.** As the NLT mg indicates, the Heb. simply says, "the river." These geographical references predict the return to their homeland of those who had gone to Assyria as deportees and to Egypt as refugees.

### COMMENTARY

The opening statement about God's defeat of the Leviathan in 27:1 actually continues from the closing verses of the preceding chapter. In this opening description of the Lord's defeat of the Leviathan monster and the deliverance of Israel, God is presented as a victorious warrior. Leviathan was a monster in Canaanite religion and tradition; here, it represents the enemy of God. The fact that Isaiah borrowed from Canaanite mythological terminology is not surprising—the biblical authors did not write in a literary vacuum but used language and imagery familiar to their audience. The Lord would not be outdone by Baal who, according to Canaanite mythology, had defeated Leviathan. The term "Leviathan" (from the root meaning to turn or twist) occurs four times in poetic settings (Job 3:8; 41:1; Ps 74:14; 104:26), and the "gliding serpent" in Job 26:13 is apparently the same creature.

However, even more significant is a reference in Revelation 12:9 where Satan is referred to as both a "dragon" (cf. 27:1) and a "serpent" in the same verse. The destruction of the dragon is depicted in Revelation 20:7-10; the definitive conquest of the dragon-monster took place in the death and resurrection of Christ, when he defeated the powers of darkness, disarmed the demonic forces, cast out the devil, and rendered him powerless (Ps 110:6; John 12:31-32; Col 2:15; Heb 2:14; Rev 12:5-10; 20:1-3). The implications of Christ's victory continue to be worked out in various increments by his people on earth (John 16:33; 1 John 2:13-14; 4:4; 5:4-5; Rev 12:11).

Next, Isaiah returns to the theme of God's vineyard (27:2-5; cf. 5:1-7)—a picture of Israel, God's covenant people (cf. John 14, where it is a picture of God's new covenant people). The vineyard in 27:2-5 is contrasted with the vineyard in 5:1-7, where God judged his people because of their rebellion and disobedience. In the earlier picture of the vineyard in chapter 5, God condemned the vineyard because it was bad, but in this song Isaiah looks forward to a time when its fruit will fill the whole earth (27:6). Although the Lord struck Israel, he did not punish her as he did the Assyrian troops when they surrounded Jerusalem in 701 BC (37:36); God had a continuing purpose and plan for his people (27:7-9). The desolate picture painted in 27:10-11 is in contrast to the depiction of the people's ultimate hope. In 27:12-13, the Lord promises to gather his people "like handpicked grain" from the most distant points.

This song (27:2-5) teaches that someday the Lord will shelter the faithful remnant of his people with his protecting hand. It describes how the Lord will watch over the vineyard, watering it carefully (27:3). Some have suggested that this watering refers to God's repeatedly sending his prophets to speak to his people (cf. Jer 7:25; 25:4). Here his anger against Israel (27:4) is gone; he burns up the briers and thorns. In contrast to the previous vineyard song, these enemies will be spared only if they turn to God for help and make peace with him (27:5). The oppressed cried out in the sinful Israel of old, but the new Israel will be secured by the Lord's gift of peace. The old vineyard was confined by hedge and wall, but the new Israel of the prophet's vision will cover the face of the earth with its yield.

In 27:6, Isaiah describes the time "when Jacob's descendants will take root," "bud and blossom," and "fill the whole earth with fruit." The messianic age is possibly in view here, with the Messiah as the true vine (John 15:1-8) and his disciples as the fruit-bearing branches. The spiritual influence of the new vineyard will be like leaven, permeating the whole world. The grain is carefully gathered ("one by one") and the harvest is extensive, "from the Euphrates River in the east to the Brook of Egypt in the west" (27:12).

After the lengthy section on judgment (ch 24) and an even longer section on restoration (25:1-27:6), Isaiah now concludes his Apocalypse with another brief section on judgment (27:7ff) and the promise of purified and unified worship at Mount Zion. Niehaus (1995:113-114) notes that a similar pattern appears in Exodus 15, where the Lord's theophanic supremacy over the sea (Exod 15:8-10) is followed by anticipation that the Lord will lead his people to "the mountain of the Lord's inheritance . . . the sanctuary, O Lord your hands established" (Exod 15:17).

## ◆ E. Pronouncement of Woes (28:1–33:24)
### 1. Woe to Ephraim (28:1–13)

What sorrow awaits the proud city of
　　Samaria—
　　the glorious crown of the drunks of
　　　Israel.*
It sits at the head of a fertile valley,
　　but its glorious beauty will fade like
　　　a flower.
It is the pride of a people
　　brought down by wine.
2 For the Lord will send a mighty army
　　against it.
　　Like a mighty hailstorm and a
　　　torrential rain,
they will burst upon it like a surging
　　flood
　　and smash it to the ground.
3 The proud city of Samaria—
　　the glorious crown of the drunks of
　　　Israel*—
　　will be trampled beneath its
　　　enemies' feet.
4 It sits at the head of a fertile valley,
　　but its glorious beauty will fade like
　　　a flower.
Whoever sees it will snatch it up,

as an early fig is quickly picked and
　　eaten.

5 Then at last the LORD of Heaven's
　　Armies
　　will himself be Israel's glorious
　　　crown.
He will be the pride and joy
　　of the remnant of his people.
6 He will give a longing for justice
　　to their judges.
He will give great courage
　　to their warriors who stand at the
　　　gates.

7 Now, however, Israel is led by drunks
　　who reel with wine and stagger with
　　　alcohol.
The priests and prophets stagger with
　　alcohol
　　and lose themselves in wine.
They reel when they see visions
　　and stagger as they render
　　　decisions.
8 Their tables are covered with vomit;
　　filth is everywhere.

9 "Who does the LORD think we are?"
  they ask.
  "Why does he speak to us like this?
  Are we little children,
    just recently weaned?
10 He tells us everything over and over—
  one line at a time,
    one line at a time,
  a little here,
    and a little there!"

11 So now God will have to speak to his
  people
    through foreign oppressors who
    speak a strange language!

12 God has told his people,
  "Here is a place of rest;
    let the weary rest here.
  This is a place of quiet rest."
    But they would not listen.
13 So the LORD will spell out his message
  for them again,
  one line at a time,
    one line at a time,
  a little here,
    and a little there,
  so that they will stumble and fall.
  They will be injured, trapped, and
    captured.

28:1 Hebrew *What sorrow awaits the crowning glory of the drunks of Ephraim,* referring to Samaria, capital of
the northern kingdom of Israel.   28:3 Hebrew *The crowning glory of the drunks of Ephraim;* see note on 28:1.

## NOTES

28:1 *What sorrow.* This section is marked by a sequence of "sorrows" (cf. 28:1; 29:1, 15;
30:1; 31:1; 33:1).

*Samaria.* Samaria was the capital of the northern kingdom of Israel; it is also called
"Ephraim."

28:3 *glorious crown.* See the NLT mg. The "crowning glory" could also refer to the city of
Samaria that encircled the crest of a prominent hill like a wreath (cf. 28:3). Although the
primary reference is surely to the city, it could also allude to the garlands worn by revelers
on festive occasions.

*drunks.* From the Heb. root *shakar* [TH7937, ZH8509], "to be drunk." The reference is easily
understood in this context of luxury and indulgence amid the rich vineyards of that area.
The prophet uses this root several times (cf. 5:11, 22; 24:9; 28:7; 56:12).

*Israel.* This translates the Heb. for "Ephraim" (so the NLT mg).

28:5 *Then at last.* This translates the Heb. for "in that day" (cf. 4:1-2; 10:20, 27; 12:1, 4;
24:21; 25:9; 26:1; 27:1-2, 12-13).

*LORD of Heaven's Armies.* The Targum gives the messianic reading, "Messiah of the Lord of
Hosts" (Levey 1974:58).

28:7 *drunks . . . priests and prophets stagger.* According to Lev 10:9, priests were forbidden by law to drink any wine or beer prior to their participation in the service of the tabernacle; the prohibition was also assumed to apply to the Temple (Ezek 44:21).

28:8 *vomit . . . filth.* "Vomit" translates Heb. *qi'* [TH6892, ZH7795], which occurs in only two
verses in Isaiah, here and 19:14. It is an onomatopoeic word, sounding like what it means
(spit, vomit). The explicit Heb. word for "filth" (*tso'ah* [TH6675, ZH7363]) is translated "dung"
in the KJV (2 Kgs 18:27; Isa 36:12), where it is parallel to "urine." However, some new versions take the combination of these two words as hendiadys (two terms with one meaning) and translate it as "filthy vomit" (NRSV, NAB, NJB, ESV).

28:10 *one line at a time . . . a little here.* Although the general idea seems clear (mimicry
and sarcasm), the Heb. is not fully understood. Probably it means that Isaiah's audience
got bored with hearing the same old prophetic warnings about their repeated sins, so they
engaged in sarcastic ridicule of the prophet's words (cf. the mocking of 5:19). Van Selms
(1973) suggests that the language reflects an Assyrian idiom.

**28:11-12** This passage is partially quoted in 1 Cor 14:21.

*strange language.* This refers to Assyrian, the language of the invaders. Although Assyrian was a Semitic language, it was eastern, whereas Heb. was western. Despite similarities, Assyrian would have sounded "strange" to the Hebrews.

**28:12** This verse is a good example of a chiasm. See the Heb. text and Watson (1981:130).

COMMENTARY

**Overview of Isaiah 28–33.** Isaiah's next literary unit is a book of the woes that lie at the heart of Isaiah's prophecies, reminding us that this is a central theme in Old Testament prophecy.

Much like chapters 1–12, this section (28:1–33:24) consists of a series of prophecies that reached their climax during Hezekiah's testing, when Sennacherib was successfully resisted. The death of Ahaz and the accession of Hezekiah to the throne brought an immediate change for the better in the religious life of the people, but Isaiah realized that there would be a new test with the new king. These "woes" make an appropriate sequel to an age of unbelief and darkness accompanied by disgrace and misery. They appear as something of a spiritual tonic for the debased standards of God's covenant people. Israel had been guilty of neglecting God and the great salvation he offered to them, and they had despised the prophet that had labored in vain among them.

The New Testament repeatedly quotes from this section (chs 28–33) of Isaiah. The following passages from Isaiah are followed by their New Testament references: Isaiah 28:11-12 (1 Cor 14:21); Isaiah 28:16 (Rom 9:33; 10:11; 1 Pet 2:6); Isaiah 29:10 (Rom 11:8); Isaiah 29:13 (Matt 15:8-9; Mark 7:6-7); Isaiah 29:14 (1 Cor 1:19).

**Woe to Ephraim.** The northern kingdom of Israel was also called Ephraim. Its capital, Samaria, was established by Ahab's father, King Omri; it was built on a prominent hill and stood out dramatically from the surrounding countryside. The city had been taken in an early Assyrian invasion and was in decline by Isaiah's time, but earlier in the eighth century it had been known for its luxury (cf. Amos 6:4-7).

This passage vividly describes Samaria's outrageous pride and sad end as "the glorious crown of the drunks of Israel" (28:1-4). Ancient Samaria was on an elevated site in a fertile valley renowned for its beautiful setting, but God will bring against them the greedy Assyrians and "its glorious beauty will fade like a flower" (28:4). "The Lord will send a mighty army against it" (28:2) and "it will be trampled beneath its enemies' feet" (28:3). It will be snatched up "as an early fig is quickly picked and eaten" (28:4).

Ultimately, the "LORD of Heaven's Armies will be Israel's glorious crown" (28:5) and he "will be the pride and joy of the remnant of his people" (28:5). However, for the present, Israel was "led by drunks" (28:7) who ridiculed the warnings from the Lord. These were probably the priests, prophets, and judges who preferred the escapism temporarily found in alcohol instead of facing the reality of the prophetic warning. Among their tables covered with "vomit," and "filth" (28:8) they boldly but blindly exclaimed, "Who does the LORD think we are?" and "Why does he speak to us like this?" (28:9). They even mimicked and ridiculed the word of warning from God (28:10), so the Lord responded that they would indeed hear the strange words of a foreign language as the Assyrians invaded their country and destroyed their capital (28:11). Because of their drunken state and spiritual obtuseness, they "will stumble and fall" and will "be injured, trapped, and captured" (28:13).

This oracle against Samaria appropriately serves as an introduction to the following oracle against Jerusalem (28:14-29).

◆ ## 2. Warning to the rulers of Judah (28:14-29)

14 Therefore, listen to this message from the LORD,
  you scoffing rulers in Jerusalem.
15 You boast, "We have struck a bargain to cheat death
  and have made a deal to dodge the grave.*
The coming destruction can never touch us,
  for we have built a strong refuge made of lies and deception."

16 Therefore, this is what the Sovereign LORD says:
"Look! I am placing a foundation stone in Jerusalem,*
  a firm and tested stone.
It is a precious cornerstone that is safe to build on.
  Whoever believes need never be shaken.*
17 I will test you with the measuring line of justice
  and the plumb line of righteousness.
Since your refuge is made of lies,
  a hailstorm will knock it down.
Since it is made of deception,
  a flood will sweep it away.
18 I will cancel the bargain you made to cheat death,
  and I will overturn your deal to dodge the grave.
When the terrible enemy sweeps through,
  you will be trampled into the ground.
19 Again and again that flood will come,
  morning after morning,

day and night,
  until you are carried away."

This message will bring terror to your people.
20 The bed you have made is too short to lie on.
The blankets are too narrow to cover you.
21 The LORD will come as he did against the Philistines at Mount Perazim
  and against the Amorites at Gibeon.
He will come to do a strange thing;
  he will come to do an unusual deed:
22 For the Lord, the LORD of Heaven's Armies,
  has plainly said that he is determined to crush the whole land.
So scoff no more,
  or your punishment will be even greater.

23 Listen to me;
  listen, and pay close attention.
24 Does a farmer always plow and never sow?
  Is he forever cultivating the soil and never planting?
25 Does he not finally plant his seeds—
  black cumin, cumin, wheat, barley, and emmer wheat—
each in its proper way,
  and each in its proper place?
26 The farmer knows just what to do,
  for God has given him understanding.

²⁷A heavy sledge is never used to thresh
  black cumin;
  rather, it is beaten with a light stick.
A threshing wheel is never rolled on
  cumin;
  instead, it is beaten lightly with
  a flail.
²⁸Grain for bread is easily crushed,

so he doesn't keep on pounding it.
He threshes it under the wheels of
  a cart,
  but he doesn't pulverize it.
²⁹The LORD of Heaven's Armies is
  a wonderful teacher,
  and he gives the farmer great
  wisdom.

28:15 Hebrew *Sheol;* also in 28:18. 28:16a Hebrew *in Zion.* 28:16b Greek version reads *Look! I am placing a stone in the foundation of Jerusalem* [literally *Zion*], */ a precious cornerstone for its foundation, chosen for great honor. / Anyone who trusts in him will never be disgraced.* Compare Rom 9:33; 1 Pet 2:6.

## NOTES

**28:15 *struck a bargain to cheat death.*** Lit., they "made a covenant with death," the meaning of which is not certain. One interpretation understands this as a possible allusion to necromancy and idol worship (cf. 8:19). Another view refers to the alliance with Egypt that was supposed to protect the nation from Assyrian aggression (cf. 20:6). Yet another possibility concerns the relationship of Judah with Assyria. Perhaps they had a secret understanding with Assyria's enemies but continued to present themselves to the Assyrian authorities as friends. Probably the point is that they presumed that death could not touch them, believing that their diplomatic skills would protect them against Sheol (the grave). Their confidence seemed to indicate that they had a document in their pockets in which these powers promised not to harm them.

***grave.*** Heb. *she'ol* [TH7585, ZH8619], as the NLT mg indicates (cf. 28:18).

**28:16 *foundation stone . . . cornerstone.*** The stacking of terms here ("foundation stone . . . firm and tested stone . . . precious stone") is for effect and emphasis. Motyer (1993:233) comments, "Note the emphasis on 'foundation' throughout; the superstructure is not yet there (see 1 Pet 2:4-8a)." The image of a cornerstone for a sure foundation is probably taken from the easily observed architecture of that time. Solomon made use of huge foundation stones at the corners of the Temple. Some of those discovered are thirty-eight feet long and weigh many tons.

***Jerusalem.*** This translates the Heb. word for "Zion" (cf. NLT mg).

**28:17 *justice . . . righteousness.*** These standards were repeatedly held up by Isaiah and his contemporary Amos.

**28:21 *Mount Perazim.*** The reference is to the mount where God "broke out" (the meaning of "Perazim") against the Philistines (2 Sam 5:20).

***Gibeon.*** This is where God sent a hailstorm to destroy the Amorites (Josh 10:10-12).

**28:25 *black cumin.*** Heb. *qetsakh* [TH7100, ZH7902]. The precise identification is uncertain. The versions vary: "dill" (NRSV, REB, ESV), "gith" (NAB), "fennel" (NJB), "fitches" (KJV), "caraway" (NIV), and "black cumin" (NJPS).

***cumin.*** Heb. *kammon* [TH3646, ZH4021]. This plant was used especially for seasoning. The versions agree on this term except for the spelling: "cummin" (KJV, NASB, NRSV, NIV) and "cumin" (TEV, ESV, NJPS).

## COMMENTARY

In this section, the "rulers in Jerusalem" are described as "scoffing," which in the Old Testament world was "the very last degree of ungodliness" (Webb 1996:121). The drunken rebels had the audacity to boast that they were safe because they had "struck a bargain to cheat death" and had "made a deal to dodge the grave" (28:15). They also thought that they had "built a strong refuge made of lies and deception" (28:15). The Lord's response to this was that he would place a "foundation stone in Jerusalem," and that "whoever believes need never be shaken" (28:16). This foundation was probably David's royal house, the bearer of God's promises (cf. 9:6). In its deepest sense, therefore, this statement refers to David's descendant, the Messiah, for it is in Christ that the royal house of David acquires its full significance (cf. Rom 9:33; 1 Pet 2:6ff). Note the reference to this verse (or to Isa 8:14) in Romans 9:33.

The Lord responded to the drunken rebels' attitude of self-justification (28:17-22). In vivid language, using the image of a building (cf. 28:16), Isaiah described how the Lord would use the "measuring line of justice and the plumb line of righteousness" (28:17) to check their foundations and the refuge in which the people put their trust. God's standards and tests for the people were based on his justice and righteousness, recurring themes found throughout Isaiah. Their refuge of lies would be blown away (28:17) as the Lord cancelled the bargain they made to avoid death and overturned their "deal to dodge the grave" (28:18). Invaders flooded them, day and night. As often as the Mesopotamian powers came by, they would take captives from Judah. The prophet had said that the Assyrian arm would "sweep into Judah, until it is chin deep . . . submerging your land from one end to the other" (8:8). The flood would come to the walls of Jerusalem but not take the city (ch 37). But the surrounding areas would be sacked and the inhabitants of Jerusalem would be confined for safety inside the city. They would discover that their bed was "too short to lie on. The blankets . . . too narrow to cover [them]" (28:20). This is similar to our expression, "You made your bed; now lie on it." In the end, the Lord would come against them "as he did against the Philistines in Mount Perazim and the Amorites at Gibeon" (28:21).

The closing paragraph (28:23-29) describes the proper way of threshing understood by the skilled and experienced farmer. Not all grains are threshed the same way, and improper threshing of certain grains could crush them and make them worthless (28:28). The "LORD of Heaven's Armies is a wonderful teacher" (28:29) and a wise judge; he uses the right form of threshing for the various grains being threshed, just as a wise farmer does.

◆       ## 3. Woe to Jerusalem (Ariel) (29:1-24)

"What sorrow awaits Ariel,* the City
    of David.
Year after year you celebrate your
    feasts.
2 Yet I will bring disaster upon you,
    and there will be much weeping and
        sorrow.
For Jerusalem will become what her
    name Ariel means—

an altar covered with blood.
3 I will be your enemy,
    surrounding Jerusalem and
        attacking its walls.
I will build siege towers
    and destroy it.
4 Then deep from the earth you
    will speak;

from low in the dust your words
  will come.
Your voice will whisper from the
  ground
like a ghost conjured up from the
  grave.

5 "But suddenly, your ruthless enemies
    will be crushed
  like the finest of dust.
  Your many attackers will be driven
    away
  like chaff before the wind.
  Suddenly, in an instant,
6   I, the LORD of Heaven's Armies,
    will act for you
  with thunder and earthquake and
    great noise,
    with whirlwind and storm and
      consuming fire.
7 All the nations fighting against
    Jerusalem*
  will vanish like a dream!
  Those who are attacking her walls
    will vanish like a vision in the
      night.
8 A hungry person dreams of eating
    but wakes up still hungry.
  A thirsty person dreams of drinking
    but is still faint from thirst when
      morning comes.
  So it will be with your enemies,
    with those who attack Mount Zion."

9 Are you amazed and incredulous?
    Don't you believe it?
  Then go ahead and be blind.
    You are stupid, but not from wine!
    You stagger, but not from liquor!
10 For the LORD has poured out on you
    a spirit of deep sleep.
  He has closed the eyes of your
    prophets and visionaries.

11 All the future events in this vision are
like a sealed book to them. When you give
it to those who can read, they will say,
"We can't read it because it is sealed."
12 When you give it to those who cannot
read, they will say, "We don't know how to
read."

13 And so the Lord says,
    "These people say they are mine.
  They honor me with their lips,
    but their hearts are far from me.
  And their worship of me
    is nothing but man-made rules
      learned by rote.*
14 Because of this, I will once again
    astound these hypocrites
  with amazing wonders.
  The wisdom of the wise will pass
    away,
    and the intelligence of the
      intelligent will disappear."

15 What sorrow awaits those who try to
    hide their plans from the LORD,
  who do their evil deeds in the dark!
  "The LORD can't see us," they say.
    "He doesn't know what's going on!"
16 How foolish can you be?
    He is the Potter, and he is certainly
      greater than you, the clay!
  Should the created thing say of the
    one who made it,
    "He didn't make me"?
  Does a jar ever say,
    "The potter who made me is
      stupid"?

17 Soon—and it will not be very long—
    the forests of Lebanon will become
      a fertile field,
    and the fertile field will yield
      bountiful crops.
18 In that day the deaf will hear words
    read from a book,
  and the blind will see through the
    gloom and darkness.
19 The humble will be filled with fresh joy
    from the LORD.
  The poor will rejoice in the Holy One
    of Israel.
20 The scoffer will be gone,
    the arrogant will disappear,
  and those who plot evil will be
    killed.
21 Those who convict the innocent
    by their false testimony will
      disappear.

A similar fate awaits those who use
trickery to pervert justice
and who tell lies to destroy the
innocent.

²²That is why the LORD, who redeemed
Abraham, says to the people of Israel,*

"My people will no longer be ashamed
or turn pale with fear.
²³ For when they see their many children

and all the blessings I have given
them,
they will recognize the holiness of the
Holy One of Israel.
They will stand in awe of the God
of Jacob.
²⁴ Then the wayward will gain
understanding,
and complainers will accept
instruction.

29:1 *Ariel* sounds like a Hebrew term that means "hearth" or "altar."   29:7 Hebrew *Ariel.*   29:13 Greek version
reads *Their worship is a farce, / for they teach man-made ideas as commands from God.* Compare Mark 7:7.
29:22 Hebrew *of Jacob.* See note on 14:1.

NOTES
29:1 The Hebrew has more lit. "woe to Ariel, Ariel, the city where David camped." The verb
translated "camp" (*khana* [TH2583, ZH2837]) is used only here and in verse 3 in Isaiah,
although it is common elsewhere.

**Ariel.** The Heb. word *'ari'el* [TH740, ZH790] occurs five times vv. 1, 2, 7 and is generally
accepted as a reference to Jerusalem. In v. 2, the word is translated as "altar covered with
blood," and in v. 7 as "Jerusalem" (cf. NLT mg). Several interpretations have been suggested for the meaning of the term. See Youngblood (1979).

29:6-7 For a detailed study of the language and imagery of these verses, see Wong (1995).

29:10 *a spirit of deep sleep.* The Lord brought about this condition. The expression *ruakh
tardemah* [TH8639, ZH9554] (sleep) is found only here in Isaiah, but it contains the same term
used in Gen 2:21 and 1 Sam 26:12. Its use in Prov 19:15 is connected with laziness.

29:13 Jesus quoted this verse when he addressed the hypocritical leaders of his day (Matt
15:8-9; Mark 7:6-7).

29:14 *wonders.* Three times in Isaiah, the root for "wonder" (*pala'* [TH6381, ZH7098]) is used
in the Heb. Here it links this oracle with 28:29. God had shown his people wonders in the
Exodus (Exod 15:11; Ps 78:12), and now he would show them wonders in judgment.

*The wisdom of the wise will pass away, and the intelligence of the intelligent will
disappear.* This is aptly quoted by Paul in 1 Cor 1:19 in connection with finite worldly
wisdom.

29:15 *their plans.* The Heb. *'etsah* [TH6098, ZH6783] probably refers to the alliance between
Ahaz and Assyria or to the one between Hezekiah and Egypt (cf. 30:1-2).

*in the dark.* The word for "dark" (*makhshak* [TH4285, ZH4743]) is used by Isaiah here and in
42:16 but is not found elsewhere in the prophetic writings.

29:16 Paul quoted this verse and Isa 45:9 in Rom 9:20.

29:18 *gloom and darkness.* This language of "gloom" (*'ophel* [TH652, ZH694]) and "darkness"
(*khoshek* [TH2822, ZH3125]) also echoes the language used in context of the coming Messiah
(9:1-2; cf. Eph 5:8; 1 Thess 5:4).

29:22 *Abraham.* Outside of the Pentateuch, Abraham is singled out only eight times,
and four of these references are in Isaiah. They are found in all three divisions of the
book (29:22; 41:8; 51:2). For a possible purpose in this distribution, see Conrad
(1988).

*ashamed.* Heb. *bosh* [TH954, ZH1017], a verb used twenty-two times in Isaiah (see 45:17; 50:7; 54:4).

**29:23 they will recognize the holiness of the Holy One of Israel.** More lit. "they shall sanctify my name, and sanctify the Holy One of Jacob" (KJV). Jacob is an alternate name for Israel, and it was just used in the preceding verse (cf. NLT mg). The title "Holy One of Israel" is a favorite of Isaiah and he often used it in some strategic way, as here. The Lord is holy and is not to be treated lightly (cf. 1:19).

## COMMENTARY

This chapter presents the next of the "sorrow" oracles in this section of Isaiah's prophecies; it is parallel to the "sorrow" against Samaria in 28:1. Having denounced Samaria briefly and Jerusalem at length in the previous chapter, the prophet now focuses on Jerusalem alone. An image is again used to express the city's character.

In 29:1-4, woe is pronounced upon Jerusalem, conveying a warning of the Assyrian siege that was God's intended punishment for his people. The opening reference, "year after year you celebrate your feasts" (29:1) could mean that a feast was the setting for this oracle. The next verse indicates what the prophet had in mind by explaining the meaning of Ariel as "an altar covered with blood" (29:2).

Suddenly the scene changes and a promise of miraculous deliverance (29:5-8) is presented in highly poetic language. Jerusalem's rescue from Sennacherib in 701 BC (cf. 37:33-37) was truly amazing. The "thunder and earthquake and great noise, with whirlwind and storm and consuming fire" (29:6) depict the Lord's supernatural intervention in delivering Jerusalem from the might of Assyria.

The people were without vision (29:9-12). The reflexive verbs in 29:9 suggest that their blindness was to some extent unconsciously self-imposed (cf. 6:9-10; 30:10-11). A spiritual stupor had come over Judah, and they staggered like blind people because the word of God had become a closed book to them. The people were responsible for their drunkenness, but the Lord had "poured out" on them "a spirit of deep sleep" and "closed the eyes" of their prophetic leaders (29:10), a passage quoted by Paul in Romans 11:8. The resulting spiritual blindness prevented them from seeing and grasping the true revelation, like someone unable to read. Neither the uneducated nor the educated were able to understand the message of God's word. Motyer (1993:239) suggests that "the theology is identical with 1 Kgs 22:22 ('a spirit of falsehood'), where Ahab's determination to embrace falsehood brought on him a judicial visitation of the very spirit he chose (cf. 2 Thess 2:9-12)." The people of God had gotten themselves into this pathetic condition.

"They honor me with their lips but their hearts are far from me" (29:13) echoes the description of the hypocritical worship in the first chapter. Jesus quotes this passage when describing the hypocrisy of the Jewish leaders of his time (Matt 15:8-9; Mark 7:6-7). The people had mocked the teachings of God (cf. 28:10) while exalting man-made rules, just as the Pharisees later emphasized human tradition (cf.

Matt 15:8-9). This "religion" eventually resulted in contempt for the Creator, whom they mocked by saying, "He doesn't know what's going on" (29:15).

Their leaders made plans without consulting God, because in their eyes human wisdom seemed sufficient. Only true worship produces wisdom; false worship destroys it. When wisdom and understanding are missing from a people, they become fools. So God will "astound these hypocrites with amazing wonders" of punishment and reveal that "the intelligence of the intelligent will disappear" (29:14), a passage quoted by Paul in 1 Corinthians 1:19.

The words of judgment continue with another "sorrow" in 29:15-16. Incredibly, those who were blind themselves actually thought, "the LORD can't see us" (29:15). Since they had completely reversed the Creator-creature relationship, it is not surprising that Isaiah pronounced woe on them and reminded them of the proper order of things. In 29:15 the people denied God's omniscience ("The LORD can't see us"), his wisdom ("He doesn't know what is going on"), and his sovereignty ("He didn't make us"). In 45:9, the prophet shows how ridiculous it would be for a pot to talk back to the potter, and in 10:15 he had compared Assyria to the absurd picture of an ax that quarreled with a woodsman. Such a confusion of the divine order of creation leads to moral confusion that cannot distinguish right from wrong (cf. 5:20). Here in 29:16 he gives the same warning, a passage quoted by Paul in Romans 9:20.

Isaiah did not dwell for long on negative matters, but shifted to a look at the glorious future transformation of God's people. Then, social wrongs will be made right, and Israel will genuinely worship the Lord. As usual, it is difficult to understand when these events are supposed to occur. These verses describe the great reversal that will take place; they change in tone from judgment to hope by looking beyond the Assyrian attacks to a happier future when God would overturn present conditions and correct injustices. "In that day" (29:18) must refer beyond Assyria's destruction to the time of Israel's restoration. The time when "the deaf will hear words read from a book, and the blind will see through the gloom and darkness" (29:18) is linked with the rule of the righteous king (32:3) and with the messianic age (35:5).

Evil people—the scoffers, the arrogant, and those who plot evil and convict the innocent—will perish. The closing paragraph (29:22-24) promises a time when "My people will no longer be ashamed or turn pale with fear" (29:22). It will be a time of blessing when they will "recognize the holiness of the Holy One of Israel" (29:23) and "the wayward will gain understanding" (29:24). If 29:23 refers to the Assyrian deportations of people from Israel to Mesopotamia, the reference to Abraham whom God brought from Mesopotamia to Canaan makes sense and the expression "see their many children" (29:23; cf. 49:20-21; 54:1-2) may refer to the return from exile (cf. 53:10). The fact that they are called "children, the work of my hands" (see the Heb. of 29:23) may be intended to remind the people of God's grace in permitting this remnant to survive (cf. 45:11; Eph 2:10).

◆      4. Woe to the Egyptian alliance (30:1–31:9)

"What sorrow awaits my rebellious
    children,"
says the LORD.
"You make plans that are contrary
    to mine.
You make alliances not directed
    by my Spirit,
    thus piling up your sins.
2 For without consulting me,
    you have gone down to Egypt for
    help.
You have put your trust in Pharaoh's
    protection.
You have tried to hide in his shade.
3 But by trusting Pharaoh, you will be
    humiliated,
    and by depending on him, you will
    be disgraced.
4 For though his power extends to Zoan
    and his officials have arrived in
    Hanes,
5 all who trust in him will be ashamed.
He will not help you.
Instead, he will disgrace you."

6 This message came to me concerning the
animals in the Negev:

The caravan moves slowly
    across the terrible desert to
    Egypt—
donkeys weighed down with riches
    and camels loaded with treasure—
    all to pay for Egypt's protection.
They travel through the wilderness,
    a place of lionesses and lions,
    a place where vipers and poisonous
    snakes live.
All this, and Egypt will give you
    nothing in return.
7     Egypt's promises are worthless!
Therefore, I call her Rahab—
    the Harmless Dragon.*

8 Now go and write down these words.
    Write them in a book.
They will stand until the end of time
    as a witness
9 that these people are stubborn rebels

who refuse to pay attention to the
    LORD's instructions.
10 They tell the seers,
    "Stop seeing visions!"
They tell the prophets,
    "Don't tell us what is right.
Tell us nice things.
Tell us lies.
11 Forget all this gloom.
    Get off your narrow path.
Stop telling us about your
    'Holy One of Israel.'"

12 This is the reply of the Holy One of
Israel:

"Because you despise what I tell you
    and trust instead in oppression and
    lies,
13 calamity will come upon you
    suddenly—
    like a bulging wall that bursts and
    falls.
In an instant it will collapse
    and come crashing down.
14 You will be smashed like a piece of
    pottery—
shattered so completely that
there won't be a piece big enough
    to carry coals from a fireplace
    or a little water from the well."

15 This is what the Sovereign LORD,
    the Holy One of Israel, says:
"Only in returning to me
    and resting in me will you be saved.
In quietness and confidence is your
    strength.
But you would have none of it.
16 You said, 'No, we will get our help
    from Egypt.
They will give us swift horses for
    riding into battle.'
But the only swiftness you are going
    to see
is the swiftness of your enemies
    chasing you!
17 One of them will chase a thousand
    of you.

Five of them will make all of you
flee.
You will be left like a lonely flagpole
on a hill
or a tattered banner on a distant
mountaintop."

<sup>18</sup> So the LORD must wait for you to come
to him
so he can show you his love and
compassion.
For the LORD is a faithful God.
Blessed are those who wait for
his help.

<sup>19</sup> O people of Zion, who live in
Jerusalem,
you will weep no more.
He will be gracious if you ask for help.
He will surely respond to the sound
of your cries.
<sup>20</sup> Though the Lord gave you adversity
for food
and suffering for drink,
he will still be with you to teach you.
You will see your teacher with your
own eyes.
<sup>21</sup> Your own ears will hear him.
Right behind you a voice will say,
"This is the way you should go,"
whether to the right or to the left.
<sup>22</sup> Then you will destroy all your silver
idols
and your precious gold images.
You will throw them out like filthy
rags,
saying to them, "Good riddance!"

<sup>23</sup>Then the LORD will bless you with rain
at planting time. There will be wonderful
harvests and plenty of pastureland for
your livestock. <sup>24</sup>The oxen and donkeys
that till the ground will eat good grain, its
chaff blown away by the wind. <sup>25</sup>In that
day, when your enemies are slaughtered
and the towers fall, there will be streams
of water flowing down every mountain
and hill. <sup>26</sup>The moon will be as bright as
the sun, and the sun will be seven times
brighter—like the light of seven days in
one! So it will be when the LORD begins to
heal his people and cure the wounds he
gave them.

<sup>27</sup> Look! The LORD is coming from far
away,
burning with anger,
surrounded by thick, rising smoke.
His lips are filled with fury;
his words consume like fire.
<sup>28</sup> His hot breath pours out like a flood
up to the neck of his enemies.
He will sift out the proud nations for
destruction.
He will bridle them and lead them
away to ruin.

<sup>29</sup> But the people of God will sing a song
of joy,
like the songs at the holy festivals.
You will be filled with joy,
as when a flutist leads a group of
pilgrims
to Jerusalem, the mountain of the
LORD—
to the Rock of Israel.
<sup>30</sup> And the LORD will make his majestic
voice heard.
He will display the strength of
his mighty arm.
It will descend with devouring
flames,
with cloudbursts, thunderstorms,
and huge hailstones.
<sup>31</sup> At the LORD's command, the Assyrians
will be shattered.
He will strike them down with his
royal scepter.
<sup>32</sup> And as the LORD strikes them with his
rod of punishment,
his people will celebrate with
tambourines and harps.
Lifting his mighty arm, he will fight
the Assyrians.
<sup>33</sup> Topheth—the place of burning—
has long been ready for the Assyrian
king;
the pyre is piled high with wood.
The breath of the LORD, like fire from
a volcano,
will set it ablaze.

## CHAPTER 31

1 What sorrow awaits those who look to
    Egypt for help,
  trusting their horses, chariots, and
    charioteers
and depending on the strength of
    human armies
  instead of looking to the LORD,
    the Holy One of Israel.
2 In his wisdom, the LORD will send great
    disaster;
  he will not change his mind.
He will rise against the wicked
  and against their helpers.
3 For these Egyptians are mere humans,
    not God!
  Their horses are puny flesh, not
    mighty spirits!
When the LORD raises his fist against
    them,
  those who help will stumble,
and those being helped will fall.
  They will all fall down and die
    together.

4 But this is what the LORD has told me:

"When a strong young lion
  stands growling over a sheep it has
    killed,
  it is not frightened by the shouts and
    noise
of a whole crowd of shepherds.
In the same way, the LORD of Heaven's
    Armies
  will come down and fight on Mount
    Zion.
5 The LORD of Heaven's Armies will hover
    over Jerusalem
  and protect it like a bird protecting
    its nest.
He will defend and save the city;
  he will pass over it and rescue it."

6 Though you are such wicked rebels, my
people, come and return to the LORD. 7 I
know the glorious day will come when
each of you will throw away the gold idols
and silver images your sinful hands have
made.

8 "The Assyrians will be destroyed,
  but not by the swords of men.
The sword of God will strike them,
  and they will panic and flee.
The strong young Assyrians
  will be taken away as captives.
9 Even the strongest will quake with
    terror,
  and princes will flee when they see
    your battle flags,"
says the LORD, whose fire burns in Zion,
  whose flame blazes from Jerusalem.

30:7 Hebrew *Rahab who sits still.* Rahab is the name of a mythical sea monster that represents chaos in ancient
literature. The name is used here as a poetic name for Egypt.

### NOTES

**30:4 Zoan.** Zoan was located in the northeastern part of the delta (cf. 19:11) where Israel
once served as slaves. For various proposals concerning the identity of Zoan, see ABD. It
may also have also been known as Tahpenes or Heracleopolis. The Aramaic Targum of
Isaiah has Tahpenes, the Egyptian fortress on Egypt's eastern frontier, near Zoan in the
north delta.

**Hanes.** This was probably a city in the Nile delta close to Zoan. Some connect it with
Heracleopolis Magna, fifty miles south of Cairo, but Kitchen suggests it should be linked
with Tanis (NBD 452).

**30:6 desert.** The Heb. word is *negeb* [TH5045A, ZH5582] (Negev); it refers to the desert area
immediately south of Judah. If the Assyrians had control of the main roads, the envoys had
to use back roads more populated by wild creatures.

**poisonous snakes.** The Heb. phrase *sarap* [TH8314, ZH8597] *me'opep* [TH5774, ZH6414] is translated in the KJV as "fiery flying serpent." The meaning of the phrase is not certain, as the

versions reflect: "darting snakes" (NIV), "flying serpent" (NRSV), "venomous flying serpent" (REB), "flying seraph" (NAB), and "flying dragon" (NJB).

**30:7 *Harmless Dragon*.** As the NLT mg indicates, the Heb. word is *rahab* [TH7294, ZH8105] (Rahab), the name of a sea monster in the literature of that time. Here it is a symbolic name for Egypt. The Heb. word can mean "arrogance."

**30:8 *write down . . . Write them in a book*.** More lit., "write it on a tablet . . . inscribe it on a scroll" (NIV). Although this is probably a case of synonymous parallelism, some would make a distinction between the two; for example, Ridderbos (1985:242) thinks that the "scroll" (*seper* [TH5612, ZH6219]) was a fuller record of this and other prophecies and that the "tablet" (*luakh* [TH3871, ZH4283]) contained only the summary of this particular prophecy.

**30:9 *stubborn rebels*.** The word "stubborn" translates Heb. *meri* [TH4805, ZH5308], a word used only here in Isaiah; however, the idea of stubbornness and rebellion is common in the book. The prophet noted this particular sin of the Lord's covenant people in the first chapter (1:2) where the Heb. is *pasha'* [TH6586, ZH7321], a word used frequently by Isaiah.

**30:10 *Tell us nice things. Tell us lies*.** This was typical of the messages of false prophets (1 Kgs 22:13; Jer 6:14; 8:11; 23:17, 26). More lit., "prophesy unto us right things, speak unto us smooth things (*khalaqoth* [TH2513, ZH2754]) prophecy deceits (*mahathalloth* [TH4123, ZH4562])" (KJV). The root meaning of the word translated "smooth" is used in both the literal and non-literal sense (cf. Dan 11:21). It is used in Prov 5:3 of the adulteress whose speech is smoother than oil.

**30:15 *returning to me*.** The reference is to repentance, the first step in reconciliation with the Holy One of Israel.

**30:22 *destroy*.** The Heb. root (*tm'* [TH2930, ZH3237]) means "defile, pollute," which was accomplished by discarding and rejecting the idols. The versions have "defile" (NASB, NRSV, ESV), "treat as unclean" (REB), "ruin for further use" (NCV), "dishonor" (GW), "treat like garbage" (CEV), "treat as unclean" (NJPS), "consider unclean" (NAB), and "hold unclean" (NJB).

***like filthy rags*.** The Heb. is *kemo dawah* [TH1739A, ZH1865], which the KJV translates as "a menstruous cloth." The NIV has, "like a menstrual cloth." The new versions are more general: "filthy rags" (NRSV, NAB), "dirty rags" (NIrV), and "polluted things" (NJB). The expression is found only here, and must be understood in light of 4:4.

**30:28 *like a flood up to the neck of his enemies*.** Similar language is used of the Assyrians (8:8).

**30:30 *display the strength of his mighty arm*.** More lit., "his arm coming down." Similar language is found in 9:12, 17, 21; 51:9.

**30:33 *Topheth*.** This was a burning site outside of Jerusalem, and a place where children had been sacrificed to Molech (2 Kgs 23:10; Jer 7:31-32; 19:6, 11-14).

**31:1 *What sorrow*.** Again we hear sorrows pronounced on those who go down to Egypt for help instead of relying on the Lord.

***help*.** This word (*'ezrah* [TH5833, ZH6476]) occurs four times in 31:1-3.

***horses, chariots, and charioteers*.** Egypt was especially noted for its horses and chariots (see 1 Kgs 10:28-29).

**31:2 *wisdom*.** Against the backdrop of the wisdom traditionally attributed to Egypt, the Lord speaks of his own wisdom. Note Paul's statement that God's wisdom judges all that passes for wisdom among mortals (1 Cor 1:18–3:23).

**31:3 horses.** The Judahites put their hope in the Egyptian cavalry (cf. 30:16). According to 1 Kgs 10:28-29, Egypt had many horses and chariots.

**puny flesh, not mighty spirits.** Grogan (1986:202) observes that "flesh" may seem so substantial to us because it is visible and tangible, whereas spirits may seem ethereal.

**raises his fist.** Similar language is also found in 5:25; 9:12, 17, 21; 10:4. This imagery has overtones of the Exodus, when the pomp and power of Egypt were overwhelmed by the Lord (Deut 4:34; 7:19). Egypt was more powerful then than it was in Isaiah's time.

**31:4 strong young lion stands growling over a sheep it has killed.** This vivid image may not be appreciated by those unfamiliar with this ancient scene, which probably took place frequently among those caring for sheep. One must picture the lion holding tightly to its prey, while from every direction shepherds appear and try to scare him away. Just as the lion knows how to hold on to its prey, the Lord can hold on to Jerusalem.

**shepherds.** This term was often used for the rulers of a country (e.g., Jer 3:15).

**31:5 hover over . . . protect . . . defend . . . rescue.** Motyer (1993:255) suggests that these four verbs may mean "on every side" and may represent sufficient surrounding help.

**pass over.** This same Heb. word (pasoakh [TH6452, ZH7173]) is found in Exod 12:13, 23, 27 (cf. Isa 37:35) and is used of the death angel who "passed over" every house in Egypt that had blood on its doorposts.

**31:8 sword of God.** The sword that would destroy the Assyrians belonged to the angel of the Lord, whose previous activity is alluded to in 31:5. According to 37:36-37, the angel struck down 185,000 Assyrian soldiers in one night. God, not the Egyptians with their horses, would defeat Assyria. The Heb. expression "to fall by the sword" can refer to any violent death, not necessarily to death by a sword.

**31:9 the strongest will quake.** "Strongest" translates the Heb. word sela' [TH5553, ZH6152] (rock), which the NLT understands as a reference to mighty ones, and as parallel to "princes" in the next line. The earlier version of the NLT had "their generals will quake." Motyer (1993:256) suggests that the reference could be to the king of Assyria in contrast to the "Rock of Israel" (cf. 30:29), and Driver (1968:52) gives examples of the cognate word for "leaders" in Arabic. Oswalt (1986:577) suggests a different translation for the word in this context: "all his confidence will pass away." The versions vary: "his rock will pass away" (NASB, cf. NRSV, ESV), "officers will be helpless" (REB), "they will run to their stronghold" (GW), "his rock shall melt" (NJPS), "he will abandon his rock" (NJB), and "he shall rush past his crag" (NAB).

**fire . . . flame.** According to the Heb., the reference to the "fire" ('ur [TH217, ZH241]) and "flame" (tannur [TH8574, ZH9486]) in Jerusalem and may correspond to "Topheth" in 30:33. This verse also has a subtle wordplay in that the Heb. 'ur (fire) is so similar to 'or [TH216, ZH240] (light).

### COMMENTARY

Another pair of woes (30:1; 31:1) is directed against those who advocated a military alliance with Egypt. They apparently had been influential enough that an envoy was on its way to Egypt, carrying the Exodus treasures across the desert to purchase the friendship of their former oppressors (30:1-5).

During the reign of Hezekiah, Judah's existence was threatened as Assyria captured Samaria in 722 BC, removing the last buffer state between the Assyrian provinces and Judah. After Pharaoh Shabako came to power in 715 BC, the small kingdoms in Palestine and Aram sought his help in resisting Assyria and there was growing pressure in Judah to join the alliance. One of Hezekiah's leading officials, Shebna, possibly had close personal ties with Egypt and may have spearheaded the move (cf. 22:15-19). Isaiah vigorously opposed it.

Judah's treaty with Egypt was worthless (30:1-7). In these verses, the Lord accused the people of making "plans that are contrary to mine" and "alliances not directed by my Spirit" (30:1). Instead of consulting the Lord, they put their "trust in Pharaoh's protection" (30:2); this was a terrible mistake, because all who trust in Pharaoh "will be ashamed" (30:5). Isaiah warned them that they were ignorant of Egypt's true character and that when the time came, Egypt would remain indifferent and helpless, bringing shame and confusion on Israel (30:7). Although, Judah's diplomats regarded their policies with Egypt as high and wise statesmanship (cf. 28:15; 29:14-15), Isaiah condemned them for refusing to "pay attention to the LORD'S instructions" (30:9).

In his mind, the prophet accompanied the envoys on their journey to Zoan and Hanes. Ironically, Zoan symbolized the awful slavery Israel had endured during her long tenure in Egypt (cf. 19:11). Egypt was a "Harmless Dragon" and her "promises are worthless" (30:7), yet the people went blindly down to Egypt without consulting the Lord's prophet. By seeking Pharaoh's protection, they hoped to be secure from the Assyrian threat. The people of Judah were willing to exchange God's protection and shelter for the refuge they thought Pharaoh could supply (cf. 25:4), but the Lord should have been their refuge (cf. 49:2; 51:16). The advocates of the pro-Egyptian party stubbornly refused to listen to the prophet, so Isaiah wrote his words of warning in a book (30:8) to be a lasting record for generations to come of their unwillingness to listen.

The wicked people actually told the prophets, "Stop seeing visions . . . Don't tell us what is right" (30:10). Instead, the rebels preferred, "Tell us nice things. Tell us lies" (30:10). The rebels had heard more than enough about the Holy One of Israel (30:11; cf. 5:19), and preferred to "trust instead in oppression and lies" (30:12). The Lord had condemned the oppression that characterized Judah's domestic policy (1:15-17, 23; 5:7; 29:21; 58:3-4; 59:3, 6-8, 13), as well as the deceit of her foreign policy (29:15; 30:1-2). Now the Lord's response was that they would be judged and become "like a bulging wall that bursts and falls" (30:13).

Isaiah urged the recall of the envoy on its way to Egypt, and he admonished the people to turn to the Lord for deliverance (30:15-17). The warning from the "Sovereign LORD, the Holy One of Israel" declared that "only in returning to me and resting in me will you be saved" (30:15). This was the kind of repentance they were to follow: to turn from the way of unbelief and worldly perspective in order to walk in the way of faith (Wong 1997). The rebels responded, "No, we will get our help from Egypt," because they thought they could get "swift horses for riding into battle" (30:16). The Lord's response to this was that "the only swiftness you are going to see is the swiftness of your enemies chasing you!" (30:16). The result of all this was that the rebels would "be left like a lonely flagpole on a hill or a tattered banner on a distant mountaintop" (30:17).

Isaiah shifts from predicted judgment to promised salvation, as 30:18-33 describes blessings for the Lord's people. The people of Zion will receive gracious help
if they ask for it (30:19), and the Lord will direct them, saying "This is the way you
should go" (30:21). Jerusalem and Zion (30:19) are where the Lord dwells (8:18),
and his prophecy represents future redemption (4:3ff; 11:9). The new covenant
message of redemption was first literally announced at these actual sites, and the
new people of God were figuratively connected to "Mount Zion, to the city of the
living God, the heavenly Jerusalem" (Heb 12:22; cf. Rev 14:1). If they followed the
Lord's intended lifestyle for them, he would bless their crops, their livestock, and all
aspects of their lives (30:23-26).

In 30:27-28, there is a graphic description of the wrath of the Lord unleashed
against his enemies. Anthropomorphic language depicts the Lord as burning with
anger, his lips filled with furious words that consume like fire. The target of his
wrath was the Assyrians, whom he would strike down "with his royal scepter"
(30:31) so that God's people "will celebrate with the music of tambourines and
harps" (30:32). Finally, even "Topheth—the place of burning" that had been prepared to receive the Assyrian king will be ignited with "the breath of the LORD,"
which is compared to the fire from a volcano (30:33). Topheth was the place in the
Valley of Hinnom, outside Jerusalem, where children were burned as offerings to
Molech (2 Kgs 23:10). New Testament "Gehenna," the place of perpetual burning,
is derived from the Hebrew that means "Valley of Hinnom." In graphic and poetic
language, the text describes Topheth as large enough to accommodate the destruction of the Assyrian nation. Topheth probably refers to a high place in the valley of
Hinnom; the name is derived from the Aramaic and Arabic root *tpt*, which means
"fireplace" (NBD, 1208).

Chapter 31 largely replicates chapter 30, compressing the same message into
only nine verses. Isaiah presents his message in a clear and succinct form, effectively summarizing his teaching about Judah's alliance with Egypt. Like the previous three chapters, this one begins with "what sorrow" (31:1), but it is not entirely
threatening in nature, as it contains some divine promises. It is a fitting climax to
Isaiah's recorded preaching about the circumstances of Hezekiah's revolt against
Assyria.

Two oracles are brought together here. The first pronounces woe upon Hezekiah's pro-Egyptian advisers (31:1-3), and the second promises Jerusalem salvation
from the Assyrian invaders (31:4-9). The first three verses condemn the proposed
alliance with Egypt, which Isaiah saw as a direct rejection of the Lord (Wong 1996).
Israel valued Egypt's help because the Egyptians had many horses and chariots (cf.
30:16). The Lord warned that destruction was certain for "those who look to Egypt
for help" because of their trusting "horses, chariots, and charioteers" and "depending on the strength of human armies" (31:1). Centuries earlier, Moses had warned
Israel not to go to Egypt for that purpose (Deut 17:16). Chariots were the tanks
of the ancient world, and both Assyria and Egypt had an ample supply. Chariots
were no match for the Lord (cf. Judg 4:15), but the men of Judah had ignored him,

forfeiting their major source of strength. They preferred to trust in weak and unreliable human strength (31:2).

These Egyptians were "mere humans, not God" (31:3). The people had to choose whether to confide in humans or in God—in "flesh" or in "spirit." In Egypt, various creatures were deified and worshiped, so the prophet noted the vast gap between humans and God, between the creature and the Creator. Furthermore, "their horses are puny flesh" and when the Lord "raises his fist against them . . . they will all fall down and die together" (31:3). This woe is uttered in the same spirit as that of chapter 30 and dates from the same period. The Israelites put their hope in the Egyptian cavalry (cf. 30:16) to help them resist Assyria, but the oracle proclaims that the "LORD of Heaven's Armies" will come down and "fight on Mount Zion" (31:4). The Assyrians would be destroyed by "the sword of God" (31:8). In 31:9, fire and flame are symbols of the Lord's consuming wrath. He dwells in Zion, spreading light that becomes a consuming fire for his enemies (cf. 10:17; 30:33; Gen 15:17). This imagery is especially clever since the Hebrew words for "light" and "fire" are so similar (see note on 31:9).

◆  ## 5. The rule of the righteous King (32:1-20)

Look, a righteous king is coming!
    And honest princes will rule under
    him.
2 Each one will be like a shelter from
    the wind
    and a refuge from the storm,
like streams of water in the desert
    and the shadow of a great rock in
    a parched land.

3 Then everyone who has eyes will be
    able to see the truth,
    and everyone who has ears will be
    able to hear it.
4 Even the hotheads will be full of sense
    and understanding.
    Those who stammer will speak out
    plainly.
5 In that day ungodly fools will not be
    heroes.
    Scoundrels will not be respected.
6 For fools speak foolishness
    and make evil plans.
They practice ungodliness
    and spread false teachings about
    the LORD.
They deprive the hungry of food
    and give no water to the thirsty.

7 The smooth tricks of scoundrels
    are evil.
    They plot crooked schemes.
They lie to convict the poor,
    even when the cause of the poor
    is just.
8 But generous people plan to do what
    is generous,
    and they stand firm in their
    generosity.

9 Listen, you women who lie around in
    ease.
    Listen to me, you who are so smug.
10 In a short time—just a little more than
    a year—
    you careless ones will suddenly
    begin to care.
For your fruit crops will fail,
    and the harvest will never take
    place.
11 Tremble, you women of ease;
    throw off your complacency.
Strip off your pretty clothes,
    and put on burlap to show your grief.
12 Beat your breasts in sorrow for your
    bountiful farms
    and your fruitful grapevines.

¹³ For your land will be overgrown with
    thorns and briers.
Your joyful homes and happy towns
    will be gone.
¹⁴ The palace and the city will be deserted,
    and busy towns will be empty.
Wild donkeys will frolic and flocks
    will graze
in the empty forts* and watchtowers
¹⁵ until at last the Spirit is poured out
    on us from heaven.
Then the wilderness will become
    a fertile field,
and the fertile field will yield
    bountiful crops.

¹⁶ Justice will rule in the wilderness
    and righteousness in the fertile field.
¹⁷ And this righteousness will bring peace.
    Yes, it will bring quietness and
    confidence forever.
¹⁸ My people will live in safety, quietly
    at home.
They will be at rest.
¹⁹ Even if the forest should be destroyed
    and the city torn down,
²⁰ the LORD will greatly bless his people.
    Wherever they plant seed, bountiful
    crops will spring up.
Their cattle and donkeys will graze
    freely.

32:14 Hebrew *the Ophel.*

## NOTES

**32:1 righteous . . . honest.** In the Heb. these twin themes of "righteousness" (*tsedeq* [ᵀᴴ6664, ᶻᴴ7406]) and "justice" (*mishpat* [ᵀᴴ4941, ᶻᴴ5477]) occur here and in 32:16; 33:5.

**righteous king.** Surely this is the Messiah (cf. 9:7; 11:4; 16:5).

**honest princes will rule under him.** Ridderbos (1985:258) notes that Christ assigns to the apostles a place in his kingdom similar to the one described here (Matt 19:28) and reminds us that we must remember that "the blessings of the messianic kingdom are here described in the colors of this earthly life."

**32:2 Each one.** Miscall (1993:81) suggests that "each" in this context and usage "downplays individual achievement and may include others besides king and princes."

**shelter from the wind . . . refuge from the storm.** The storm imagery may refer to the violence of the oppressors (cf. 25:4-5).

**streams of water in the desert.** See 30:25; 35:6-7; 41:18; 49:10.

**32:5 Scoundrels.** The Heb. *kila* [ᵀᴴ3596, ᶻᴴ3964] is found only here and in 32:7. Both the term and its assonance (with *kela* in 32:7) are typical of Isaiah. The versions differ on its translaton: "scoundrel" (NIV, TEV, ESV, GW), "wicked" (NCV), "villain" (NRSV, REB), "rogue" (NASB), "crook" (CEV), and "knave" (NJPS).

**32:7 smooth tricks of scoundrels.** Heb. *kela kelayw* [ᵀᴴ3596, ᶻᴴ3964] involves a wordplay difficult to capture in English: "the villainies of villains" (NRSV); "the villain's tactics are villainous" (REB); "the trickster uses wicked trickery" (NAB); and "as for the knave, his tools are knavish" (NJPS).

**32:9 you women.** Cf. the earlier reference to women in 3:16–4:1.

**32:10 a little more than a year.** The language is cryptic and the translations vary: "at the turn of the year" (REB), and "within one year and a few days" (NJB).

**32:11 Strip off your pretty clothes.** Kaiser (1974:330) suggests that this means to bare only the breasts and mentions such a portrayal on the coffin of the Phoenician King Ahiram of Byblos.

**32:12 Beat your breasts.** Cf. Nah 2:7.

**32:15 the Spirit is poured out.** Elsewhere, the pouring out of the Spirit is connected with prosperity (cf. 44:3).

COMMENTARY

This oracle interrupts the sequence of "sorrow" oracles that began at 28:1 and resumes at 33:1. Chapter 32 is the only one in this six-chapter cluster (chs 28–33) that does not begin with "what sorrow."

In chapters 32–33, Isaiah refers to the kingship of the coming King who will rule over Zion as a righteous and splendid king (32:1; 33:17). These factors indicate that Isaiah had a messianic King in mind, an interpretation borne out by the levels of righteousness and peace that Isaiah predicted. There have already been numerous allusions to the messianic period (e.g. 16:5; 28:16; 29:22-24; 30:23-26), but no direct reference to the Messiah himself since chapters 9 and 10, where we hear the Immanuel prophecies that describe the son called the Branch of Jesse (11:1-10) who will rule on the throne of David (9:6-7).

In the Hebrew text of this passage, the twin themes of righteousness and justice are found in 32:1 (see note); 32:16; and 33:5. Each of these verses is then followed by a reference to the peace and security that Zion will enjoy under the righteous king (32:17-18; 33:6). His strong protection is also emphasized in verses filled with encouraging and comforting terms such as "shelter," "refuge," "shadow of a great rock" (32:2), "quietness and confidence" (32:17), "safety, quietly at home . . . be at rest" (32:18).

The Hebrew of 32:3-4 describes how eyes, ears, heart, and tongue will be affected. The NLT obscures these anatomical terms, used here intentionally to show the totality of God's healing. The text more lit. reads, "the eyes of those who see will no longer be closed, and the ears of those who hear will listen. The mind [heart] of the rash will know and understand, and the stammering tongue will be fluent and clear" (NIV). This situation reverses the conditions described in 6:10, where blindness, deafness, and general spiritual dullness affected their encounter with the prophetic word. Obedience to God's standards always brings spiritual clarity and improved life, but rebellion is a sure prescription for inability to discern between good and evil. Although the immediate reference is to a renewed and improved political situation, surely the ultimate reference is to the Messiah, the One who makes illumination and empowerment possible. Motyer (1999:204) says the reference is to "the messianic king of chapters 9 and 11." Concerning the description of the righteous king of the preceding verses, Oswalt (1986:580) says, "Nowhere is this better typified than in Jesus the Good Shepherd who gives his life for his sheep (John 10:11), the Servant who did not come to be ministered to, but to minister (Matt 20:28)." With the initiation of his messianic kingdom, the Righteous King makes possible a spiritual insight and awareness not previously experienced that in turn enable more articulate witness (cf. 1 Pet 3:15; 4:11; 1 Cor 1:10).

The next section (32:9ff) addresses the "women who lie around in ease" and "who are so smug." They are warned, "you careless ones will suddenly begin to care" (32:10). These women are told to "strip off your pretty clothes, and put on burlap" (32:11). The time was soon to come when their "bountiful farms" would be gone (32:12), and their land overgrown with thorns and briers (32:13). The formerly busy towns will be empty (32:14). The invasion referred to may be that of Sennacherib in 701 BC, which resulted in widespread destruction of crops.

The next section (32:15ff) uses imagery of things already known to express God's new things to come. No human king will inaugurate this era because it will take place when "at last the Spirit is poured out on us from heaven" (32:15; cf. Joel 2:28; Acts 2:16). At that time, fertility and lush growth will resume, "justice will rule in the wilderness and righteousness in the fertile field" (32:16), and "the LORD will greatly bless his people" (32:20). As a result, "bountiful crops will spring up" and "their cattle and donkeys will graze freely" (32:20).

◆     ## 6. Woe to Assyria (33:1-24)

What sorrow awaits you Assyrians,
    who have destroyed others*
but have never been destroyed
    yourselves.
You betray others,
    but you have never been
    betrayed.
When you are done destroying,
    you will be destroyed.
When you are done betraying,
    you will be betrayed.
2 But LORD, be merciful to us,
    for we have waited for you.
Be our strong arm each day
    and our salvation in times
    of trouble.
3 The enemy runs at the sound of your
    voice.
When you stand up, the nations
    flee!
4 Just as caterpillars and locusts strip
    the fields and vines,
so the fallen army of Assyria will
    be stripped!

5 Though the LORD is very great and
    lives in heaven,
he will make Jerusalem* his home
    of justice and righteousness.
6 In that day he will be your sure
    foundation,
providing a rich store of salvation,
    wisdom, and knowledge.
The fear of the LORD will be your
    treasure.

7 But now your brave warriors weep
    in public.
Your ambassadors of peace cry in
    bitter disappointment.
8 Your roads are deserted;
    no one travels them anymore.
The Assyrians have broken their
    peace treaty
and care nothing for the
    promises they made before
    witnesses.*
They have no respect for anyone.
9 The land of Israel wilts in mourning.
    Lebanon withers with shame.
The plain of Sharon is now a
    wilderness.
Bashan and Carmel have been
    plundered.

10 But the LORD says: "I will stand up
    and show my power and might.
11 You Assyrians produce nothing but
    dry grass and stubble.
Your own breath will turn to fire
    and consume you.
12 Your people will be burned up
    completely,
like thornbushes cut down and
    tossed in a fire.
13 Listen to what I have done, you
    nations far away!
And you that are near, acknowledge
    my might!"
14 The sinners in Jerusalem shake
    with fear.

Terror seizes the godless.
"Who can live with this devouring
fire?" they cry.
"Who can survive this all-
consuming fire?"
15 Those who are honest and fair,
who refuse to profit by fraud,
who stay far away from bribes,
who refuse to listen to those who plot
murder,
who shut their eyes to all
enticement to do wrong—
16 these are the ones who will dwell on
high.
The rocks of the mountains will be
their fortress.
Food will be supplied to them,
and they will have water in
abundance.

17 Your eyes will see the king in all his
splendor,
and you will see a land that
stretches into the distance.
18 You will think back to this time of
terror, asking,
"Where are the Assyrian officers
who counted our towers?
Where are the bookkeepers
who recorded the plunder taken
from our fallen city?"

19 You will no longer see these fierce,
violent people
with their strange, unknown
language.
20 Instead, you will see Zion as a place
of holy festivals.
You will see Jerusalem, a city quiet
and secure.
It will be like a tent whose ropes are
taut
and whose stakes are firmly fixed.
21 The LORD will be our Mighty One.
He will be like a wide river of
protection
that no enemy can cross,
that no enemy ship can sail upon.
22 For the LORD is our judge,
our lawgiver, and our king.
He will care for us and save us.
23 The enemies' sails hang loose
on broken masts with useless
tackle.
Their treasure will be divided by the
people of God.
Even the lame will take their
share!
24 The people of Israel will no longer
say,
"We are sick and helpless,"
for the LORD will forgive their sins.

33:1 Hebrew *What sorrow awaits you, O destroyer.* The Hebrew text does not specifically name Assyria as the object of the prophecy in this chapter.   33:5 Hebrew *Zion;* also in 33:14.   33:8 As in Dead Sea Scrolls; Masoretic Text reads *care nothing for the cities.*

## NOTES

**33:1** The Heb. of this verse effectively uses assonance by repeating two different roots four times each. Pairs of terms for "destroy" (*shadad* [TH7703, ZH8720]) and "betray" (*bagad* [TH898, ZH953]) alternate in successive couplets. The "traitor/betray" root (*bagad*) occurred earlier in 24:16, and the word for "destroyed" (*shadad*) is also found elsewhere in Isaiah (15:1; 16:4; 21:2; 23:1, 14).

**33:4** *locusts.* The Heb. has two terms and probably refers to "young locusts" (*khasil* [TH2625, ZH2885]) and a "swarm of locusts" (*gebim* [TH1357, ZH1466]), which represent the dreaded insects that came swiftly and devoured all in their path. This was graphic imagery that the hearers were quick to recognize (see 7:18).

**33:5** *Jerusalem.* The Heb. here is "Zion," not "Jerusalem" (so the NLT mg).

*justice and righteousness.* The terms "justice" (*mishpat* [TH4941, ZH5477]) and "righteousness" (*tsedaqah* [TH6666, ZH7407]) refer to God's essence as revealed through his deeds (cf. 32:16; Ps 89:14; 97:2).

**33:6 sure foundation.** The Heb. (*'emunah* [TH530, ZH575]) comes from the same Heb. root as "Amen."

**will be your treasure.** The Heb. (*hi' 'otsaro* [TH214, ZH238]) behind this phrase is enigmatic. English versions vary in their renderings: "is Zion's treasure" (NRSV), "her treasure is" (REB), "is her treasure" (NAB), and "is his treasure" (KJV, NJB). The phrase could also be rendered, "a treasure from him."

**33:8 witnesses.** The reading of the DSS (cf. NLT mg). The DSS Heb. has "witnesses" (*'edim* [TH5707, ZH6332]) in contrast to the Masoretic Text that has "cities" (*'arim* [TH5892, ZH6551]). The DSS manuscripts are followed by most modern English versions (NRSV, REB, NAB, NJB). The KJV has "despised the cities."

**33:9 Lebanon . . . Sharon . . . Bashan and Carmel.** Lebanon was famous for its cedars (2:13); Sharon, along the Mediterranean Coast, was known for its beautiful foliage and excellent grazing land (1 Chr 27:29); and Bashan was famous for its oak trees (2:13). The name Carmel means "fertile place" (cf. 16:10; 29:17; 32:15) and is associated with verdant pasturelands (35:2; Mic 7:14).

**33:10 the LORD.** The NLT does not show the striking threefold repetition of the almost explosive sounding "now" (*'attah* [TH6258, ZH6964]), as the Lord indicated that the time for action had finally come, and he would be "exalted" and "lifted up" as a result of his judgment. The KJV preserves this: "Now will I rise . . . now will I be exalted . . . now will I lift up myself." The theme of the Lord's being exalted is pervasive in Isaiah (cf. the thrice-exalted Servant of the Lord in 52:13).

**33:11 produce nothing but dry grass and stubble.** The Heb. says "you conceive chaff but give birth to straw" (cf. 26:28), which is like saying that although pregnant with grandiose ideas, plans, and schemes, their plans to destroy Jerusalem will come to nothing.

**33:12 burned up completely.** Lit., "burned to lime" (*sid* [TH7875, ZH8487]). Heating calciferous material red hot produces lime, a white powder. Moab was charged with burning the bones of the king of Edom into lime (Amos 2:1). Here the mighty army of the Assyrians, composed of soldiers from many nations (cf. 8:9), will become one burning, melting mass.

**33:14 sinners in Jerusalem.** The literal "sinners in Zion" is disturbing, because Zion is God's city, "the place where there was a concentration of the OT means of grace" (Grogan 1986:212).

**33:15 Those who are honest and fair.** More lit., "walks righteously and speaks uprightly." The Heb. includes two participles of action. "Honest" translates the plural noun (*tsedaqoth* [TH6666, ZH7407]). This usage by Isaiah (found only here and in 45:24) does not appear elsewhere in the prophets. "Fair" translates Heb. *mesharim* [TH3596, ZH3964] from the root "to be straight." Most translations retain the verbs: "behaves properly and speaks the truth" (REB), "walks righteously and speaks with sincerity" (NASB), "does what is right and speaks the truth" (GW), "walk righteously and speak uprightly" (NRSV, ESV), "live right and tell the truth" (CEV), and "walks in righteousness, speaks uprightly" (NJPS).

**those who plot murder.** See 1:15 and Prov 1:11.

**33:16 rocks of the mountains.** The Heb. is lit., "Masada of cliffs" (*metsadoth sela'im* [TH4679/ 5553, ZH5171/6152]). Their defense will be in the security of an inaccessible mountain.

**33:17 the king.** The Heb. does not use the definite article with "king," so it should probably be understood as a generic or ideal reference, as in Ps 45.

**33:18 terror.** The word (*'eymah* [TH367, ZH399]) is a strong one (cf. Gen 15:12; Job 41:6).

**officers.** The Heb. uses three different terms for the officials in this verse.

**33:19 fierce, violent.** This translates the Heb. word *no'az* [TH3267A, ZH3594], a word found only here but probably from the root *ya'az* [TH3267, ZH3594], meaning "arrogant."

**33:20** *will see.* This translates the Heb. *khazeh* [TH2372, ZH2600], a term used by Isaiah in this form only here and in 48:6; the same word in another grammatical form is used in 33:17.

*ropes.* The same Heb. word, *khebel* [TH2256A, ZH2475] is used in 33:23 where it is translated as "tackle."

### COMMENTARY

In chapter 33, the prophet brings the section (chs 29–32) to a close by repeating many of the preceding themes and images. Most agree that this woe was pronounced against the Assyrian Sennacherib when his army threatened Jerusalem (701 BC), although some understand it to apply to all destroyers at all times (cf. 16:4; 21:2; 24:16). Assyria had been appointed by God to punish Israel, but when its task was completed, it would be judged. The destiny of the Assyrian king and his nation was not in his own hands, but in the hands of God, who "decided beforehand which [nations] should rise and fall, and . . . determined their boundaries" (Acts 17:26).

The historical background of this chapter is recorded in 2 Kgs 18–19 and Isa 36–37. Hezekiah had given Sennacherib tribute in the amount of 300 talents (about eleven tons) of silver and thirty talents (about one ton) of gold, depleting the treasury and stripping the Temple of its treasure. The Assyrian then immediately sent three of his chief military officers to demand the surrender of the city (cf. 2 Kgs 19:13-35).

**Oracle against Assyria.** The chapter opens by warning the Assyrians that although they have defeated and destroyed others, now it is their turn to be betrayed and destroyed (33:1), terms which could refer to Sennacherib's death at the hand of his own sons some years after returning to Nineveh.

In contrast, 33:2-6 contains a prayer asking the LORD to be merciful to the Judahites with whom the prophet identified. The prophet and people had been praying together, but now he prayed for his people. Because God had promised to be gracious to his people (30:18), Isaiah interceded on their behalf, and they waited patiently for God to act (cf. 8:16-18; 25:9). The promise and prediction were that the "fallen enemy of Assyria will be stripped" (33:4). The prophet does not say that the Lord "becomes great" but that he "is very great" (33:5), a depiction that is pervasive throughout the book of Isaiah (3:13; 6:1; 30:18; 57:15; 63:15). In 33:5-6, Isaiah describes how the Lord will fill Zion (see note) with justice and righteousness, qualities reflecting his essence as revealed through his actions (cf. 32:16; Ps 89:14; 97:2; for more on the Zion tradition throughout this passage, see Roberts 1983). Isaiah knew that God was in control and that he was the "sure foundation" (33:6) that would provide justice and stability to Jerusalem.

In 33:7-9, the prophet returns to a description of the pathetic condition of the people and the land of Judah, as he notes the weeping ambassadors (33:7), the deserted roads (33:8), and the impoverished land (33:9). The "ambassadors" (33:7) may be the negotiators mentioned in 36:3, 22 that reported to Hezekiah during deep mourning. They "cry in bitter disappointment" because the "Assyrians have broken their peace treaty" (33:7-8). This breach in peace terms was the reason that the prophet now focused his attention on all the destruction the Assyrians had left in their wake and were still bringing about. The forests of Lebanon suffered at the hands of the Assyrians (37:24; cf. 14:8), and Sennacherib, on his march through the land of the Philistines, did pass through the plain of Sharon. In each case, the invading armies lived off the land as they moved through it.

The scene shifts again as the Lord declares, "I will stand up and show my power and might" (33:10). This is contrasted with the Assyrians, who "produce nothing but dry grass and stubble" (33:11). The very graphic expression that their "own breath will turn to fire and consume [them]" (33:11) means that what they produced only resulted in their own swift destruction, here represented by consuming fire. The Lord called on all, both those who were "far away" (the nations; cf. 49:1; 57:19; Acts 2:39; Eph 2:13, 17), and those who were "near" (Judah; 33:13) to comprehend the great thing the Lord had done and to observe the power he had demonstrated (cf. 18:3).

In yet another image, the people are compared with "thornbushes cut down and tossed in a fire" (33:12; cf. 5:24; 9:18); "sinners in Jerusalem" (33:14) will be consumed in the fire. The righteous "shut their eyes to all enticement to do wrong" (33:15) and will have no fear of the devouring fire; rather, "the rocks of the mountains will be their fortress" (33:16). They will have food and water in abundance.

In 33:13-16, Isaiah notes the kind of people who will be saved, in contrast to the destruction he had just described, and in the next section (33:17-24), the land in which they will live is described. The focal point of the passage is 33:17a ("will see the king in all his splendor") and the last phrase of 33:15 is indispensable for understanding it. Isaiah challenged all the Judahites to live pure lives, and 33:15 identifies those who are "honest and fair" as those who refuse fraud, bribes, and murder. The fierce and violent Assyrians will disappear from this future scene (33:18-19).

The officers who "counted our towers" (33:18) probably were those who looked for points of weakness at which to attack the city. God's people will no longer see the enemy that is characterized as a "people with their strange, unknown language" (33:19; this probably refers to Isaiah's contemporaries who never saw the Assyrians again). The language of the Assyrians was a cognate Semitic language of the eastern branch, in contrast to Hebrew (and Aramaic), that were western Semitic languages. Assyrian script was completely different from Hebrew script—Hebrew was written alphabetically, and Assyrian writing was syllabic. No wonder the Assyrian language seemed so different! The similarities and dissimilarities of the language would have frustrated the Hebrews.

The new scene is of "Zion as a place of holy festivals" that is "quiet and secure" (33:20). Each year the people journeyed to Mount Zion to celebrate the feasts of Passover, Pentecost, and Tabernacles, the special events that gave the city its distinctiveness. During the Feast of Tabernacles, the people lived in tents, but some day Jerusalem will be like a tent that never has to be moved (cf. 54:2)—the tents will be pegged down forever (Heb 11:9-10).

Zion's security depends on the Lord, who will separate Jerusalem from her enemies by a wide river "that no enemy can cross" (33:21). Considering the mountainous terrain of Jerusalem and Zion, this imagery seems rather strange, but in fact it is filled with meaning for anyone living in the ancient Near East. Calling upon background awareness of world cities such as Nineveh, Babylon, and Thebes (cf. Nah 3:8) that were protected and served by rivers, canals, and moats, the prophet pictures Jerusalem as surrounded and served by the abundance of flowing water that will characterize Jerusalem in the days of the Messiah. Grogan (1986:214) suggests that Jerusalem is depicted here as an ancient Near Eastern Venice or Amsterdam. The messianic age again seems to be the primary reference. The Lord will be a "wide river of protection" (33:21), keeping the place safe from its enemies; he will be judge, lawgiver, and king combined (33:22)—Isaiah stacks these terms for effect. The spoils from the enemy will be "divided by the people of God" (33:23), and the Lord will forgive everyone, including the "sick and helpless" (33:24).

In 33:20, Jerusalem is compared to a tent, but in 33:23, the figure is of a ship. The Hebrew word for the ropes that hold the tent secure (33:20) provides a verbal link between the two passages; in 33:23, the same word refers to the ropes on a ship (see note). In contrast to the New Jerusalem, the glorious Zion of the future, Isaiah looks back on the old physical city and compares it to a dilapidated ship with broken masts (33:23), unfit for battle. Even the lame will share in looting it (33:23; cf. 2 Sam 5:6). The passage closes with the promise of a time when "Israel will no longer say, 'We are sick and helpless'" (33:24; cf. 1:5).

◆    ## F. Indignation and Glory (34:1–35:10)
### 1. The Lord's great anger (34:1-17)

Come here and listen, O nations of the
  earth.
Let the world and everything in it
  hear my words.
2 For the LORD is enraged against the
  nations.
His fury is against all their armies.
He will completely destroy* them,
  dooming them to slaughter.
3 Their dead will be left unburied,
  and the stench of rotting bodies
  will fill the land.
The mountains will flow with their
  blood.
4 The heavens above will melt away
  and disappear like a rolled-up scroll.
The stars will fall from the sky
  like withered leaves from a grapevine,
  or shriveled figs from a fig tree.

5 And when my sword has finished
  its work in the heavens,
it will fall upon Edom,
  the nation I have marked for
  destruction.
6 The sword of the LORD is drenched
  with blood
  and covered with fat—
with the blood of lambs and goats,
  with the fat of rams prepared for
  sacrifice.
Yes, the LORD will offer a sacrifice
  in the city of Bozrah.
He will make a mighty slaughter
  in Edom.
7 Even men as strong as wild oxen will
  die—
  the young men alongside the
  veterans.

The land will be soaked with blood
and the soil enriched with fat.

8 For it is the day of the LORD's revenge,
the year when Edom will be paid
back for all it did to Israel.*
9 The streams of Edom will be filled
with burning pitch,
and the ground will be covered
with fire.
10 This judgment on Edom will never end;
the smoke of its burning will rise
forever.
The land will lie deserted from
generation to generation.
No one will live there anymore.
11 It will be haunted by the desert owl
and the screech owl,
the great owl and the raven.*
For God will measure that land
carefully;
he will measure it for chaos and
destruction.
12 It will be called the Land of Nothing,
and all its nobles will soon be gone.*
13 Thorns will overrun its palaces;
nettles and thistles will grow in its
forts.

The ruins will become a haunt for
jackals
and a home for owls.
14 Desert animals will mingle there
with hyenas,
their howls filling the night.
Wild goats will bleat at one another
among the ruins,
and night creatures* will come there
to rest.
15 There the owl will make her nest and
lay her eggs.
She will hatch her young and cover
them with her wings.
And the buzzards will come,
each one with its mate.

16 Search the book of the LORD,
and see what he will do.
Not one of these birds and animals
will be missing,
and none will lack a mate,
for the LORD has promised this.
His Spirit will make it all come true.
17 He has surveyed and divided the land
and deeded it over to those creatures.
They will possess it forever,
from generation to generation.

34:2 The Hebrew term used here refers to the complete consecration of things or people to the LORD, either by destroying them or by giving them as an offering; similarly in 34:5. 34:8 Hebrew *to Zion.* 34:11 The identification of some of these birds is uncertain. 34:12 The meaning of the Hebrew is uncertain. 34:14 Hebrew *Lilith,* possibly a reference to a mythical demon of the night.

## NOTES

**34:2 *destroy.*** The Heb. uses the term *kherem* [TH2763, ZH3049] signifying destruction that was dedicated to the Lord (cf. NLT mg). This echoes the extermination language used with reference to the Canaanites during the Israelite conquest (cf. Lev 27:28ff; Josh 6:17, 21).

**34:4 *heavens . . . stars.*** Such cosmic disturbances represent the day of the Lord (cf. 13:10; Ezek 32:7-8; see also Matt 24:29; Rev 6:13-14).

***disappear like a rolled-up scroll.*** It has been suggested that this cosmic imagery is derived from the appearance of the sky before and during a storm as it darkens with clouds rolling over it. Whatever the origin may be, this language was often used to depict the fall of political and economic systems.

**34:5 *Edom.*** Like Moab in 25:10-12, Edom may refer symbolically to all enemies of God.

**34:6 *Bozrah.*** This leading city and capital of Edom was located about twenty-five miles southeast of the southern end of the Dead Sea (cf. 63:1; Gen 36:33; Amos 1:2) and thirty miles northeast of Petra. Its name could mean "grape-gathering," which would fit this context. The Heb. *botsrah* [TH1224, ZH1313] is usually seen as related to the root *btsr* I [TH1219, ZH1305], "to gather grapes," and probably related to Akkadian *batsaru* "to bite, tear off" (HALOT 1:148), but a different root *batsar* III [TH1219B, ZH1307] ("to be inaccessible") is also a possibility.

*fat.* This is mentioned three times in the Heb. of 34:6-7, probably because it was considered the best part of the meat.

**34:7 *men as strong as wild oxen . . . young men . . . veterans.*** The Heb. is lit. "wild oxen . . . bull calves . . . great bulls." The NLT understands this as animal imagery to represent human leaders. The same is done in English. Political leaders may be classified as "doves" or "hawks" based on their attitudes about war. Aggressive leaders in various fields may be called "tigers" or "sharks." Countless examples are also found for groups of persons: the Lions or Elks clubs, the Philadelphia Eagles or the University of Michigan Wolverines, etc. Besides the NLT, only the CEV translates with clear reference to human leaders: "Edom's leaders are wild oxen. They are powerful bulls."

**34:8 *Israel.*** The Heb. is "Zion" (cf. NLT mg).

**34:9 *burning pitch . . . covered with fire.*** The language of destruction here compares with that used of Sodom and Gomorrah (cf. Gen 19:24; Jer 49:17-18).

**34:11 *desert owl . . . screech owl . . . great owl . . . raven.*** These were ceremonially unclean birds (cf. Deut 14:14-17), also associated with the ruins of Babylon (13:2) and Nineveh (Zeph 2:14).

***chaos and destruction.*** The same two Heb. words (*tohu* [TH8414, ZH9332] and *bohu* [TH922, ZH983]) are used in Gen 1:2.

**34:14 *Wild goats.*** This Heb. word (*sa'ir* [TH8163, ZH8539]) can also refer to demons (cf. 13:21). The KJV translates it "satyr." It is translated "demon" here in the TEV and CEV; the NJPS uses "goat-demons."

***night creatures.*** As the NLT mg indicates, this could possibly refer to the famous Lilith of tradition, a demon of the night (HALOT 1:528-529). This creature was known in earlier Semitic literature, as well as in Jewish literature and tradition after Isaiah.

**34:15 *owl . . . buzzards.*** These were ceremonially unclean birds (cf. Deut 14:13, 15-17).

C O M M E N T A R Y

Sections of Isaiah often recapitulate preceding material, as for example, chapter 12 summarizes much of chapters 1-11. It is obvious that chapters 34 and 35 belong together and complement one another, and that they relate to chapters 28–33 in a way similar to how chapters 24–27 relate to chapters 13–23. In both cases, the concluding chapters constitute a kind of conclusion in which notes of both judgment and redemption are repeated.

In chapters 34–35, the first half of the book is summarized, preparing for the historical interlude of chapters 36–39 and their language in turn nicely prepares the way for chapters 40–66. The opening imperatives are similar to those used in 48:16 and 49:1. The Lord's sacrifice in Bozrah (34:6) is similar to Bozrah's symbolic winepress (63:1-3). In 34:8 and in 35:4, the coming of the Lord is associated with vengeance and retribution, and the same themes are found in 40:10; 62:11; and 63:4. Israel's return from exile lies at the heart of the last part of the book of Isaiah. This theme is also emphasized in 35:8-10. Isaiah 34:10 is repeated verbatim in 51:11. These thematic and lexical links affirm the unity of the book.

**The Lord's great anger (34:1-17).** This chapter is the most vivid picture of destruction and desolation encountered thus far in the book of Isaiah, and the first four verses refer to judgment on the entire world. When Edom is mentioned in 34:5, 6,

8, and 9, we should remember Edom's (Esau's) sensual character, his contempt for that which is holy, his treatment of Israel, and his scorn of the Lord. In spite of how Israel may have felt toward his brother nation, this chapter is not an expression of Israel's judgment. Rather, the chapter relates the outpouring of God's wrath against all that is profane and antagonistic to him and his kingship. Edom/Esau symbolizes the wicked giving vent to earthly character and hatred of God, his people, and everything spiritual.

Obadiah, thought by some to be the earliest of the writing prophets, charged Edom with doing violence to his brother Jacob, putting himself on the side of the destroyers of Israel, and rejoicing in Jacob's calamity (Obad 10-15). Also Amos charged Edom with receiving whole villages from Gaza and Tyre as captives, pursuing his brother nation with the sword (Amos 1:6, 9, 11).

The chapter begins with strong language that describes the Lord as giving vent to his holy wrath by pouring it out on the nations of the earth (34:1). God is said to be enraged against them, and his fury is against all their armies (34:2). They are doomed to complete destruction, and their rotting and unburied bodies will fill the land with stench and blood (34:3). The gruesome language describing this disgusting scene emphasizes the mortality of those under the judgment of Almighty God. The cosmic phenomena described in 34:4 convey the widespread nature of this judgment. In typical cosmic language of judgment, the stars of the heavens dissolve, and the immense expanse of sky is rolled up like a scroll (Rev 6:14). The "stars will fall from the skies" as withered leaves (34:4) fall and crumble into mulch and decay (cf. Matt 24:29). This imagery of a collapsing universe is used elsewhere to describe great political upheaval and economic disaster (cf. 13:10ff; Ezek 32:7-8; Rev 6:13-14). It is sometimes called "de-creation" terminology and refers to the time when God's wrath and indignation will come against the nations that oppose and fight him, as their universe of existence comes to an end and their world as they knew it is gone (cf. 51:4-6, 16; 65:16-18; 66:22-24).

The universal language then shifts to a local focus (34:5), and Edom is singled out from among the nations and used to represent all that is profane and ungodly. By virtue of its descent from Esau, this nation was closely connected to Israel, and from the earliest times, Israel had been commanded to treat it fraternally (Num 21:4; Deut 2:1ff; 23:7-8), an attitude not reciprocated by Edom (Num 20:14ff). The diverse destiny of the two nations strikingly demonstrates God's sovereign good pleasure in loving Jacob and hating Esau (Mal 1:2-3). In prophecy, Edom is often the object of judgment (Isa 63; Amos 1:11-12), especially because of its hostility against Judah (cf. Obadiah).

The Lord, with his sword dripping blood, will in judgment "offer a sacrifice in the city of Bozrah" and "make a mighty slaughter in Edom," including men "as strong as wild oxen," "young men," and "veterans" (34:5-7). In view of the highly figurative language used in the preceding verses, the larger animals listed here (see note) can also be understood (as the NLT does) as representing human leaders. The Old Testament uses such language elsewhere, and even English does this to denote certain kinds of people. There seems to be a progression from smaller to larger animals in 34:5-7.

All this dreadful judgment occurs on "the day of the LORD's revenge" (34:8), a term also found in 61:2 and 63:4. This time is also sometimes called a "year of retribution" (retribution and revenge or vengeance are also joined in 35:4 and 59:17-18). The reference is to a certain period of time, not precisely delimited as to duration, in which injustice will be avenged (cf. 61:2; 63:4). In contrast to Zion, a place of salvation, Edom is described as a place of desolation, not unlike the cities of Sodom and Gomorrah (cf. 1:9, 10; 3:9). As the Zion of chapter 35 is the ideal "city of God," so the Edom of chapter 34 includes all who hate and persecute the mystical Zion. The extermination of the Edomites is accompanied by the destruction of the land.

The land of Edom will become a ghostlike habitation for wild creatures of the desert (34:11ff; some of the creatures mentioned here are also mentioned in chapter 13). In contrast to the way that God will construct the walls of Zion (28:17), God will stretch out over Edom the measuring line "for chaos and destruction" (34:11). Although measuring and plumb lines were used in construction, they can also be used for destruction (cf. 2 Chr 21:14; Lam 2:8; Amos 7:7-9). Perhaps the point is that the judgment of destruction will be executed with the same deliberation and precision that characterizes the construction of a master builder.

More animals are mentioned in 34:14-15, making this a desolate and foreboding scene. All of this pictures the life that God has abandoned to sin. There is nothing beautiful or pleasant in this chapter, and virtually all of the animals and birds listed were categorized by law as unclean. The life separate from God is defiled and unlovely, confused and empty.

The "book of the LORD" (34:16) undoubtedly refers to these prophecies from Isaiah (cf. 8:16; 30:8), and the expression "the LORD has promised this" (34:16) probably reflects the prophet's awareness of the authority of the message. The prophet looks ahead to the time when "his Spirit will make it all come true" (34:16).

◆    ## 2. The Lord's great grace (35:1-10)

Even the wilderness and desert will be
glad in those days.
The wasteland will rejoice and
blossom with spring crocuses.
²Yes, there will be an abundance of
flowers
and singing and joy!
The deserts will become as green as
the mountains of Lebanon,
as lovely as Mount Carmel or the
plain of Sharon.
There the LORD will display his glory,
the splendor of our God.
³With this news, strengthen those who
have tired hands,
and encourage those who have weak
knees.
⁴Say to those with fearful hearts,
"Be strong, and do not fear,
for your God is coming to destroy your
enemies.
He is coming to save you."

⁵And when he comes, he will open the
eyes of the blind

and unplug the ears of the deaf.
⁶The lame will leap like a deer,
and those who cannot speak will
sing for joy!
Springs will gush forth in the
wilderness,
and streams will water the
wasteland.
⁷The parched ground will become a
pool,
and springs of water will satisfy the
thirsty land.
Marsh grass and reeds and rushes will
flourish
where desert jackals once lived.

⁸And a great road will go through that
once deserted land.

It will be named the Highway of
Holiness.
Evil-minded people will never travel
on it.
It will be only for those who walk
in God's ways;
fools will never walk there.
⁹Lions will not lurk along its course,
nor any other ferocious beasts.
There will be no other dangers.
Only the redeemed will walk on it.
¹⁰Those who have been ransomed by the
LORD will return.
They will enter Jerusalem* singing,
crowned with everlasting joy.
Sorrow and mourning will disappear,
and they will be filled with joy and
gladness.

35:10 Hebrew *Zion.*

NOTES

**35:2 Carmel . . . Sharon.** These locations represent fertility and lush growth.

**35:3-4 hands . . . knees . . . hearts.** Notice that three more parts of the body are mentioned in the Heb. of 35:5-6 (eyes, ears, and tongue [the NLT omits "tongue" in v. 6]; cf. 32:3-4).

**35:8 great road.** The Heb. *maslul* [TH4547, ZH5020] refers to a road built up to make travel easier and safer (see 11:16; 40:3).

*Highway of Holiness.* In the culture of the ancient Near East, certain roads between temples were sometimes open only to those who were ceremonially clean.

**35:9 Lions will not lurk along its course.** Wild animals made cross-country travel dangerous at that time.

**35:10** This verse is repeated in 51:11.

COMMENTARY

Chapters 34–35 form an appendix to the preceding parts of the book; they contrast the storm of God's wrath with the blessings yet to come. From judgment, the prophet turns to the redemption of Israel. The somber picture of death and destruction in chapter 34 is transformed into one of vibrant life and rejoicing in chapter 35.

Contrast—the setting of one condition or situation against another—was Isaiah's favorite method of teaching. In chapters 2–4, he contrasted the ideal Zion of the messianic age with the moral corruption of the real Zion (Jerusalem) of his day. In chapters 9–11, he set the terrible treatment of Israel and Judah at the hands of Assyria over against the future glory and permanence of the redeemed remnant under the Messiah, the Root of Jesse. Now he contrasts the deserts of Edom, filled with hyenas and wild goats (34:14), with Israel's blooming desert (35:1-2). This change is symbolized by the blooming of the desert as nature enters into the joy of God's redeemed people.

In contrast to the doom just pronounced on Edom, the prophet now predicts a glorious future for Zion, when nature will display the glory and splendor of God (35:1-3) and the disadvantaged and fearful will be encouraged as God destroys their enemies and saves them (35:3-5). Three parts of the body are mentioned in 35:3-4, and three more appear in 35:5-6. The description of the coming of the Lord ("God will come") has several parallels with Isaiah's description of the second coming of Christ (62:11; cf. Rev 22:12).

God comes to the aid of the blind, deaf, and lame (35:5-6). The similarity between 35:5-7 and Jesus' response to John the Baptist's question from prison has led many to believe that Jesus had Isaiah's words in mind when he sent his reply to John (Matt 11:2-6). The strong likeness is sufficient reason to conclude that Isaiah's words clearly point to the Messiah who would come. Israel was blind and deaf to the word of God that Isaiah proclaimed (cf. 6:9-10), but in the future, her spiritual perception will be restored. These were signs of the messianic age (cf. Matt 12:22; Acts 3:7-8). Christ's healing of the blind and the lame proved that he could also forgive sin (Matt 11:5; cf. Acts 3:18; 14:10). Even nature would benefit (35:6-7; for "springs . . . streams" see 32:2, and note God's provision of water in Exod 17:6 and 2 Kgs 3:15-20). Spiritual and physical healing are linked in Christ's ministry (Matt 11:5). In chapter 34, the streams of Edom were filled with pitch, and wild animals roamed the ruins. Now those creatures are gone, and streams of water irrigate the desert. The reeds and rushes associated with well-watered areas are now bountiful there (35:7). The Messiah has become the unending source of living water (John 4:14).

Granted new courage and spiritual power, the Israelites are pictured as ready to make a new entrance into Palestine, for God will prepare a great road named the "Highway of Holiness" that will be safe from evil-minded people, lions, and other dangers (35:8-9). The great road prepared for this purpose is described in 35:8-10. It is a highway leading to the Zion of God, a way of holiness for travelers. In Isaiah's day, the roads were dangerous and deserted (cf. 33:8), but this highway of the future will be completely secure. The "redeemed" (35:9) are those the Lord has delivered from bondage (cf. 1:27; 51:10; 62:12; Lev 25:47-48; Deut 7:8). The beautiful themes of 35:10 are repeated in 51:11, a passage that compares the future return from Babylon to the road that God made through the Red Sea at the Exodus.

This passage pictures the glories ultimately to come under the Messiah by whom we now come into Zion (Heb 12:22; cf. Rev 14:1) by a new and living way (Heb 10:19-20). It is only the redeemed and "those who have been ransomed by the LORD" that will "enter Jerusalem singing, crowned with everlasting joy" and will be "filled with joy and gladness" (35:10).

◆ II. A Historical Interlude (36:1–39:8)
   A. God's Deliverance of Jerusalem from Sennacherib (36:1–37:38)
      1. Sennacherib and Jerusalem (36:1–37:4)

In the fourteenth year of King Hezekiah's reign,* King Sennacherib of Assyria came to attack the fortified towns of Judah and conquered them. ²Then the king of Assyria sent his chief of staff* from Lachish with a huge army to confront King Hezekiah in Jerusalem. The Assyrians took up a position beside the aqueduct that feeds water into the upper pool, near the road leading to the field where cloth is washed.*

³These are the officials who went out to meet with them: Eliakim son of Hilkiah, the palace administrator; Shebna the court secretary; and Joah son of Asaph, the royal historian.

⁴Then the Assyrian king's chief of staff told them to give this message to Hezekiah:

"This is what the great king of Assyria says: What are you trusting in that makes you so confident? ⁵Do you think that mere words can substitute for military skill and strength? Who are you counting on, that you have rebelled against me? ⁶On Egypt? If you lean on Egypt, it will be like a reed that splinters beneath your weight and pierces your hand. Pharaoh, the king of Egypt, is completely unreliable! ⁷"But perhaps you will say to me, 'We are trusting in the LORD our God!' But isn't he the one who was insulted by Hezekiah? Didn't Hezekiah tear down his shrines and altars and make everyone in Judah and Jerusalem worship only at the altar here in Jerusalem?

⁸"I'll tell you what! Strike a bargain with my master, the king of Assyria. I will give you 2,000 horses if you can find that many men to ride on them! ⁹With your tiny army, how can you think of challenging even the weakest contingent of my master's troops, even with the help of Egypt's chariots and charioteers? ¹⁰What's more, do you think we have invaded your land without the LORD's direction? The LORD himself told us, 'Attack this land and destroy it!'"

¹¹Then Eliakim, Shebna, and Joah said to the Assyrian chief of staff, "Please speak to us in Aramaic, for we understand it well. Don't speak in Hebrew,* for the people on the wall will hear."

¹²But Sennacherib's chief of staff replied, "Do you think my master sent this message only to you and your master? He wants all the people to hear it, for when we put this city under siege, they will suffer along with you. They will be so hungry and thirsty that they will eat their own dung and drink their own urine."

¹³Then the chief of staff stood and shouted in Hebrew to the people on the wall, "Listen to this message from the great king of Assyria! ¹⁴This is what the king says: Don't let Hezekiah deceive you. He will never be able to rescue you. ¹⁵Don't let him fool you into trusting in the LORD by saying, 'The LORD will surely rescue us. This city will never fall into the hands of the Assyrian king!'

¹⁶"Don't listen to Hezekiah! These are the terms the king of Assyria is offering: Make peace with me—open the gates and come out. Then each of you can continue eating from your own grapevine and fig tree and drinking from your own well. ¹⁷Then I will arrange to take you to another land like this one—a land of grain and new wine, bread and vineyards.

¹⁸"Don't let Hezekiah mislead you by saying, 'The LORD will rescue us!' Have the gods of any other nations ever saved their people from the king of Assyria? ¹⁹What happened to the gods of Hamath and Arpad? And what about the gods of Sepharvaim? Did any god rescue Samaria from my power? ²⁰What god of any nation has ever been able to save its people from my

power? So what makes you think that the LORD can rescue Jerusalem from me?"

²¹But the people were silent and did not utter a word because Hezekiah had commanded them, "Do not answer him."

²²Then Eliakim son of Hilkiah, the palace administrator; Shebna the court secretary; and Joah son of Asaph, the royal historian, went back to Hezekiah. They tore their clothes in despair, and they went in to see the king and told him what the Assyrian chief of staff had said.

## CHAPTER 37

When King Hezekiah heard their report, he tore his clothes and put on burlap and went into the Temple of the LORD. ²And he sent Eliakim the palace administrator, Shebna the court secretary, and the leading priests, all dressed in burlap, to the prophet Isaiah son of Amoz. ³They told him, "This is what King Hezekiah says: Today is a day of trouble, insults, and disgrace. It is like when a child is ready to be born, but the mother has no strength to deliver the baby. ⁴But perhaps the LORD your God has heard the Assyrian chief of staff,* sent by the king to defy the living God, and will punish him for his words. Oh, pray for those of us who are left!"

36:1 The fourteenth year of Hezekiah's reign was 701 BC.   36:2a Or *the rabshakeh;* also in 36:4, 11, 12, 22.
36:2b Or *bleached.*   36:11 Hebrew *in the dialect of Judah;* also in 36:13.   37:4 Or *the rabshakeh;* also in 37:8.

NOTES

36:1 *fourteenth year.* This event can be dated to 701 BC.

36:2 *chief of staff.* As the NLT mg indicates, this translates Heb. *rab-shaqeh* [TH7262, ZH8072], formerly thought to be a personal name, Rabshakeh (cf. older English versions and see 36:4, 11, 12, 22). It is now understood to have been an Assyrian title (cf. "chief officer," REB; "commander," NAB; "cupbearer-in-chief," NJB). The NRSV and NJPS transliterate the term but treat it as a title: "the Rabshakeh."

*Lachish.* This strategically located city was about twenty-five miles southwest of Jerusalem. Extensive archaeological excavations have been conducted on the site and important written documents ("Lachish Letters") have been found there.

36:3 *Eliakim . . . Shebna.* Their previous mention in 22:15-25 indicates that next to the king, they held the highest offices in the land. Their responsibilities probably approximated those of a modern-day prime minister and secretary of state, but the details remain unknown to us.

36:6 *reed.* Egypt is similarly presented in Ezek 29:6-7.

36:7 *shrines and altars.* Hezekiah had destroyed many of the sacred sites of Baal worship (cf. 2 Kgs 18:4; 2 Chr 31:1).

36:8 *2,000 horses.* These would have been very desirable at this time. In light of 36:9, the reference is probably to horses for chariots, since cavalry was probably not used at this time.

36:11 *Aramaic.* Aramaic, the diplomatic language of that time, was not understood by the common people of Jerusalem who used Hebrew. Aramaic and Hebrew are both western Semitic languages, in contrast to Assyrian, which is eastern Semitic.

36:16 *Eating from your own grapevine and fig tree.* Lit., "eating from his own vine and fig tree." These were symbols of well-being (cf. 1 Kgs 4:25; Mic 4:41).

36:17 *take you to another land.* This refers to the policy of deportation used by the Assyrians to break up the patriotism and resistance of conquered peoples (cf. 2 Kgs 15:29; 17:6).

36:19 *Hamath and Arpad.* These sites were in Aram. Hamath was an object of the Assyrian conquest, and some of its inhabitants were exiled and settled in Israel (2 Kgs 17:24). The site is very old and is referred to in the ancient Ebla texts as Ematu, according to

ABD (3:33). Arpad was a city in northern Syria, referred to in 2 Kgs 18:34; 19:13; Isa 10:9; 37:13; and Jer 49:23. According to ABD, before its conquest by Assyria, Arpad was the capital of the land of Bit-Agusi (1:401).

**Sepharvaim.** This location remains uncertain but it was probably in the Hamath area of Aram. We know from 2 Kgs 17:24 that Sargon II settled captives from Sepharvaim in Samaria.

**Did any god rescue Samaria?** Apparently, the Assyrians did not associate the God of Judah with Samaria. They probably assumed separate deities for different areas of Israel and Judah.

**37:1 tore his clothes and put on burlap.** It was customary to tear one's clothes during times of duress or mourning. "Burlap" translates the Heb. *saq* [TH8242, ZH8566], traditionally "sackcloth," a rough garment of poor quality. These two customs often went together (cf. Gen 37:34).

**into the Temple of the LORD.** An especially solemn place for prayer (cf. 1 Kgs 8:33).

**37:2 Eliakim . . . Shebna.** See the note on 36:3.

### COMMENTARY

With this passage, we move into a new section in Isaiah that can be called "A Historical Interlude." Beginning at 36:1 and ending at 39:8, this section consists of a historical narrative about King Hezekiah and the Assyrian siege of Jerusalem. This was a critical period in the life of Israel and, except for 38:9-20, has parallel material in 2 Kings 18:13–20:19. The events described in Isaiah 36:1–37:38 record God's miraculous deliverance of Jerusalem from King Sennacherib of Assyria in the "fourteenth year of King Hezekiah's reign" (36:1), or 701 BC. In response to Hezekiah's insubordination, Sennacherib invaded Judah and captured forty-six towns of Judah.

To avoid further bloodshed, the Assyrians pressed for a peace treaty with Jerusalem. As Hezekiah wavered, he heard a message from Isaiah warning him not to worry but to put his trust in God. The final outcome was miraculous. The Lord intervened to destroy the Assyrian army camped outside Jerusalem. The text tells us that the "angel of the LORD" killed 185,000 Assyrian soldiers (37:36).

**Sennacherib and Jerusalem.** During the year 701 BC, the mighty Assyrian king Sennacherib reached Palestine in an attempt to suppress a widespread rebellion. As the Assyrians swept down from the north, city after city capitulated, and soon the enemy had made its way into Judah.

The Assyrians camped at Lachish, located about twenty-five miles southwest of Jerusalem, and on the main approach to that city. Hezekiah had sent envoys to Lachish to acknowledge that he was wrong to have revolted against Assyria (2 Kgs 18:14ff). Sennacherib accepted a sizeable tribute payment, but then decided to punish Jerusalem anyhow.

The historical setting of the situation is given in 36:1-3, and 36:4-10 gives the message communicated by the Assyrian officer to Hezekiah. The field commander showed great insight into Judah's faith and life and a rude and arrogant contempt for both. He began his speech by casting aspersions on Judah's faith and ridiculing their God. He addressed his message to Hezekiah, and he intimidated and belittled him by not recognizing his kingship and by referring to his own king as "the great king of Assyria" (36:4). Assyrian inscriptions show that this was indeed the way that Assyrian kings were referred to. The commander then quoted his king as inquiring of Hezekiah, "What are you trusting in that makes you so confident?" (36:4).

The commander then charged Hezekiah with deceiving himself and his people by rebelling against the Assyrians, "Who are you counting on, that you have rebelled against me?" (36:5). He reminded Hezekiah that he had only two sources of strength, Egypt and the Lord—both of no help to him. The commander charged that leaning on Egypt was like leaning upon a "reed that splinters beneath your weight and pierces your hand" (36:6; cf. 42:3). This was true not only for Hezekiah, but for all who depended on Egypt.

Because Hezekiah claimed to be relying on the Lord, the Assyrian officer observed that Hezekiah must have incurred God's disfavor by removing many of the high places. These cultic centers of worship were popular throughout Israel, and the people probably feared the results of their destruction. In spite of some insight into the worldview and lifestyle of the Judahites, the officer erred again, mistakenly believing Hezekiah's reforms (cleansing the temple and destroying idols) to be acts against the Lord, whereas they were actually just the opposite! The "shrines and altars" that the king had destroyed were popular sites dedicated to Baal worship, and "the altar here in Jerusalem" refers to Solomon's temple (36:7).

After pointing out the futility of trusting in Egypt or the Lord, the Assyrian officer urged Hezekiah to make a bargain with Sennacherib, the king of Assyria. Unable to resist yet another word of contempt for Judah's weakness and lack of militia, he offered 2,000 horses—if only they could find horsemen for them! With biting sarcasm, the commander heaped insult upon insult as he continued, "how can you think of challenging even the weakest contingent of my master's troops?" (36:9). The Assyrian officer was familiar with propaganda warfare and was using it to break the spirit of Hezekiah and the Judahites. He made one more bold attempt to neutralize their faith in the Lord, by asserting that Judah's God had directed Assyria to attack Judah (36:10). In the light of Isaiah's earlier messages (10:5-6), we know that Assyria did indeed serve as the Lord's tool for punishing other nations, and that made the officer's bold claim sound even more plausible.

Realizing the potential bad effects of his speech, the three Judahite officials interrupted the officer, requesting that he speak in Aramaic rather than in Hebrew since Aramaic was the recognized international diplomatic language and the officer should have followed protocol (36:11). The officer, however, was intentionally trying to stir up the people, so he (or his interpreter from Assyrian to Hebrew) continued to use Hebrew and spoke even more loudly. In 36:4-10, he pretended to speak to Hezekiah, but in 36:13-20, he openly addressed "the people on the wall" with his filthy and vile remarks that they would "eat their own dung and drink their own urine" (36:12). This was a crude way of describing the horrible results of the famine that would follow a prolonged siege of the city.

In 36:13-17, the proud Assyrian described in Hebrew the alternatives facing the people of Jerusalem. It is possible that the officer was able to speak in several related Semitic languages. Surely he would have known Aramaic, the international language at that time and its closely related dialect of Hebrew. However, he warned the people publicly in their own language and sarcastically quoted Hezekiah's promise to the people that the Lord would rescue them and that they would never be handed over to the Assyrian king (36:15).

The commander reviewed the people's possible options. They could "continue eating from [their] own grapevine and fig tree and drinking from [their] own well" (36:16), or they could "eat their own dung and drink their own urine" (36:12). He said that the Judahites could continue to enjoy their familiar good life until the Assyrians took them into captivity, and he described this in pleasant terms (36:17). Nothing is mentioned about the hardships to be suffered, the deprivations experienced during the long trip to Assyria or the Judahites' status there.

The next part of the officer's speech combines arguments from theology and history (36:18-20). Since other gods had not been able to rescue their followers from the king of Assyria, why should the Judahites expect any different results (36:18)? In the ancient Near East, war was viewed as a battle between the gods of respective nations, and it appeared that the gods of Assyria were winning. Despite the officer's remarkable understanding of the Judahites, he did not know God Almighty, Creator of heaven and earth, and he confused the idols of the nations with the true God of the covenant people. Little did he realize that the Lord was using him as the rod of his anger, and when this work was completed, he too would be destroyed by the one true and holy God (cf. 10:5-6, 25-27).

At several points in his speech, the Assyrian officer attempted to pit the power and integrity of the great king of Assyria (36:4, 13) against Hezekiah's weakness and deceitfulness. Graft and corruption were common in ancient Near Eastern governments, and the officer strongly insinuated that Hezekiah was deceiving his people (cf. 36:14-16, 18). Mention of Samaria, the capital of the northern kingdom of Israel, was designed to strike terror into the hearts of the Judahites because they worshiped the same God as the Israelites (36:19) and war was understood to be a battle between the various national gods.

Chapter 37 records Hezekiah's response to the situation. When Hezekiah heard the report from the three men, he not only "tore his clothes and put on burlap," but went in anguish into the temple to pray (37:1). Desperate over the nation's condition and conscious of his need for divine help, he went into the Lord's house, a place of prayer and meditation. Next he sent an impressive array of dignitaries to Isaiah—Eliakim (palace administrator), Shebna (secretary; cf. 22:15-25), and the leading priests—all dressed in burlap (37:2).

Isaiah's prophetic warnings to the people through the years were now being recognized by the king and his men of state. It was a "day of trouble, insult, and disgrace" (37:3). The people were in a desperate situation; the king had been openly rebuked before them, and the great God of Israel had been blasphemed by an arrogant Assyrian. Their condition was compared to a woman who was giving birth but did not have enough strength—a figure representing great difficulty (37:3; cf. Hos 13:13). In speaking to Isaiah of the "LORD your God" (37:4), Hezekiah and his representatives were not necessarily failing to acknowledge him as their God also; they were probably focusing on Isaiah's personal faithfulness to the Lord as compared to their own wavering faith. For the Lord to hear meant for him to take note and act upon the blasphemous words of the Assyrian field commander who had defied and challenged the omnipotence and absolute deity of the living God, who lives in contrast to the lifeless idols of the nations.

Hezekiah and his men then requested Isaiah to "pray for those of us who are left" (37:4). Jerusalem was probably characterized as part of the "remnant," because most of Judah's cities had already been captured, and many of her citizens had been taken captive. Her desperate plight recalls Isaiah's words in 1:7-9.

◆      ## 2. Jerusalem's deliverance foretold (37:5-13)

⁵After King Hezekiah's officials delivered the king's message to Isaiah, ⁶the prophet replied, "Say to your master, 'This is what the LORD says: Do not be disturbed by this blasphemous speech against me from the Assyrian king's messengers. ⁷Listen! I myself will move against him,* and the king will receive a message that he is needed at home. So he will return to his land, where I will have him killed with a sword.'"

⁸Meanwhile, the Assyrian chief of staff left Jerusalem and went to consult the king of Assyria, who had left Lachish and was attacking Libnah.

⁹Soon afterward King Sennacherib received word that King Tirhakah of Ethiopia* was leading an army to fight against him. Before leaving to meet the attack, he sent messengers back to Hezekiah in Jerusalem with this message:

¹⁰"This message is for King Hezekiah of Judah. Don't let your God, in whom you trust, deceive you with promises that Jerusalem will not be captured by the king of Assyria. ¹¹You know perfectly well what the kings of Assyria have done wherever they have gone. They have completely destroyed everyone who stood in their way! Why should you be any different? ¹²Have the gods of other nations rescued them—such nations as Gozan, Haran, Rezeph, and the people of Eden who were in Tel-assar? My predecessors destroyed them all! ¹³What happened to the king of Hamath and the king of Arpad? What happened to the kings of Sepharvaim, Hena, and Ivvah?"

37:7 Hebrew *I will put a spirit in him.*   37:9 Hebrew *of Cush.*

NOTES

**37:6 messengers.** This is not the usual word for 'messenger" or "servant" but one (*na'ar* [TH5288, ZH5853]) that usually means "lad" or "young man." Perhaps in this context it means something like "underlings" (NIV). The REB and NJB use "minions."

**37:7 I myself will move against him and the king will receive a message.** The more lit. rendering is, "I am going to put a spirit in him so that when he hears a certain report." The word "spirit" can in certain contexts refer to "attitude," as in the English expression, "spirit of bitterness."

**37:8 *Lachish.*** Scenes of Sennacherib's siege of Lachish are preserved in a variety of sculptured pictures (reliefs) found by archaeologists at the Assyrian capital.

***Libnah.*** At the time of Hezekiah's reign and Sennacherib's campaign, Libnah was under Judah's control (cf. 2 Kgs 19:8). No ancient non-biblical references to Libnah are known, and the location of the site is disputed. At least three alternatives are proposed (cf. ABD).

**37:9 *Tirhakah.*** This king of Egypt was of Sudanese origin, the third member of the 25th Dynasty (690–664 BC). He is mentioned only here and in the parallel in 2 Kgs 19:9.

**37:12 *Gozan, Haran, Rezeph . . . Eden . . . Tel-assar.*** These are all sites in ancient Aram. Gozan is the biblical name for a place on the Habor River where some Israelites deported from Samaria settled. Assyrian documents recovered at Gozan (Akkadian *guzana*, modern Tell Halaf) contain some personal Israelite names that undoubtedly belonged to some of the exiles who lived there. Haran is west of Gozan and north of the confluence of the Euphrates and the Balikh (a tributary of the Upper Euphrates); it is east of the city of Carchemish on the winding upper Euphrates River. Rezeph is located between Haran and the Euphrates River. Eden refers to Bit Adini located between the Euphrates and Balikh Rivers (cf. ABD). The location of Tel-Assar is uncertain, but Wiseman (NBD 1167) mentions a Tell-Avvur named in the annals of Tiglath-pileser III and Esarhaddon that was apparently near the Assyrian border with Elam.

**37:13 *Hamath . . . Arpad . . . Sepharvaim . . . Hena . . . Ivvah.*** Hamath (modern Hama, on the Orontes River) is 120 miles north of Damascus (see 10:9). Arpad is nineteen miles north of Aleppo. The locations of Sepharvaim (cf. 36:19; Ezek 47:16), Hena, and Ivvah are not identified with certainty.

### COMMENTARY

Apparently Isaiah had already been praying, for when the entourage from the king reached Isaiah, he had an answer from the Lord (37:6) similar to what the Lord had earlier told Isaiah to tell Ahaz (cf. 7:4). The prophet said to Hezekiah, "Do not be disturbed by this blasphemous speech against me from the Assyrian king's messengers" (37:6).

The encouraging message was that the king of Assyria would soon return to his homeland, where he would be killed (37:7). To believe this required great faith on Hezekiah's part, because the Lord did not reveal how the prophecy would be fulfilled. This event would take place because "the king will receive a report from Assyria telling him that he is needed at home" (37:7). Since the content of the report is not stated, commentators have made many suggestions. Some think it concerned Tirhakah's plan (37:9), or perhaps was a report about internal problems at home, or about other problems in his western campaigns. Probably it included a sense of defeat after the death of his 185,000 men and the realization that he could not cope with Israel's God (cf. 37:36-38). At any rate, the Assyrian officer and his contingent returned to the king, who was at that time attacking Libnah (37:8). Not only would the sovereign God of the Judahites cause him to leave Judah and return home, but he would be "killed with the sword" (37:7).

In 37:8-13, we find a renewed effort by the Assyrians to persuade Hezekiah. Unable to dispose quickly of Jerusalem, the Assyrian officer withdrew and rejoined Sennacherib at Libnah, about ten miles north of Lachish (37:8). Sennacherib received a report that Tirhakah, the Cushite king of Egypt, was approaching to fight him. Since Tirhakah was only a young prince at the time (he assumed the throne in 690 BC), the title "king" is probably used in an anticipatory sense (37:9).

The Assyrian officer had warned the people not to be deceived by Hezekiah. Now Sennacherib repeated his warning to Hezekiah, "Don't let your God, in whom you trust, deceive you with promises" (37:10). He again warned Hezekiah not to be so naive as to think his God could deliver him.

◆     3. Hezekiah's prayer (37:14-20)

¹⁴After Hezekiah received the letter from the messengers and read it, he went up to the LORD's Temple and spread it out before the LORD. ¹⁵And Hezekiah prayed this prayer before the LORD: ¹⁶"O LORD of Heaven's Armies, God of Israel, you are enthroned between the mighty cherubim! You alone are God of all the kingdoms of the earth. You alone created the heavens and the earth. ¹⁷Bend down, O LORD, and listen! Open your eyes, O LORD, and see! Listen to Sennacherib's words of defiance against the living God.

¹⁸"It is true, LORD, that the kings of Assyria have destroyed all these nations. ¹⁹And they have thrown the gods of these nations into the fire and burned them. But of course the Assyrians could destroy them! They were not gods at all—only idols of wood and stone shaped by human hands. ²⁰Now, O LORD our God, rescue us from his power; then all the kingdoms of the earth will know that you alone, O LORD, are God.*"

37:20 As in Dead Sea Scrolls (see also 2 Kgs 19:19); Masoretic Text reads *you alone are the LORD.*

NOTES

**37:16 Heaven's Armies.** The Heb. *tseba'oth* [TH6635, ZH7372] is traditionally rendered "hosts."

*enthroned between the mighty cherubim.* This phrase is often used of God (cf. 1 Sam 4:4; 2 Sam 6:2; 2 Kgs 19:15; 1 Chr 13:6; Ps 80:1; 99:1). The cherubim at each end of the mercy seat gazed inwards and downwards (Exod 37:6-9) and were probably viewed as the pedestals of the invisible throne of the God of Israel (Ezek 1:22-28).

**37:16 created.** The concept of God as Creator is also noted in 40:26, 28; 42:5; 45:12.

**37:17 listen. . . . Open your eyes.** Notice the similarity of language in Solomon's prayer (1 Kgs 8:52; 2 Chr 6:40).

*the living God.* The Heb. is indefinite ("living God"), but most versions treat the expression as definite ("the living God") to suit English style. Motyer (1986:281) suggests that the indefiniteness is actually for the sake of emphasis. "The LORD is set apart as in a different category from all other claimants to deity."

**37:19 idols of wood and stone.** Cf. 2:8; 44:9-20.

**37:20 you alone, O LORD, are God.** The MT reads, "you alone are the LORD" (cf. NLT mg). The DSS here agree with the parallel passage in 2 Kgs 19:19. The idea may be that just as the Lord is God, it can also be said that God is the Lord.

COMMENTARY

After Hezekiah received the renewed threat from the Assyrians, he took it before the Lord (37:14), and in words of praise and supplication requested divine deliverance (37:16-20). In his prayer, he acknowledged that the God "enthroned between the mighty cherubim" was indeed the "God of all the kingdoms of the earth" (37:16). His prayer was not just for personal help, but was concerned with "Sennacherib's words of defiance against the living God" (37:17); he prayed that "all the kingdoms of the earth will know that you alone, O LORD, are God" (37:20).

Hezekiah's response to the messengers is noteworthy, and perhaps even shocked them. Rather than a knee-jerk reaction of fright, he took the letter, read it, and then once more went to the Temple to pray (cf. 37:1, 14) and to "spread [the message] out before the LORD" (37:14). In 1:15, the Lord had said that he would not listen to the people when they spread out their hands to pray, but when Hezekiah spread the letter out before him, God graciously listened.

Hezekiah's prayer (37:15-20) reveals theological insight and anticipates some of the key teachings of chapters 40–66. In devout and lofty language, the king's prayer manifests a firm trust in God and total dependence upon him to deal with the situation. The prayer is majestic and acknowledges God not only as the "LORD of Heaven's Armies, God of Israel . . . enthroned between the mighty cherubim," but also as the "God of all the kingdoms of the earth" (37:16). He acknowledged Israel's God as the Creator, the one who "created the heavens and the earth," (37:16) and as the one who was able to save his people from their sins and from their enemies. In 37:17, Hezekiah presented the petitions of his prayer in several requests: (1) "Bend down . . . and listen," (2) "Open your eyes . . . and see," and (3) "Listen to Sennacherib's words of defiance against the living God." Since God was the only true God and sovereign over all the nations, Sennacherib's claim that he had vanquished the deities of other nations was false (37:19). Hezekiah acknowledged the claim of Sennacherib that the Assyrian kings had laid waste the various sites mentioned and had "thrown the gods of these nations into the fire and burned them"; he then noted that "they were not gods at all, only idols of wood and stone shaped by human hands" (37:19). Should the Almighty Lord of all creation be compared to such nonentities?

On an earlier occasion, the uncircumcised heathen Goliath had defied the armies of the living God" (1 Sam 17:36) and "cursed David by the names of his gods" (1 Sam 17:43), but the shepherd boy defeated him "in the name of the LORD of Heaven's Armies, the God of the armies of Israel" (1 Sam 17:45). In both cases, God defeated those who insulted, defied, and cursed him.

Having unburdened his heart before the Lord, the king then made his earnest request for the people. He asked God to deliver his people so that all the kingdoms on earth might know that only the Lord is God (37:20; cf. 43:11; 45:18, 21-22).

## ◆    4. The Lord's answer to Hezekiah's prayer (37:21-29)

²¹Then Isaiah son of Amoz sent this message to Hezekiah: "This is what the LORD, the God of Israel, says: Because you prayed about King Sennacherib of Assyria, ²²the LORD has spoken this word against him:

"The virgin daughter of Zion
    despises you and laughs at you.
The daughter of Jerusalem
    shakes her head in derision as
    you flee.

²³ "Whom have you been defying and
        ridiculing?
    Against whom did you raise your
        voice?
    At whom did you look with such
        haughty eyes?
    It was the Holy One of Israel!
²⁴ By your messengers you have defied
        the Lord.
    You have said, 'With my many
        chariots
    I have conquered the highest
        mountains—
        yes, the remotest peaks of Lebanon.
    I have cut down its tallest cedars
        and its finest cypress trees.
    I have reached its farthest heights
        and explored its deepest forests.
²⁵ I have dug wells in many foreign
        lands*
    and refreshed myself with their
        water.

With the sole of my foot,
    I stopped up all the rivers of Egypt!'

²⁶ "But have you not heard?
    I decided this long ago.
Long ago I planned it,
    and now I am making it happen.
I planned for you to crush fortified
        cities
    into heaps of rubble.
²⁷ That is why their people have so little
        power
    and are so frightened and confused.
They are as weak as grass,
    as easily trampled as tender green
        shoots.
They are like grass sprouting on
        a housetop,
    scorched* before it can grow lush
        and tall.

²⁸ "But I know you well—
        where you stay
    and when you come and go.
    I know the way you have raged
        against me.
²⁹ And because of your raging
        against me
    and your arrogance, which I have
        heard for myself,
    I will put my hook in your nose
        and my bit in your mouth.
    I will make you return
        by the same road on which you
        came."

37:25 As in Dead Sea Scrolls (see also 2 Kgs 19:24); Masoretic Text lacks *in many foreign lands.*  37:27 As in Dead Sea Scrolls and some Greek manuscripts (see also 2 Kgs 19:26); most Hebrew manuscripts read *like a terraced field.*

### NOTES

**37:22** *virgin daughter of Zion . . . daughter of Jerusalem.* These are personifications of the city of Jerusalem. Isaiah also refers to the "Virgin Daughter of Sidon" (23:12) and the "Virgin Daughter of Babylon" (47:1). In each instance, he was referring not to the purity of the people, but to the fact that these cities had not been cast down or "raped" by a conqueror.

*shakes her head.* The figure is found in Pss 22:7; 44:14.

**37:24** *your messengers.* This undoubtedly refers to the supreme commander, chief officer, and field officer mentioned in 2 Kgs 18:17.

*many chariots.* Cf. 36:8.

*Lebanon . . . tallest cedars.* The cedars of Lebanon were highly valued as building material by the kings of the ancient Near East (cf. 1 Kgs 5:8-10). The actions listed by the Assyrians in their boasting have been remarkably attested and illuminated in pictorial representations found by archaeologists. We can see pictures of Assyrian soldiers climbing steep mountains and cutting down trees. We also know that the Assyrians used cedars and pines for the construction of ships and siege works (cf. 14:8).

**37:25** Both the style and the content of this verse closely resemble the language of subsequent chapters (cf. 40:12; 41:26).

*the rivers of Egypt.* This probably refers to the many branches of the Nile.

**37:27 *They are as weak as grass.*** The people are likened to such perishables as "grass" and "tender green shoots."

*grass sprouting on a housetop.* In ancient Israel, the roofs of the simpler clay houses were made of logs and branches with a layer of earth on top. The grass that sometimes grew there withered easily.

**37:29 *hook in your nose.*** This was used by the Assyrians to lead away captives (cf. 1 Kgs 19:28). Pictures of this are preserved on reliefs.

*bit in your mouth.* The bit for controlling animals is also mentioned in 30:28.

COMMENTARY

This passage contains the message that Isaiah sent to Hezekiah concerning King Sennacherib of Assyria; it is parallel to 2 Kings 19:20-32. It begins with the Lord's response to Isaiah that he passed on to Hezekiah. God's answer to Hezekiah came in the form of an extended taunt against the king of Assyria (37:22-29), and the content of this taunt closely resembled Isaiah's condemnation of the king of Babylon in chapter 14.

The "virgin daughter of Zion" and the "daughter of Jerusalem" are obvious parallels, each referring to the city and its people (37:22). Jerusalem/Zion "scoffs, shaking her head" (37.22) in contempt for those who would seduce her. In this poem against the king of Assyria, the Lord promised that Jerusalem would not be destroyed by Assyria. She would remain untouched, like a virgin. The message from God reminded them of who he is. In contrast to the idol-gods who were thrown into the fire and destroyed, he is the Holy One of Israel! Sennacherib's doom was certain because he was guilty of blaspheming the "Holy One of Israel," and of "defying and ridiculing" him (37:23). Assyria's great pride is described in 37:23-25, a passage that is parallel to 10:12-14 and 14:13-14. According to 37:23-25, the Assyrians believed that no obstacle could stand in their way because their chariots "conquered the highest mountains" (37:24). Apparently, they even thought of Sennacherib as divine and said that he "stopped up all the rivers of Egypt" with his foot (37:25; throughout these verses, we encounter strong poetic imagery, combining anthropomorphism, synecdoche, and hyperbole).

The Assyrians were unaware that all their victories were part of God's plan, for he had decreed the collapse of kingdoms and the shattering of peoples (cf. 25:1-2). God, not Assyria or Babylon, was in control of history. A couple of proverbs bear out this truth of God's sovereign control: "The king's heart is like a stream of water directed by the LORD; he turns it wherever he pleases" (Prov 21:1) and "The horse is prepared for the day of battle, but the victory belongs to the LORD" (Prov 21:31).

God is both omnipotent and omniscient, knowing every move and every attitude. He thoroughly understood Assyria's attitudes and plans, and especially their raging against him, and he would punish them for such arrogance. He would snag the Assyrian leader like a fish or untamed beast and take him back powerless by the way that he came (37:28-29).

◆     5. The message of assurance to Hezekiah (37:30-38)

³⁰Then Isaiah said to Hezekiah, "Here is the proof that what I say is true:

"This year you will eat only what
  grows up by itself,
and next year you will eat what
  springs up from that.
But in the third year you will plant
  crops and harvest them;
you will tend vineyards and eat
  their fruit.
³¹And you who are left in Judah,
  who have escaped the ravages
    of the siege,
will put roots down in your own soil
  and grow up and flourish.
³²For a remnant of my people will
  spread out from Jerusalem,
a group of survivors from Mount
  Zion.
The passionate commitment of the
  LORD of Heaven's Armies
  will make this happen!

³³"And this is what the LORD says about the king of Assyria:

"'His armies will not enter Jerusalem.
  They will not even shoot an arrow
    at it.

They will not march outside its gates
  with their shields
  nor build banks of earth against
    its walls.
³⁴The king will return to his own
  country
  by the same road on which he
    came.
He will not enter this city,'
  says the LORD.
³⁵'For my own honor and for the sake
  of my servant David,
  I will defend this city and protect it.'"

³⁶That night the angel of the LORD went out to the Assyrian camp and killed 185,000 Assyrian soldiers. When the surviving Assyrians* woke up the next morning, they found corpses everywhere. ³⁷Then King Sennacherib of Assyria broke camp and returned to his own land. He went home to his capital of Nineveh and stayed there.

³⁸One day while he was worshiping in the temple of his god Nisroch, his sons Adrammelech and Sharezer killed him with their swords. They then escaped to the land of Ararat, and another son, Esarhaddon, became the next king of Assyria.

37:36 Hebrew *When they.*

NOTES

37:31 *put roots down . . . flourish.* See 4:2; 11:1, 10; 27:6.

37:32 *remnant.* This is an important concept in Isaiah and in the rest of the OT (cf. 1:9; 2 Kgs 19:4, 30-31).

37:33 *build banks of earth against its walls.* These were known as siege ramps; they enabled those besieging the city to bring battering rams up against the walls (cf. 2 Sam 20:15).

**37:35 defend.** Heb. *ganan* [TH1598, ZH1713], a word used only eight times in the OT and half of those are in Isaiah. Cf. 31:5 where "protect" translates the same Heb. word.

**37:36 angel of the LORD. . . killed.** See Exod 12:12; 2 Sam 24:16. The parallel account in 2 Kgs 20:25 also has "the angel of the LORD," but 2 Chr 32:20 reads simply, "an angel." Possibly the reference here is not to "the angel of the LORD" that appears in many passages of the OT as a theophany, particularly of the second person of the Trinity, but rather a created angel by whose agency the judgment of God was executed (cf. Ps 91:11). The Assyrian account of what happened to Sennacherib and Hezekiah at Jerusalem is given in the "Taylor Prism," a six-sided clay column that records the military campaigns of Sennacherib against Aram, Phoenicia, and Judah, including the siege of Jerusalem in which Sennacherib claimed that he made Hezekiah "a prisoner in Jerusalem, his royal residence, like a bird in a cage."

**killed.** "Put to death" translates the Heb. word *nakah* [TH5221, ZH5782], a common word for "smite, strike." It is general and can mean everything from "pursue" to "kill." The parallel passage in 2 Chr 32:21 uses the Heb. *kakhad* [TH3582, ZH3948], often rendered as "cut off."

**surviving Assyrians . . . found corpses.** As the NLT mg indicates, the literal Heb. is "when they woke up they were all dead." This cryptic Heb. is variously rendered in the new versions as "when men rose early in the morning, behold, all these were dead" (NASB), "they were all dead bodies" (NRSV), "there they all lay dead" (REB), "there they were, all the corpses of the dead" (NAB), "there they lay, so many corpses" (NJB), "when people arose early in the morning, behold these were all dead bodies" (ESV), and "the following morning they were all dead corpses" (NJPS).

**37:38 in the temple.** While Hezekiah went to the temple of the Lord to gain strength, Sennacherib went to the temple of his god Nisroch and was killed.

**Nisroch.** The place of this assassination is also mentioned in the Assyrian records Possibly the name Nisroch is a rendering of the name of the Assyrian national god (NBD 837).

**Adrammelech and Sharezer.** This event, which took place in 681 BC, is also recorded in 2 Kgs 19:37 and in the Babylonian Chronicle (NBD 17).

COMMENTARY

This oracle directly addresses Hezekiah, for whom it was the answer to prayer. As proof that the Assyrians would leave Judah never to threaten Jerusalem again, the Lord gave Hezekiah a sign. This three year sign (37:30) covers the same time period as the one in 20:3. By the end of this time, the planting and harvesting of crops would return to normal (37:30). During the Assyrian invasion, the fields were ruined by neglect and destruction, but improvement could now be expected. Three years seemed like a long time since the Assyrians would soon be destroyed, but probably the "second year" was due to begin within a few months of the prophecy, so the total period would have been considerably less than thirty-six months (similarly, Christ's three days in the grave covered one full day and parts of two others). Whatever the exact length of time may have been, recovery from such severe devastation was not easy. Hezekiah had requested prayer for "the remnant that is left" (37:4b), and 37:31-32 contains the promise that the "remnant" would be fruitful. The fields and vineyards would be restored and the depleted population replenished. The survivors would be able to repopulate Judah and thereby assure the continuation of the nation.

The imagery of putting roots down and flourishing (37:31) recalls 4:2-3 and 11:10-11, passages that describe the future situation of the remnant after the Babylonian destruction of 586 BC. The last sentence in 37:32 is identical to the final words of 9:7. Both verses contain promises about Israel's future, as guaranteed by God's faithful love for his covenant people and for his servant David. In 37:33-35, the Lord repeated the promise he gave in 37:29: Sennacherib would not subject Jerusalem to the horrors of a long siege. Using the words of 31:5, God promised to "defend" Jerusalem (37:35) and to save it out of the hands of the enemy. The Lord would defend the city for his own sake and for the sake of David, whose seed he had sworn to preserve until the coming of him who would fulfill the promise (cf. 2 Sam 7:11-16).

The dramatic fulfillment of this prophecy is concisely given in 37:36-38. The "angel of the LORD" (like the angel of death who had slain the firstborn of Egypt) struck again, and one of the most formidable armies of the ancient world was broken. Since details are not given, many have speculated as to when, where, and how this took place. The parallel account in 2 Chronicles 32:20-21 gives the impression that the Lord sent his angel when Hezekiah and Isaiah prayed. The other parallel account (2 Kgs 19:35) adds "that night," which suggests that the Assyrians were broken immediately after the delivery of Isaiah's message.

We have even fewer clues in the text as to where this took place; it simply says, "the Assyrian camp" (37:36). Although most readers probably assume that the camp was right outside Jerusalem, this is not stated in the narrative. Some think that the main camp was still at Libnah, and only a smaller detachment was at Jerusalem. If so, was Sennacherib at the main camp or with the detachment in Jerusalem? Others think that the Assyrian king was on his way to Egypt to meet Tirhakah.

As to the "how" of the event, details are not provided for the curious. The text simply states that "the angel of the LORD . . . killed [them]," and the parallel in 2 Chr 32:21 says that they were "destroyed." Sennacherib's report preserved on the Taylor Prism (ANET 288-289) omits the defeat and losses. Probably the most common theory is that the Lord used something like a bubonic plague to accomplish this, and attention is directed to a somewhat similar plague also involving an angel (2 Sam 24:15ff). The Greek historian Herodotus (*Histories* 2.141) relates that while Sennacherib was marching against Egypt, field mice destroyed the quivers, bows, and shield straps of the Assyrians, so that they were forced to flee and many of them were killed. Some think that this may be a garbled reminiscence of the disaster that struck Sennacherib's army, and then argue the understandable tendency on the part of Egyptian priests (sources used by Herodotus) to relate history as much as possible to their own country. At any rate, the end came swiftly and decisively. In 31:8, it was predicted that Assyria would fall "not by the swords of men" because the sword of God will strike them." The mighty storm had struck (30:27-33), and the mighty tree of Assyria had fallen (10:33-34).

The closing statement of 37:36 is unusual (see note). The KJV gives an example of a literal translation: "when they arose early in the morning, they were all dead corpses." The NLT translates this as, "when the surviving Assyrians woke up the next morning, they found corpses everywhere."

The narrative relates how this divine act caused Sennacherib to break camp and withdraw (37:37). He and the few troops that survived had to abandon the campaign and return to Nineveh, the Assyrian capital. In his later report on what happened, he mentioned that he "shut up Hezekiah in Jerusalem like a bird in a cage" and received tribute from him (ANET 288-289). He does not mention any capture of the city or anything about scaling the walls of the city, as he does with other cities that he defeated. Twenty years later (681 BC), two of his sons (Adrammelech and Sharezer) "killed him with their swords" while he was worshiping "in the temple of his god Nisroch" (37:38). This event is also preserved in the Assyrian inscriptions, but these mention just one son, who must have been in charge. It is significant that Hezekiah went to the temple of his God and found help, while Sennacherib went to the house of his god and was destroyed (cf. 37:7). Through it all, the God of Israel was vindicated, the gods of Assyria were violated, and Isaiah's role as a true prophet was validated.

◆   **B. Hezekiah's Sickness and Recovery (38:1-22)**
      **1. Hezekiah's prayer for healing (38:1-8)**

About that time Hezekiah became deathly ill, and the prophet Isaiah son of Amoz went to visit him. He gave the king this message: "This is what the LORD says: 'Set your affairs in order, for you are going to die. You will not recover from this illness.'"

²When Hezekiah heard this, he turned his face to the wall and prayed to the LORD, ³"Remember, O LORD, how I have always been faithful to you and have served you single-mindedly, always doing what pleases you." Then he broke down and wept bitterly.

⁴Then this message came to Isaiah from the LORD: ⁵"Go back to Hezekiah and tell him, 'This is what the LORD, the God of your ancestor David, says: I have heard your prayer and seen your tears. I will add fifteen years to your life, ⁶and I will rescue you and this city from the king of Assyria. Yes, I will defend this city.

⁷"And this is the sign from the LORD to prove that he will do as he promised: ⁸I will cause the sun's shadow to move ten steps backward on the sundial* of Ahaz!'" So the shadow on the sundial moved backward ten steps.

38:8 Hebrew *the steps.*

NOTES
**38:1 *About that time.*** Lit., "in those days."

***Set your affairs in order.*** Lit., "put your house in order." The prophet Elisha similarly predicted Ben-hadad's death (2 Kgs 8:9-10).

**38:7-8** At this point, between 38:7 and 38:8, the parallel account in 2 Kgs 20:7-11 contains additional material.

***sign.*** The Heb. word *'ot* [TH226, ZH253] is often used of a miraculous sign (cf. Isa 7:14; Exod 3:12).

***move . . . backward.*** Cf. Josh 10:12-14.

*steps backward on the sundial.* The Heb. is not precise. Oswalt (1986:672) notes that the Qumran scroll 1QIsaᵃ has "the steps of the upper chamber of Ahaz" and the LXX has "steps of the house of Ahaz." The KJV has "sun dial," and the modern versions vary in their understanding of this. Most refer to a "stairway" (NASB, REB, TEV, GW, CEV, NCV), but some have "dial" (NRSV, ESV). The NJPS has "steps" with a note indicating a model of a dial with steps has been discovered in Egypt.

### COMMENTARY

Interpreters generally agree that the events described in chapters 38 and 39 precede the invasion of 701 BC. Oswalt (1986:674) suggests that "if Hezekiah began to reign in 716/15 and reigned for twenty-nine years (2 Kgs 18:2, 13), then this event (whereby fifteen years were added) would have occurred around 701, at the time of Sennacherib's invasion." Second Kings 20:1-11, which runs parallel to the first eight verses of chapter 38, bears out the view that the Assyrian siege and Hezekiah's illness were simultaneous. However, others date these events in 703 BC or as early as about 712 BC. The phrase "about that time" refers to the general period of Hezekiah's involvement with the Assyrian armies, regardless of who the Assyrian king was.

**Hezekiah's Prayer for Healing.** The opening verses of this chapter give a brief account of Hezekiah's illness and recovery. The king was informed by the Lord through Isaiah that he would soon die, just as Elisha was able to predict the death of Ben-hadad (2 Kgs 8:10). The words "set your affairs in order" (38:1) warn him to make the necessary preparations for his death. Hezekiah's reaction was a natural one; he pleaded with the Lord to change his mind. Instinctively, he turned to God in prayer, facing the wall, apparently to shut out any distraction (38:2). The king reminded God that he (Hezekiah) had been faithful and served him "single-mindedly, always doing what pleases you" (38:3). Very few kings since David could have made these claims, but Hezekiah had instituted a thorough reform that included the removal of the high places and the curtailment of idolatry (cf. 2 Kgs 18:3-6). He felt that he deserved to live longer. Another concern may have been his need for an heir. Since Manasseh, the next king, was not born until three years later (2 Kgs 21:1), Hezekiah may have been concerned about the continuation of the Davidic line.

The Lord responded, "I have heard your prayer and seen your tears" (38:5). The God of David granted Hezekiah time to sire a son through whom the promise made to David would be fulfilled, and Manasseh was born three years later (2 Kgs 21:1). Although Isaiah did not say "for the sake of my servant David," as in 37:35, the reference to "your ancestor David" (38:5) and the inclusion of the phrase in the parallel passage in 2 Kgs 20:6 make it clear that the Davidic promise was involved. The answered prayer included an additional fifteen years of life and the promise that Jerusalem would not fall to the Assyrians. When the armies of Sennacherib closed in, Hezekiah believed that prayer changes things and that God works miracles.

In 38:7-8, the Lord gave a sign to confirm his word through Isaiah. Unlike the signs described in 20:3 and 37:30, this one involved a miracle. The NLT associates the "steps" with the "sundial of Ahaz" (38:8), but some scholars understand them as referring to the "stairway of Ahaz" (NIV); perhaps they were steps to an upper room (cf. 2 Kgs 23:12). According to 2 Kings 20:8, Hezekiah requested a sign of confirmation. Several commentators note the contrast to Ahaz, who refused to accept a sign when one was offered. The two Judahite kings had opposite attitudes.

◆ ## 2. Hezekiah's healing and his poem of thanks (38:9-22)

9When King Hezekiah was well again, he wrote this poem:

10I said, "In the prime of my life,
    must I now enter the place of the
    dead?*
    Am I to be robbed of the rest of my
    years?"
11I said, "Never again will I see the
    LORD GOD
    while still in the land of the living.
Never again will I see my friends
    or be with those who live in this
    world.
12My life has been blown away
    like a shepherd's tent in a storm.
It has been cut short,
    as when a weaver cuts cloth from
    a loom.
Suddenly, my life was over.
13I waited patiently all night,
    but I was torn apart as though
    by lions.
Suddenly, my life was over.
14Delirious, I chattered like a swallow
    or a crane,
and then I moaned like a mourning
    dove.
My eyes grew tired of looking to
    heaven for help.
I am in trouble, Lord. Help me!"

15But what could I say?
    For he himself sent this sickness.

Now I will walk humbly throughout
    my years
    because of this anguish I have felt.
16Lord, your discipline is good,
    for it leads to life and health.
You restore my health
    and allow me to live!
17Yes, this anguish was good for me,
    for you have rescued me from death
    and forgiven all my sins.
18For the dead* cannot praise you;
    they cannot raise their voices in
    praise.
Those who go down to the grave
    can no longer hope in your
    faithfulness.
19Only the living can praise you as
    I do today.
Each generation tells of your
    faithfulness to the next.
20Think of it—the LORD is ready to
    heal me!
I will sing his praises with
    instruments
every day of my life
    in the Temple of the LORD.

21Isaiah had said to Hezekiah's servants, "Make an ointment from figs and spread it over the boil, and Hezekiah will recover." 22And Hezekiah had asked, "What sign will prove that I will go to the Temple of the LORD?"

38:10 Hebrew *enter the gates of Sheol?* 38:18 Hebrew *Sheol.*

NOTES

38:10 *place of the dead.* Lit., "gates of Sheol" (cf. NLT mg).

38:18 *grave.* The Heb. *sheol* [TH7585, ZH8619] refers to the realm of the dead, whether the grave where their bodies lie, or the place where their spirits live.

**38:21-22 *Isaiah had said . . . Hezekiah had asked.*** Many commentators and several translations follow the account in 2 Kgs 20 by inserting these two verses (38:21-22) between 38:6 and 38:7, where they logically belong. The NLT and other versions (cf. the NIV) try to soften the difficulty of this placement by translating the verbs as past perfect: "Isaiah had said" and "Hezekiah had asked."

***Hezekiah's servants.*** The Heb. does not specify those addressed, but since the verbs are in the plural, it is probably the "servants" or court physicians.

***ointment from figs.*** The Heb. says more lit., "a lump of figs" (*debeleth te'enim* [TH1690, ZH1811]) and "spread it over the boil." This was probably more of a poultice of figs than an ointment. The versions vary: "cake of figs" (NASB, ESV, NJPS), "lump of figs" (NRSV), "fig-plaster" (REB), "paste from figs" (NCV), "paste made from figs" (TEV), and "fig cake" (GW). The medicinal function of the figs remains uncertain, but the use of figs for horse ailments is now attested at Ugarit (Gordon 1949:129).

**38:22 *sign.*** Heb. *'ot* [TH226, ZH253]. The sign may indicate the healing, but it could also point to the Lord, who did the healing. In other words, the procedure was a "visible symbol of the healing power of God, an 'acted oracle'" (Motyer 1999:239).

### COMMENTARY

In response to his divine healing, King Hezekiah wrote the poem that takes up most of the remainder of the chapter. The parallel passage in 2 Kings does not include the poem. The king described the horror and grief he experienced as he faced the specter of death. According to 2 Chronicles 29:30, the king had shown deep interest in the Psalms of David and Asaph, and this hymn of thanksgiving in two stanzas preserves one of his own compositions. The hymn begins with a description of Hezekiah's agony in the face of imminent death (38:10-14). Hezekiah certainly had confidence in a life beyond death, but to him the "place of the dead" (38:10) was a completely sealed off realm where praise, celebration of fellowship, and truth could not be found. The king called upon all who were truly alive in this life to join him in praise to God. He urged fathers to pass on the truth of the Lord's great faithfulness to their children. In the Old Testament, individual hymns of thanksgiving often conclude with a vow of praise like the one here. The person whose prayer had been heard gave his testimony in front of the assembly, and the people joined him in praising the Lord (Ps 116:18-19).

Hezekiah's feelings differed sharply from those of Paul, who said "sometimes I long to go and be with Christ" (Phil 1:23). The Christian concept of the dead transcends the Old Testament concept because of Christ's victory over the grave. Like David, Hezekiah possessed the more limited revelation of the old covenant, so he was more interested in knowing and serving the Lord in his present life. He preferred to be with his friends and "with those who live in this world" (38:11). Since Sheol, the place where the dead would reside, was little known, it is understandable that Hezekiah thought it better to praise God during his life among the living than to go down to Sheol.

Death is compared to the taking down of a tent, a figure used in an opposite way in 33:20. Like a shepherd's tent that is moved from one place to another after the pasturage is consumed, so Hezekiah's earthly dwelling would be moved along (38:12). A second image (38:12) refers to the slender thread of life, which is compared to the cloth a weaver cuts from a loom. After this life is spun, God will cut it off of the loom. Knowing he was about to be cut off, Hezekiah begged the Lord to intervene personally on his behalf (38:14; cf. Ps 119:122).

God did intervene, and 38:15-19 is a reflection on God's faithfulness. The NLT correctly indicates a new strophe here, as the mood clearly shifts with Hezekiah focusing on the blessings that had come out of his suffering. The tone was now one of pleased surprise at God's deliverance and the new joy of life. Hezekiah's health was restored, and he was allowed to live. Like Job, Hezekiah found a new concept of God through suffering (cf. Job 42:5), and he observed how beneficial this difficult experience had turned out to be. He acknowledged that the Lord's "discipline is good" (38:16) and that "this anguish was good for me" (38:17). He praised God for his love that kept him from death and the grave. Hezekiah thanked God that his health was restored, that he was allowed to continue living, and that God had forgiven all his sins (38:17).

The poem began with mourning and crying (38:10-14), but ended with music and singing (38:15-20). Hezekiah loved the "Temple of the LORD," and it was his desire to spend the rest of his life near its courts (38:20; cf. Ps 23:6). With his life extended, the Assyrians defeated, and true worship restored, Hezekiah's life could now be what it should be.

◆    ## C. Envoys from Babylon (39:1-8)
### 1. Hezekiah's reception of the envoys (39:1-2)

Soon after this, Merodach-baladan son of Baladan, king of Babylon, sent Hezekiah his best wishes and a gift. He had heard that Hezekiah had been very sick and that he had recovered. ²Hezekiah was delighted with the Babylonian envoys and showed them everything in his treasure-houses— the silver, the gold, the spices, and the aromatic oils. He also took them to see his armory and showed them everything in his royal treasuries! There was nothing in his palace or kingdom that Hezekiah did not show them.

### NOTES
**39:1 *Soon after this.*** The Hebrew is *ba'eth hahi'* (at that time); it focuses more on the significance of the occasion, and refers to more chronological information.

***Merodach-baladan.*** Akkadian (Babylonian) Marduk-apal-iddina means "Marduk has given a son." Merodach-baladan reigned from 721–710 BC. Motyer (1993:296) gives details on the historical background and concludes that Merodach-baladan offered a "credible alternative to the power of the ascendant Assyria."

**39:2 *was delighted with.*** The Heb. text has *wayyismakh* [TH8055, ZH8523], which means "and he rejoiced" over them. The more formal parallel language in 2 Kgs 20:13 has *wayyishma'* [TH8085, ZH9048], "and he heard" them. Perhaps Isaiah was exposing Hezekiah's heart attitude with this choice of language.

COMMENTARY

Chapter 39 records an important sequel to Hezekiah's illness. The king of Babylon, Merodach-baladan, chose the occasion of Hezekiah's recovery to send him a letter of congratulations and a gift. This is the second reference in this historical interlude to a letter from a Mesopotamian king, but its contents were different from the letter Sennacherib had sent (cf. 37:14). Merodach-baladan was a prince who never tired of stirring up revolts against the Assyrians. He ruled Babylon from 721–710 BC, and it was probably toward the end of this period that he sent his envoys to Hezekiah. Sargon II was preparing his Assyrian troops for an attack on Babylon, and Merodach-baladan was eager to enlist the support of other nations for Babylon, including the kingdom of Judah.

"Soon after this" (39:1) refers to the time of Hezekiah's recovery. It is impossible to know the exact date of the messengers and envoys from the Babylonian king. Merodach-baladan is remembered as a clever and ambitious king who was the bitter enemy of the Assyrian kings Sargon II and Sennacherib. Sending envoys from one country to another for political reasons was not unusual (cf. 18:10-3; 30:1-7); however, it was most unusual for a king to send congratulatory letters and a present to a far distant king on his recovery from illness. Also, there was a vast difference in stature and rank between the king of Babylon and Hezekiah of Judah. There are two probable reasons for this visit from the Babylonian envoys. One was to investigate the miracle of the sundial, because Merodach-baladan had heard "that Hezekiah had been very sick and that he had recovered" (39:1). The parallel account in 2 Chronicles 32:31 adds that they came to ask him about the miraculous sign that had occurred in the land. Another reason generally assumed is that the Babylonian king needed all the assistance against Assyria that he could get. Hezekiah was also eager to get help against the Assyrian threat, so they were both using each other for their own interests.

Hezekiah "was delighted with" the Babylonian envoys (39:2). Merodach-baladan had recently defeated the armies of Sennacherib, which helps shed light on Hezekiah's now putting his hopes in Babylon. Without consulting either the Lord or Isaiah, he showed the envoys his vast treasures, his abundant food supplies, and his military provisions. God had given Hezekiah great wealth, so the visitors were impressed (2 Chr 32:27-29). Apparently, since paying the heavy tribute to Sennacherib, he had accumulated considerable wealth, the extent of which is indicated in 2 Chronicles 32:27-29. Much of this may have been from gifts sent to him following his sickness (2 Chr 32:23). By showing the men from Babylon all his wealth, it appears that he was trying to impress upon them that he was a king worthy of high regard. "Kingdom" probably does not refer to a tour of his territory but to his administration.

It is difficult to picture a king gladly showing a potential enemy his whole arsenal and wealth, but such is the power of flattery. Just as his forefather David succumbed to the lust of the flesh, and Solomon yielded to vanity and pomp, so Hezekiah, one of Judah's most admired kings, yielded to flattery and pride.

◆      ## 2. Isaiah's counsel to Hezekiah (39:3-8)

³Then Isaiah the prophet went to King Hezekiah and asked him, "What did those men want? Where were they from?"

Hezekiah replied, "They came from the distant land of Babylon."

⁴"What did they see in your palace?" asked Isaiah.

"They saw everything," Hezekiah replied. "I showed them everything I own—all my royal treasuries."

⁵Then Isaiah said to Hezekiah, "Listen to this message from the LORD of Heaven's Armies: ⁶'The time is coming when everything in your palace—all the treasures stored up by your ancestors until now—will be carried off to Babylon. Nothing will be left,' says the LORD. ⁷'Some of your very own sons will be taken away into exile. They will become eunuchs who will serve in the palace of Babylon's king.'"

⁸Then Hezekiah said to Isaiah, "This message you have given me from the LORD is good." For the king was thinking, "At least there will be peace and security during my lifetime."

### NOTES

**39:3** *the prophet went to King Hezekiah.* Nathan the prophet similarly confronted King David (2 Sam 12:1, 7).

*from the distant land of Babylon.* It probably fed Hezekiah's pride to observe that these visitors came from so far away to see his holdings.

**39:4** *everything.* This is matched by the "everything" in 39:6.

**39:5** *LORD of Heaven's Armies.* This title is missing in the parallel text of 2 Kgs 20:16.

**39:6** *carried off to Babylon.* This is the first explicit mention of Babylon as Jerusalem's conqueror, although the Babylonian captivity is implied in 14:3-4.

**39:7** *your very own sons.* King Jehoiachin was one of them (2 Kgs 24:15).

*eunuchs.* Heb. *saris* [TH5631, ZH6247]; the term came to be used of officials in general, apart from the issue of castration.

### COMMENTARY

After the envoys departed, Isaiah questioned the king about his guests. Perhaps the full titles ("Isaiah the prophet" and "King Hezekiah") are used here because one was the spokesman for the Lord, and the other was the head of political affairs (39:3). The prophet straightforwardly asked about the origin of the men and what they had said. Hezekiah responded with pride, "They came from the distant land of Babylon" (39:3). In other words, he imagined that they had come all the way from distant Babylon to see him.

Isaiah then asked the king, "What did they see in your palace?" (39:4). Hezekiah admitted that he had shown them everything; he had given them a complete sight-seeing tour of all the treasures and resources of Judah, but he had never asked for guidance from the Lord.

Isaiah had denounced the alliances of Ahaz with Assyria and of Judah's politicians with Egypt, and he was just as ready to denounce any alliance or relationship of Hezekiah with Babylon. From the perspective of the prophet (speaking for God), all such associations of God's people with the world were a sinful rejection of their dependence on the Lord.

Hezekiah engaged in a rash display of pride when he showed off everything in his treasure-houses to the pagan envoys. The men from Babylon would not forget about all the silver and gold they had seen, and one day they would return to claim it. The prophet predicted, "all the treasures stored up by your ancestors until now— will be carried off to Babylon" (39:6) and "some of your very own sons will be taken away into exile" (39:7). This was Isaiah's first unmistakable reference to Babylon as the land of captivity. Isaiah's predictions about Assyria came true in 701 BC and this prophecy about Babylon would also be fulfilled (over a century later).

Hezekiah's treasures would be carried off to Babylon, and the people of Judah, including some of Hezekiah's own descendants, would be taken away and "become eunuchs who will serve in the palace of Babylon's king." Although "eunuchs" (39:7) can refer specifically to castrated men, it is undoubtedly used here of government officers in general.

Hezekiah's reply that "This message you have given me from the LORD is good" (39:8) sounds puzzling in view of the content of the message, but the good news was that the judgment would not come within Hezekiah's lifetime. Despite this element of selfishness in his response, the king undoubtedly was also grateful that the nation would now have peace and that he could end his reign in tranquility. Until the destruction of Sennacherib's army, however, neither the king nor his people enjoyed much peace or security.

## ◆ III. God's Comfort for His People (40:1–66:24)
### A. God's Deliverance for His People (40:1–48:22)
#### 1. God's comfort for Israel (40:1-31)

"Comfort, comfort my people,"
  says your God.
2 "Speak tenderly to Jerusalem.
  Tell her that her sad days are gone
    and her sins are pardoned.
  Yes, the LORD has punished her
    twice over
    for all her sins."

3 Listen! It's the voice of someone
    shouting,
"Clear the way through the wilderness
  for the LORD!
Make a straight highway through
  the wasteland
  for our God!
4 Fill in the valleys,
  and level the mountains and hills.
Straighten the curves,
  and smooth out the rough
    places.

5 Then the glory of the LORD will be
  revealed,
and all people will see it together.
The LORD has spoken!"*

6 A voice said, "Shout!"
  I asked, "What should I shout?"

"Shout that people are like the grass.
  Their beauty fades as quickly
  as the flowers in a field.
7 The grass withers and the flowers fade
  beneath the breath of the LORD.
  And so it is with people.
8 The grass withers and the flowers fade,
  but the word of our God stands
    forever."

9 O Zion, messenger of good news,
  shout from the mountaintops!
Shout it louder, O Jerusalem.*
  Shout, and do not be afraid.

Tell the towns of Judah,
  "Your God is coming!"
[10] Yes, the Sovereign LORD is coming
    in power.
  He will rule with a powerful arm.
  See, he brings his reward with him
    as he comes.
[11] He will feed his flock like a shepherd.
  He will carry the lambs in his arms,
  holding them close to his heart.
  He will gently lead the mother sheep
    with their young.

[12] Who else has held the oceans in his
    hand?
  Who has measured off the heavens
    with his fingers?
  Who else knows the weight of the earth
    or has weighed the mountains and
    hills on a scale?
[13] Who is able to advise the Spirit of the
    LORD?*
  Who knows enough to give him
    advice or teach him?
[14] Has the LORD ever needed anyone's
    advice?
  Does he need instruction about
    what is good?
  Did someone teach him what is right
    or show him the path of justice?

[15] No, for all the nations of the world
    are but a drop in the bucket.
  They are nothing more
    than dust on the scales.
  He picks up the whole earth
    as though it were a grain of sand.
[16] All the wood in Lebanon's forests
    and all Lebanon's animals would
    not be enough
  to make a burnt offering worthy
    of our God.
[17] The nations of the world are worth
    nothing to him.
  In his eyes they count for less than
    nothing—
  mere emptiness and froth.

[18] To whom can you compare God?
  What image can you find to
    resemble him?

[19] Can he be compared to an idol formed
    in a mold,
  overlaid with gold, and decorated
    with silver chains?
[20] Or if people are too poor for that,
    they might at least choose wood
    that won't decay
  and a skilled craftsman
  to carve an image that won't fall
    down!

[21] Haven't you heard? Don't you
    understand?
  Are you deaf to the words of God—
  the words he gave before the world
    began?
  Are you so ignorant?
[22] God sits above the circle of the earth.
  The people below seem like
    grasshoppers to him!
  He spreads out the heavens like
    a curtain
  and makes his tent from them.
[23] He judges the great people of the
    world
  and brings them all to nothing.
[24] They hardly get started, barely taking
    root,
  when he blows on them and they
    wither.
  The wind carries them off like chaff.

[25] "To whom will you compare me?
  Who is my equal?" asks the
    Holy One.

[26] Look up into the heavens.
  Who created all the stars?
  He brings them out like an army,
    one after another,
  calling each by its name.
  Because of his great power and
    incomparable strength,
  not a single one is missing.
[27] O Jacob, how can you say the LORD
    does not see your troubles?
  O Israel, how can you say God
    ignores your rights?
[28] Have you never heard?
  Have you never understood?
  The LORD is the everlasting God,

the Creator of all the earth.
He never grows weak or weary.
No one can measure the depths
of his understanding.
<sup>29</sup> He gives power to the weak
and strength to the powerless.
<sup>30</sup> Even youths will become weak
and tired,

and young men will fall in
exhaustion.
<sup>31</sup> But those who trust in the LORD
will find new strength.
They will soar high on wings
like eagles.
They will run and not grow weary.
They will walk and not faint.

**40:3-5** Greek version reads *He is a voice shouting in the wilderness, / "Prepare the way for the LORD's coming! / Clear a road for our God! / Fill in the valleys, / and level the mountains and hills. / And then the glory of the LORD will be revealed, / and all people will see the salvation sent from God. / The LORD has spoken!"* Compare Matt 3:3; Mark 1:3; Luke 3:4-6. **40:9** Or *O messenger of good news, shout to Zion from the mountaintops! Shout it louder to Jerusalem.* **40:13** Greek version reads *Who can know the LORD's thoughts?* Compare Rom 11:34; 1 Cor 2:16.

## NOTES

**40:2** *speak tenderly.* Lit., "speak to the heart." Other renderings are, "speak kindly" (NASB, REB, NCV, CEV), and "encourage" (TEV). This idiom, which occurs nine times in the OT, is an expression of encouragement, reassurance, and renewed hope. Five of these occurrences describe a lover wooing his beloved.

*sins . . . pardoned.* The noun *'awon* [TH5771, ZH6411] (sins) and verb *ratsah* [TH7521A, ZH8355] (pardoned), appear in Lev 26:41, 43, meaning "to accept punishment for iniquity."

*twice over.* The Heb. says that the people received double from the Lord for all their sins, which is perhaps a reference to 51:19. Perhaps this double payment reflected the double calamities described in 51:19. The expression seems to refer to what is amply sufficient (cf. Jer 17:18; Rev 18:6). Motyer (1993:299) notes that the unusual "double" is a dual form of the noun from the root *kepel* [TH3718, ZH4101], meaning "to fold double" (cf. Exod 26:9; 28:16; 39:9; Ezek 21:19). Some other translations are, "double" (NASB, NRSV, NIV, GW, CEV, ESV, NJPS), "double measure" (REB), "twice" (NCV), and "in full" (TEV).

**40:5** *glory of the LORD will be revealed.* Some distinguish epiphany (God's presence precipitating dramatic disruptions in nature) from theophany (God's appearance to reveal his will by speech). In an epiphany, God usually approaches from a distant place on earth, but in a theophany, God descends from an exalted height to a sacred place on earth. The latter is the case here, and the "central fulfillment lies in the coming of Christ, the effulgence of the glory of God (Heb 1:3), by whom we have knowledge of God (2 Cor 4:6)" (Ridderbos 1985:340). John the Baptist claimed only to be the heralding voice (John 1:23) that introduced the one in whom the glory of God would be revealed, "the glory of the only Son of the Father" (John 1:14).

*all people.* Lit., "all flesh." This is used of people elsewhere, in the same sense (cf. Joel 2:28).

*the LORD has spoken.* The Heb. has "for the mouth of the LORD has spoken" (*ki pi yhwh dibber*). This exact Heb. phrase is also found in 1:20 and 58:14. Outside of Isaiah, it is found only in 1 Kgs 14:11; Joel 3:8 [4:8]; Obad 18; and Mic 4:4.

**40:7** *And so it is.* This translates the Heb. *'aken* [TH403, ZH434] ("surely"), a particle often used to emphasize the unexpected. Note the renderings in the modern versions: "Surely" (NIV), "Indeed" (NJPS), and "So then" (NAB). See the use of this particle in Gen 28:16; Exod 2:14.

*people.* The imagery of mortal life as perishing vegetation is also found in Job 5:25; Ps 90:5; 92:7; 103:15.

**40:9** *messenger of good news.* Heb. *mebassereth* [TH1319B, ZH1413]. Although the root for "good news" can be used of bad news (1 Sam 4:17), it generally means "good news" and matches the NT word for "gospel." Since Isaiah used the feminine form, the NLT presents the picture of Zion receiving the news and running with it to the surrounding townships (but cf. the NLT mg: "O messenger . . . shout to Zion"). The NAB also makes Zion the subject and herald of the good news. The REB has "you that bring good news to Zion." The NJB has the ambiguous, "Go up on a high mountain, messenger of Zion. Shout as loud as you can, messenger of Jerusalem!" At any rate, Jerusalem and Zion are certainly parallel here.

**40:10** *Sovereign LORD.* This translates the Heb. (*'adonay yhwh* [TH136/3068, ZH151/3378]), which is, lit., "Lord Yahweh" but has been traditionally rendered "Lord GOD" (KJV, NASB, NRSV, REB, ESV, NJPS), but is also translated "Sovereign LORD" (NIV, TEV), and "Almighty LORD" (GW). The problem arises in English because two different Heb. words are both translated Lord and LORD. The NJB, which regularly uses "Yahweh" for LORD, is able to solve the English problem by using "Lord Yahweh" here.

*powerful arm.* This imagery appears more often in Isaiah than in any other prophet (cf. 48:14; 51:5, 9; 52:10; 53:1; 59:16; 62:8; 63:5, 12)

**40:13** *Spirit of the LORD.* Although "Spirit" is capitalized in the KJV, "spirit" is the rendering used by the NEB, REB, JB, NJB, and NAB. The RSV had "Spirit" but the NRSV changed it to "spirit." The NIV has "mind" in the text, with a footnote indicating the possibility of "spirit" or "Spirit." The NJPS has "who has plumbed the mind of the LORD," and the NCV has "who has known the mind of the LORD."

*Who knows enough to give him advice or teach him?* Paul refers to this verse at the end of his survey of God's dealings with Israel (Rom 11:34) and in 1 Cor 2:16, which concludes an apologetic discourse containing other allusions to Isaiah. In the course of his lengthy discussion in Rom 9–11, Paul quotes Isa 1:9; 6:9; 8:14; 10:22-23; 28:16, 22; 53:1; and 65:1-2 to illustrate Israel's fall, and 27:9; 52:7; 59:20 as evidence of their final recovery.

**40:15** *drop in the bucket.* The Heb. is imprecise but the point is clear: the nations are insignificant as compared to the creator God. The versions use "drop of a bucket" (KJV), "drop of the bucket" (NAB), "drop from a bucket" (NRSV), "drops from a bucket" (REB), "drop in a bucket" (NJB, NJPS), and "drop of water" (TEV).

*whole earth.* The Heb. *'iyim* [TH339, ZH362] is usually translated "islands" or "coastlands" to indicate distant or remote lands. New versions try to capture this: "islands" (NIV), "coasts and islands" (REB, NJB), and "coastlands" (NAB, NJPS).

**40:22** *circle of the earth.* This seems to be unique language in the imagery of the ancient Near East and the noun is found only here in Isaiah (elsewhere only in Prov 8:27 and Job 22:14). Motyer (1993:306) suggests that the reference here is to the "heavens or the horizon, both of which are circular to the observer's eye."

**40:26** *all the stars.* It is said that on a clear, moonless night about 3,000 stars are visible to the unaided eye. A small telescope increases the number to 100,000. These stars are all in our Milky Way galaxy, which numbers about 100 billion stars. Around 100 billion of such galaxies are known to exist. What an incredible way for the Creator to reveal his glory!

**40:31** *trust in the LORD.* Probably the more literal reading is something like "hope in the LORD," but this sounds weaker in English than in the Heb., which means "look to in trust and confidence." The Heb. root (*qwh* [TH6960, ZH7747]) is found in the name of the national anthem of Israel, "The Hope" (Hatikvah).

*will find new.* Heb. *khalap* [TH2498, ZH2736] is used again with the same object in the next verse (41:1) where it is translated "bring your strongest arguments." The verb is used in 24:5, where Isaiah uses it of changing laws. It is used of changing clothing in Ps 102:26 [27].

*strength.* Heb. *koakh* [TH3581, ZH3946]. A word found 125 times in the OT, a dozen times in Isaiah. The idea of "new" comes from the verb.

*run.* Heb. *ruts* [TH7323, ZH8132]. The common word for "run, rush" found about 102 times in the OT but only three times in Isaiah.

*grow weary.* Heb. *yaga'* [TH3021, ZH3333]; found about 26 times in the OT, twelve of these in Isaiah. The root idea is weariness or being worn out (cf. Prov 23:4; Ps 6:6).

*faint.* Heb. *ya'ap* [TH3286, ZH3615]. The idea is "fatigue, exhaustion." It is used four times in this chapter.

## COMMENTARY

**Overview of Isaiah 40–66.** The last section of Isaiah (chs 40–66), is rich in theological insight and spiritual treasure. It is generally recognized as one of the great masterpieces in world literature and is often quoted. The passion and evangelical concern found here helped earn for Isaiah the title, "Evangelist of the Old Testament."

In contrast to the first part of Isaiah (chs 1–39), which emphasizes judgment, the last part of the book emphasizes comfort and restoration. These final chapters can be divided into three sections of nine chapters each (chs 40–48; 49–57; 58–66). The first two sections each conclude with the statement, "There is no peace for the wicked" (48:22; 57:21). The first section focuses on the theme of the deliverance of God's people through the instrumentality of Cyrus, the second on the theme of the Suffering Servant and the glory of Zion. The third and concluding section summarizes the future blessed condition of the true Israel in contrast with the doom and miserable condition of apostates. It has been suggested that these three parts correspond to and develop the idea of each of the three phrases describing the condition of Jerusalem in 40:2. Thus, following the structure of 40:2, "her sad days are gone" (cf. chs 40–48); "her sins are pardoned" (cf. chs 49–57); and "the LORD has punished her twice over for all her sins" (cf. chs 58–66).

Isaiah 40:1–48:22 focuses on God as Creator and Redeemer. The section includes the grand themes of God's comfort, power, and purpose. Special attention is given to Israel's liberation and restoration. The comfort that comes from confidence in the eventual return from exile depends on God's ability to keep his promise. As proof of his power and claim to sovereignty, attention is given to his ability to predict events and then bring them to pass.

Throughout these chapters, the Lord is presented as great and glorious in contrast with the dumb idols; he is victorious in his conflict with them. Since only he can foretell the end from the beginning, the Lord asserts his right to Israel's faith. His covenant name, Yahweh, occurs sixty-six times in these chapters, and is most appropriate in this context.

These chapters introduce three individuals that the Lord called to his service. God would raise up Cyrus, his shepherd, from the east to deliver his people from Babylon. Israel was his blind and deaf servant, and the third, the perfect Servant, was the one in whom his purpose would be fulfilled. The prediction and fulfillment of the captivity and the return of Judah, the raising up of Cyrus over a century yet in the future, and finally, the appearance of the messianic Servant several hundred years in the future, would all be decisive proof of the Lord's omniscience and omnipotence. Only the absolute sovereignty of God could predict and bring such things to pass, in contrast to the impotence of the pagan deities. Manufactured idols are helpless to assist those who look to them for salvation, and they are unable to hinder or frustrate the Lord's sovereign purposes.

**Comfort for God's People.** The opening verses of Isaiah 40 set the tone for the remainder of the book. The call is urgent, as reflected in the use of the imperative and of repetition for emphasis (Geller 1984:413). "Comfort" (40:1) is the first in a series of imperatives in the Hebrew: "comfort . . . speak tenderly . . . tell her," and it is repeated for emphasis. The expression "says your God" (40:1) is a reminder that the comfort comes from their God and is based on their relationship to him. The expression "Speak tenderly to Jerusalem" (40:2) is lit. "speak to the heart of" (cf. Gen 34:3; Ruth 2:13). From this point on, the terms "Jerusalem" and "Zion" are increasingly used as references to God's covenant people.

The good news is that "her sad days are gone" (the 70-year captivity was seen as almost over), and "the LORD has punished her twice over for all her sins" (40:2). This means that God had accepted the punishment of their sin as satisfactory; the passive of the verb is used elsewhere only of God's acceptance of the Levitical bloody offerings (Lev 1:4; 7:18; 19:7; 22:23, 25, 27; cf. Motyer 1993:299).

The passage opens with a human voice ("someone shouting"; 40:3a) but ends with a word from the LORD (40:5). It contrasts the present scene—"clear the way through the wilderness" (40:3)—with the future "glory of the LORD [that] will be revealed" (40:5). "The voice of someone shouting" (40:3) comes from a messenger that will appear in the power and spirit of Elijah the prophet, fulfilled by John the Baptist (Matt 11:13-14). The gospel writers apply Isaiah 40:3 to him (Matt 3:1-4; Mark 1:1-4; Luke 1:76-78).

Ancient Near Eastern monarchs would sometimes employ special agents to clear the roadways before their approach. This would include cutting trees, leveling and smoothing the road, and often much more. Many examples could be given of this practice of literally leveling hilly areas and filling in low areas (at very great cost) to prepare the way for a dignitary. Even in modern construction, the terms "level down" and "fill in" are used with reference to building roads through mountainous terrain. It is especially noteworthy that the writer of this chapter used the language "make straight," since Babylonia is in an alluvial plain unlike the rugged terrain of Israel. This would be unusual imagery coming from a Deutero-Isaiah living on the flat plains of Mesopotamia.

When God appeared among his people, it was often said that the glory of the Lord was revealed to them (cf. Exod 16:7, 10; 24:15), but here we read that when the "glory of the LORD will be revealed . . . all people will see it together" (40:5). In contrast, the frailty of humans is compared to temporary, withering foliage—the kind of glory found in the "flowers in a field" (40:6-8; cf. 37:27). In the graphic expression, "beneath the breath of the LORD" (40:7; cf. 40:24), the Hebrew for "breath" can also mean "spirit"—a convenient double meaning for the work of the Lord's spirit on humankind as compared to an abrasive wind in nature (cf. Ps 139:7). In contrast to the passing glory of man, "the word of our God stands forever" (40:8) as a basis for the previous promises (40:2, 5). The words of 40:6-8 are quoted in 1 Pet 1:24-25.

According to custom, a messenger of good news from a battle scene would go to the city to report the results of a crucial conflict (2 Sam 18:26). In this instance, however, the herald shouts from the mountaintops to tell Jerusalem and the towns of Judah the good news that, "Your God is coming" (40:9) and that he will rule "with a powerful arm" (40:10). This is the first reference to the Lord's "arm" in this major section (chs 40ff); it depicts personal strength in action, but in contrast "arms" are used in the very next verse to describe how the Lord will compassionately "carry the lambs in his arms" (40:11). God revealed his superior power by defeating Babylon (cf. 52:7-11), and the "reward" (40:10) probably refers to the people God was bringing with him (cf. 62:11).

God's covenant people are appropriately called a "flock" (40:11), and the Lord is depicted as a kind shepherd who is careful not to drive the sheep faster than they can go—a vivid and true picture of the good shepherd who tenderly yet strongly cared for his sheep. This shepherd imagery is also found in 49:9-10 as well as in the Psalms (Pss 77:20; 78:52; 80:1). Tenderness and compassion reflect well the theme of comfort introduced in 40:1 and 2.

In 40:12-14, Isaiah describes the infinite power and wisdom of God who controls the whole universe with effortless ease (cf. Rev 4:11), and the question is raised, "Who else has held the oceans in his hand?" (40:12). The measurement of the earth's waters must be precise—there must be enough but not too much (cf. Job 28:25; 38:8). The expression "in his hand" (40:12; lit., "in the hollow of his hand") is an anthropomorphism that fits with the expression "his arm" (40:10; cf. Prov 30:4, which describes God who "holds the wind in his fists").

In the question, "Who is able to advise the Spirit of the LORD?" (40:13), if the Holy Spirit is the referent, the language may reflect the creation and the Spirit's role in it (for more on the Holy Spirit in Isaiah, see Wonsuk 1989). Paul quotes this verse in Romans 11:34 and 1 Cor 2:16. The Lord doesn't "need instruction about what is good" (40:14). The theme of the preceding verse is continued in 40:14, "has the LORD ever needed anyone's advice?" The obvious answer is that no one taught God how to create the universe! When we come to the Lord, we have reached the absolute in wisdom and power.

Beginning with 40:15, the glory of God is contrasted with that of mortals (40:15-17, 23, 28-31), with idols (40:19-20), and with nature (40:21-22, 26). The effectiveness of Isaiah's description is enhanced by the use of a series of rhetorical questions at the beginning of the various paragraphs. The structure of 40:12-31 is similar to that of many psalms of praise that extol God's majesty (40:11-26) and his goodness to mankind (40:27-31).

For the Lord, the nations are but "a drop in a bucket," or mere "dust on the scales"; "he picks up the whole earth as though it were a grain of sand" (40:15). All the famous trees of Lebanon and all its sacrificial animals were insufficient to pre-sent him adequate sacrifice (40:16), and all "the nations of the world are worth nothing to him" (40:17).

A contest between the Lord and the idols is introduced in 40:18-20, and this theme continues into chapter 48. God is not only greater than the nations, but is also superior to the idols that the nations worship. Isaiah repeatedly denounced the idolatry practiced in Israel (cf. 1:31; 2:18, 20; 10:11; 17:8, 10; 27:9; 30:22; 31:6, 7). Idols can be made beautiful if several craftsmen carefully labor over them, but then they must be careful not to let the idols topple or collapse. Next Isaiah focuses on the homemade character of these idols; they are fashioned and "overlaid with gold, and decorated with silver chains" by the workers who make them (40:19). The prophet ironically presses the point that these fancy images representing their gods originated in the shops of those who manufactured them. This note of sarcasm is developed more fully in chapter 44.

In 40:22-28, a series of blunt questions is put to the people to turn them back to what they should have known from the beginning. This seems to be an appeal to history. From the beginning, Israel had been warned against idolatry (Exod 20:4-6; Deut 5:8-10), and had repeatedly witnessed the inability of idols to save them from disaster. However, the people continued to worship the product of their own minds instead of the one true and perfect God who created and sustains the universe. In contrast to the lifeless idols that must be fixed on a stand, "God sits above the circle of the earth" (40:22) and "spreads out the heavens like a curtain" (cf. Ps 104:2). The people, like grasshoppers (40:22), were small and insignificant (cf. Num 13:33). In 40:15-17, God's sovereignty over the nations was emphasized; 40:22-24 stresses his full control over the rulers of those nations. Whether Sennacherib or Nebuchad-nezzar, all rulers come under his control and will reign only as long as the Lord decrees (cf. 40:6-7). The incomparable God "judges the great people of the world and brings them all to nothing" (40:23). They are like plants that have barely taken root and begun to grow when "he blows on them and they wither" (40:24), and are blown away like chaff in the wind (cf. 17:13). The typical whirlwind of the region sweeps along the country, often raising sand, straw, and other stubble to great heights before dispersing them. Travelers to the Middle East in the past have written vivid accounts of these miniature tornadoes.

Once again (40:25ff), the conclusion is drawn that no appropriate likeness can be compared to such a majestic God (cf. 40:18). The question, "to whom will you compare me?" comes from the mouth of the Holy One (40:25). Since God is supe-rior to idols (40:19-20), nature (40:22), and mortals (40:23-24), to whom can he be compared? The Holy One is without equal. Since people were prone to worship the stars in the sky and to believe that they controlled human lives, 40:25-26 deals with this subject. The Lord created all the stars and fully controls their orderly march across the heavens (cf. Job 38:32). Not one star is missing or out of place (cf. Isa 34:16); not one fails to make muster when God marshals their host. Such fantas-tic power defies description, and 40:26 uses four different expressions ("created . . .

brings them out . . . calling each by its name . . . not a single one is missing") to convey God's sovereign control.

In light of the description of God in 40:12-26, the people of Israel should have had no doubts about his ability to fulfill his promises, yet there was a feeling that God had overlooked Israel's plight and was unconcerned about her fate. How easy it is to believe in the infinite power of God and at the same time to feel that he is unable to meet our personal needs. Isaiah had to remind Israel of God's greatness—again, by asking whether they had "heard" or "understood" (40:28; cf. 40:21).

Then Isaiah makes his grand statement: "The LORD is the everlasting God, the Creator of all the earth" (40:28). Because he is the Creator, he is the inexhaustible source of strength for his people, so that in all their weariness, he renews their strength (40:29). Even young people eventually become weary, but those who find their strength in the Lord "will soar high on wings like eagles" (40:31; cf. Ps 103:5; for the metaphor for strength, cf. Exod 19:4; Deut 32:11).

◆     ## 2. God's power in history (41:1-29)

"Listen in silence before me, you lands
   beyond the sea.
Bring your strongest arguments.
Come now and speak.
   The court is ready for your case.

2 "Who has stirred up this king from
   the east,
   rightly calling him to God's service?
Who gives this man victory over many
   nations
   and permits him to trample their
     kings underfoot?
With his sword, he reduces armies
   to dust.
   With his bow, he scatters them like
     chaff before the wind.
3 He chases them away and goes on
   safely,
   though he is walking over
     unfamiliar ground.
4 Who has done such mighty deeds,
   summoning each new generation
     from the beginning of time?
It is I, the LORD, the First and the Last.
   I alone am he."

5 The lands beyond the sea watch
   in fear.
   Remote lands tremble and mobilize
     for war.

6 The idol makers encourage one
   another,
   saying to each other, "Be strong!"
7 The carver encourages the goldsmith,
   and the molder helps at the anvil.
"Good," they say. "It's coming along
   fine."
Carefully they join the parts together,
   then fasten the thing in place so it
     won't fall over.

8 "But as for you, Israel my servant,
   Jacob my chosen one,
   descended from Abraham my
     friend,
9 I have called you back from the ends
   of the earth,
   saying, 'You are my servant.'
For I have chosen you
   and will not throw you away.
10 Don't be afraid, for I am with you.
   Don't be discouraged, for I am
     your God.
I will strengthen you and help you.
   I will hold you up with my victorious
     right hand.

11 "See, all your angry enemies lie there,
   confused and humiliated.
Anyone who opposes you will die
   and come to nothing.

¹²You will look in vain
    for those who tried to conquer you.
Those who attack you
    will come to nothing.
¹³For I hold you by your right hand—
    I, the LORD your God.
And I say to you,
    'Don't be afraid. I am here to help
    you.
¹⁴Though you are a lowly worm, O Jacob,
    don't be afraid, people of Israel,
    for I will help you.
I am the LORD, your Redeemer.
    I am the Holy One of Israel.'
¹⁵You will be a new threshing
    instrument
    with many sharp teeth.
You will tear your enemies apart,
    making chaff of mountains.
¹⁶You will toss them into the air,
    and the wind will blow them all
    away;
    a whirlwind will scatter them.
Then you will rejoice in the LORD.
    You will glory in the Holy One of
    Israel.

¹⁷"When the poor and needy search for
    water and there is none,
    and their tongues are parched from
    thirst,
then I, the LORD, will answer them.
    I, the God of Israel, will never
    abandon them.
¹⁸I will open up rivers for them on the
    high plateaus.
    I will give them fountains of water
    in the valleys.
I will fill the desert with pools of water.
    Rivers fed by springs will flow
    across the parched ground.
¹⁹I will plant trees in the barren desert—
    cedar, acacia, myrtle, olive, cypress,
    fir, and pine.
²⁰I am doing this so all who see this
    miracle
    will understand what it means—
that it is the LORD who has done this,
    the Holy One of Israel who created it.

²¹"Present the case for your idols,"
    says the LORD.
"Let them show what they can do,"
    says the King of Israel.*
²²"Let them try to tell us what happened
    long ago
    so that we may consider the
    evidence.
Or let them tell us what the future
    holds,
    so we can know what's going to
    happen.
²³Yes, tell us what will occur in the
    days ahead.
    Then we will know you are gods.
In fact, do anything—good or bad!
    Do something that will amaze and
    frighten us.
²⁴But no! You are less than nothing
    and can do nothing at all.
    Those who choose you pollute
    themselves.

²⁵"But I have stirred up a leader who
    will come from the north.
    I have called him by name from
    the east.
I will give him victory over kings
    and princes.
    He will trample them as a potter
    treads on clay.
²⁶"Who told you from the beginning
    that this would happen?
Who predicted this,
    making you admit that he
    was right?
    No one said a word!
²⁷I was the first to tell Zion,
    'Look! Help is on the way!'*
    I will send Jerusalem a messenger
    with good news.
²⁸Not one of your idols told you this.
    Not one gave any answer when
    I asked.
²⁹See, they are all foolish, worthless
    things.
    All your idols are as empty as
    the wind.

41:21 Hebrew *the King of Jacob.* See note on 14:1.   41:27 Or *'Look! They are coming home.'*

## NOTES

**41:2 *stirred up this king from the east, rightly calling him to God's service.*** This Heb. clause is variously translated in the modern translations: "stirred up one from the east calling him in righteousness" (NIV); "roused a victor from the east, summoned him to service" (NRSV); "raised up . . . greeted by victory wherever he goes" (REB); "stirred up . . . the champion of justice" (NAB); and "raised . . . him whom saving justice summons in its train" (NJB). The KJV has "raised up the righteous man from the east, called him to his foot." The Hebrew *tsedeq* [TH6664, ZH7406] has a great range of meaning from "righteous" to "victorious" (NIDOTTE 3:744-769).

**41:5 *lands beyond the sea.*** This translates one Heb. term (*'iyim* [TH339, ZH362]) that is often translated "islands." It is found fifteen times in the OT, fourteen of them in Isaiah. The reference is to the coastlands of the Mediterranean, and the whole verse (including the next line, "remote lands") indicates the known world at that time.

**41:8 *Jacob my chosen one.*** The terms "Israel . . . Jacob" in the first two lines are parallel expressions (cf. 41:14; 40:27; 42:24; 43:1, 22, 28; 44:1, 5, 21, 23; 45:4; 46:3; 48:1, 12; see also Deut 4:37; 7:6-7; Rom 11:5).

**Abraham my friend.*** The Heb. *'ohabi* [TH157A, ZH170] means "my loving one." The root for the word "love" is a term sometimes used in covenant language that refers to alignment of loyalty. The Arabic term, *khalil-ullah*, "Friend of God," is a title for Abraham in Islam (Quran 4:124). Most translations use "friend" although the word sounds weak in English.

**41:10 *my victorious right hand.*** The traditional lit. rendering is "right hand of my righteousness" (KJV). Modern versions, recognizing the semantic range of the Heb. word *tsedeq* [TH6664, ZH7406], have "my righteous right hand" (NASB), "my victorious right hand" (NRSV, GW, REB, NJPS), "my right hand of justice" (NAB), and "my saving right hand" (NJB).

**41:14 *lowly worm, O Jacob.*** The Heb. word *tole'ah* (worm) also appears in 14:11 and 66:24. Here its weakness is in view as it is trodden underfoot (cf. Job 25:6; Ps 22:6); it probably refers to the weak and oppressed condition of the Israelites in exile.

**people of Israel.*** The verse involves a parallel between the worm (*tole'ah* [TH8438A, ZH9357] of Jacob and the people (*methey* [TH4962, ZH5493]) of Israel. The meaning of Heb. *methey* is uncertain. Some understand the meaning to be "dead men" of Israel (cf. Aquila, Theodotion, Jerome, and DSS). Possibly the Akkadian cognate *mutu* (man) is involved here. Modern translations vary: "men" (NJPS, ESV), "insect" (NRSV), "maggot" (REB, NAB), "little handful" (NJB), "louse" (NEB). A close parallel in Gen 34:30 and Deut 4:27 suggests "few in number," which may be supported by the LXX (cf. NIV's "little").

**Redeemer.*** The Heb. word *go'el* [TH1350B, ZH1457] refers to the nearest relative who bought back (redeemed) alienated property (Lev 25:14, 23-25; Ruth 3:11-12; 4:1-6) or an enslaved person (Lev 25:48). It is used as a metaphor for Israel's redemption from Egypt (Exod 6:6) or from the Exile, with the Lord as the Redeemer.

**Holy One of Israel.*** First appearing in 1:4, this is a favorite title for God used by Isaiah throughout his book (see 43:14-15; 45:11; 47:4; 48:17; 49:7; 54:5; 57:15).

**41:19 *trees.*** Seven trees are listed, which could reflect the idea of fullness. Isaiah has a rich vocabulary of plant names, some of which may never be identified with certainty. Forests were not part of the Babylonian landscape, but Israel was heavily forested; the setting is clearly Palestinian, not Mesopotamian. The one tree that was typical of Babylonia, the palm, is not mentioned. The writer had to have been familiar with Israel.

**41:22 *what happened long ago.*** Lit., "former things" (cf. 42:9; 43:9; 46:9; 48:3), with special reference to God's prophecies about his people in chs 1-39.

*what's going to happen.* Lit., "things to come" (cf. 42:23; 44:7; 45:11; 46:10), with special reference to the Lord's future plans for his new Zion as described in chs 40–66.

**41:25 *from the north . . . from the east.*** A "king from the east" is mentioned in 41:2 and is now described as coming "from the north and east" (the Heb. has only "north" in this verse). This was true of Cyrus, who was from Anshan, a region of eastern Elam, east of Babylon. After becoming king of Persia, Cyrus conquered Media to the north, uniting the Medes and Persians, so he was from both the east and the north.

## COMMENTARY

The preceding chapter (Isa 40) contains the great promise of the exiles' return to Judah; in 41:2 we are introduced to the agent whom God will raise up to accomplish this deliverance. God demonstrated his superiority over the idolaters and their idols by his ability to predict the rise to power of Cyrus, king of Persia.

In this chapter and the following one, we are introduced to a series of servants through whom God would accomplish his work. First we meet Cyrus, through whom the Lord would deliver his people from Babylon (41:2-7, 25; 44:26-45; 46:11; 48:15). Next, Israel is introduced (41:8-10; 42:18-25; 43:8-13; 44:1-5, 21-28; 45:4; 48:20-22), and at the beginning of the next chapter, the third and greatest is presented—the perfect Servant, who holds a prominent place in the remainder of the book (42:1-9; 49:1-13; 50:4-11; 52:13–53:12).

The great Persian ruler Cyrus is referred to a number of times between 41:2 and 48:14; the emphasis is not on his pomp and splendor, but on the power of God who raised him up. From east of Babylon, in what is now Iran, Cyrus moved through country after country, conquering every king in his path. Shortly after 550 BC, Cyrus was able to unify the Medes and Persians and to defeat the powerful kingdom of Lydia in Asia Minor. Then he turned south to conquer Babylon in 539 BC (for more on Cyrus the Great, see Yamauchi 1990:72-92).

The chapter opens with God as the speaker, and the solemnity of the situation is reflected in the words, "listen in silence before me" (41:1). This is addressed to Israel and to the Gentiles ("you lands beyond the sea"). The scene is a courtroom, in which the people were to examine the facts submitted to them and take note of the deliverer God had raised up for his people.

The king who is stirred from the east is not named here (41:2). The Targums and some commentators apply this reference to Abraham, but the word rendered "stirred up" is used (41:5; 45:13) of Cyrus (cf. Ezra 1:1; Isa 13:17; Jer 41:11), and Cyrus is mentioned by name in 44:28 and 45:1. The raising of Cyrus is prophetically foretold in a past tense that regards a future event as just as certain of accomplishment as if it had already taken place. Nothing will stop his conquests, because God "gives this man victory over many nations" (41:2). He is said to come from the east (41:2) and also from the north (41:25). This was true of Cyrus because he was connected with Persia in the east (because he was Persian) and with Media to the north (by having subdued it).

In 41:4, the Lord is presented as "I, the LORD, the First and the Last. I alone am he," a significant self-identification (41:4; cf. 41:13; 42:8; 43:3, 10, 13, 15; 44:24;

45:3, 5, 6; 46:4; 48:17; 49:23; 51:15; 60:22). Jesus made similar "I am" proclamations (John 6:35; 8:12, 58; 9:5; 10:7, 9, 11,14; 11:25; 14:6; 15:1, 5). The fundamental truth is that God the Creator, the incomparable who is eternally the same, is repeatedly presented in these chapters (cf. 45:6; 46:9, 10; 48:12; also cf. Rev 1:8, 11, 17; 2:8; 21:6; 22:13). As the Creator of all things, he is before all things and therefore first (see Col 1:15); but when the last generation appears, he still is God. He will outlast human history, for he is the eternal God (40:28) and acts in accordance with his sovereign good pleasure (cf. 40:22ff). Therefore, the astonishing conquests of Cyrus are the work of God.

The international threat posed by Cyrus' conquests called for acceleration of idol manufacturing. In seemingly total confusion, they "encourage one another" (41:6) in making idols. The "carver encourages the goldsmith" and the "molder helps at the anvil" (41:7). They carefully "join the parts together" and fix it in its place "so it won't fall over" (41:7). But the mutual support described here is in vain, because instead of turning to the true God, these idolatrous people became more and more involved in futile idolatry. Despite the expertise of the craftsmen, the idols they constructed needed support, lest they topple like Dagon (1 Sam 5:4) or fall on their faces!

In the description of the victorious servant (41:8-13), the imagery of the courtroom and the trial between the Lord and the Gentiles is dropped, to be picked up again in 41:21. Israel is being addressed, but the other nations are involved because of the confusion brought about by the approach of Cyrus. Israel is told not to fear, for they will experience deliverance. The Lord, still speaking, addresses the people of Israel with words of encouragement and promises of salvation in the midst of the general alarm and confusion. He speaks of "Israel my servant" (41:8), and here it is obvious that "my servant" refers to Israel (cf. 42:19). As such, it describes the relationship between the Lord and his people in Old Testament fashion, but still very intimately. God chose Israel to be his covenant people and his servant to do his will, a frequent theme in the closing chapters of Isaiah (41:8-9; 42:1; 43:10, 20; 44:1-2; 45:4; 49:7; 65:9, 15, 22). In this position, Israel sustained a close relationship to him, reflecting the covenant. "Jacob my chosen one" bears witness to the position and the privilege Israel enjoyed, and "descended from Abraham my friend" further emphasizes this (41:8).

After this mention of the intimate relationship of the Lord with his servants and their descendants, the prophet describes them as called back "from the ends of the earth" (41:9), meaning that they were very far away. Although some have connected this language with the Exodus and others with the return from captivity, possibly Abraham, who was just mentioned in the previous verse (41:8) is in view in this context. To the Judahites, Ur of the Chaldees was viewed as at the "ends of the earth" (41:9). In the light of the Lord's election and purpose, he encourages his people with rich promises: "Don't be afraid, for I am with you" and "Don't be dismayed, for I am your God" (41:10; cf. 13). The latter part of the verse promises the strength and resources needed to encourage and support the people by promising that God will "strengthen . . . help . . . hold you up" with his "victorious right hand" (41:10).

These comforting and reassuring words are accompanied by a message about how the Lord will deal with the servant's enemies; those who oppose the servant will be "confused and humiliated . . . and come to nothing" (41:11). To speak of holding the servant's "right hand" (41:13; instead of his left) is a strange picture by our logic (unless the Lord is left-handed), but this is poetry, not physical accuracy (also note that "right hand" was just mentioned in 41:10). Probably right hand is simply used in the sense of propriety or strength. In the Hebrew, 41:14 opens with a twofold parallel reference to the miserable condition of the people ("worm, O Jacob" // "people of Israel"), contrasted with "the Holy One of Israel." The imagery of the threshing sledge is introduced in 41:15, followed in 41:16 by the picture of winnowing, during which the chaff is caught up by the wind and blown away.

Since the mountains (41:15) are obviously figurative here, this could refer to the word of God defeating empires and kingdoms, that is, the conquest of pagans by the spread of the Messiah's gospel. As noted earlier, mountains can refer to kingdoms in Semitic imagery (cf. 2:2-4).

Help for the poor and needy is the topic of 41:14-20. The scene is of the redemption promised to the Judahites, who are described as poor and needy (41:17) and as living in distress and great difficulty. This is especially well presented by the picture of extreme thirst (41:17-18), an image easily understood by people living in that arid part of the world. The need addressed is spiritual (cf. Ps 42:1), a point made also in 55:1 (cf. John 4:14; 7:37-38). But God will provide "rivers . . . fountains of waters . . . pools of water . . . rivers fed by springs" (41:18). The sevenfold variety of trees mentioned in 41:19 is probably intended to represent fullness, which in this case represents the richness of God's provision so that "all who see this miracle will understand . . . that it is the LORD who has done this" (41:20).

In this courtroom setting (41:21ff), the Lord and his worshipers are on one side, and the idols and their worshipers are on the other. The idols and their followers were challenged to tell "what happened long ago so that we may consider the evidence" (41:22), which in this context probably refers to past predictive prophecies that were later fulfilled. The Lord challenged the idols to produce examples of fulfilled predictions or to give indications of their power, either good or bad (41:22-23; cf. Jer 10:5; Zeph 1:12). If they could do neither, they were "less than nothing and can do nothing at all" and their followers only polluted themselves (41:24).

The things required of the idols were precisely what the Lord had done and was doing. The idols were not necessarily being challenged to make pronouncements regarding Cyrus; rather, they were being challenged to tell of any purpose they might once have had (or may now have) for their followers. Surely, the idols must have had some purpose that they had already revealed and which could now be evaluated as to whether or not it had been fulfilled. If not, they should make known any present purpose of theirs that would have some bearing on the future. If the idols were gods, they could declare what would happen to the nations that served them, whether in salvation or judgment. Surely any true deity could reveal his plans and carry them through! The idols, however, remained lifeless, so the Lord broke the silence with a scornful charge.

Next the prophet returned to the leader from the north and the east (41:25) and the argument about reliable predictions. The God of Israel was able to reveal his faithfulness and power by prediction. The one "stirred up" (41:25) is described as one who will call on the Lord's name, but this expression does not necessarily refer to his personal faith or mean that he was a believer in the Lord. In this context, it simply means that he recognized that it was the Lord who gave him "all the kingdoms of the earth . . . and appointed" him to build a temple for the Lord in Jerusalem (2 Chr 36:23; Ezra 1:2).

Only God could predict such a thing; "no one said a word!" (41:26). God was the first to tell them that help was on the way (41:27). Not one of their idols told them this; "not one gave any answer when I asked" (41:28).

Again, a hushed silence fell over the courtroom because there was no one to accept the challenge, and no prophet of the idols offered any counsel. There was only a deafening silence. Finally, the verdict was rendered: "they are all foolish, worthless things" and "empty as the wind" (41:29). The Lord is the true God, and all idols are false gods, amounting to nothing (cf. 41:7, 21-24; 44:9).

◆     ### 3. God's chosen servant (42:1-9)

"Look at my servant, whom I
    strengthen.
He is my chosen one, who pleases me.
I have put my Spirit upon him.
    He will bring justice to the nations.
² He will not shout
    or raise his voice in public.
³ He will not crush the weakest reed
    or put out a flickering candle.
    He will bring justice to all who have
        been wronged.
⁴ He will not falter or lose heart
    until justice prevails throughout
        the earth.
    Even distant lands beyond the sea
    will wait for his instruction.*"

⁵ God, the LORD, created the heavens
    and stretched them out.
    He created the earth and everything
        in it.
He gives breath to everyone,
    life to everyone who walks the
        earth.
And it is he who says,

⁶ "I, the LORD, have called you to
    demonstrate my righteousness.
    I will take you by the hand and
        guard you,
    and I will give you to my people,
        Israel,
    as a symbol of my covenant with
        them.
And you will be a light to guide
    the nations.
⁷ You will open the eyes of the blind.
You will free the captives from
    prison,
    releasing those who sit in dark
        dungeons.

⁸ "I am the LORD; that is my name!
    I will not give my glory to anyone
        else,
    nor share my praise with carved
        idols.
⁹ Everything I prophesied has come true,
    and now I will prophesy again.
    I will tell you the future before it
        happens."

**42:4** Greek version reads *And his name will be the hope of all the world.* Compare Matt 12:21.

NOTES

**42:1 Look.** This translates the Heb. word traditionally translated "behold"; it is an attention-getting term that seems especially significant here.

*my servant.* The role of the servant is ultimately fulfilled in Jesus (Matt 12:15-21). "My servant" implies royal association in this context (41:21; cf. 43:15; 44:6).

*chosen one.* The Targum applies this reference to the Messiah (Levey, 1974:59).

*who pleases me.* More lit. "in whom my soul delights" (KJV). Variously rendered as, "in whom my soul delights" (NASB, NRSV), "with whom I am pleased" (TEV, GW), in whom I take delight" (REB), and "in whom I delight" (NIV, NJPS).

*bring justice to the nations.* Justice (*mishpat* [TH4941, ZH5477]) is a key concept in the first servant song, used three times to emphasize the totality of the servant's task.

**42:2 not shout or raise his voice.** The verb "shout" (*tsa'aq* [TH6817, ZH7590]) is used of crying out to God in lamentation, a cry for relief or justice, for deliverance in deep need or trouble (cf. Exod 14:10; 17:4; Judg 4:3; Ps 107:6; Lam 2:18). The second verb (*nasa'* [TH5375, ZH5951], raise) lit. means "to lift up [the voice]" as in a cry of protest (cf. Gen 21:16; Num 14:1; Judg 2:4), although it can also be used of a cry of joy (Isa 24:14; 52:8). This may reflect the custom of an unhappy loser in a court case at the city gate, who purposely repeated the facts of his lost case to a companion who was following him through the city streets, in a voice loud enough for all to hear.

**42:3 bring justice to all who have been wronged.** More lit., "in faithfulness he will bring forth justice." The versions render "faithfully bring forth justice" (NASB, NRSV), "unfailingly he will establish justice" (REB), "faithfully he presents fair judgment" (NJB), "bring forth the true way" (NJPS), "truly bring justice" (NCV), "bring lasting justice" (TEV), and "faithfully bring about justice" (GW).

**42:4 distant lands beyond the sea.** The Heb. is used of geographical extremities. In 42:1, God says that he will bring justice to the nations.

*will not falter or lose heart.* "Falter" translates the Heb. word *kahah* [TH3543, ZH3908], and "lose heart" translates the Heb. *yaruts,* a similar sounding word to "bruised (*ratsuts*) reed" (cf. 42:3). Both Heb. words involve the root *ratsats* [TH7533, ZH8368], meaning "splintered, broken."

*justice.* In the Heb. of 42:1-4, the threefold use of this word is probably intended for emphasis.

**42:5 God, the LORD.** Heb. *ha'el yhwh.* This title is found only here in Isaiah.

**42:6 to demonstrate my righteousness.** The lit. phrase "in righteousness" (*betsedeq* [TH6664, ZH7406]) that describes the call is also used in 41:2 (cf. 45:13) to describe the Lord's call of Cyrus. This is also similar to the language of the Lord's call of the nation Israel as his servant in 41:9-10.

**42:7 those who sit in dark dungeons.** Ancient Near Eastern prisons were notoriously dark and dismal places.

**42:8 share my praise with carved idols.** There are frequent speeches against idolatry in Isa 40–55 (see 41:1-7, 21-29; 43:8-13; 44:6-8; 45:20-25).

COMMENTARY

This chapter begins with the first of Isaiah's "Servant Songs" found in chapters 40–55. The expression "servant of the Lord" (or "servant of God") occurs repeatedly in

Isaiah 40–66. When the eunuch, reading the book of Isaiah, asked Philip (Acts 8:34), "Who is the prophet talking about?" he voiced a common question.

Sometimes the servant of the Lord represents a group, rather than an individual. Sometimes it is used in the plural for the faithful worshipers of the Lord (54:17; 63:17; 65:8-9; 66:14); and sometimes it is used in the singular for the people of Israel (41:8-9; 42:19; 43:10; 44:1-2, 21; 45:4; 48:20). In 44:26, it may refer to the prophets. Some would limit the reference to the faithful among the people or to the ideal people of Israel. Since both Israel (41:8; 42:19; 43:10; 44:1-2, 21; 45:4; 48:20) and the Messiah are called the servant (49:3, 5-7; 50:10; 52:13; 53:11), the servant referred to in any given passage must be deduced from the context and usage. Israel as God's servant failed to bring the knowledge of God to the world, so the Messiah, the Lord's Servant, would accomplish this.

The opening verse of this chapter introduces the servant as "my chosen one," anointed by the Spirit (42:1). As indicated by Payne, "the language seems to link kingly and prophetic characteristics in a role reminiscent of that of Moses" (1986:749). It is as if to say that the second Exodus (a major theme in chs 40–55) will require a second Moses. Westermann (1969:97) suggests that the functions of prophet (mediator by word of mouth) and king (mediator by action) parted company after Moses' time but were reunited in the Servant.

The phrase "who pleases me" (42:1) is, lit., "in whom my soul delights," with the verb in the perfect (completed) tense. Both Israel and Cyrus will find an antitype in the Servant, for he will be truly what Israel was ideally. He will be to mankind at large, in regard to their spiritual condition, what Cyrus was politically to the captive Jews, their liberator from darkness. Although some contend that "my servant" refers to Israel, the statements in 42:1b-4 suggest that here the servant is the Messiah. The Targum Jonathan translates, "Behold, my servant, the Messiah" (Levey 1974:59). Also note that Matthew (12:18-21) quotes Isaiah 42:1-4 with some minor variations, applying it to Jesus and his activity in Israel. Furthermore, Matthew 3:17 and 17:5 seem to take this passage as messianic. The designation "my servant" is highlighted by the addition of "my chosen one," language also used of Moses (Ps 106:23) and Saul (2 Sam 21:6). He is the effective mediator through whom a new Israel will be formed that will continue to bear the title "my chosen" (43:20; 45:4; cf. 65:9, 15, 22; Eph 1:4).

The reference to the anointing ("put my Spirit upon him") with the Spirit (42:1) reflects the prophetic office of the servant and the sustained success of the servant's mission. He is characterized as having the Spirit of God on him (cf. 11:2; 61:1) and as bringing justice to the nations (cf. 9:7; 11:3-4; 16:5). The results of the endowment with the Lord's Spirit are described in Isaiah 11:2-4, a messianic passage containing concepts found in the Servant Songs. Another messianic passage (61:1-3; cf. Luke 4:17-21) describes the divine empowering by the Spirit for an anointed one entrusted with a task. Such an endowment with the Spirit of the Lord is typical of the special gift of the Spirit often given to empower the leaders of Israel, especially the Davidic kings (1 Sam 11:6; 16:13; cf. Isa 11:2).

The expression "he will bring justice to the nations" (42:1) refers to the servant's task of correcting all aspects of human existence—moral, religious, spiritual, political, social, economic—in order to fulfill the prayer, "Your kingdom come, your will be done on earth as it is in heaven" (Matt 6:10). The Lord's affirmation of his servant's success (42:3b) is preceded by a description of the servant's mission (42:2-3a). Odendaal (1970:129) convincingly argues that "the identification of the Suffering Servant and the Messiah did not take place for the first time in the self-consciousness of Jesus, but it was there from the beginning." Odendaal also recognizes that the terminology describing the Servant is not completely royal, for in the Servant, "the priestly and prophetic offices find their divinely ordained integration in and subordination to the royal office" (1970:134).

It is said of the Servant that he will not "shout or raise his voice in public" (42:2). This language has been understood two different ways. It could mean that "He will not . . . raise his voice in the streets" because the streets are a place for weeping and mourning (15:3; 24:11; 33:7), or it could mean that the servant never laments from discouragement or becomes defeated but rather perseveres in the task of administering justice. The New Testament usage of the passage favors the first interpretation (Matt 12:19). The Servant will not use force (42:3; "he will not crush the weakest reed or put out a flickering candle"). The manner in which the Servant fulfills his role is described in terms probably intended to contrast him with Cyrus and his conquests by external means.

Since a reed is very fragile, a bruised or cracked reed is an even more striking image of weakness and uselessness. It may be that ancient shepherds entertained themselves with the music from a reed-pipe, but when it became "bruised" or split, they destroyed it or threw it away as useless. The "flickering candle" pictures the life that is nearly dead—those who are losing hope. If the head of a torch (cf. 43:17) or the wick of a lamp gave only a feeble light, he would trim it and supply it with fresh oil (cf. 61:3) rather than extinguish it. Matthew (12:20) applies this to the Messiah's acts of healing (cf. 50:4; Matt 11:28)

The expression "he will not falter or lose heart until justice prevails throughout the earth" (42:4) signifies that the Servant, unlike those to whom he ministers, will not be weak or unsuccessful but will accomplish his task. The unusual word selection in the Hebrew grows out of Isaiah's play on words in 42:3 and 4 (see notes). The Servant who does not promote violent destruction will himself persist with unfailing endurance; despite oppression, he will not fail to complete his task. Delitzsch (1949 2:176) says that "His zeal will not be extinguished, nor will anything break his strength till he shall have secured for right a firm standing on the earth." He will bring truth and righteousness to weak and faltering peoples everywhere. The standard of this justice and righteousness was revealed earlier in the laws given to Israel. True justice is that which is based on the knowledge of the true God, so justice, like law, (cf. 42:4, where "law" is parallel with "justice") is the revelation of God and his standards. This is what the Servant will bring to the nations.

The themes of law and justice are presented in various ways throughout Isaiah.

The repeated reference to the concept of a worldwide just order in 42:1 and 4 is stylistically an inclusio that helps to mark off 42:1-4 as the first strophe of this Servant Song. The word "justice" describes the totality of the just order that the Servant will cause to prevail on the earth and is the theological center of these verses. "Even distant lands beyond the sea will wait for his instruction" (42:4). The parallelism of "justice" and "law" (instruction) is found often elsewhere (Hab 1:4; Ps 89:31; Isa 51:4). "Law" is a pregnant term including the idea of authoritative instruction for life; it was given first by God through Moses, and later through priests or prophets (Jer 26:4-5).

After being introduced as the Creator in order to demonstrate his incomparable ability to empower his Servant (42:5), the Lord affirms his divine call of the Servant (42:6a), promises divine aid (42:6b), and outlines his task (42:6c-7). The speaker is appropriately identified as "God, the LORD" (42:5), as the passage continues with a vivid description of his greatness and majesty.

The high calling of the Servant (42:1-4) corresponds to the majesty of the One calling him, the One who is Creator. The Lord's creative power is evidence that he can empower the Servant to perform his mission as described in 42:1-4 and as partially repeated and clarified in 42:6-7. The language of stretching out the heavens (42:5) suggests stretching out a curtain or tent, or the activity of a goldsmith or silversmith who pounds out the malleable metal with his tools. The creation of the heavens and the earth is probably a merism ascribing to God the creation of all things everywhere (cf. Gen 1:1). "Breath" and "life" (42:5) are used in poetic parallelism to describe the natural life that the Creator imparts to all mankind. The greatness of God in creation and the moral character of the Lord are mentioned: "I, the Lord, have called you to demonstrate my righteousness" (42:6).

The task assigned to this Servant as described in 42:6-7 is more far-reaching and spiritual than any task the Lord purposed or accomplished through Cyrus, and because it was done on Israel's behalf, it could not have been accomplished by Israel. The Lord gave Cyrus the military task of subduing nations (45:1) and of setting Israel free from Babylonian Exile (45:13), but Cyrus did not bring the light of salvation to the Gentiles, nor was he a covenant for the people of Israel (42:6).

The relationship of the Creator with his Servant is further described with the words, "I will take you by the hand and guard you" (42:6). They are to "be a light to guide the nations" (42:6) to their covenant Lord. The expression occurs again in 49:8, where the context (42:5-7) implies that those who are constituted a "people" by this new covenant are in large measure Gentiles. They are new light-bearers in a dark world (9:2; 49:6; 51:4; 60:1-3; Luke 2:30-32; Acts 26:17-18, 23). To seal such a covenant, a mightier Servant of the Lord was needed (cf. Luke 22:20; Heb 13:17). The Servant is described as "a light to guide the nations," and one who "will open the eyes of the blind" (42:6-7). "Light" stands for "salvation" here; the two are used synonymously in 49:6. But the emphasis is on spiritual illumination, as brought out by "open the eyes of the blind." Since the blindness was not literal, it is likely that the prison and dungeon are also figurative. The continued description, to "free the captives from prison, releasing those who sit in dark dungeons" may refer to the conditions of the literal captivity (cf. 42:22, 24-25), but may also include the spiritual sense of those dwelling in the dark dungeon of sin and ignorance (cf. 9:2). The imprisonment may refer to the nation in the Babylonian captivity (the background for Isa 40–66), the spiritual blindness being due to idolatry (cf. 40:18-20; 46:5; 48:4-5). The Gentiles were also blinded by idolatry (41:5-7) and so were unable to perceive that the Lord is the true God and that their idols were worthless (41:25-29). The Lord directed glory to himself by asserting his uniqueness. He affirmed his name: "I am the LORD; that is my name!" (42:8). Then he asserted his refusal to share his glory: "I will not give my glory to anyone else" (42:8; cf. 48:9-11), which echoes the idolatry references of 41:21-29. The expression, "I am the Lord; that is my name" (42:8) also echoes judgment on all the gods of Egypt (Exod 12:12). The covenant Lord of Israel had given the predictions recorded in 42:6-7, and he would not let idols take credit for it; no other god can foretell such things.

Verse 9 draws the Servant poem to a climax and indicates its close relationship to the context. In it, the Lord directs attention to his use of predictive prophecy, namely, that just as the first predictions ("the former things") had been fulfilled, new predictions—the prophecies concerning the messianic Servant—would likewise be fulfilled. If, as some allege, someone other than Isaiah wrote chapters 40–66 after the Jewish captives were released by Cyrus, then the point made here is destroyed. However, in contrast to idols, God can predict the future. "I will tell you the future before it happens" (42:9) includes the voluntary restoration of a captive people, something contrary to the prerogatives of a sovereign power, as vividly depicted in Exodus 5-15. It also included the new conditions associated with the righteous order that the messianic Servant will cause to prevail on the whole earth.

The anonymous servant of 42:1-9 cannot be Israel or Cyrus or any person other than the royal Davidic Messiah, the Lord Jesus Christ. The first Servant Song introduces the Servant and highlights the successful completion of the task to which he has been divinely called.

◆     ## 4. A song of praise to the Lord (42:10-17)

10 Sing a new song to the LORD!
   Sing his praises from the ends
      of the earth!
   Sing, all you who sail the seas,
      all you who live in distant
      coastlands.
11 Join in the chorus, you desert towns;
   let the villages of Kedar rejoice!
   Let the people of Sela sing for joy;
      shout praises from the
      mountaintops!
12 Let the whole world glorify the LORD;

let it sing his praise.
13 The LORD will march forth like
   a mighty hero;
   he will come out like a warrior,
      full of fury.
   He will shout his battle cry
      and crush all his enemies.

14 He will say, "I have long been
   silent;
   yes, I have restrained myself.
   But now, like a woman in labor,
      I will cry and groan and pant.

<sup>15</sup> I will level the mountains and hills
and blight all their greenery.
I will turn the rivers into dry land
and will dry up all the pools.
<sup>16</sup> I will lead blind Israel down a new
path,
guiding them along an unfamiliar
way.

I will brighten the darkness before them
and smooth out the road ahead of
them.
Yes, I will indeed do these things;
I will not forsake them.
<sup>17</sup> But those who trust in idols,
who say, 'You are our gods,'
will be turned away in shame.

### NOTES

**42:10 *new song.*** This expression is frequent in the Psalms (33:3; 96:1; 98:1; 144:9; 149:1).

**42:11 *desert.*** This should not be taken too lit. in the sense of the modern usage of the word. Sometimes "desert" is used of areas inhabited by more than roving Bedouin. Nabal lived in the "desert" with 3,000 sheep and 1,000 goats (1 Sam 25:2).

**42:13 *march forth.*** The Heb. expression is often used for embarking on a military campaign.

***mighty hero.*** This Heb. word (*gibbor* [<sup>TH</sup>1368A, <sup>ZH</sup>1475]) is sometimes used for "warrior" (cf. 9:5[7]; 10:21). Here the same Heb. root begins the verse as a noun ("mighty man") and ends the verse as a verb ("he will crush").

***full of fury.*** Lit., "he shall stir up [his] jealousy." God is a jealous God (Exod 20:5), so much so that his very name is "Jealous" (Exod 34:14).

***shout his battle cry.*** The Heb. consists of two verbs, "shout" and "raise," which are linked by Heb. *'ap* [<sup>TH</sup>637, <sup>ZH</sup>677], the particle of cumulative emphasis (cf. 40:24; 41:10). The idea is something like, "He will shout—oh, how he will raise!" The versions have "he will utter a shout, yes, he will raise a war cry" (NASB); "he cries out, he shouts aloud" (NRSV); "he will shout, he will raise the battle cry" (REB); "with a shout he will raise the battle cry" (NIV); "he shouts, gives the battle cry" (GW); and "He yells, He roars aloud" (NJPS).

**42:14 *cry and groan and pant.*** Heb. *'ep'eh 'eshom we'esh'ap,* is probably intended onomatopoeic language with its gutturals and aspirates. The words are not common. The first two words, *pa'ah* [<sup>TH</sup>6463, <sup>ZH</sup>7184] and *nasham* [<sup>TH</sup>5395, <sup>ZH</sup>5971] are found only here in the entire OT, and *sha'ap* [<sup>TH</sup>7602A, <sup>ZH</sup>8634] is found only here in Isaiah and ten times elsewhere.

### COMMENTARY

This song of praise ("from the ends of the earth"; 42:10) follows naturally on the announcement of new things in the preceding verse. The entire world (which God, after all, created) is invited to join in praise.

Although some commentators understand this passage as reflecting the world's joy over what the Lord will do for Israel (as in Pss 96–98), it seems better to understand it as a call for worldwide praise in response to the global work of the Servant (42:1-4, 5-9). The same broad themes continue: "earth" and "distant lands" (42:4; cf. v. 10), "earth and everything in it" and "everyone who walks on the earth" (42:5).

In particular, the Lord's controversy with the idols continues. His refusal to share the praise due to him (42:8) is matched by his call for the world to give him praise

(42:12), and his enmity against false gods is carried to its conclusion (cf. 42:13, 17).

The introductory section of this hymn of praise (42:10-12) is bracketed by the inclusio, "his praises from the ends of the earth" (42:10) and "Let the whole world glorify the LORD" (42:12). In a balanced arrangement, the whole Gentile world is brought into this summons to sing. Those addressed include the pairing of those who "sail the seas" (42:10) with those who "shout praises from the mountaintops" (42:11), the whole Gentile world from those in the nearby desert of Kedar (42:11) to those in the "distant coastlands" (42:10). All of humanity is called upon to sing a "new song to the LORD" (42:10) because of the new things ascribed to the Lord. The conqueror of 41:1-4 provoked an international reaction of terror and a flight to idol-making, but the Servant inspires an outburst of song and a turning to the Lord. All creation is caught up in praise because the bondage of corruption is over. With the whole world now brought into covenant with the Lord (42:7), creation's groans are turned to song (cf. Rom 8:19ff).

Specific reference is also made to those who live in "desert towns" (42:11). The people of Kedar (cf. 21:17) were the most important Ishmaelite Arabian tribe after the Nabateans; they lived in North Arabia. The people of Sela (cf. 16:1), capital of Edom, were also summoned to "shout praises from the mountaintops" (42:11). The fact that Edom, the inveterate enemy of God's people, should participate in the joy shows the complete triumph of the Lord over all hostility.

In 42:13, terrifying anthropomorphic language (cf. Exod 1:3; Ps 24:8) represents the warrior-like attitude with which the Lord God will take up the cause of his people. He will come out for battle "full of fury" (42:13). The Lord had restrained himself long enough; now he was about to "cry and groan and pant" like a woman in labor (42:14; this is one of the few times that female imagery is used of the Lord). For a long time, the Lord held his purpose against idols and wickedness in check, but now he would destroy idolatry and bring in a new age. Was he referring here only to the return of his people from captivity in Babylon, or does this represent a larger, more inclusive view that includes the Servant's appearance and what he will do? The latter seems to fit the context better. The Lord's wrath against his enemies is represented in the devastation he brings about in nature (42:15). In contrast, 46:16 describes the compassion he has for his people, who are called blind because they are not able to see the way of salvation for themselves (cf. 42:7). The language is so general that it could equally well apply to deliverance from captivity or to salvation in a spiritual sense, which the deliverance from captivity illustrates.

The passage closes with pictures of the Lord as a warrior and as a woman in childbirth (42:14), which remind us that redemption is accomplished only with effort and pain. God will not forsake his people (42:16). In contrast, the praise of idols is pathetic, and those who call them gods "will be turned away in shame" (42:17).

◆     5. Israel's failure to see and listen (42:18-25)

18 "Listen, you who are deaf!
    Look and see, you blind!
19 Who is as blind as my own people,
    my servant?
Who is as deaf as my messenger?
Who is as blind as my chosen people,
    the servant of the LORD?
20 You see and recognize what is right
    but refuse to act on it.
You hear with your ears,
    but you don't really listen."

21 Because he is righteous,
    the LORD has exalted his glorious law.
22 But his own people have been robbed
    and plundered,
    enslaved, imprisoned, and trapped.
They are fair game for anyone
    and have no one to protect them,
    no one to take them back home.

23 Who will hear these lessons from
    the past
    and see the ruin that awaits you
    in the future?
24 Who allowed Israel to be robbed and
    hurt?
    It was the LORD, against whom we
    sinned,
    for the people would not walk in his
    path,
    nor would they obey his law.
25 Therefore, he poured out his fury
    on them
    and destroyed them in battle.
They were enveloped in flames,
    but they still refused to
    understand.
They were consumed by fire,
    but they did not learn their lesson.

NOTES

42:18 *deaf . . . blind.* See 6:10.

42:21 *exalted his glorious law.* For the glorified law of God, see Exod 34:29.

42:22 *robbed and plundered.* The Lord was punishing his people (Isa 40:17-18; 1 Kgs 20:23). The people were plundered by both the Assyrians (10:6) and the Babylonians (39:6).

COMMENTARY

This passage interrupts the announcement of coming redemption and gives a broad description of Israel's condition in exile, stressing that Israel's own sin was the cause of it. The voice of compassion calls Israel "blind" (three times in 42:18-19) and describes the plight of the people, a condition from which they will be redeemed. In contrast to the earlier servant, this servant is deaf and blind Israel, a theme which will continue through chapter 45.

God's people were called his "messenger" (42:19) because they received his message and "glorious law" (42:21). No one is as blind as the Lord's servant Israel (cf. 41:1, 8). Having been given a privileged place above all other nations, they also bore more responsibility. Although Israel was privileged to witness much, they paid no attention; although they saw and understood what was right, they refused to act on it (42:20). They had received the Lord's law (Torah or teaching), which refers here to the entire divine revelation given by way of Moses and the prophets (cf. 42:4).

The people are described as "robbed and plundered, enslaved, imprisoned, and trapped" (42:22). In 42:23-25, it is clear that Israel was plundered because God was punishing them, not because he was unable to protect them. In the statement "It was the LORD, against whom we sinned" (42:24), Isaiah included himself among the disobedient. God "poured out his fury on them and destroyed them in battle" (42:25) because of the people's sin. Despite the destruction they experienced, they failed to understand and take it to heart. This section seems preparatory to 43:1-7, where God again proclaims mercy to Israel.

This shocking passage is designed to get the attention of the wayward people. Unlike the Servant-Messiah earlier in this chapter, this servant is the people of Israel (cf. 41:8-9), contrasted with the faithful servant (42:19). The people are described as deaf and blind (42:18); they refused to hear words of encouragement (42:20; cf. 6:9-10). Although the Lord had "exalted his glorious law" (42:21), they would not obey him (42:24). As a result, God handed them over first to the Assyrians (10:5-6) and then to the Babylonians (39:6). In spite of all this judgment, they refused to repent and return to the Lord. What a contrast this is to the preceding song of praise! These rebellious people were more capable of complaint than of praise (cf. 40:27). They were deaf to God's message and blind to his plan; they were no better than their ancestors (42:23-25).

◆     ## 6. Redemption and the new exodus (43:1-28)

But now, O Jacob, listen to the LORD
  who created you.
O Israel, the one who formed you
  says,
"Do not be afraid, for I have ransomed
  you.
  I have called you by name; you are
  mine.
² When you go through deep waters,
  I will be with you.
When you go through rivers of
  difficulty,
  you will not drown.
When you walk through the fire
  of oppression,
  you will not be burned up;
  the flames will not consume you.
³ For I am the LORD, your God,
  the Holy One of Israel, your Savior.
I gave Egypt as a ransom for your
  freedom;
  I gave Ethiopia* and Seba in
  your place.
⁴ Others were given in exchange
  for you.
I traded their lives for yours
because you are precious to me.
  You are honored, and I love you.

⁵ "Do not be afraid, for I am with you.
  I will gather you and your children
  from east and west.
⁶ I will say to the north and south,
  'Bring my sons and daughters back
  to Israel
  from the distant corners of the
  earth.
⁷ Bring all who claim me as their God,
  for I have made them for my glory.
  It was I who created them.'"

⁸ Bring out the people who have eyes
  but are blind,
  who have ears but are deaf.
⁹ Gather the nations together!
  Assemble the peoples of the world!
Which of their idols has ever foretold
  such things?
  Which can predict what will happen
  tomorrow?
Where are the witnesses of such
  predictions?
  Who can verify that they spoke
  the truth?
¹⁰ "But you are my witnesses, O Israel!"
  says the LORD.
  "You are my servant.

You have been chosen to know me,
believe in me,
and understand that I alone
am God.
There is no other God—
there never has been, and there
never will be.
<sup>11</sup> I, yes I, am the LORD,
and there is no other Savior.
<sup>12</sup> First I predicted your rescue,
then I saved you and proclaimed
it to the world.
No foreign god has ever done this.
You are witnesses that I am the
only God,"
says the LORD.
<sup>13</sup> "From eternity to eternity I am God.
No one can snatch anyone out of
my hand.
No one can undo what I have done."

<sup>14</sup> This is what the LORD says—your
Redeemer, the Holy One of Israel:

"For your sakes I will send an army
against Babylon,
forcing the Babylonians* to flee in
those ships they are so proud of.
<sup>15</sup> I am the LORD, your Holy One,
Israel's Creator and King.
<sup>16</sup> I am the LORD, who opened a way
through the waters,
making a dry path through the sea.
<sup>17</sup> I called forth the mighty army of
Egypt
with all its chariots and horses.
I drew them beneath the waves, and
they drowned,
their lives snuffed out like a
smoldering candlewick.

<sup>18</sup> "But forget all that—
it is nothing compared to what
I am going to do.
<sup>19</sup> For I am about to do something new.
See, I have already begun! Do you
not see it?
I will make a pathway through the
wilderness.

I will create rivers in the dry
wasteland.
<sup>20</sup> The wild animals in the fields will
thank me,
the jackals and owls, too,
for giving them water in the desert.
Yes, I will make rivers in the dry
wasteland
so my chosen people can be
refreshed.
<sup>21</sup> I have made Israel for myself,
and they will someday honor me
before the whole world.

<sup>22</sup> "But, dear family of Jacob, you refuse
to ask for my help.
You have grown tired of me,
O Israel!
<sup>23</sup> You have not brought me sheep or
goats for burnt offerings.
You have not honored me with
sacrifices,
though I have not burdened and
wearied you
with requests for grain offerings
and frankincense.
<sup>24</sup> You have not brought me fragrant
calamus
or pleased me with the fat from
sacrifices.
Instead, you have burdened me with
your sins
and wearied me with your faults.

<sup>25</sup> "I—yes, I alone—will blot out your sins
for my own sake
and will never think of them again.
<sup>26</sup> Let us review the situation together,
and you can present your case to
prove your innocence.
<sup>27</sup> From the very beginning, your first
ancestor sinned against me;
all your leaders broke my laws.
<sup>28</sup> That is why I have disgraced your
priests;
I have decreed complete
destruction* for Jacob
and shame for Israel.

43:3 Hebrew *Cush.* 43:14 Or *Chaldeans.* 43:28 The Hebrew term used here refers to the complete
consecration of things or people to the LORD, either by destroying them or by giving them as an offering.

NOTES

**43:1** *Do not be afraid.* This theme runs like a continuous thread through these oracles (cf. 40:9; 43:5; 44:2; 54:4).

*ransomed.* Heb. *ga'al* [TH1350, ZH1453] whose participial form gives us the word "redeemer." This word for "ransom" or "redeem" occurs in 43:1, 3, and 14 and also in 44:6, 22, 23, 24. This remarkable love of God for his people is also expressed in other prophets (cf. Hos 11:1; Jer 31:20).

*I have called you by name.* This highlights Israel's special covenant relationship with the Lord (cf. 48:12). It could be compared to the shepherd who calls his sheep by name. The idiom "to call by name" signifies that they were chosen and appointed for a very special purpose. Note its use in Exod 31:2; 35:30; Isa 45:4. In 58:12, Israel is referred to as "called."

**43:2** *go through rivers of difficulty.* More lit., this is "go through rivers," here parallel to "deep waters." Passing through the waters was lit. fulfilled at the Red Sea (Exod 14:21-22) and the Jordan River (Josh 3:14-17), but of course it could include metaphorical use; in Isa 8:7, the king of Assyria with all his pomp is referred to as "a mighty flood from the Euphrates River."

**43:3** *Ethiopia.* This was the ancient land of Cush, south of Egypt.

*Seba.* Seba was probably near Cush and associated with Sheba (cf. Ps 72:10). Seba may have been in Africa or may refer to Sheba in Arabia (cf. 60:6; Job 6:19; 1 Kgs 10:1-13), where the Sabeans lived (cf. Job 1:15; Isa 45:14; Ezek 23:42; Joel 3:8). It was only under Cambyses that the Persians were able to conquer these lands.

**43:5-6** *gather . . . east and west . . . north and south.* History reveals that by the sixth century BC, God's people were already widely scattered. Some had fled to Egypt (Jer 43), and some had founded a colony there at Elephantine, near the first Cataract (cf. 49:12). A group from the northern tribes had earlier been deported to Assyria. Other migrations and deportations may have occurred that are not yet known from history. The word translated "gather" in 43:5 is derived from the same root as the modern Heb. word kibbutz, which designates a form of collective settlement.

**43:8** *eyes . . . blind . . . ears . . . deaf.* Cf. 48:8; 59:10; Deut 28:29.

**43:10** *my servant.* Targum Jonathan renders this as "my servant is the Messiah" (Levey 1974:62, 155).

**43:11** *Savior.* Heb. *moshia'.* This is another title for God that Isaiah uses frequently (17:10; 43:3; 45:15, 21; 49:26; 60:16; 62:11; 63:8). It is not always translated as a noun and here a couple modern versions translate otherwise: "one who can save you" (TEV) and "can rescue you" (CEV).

**43:14** *This is what the LORD says.* Isaiah uses this statement frequently in the second major division of his book (43:14, 16; 44:2, 6, 24; 45:1, 11, 14; 48:17; 49:7-8; 50:1; 52:4; 56:1, 4; 65:8, 13; 66:1, 12) to emphasize the divine authority of his words.

**43:14** *Holy One of Israel.* See 1:4; 41:14.

*those ships.* The reference to Babylonian ships may seem strange with reference to an essentially desert people, but they used the Persian Gulf as well as the Tigris and Euphrates rivers. Their famous ships (see 2:16) would be used for escape from the enemy. It is ironic that the very vessels that had once brought them wealth would become the means of disgrace and humiliating flight.

**43:15** *King.* God is also called "King" in Deut 33:5.

**43:17 snuffed out like a smoldering candlewick.** The destroyed forces of the Pharaoh are compared to a wick that has been snuffed out. Since candles did not exist at this time in history, the meaning is not candlewick but just "wick" (NIV).

**43:20 wild animals in the fields will thank me.** Isaiah excels in such language (cf. "the mountains and hills will burst into song, and the trees of the field will clap their hands!" 55:12). Similar poetic imagery can also be found elsewhere (cf. Ps 96:12; Job 38:7). Desert animals (cf. 13:21-22) are used as examples following the mention of the desert.

**jackals and owls.** These are desert creatures. The Heb. (*benot ya'anah* [TH3284, ZH3613]) translated "owls" is uncertain. Other versions have "ostriches" (NASB, NRSV, TEV, GW, ESV, NJPS), "desert-owl" (REB), and "owls" (KJV, NIV, NCV, CEV).

**43:24 pleased me with the fat from sacrifices.** The fat parts of the sacrifices were especially well-pleasing to the Lord.

**faults.** Heb. *'awon*, often translated "iniquity" or "guilt," is used in Isaiah about 25 times. "Fault" may sound weak, but, if understood in the sense of inherent defect, is accurate.

## COMMENTARY

With typical abruptness, Isaiah returns to the subject of restoration. Such sudden shifts between judgment and salvation are common in chapters 28–33. This long and complex section includes an indictment of Israel for their sins and their failures to be the witness God expected; it also promises a servant who is far greater and will not fail. Promise of deliverance, the certainty of God's promise, the new exodus, and God's grace despite Israel's indifference are all found in these verses.

God as Creator and Redeemer is constantly in the background of his activity for and through his covenant people. He had introduced himself as the Creator of heaven and earth in 42:5; he now introduces himself as the Creator of Israel (43:1). Just as in the past he had brought their ancestors through the waters of the Red Sea and the Jordan River (43:16), he was ready to perform similar miracles for his people once again (43:2). They might falter and fail, but the true God cannot and will not fail.

The indictment of Israel at the end of the previous chapter is followed by words of promise and hope. The Lord who created his covenant people now encouraged them with the words, "Do not be afraid, for I have ransomed you . . . you are mine" (43:1). They were called by name (43:1), as Cyrus was later called by name (45:4). When they "go through deep waters" they will not drown, and when they go "through the fire of oppression" they will not be consumed by its flames (43:2). Although Israel had felt God's burning anger (42:25), the flames of oppressors would not harm them (43:2). Under God's protection, Israel will be safe from fire and flood (cf. Ps 66:12). The statement that God gave Egypt, Ethiopia, and Seba as a ransom (43:3) for his people probably refers to the expanded empire granted to Cyrus as reward for his release of the captives (the same three nations are mentioned together in 45:14 in relation to Israel). God loved his people so much that he said that "others were given in exchange for you" (43:4). The Lord's power and sovereignty enabled him to work out his purposes providentially through the nations.

The ingathering of the exiles is a recurring theme (cf. 49:12, 18, 22). Since the Zionist movements of modern times, such texts have been applied to the immigration to the modern state of Israel of Jews from South America, China, the United States, Russia, and almost every part of the world (Sawyer 1996:74). Zionist interpretation takes such predictions primarily in a political sense.

God will restore his people because he has made them for his glory (43:7). The sons and daughters of the covenant are referred to in this verse as "all who claim me as their God" (43:7), which is usually translated, "everyone called by my name" (KJV). These were created or given birth by the Lord for his own glory, so there was no room for nationalistic or ethnic pride. The Lord's ultimate goal was his own glory, not that of Israel. In reflecting the certainty of God's promises, 43:8-13 picks up the legal language that was so prominent in chapter 41. The Lord had previously called the gods of the nations to court to examine their claims of deity (41:1-7, 21-24). Now the trial speech of this passage develops the legal imagery of 43:3-4 and uses it to argue that there is no Savior apart from the Lord.

The nations were challenged to produce evidence that they and their idols have been able to predict the future, even "what will happen tomorrow" (43:9; cf. 41:22-23). In contrast, God's covenant people had witnessed his revelation and activity in their midst. "My servant" (43:10) is here interpreted by some, including the Targums (Levey 1974:62) as messianic. The servant is distinguished from the nation as in 49:6, and was especially to be a witness (cf. 55:4) with God's people.

In bold language, the Lord says, "I, yes I, am the LORD, and there is no other Savior" (43:11; cf. 44:6, 8; 45:5-6, 18). His people were witnesses to God's promised deliverance and saw him fulfill it (43:12; 44:8). They had witnessed something that no "foreign god has ever done" (43:12). Since God rules from eternity past to eternity future, no one can reverse his actions (43:13). He existed before any gods were made, and he will continue to exist long after the last idol is gone.

In 43:14-21, the focus shifts from the former work of God to his new work. As their "Redeemer, the Holy One of Israel," God predicted and promised to send "an army against Babylon" (43:14). As if to further emphasize his glory and power, 43:15 also uses a full title for God: "the LORD, your Holy One, Israel's Creator and King." He delivered them from the "mighty army of Egypt," and the Egyptians' lives were "snuffed out like a smoldering candlewick" (43:17). In the past, in the first Exodus, God brought Israel out of Egypt, and now he was about to bring about a new Exodus as he brought his people back home from another captivity. This new Exodus theme is found in many passages in Isaiah (cf. 40:3-5; 41:17-20; 42:14-16; 43:14-21; 48:20-21; 49:8-12; 51:9-10; 52:11-12; 55:12-13).

The reference to the King (43:15) again reminds the people that God is their ruler. The past Exodus was nothing compared to the "something new" the Lord was now going to do (43:18). He "will make a pathway through the wilderness" for his people's return home (43:19). Their return and restoration includes water in the desert (43:20); even the wild animals in the fields will take note and thank the Lord

(43:20). All this will occur because the Lord said, "I have made Israel for myself and they will someday honor me before the whole world" (43:21).

The contrast between Israel's indifference and God's grace is highlighted in 43:22-28. This passage interrupts with a consideration of Israel's unworthiness: "You refuse to ask for my help" (43:22). The adversative "but" indicates that what is said here of Israel forms a contrast with the soon-to-be-resumed promise of salvation (44:1), even as it does with the promises given in the preceding verses. Israel might have been expected to call on the Lord in their distress, but this had not happened. The Lord took the initiative, freely and graciously calling Israel in order to lead them from exile (43:1), as earlier he had called them from the ends of the earth (41:9) to be his servants.

Despite this personal attention and special grace and favor shed on God's covenant people, they grew tired of him and refused to ask him for help (43:22). They did not honor him with sacrifices and offerings (43:23); instead, they burdened the Lord with their sins and wearied him with their faults (43:23). By contrast, God did not burden or weary them with his requests, which probably means that he did not make excessive demands on his people (43:23). Oswalt (1998:159n64), noting examples from ANET (343, 358-361, 445), points out that "by comparison with the rituals practiced by their neighbors, Israel's seem to have been rather simple." Although God had to punish them for their sins, the Lord himself would blot out their sins and "never think of them again" (43:25; cf. 1:8; 44:22). This was good news to captives separated from the Temple and its sacrificial system, without which they could not carry out the required shedding of blood. Without offerings, their sins were not dealt with; they piled up, resulting in disgrace and shame for Israel (43:28).

◆       **7. God's power versus powerless idols (44:1-28)**

"But now, listen to me, Jacob my
    servant,
Israel my chosen one.
2 The LORD who made you and helps
    you says:
Do not be afraid, O Jacob, my servant,
O dear Israel,* my chosen one.
3 For I will pour out water to quench
    your thirst
and to irrigate your parched fields.
And I will pour out my Spirit on your
    descendants,
and my blessing on your children.
4 They will thrive like watered grass,
like willows on a riverbank.
5 Some will proudly claim, 'I belong
    to the LORD.'

Others will say, 'I am a descendant
    of Jacob.'
Some will write the LORD's name
    on their hands
and will take the name of Israel
    as their own."

6 This is what the LORD says—Israel's King and Redeemer, the LORD of Heaven's Armies:

"I am the First and the Last;
    there is no other God.
7 Who is like me?
    Let him step forward and prove
        to you his power.
Let him do as I have done since
    ancient times

when I established a people and
explained its future.
⁸ Do not tremble; do not be afraid.
Did I not proclaim my purposes for
you long ago?
You are my witnesses—is there any
other God?
No! There is no other Rock—not one!"

⁹ How foolish are those who
manufacture idols.
These prized objects are really
worthless.
The people who worship idols don't
know this,
so they are all put to shame.
¹⁰ Who but a fool would make his own
god—
an idol that cannot help him one bit?
¹¹ All who worship idols will be disgraced
along with all these craftsmen—
mere humans—
who claim they can make a god.
They may all stand together,
but they will stand in terror and
shame.

¹² The blacksmith stands at his forge
to make a sharp tool,
pounding and shaping it with all
his might.
His work makes him hungry and weak.
It makes him thirsty and faint.
¹³ Then the wood-carver measures
a block of wood
and draws a pattern on it.
He works with chisel and plane
and carves it into a human figure.
He gives it human beauty
and puts it in a little shrine.
¹⁴ He cuts down cedars;
he selects the cypress and the oak;
he plants the pine in the forest
to be nourished by the rain.
¹⁵ Then he uses part of the wood to make
a fire.
With it he warms himself and bakes
his bread.
Then—yes, it's true—he takes the rest
of it

and makes himself a god to worship!
He makes an idol
and bows down in front of it!
¹⁶ He burns part of the tree to roast his
meat
and to keep himself warm.
He says, "Ah, that fire feels good."
¹⁷ Then he takes what's left
and makes his god: a carved idol!
He falls down in front of it,
worshiping and praying to it.
"Rescue me!" he says.
"You are my god!"

¹⁸ Such stupidity and ignorance!
Their eyes are closed, and they
cannot see.
Their minds are shut, and they
cannot think.
¹⁹ The person who made the idol never
stops to reflect,
"Why, it's just a block of wood!
I burned half of it for heat
and used it to bake my bread and
roast my meat.
How can the rest of it be a god?
Should I bow down to worship
a piece of wood?"
²⁰ The poor, deluded fool feeds on ashes.
He trusts something that can't help
him at all.
Yet he cannot bring himself to ask,
"Is this idol that I'm holding in
my hand a lie?"

²¹ "Pay attention, O Jacob,
for you are my servant, O Israel.
I, the LORD, made you,
and I will not forget you.
²² I have swept away your sins like
a cloud.
I have scattered your offenses
like the morning mist.
Oh, return to me,
for I have paid the price to set
you free."

²³ Sing, O heavens, for the LORD has done
this wondrous thing.
Shout for joy, O depths of the
earth!

Break into song,
  O mountains and forests and every
    tree!
For the LORD has redeemed Jacob
  and is glorified in Israel.
<sup>24</sup>This is what the LORD says—
  your Redeemer and Creator:
"I am the LORD, who made all things.
  I alone stretched out the heavens.
Who was with me
  when I made the earth?
<sup>25</sup>I expose the false prophets as liars
  and make fools of fortune-tellers.
I cause the wise to give bad advice,
  thus proving them to be fools.

<sup>26</sup>But I carry out the predictions of my
    prophets!
By them I say to Jerusalem, 'People
    will live here again,'
and to the towns of Judah, 'You will
    be rebuilt;
  I will restore all your ruins!'
<sup>27</sup>When I speak to the rivers and say,
    'Dry up!'
  they will be dry.
<sup>28</sup>When I say of Cyrus, 'He is my
    shepherd,'
  he will certainly do as I say.
He will command, 'Rebuild Jerusalem';
  he will say, 'Restore the Temple.'"

44:2 Hebrew *Jeshurun*, a term of endearment for Israel.

## NOTES

**44:2 Israel.** Lit., "Jeshurun" (cf. NLT mg), a variant for Israel found elsewhere only in Deut 32:15; 33:5, 26. From the Hebrew root meaning straight or upright.

**44:9 manufacture.** Heb. *yatsar* [TH3335, ZH3670]. Although the English word seems anachronistic and appears to reflect the industrial age, the etymology of "manufacture" is "to make with the hands," which is exactly how the idols came into being.

**44:14 cedars . . . cypress.** These were the most valuable kinds of wood in that culture.

**44:15 He makes an idol and bows down in front of it!** This idea is repeated in 44:17, 19.

**44:18 eyes are closed . . . minds are shut.** This is the condition of both the idols and those who worship them.

**44:19 How can the rest of it be a god?** More lit., "I make the rest of it into an abomination" (NASB). The NLT omits the reference to this "abomination" (*to'ebah* [TH8441, ZH9359]), which is a particularly strong word denouncing idols (cf. Deut 27:15; 1 Kgs 11:5, 7; 2 Kgs 23:13).

**44:22 swept away your sins.** This would be accomplished by the suffering servant (cf. 43:25).

**44:23 Sing, O heavens . . . Shout . . . O . . . earth!** All of nature is called upon to sing in praise to the Lord (cf. 49:13; 55:12).

**44:25 fortune-tellers.** The word *qosemim* [TH7080, ZH7876] is used of Balaam in Josh 13:22. Elsewhere in Isaiah it is found only in 3:2. It is used of sorcery and soothsaying and not to be confused with modern fortune-tellers. Modern versions use a variety of terms: "diviners" (NASB, NRSV, NIV, REB, NJPS), "those who do magic" (NCV), and "fortune-tellers" (TEV, CEV).

**44:27 Dry up.** This is used of the Red Sea elsewhere (cf. 11:15; 37:25; 43:16-17).

**44:28 Rebuild Jerusalem. . . . Restore the Temple.** Cyrus gave permission to rebuild the temple, which led to the eventual restoration of Jerusalem.

## COMMENTARY

In the opening section, God's words of hope follow the immediately preceding words about the disgrace of God's people (43:22-28). Twice the Lord speaks of

Jacob and Israel as his chosen (44:1-2); on the second occasion (44:2) he uses the name Jeshurun (in the Heb. text; Israel in the NLT) for Israel, and addresses them as their Creator ("the LORD who made you"). In the desert during the first Exodus, God provided water for the thirsty people, but now the people themselves were the dry ground (cf. 41:17-18; 43:20). "I will pour out my Spirit on your descendents, and my blessings on your children" (44:3) is appropriate language for portraying the Holy Spirit's blessing on what would otherwise be barren ground. The promise of refreshing water is often linked with the promise of the Spirit. The language of being poured out (44:3) links this and other passages (cf. 32:15; Ezek 39:29; Joel 2:28ff; Zech 12:10) with the fulfillment that will come on the day of Pentecost (Acts 2:16-17). The blessings then resulted in the children thriving like "watered grass, like willows on a riverbank" (44:4). They will "proudly claim, 'I belong to the LORD' or 'I am a descendant of Jacob'" (44:5). They will even "write the LORD's name on their hands and will take the name of Israel as their own" (44:5).

The rest of the chapter challenges the idolaters; it opens with a full title of Israel's God: "the LORD says, Israel's King and Redeemer, the LORD of Heaven's Armies," to which is then added, "I am the First and the Last; there is no other God" (44:6). The Lord's case against the worship of idols (which began in ch 41) is brought to a climax in chapter 44. Every chapter from 40 to 48 contains some reference to idols, images, or pagan worship, but chapter 44 presents the strongest attack against them.

Once again the claim is made that only the Lord can predict the future, and the lifeless idols are challenged to prove their power and "do as I have done since ancient times" (44:7). The challenge rings throughout this section (chs 40–48), but it receives no response, and the Lord remains unchallenged as the only God. He encourages his people with the words, "Do not tremble; do not be afraid," and reminds them that "There is no other Rock—not one!" (44:8).

Those who "manufacture" idols are ridiculed for their foolishness because the "prized objects are really worthless" (44:9). Only a fool "would make his own god, an idol that cannot help him one bit" (44:10), and "all who worship idols will be disgraced" (44:11). The word translated "manufacture" is rendered "created" when it describes God as the Creator of Israel (43:1). God created mortals, but how can a mortal create the immortal God? The very suggestion reveals the impossibility of such an undertaking. One would have to be blind and ignorant to attempt it. The prophet ridicules humans who think they can make something higher than themselves (44:11).

The bitter ridicule of those who try to make their own gods continues in 44:12-18. The blacksmith who labors at his forge and the wood-carver carefully making his measurements are described in detail, but their idols are motionless and mute. Fine wood (cedar, cypress, oak) is cut down and used either for firewood or for making gods (44:14). The carpenter can only shape his materials, not create them, for these beautiful trees depend on rain to make them grow, and if the Creator withholds the rains, there will be no material for making an idol (44:14). Attention may have been given especially to the wooden idols that were less expensive and therefore more common. The creator of his little god then falls down before the god he has made and says, "Rescue me . . . you are my god" (44:17). No wonder God detests idols (Deut 27:15) and calls them a fraud (Jer 10:14). So much stupidity and ignorance is reflected in making something that cannot see or think (44:18). Those involved in idolatry are both ignorant and irrational; "they cannot see . . . they cannot think," any more than the lifeless idols (44:18). "Their minds are shut" (44:18) and they never consider the fact that their god is only "a block of wood" (44:19). The idolater never thinks to ask, "Is this idol that I'm holding in my hand a lie?" (44:20). When the creature fails to acknowledge and worship the Creator, he exchanges the truth for a lie, and attempts to fill the void by worshiping a creature.

The closing words (44:21-28) of this passage speak of the restoration of Jerusalem. In contrast to idols, God is a powerful Redeemer who forgives his people. They had paid for their sins by going into exile, and God would bring them home to Israel. This joyful news elicits praise even from the mountains and trees (44:23; cf. 49:13).

Israel is here called the Lord's servant whom he will not forget to help (44:21) because he has "swept away" Israel's sins and "scattered" their offenses (44:22). Nature ("mountains . . . forests . . . every tree") is admonished to sing and break out in praise (44:23; cf. 49:13). The Lord is identified as their Redeemer and Creator "who made all things" (44:24); he brought them forth by his word (Ps 33:6), and by his wisdom set them in order (Prov 8:22-31). He is the One who stretched forth the heavens from infinity to infinity and who spread out the earth from east to west. He also "exposes the false prophets" and causes "the wise to give bad advice" (44:25), but the Lord will bring to pass the predictions of his prophets (44:26).

The Lord controls all nature and all people. Isaiah 44:27 may refer to the dividing of the Sea (cf. 43:16, 19) that allowed Israel to pass through on dry land, to the crossing of the Jordan River, which "piled up in a heap" (Josh 3:16), providing dry ground on which the Israelites could cross, or to the taking of Babylon when Cyrus diverted the flow of the Euphrates River so that he could use the dry riverbed as a passageway under the wall of the city. It has also been applied to the drying of the Euphrates (cf. Jer 51:36) in the sense that the river represented the empire of Babylon. Of course, the language could be metaphoric to express God's power to overcome all obstacles that might stand in opposition to his will; there are no barriers that he cannot move.

Up to 44:28, the deliverer has not been identified. But now the Lord does a thing unheard of among the nations: he names (here and in 45:1) the one that he will raise up to deliver his people years in the future. His name is Cyrus. Although unusual, it is not without parallel; Josiah was announced by name centuries before his birth (1 Kgs 13:2). In this announcement, the prophet reaches the climax toward which he has been moving since his prophecy in 41:1-7. Cyrus will act as the Lord's shepherd, seeing that the flock is restored to their home, while not involving himself in the actual rebuilding of Jerusalem, which is not to be done by a Gentile but by God's people. Although mentioned by name, no commentary is given about him; secular history does that.

◆    ## 8. God's purpose through Cyrus (45:1-25)

This is what the LORD says to Cyrus,
    his anointed one,
    whose right hand he will empower.
Before him, mighty kings will be
    paralyzed with fear.
Their fortress gates will be
    opened,
    never to shut again.
² This is what the LORD says:

"I will go before you, Cyrus,
    and level the mountains.*
I will smash down gates of bronze
    and cut through bars of iron.
³ And I will give you treasures hidden
    in the darkness—
    secret riches.
I will do this so you may know that
    I am the LORD,
    the God of Israel, the one who calls
    you by name.

⁴ "And why have I called you for this
    work?
Why did I call you by name when
    you did not know me?
It is for the sake of Jacob my servant,
    Israel my chosen one.
⁵ I am the LORD;
    there is no other God.
I have equipped you for battle,
    though you don't even know me,
⁶ so all the world from east to west
    will know there is no other God.
I am the LORD, and there is no other.
⁷   I create the light and make the
    darkness.
I send good times and bad times.
    I, the LORD, am the one who does
    these things.

⁸ "Open up, O heavens,
    and pour out your righteousness.
Let the earth open wide
    so salvation and righteousness can
    sprout up together.
    I, the LORD, created them.

⁹ "What sorrow awaits those who argue
    with their Creator.

Does a clay pot argue with its
    maker?
Does the clay dispute with the one
    who shapes it, saying,
    'Stop, you're doing it wrong!'
Does the pot exclaim,
    'How clumsy can you be?'
¹⁰ How terrible it would be if a newborn
    baby said to its father,
    'Why was I born?'
or if it said to its mother,
    'Why did you make me this way?'"

¹¹ This is what the LORD says—
    the Holy One of Israel and your
    Creator:
"Do you question what I do for my
    children?
Do you give me orders about the
    work of my hands?
¹² I am the one who made the earth
    and created people to live on it.
With my hands I stretched out the
    heavens.
All the stars are at my command.
¹³ I will raise up Cyrus to fulfill my
    righteous purpose,
    and I will guide his actions.
He will restore my city and free my
    captive people—
    without seeking a reward!
    I, the LORD of Heaven's Armies,
    have spoken!"

¹⁴ This is what the LORD says:

"You will rule the Egyptians,
    the Ethiopians,* and the
    Sabeans.
They will come to you with all their
    merchandise,
    and it will all be yours.
They will follow you as prisoners
    in chains.
They will fall to their knees in front
    of you and say,
'God is with you, and he is the only
    God.
There is no other.'"

15 Truly, O God of Israel, our Savior,
  you work in mysterious ways.
16 All craftsmen who make idols will
    be humiliated.
  They will all be disgraced together.
17 But the LORD will save the people
    of Israel
  with eternal salvation.
  Throughout everlasting ages,
    they will never again be humiliated
    and disgraced.

18 For the LORD is God,
  and he created the heavens and
    earth
  and put everything in place.
  He made the world to be lived in,
    not to be a place of empty chaos.
  "I am the LORD," he says,
    "and there is no other.
19 I publicly proclaim bold promises.
  I do not whisper obscurities in
    some dark corner.
  I would not have told the people
    of Israel* to seek me
  if I could not be found.
  I, the LORD, speak only what is true
  and declare only what is right.

20 "Gather together and come,
  you fugitives from surrounding
    nations.

What fools they are who carry around
    their wooden idols
  and pray to gods that cannot save!
21 Consult together, argue your case.
  Get together and decide what to say.
  Who made these things known so long
    ago?
  What idol ever told you they would
    happen?
  Was it not I, the LORD?
  For there is no other God but me,
  a righteous God and Savior.
  There is none but me.
22 Let all the world look to me for
    salvation!
  For I am God; there is no other.
23 I have sworn by my own name;
  I have spoken the truth,
  and I will never go back on my
    word:
  Every knee will bend to me,
    and every tongue will confess
    allegiance to me.*"
24 The people will declare,
  "The LORD is the source of all my
    righteousness and strength."
  And all who were angry with him
    will come to him and be ashamed.
25 In the LORD all the generations of
    Israel will be justified,
  and in him they will boast.

45:2 As in Dead Sea Scrolls and Greek version; Masoretic Text reads *the swellings.*  45:14 Hebrew *Cushites.*
45:19 Hebrew *of Jacob.* See note on 14:1.  45:23 Hebrew *will confess;* Greek version reads *will confess and give praise to God.* Compare Rom 14:11.


NOTES

45:1 *anointed.* Used in reference to kings (2 Sam 5:3), this is the word from which "Messiah" comes.

45:2 *gates of bronze . . . bars of iron.* Gates of some towns were secured by iron bars, the strongest material available to the Babylonians. Herodotus (*Histories* 1.179) reported that the gates of Babylon were of bronze, but on that fateful night, the gates on the bank of the river were left unbarred. Although they may have appeared to be solid bronze, the examples discovered are bronze-plated wood.

45:3 *treasures hidden in the darkness.* May refer to the origins of precious metals in deep mines (see Job 28:1-6).

45:7 *I create the light and make the darkness.* In this context, this could also refer to the darkness that plagued the Egyptians (Exod 10:21-23; Ps 105:28; cf. Isa 47:11; Amos 3:6).

45:8 *pour out your righteousness.* This is a remarkable picture of righteousness being poured down from on high as it also springs up from below (cf. 44:23). Heaven and earth are summoned to participate in the glory of Israel's redemption and restoration. God's final goal is that the kingdom of heaven (righteousness, justice, salvation) be planted upon earth (cf. 61:3b). Cf. the prayer of Jesus, "Your will be done on earth as it is in heaven."

**45:15** *you work in mysterious ways.* Lit., "God who hides himself" (*'el mistatter*). This could mean that God might not be available when needed (8:17; 54:8) or that his ways are mysterious and he is not accountable to anyone (55:8-9; Ps 77:19; Rom 9:20; 11:33-34). The versions have "God who hides himself" (NASB, NRSV, NIV, REB), "God who hides yourself" (ESV), "God who has hidden himself" (GW), "God who conceals himself" (TEV), "God that people cannot see" (NCV), "your God is a mysery" (CEV), and "God who concealed Himself" (NJPS).

**45:18** *empty chaos.* The Heb. is *tohu* [TH8414, ZH9332] (cf. 24:10); this would not be a good place to live.

**45:19** *dark corner.* In contrast to pagan oracles often associated with caves and dark recesses, the Lord spoke openly on Mount Sinai.

**45:23** *sworn by my own name.* The Lord could swear by none greater (cf. 62:8; Gen 22:16; Jer 22:5; Rom 14:11; Heb 6:13-20).

*Every knee will bend to me.* Paul uses this language in Rom 14:11 and Phil 2:10-11.

COMMENTARY

Isaiah first alluded to a king who met victory at every step in 41:2; now, in two successive verses, he mentions this king specifically by name (44:28; 45:1). The ability to name Cyrus 150 years before his time underscores God's creative power (45:24). Other kings were also named beforehand in view of a special commission, such as Jehu (1 Kgs 19:16), and Josiah (1 Kgs 13:2). This predictive ability should not seem unusual in a deity who also defeated false religious leaders (44:25), fulfilled his prophets' words (44:26), and dried up the Red Sea (44:27; cf. 43:16-17)!

In the preceding verse (44:28), Cyrus is called "my shepherd," with the notation that he would certainly do as God said regarding the rebuilding of Jerusalem and restoration of the Temple. For this work, Cyrus received the additional title, "anointed," even as Hazael and Jehu were anointed for their work. He was to be empowered as Israel was (41:13; 42:6), but nothing was said of a "house of Cyrus." He stands as a solitary individual, an object of wonder almost like Melchizedek. The unusual attribution of "anointed" (45:1) to someone outside Israel must have shocked Isaiah's audience. The Lord would use the anointed Persian king Cyrus (cf. Dan 4:17) to accomplish his sovereign purposes among the nations of that world just as he used the Assyrians (10:5-11) and the Babylonians (Hab 1:5-6).

It was said of this anointed servant that "mighty kings [would] be paralyzed with fear" before him (45:1). The Lord would go before Cyrus to "level the mountains" and "cut through bars of iron" (45:2). The Lord would give treasures and riches to Cyrus (45:3), and all of this would be done so people would know that God is "the LORD, the God of Israel" (45:3) and "for the sake of Jacob, [God's] servant" (45:4). Although Cyrus would not be aware of it, he would be used of God for sovereign purposes so that "all the world from east to west will know there is no other God" (45:5-6).

Cyrus would be used by the one who created light and darkness and sends good times as well as bad (45:7). The Creator commanded the heavens and the earth to obey him because he was the one who created them (45:8). Salvation and righteousness (45:8) seems to refer to an ethical and moral standard in accordance with God's nature; they include deliverance, safety, and freedom from distress.

In 45:9-13, the Lord's sovereignty in sending Cyrus is revealed. The will of God, the sovereign Lord of the universe, will be done, and "what sorrow awaits those who argue with their Creator" (45:9). Can one imagine a clay pot in dispute with its maker? (45:9). Can a newborn baby ask its parents, "Why did you make me this way?" (45:10). Similar perspective is found elsewhere (29:16; cf. 10:15), and Paul uses this language in Romans 9:20.

"The Holy One of Israel and your Creator" (45:11) is the one who "made the earth and created people to live on it" and has "all the stars at [his] command" (45:12). He will raise up Cyrus to fulfill his righteous purpose and guide his actions (45:13). The Lord of Heaven's Armies will use Cyrus to restore his city and free his captive people (45:13).

The nations and the Lord's people are described in 45:14-17. In the future, the nations that come with all their wealth and fall on their knees before God's people, confessing that "God is with you, and he is the only God" (45:14) will become converted. God will be working in "mysterious ways" (45:15) that are not grasped by human minds (cf. 40:28; 55:9; Prov 25:2; Rom 11:33). He is the Redeemer from all forms of anguish; he is the LORD that will save his people with "eternal salvation" so they will "never again be humiliated and disgraced" (45:17). Isaiah viewed Israel's return from exile as the beginning of a great time of salvation that would never end.

This section concludes by addressing God's purpose in creation (45:18-25). In 45:18-19, the Lord points to his two great witnesses, creation and revelation. The Lord did not make the earth a "place of empty chaos" (45:18), but a place to be inhabited. After the introductory expression, "I am the LORD . . . and there is no other" (45:18), God says that he did not "whisper obscurities in some dark corner" (45:19). This could be an allusion to the clandestine ways of mediums and spiritists (cf. 8:19; 29:4). In contrast to the frequently devious and evasive pagan oracles, the Lord spoke the truth clearly and directly (cf. Deut 30:11-14). He spoke "only what is true" and "only what is right" (45:19).

The Lord then invited the "fugitives from surrounding nations" to "gather together and come" (45:20). Idolaters were again confronted and challenged: "consult together, argue your case . . . decide what to say" (45:21). They needed to admit that "there is no other God" but the Lord (45:21), and comply with God's admonition to "let all the world look to me for salvation!" (45:22). This invitation was issued to "all the world"—that is, to all of humanity. The idol gods could not save (45:20), and there is no other Savior than the Lord (45:21).

This salvation was not for Israel alone, but through Israel; it was intended for the benefit of the whole world. Heathenism was breaking up. As time passed and the prophecies concerning the nations came to pass (cf. chs 13–23), and as the prophecies about Cyrus, Babylon, Israel, and the servant were fulfilled, the Lord's case would be established and confirmed. Let the nations declare and present their proofs (cf. 41:21), and let them consult and help each other to that end. It would be of no avail, for the all-decisive question concerns the one who declared this in advance.

The Lord will never go back on his word and ultimately "every tongue will confess allegiance" to him (45:23), a verse cited by Paul in Rom 14:11. The people will declare, "The LORD is the source of all my righteousness and strength" (45:24). He will be their justification and "in him they will boast" (45:25). This is the goal of all redemptive history.

◆     ## 9. Babylon's false gods (46:1-13)

Bel and Nebo, the gods of Babylon,
  bow as they are lowered to the
  ground.
They are being hauled away on
  ox carts.
The poor beasts stagger under
  the weight.
2 Both the idols and their owners are
  bowed down.
The gods cannot protect the people,
and the people cannot protect the
  gods.
They go off into captivity together.

3 "Listen to me, descendants of Jacob,
  all you who remain in Israel.
I have cared for you since you were
  born.
Yes, I carried you before you were
  born.
4 I will be your God throughout your
  lifetime—
until your hair is white with age.
I made you, and I will care for you.
I will carry you along and save you.

5 "To whom will you compare me?
  Who is my equal?
6 Some people pour out their silver and
  gold
and hire a craftsman to make a god
  from it.
Then they bow down and worship it!

7 They carry it around on their
  shoulders,
and when they set it down, it stays
  there.
It can't even move!
And when someone prays to it, there is
  no answer.
It can't rescue anyone from trouble.

8 "Do not forget this! Keep it in mind!
  Remember this, you guilty ones.
9 Remember the things I have done in
  the past.
For I alone am God!
I am God, and there is none like me.
10 Only I can tell you the future
  before it even happens.
Everything I plan will come to pass,
  for I do whatever I wish.
11 I will call a swift bird of prey from
  the east—
a leader from a distant land to come
  and do my bidding.
I have said what I would do,
  and I will do it.

12 "Listen to me, you stubborn people
  who are so far from doing right.
13 For I am ready to set things right,
  not in the distant future, but right
  now!
I am ready to save Jerusalem*
  and show my glory to Israel.

46:13 Hebrew *Zion.*

NOTES

**46:1 Bel.** Bel means "lord" and is equivalent to the Canaanite "Baal"; this title of honor was assigned to the chief Babylonian god Marduk, the city god of Babylon and head of the Babylonian pantheon. It was used as a theophoric element in the names of Babylonian kings, for example, Belshazzar.

**Nebo.** Nebo, the son of Marduk (Bel), was the god of learning and writing. His name was also used as a theophoric element in the names of three of the most significant kings of the final dynasty—Nabopolassar, Nebuchadnezzar, and Nabonidus. This shows the status that Nebo/Nabu enjoyed in the royal house.

**46:10 *Everything I plan will come to pass.*** God's purpose (cf. 14:24) would stand, and his plans regarding Israel and Babylon would be carried out (cf. Ps 33:11; Job 23:13; Isa 14:26).

**46:11 *bird of prey.*** Heb. *'ayit* [TH5861, ZH6514] refers to a kind of bird of prey, used elsewhere in Isaiah only in 18:6. No particular species is indicated, although its use (cf. 18:6; Gen 15:11; Ezek 39:4) suggests some form of scavenger whose swiftness and power are in view (cf. 8:8; Jer 49:22; Dan 8:4). The reference here is to Cyrus, king of Persia (cf. 41:2). He was noted for his ensign, a golden eagle standing with outstretched wings on the top of his spear (cf. Xenophon *Cyropaedia* 7.1, 4 and *Anabasis* 1.10, 12).

**46:12 *stubborn.*** Heb. *'abbirey leb* [TH47/3820, ZH52/4213], lit., "strong of heart." The NIV renders it "stubborn-hearted," and Oswalt translates it "hard-hearted" (1998:233). Motyer (1993:370) defines it as "rigid in mind, intractable in emotions, and unbiddable in will."

COMMENTARY

Chapters 46 and 47 reveal the impending doom of Babylon. The call and mission of Cyrus had been presented, and now the Lord was ready to make known the fall of the great pagan metropolis of Babylon. This section is somewhat repetitious, as particular themes are emphasized. Much is an elaboration of 45:20.

In contrast to the Babylonian worshippers who must carry their gods, the Lord of Israel carries his people. With sarcasm, Isaiah described the idol-gods of Babylon as "being hauled away on ox carts" (46:1); the dead weight of the lifeless idols was a load to the idols and to the ones moving them—they were both "bowed down" (46:2). The sad fact was that neither could help the other as they went "off into captivity together" (46:2). Since they were unable to save the people, the helpless idols must also go into captivity with them (cf. Jer 48:7; 49:3; Hos 10:5; Amos 1:15). The famous Cyrus Cylinder (ANET 316) depicts the Persian conqueror accepting Babylon's gods and doing homage to them. Although idols were adored beyond the fall of Babylon, they eventually disappeared into oblivion.

In contrast to the dead deities of Babylon, the Lord had created his people and had cared for them since birth (46:3). He especially cared for the remnant that was left in Israel, and this becomes a significant theological theme. The word "remnant" generally suggests something pitifully small (see 44:16ff; Amos 1:8; 5:15; Jer 42:2). The theme of the remnant communicates overtones of God's love and compassion and was used by preexilic prophets such as Amos (5:15) and Micah (2:12).

In contrast to the idol worshipers must carry their helpless gods, the Lord carries his people (46:4). In view of this, the challenge is made: "Who is my equal?" "To whom will you compare me?" (46:5). The lifeless and helpless idols had no power to rescue anyone from trouble (46:7). With repetition for emphasis, the covenant people were warned to "remember the things I have done in the past" (46:9). There is no one else like God, and only he "can tell . . . the future" (46:10).

A "swift bird of prey from the east" (46:11) will appear in response to the Lord's call. This seems an appropriate image for Cyrus's swift conquest (cf. 41:2; Jer 49:22). The Lord was ready to save Jerusalem and bring glory to his people (46:13).

## ◆   10. Babylon's fall (47:1-15)

"Come down, virgin daughter of
  Babylon, and sit in the dust.
For your days of sitting on a throne
  have ended.
O daughter of Babylonia,* never again
  will you be
the lovely princess, tender and
  delicate.
2 Take heavy millstones and grind flour.
  Remove your veil, and strip off your
  robe.
Expose yourself to public view.
3 You will be naked and burdened with
  shame.
I will take vengeance against you
  without pity."

4 Our Redeemer, whose name is the
  LORD of Heaven's Armies,
is the Holy One of Israel.

5 "O beautiful Babylon, sit now in
  darkness and silence.
Never again will you be known as
  the queen of kingdoms.
6 For I was angry with my chosen
  people
and punished them by letting them
  fall into your hands.
But you, Babylon, showed them no
  mercy.
You oppressed even the elderly.
7 You said, 'I will reign forever as queen
  of the world!'
You did not reflect on your actions
  or think about their consequences.

8 "Listen to this, you pleasure-loving
  kingdom,
living at ease and feeling secure.

You say, 'I am the only one, and there
  is no other.
I will never be a widow or lose
  my children.'
9 Well, both these things will come
  upon you in a moment:
widowhood and the loss of your
  children.
Yes, these calamities will come
  upon you,
despite all your witchcraft and
  magic.

10 "You felt secure in your wickedness.
  'No one sees me,' you said.
But your 'wisdom' and 'knowledge'
  have led you astray,
and you said, 'I am the only one,
  and there is no other.'
11 So disaster will overtake you,
  and you won't be able to charm
  it away.
Calamity will fall upon you,
  and you won't be able to buy your
  way out.
A catastrophe will strike you suddenly,
  one for which you are not prepared.

12 "Now use your magical charms!
  Use the spells you have worked
  at all these years!
Maybe they will do you some good.
Maybe they can make someone
  afraid of you.
13 All the advice you receive has made
  you tired.
Where are all your astrologers,
those stargazers who make predictions
  each month?

Let them stand up and save you
from what the future holds.
<sup>14</sup>But they are like straw burning in a
fire;
they cannot save themselves from
the flame.
You will get no help from them at all;

their hearth is no place to sit for
warmth.
<sup>15</sup>And all your friends,
those with whom you've done
business since childhood,
will go their own ways,
turning a deaf ear to your cries.

47:1 Or *Chaldea;* also in 47:5.

### NOTES

**47:1 *virgin daughter of Babylon.*** The form of address, "virgin daughter," does not refer to moral chastity, but to the fact that since she became a world power, she had not been "violated"; no one had yet breached her walls. According to Herodotus (*Histories* 1.29), Babylon was very proud of the fact that she had never been breached or captured. This same expression is used of Tyre in 23:12.

*sit in the dust.* This was a picture of desolation and mourning (cf. 3:26).

**47:2 *Take heavy millstones and grind flour.*** This refers to lowly work, usually done by women.

***Remove your veil, and strip off your robe. Expose yourself to public view.*** The Heb. has something more like, "Lift up your skirts, bare your legs, and wade through the streams" (NIV). The language of "lift your skirts" and "bare your legs" can be understood as describing women doing menial tasks (such as washing clothes in the streams) or it could possibly refer to preparation for wading through streams on their way to exile (Knight 1965:156). Such language—including "take off your veil"—can also refer to the exposure of a proud woman's body and therefore to her humiliation (cf. Hos 2:10; Isa 20:4; Nah 3:8; Jer 13:22, 26).

**47:3 *naked and burdened with shame.*** This is not the picture of a queen but that of a debased woman.

### COMMENTARY

In chapter 14, Isaiah dealt with the arrogant boast and fall of the Babylonian king; in chapter 46, he revealed the divine judgment against the idols of Babylon. Here in chapter 47, he points to the fall of the queen city. Chapter 46 described Babylon's impotent idols, and chapter 47 describes her dethroned queen.

The text is in the form of a "taunt song" dealing with Babylon's wicked king. This genre occurs elsewhere in the Old Testament (see, for example, Isaiah 13–14 and Jeremiah 50–51). Isaiah 47 is an elegy on the overthrow of Babylon and can be divided into four strophes: 47:1-4, 5-7, 8-11, 12-15.

**Taunt Song of Babylon's Fall.** The first three verses graphically describe the shame of Babylon's downfall. The time had come for the unconquered one to strip herself, expose herself to public view, and sit in the dust. She would be left "naked and burdened with shame" (47:3). From near the dawn of human history, Babylon had been considered proud and arrogant. The tower erected at Babel (the forerunner of Babylon) after the Deluge (Gen 11:1-9) was an expression of man's desire to have his own god and a religion fashioned after his own fallen nature. This Babylon had to fall—it was God's design.

At 47:4, a full and elaborate name for God is proclaimed. This God is behind all of history, and his name reflects his nature and purpose: "our Redeemer . . . the LORD of Heaven's Armies, the Holy One of Israel." Babylon is then described as she is stripped of her power, wealth, and glory. She will appear before the nations in her nakedness and shame, to be stared at and mocked by them. Never again will she be known as the "queen of kingdoms" (47:5). Humiliated by the shame of her fall, the proud queen must sit in silence, no longer boasting of her greatness but sinking away into the darkness of obscurity and oblivion. In contrast, she had earlier been known as chief among the nations.

Although God purposely let his people be punished by Babylon, she went too far and did not consider the consequences of her actions (47:7). Her boasting is reminiscent of the words of Nebuchadnezzar in Daniel 4:30, and she was given to revelry, orgies, drunkenness, and debauchery (cf. Herodotus *Histories* 1:199; Bar 6:43). She considered herself beyond God's reach, and assumed a place for herself in the divine realm.

The pleasure-loving (47:8) Babylon's lofty opinion of herself is contrasted with the lowly position assigned to her by God in 47:8-10. Twice, Babylon boasts, "I am the only one, and there is no other," a claim similar to the one the Lord himself made (47:8, 10; 43:11; 45:5-6). She was lounging in false security (cf. 32:9, 11), for eventually the queen would become a widow and lose all her children (cf. 13:16, 18). Despite all her witchcraft and magic, she experienced the calamities of "widowhood and the loss of children" (47:9). Babylon was noted for its many magic and occult practices (cf. Dan 2:2), but the words "no one sees me" (47:10) are an admission of the non-reality of their gods. Babylon practiced a practical atheism.

A "calamity" and "catastrophe" (47:11) arose so fast that Babylon did not know what had hit her (47:11-15). God taunted the city to use its magical charms. "Use the spells you have worked at all these years!" (47:12). Since the city had so many occult advisers, "Let them stand up and save you from what the future holds" (47:13). Since they could not even save themselves, Babylon would "get no help from them at all" (47:14). The Babylonians would burn under the wrath of God as rapidly as stubble or dry grass, one of Isaiah's favorite metaphors (47:14; cf. 5:24; 10:17; 40:24; Mal 4:1). Former friends will "go their own ways, turning a deaf ear to your cries" (47:15).

◆    ## 11. God's reminder to his stubborn people (48:1-22)

"Listen to me, O family of Jacob,
you who are called by the name
of Israel
and born into the family of Judah.
Listen, you who take oaths in the
name of the LORD
and call on the God of Israel.
You don't keep your promises,

2    even though you call yourself the
holy city
and talk about depending on the God
of Israel,
whose name is the LORD of Heaven's
Armies.
3 Long ago I told you what was going
to happen.

Then suddenly I took action,
and all my predictions came true.
⁴For I know how stubborn and
obstinate you are.
Your necks are as unbending as
iron.
Your heads are as hard as bronze.
⁵That is why I told you what would
happen;
I told you beforehand what I was
going to do.
Then you could never say, 'My idols
did it.
My wooden image and metal god
commanded it to happen!'
⁶You have heard my predictions and
seen them fulfilled,
but you refuse to admit it.
Now I will tell you new things,
secrets you have not yet heard.
⁷They are brand new, not things from
the past.
So you cannot say, 'We knew that
all the time!'

⁸"Yes, I will tell you of things that are
entirely new,
things you never heard of before.
For I know so well what traitors you
are.
You have been rebels from birth.
⁹Yet for my own sake and for the honor
of my name,
I will hold back my anger and not
wipe you out.
¹⁰I have refined you, but not as silver
is refined.
Rather, I have refined you in the
furnace of suffering.
¹¹I will rescue you for my sake—
yes, for my own sake!
I will not let my reputation be
tarnished,
and I will not share my glory
with idols!

¹²"Listen to me, O family of Jacob,
Israel my chosen one!
I alone am God,
the First and the Last.

¹³It was my hand that laid the
foundations of the earth,
my right hand that spread out
the heavens above.
When I call out the stars,
they all appear in order."

¹⁴Have any of your idols ever told you
this?
Come, all of you, and listen:
The LORD has chosen Cyrus as his ally.
He will use him to put an end to the
empire of Babylon
and to destroy the Babylonian*
armies.

¹⁵"I have said it: I am calling Cyrus!
I will send him on this errand and
will help him succeed.
¹⁶Come closer, and listen to this.
From the beginning I have told you
plainly what would happen."

And now the Sovereign LORD and his
Spirit
have sent me with this message.
¹⁷This is what the LORD says—
your Redeemer, the Holy One of
Israel:
"I am the LORD your God,
who teaches you what is good
for you
and leads you along the paths
you should follow.
¹⁸Oh, that you had listened to my
commands!
Then you would have had peace
flowing like a gentle river
and righteousness rolling over you
like waves in the sea.
¹⁹Your descendants would have been
like the sands along the
seashore—
too many to count!
There would have been no need for
your destruction,
or for cutting off your family name."

²⁰Yet even now, be free from your
captivity!
Leave Babylon and the Babylonians.*

Sing out this message!
Shout it to the ends of the earth!
The LORD has redeemed his servants,
the people of Israel.*
²¹They were not thirsty
when he led them through the desert.

He divided the rock,
and water gushed out for them
to drink.
²²"But there is no peace for the
wicked,"
says the LORD.

48:14 Or Chaldean.   48:20a Or the Chaldeans.   48:20b Hebrew his servant, Jacob. See note on 14:1.

## NOTES

**48:1 born into the family of Judah.** Lit., "come out of the waters of Judah," indicating that their tribe of origin was Judah, the headwaters and chief tribe of the southern kingdom.

**48:2 call yourself the holy city.** The Heb. is cryptic, lit., "of the holy city they call themselves." The versions have "you who call yourselves citizens of the holy city" (NIV, REB, GW), "call themselves after the holy city" (NASB, NRSV), and "for you are called after the holy city" (NJPS).

**48:3 Long ago I told you what was going to happen.** The Heb. speaks of the "former things" (ri'shonoth [TH7223A, ZH8037]), which apparently is a general reference to all the acts of redemption the Lord had performed in earlier times that were in keeping with what he had foretold (see 41:22; 42:9; 43:18; 44:7-8; 45:21; 46:9-10). Numerous events had been declared in advance and fulfilled by that time. The people could examine the evidence—the prophecies and their fulfillment—for themselves.

*suddenly.* The suddenness was additional proof that it was the hand of the Lord that was at work (cf. 17:14; 37:35).

**48:4 Your heads are as hard as bronze.** This specific expression (lit. "bronze forehead") does not occur elsewhere in Scripture, but similar ideas are found in such passages as Jer 6:28, which describes the people as hardened rebels of "bronze and iron," and Ezek 3:7, which calls them "hard-hearted and stubborn," requiring the Lord to make the prophet "as hard and stubborn as they are."

**48:5 wooden image and metal god.** This is a reference to idols carved from wood and cast in metal.

**48:8** In the Heb., this verse opens with emphasis on the obtuseness of the rebellious people: "You have neither heard nor understood; from of old your ear has not been opened" (NIV). The three statements—"heard," "understood" and "been open"—are each prefaced by *gam* [TH1571, ZH1685], a particle of addition or emphasis.

*traitors.* The Heb. root *bagad* [TH898, ZH953] includes ideas of faithlessness, disloyalty, and spiritual prostitution. The verb appears a dozen times in Isaiah and a cognate noun is found in 24:16.

**48:13 laid the foundations of the earth.** This is probably a reference to its being firmly fixed in place, for Job had said, "he suspends the earth over nothing" (Job 26:7), indicating that there is no material substance on which it rests, a cosmology apparently unique to Israel. For the idea of "firmly established," see also Ps 96:10.

*When I call out the stars.* This is probably a reference to the creation of the stars. Isaiah often refers to God as Creator (40:21-22; 42:5; 51:13).

**48:14 his ally.** Lit., "whom the Lord loves." In Heb., the verb "to love" can mean "to be in alliance with" (NIDOTTE 1:285).

**48:16 I have told you plainly.** See the words of Christ in John 18:20.

***Spirit.*** The translator must decide whether to capitalize this word or not. It is capitalized in the NIV, NASB, and RSV, but is rendered "spirit" in the KJV, NRSV, NEB, REB, NJB, and NAB. (The RSV used "Spirit," but the NRSV changed it to "spirit.")

***have sent me with this message.*** These words have noteworthy parallels in the experience of Moses (Exod 2:14-15; 7:16) and Jesus (John 5:24; 6:44, 57; 8:42).

**48:18 *peace.*** The Heb. word for "peace" (*shalom* [TH7965, ZH8934]) means more than cessation of hostilities; it also includes the ideas of well-being and prosperity. Here it is compared to the good influence of a constant river, like the Euphrates.

## COMMENTARY

Chapter 48 concludes a section that is primarily about the Lord's controversy with idols and his plan involving Cyrus for the destruction of Babylon. God's purpose was twofold: to strengthen Israel's faith in him, and to expose the folly of worshiping idols, which were impotent and unreal.

The perspective of these chapters seems to be that of the Babylonian captivity. From Babylon, the prophet looked back at the causes for the captivity and forward to deliverance by Cyrus. The Lord was speaking through Isaiah to reveal what was still in the future.

Israel's hypocrisy and stubbornness are described in 48:1-11. Although Israel prayed to God and appeared to rely on him, the nation had, in reality, acted hypocritically. All too frequently, the people failed to worship God, instead worshiping the idols that Isaiah so strongly condemned.

God's people are addressed fully as the "family of Jacob . . . called by the name of Israel . . . family of Judah" (48:1). Although they called themselves "the holy city" and took "oaths in the name of the LORD" while calling on the God of Israel, they were unfaithful and disobedient (48:1-2). For his part, God was faithful in warning them of impending judgment before he took action (48:3). For the captives in Babylonia, the holy city of Jerusalem (which now lay in ruins; 48:2) was only symbolic of what they longed for—the special presence of God in their midst.

The rebels are described as "stubborn and obstinate," with necks "as unbending as iron" and heads "as hard as bronze" (48:4). But despite the people's hypocrisy, stubbornness, and trust in idols, God would not cut the nation off at this time, for that would defeat his purpose of bringing the Servant in through Israel. By suffering, this Servant would deliver all who looked to him for salvation (49:1-13; 53). According to chapter 54, the "new things" included the enlargement and glory of the redeemed Zion and a completely new order—a new heaven and a new earth (65:16-17, 25).

How and in what sense were these "things that are entirely new" created (48:7)? In both Isaiah (cf. 46:10) and the New Testament (Rom 8:28; 9:11; Eph 1:9-11; 3:11; 2 Tim 1:9; 1 Pet 1:10-12, 20), God's plan of redemption, which includes the work of the Servant, was in his design from the beginning. The immediate unfolding of God's plan concerned the return and restoration of the Jews through Cyrus. However, the reference is not only to old Jewish history, but to a higher order of things, a new creation that was already depicted as a reality in Isaiah's prophecies.

God would restore Israel, and the messianic age would come (cf. 65:17) even though Israel did not deserve it.

The people were told of "things that are entirely new," despite the fact that they had been traitors and rebels from birth (48:8). Like silver, they had been refined in the furnace of suffering (48:9-10), and Egypt is referred to as a "burning furnace" (Deut 4:20; 1 Kgs 8:51; Jer 11:4). The experience of God's people in Babylon was similar to the testing in Egypt, but despite Israel's sin, God would be faithful to his covenant (cf. 55:3) and would act for his own sake.

The message of 48:9 is reiterated in 48:11, probably for emphasis. The Lord would not destroy Israel as they deserved, nor would he allow weakness to be charged against him on the grounds that he had overlooked their sins. He rebuked the nation for its hypocrisy, but did not terminate his covenant people. The fall of Jerusalem and the exile of his people brought dishonor to the Lord's name (Ezek 36:20-23).

In spite of the rebellion and unbelief of his covenant people, God would rescue them for his own sake (48:11). As Israel's collapse dishonored God's name (48:11), so her restoration would cause it to be praised (cf. 42:8). This way, God said, "I will not let my reputation be tarnished" or "share my glory with idols" (48:11).

The closing verses (48:12-22) speak of God's faithfulness in carrying out his purposes against Babylon. The Lord again reminded the people that "I alone am God, the First and the Last" (48:12), a statement reinforced with the reminder that he was the Creator who "spread out the heavens above" with the palm of his right hand (48:13). He simply spoke, and they all appeared in their places (48:13). No idols ever made such claims of creative activity (48:14). After this introduction to his identity came the statement, "the LORD has chosen Cyrus as his ally." God would use Cyrus "to put an end to the empire of Babylon" (48:14). The Lord said three things about Cyrus: (1) "I am calling Cyrus!" (2) "I will send him on this errand," and (3) "[I] will help him succeed" (48:15). This is the last mention of Cyrus.

Isaiah's message came from the "Sovereign LORD and his Spirit" (48:16). The one sent is not explicitly identified here but it is undoubtedly the Servant, introduced earlier in this section (42:1-13) and prominent in the following text (49:1-13; 50:4-11; 52:13–53:12) and in 61:1-3. This being the case, the verse speaks of three persons: (1) the Sovereign LORD, (2) his Spirit, and (3) the Servant who is sent with the message.

The next verse elaborates on the identity of God as "your Redeemer, the Holy One of Israel . . . the LORD your God" (48:17). If only the people had listened to God's commands, they would have enjoyed peace and righteousness (48:18), for God's commands were righteous (Ps 119:172). They could have "been like the sands along the seashore—too many to count" (48:19), but instead only a meager remnant was preserved by God's grace.

The captive people had entered Babylonia weeping and had hung up their lyres on the branches of the willow trees (Ps 137:1-4), unable to sing in a foreign land. Now they were to leave that land singing and shouting to the ends of the earth that

"The LORD has redeemed his servants, the people of Israel" (48:20). God's people may obey him, enjoy peace, and have their thirst quenched, but "there is no peace for the wicked," (48:22).

◆     **B. The Servant of the Lord (49:1–57:21)**
      **1. The commission of the servant (49:1-13)**

Listen to me, all you in distant lands!
Pay attention, you who are far away!
The LORD called me before my birth;
  from within the womb he called me
  by name.
2 He made my words of judgment as
  sharp as a sword.
He has hidden me in the shadow of
  his hand.
I am like a sharp arrow in his quiver.

3 He said to me, "You are my servant,
  Israel,
and you will bring me glory."

4 I replied, "But my work seems so
  useless!
I have spent my strength for
  nothing and to no purpose.
Yet I leave it all in the LORD's hand;
  I will trust God for my reward."
5 And now the LORD speaks—
  the one who formed me in my
  mother's womb to be his servant,
who commissioned me to bring
  Israel back to him.
The LORD has honored me,
  and my God has given me strength.
6 He says, "You will do more than
  restore the people of Israel to me.
I will make you a light to the
  Gentiles,
and you will bring my salvation to
  the ends of the earth."
7 The LORD, the Redeemer
  and Holy One of Israel,
says to the one who is despised and
  rejected by the nations,
to the one who is the servant
  of rulers:
"Kings will stand at attention when
  you pass by.

Princes will also bow low
because of the LORD, the faithful one,
  the Holy One of Israel, who has
  chosen you."

8 This is what the LORD says:

"At just the right time, I will respond
  to you.*
On the day of salvation I will help
  you.
I will protect you and give you to the
  people
  as my covenant with them.
Through you I will reestablish the land
  of Israel
  and assign it to its own people
  again.
9 I will say to the prisoners, 'Come out
  in freedom,'
and to those in darkness, 'Come into
  the light.'
They will be my sheep, grazing in
  green pastures
  and on hills that were previously
  bare.
10 They will neither hunger nor thirst.
  The searing sun will not reach them
  anymore.
For the LORD in his mercy will lead
  them;
  he will lead them beside cool
  waters.
11 And I will make my mountains into
  level paths for them.
The highways will be raised above
  the valleys.
12 See, my people will return from far
  away,
  from lands to the north and west,
  and from as far south as Egypt.*"

| | |
|---|---|
| <sup>13</sup>Sing for joy, O heavens!<br>   Rejoice, O earth!<br>   Burst into song, O mountains! | For the LORD has comforted his people<br>   and will have compassion on them<br>   in their suffering. |

**49:8** Greek version reads *I heard you.* Compare 2 Cor 6:2.   **49:12** As in Dead Sea Scrolls, which read *from the region of Aswan,* which is in southern Egypt. Masoretic Text reads *from the region of Sinim.*

## NOTES

**49:3 *bring me glory.*** Heb. *'asher beka 'etpa'ar,* which is translated in a variety of ways: "in whom I will show my glory" (NASB), "in whom I will display my splendor" (NIV), "in whom I will be glorified" (NRSV), "I will display my glory through you" (GW), "because of you people will praise me" (TEV), "in whom I glory" (NJPS), and "you will bring me glory" (ESV). The expression occurs thirteen times in the OT, nine of which are in Isaiah. Elsewhere, the plural is used of those in whom the Lord shows his beauty, but here the servant (singular) is the focus. This was never said to any prophet or individual, or to Israel or any group within Israel. Isaiah is saying a unique thing about a unique person (Motyer 1993:386). Paul applies 49:6 specifically to Christ, the Redeemer of the Gentiles (see Acts 13:47).

**49:6 *light.*** This is a rich figure representing the light of life (Job 3:20; 18:5; Ps 36:9; 56:13 [14]) and the light of truth (Ps 43:3). Isaiah speaks of the light of the revealed way of the Lord (2:5; 42:6; 51:4; 60:1, 3), of hope (5:30; 42:16; 45:7; 58:8, 10; 59:9), of the Lord (10:17; 60:19-20), and of the day of the Lord (30:26). Isaiah alone uses "light" for moral integrity (5:20) and for the messianic hope (9:2; 42:6; 49:6; 60:1, 3).

***Gentiles.*** Heb. *goyim* [<sup>TH</sup>1471, <sup>ZH</sup>1580], a common word referring in a general way to the nations apart from Israel. The English word "Gentile" seems somewhat anachronistic in the OT (though it is used here by the NIV and KJV); in the NT where it clearly distinguishes between Jews and non-Jews it seems more appropriate. Most modern translations use "nations" (NASB, NRSV, TEV, NCV, GW, CEV, NJPS, ESV) here and elsewhere in the OT.

**49:8 *as my covenant with them.*** This picks up the language of 42:6.

## COMMENTARY

The preceding section (chs 40–48) was about the court scene between the Lord and the heathen idols, the anointed of the Lord, who would deliver Israel from captivity, and the fall of Babylon. That section also presented the glory of the Lord and Israel's attention to him as his servant and witness in the midst of a heathen world. Zion is mentioned only a few times in passing, but from now on it will be an important part of Isaiah's message.

After chapter 48 there are no further references to Cyrus, the Persian king who delivered Israel from Babylon. Instead, chapters 49–57 focus on the greater deliverer, the Messiah-Servant of the Lord who would bring salvation to the world (cf. ch 42). Chapters 49–53 contain three more Servant Songs that describe the servant's work.

The Servant Song of 49:1-13 presents the servant as an individual with a worldwide mission of redemption. The climax of the song describes the servant's death in atonement for sin that will make salvation available to the whole world (53:11-12; cf. 55:1; 56:6-7). There are significant parallels between this song and the one in 42:1-7. There the mission of the servant of the Lord was first announced, and this fuller section introduces the theme of opposition to the servant (49:4, 7).

Speaking in the first person, the servant addresses the "far-off lands" (49:1).

"Listen to me" (49:1) is personal language used in an unusually stark way. Neither Jeremiah, though appointed a prophet to the nations (1:5), nor any other prophet ever said, "listen to me" like this, so this language distinguishes the Servant from the nation. Only Isaiah uses the expression, "to me," and he uses it only of the Lord (46:3, 12; 48:12; 51:1, 7; 55:2). Commentators often compare this with the "Hear him" of Mark 9:7.

The servant announces that he was called before his birth, "from within the womb" (49:1). Isaiah 66:7-8 describes Zion as giving birth to a son, and Micah 4:10 (cf. the Heb. and NIV) speaks of Zion as a woman in labor, who after her rescue from Babylon will give birth to a ruler (Mic 5:2; cf. Rev 12:1-5). According to Isaiah, he received his commission later in life, but the Messiah was still in the womb when he was designated for his office (Luke 1:31-33) and when the name "Jesus" was assigned to him (Matt 1:21; Luke 1:31; also note the echo of this language in Gal 1:15).

The servant was "hidden . . . in the shadow" of the Lord's hand until God's appointed time for him to be revealed (cf. Isa 64:3-4; 1 Cor 2:9-13; Gal 4:4). This Servant would use a different sword than that used by Cyrus and his army in their conquests. The servant's mouth is "sharp as a sword" (cf. Eph 6:17; Heb 4:12; Rev 1:16; 21:12, 16). In 11:4, a powerful rod comes from the mouth of the Messiah. In Revelation 1:16, the one "like a son of man" has a sharp sword in his mouth that represents his authority. The "sharp arrow" indicates that the servant will be used by the Lord to penetrate the hearts of his enemies, either bringing them under his dominion or spreading a judgment of death and destruction on them (cf. Ps 45:3-5; 110; Hab 3:11-13).

The servant is identified as God's servant, Israel who will bring him glory (49:3). This refers to the redemption that he will accomplish (cf. 35:2; 40:5). Although the servant is called "Israel," this cannot refer to the nation of Israel because in 49:5 this servant has a mission to Israel (some commentators apply this reference to national Israel, or at least to some part of it, but most acknowledge that in some way it refers to the Messiah of the New Testament). The name Israel (prince of God) implies conquest or victory and is appropriate for this victorious servant, the Messiah who, in a truer sense than any other, would be an "Israel," that is, a "Prince with God." This servant represents the ideal Israel, in whom God will be glorified.

The servant's response is, "my work seems so useless! . . . Yet I leave it all in the LORD's hand" (49:4). This expression of apparent vanity and lack of purpose in his work probably means that just as the nation Israel had toiled in vain (cf. 65:23), so Christ would encounter strong opposition during his ministry and would temporarily suffer apparent failure. The "suffering servant" theme is developed in the third and fourth Servant Songs (50:4-9 [11]; 52:13–53:12). Yet he knew his reward would eventually come. The "reward" (49:4) probably refers to the servant's spiritual offspring (cf. 53:10), the people who would believe in the Messiah.

The servant's work is described in greater detail in 49:5-6. The one God so tenderly led (cf. 44:2) would indeed be involved in the restoration of Israel, but also in the greater mission of being a light to the nations and of providing opportunity for them to come to the light of salvation. The light for the nations (NLT, "light to the Gentiles") is continued from 42:6; in 45:7, we learn that God, not man, creates the light (cf. 60:3). The Servant is a light so that those in darkness can see (cf. 29:18; 35:5) and "walk in the light of the LORD" (2:5). The language of 49:6 is sometimes referred to as the "Great Commission" of the Old Testament; it was used by Paul and Barnabas in their Christian witness at Pisidian Antioch (Acts 13:47). The Lord's purpose was not just to exalt Jacob, or only to preserve Israel, but to provide a light for the Gentiles. Cyrus was responsible for the physical return of the people to their homeland; the servant is responsible for their spiritual turning to the Lord. "The LORD has demonstrated his holy power before the eyes of all the nations. All the ends of the earth will see the victory of our God" (52:10).

The Lord promised that the "one who is despised and rejected by the nations" would see kings "stand at attention" as he passed by. "Princes will also bow low" because the Lord had chosen him (49:7). Although this is sometimes applied to Israel (Zion was despised by the nations in 60:14), the same language is used of the personal suffering servant of Isaiah 53:3, who was also "despised and rejected." Even kings would be astonished at his suffering and subsequent glory (52:15). As such, this passage is the first in Isaiah in which the Messiah's sufferings are presented. When applied to the personal servant, "servant of rulers" (49:7) could refer to his treatment by such rulers as Herod (Luke 23:11) and Pontius Pilate (John 19:1, 16).

The return to the homeland is the focus of 47:8-12. In 61:2, the Year of Jubilee is compared to "the time of the LORD's favor." Just as the Year of Jubilee was to be a time of freedom and rejoicing, so this release from captivity would return the people to their beloved land. The Lord also promised that "at just the right time," on the day of salvation he would give the servant "as my covenant with them" (47:8). Paul (2 Cor 6:2) understood this verse to refer to salvation through Christ. The mention of a covenant or pledge ties in well with Paul's use of the verse because the servant was called a covenant for the people (42:6). As with "servant" (49:5), "covenant" (49:9) may include the faithful in Israel, those who deserved to repossess the land that God promised Abraham when he made his covenant with him (Gen 15:18). The land had lain desolate for decades, but the tribes and families would again live on their allotted portions. Those who had been captive in Babylon would at last be free.

Through the servant, prisoners were beckoned to come out and enjoy freedom (49:9). They will be like "sheep, grazing in green pastures" (49:9), as echoed in John 10:11-16; 21:15-17. The freed prisoners "will neither hunger nor thirst" (49:10; cf. Rev 7:16), and the "searing sun will not reach them anymore" (49:10). The way will be prepared for the people as they return from distant lands (49:12). The Lord speaks of "my mountains" (49:11), showing that he can do with them as he pleases. God would remove the obstacles that separated Israel from her homeland (cf. 35:8; 40:3-4). The song ends with highly poetic imagery wherein the heavens and earth rejoice and burst into song because the Lord has "comforted his people and will have compassion on them in their suffering" (49:13).

## 2. The Lord remembers Zion (49:14-26)

¹⁴Yet Jerusalem* says, "The LORD has
    deserted us;
    the Lord has forgotten us."

¹⁵"Never! Can a mother forget her
    nursing child?
Can she feel no love for the child
    she has borne?
But even if that were possible,
    I would not forget you!
¹⁶See, I have written your name on the
    palms of my hands.
Always in my mind is a picture of
    Jerusalem's walls in ruins.
¹⁷Soon your descendants will come
    back,
    and all who are trying to destroy
    you will go away.
¹⁸Look around you and see,
    for all your children will come back
    to you.
As surely as I live," says the LORD,
    "they will be like jewels or bridal
    ornaments for you to display.

¹⁹"Even the most desolate parts of your
    abandoned land
    will soon be crowded with your
    people.
Your enemies who enslaved you
    will be far away.
²⁰The generations born in exile will
    return and say,
    'We need more room! It's crowded
    here!'
²¹Then you will think to yourself,
    'Who has given me all these
    descendants?
For most of my children were killed,
    and the rest were carried away
    into exile.

I was left here all alone.
    Where did all these people come
    from?
Who bore these children?
    Who raised them for me?'"

²²This is what the Sovereign LORD says:
    "See, I will give a signal to the
    godless nations.
They will carry your little sons back
    to you in their arms;
    they will bring your daughters on
    their shoulders.
²³Kings and queens will serve you
    and care for all your needs.
They will bow to the earth before you
    and lick the dust from your feet.
Then you will know that I am
    the LORD.
Those who trust in me will never
    be put to shame."

²⁴Who can snatch the plunder of war
    from the hands of a warrior?
Who can demand that a tyrant* let
    his captives go?
²⁵But the LORD says,
    "The captives of warriors will be
    released,
    and the plunder of tyrants will
    be retrieved.
For I will fight those who fight you,
    and I will save your children.
²⁶I will feed your enemies with their
    own flesh.
They will be drunk with rivers
    of their own blood.
All the world will know that I,
    the LORD,
    am your Savior and your Redeemer,
    the Mighty One of Israel.*"

**49:14** Hebrew *Zion.* **49:24** As in Dead Sea Scrolls, Syriac version, and Latin Vulgate (also see 49:25); Masoretic Text reads *a righteous person.* **49:26** Hebrew *of Jacob.* See note on 14:1.

NOTES

**49:14** *Jerusalem.* As the NLT mg indicates, the Hebrew is "Zion," which stands for "daughter of Zion" or "people of Zion," the more common usage.

**49:15** *Can a mother forget her nursing child?* This is very strong imagery, yet during the siege of Samaria by King Ben-hadad of Aram, a mother cooked her child for food (2 Kgs

6:28-29). Although some mothers might abandon their children (Ps 27:10), God will never abandon his. God's love for Zion far exceeds any form of human love.

**49:16 written your name on the palms of my hands.** This imagery is possibly derived from the widespread use of tattoos in the Middle East. The hand or arm was punctured or burned and colored substances were rubbed into the scars to preserve the mark. In Israel, the practice was prohibited (Lev 19:28), but the prophet could still derive a metaphor from it (cf. Gal 6:17).

**49:17 your descendants.** The picture of the city as the mother of her inhabitants often recurs in the sequel (cf. 49:20-21; 54:1).

**49:18 bridal ornaments.** The imagery of the new people of God as a bride is common in the NT (2 Cor 11:2; Eph 5:29, 32; Rev 21:2, 9; 22:17).

**49:20 generations born in exile.** More lit., "children born during your bereavement," because during the Babylonian exile, Israel was viewed as a widow bereft of her children (cf. 54:10).

**49:22 give a signal.** This telescopes two separate Heb. expressions, "beckon" and "lift up my banner." The Lord will lift or wave his hand, either to signal those nearby or to point to the ensign, a banner or standard that indicated a rallying point for people at a distance (cf. 11:10, 12). The Heb. word translated "banner" (*nes* [TH5251, ZH5812]) is a favorite of Isaiah, occurring eight times in the first part of his book and twice in the second. The combination of "beckon" (or "wave the hand") and "lift up the banner" is found only here and in 13:2.

**49:23 Kings and queens will serve you.** The NLT collapses the fuller Heb. parallelism, "kings will be your foster fathers, and their queens your nursing mothers." This refers to the care provided to Zion's children by kings and queens, the way that a small child is cared for by his nurse (cf. Num 11:12). From the lowly state of being forced to serve others, Zion had now come to be "nursed" by kings and queens.

COMMENTARY

In this section of the poem, the new theme of Jerusalem's restoration and glorification gets attention. The focus is on Zion, which becomes increasingly integral to Isaiah's message. Cyrus and the capture of Babylon are no longer mentioned in this or the following sections, nor do we read of the sharp contest between the Lord and the gods. The exodus from Babylon is still referred to, but not by name (cf. 52:11).

Although the people of Jerusalem [Zion] may think that the Lord had forgotten [them] (49:14), the Lord responds, "I would not forget you!" (49:15). Using the graphic imagery of a mother nursing her child, Isaiah illustrates the love God feels for his people (49:15). The Lord also says, "I have written your name on the palms of my hands" (49:16). He promises that their "descendants will come back" and that "all who are trying to destroy [them] will go away" (49:17).

The most desolate parts of the land will become so "crowded with . . . people" (49:19) that those returning will say, "We need more room! It's crowded here!" (49:20). This is typical of Isaiah's poetic flair. In continuing vivid imagery, the returnees are described as receiving help even from the godless nations, who will help carry the children on the trip back home (49:22). Even kings and queens will serve them and care for all their needs; they will "lick the dust from [their] feet" (49:23). That they bow to the earth indicates that the royalty of Zion and her children is of superior quality; they are a royal priesthood (1 Pet 2:9; cf. Heb 2:11-12). The description of kings and queens serving Zion indicates a reversal of circumstances. If the warrior thinks he can retrieve the freed captives, he must face the Lord who fights for his children (49:24). He has declared, "I will fight those who fight you, and I will save your children" (49:25). In fact, the Lord would so arrange it that the enemies will eat their own flesh and drink their own blood (49:26).

The chapter closes with a reference to the "Mighty One of Israel/Jacob," a title first mentioned in Gen 49:24. The term "mighty" ('abir [TH46, ZH51]) is cognate to a word for "bull" and suggests a positive expression of virility and power, contrary to what the word often implies in English usage. In many cultures, including ancient Canaan, bulls represented strength and might (cf. 34:7). Motyer (1993:396) observes that the "form here ('abir) may have been specially devised to focus on the absolute power of the Lord free from any taint of bull worship or suggestion of merely brute strength. Apart from Genesis 49:24 and Psalm 132:2, the word is used only in Isaiah of the Lord (1:24; 60:16)."

The words "Savior" and "Redeemer" in this context indicate the victorious salvation accomplished by God when "all the world will know that I . . . am your Savior and your Redeemer" (49:26; cf. 1:24; 60:16). The immediate passage (49:8-26) has been about the restoration of ancient Israel from captivity, but beginning with chapter 40 and through the following chapters, increasing attention will be given to Zion, God's people in a larger sense. God will preserve his remnant, his people, and will ultimately be glorified as their mighty Savior and Redeemer.

◆     ## 3. Israel's sin and the servant's obedience (50:1-11)

This is what the LORD says:

"Was your mother sent away because
    I divorced her?
Did I sell you as slaves to my
    creditors?
No, you were sold because of your sins.
And your mother, too, was taken
    because of your sins.
²Why was no one there when I came?
Why didn't anyone answer when
    I called?
Is it because I have no power to rescue?
No, that is not the reason!
For I can speak to the sea and make
    it dry up!
I can turn rivers into deserts covered
    with dying fish.
³I dress the skies in darkness,
    covering them with clothes of
    mourning."

⁴The Sovereign LORD has given me his
    words of wisdom,
    so that I know how to comfort the
    weary.
Morning by morning he wakens me
    and opens my understanding to
    his will.
⁵The Sovereign LORD has spoken to me,
    and I have listened.
    I have not rebelled or turned away.
⁶I offered my back to those who beat
    me
    and my cheeks to those who pulled
    out my beard.
I did not hide my face
    from mockery and spitting.
⁷Because the Sovereign LORD helps me,
    I will not be disgraced.
Therefore, I have set my face like
    a stone,

determined to do his will.
And I know that I will not be put
to shame.
⁸He who gives me justice is near.
Who will dare to bring charges
against me now?
Where are my accusers?
Let them appear!
⁹See, the Sovereign LORD is on
my side!
Who will declare me guilty?
All my enemies will be destroyed
like old clothes that have been
eaten by moths!

¹⁰Who among you fears the LORD
and obeys his servant?
If you are walking in darkness,
without a ray of light,
trust in the LORD
and rely on your God.
¹¹But watch out, you who live in your
own light
and warm yourselves by your own
fires.
This is the reward you will receive
from me:
You will soon fall down in great
torment.

# NOTES

**50:1 your mother.** This probably refers to Israel's ancestry.

*I divorced her.* The Heb. *seper kerithuth 'immekem* refers to a "bill of your mother's divorcement" (KJV). *kerithuth* [TH3748, ZH4135] occurs only in Deut 24:1-4; Jer 3:8; and here. "Divorce" is from the root *karath* [TH3772, ZH4162] meaning "to cut off"; it was used of a husband's dismissal of his wife. Within the community of Israel, it was only the husband who could divorce his wife; no divorce therefore became legal unless the husband presented his wife with such a certificate. Husband-wife imagery for God and his people is often used in the Bible (see 45:5; 62:5; Jer 3:14; Rev 21:9).

*you were sold.* The language of selling Israel into the hands of the enemy occurs several times in the book of Judges (Judg 3:8; 4:2; 10:7).

**50:2 Is it because I have no power to rescue?** The Heb. has "was my arm too short to rescue you?" Varous translations are used to convey the meaning: "is my hand shortened that it cannot redeem?" (NRSV), "was my arm too short to ransom you?" (NIV), "can my arm not reach out to deliver?" (REB), "am I too weak to save them?" (TEV), "am I too weak to reclaim you?" (GW), "do you think I am not able to save you?" (NCV), and "have I lost my power to rescue and save?" (CEV).

*I can speak to the sea and make it dry up!* This undoubtedly refers to the time that God dried up the Red Sea for the Israelites to pass through (cf. 43:16-17). The reference to dying fish supports this and may indicate one of the plagues on Egypt (19:5-8; Exod 7:18).

**50:3 I dress the skies in darkness.** The Heb. word *qadruth* [TH6940, ZH7725] (darkness) is found only here and implies mourning. It is parallel with *saq* [TH8242, ZH8566] (clothes of mourning).

**50:4 Sovereign LORD.** Heb. *'adonay yhwh.* This title occurs only in this particular Servant Song.

*how to comfort the weary.* The language is somewhat enigmatic. The KJV has "speak a word in season to him that is weary." The modern versions vary: "sustain the weary with a word" (NRSV), "console the weary with a timely word" (REB), "speak to the weary a word that will rouse them" (NAB), "give a word of comfort to the weary" (NJB), and "the word that sustains the weary" (NIV).

*opens my understanding to his will.* The NLT paraphrases the end of this verse. The Heb. ends the verse, lit., "to hear like the learned" (*limmudim* [TH3928A, ZH4341]). This word is used as a substantive only in Isaiah and is found in both parts of the book. Its first occurrence is at 8:16-17.

**50:5** *spoken to me.* The Heb. is lit., "opened my ear," which means to prepare one to receive instruction or information. It is a common image in the Bible.

*listened.* The Heb. verb *shama'* [TH8085, ZH9048], traditionally rendered "hearken," can also mean "obey" and is often translated this way in new translations.

**50:6** *beat me.* Beatings were for criminals or fools (cf. Prov 10:13; 19:29; 26:3; Matt 27:26; John 19:1).

*pulled out my beard.* Although the Heb. is unusual and the DSS have a variant (Oswalt 1998:321), we can assume that this is an act of disgrace. Most new versions keep the traditional idea. Bedouin, who are often very sensitive about care of the beard, use expressions such as "Beg by the beard" or "Swear by the beard." The NCV has "pulled my beard" and the GW has "pluck hairs out of my beard," but most versions have the traditional idea of pulling out the beard.

*spitting.* To spit upon another was an act of ritual defilement and contempt (Lev 15:8; Num 12:14; Deut 25:9; Job 17:6; Matt 27:30).

**50:9** *Sovereign LORD.* This particular title is composed of the two words that are normally translated "Lord" (*'adonay* [TH136, ZH151]) and "LORD" (*yhwh* [TH3068, ZH3378]). When they occur together, these two names for God emphasize his sovereign control over the nations and his covenant relationship with Israel. This dual title is found in 7:7; 25:8; 28:16; 30:15; 40:10; 48:16; 49:22; 50:4-5, 7, 9; 52:4; 56:8; 61:1, 11; 65:13, 15. The extended title "the Lord, the LORD Almighty" is found in 3:15; 10:23-24; 22:5, 12, 14-15; 28:22.

*moths.* In the ancient Near East, where so much clothing was made from wool, the moth was highly feared.

## COMMENTARY

The passage opens with a question to the exiles, "Did I sell you as slaves to my creditors?" (50:1). If a man did not pay his debts, his children could legally be sold as slaves (Exod 21:7; Neh 5:5; 2 Kgs 4:1). But the Lord was not in debt to Babylon; he did not have any creditors, nor did he receive anything when he sent his people into captivity (52:3). They alone were responsible for their captivity because of their rebellion and rejection of the Lord's authority and rule over them.

The Lord's opening question is followed by a sequence of questions provoking the people to remember who God is and what he had done. These opening verses explain that Israel was not taken into exile because God was unable to prevent it, for he is the One who could "speak to the sea and make it dry up" (50:2) and "turn rivers into deserts" (50:2; cf 42:15). The reason for the exile was Israel's sin, which resulted in the nation's spiritual deafness (cf. 6:10).

The Lord addressed Zion as a mother in 49:14-22, and now in 50:1 the mother is referred to in the third person. He returned to the charge made against him in 49:14 and answered it by challenging the exiled children to produce a certificate of divorce to prove that he had cast off their mother. Viewing the exile as a divorce, another penetrating question is made: "Was your mother sent away because I divorced her?" God was thereby saying to Zion's children: "I didn't divorce your mother [when I sent Zion into exile]" (50:1). Perhaps the rhetorical question here is a way of putting the blame for the divorce on the rebellious and disobedient people. They broke the relationship by sinning against God; he did not initiate the divorce.

Another question follows: "Why didn't anyone answer when I called?" (50:2). This apparently refers to God's call to his people through his prophets (Jer 25:4), but no one could answer because of their blindness, deafness, and hard hearts (6:9-10; 42:18-20). Then the Lord sarcastically asks a rhetorical question: "Is it because I have no power to rescue?" (50:2). In the Hebrew, this is an idiom using "arm" to indicate a waning or diminishing of strength (see note on 50:2).

Another expression of God's infinite power is presented in 50:3 with the words, "dress the skies in darkness." The Hebrew text includes a reference to "sackcloth," a coarse and dark cloth that was usually worn as an emblem of mourning (the same imagery is found in Rev 6:12). To say that the sky was clothed with sackcloth is a striking figure that reflects the plague of darkness in Egypt (Exod 10:21).

**The Servant Song.** The third Servant Song (50:4-11) is included in a passage in which Isaiah shows the difference between the responsiveness of the servant and the sin of the nation. In contrast to the stubborn and rebellious attitude of Israel (48:8), the servant is obedient and submissive. He also knows "how to comfort the weary" (50:4) and he has not "rebelled or turned away" from the Lord (50:5). By contrast, Moses shrank from his call (Exod 4:1, 10, 13), Jonah fled from the responsibility imposed upon him (Jon 1:3), and Jeremiah complained of his task and calling (Jer 15:15-18; 20:7-18). The New Testament describes the Messiah as submissive to the will and instruction of his divine Teacher, the Father (Luke 22:42; John 6:38; Heb 10:4-10; cf. Ps 40:7-8). The Messiah spoke only what he was instructed to teach (cf. John 7:16; 8:28b; 12:49). The true prophet or teacher speaks only what is revealed from God.

The servant would undergo suffering and humiliation as he offered his back to those who beat him, a statement that could hardly be applied to anyone but Jesus the Messiah (50:6; cf. Matt 27:26; Luke 18:33). His beard would be pulled out as a sign of the people's contempt of him (cf. 2 Sam 10:4-5; Neh 13:25). This act was one of the highest insults that could be imagined in the Middle East. It was also an expression of wrath or moral outrage. In indignation, Ezra pulled out his own hair (Ezra 9:3), and in a similar attitude, Nehemiah pulled out the hair of Jews who intermarried with heathen (Neh 1:25). The "mockery and spitting" (50:6) were also intended to insult and disgrace the Servant (Matt 26:67; 27:30). In the Old Testament, such actions were used to show hatred (Job 30:10) or insult (Deut 25:9; Job 17:6). Westermann, as reported by Oswalt (1998:325-326), notes that in ancient Near Eastern culture, submission to such public humiliation implied guilt. However, the servant made charges ("Where are my accusers? . . . Who will declare me guilty?") and claimed innocence (50:8-9). All such abusive treatment of the servant anticipates his ultimate suffering as described in 52:13–53:12.

Such language is eminently applicable to Jesus the Messiah, and many of the details that might have seemed like natural imagery in the larger picture had a literal fulfillment (cf. Matt 26:67; 27:30; Luke 18:31-33). Luke 18:32 says that such prophecies were fulfilled in Jesus' being spit upon. This entire description is a preview of the beating and mockery that Jesus Christ endured prior to his death on Calvary (cf.

Matt 27:2, 30-31). The Roman guards made sport of him, beating his face and hitting him with clubs, but the submissive Servant did not rebel or attempt to escape this dishonor and humiliation (cf. Matt 26:67; 27:30).

With the Lord's help, the servant "will not be disgraced," inasmuch as he was "determined to do [God's] will" (50:7). He was able to proclaim, "the Sovereign LORD is on my side! Who will declare me guilty?" (50:9). The beating and mocking of the Servant were not the end, for he had the confidence to know that he would "not be put to shame" (50:7). Like the prophets before him, the Servant stood firm and prevailed against his opponents (cf. Ezek 3:8-9). The Servant set his "face like a stone" (50:7) to do the will of God (cf. Jer 26:10; Luke 9:51), and gave his life for the sins of the world in a death that ultimately resulted in great honor and glory (cf. 52:13). The phrase "gives me justice" (50:8) means that the Lord God would find the Servant to be righteous (cf. 45:25). The Servant could thereby challenge his accusers: "Who will dare to bring charges against me now? . . . Let them appear!" (50:8). The Messiah Jesus flung this very challenge into the teeth of his enemies (John 8:46), and they were not able to oppose him (Mark 14:55-56).

The title "Sovereign LORD" (see note) is used four times in 50:4-9, emphasizing that the Sovereign LORD was on the side of the righteous Servant. If the Lord was his defender, who could accuse him? The apostle Paul cited this verse to show that the Lord also defended those who belonged to Jesus (Rom 8.31). None of the servant's opponents would last long, and those who brought false charges against the righteous would be "destroyed like old clothes that have been eaten by moths" (50:9; cf. 51:8), an apt picture of corruption working slowly from within.

Verses 10 and 11 challenge the entire nation to follow the lead of the Servant who testified of his close relationship with the Lord. The Servant warned them against attempting to live by their own light or warm themselves by their own fires (50:11). Rather than turning in repentance to the Lord and his revelation for light and direction, the wayward people preferred their own ideas and plans for help. These unspecified ideas were contrived by spiritually blind and ignorant rebels.

Since fire is a frequent figure of punishment (cf. 1:31), it is ironic that they would attempt "to warm [themselves] by [their] own fire." Instead, they would be warmed by God's fire in another sense! Because they had rejected the light of God's word, they would face terrible punishment. God is the real furnace of judgment (cf. 30:33; 31:9; 42:25; 47:14; 66:24), and he is both fire and light. The closing words of the chapter promise that the rebels will "soon fall down in great torment" (50:11).

◆     ### 4. The Lord's promise to comfort his people (51:1-16)

"Listen to me, all who hope for
    deliverance—
all who seek the LORD!
Consider the rock from which you
    were cut,

the quarry from which you were
    mined.
²Yes, think about Abraham, your
    ancestor,

and Sarah, who gave birth to your
nation.
Abraham was only one man when
I called him.
But when I blessed him, he became
a great nation."

³ The LORD will comfort Israel* again
and have pity on her ruins.
Her desert will blossom like Eden,
her barren wilderness like the
garden of the LORD.
Joy and gladness will be found
there.
Songs of thanksgiving will fill
the air.

⁴ "Listen to me, my people.
Hear me, Israel,
for my law will be proclaimed,
and my justice will become a light
to the nations.
⁵ My mercy and justice are coming
soon.
My salvation is on the way.
My strong arm will bring justice to
the nations.
All distant lands will look to me
and wait in hope for my powerful
arm.
⁶ Look up to the skies above,
and gaze down on the earth below.
For the skies will disappear like
smoke,
and the earth will wear out like
a piece of clothing.
The people of the earth will die like
flies,
but my salvation lasts forever.
My righteous rule will never end!

⁷ "Listen to me, you who know right
from wrong
you who cherish my law in your
hearts.
Do not be afraid of people's scorn,
nor fear their insults.
⁸ For the moth will devour them as it
devours clothing.
The worm will eat at them as it
eats wool.

But my righteousness will last
forever.
My salvation will continue from
generation to generation."

⁹ Wake up, wake up, O LORD! Clothe
yourself with strength!
Flex your mighty right arm!
Rouse yourself as in the days of old
when you slew Egypt, the dragon
of the Nile.*
¹⁰ Are you not the same today,
the one who dried up the sea,
making a path of escape through the
depths
so that your people could cross
over?
¹¹ Those who have been ransomed by the
LORD will return.
They will enter Jerusalem* singing,
crowned with everlasting joy.
Sorrow and mourning will disappear,
and they will be filled with joy and
gladness.

¹² "I, yes I, am the one who comforts you.
So why are you afraid of mere
humans,
who wither like the grass and
disappear?
¹³ Yet you have forgotten the LORD, your
Creator,
the one who stretched out the sky
like a canopy
and laid the foundations of the
earth.
Will you remain in constant dread of
human oppressors?
Will you continue to fear the anger
of your enemies?
Where is their fury and anger now?
It is gone!
¹⁴ Soon all you captives will be released!
Imprisonment, starvation, and death
will not be your fate!
¹⁵ For I am the LORD your God,
who stirs up the sea, causing its
waves to roar.
My name is the LORD of Heaven's
Armies.

<sup>16</sup>And I have put my words in your mouth
   and hidden you safely in my hand.
I stretched out* the sky like a
   canopy

and laid the foundations of the
   earth.
I am the one who says to Israel,
   'You are my people!'"

51:3 Hebrew *Zion;* also in 51:16.    51:9 Hebrew *You slew Rahab; you pierced the dragon.* Rahab is the name of
a mythical sea monster that represents chaos in ancient literature. The name is used here as a poetic name for
Egypt.    51:11 Hebrew *Zion.*    51:16 As in Syriac version (see also 51:13); Hebrew reads *planted.*

### NOTES

**51:1** *the rock.* God is also sometimes called a "rock" (see Deut 32:4).

**51:1-2** The Heb. uses striking parallelism here: "rock from which you were cut // the
quarry from which you were mined" is a couplet parallel to "Abraham, your ancestor //
and Sarah, who gave birth to your nation."

*Sarah.* This is the only occurrence of her name in the OT outside of Genesis. Here the use
supplies the variety necessary to balance the poetic parallelism of 51:1b-2a.

**51:3** *blossom like Eden.* The contrast between the lush garden of Eden and the arid desert
is also found in Joel 2:3 (cf. Gen 2:8, 10).

**51:4** *Listen.* This is not the usual word for "listen," but Heb. *qashab* [TH7181, ZH7992], which
means something more like "be attentive to me" (NAB) or "pay heed to me" (REB). Cf.
Prov 7:24.

*Israel.* Lit., "my people," which is not used of Israel elsewhere (Gen 25:23 is different).

*law.* The Heb. for "law" (*torah* [TH8451, ZH9368]) comes from the root "to teach"; the term
was used (especially by the prophets) for the general message and revelation of God given
to Israel in the form of instructions for the highest good in life.

*justice.* In this context, parallel with "law," Heb. *mishpat* [TH4941, ZH5477] refers to the
proper and best way of life.

**51:9** *Flex your mighty right arm!* This language comes from the Exodus event (Exod 6:6;
Deut 4:34; 5:15; 7:19). Of the twenty-eight occurrences of this phrase in the OT, eleven are
in Isaiah (30:30; 40:10; 48:14; 51:5, 9; 52:10; 53:1; 59:16; 62:8; 63:5, 12).

*dragon of the Nile.* The Heb. refers to two different creatures here: "Rahab" (here called
"the Nile"; Heb. *rahab* [TH7293, ZH8105]), and "dragon" (Heb. *tannin* [TH8577, ZH9490]). The
Heb. word *rahab* refers to an arrogant and haughty attitude reflected in proud behavior.
The two are in parallel here: "cut Rahab in pieces . . . pierced the dragon" (NASB), "cut
Rahab to pieces . . . pierced that monster through" (NIV, NRSV), "hacked Rahab in pieces
. . . pierced the Dragon" (NJPS).

**51:15** Much of this verse is also found in Jer 31:35b (cf. Job 26:12).

**51:16** *hidden you safely in my hand.* This expression is also used of the Servant of the
Lord in 49:2.

*stretched out the sky like a canopy.* This image appears repeatedly in Isaiah's cosmic language; it emphasizes the Lord's work as Creator (cf. 37:16; 40:22; 42:5; 45:12, 18; 48:13).

### COMMENTARY

The first part of this chapter (51:1-11) concerns the people and their pilgrimage; the
next part (51:12-16) has more to do with their covenant God and his commitment
to them. The first part of the passage is introduced with a series of imperatives (51:1,
4, 7) that tell the people to listen to the Lord. Isaiah 51:1-8 mostly address the
believing remnant, those people that were obedient to the Lord. They hoped for

deliverance (51:1) and cherished God's law (51:7). Since the goal for this remnant was their return to Zion (51:11; NLT mg), these verses describe the pilgrimage, including the trials and joys that accompanied the people. The covenant between the Lord and his people is affirmed in 51:12-16, using some of the same language as at the Exodus event when God claimed Israel for his own (Exod 20:2; Lev 26:12).

The opening verses of this passage are mainly addressed to the believing remnant that, like the Servant in chapter 50, were obedient to the Lord. In contrast to those who lived by their own light (50:11), a faithful remnant remained, although few in number. These were descendants of "Abraham, your ancestor, and Sarah, who gave birth to your nation" (51:2). Since Sarah's faith is hardly mentioned in Scripture in comparison to the proverbial faith of Abraham, it may be more than poetically significant in this parallelism. In Old Testament times, a man was viewed as being one with his wife; his children, and even his slaves and possessions were regarded as a unit. This contrasts with the perspective of modern American individualism.

There are several other links with previous descriptions of the messianic age in 51:3-8. Zion (51:3; NLT mg), although barren like Sarah (49:21), will become a fruitful (54:1) paradise full of joy and gladness (51:3), and "justice will become a light to the nations" (51:4). The mighty God who can dry up seas and rivers, making them a desert (50:2), can reverse the order and restore the desolate ruins of Zion, whether physical or spiritual. In addition to joy and gladness, the promise includes God's law and his justice, which must go together (51:4). The law will go forth from the Lord (not from Israel) and his "justice will become a light to the nations" (51:4). Under the Servant (42:1-4), it will be a "law of the Spirit of life" (Rom 8:1-2; for "light to the nations" in 51:4, see its use in connection with the Servant in 42:6 and 49:6).

The promise that "mercy and justice are coming soon" (51:5; traditionally, "righteousness and salvation") probably refers to deliverance from the exile, but the Messiah will ultimately bring salvation to all nations (cf. 46:13). These terms are also parallel in 51:8 and include the deliverance from Babylon that God brought about through Cyrus (cf. 46:13). However, a far richer salvation will be accomplished through the Servant-Messiah. The skies and the earth, which represent the entire world, will eventually wear out and disappear, in contrast to God's "salvation [that] lasts forever" (51:6). This cosmic imagery is similar to other descriptions of the last days (24:4; 34:4).

The prophet encouraged those who cherished God's law in their hearts to not be "afraid of people's scorn nor fear their insults" (51:7). Those who opposed the Servant and God's people would fall prey to destruction like clothing eaten by moths (51:8; cf. 50:9; 51:6). In contrast, the righteousness and salvation of the Lord "will continue from generation to generation" (51:8; cf. 51:6).

Isaiah cried out to the Lord for immediate action. The repeated use of "wake up" reflects the urgency of the plea (51:9), as Isaiah called on the Lord to robe himself with strength and rouse himself as in the days of old (51:9). As long as the Lord permitted the nations to oppress Israel, it seemed as though he were indifferent. Isaiah called upon him to act, to intervene (cf. 18:4ff).

As God was called upon once more to rouse himself, his deliverance of his people in the Exodus event was evoked. The defeat of Egypt is described as "slaying the dragon of the Nile." The NLT margin explains that this is a reference to Rahab the dragon, a poetic name for Egypt. Just as God in the Exodus event dried up the sea, so he could again provide a path of escape for his people.

Isaiah affirmed that the "ransomed" would return to Jerusalem (Zion), "singing songs of everlasting joy" (51:11). The word "ransomed" or "redeemed" was used in 35:9, and it may have prompted Isaiah to repeat 35:10 in its entirety in 51:11.

The Lord's response to Isaiah's cry was encouraging. The use of the double "I, yes I, am the one" (51:12) emphasizes the Lord's claim to be the deliverer and the source of Israel's comfort. The Lord was the one speaking as he asked them, "Why are you afraid of mere humans who wither like the grass and disappear" (51:12)? He reminded them that he was "the LORD, your Creator," as well as "the one who stretched out the sky like a canopy" (51:13). In light of this, why would they "remain in constant dread" and continue to fear their enemies (51:13)? When the Lord blew upon the strong of the earth, they were carried away like stubble (cf. 40:24). Therefore, "the captives will be released" (51:14). The Lord God, who controls the elements of nature, is "the LORD of Heaven's Armies"; this message is repeated and reinforced in 51:15 (cf. 1.19, 44.6). The one who "stretched out the sky like a canopy" is the same one who put his words in Isaiah's mouth and who says to Israel, "You are my people!" (51:16). God did indeed put his words in the mouth of Israel and they received this revelation (cf. 59:21), so that they might proclaim it (cf. Deut 30:14).

◆   ## 5. Jerusalem's redemption (51:17–52:12)

¹⁷Wake up, wake up, O Jerusalem!
　You have drunk the cup of the
　　LORD's fury.
You have drunk the cup of terror,
　tipping out its last drops.
¹⁸Not one of your children is left alive
　to take your hand and guide you.
¹⁹These two calamities have fallen
　on you:
　desolation and destruction, famine
　and war.
And who is left to sympathize with
　you?
Who is left to comfort you?*
²⁰For your children have fainted and
　lie in the streets,
　helpless as antelopes caught in
　a net.

The LORD has poured out his fury;
　God has rebuked them.

²¹But now listen to this, you afflicted
　ones
who sit in a drunken stupor,
　though not from drinking wine.
²²This is what the Sovereign LORD,
　your God and Defender, says:
"See, I have taken the terrible cup
　from your hands.
You will drink no more of my
　fury.
²³Instead, I will hand that cup to your
　tormentors,
　those who said, 'We will trample
　you into the dust
　and walk on your backs.'"

# CHAPTER 52

¹Wake up, wake up, O Zion!
　Clothe yourself with strength.
Put on your beautiful clothes, O holy
　city of Jerusalem,
for unclean and godless people will
　enter your gates no longer.
²Rise from the dust, O Jerusalem.
　Sit in a place of honor.
Remove the chains of slavery from
　your neck,
O captive daughter of Zion.
³For this is what the LORD says:
"When I sold you into exile,
　I received no payment.
Now I can redeem you
　without having to pay for you."

⁴This is what the Sovereign LORD says: "Long ago my people chose to live in Egypt. Now they are oppressed by Assyria. ⁵What is this?" asks the LORD. "Why are my people enslaved again? Those who rule them shout in exultation. My name is blasphemed all day long.* ⁶But I will reveal my name to my people, and they will come to know its power. Then at last they will recognize that I am the one who speaks to them."

⁷How beautiful on the mountains
　are the feet of the messenger who
　brings good news,
the good news of peace and salvation,
　the news that the God of Israel*
　reigns!
⁸The watchmen shout and sing with joy,
　for before their very eyes
they see the LORD returning to
　Jerusalem.*
⁹Let the ruins of Jerusalem break into
　joyful song,
for the LORD has comforted his
　people.
He has redeemed Jerusalem.
¹⁰The LORD has demonstrated his holy
　power
before the eyes of all the nations.
All the ends of the earth will see
　the victory of our God.

¹¹Get out! Get out and leave your
　captivity,
where everything you touch is
　unclean.
Get out of there and purify
　yourselves,
you who carry home the sacred
　objects of the LORD.
¹²You will not leave in a hurry,
　running for your lives.
For the LORD will go ahead of you;
　yes, the God of Israel will protect
　you from behind.

51:19 As in Dead Sea Scrolls and Greek, Latin, and Syriac versions; Masoretic Text reads *How can I comfort you?*
52:5 Greek version reads *The Gentiles continually blaspheme my name because of you.* Compare Rom 2:24.
52:7 Hebrew *of Zion.*   52:8 Hebrew *to Zion.*

## NOTES

**51:23 *trample . . . walk on your backs.*** Victors sometimes put their feet on the necks of the vanquished (cf. Josh 10:24).

**52:3 *sold.*** The book of Judges reveals that such a sale was not an irrevocable transaction but merely expressed passing into other ownership (cf. Judg 2:14; 3:8; 4:2). The property still belonged to the Lord, and he could recover it at will.

**52:3-4** Note that these verses both begin with "This is what the Sovereign LORD says" and 52:5 has "declares the LORD" twice.

***to live.*** The Heb. *gur* [TH1481, ZH1591] refers to temporary residence as an alien and was the term used of Israel's "sojourn" in Egypt. Although Israel had entered Egypt at the Pharaoh's invitation (Gen 45:16ff), the original situation of hospitality eventually changed to the threat of genocide.

**52:5 What is this?** This Heb. idiom is wide-ranging in meaning. It could be ironic here ("What am I playing at?") or simply "Does this matter to me?" The NIV translates, "What do I have here?"

**52:10 demonstrated his holy power.** More lit., "lay bare his holy arm."

**52:11 Get out of there.** The Heb. is *misham*, "from there."

**52:12 in a hurry.** The Heb. *bekhippazon* [TH2649, ZH2906] is found elsewhere only in Exod 12:11, where it is used of the urgency with which the Passover meal must be eaten.

C O M M E N T A R Y

There is a contrast between 51:17-23 and the preceding section (51:9) in which the Lord was urged to "wake up." Now it was Jerusalem's turn to be roused (52:1). The pathetic condition of the city is described. The symbolic mother of his people lay in ruins, having "drunk the cup of the LORD's fury" (51:17), something normally reserved for wicked nations (Jer 25:15-26; cf. Isa 63:6). Jerusalem had no children left alive to take her hand to guide her (51:18). In that culture, when parents became old, it was the responsibility of their children to steady them and keep them from injury (Gordon 1965:95).

As in a song of lament, the prophet adds, "Who is left to sympathize with you? Who is left to comfort you?" (51:19). There was no one who cared, while there were many who took pleasure in her downfall (Ps 137:7). The second calamity mentioned above is expanded upon in 51:20, as the prophet presents a graphic description of the cup of wrath that left Jerusalem in ruins. Like "antelopes caught in a net," her snared children were helplessly lying in the streets (51:20). Then the good news came: "you will drink no more of my fury" (51:22). Jerusalem had been afflicted (cf. 54:11) for many years, but the Lord would reverse her fortunes. Her Babylonian tormentors must themselves drink the cup of wrath (cf. Jer 25:26).

A call to "wake up, wake up" begins chapter 52, introducing a new section (52:1; cf. 51:17). It is addressed to a city in ruins that is now aroused to enjoy a new condition. After the removal of divine wrath (cf. 51:17-23), the holy city of Jerusalem is called upon to put on "beautiful clothes" (52:1) and to "sit in a place of honor" (52:2). Of course, this provokes questions as to why things have changed; the following explanation is introduced with "For" in 52:3.

The attitude of the Lord who promises free redemption (52:3) is seen in verses 3-6 because he can no longer tolerate seeing his people in bondage (52:4-5). Jerusalem will be free because the Lord will redeem his people without needing to pay for them, since when they were sold into exile, the Lord "received no payment" (52:3; cf. 50:1). Israel had suffered at the hands of Egypt and Assyria, and now Babylon had taken them captive. In 52:4, the divine title is amplified ("Sovereign LORD"), perhaps for further assurance. The LORD (Yahweh) was the great Redeemer of the Exodus event (Exod 6:6-7); the added "Sovereign" seems to heighten the effect. (The end of 52:5 is cited by Paul in Rom 2:24).

The Hebrew of 52:6 has "therefore" twice (not translated in the NLT), probably for emphasis. Motyer (1993:418) says, the repetition "indicates a high degree of excitement." However, Oswalt (1998:364) interprets the twofold use as indicating two separate consequences. The Hebrew is cryptic, lit. "therefore my people will know my name; therefore in that day that I am he, the one speaking, 'Behold me.'" In the culture of the Old Testament, a name stood for a person. To know the name of the Lord was to know the Lord himself. At the time of the Exodus, the name of Israel's covenant God, "the LORD" (*yhwh* [TH3068, ZH3378]) was revealed in a special way to Moses at the burning bush (Exod 3; cf. Exod 19:9). Moses was then the mediator in communicating that name to the people as he identified the one who commissioned him. However, the time was coming when God's revelation of himself would be more direct, as he says, "Behold me" (*hinneni* [TH2009, ZH2180]; cf. 58:9). In the great day of redemption, God's people will personally experience in a new way what is included in that name. It will be the time of Zion's beauty and strength.

In 52:7-10, the story goes beyond the Lord's victorious action to the triumphal entry into Zion. As in 40:9, the picture of a messenger that returns from a battle scene to an anxious people is the background of this section (cf. 1 Sam 4:17; 2 Sam 18:26). Isaiah 52:7 is quoted by Paul in Romans 10:15. The news that Israel would be released is good news indeed, and the lone runner shouts, "the God of Israel reigns" (cf. the familiar cry in Pss 93:1; 97:1; 99:1), as the "watchmen shout and sing with joy" (52:8) because the Lord has "demonstrated his holy power" (52:10).

The parallel section of 51:4-6 promised worldwide revelation and universal salvation; this section tells us it has happened—another example of Isaiah's literary skill in suspense and creativity. The striking, graphic imagery of 52:10 (see note) is unique. Although the "arm of the Lord" has been mentioned before, this is the first (and only) place that we read that the Lord will, lit., "lay bare his holy arm," to be revealed "before the eyes of all the nations" (52:10; cf. 51:9). The Lord is rolling up his sleeves to facilitate his work and win the victory. The Lord's arm, which stands for the whole person, was first mentioned in 40:10. It is part of the Exodus language used in this section (cf. 51:9, where the "arm" is the agent in the Exodus that will rise to fulfil the promises of 51:1-8). The expression "see the victory of our God" (52:10) means to experience salvation. This verse and the next include instruction and information about the return.

When they departed, the people were not to touch anything that was "unclean" (52:11). This was probably a warning for them not to take with them any religious objects that could lead to idolatry. The twofold call to holiness is both negative ("get out" from where "everything you touch is unclean") and positive ("purify yourselves"). The prepositional phrase "of there" (52:11) poses a great difficulty for all commentators who propose a Babylonian location and perspective for the author of these words. If the author were in Babylon, he would have said, "from here." The expression, "of there," however, shows that the writer was an outsider.

The message is that the people had to leave behind their sinful lifestyle in which "everything they touched was unclean" (52:11), a verse quoted by Paul in 2 Corinthians 6:17. At the time of the Exodus, the people were commanded to load themselves with the treasures of Egypt (Exod 12:35). Not long after the Exodus, Israel made a golden calf out of these treasures and worshiped it, undoubtedly under the influence of Egyptian bull worship. This time the nation was encouraged to be pure, especially the priests and Levites that carried the articles that Nebuchadnezzar had seized from the Temple (cf. Ezra 1:7-11). During this exodus, the exiles would not have to flee from Babylon, for they were assured of the Lord's protection. He would superintend their journey, as he did by means of the angel and the pillar of cloud and fire during the Exodus (cf. Exod 13:21; 14:19-20). He would go ahead of them while also protecting them from behind (52:12).

◆   **6. The Lord's suffering servant (52:13–53:12)**

13 See, my servant will prosper;
   he will be highly exalted.
14 But many were amazed when they
   saw him.*
His face was so disfigured he
   seemed hardly human,
and from his appearance, one would
   scarcely know he was a man.
15 And he will startle* many nations.
   Kings will stand speechless in his
   presence.
For they will see what they had not
   been told;
they will understand what they had
   not heard about.*

## CHAPTER 53

1 Who has believed our message?
   To whom has the LORD revealed his
   powerful arm?
2 My servant grew up in the LORD's
   presence like a tender green
   shoot,
like a root in dry ground.
There was nothing beautiful or
   majestic about his appearance,
nothing to attract us to him.
3 He was despised and rejected—
   a man of sorrows, acquainted with
   deepest grief.
We turned our backs on him and
   looked the other way.
He was despised, and we did not
   care.

4 Yet it was our weaknesses he carried;
   it was our sorrows* that weighed
   him down.

And we thought his troubles were
   a punishment from God,
   a punishment for his own sins!
5 But he was pierced for our rebellion,
   crushed for our sins.
He was beaten so we could be whole.
He was whipped so we could be
   healed.
6 All of us, like sheep, have strayed
   away.
We have left God's paths to follow
   our own.
Yet the LORD laid on him
   the sins of us all.

7 He was oppressed and treated harshly,
   yet he never said a word.
He was led like a lamb to the
   slaughter.
And as a sheep is silent before the
   shearers,
he did not open his mouth.
8 Unjustly condemned,
   he was led away.*
No one cared that he died without
   descendants,
that his life was cut short in
   midstream.*
But he was struck down
   for the rebellion of my people.
9 He had done no wrong
   and had never deceived anyone.
But he was buried like a criminal;
   he was put in a rich man's grave.

10 But it was the LORD's good plan to
   crush him
   and cause him grief.

Yet when his life is made an offering
for sin,
he will have many descendants.
He will enjoy a long life,
and the LORD's good plan will
prosper in his hands.
¹¹ When he sees all that is accomplished
by his anguish,
he will be satisfied.
And because of his experience,

my righteous servant will make
it possible
for many to be counted righteous,
for he will bear all their sins.
¹² I will give him the honors of a
victorious soldier,
because he exposed himself to death.
He was counted among the rebels.
He bore the sins of many and
interceded for rebels.

52:14 As in Syriac version; Hebrew reads *you.*   52:15a Or *cleanse.*   52:15b Greek version reads *Those who have never been told about him will see, / and those who have never heard of him will understand.* Compare Rom 15:21.   53:4 Or *Yet it was our sicknesses he carried; / it was our diseases.*   53:8a Greek version reads *He was humiliated and received no justice.* Compare Acts 8:33.   53:8b Or *As for his contemporaries, / who cared that his life was cut short in midstream?* Greek version reads *Who can speak of his descendants? / For his life was taken from the earth.* Compare Acts 8:33.

# NOTES

**52:13 *my servant.*** Levey (1974:63) notes that the Targum on 52:13 renders: "My servant the Messiah." He also refers to a Rabbinic parallel, "this is the King Messiah . . . he shall be exalted above Abraham . . . and lifted, above Moses . . . and very high, above the ministering angels" (Yalkut Shimeoni on Isa 52:13; cited in Levey 1974:67).

**53:1 *our message.*** Heb. *shmu'ah* [TH8052, ZH9019] is used here of the word given to the prophet by God (28:9, 19; Jer 49:14). It is widely used elsewhere for "news" or "information" (1 Sam 2:24; 4:19).

**53:2 *tender green shoot.*** The Heb. is "suckling" (*yoneq* [TH3126, ZH3437]) from the root *yanaq* [TH3243, ZH3567], "to suck," used of a child nursing.

***beautiful . . . appearance.*** The words translated "beautiful" (*to'ar* [TH8389, ZH9307]) and "appearance" (*mar'eh* [TH4758, ZH5260]) are also used of Rachel in Gen 29:17—she was "lovely in form and beautiful."

**53:3 *despised.*** The repetition of "despised" in the first and last lines is a typical stylistic construction in Isaiah. The verb "despise" (*bazah* [TH959, ZH1022]) is not used elsewhere in Isaiah.

***rejected.*** The Heb. has the fuller "rejected of men" (*khadal 'ishim* [TH2310, ZH2534]). This is an unusual use of the root *khadal* [TH2308, ZH2532], which can convey a variety of meanings, such as "cut off, cease." The modern versions generally agree on the rendering of the verb as "rejected" (NRSV), "shunned" (REB; NJPS), "avoided" (NAB), but note "lowest of men" (NJB). The rare plural "men" (*'ishim*) is found elsewhere only in Ps 141:4 and Prov 8:4 and seems to be used for poetic assonance with the immediately following singular (*'ish* [TH376, ZH408]), thus throwing into prominence the isolated individuality of the servant who continued to be the "one" in contrast to the "many" (Motyer 1993:428).

***we did not care.*** Traditionally and more lit., "we esteemed him not." The Heb. verb is *khashab* [TH2803, ZH3108], which is used as an accounting word. "Thus the contemporaries of the servant so totally despised and devalued him that they ranked him as 'zero'" (Lindsey 1985:117).

**53:4 *Yet.*** Heb. *'aken* [TH403, ZH434] can be either emphatic or adversative (HALOT 1:47), traditionally, "surely." Whatever people may have thought about the sorrows and sufferings they saw, the truth was dramatically different. Perhaps it could be paraphrased, "But the truth of the matter is this" (Lindsey 1985:118).

*weaknesses.* The Heb. *kholi* [TH2483, ZH2716], traditionally "infirmities," refers to sins as well as to physical diseases. Matthew understood Jesus' healing ministry as the fulfillment of Isa 53:4, which he quoted in Matt 8:17.

*he.* This pronoun is represented in the Heb. by an independent pronoun, probably used here for emphasis. He was the one who suffered for us. The language is vivid in the original Heb. word order and contrasts the emphatic pronoun "he," which identifies the servant, with the pronoun "our," referring to the speakers.

*carried . . . weighed him down.* The Heb. for "carried" or "took up" (*nasa'* [TH5375, ZH5951]), and "weighed him down" (*sabal* [TH5445, ZH6022]) suggest that the Servant experienced the weight of the guilt and consequences of sin, a frequent concept in the OT (cf. Gen 4:13; Exod 28:43; Lev 17:16; 22:9; 24:15).

**53:4-5 a punishment . . . pierced . . . crushed.** This corresponds to the KJV rendering: "we considered him stricken (*naga'* [TH5060, ZH5595]), smitten (*nakah* [TH5221, ZH5782]) of God, and afflicted" (*'anah* [TH6031, ZH6700]). Motyer (1993:430) points out that the Heb. *nega'* [TH5061, ZH5596]) is used sixty times in Lev 13–14, not of the disease of leprosy but of the infliction or "blow" of it (cf. 1 Kgs 8:37-38 and Ps 73:14, the only other places where precisely this form of the verb occurs).

**53:5 But.** The opening conjunction (Heb. *waw*) may be taken in an adversative sense ("but"—so NLT, NRSV, REB, NAB, NIV). The NJB uses "whereas."

*pierced.* Heb. *mekholal* [TH2490A, ZH2726], one of the strongest words in the Heb. language, describes a violent and painful death; it conveys the idea of "pierced through," or "wounded to death" (cf. Deut 21:1; Isa 51:9; see also Ps 22:16; Zech 12:10; John 19:34). It is used when a man is run through with a sword or spear (cf. Ezek 28:7; Num 25:8). Other Heb. passages referring to the piercing of the Messiah are Ps 22:16 and Zech 12:10. "Pierced" is found elsewhere in Isaiah only in 51:9, where it is used of the death wound to the dragon. It usually means "to pierce fatally" (Job 26:13; Ps 109:22).

*rebellion.* The Heb. root (*pesha'* [TH6588, ZH7322]) refers to the rebellious nature of sin against God and his law.

*crushed.* The Heb. *daka* [TH1792, ZH1917] is used for "broken to pieces, shattered"; it probably refers to the psychological and spiritual suffering the servant endured. It is used consistently (except in Deut 23:1) in a metaphorical sense of a "crushed spirit" (57:15) or a "crushed heart" (Ps 51:17). Even David's petition, "Let the bones you have crushed rejoice" (Ps 51:8, lit.) is clearly a figurative reference to emotional rather than physical crushing (TDOT 3:195-208).

*sins.* Heb. (*'awon* [TH5771, ZH6411]) is one of the basic words for sin and denotes "bent, twisted, perverted."

*be whole.* This translates the Heb. *shalom* [TH7965, ZH8934] (peace), a very rich term in Heb., which refers to more than cessation of hostility. It can refer to a full life (Gen 15:15; 2 Kgs 22:20); personal well-being, peace of mind and satisfaction (Gen 43:23, 27; 1 Sam 1:17); harmony (Gen 26:29, 31; 1 Sam 16:4); and peace with God (Num 25:12; Judg 6:23; Ps 85:8; Isa 27:5; 48:22; 57:2).

**53:6 strayed away . . . left God's paths to follow our own.** Clear internal rhyme is heard in the Heb. (*ta'inu . . . paninu*). This language and imagery refer to wandering in the wilderness of sin (cf. Ps 119:176). The verb is used elsewhere of Israel's aberration (Ps 95:10; 2 Chr 33:9; Ezek 44:10); it occurs frequently in Isaiah (3:12; 9:16; 19:13; 47:15; 63:17).

*laid.* Heb. *pagha'* [TH6293, ZH7003] means "to meet, reach," but the causative form can mean "to cause to arrive at" or "to make to meet."

**53:7 lamb.** The Heb. *seh* [TH7716, ZH8445] is the term used regularly in the cultic laws (Gen 22:7-8; Exod 12:3, 5; Lev 5:7).

*did not open his mouth.* See Matt 26:63; 27:12-14; Mark 15:5; Luke 23:9; John 19:9, which tell us that Jesus did not open his mouth before his accusers.

**53:8 Unjustly condemned.** More lit., "he was taken from prison and from judgment." The NLT's "unjustly" translates the Heb. "from judgment" (*mishpat* [TH4941, ZH5477]), a word that has a wide range of meaning. Motyer (1993:433) summarizes: (1) a person's right (Deut 18:3; 21:17); (2) the practice of law or due process (Num 27:21; Deut 1:17); (3) legal enactment or sentence (Exod 21:1, 31); (4) bringing a lawsuit (Num 27:5). All this leaves the translator with several possibilities. Is it "from justice" in the sense of "from the court of law" or "from due trial and sentencing," or is it "without justice, ignoring rights, without a proper trial"? In other words, we can underline the fact by saying "from arrest and sentence" or the victim by saying "without restraint and without right," or the injustice by saying "without restraint and without justice" (Motyer 1993:434). D. F. Payne (1971:135) thinks the phrase is a set formula like "due process of law." The versions handle the language here in several ways: "by oppression and judgment" (NASB, NIV, ESV), "by a perversion of justice" (NRSV), "he was arrested and sentenced" (TEV, REB), "arrested, taken away, and judged" (GW), "condemned to death without a fair trial" (CEV), and "by oppressive judgment" (NJPS). The NLT mg indicates the Greek version's reading and compares Acts 8:33.

*he was led away.* The Heb. only says "taken away," which Calvin, in his Commentary on the passage, understands to refer to rescue by resurrection (i.e., taken away into glory). But this seems contextually inappropriate; there is no alleviation of the gloom as yet. In the light of the context, it must mean "taken away to die by punishment" (Young 1972:3.351). The verb can be elliptical for "taken out to die" (cf. Prov 24:11; Ezek 33:4). In summary, the servant "was the victim of a judicial murder" (MacRae 1977:140).

**53:10 have many descendants.** Lit., "he shall see his seed" (so the KJV).

*enjoy a long life.* More lit., "prolong his days." This or similar expressions occur twenty-one times in the OT (e.g. Deut 5:30 [33]). Note the similar expression, "length of days," which occurs nine times (e.g., Deut 30:20).

**53:11 sees all that is accomplished.** The NLT paraphrases the first part of this verse. The Heb. (with the DSS; cf. the LXX) says, "sees [the light]," and most modern versions supply "light," which is still rather cryptic. It could mean something like our expression "light at the end of the tunnel" or some similar idea of an end in sight. The Heb. could be interpreted in the sense of "see the result of the suffering of his soul and be satisfied," or as the NLT has summarized it (cf. the NIV text and mg). For more on the expression, "see light," see Job 33:28; 37:21; Ps 36:9 [10]; Isa 9:2 [1].

*because of his experience, my righteous servant will make it possible for many to be counted righteous.* Lit., "by his knowledge my righteous servant will justify many."

*my righteous servant.* Lit., "the righteous one, my servant"; the emphasis of the construction is on "the righteous one." This is the rendering of the NRSV; the NJB has "the upright one, my servant."

*many.* This refers to a specific group that is numerous, but not all-inclusive, that he clothes in his righteousness. In 51:1, the remnant is described as those "who hope for salvation."

*bear.* This translates Heb. *sabal* [TH5445, ZH6022], which appears earlier in 53:4b.

**53:12 honors.** The Heb. refers to a designated portion, lot, or inheritance.

**because.** *takhath 'asher*; a strong causative construction in Heb. that means something like "because of the fact that."

**exposed himself to death.** Lit., "he bared his soul unto death," a Heb. expression found elsewhere only in Ps 141:8. The verb is the hiphil form of the root *'arah* [TH6168, ZH6867] (expose, lay bare).

**interceded.** The Heb. *paga'* [TH6293, ZH7003] (touch) is in the hiphil here. In 53:6, the same word is translated "laid on him."

## COMMENTARY

This outstanding passage on the Lord's suffering servant begins at the end of chapter 52 and continues through the end of chapter 53. For a detailed study of the use of this important passage in the NT, see Litwak (1983). Ryken (1987:309) calls this passage, "the most unusual and paradoxical encomium ever written." A paradox is an apparent contradiction that needs to be resolved, and this passage opens with one: the servant is said to be exalted (52:13) but the rest of the passage speaks of his suffering and degradation. Perhaps today this would be called by some an oxymoron—an internal contradiction. In this case, the servant is of low social standing, but is spiritually exalted. The passage praises the servant for the unlikely reason that he was so severely treated, much as the book of Revelation praises the Lamb because it was slain (Rev 5:12).

The twofold theme of "the sufferings of the servant [Christ] and the glories that would follow" (1 Pet 1:11) draws together the prominent thematic threads of the preceding Servant Songs. The first two songs (42:1-9; 49:1-13) emphasize the ultimate success of the Lord's Servant-Messiah while alluding to his sufferings (42:4; 49:4), and the third song (50:4-11) emphasizes the sufferings and endurance of the servant while implying his ultimate vindication or exaltation (cf. 50:7-9). The distinctive contribution of the fourth song is to present the details and purpose of the servant's sufferings and death, particularly as they relate to his exaltation and the ultimate success of his mission.

The passage opens with an introduction to the prosperous and successful servant. Westermann (1969:258) correctly notes the identification between the opening words in this verse ("See, my servant") and the opening words of the first servant song in 42:1. But though the opening statement introduces the servant who "will prosper" (52:13) and be "highly exalted," it immediately changes the mood and focus: "his face was so disfigured he seemed hardly human" (52:14). The seemingly reverse order of events is noted in von Rad's (1968:223) observation that "the unusual aspect of this great poem is that it begins with what is really the end of the whole story, the servant's glorification and the recognition of his significance for the world."

The last line of 52:13 describes the servant's exaltation, as does 53:12 and the New Testament (Acts 2:33; Phil 2:9-11). The NLT telescopes three different verbs of exaltation ("raised and lifted up and highly exalted," NIV) into "highly exalted." The first two of the Hebrew verbs are reminiscent of the exaltation of the Lord in Isaiah 6:1 and describe the servant's "superlative degree of success" (Leupold

1971:2.224). It is difficult to know if this stacking of terms is to be understood as synonymous or sequential. Those who view them as sequential suggest that they describe something like the announcement, the continuation, and the result or climax of the exaltation. Motyer (1993:424) says, "The threefold exaltation (raised . . . lifted up . . . highly exalted) expresses a dignity beyond what any other merits or receives and is surely intended as a clue leading to the identity of the servant. It is impossible not to be reminded of the resurrection, ascension and heavenly exaltation of the Lord Jesus."

The scene immediately switches to the suffering servant whose "face was so disfigured he seemed hardly human." In fact, "from his appearance, one would scarcely know he was a man" (52:14). The whole scene and situation is one that "will startle many nations" and even "kings will stand speechless" before him (52:15; the latter part of this verse is quoted by Paul in Rom 15:21). The only reason for such a response is given in the cryptic expression, "they will see what they had not been told" and "understand what they had not heard about" (52:15).

The statement "stand speechless" (lit., "shut their mouths") has been understood in three different senses: (1) they keep their mouths firmly closed to avoid contamination from the servant (North 1964:235); (2) they are speechless from "their inability to say anything by way of self-justification" (Archer 1962:646); and (3) they are silent in reverential awe and honor before the Servant (Young 1972:3.339). This latter view seems the best in this context where the last part of the verse states the reason for action. They will come to comprehend "what they had not heard about."

The three opening verses of chapter 53 take up the suffering servant's origin; he is described as one who grew up "like a tender green shoot" and also like a "root in dry ground" (53:2). These verses emphasize the lowliness of the Servant and the superficial estimation of him. He was totally misunderstood and unappreciated because of his apparent insignificance. His appearance was "nothing beautiful or majestic" and certainly nothing "to attract us to him" (53:2). "They wanted a king, but they got a carpenter" (Culver 1958:52). In fact, he was "despised and rejected," and acquainted with sorrows and deep grief (53:3). This was so much the case that "we turned our backs on him and looked the other way" (53:3); he was despised and no one cared. The words "we did not care" (53:3) translate the Hebrew traditionally rendered "esteemed him not," which is an accounting word, a reckoning up of value. "Thus the contemporaries of the servant so totally despised and devalued him that they ranked him as 'zero'" (Lindsey 1985:117), or "reckoned him as nothing" (McKenzie 1968:129).

In sharp contrast and strong contradiction to the misunderstanding and lack of appreciation of the servant (53:1-3), the nature of the servant and his sufferings are set forth in 53:4-6, which focus on what the servant did for others. "It was our weaknesses he carried" and it "was our sorrows that weighed him down," not the mistaken opinion that he received "a punishment from God" as a "punishment for his own sins!" (53:4; a verse quoted in Matt 8:17). "Punishment from God" is, more lit., "stricken by God." Motyer (1993:430) points out that "stricken" is used sixty times in Leviticus 13–14, not of the infection of leprosy, but of the infliction or the "blow" of it.

In 53:4, the verbs "carried" and "weighed him down" suggest that the servant felt the guilt and the consequences of sin as a burden to be borne, a frequent concept in the Old Testament (cf. Gen 4:13; Exod 28:43; Lev 17:16; 22:9; 24:15). The unusual feature here is that the servant would take guilt and punishment for sin upon himself on behalf of others. The terms "weaknesses" and "sorrows" (53:4) are general terms for all suffering that is viewed as the result of sin. Lindsey (1985:119) suggests that these should be identified as a metonymy of effect for cause, and Young (1972:3.346) indicates that "when it is said that he bore our sicknesses, what is meant is not that he became a fellow sufferer with us, but that he bore the sin that is the cause of the evil consequences, and thus became our substitution."

He was pierced, crushed, beaten, and whipped so that we could be healed and made whole (53:5; for "crushed," see the note on 53:5). In this context, "crushed" is parallel to "wounded," which refers to the servant's physical death, so it is possible that "crushed" also refers to the servant's physical condition. But it is more consistent with Old Testament usage to understand it as referring to his emotional hurt in bearing sin for guilty sinners. All the sins of the world were placed on him in those awful hours that Jesus became sin for us. "Crushed" appears alongside "brokenhearted" in Psalm 34:18 and "humble" in Isaiah 57:5. Hatred of the servant is also described in 50:5, where mocking and beating are mentioned (cf. Ps 22:5-7).

We are the wayward sheep that have strayed away and "left God's paths to follow our own" (53:6). This language and imagery refer to wandering in the wilderness of sin (cf. Ps 119:176). The verb is used elsewhere of Israel's aberration (Ps 95:10; 2 Chr 33:9; Ezek 44:10) and it occurs frequently in Isaiah (3:12; 9:16; 19:13; 47:15; 63:17). The simile "like sheep" pictures the helplessness of people without a shepherd. This verse and the next compare people and the servant to sheep, but the comparisons are vastly different. People are like sheep because they wander off so easily and stray into sin, and the Bible stresses the peril of sheep without a shepherd. In contrast, the servant is the lamb that suffered as a substitute for our sins (Lev 1:4; John 1:29). That each individual turned to his own way means that they were all in opposition to God's ways (cf. 40:3; 55:7-9). Nevertheless, the Lord laid on the suffering servant "the sins of us all" (53:6). By divine decree, the servant was the provision of God, who himself superintended the priestly task (Lev 16:21) of transferring the guilt of the guilty to the head of the Servant, giving notice that this was an acceptable satisfaction for sin (Motyer 1993:431).

The servant's condition is described as similar to the condition of Israel in 1:5-6, where Israel's moral and spiritual collapse is compared to wounds and illness. A number of terms found in 1:5-6 correspond to words in 53:4-5. Lindsey (1985:119) lists several items that he believes support the view that this was a full vicarious atonement, that is, that the servant was not merely participating in the sufferings of others, nor simply removing their sin and sufferings, but that he rather took their sin and guilt away from them and upon himself and bore it as a burden: (1) the significance of the verbs (in 53:4-6, 8, 11, 12); (2) their close verbal similarities to the Day of Atonement ritual (Lev 16); (3) the contrast between the pronouns "he" and "us/our" (53:4-6; cf. 53:8, 11-12); and (4) the specific identification of the servant as a guilt offering (53:10).

The remaining verses (53:7-12) of the chapter further describe the treatment of the servant who not only was "treated harshly" but was "led like a lamb to the slaughter" (53:7). Despite this, "he did not open his mouth" and "never said a word" (53:7). Although his suffering was caused by others, he remained silent as he was led like a "lamb to the slaughter" (53:7). He suffered silently, in submission to the will of the Lord. Although animals go as uncomprehendingly to slaughter as to shearing, the servant went to his horrible death in full awareness. Isaiah 53:7-8 is the passage explained by Philip to the Ethiopian eunuch (Acts 8:32-33).

The Hebrew behind "unjustly condemned" (53:8) has been understood in different ways. Lit., it reads something like, "from prison and trial he was led away." The most likely understanding suggests that violent action was taken against the servant within a legal context (Westermann 1969:265). Some scholars understand a hendiadys here that means, "by reason of an oppressive sentence," "a perverted judgment," or "judicial violence" (North 1964:241). However, Payne (1971:139) is probably correct that there is "some fixed legal idiom here, either 'after arrest and sentence' or 'from prison and lawcourt.'" Motyer (1993:433) suggests two possibilities: (1) "from restraint" (from having been imprisoned) or (2) "without restraint" (with all ordinary restraints and protection removed).

The vivid and detailed description of maltreatment includes such pertinent data as "his life was cut short in midstream" (53:8), "buried like a criminal," and "put in a rich man's grave" (53:9). That "he was struck down for the rebellion of my people" (53:8) makes clear the distinction between "my people" and the servant. The servant is not Israel. The Lord's servant silently submitted himself to a death his contemporaries did not understand (53:8) and that was followed by an honorable burial despite the intentions of his enemies (53:9). The latter part of verse 9 is quoted in 1 Peter 2:22.

He ended up "buried like a criminal," which means, more lit., that he was "assigned a grave with the wicked ones." Yet the significant added detail is that "he was put in a rich man's grave" (53:9). The Jews placed great importance on a person's burial (cf. 22:16), and Jesus was originally assigned an ignominious grave with the two rebels who were crucified with him (Matt 27:38). Due to the intervention of Joseph of Arimathea, he received an honorable burial when his body was laid in the tomb of that wealthy Jewish leader (Matt 27:57-60). Motyer (1993:436) summarizes the enigma of 52:13-15 as, "How could such suffering lead to such exaltation?" and of 53:1-3 as, "How could one so plainly human be the 'arm of the Lord'?" Such striking language has obviously provoked much discussion through the centuries. Delitzsch (1949:2.327) simply summarizes the issue by saying, "Without the commentary supplied by the fulfillment, it would be impossible to understand verse 9 at all." God overruled the intentions of the wicked and ordained that his servant should have a splendid tomb.

The concluding verses of this section (53:10b-12) describe the servant's victorious accomplishments and return to the theme of exaltation that began in 52:13. The amazing truth revealed in these verses is that the servant's vindication and victory came after his death. Only then was he is enabled to witness his "many descendants," to "enjoy a long life" (53:10), and to witness all that was "accomplished by his anguish" (53:11). The fourth Servant Song both begins and ends with a divine oracle in which the Lord announces the exaltation of his servant (52:13-15; 53:10-12). The truth announced in these verses concerns the servant's vindication and victory after death.

Incredibly, we are told that it was "the LORD's good plan to crush him and cause him grief" (53:10). This entire event was not by chance or accident and the servant is promised "many descendants" (53:10). This answers the question of 49:21 where Zion asks, "Who bore these children? Who raised them for me?" These "descendants" result because his life was "made an offering for sin" (53:10).

Part of the suffering servant's victory is that "he will enjoy a long life," and "the LORD's good plan will prosper in his hands" (53:10). "Enjoy a long life" is a typical Hebrew reference to prolonged earthly life, but its usage here in reference to one who had already died is unusual. The Old Testament testifies that the dead will "rise up" and live on (Dan 12:2), and in this sense it is no surprise to find the servant alive after death, but things are said about him after death that set him apart from all others. Jacob sees his children (29:23) as the servant sees his seed, but Jacob does so as a mere watcher from the sidelines of history. For the servant, there is "long life," and "the LORD's good plan will prosper in his hands" (53:10). The servant who was crushed under the will of the Lord lives on as the executor of that will. In 14:9-17, Isaiah depicted earth's royalty in Sheol, dethroned by death. In the case of the servant, however, death ushers him into sovereign dignity and power, with his own hand administering the saving purposes of the Lord, and as a victor taking the spoil (53:12). Westermann (1969:267) confesses, "There is no doubt that God's act in restoring the Servant, the Latter's exaltation, is an act done upon him after death and on the far side of the grave." In 53:10 there is an affirmation that the Lord's purpose through the mediation of his servant has been completely accomplished. As he did with Joseph in Egypt (Gen 39:3-4), so the Lord would cause the servant to be successful in all his undertakings.

It will be his privilege to "see all that is accomplished by his anguish" and "be satisfied," and he "will make it possible for many to be counted righteous" (53:11). In fact, he will enjoy "the honors of a victorious soldier" (53:12). What appeared as a pitiful display of weakness turns out to be a victory of massive proportions, described in vivid and graphic language.

The suffering servant's postmortem satisfaction includes more than just having "many descendants" (53:10); he will also "be satisfied" (53:11) as he makes it possible "for many to be counted righteous" (53:11). Motyer (1993:440) writes,

"Those who become the servant's beneficiaries through the reparation-offering become his children (his offspring/'seed')." These verses thus provide the answer to the question asked in 49:21, "Who has given me all these descendants? . . . Who bore these children? Who raised them for me?"

Isaiah 53:11 contains an expression that is literally something like, "he will see and be satisfied," which is usually taken as a reference to the servant's resurrection (cf. 1 Cor 15:4). Young (1972:3.356) views the verbs "see" and "be satisfied" as a hendiadys meaning, "he shall see with abundant satisfaction," but the two verbs here should probably be treated separately as forming a climax. "Be satisfied" (53:11a) translates a word also used in 1:11, where it means not being satisfied with the empty ritual of the wayward people. What the multitude of sacrifices could not accomplish in 1:11, the one perfect sacrifice of the servant accomplishes in this passage.

The expression "because of his experience" (53:11b) is traditionally "by his knowledge" and is based on the fact that the verb "to know" in Hebrew often means "to experience." The reference is to the servant's experience of suffering and sin-bearing, which is explicated in the following verses. Since the Hebrew construction, "experience of him," can mean either "his own experience" (subjective genitive) or "the experience of him" (objective genitive) by others, there has been much discussion on this (for a full discussion of this issue, see Murray 1959:1.375-383).

"My righteous servant" (53:11b) is, lit., "the righteous one, my servant." This construction places emphasis on the righteous character of the servant. This prepares for the reference to the servant's necessary qualification for the work of sin-bearing in 53:11d by underlining his moral fitness for the task. "Many" (53:11c) refers to a specific group, a numerous but not all-inclusive group that he clothes in his righteousness. In 51:1, the remnant was described as those who "hope for deliverance . . . who seek the Lord"; now the servant meets their quest. The promise had been given in 51:5 that "my mercy and justice are coming soon."

The expression "he will bear" (53:11c) has the pronoun "he" in the emphatic position in Hebrew; it is "he himself" who will bear all their sins. Because of all this suffering culminating in death, the servant will enjoy the "honors of a victorious soldier" (53:12). What appeared to be a pitiful defeat becomes a victory of massive proportions described in military language. He will enjoy this reward and honor only because he allowed himself to be "counted among the rebels" and "exposed himself to death" (53:12; cf. Matt 27:38; Luke 22:37). Because of his unique death, "he bore the sins of many and interceded for rebels" (53:12b; cf. Heb 7:25). The expression "exposed himself to death" (lit., "he bared his soul to death") contains a Hebrew expression found elsewhere only in Ps 141:8. The servant Jesus was both the agent and the substance of this outpouring. No one took his life from him; he laid it down of his own choice (John 10:18; Phil 2:7). He personally identified himself with those he came to save. He was willing to be counted with the "rebels" as he "bore the sins of many." Because of his unique vicarious death, the victorious servant was able to intercede for his own (Heb 7:25).

## ◆ 7. Zion's future glory (54:1-17)

"Sing, O childless woman,
you who have never given birth!
Break into loud and joyful song,
O Jerusalem,
you who have never been in labor.
For the desolate woman now has more children
than the woman who lives with her husband,"
says the LORD.
<sup>2</sup> "Enlarge your house; build an addition.
Spread out your home, and spare no expense!
<sup>3</sup> For you will soon be bursting at the seams.
Your descendants will occupy other nations
and resettle the ruined cities.

<sup>4</sup> "Fear not; you will no longer live in shame.
Don't be afraid; there is no more disgrace for you.
You will no longer remember the shame of your youth
and the sorrows of widowhood.
<sup>5</sup> For your Creator will be your husband;
the LORD of Heaven's Armies is his name!
He is your Redeemer, the Holy One of Israel,
the God of all the earth.
<sup>6</sup> For the LORD has called you back from your grief—
as though you were a young wife abandoned by her husband,"
says your God.
<sup>7</sup> "For a brief moment I abandoned you,
but with great compassion I will take you back.
<sup>8</sup> In a burst of anger I turned my face away for a little while.
But with everlasting love I will have compassion on you,"
says the LORD, your Redeemer.

<sup>9</sup> "Just as I swore in the time of Noah
that I would never again let a flood cover the earth,
so now I swear
that I will never again be angry and punish you.
<sup>10</sup> For the mountains may move
and the hills disappear,
but even then my faithful love for you will remain.
My covenant of blessing will never be broken,"
says the LORD, who has mercy on you.

<sup>11</sup> "O storm-battered city,
troubled and desolate!
I will rebuild you with precious jewels
and make your foundations from lapis lazuli.
<sup>12</sup> I will make your towers of sparkling rubies,
your gates of shining gems,
and your walls of precious stones.
<sup>13</sup> I will teach all your children,
and they will enjoy great peace.
<sup>14</sup> You will be secure under a government
that is just and fair.
Your enemies will stay far away.
You will live in peace,
and terror will not come near.
<sup>15</sup> If any nation comes to fight you,
it is not because I sent them.
Whoever attacks you will go down in defeat.

<sup>16</sup> "I have created the blacksmith
who fans the coals beneath the forge
and makes the weapons of destruction.
And I have created the armies that destroy.
<sup>17</sup> But in that coming day
no weapon turned against you will succeed.
You will silence every voice raised up to accuse you.
These benefits are enjoyed by the servants of the LORD;
their vindication will come from me.
I, the LORD, have spoken!

NOTES

**54:4 shame of your youth.** Probably refers to the time of bondage in Egypt (cf. Jer 31:19; Ezek 16:60).

**sorrows of widowhood.** Probably refers to the time of the Exile, although it is parallel to the preceding.

**54:6 young wife abandoned by her husband.** Probably Israel's experience in exile.

**54:7 brief moment.** Compared to the many years in Egyptian bondage, the years of the Exile were relatively brief.

**54:9 never again let a flood cover the earth.** See Gen 9:11.

**54:10 covenant of blessing.** This refers to one of the covenants made with Israel (cf. 55:3).

**54:12 towers.** Traditionally, "battlements"; this is a reference to the parapets on the tops of walls.

COMMENTARY

In contrast to the grief and suffering of the Servant depicted in the preceding passage (52:13–53:12), this chapter depicts the glorious redemption accomplished by his suffering. Chapter 54 turns to the work of God in accomplishing his ultimate plan of salvation for all who are willing to partake of its blessings. God's plan for his people was not an afterthought (cf. Eph 3:9-11). The Lord's symbolic wife in this chapter is Jerusalem (Zion). Although depicted as a fallen and disgraced woman in 51:17-18, she is restored here to a place of glory.

The first five verses develop 49:14-23. The childless lady Zion was separated (not divorced) during the time of her captivity, but now all that is over, and she is told to "Break into loud and joyful song" (54:1). The New Testament applies this verse to the "Jerusalem that is above" (Gal 4:26) and speaks of a "heavenly Jerusalem, the city of the living God . . . the church of the firstborn" (Heb 12:22-23), and Paul applies this verse to Sarah in Galatians 4:27, where he contrasts Hagar and Sarah (Gal 4:21-31).

Sarah's children number more than those of "the woman who lives with her husband" (54:1), and therefore she must enlarge her house and build an addition (54:2). Jerusalem is viewed as a woman living in her tent (the work of setting up and taking down a tent was the work of women). Her children will eventually "occupy other nations and resettle the ruined cities" (54:3), not by military might but by spiritual conquest through a renewed spiritual people, a holy nation (cf. 1 Pet 2:9). Paul compared the land to Sarah (Gal 4:26-27) because she had endured the same barrenness. Just as Sarah became the mother of a whole nation, so Israel would again be filled with people, and her borders would have to be enlarged because her tent could not hold all her children (54:2). The scope of this magnificent restoration extends far beyond Israel's return from Babylon to include the spiritual descendants of the old covenant people. From Paul's allegory involving Sarah and Hagar, where he quotes this verse (Gal 4:21-31), we conclude that the prophet was speaking of the children to be born of the spiritual promise (Gen 12:3) rather than those born of the fleshly promise (Gen 12:2).

The shame of her youth and the "sorrows of widowhood" will be remembered no more (54:4). The widowhood of Zion was only a temporary aberration because, "Your Creator will be your husband," the "LORD of Heaven's Armies" (54:5). The verse goes on to describe him as "your Redeemer, the Holy One of Israel, the God of all the earth." As the "Holy One of Israel," he judged sinful Israel, but he was also Israel's "Redeemer." The point of the elaborate parallelism in this verse seems designed to show that Judah's husband is none other than the Holy One of Israel. He is also "God of all the earth" (54:5), and as such, he will ultimately be recognized by all of earth's inhabitants (Rom 3:29).

God promises in 54:7 that "with great compassion" he will take back his formerly abandoned wife. Although in a moment of anger he had turned his face from her, he will "with everlasting love" have compassion on her (54:8). He had left her (Ezek 11:23) because he hated her sinful ways. Her exile in Babylonia was a brief time in comparison to the total history of the relationship (cf. 26:20). Psalm 30:5 reflects the fact that God's anger is but for a moment, but his favor endures for a lifetime. Although there is weeping in the night, joy comes with the morning. This is an eternal principle with God.

Noah is the subject of 54:9-10. Just as God had promised Noah not to destroy the world by a flood again, so he now promised: "My covenant of blessing will never be broken" (54:10). Once again, God's judgment purged his people and restored the remnant as his wife. The promise did not exclude persecution, but it did mean that the true people of God would not be destroyed. God's loyal oath is more permanent than features of the terrain such as mountains, so a more permanent foundation stands (cf. Heb 12:28). The covenant of peace sealed by the servant's blood will not pass away (Matt 24:35; 26:28).

In 54:11-15, Jerusalem's glory is described in vivid, figurative language. The new Zion is brilliantly depicted as being built on "foundations from lapis lazuli" (54:11), with "towers of sparkling rubies" and "gates of shining gems" (54:12), indicating that the city will be both beautiful and permanent. Some of these stones are the same as those used in the foundations, walls, and gates of the New Jerusalem (Rev 21:18-21). They undoubtedly allude to Eden (cf. the precious stones of the earth in Gen 2:11-12). Isaiah's highly figurative description may also be based on Solomon's beautiful Temple, which also contained various precious stones (1 Chr 29:2). The sparkling, brilliant gems of the new city reflect her glorious and permanent nature, and ultimately the glory of her heavenly architect. All of this indicates paradise restored.

The picture portrays the riches of the glory of God in his people (Eph 1:18). The people of this new city will enjoy the benefits of peace and they will prosper "under a government that is just and fair" (54:14). The promise is made that "whoever attacks you will go down in defeat" (54:15). Although some of this surely applies to the restored old city of Jerusalem after the return, giving immediate hope to the people at that time, some of it undoubtedly refers to the future heavenly Jerusalem of Revelation 21:9ff. All of it refers to God's dwelling among his covenant people.

This section (54:16-17) closes with a description of God's protective care. As protector of his people, God reminds them that he was the one who "created the blacksmith who fans the coals beneath the forge" to make weapons for the "armies that destroy" (54:16). God raised up nations such as Assyria and Babylonia to punish Israel (cf. 10:5; 33:1); without his sovereign control, every weapon would fail. Finally, God promised that in the future, "no weapon turned against you will succeed" (54:17). This assurance of divine protection is a permanent possession of God's people.

◆      ## 8. The great invitation (55:1-13)

"Is anyone thirsty?
　　Come and drink—
　　even if you have no money!
　　Come, take your choice of wine or
　　　milk—
　　it's all free!
2 Why spend your money on food that
　　does not give you strength?
　　Why pay for food that does you
　　no good?
　　Listen to me, and you will eat what
　　is good.
　　You will enjoy the finest food.

3 "Come to me with your ears wide open.
　　Listen, and you will find life.
　　I will make an everlasting covenant
　　with you.
　　I will give you all the unfailing love
　　I promised to David.
4 See how I used him to display my
　　power among the peoples.
　　I made him a leader among the
　　nations.
5 You also will command nations you
　　do not know,
　　and peoples unknown to you will
　　come running to obey,
　　because I, the LORD your God,
　　the Holy One of Israel, have made
　　you glorious."

6 Seek the LORD while you can find him.
　　Call on him now while he is near.
7 Let the wicked change their ways
　　and banish the very thought of
　　doing wrong.
　　Let them turn to the LORD that he may
　　have mercy on them.

Yes, turn to our God, for he will
　　forgive generously.

8 "My thoughts are nothing like your
　　thoughts," says the LORD.
　　"And my ways are far beyond
　　anything you could imagine.
9 For just as the heavens are higher
　　than the earth,
　　so my ways are higher than your
　　ways
　　and my thoughts higher than your
　　thoughts.

10 "The rain and snow come down from
　　the heavens
　　and stay on the ground to water
　　the earth.
　　They cause the grain to grow,
　　producing seed for the farmer
　　and bread for the hungry.
11 It is the same with my word.
　　I send it out, and it always produces
　　fruit.
　　It will accomplish all I want it to,
　　and it will prosper everywhere
　　I send it.
12 You will live in joy and peace.
　　The mountains and hills will burst
　　into song,
　　and the trees of the field will clap
　　their hands!
13 Where once there were thorns, cypress
　　trees will grow.
　　Where nettles grew, myrtles will
　　sprout up.
　　These events will bring great honor
　　to the LORD's name;
　　they will be an everlasting sign of
　　his power and love."

NOTES

**55:1 thirsty.** Thirst can be of the body for water, of the mind for knowledge or culture, of the heart for affection, fellowship, or friends, or of the soul for spiritual satisfaction. The last seems to be the focus in this context (cf. 41:17; 44:3; Ps 42:1-2; 63:1), although not completely exclusive of the others.

**Come and drink.** These opening words remind us of those spoken by the Messiah to the Samaritan woman at Jacob's well in Sychar. Jesus said, "People soon become thirsty again after drinking this water. But the water I give them takes away thirst altogether" (John 4:13-14). The invitation to "come" is found three times in the Heb. Motyer (1993:452) observes that this is followed by a threefold "listen" (55:2c, 3ab), and that the section concludes with a threefold guarantee by the covenant (55:3c), the king (55:3d-5b), and the Lord (55:5c-e).

**Come, take your choice.** This reminds us of Jesus' parable of the great banquet that ends with an invitation to "Go quickly into the streets and alleys of the city and invite the poor, the crippled, the lame, and the blind" (Luke 14:21). Sinners have no way of bargaining with God for their salvation. They are spiritually dead (Eph 2:1).

**wine or milk.** These are symbols of abundance and pleasure (Song 5:1; Joel 3:18).

**55:2 Listen.** This is an infinitive absolute following its cognate finite verb, a construction meaning "listen persistently" or "keep on listening."

**enjoy the finest food.** The Heb. says "let your soul delight itself in fatness" (KJV). In that culture, fat was considered a great treat. Spiritual blessings are often compared to a banquet (Pss 22:26; 34:8; Jer 31:14).

**55:3 unfailing love I promised to David.** "Unfailing love" translates the plural form of the Heb. *khesed* [TH2617, ZH2876], a form found only thirteen times in the OT. The KJV translation here is "sure mercies of David." Again, translators handle this in various ways: "faithful mercies shown to David" (NASB), "enduring loyalty promised to David" (NJPS), "my steadfast, sure love for David" (NRSV, ESV), "love you faithfully as I loved David" (REB), "faithful love promised to David" (NIV), and "the blessings I promised to David" (GW).

**55:4 leader.** The Heb. has *nagid umetsawweh* (leader and commander). *nagid* [TH5057, ZH5592] (leader) is applied to David in 1 Sam 13:14; 25:30 and to the Messiah (Dan 9:25). The NLT, instead of translating the second word in 55:4 as a noun, apparently carries it over into the next verse where it is translated with the verb "command." The Heb. *metsawweh* [TH6680, ZH7422] is used only here as a title expressing authority.

**55:6 Seek.** This is not used in the sense of looking for what is lost but of coming with commitment to one known to be there (e.g. Deut 12:5).

**near.** Heb. *qarob* [TH7138, ZH7940]. This is a kinship vocabulary word (Ruth 2:20; 3:12; 4:4). In Lev 25:25, it is used with the "kinsman-redeemer" *go'el* [TH1350B, ZH1457]). Its use here is probably deliberate.

**55:7 wicked.** This is *rasha'* [TH7563, ZH8401], a broad-meaning word as wicked is in English. The Heb. here has it parallel to "evil" ('*awen* [TH205, ZH224]; "wrong" in the NLT). Both are generic in this context and refer to sinful people in general.

**mercy.** *rakham* [TH7355, ZH8163] refers to the compassionate love of a personal God. The Heb. word for "womb" (*rekhem*) shares the same root.

COMMENTARY

We can observe the progression leading up to this chapter, as chapter 53 built on chapters 40–52, and 54 built on 53. The servant of chapter 53 was promised "many descendants" (53:10) and chapter 54 describes a family and home so large that it is "bursting at the seams" (54:3). Now the growing family of God in Isaiah 54 is followed by the great invitation of Isaiah 55, an urgent and passionate call to the lost.

This is one of the most attractive chapters of the Bible, as it presents a striking invitation in a jubilant and victorious style. This great invitation is often compared with Matthew 11:28-29 and Revelation 22:17. In arresting language, God is portrayed as a merchant in a marketplace where people are selling and buying. He extends the invitation to "Come and drink" and enjoy "your choice of wine or milk" because "it's all free!" (55:1). People who crossed the desert often suffered from thirst (cf. 41:17-18), but those without God are spiritually thirsty. To them, God offers the water of life so that streams of living water can flow from within them (John 4:14; 7:37). Earlier (41:17-18), the Lord had promised that he would provide water for the thirsty. Here he presents a gracious invitation to a great banquet, a very rich and wonderful meal consisting of the finest foods, to which great spiritual blessings are often compared (Pss 22:26; 34:8; Jer 31:14). Elsewhere in Isaiah, God invites all to the great salvation banquet: "Let all the world look to me for salvation! For I am God; there is no other" (45:22).

What God offers is a free gift, and it is primarily the gift of God himself. The rhetorical question is raised as to why anyone would want to spend money on "food that does not give you strength" (55:2). Why waste time and strength on what is not lasting or significant (cf. 44:20)?

The promise is given, "Listen to me . . . and you will enjoy the finest food" (55:2), a promise that includes "an everlasting covenant" and the "unfailing love I promised to David" (55:3). This refers to the royal establishment of David's Seed, the Messiah (cf. 9:6-7). David had been promised an unending dynasty, one that would culminate in the Messiah (cf. 9:7; 54:10; 61:8; 2 Sam 7:14-16). Paul quoted this Scripture (see Acts 13:34) to show the faithfulness of God and that the resurrection of Christ was the fulfillment of God's promises to David. Since "the LORD your God, the Holy One of Israel" had made his people glorious, "peoples unknown to you will come running to obey" (55:5). This picture of the nations coming to Zion is similar to Isaiah's earlier descriptions of the nations being attracted to Jerusalem and to the God of Israel (2:2-4; 45:14). During the Exile, Israel was sent to nations she did not know (cf. Deut 28:36), but someday the reverse would be true. Like the Moabite Ruth (cf. Ruth 2:11), Gentiles would become part of the new covenant people.

The invitation changed to admonition as the people were told, "Seek the LORD while you can find him. Call on him now while he is near" (55:6). They should not even think of doing wrong but should "turn to the LORD that he may have mercy on them" (55:7). The entire passage of 55:6-13 is a call to repentance. Motyer (1993:456) sees a three-part call on the theme of repentance (55:6-7), followed by a three-part substantiation of the call (55:8-9, 10-11, 12-13).

God's thoughts are as different from those of mortals as the "heavens are higher than the earth" (55:9). The history of philosophy reflects finite thinking about God. This is not just a statement about logic but about the way of salvation itself. It is

God's word, not theirs, that "produces fruit" (55:11) and accomplishes God's will. In 40:8, Isaiah said, "The word of our God stands forever," and this verse expands on that concept. God's plans and purposes will be accomplished as surely as the rain waters the earth and makes it fruitful (55:10; cf. 30:23).

The chapter closes with a glorious figurative description of the response of nature to all this good news: "the trees of the field will clap their hands" and the "hills will burst into song" (55:12). The disappearance of "thorns" and "briers" (55:13) symbolizes the removal of the curse that follows sin (Gen 3:17ff). It is a transformation of nature that reverses the curse. The symbols of death and the curse are replaced by those of life. All this will signal his "power and love" (55:13). The Bible foretells the "regeneration" of the world (cf. Matt 19:28; Titus 3:5). The present world is wearing out like a garment and will be rolled away and changed (Ps 102:26; Heb 1:11-12). The vision of the future includes a new earth and a new heaven in which righteousness dwells (2 Pet 3:13; Rev 21:1-4). Eventually, creation will be liberated from its bondage to decay and brought into the glorious freedom of the children of God (Rom 8:21).

◆ ## 9. Blessings for all people (56:1-8)

This is what the LORD says:

"Be just and fair to all.
Do what is right and good,
for I am coming soon to rescue you
and to display my righteousness
among you.
²Blessed are all those
who are careful to do this.
Blessed are those who honor my
Sabbath days of rest
and keep themselves from doing
wrong.

³"Don't let foreigners who commit
themselves to the LORD say,
'The LORD will never let me be part
of his people.'
And don't let the eunuchs say,
'I'm a dried-up tree with no children
and no future.'
⁴For this is what the LORD says:
I will bless those eunuchs
who keep my Sabbath days holy
and who choose to do what pleases me
and commit their lives to me.
⁵I will give them—within the walls of
my house—

a memorial and a name
far greater than sons and daughters
could give.
For the name I give them is an
everlasting one.
It will never disappear!

⁶"I will also bless the foreigners who
commit themselves to the LORD,
who serve him and love his name,
who worship him and do not desecrate
the Sabbath day of rest,
and who hold fast to my
covenant.
⁷I will bring them to my holy mountain
of Jerusalem
and will fill them with joy in my
house of prayer.
I will accept their burnt offerings and
sacrifices,
because my Temple will be called a
house of prayer for all nations.
⁸For the Sovereign LORD,
who brings back the outcasts of
Israel, says:
I will bring others, too,
besides my people Israel."

NOTES

**56:1** *just . . . right.* Lit., "justice" and "righteousness," the combination of which is found more often in Isaiah than in any other book. A third of the total occurrences are in Isaiah, with twelve in chs 1–33 and four in chs 56–66.

**56:2** *those.* This is an inclusive translation of "man." The Heb. here is "man" (*'enosh* [TH582, ZH632]), a word used to designate naturally weak mortals.

**56:3** *eunuchs.* Heb. *saris* [TH5631, ZH6247]. The idea of castration is obvious in this context but the word more often has the extended meaning of some kind of official—whether castrated or not. The same idea carries over into the NT where castration may be involved (Matt 19:12), or both meanings are possible (Acts 8:27).

**56:4** *Sabbath.* Isaiah will elaborate on this in 58:13-14.

**56:5** *memorial.* The Heb. is *yad* [TH3027, ZH3338] (hand), often used to signify power and strength.

**56:6** *foreigners.* The Heb. means "foreigners" or "sons of strangers." The "foreigners" were from various nations and had come to live among the Israelites. They were excluded from worship for several generations (cf. Exod 12:43; Deut 23: 3, 7-8), but the work of the servant of the Lord would change this (49:19-20; 54:17; 60:10).

COMMENTARY

Chapter 56 begins a new section. Chapters 40–55 were concerned primarily with events relating to the Babylonian captivity and consequent homecoming, and now the rest of Isaiah focuses on this homeland, from its present corruption (chs 56–59) to its devastation when the Avenger comes to destroy it (chs 63–64), to its eventual rescue (chs 60–62) and ultimate glory (chs 65–66). When we move from chapter 55 to chapter 56, we recognize a difference in historical background and some differences in style, structure, and tone. These have caused some to suggest that a new author is behind this material, but it should be remembered that language naturally changes with subject matter, perspective, and mood.

Isaiah separated the kingdom of God from the nation, projected it into the future, and identified it with the remnant. He believed in the "sure" house of David and was convinced that from that house would come a messianic King (cf. 9:1-7; 11:1-9) who would rule over the remnant, the community of faith, the kingdom of God. He would be God's representative, and under his leadership the reign of God would become a glorious reality.

This chapter opens with the promise of blessings for the nations (56:1-8) and closes with the condemnation of sinful leaders (56:9-12). The passage looks to a time when God will accept those outside his old covenant people, and not consider them second-class citizens (56:3). Even the "eunuchs" (56:3-4) are his, and the Lord promises to "bless the foreigners" (56:6). According to the law, eunuchs could not participate in the assembly of the Lord (cf. Deut 23:1, 3, 7-8); however, a new era was coming in which even eunuchs would be graciously accepted. The Old Testament was never exclusive on a purely national basis. Exodus 12:48-49 expresses the position that a stranger was always a welcome convert into the covenant community. Ezra and Nehemiah have been misunderstood as practicing exclusivism.

Their concern was to preserve the identity of God's covenant people in a religious sense, not a mere ethnic sense.

The background to "a memorial and a name" (56:5) is found in 2 Samuel 18:18, where the childless Absalom sought to perpetuate himself by a memorial stone that would last beyond his own lifespan. In 55:13, by gathering in a world-wide people, the Lord made for himself a name that will not be cut off. He shares that reality with those who were formerly excluded but have now become members of his house.

The reference to bringing foreigners "to my holy mountain of Jerusalem" (56:7) recalls Isaiah 2:2-3 (cf. 66:20). Zion will be a "house of prayer for all nations" (56:7). Although foreigners and eunuchs were formerly rejected, the Lord would now bring into his holy mountain all those from outside who will join themselves to him. It is plain from the succeeding words that the proselytes' access to the Temple will be free. Because of their commitment to the covenant, they will be invited to the holy mountain of Zion. Reference is made to 56:7 in all three synoptic gospels (Matt 21:13; Mark 11:17; Luke 19:46).

◆     10. Sinful leaders and idolatry condemned (56:9–57:12)

⁹Come, wild animals of the field!
   Come, wild animals of the forest!
   Come and devour my people!
¹⁰For the leaders of my people—
   the LORD's watchmen, his
      shepherds—
   are blind and ignorant.
They are like silent watchdogs
   that give no warning when danger
      comes.
They love to lie around, sleeping and
   dreaming.
¹¹   Like greedy dogs, they are never
      satisfied.
They are ignorant shepherds,
   all following their own path
   and intent on personal gain.
¹²"Come," they say, "let's get some wine
   and have a party.
Let's all get drunk.
Then tomorrow we'll do it again
   and have an even bigger party!"

CHAPTER 57

¹Good people pass away;
   the godly often die before their time.
But no one seems to care or wonder
   why.

No one seems to understand
   that God is protecting them from
   the evil to come.
²For those who follow godly paths
   will rest in peace when they die.

³"But you—come here, you witches'
      children,
   you offspring of adulterers and
      prostitutes!
⁴Whom do you mock,
   making faces and sticking out
      your tongues?
You children of sinners and liars!
⁵You worship your idols with great
      passion
   beneath the oaks and under every
      green tree.
You sacrifice your children down
   in the valleys,
   among the jagged rocks in
      the cliffs.
⁶Your gods are the smooth stones
   in the valleys.
You worship them with liquid
   offerings and grain offerings.
They, not I, are your inheritance.
Do you think all this makes me
   happy?

⁷You have committed adultery on every
    high mountain.
There you have worshiped idols
    and have been unfaithful to me.
⁸You have put pagan symbols
    on your doorposts and behind your
    doors.
You have left me
    and climbed into bed with these
    detestable gods.
You have committed yourselves to
    them.
You love to look at their naked
    bodies.
⁹You have given olive oil to Molech*
    with many gifts of perfume.

You have traveled far,
    even into the world of the dead,*
    to find new gods to love.
¹⁰You grew weary in your search,
    but you never gave up.
Desire gave you renewed strength,
    and you did not grow weary.

¹¹"Are you afraid of these idols?
    Do they terrify you?
Is that why you have lied to me
    and forgotten me and my words?
Is it because of my long silence
    that you no longer fear me?
¹²Now I will expose your so-called
    good deeds.
None of them will help you.

57:9a Or to the king.  57:9b Hebrew into Sheol.

NOTES

56:9 *wild animals.* The appearance of these animals is perhaps intended to reflect departure from the law of the Lord (Lev 26:22; Deut 28:26; 32:24; 2 Kgs 17:25).

56:10 *lie around.* This translates the Heb. participle *shokebim* [TH7901, ZH8886], which is not used elsewhere.

57:2 *rest in peace.* Lit., "rest in their beds." The NIV has "find rest as they lie in death" and other versions vary on how to render the Heb. of this line: "rest in their beds" (KJV, NASB), "have rest on his couch" (NJPS), "rest on their couches" (NRSV), "lie on their deathbeds" (REB), "rest on his own bed" (GW), and "rest in death" (TEV).

57:4 *making faces and sticking out your tongues.* These are signs of derision, as in Ps 22:7. Gestures in that ancient culture are not always clearly understood by us today. Translations vary: "open wide your mouth and stick out your tongue" (NASB, cf. NRSV), "open your mouths and stick out your tongues" (REB, NJPS).

57:6 *Your gods are the smooth stones in the valleys.* They are possibly smooth because of pagan oil libations poured on them, or stones worn by the stream to resemble deities. Since the Heb. for "smooth" can also mean "slippery," Isaiah may be using a deliberate wordplay. The translations vary: "[the idols] among the smooth stones of the ravines are your portion" (NIV), "among the smooth stones of the valley is your portion" (NRSV), "among the smooth stones of the ravine is your portion" (NASB), "your place is with the deceitful gods of the wadi" (REB), and "you take smooth stones from there and worship them as gods" (TEV).

57:7 *high mountain.* This is undoubtedly a reference to the high places or pagan mountain shrines (Jer 3:6; Ezek 16:16; 22:9).

57:8 *pagan symbols.* The Heb. *zikkaron* [TH2146, ZH2355] with the suffix is unusual. The Heb. term usually refers to a "memorial," which doesn't fit well here. Some suggest that this reference is to some small image posted at the door (like a cross in some Christian homes). Since the Heb. root is the same as the one that denotes "male," some suggest that some kind of phallic symbol is intended. The NAB translates it "indecent symbol," and the NRSV has the alternate translation "on their phallus" in its mg.

*You love to look at their naked bodies.* More lit., "you love their bed [where] you saw a hand." Since the same word for "hand" (*yad* [TH3027, ZH3338]) in Ugaritic can sometimes denote the male organ, some think that this may be the case here for the Heb. Motyer (1993:473) thinks the "hand" may refer to financial resources, something of interest to a prostitute.

**57:9 Molech.** This translation is based on a different vocalization of the Heb.; the received text has *melek* [TH4428, ZH4889] ("king"; cf. NLT mg). The worship of the Canaanite deity Molech apparently sometimes involved the sacrifice of children (Jer 19:5). Molech (*molek* [TH4432, ZH4891]) was the leading deity of the Ammonites and was worshiped by Solomon in his later years (1 Kgs 11:5). Child sacrifice took place in Topheth, in the Valley of Hinnom south of Jerusalem; perhaps the "ravines" of 57:5 included Topheth. According to 2 Chr 28:3, King Ahaz sacrificed his sons in the Valley of Ben Hinnom.

***olive oil . . . gifts of perfume.*** For the concept of using olive oil and perfume to allure lovers, see Ezek 23:40. Olive oil was used as an ointment for perfume (cf. Songs 4:10, where the word for "oil" is translated "perfume").

***traveled far.*** The Heb. *shapel* [TH8213, ZH9164] (be low) here means "to descend, go down." It could refer to debasing service. The KJV translates it as "debase."

**57:10 Desire gave you renewed strength.** This translates the unique Heb. phrase *khayyath yadek matsa'th* [TH2416C, ZH2652], which is, lit., "you found the life of your hand." The Heb. *yad* [TH3027, ZH3338] can mean strength or power (HALOT 1:388) and the meaning here would then be "found your strength." As observed in the note on 57:8, *yad* can also refer to the male sexual organ, which undoubtedly connotes virility and potency (cf. HALOT 1:387). The NJPS translation, "you found gratification for your lust," reads too much into the language.

## COMMENTARY

Isaiah was fond of sharp transitions (cf. 9:8), and here he returns to the theme of judgment. In 52:1–56:8, Isaiah reveled in God's good news for Israel and the nations based on the work of the Servant-Messiah. From 56:9–59:15, he concentrates once again on the sins of Israel. The first section of this passage (56:9-12) contains a condemnation of self-seeking leadership, and the second section (57:1-12) exposes the tension between "the godly" (57:1) and those who have joined cults and have forgotten the Lord (57:11).

The Lord's watchmen, who should have been alert "watchdogs" (56:10), had become "greedy dogs" (56:11). The sinful leaders were only intent on their personal gain and were never satisfied (56:11). Motyer (1993:468) describing this situation, says "The eyes of the leaders, which should be turned outwards, whether in guardianship (10a-d) or in care (11c-f), are turned inwards to their own welfare."

Chapter 57 opens with good news about the good people who "die before their time" because "God is protecting them from the evil to come" (57:1). Some of the righteous mercifully died preceding the judgment that God brought on the whole people, yet the death of those who were righteous only caused conditions to deteriorate more. Condemnation of idolatry is resumed in 57:3, and in biting language, the wicked are described as "witches' children" and "offspring of adulterers and prostitutes" (57:3) who mock and make faces while sticking out their tongues (57:4). They even sacrifice their children "down in the valleys" (57:5). They "climbed into bed with these detestable gods" and are thereby castigated because they "love to look at their naked bodies" (57:8).

Judah feared people more than God (57:11; cf. 51:12). Since they had not witnessed any activity of God for years ("Is it because of my long silence?"), they easily forgot him. They lied to him, forgot him and his words, and no longer feared him. In 57:12-13, the utter folly of idolatry is again exposed in contrast to "whoever trusts in me." These "will inherit the land and possess my holy mountain." When Almighty God exposes their "so-called good deeds" (57:12; cf. the description of "filthy rags" in 64:6), their feeble idols will be unable to help them. They are so helpless that "a puff of wind can knock them down" (57:13; cf. Judg 10:14). The land was given to the people to be their possession (Exod 32:13) in fulfillment of the promise made to Abraham (Gen 12:7), but they had also been warned that if they turned away from the Lord, they would be taken away from the land and scattered (Deut 28:63-64). When Isaiah addressed them, there was still a chance for them to renounce their idols, repent, and continue to possess the land, including the heritage of his holy mountain.

◆      ## 11. Healing and comfort for the repentant (57:13-21)

13 Let's see if your idols can save you
     when you cry to them for help.
Why, a puff of wind can knock them
     down!
     If you just breathe on them, they
     fall over!
But whoever trusts in me will inherit
     the land
     and possess my holy mountain."

14 God says, "Rebuild the road!
     Clear away the rocks and stones
     so my people can return from
     captivity."
15 The high and lofty one who lives in
     eternity,
     the Holy One, says this:
"I live in the high and holy place
     with those whose spirits are contrite
     and humble.
I restore the crushed spirit of the
     humble
     and revive the courage of those with
     repentant hearts.
16 For I will not fight against you forever;

I will not always be angry.
     If I were, all people would pass away—
     all the souls I have made.
17 I was angry,
     so I punished these greedy people.
I withdrew from them,
     but they kept going on their own
     stubborn way.
18 I have seen what they do,
     but I will heal them anyway!
     I will lead them.
     I will comfort those who mourn,
19      bringing words of praise to their
     lips.
May they have abundant peace, both
     near and far,"
     says the LORD, who heals them.
20 "But those who still reject me are
     like the restless sea,
     which is never still
     but continually churns up mud
     and dirt.
21 There is no peace for the wicked,"
     says my God.

NOTES

57:18 *mourn.* This refers to those who were mourning the fall of Jerusalem and the sin that caused it (cf. 66:10).

57:19 *bringing words of praise to their lips.* Lit., "creating the fruit of the lips." The word "create" is the same here as in the Genesis creation account.

*abundant peace.* Lit., "peace, peace"; the repetition is for emphasis. Similar examples are found in Gen 14:10; Deut 16:20.

**57:20 churns up.** The Heb. is *garash* [TH1644A, ZH1764], which means "to disturb, stir up" (cf. Jer 49:23).

COMMENTARY

This passage is about the healing and restoration of Israel. The opening verse speaks of those who "inherit the land and possess [God's] holy mountain." This, in turn, leads again to the theme of preparing a highway so that God's people can return from captivity (57:14). The remainder of the passage (57:15-21) describes God's forgiveness for the repentant.

The "high and lofty one who lives in eternity, the Holy One" (57:15a; cf. 6:1) is the same one who can "restore the crushed spirit of the humble and revive the courage of those with repentant hearts" (57:15b). The contrite are "crushed in spirit" (57:15; Ps 34:18). Their hearts have been broken, humbled by the sin they have committed (66:2), just like David, who committed adultery and murder (Ps 51:17). The Lord will comfort those who mourn (57:18), but those who reject him will become "like the restless sea" (57:20) because "there is no peace for the wicked" (57:21).

Isaiah compares the condition of the wicked to the continually churning sea because the wicked are forever dredging up evil thoughts and schemes. For the wicked, "there is no peace" (57:21) by divine mandate. The wicked do not have peace with God during their lives nor do they enter into peace at death. This major section closes on the same note as did the first (48:22): "There is no peace for the wicked."

◆    C. The Glorious Consummation (58:1–66:24)
       1. True and false worship (58:1-14)

"Shout with the voice of a trumpet
     blast.
Shout aloud! Don't be timid.
Tell my people Israel* of their sins!
² Yet they act so pious!
They come to the Temple every day
     and seem delighted to learn all
     about me.
They act like a righteous nation
     that would never abandon the laws
     of its God.
They ask me to take action on their
     behalf,
     pretending they want to be
     near me.
³ 'We have fasted before you!' they say.
     'Why aren't you impressed?
We have been very hard on ourselves,
     and you don't even notice it!'

"I will tell you why!" I respond.
     "It's because you are fasting to
     please yourselves.
Even while you fast,
     you keep oppressing your workers.
⁴ What good is fasting
     when you keep on fighting and
     quarreling?
This kind of fasting
     will never get you anywhere
     with me.
⁵ You humble yourselves
     by going through the motions
     of penance,
bowing your heads
     like reeds bending in the wind.
You dress in burlap
     and cover yourselves with ashes.
Is this what you call fasting?

Do you really think this will please
the LORD?

6 "No, this is the kind of fasting I want:
Free those who are wrongly
imprisoned;
lighten the burden of those who
work for you.
Let the oppressed go free,
and remove the chains that bind
people.
7 Share your food with the hungry,
and give shelter to the homeless.
Give clothes to those who need them,
and do not hide from relatives who
need your help.

8 "Then your salvation will come like
the dawn,
and your wounds will quickly heal.
Your godliness will lead you forward,
and the glory of the LORD will
protect you from behind.
9 Then when you call, the LORD will
answer.
'Yes, I am here,' he will quickly reply.

"Remove the heavy yoke of oppression.
Stop pointing your finger and
spreading vicious rumors!
10 Feed the hungry,
and help those in trouble.

Then your light will shine out from
the darkness,
and the darkness around you will
be as bright as noon.
11 The LORD will guide you continually,
giving you water when you are dry
and restoring your strength.
You will be like a well-watered
garden,
like an ever-flowing spring.
12 Some of you will rebuild the deserted
ruins of your cities.
Then you will be known as a
rebuilder of walls
and a restorer of homes.

13 "Keep the Sabbath day holy.
Don't pursue your own interests
on that day,
but enjoy the Sabbath
and speak of it with delight as the
LORD's holy day.
Honor the Sabbath in everything you
do on that day,
and don't follow your own desires or
talk idly.
14 Then the LORD will be your delight.
I will give you great honor
and satisfy you with the inheritance
I promised to your ancestor Jacob.
I, the LORD, have spoken!"

58:1 Hebrew *Jacob.* See note on 14:1.

NOTES

58:1 *Israel.* The Heb. has "Jacob" (cf. NLT mg).

58:5 *like reeds bending in the wind.* A sign of weakness and humility (see 43:3).

*burlap.* Heb. *saq* [TH8242, ZH8566], which is probably (through Gr. *sakkos*) the origin of English "sack," and the Heb. sometimes carries this meaning (Gen 42:27). Traditionally translated "sackcloth," this coarse cloth (probably of black goat's hair) is mentioned thirty-three times in the Bible in connection with mourning and self-abasement before the Lord (see comments at 15:3; 20:2; 37:1). In ancient Near Eastern culture, it was the outward demonstration of inner grief and sorrow.

*please the LORD.* Lit., "a day acceptable to the LORD," where "acceptable" translates the Heb. *ratson* [TH7522, ZH8356], a term often applied to sacrifices (see 56:7; 60:7; Lev 1:3).

58:8 *your salvation.* Lit., "your light," which is symbolic for the joy, prosperity, and salvation that come from the Lord (cf. 9:2; 60:1-3).

*glory of the LORD.* This probably recalls the pillars of cloud and fire that shielded the Israelites during their dangerous travels through the desert (cf. 4:5-6; Exod 13:21–14:20).

**58:9** *Stop pointing your finger.* This expression is not found elsewhere, although the context reveals the general meaning.

**58:10** *help those in trouble.* Lit., "draw out thy soul to the hungry" (KJV). The Heb. verb translated "draw out" is the hiphil of *puq* [TH6329, ZH7049], which can mean something like "to cause to receive, obtain." It seems to indicate a sharing of one's self by sympathizing, comforting, and bearing the burdens of those afflicted with inward pain.

**58:11** *well-watered garden.* Isaiah was fond of using the figure of a "well-watered garden" (30:25; 33:21; 35:6-7; 41:17-18; 43:20; 44:4; 48:21; 49:10).

**58:13** *talk idly.* Heb. *dabber dabar,* an expression found elsewhere only in Deut 18:20, where it is used of "chit-chat." Cf. "speaking idle words" (NIV), "talking idly" (GW, TEV, ESV), and "pursuing your own affairs" (NRSV).

**58:14** *the LORD will be your delight.* Elsewhere we read that God's people were to delight themselves in the Lord (Ps 37:4) and in his law (Ps 1:2).

## COMMENTARY

**The Final Section of Isaiah.** These last nine chapters of Isaiah comprise the third and final part of the section on God's Comfort for his People (40:1–66:24). They focus on the culmination of God's work among his people. The shift from the preceding material is more subtle than with many of Isaiah's transitions, and the close relationship between chapters 57, 58, and 59 makes it difficult to distinguish clearly where one section ends and the next begins.

Although I assume that Isaiah was addressing the people of his own day, some scholars suggest that this material was written by a Deutero-Isaiah writing during the captivity, or even a Trito-Isaiah writing in the period following the exile (see Introduction). After revealing the captivity to come, the return of the remnant, the suffering Servant, and the glory of the future Zion, the prophet turns again to present conditions.

The subject of the first half of chapter 58 (58:1-12) is the sin of hypocrisy, especially as it relates to fasting. This passage has many parallels with 1:10-20. Both passages expose the folly of religious hypocrisy—thinking that one can be truly religious but socially indifferent. Smart (1965:247) puts it succinctly, "One of the unique features of the Biblical faith is that there is no genuine relation with God that is not at the same time a relation with the brother." True faith is depicted in 58:13-14: God's laws are to be kept, but not in a legalistic fashion. People are to enjoy the Sabbath and speak of it with delight (58:13). Serving the Lord is to be a joyful experience (58:14), not a grudging one.

**Warnings against Sin.** Israel was asleep in sin, but was about to be awakened with "the voice of a trumpet blast" (58:1). They appeared "so pious" and seemed "delighted to learn all about [God]" as they regularly observed their religious rituals (58:2). In fact, the people were pretending that they wanted to be near God (58:2), as they claimed, "we have fasted" and "been very hard on ourselves" (58:3). Their religious actions were mechanical and superficial (cf. 1:11-15). True humility shows itself in a willingness to turn away from sin and towards God, an attitude that was obviously lacking in Judah's attitude toward worship at this time. People look at the outward appearance, but the Lord looks on the heart (1 Sam 16:7); the formalities of religion do not impress him. When they complained to God, "Why aren't you impressed" (58:3), he responded that the problem was that they persisted in "oppressing [their] workers" (58:3; cf. 3:14-15; 10:2) and "fighting and quarrelling" (58:4) even as they observed the outward rituals of their faith. The psalmist observed, "If I had not confessed the sin in my heart, my Lord would not have listened" (Ps 66:18).

The kind of observance God desired was for them to "free those who are wrongly imprisoned" and "lighten the burden of those who work for you" (58:6). God wanted them to "share [their] food with the hungry," "give shelter to the homeless," and "give clothes to those who need them" (58:7). If they did such things, their salvation and healing would come quickly. The Lord did not reject the practice of fasting per se, but insisted that it be accompanied by social works, an issue that was still a matter of concern during the time of Jesus when the Pharisees paraded about on their fast days (Matt 6:16-18). Jesus insisted that humility and mercy must go hand-in-hand with fasting (Matt 5:3-9). If God's people will practice social justice and observe religious rituals, then their "light will shine out from the darkness" (58:10). They should "enjoy the Sabbath and speak of it with delight" (58:13). It was instituted as a day set apart to the Lord, a time when the people were to take delight in the Lord and in his word (Exod 20:8; Pss 1:2; 37:4). Since it had become a day for personal amusement and for pursuing business interests, Isaiah urged the people to restore the Sabbath to its rightful place.

The chapter closes with the encouraging words that the Lord would give them "great honor" and "satisfy [them] with the inheritance I promised to your ancestor Jacob" (58:14).

## ◆  2. Warning against sin (59:1-21)

Listen! The LORD's arm is not too weak
    to save you,
nor is his ear too deaf to hear you
    call.
2 It's your sins that have cut you off
    from God.
Because of your sins, he has turned
    away
and will not listen anymore.
3 Your hands are the hands of
    murderers,
and your fingers are filthy with sin.
Your lips are full of lies,
    and your mouth spews corruption.

4 No one cares about being fair and
    honest.

The people's lawsuits are based
    on lies.
They conceive evil deeds
    and then give birth to sin.
5 They hatch deadly snakes
    and weave spiders' webs.
Whoever falls into their webs will die,
    and there's danger even in getting
    near them.
6 Their webs can't be made into
    clothing,
    and nothing they do is productive.
All their activity is filled with sin,
    and violence is their trademark.
7 Their feet run to do evil,
    and they rush to commit murder.
They think only about sinning.

Misery and destruction always
follow them.
⁸They don't know where to find peace
or what it means to be just and good.
They have mapped out crooked roads,
and no one who follows them knows
a moment's peace.
⁹So there is no justice among us,
and we know nothing about right
living.
We look for light but find only
darkness.
We look for bright skies but walk
in gloom.
¹⁰We grope like the blind along a wall,
feeling our way like people without
eyes.
Even at brightest noontime,
we stumble as though it were dark.
Among the living,
we are like the dead.
¹¹We growl like hungry bears;
we moan like mournful doves.
We look for justice, but it never comes.
We look for rescue, but it is far
away from us.
¹²For our sins are piled up before God
and testify against us.
Yes, we know what sinners we are.
¹³We know we have rebelled and have
denied the LORD.
We have turned our backs on our
God.
We know how unfair and oppressive
we have been,
carefully planning our deceitful lies.
¹⁴Our courts oppose the righteous,
and justice is nowhere to be found.
Truth stumbles in the streets,
and honesty has been outlawed.
¹⁵Yes, truth is gone,

and anyone who renounces evil is
attacked.

The LORD looked and was displeased
to find there was no justice.
¹⁶He was amazed to see that no one
intervened
to help the oppressed.
So he himself stepped in to save them
with his strong arm,
and his justice sustained him.
¹⁷He put on righteousness as his body
armor
and placed the helmet of salvation
on his head.
He clothed himself with a robe of
vengeance
and wrapped himself in a cloak
of divine passion.
¹⁸He will repay his enemies for their
evil deeds.
His fury will fall on his foes.
He will pay them back even to the
ends of the earth.
¹⁹In the west, people will respect the
name of the LORD;
in the east, they will glorify him.
For he will come like a raging flood
tide
driven by the breath of the LORD.*

²⁰"The Redeemer will come to Jerusalem
to buy back those in Israel
who have turned from their sins,"*
says the LORD.

²¹"And this is my covenant with them,"
says the LORD. "My Spirit will not leave
them, and neither will these words I have
given you. They will be on your lips and on
the lips of your children and your children's children forever. I, the LORD, have
spoken!

59:19 Or *When the enemy comes like a raging flood tide, / the Spirit of the LORD will drive him back.*
59:20 Hebrew *The Redeemer will come to Zion / to buy back those in Jacob / who have turned from their sins.*
Greek version reads *The one who rescues will come on behalf of Zion, / and he will turn Jacob away from
ungodliness.* Compare Rom 11:26.

NOTES

**59:1** *The LORD's arm is not too weak.* Lit., "the arm of the LORD is not too short" (cf.
51:9). "Arm" and "hand" in Semitic idioms often refer to power.

**59:3 *Your hands are the hands of murderers.*** The Heb. vividly says, "your hands are stained with blood."

***mouth.*** Lit., "tongue" (see 3:8; 32:4; 35:6; 57:14).

**59:5 *weave spiders' web.*** This image conveys weakness and fragility (cf. Job 8:14-15).

**59:7 *feet run to do evil.*** The same image is found in Prov 1:16.

**59:8 *peace.*** Lit., "way of peace"; this expression is also found in 26:3, 12; 57:20-21; Luke 1:79.

**59:10 *Among the living.*** The Heb. word *'ashmannim* [TH820, ZH875] is found only here; its translation is uncertain, as reflected in the versions: "among the vigorous" (NRSV), "in the desolate underworld" (REB), "in Stygian darkness" (NAB), "among the robust" (NJB), "among the strong" (NIV), and "among the sturdy" (NJPS).

**59:12 *our sins.*** The NLT compresses the text; the Heb. has three basic words for sin here: *pesha'* [TH6588, ZH7322], *khatta'th* [TH2403A, ZH2633], and *'awon* [TH5771, ZH6411].

**59:14 *justice is nowhere to be found.*** More lit., "justice is driven back" (NIV). Cf. 59:9; contrast 46:13.

**59:16 *stepped in to save them with his strong arm.*** More lit., "his own arm worked salvation for him" (NIV; cf. 51:9; 52:10). Other versons have "his own might brought him the victory" (REB), "with his own power he wins a victory" (GW), "his victorious right hand supported him" (NJPS), and "with his own powerful arm he won victories for truth" (CEV).

**59:17 *a robe of vengeance.*** Cf. the blood-spattered garments of 63:1-3, a parallel passage.

## COMMENTARY

The preceding passage (58:1-14) exposed rebellion and sin; chapter 59 contains further charges (59:1-8), which are followed by a confession of guilt and helplessness (59:9ff). Within this context, 59:3-7 mentions various parts of the body that are involved in sin, revealing its pervasive nature, and 59.9-11 depicts some of the sad results of sin. The Lord's intervention to save his covenant people is the focus of 59:16-21.

The chapter opens with warnings about the high cost of sin. The problem was that their sins had cut them off from God, and because of their sin, God has "turned away and will not listen anymore" (59:2). In graphic language, sinners are described as "murderers"; their hands, fingers, lips, and mouth are all tainted with corruption (59:3). Paul picks up on this passage (see Rom 3:15-17) in his own description of human sinfulness. His conclusion is that such sinners have no fear of God to restrain them (Rom 3:18). Their pollution renders them unfit for being in God's presence or doing God's work.

All of society is permeated with sin, so that "nothing they do is productive" (59:6). They "think only about sinning," with the result that "misery and destruction always follow them" (59:7). The wicked do not enter into evil in a leisurely way; "their feet run to do evil, and they rush to commit murder" (59:7; cf. Prov 1:16).

These blind and rebellious people miss the meaning of true peace and what it means to be just and good (59:8). They also miss God's protection from their enemies (59:9), as their "sins are piled up before God and testify against [them]"

(59:12). The reference in 59:9 to darkness and gloom probably reflects the absence of justice. Such terms were used to describe the distress caused by the Assyrian invasions (5:30; 8:21-22; 9:1-2). The metaphorical use of light and darkness is not as common in Isaiah as one might expect (but cf. 2:5; 5:20, 30; 42:6, 16; 45:7; 51:4; 59:8, 10). It is so dark that sinners "grope like the blind" and stumble about at midday, a plight mentioned in Deuteronomy 28:29 as a curse for disobedience (59:10; cf. Job 5:14). Like Ezra (Ezra 9:6-7), Isaiah confessed the sins of the nation, and in 59:12 alone (see note), he used the three most common Hebrew words for sin.

The picture painted by Isaiah is indeed a gloomy one, but suddenly the Lord bursts upon the scene, and all is changed (59:15b-21). God himself steps in to "help the oppressed" (59:16). He is described in very graphic language as a mighty warrior in the body armor of righteousness, with a helmet of salvation, and "a robe of vengeance." He is wrapped "in a cloak of divine passion" (59:17). The breastplate of righteousness and the helmet of salvation are mentioned in Ephesians 6:14, 17. There Paul describes the Christian's armor in the war against Satan, but neither the garments of vengeance nor the cloak of zeal have a place in Ephesians. The picture of the Lord as the divine Warrior must be studied against the background of passages such as Psalms 18:9-15 and 104:1-4. Isaiah now takes up this image (and he will do so again in 63:2-3). The vision is the same as the one John gives of the Messiah in Revelation 19:11-21 when he depicts him as the Warrior who comes to judge the world at the last day.

When the divine Warrior's fury falls on his foes, he will be respected and glorified (59:19). The last part of 59:19 describes the coming of the Lord as a flood tide, a rushing, irresistible torrent that overwhelms the enemy (cf. 30:28). In 30:27-28, similar imagery is used to depict the Lord's appearance as he overwhelms Assyria, whose invasion of Israel had been similarly compared (cf. 8:7).

In Isaiah, the deliverance refers initially to the nation's rescue from captivity, as it did in 52:10, where the mighty arm of the Lord is also described as going into action. But spiritual salvation is not to be excluded from the meaning of the words in 59:15b-21, for Paul quoted 59:20 in connection with the salvation of "all Israel" by the appearing of Christ (Rom 11:26).

The chapter closes with the Redeemer coming to Jerusalem "to buy back those in Israel" (59:20). Paul relates 52:7 and 59:20 to the coming of Christ (Rom 10:15; 11:26) because redemption in its fullest sense awaited his work on Calvary. Salvation through Christ is good news that surpasses release from the Babylonian exile. Those who returned to Jerusalem would be repentant and responsive to the word of God. So, in contrast to several previous chapters that had ended with a word of warning (cf. 48:22; 57:20-21; 59:21), this one ends with a word of blessing to the repentant (cf. 59:20-21). The Redeemer will come to save his people according to the covenant of God (59:21).

The covenant recalls the "covenant with them" that is associated with the work of the Servant of the Lord in 42:6 and in 49:8. It may also be related to the "new covenant" predicted in Jeremiah 31:31-34, a passage that emphasizes wholehearted reception of the word of God. Jeremiah mentions the implanting of the law on the people's minds and hearts, and Isaiah draws attention to the mouth that will never cease to speak God's Word.

The promise given was that God's Spirit would not leave them and that his words would be on the lips of that generation and the generations to follow (59:21). The reference to God's Spirit (59:21) is similar to another great passage about restoration, Ezekiel 36:26-27. There, the Spirit provides the power to follow God's decrees and laws. Elsewhere in Isaiah, the Spirit of God is linked with the Messiah or with his era (11:2; 32:15; 44:3). The covenant referred to here includes the promise of the Holy Spirit and his word of truth. God's new people are to be marked by holiness and obedience to God's ways—things evidently lacking in the prophet's own day.

## ◆ 3. The glory of Zion (60:1-22)

"Arise, Jerusalem! Let your light shine
　　for all to see.
　For the glory of the LORD rises to
　　shine on you.
2 Darkness as black as night covers all
　　the nations of the earth,
　but the glory of the LORD rises and
　　appears over you.
3 All nations will come to your light;
　mighty kings will come to see your
　　radiance.

4 "Look and see, for everyone is coming
　　home!
　Your sons are coming from distant
　　lands;
　your little daughters will be carried
　　home.
5 Your eyes will shine,
　and your heart will thrill with joy,
　for merchants from around the world
　　will come to you.
　They will bring you the wealth of
　　many lands.
6 Vast caravans of camels will converge
　　on you,
　the camels of Midian and Ephah.
　The people of Sheba will bring gold
　　and frankincense
　and will come worshiping the LORD.
7 The flocks of Kedar will be given to
　　you,
　and the rams of Nebaioth will be
　　brought for my altars.

I will accept their offerings,
　and I will make my Temple glorious.

8 "And what do I see flying like clouds
　　to Israel,
　like doves to their nests?
9 They are ships from the ends of the
　　earth,
　from lands that trust in me,
　led by the great ships of Tarshish.
　They are bringing the people of Israel
　　home from far away,
　carrying their silver and gold.
　They will honor the LORD your God,
　the Holy One of Israel,
　for he has filled you with
　　splendor.

10 "Foreigners will come to rebuild your
　　towns,
　and their kings will serve you.
　For though I have destroyed you in
　　my anger,
　I will now have mercy on you
　　through my grace.
11 Your gates will stay open around
　　the clock
　to receive the wealth of many lands.
　The kings of the world will be led as
　　captives
　in a victory procession.
12 For the nations that refuse to serve
　　you
　will be destroyed.

13 "The glory of Lebanon will be yours—
the forests of cypress, fir, and pine—
to beautify my sanctuary.
My Temple will be glorious!
14 The descendants of your tormentors
will come and bow before you.
Those who despised you
will kiss your feet.
They will call you the City of the LORD,
and Zion of the Holy One of Israel.

15 "Though you were once despised and
hated,
with no one traveling through you,
I will make you beautiful forever,
a joy to all generations.
16 Powerful kings and mighty nations
will satisfy your every need,
as though you were a child
nursing at the breast of a queen.
You will know at last that I, the LORD,
am your Savior and your Redeemer,
the Mighty One of Israel.*
17 I will exchange your bronze for gold,
your iron for silver,
your wood for bronze,
and your stones for iron.
I will make peace your leader
and righteousness your ruler.
18 Violence will disappear from
your land;

the desolation and destruction of
war will end.
Salvation will surround you like city
walls,
and praise will be on the lips of
all who enter there.

19 "No longer will you need the sun
to shine by day,
nor the moon to give its light by
night,
for the LORD your God will be your
everlasting light,
and your God will be your glory.
20 Your sun will never set;
your moon will not go down.
For the LORD will be your everlasting
light.
Your days of mourning will come
to an end.
21 All your people will be righteous.
They will possess their land forever,
for I will plant them there with my
own hands
in order to bring myself glory.
22 The smallest family will become
a thousand people,
and the tiniest group will become
a mighty nation.
At the right time, I, the LORD, will
make it happen."

60:16 Hebrew *of Jacob.* See note on 14:1.

NOTES

60:1 *Arise . . . shine.* In the Heb., the imperatives "arise" and "shine" and the pronouns "you" and "your" are in the feminine singular form and apply to Jerusalem.

*light.* Isaiah is the only prophet who uses the metaphor of "light" to any extent (2:5; 5:20; 9:2 [1]; 10:17; 42:6; 49:6; 51:4). Jeremiah uses it once (13:16); Amos (5:18, 20) used it in connection with the day of the Lord, which will be "darkness," not "light." Micah used it twice in Mic 7:8-9.

*glory.* Motyer observes that two different words are used for the broad idea of "glory" in this chapter. The *kabod* [TH3519, ZH3883] group (60:1-2, 13), has the idea of "weight" and so of importance or influence; in the other group (60:7, 9, 13, 19, 21), the idea is of "beauty." Motyer (1993:495) suggests that these two groups "express the glory that impresses and the glory that attracts."

60:4 *carried home.* The Heb. has *tsad* [TH6654, ZH7396] "side." Some versions (e.g., the NIV) have "carried on the arm," but the Heb. probably refers to the practice of mothers carrying little ones on the hip, as is often seen in our society. The NJB has "daughters carried on the hip." REB's "walking beside them" seems unlikely. Zion's delicate daughters were carefully carried.

**60:5 *wealth of many lands.*** For Jerusalem (Zion) being enriched by the nations, see ch 11; 61:6; 66:12; and 18:7; 23:18; 45:14.

**60:6 *camels of Midian.*** It is ironic that these are mentioned, since the camel-riding Midianites had devastated Israel before Gideon drove them off (Judg 6:5; Isa 9:4). The former plunderers were now worshipers. Midian was Abraham's son through Keturah (Gen 25:2), and Ephah was a son of Midian (Gen 25:4). At one time Moses found refuge among the Midianites (Exod 2:15-21). The Midianites roamed the deserts of what is now Jordan.

***Sheba.*** His dwelling place was the southwest tip of Arabia; he was a grandson of Abraham by Keturah (Gen 25:1-3).

***gold and frankincense.*** In this context, the reference is to the visit of the queen of Sheba, who was overwhelmed by Solomon's riches and offered praise to the Lord (cf. 1 Kgs 10:2, 9). Sheba was a wealthy land in southern Arabia, perhaps roughly equivalent to modern Yemen (cf. Gen 25:3; 1 Kgs 10:1-2).

**60:7 *Kedar.*** He was a son of Ishmael, who was the son of Abraham by Hagar the handmaid (Gen 25:3). Kedar's land lay northeast of Jerusalem in the desert between Judah and Babylon.

**60:9 *great ships of Tarshish.*** The very same ships that were judged in 2:16 (translated "trading ships" in the NLT), here become instruments of service (Ps 48:7 also speaks of God's judgment on the ships of Tarshish). The judgment is purifying. Mouw (1983:13) suggests that the "destroying" of the ships was more like the breaking of a horse than the breaking of a vase. The ships will be harnessed for service in the holy city, Jerusalem. Their pagan function will be destroyed, and they will be renewed. The famous ships of Tarshish were used to bring silver and gold to Solomon every three years (cf. 1 Kgs 10:22). It is uncertain if these ships were from the city of Tarshish, or if the name simply denoted a certain kind of trading vessel.

**60:10 *towns.*** The Heb. is actually the word for "wall" (*khomah* [TH2346, ZH2570]) in the plural. The NLT translators possibly understand this as a figure where the part stands for the whole. Most translations use "walls" here but the CEV has "city walls."

**60:13 *glory of Lebanon.*** This refers to the famous cedars that were abundantly used in Solomon's Jerusalem (Lipinski 1973:358).

***My Temple will be glorious!*** Lit., "I will glorify the place of my feet." This refers to the site that is called the "footstool of God" in 1 Chr 28:2 (cf. Ps 132:7), where the transcendent and holy God touched earth, in the Temple, especially at the Ark of the Covenant (Pss 99:1; 132:7; Isa 66:1; Lam 2:1).

**60:14 *your . . . you.*** The Heb. is feminine singular throughout this verse, referring to the city of Jerusalem.

**60:16 *Powerful kings and mighty nations will satisfy your every need, as though you were a child nursing at the breast of a queen.*** Or, "You will drink the milk of nations and be nursed at royal breasts" (NIV). Milk is rich nourishment, and breasts provide intimate, maternal attention.

**60:21 *I will plant them.*** The Heb. is unusual: "branch of my planting" (*netser matta'aw* [TH5342, ZH5916]) and may have background meaning from the famous "divine plant" of the ancient Near East (cf. 61:1-3, 11; for discussion of usage in the DSS, see Tiller 1997).

**60:22 *will make it happen.*** This translates the Heb. verb *khush* [TH2363, ZH2590], which is usually understood to reflect two separate roots with different meanings, either "to hasten" or "to enjoy." The new versions seem to keep the traditional understanding: "accomplish it quickly" (NRSV), "bring this swiftly to pass" (REB), "will swiftly accomplish these things"

(NAB), "shall quickly bring it about" (NJB), and "do this swiftly" (NIV). Motyer (1993:499) suggests that Isaiah deliberately chose this verb with a double meaning.

### COMMENTARY

Chapters 60–62 focus on the glory of God's future people, and much of what follows echoes 59:20. Although the old covenant people experienced an initial fulfillment, the discussion here goes beyond that to the new covenant people. Revelation 21, with its picture of the New Jerusalem, draws heavily on Isaiah 60. Ultimately, this is a description of the glory of heaven. Both Isaiah and John entertain the same hope of the new city of God, characterized by righteousness.

Chapter 60 has parallels with 2:12-17, another list of items that are a source of pagan pride. Many of the same things are mentioned, such as costly lumber from Lebanon and commercial vessels. Even particular kinds of military protection are noted in both places, such as hills, mountains, and towers. Although people trusted in these things for security and regarded them as signs of their corporate strength, only the Lord will be exalted on the final day.

The opening scene in chapter 60 assumes the continuing picture of Jerusalem as lying prostrate in a drunken stupor (cf. 51:17). She had been depicted as a barren wife who would, nevertheless, some day break forth into singing because of her children (60:1). Suddenly, the glory of the LORD will rise to shine on her (60:2), and this light will attract "mighty kings" and "all nations" (60:2-3). This bright, attractive light will result from God's presence among his people as he graciously comes to Zion (cf. 59:20), for the Servant of the Lord will be a light for all peoples (42:6; 49:6). What he does for Zion, he does for the world.

The brightness of this light in a world of moral and spiritual darkness will cause mighty kings to come to see God's radiance (60:3). Drawn by this illuminating and guiding light, they will come to learn of the Lord's ways and to walk in them (cf. 2:2-3; 40:5). Motyer (1993:494) observes that missionary outreach was found in Old Testament times, but the nations seemed more attracted to Israel's witness when God blessed them and used them for his glory (cf. Deut 4:5-8). Examples of this may be observed with Rahab (Josh 2:10) and Naaman (2 Kgs 5).

The return of God's sons and daughters is described (60:4-7) in the language of merchants with expensive merchandise. The NLT rendering "around the world" stands in place of the more literal "of the sea" (60:5), which seems to refer to wealth by sea from the West as opposed to the wealth of the desert regions in the East mentioned in 60:6. God promised to make his Temple glorious, but the main thrust of 60:7 seems to be the acceptance of animals from heathen nations as offerings to the Lord. This is not in the sense of Ezra 6:9-10, where a Gentile ruler provided animals for sacrifice by Israel, but in their partaking of the benefits of the altar in their own right. The descendants of Abraham by Hagar and Keturah will share with his descendants by Sarah—that is, with the seed of Isaac—in glorifying God's spiritual house. God will adorn his glorious Temple by receiving Abraham's cast-off descendants and their gifts.

This returning group is described as clouds flying to Israel or doves returning to their nests (60:8). The returnees are described as "carrying their silver and gold" with them (60:9), which will bring great honor to the "Holy One of Israel" (60:9). The most remote regions are indicated (60:8-9), especially if the "ships of Tarshish" are from a location in Spain.

Similar verses about the restoration of Jerusalem are found elsewhere in the book of Isaiah; the nations are described as bringing riches to Jerusalem (18:7; 45:14; 61:6; 66:12) as in Haggai 2:7 and Zechariah 14:14. The assistance given to the returning exiles by the Persian government may have been an initial fulfillment of these passages, especially since the Persian king Darius helped to pay for the rebuilding of the Temple and even supplied animals for sacrifices (Ezra 6:8-10). With Darius's help, Zerubbabel was eventually able to complete the Temple by 516 BC. Isaiah mourned the destruction of the Temple in 63:18 and 64:11, but here he reflected on its glorious renewal, which symbolized the nation's physical and spiritual revival, and brought honor to the Lord (60:9; cf. 55:5).

The rebuilding of the walls (60:10; cf. the Heb.) is also described as the work of foreigners. Probably this is somewhat related to the period after the return from exile when King Artaxerxes issued a decree in 445 BC that allowed Nehemiah to rebuild the walls of Jerusalem (Neh 2:8). However, this did not produce the spectacular results described in 60:11-16, which must therefore refer to the future city of God (cf. Acts 15:14-16). Isaiah elsewhere describes the strong city where "God makes salvation its walls and ramparts" (26:1, NIV); also, later in this chapter, see "salvation will surround you like city walls" (60:18).

Their income will be so great that the "gates will stay open around the clock to receive the wealth of many lands" (60:11), and nations that refuse to support them will be destroyed. Perhaps these open gates are like the gates of the New Jerusalem (Rev 21:25-26), whose gates will never be shut, "for there will be no night there." When Nehemiah rebuilt the walls of Jerusalem, special emphasis was placed on repairing the gates and opening the gates only at specified times (Neh 7:3). In contrast, Isaiah said, "Open the gates to all who are righteous" (26:2), and it is possible that the gates were to be left open because the incoming wealth was so great and continuous that the caretakers of the city had no opportunity to close them. Zion was the place where divine wrath had become divine compassion (60:12). Only the nations that come and build in this "City of the LORD" by serving the Lord of Zion will survive; all others will be destroyed. Isaiah's contemporary, Micah, said that the Lord would pour out his wrath on all the nations that did not obey him (Mic 5:15).

The result of all this is that the Lord's "Temple will be glorious" (60:13); Jerusalem will be called "the City of the LORD," and the "Zion of the Holy One of Israel" (60:14). Although Zion (Jerusalem) was once despised and hated, the future will bring joy and beauty as the kings and nations satisfy their every need (60:16). When the Lord in his holiness is enshrined in his people, the world will be attracted. The nations will know the Lord as "Savior and . . . Redeemer, the Mighty One of Israel" (60:16).

A series of "transformation" phrases indicates that the new is better than the old (60:27; cf.1 Kgs 10:21, 27), and may indicate strength as well as value. Everything is better than it was before; the word "better" is used thirteen times in the book of Hebrews, indicating the superiority of the new covenant over the old. This verse concludes with a striking personification of peace as their leader and of righteousness as their ruler— both of which are present in the rule of the messianic king in 9:7 (cf. 48:18).

In using these three names for God—"Savior, Redeemer, and the Mighty One of Israel/Jacob"—Isaiah indicates that Israel will come to recognize their God (60:19). "Savior" is used of the obvious saving work of God. "Redeemer" is a term based on the kinsman-redeemer cultural practice of redemption in ancient Israel. "Mighty" is a word that stresses power (cf. 1:24). The citizens of Zion will know God on these terms.

This chapter began with a picture of the light of the Lord's glorious presence in his kingdom; it concludes with the promise that the Lord will be their "everlasting light" and "glory" as the days of her mourning come to an end (60:20). Having introduced this picture in earlier prophecies as well (24:23; 30:26), the prophet now returns to it. In the old, natural order of things, everyday life was ruled by the regularly alternating light of sun and moon (Gen 1:16) that dictated the activities of the people. In the new city here described, no sun or moon will be needed. According to Revelation 21:23 and 22:5, light will no longer be needed in the New Jerusalem, since God and the Lamb will be the "everlasting light" (60:20). With the Lord as the light of Zion, there will be no night there (cf. Rev 22:5), only the light of joy and salvation (cf. 58:8). The light of the Messiah's glory, revealed briefly at the transfiguration, will then shine with dazzling brilliance (cf. Luke 9:29; John 1:14). Revelation 21:23 and 22:5 confirm that Isaiah's vision transcends anything that we have ever seen in this world.

The promise for future prosperity includes a burgeoning population as the "tiniest group" becomes a "mighty nation." The Lord will bring all of this to pass at just the right time (60:22). In Genesis 12:2, the Lord promised to make Abraham's descendants into a great nation (cf. 51:2). That greatness is described clearly in this chapter, as the citizens of Zion are multiplied.

◆     ### 4. Good news for the oppressed (61:1-11)

The Spirit of the Sovereign LORD is
    upon me,
for the LORD has anointed me
to bring good news to the poor.
He has sent me to comfort the
    brokenhearted
and to proclaim that captives will be
    released
and prisoners will be freed.*

2 He has sent me to tell those who
    mourn
that the time of the LORD's favor
    has come,*
and with it, the day of God's anger
    against their enemies.
3 To all who mourn in Israel,*
he will give a crown of beauty for
    ashes,

a joyous blessing instead of
     mourning,
festive praise instead of despair.
In their righteousness, they will be like
     great oaks
     that the LORD has planted for his
     own glory.

⁴They will rebuild the ancient ruins,
     repairing cities destroyed long ago.
They will revive them,
     though they have been deserted for
     many generations.
⁵Foreigners will be your servants.
     They will feed your flocks
and plow your fields
and tend your vineyards.
⁶You will be called priests of the LORD,
     ministers of our God.
You will feed on the treasures of the
     nations
and boast in their riches.
⁷Instead of shame and dishonor,
     you will enjoy a double share of
     honor.
You will possess a double portion of
     prosperity in your land,
and everlasting joy will be yours.

⁸"For I, the LORD, love justice.
     I hate robbery and wrongdoing.
I will faithfully reward my people for
     their suffering
and make an everlasting covenant
     with them.
⁹Their descendants will be recognized
     and honored among the nations.
Everyone will realize that they are
     a people
     the LORD has blessed."

¹⁰I am overwhelmed with joy in the LORD
     my God!
For he has dressed me with the
     clothing of salvation
and draped me in a robe of
     righteousness.
I am like a bridegroom in his wedding
     suit
or a bride with her jewels.
¹¹The Sovereign LORD will show his
     justice to the nations of the
     world.
Everyone will praise him!
His righteousness will be like a garden
     in early spring,
with plants springing up everywhere.

61:1 Greek version reads *and the blind will see.* Compare Luke 4:18.    61:2 Or *to proclaim the acceptable year of the LORD.*    61:3 Hebrew *in Zion.*

## NOTES

61:1 *Sovereign* LORD. The Heb. *'adonay yhwh* [TH136/3068, ZH151/3378] can be translated lit., "Lord LORD." This is the same title as in 50:4-5, 7, 9. This title especially notes the sovereignty or lordship of Jehovah (the LORD). It is the Spirit of this God that rests on the Anointed One (Messiah) so that he can work the works of God.

*anointed.* Heb. *mashakh* [TH4886, ZH5417] (anoint), the word from which we get Messiah (Anointed One).

*bring good news.* The Heb. verb is *basar* [TH1319, ZH1413], as in 40:9.

*poor.* The poor (*'anawim* [TH6035, ZH6705]) are the downtrodden, the disadvantaged, and all those held back from success or progress.

*proclaim that captives will be released.* The Heb. *liqro' lishebuyim deror* is connected with Leviticus and the great manumission of the Jubilee Year (cf. Lev 25:10; Jer 34:8). The Heb. word *deror* [TH1865A, ZH2002] (freedom) is the technical word used for the restoration of the Year of Jubilee (Lev 25:10; cf. Isa 49:8).

*prisoners will be freed.* More lit., "release from darkness for the prisoners." The verbal form *peqakh-qoakh* [TH6495, ZH7223] is found only here, but the root, *paqakh* [TH6491, ZH7219] normally refers to opening the eyes or ears (42:20), and in 42:7 this is associated with bringing people out of the darkness of prison.

**61:3 *crown of beauty for ashes*.** The phrase involves a wordplay typical of Isaiah, *pe'er takhath 'eper* ("beauty" for "ashes"). Motyer (1993:501) observes that the Lord replaces the hurt with the remedy, and since the ashes of mourning were smeared on the head, he applies his cure precisely to the point of need.

***joyous blessing*.** Lit., "oil of gladness." Oil was used for times of gladness (Ps 23:5; 45:7; 104:15; 133:1-2), not times of sorrow (2 Sam 14:2). The Anointed One replaces mourning with fresh life.

***great oaks*.** Heb. *'ayil* [TH8334, ZH9250] does not indicate a particular species of tree, only that it is a "large tree" (cf. 1:29; 57:5).

**61:6 *ministers*.** From the Heb. root *sharath* [TH8334, ZH9250], this is the verb regularly used of Levitical service.

**61:7 *double share of honor*.** The firstborn received a double share of the inheritance (Deut 21:17; Zech 9:12).

**61:10 *I am overwhelmed with joy*.** Based on the context, the unnamed speaker is the Anointed One (Motyer 1993:504). He is filled with joy because he is dressed with salvation and righteousness.

### COMMENTARY

The glorious themes of salvation and restoration continue into chapter 61 from chapter 60, although they are less sharply presented there. The first two verses of chapter 61 are especially noteworthy because Jesus quoted them in the synagogue at Nazareth (Luke 4:18-19), adding, "This Scripture has come true today before your very eyes" (Luke 4:21).

In addition to the servant (the speaker), the Spirit and the LORD are also mentioned in 61:1: "The Spirit of the Sovereign LORD is upon me    to bring good news to the poor." In the New Testament, the Spirit of God rested on Jesus at his baptism; here, the Spirit rests on the servant of the Lord (cf. 42:1). The servant describes his mission as one of comforting the broken-hearted, announcing the release of captives, and freeing prisoners. This was not limited only to the physically outcast and oppressed by society. Jesus did minister to such people, but in a broader and deeper sense, this passage is speaking of the spiritually poor, the spiritually imprisoned, and the spiritually blind and bruised.

In 61:2, the servant continues to describe his mission as including the announcement of "the time of the LORD's favor" to those who mourn. This time will also be "the day of God's anger" against the enemies of God's people. God's wrath is against all who imprison or oppose God's people. Ridderbos (1985:545) suggests that the "year of the LORD's favor" alludes to the Year of Jubilee (Lev 25), a time observed every fiftieth year when debtors were freed from their slavery (Lev 25:39ff; cf. Ezek 46:17).

The remaining verses of this chapter (61:3-11) describe the activities of the returnees from Babylon and their rebuilding of Jerusalem and the surrounding areas. Although their Babylonian conquerors had oppressed and exploited them, their faithful Lord would bless them again (61:9) and Zion will respond with gratitude and praise (61:10-11).

The returnees will be planted in Zion and therein glorify the Lord. "In their righteousness, they will be like great oaks" (61:3; cf. 60:21) refers to their being planted by the Lord to take root, blossom, and bear the fruit of righteousness. This time they are compared to sturdy oaks rather than to a shoot (cf. Ps 92:12-13). The other two references in Isaiah to "large trees" (not necessarily oak trees) associate them with false religion. In this case, they have been recovered by the Lord, transplanted, and rooted in his garden.

The promise comes again of "repairing cities" that were "destroyed long ago" (61:4; cf. 44:26; 58:12); this includes a new situation in which foreigners will serve the returnees (61:5). This should not be understood as a picture of a slave state, but as the voluntary and glad cooperation of former outsiders that now take their place in the life of the people. Oswalt notes that "the figure of speech that the prophet uses is of farmworkers" and states that "without question the roles identified—shepherds, plowmen, and vinedressers—are of the lower social classes" (1998:571). The expression "foreigners" (61:5) is the same as in 56:3, which refers to participation in the covenant. There is no record that after the return from Babylon foreigners tended the flocks, plowed the fields, or took care of the vineyards of the Jews. The thought seems to be that Jews and the nations would work together in building the new Zion. In fact, when the nations and Jews come to Zion, they will all be called "priests of the LORD, ministers of our God" (61:6); there will be no distinction between them, for all will be priests and ministers of God (61:6; cf. Exod 19:6, which refers to a "kingdom of priests" among the nations). This high position is one of responsibility, as that of a priest, a mediator between God and people. The nations come to God through Israel (the true heirs of Abraham), and there will be no special priesthood apart from all the citizens of the new city, for each will be a priest. Certain passages such as 1 Peter 2:9 indicate that early Christians understood these words as applying to themselves as heirs of OT religion (cf. 1 Pet 2:5, 9-10; Rev 1:6; 5:9-10).

Isaiah depicts Israel's redemption as the rebuilding of Jerusalem (cf. 35:1-10; 58:12). From 49:1 onwards, the picture of the return from Babylon into a desolate country seems to depict a greater recovery, an entrance into the true kingdom of God, the land of spiritual inheritance. All this will be because the Lord loves justice and will make an everlasting covenant with his people (61:8). The background of "everlasting covenant" is 54:10 and 55:3 (where the same words are used), but the main reference must be 59:21, where God's promise is given that his "Spirit will not leave them and neither will these words" he has given them.

The theme of God's goodness to his people is further developed in 61:8-9. In exile, Israel had been mistreated and oppressed (cf. 42:24), but all this would be changed as the Lord confirmed the "everlasting covenant" he had made with Abraham (61:8; Gen 12:1-3) and with David (cf. 55:3). Jeremiah and Ezekiel also speak of the "new covenant" (Jer 31:27-44; 50:4-5; Ezek 16:60-63; 37:15-28). This "everlasting covenant" should probably be associated with the covenant referred to in Jeremiah 32:40 (cf. Isa 59:21). The close connection between the everlasting covenant and the "new covenant" in these passages reminds us that God brought to a climax what had been there all along in the old covenant.

Ultimately, this chapter has in view the new Zion. The imagery of the rebuilt city and the restored people informs the prophet's predictive language, as Isaiah saw how the work of the Messiah would appear. Motyer (1993:504) applies this scene to the status of God's new covenant people between the two comings of the Messiah.

◆   **5. Isaiah's prayer for Zion (62:1-12)**

Because I love Zion,
   I will not keep still.
Because my heart yearns for
      Jerusalem,
   I cannot remain silent.
I will not stop praying for her
   until her righteousness shines
      like the dawn,
   and her salvation blazes like
      a burning torch.
² The nations will see your
      righteousness.
   World leaders will be blinded
      by your glory.
And you will be given a new name
   by the LORD's own mouth.
³ The LORD will hold you in his hand
      for all to see—
   a splendid crown in the hand of God.
⁴ Never again will you be called "The
      Forsaken City"*
   or "The Desolate Land."*
Your new name will be "The City of
      God's Delight"*
   and "The Bride of God,"*
for the LORD delights in you
   and will claim you as his bride.
⁵ Your children will commit themselves
      to you, O Jerusalem,
   just as a young man commits
      himself to his bride.
Then God will rejoice over you
   as a bridegroom rejoices over his
      bride.

⁶ O Jerusalem, I have posted watchmen
      on your walls;
   they will pray day and night,
      continually.

Take no rest, all you who pray to
   the LORD.
⁷ Give the LORD no rest until he
   completes his work,
   until he makes Jerusalem the pride
      of the earth.
⁸ The LORD has sworn to Jerusalem by
   his own strength:
"I will never again hand you over
   to your enemies.
Never again will foreign warriors come
   and take away your grain and new
      wine.
⁹ You raised the grain, and you will
   eat it,
   praising the LORD.
Within the courtyards of the Temple,
   you yourselves will drink the wine
   you have pressed."

¹⁰ Go out through the gates!
   Prepare the highway for my people
      to return!
Smooth out the road; pull out the
      boulders;
   raise a flag for all the nations
      to see.
¹¹ The LORD has sent this message
   to every land:
   "Tell the people of Israel,*
'Look, your Savior is coming.
   See, he brings his reward with him
      as he comes.'"
¹² They will be called "The Holy People"
   and "The People Redeemed by the
      LORD."
And Jerusalem will be known as "The
      Desirable Place"
   and "The City No Longer Forsaken."

62:4a Hebrew *Azubah,* which means "forsaken."   62:4b Hebrew *Shemamah,* which means "desolate."
62:4c Hebrew *Hephzibah,* which means "my delight is in her."   62:4d Hebrew *Beulah,* which means "married."
62:11 Hebrew *Tell the daughter of Zion.*

## NOTES

**62:1 *keep still.*** Heb. *khashah* [TH2814, ZH3120] refers as much to action (Judg 18:9; Ps 107:29) as to words (Pss 28:1; 39:2 [3]; cf. Isa 42:14; 57:11; 62:6; 64:12 [11]; 65:6).

***remain silent.*** The reference to keeping silent is close to the thoughts expressed in 42:14 and in 57:11, where the long period of exile is described as "the time when God was silent."

***righteousness . . . salvation.*** As in 61:10, Isaiah joins righteousness with salvation, but in the next verse, righteousness is joined with glory, much as in 58:8.

***shines like the dawn.*** The Heb. is *yetse' kannogah* ("goes out like the shining"). Interestingly, the Heb. *nogah* [TH5051, ZH5586] is never used of "dawn" but always of clear, sharp brightness (cf. 4:5; 50:10; 60:3, 19; Joel 2:10). The versions have "goes forth as brightness" (KJV, cf. NASB), "shines out like the dawn" (NRSV, NIV), "shines forth like the sunrise" (REB), and "shines like a torch in the night" (TEV).

**62:4 *The Forsaken City.*** Other translation have "Deserted" (NIV, GW), "Forsaken" (NASB, NRSV, REB, TEV, NJPS), and "The Deserted Wife" (TEV). The various translations for the four names in this verse reveal inconsistency in treating them as common nouns or proper nouns.

***The Desolate Land.*** Other translations have "Desolate" (NASB, NRSV, NIV, REB, NJPS) or "Destroyed" (GW).

***The City of God's Delight.*** Heb. *kheptsi-bah* [TH2657A, ZH2915], lit. "my delight is in her," as the NLT mg indicates. At one time in the past, this was a popular female name (Hephzibah) in English. Other translations have "Hephzibah" (NIV), "my delight is in her" (NASB), "My Delight is in Her" (NRSV), "My Delight" (GW), "God is Pleased With Her" (TEV), and "I delight in her" (NJPS).

***The Bride of God.*** Heb. *be'ulah* [TH1166B, ZH1241] ("married") is the Beulah (see NLT mg) popularized by the KJV and found in music, names of churches, and even names of towns. In the ancient Near East, a sovereign was sometimes described as married to his land since they were mutually dependent on each other. Other translations have "Beulah" (NIV), "Married" (NASB, NRSV, GW), "Happily Married" (TEV), and "Espoused" (NJPS).

**62:8 *sworn . . . by his own strength.*** Lit., "sworn by his right hand and by his mighty arm."

**62:11 *reward.*** Heb. *sakar* [TH7939, ZH8510]. The NLT omits the parallel term, "recompense" (*pe'ullah* [TH6468, ZH7190]). Motyer (1993:508) notes that when a craftsman commissioned to make a piece of furniture is paid for it, that is his "reward," and the completed article is his "recompense," or the fruit of his work. The Messiah's saved people are both what he has earned and what he has accomplished—in terms of 53:12, both his portion and his spoil.

## COMMENTARY

The great scene of Israel's restoration, introduced in chapter 40, reaches a climax in chapter 62 as several themes from the earlier chapter are repeated and amplified here (cf. 62:2 with 40:5, 62:10 with 40:3-4, and 62:11 with 40:9-10), as noted by Wolf (1985:240). The first five verses present what could be called the bridal beauty of Zion.

The chapter opens with Isaiah saying, "I will not stop praying . . . because I love Zion" (62:1). The first five verses then describe the bright glory of the new Zion, whose "righteousness shines like the dawn" and whose "salvation blazes like a burning torch" (62:1) so that "world leaders will be blinded" by their glory (62:2). This could be compared to Malachi's description of the Messiah's coming, when he says, "The sun of righteousness will rise with healing in his wings" (Mal 4:2).

Never again will Zion be called "The Forsaken City" or "The Desolate Land" because God holds her in his hands (62:4). Jerusalem's change in status will bring her new names, particularly, "The City of God's Delight" (Hephzibah), "The Bride of God" (Beulah), "The Desirable Place," and "The City No Longer Forsaken" (62:4, 12). Although the old people of Jerusalem had forsaken the Lord, he had never completely abandoned them. As wives change their names after marriage, so Jerusalem will be called "Hephzibah" as opposed to "Forsaken," and the land in which she lives will be called "Beulah" instead of "Desolate" (62:4). The imagery of God rejoicing over the new Zion "as a bridegroom rejoices over his bride" (62:5) continues the marriage metaphor, using terms similar to those used in 54:5-8. The picture is also extended to the sons of Israel, who will "marry" the land by taking possession of the long-deserted country (cf. 54:1-2).

The protection of the new Zion is described in 62:5. On her walls will be watchmen who pray to the Lord day and night for the fulfillment of his promises (62:6). Furthermore, the Lord had "sworn to Jerusalem by his own strength" that he would never abandon her to her enemies (62:8). Earlier, God had warned that his people's produce would be handed over to their enemies if they disobeyed him (Lev 26:16; Deut 28:33), but that awful curse will not be repeated. Instead, the people will eat and drink as they formerly did during a festival or when they brought their tithes to the house of the Lord (cf. Lev 23:39; Deut 14:23).

The last two verses (62:11-12) of the chapter speak of salvation in Zion and of the preparation for all who would enter her. The commands to go out and "prepare the highway for my people to return" (62:10; cf. 40:3; 49:11; 57:14), along with the raising of a flag or banner for the nations to see, are also linked with the return of the exiles in 11:12 and in 49:22. The invitation includes the message, "Look, your Savior is coming," and he will bring "his reward with him"(62:11). The last two lines of 62:11 are identical to 40:10, and both passages indicate that the "reward" refers to the people that God will bring back to Jerusalem. The Lord is called "Savior" because he had saved his people from captivity (cf. 52:7-8). John possibly alluded to this verse in his description of the second coming of Christ (Rev 22:12).

The citizens of the city will be called "the Holy People and the People Redeemed by the LORD" (62:12). In addition to the name "Hephzibah" mentioned in the Hebrew of 62:4, Isaiah mentions four more names in 62:12: two names for God's people ("The Holy People" and "The People Redeemed by the LORD") and two for the city of Jerusalem ("The Desirable Place" and "The City No Longer Forsaken"). The expression "The Holy People" is closely associated with the designation, "priests of the Lord" in 61:6; both are derived from Exodus 19:6, God's blueprint for his people. Holiness is to be their dominant characteristic. The title "The People Redeemed by the LORD" probably echoes God's rescue of Israel from Egypt (cf. 35:9-10; 51:10-11), but now it is applied to the release of those who had been captive in Babylon (cf. 50:1-2). Their debts paid, they now belong to the Lord (cf. 35:9-10). The two names for Jerusalem (62:12) are the reverse of "The Forsaken City" and "The Desolate Land" (62:4) and thereby emphasize how much the city will be loved.

◆     ## 6. Judgment and deliverance (63:1-14)

Who is this who comes from Edom,
  from the city of Bozrah,
  with his clothing stained red?
Who is this in royal robes,
  marching in his great strength?

"It is I, the LORD, announcing your
    salvation!
  It is I, the LORD, who has the power
    to save!"

2 Why are your clothes so red,
  as if you have been treading out
    grapes?

3 "I have been treading the winepress
    alone;
  no one was there to help me.
In my anger I have trampled my
    enemies
  as if they were grapes.
In my fury I have trampled my foes.
  Their blood has stained my clothes.
4 For the time has come for me to
    avenge my people,
  to ransom them from their
    oppressors.
5 I was amazed to see that no one
    intervened
  to help the oppressed.
So I myself stepped in to save them
    with my strong arm,
  and my wrath sustained me.
6 I crushed the nations in my anger
  and made them stagger and fall to
    the ground,
  spilling their blood upon the earth."

7 I will tell of the LORD's unfailing love.
  I will praise the LORD for all he has
    done.

I will rejoice in his great goodness
    to Israel,
  which he has granted according
    to his mercy and love.
8 He said, "They are my very own
    people.
  Surely they will not betray me
    again."
And he became their Savior.
9 In all their suffering he also suffered,
  and he personally* rescued them.
In his love and mercy he redeemed
    them.
He lifted them up and carried them
  through all the years.
10 But they rebelled against him
  and grieved his Holy Spirit.
So he became their enemy
  and fought against them.

11 Then they remembered those days
    of old
  when Moses led his people out
    of Egypt.
They cried out, "Where is the one who
    brought Israel through the sea,
  with Moses as their shepherd?
Where is the one who sent his Holy
    Spirit
  to be among his people?
12 Where is the one whose power was
    displayed
  when Moses lifted up his hand—
the one who divided the sea before
    them,
  making himself famous forever?
13 Where is the one who led them
    through the bottom of the sea?
  They were like fine stallions

| | |
|---|---|
| racing through the desert, never stumbling. | the Spirit of the LORD gave them rest. You led your people, LORD, |
| ¹⁴As with cattle going down into a peaceful valley, | and gained a magnificent reputation." |

63:9 Hebrew *and the angel of his presence.*

## NOTES

**63:1 *Edom.*** This is the same nation that was used to represent God's enemies in 34:5 (cf. Ps 137:7; Ezek 35:1-15; Amos 1:11-12). In addition, the area named Edom (*'edom* [TH123A, ZH121]) and the reddened (*'adom* (cf. 63:2) [TH122, ZH137]) garments provide a striking wordplay. Where better to get "reddened" garments than in the "red" land?

**Bozrah.** As in 34:6, the important city of Bozrah is singled out because its name means "grape-gathering," and Isaiah makes use of a comparison between treading grapes and pouring out blood. Bozrah is also related to the "vintage," an appropriate place for a winepress. However, there are at least four homographs of this root.

**red.** The translations have "red" (REB, TEV, NCV, CEV), "bright red" (GW), "glowing colors" (NASB), and "crimson" (NRSV, NJPS, ESV).

**63:2 *treading out grapes.*** Grapes were placed in a vat that had been hollowed out of rock. Then they were trampled on and the juice would run through channels cut into the rock and into another vat. The workers who trampled the grapes would have their clothes stained from the grape juice.

**63:3 *alone.*** As in 59:16, God does the work alone.

**anger . . . fury.** God's "anger," and "fury" are linked with the Day of the Lord in 13:3 and 34:2. They characterize his righteous response to the horrors of sin.

**Their blood has stained.** The phrase contains the word *'eg'aleti* [TH1351, ZH1458] (I have stained), found only here; it does not specify the color, which must be determined by the context. The color must be red or crimson, the color of both blood and grape juice. The new translations keep the traditional "crimson" (NRSV, NIV, NAB, NJB) or use "red" (REB). "Stained" represents an abridgment of the Heb., which has two verbs: "spattered" (*nazah* [TH1351, ZH1458]) and "stained" (*ga'al* [TH1351, ZH1458]). The latter term is used of staining by defilement, that is, by pollution. The first verb is found elsewhere in Isaiah only in 52:15, where it is said of the Suffering Servant that he will "sprinkle" many nations. The word is also used of sprinkling blood in the sacrificial system (Lev 4:6, 17; 5:9; 14:7; Num 19:4, 18-19).

**63:4 *to ransom them from their oppressors.*** The Heb. reads, "the year of my redemption has come," and it has been observed that "my redemption" has the same root letters (*ge'ulim* [TH1350A, ZH1453]) as "stained" in 63:3 (*gimel, aleph, lamedh*). Knowing Isaiah's style, this is surely not coincidental.

**63:7 *unfailing love.*** The first and last word of this verse in Heb., *khesed* [TH2617, ZH2876], is used often for the faithful and loyal love of the covenant.

**63:8 *Savior.*** Heb. *moshia'*. The word has a broad range of meaning and usage in the OT, including deliverance of the Hebrews from oppression in Egypt.

**63:9 *he personally rescued them.*** The Heb. says, "the angel of his presence (face) rescued them." This is the angelic being that made the Lord's presence recognizable among his people; he is equivalent to the Angel of the Covenant. During the Egyptian oppression, God's people cried out and the Lord sent "the angel of his presence" (cf. the Heb. of Exod 33:14-15) to secure their release from bondage. This redemption lies at the heart of Isaiah's message (cf. 35:9; 41:14; 43:1-3). Motyer (1993:514) suggests that it is "distinct from God only insofar as God-in-revelation is different from God-in-himself."

*mercy.* The Heb. *khemlah* [TH2551, ZH2799], found only here and in Gen 19:16, is from a root word meaning "to spare, have pity."

*he redeemed them.* This work of redemption lies at the very heart of Isaiah's message (cf. 35:9; 41:14; 43:1-3). See Winter (1954).

*He lifted them up and carried them.* This is probably an example of hendiadys—two verbs with one basic meaning. Other examples include, "lift up the eyes and look," or "lift up the ears and listen."

**63:10 rebelled.** The Heb. *marah* [TH4784, ZH5286], "to be obstinate," is a strong word; it indicates grievous rebellion (cf. 1:20; 3:8; 50:5).

*he became their enemy.* The Heb. says, "he turned and became their enemy." Although this looks like a simple use of hendiadys (one meaning combined in two verbs), the word for "turned" (*hapak* [TH2015, ZH2200]) is unusually strong and refers to "overturning," as when God destroyed Sodom. Some versions try to bring out this meaning: "he turned and became their enemy" (NIV), "turned Himself to become their enemy" (NASB), "turned hostile to them and himself fought against" (NRSV), and "turned against them as their enemy" (GW).

**63:12 whose power was displayed.** More lit., "glorious arm of power" (NIV). Modern translations vary as to the best way to handle this expression: "glorious arm" (NRSV, NAB, NJB), or "glorious power" (REB). In Heb. language and culture, the arm signified power.

**63:14 rest.** Here the reference is probably to the Israelites' long-awaited arrival in Canaan (Deut 12:9; Josh 1:13), where they found abundant pastures and water for their livestock.

*magnificent reputation.* More lit., "name of beauty." This probably refers to everything attractive about the Lord; he will still work so that his name (representing himself) will be seen in all its beauty.

COMMENTARY

Chapters 60–62 spoke of the restoration and glory of Jerusalem and her people. In chapter 63, a passage closely related to 59:16-20, Isaiah returns to the judgment of the ungodly that must precede the redemption of God's people. The chapter opens with a graphic picture of a royal warrior striding forward in "his great strength," and immediately he is identified: "It is I, the LORD" (63:1). This avenging warrior is in royal robes stained red; he is characterized by the same awesome power that was described in 40:26. As the Lord saves, he does so "in righteousness" (63:1; omitted in the NLT), and these two concepts—salvation and God's righteousness—are joined in 41:2, 46:13, and 59:16. God will set things right as he saves his people.

The Lord also claims, "In my fury I have trampled my foes. Their blood has stained my clothes" (63:3). Isaiah opened his prophecy with a description of Israel's sins as being "red as crimson" (1:18). He now combines this color imagery with the process of making wine (63:3). Wine is made by treading and crushing grapes with bare feet. The red grape juice flows into a receptacle, and the clothing of those treading out the wine is spattered with red stains. The blood-spattered garments are mentioned in each of the first three verses and correspond to the "robe of vengeance" in 59:17. All this fits in with Edom (red) and Bozrah, a name that reflects viticulture.

There is hardly a more graphic portrayal of God's wrath in the Bible than this one. John takes it up in Revelation 14:17-20 and makes it clear that the divine Warrior is none other than Jesus the Lamb of God, who will come on a white horse to subjugate all enemies, including Satan (cf. Rev 19:11-20; 20:11-15).

In Isaiah 63, the Lord says, "no one intervened to help the oppressed. So I myself stepped in to save them with my strong arm" (63:5). Judgment on the nations resulted in redemption for God's people. Isaiah 61:1-2 also discusses this interrelationship between salvation and judgment. Isaiah 63:5 repeats 59:16 very closely, a fact that helps in the interpretation of 63:1-6. The Lord looked closely, expecting to discover among the people an individual or a nation on his side; he was amazed and appalled to find none (cf. 59:16-17). The Messiah, who came to announce the Lord's Day (61:2) and to do the Lord's work (61:10), now speaks with the Lord's voice.

The future for God's people is glorious, but the future of the unrepentant is not. When God's patience runs out, he will put on his clothes and weapons of war and crush the nations in his anger, making them "stagger and fall to the ground" (63:6). Suffering from God's vengeance will be like staggering and falling in a drunken state. The idea looks back to 51:17, 21-22, where the cup that intoxicates is the cup of the Lord's wrath. There it is taken from the hand of Zion and put into the hand of their foes. In 51:17, Jerusalem had to drink "the cup of the LORD'S fury," but usually it was the nations who suffered God's anger (cf. Zech 12:2; Rev 14:10; 16:19). Just as the blood of animals was poured out at the base of the altar (Lev 8:15), so the blood of soldiers will be shed on the battlefield (cf. 34:6).

The next section (63:7ff) begins with Isaiah's praise for the Lord's unfailing love and for his great deliverance. The glories of chapters 60–62 and the decisive action in 63:1-6 lead to one of the most eloquent passages of praise and intercession in the Bible as the prophet surveys the past goodness of God and the present difficulties of his people. The statement, "they are my very own people" (63:8), refers to the covenant status of God's people and is linked to the "unfailing love" (the Heb. for "covenant love") of 63:7.

"In his love and mercy he redeemed" his people and "carried them through all the years" (63:9). During their travels, God lifted them up and carried them as a father carries his little children (cf. Deut 1:31). In response to this show of divine favor, his people rebelled against him in the wilderness (cf. Num 20:10). Their repeated grumbling grieved him deeply (cf. Ps 106:32-33) and probably provided the background for Paul's admonition to believers not to grieve the Holy Spirit (Eph 4:30). The statement that "in all their suffering he also suffered" (63:9) presents the Lord's side as he suffered with his people. They were God's own people, so when they suffered under Egyptian oppression, he suffered with them. Later, during the period of the Judges, we read that the Lord "was grieved by their misery" (Judg 10:16), a perspective that should remind Christians that we have a high priest who "understands our weaknesses" (Heb 4:15). "He lifted them up and carried them" (63:9) as a father carries his little children (cf. Deut 1:31). But in response to his love, the Israelites rebelled against him (cf. Num 20:10), and when "they rebelled against him, . . . he became their enemy" (63:10; cf. Lev 26:24, 28).

The people cried out for the good old days when their God was there to save them and help them in their distress. "When Moses led his people out of Egypt" recalls the time when Moses, as their shepherd, led them out of Egypt and "through the sea" (63:11; Exod 14:16). The third reference to the Holy Spirit in this passage is in 63:14 (cf. 63:10, 11) where we read that he enabled Moses and the seventy elders to govern the complaining Israelites and to lead them to the Promised Land (Num 11:17, 25, 29; Hag 2:5). The work of the Holy Spirit during the time of the old covenant is mentioned in Nehemiah 9:20, which records that God "gave his good Spirit to instruct them" during their wanderings in the desert.

### ◆ 7. Prayer for mercy and help (63:15–64:12)

15 LORD, look down from heaven;
    look from your holy, glorious home,
    and see us.
Where is the passion and the might
    you used to show on our behalf?
Where are your mercy and
    compassion now?
16 Surely you are still our Father!
    Even if Abraham and Jacob* would
    disown us,
LORD, you would still be our Father.
    You are our Redeemer from ages
    past.
17 LORD, why have you allowed us to turn
    from your path?
Why have you given us stubborn
    hearts so we no longer fear you?
Return and help us, for we are your
    servants,
    the tribes that are your special
    possession.
18 How briefly your holy people
    possessed your holy place,
    and now our enemies have
    destroyed it.
19 Sometimes it seems as though we
    never belonged to you,
    as though we had never been known
    as your people.

## CHAPTER 64

1* Oh, that you would burst from the
    heavens and come down!
How the mountains would quake
    in your presence!

2* As fire causes wood to burn
    and water to boil,
    your coming would make the nations
    tremble.
Then your enemies would learn the
    reason for your fame!
3 When you came down long ago,
    you did awesome deeds beyond our
    highest expectations.
And oh, how the mountains quaked!
4 For since the world began,
    no ear has heard,
and no eye has seen a God like you,
    who works for those who wait
    for him!
5 You welcome those who gladly do
    good,
    who follow godly ways.
But you have been very angry with us,
    for we are not godly.
We are constant sinners;
    how can people like us be saved?
6 We are all infected and impure with
    sin.
When we display our righteous
    deeds,
    they are nothing but filthy rags.
Like autumn leaves, we wither and fall,
    and our sins sweep us away like the
    wind.
7 Yet no one calls on your name
    or pleads with you for mercy.
Therefore, you have turned away
    from us
    and turned us over* to our sins.

⁸And yet, O LORD, you are our Father.
We are the clay, and you are the
    potter.
We all are formed by your hand.
⁹Don't be so angry with us, LORD.
Please don't remember our sins
    forever.
Look at us, we pray,
    and see that we are all your
    people.
¹⁰Your holy cities are destroyed.

Zion is a wilderness;
yes, Jerusalem is a desolate ruin.
¹¹The holy and beautiful Temple
where our ancestors praised you
has been burned down,
and all the things of beauty are
    destroyed.
¹²After all this, LORD, must you still
    refuse to help us?
Will you continue to be silent and
    punish us?

63:16 Hebrew *Israel.* See note on 14:1.   64:1 Verse 64:1 is numbered 63:20 in Hebrew text.   64:2 Verses
64:2-12 are numbered 64:1-11 in Hebrew text.   64:7 As in Greek, Syriac, and Aramaic versions; Hebrew reads
*melted us.*

## NOTES

**63:15** *holy, glorious home.* More lit., "the house of your holiness and beauty." The Heb.
*zebul* [TH2073, ZH2292] (house) is found only here in Isaiah, and its use elsewhere indicates
some kind of exalted dwelling. The word translated "glorious" is *tip'ereth* [TH8597, ZH9514],
a word favored by Isaiah and used by him about eighteen times.

**63:16** *Abraham and Jacob.* These were the fathers of the covenant against which the people rebelled.

*Father.* The tendency of later Judaism to avoid explicit references to God as Father is
reflected in the Targums that render this passage, "Thou art he whose compassions towards
us are more than those of a father towards his children" (McNamara 1972:115).

*Redeemer.* Heb. *go'el* [TH1350, ZH1457]. The first appearance of this term as a name of God is
in Job 19:25; it is also used in the Psalms (19:14; 78:35). It occurs thirteen times in the latter part of Isaiah.

**63:17** *given us stubborn hearts.* Cf. the case of the Pharaoh of the Exodus (Exod 4:21) and
the pattern in Rom 1:21-32.

**63:19** *known as your people.* Lit., "called by your name" (cf. 43:7). The English verses are
numbered one verse ahead of the Heb. in this section (63:19b–64:12). At 65:1, the two
agree again. This commentary follows the English versification and includes the Heb. in
brackets.

**64:1 [63:19b]** *burst from the heavens.* The Heb. says "rend" or "tear the heavens." In OT
imagery, the sky is compared to a tent curtain (cf. 40:20). For other cosmic effects of
God's coming in judgment and redemption, see Judg 5:4-5; Pss 18:7-15; 144:5; Nah 1:5;
Hab 3:3-7.

**64:3 [2]** *awesome deeds.* This is probably a reference to OT miracles done by the Lord on
behalf of his covenant people.

**64:4 [3]** *wait for him.* The Heb. verb translated "wait" is *khakah* [TH2442, ZH2675]; it suggests "an attitude of earnest expectation and confident hope" (TWOT 1:282).

**64:5 [4]** *us . . . we . . . we . . . us.* By using first person pronouns, Isaiah identified with
sinful Israel (cf. 59:12-13).

**64:6 [5]** *filthy rags.* Heb. *beged 'iddim* [TH5708, ZH6340] (probably "time/periodic cloth";
cf. HALOT 1:790). "Filthy rags" (KJV) is also the translation of the NJB, while the singular
"filthy rag" is used by the NEB, CEV and NJPS. Other versions use "filthy garment" (NASB),
"filthy cloth" (NRSV), "polluted garment" (RSV), "filthy pieces of cloth" (NCV), or "pol-

luted rags" (NAB). If this refers to the menstrual cloth used by women who were ceremonially unclean during their periods (cf. Lev 15:19-24), the picture is of a defiled people viewed as repulsive and disqualified from God's presence.

**64:8 [7]** *Father.* Although the pathetic people do not deserve God's favor, they appeal to him as a child does to a loving parent.

### COMMENTARY

In Isaiah 63:11-14, the people cry out for the good old days when God was there to save them and help them in their distress. "When Moses led his people out of Egypt" recalls the time when Moses, as their shepherd, with staff extended, led them out of Egypt and "through the sea" (63:11; Exod 14:16). Now the outcry was for "mercy and compassion" (63:15). Even though their fathers Abraham and Jacob "would disown" them, their confidence was that the Lord would still be their father since he was their "Redeemer from ages past" (63:16). Not even these patriarchal fathers loved Israel as much as God did, so Isaiah referred to God as Israel's "Father" (63:16; cf. 64:8), and in 49:15 and 66:13, he compared God's love for Israel to the love of a mother for her child.

The basis of the plea is that Israel claimed to be God's "servants [and] special possession" (63:17). Both terms express a special relationship with the Lord. The former implies obedience, and the latter implies the privilege of what the Lord has given to "possess" them. Since God's covenant people were his inheritance as well as his servants, how could the Lord continue to ignore them? Out of all the nations, Israel alone bore God's name because she belonged exclusively to him (63:19; cf. 43:7).

Chapter 63 concludes with Isaiah reminding God of what had happened to his "holy place" (63:18), even with the people wondering why God acted as though they had never belonged to him (63:19). The Lord's very dwelling place, the Temple built by Solomon, had been destroyed by enemies (cf. Ps 74:3-7), and this was a challenge to God's honor. So Isaiah pleaded for God to notice and take action.

Chapter 64 continues the prayer that began in 63:15. As the prophet continued his intercession, its power and urgency increased in keeping with the intense distress of the people. He desired nothing less than that God would "burst from the heavens" (behind which he was hidden) and come down so that he might to put an end to the misery of God's covenant people (64:1). Mountains that "would quake in [his] presence" (64:1) may refer to the mighty revelation of God at Mount Sinai. If only God would "make the nations tremble." Then "[his] enemies would learn the reason for [his] fame!" (64:2).

The Lord had challenged the idols to speak or to act or do something (41:21-24), but they only brought shame to their followers by their inability to comply (44:9). In contrast, "no eye has seen a God like you, who works for those who wait for him!" (64:4; cf. 30:18; 40:31). This contrasts with what the sovereign God of his covenant people had done for them in comparison to the helpless gods of the nations who were unable to save their people from powerful enemies (this verse is quoted by Paul in 1 Cor 2:9).

In 64:5, Isaiah acknowledges God's justice in response to the sin of the people ("you have been angry with us . . . we are constant sinners"). He then confesses that all Israel had become "infected and impure," ceremonially unclean and defiled by sins (64:6; cf. Lev 13:45). The "righteous deeds" of the people were no more genuine than those of the scribes and Pharisees (64:6; cf. Matt 5:20). Isaiah called such good deeds "filthy rags" (64:6), possibly with reference to the stained menstrual cloths of a woman during her period, a time when she was ceremonially unclean (cf. Lev 15:19-30, 33; Ezek 36:17). Sin makes one polluted and defiled (cf. Lev 15:19-24).

In 64:8-12, Isaiah continues to press his plea, again calling God their Father as well as their "potter" (64:8). A potter can mold a vessel only as the clay yields itself in his hand; if he is unable to make an honorable vessel, then he makes a dishonorable one (Jer 18:1-4). God is the Creator and has the right to do as he pleases with his creatures.

The prophet's intercession reaches a climax in 64:10-11, where he returns to the subject of the destruction of the Temple. The "holy cities are destroyed" and "Jerusalem is a desolate ruin" (64:10). Some scholars insist that this kind of language betrays a late date for the passage, but Scripture does contain examples of speaking of events before they take place and of describing them as though they had already taken place. Certainly David (Ps 22) and Isaiah (ch 53) had clear foresight of certain aspects of the trial and crucifixion of Jesus.

◆     ## 8. The Lord's response (65:1-25)

The LORD says,

"I was ready to respond, but no one
    asked for help.
I was ready to be found, but no one
    was looking for me.
I said, 'Here I am, here I am!'
    to a nation that did not call on my
    name.*
2 All day long I opened my arms to a
    rebellious people.*
But they follow their own evil paths
    and their own crooked schemes.
3 All day long they insult me to my face
    by worshiping idols in their sacred
    gardens.
They burn incense on pagan altars.
4 At night they go out among the
    graves,
    worshiping the dead.
They eat the flesh of pigs
    and make stews with other
    forbidden foods.

5 Yet they say to each other,
    'Don't come too close or you will
    defile me!
    I am holier than you!'
These people are a stench in my
    nostrils,
    an acrid smell that never goes
    away.

6 "Look, my decree is written out* in
    front of me:
I will not stand silent;
I will repay them in full!
    Yes, I will repay them—
7 both for their own sins
    and for those of their ancestors,"
    says the LORD.
"For they also burned incense on the
    mountains
    and insulted me on the hills.
I will pay them back in full!

8 "But I will not destroy them all,"
    says the LORD.

"For just as good grapes are found
   among a cluster of bad ones
   (and someone will say, 'Don't throw
      them all away—
   some of those grapes are good!'),
so I will not destroy all Israel.
   For I still have true servants there.
9 I will preserve a remnant of the people
      of Israel*
   and of Judah to possess my land.
Those I choose will inherit it,
   and my servants will live there.
10 The plain of Sharon will again be filled
      with flocks
   for my people who have searched
      for me,
   and the valley of Achor will be
      a place to pasture herds.

11 "But because the rest of you have
      forsaken the LORD
   and have forgotten his Temple,
and because you have prepared feasts
      to honor the god of Fate
   and have offered mixed wine to the
      god of Destiny,
12 now I will 'destine' you for the sword.
   All of you will bow down before the
      executioner.
For when I called, you did not
      answer.
   When I spoke, you did not listen.
You deliberately sinned—before my
      very eyes—
   and chose to do what you know I
      despise."

13 Therefore, this is what the Sovereign
      LORD says:
   "My servants will eat,
      but you will starve.
My servants will drink,
      but you will be thirsty.
My servants will rejoice,
      but you will be sad and ashamed.
14 My servants will sing for joy,
      but you will cry in sorrow and
      despair.
15 Your name will be a curse word among
      my people,

for the Sovereign LORD will destroy
      you
   and will call his true servants by
      another name.
16 All who invoke a blessing or take an
      oath
   will do so by the God of truth.
For I will put aside my anger
   and forget the evil of earlier days.

17 "Look! I am creating new heavens and
      a new earth,
   and no one will even think about
      the old ones anymore.
18 Be glad; rejoice forever in my creation!
   And look! I will create Jerusalem as
      a place of happiness.
   Her people will be a source of joy.
19 I will rejoice over Jerusalem
   and delight in my people.
And the sound of weeping and
      crying
   will be heard in it no more.

20 "No longer will babies die when only
      a few days old.
   No longer will adults die before they
      have lived a full life.
No longer will people be considered
      old at one hundred!
   Only the cursed will die that young!
21 In those days people will live in the
      houses they build
   and eat the fruit of their own
      vineyards.
22 Unlike the past, invaders will not take
      their houses
   and confiscate their vineyards.
For my people will live as long as
      trees,
   and my chosen ones will have time
      to enjoy their hard-won gains.
23 They will not work in vain,
   and their children will not be
      doomed to misfortune.
For they are people blessed by the LORD,
   and their children, too, will be
      blessed.
24 I will answer them before they even
      call to me.

| | |
|---|---|
| While they are still talking about | The lion will eat hay like a cow. |
| their needs, | But the snakes will eat dust. |
| I will go ahead and answer their | In those days no one will be hurt |
| prayers! | or destroyed on my holy |
| 25 The wolf and the lamb will feed | mountain. |
| together. | I, the LORD, have spoken!" |

65:1 Or *to a nation that did not bear my name.* 65:1-2 Greek version reads *I was found by people who were not looking for me. / I showed myself to those who were not asking for me. / All day long I opened my arms to them, / but they were disobedient and rebellious.* Compare Rom 10:20. 65:6 Or *their sins are written out;* Hebrew reads *it stands written.* 65:9 Hebrew *remnant of Jacob.* See note on 14:1.

## NOTES

**65:2 *opened my arms.*** The Heb. says, "held out my hands." Some readers may find a difference in these two gestures. The gesture in the text is one of appeal, as one in prayer lifts his hands toward the Lord. Most versions use the idea of hands held out (NASB, NRSV, REB, GW) but others vary: "stood ready to accept" (NCV), "ready to welcome" (TEV), and "reached out to" (CEV).

**65:3 *sacred gardens.*** Pagan religious practices often took place in groves of trees and in areas of luxuriant growth.

***pagan altars.*** The Heb. says, "on altars of brick," an expression that could refer to the altars that were built on the flat roofs of houses (2 Kgs 23:12), or to the worship of the "Queen of Heaven" described in Jer 44:17.

**65:4 *they go out among the graves, worshiping the dead.*** This practice of necromancy is specifically condemned in 8:19 (see Lev 19:31; Deut 18:10-12).

***eat the flesh of pigs.*** A practice specifically forbidden in Lev 11:7-8 and Deut 14:8; cf. Isa 66:3, 17.

**65:5 *stench in my nostrils.*** The smoke from the pagan rituals was distasteful to God.

**65:6 *Yes, I will repay them.*** The Heb. has the graphic, "pay it back into their laps" (also repeated in 65:7).

**65:7 *mountains . . . hills.*** These "high places" had been favorite sites for erecting altars on which to offer sacrifices to idols. These sacrifices, accompanied by immoral practices, had blasphemed God by bringing reproach upon his holy name (cf. 57:7; Hos 4:13). The reference here is undoubtedly to Baal worship.

**65:8 *I will not destroy them all.*** This is another reminder that God would preserve a faithful remnant.

**65:10 *plain of Sharon.*** This lay along the Mediterranean coast between Mount Carmel and Joppa.

***valley of Achor.*** Located near Jericho (cf. Josh 7:24, 26).

**65:11 *god of Fate . . . god of Destiny.*** "Fate" (Heb. *gad* [TH1409, ZH1513]) and "Destiny" (Heb. *meni* [TH4507, ZH4972]) were the pagan deities of good fortune and fate. "Fate" was possibly the name of a Canaanite deity because when Israel entered the land, at least two towns bore the element *gad*: Baal Gad (Josh 11:17) and Migdal Gad (Josh 15:37). "Fortune" and "Destiny" are the renderings used in the NRSV and NAB; the REB reads "Fate" and "Destiny." The NJB transliterates these as "Gad" and "Meni." The rebellious people preferred to give allegiance to such gods rather than to the Sovereign Lord (65:15) of their covenant.

**65:12 *destine.*** Heb. *manah* [TH4487, ZH4948], a verb which picks up on the noun "Destiny" in the preceding verse. The words are cognate in Heb.

**65:15 *by another name.*** In the OT, a name change was often connected with a status change.

**65:16 *God of truth.*** The pagan idols were gods of falsehood.

**65:18 *create.*** Heb. *bara'* [TH1254, ZH1343], a distinctive word used also in Gen 1:1.

**65:21 *eat the fruit of their own vineyards.*** Cf. 62:8-9.

### COMMENTARY

This passage seems to be the Lord's response to the preceding prayer, as he promises to break his silence and act (65:6; "I will not stand silent"). Although the Lord will reject ungodly people, he will save a remnant. The present order will pass away, but he will create a new order. God's answer to his servant includes judgment as well as mercy. The Lord's people will be blessed by him (65:13-16), but much of the blessing described here will take place in the more remote future (65:17-25).

The nation of Israel had prayed to God for help on the grounds that they belonged to him. The Lord responded that he "was ready to be found, but no one was looking" for him (65:1). He said, "Here I am, here I am!" (65:1; cf. 55:5). Paul quotes from these verses in Romans 10:20-21 and applies 65:1 to the Gentiles who did not seek God. Although in the context of the book of Isaiah both verses probably refer to Israel, it is true that in 56:6-8 Isaiah had already spoken of God's acceptance of Gentiles (cf. 54:17). In Romans 9:6, Paul notes that not all who are descended from Israel are true Israelites, and that what distinguishes the true believer is not the division between Jew and Gentile, but the bigger division between those who seek God and those who forsake him (65:10-11).

A combination of judgment and salvation takes place as God distinguishes between disobedient and obedient people. The obstinate old covenant people rebelled and followed their own plans (65:2), an attitude that persisted into the time of the new covenant (cf. Acts 7:51). Again, the Lord recounted the terrible sins of Israel that had brought about their banishment into exile, and explained why sinners who refuse to repent must face judgment.

The next section (65:3ff) catalogs some of the sins of the people, and Isaiah did not hesitate to identify specific sins. The list includes idolatry and various pagan rituals that took place in "sacred gardens" (cf. 1:29; 57:5; 66:17), where they indulged in burning incense on pagan altars and even resorted to consulting spirits of the dead. It is not surprising that they were said to "eat the flesh of pigs and make stews with other forbidden foods" (65:4). Yet they had the pride and audacity to say to each other, "I am holier than you!" (65:5). A similar claim was made by the Pharisees of Jesus' day (cf. Luke 7:39; 18:9-12), and this was as irritating to God as smoke in his nostrils—"a stench" and "acrid smell that never goes away" (65:5). He would repay them for their sins and they would receive what they deserveed (cf. 59:18).

Not all of the people had to face judgment, however, and 65:8-10 introduces the believing remnant of the nation, called God's "true servants" (65:8b). Although this term was used earlier in 54:17 and in 63:17, its significance is developed most fully in chapter 65. The reference is probably to the remnant that would survive God's judgment and return to their homeland. God had promised a blessing to all nations through the seed of Abraham (Gen 12:3; 22:18; cf. also the promise to Isaac and Jacob in Gen 26:2-5; 28:14), and for his name's sake it would be fulfilled. Not everyone would be cut off (48:9). Both Israel and Judah went into captivity and both ceased to exist as political kingdoms, but from them the Lord would redeem his remnant.

The fate and destiny (65:11b) of the people did not rest in the hands of idols, but with the overruling providence of God. Although the Lord repeatedly called the nation through the prophets, the people turned a deaf ear (65:12; cf. 50:2; Jer 25:4). Israel chose what displeased God, unlike the often-despised eunuchs of 56:4.

The contrast between God's servants and unbelieving Israel reaches its peak in 65:13-16, where Isaiah underlines the sharp contrast between the fate of the wicked and the true remnant of God. The redeemed of the Lord can expect to eat, drink, rejoice, and sing. The future for unbelievers is the opposite: they will starve, be thirsty, and cry in sorrow and despair. God announces that he is "creating new heavens and a new earth" that will be so wonderful that "no one will even think about the old ones anymore" (65:17; cf. 2 Pet 3:13). Earlier, Isaiah contrasted the former things with the new things (42:9; cf. 43:18-19; 48:3, 6-7). The new things include the return of the exiles to the newly created Jerusalem and the work of the servant of the Lord. In 48:7, the Lord said, "They are brand new, not things from the past." Just as chapter 54 began with a description of the repopulation of Jerusalem after the exile and then described the New Jerusalem (65:11-14), so the context of 65:17-19 may begin in the present before leading far into the future. The apostle John spoke of the new heaven and new earth in connection with the "new Jerusalem, coming down from God out of heaven" (Rev 21:2). Like Isaiah (65:19), John (who drew heavily on 25:8) proclaimed that crying and mourning will be gone because "the old world and its evils are gone forever" (Rev 21:4).

In this new setting, "invaders will not take their houses" (65:22) as they did in the past (cf. Deut 28:30; Amos 5:11), nor will they will work in vain (65:23), as they did when the people labored for that which did not satisfy (55:2) and wearied themselves in following their own ways (57:10). When they are about to pray, God will "answer them before they even call to [him]" (65:24; cf. 30:19; 58:9). In his promise to answer prayer before it is made, the Lord even goes beyond what is pledged in 58:9 and Psalm 145:18-19. Before his saints even call on him, the Lord, knowing their needs (Matt 6:8), will make provision for them. How different from the days when the sins of the people made it impossible for God to hear them and respond (cf. 59:1-2).

The chapter closes (65:25 ) with reference to the peace that will characterize the world, using the imagery of change in animal instincts (cf. 11:6-9) and recalling the conditions of paradise. Lines one and two are very similar to Isaiah 11:6-7, and the last sentence is identical to the first part of 11:9 (see commentary on Isa 11).

◆     9. Conclusion and summary (66:1-24)

This is what the LORD says:

"Heaven is my throne,
and the earth is my footstool.
Could you build me a temple as good
as that?
Could you build me such a resting
place?
2 My hands have made both heaven and
earth;
they and everything in them are
mine.*
I, the LORD, have spoken!

"I will bless those who have humble
and contrite hearts,
who tremble at my word.
3 But those who choose their own ways—
delighting in their detestable sins—
will not have their offerings
accepted.
When such people sacrifice a bull,
it is no more acceptable than
a human sacrifice.
When they sacrifice a lamb,
it's as though they had sacrificed
a dog!
When they bring an offering of grain,
they might as well offer the blood
of a pig.
When they burn frankincense,
it's as if they had blessed an idol.
4 I will send them great trouble—
all the things they feared.
For when I called, they did not answer.
When I spoke, they did not listen.
They deliberately sinned before my
very eyes
and chose to do what they know
I despise."

5 Hear this message from the LORD,
all you who tremble at his words:
"Your own people hate you
and throw you out for being loyal to
my name.
'Let the LORD be honored!' they scoff.
'Be joyful in him!'
But they will be put to shame.

6 What is all the commotion in the city?
What is that terrible noise from the
Temple?
It is the voice of the LORD
taking vengeance against his
enemies.

7 "Before the birth pains even begin,
Jerusalem gives birth to a son.
8 Who has ever seen anything as
strange as this?
Who ever heard of such a thing?
Has a nation ever been born in a
single day?
Has a country ever come forth in a
mere moment?
But by the time Jerusalem's* birth
pains begin,
her children will be born.
9 Would I ever bring this nation to the
point of birth
and then not deliver it?" asks the
LORD.
"No! I would never keep this nation
from being born,"
says your God.

10 "Rejoice with Jerusalem!
Be glad with her, all you who
love her
and all you who mourn for her.
11 Drink deeply of her glory
even as an infant drinks at its
mother's comforting breasts."

12 This is what the LORD says:
"I will give Jerusalem a river of peace
and prosperity.
The wealth of the nations will flow
to her.
Her children will be nursed at her
breasts,
carried in her arms, and held on
her lap.
13 I will comfort you there in Jerusalem
as a mother comforts her child."

14 When you see these things, your heart
will rejoice.
You will flourish like the grass!

Everyone will see the LORD's hand of
blessing on his servants—
and his anger against his enemies.
15 See, the LORD is coming with fire,
and his swift chariots roar like a
whirlwind.
He will bring punishment with the
fury of his anger
and the flaming fire of his hot
rebuke.
16 The LORD will punish the world by fire
and by his sword.
He will judge the earth,
and many will be killed by him.

17 "Those who 'consecrate' and 'purify'
themselves in a sacred garden with its
idol in the center—feasting on pork and
rats and other detestable meats—will
come to a terrible end," says the LORD.
18 "I can see what they are doing, and I
know what they are thinking. So I will
gather all nations and peoples together,
and they will see my glory. 19 I will perform
a sign among them. And I will send those
who survive to be messengers to the nations—to Tarshish, to the Libyans* and
Lydians* (who are famous as archers), to
Tubal and Greece,* and to all the lands beyond the sea that have not heard of my
fame or seen my glory. There they will declare my glory to the nations. 20 They will
bring the remnant of your people back
from every nation. They will bring them to
my holy mountain in Jerusalem as an
offering to the LORD. They will ride on
horses, in chariots and wagons, and on
mules and camels," says the LORD. 21 "And I
will appoint some of them to be my priests
and Levites. I, the LORD, have spoken!

22 "As surely as my new heavens and
earth will remain,
so will you always be my people,
with a name that will never
disappear,"
says the LORD.
23 "All humanity will come to
worship me
from week to week
and from month to month.
24 And as they go out, they will see
the dead bodies of those who have
rebelled against me.
For the worms that devour them will
never die,
and the fire that burns them will
never go out.
All who pass by
will view them with utter horror."

66:2 As in Greek, Latin, and Syriac versions; Hebrew reads *these things are.*   66:8 Hebrew *Zion's.*   66:19a As in
some Greek manuscripts, which read *Put* [that is, *Libya*]; Hebrew reads *Pul.*   66:19b Hebrew *Lud.*
66:19c Hebrew *Javan.*

NOTES

66:1 *footstool.* Cf. 40:22; Pss 11:4; 103:19. The term is applied to the Ark of the Covenant
in the Holy of Holies (1 Chr 28:2).

66:3 *dog . . . pig.* A dog was ceremonially unclean and could not be used in offerings, and
pigs (cf. 66:17 and 65:4) were also unacceptable as sacrificial animals (Lev 11:7-8).

*sacrificed a dog.* The Heb. says, "breaks a dog's neck." Note the law about breaking a donkey's neck in Exod 13:13.

*it is as if they had blessed an idol.* Lit., "their souls delight in their abominations" (NIV).
The Heb. for "abominations" (*shiqquts* [TH8251, ZH9199]) is a very strong word here; it is
used elsewhere for idols (2 Kgs 23:24), heathen gods (1 Kgs 11:5), various forbidden practices or foods (Zech 9:7), and all that is contrary to the worship of the Lord.

66:5 *Let the LORD be honored!* This is sarcasm from the lips of the wicked who taunt the
righteous for their hope in the Lord.

66:12 *held on her lap.* Or, "dandled on her knees" (NIV, NRSV, REB). Similar language is
found in 49:22; 60:4. Other versions have "fondled on her knees" (NASB), "treated with
love" (TEV), "cuddled on her knees" (GW), and "hold you in her lap" (CEV).

**66:13** *as a mother comforts her child.* The last half of the book of Isaiah begins with the command, "Comfort, comfort my people" (40:1). That comfort is now complete (in the Heb. the word is found three times in this verse).

**66:14** *You will flourish.* The Heb. is fuller: "your bones will flourish," a Semitism indicating the depths of human nature. The bones, as the firmest parts of the body, can be used to represent the entire body or the whole person (cf. Pss 31:10; 32:3).

*grass.* Although used elsewhere in Isaiah for what is temporal and weak (cf. 37:32; 40:6-8), it is used here to depict what is flourishing.

**66:17** *feasting on pork and rats.* Such things were forbidden in the law and were associated with Israel's pagan neighbors (cf. 65:3-4; Lev 7:21; 11:29).

*detestable.* The Heb. word *sheqets* [TH8263, ZH9211] is used in Lev 11:41 of every creature that creeps on the ground. The KJV translates it as "abomination" and the NIV has "abominable things."

**66:19** *Tarshish.* This city is usually identified with Tartessus in Spain, which is believed to have been near the modern city of Cadiz.

*Tubal.* This was located in the far north (cf. Ezek 39:1-5).

**66:20** *remnant of your people.* Lit., "all your brothers."

*offering.* The Heb. *minkhah* [TH4503, ZH4966] was widely used in the terminology of offerings, especially grain offerings (cf. Lev 2). It had the general meaning of "gift." Here it may refer to Gentile believers, who represent part of the fulfillment of the visions of 2:2-4; 60:1-14.

**66:23** *from week to week and from month to month.* More lit., "From one New Moon to another and from one Sabbath to another" (NIV).

**66:24** *rebelled.* Heb. *pasha'* [TH6586, ZH7321]; also found in 1:2, 28; 43:27; 46:8; 48:8; 53:12; 66:24. The noun form is found in 24:20; 43:25; 44:22; 50:1; 53:5, 8; 57:4; 58:1; 59:12, 20. Isaiah uses this word more than any other prophet.

*view them with utter horror.* The Heb. word *dera'on* [TH1860, ZH1994], here translated "horror," is translated as "contempt" in Dan 12:2, where the picture is of unbelievers being raised from the dead, but excluded forever from the city of God. Isaiah is clear about the existence of such a place. A comparison with Jer 7:32–8:3 suggests that the background imagery is of the Valley of Hinnom, or Gehenna (cf. Mark 9:48).

### COMMENTARY

The final chapter of Isaiah summarizes many of the key themes of this magnificent prophecy, as Isaiah emphasizes the greatness of God the Creator who would come with fire to judge sinners, but who also comforts his people and brings rejoicing to Jerusalem. These twin themes of salvation and judgment reach a climax in 66:22-23.

The opening verses depict a throne greater than any that could ever be built by mortals, one for which the earth is God's "footstool" (66:1). Both "heaven and earth" (66:2) were created by and belong to the Creator. According to Acts 7:49-50, Stephen quoted 66:1-2, agreeing with Solomon and Isaiah about the greatness of God the Creator (Thornton 1974).

In view of such glory and majesty, mere humans are admonished to "have humble and contrite hearts" (66:2). But those who "choose their own ways . . . will not have their offerings accepted" (66:3). The reason for God's rejection of their offerings is because they have chosen their own ways rather than obeying God—in fact, they chose to do what they know God despises (66:4; the last lines of this verse are almost identical with 65:12). A division between the obedient and the disobedient people is clearly seen in 66:5.

The birth of the nation is described in 66:7-9 in the image of a newborn infant. In words similar to those of 54:1, Isaiah speaks of Zion as painlessly giving birth to children. Before her pains come upon her, Jerusalem will give birth to a son (cf. 49:20-21; 54:1); all at once she will again have inhabitants. All who love Jerusalem are thereby encouraged to rejoice, be glad (66:10), and delight in her, because God "will give Jerusalem a river of peace and prosperity" (66:12). This speaks of the nations coming to Jerusalem. In 60:16, Jerusalem is described as drinking the milk of the nations, as the riches of the nations come to her (cf. 60:5) like a flowing stream (48:18), unlike the destructive flood of Assyria's armies (8:7-8). The peace (66:12) that she will enjoy is linked with the righteous rule of the Messiah (9:7).

The statement in 66:18 ("gather all nations and peoples together") is language typically used of God's redemptive work for all the nations (cf. 2:2-4; 11:10; 60:1-14; 62:2). This gathering is linked with a sign (66:19) from God, which though not specified, must be connected with the birth mentioned in 66:7-8 (cf. the sign and special birth mentioned in 7:14). The various returnees will bring the remnant (lit., "all your brothers") to the "holy mountain in Jerusalem as an offering to the LORD" (66:20). This remnant is not just fellow Israelites, nor are they the priests and Levites (66:21) of the old order—rather, they represent the new royal priesthood of the new messianic order (cf. 1 Pet 2:9; Rev 5:9-10). All this refers to the new order and new age, which must be inclusive (cf. John 11:52) and must be described in language familiar to the readers of that age. The list of nations (66:19) as well as the list of means of transportation (66:20) is impressionistic (Motyer 1993:542; cf. 19:24-25; 45:14-25). The various places mentioned were obviously known to the world of that era and represented the whole world (66:20; cf. 49:12). The harvest from all nations will be brought as a bloodless offering to the Lord's "holy mountain in Jerusalem" (66:20; cf. 2:2-4; 56:7; 57:13).

The book closes with a promise that God's people will be as permanent as the "new heavens and earth" (66:22; cf. 65:17). In 66:23, this condition of God's new people is described in the worship language of the Old Testament. Two previous sections of Isaiah (48:22; 57:20) both closed with the words, "there is no peace for the wicked"; this final section closes with an even more dreadful picture of the lot of the wicked, who are said to be forever devoured by worms and burned with everlasting fire (cf. Mark 9:43-48).

Oswalt (1998:691) observes that the old heavens and earth witnessed judgment from God (1:2) but also sang over the salvation from God made possible by the Servant's work (44:23; 49:13). Now the "new heavens and earth" are mentioned (65:17; 66:22) as part of the complex of "new things" Isaiah promised (42:9; 48:6). This includes the messianic age, the time when victory will be accomplished through the good news of the Messiah and his victorious work. This good news is not only for the people of Israel but for "all humanity" who come from everywhere to worship the Lord (66:23). Later, the apostle John used the language of the new heaven and new earth in connection with the "new Jerusalem, coming down from God out of heaven" (Rev 21:2). This builds on and goes beyond the message of Isaiah, and refers to a time when weeping will cease and the old world and its evils will be gone forever (Rev 21:4). For Isaiah, Jerusalem includes the old city to which the exiles returned and also the new city that will involve the salvation promised to the whole earth. The last verse in the book refers to the "worms that devour" but "never die" and the "fire that burns" but never goes out, language echoed in Mark 9:48.

The long book of Isaiah covers the whole range of the drama of salvation and redemption. It is the story of rebellious sinners judged by a just and holy God, but it is also the story of a loving and gracious God who forgives repentant sinners. It is the story of the covenant Lord who preserves the remnant of his covenant people, and it is the story of the Messiah who is both the suffering servant and the reigning sovereign, and it concludes with the story of the glorious Zion of the new, messianic age, when God will reign in victory in the midst of his people. All of these themes, and more, are woven together in a tapestry of vivid language revealing the work of the Creator. All of this is depicted against a religious background that denied the Creator and involved the worship of mute and lifeless idol-gods, created by humans for human convenience.

# BIBLIOGRAPHY

Alexander, Joseph A.
1992 *Commentary on Isaiah*. Editor, John Eadie. Grand Rapids: Kregel. (Orig. Pub. c1875.)

Archer, Gleason A.
1962 Isaiah. Pp. 605-654 in *The Wycliffe Bible Commentary*. Editors, Charles F. Pfeiffer and Everett F. Harrison. Chicago: Moody Press.

Avigad, N.
1953 The Epitaph of a Royal Steward from Siloam Village. *Israel Exploration Journal* 3:137-152.

Baldwin, Joyce G.
1964 Semah as a Technical Term in the Prophets. *Vetus Testamentum* 14:93-97.

Bellinger, William H. and William R. Farmer
1998 *Jesus and the Suffering Servant: Isaiah 53 and Christian Origins*. Harrisburg, PA: Trinity.

Bright, John
1981 *History of Israel*. 3rd ed. Philadelphia: Westminster.

Brueggemann, Walter
1998 *Isaiah*. 2 vols. Louisville: Westminster John Knox.

Caird, G. B.
1980 *The Language and Imagery of the Bible*. Philadelphia: Westminster.

Calvin, John
1948 *Commentary on the Book of the Prophet Isaiah*. 4 vols. Translator, W. Pringle. Grand Rapids: Eerdmans. (Orig. Pub. c1560.)

Chi, Chung Hsin
1974 Concept of Hardening of the Heart in the Old Testament with Special Reference to Isaiah 6. *South East Asia Journal of Theology* 15:116-117.

Childs, B. S.
1974 *The Book of Exodus: A Critical, Theological Commentary*. Philadelphia: Westminster.

2000 *Isaiah*. Louisville: Westminster John Knox.

Chilton, Bruce D.
1985 Three Views of the Isaiah Targum. *Journal of the Study of the Old Testament* 33:127-128.

Chisholm, Robert B.
1996 Divine Hardening in the Old Testament. *Biblia Sacra* 153:410-434.

Christensen, D. L.
1976 The March of Conquest in Isaiah X 27c-34. *Vetus Testamentum* 26:385-399.

Clifford, R. J.
1966 The Use of HOY in the Prophets. *Catholic Biblical Quarterly* 28:458-464.

Clines, David J. A.
1992 Was There an *abl* 'be dry' in Classical Hebrew? *Vetus Testamentum* 42:1-10.

Compstonk, H. F. B.
1926/1927 Ladies' Finery in Isaiah III 18-23. *Church Quarterly Review* 103:316-330.

Conrad, Edgar W.
1988 Isaiah and the Abraham Connection. *Asia Journal of Theology* 2.2:382-393.

1991 *Reading Isaiah*. Minneapolis: Fortress.

Cross, F. M.
1975 Evolution of a Theory of Local Texts. Pp. 306-320 in *Qumran and the History of the Biblical Text*. Editors, F. M. Cross and S. Talmon. Cambridge, MA: Harvard University Press.

Culver, R. D.
1958 *The Sufferings and the Glory of the Lord's Righteous Servant*. Moline, IL: Christian Service Foundation.

Day, John N.
1998 God and Leviathan in Isaiah 27:1. *Bibliotheca Sacra* 155:423-436.

**DeBoer, P. A. H.**
1956 *Second-Isaiah's Message.* Leiden: Brill.

**Delitzsch, Franz.**
1949 *Commentary on Isaiah.* 2 vols. Grand Rapids: Eerdmans.

**Driver, G. R.**
1968 Isaiah 1–39: Textual and Linguistic Problems. *Journal of Semitic Studies* 13:36-57.

**England, Archie**
1994 Resurrection Language and Imagery in the Old Testament and Ancient Near East. PhD diss., Mid-America Baptist Seminary.

**Evans, Craig A.**
1989 *To See and Not Perceive: Isaiah 6:8-10 in Early Jewish and Christian Interpretation.* Journal for the Study of the Old Testament Supplement Series 64. Sheffield: Sheffield Academic Press.

**Geller, S.**
1984 A Poetic Analysis of Isaiah 40:1-2. *Harvard Theological Review* 77:413-420.

**Gitay, Yehoshua**
1984 The Effectiveness of Isaiah's Speech. *Jewish Quarterly Review* 75:162-172.

**Glueck, J. J.**
1970 Paronomasia in Biblical Literature. *Semitics* 1:50-78.

**Goldingay, John**
1998 Isaiah 1:1 and 2:1. *Vetus Testamentum* 48:326-332.

**Gordon, Cyrus**
1949 *Ugaritic Literature.* Rome: Pontifical Biblical Institute.

1965 *The Ancient Near East.* 3rd ed. New York: W. W. Norton.

**Goshen-Gottstein, M. H.**
1960 Prolegomena to a Critical Edition of the Peshitta. *Text and Language in Bible and Qumran.* Jerusalem/Tel Aviv: Orient Publishing House.

1965 *The Book of Isaiah, Sample Edition.* The Hebrew University Bible Project. Jerusalem: Magnes Press.

1976 (editor) *The Aleppo Codex: Part I (plates).* Jerusalem: Magnes Press.

**Graham, Pat**
1976 The Remnant Motif in Isaiah. *Restoration Quarterly* 19:217-228.

**Grelot, Pierre**
1992 *What are the Targums?* Collegeville, MN: Liturgical Press.

**Grogan, Geoffrey W.**
1986 *Isaiah.* Pp. 1-354 in *Expositors Bible Commentary,* vol. 6. Editor, Frank Gaebelein. Grand Rapids: Zondervan.

**Harrison, R. K., editor**
1985 *Major Cities of the Biblical World.* Nashville: Nelson.

**Hayes, Daniel J.**
1996 The Cushites: A Black Nation in Ancient History. *Biblica Sacra* 153:270-280, 396-409.

**Hoerth, Alfred, Gerald L. Mattingly, and Edwin Yamauchi**
1994 *Peoples of the Old Testament World.* Grand Rapids: Baker.

**Holladay, W.**
1968 Isa III 10-11: An Archaic Wisdom Passage. *Vetus Testamentum* 18:481-487.

1971 *A Concise Hebrew and Aramaic Lexicon of the Old Testament.* Grand Rapids: Eerdmans; Leiden: Brill.

**Hollenbach, Bruce**
1983 Lest They Should Turn and Be Forgiven: Irony in Is. 6:10. *The Bible Translator* 34:312-321.

**Huffmon, H. B.**
1959 The Covenant Lawsuit in the Prophets. *Journal of Biblical Literature* 78:288-295.

**Hurowitz, V.**
1989 Isaiah's Impure Lips and their Purification in Light of Akkadian Sources. *Hebrew Union College Annual* 60:39-89.

Joines, K. R.
1967 Winged Serpents in Isaiah's Inaugural Vision. *Journal of Biblical Literature* 86:410-15.

Kaiser, Otto
1974 *Isaiah 13–39.* Philadelphia: Westminster.

Kidner, Derek
1994 *Isaiah.* Downers Grove: InterVarsity.

Kissane, Edward J.
1941 *The Book of Isaiah.* Dublin: Richview.

Knight, G. A. F.
1965 *Deutero-Isaiah: A Theological Commentary on Isaiah 40–55.* Nashville: Abingdon.
1985 *New Israel: A Commentary on the Book of Isaiah 56–66.* Grand Rapids: Eerdmans.

Korpel, Marjo C. A.
1996 Metaphors in Isaiah LV. *Vetus Testamentum* 46:43-55.

Lacheman, E.
1968 Seraphim of Isaiah 6. *Jewish Quarterly Review* 59:71-72.

Leupold, H. C.
1971 *Exposition of Isaiah.* 2 vols. Grand Rapids: Baker.

Levey, Samson H.
1974 *The Messiah: An Aramaic Interpretation.* Cincinnati: Hebrew Union College-Jewish Institute of Religion.

Lindsey, Duane
1985 *The Servant Songs.* Chicago: Moody Press.

Lipinski, E.
1973 Garden of Abundance, Image of Lebanon Is 60. *Zeitschrift für die Alttestamentliche Wissenschaft* 85:358-359.

Litwak, Kenneth D.
1983 The Use of Quotations from Isaiah 52:13–53:12 in the New Testament. *Journal of the Evangelical Theological Society* 26:385-94.

Lowenstamm, S. E.
1972 Isaiah I 31. *Vetus Testamentum* 22:246-248.

MacRae, Allan A.
1977 *The Gospel of Isaiah.* Chicago: Moody Press.

McKenzie, John L.
1968 *Second Isaiah: The Anchor Bible.* Garden City, NY: Doubleday.

McLaughlin, John L.
1994 Their hearts were hardened: The Use of Isaiah 6:9-10 in the Book of Isaiah. *Biblica* 75:1-25.

McNamara, Martin
1972 *Targum and Testament.* Grand Rapids: Eerdmans.

Marshall, R. J.
1962 The Structure of Isaiah 1–12. *Biblical Research* 7:19-32.

Melugin, R.
1976 *The Formation of Isaiah 40–55.* Beihefte zur Zeitschrift für die Alttestamentliche Wissenschaft 141. Berlin: de Gruyter.

Milgrom, J.
1964 Did Isaiah Prophesy During the Reign of Uzziah? *Vetus Testamentum* 14:164-182.

Millar, W.
1976 *Isaiah 24–27 and the Origin of the Apocalyptic.* Missoula, MT: Scholars Press.

Miscall, Peter D.
1993 *Isaiah.* Sheffield: Journal for the Study of the Old Testament Press.

Motyer, J. Alec
1993 *The Prophecy of Isaiah: An Introduction and Commentary.* Downers Grove: InterVarsity.
1999 *Isaiah: An Introduction and Commentary.* Tyndale Old Testament Commentaries. Downers Grove: InverVarsity.

**Mouw, Richard J.**
1983 *When the Kings Come Marching In.* Grand Rapids: Eerdmans.

**Murray, John**
1959 *The Epistle to the Romans.* vol. 1. Grand Rapids: Eerdmans.

**Niehaus, Jeffrey J.**
1995 *God at Sinai.* Grand Rapids: Zondervan.

**North, C. R.**
1964 *The Second Isaiah: Introduction, Translation and Commentary to Chapters 40–55.* Oxford:
       Oxford University Press.

**Odendaal, Dirk**
1970 *The Eschatological Expectation of Isaiah 40–66 with Special Reference to Israel and the Nations.*
       Nutley, NJ: Presbyterian and Reformed Pub. House.

**Oswalt, John**
1986 *The Book of Isaiah: 1–39.* Grand Rapids: Eerdmans.

1998 *The Book of Isaiah: 40–66.* Grand Rapids: Eerdmans.

**Payne, David F.**
1971 The Servant of the Lord: Language and Interpretation. *Evangelical Quarterly* 43:131-143.

1986 *Isaiah.* Pp. 714-763 in *The International Bible Commentary,* rev. ed. Editor, F. F. Bruce.
       Grand Rapids: Zondervan.

**Platt, Elizabeth E.**
1979 Jewelry of Bible Times and the Catalog of Isaiah 3:18-23. *Andrews University Seminary Studies*
       17:71-84, 189-202.

**Ridderbos, J.**
1985 *Isaiah: Bible Student's Commentary.* Translator, John Vriend. Grand Rapids: Zondervan.

**Ridenhour, Thomas E.**
1976 Immortality and Resurrection in the Old Testament. *Dialog* 15:104-9.

**Roberts, J. J. M.**
1983 Isaiah 33: An Isaianic Elaboration of the Zion Tradition. Pp. 15-25 in *The Word of the Lord
       Shall Go Forth: Essays in Honor of David Noel Freedman in Celebration of his Sixtieth Birthday.*
       Editors, C. L. Meyers and M. O'Conner. Winona Lake: Eisenbrauns.

1992 Double Entendre in First Isaiah. *Catholic Biblical Quarterly* 54:39-48.

**Russell, John Malcolm**
1991 *Sennacherib's Palace Without Rival at Nineveh.* Chicago: University of Chicago Press.

**Ryken, Leland**
1987 *Words of Delight: A Literary Introduction to the Bible.* Grand Rapids: Baker.

**Sawyer, John J. A.**
1996 *The Fifth Gospel.* Cambridge: Cambridge University Press.

**Schoekel, Luis Alonso**
1963 *Estudios de Poetica Hebrea.* Barcelona: J. Flors.

**Smart, J. D.**
1965 *History and Theology in Second Isaiah.* Philadelphia: Westminster.

**Smick, Elmer B.**
1968 The Bearing of New Philological Data on the Subjects of Resurrection and Immortality
       in the Old Testament. *Westminster Theological Journal* 31:12-21.

**Stenning, J. F.**
1949 *The Targum of Isaiah.* Oxford: Clarendon.

**Tadmor, H.**
1958 The Campaigns of Sargon II of Assar: A Chronological-Historical Study. *Journal of Cuneiform Studies*
       12:33-40.

1966 Philistia under Assyrian Rule. *Biblical Archaeologist* 29:86-102.

**Thomas, Derek**
1991 *God Delivers.* Durham: Evangelical Press.

Thornton, Timothy C. G.
1974 Stephen's Use of Isaiah 66:1. *Journal of Theological Studies* 25:432-434.

Tiller, P. A.
1997 The "Eternal Planting" in the Dead Sea Scrolls. *Dead Sea Discoveries* 4:312-335.

Tov, Emmanuel
1992 *Textual Criticism of the Hebrew Bible.* Minneapolis: Fortress Press.

1997 The Text of Isaiah at Qumran. Pp. 491-511 in *Writing and Reading the Scroll of Isaiah.*
     Editors, Craig C. Broyles and Craig A. Evans. Leiden: Brill.

Tsevat, M.
1969 Isaiah I 31. *Vetus Testamentum* 19:261-263.

Van Selms, A.
1973 Isaiah 28:9-13: An Attempt to Give a New Interpretation. *Zeitschrift für die Alttestamentliche
     Wissenschaft* 85:332-339.

VanGemeren, Willem.
1990 *Interpreting the Prophetic Word.* Grand Rapids: Zondervan.

Von Rad, Gerhard
1968 *The Message of the Prophets.* New York: Harper & Row.

Walker, Larry L.
1991 Notes on the Language of Isaiah. *Mid-America Theological Journal* 15:104-108.

Walsh, Carey Ellen
1998 God's Vineyard: Isaiah's Prophecy as Vintner's Textbook. *Biblical Research* 14:42-49, 52-53.

Watson, G. E. Wilfred
1976 Tribute to Tyre Is. 23:7. *Vetus Testamentum* 26:371-374.

1981 Chiastic Patterns in Biblical Hebrew Poetry. Pp. 118-168 in *Chiasmus in Antiquity.*
     Editor, John Welch. Hildesheim: Gerstenberg Verlag.

Watts, John D. W.
1985 *Isaiah,* vol 1. Waco: Word.

1987 *Isaiah,* vol 2. Waco: Word.

Webb, Barry G.
1996 *The Message of Isaiah.* Downers Grove: InterVarsity.

Weiss, Meir
1984 *The Bible from Within.* Jerusalem: Magnes Press.

Weren, W. J. C.
1998 The Use of Isaiah 5:1-7 in the Parable of the Tenants Mark 12:1-12; Matthew 21:33-46.
     *Biblica* 79:1-26.

Westermann, Claus
1969 *Isaiah 40-66.* Old Testament Library. Philadelphia: Westminster.

Whybray, R. N.
1981 *Isaiah 40-66.* Grand Rapids: Eerdmans.

Wildberger, Hans
1991 *Isaiah 1-12.* Translator, Thomas A. Trapp. Minneapolis: Fortress.

Williams, J. G.
1967 The Alas-oracles of the Eighth Century Prophets. *Hebrew Union College Annual* 39:750-791.

Willmington, Harold L.
1985 Shakespeare of the Prophets. *Fundamentalist Journal* 4:482-488.

Winter, Paul
1954 Isaiah 63:9 Gk and the Passover Hagadah. *Vetus Testamentum* 4:439-441.

Wiseman, D. J.
1973 *Peoples of Old Testament Times.* Oxford: Clarendon.

Wolf, Herb M.
1985 *Interpreting Isaiah: The Suffering and Glory of the Messiah.* Grand Rapids: Zondervan.

1986 The Relationship Between Isaiah's Final Servant Song 52:13–53:12 and Chapters 1–6.
Pp. 251-259 in *A Tribute to Gleason Archer.* Editors, Walter C. Kaiser, Jr. and Ronald F. Youngblood.
Chicago: Moody Press.

**Wong, G. C. I.**
1995 On "visits" and "visions" in Isa XXIX 6-7. *Vetus Testamentum* 45:370-376.

1996 Isaiah's Opposition to Egypt in Isaiah XXXI 1-3. *Vetus Testamentum* 46:392-400.

1997 Faith and Works in Isaiah XXX:15. *Vetus Testamentum* 47:236-246.

**Wonsuk, Ma**
1989 The Spirit Ruah of God in Isaiah 1–39. *Asia Journal of Theology* 3:582-596.

**Yamauchi, Edwin**
1980 The Archaeological Background of Ezra. *Bibliotheca Sacra* 137:195-221.

1988 *Ezra, Nehemiah.* Pp. 563-771 in *The Expositor's Bible Commentary,* vol. 4. Editor, F. E. Gaebelein.
Grand Rapids: Zondervan.

1990 *Persia and the Bible.* Grand Rapids: Baker.

**Young, E. J.**
1949 *Introduction to the Old Testament.* London: Tyndale.

1956 *The Book of Isaiah,* vol 1. Grand Rapids: Eerdmans.

1958 *Who Wrote Isaiah?* Grand Rapids: Eerdmans.

1969 *The Book of Isaiah,* vol. 2. Grand Rapids: Eerdmans.

1972 *The Book of Isaiah,* vol. 3. Grand Rapids: Eerdmans.

**Youngblood, R. F.**
1979 Ariel, City of God. Pp. 457-462 in *Essays on the Occasion of the Seventieth Anniversary of
the Dropsie University 1909-1979.* Editors, Abraham I. Katsch and Leon Nemoy. Philadelphia:
Dropsie University.

1993 *The Book of Isaiah.* Grand Rapids: Baker.

1998 Fallen Star: The Evolution of Lucifer. *Bible Review* 14:22-31.

# *Jeremiah*

## ELMER A. MARTENS

# *Jeremiah*

JEREMIAH spoke from within the cultural context of a society in upheaval. When eras are in transition, as from modernity to post-modernity, Jeremiah is the handbook of choice, for this book addresses uncertainty and large-scale shifts. The word of God came then, as it comes now, to rebuke, to console, and to affirm such constants as God's anger against sinful excesses and his promise of everlasting love (31:30).

When individuals wonder what it means to know God, they will find answers in Jeremiah, but they will not be cliched directions such as "read the Bible and pray" (see 9:23-24). Devotion to God may mean going against the cultural grain. Jeremiah's courage in confronting religious and political establishments inspires those who want to know and follow God and God alone.

## AUTHOR

By word count, Jeremiah is the longest book in the Bible. Its author, a prophet, lived in Palestine, the land of Israel in the seventh and sixth centuries BC. His ministry was primarily to the people of Judah before, during, and after the Babylonian siege, which culminated in the capture of Jerusalem in 587 BC.

Jeremiah came from a family of priests whose hometown was Anathoth, located two or three miles northeast of Jerusalem. Abiathar, a priest in David's time, had lived there (1 Kgs 2:26); the place seems to have been the preferred residence for priests of Judah. Around 640 BC, Jeremiah was born in Anathoth to parents of priestly lineage. His public ministry began in 627, spanned at least forty years, and concluded in Egypt among the remnant that had gone there after 587. Little is known of Jeremiah's youth apart from his divine call to be a prophet, which came during his teenage years and meant that his vocation would not be priestly but prophetic. (In suggesting a date of birth, I agree with Lundbom 1999:107 in taking *na'ar* to indicate a "boy" of thirteen to fourteen years; cf. the boy Samuel.)

Jeremiah's ministry was characterized throughout by opposition, no doubt because he confronted his nation with its evil and, at God's directive, threatened the nation with God's judgment in the form of a military invasion. His fellow-citizens, if not also his family, planned to kill him (11:18-23). The priestly group, on at least one occasion, took exception to his message and imprisoned him (20:1-6). Jeremiah was also in constant conflict with false prophets, about whom he warned the people of Judah (23:9-40). His verbal duel with Hananiah, a prophet from Gibeon, is recounted in detail (28:1-17). Jeremiah singled out two false prophets, Ahab and

Zedekiah, who lived among the exiled Jews in Babylon (29:20-23). His heated exchanges with royalty, sometimes through writings, are also notable. He delivered oracles against the last four kings of Judah (22:10-23:6) and was definitely at odds with King Jehoiakim, who trivialized Jeremiah's written message by cutting up the columns as the scroll was read (36:21-26). He also met in person with King Zedekiah, for whom he had scarcely a consoling word (38:14-28). Opposition to his ministry landed him in custody (37:11-16), then in a terrible dungeon (38:1-6), and eventually in court confinement (38:13, 28). Most of his relationships were adversarial, and there were times, as shown by his laments, when he felt that even God was against him (20:7-13).

Many personal details about Jeremiah remain unknown, but he disclosed more of his emotional life than any other prophet. He was deeply pained by the recalcitrance of his listeners. He told of his inward agony over their refusal to change their ways, and he wished at one point that his head were a wellspring of tears so that he might weep nonstop for his people (8:18-23). His "confessions" or "laments" reveal a prophet of great sensitivity who experienced much disappointment in his life (11:18-23; 12:1-6; 15:10-14, 15-21; 17:14-18; 18:18-23; 20:7-13, 14-18). He boldly complained to God about the evil around him (12:1-4) and in even bolder language, charged God with being deceptive and not delivering on his promises (15:15-21). With remarkable audacity, he accused God of misusing him (see comments on 20:7-13). Details about Jeremiah's physical appearance are lacking, but given the emotional disclosures, artists have been eager to capture something of the pathos that marks this prophet in their representations. He may be remembered popularly as a weeping prophet, but given his lifelong, uphill struggle against unrelenting opposition from virtually every quarter, he can more accurately be characterized as a courageous prophet.

He had only a few friends to support him that we know of. Some officials— members of Shaphan's family (26:24) and Ebed-melech (38:7-13)—were sympathetic to him. From the account of his real estate purchase from his uncle (32:1-25), it is clear that there was an extended family, not all of whom had written him off. Following a divine order, he remained unmarried (16:1-2). When Jeremiah was silenced in public ministry, his message was still disseminated, thanks to Baruch, Jeremiah's scribe and associate (36:1-8).

## DATE AND OCCASION OF WRITING

The diverse style and organizational problems of the book of Jeremiah have led to many theories about its composition and date (e.g., Parke-Taylor 2000; cf. Sommer 1999). An extreme position, best described as historically minimalist, is represented by Robert Carroll (1981:8-14), who is cautious to the point of ascribing hardly any material to a man named Jeremiah. His view is that there were people of various orientations and vocations who drew inspiration from a prophet by that name, about whom we know nothing. These groups compiled materials over several centuries that were eventually edited long after the exile. A somewhat less extreme view would suggest that core materials originated with Jeremiah and were then developed at a later time, mostly by adapting the prose sections to make them relevant to a new social context (Nicholson 1970:136-138). In this view, much is made of the Deuteronomic influence. Others, however, Weippert (1973:78, 323-333) among them, argue that the language of Jeremiah is sixth-century prose. She and John Bright attribute the bulk of the Jeremiah text to the prophet himself (Bright 1951:26). Traditionally, the contents of the book have been dated to the forty-year ministry of the prophet, 627-586 BC (Jer 1:1-3), but that ministry may have continued as late as 570 BC (cf. 44:30).

That the book was edited during and after Jeremiah's lifetime, possibly by Baruch, is virtually certain, given the initial dating (1:2-3). The opening verses specify the time period as occurring during the reigns of Josiah, Jehoiakim, and Zedekiah, but some material in the book falls outside these dates, such as the trek of the emigrants to Egypt after 586 BC (chs 43-44). The collection and arrangement of materials by editors is also likely, given the changes of speakers. In chapters 2-25, Jeremiah speaks in the first person, "The word of the LORD came to me saying . . ." (1:4). In other parts, as in the last half of the book, Jeremiah is referred to in the third person: "The LORD gave a message to Jeremiah" (40:1; cf. 7:1). Assuming that much of the book is from Jeremiah, a date for it might be about 570 BC, but with the strong possibility of later editing, a date for the book as we have it is certainly later, but can hardly be specified.

Although the stages of that composition cannot be known, there is no shortage of speculation. One may theorize, for example, on the dating of the Book of Comfort (chs 30-31). Was it written before or after the catastrophic fall of Jerusalem? Can the second scroll that Jeremiah wrote following Jehoiakim's burning of the first one (36:27-32) be identified within the current book? Do the early chapters (e.g., 2-25) comprise the scroll that Jehoiakim burned? Can any of the material be dated to Josiah's time? Were the oracles against the nations, now appearing in a block (chs 46-51), at one time isolated oracles? It is claimed that by identifying text blocks and historical frameworks, the interpreter can better understand the text. Generally, however, interest in identifying sources for various parts is waning, as scholars have increasingly gravitated away from preoccupation with the person of Jeremiah and the process of composition to the literary shape of the book as it now appears in the canon.

The occasion for Jeremiah's messages, and hence for the book, had much to do with Judah's spiritual condition and political situation at the end of the seventh century BC. In brief, Judah had seriously drifted away from Yahweh, who now warned and threatened his people. Politically, the Babylonians from the east were extending their territorial domain and would become Yahweh's agents in punishing Judah for its sin (as Jeremiah proclaimed).

The Mediterranean world was politically stable in the middle of the seventh century BC. Assyria's empire was then at its zenith, extending westward to Syria and southward to Egypt, its vassal state. A century earlier, Samaria in Northern Israel had been swallowed up in the Assyrian advance. Judah was spared, but like many other nations was forced to pay tribute to Assyria. Assyria's major political and cultural achievements came in Ashurbanipal's reign (668–626 BC), during which time Jeremiah was born in distant Israel. Soon thereafter, the 200-year-old empire was beset with difficulties, and the downward spiral was swift. Egypt broke away. Nabopolassar of Babylon, to the south, challenged the mighty empire by attacking and capturing Nineveh (612 BC).

This change of events altered political alignments and soon created a crisis in Judah as the Babylonians moved swiftly westward. Josiah was killed in a battle at Megiddo (609 BC) while trying to prevent the Egyptians from moving through Israel to halt the Babylonians. In a major battle at Carchemish a few years later, the Egyptians were defeated and Babylon became the new political power in the Mediterranean region. Judah's king Jehoiakim faced the encroachment of this emerging power when, under Nebuchadnezzar, Judah's coastal city Ashkelon was taken (604 BC). In 597, the Babylonians took Jehoiachin, the successor to Jehoiakim, captive and appointed a puppet ruler, Zedekiah, in his place. His political stance vacillated during his ten-year rule as loud voices urged alliance with Egypt in order to shake off Babylonian control. Such a move, which may have seemed justified in 594/593 when the Babylonians had internal problems, proved highly problematic. Nebuchadnezzar dealt with this disloyal vassal in no uncertain terms. Babylon besieged Judah's capital, Jerusalem, and sacked it in 586 BC.

The period preceding this calamity was critical for the small country of Judah. These were strange and wonderful times the world over. Karl Jaspers, a philosopher, has proposed that the sixth and fifth centuries were an axial period in world history. There were great religious and ideological stirrings: In Asia, Confucius and Gautama Buddha were founding religious movements. In Greece, Plato and Aristotle were laying the groundwork for Western civilization. A paradigm shift was underway during this hinge point in history. The Old Testament Scriptures mark that shift in the prophetic figures of Jeremiah, Habakkuk, Zephaniah, and Ezekiel. God was speaking a word in these changing times. Judah's disregard of God's message put her well-being at risk and soon landed her in exile.

Jeremiah's assignment was to arrest the downward spiritual spiral of the people. He characterized Judah as "ever turning," but mostly in the direction away from God (3:6-10). Judah did not profit from the example of nearby Israel, which had been subjugated by the Assyrians a century earlier due to her spiritual waywardness. Jeremiah's "temple sermon" addressed Judah's twofold evil: misplaced confidence and social injustice (7:1-15). To these charges could be added idolatry (7:30–8:3), living a lie (9:3-6), and spiritual adultery (2:23-25; 3:1-5). Jeremiah warned that chaos and death were imminent if the people did not change. He urged Judah (and former Israel) to repent of their sins and turn to Yahweh their God. He assured them that salvation was God's intent (31:3-9) and urged, in what must have seemed a traitorous gesture, that Judah submit to the King of Babylon. Both religiously and politically, Jeremiah was very much within the fray.

## AUDIENCE

For whom was the book intended? That question can be answered in two ways. The prophet's oracles are primarily addressed to the people of Jerusalem and Judah (e.g., 4:3-4). The famous temple sermon, for example, is given at the temple in the capital city (7:1-15). However, parts of the book are addressed to Israel, a political designation that distinguishes the northern ten tribes from the two southern tribes known as Judah (see 3:12-18; the name "Israel" can also have a theological meaning as the "people of God," in which case both the northern and southern kingdoms are included). Sometimes both Israel and Judah are recognized in the word of address (31:31-34). It is possible, as some have argued, that a word addressed to the north (for example, in the Book of Comfort) was later adapted, especially after the exile, to include a message to the south. Such a process, while not unlikely, cannot now be unraveled into its successive stages or times.

The question of audience takes a different cast when it is construed as asking for whose benefit the book containing Jeremiah's messages was compiled. If Jeremiah (essentially the words of the prophet) was brought into its present form after the exile, as is most likely, then the oracles of warning about an enemy from the north were no longer existentially relevant. Yet the messages would still have been relevant for the people in exile or thereafter inasmuch as they confirmed the reality of divine prediction and supported the prophet's credibility. At the same time, a chronicle of Jeremiah's message would show that not all prophets could be believed. Hananiah (ch 28), as could now be shown historically, was a false prophet. Moreover, disputes about the reasons for captivity would be resolved, for Jeremiah laid them out in his book with utmost clarity. The nation of Judah was expelled from its land because its inhabitants had sinned. The reason for the captivity was theological, not political. The main audience of the book was not Jeremiah's contemporaries, but people of subsequent generations. As the word of God, Jeremiah's messages remain instructive about God and his ways with humanity (2 Tim 3:16-17). This is why John Calvin, the eminent reformer, could preach 300 sermons from the book of Jeremiah (Calvin 1990:iii).

## CANONICITY AND TEXTUAL HISTORY

The Hebrew Scriptures arrange the Prophets in two groups: Former and Latter. In this ordering, Jeremiah is second of the four Latter Prophets (Isaiah, Jeremiah, Ezekiel, The Twelve). In some listings Jeremiah appears first, which may explain a quotation attributed to him (as giving his name to the prophetic corpus) that is actually from Zechariah (Matt 27:9). In the Greek arrangement of books (also followed in English Bibles), the book of Lamentations follows Jeremiah, on the hardly supportable basis that Jeremiah was the author of Lamentations. To be sure, the tragedy of Jerusalem's destruction, detailed in Jeremiah, receives further reflection in Lamentations, but the book is likely by another author.

The New Testament writers quote Jeremiah directly and allude to his book as many as forty times, according to one count. Matthew reports Herod's slaughter of the infants as the fulfillment of Rachel's weeping for her lost children (31:15). "Fulfillment" must not be understood here as prediction and verification, but in the sense of correspondence. In the Greek language, the word for "fulfill" has a larger range of meanings than the English counterpart. In the historical flow of events, the trauma brought on by Herod recalls the traumatic experience of Rachel, personified as Israel. The longest quote from the Old Testament found in the New Testament is in the book of Hebrews, where the famous "new covenant" passage in Jeremiah 31:31-34 is quoted twice. In making the argument that Christ is the mediator of a new covenant, the author cites the entire passage (Heb 8:8-12). In the second instance, a quotation of part of the new covenant passage supports a discussion about forgiveness (Heb 10:16-17). Many quotations and allusions to Jeremiah are also found in the book of Revelation (cf. Jer 51:7, 9 with Rev 17:4, 18:5; Jer 16:18 with Rev 18:6).

Leaving aside other quotations, the New Testament list of allusions to Jeremiah includes the popular belief that Jesus had similarities to Jeremiah or even was a resurrected Jeremiah (Matt 16:14). The affinities are striking: Jesus was unmarried and was rejected and misunderstood by his own people. He preached a message of repentance, had a small following, was opposed by religious leaders seeking his death, and was vindicated in the end.

The book of Jeremiah mirrors the larger story of the Bible in compressed form. Israel, like all humanity, is alienated from God. God continually reaches out with invitations for repentance and return. The message falls mostly on deaf ears, and people try to destroy the messenger, but even the people's rejection cannot frustrate God's gracious work of salvation, and a new covenant (for Israel) is inaugurated with the coming of Jesus, the Messiah. Thus, in both its specific and its general message, Jeremiah's fit in the canon is comfortable and without controversy.

By contrast, the textual history of the book is highly convoluted, mostly because of two differing versions, the Masoretic Text (Hebrew), and the Septuagint (Greek). The Septuagint version of Jeremiah is one-seventh shorter than the Masoretic Text, on which English translations are generally based. Several verses (e.g., 29:16-20) or parts of verses in the Masoretic Text do not appear in the Septuagint. This discrepancy between the two versions poses the question of whether the Septuagint is an abridgment of the Masoretic Text, or the Masoretic Text an expansion of the Septuagint. Alternatively, each could have a separate baseline text (*Vorlage*), as suggested by the evidence from the Dead Sea scrolls. While some scholars regard the Septuagint as more likely to be the authentic version, others (e.g., Fischer 1998) argue for the Masoretic Text. Soderlund (1985:246-248) acknowledges that the Septuagint had a Hebrew *Vorlage* but does not conclude as readily as some that this *Vorlage* was both shorter than and superior to that which became the Masoretic Text. Waltke (1989:93-108) sides with Emanuel Tov who holds to two different editions of the book, both produced by Jeremiah himself. Research will no doubt continue. Since the Septuagint mostly omits repetitive material, the story line and message of the two are essentially the same.

The material in the Septuagint is arranged differently than in the Masoretic Text. The most noticeable difference is that the oracles against the nations (chs 46–51 in the MT) are located after Jeremiah 25:13 in the Septuagint. The significance of this placement is that it gives the Masoretic Text a trans-historical, apocalyptic flavor. In that end-time, nations will not be regarded as God's agents, but as God's enemies to be destroyed. The Septuagint's arrangement suggests that within history, God's judgment of the nations will spell salvation for Israel.

## LITERARY STYLE

**Stylistic Features.**   Jeremiah is written in both poetry and prose, though the demarcation is not always clear. Most of the book is poetry. Like poetry in general, Hebrew poetry is more concise and incisive than prose, and, as illustrated in Jeremiah 30–31, is characterized by parallelism (*parallelismus membrorum*), which is the repetition of the meaning of one line by a varied statement of that same meaning in the following line (e.g., 30:12; 31:14). Recent studies have clarified that the so-called "repetition" consists of refinement. That is, the second line sharpens, intensifies, and in other ways carries forward the thought of the first. Poets use figurative language, and Jeremiah frequently uses metaphors like those chosen by his predecessor Hosea (e.g., Jer 4:3; Hos 10:12). Interpreters who seek the connections between a given text and other texts (intertextuality) have noted the strong associations between Jeremiah and Hosea, and also between Jeremiah and Isaiah (cf. Sommer 1998).

If the poetry of Jeremiah draws on material from Hosea and strongly resembles Isaiah, the sermonic prose (e.g., 7:1-15; 11:1-13), shares stylistic characteristics of wordiness, expansiveness, and repetitiveness with Deuteronomy (e.g., 28:45-68) and the narrative prose of the historical books Joshua and Kings. Sigmund Mowinckel (1914) distinguished three kinds of writing in Jeremiah (prophetic oracles, usually in poetry; biographical/historical material; and prose material) and emphasizes the affinities of the exhortative material with Deuteronomistic literature. More recent research, however, has focused on other literary genres within Jeremiah, such as rhetorical niceties and narrative criticism.

The genre of the judgment oracle occurs frequently, and usually includes accusation and announcement (5:10-17). Other genres represented are the salvation oracle (30:17b-22), lament (15:15-21), sermon (7:1-15), and record of symbolic action (13:1-11). Interpreters have also noted Jeremiah's penchant for rhetorical questions (e.g., 2:11-12) and quotes by the audience (e.g., 18:12).

**Organization.**   The book of Jeremiah is framed by two narratives. Chapter 1 is largely a personal account, and chapter 52 is a historical appendix that summarizes some national matters, similar to and sometimes identical with parts of 2 Kings 24:18–25:30. Between these two narratives is extensive material about the coming judgment on God's people, their eventual deliverance, and the historical realities of judgment (chs 2–45), followed by seven chapters of oracles about other nations (chs 6–51). While prophetic oracles, either for judgment (e.g., 7:1-15) or salvation (e.g., the Book of Comfort, chs 30–31) make up most of the book, some narrative portions chronicle events in the prophet's life (e.g., 26:1-24; 37:11–38:28).

Although dates are provided for certain oracles, the book is not in chronological order. For example, chapter 34 is dated in the time of Zedekiah, and from what is known about Egyptian/Babylonian clashes, more specifically to 589 BC. The following chapter, however, is dated to Jehoiakim's reign, 605 BC, more than a decade earlier. The arrangement of some narratives, it has recently been argued, may be more theological than chronological. Thus, chapters 34–35 have a structure parallel to chapters 36–38 to emphasize the importance of obedience and the people's disregard for God's message, whether spoken or written (Martens 1987, and see especially the episodic parallelism within Jer 34–44 detailed by Ho 1999:186-263). For the overall flow of the material, see the outline below.

## MAJOR THEMES AND THEOLOGICAL CONCERNS

Like any biblical book, Jeremiah can be read for its story line or for basic data. In the latter kind of reading, one learns facts from Jeremiah about himself and about the times before, during, and after the Babylonian invasion of Israel. The reader encounters God's appeals to Israel to repent, a frequent litany of evils for which Israel was held accountable, and many threats by the Almighty to bring destruction.

A more penetrating way to read a biblical book is to ask, "What contribution does this book make to my understanding of the ways of God in the world?" This question asks for the theology of the book. There are several valid ways to answer this question. One effective way is to be alert to statements in the book that offer clues or suggest how an answer might be formulated. To condense a biblical book—and the longest book in the Bible at that—to a single sentence may be considered ambitious, if not foolhardy. Not all the nuances will be registered in such a summary, but the basic message will be made clear. With that message in mind, the book can profitably be reread for its special nuances.

Jeremiah 9:23-24 might serve as such a summary of the book. "This is what the LORD says: 'Don't let the wise boast in their wisdom, or the powerful boast in their power, or the rich boast in their riches. But those who wish to boast should boast in this alone: that they truly know me and understand that I am the LORD who demonstrates unfailing love and who brings justice and righteousness to the earth, and that I delight in these things. I, the LORD, have spoken!'" Brueggemann supports this approach, noting that "It is not too much to suggest that 9:22-23 might provide a screen through which Jeremiah can be understood more generally" (1992a:295).

**Knowing and Understanding God.** The very idea of comprehending God is daunting. God is the Almighty, the transcendent One. He also addresses human beings: "I the LORD have spoken!" God may be known or experienced in his speech and actions. The Hebrew verb "to know" (*yada'* [TH3045, ZH3359]) entails having information or experiential familiarity with someone or something. The book of Jeremiah makes a theological contribution by distinctively portraying ways in which the individual, the people of God, and the nations gain understanding about God and his ways in the world.

The book opens with the account of God calling an individual to be his prophet (1:4-10), so whatever is said later about God's dealing with Israel and other nations, the individual person is also an object of God's concern. God's foreknowledge and his intentions concerning Jeremiah are mentioned. God assures the prophet that he will accompany him in his life and vocation and promises him the wisdom and guidance needed for his divinely-assigned task.

If we follow the thread of God's involvement with individuals throughout the book, we soon learn that experiencing God takes a person on a convoluted journey. In Jeremiah, the reader has access to the prophet's spiritual journal, in which he testifies to great moments, such as when he experienced God's presence (20:11). When he was about to be lynched (26:7-24), God rescued him through the agency of the palace officials. Jeremiah had the experience of being a divine spokesman, speaking with God-given authority (15:16). Jeremiah's experience of God was also uncertain and confusing at times. Like John the Baptist, who during his imprisonment felt bewildered about what Jesus was doing, Jeremiah asked how a God of justice could allow the troubles inflicted on him, even by his own people (11:18-23). Worse, Jeremiah sometimes felt forsaken, even by God. In his laments, the prophet complained about God's absence (15:18). He became so disillusioned at times that he spoke as one for whom life had no meaning and even wished for utter annihilation (20:14-18). The prophet's diary discloses the tensions that emerge for someone engaged with God.

Most of the book probes the experience of a community with its God. The people of Judah, God's people, experienced God as an *inviting God*. God urges all Israel to turn from evil and return to God, their covenant partner (3:11-14; 3:19-22a). With passion, intensity, and considerable personal pain, God speaks as a husband inviting his unfaithful spouse to be reconciled to him. God reasons with his people, elaborating the specific parameters of what he requires from them (2:1–4:4). The tears of the prophet, if not those of God himself, punctuate this appeal.

Because Judah failed to respond, the people soon experienced God as a *threatening God*. He would not let them continue in their evil ways. He threatened them with drought and other catastrophes, including the ominous destruction that would be brought on by the enemy from the north. The projected devastation is described in spine-tingling detail, including the clatter of cavalry, the shouts of captains, and the clashing of swords (6:1-6). The threat is aggravated in its seriousness because it is the venting of God's anger (21:5). That wrath, a major emphasis of the book, is not a vengeful, arbitrary outrage but rather the just outpouring of God's displeasure against a recalcitrant people whose only and repeated answer to him is "No."

Soon, Judah would experience God as a *destructive God*. His was not an empty threat. The details of the siege are first imagined, with the devastation chronicled in broad strokes. The destruction is vast and terrible, like a nuclear winter (4:23-26).

Yet for all its terror, the catastrophe is not as total as might be inferred from the threats. As in the story line of Genesis 1–11, this judgment (like those against Adam and Eve, Cain, the people of the flood, the tower builders) is mellowed by a promise of grace. A remnant would remain alive in the territory, although king, city, and temple would be gone.

Still, God delights in life, not in death, and no one can read Jeremiah without discovering that God is a *saving* God. Deliverance is historically displayed as some people, Jeremiah included, are spared from death from the Babylonians. This is especially affirmed in oracles of salvation to the faithful (e.g., Ebed-melech, 39:16; Baruch, 45:5) and to the nation. The saving acts of God on behalf of his people are depicted most graphically and exuberantly in the so-called Book of Comfort (chs 30–31). Here God is depicted as one who rescues from trouble (31:2-3), and who saves his people and provides for them abundantly. This includes the material abundance of grain, oil, and wine (31:10-14) and the restoration of those separated from home and land (31:15). It is all that the covenant represents, including forgiveness by a gracious God (31:31-34).

Finally, readers of Jeremiah must acknowledge that, as intimate as God is with his own people, he is not thereby unaware of or unconcerned about peoples elsewhere. The oracles about the nations (chs 46–51) depict a God who holds nations large and small accountable to him. So, for example, the superpowers Egypt and Babylon were given elaborate threats. Little is said about what they did wrong, but much is said about the dire things that will result from their wrongdoing (such as Egypt's shame when handed over to the people of the north, 46:24). While the threats against the nations are extensive and dark, the accusations are few and reducible to the common denominator of pride and arrogance (e.g., 50:31; cf. 48:29). Much like Israel, these nations experience God as the *inviting* God (in that God counsels nations for their good, 27:5-11), the *threatening* God (50:35-40), the *destroying* God (51:50-58), and, in more muted tones, the *saving* God (49:6, 39).

**God s Passions and Delights.** The foregoing comments view the book "from below," that is, from the human side of encountering God. The summary verses of Jeremiah 9:23-24, however, present the view "from above" in which God's side of the story is told. Here we learn that God delights in justice, righteousness, and unfailing love. The book of Jeremiah narrates how people experience God, experiences that are made possible by the self-proclaimed identity of the Lord. To be in touch with justice, righteousness, and unfailing love is to hear God's heartbeat. The word "delight" further suggests the affective dimension of the Almighty. God's emotions are strongly emphasized in Jeremiah 2–3, where Israel is portrayed as a faithless and promiscuous spouse whose departure deeply wounds God, her husband and covenant partner. His hurt and his passion for justice, righteousness, and unfailing love are equally intense.

**Justice and Injustice.** Justice and injustice are remarkably pervasive topics in Jeremiah. Among the prophets, Amos and Isaiah are most often associated with concern for justice. Jeremiah is commonly cast as a prophet of the new covenant, or as the prophet given to lamenting. But the data supports Jean-Pierre Prévost in saying that Jeremiah is one of the prophets who "presses furthest the demands for social justice. . . . Of all these prophets [Amos, Hosea, Isaiah], [Jeremiah] is the one who offers the most complete and systematic analysis of social injustice" (1998:89). That discussion of justice and injustice is germane to the people, religious leaders, and civil leaders.

Jeremiah was commissioned to search for one person of integrity in the city of Jerusalem. God said, "If you can find even one just and honest person, I will not destroy the city" (5:1). Jeremiah's search of the lower classes turned up empty, for they didn't know the ways of the Lord (5:4)—God's ways are later characterized as ways of justice (9:24). If Jeremiah hoped that the situation among the upper classes would be better, he was disappointed, for there, too, no one walked in the ways of the Lord. With his focus still on the people, Jeremiah noted that among them were wicked persons, whose homes, like cages of birds, were filled with evil plots. They had become sleek and wealthy, refusing justice to orphans and denying the rights of the poor (5:28). Injustice prevailed between family members who, like the citizenry of Jerusalem, were given to falsehood (9:4-6; cf. 5:2). Two basic conclusions can be drawn: justice has to do with truth and with compassion for the poor. Given God's passion for justice, the prophet raised the banner of justice throughout the land, only to learn that no one would rally to it.

The crucial agenda of justice was laid before the religious leaders, but these also came up short. "Even the priests and prophets are ungodly, wicked men" (23:11). These prophets aligned themselves with evildoers, lived unethically and adulterously, and prophesied falsely. They had not stood in the council of Yahweh (23:18), where the concern is clearly for justice (Ps 82:2-4).

Kings are notable among those castigated for injustice, and none more so than Jehoiakim (609-598 BC). This greedy ruler built an ostentatious, vermillion-painted palace without paying his workers. Jeremiah contrasted him with his father Josiah, who, though he knew the privileges of royalty, interested himself in caring for the poor and knowing the Lord (22:16). In fact, the entire panel of speeches in which Jeremiah assesses the roster of kings within his lifetime opens by setting justice as the standard of measurement. In two parallel segments (21:11-14; 22:1-5) he delineates the requirement that royalty be committed to justice: "Give justice each morning to the people you judge!" (21:12). That general requirement is further defined as defending the interests of the oppressed. Whatever else justice means, it cannot be disassociated from concern for the disadvantaged.

**Righteousness.** The distinction between justice and righteousness is not always clear, and the two words often appear together (Amos 5:24; Isa 5:7; Jer 9:23-24). One useful view is that righteousness pertains to an interior disposition to do what is right (as defined by God), and justice to the actions that flow from this disposition. God is both righteous and just. "You will be in the right, O LORD" (12:1, NRSV; cf. Hebrew tsadiq 'attah [cf. "just" TH6662, ZH7404]; NLT, "LORD, you always give me justice"). Righteousness is a passionate characteristic of the Almighty; he desires people to be righteous and full of integrity.

**Unfailing Love.** God's passion is to extend unfailing love to his people. The term *khesed* [TH2617, ZH2876] carries overtones of love and loyalty, with the staying power of a covenant. Older translations that used the word "mercy" were correct in that *khesed* can also signify the emotional component that motivates and accompanies help for those in need. Recent research points to the term *khesed* as a generous response by a person of means to another who is needy. It is in God's nature to put his resources at the disposal of the disadvantaged.

That aspect of God is set forth early in Jeremiah through the marriage metaphor. God can speak of the happy relationship of love that he and Israel enjoyed during their honeymoon (2:2-3). This affection and attachment on God's part is not episodic but enduring. When Israel grew distant to the point of taking up with other lovers (gods), God in his unfailing love pursued her and invited her back. Accordingly, God's appeals for her to return display strong emotions (3:19-22a).

Later in the book, the language, now more formal, is about covenant. God asks his people to remember his covenant with them (11:6), a covenant that Jeremiah charges they have broken (11:10). A covenant is a formal instrument for displaying and ensuring bondedness. The covenant formula, "I will be your God and you will be my people" appears often in the narrative of the Exodus (Exod 6:7) and in the priestly legislation (Lev 26:12), but in no book so frequently as in Jeremiah (7:23; 11:4; 24:7; 30:22; 31:1, 33; 32:38). This formula represents God's commitment to his people, and his unfailing love is demonstrated by his working to restore that bond despite the stubbornness of his covenant partner. At a high point, God even declares that he will make a new covenant (31:31-34) to maintain this bond and lavish goodness on his people.

God's unfailing love for his people is demonstrated in his many promises to them. He will make good on his gift of land, for example, and even when they are removed from it because of sin, he will eventually return them to it (e.g., 24:6; 30:3; 33:10-11). This was an initial promise to his people, and one that God intends to keep (11:5). In addition, the Book of Comfort (chs 30–31) is filled with prospects of material prosperity, healing of broken relationships, high moments of worship, and spiritual intimacy. Unfailing love is not sloppy love. God's expectation is for his people to obey him (11:7), but his stance toward them is clear: "I have loved you, my people, with an everlasting love. With unfailing love I have drawn you to myself" (31:3).

So large is the Almighty's embrace of love that while it enfolds his people closely to him in covenant, it is sufficiently generous to embrace other peoples as well. So, for example, good things are promised to Moab. For all the evils that God declares upon them, the final word for Moab is that he will restore their fortunes (48:47). To Edom he says, "But I will preserve the orphans who remain among you. Your widows, too, can depend on me for help" (49:11). The Almighty's declaration that he is a God of unfailing love (9:24) is repeatedly and effectively demonstrated both for his people and for other nations.

The Lord's disclosure of his passions and his desire for people to experience him in these dimensions (9:24) captures the heart of this book. These divine priorities speak to every age, including ours, about the ways of God in the world.

OUTLINE

I. Preface (1:1-3)
II. God's Personal Message to Jeremiah (1:4-19)
  A. Jeremiah's Call to Ministry (1:4-10)
  B. Divine Encouragement for Ministry (1:11-19)
III. Sermons Warning of Disaster (2:1-10:25)
  A. A Troubled Marriage (2:1-3:5)
    1. Honeymoon delights (2:1-3)
    2. Law court proceedings (2:4-13)
    3. Probing questions (2:14-37)
    4. Talk of divorce (3:1-5)
  B. Calling Home the Wayward Children (3:6-4:4)
    1. Two guilty sisters (3:6-10)
    2. The first call to fickle Israel: come home (3:11-18)
    3. Children who disappoint God (3:19-21)
    4. Second call to wayward children: come home (3:22-4:4)
  C. Calamity from the North (4:5-6:30)
    1. Sound the alarm (4:5-21)
    2. A land in ruins (4:22-31)
    3. Taking a public poll (5:1-19)
    4. Treachery and trouble (5:20-6:9)
    5. Alert! Invasion imminent (6:10-30)
  D. Sermons about Worship (7:1-8:3)
    1. The Temple sermon (7:1-15)
    2. Censuring worship abuses (7:16-8:3)
  E. A People's Sins, an Enemy's Siege, and a Prophet's Sorrow (8:4-10:25)
    1. Hurtling down the path of sin (8:4-9:2)
    2. No one tells the truth (9:3-26)
    3. A study in contrasts: idols and Yahweh (10:1-25)
IV. Stories about Wrestling with Both People and God (11:1-20:18)
  A. Preaching to People and Protesting before God (11:1-12:17)
    1. Covenant talk (11:1-17)
    2. An endangered prophet (11:18-23)
    3. Audience with the Almighty (12:1-17)

# COMMENTARY ON
# *Jeremiah*

## ◆ I. Preface (1:1–3)

These are the words of Jeremiah son of Hilkiah, one of the priests from the town of Anathoth in the land of Benjamin. ²The LORD first gave messages to Jeremiah during the thirteenth year of the reign of Josiah son of Amon, king of Judah.* ³The LORD's messages continued throughout the reign of King Jehoiakim, Josiah's son, until the eleventh year of the reign of King Zedekiah, another of Josiah's sons. In August* of that eleventh year the people of Jerusalem were taken away as captives.

1:2 The thirteenth year of Josiah's reign was 627 BC.   1:3 Hebrew *In the fifth month*, of the ancient Hebrew lunar calendar. A number of events in Jeremiah can be cross-checked with dates in surviving Babylonian records and related accurately to our modern calendar. The fifth month in the eleventh year of Zedekiah's reign occurred within the months of August and September 586 BC. Also see 52:12 and the note there.

### NOTES

**1:1 Jeremiah.** The name could mean "May the LORD [Yahweh] throw," if the root is *ramah* [TH7411, ZH8227], or more likely, "May the Lord lift up," or even, "The Lord has lifted up," from the root *rum* [TH7311, ZH8123]. Like some other prophets (e.g., Ezek 1:3), Jeremiah was of a priestly line.

**Hilkiah.** It is debatable whether the Hilkiah of 2 Kgs 22:4 is Jeremiah's father.

**Anathoth.** Anathoth, modern Anata, lay three miles northeast of Jerusalem in the region of Benjamin. Here Abiathar, one of two priests in David's time, was exiled by Solomon (1 Kgs 2:26-27).

**1:2 LORD . . . gave messages.** Known technically as the "prophetic revelation formula," this clause in Heb. depicts the *dabar* [TH1697, ZH1821] (message) as a distinct entity, almost as a thing whose coming is an event, a happening (cf. 2:1; 14:1; 21:1; 27:1).

**thirteenth year.** Some see this date, 627 BC, as the date of Jeremiah's birth (1:5) since no oracles are clearly dated between 627 and 609 BC (e.g., Holladay 1989:25-26). Most, however, regard the date as marking the beginning of the prophet's ministry.

**Josiah.** This good king, noted for initiating a spiritual renewal, reigned over Judah for 31 years (640–609 BC; 2 Kgs 21:24).

**1:3 Jehoiakim.** During Jehoahaz's three-month rule, Jeremiah was apparently silent; thus, he is not listed and we read immediately of Jehoiakim, whom Pharaoh Neco put on the throne in place of Jehoahaz, whom he imprisoned. He ruled for eleven years (609–598 BC; 2 Kgs 23:36) and was severely censured by the prophet (Jer 22:13-19; cf. oracles dated to his reign, e.g., 26:1; 36:1).

**the eleventh year of the reign of King Zedekiah.** Zedekiah, Judah's last king, ruled from 597–586 BC. The book of Jeremiah includes oracles subsequent to King Zedekiah's death (586 BC); these are explained as additions by later editors (e.g., chs 40–44).

COMMENTARY

The opening paragraph, the preface to this book, presents a conundrum. On one level, the book's content is attributed to a man named Jeremiah. Like other books, this one is stamped by a personality and shaped by an individual mind. But the second sentence qualifies the first. This book has not one author, but two. God stands behind and beyond the human author, Jeremiah. The prophetic formulas ("The word of the LORD came," e.g., 2:1; 18:5) and messenger formulas ("This is what the LORD says," e.g., 31:15) are constant reminders that the content originates with God. Thus the message partakes of both a divine and a human element, not unlike the dual nature of the incarnate Christ. God superintended the presentation of the message so that the human language formulations corresponded to the divine intent (2 Tim 3:16).

The preface teaches that divine revelation to humans is anchored in history. God's communication comes to us within the flow of human experience with its concomitant politics, significant dates, and key events. The names of the kings Jehoiakim and Zedekiah foreshadow the prophet's role in engaging, admonishing, and challenging them. God's word is grounded in the affairs of human beings living out their days. It was mostly prior to the catastrophe of Jerusalem's capture that Jeremiah spoke God's words to Israel, giving warning and counsel both to civil and religious leaders and to the general public.

◆ II. God's Personal Message to Jeremiah (1:4-19)
   A. Jeremiah's Call to Ministry (1:4-10)

⁴The LORD gave me this message:

⁵"I knew you before I formed you in
   your mother's womb.
Before you were born I set you apart
   and appointed you as my prophet to
   the nations."

⁶"O Sovereign LORD," I said, "I can't speak for you! I'm too young!"

⁷The LORD replied, "Don't say, 'I'm too young,' for you must go wherever I send you and say whatever I tell you. ⁸And don't be afraid of the people, for I will be with you and will protect you. I, the LORD, have spoken!" ⁹Then the LORD reached out and touched my mouth and said,

"Look, I have put my words in your
   mouth!
¹⁰Today I appoint you to stand up
   against nations and kingdoms.
Some you must uproot and tear
   down,
   destroy and overthrow.
Others you must build up
   and plant."

NOTES

1:5 *I knew you.* The Heb. *yada'* [TH3045, ZH3359] indicates intimate familiarity with another person (see Gen 4:1, 17, KJV), as well as possessing information.

*formed.* God formed (*yatsar* [TH3335, ZH3670]) the earth (Isa 45:18, NRSV), as well as the first human (Gen 2:8, KJV). The related noun *yotser* [TH3335A, ZH3450] means "potter" (18:2; cf. Isa 29:16).

*set you apart.* The root *qadash* [TH6942, ZH7727] in the causative (hiphil) form has the sense of making holy—i.e, cleansing, sanctifying, and consecrating (e.g., priests, Exod 20:23-26; temple, 2 Chr 29:5). The term *nabi'* [TH5030, ZH5566] (prophet) is used of Abraham (Gen 20:7), Moses (Deut 34:10), Samuel (1 Sam 3:20), and of the writing prophets such as Isaiah (37:2), Habakkuk (1:1), Zechariah (1:1), and others. Speaking for God was a major function of the *navi'* (Exod 7:1), but prophets were also intercessors (1 Sam 12:23; Jer 14:11) and analysts of their society (Amos 5:7-8).

**1:6 *I'm too young.*** The term *na'ar* [TH5288, ZH5853] can refer to an infant (Exod 2:6), a child just weaned (1 Sam 1:24), or a youth (Gen 37:2); in this context, its nuance may indicate Jeremiah's lack of experience. Almost certainly, given what is known of the length of Jeremiah's ministry, the term here designates a teenager, perhaps 15–18 years old.

**1:8 *don't be afraid.*** The prohibition against fearing the people anticipates later opposition (e.g., his own family and townspeople; Jer 11:21). Fear, rather than youthfulness, may have been the real cause of his hesitation.

***I will be with you.*** This "divine assistance formula" first occurs as a word to Jacob (Gen 28:15) and then to others (e.g., Gideon, Judg 6:12). It is frequent in Jeremiah (15:20; 30:11; 42:11; 46:28; cf. Matt 28:20).

**1:9 *the LORD . . . touched my mouth.*** In the symbolic installation service (cf. Isa 6:7), God further addresses Jeremiah's objection about his inability to speak (cf. Deut 18:18).

**1:10 *uproot and tear down.*** Jeremiah is to be something of a verbal wrecking ball; he will demolish wrong-headed notions and misapplied traditions (cf. 7:1-15). While the book contains reassuring oracles (e.g., chs 30–33), it is more often a critique of the people and their ways than a book about future hope.

***build up and plant.*** This word combination occurs frequently in Jeremiah (18:7-9; 24:6; 31:28; 42:10; 45:4; cf. Ezek 36:36).


COMMENTARY

God's messages frequently address religious or political groups, but that does not mean that God is inattentive to individuals, even before they are born (Jer 1:5; cf. Ps 139:6, 13-16). God is concerned with cosmic galaxies (Ps 113:5, 6, 9) and with the smallest details of human life. God's attentiveness to the unborn is a strong consideration in the debate about abortion, for it means that a fetus is alive and that God knows it as a living person.

God claims a person's life in the full knowledge of who that person is. Many persons called to fulfill a divinely appointed task (and what Christian is not?) recognize, as Paul did, that God's involvement in their lives began very early (Gal 1:15). John Goldingay, a British Old Testament theologian and scholar, chronicled his life in the introduction to one of his books (e.g., "Age 12: decide to learn Greek instead of German"). His first entry reads: "Age 0: chosen, called to be a theologian, born, baptized" (1998:14). Similarly, Wilbur Smith, a twentieth-century preacher, recounts, "One morning when I was standing in my bedroom on the third floor of our home, the Lord suddenly hit me. I wasn't praying. I wasn't weeping for my sins; I was rather perplexed as to what I should do, and the Lord just suddenly said to me, 'You are to go into the Christian ministry.' I can't explain it; it was just overwhelming, and it was from the Lord."

In a culture in which age was revered and youth frequently disparaged as unimportant, God moved counter-culturally by selecting a youth for his service. The Scriptures identify a number of God's servants as young at the time of their calling: Joseph (Gen 37–41), Samuel (1 Sam 2:18–3:21), Daniel (Dan 1:4-7), Mary (Luke 1:27), and Timothy (1 Tim 4:12). The times when God chooses inexperienced and insignificant persons over those who are experienced and favored are so numerous as to call for careful reflection, especially by leaders and institutions.

When God called Jeremiah, he hesitated. One would think that the initial human response to God's commissioning would be exuberance, but more often there is hesitation or even refusal (cf. Moses, Exod 3:1-12; Isaiah, Isa 6:1-13; Ezekiel, Ezek 1:28–3:11). The objections are frequently superficial. That Jeremiah's objection misses the heart of the matter is suggested by God's remonstrance, "Don't be afraid." With that remark, God identifies the unspoken excuse as fear. God does not ignore the objections raised; he answers them (cf. 1 Sam 16:1-3; Acts 9:10-16).

Jeremiah's ministry was not grounded in human abilities, but in God's sovereign knowledge and purposes (1:5). God takes the initiative in calling someone to ministry; he also takes ownership of the follow-through (1:7). He will not leave his servant stranded, but promises direction and protection, as well as the content of the message and the know-how to present it. God does not call people without also equipping them.

Jeremiah's call includes a ministry to the nations (1:10). It may have been the projected scope of his ministry that was the reason for his reluctance. Most prophets were appointed to address Israel; a few such as Obadiah and Nahum had other nations as their primary subject matter. Jeremiah was an international prophet as the later oracles indicate (46–51). Overall, his job consisted of demolition activities, not unlike that of a wrecker ball. He hammered away at false theologies, for example (7:3). Yet after his many critiques and dire warnings with the threat of exile, there would be a time to be constructive. Israel would return to her land (24:6). His message would yet be one of hope and comfort (cf. 30–33).

◆   ## B. Divine Encouragement for Ministry (1:11-19)

¹¹Then the LORD said to me, "Look, Jeremiah! What do you see?"

And I replied, "I see a branch from an almond tree."

¹²And the LORD said, "That's right, and it means that I am watching,* and I will certainly carry out all my plans."

¹³Then the LORD spoke to me again and asked, "What do you see now?"

And I replied, "I see a pot of boiling water, spilling from the north."

¹⁴"Yes," the LORD said, "for terror from the north will boil out on the people of this land. ¹⁵Listen! I am calling the armies of the kingdoms of the north to come to Jerusalem. I, the LORD, have spoken!

"They will set their thrones
at the gates of the city.
They will attack its walls
and all the other towns of Judah.
¹⁶I will pronounce judgment
on my people for all their evil—
for deserting me and burning incense
to other gods.
Yes, they worship idols made with
their own hands!

<sup>17</sup> "Get up and prepare for action.
  Go out and tell them everything
    I tell you to say.
  Do not be afraid of them,
    or I will make you look foolish in
    front of them.
<sup>18</sup> For see, today I have made you strong
  like a fortified city that cannot be
  captured,

like an iron pillar or a bronze wall.
  You will stand against the whole
    land—
  the kings, officials, priests, and
    people of Judah.
<sup>19</sup> They will fight you, but they will fail.
  For I am with you, and I will take
  care of you.
  I, the LORD, have spoken!"

1:12 The Hebrew word for "watching" *(shoqed)* sounds like the word for "almond tree" *(shaqed)*.

NOTES

**1:11-12 *What do you see?*** God's approach is sometimes interactive (cf. 24:3; Amos 7:7-8; 8:1-2).

*I see a branch.* A word play is evident in the Heb.: *shaqed* [TH8247, ZH9196] (almond branch) and *shoqed* [TH8245, ZH9193] (watching). The almond tree is appropriately called *shaqed* since it is the first of the nut and fruit trees to blossom (figuratively "peek, watch") in the spring. The *shaqed* blossom (watcher) confirmed visually that God would be on the lookout to ensure that his announcement (*dabar* [TH1697, ZH1821], "word"), linked either to Jeremiah's call (1:4-10) or to the nation's future, would be fulfilled (see 1:13).

**1:13 *again.*** Usually *again* (lit., "a second time") is understood as indicative of a new vision that directly follows the vision of the almond branch. Lundbom (1999:227-230, 238) proposes that the call vision of 1:4-10 concludes with the story of the almond branch in 1:12, thus making the second vision of the boiling pot a sequel to the first vision. Support for this view is found in Heb. paragraphing and thematic fit. The first vision is primarily about Jeremiah's vocation; the second concerns the substance of Jeremiah's message, so that the "word" over which God watches (and which he guarantees) concerns the coming enemy (1:14-15).

*pot of boiling water, spilling from the north.* The boiling pot, presumably over an outdoor stone firepit, may have been in close proximity to the almond tree, also in the courtyard.

**1:14 *terror from the north.*** Invasions of Israel came either from the south (e.g., from Egypt), or from the north (e.g., Assyria, Babylon). The desert to the east spelled doom for travelers, so merchants and armies from the east followed the river routes and entered the land of Israel from the north. The unidentified enemy from the north was earlier thought to be the Scythian people. The current consensus is that this indefinite designation, here and certainly later in the book, refers to the Babylonians (25:9; cf. 6:1, 22; 10:22). Alternatively, the "terror from the north" may be Yahweh or something related to his dwelling place (cf. E. H. Roshwalb 1998; D. J. Reimer 1989).

**1:15 *They will set their thrones at the gates of the city.*** This announcement anticipates the later Babylonian occupation of the city (39:3).

**1:16 *for all their evil.*** The evil of deserting God is singled out early in the book (2:13). There will be more than one diatribe against idolatry (7:17 20; 7:30–8:3), sometimes delivered with scathing sarcasm (10:1-16).

**1:17 *prepare for action.*** This lit. means "fasten your belt," in the sense of girding oneself for war. This is appropriate to the following job description with its adversarial tone (1:18).

*Go out and tell them.* Several phrases from the "calling" section (1:4-10) are echoed in this segment (1:11-19). The directive "say whatever I tell you" of 1:7 is repeated in 1:17, and "Do not be afraid of them" in 1:17 echoes a similar earlier command (1:8). The assistance formula, "I will be with you," is found in both sections (1:8, 19), as is the signature statement *ne'um Yahweh* [TH5002/3068, ZH5536/3378], cf. "says/LORD" and "I, the LORD, have spoken" (1:8, 19).

**1:18** *fortified city . . . iron pillar . . . bronze wall.* These are images of defense and solidity (cf. 15:20). Jeremiah's ministry will be characterized by contests and struggles with people in authority.

## COMMENTARY

As a follow-up to his call, God gave Jeremiah visions (1:11-16) and a directive (1:17-19; see notes on 1:13). Both were divine encouragements. Within the frame of the book, both the vision and the directive are programmatic—they are about large threats and large promises.

**Two Visions (1:11-16).**   If the entire chapter is regarded as a unified account of a one-day event, one can imagine Jeremiah's contemplating the divine call as he strolled in the courtyard or in the orchard. There God engaged the prophet in dialogue about a blossoming almond branch. Questions have a way of pinning down rambling thoughts, and a memorable place, or even an object such as a branch, can be a significant hook on which to hang promises. Conceivably, each year in the spring when the prophet saw a blossoming almond branch, he would remember that God was taking care of matters and that he would fulfill his word, both the promises and the threats. Whatever his misgivings, Jeremiah would be reassured about God's credibility.

In a second divine-human interaction concerning a boiling pot, God gave Jeremiah a clue about the content of his message by filling in some details of his job description. In much the same way, other prophets were helped to understand what lay ahead at the time of their call (Isa 6:9-13; cf. Ezek 2:1-10). The message might be grim, but the prophet was encouraged by the reliability of a God who would be watching over his word.

God's punitive action, as Jeremiah would insist throughout his career, was not capricious or triggered by temperamental whims. If there was judgment in the overall forecast, it was because the people's evil called for it. Jeremiah will harp on the theme of the people's deserting the Lord (2:13, 19; 5:7, 19; 16:11; 17:13). The remedy for the impending catastrophe is a return to God, so it is not surprising if Jeremiah's message is punctuated with shrill calls for the people's repentance.

**A Divine Directive (1:17-19).**   God's directive to Jeremiah was to put aside his fear and get going. "Don't lose your nerve because of them, lest I shatter your nerve right before them." Jeremiah would stand firm, because God took responsibility for outfitting the prophet for his job. God would work in advance of the problems the prophet would encounter, not by forestalling the problems (though that was an option) but by empowering his servant.

## ◆ III. Sermons Warning of Disaster (2:1-10:25)
### A. A Troubled Marriage (2:1-3:5)
#### 1. Honeymoon delights (2:1-3)

The LORD gave me another message. He said, 2"Go and shout this message to Jerusalem. This is what the LORD says:

"I remember how eager you were to please me
as a young bride long ago,
how you loved me and followed me

even through the barren wilderness.
3 In those days Israel was holy to the LORD,
the first of his children.*
All who harmed his people were declared guilty,
and disaster fell on them.
I, the LORD, have spoken!"

2:3 Hebrew *the firstfruits of his harvest.*

NOTES

2:2 *Go and shout.* Private directives to the prophet also occur elsewhere (3:12; 13:1; 19:l; 28:13; 34:2).

*I remember how eager you were to please me . . . how you loved me and followed me.* This expression speaks of (1) eagerness to please, devotion (*khesed* [TH2617, ZH2876]; cf. Hos 6:4, 6); (2) love (*'ahavah* [TH160, ZH173]; cf. Deut 11:1); and (3) faithful following (*halak* [TH1980, ZH2143]; cf. Jer 2:5, 25).

2:3 *All who harmed his people.* The Amalekites and the Midianites were among those who came to grief (Exod 17:8ff; Num 25:16ff).

COMMENTARY

The metaphor of marriage between God and Israel is first developed in Hosea, from which Jeremiah frequently borrows (Hos 1-3; especially 2:14-16). The "marriage ceremony" is properly placed at Sinai, where God "proposed" and Israel responded, "We will certainly do everything the LORD asks of us" (Exod 24:7; cf. Jer 19:8; for studies of the marriage metaphor, see Ortlund 1996 and Abma 1999).

William Holladay (1976:123-142) has characterized 2:2 as a "seed oracle," since the theme of marriage dominates the opening chapters. This marriage imagery is daring because sexual language pervaded the neighboring Canaanite Baal religion. In marriage, the primary commitment is to loyalty, a key issue in what immediately follows. The New Testament develops the image of marriage between Christ and the Church (Eph 5:25-33).

That Jeremiah's lead oracle should revolve around delight, as in a marriage, emphasizes God's intent to lead his people into joy (32:40-41). Though not elaborated, the positive aspects of the wilderness honeymoon era might be (1) Israel's commitment to fully observe God's ways (Exod 24:7); (2) the absence of idolatry, except for the short-lived golden calf incident (Exod 32); (3) sharing God's will and purpose at Sinai; (4) the absence of interference by neighboring peoples with their temptations to reach for substitute deities; (5) the people's loyalty in constructing the tabernacle; and (6) progress toward the land of promise.

## ◆ 2. Law court proceedings (2:4-13)

4Listen to the word of the LORD, people of Jacob—all you families of Israel! 5This is what the LORD says:

"What did your ancestors find wrong
with me
that led them to stray so far from
me?
They worshiped worthless idols,
only to become worthless
themselves.
6They did not ask, 'Where is the LORD
who brought us safely out of Egypt
and led us through the barren
wilderness—
a land of deserts and pits,
a land of drought and death,
where no one lives or even travels?'

7"And when I brought you into a
fruitful land
to enjoy its bounty and goodness,
you defiled my land and
corrupted the possession I had
promised you.
8The priests did not ask,
'Where is the LORD?'
Those who taught my word ignored me,
the rulers turned against me,
and the prophets spoke in the name of
Baal,
wasting their time on worthless idols.

9Therefore, I will bring my case against
you,"
says the LORD.
"I will even bring charges against your
children's children
in the years to come.
10"Go west and look in the land of
Cyprus*;
go east and search through the land
of Kedar.
Has anyone ever heard of anything
as strange as this?
11Has any nation ever traded its gods for
new ones,
even though they are not gods at
all?
Yet my people have exchanged their
glorious God*
for worthless idols!
12The heavens are shocked at such a
thing
and shrink back in horror and
dismay,"
says the LORD.
13"For my people have done two evil
things:
They have abandoned me—
the fountain of living water.
And they have dug for themselves
cracked cisterns
that can hold no water at all!

2:10 Hebrew *Kittim.* 2:11 Hebrew *their glory.*

NOTES

2:5 *What did your ancestors find wrong with me?* Questions are prominent throughout this segment (e.g., 2:11, 14, 17, 18, 21, 23, 24, 28, 29, 31; 3:1, 5). Among the several derogatory words for idols is the term *hebel* [TH1892, ZH2039] (empty, worthless), which is similar in sound to "Baal." With this in mind, one could render the last sentence of this verse, "They worshiped empty-headed idols which in turn made them empty headed."

2:6 *They did not ask.* The ancestors were dismissive of God's power (e.g., the Exodus) and protective guidance (e.g., the wilderness travels).

2:7 *defiled my land.* The land could become unclean (cf. 3:1, 2, 9; 16:18) through the people's failure to deal properly with criminals (Deut 21:23), through child sacrifice (Ps 106:38), because of marriage irregularities (Deut 24:1-4; Jer 3:1), through idolatry (Ezek 36:18), and by sexual sins of incest and sodomy (Lev 18:19-30).

2:8 *priests did not ask.* The issue is their orientation, not their need for information (cf. Mal 2:7).

**2:9 I will bring my case.** A rib [TH7379, ZH8190] (case, lawsuit) entailed accusations by the plaintiff, a call for witnesses, a recital of God's acts (often), and a judicial sentence (cf. Hos 4:1).

**2:10 Cyprus.** The islands (Heb. kittiyyim [TH3794, ZH4183]) of the Mediterranean represented distant countries to the west.

**Kedar.** Kedar was far to the east in northern Arabia. Both Cypress and Kedar were known for the bartering skills of their people (cf. 2:11).

**2:13 cracked cisterns.** Cisterns dug into porous limestone were lined with plaster.

COMMENTARY

From the joys of a honeymoon, the narrative plunges into the adversarial relationship of a dysfunctional marriage and the subsequent court proceedings. The opening question is shocking: Would God commit injustice? This rhetorical question "forces the listener to conceive the inconceivable—that Yahweh might have a defect" (Holladay 1986:85). The reflective question is filled with pathos; God has an emotional side (cf. Gen 6:6) and he now has ingrates on his hands—some thanks for his exertions on their behalf!

In this section, God resorts to straightforward calculation. Israel's actions are repeatedly characterized as being of no benefit or profit. It is clearly unreasonable to trade a gushing water supply (God), from which one may effortlessly secure water, for self-made cisterns that are cracked and leaking. Why would anyone foolishly shortchange himself by such wrong-headed decisions?

Although God is pained like a lover spurned by his chosen bride, he also functions as a litigant who will hold his spouse accountable before a court of law. Israel may ignore him as her lover. She will find, however, that she cannot escape facing him as a plaintiff in court. God, as lover, benefactor, or plaintiff, is not to be trifled with.

◆     3. Probing questions (2:14-37)

14 "Why has Israel become a slave?
    Why has he been carried away as
        plunder?
15 Strong lions have roared against him,
    and the land has been destroyed.
The towns are now in ruins,
    and no one lives in them anymore.
16 Egyptians, marching from their cities
        of Memphis* and Tahpanhes,
    have destroyed Israel's glory and
        power.
17 And you have brought this upon
        yourselves
    by rebelling against the LORD your
        God,
    even though he was leading you
        on the way!

18 "What have you gained by your
        alliances with Egypt
    and your covenants with Assyria?
What good to you are the streams
        of the Nile*
    or the waters of the Euphrates
        River?*
19 Your wickedness will bring its own
        punishment.
    Your turning from me will shame
        you.
You will see what an evil, bitter thing
        it is
    to abandon the LORD your God and
        not to fear him.
    I, the Lord, the LORD of Heaven's
        Armies, have spoken!

²⁰ "Long ago I broke the yoke that
    oppressed you
and tore away the chains of your
    slavery,
but still you said,
    'I will not serve you.'
On every hill and under every green
    tree,
    you have prostituted yourselves by
    bowing down to idols.
²¹ But I was the one who planted you,
    choosing a vine of the purest stock—
    the very best.
How did you grow into this corrupt
    wild vine?
²² No amount of soap or lye can make
    you clean.
    I still see the stain of your guilt.
    I, the Sovereign LORD, have spoken!

²³ "You say, 'That's not true!
    I haven't worshiped the images
    of Baal!'
But how can you say that?
    Go and look in any valley in the land!
Face the awful sins you have done.
    You are like a restless female camel
    desperately searching for a mate.
²⁴ You are like a wild donkey,
    sniffing the wind at mating time.
Who can restrain her lust?
    Those who desire her don't need
    to search,
    for she goes running to them!
²⁵ When will you stop running?
    When will you stop panting after
    other gods?
But you say, 'Save your breath.
    I'm in love with these foreign gods,
    and I can't stop loving them now!'

²⁶ "Israel is like a thief
    who feels shame only when he gets
    caught.
They, their kings, officials, priests, and
    prophets—
    all are alike in this.
²⁷ To an image carved from a piece of
    wood they say,
    'You are my father.'

To an idol chiseled from a block of
    stone they say,
    'You are my mother.'
They turn their backs on me,
    but in times of trouble they cry
    out to me,
    'Come and save us!'
²⁸ But why not call on these gods you
    have made?
When trouble comes, let them save
    you if they can!
For you have as many gods
    as there are towns in Judah.
²⁹ Why do you accuse me of doing wrong?
    You are the ones who have
    rebelled,"
    says the LORD.
³⁰ "I have punished your children,
    but they did not respond to my
    discipline.
You yourselves have killed your
    prophets
    as a lion kills its prey.

³¹ "O my people, listen to the words of
    the LORD!
Have I been like a desert to Israel?
Have I been to them a land of
    darkness?
Why then do my people say, 'At last
    we are free from God!
    We don't need him anymore!'
³² Does a young woman forget her
    jewelry?
Does a bride hide her wedding dress?
Yet for years on end
    my people have forgotten me.

³³ "How you plot and scheme to win your
    lovers.
Even an experienced prostitute
    could learn from you!
³⁴ Your clothing is stained with the blood
    of the innocent and the poor,
    though you didn't catch them
    breaking into your houses!
³⁵ And yet you say,
    'I have done nothing wrong.
    Surely God isn't angry with me!'
But now I will punish you severely

because you claim you have not
sinned.
36 First here, then there—
you flit from one ally to another
asking for help.
But your new friends in Egypt will
let you down,

just as Assyria did before.
37 In despair, you will be led into
exile
with your hands on your heads,
for the LORD has rejected the nations
you trust.
They will not help you at all.

2:16 Hebrew *Noph.*  2:18a Hebrew *of Shihor,* a branch of the Nile River.  2:18b Hebrew *the river?*

### NOTES

**2:14** *Why has Israel become a slave?* In the Hebrew, there is another question within this one about the lack of freedom: "How come you are a servant in your own house?" Her identity as a slave contrasts with her earlier identity as a bride (2:2).

**2:15** *lions.* This is a reference to political empires such as Assyria or, as some suggest, Babylon (Holladay 1986:93).

**2:16** *Memphis.* This is the capital of Egypt's Old and Middle kingdoms; it was some fourteen miles south of Cairo on the Nile.

*Tahpanhes.* This city was on the border of the eastern Nile delta region.

*destroyed Israel's glory and power.* The Heb. idiom is graphic and sarcastic: Egyptians have shaved (grazed off) the crown of the head (Israel's grassy highland plateaus). Figuratively, Egypt has removed Israel's king, the governing head.

**2:18** *What have you gained?* The Nile is the lifeline of Egypt, just as the Euphrates is the main river of Assyria. Drinking at the waters of Egypt and Assyria metaphorically contrasts the resources of these two countries with the fountain of living waters, the Lord (2:13).

**2:19** *Your wickedness will bring its own punishment.* Four key Heb. words appear in an a/b/b/a pattern: (a) will discipline (*yasar* [TH3256, ZH3579]) you; (b) your wrongdoing (*ra'ah* [TH7451B, ZH8288]); (b) your apostasy (*meshubah* [TH4878, ZH5412]); (a) will correct (*yakakh* [TH3198, ZH3519]) you.

**2:20** *Long ago I broke the yoke.* Holladay (1986:52) argues from context and from archaic personal endings for "you broke your yoke" (cf. NRSV, NIV). Bozak (1996), however, endorses God as the first person subject. Following this, the people's response is straightforward but jarring: *I will not serve.* Jeremiah frequently cites people's speech—more than 100 times, by one count (e.g., 2:6, 8, 20, 23, 27 [3 times] 25, 31, 35 [2 times]). For studies of Israel's harlotry in Jeremiah, see Ortlund (1996:83-99).

**2:21** *choosing a vine.* For imagery of Israel as a vine, see Ps 80:8 and Isa 5:1-6.

**2:22** *soap or lye.* The ancient cleansing agents were soda, nitre, and potash. Nitre (*nether* [TH5427, ZH6003]) was likely an import from Egypt, and potash (*borith* [TH1287, ZH1383]) was available locally and was made from the ash of the soda plant (Holladay 1986:99).

**2:25** *When will you stop running?* The tone may be one of inquiry, but the grammar is in the imperative: "refrain from running about barefoot; discipline your thirst."

*Save your breath.* Holladay (1971:126) sees *no'ash lo'* [TH2976, ZH3286], which is rendered here politely, as an interjection having the force of "to hell with it" (cf. 18:12).

**2:29** *rebelled.* In its secular usage, the term *pesha'* [TH6588, ZH7322] (revolt, breach) is associated with political insubordination and the revolt of vassal states (1 Kgs 12:19).

**2:30** *they did not respond to my discipline.* Lit., "they did not receive correction" (*musar lo' laqakhu* [TH4148, ZH4592] "discipline"). The expression, which may have a wisdom setting

(Prov 1:3; 24:32, NRSV), occurs three times in Jeremiah as an accusation of disobedience and recalcitrance (cf. 2:30; 7:28; 32:33 in Heb.).

**2:31** *listen to the words of the* LORD. Lit., "see the word of Yahweh," perhaps in the sense of perceiving it. God's questions are ironic, for he has been living water to them, not a desert (2:13), and a light of glory (2:11), not darkness.

**2:32** *years on end.* This possibly refers to the situation prior to Josiah's reform, or to the rule of Manasseh (seventh century BC; 2 Kgs 21:11). However, spiritual amnesia might be said to characterize Israel's total history (cf. 2:8).

**2:33** *How you plot.* The twist is sarcastic: "How nicely you go about seeking love!"

**2:36** *Egypt . . . Assyria.* Israel often courted both of these world powers for political security.

*will let you down.* The Heb. here involves more than political disappointment; it includes embarrassment, being shamed (*bosh* [TH954, ZH1017]).

**2:37** *your hands on your heads.* Though some take the gesture to be one of shame (e.g., Kruger 1996); others hold it to be a gesture by mourners.

COMMENTARY

God's questions thread their way through this segment (cf. 2:14, 18, 21). As in God's question to Adam, "Where are you?" these questions are not aimed at gathering information, but at confronting those questioned about their actions.

The first question (2:14) calls attention to invasions by foreign powers, such as those by the Assyrians, beginning with Tiglath-pileser III (744–727 BC; 2 Kgs 15:29) and continuing through the pillage and capture of Samaria under Shalmaneser V (722 BC; 2 Kgs 17:5). A century later, the Egyptians came through the land of Israel headed toward Carchemish, where they hoped to block a Babylonian advance. Egypt controlled Israel, deposing Israel's king Jehoahaz and placing Jehoiakim on the throne as an Egyptian vassal. Should not these incursions by foreign powers and the resulting troubled times (2:17) bring about some self-examination on Israel's part? Why flirt with foreign alliances? The evil of walking out on God quickly led to illicit associations with Canaanite deities and to the adoption of flabby morals in which prostitution was tolerated (2:20).

God was perplexed about what had gone wrong (2:21), for he had acted with the utmost care (cf. Isa 5:1-7). What accounted for such a disappointing turn of events? The very notion that God might be blameworthy points to the gravity of the situation (cf. 2:5).

In 2:23-30, God is seen as a prosecuting attorney, who becomes more aggressive in pressing charges and in refuting the defendant's position. Israel's denial of her involvement with Baal, a young deity in the Canaanite pantheon around whom a fertility cult was built, flies in the face of evidence. Israel had, in fact, built shrines to Baal (19:5), burnt incense to Baal (11:13), sworn by Baal (12:16), and prophesied in the name of Baal (2:8). Israel had bowed to wood and stone, and, in keeping with animistic religion, even ascribed her origin to these immaterial objects! Israel's forthright statement was the final incriminating evidence: "I have fallen in love with these foreign gods" (2:25).

But the prosecution was interested in more than establishing a "guilty" verdict. God, as prosecutor, was still Israel's "husband." Desiring to effect a change in Israel's behavior, God shifted to the tactic of shaming Israel. In an honor/shame culture, to be considered a source of shame would be quite embarrassing (2:24-28). Shameful behavior calls a person's ability into question, and, more seriously, is cause for diminishing respect. A frustrated husband might use embarrassment to win back an estranged spouse.

In the last part of this section (2:31-37), we see analogies formed as questions. God reflectively asks himself whether he had failed his people by being desert-like (boring?) to them, or even worse, whether he was somehow to blame for their confusion and darkness (2:31). The passage reads like a counselor trying to figure out where a problem lies and finding the problem so unusual that it defies common explanations.

The allusion to brides and weddings is apt because it keeps the marriage analogy with which God's speech began at the forefront (2:32; cf. 2:2-3). A bride is identified by her apparel to such an extent that for her to overlook her bridal gown would be unthinkable. Just so, for Israel to forget the God who is so critical to her identity was beyond belief.

After this reverie, God's speech becomes direct and adversarial, charging that Israel was preoccupied with other lovers. Indeed, so keen was she in securing their favors that a prostitute could learn a technique or two from her. Earlier accusations were about religious defection (2:32); God now points to sins of social injustice. Innocents have been killed (2:34). Israel has loved neither God nor neighbor. Yet Israel claims she has not sinned. Failure to see evil for what it is is itself an evil.

◆     ## 4. Talk of divorce (3:1-5)

"If a man divorces a woman
and she goes and marries someone
    else,
he will not take her back again,
    for that would surely corrupt the
    land.
But you have prostituted yourself with
    many lovers,
    so why are you trying to come back
    to me?"
says the LORD.
2 "Look at the shrines on every hilltop.
    Is there any place you have not been
    defiled
by your adultery with other gods?
You sit like a prostitute beside the
    road waiting for a customer.

You sit alone like a nomad in the
    desert.
You have polluted the land with your
    prostitution
    and your wickedness.
3 That's why even the spring rains have
    failed.
For you are a brazen prostitute and
    completely shameless.
4 Yet you say to me,
    'Father, you have been my guide
    since my youth.
5 Surely you won't be angry forever!
    Surely you can forget about it!'
So you talk,
    but you keep on doing all the evil
    you can."

NOTES

**3:1** *you have prostituted yourself with many lovers.* This refers metaphorically to attachments to deities other than Yahweh; possibly it is a double entendre that includes physical acts of sexual adultery.

*so why are you trying to come back to me?* Scholarly opinion varies as to whether this is a forthright statement or is intended as a question. The Heb. *shob* [TH7725, ZH8740] is a verbal infinitive absolute which leaves the subject unspecified. The LXX reads "will [she] return to him?" Holladay (1986:57) translates, "and to think you would return to me!" Lundbom (1999:298), like the NRSV, renders, "and would you return to me?" The immediate context might suggest that, given the law on divorce, the possibility of Israel's return to God was legally out of the question (so Holladay 1986:113; Clements 1988:33). But it is preferable, since there are invitations elsewhere for Israel to return to God (3:22), to read the sentence not as a question or sarcastic innuendo ("to think you would return to me!") but as an assertion; in a stunning move, God invites Israel to return to him!

**3:2** *Look at the shrines on every hilltop.* The original is more graphic: "see the tracks, the deeply worn ruts (*shepayim* [TH8205, ZH9155]) that you have followed."

*sit alone like a nomad.* Lit., "sit alone like an Arab." This points to the practice of waylaying people for financial or other gain. From the context, it would seem that, contrary to custom, a lone woman (Israel) was intent on ambushing men for her lustful purposes.

**3:3** *the spring rains have failed.* Hosea forcefully makes the point that sins—adultery in this case (either spiritual defection from Yahweh or sexual infidelity to a spouse)—have an adverse effect on the environment (Hos 4:1-3; cf. Jer 2:7).

*you are a brazen prostitute.* This is a rendering of the more literal, "you have the mark (*metsakh* [TH4696, ZH5195]) of a woman of prostitution."

COMMENTARY

The marriage analogy that began in the seed oracle (2:2-3) and continued with questions about wedding dress and jewelry (2:30-37) here concludes with discussion about divorce (3:1-5). If in 2:30-37 God appeared as a frustrated husband and counselor, he is now depicted as a lawyer reaching for precedent. This precedent is found in a divine regulation about divorce from Deuteronomy 24:1-4.

Jeremiah's use of Deuteronomy is a striking case of intertextuality—that is, of employing an earlier text in a new context with changed meanings (cf. Fishbane 1985:307-312). A text about human marriage and divorce becomes a text about God and Israel. The Deuteronomy text forbade a first husband to take his first wife, whom he once divorced, back to himself after she had remarried and once again became available by her new husband's death or a second divorce. The law presupposed that the husband had initiated the divorce, but in Jeremiah, it is Israel who is separating from God. While there is no explicit statement of Israel divorcing God, her actions of adultery and the fact that she has "abandoned the LORD" (2:19) suggest a divorce mentality. In the earlier law, the divorced woman remarried legitimately, but Israel had quite illegally and immorally allied herself with other lovers. The law from the Torah addresses physical concerns; God's speech in Jeremiah is about spiritual matters. The law spoke of a physical return; now the return was that of repentance. Most startling is that whereas the law precluded the possibility of a return once the divorce was in effect, God suspended his own regulation and in grace invited Israel to return!

Although the discussion is about legalities, the speech is charged with emotion. God, as the marriage partner, was deeply wounded by Israel's behavior. The question, "Where have you not been defiled by your adulteries?" is accusatory, of course, but it is also a question of pathos. By flirting elsewhere, Israel had spurned her covenantal spouse. It had not been a clandestine affair; Israel did not even care how publicly her behavior was known. She was not overcome by temptation—she sought it out! Her brazenness in search of intimate pleasures outside those offered by her mate reflected badly on God, her spouse. Divorce is almost always painful for both parties, but here Israel seems nonchalant, almost flippant. By contrast, God is very troubled.

Israel's response to God is odd. The change in metaphor by which Israel calls God "Father" is strange. Jeremiah uses both metaphors—marriage and parenting—to describe a bonded relationship. Their use in such close proximity reminds us that these are metaphors, and that neither should be pressed too far. That Israel addresses God as a parent perhaps suggests that she has not understood the covenant and the resulting partnership, but sees herself as a minor, not to be held responsible.

The situation is ironic. The flirting wife seeks to smooth over any ruffles created by her misbehavior with sweet talk, overplaying the husband's role as though he were a parent. In addressing God as Father, Israel plays on the indulgence of a father and hopes thereby to sidestep the jealousy of a thwarted lover. The hope that God as Father will be soft in responding to her dalliance is perhaps encouraged by God's past patience and tolerance (e.g., Judah had thus far escaped foreign invasion). Judah counts on God's being a permissive parent who will not bring her to account.

Accountability is part of the equation, however, whether in a marriage or in a parent-child relationship. Already, the effects of her moral evil had set in. The land was polluted by the sin of spiritual infidelity, as it was also polluted by sins of murder, deceit, violence, incest, and social injustice (2:34; 3:2). The connection between human evil and the harm brought to the soil may not be immediately clear, but one link is given in this text. As a punishment for sin, God withheld the rain (3:3; cf. Lev 26:19; 1 Kgs 17-19; Amos 4:6ff), so the land experienced drought.

◆    ## B. Calling Home the Wayward Children (3:6–4:4)
### 1. Two guilty sisters (3:6–10)

⁶During the reign of King Josiah, the LORD said to me, "Have you seen what fickle Israel has done? Like a wife who commits adultery, Israel has worshiped other gods on every hill and under every green tree. ⁷I thought, 'After she has done all this, she will return to me.' But she did not return, and her faithless sister Judah saw this. ⁸She saw that I divorced faithless Israel because of her adultery. But that treacherous sister Judah had no fear, and now she, too, has left me and given herself to prostitution. ⁹Israel treated it all so lightly—she thought nothing of committing adultery by worshiping idols made of wood and stone. So now the land has been polluted. ¹⁰But despite all this, her faithless sister Judah has never sincerely returned to me. She has only pretended to be sorry. I, the LORD, have spoken!"

NOTES

**3:6 the reign of King Josiah.** Josiah had a long reign (640–609 BC), during which time he initiated a remarkable reform movement (622 BC; 2 Kgs 22–23).

**fickle.** The Heb. is *meshubah* [TH4878, ZH5412], from the root *shub* [TH7725, ZH8740] ("turn"; cf. Holladay 1986:58). "Turncoat Israel" defected from Yahweh and resorted to hills and groves marked by Canaanite Baal shrines.

**3:7 she will return.** Much in this segment plays on the word *shub* [TH7725, ZH8740]. Theologically, "to turn" means to redirect oneself, either toward God (devotion), or away from him (apostasy).

**faithless.** Judah is described as faithless, from the root *bagad* [TH898, ZH953], meaning to "betray," "deal deceitfully," or even "deal treacherously."

**3:8 She saw.** This is the reading of the LXX and Syriac; the Heb. reads, "I saw."

**3:9 Israel treated it all so lightly.** Israel's trivializing of her own behavior (cf. 3:4) is in stark contrast to God's assessment that it is grounds for divorce.

**the land has been polluted.** This was caused by Israel's spiritual adultery (cf. Deut. 24:1 and commentary at 3:1-5).

**3:10 never sincerely . . . only pretended.** Lit., "not with all her heart . . . but in deceit." The Heb. *sheqer* [TH8267, ZH9214] ("lie," "deceit"; here, "pretend") is a signature word for the book, occurring in 34 verses (see, e.g., 5:31; 13:25; 23:14; 29:9).

COMMENTARY

The Lord's accusations are telling, but his invitation for the wayward to return is even more striking. Two discussions about guilt and failure (3:6-10, 3:19-21) are each followed by appeals for a return to God, their spiritual home (3:11-18; 3:22–4:2). The final threat, however, must also be heard (4:3-4).

This block of speeches opens with a question, as did the first block (cf. 2:5). The marriage analogy continues (cf. 2:32; 3:1) as a forceful and graphic way of specifying the evil of spiritual apostasy and conveying God's abhorrence. Ascribing total knowledge of all things to God easily immunizes us from understanding that God's involvement in human decision-making is highly emotional. When a people or an individual treat a spiritual commitment lightly, God is hurt. God had hoped—as humans sometimes hope in the face of contrary evidence—that Israel would return to her true Lover. Instead, God found to his dismay, disappointment, and humiliation that she did not care to return.

God's disappointment was also keen because Israel saw nothing seriously wrong with devoting herself to the worship of wood and stone. Sin has a domino effect. The land, and the natural environment generally, would fail her (3:3). It is painful for a parent, including the divine Parent, to witness a child launched on a path of self-harm. God was saddened over Judah's learning deficit, for she failed to learn from the mistakes of others. Judah's spiritual obtuseness dashed God's high hopes that she would be an improvement over Israel. God's disappointment extended to both sisters—Israel and Judah.

Judah was to have learned from Israel's disregard of covenant loyalty. The language is strong: God divorces faithless Israel (3:8), which raises the question of whether God's covenant with her is terminated. Covenant language plays a significant role in

Jeremiah, and so does language about a broken covenant (e.g., Jer 11:10). Easy generalizations about unconditional covenants may need to be revisited.

◆   ## 2. The first call to fickle Israel: come home (3:11-18)

11Then the LORD said to me, "Even faithless Israel is less guilty than treacherous Judah! 12Therefore, go and give this message to Israel.* This is what the LORD says:

"O Israel, my faithless people,
come home to me again,
for I am merciful.
I will not be angry with you forever.
13Only acknowledge your guilt.
Admit that you rebelled against the
LORD your God
and committed adultery against him
by worshiping idols under every
green tree.
Confess that you refused to listen to
my voice.
I, the LORD, have spoken!

14"Return home, you wayward children,"
says the LORD,
"for I am your master.
I will bring you back to the land of
Israel*—

one from this town and two from
that family—
from wherever you are scattered.
15And I will give you shepherds after my
own heart,
who will guide you with knowledge
and understanding.

16"And when your land is once more filled with people," says the LORD, "you will no longer wish for 'the good old days' when you possessed the Ark of the LORD's Covenant. You will not miss those days or even remember them, and there will be no need to rebuild the Ark. 17In that day Jerusalem will be known as 'The Throne of the LORD.' All nations will come there to honor the LORD. They will no longer stubbornly follow their own evil desires. 18In those days the people of Judah and Israel will return together from exile in the north. They will return to the land I gave their ancestors as an inheritance forever.

3:12 Hebrew *toward the north.*   3:14 Hebrew *to Zion.*

### NOTES

**3:11** *less guilty.* Israel, though fickle (*meshubah* [TH4878, ZH5412]), is more righteous (*tsiddeqah* [TH6663, ZH7405]) than treacherous (*bogedah* [TH898, ZH953]) Judah. There are degrees of guilt.

**3:12** *come home to me again.* The play on words continues: "return (*shub* [TH7725, ZH8740], come home) O ever-turning one" (*meshubah* [TH4878, ZH5412], faithless one).

*merciful.* khasid [TH2623, ZH2883] is the adjectival form of *khesed* [TH2617, ZH2876], a significant OT theological term with overtones of loving-kindness, faithfulness in response to need, and covenant loyalty.

*I will not be angry with you forever.* Two Heb. assertions are conflated in this statement. The first is, lit., "I will not cause my face to fall (hiphil of *napal* [TH5307, ZH5877], "fall") on account of you." This is rendered by Holladay (1986:119) as "I will not frown at you" (cf. NIV). In the second assertion, also idiomatic, the object of "I will not maintain" (*natar* [TH5201A, ZH5758]) is unstated, but is inferred to be "anger" or "grudge." The word *natar* (guard) occurs twice in the DSS (NIDOTTE 3:98; cf. also Ps 103:9; Jer 3:5; Nah 1:2).

**3:13** *acknowledge your guilt.* The Heb. 'awon [TH5771, ZH6411] ("perversity"; here, "guilt") is illustrated by Israel's playing the field of lovers (idols)—lit., "you scattered your ways among strangers" (3:13b).

*you rebelled.* See 2:20. A synonym for *'awon* is *pesha'* [TH6588, ZH7322] (rebel), a term used in the political world of treaties between nations (cf. 1 Kgs 12:19) and illustrated by Israel's refusal to follow her covenant partner (lit., "you have not obeyed my voice," 3:13e, an idiom found eighteen times in Deuteronomy and often in Jeremiah; see, e.g., 32:23).

**3:14 *wayward children.*** The adjective *shobabim* ([TH7726, ZH8743] "ever-turning"; here, "wayward") is from the root *shub* [TH7725, ZH8740] (turn). It is found only in Jeremiah and in Isa 57:17.

*I will bring you back to the land of Israel.* This is the first of many such promises in the book (e.g., 24:6; 31:17; 32:41).

**3:16 *the Ark of the LORD's Covenant.*** This wooden box, inside which were the two tables of the Law and Aaron's rod, was a feature of the tabernacle in the wilderness (Exod 25:10-17). The ark was later located at Shiloh (1 Sam 4:3) and was eventually moved to Jerusalem and situated in Solomon's temple (1 Kgs 8:6). It was probably destroyed along with the Temple in 586 BC. Quite possibly, then, this oracle could be dated after that event.

**3:17 *The Throne of the LORD.*** The ark symbolized God's presence, as the Philistines rightly understood (1 Sam 4:3-4).

COMMENTARY

That God should invite a fickle partner to return to him is amazing, especially in light of the talk about divorce (3:8), the restrictions God had placed on divorce and remarriage, and the humiliation which a spouse's flirtations bring. God overrides his own restrictions (3:1)—indicating his intense desire for reconciliation.

God was steadfast (*khesed* [TH2617, ZH2876]) in his commitment, in contrast to Israel's lack of staying power (see notes, 3:12). The language of *khesed* and the mention of anger hark back to Exodus 34:6, a foundational credo regarding God's identity (cf. Deut 7:9; Neh 1:5). It would be right for Israel to come home since God was Israel's lawful husband and true covenant partner by election and redemption.

God made promises to them about their return. These included a homeland for those in exile (3:14), good leaders (in contrast to the unreliable ones they had before—3:15), a new experience of God's presence as symbolized by the city of Jerusalem, and the unity of the entire people in place of their current disjointedness and dispersion.

The motivation of a person's spiritual choices is critical. Ministers and others who are called to guide people to repentance should look carefully at God's invitational approach. As in Jesus' conversation with the Samaritan woman, the first line of persuasion is positive. He set out an image of a different future, with all its benefits. God's goodness, whether past or promised, can lead to repentance (Rom 2:4). Unfortunately, where promises fail as an incentive, it may be necessary to use threats (Jer 4:4). The second cycle of the longer speech will expand on the directives for return (see comments at 3:22-4:1).

◆     ### 3. Children who disappoint God (3:19-21)

19 "I thought to myself,
   'I would love to treat you as my own
    children!'
I wanted nothing more than to give
   you this beautiful land—
   the finest possession in the world.
I looked forward to your calling me
   'Father,'
and I wanted you never to turn
   from me.
20 But you have been unfaithful to me,
   you people of Israel!

You have been like a faithless wife
   who leaves her husband.
I, the LORD, have spoken."

21 Voices are heard high on the
   windswept mountains,
   the weeping and pleading of
   Israel's people.
For they have chosen crooked
   paths
   and have forgotten the LORD their
   God.

### NOTES

**3:19** *the finest possession.* Lit. "beauty of beauties" if the second word (*tsib'oth*) is construed as a cognate of the first (*tsebi* [TH6643, ZH7382], "ornament," "glory"). If, however, *tseba'oth* [TH6635, ZH7372] (hosts) is read, then the nuance is "the inheritance of the beauty/glory of the hosts of the nations."

**3:20** *like a faithless wife.* The writer betrays no discomfort here or in 3:1-5, where the marriage and the parent metaphor are juxtaposed.

**3:21** *Voices . . . weeping and pleading.* The prophet pictures the misery of a misguided people. The places might be unfamiliar, though the mention of "wind-swept mountains" may allude to the idolatrous hillside practices with their Canaanite shrines.

### COMMENTARY

The image of God as parent is poignantly developed (cf. 3:4; 31:9). Parental pathos and emotional involvement are sketched in two ways. First, like human parents, the divine Parent wanted to develop a bond with the child in the course of the child's growing up. Psychologists describe this as a process of attachment. Second, just as a human parent delights in lavishing good gifts, so did God. God's purpose was to give Israel a homeland. The praises of this special gift would often be sung (cf. Deut 8:7-10).

In the mouth of God, the word "Father" means something very different than when Israel, in her frivolous way, blurts it out (3:4). The profound understanding that God the Father is loving brings a lump to one's throat. But Israel didn't understand this. God was disappointed about forfeiting an anticipated set of pleasures. God was also disappointed at Israel's defection from him. Israel forgot God (2:32) and took a wrong path (2:36). The pain of this unabashed affront is particularly sharp because of the emotional investment God had already made in his partner. Israel's action humiliated God, the covenant partner, by broadcasting the message that someone other than God was more desirable. God's anguish and yearning, while given in anthropomorphic language, is not for that reason to be dismissed. God knows the pain of disappointment firsthand.

◆ **4. Second call to wayward children: come home (3:22–4:4)**

22"My wayward children," says the LORD,
"come back to me, and I will heal
your wayward hearts."

"Yes, we're coming," the people reply,
"for you are the LORD our God.
23Our worship of idols on the hills
and our religious orgies on the
mountains
are a delusion.
Only in the LORD our God
will Israel ever find salvation.
24From childhood we have watched
as everything our ancestors worked
for—
their flocks and herds, their sons and
daughters—
was squandered on a delusion.
25Let us now lie down in shame
and cover ourselves with dishonor,
for we and our ancestors have sinned
against the LORD our God.
From our childhood to this day
we have never obeyed him."

**CHAPTER 4**
1"O Israel," says the LORD,
"if you wanted to return to me,
you could.

You could throw away your detestable
idols
and stray away no more.
2Then when you swear by my name,
saying,
'As surely as the LORD lives,'
you could do so
with truth, justice, and
righteousness.
Then you would be a blessing to the
nations of the world,
and all people would come and
praise my name."

3This is what the LORD says to the people of Judah and Jerusalem:

"Plow up the hard ground of your
hearts!
Do not waste your good seed among
thorns.
4O people of Judah and Jerusalem,
surrender your pride and
power.
Change your hearts before
the LORD,*
or my anger will burn like an
unquenchable fire
because of all your sins.

**4:4** Hebrew *Circumcise yourselves to the LORD, and take away the foreskins of your heart.*

NOTES

**3:22** *come back.* The imperative (lit., "turn," *shub* [TH7725, ZH8740]) is addressed to the back-sliding ones (*shobabim* [TH7726, ZH8743], from the root *shub*). This standard Heb. term for "repent" indicates a directional change, an about-face or a U-turn made by a person headed in a wrong direction.

*heal.* The use of this word characterizes Judah's flighty nature as a disease.

**3:23** *religious orgies.* The noise and hubbub (*hamon* [TH1995, ZH2162]) on the mountains are reminiscent of the prophets of Baal shrieking for their god to hear.

**3:24** *squandered on a delusion.* The Heb. idiom means that the thing of shame (*bosheth* [TH1322A, ZH1425], a reference to the god Baal) had consumed whatever was produced and offered to him (cf. Hos 9:10). Nothing good had come from that experiment.

**3:25** *Let us now lie down in shame.* The repetition of "shame" (*bosheth* [TH1322, ZH1425]) underlines the embarrassment that accompanied the distance that Israel had put between herself and her Lord.

**4:1** *if you wanted to return to me, you could.* Verses 1 and 2 contain an "if . . . then" con-struction, but translations differ on how far the protasis (the "if clause" or condition) extends. The RSV and NIV supply a "when" or an "if" in 4:2 to continue the list of conditions, which leads into a "then" conclusion at the end of 4:2. In that case the entire list following the clause "if you wanted . . ." can be read as a clarification of what returning to God means (so also Unterman 1987:23-36). The readings of the Vulgate, Syriac, and Targum offer another option. These versions omit the conjunction in the phrase *welo' thanud* [TH5110, ZH5653] "and not go astray" (4:1). Thus they limit the protasis (condition) to "throw away your detestable idols," so that the apodosis (conclusion) immediately follows, "[then] you shall not [go astray]." The third option, followed by NLT and preferable, is to consider v. 1 as the protasis (with its *'im*, "if") and v. 2 as the apodosis. Israel's restored integrity and her being a blessing to nations would then be among the results that would follow from her repentance.

**4:2 *swear by my name*.** Departure from idolatry means invoking the Lord God, not the gods represented by the idols. God's original intention was for Israel to be a channel of blessing to the nations (Gen 12:1-3; 18:18; 26:4).

**4:4 *Change your hearts*.** Lit., "circumcise yourselves to the LORD and remove the foreskin of your hearts" (cf. NLT mg). Circumcision was the physical sign of the covenant, an identity marker of one belonging to the Lord (Gen 17:9-11).

***my anger*.** God's wrath, a frequent theme in Jeremiah (15:14; 33:5; cf. 25:15-38), is not released on a whim but for a defined reason, the evil of their deeds.

COMMENTARY

The accusations in the speech of 3:19-21 are followed by God's invitation for his children to return (3:22–4:2), just as in the first cycle the accusations (3:6-10) are followed by an appeal to return (3:11-18). This parallelism reinforces the message.

|  | Jeremiah 3:6–18 | Jeremiah 3:19–4:2 |
|---|---|---|
| Comparison | between Judah and Israel (3:11) | between God's intended relationship with his people and the actual situation (3:19-20) |
| Accusations | adultery (3:8) | faithlessness in marriage (3:20) |
|  | worship of wood and stone (3:9) | betrayal (3:20) |
|  | no interest in returning (3:7) | non-remembrance of God (3:21) |
| Appeal | return (3:14) | return (3:22; 4:1) |
|  | clarification of process (3:13) | clarification of process amplified (3:22–4:2) |
|  | incentive of promises (3:14-18) | incentive of a desired prospect or threat of God's anger (4:2, 4) |

**The Repentance Protocol (3:22b–4:2).** In the first appeal (3:11-18), emphasis is on the incentives for return. The second appeal (3:22b–4:2) focuses on the acceptable process for doing so. Whether the "confession" of 3:22b-25 is the prophet's (or God's) wishful thinking, a bona fide statement by the people, or part of a repentance ritual, the verses clarify what repentance looks like. The steps in returning are to (1) affirm that God is the true God (3:22b; 23b); (2) admit wrongful actions (3:23a) without offering any excuse; (3) acknowledge the adverse consequences of their actions (3:24); and (4) accept without debate the resulting shame, embarrassment, and judgment (3:25).

These moves would put Israel on the right track, but repentance would not yet be complete. The Lord insisted that the repentance process not be short-circuited. To the above steps are added (5) abandonment of evil ways (4:1); and (6) adoption of a new orientation characterized by integrity and justice (4:2). True repentance, a turning to God (cf. the prodigal son, Luke 15:11-32; 1 Thess 1:9), is followed by a practice of justice in truth and honesty.

**A Metaphor for Repentance (4:3-4).** Hardness and obstinacy often preclude a spiritual turnabout. Jeremiah employs hard ground as a metaphor for the people's hearts: just as natural seeds will not grow on pavement-like soil, so the spiritual fruit of righteousness cannot grow in a spiritually-resistant heart. Hosea, Jeremiah's predecessor, spells out the metaphor further and calls for action: "now is the time to seek the LORD" (Hos 10:12).

So, while one part of the metaphor deals with soil preparation, the second part of the metaphor, also from Hosea, deals with the seed. Hosea put it positively: "Plant the good seeds of righteousness" (Hos 10:12), and Jeremiah states it negatively: "Do not waste your good seed among thorns." The plowing and sowing metaphor, a wisdom motif, is also used by Isaiah to compare the timing of the farmer's activities and harvest to God's timing, when in his burning anger he will deal with evil deeds (Isa 28:23-29; cf. Jer 4:4). In sum, drawing from the realm of nature (plowing/sowing) and from redemptive history (circumcision/covenant), the prophet clinches his explanation of what repentance entails.

**Motivations for Repentance.** Because repentance is volitional, two persuasive techniques are needed. One is persuasion by promise and invitation (3:6-18). Good things will follow repentance (3:15-18). Judah, the more recalcitrant of the two sisters, requires the second persuasive technique, that of threat, the fire of God's wrath. (4:3-4).

The instruction about what repentance entails is ignored to everyone's peril. The common misconception is that blurting "I am sorry" qualifies as repentance and deserves forgiveness. However, stating regret is not the same as saying, "I have sinned"—perhaps the most difficult of any three words to say. Repentance cannot be reduced to a recipe, but the elements in repentance are not negotiable, though they may be variously expressed.

What must not be missed in this discussion is God's eagerness to restore wholesome relationships. He is most solicitous in his desire for the return home of a wayward family member. He invites; he appeals. But the God who has been offended, whose love has been rebuffed, and who is pained, is also the One who rightly threatens disastrous consequences when sinners remain unrepentant.

◆   C. Calamity from the North (4:5–6:30)
      1. Sound the alarm (4:5-21)

⁵"Shout to Judah, and broadcast to
      Jerusalem!
Tell them to sound the alarm
      throughout the land:
'Run for your lives!
Flee to the fortified cities!'
⁶Raise a signal flag as a warning for
      Jerusalem*:
'Flee now! Do not delay!'
For I am bringing terrible destruction
      upon you
from the north."

⁷A lion stalks from its den,
      a destroyer of nations.
It has left its lair and is headed your
      way.
It's going to devastate your land!
Your towns will lie in ruins,
      with no one living in them
      anymore.
⁸So put on clothes of mourning
      and weep with broken hearts,
for the fierce anger of the LORD
      is still upon us.

⁹"In that day," says the LORD,
      "the king and the officials will
      tremble in fear.
The priests will be struck with
      horror,
and the prophets will be appalled."

¹⁰Then I said, "O Sovereign LORD,
      the people have been deceived by
      what you said,
for you promised peace for Jerusalem.
But the sword is held at their
      throats!"

¹¹The time is coming when the LORD
      will say
to the people of Jerusalem,
"My dear people, a burning wind is
      blowing in from the desert,
and it's not a gentle breeze useful
      for winnowing grain.
¹²It is a roaring blast sent by me!

Now I will pronounce your
      destruction!"

¹³Our enemy rushes down on us like
      storm clouds!
His chariots are like whirlwinds.
His horses are swifter than eagles.
How terrible it will be, for we are
      doomed!
¹⁴O Jerusalem, cleanse your heart
      that you may be saved.
How long will you harbor
      your evil thoughts?
¹⁵Your destruction has been announced
      from Dan and the hill country of
      Ephraim.

¹⁶"Warn the surrounding nations
      and announce this to Jerusalem:
The enemy is coming from a distant
      land,
raising a battle cry against the
      towns of Judah.
¹⁷They surround Jerusalem like
      watchmen around a field,
for my people have rebelled
      against me,"
says the LORD.
¹⁸"Your own actions have brought this
      upon you.
This punishment is bitter, piercing
      you to the heart!"

¹⁹My heart, my heart—I writhe in pain!
My heart pounds within me!
      I cannot be still.
For I have heard the blast of enemy
      trumpets
and the roar of their battle cries.
²⁰Waves of destruction roll over the
      land,
until it lies in complete desolation.
Suddenly my tents are destroyed;
      in a moment my shelters are
      crushed.
²¹How long must I see the battle flags
      and hear the trumpets of war?

4:6 Hebrew *Zion.*

NOTES

**4:5 sound the alarm.** Lit., "blow the trumpet" (*shopar* [TH7782, ZH8795]), an instrument used by watchmen to alert the people to danger and by commanders to mobilize troops (Judg 3:27; Jer 51:27). The verse has eight imperatives; those not represented in the NLT are, "cry" (*qara'* [TH7121, ZH7924]); "be full" (*male'* [TH4390, ZH4848], "full-throated" or "aloud"); and "gather together" (*'asaph* [TH622, ZH665]).

**4:6 Raise a signal flag.** Hoisted banners became rallying points for soldiers during combat, or alternatively, for escapees during flight (NIDOTTE 3:110-111).

*from the north.* The foe from the north, thought by earlier scholars to be the Scythians, remains unnamed until 27:6 (cf. note on 1:14).

**4:8 the fierce anger of the LORD is still upon us.** Lit., it "has not turned from us." The image is of God's anger as punishment. Unleashed like a missile hurtling towards its target, it may still be intercepted or recalled (cf. Amos 1:3, 6).

**4:10 you promised peace.** This may refer to the Assyrian experience a century earlier (cf. Isa 26:3; 37:33-35); it may be a jab at the false prophets with their message of peace (Jer 14:13; 23:17); or it may be a quotation by the people (cf. LXX, "they said").

**4:12 I will pronounce your destruction!** Lit., "I will speak decisions (*mishpatim* [TH4941, ZH5477]) with them," i.e., "sentences of judgment with them."

**4:15 from Dan and . . . Ephraim.** Dan, to the far north, as well as Ephraim, the near neighbor tribe to Judah, was occupied by Assyria (721 BC), but Babylon would overrun those territories en route to Jerusalem.

**4:19 My heart, my heart.** Lit., "my guts, my guts." In Heb. thought, emotions were physically localized in the inward parts. Cf. "my bowels, my bowels" (KJV) and "oh, my anguish, my anguish" (NIV). The speaker is Jeremiah, though some suggest a personified Jerusalem or even God (for proposals by various scholars see Lundbom 1999:350). The blast of trumpets (*shopar* [TH7782, ZH8795]) could come from enemies, but is more likely that of Israelite watchmen (cf. comment at 4:5).

COMMENTARY

God made earnest appeals for his people to repent, using the language of marriage (3:22–4:4). The subsequent chapters use military language, and are largely variations on the themes of coming disaster, continued diagnosis of Israel's sin, and an occasional plea for change. The theme of approaching catastrophe holds center stage in 4:5-21, with sights and sounds of war both beginning and ending the unit (4:5, 21). Interwoven in a deft description of the coming invasion are poignant explanations, earnest admonitions, and Jeremiah's emotional outbursts. Behind each lies a theology.

The description of the coming invasion shows confusion in the rural areas as people hurry to fortified cities (4:5-6), where political and religious leaders huddle in consternation (4:9). The unnamed enemy from the north is described as a lion (4:7), a desert storm—the well-known sirocco (4:11), and as horses swifter than eagles who will soon surround Jerusalem as watchmen surround a field (4:13, 17). This invasion can be interpreted politically as a greedy empire's hurrying to swallow one more territory (4:7), but theologically the invasion expresses God's fierce anger (4:8). Prophets look behind the headlines and see God at work. They reckon with God's wrath as well as with his compassion.

The explanation for the invasion is more moral than political. "Your actions have brought this upon you" (4:18). "Your actions" is more literally rendered, "your ways and your deeds," a common phrase referring both to a general way of being in the world and to specific actions (e.g., 7:5; 23:22). Details about Israel's rebellion (4:17) have been given earlier (2:13, 20, 27, 32; 3:6). Jeremiah operated with the theological conviction that sinful actions result in bitter consequences.

With his admonitions, the prophet puts before his hearers the option of another way of being in the world, one that is humble and submissive before God. The prophet exhorts his hearers to give tangible expression to their contrition by wearing mourner's clothes (4:8; cf. 2 Sam 3:31; Lam 2:10). He urges the people of Jerusalem to cleanse their hearts so they may be saved (4:14; cf. 4:4). The sinner is not altogether at the mercy of an inexorable law of sin with its evil consequences. The theology behind this plea will be clarified later in the sign-act of the potter—namely, that God is prepared to change his decreed course of action if people repent (18:7-8).

Jeremiah's emotional outbursts indicate that his announcements do not arise out of personal vindictiveness. Rather, Jeremiah hurts for his people, and one can imagine him as doubled over with grief because of what the future holds for them (4:19). A messenger does not remain unaffected by his or her message. Jeremiah was not the last to agonize over the messages of doom and destruction that he was called to give.

◆     ## 2. A land in ruins (4:22-31)

22 "My people are foolish
      and do not know me," says the LORD.
   "They are stupid children
      who have no understanding.
   They are clever enough at doing
         wrong,
      but they have no idea how to
         do right!"

23 I looked at the earth, and it was empty
      and formless.
   I looked at the heavens, and there
      was no light.
24 I looked at the mountains and hills,
      and they trembled and shook.
25 I looked, and all the people were gone.
   All the birds of the sky had flown
      away.
26 I looked, and the fertile fields had
      become a wilderness.
   The towns lay in ruins,
      crushed by the LORD's fierce anger.

27 This is what the LORD says:
   "The whole land will be ruined,
      but I will not destroy it completely.
28 The earth will mourn
      and the heavens will be draped
         in black
   because of my decree against my
         people.
   I have made up my mind and will
      not change it."

29 At the noise of charioteers and
      archers,
   the people flee in terror.
   They hide in the bushes
      and run for the mountains.
   All the towns have been abandoned—
      not a person remains!
30 What are you doing,
      you who have been plundered?
   Why do you dress up in beautiful
      clothing

and put on gold jewelry?
Why do you brighten your eyes with
    mascara?
Your primping will do you no
    good!
The allies who were your lovers
    despise you and seek to kill you.

4:31 Hebrew *the daughter of Zion.*

<sup>31</sup> I hear a cry, like that of a woman in
    labor,
the groans of a woman giving birth
    to her first child.
It is beautiful Jerusalem*
    gasping for breath and crying out,
    "Help! I'm being murdered!"

NOTES

4:22 God's accusation against his people abounds with terms found in wisdom literature: *'ewil* [TH191, ZH211] (foolish); *sakal* [TH5530A, ZH6119] (stupid); *bin* [TH995, ZH1067] (discerning, understanding); and *khakam* [TH2450A, ZH2682] (wise, clever). The first and last cola in the Heb. end with "know" (*yada'* [TH3045, ZH3359]). Judah does not know Yahweh (for ramifications, cf. 9:23-24) or know how to do good.

4:23 *empty and formless.* The words *tohu* [TH8414, ZH9332] (without form) and *bohu* [TH922, ZH0983] (empty) are onomatopoeic; they recall Gen 1:2 and describe the results of an "uncreation." In Heb. each of the four verses (4:23-26) includes the word *hinneh* [TH2009, ZH2180] (behold), a word that calls attention each time to a fresh reality.

4:26 *fertile fields had become a wilderness.* Throughout, the language is reminiscent of the day of the Lord (Isa 13:1-10; Joel 2:30-31). About the Lord's anger (*kharon 'aph* [TH2740/639, ZH3019/678], "fierce anger"), see comments on 25:15-38.

4:27 *I will not destroy it completely.* God stops short of annihilation (cf. 5:10, 18; 30:11, 46:28), though John Calvin, in harmony with what has preceded, explains that God has not yet made an end to the devastation, but will do so (cited in Brueggemann 1998:60). Some emend the text to read, "I will make a full end of it."

4:28 *I have made up my mind and will not change it.* The Heb. is staccato: "I have spoken; I have purposed; I will not relent; I will not turn back."

4:30 *you brighten your eyes with mascara.* Cf. Jezebel, 2 Kgs 9:30.

*Your primping will do you no good!* This has the nuance, "you beautify yourself to no profit." For a view on feminine imagery in Jeremiah, see Bauer 1999:293-305.

4:31 *gasping for breath.* This phrase is followed in the Heb. by "stretching her hands"; this is left untranslated in the NLT.

COMMENTARY

This chapter has two panels hinged by 4:22, the Lord's summary of the problem. The first panel (4:5-21) is complemented with variations on the same theme by the second panel (4:23-31).

Two features call for comment, the first of which is the cause for the coming catastrophe. Unlike the first panel, the second panel does not point to the people's shortcomings, except for a brief note on Judah's misreading of her situation (4:30). The hinge verse gives the rationale for the coming catastrophe (4:22). Here Judah's evils are cast, not as infractions of the Torah, but as folly. Judah is without sense (cf. her response, 4:30). Ignoring the basic elements of even human wisdom, she has chosen what is wrong instead of what is right. In the first panel, by contrast, the talk about cleansing the heart (4:14) and about evil actions (4:18) is more deuteronomistic.

| Jeremiah 4:5-21 | Jeremiah 4:23-31 |
|---|---|
| disaster approaches (Judah) 4:5-6 | disaster approaches (cosmic) 4:23-26 |
| people in flight 4:5c-d, 6a | people running for refuge 4:29c-d |
| towns in ruins, no inhabitant 4:7 | towns in ruin, no inhabitant 4:26b, 29e-f |
| root cause: God's anger 4:8c | root cause: God's anger 4:26c |
| call for mourning 4:8a | earth will mourn 4:28a |
| war chariots, horses 4:13b-c | charioteers and archers 4:29a |
| Judah doomed 4:13d | Judah's allies turn traitor 4:30d |
| destruction announced 4:15 | God decrees judgment versus Israel 4:28c-d |
| people rebelled 4:17a | people do wrong 4:22 |
| people harbor evil thoughts 4:14c | Judah is self-absorbed 4:30a-f |
| Jeremiah's cry of agony 4:19-21 | Jerusalem's cry for help 4:31 |

A second comment is about the gravity of the situation. God will "unmake" both his creation of a world and his creation of a people. Jeremiah 4:23-26 describes a reversal of Genesis 1 (cf. Zeph 1:2-3). The earth returns to chaos, and the life of humans and wildlife ceases. The account, as has been noted, does not end with the Sabbath, but with wrath. God not only unmakes his creative work in the universe, but he moves counter to his own elective purposes for his people (4:28). Sin plunges the universe into chaos and jeopardizes divine election. Despite this crisis, Judah, a prostitute dressed in scarlet and jewels, nonchalantly puts on cosmetics, preparing to go to a party (4:30)! Even more tragic than the evils themselves is the people's blindness to the emergency their sin has precipitated. The Laodicean church is another case in point (Rev 3:14-17). Such self-delusion continues in churches to this day.

### ◆ 3. Taking a public poll (5:1-19)

"Run up and down every street in
  Jerusalem," says the LORD.
  "Look high and low; search
    throughout the city!
If you can find even one just and
  honest person,
  I will not destroy the city.
²But even when they are under oath,
  saying, 'As surely as the LORD lives,'
  they are still telling lies!"

³LORD, you are searching for honesty.
  You struck your people,

but they paid no attention.
  You crushed them,
  but they refused to be corrected.
They are determined, with faces set
  like stone;
  they have refused to repent.

⁴Then I said, "But what can we expect
  from the poor?
  They are ignorant.
They don't know the ways of the LORD.
  They don't understand God's laws.
⁵So I will go and speak to their leaders.

Surely they know the ways of the
LORD
and understand God's laws."
But the leaders, too, as one man,
had thrown off God's yoke
and broken his chains.
⁶So now a lion from the forest will
attack them;
a wolf from the desert will pounce
on them.
A leopard will lurk near their towns,
tearing apart any who dare to
venture out.
For their rebellion is great,
and their sins are many.

⁷"How can I pardon you?
For even your children have turned
from me.
They have sworn by gods that are not
gods at all!
I fed my people until they were full.
But they thanked me by committing
adultery
and lining up at the brothels.
⁸They are well-fed, lusty stallions,
each neighing for his neighbor's
wife.
⁹Should I not punish them for this?"
says the LORD.
"Should I not avenge myself against
such a nation?

¹⁰"Go down the rows of the vineyards
and destroy the grapevines,
leaving a scattered few alive.
Strip the branches from the vines,
for these people do not belong to
the LORD.
¹¹The people of Israel and Judah
are full of treachery against me,"
says the LORD.
¹²"They have lied about the LORD
and said, 'He won't bother us!
No disasters will come upon us.

There will be no war or famine.
¹³God's prophets are all windbags
who don't really speak for him.
Let their predictions of disaster fall
on themselves!'"

¹⁴Therefore, this is what the LORD God of
Heaven's Armies says:

"Because the people are talking like
this,
my messages will flame out of your
mouth
and burn the people like kindling
wood.
¹⁵O Israel, I will bring a distant nation
against you,"
says the LORD.
"It is a mighty nation,
an ancient nation,
a people whose language you do not
know,
whose speech you cannot
understand.
¹⁶Their weapons are deadly;
their warriors are mighty.
¹⁷They will devour the food of your
harvest;
they will devour your sons and
daughters.
They will devour your flocks and herds;
they will devour your grapes and
figs.
And they will destroy your fortified
towns,
which you think are so safe.

¹⁸"Yet even in those days I will not blot
you out completely," says the LORD.
¹⁹"And when your people ask, 'Why did
the LORD our God do all this to us?' you
must reply, 'You rejected him and gave
yourselves to foreign gods in your own
land. Now you will serve foreigners in a
land that is not your own.'

NOTES

5:1 *If you can find even one just and honest person.* Justice (*mishpat* [TH4941, ZH5477]) is
one of God's topmost priorities (Isa 5:7; 61:8), as is honesty (*'emunah* [TH530, ZH575], "faithfulness," "reliability"). Ps 89:14 is a good example for comparison; there, *mishpat* (justice)
and *'emet* (truth) [TH571, ZH622] are found together.

*I will not destroy the city.* This is an interpretive rendering of "I will pardon her."

**5:3 they refused to be corrected.** Lit., "they refused to accept discipline" (*musar* [TH4148, ZH4592], primarily "instruction," but also "correction"). This is a frequent accusation against God's people (7:28; 17:23; 32:33; 35:13).

**5:6 their sins are many.** Lit., "their turnings away from are many"—(cf. "backslidings," NIV, and "apostasies," NRSV). In a meditation on Jer 5:1-6, Achtemeier (1984:35) observes that in Jeremiah there is no romanticizing of the poor because they are poor.

**5:8 each neighing for his neighbor's wife.** Men are described as stallions, "hot and lusty" (Craigie et al. 1991:86). For neighing associated with adultery, see 13:27 (NRSV); for comparisons of Israel with other animals, camels, and donkeys, see 2:23-24.

**5:10 leaving a scattered few alive.** The principle of vast destruction without annihilation is also enunciated elsewhere (see comment at 4:27; cf. 5:18, which forms an inclusio with 5:10; 30:11; 46:28). Mention of vineyards recalls Israel, portrayed as a choice vine (Isa 5:1-6; Ps 80:8). Pruning is ultimately beneficial.

**5:12 He won't bother us!** The Heb. cryptically says, "Not he," apparently with the sense of "Never mind him."

**5:15 It is a mighty nation.** The word for "mighty" (*'ethan* [TH386, ZH419], "ever-flowing"), is applied to perennial streams (Deut 21:4; Ps 74:15), but here it means "enduring" and is applied to an unnamed, powerful enemy, probably Babylon (27:6).

**5:17 they will destroy your fortified towns.** The Heb. adds, "with a sword" (*khereb* [TH2719, ZH2995]), meaning "through war."

COMMENTARY

Central to the material in 5:1-6:9 is an underlying question placed roughly in the middle of the section, "Why has the LORD our God done this to us?" (5:19). "This" refers to the threat that a foreign power will decimate the land. The four sections alternate, broadly speaking, between sets of accusations and threats of punishment. The first accusation (5:1-9) is followed by the threat of punishment in the form of an enemy invasion (5:10-18), then a second list of accusations (5:20-31) is followed once again by the threat of an enemy invasion (6:1-9). The question, Why? is more than adequately answered.

The short answer is a single word, sin. The longer answer verifies and explains such things as What sin? How much sin? and Where is the evidence? The evidence is statistical. Jeremiah takes a public poll, which shows that all, poor and rich, are playing with the truth. They have "thrown off the yoke," an action that is explained in another context to mean, "I will not serve" (2:20). Since it is pragmatically and existentially shown that the city is without justice or honesty, God is justified in punishing them.

An analysis of this data-gathering offers three insights, the first of which is how far God will go in order to spare the city. Like Sodom and Gomorrah when the ax of judgment was about to fall, Jerusalem was ripe for judgment. Abraham asked whether God would spare Sodom if there were ten righteous people in the city (Gen 18:16-33). The answer was affirmative. How much more bargaining would God tolerate? The answer is that for the sake of one just person, God would forgive this grossly sinning city and spare her the deserved punishment (see note on 5:1). Sin will bring evil consequences, but the good news from both the Sodom story and Jeremiah's census is that the sin-consequence chain can be broken. Judah was invited to experience a forgiving God. However, "forgiveness still requires coming to terms with Yahweh" (Brueggemann 1998:63). Forgiveness always comes with a price—in this instance, one righteous person. The principle will be most profoundly illustrated in the one just man, Jesus.

A second observation pertains to the pervasiveness, dominance, and ugliness of sin. How mean and destructive this spiritual virus is! It affects an entire population, and so penetrates it that every person becomes a liar or a rebel or both. Sin is vicious and so infects individuals that they set themselves deliberately to continue in it, spurning invitations to repent (5:3). Sin assumes ugly forms. People have no gratitude to God (5:7; cf. Rom 1:21) and they turn to other gods. Adultery and sexual promiscuity are unchecked. Sin so corrupts people's sensitivities that they trivialize their situation and even dismiss God as a factor in any consequence, saying, "He won't bother us" (5:12).

The third observation turns on Yahweh's question, "Should I not punish them for this?" (5:9). Given the litany of corruption, lack of integrity (to be expanded in 9:3-9), refusal to submit to God, search for substitute gods, adultery, subversive behavior (5:11), and indifference to God's messengers (5:12-13), should the question of punishment even be an issue? And yet God is so disposed to forgive that he ponders his course of action by searching for a way to avoid the inevitable. The question, reiterated for emphasis in the second round of announcements and punishments in 5:29, makes categorically clear that God is anything but a callous judge who only awaits an excuse to pronounce a verdict of damnation. But divine integrity cannot be compromised. The decision is not arbitrary but reasoned. Sufficient evidence has been marshaled to justify the verdict for punishment, so the instruction is issued in figurative language: destroy the vineyard (5:10) by bringing in a distant nation (5:15) who will devour all (5:16-17). But in the end, even the vast destruction is curbed. "Not completely" is the divine word (5:18), and therein lies hope.

◆     ## 4. Treachery and trouble (5:20–6:9)

20 "Make this announcement to Israel,*
    and say this to Judah:
21 Listen, you foolish and senseless people,
    with eyes that do not see
    and ears that do not hear.
22 Have you no respect for me?
    Why don't you tremble in my
        presence?
I, the LORD, define the ocean's sandy
        shoreline
    as an everlasting boundary that the
        waters cannot cross.

The waves may toss and roar,
    but they can never pass the
        boundaries I set.
23 But my people have stubborn and
        rebellious hearts.
    They have turned away and
        abandoned me.
24 They do not say from the heart,
    'Let us live in awe of the LORD
        our God,
    for he gives us rain each spring
        and fall,

assuring us of a harvest when the
time is right.'
25 Your wickedness has deprived you of
these wonderful blessings.
Your sin has robbed you of all these
good things.

26 "Among my people are wicked men
who lie in wait for victims like a
hunter hiding in a blind.
They continually set traps
to catch people.
27 Like a cage filled with birds,
their homes are filled with evil plots.
And now they are great and rich.
28 They are fat and sleek,
and there is no limit to their wicked
deeds.
They refuse to provide justice to
orphans
and deny the rights of the poor.
29 Should I not punish them for this?"
says the LORD.
"Should I not avenge myself against
such a nation?
30 A horrible and shocking thing
has happened in this land—
31 the prophets give false prophecies,
and the priests rule with an iron
hand.
Worse yet, my people like it that way!
But what will you do when the end
comes?

## CHAPTER 6

1 "Run for your lives, you people of
Benjamin!
Get out of Jerusalem!
Sound the alarm in Tekoa!
Send up a signal at Beth-hakkerem!
A powerful army is coming from the
north,

coming with disaster and
destruction.
2 O Jerusalem,* you are my beautiful
and delicate daughter—
but I will destroy you!
3 Enemies will surround you, like
shepherds camped around the city.
Each chooses a place for his troops
to devour.
4 They shout, 'Prepare for battle!
Attack at noon!'
'No, it's too late; the day is fading,
and the evening shadows are falling.'
5 'Well then, let's attack at night
and destroy her palaces!'"

6 This is what the LORD of Heaven's
Armies says:
"Cut down the trees for battering
rams.
Build siege ramps against the walls
of Jerusalem.
This is the city to be punished,
for she is wicked through and
through.
7 She spouts evil like a fountain.
Her streets echo with the sounds of
violence and destruction.
I always see her sickness and sores.
8 Listen to this warning, Jerusalem,
or I will turn from you in disgust.
Listen, or I will turn you into a heap of
ruins,
a land where no one lives."

9 This is what the LORD of Heaven's
Armies says:
"Even the few who remain in Israel
will be picked over again,
as when a harvester checks each vine
a second time
to pick the grapes that were
missed."

5:20 Hebrew to the house of Jacob. The names "Jacob" and "Israel" are often interchanged throughout the Old
Testament, referring sometimes to the individual patriarch and sometimes to the nation.  6:2 Hebrew Daughter
of Zion.

NOTES

5:20 **Make this announcement to Israel.** Lit., "Declare this to Israel." What follows is more
an accusation than an announcement.

**5:22 Have you no respect for me?** "Respect" translates the Heb. verb *yare'* [TH3372, ZH3707] (to fear, be in awe, revere).

**5:24 he gives us rain.** Fall rains come in October/December; spring rains in March/April.

**5:28 They refuse to provide justice to orphans.** The Heb. uses the verb *din* [TH1777, ZH1906] ("redress a wrong," "administer justice"; Ps 72:2) with its cognate noun *din* [TH1779, ZH1907] (a "cause" or "case") in a generalization: "they do not adjudicate cases fairly." Then a specific example is given: they do not prosecute the case of an orphan energetically. The word *din* is parallel with *mishpat* [TH4941, ZH5477] in the last half of the verse; it "refers primarily to the *cause* or *case* of the one seeking judgment, while *mishpat* refers to one's rights" (NIDOTTE 1:940).

**5:31 and the priests rule with an iron hand.** Lit., "the priests rule upon their hand," an idiom that might mean that the priests do nothing (cf. "they sit upon their hands," Craigie et al. 1991:95); "the priests rule by their own authority" (NIV); or "the priests rule as the prophets direct" (NRSV).

**6:1 Run for your lives.** Cf. 4:5-6 for some of the same vocabulary: *'uz* [TH5756, ZH6395] (take refuge); *tiq'u shophar* [TH8628/7782, ZH9546/8795] ("blow the trumpet," i.e., sound the alarm), except that in 4:5, the plea was to flee to the fortified cities, such as Jerusalem. Now the appeal is to escape from Jerusalem, possibly southward to the desert.

*Tekoa.* Tekoa, the home of Amos, lay twelve miles south of Jerusalem. Craigie (1991:98) captures the assonance of Tekoa and blow (*tiq'u*) with the rendering, "toot the trumpet in Tekoa."

*Beth-hakkerem.* Lit., "house of vineyards." While its location is uncertain, it is perhaps south toward Bethlehem. Mention of the "army from the north" punctuates 4:5-6:30 (cf. 4:6; 6:22).

**6:2 I will destroy you.** The Heb. text is difficult, with scholars divided. NLT takes *damah* [TH1820A, ZH1950] to mean "destroy" (cf. NIV, NASB, RSV); others (KJV, NRSV) render it as "to be like." The decision can affect the interpretation of 6:3 as either a menacing or a peaceful pastoral scene (Craigie et al. 1991:98).

**6:4 Prepare for battle!** Lit., "Consecrate a battle against her [Jerusalem]." Conventionally, fighting began at dawn, but so eager was the enemy to fight that that strategy was set aside.

**6:6 Cut down the trees.** The Heb. text leaves the purpose unspecified. Trees were used for battering rams, in the building of ramps, and as wood to set fires. Yahweh, as commander in chief, is now aligned with the enemy and gives the orders (cf. 21:4).

**she is wicked through and through.** This renders two Heb. words *'osheq beqirbah* [TH6233, ZH6945] ("oppression within," viz., at the core).

**6:7 She spouts evil like a fountain.** Hess (1991), noting the hiphil forms of *qarar* [TH6979C, ZH7981], reads, "As a well overflows with its water/So [Jerusalem] overflows with its evil."

**6:8 Listen to this warning.** The niphal imperative is with the root *yasar* [TH3256, ZH3579] (receive discipline). Cf. 2:30; 5:3, and notes.

COMMENTARY

The two panels—accusation (5:20-31) and announcement (6:1-9)—replay the panels just completed (accusation, 5:1-19; announcement, 5:20-31; see commentary at 5:1), like a radio commercial that has no sooner ended than it is aired again. Now the accusations take on fresh nuances, and the announcement pictures the enemy as being on the scene.

**Accusations (5:20-31).** The accusations cluster around two pivots, one theological (strictly pertaining to God, 5:20-25) and the other social (5:26-31). The two parts systematically exposit the opening characterization of the people as foolish and senseless. In their folly, the people discounted God's greatness—without awe or reverence for him (5:22, 24; cf. 32:40; Prov 1:7).

Such irreverence toward God is the more reprehensible since God, the creator, enforces order. He has drawn a line in the sand; he has set boundaries for the ocean (5:22). The ocean's waters, however chaotic, will not get out of hand by violating the parameters God has set for them. On land, rain comes at the right time by his decree (5:24). God, whom the people dismissively disrespect, is the God who orchestrates nature (as, elsewhere, he orchestrates history).

This failure to relate rightly to God spills over into Israel's failure to relate appropriately to others (5:26-31). Now the exposition takes up the second point: the people are "without sense" (lit. "heartless," 5:23a). Treachery expresses itself in devious schemes for entrapping and exploiting other persons. These cunning individuals do not fall into temptation; they actively seek out sin by devices as numerous and varied as birds in a cage (5:27a), and some of them even become rich (5:27c).

Even when the prophet highlights exploitation of the poor in court (5:28), he does not seem so much to be invoking law (though he could, cf. Exod 22:22; Deut 16:18) as deploring the inhumanity toward fellow humans that results from excessive greed. The conclusion is that God is warranted in punishing them (5:29). Judah's evil is elemental (irreverence for God, maltreatment of others), behavior over which God as creator (quite apart from God as lawgiver) stands guard. Ethicists ask whether a person will do good if he or she has no belief in God. In answer, at least this much may be said: "Where covenant with Yahweh is betrayed, covenant values in social relationships cannot be sustained" (Brueggemann 1998.69).

**Announcements (6:1-9).** If God is warranted in moving against his people in punishment, the question becomes, By what means will he do so? The second panel, consisting largely of announcements, answers that question: by war. The code words are already familiar from the previous panel (5:20-31; see note on 6:1). The prophet wanted listeners to imagine themselves at the scene. They hear the commander's order to attack (6:4) and witness the alien army setting out for a second "gleaning" to ensure that the destruction was thorough and no opportunity to destroy or plunder had been missed (6:9; cf. 5:10). The army divisions advance irresistibly, taking their spoil (6:3). Siege ramps are under construction and Jerusalem's walls will soon provide no safety (6:6). The listeners overhear Yahweh saying, "Should I not punish them for this?" (5:29). Deep within their hearts, they are forced to acknowledge that the city spawns evil as surely as a fountain spouts water (6:7). Yet the divine invitation to listen and to change is still audible (6:8). When sin is so obvious and blatant, what God is this who still wrestles with a decision to punish? What God would invite his hearers to think with him, "What would you do?" God painstakingly sketches the details of his punitive action in the hope that his people will yet be warned and alter their ways. Certainly he is not a God who takes pleasure in punishment!

◆ 5. Alert! invasion imminent (6:10-30)

¹⁰To whom can I give warning?
Who will listen when I speak?
Their ears are closed,
and they cannot hear.
They scorn the word of the LORD.
They don't want to listen at all.
¹¹So now I am filled with the LORD's fury.
Yes, I am tired of holding it in!

"I will pour out my fury on children playing in the streets
and on gatherings of young men,
on husbands and wives
and on those who are old and gray.
¹²Their homes will be turned over to their enemies,
as will their fields and their wives.
For I will raise my powerful fist
against the people of this land,"
says the LORD.
¹³"From the least to the greatest,
their lives are ruled by greed.
From prophets to priests,
they are all frauds.
¹⁴They offer superficial treatments
for my people's mortal wound.
They give assurances of peace
when there is no peace.
¹⁵Are they ashamed of their disgusting actions?
Not at all—they don't even know how to blush!
Therefore, they will lie among the slaughtered.
They will be brought down when I punish them,"
says the LORD.

¹⁶This is what the LORD says:
"Stop at the crossroads and look around.
Ask for the old, godly way, and walk in it.

Travel its path, and you will find rest for your souls.
But you reply, 'No, that's not the road we want!'
¹⁷I posted watchmen over you who said,
'Listen for the sound of the alarm.'
But you replied,
'No! We won't pay attention!'

¹⁸"Therefore, listen to this, all you nations.
Take note of my people's situation.
¹⁹Listen, all the earth!
I will bring disaster on my people.
It is the fruit of their own schemes,
because they refuse to listen to me.
They have rejected my word.
²⁰There's no use offering me sweet frankincense from Sheba.
Keep your fragrant calamus
imported from distant lands!
I will not accept your burnt offerings.
Your sacrifices have no pleasing aroma for me."

²¹Therefore, this is what the LORD says:
"I will put obstacles in my people's path.
Fathers and sons will both fall over them.
Neighbors and friends will die together."

²²This is what the LORD says:
"Look! A great army coming from the north!
A great nation is rising against you
from far-off lands.
²³They are armed with bows and spears.
They are cruel and show no mercy.
They sound like a roaring sea
as they ride forward on horses.
They are coming in battle formation,
planning to destroy you, beautiful Jerusalem.*"

²⁴We have heard reports about the
    enemy,
    and we wring our hands in fright.
Pangs of anguish have gripped us,
    like those of a woman in labor.
²⁵Don't go out to the fields!
    Don't travel on the roads!
The enemy's sword is everywhere
    and terrorizes us at every turn!
²⁶Oh, my people, dress yourselves in
    burlap
    and sit among the ashes.
Mourn and weep bitterly, as for the
    loss of an only son.
For suddenly the destroying armies
    will be upon you!

²⁷"Jeremiah, I have made you a tester of
    metals,*
    that you may determine the quality
    of my people.
²⁸They are the worst kind of rebel,
    full of slander.
They are as hard as bronze and iron,
    and they lead others into
    corruption.
²⁹The bellows fiercely fan the flames
    to burn out the corruption.
But it does not purify them,
    for the wickedness remains.
³⁰I will label them 'Rejected Silver,'
    for I, the LORD, am discarding
    them."

**6:23** Hebrew *daughter of Zion.*   **6:27** As in Greek version; Hebrew reads *of metals in my people a fortress.*


NOTES

**6:10** *Their ears are closed.* Lit., "their ears are uncircumcised." J.G. Eichhorn renders this "they have skin over their ears" (quoted by Holladay 1986:214; cf. "uncircumcised hearts" in Acts 7:51).

*scorn the word.* See Jer 36:20-26.

**6:11** *I am filled with the LORD's fury.* In Heb., "pour out" is in the imperative (cf. Hos 5:10). Either Jeremiah is addressing God, or, more likely, God is answering Jeremiah's question about his assignment (6:10a).

**6:12** *their fields and their wives.* The conventional phrase is "fields and vineyards" (Ps 107:37; Jer 32:15; 39:10); the substitution of "wives" for "vineyards" is a shock technique (Jer 6:12-15a is almost identical to Jer 8:10-12).

**6:13** *they are all frauds.* Lit., "they practice deceit." Jeremiah repeatedly accuses people (Heb. of 3:10; 5:2; 9:3, 5) and prophets (14:14; 23:14, 26; 27:10, 14-16; 29:9) of deceit (*sheqer* [TH8267, ZH9214]).

**6:16** *No, that's not the road we want!* The two-word reply in Heb. (*lo' nelek*) is more defiant, similar to the parallel response in 6:17, "No! We won't pay attention!" The old, godly way is the Torah given by Moses (Ps 103:7).

**6:20** *I will not accept your burnt offerings.* For sacrifices in the absence of moral rectitude, see Isa 1:4-13; Amos 5:21-27; Hos 6:6; Mic 6:6-8; Matt 9:13; 12:7. Forests of frankincense were located in Sheba in the southwest part of the Arabian Peninsula, as well as in east Africa, now Somaliland (Holladay 1986:222).

**6:25** *The enemy's sword . . . terrorizes us at every turn!* The phrase, *magor missabib* [TH4032, ZH4471] (terror all around), is used elsewhere as Pashhur's surrogate name (20:3); it is also mockingly applied to Jeremiah (20:10; cf. 46:5; 49:29).

**6:27** *I have made you a tester of metals.* For the metaphor from metallurgy, see Job 23:10; Ezek 22:18-22; Zech 13:9; Mal. 3:2-3. Silver is separated from lead ore, usually only in small amounts, through smelting or through cupellation—all described in detail by Holladay (1986:230-232).

COMMENTARY

This section has an air of finality about it. Components of the conventional prophetic judgment speech—the accusation and the announcement—tumble about rather than appear in proper order. Jeremiah, the people, and God each get to say their last word. The ominous note of alarm had sounded as a threat (4:5-6). Now it has morphed into the sound of a refiner's bellows, above which is heard the voice of the assayer, "Reject" (6:30). Within the longer section (4:5-6:30), one can trace a development in the positions taken by each of the characters, Jeremiah, the people, and God.

**Jeremiah.** Jeremiah initially protested God's putting the land in ruins by an enemy's hands, charging that God had deceived the people (4:10). If Jeremiah was asking about a warrant for God's punitive action, the divine answer came in a litany of Judah's evils followed by rhetorical questions: "Shall I not punish them for this? Should I not avenge myself against such a nation?" (5:9, 29). Jeremiah then became emotional and wept because of the destiny now envisioned for Judah (4:19-21). The public poll that God asked Jeremiah to conduct put the prophet directly in touch with the evil in the land (5:1-5). After further dialogue with God, and his own experience of having no one listen as people scorned the word of the Lord (6:10), Jeremiah, like God, reached the point of exasperation. "So now I am filled with the LORD's fury. Yes, I am weary of holding it in!" (6:11).

The prophet was not immediately in sync with God's perspective. Eventually, however, he saw the situation as God did. Because many factors enter to cloud the vision of God's messengers, continual vigilance is necessary for the church and those who speak for God. Are they fully aligned with God's point of view? Preachers speak not only to the church but on behalf of the church against evil. Will the church be subverted by cultural pressures to be more accommodating to evil? Will the church flinch from speaking about the seriousness of evil or its ultimate consequences? Will the church and its representatives become soft when the divine message is foreboding? Or will the church side fully with God and faithfully say what God says?

**The People.** The people increasingly hardened themselves against God. They were nonchalant, saying about God that "He won't bother us" (5:12). They did not live in awe before God (5:24). When admonished to seek the old, godly path, they said, "No" (see note on 6:16). When invited to pay attention, their final retort was, "No! We won't pay attention!" (6:17). The people were initially indicted for dishonesty and adultery (5:2, 8), and later for disregarding and disdaining the prophets (5:12-13). More serious was the people's disrespect for God (5:22), and their endorsement of corruption and social injustice (5:27-28). In the end, they scorned God's word (6:10) and became "the worst kind of rebel," with evil so ingrained that no refining would remove it (6:27-29). They were incorrigibly rebellious.

The human bent on evil, unless checked, only becomes more vicious. Failure to acknowledge God soon leads to carelessness about the things of God, and then to determined obstinacy and scorn for God's word. Evil is a dangerous moral and spiritual cancer. Like yeast, it infects the whole lump. Most lamentably, people become totally comfortable in their evil ways. Evil people callously dismiss warnings because they like things the way they are. There is no embarrassment, for example, about exploitation or sexual perversion. As sad as this downward spiral is for an individual, there is something even more tragic about an entire society that trivializes evil and so hurtles, as did Judah, toward their own destruction.

**God.**    A parallel movement—from the mild to the harsh—can also be seen as God responds to Israel. At first, the order to go down the rows of the vineyard and destroy it was softened by "but leave a scattered few alive" (5:10). When destruction was threatened by the enemy invader, God said, "I will not blot you out completely" (5:18). But before long, God's position also hardened: "O Jerusalem, you are my beautiful and delicate daughter, but I will destroy you" (6:2). He warned them that he might turn from them in disgust (6:8) and then did so by raising "his powerful fist against the people of this land" (6:12) and finally discarding them (6:30). Pity does not always override anger.

A closer look at God's way of working here offers both a warning and an encouragement. The warning is that God's patience is not infinite. The time for repentance is lengthy, as in the story of Noah, but after years of fruitless waiting for repentance, the flood of judgment comes. Grain and weeds may grow together, as Jesus said, but the day of harvest is scheduled. God is patient, says Peter, but not forever (2 Pet 3:7-10). The encouragement can be read from nature. As God has set limits for the ocean so that the water in its boisterous raging cannot pass beyond the shore, so the massive waves of evil can proceed only so far and no further.

◆   **D. Sermons about Worship (7:1–8:3)**
      **1. The Temple sermon (7:1–15)**

The LORD gave another message to Jeremiah. He said, ²"Go to the entrance of the LORD's Temple, and give this message to the people: 'O Judah, listen to this message from the LORD! Listen to it, all of you who worship here! ³This is what the LORD of Heaven's Armies, the God of Israel, says:

"'Even now, if you quit your evil ways, I will let you stay in your own land. ⁴But don't be fooled by those who promise you safety simply because the LORD's Temple is here. They chant, "The LORD's Temple is here! The LORD's Temple is here!" ⁵But I will be merciful only if you stop your evil thoughts and deeds and start treating each other with justice; ⁶only if you stop exploiting foreigners, orphans, and widows; only if you stop your murdering; and only if you stop harming yourselves by worshiping idols. ⁷Then I will let you stay in this land that I gave to your ancestors to keep forever.

⁸" 'Don't be fooled into thinking that you will never suffer because the Temple is here. It's a lie! ⁹Do you really think you can steal, murder, commit adultery, lie, and burn incense to Baal and all those other new gods of yours, ¹⁰and then come here and stand before me in my Temple and chant, "We are safe!"—only to go right back to all those evils again? ¹¹Don't you yourselves admit that this Temple, which bears my name, has become a den of thieves? Surely I see all the evil going on there. I, the LORD, have spoken!

¹²" 'Go now to the place at Shiloh where

I once put the Tabernacle that bore my name. See what I did there because of all the wickedness of my people, the Israelites. 13While you were doing these wicked things, says the LORD, I spoke to you about it repeatedly, but you would not listen. I called out to you, but you refused to answer. 14So just as I destroyed Shiloh, I will now destroy this Temple that bears my name, this Temple that you trust in for help, this place that I gave to you and your ancestors. 15And I will send you out of my sight into exile, just as I did your relatives, the people of Israel.*'

7:15 Hebrew of Ephraim, referring to the northern kingdom of Israel.


## NOTES

**7:2 Go to the entrance of the LORD's Temple.** The date is possibly 609–608 BC, assuming that ch 26 refers to this Temple sermon (a misnomer, according to Lundbom 1999:458). Priests at the gate would inquire about the spiritual condition of the people (Pss 15:1-5; 24:3-4).

**7:3 if you quit your evil ways.** The Heb. text is hiphil imperative of *yatab* [TH3190, ZH3512] (cause to make good, amend); thus, "Correct your ways and your deeds."

*I will let you stay in your own land.* So also 7:7, but a slight revocalization of piel to the Heb. qal verb *shakan* [TH7931, ZH8905] and *'ethekem* ("you" with the accusative marker) to *'ittekem* (with you) as in some versions (Aquila, Vulgate), yields, "I will dwell with you" in this place (Temple). Holladay (1986:236-37), who proposes this reading for 7:3, affirms the reading of the MT for 7:7. His proposal, which I commend, yields, "I will dwell with you" (7:3, cf. NRSV) and "I will let you stay in this land" (7:7).

**7:4 The LORD's Temple is here!** In 722 BC, the Assyrians took Samaria but not Jerusalem. When King Hezekiah of Judah later faced Assyria's Sennacherib in 701 BC, Isaiah's assurance of protection to Hezekiah was connected with God's presence in the Temple (Isa 31:4-5; 37:33-35; cf. Ps 132:13-14). But to make the same claim now was *sheqer* [TH8267, ZH9214] (deception, delusion). Of the 113 occurrences of *sheqer* in the OT, 37 are in Jeremiah (so Joelle 1999, who justifies "illusion" as a rendering for *sheqer*). For other threefold repetitions (as "Lord's Temple" is repeated here), see Isa 6:3; Jer 22:29; Ezek 21:27.

**7:6 if you stop your murdering.** Lit., "not pour out innocent blood," i.e., blood of innocent persons (Deut 19:10). Both judicial malpractice and violence are in view. According to the Talmud, the prohibition against oppressing others is found in 36 places in the Torah (so Lundbom 1999:443, citing H. Freedman; cf. Exod 22:21; Deut 24:17).

**7:7 I will let you stay in this land.** Lit., "I will let you stay in this place." It is amplified here to mean "land," but cf. 7:3 and 7:12, where "this place" is "Temple."

**7:12 Go now to the place at Shiloh.** Shiloh, eighteen miles north of Jerusalem, was an early cult center (cf. Eli, 1 Sam 3:21; Ps 78:56-64, 67-68). According to Danish archaeologists, it was destroyed after 1050 BC, likely by the Philistines (cf. 1 Sam 4), with ruins possibly still exposed 450 years later in Jeremiah's time (Craigie et al. 1991:121-22; cf. also the excursus by Keown et al. 1995:16-19).


## COMMENTARY

Jeremiah's sermon has two points that correspond to "ways and deeds" (see note on 7:3): change your way of thinking, and change your behavior (7:3-4). Each of these points is expounded in turn (behavior, 7:5-7; bad reasoning, 7:8-11), an illustration is offered from Israel's history (7:12), and a judgment oracle (accusation/announcement) concludes the sermon (7:13-15). This sermon about worship was given at the entrance to the place of worship, possibly at one of Israel's week-long festivals (Deut 16:16). It was so probing that the audience called for the preacher's death (Jer 26:11; cf. Stephen's sermon, also about the Temple, Acts 7:59, and Jesus' death associated with the Temple, Mark 14:58).

Jeremiah's sermon issues a call for God's people to amend their ways in accordance with God's demand for justice. While justice includes fairness and equity, it is much more than these. Biblically understood, justice means observing honorable relations as defined by God in every sphere of human interaction, whether domestic, commercial, political, or religious. Justice means practicing reconciliation and right behavior in every relationship (Ezek 18:5-9). While Westerners speak of "getting justice," the Bible speaks of "doing justice" through concrete actions (7:6; cf. Exod 22:21; 23:9; Deut 24:19-21).

Jesus echoed Jeremiah's message that worship and unjust practices do not cohere. During the civil rights movement, Clarence Jordan went with an African-American to a white church. After being violently evicted, Jordan wryly noted: "Well, everything is integrated now, except the churches and jails—and I have hope for the jails" (cited in Boers 1999:89).

The call to alter theological thinking was startling, even offensive. The chant about the Temple where God had promised to take up residence was based on past experience and tradition (see note on 7:4). That same theological promise of God's presence was now captured in a cliche, "The LORD's Temple is here!" Jeremiah was saying, in effect, that a particular theology of God's presence, while true at one time in history, may be false when misapplied at another time. Given Judah's spiritual apostasy, the earlier promise no longer applied. Jeremiah pointed out Judah's failure to observe several of the Ten Commandments (7:9) in order to show that ethics had been separated from worship (7:8-11). The worship was a sham, since true worship cannot be divorced from godly behavior (Matt 5:23-24; Luke 19:46).

In making his two points, Jeremiah referred directly or obliquely to the covenant with Abraham ("land that I gave to your ancestors," 7:7), the Sinai covenant with Moses ("steal, murder, commit adultery," 7:9), and the covenant with David ("The LORD's Temple is here!"). Judah was misrepresenting each of them. The covenant with Abraham was being perceived as guaranteeing possession of the land, apart from ethics. However, if the promise of land to Abraham was unconditional (as many assert), its possession was definitely conditional (Ezek 33:23-29). Regarding the covenant with Moses at Sinai, ethics (i.e., keeping the commandments) had been divorced from worship. God's covenant with David was also being misunderstood; the people presumed on God's presence in the Temple as though it were some kind of magic.

The church can readily get caught in a set of cliches which, while true in certain situations, can become misleading or meaningless. Some such cliches are "being born again" (an expression used also of a new paint job on a car), "having eternal security," and "it's in the Bible." Whole systems of theology can become shibboleths. God's servants are called to identify evil behavior, and, on occasion, they must attack entire thought systems. To *orthodoxy* (correct thinking) must be added *orthopraxy* (correct practice) and *orthokardia* (right heart and right attitudes). Cranfield (1953:193) aptly exhorts, "If we imagine that every denominational tradition and every ecclesiastical vested interest and every bit of ecclesiastical pomp and circumstance are entitled to luxuriate behind the promise that 'the gates of Hades shall not prevail against it' we are like those who fondly repeated, 'The Temple of the Lord, the temple of the Lord, the temple of the Lord are these.'"

◆　　　## 2. Censuring worship abuses (7:16–8:3)

[16]"Pray no more for these people, Jeremiah. Do not weep or pray for them, and don't beg me to help them, for I will not listen to you. [17]Don't you see what they are doing throughout the towns of Judah and in the streets of Jerusalem? [18]No wonder I am so angry! Watch how the children gather wood and the fathers build sacrificial fires. See how the women knead dough and make cakes to offer to the Queen of Heaven. And they pour out liquid offerings to their other idol gods! [19]Am I the one they are hurting?" asks the LORD. "Most of all, they hurt themselves, to their own shame."

[20]So this is what the Sovereign LORD says: "I will pour out my terrible fury on this place. Its people, animals, trees, and crops will be consumed by the unquenchable fire of my anger."

[21]This is what the LORD of Heaven's Armies, the God of Israel, says: "Take your burnt offerings and your other sacrifices and eat them yourselves! [22]When I led your ancestors out of Egypt, it was not burnt offerings and sacrifices I wanted from them. [23]This is what I told them: 'Obey me, and I will be your God, and you will be my people. Do everything as I say, and all will be well!'

[24]"But my people would not listen to me. They kept doing whatever they wanted, following the stubborn desires of their evil hearts. They went backward instead of forward. [25]From the day your ancestors left Egypt until now, I have continued to send my servants, the prophets—day in and day out. [26]But my people have not listened to me or even tried to hear. They have been stubborn and sinful—even worse than their ancestors.

[27]"Tell them all this, but do not expect them to listen. Shout out your warnings, but do not expect them to respond. [28]Say to them, 'This is the nation whose people will not obey the LORD their God and who refuse to be taught. Truth has vanished from among them; it is no longer heard on their lips. [29]Shave your head in mourning, and weep alone on the mountains. For the LORD has rejected and forsaken this generation that has provoked his fury.'

[30]"The people of Judah have sinned before my very eyes," says the LORD. "They have set up their abominable idols right in the Temple that bears my name, defiling it. [31]They have built pagan shrines at Topheth, the garbage dump in the valley of Ben-Hinnom, and there they burn their sons and daughters in the fire. I have never commanded such a horrible deed; it never even crossed my mind to command such a thing! [32]So beware, for the time is coming," says the LORD, "when that garbage dump will no longer be called Topheth or the valley of Ben-Hinnom, but the Valley of Slaughter. They will bury the bodies in Topheth until there is no more room for them. [33]The bodies of my people will be food for the vultures and wild animals, and no one will be left to scare them away. [34]I will put an end to the happy singing and laughter in the streets of Je-

rusalem. The joyful voices of bridegrooms and brides will no longer be heard in the towns of Judah. The land will lie in complete desolation.

## CHAPTER 8

"In that day," says the LORD, "the enemy will break open the graves of the kings and officials of Judah, and the graves of the priests, prophets, and common people of Jerusalem. ²They will spread out their bones on the ground before the sun, moon, and stars—the gods my people have loved, served, and worshiped. Their bones will not be gathered up again or buried but will be scattered on the ground like manure. ³And the people of this evil nation who survive will wish to die rather than live where I will send them. I, the LORD of Heaven's Armies, have spoken!

### NOTES

**7:16 Pray no more for these people.** A prophet's ministry included intercession (Amos 7:1-6; cf. Jer 11:14; 14:11; 15:1). The prohibition ("do not pressure me," Lundbom 1999:473) is an argument for the effectiveness of prayer, since God, now determined to act, guards himself against being dissuaded.

**7:18 make cakes to offer to the Queen of Heaven.** This is probably Ishtar, an astral goddess of love (Venus, in the Targum) worshiped by the Babylonians, and later by the Assyrians, who in Jeremiah's time occupied the territory of northern Israel. The cakes might bear her symbol, a star (44:19).

**7:19 Am I the one they are hurting?** "Hurting" translates ka'as [TH3708, ZH4088] (anger, irritability). The word is paired with kharah [TH2734, ZH3013] (become angry) in Neh 4:1 [3:33], and with the verb "to make jealous," qana' [TH7065, ZH7861] (Ps 78:58).

**7:20 I will pour out my terrible fury.** Some forty-six verses or passages in Jeremiah deal with God's anger (e.g., 4:4, 8, 26; 12:13; 30:24). Baloian (1992:203-205) identifies thirty-seven of these in which a form of rebellion against God is the motivation for God's wrath. For a discussion of 'aph [TH639, ZH678] (anger), khemah [TH2534, ZH2779] (hot displeasure), and wrath generally, see commentary at 25:15-38.

**7:21 Take your burnt offerings.** Most see irony here because of yasap [TH3254, ZH3578] (add): "Go ahead, add your burnt offerings to your other sacrifices" (NIV). The sense is that already the sacrifices were not acceptable because of their contrary lifestyle (7:9), so they might as well add to the number and kind of offerings (cf. Amos 4:4-5). Sarcasm is evident later in the verse as well, since burnt offerings were to be totally consumed, not eaten (Lev 1:3-9).

**7:22 When I led your ancestors out of Egypt, it was not burnt offerings and sacrifices I wanted from them.** Lit., "I did not speak with your fathers or command them on the day I brought them from the land of Egypt about burnt offerings and sacrifices." The statement is false as it stands, so it must be taken with 7:23 to capture the meaning (as the NLT correctly does). For modern examples of this rhetorical device ("idiom of exaggerated contrast"), see Lundbom (1999:488-489), who illustrates from a poster at a Berkeley, California seminary in the 1970s: "It is not a time for building justice; it is a time for confronting injustice."

**7:26 They have been stubborn and sinful.** The idiom qashah 'orep [TH6203, ZH6902] (harden the neck) is found eleven times in the OT; "hardness of neck" (stiff-necked) occurs seven times in the OT (cf. Jer 17:23; 19:15).

**7:31 They have built pagan shrines at Topheth.** "Pagan shrines" translates bamoth. A bamah [TH1116, ZH1195] (height, ridge) was often a man-made platform used for cultic purposes. They were usually on mountain ridges, but here were located in a valley,

Topheth. Josiah's reform closed down such centers (2 Kgs 23:10-13). Topheth signifies "oven" or "fireplace."

*valley of Ben-Hinnom.* This lies southwest of Jerusalem. Sacrificing children was prohibited (Lev 18:21; 20:2-5) but was practiced by Ahaz and Manasseh (2 Kgs 16:3; 21:6). Despite Josiah's reform, it may have been reinstituted by King Jehoiakim.

**8:2** ***They will spread out their bones on the ground.*** This practice was regarded as a major insult (Amos 2:1). Not being buried at all was perhaps even more shameful (cf. 22:19).

### COMMENTARY

Like the preceding sermon, these verses are in prose and they continue the emphasis on all that is wrong with Judah's worship. Interspersed are several private instructions to the prophet. Three specific worship practices, probably common both in the countryside and in the capital, are attacked: astral worship, absence of genuine devotion, and manipulation.

**Astral Worship.** Astral worship had been common since early civilization in the ancient Near East (cf. Ezek 8:16). To it was added Baal worship, appropriated from the neighboring Canaanites. If the sermon (7:1-15) attacks Temple worship, these oracles censure family practices of apostasy. God's fury is intense against such practices because they fly in the face of the fundamental claim in Israelite faith: "Listen, O Israel! The LORD is our God, the LORD alone" (Deut 6:4; cf. Exod 20:3). The punishment will fit the crime: human corpses will lie unburied, exposed to sun, moon, and stars—the deities they had worshiped (8:2).

**Absence of Genuine Devotion.** Israelite worship through the sacrificial system was flawed by the absence of devotion, despite the practice of proper sacrificial techniques. Israel's disobedience is mentioned four times (7:24, 26, 27, 28). God sarcastically gives instruction about divine priorities. Despite all the elaborate "how to" prescriptions (e.g., Leviticus), offerings and sacrifices are less central to worship than obedience. Obedience and the careful guarding of an intimate relationship with God are far more important than sacrificial technique (7:23; 1 Sam 15:22; Isa 1:11-13; Amos 5:21-22; cf. Matt 23:23). God did not need sacrifices as the Queen of Heaven required cakes. God's purposes are of quite another order, as expressed in the covenant formula, "I will be your God, and you will be my people" (see 11:4; 24:7; 30:22; 31:1, 33; 32:38; cf. Lev 26:12).

Judah was caught in a perverted theology about how to ensure its well-being. People no doubt looked to the astral deities to show them favor so that it would go well with them (cf. modern horoscopes). God also had in mind that things should go well, but the condition was obedience to him (7:23). Obedience entails willingness to be taught and to speak the truth (7:28). God's people did not even try to hear, let alone to learn (7:26). As God's fury was directed against pagan worship (7:20), so it would be directed against flawed Israelite worship (7:29).

**Manipulation.** The third worship practice that God censured derived from an imported notion (likely held by Israel's neighbors, the Moabites) that sacrifice is all about gifts, and that the more precious the gift, the more effective the gift will be (i.e., the gift is a bribe). However, to offer sons and daughters by fire as a sacrifice is a wrong-headed invention, for God never intended this (7:31). The punishment fit the crime; just as human bodies were mutilated in sacrifice, so human corpses would be decimated by vultures and animals.

**True Worship.** The passage gives instruction about the difficulties surrounding true worship. Two dangers beset God's people. One of them is syncretism. Living in cultures where gods other than Yahweh were revered, there was always the risk that pagan values would enter Israelite worship by osmosis, as it were. Concern about technique replaced obedience, for example. Attention strayed from God as tangible things were substituted for the mystery and awesomeness of God.

The second danger is that people will respond at a surface level (e.g., baptism, church-going) without engaging Scripture long enough to understand God and his requirements. God yearns to shape a people, but families often prefer to do their own thing. Even when rituals are observed, the bonding of a people to their God may lapse or God's past actions may be misinterpreted. For example, Abraham's willingness to sacrifice his son (Gen 22) may be translated into a universal command (cf. Exod 22:29-30; for an extensive hermeneutical and theological treatment of Gen 22, see Moberly 2000). Bad theology, such as that held by the worshipers in Israel, is spiritually destructive.

◆ E. A People's Sins, an Enemy's Siege, and a Prophet's Sorrow
   (8:4–10:25)
   1. Hurtling down the path of sin (8:4–9:2)

4"Jeremiah, say to the people, 'This is what the LORD says:

"'When people fall down, don't they
     get up again?
When they discover they're on the
     wrong road, don't they turn back?
5 Then why do these people stay on
     their self-destructive path?
Why do the people of Jerusalem
     refuse to turn back?
They cling tightly to their lies
     and will not turn around.
6 I listen to their conversations
     and don't hear a word of truth.
Is anyone sorry for doing wrong?
Does anyone say, "What a terrible
     thing I have done"?
No! All are running down the path
     of sin
     as swiftly as a horse galloping
     into battle!

7 Even the stork that flies across
     the sky
     knows the time of her migration,
as do the turtledove, the swallow,
     and the crane.*
They all return at the proper time
     each year.
But not my people!
     They do not know the LORD's laws.

8 "'How can you say, "We are wise
     because we have the word of the
     LORD,"
when your teachers have twisted
     it by writing lies?
9 These wise teachers will fall
     into the trap of their own
     foolishness,
for they have rejected the word of
     the LORD.
Are they so wise after all?
10 I will give their wives to others

and their farms to strangers.
From the least to the greatest,
    their lives are ruled by greed.
Yes, even my prophets and priests
    are like that.
They are all frauds.
¹¹ They offer superficial treatments
    for my people's mortal wound.
They give assurances of peace
    when there is no peace.
¹² Are they ashamed of these disgusting
    actions?
    Not at all—they don't even know
    how to blush!
Therefore, they will lie among the
    slaughtered.
They will be brought down when
    I punish them,
    says the LORD.
¹³ I will surely consume them.
    There will be no more harvests
    of figs and grapes.
Their fruit trees will all die.
    Whatever I gave them will soon
    be gone.
I, the LORD, have spoken!'

¹⁴ "Then the people will say,
    'Why should we wait here to die?
Come, let's go to the fortified towns
    and die there.
    For the LORD our God has decreed
    our destruction
and has given us a cup of poison to
    drink
    because we sinned against the
    LORD.
¹⁵ We hoped for peace, but no peace came.
    We hoped for a time of healing, but
    found only terror.'

¹⁶ "The snorting of the enemies'
    warhorses can be heard
all the way from the land of Dan in
    the north!
The neighing of their stallions makes
    the whole land tremble.

They are coming to devour the land
    and everything in it—
cities and people alike.
¹⁷ I will send these enemy troops among
    you
like poisonous snakes you cannot
    charm.
They will bite you, and you will die.
    I, the Lord, have spoken!"

¹⁸ My grief is beyond healing;
    my heart is broken.
¹⁹ Listen to the weeping of my people;
    it can be heard all across the land.
"Has the LORD abandoned Jerusalem?*"
    the people ask.
"Is her King no longer there?"

"Oh, why have they provoked my anger
    with their carved idols
    and their worthless foreign gods?"
    says the LORD.

²⁰ "The harvest is finished,
    and the summer is gone," the
    people cry,
"yet we are not saved!"

²¹ I hurt with the hurt of my people.
    I mourn and am overcome with
    grief.
²² Is there no medicine in Gilead?
    Is there no physician there?
Why is there no healing
    for the wounds of my people?

## CHAPTER 9

¹* If only my head were a pool of water
    and my eyes a fountain of tears,
I would weep day and night
    for all my people who have been
    slaughtered.
²* Oh, that I could go away and forget
    my people
    and live in a travelers' shack in the
    desert.
For they are all adulterers—
    a pack of treacherous liars.

---

**8:7** The identification of some of these birds is uncertain.   **8:19** Hebrew *Zion?*   **9:1** Verse 9:1 is numbered 8:23
in Hebrew text.   **9:2** Verses 9:2-26 are numbered 9:1-25 in Hebrew text.

## NOTES

**8:4** *don't they turn back?* The wordplay on *shub* [TH7725, ZH8740] (turn), which character-izes 8:4-6 (occuring six times), is introduced lit. with "if he will turn [away], will he not turn [back]?" The term (*shub*) appears again in 8:6: "All of them turn to their own course" (NRSV). For an earlier wordplay, see the Heb. of 3:10-14; 3:22–4:1 (cf. 31:15-22).

**8:7** *laws.* This word is not *torah* [TH8451, ZH9368] (law), but *mishpat* [TH4941, ZH5477] (justice, doing what is right and honorable). Berkovitz (cited in Craigie et al. 1991:86) proposes "manner" for the biblical meaning of justice.

*the time of her migration.* For great detail on the "manner" of birds and their migratory routes, see Lundbom (1999:510-516), who notes that in North America, migrating swal-lows arrive annually at Mission San Juan Capistrano in southern California on March 19 and leave on October 23.

**8:9** *will fall into the trap of their own foolishness.* The Heb. speaks of being captured (*lakad* [TH3920, ZH4334]) here, but also of being shamed (*bosh* [TH954, ZH1017]), and being shattered (*khathath* [TH2865, ZH3169]). The "unwise wise" (so Craigie et al. 1991:130) reject the word of the Lord, while the truly wise begin with it (Prov 1:7).

**8:10** *I will give their wives to others.* The oracle of 8:10-12 is almost identical to 6:13-15 (see comments). For other parallel texts, see 8:15 and 14:19; 10:12-16 and 51:15-19; 16:14-15 and 23:7-8.

**8:13** *I will surely consume them.* Lit., "Gathering, I will end them" (so Lundbom 1999:523). "Gathering" can have the meaning of "gathering to destroy" (Judg 18:25; 1 Sam 15:6), which, together with the context of 8:12, justifies the NLT reading. But "gathering," especially with '*osepam* [TH625, ZH668] (their harvest), a revocalization preferred here by many interpreters using the LXX, can mean "ingathering" (cf. NRSV; Bright [1965:61], "Ah, but I'll harvest them").

**8:14** *has given us a cup of poison to drink.* Specifically, this is the cup of wrath (25:15; see McKane 1980). Others suggest an enemy poisoning the drinking water, or the bitter-ness of siege. Jer 8:14-17 sketches a vignette of escapees seeking refuge from an invading army.

**8:17** *I will send these enemy troops among you like poisonous snakes.* The NLT supplies the referent of this metaphor; in Heb., the announcement is simply, "I am sending poison-ous snakes among you" (cf. Num 21:6; cf. Deut 32:24; Eccl 10:11).

**8:18** *My grief is beyond healing.* The first line is variously translated, depending on word separations and revocalization of the Heb., "O my Comforter in sorrow" (NIV) or "My joy is gone" (NRSV). The unnamed speaker is likely Jeremiah, though some say it is God (e.g., O'Connor 1988; Roberts 1992). The NLT, largely following Holladay (1986:287-88), sup-plies speakers in 8:19-20.

**8:21** *I mourn and am overcome with grief.* Jeremiah says, lit., "Horror has seized me."

**8:22** *Is there no medicine in Gilead?* Yahweh asks a rhetorical question about spiritual balm to indicate that help is available. This medicine, the resin from a tree in the moun-tainous region east of Jordan, was a trade commodity (Ezek 27:17). The plant was also cul-tivated at En-gedi near Qumran (King 1993:113). Jeremiah responds with a follow-up question in 8:22b (so Holladay 1986:294). For more on the illness metaphor, see 30:12.

**9:2 [1]** *Oh, that I could go away.* Craigie et al. (1991:140-143) and Holladay (1986:299) think that God is speaking in 9:2, but it is better, following Lundbom (1999:537), to understand that Jeremiah is concluding his lament here. Yahweh's accusation begins in 9:3. William Cowper, British poet, captures the sentiment of revulsion that evil brings to sensi-tive persons:

Oh for a lodge in some vast wilderness,
Some boundless contiguity of shade,
Where rumour of oppression and deceit,
Of unsuccessful or successful war,
Might never reach me more! My ear is pained,
My soul is sick, with every day's report
Of wrong and outrage with which earth is filled.

## COMMENTARY

The larger unit (8:4–10:25) can be broken down into three movements (8:4–9:2b; 9:2c-22; 10:1-25). Each movement addresses three themes in the same order: sin, siege, and sorrow. Thus the movements can be further broken down as follows: first, 8:4-13; 8:14-17; 8:18–9:2b; second, 9:2c-9; 9:10-16; 9:17-22; and third, 10:1-16; 10:17-18; 10:19-25.

Jeremiah 8:4-17 includes the familiar elements of the prophetic judgment speech, accusation (8:4-12a) and announcements (8:12b-17). Jeremiah, however, changes his strategy in elaborating on the accusations.

Earlier, Jeremiah's persuasive strategy was built around covenant stipulations (cf. the covenant formula of 7:23). Now the argument shifts from covenant, to common sense, to wisdom generally. Jeremiah's appeal for Israel's return is drawn from everyday experience, the habits of wildlife, and logic. Common sense teaches that it is foolish for someone who discovers that he is on the wrong track to continue on it (8:4b). Oddly, it was not so with Judah (8:9).

The argument from the habits of migratory birds is even more telling (cf. the habits of domestic animals, Isa 1:2-3). In arguing from nature and experience, the prophet is searching for argumentative common ground. Birds are at home in their environment and know how to negotiate the demands made on them. "What left Jeremiah in awe was that among living creatures, humans seem to be the only ones in whom the built-in mechanism that allows all beings to keep in tune with creation was apparently malfunctioning" (Weiss 1986:45).

Jeremiah also used logic to press home the charge of inconsistency (8:8). The spotlight was on the scribes, who claimed to possess God's word. What help is there for the one who has the proper medicine but does not take it? The prophets and priests came under the same censure, for to continue the medical metaphor, they treated symptoms of the disease, but not the disease itself (8:11). They are charged with inconsistency, and beyond that, with outright fraud (8:10).

To ensure that God's warning was heard, Jeremiah used new images from the wisdom tradition. Speech about God is necessarily analogical. A major challenge for God's messengers in any time period is to find the words and images that will convey the essence of their message. Drawing upon the field of ethics, Jeremiah asks if a relationship between persons can exist, let alone flourish, when truth-telling is habitually violated (cf. 9:3-9). Can a society endure when honesty is more often ignored than observed? To recast a cartoon entitled "Lord of the Dance," are unscrupulous politicians and hypocritical religious leaders madly tap-dancing around an emblem marked "Truth"? The incident of Ananias and Sapphira in the early church shows how easily dishonesty can lurk even (or especially) in the robes of piety, and how swift and radical is God's reaction to spoken or enacted falsehood (Acts 5). Undesirable consequences follow when people refuse to admit their deceit or to repent of their dishonesty. For Judah, the consequences were crop failures (8:13), the horrors of war (8:14-16), and an epidemic of poisonous snakes (8:17).

The prophet could not but grieve and weep over the people's stubbornness and their resultant punishment (8:18; 9:1). Prophets know about people's pathos and pain (cf. 2 Kgs 8:11), as does Jesus (Luke 19:41). As one preacher put it, "The Son of man casts no rebel into hell for whom he has not wept." God's messengers, precisely because they are solicitous of a people's well-being, speak of warning and judgment (cf. Lam 2:11; Acts 20:31). When punishment arrives, they do not gloat but weep.

◆      ## 2. No one tells the truth (9:3-26)

3 "My people bend their tongues like
    bows
  to shoot out lies.
They refuse to stand up for the truth.
  They only go from bad to worse.
They do not know me,"
  says the LORD.

4 "Beware of your neighbor!
  Don't even trust your brother!
For brother takes advantage of
    brother,
  and friend slanders friend.
5 They all fool and defraud each other;
  no one tells the truth.
With practiced tongues they tell lies;
  they wear themselves out with all
    their sinning.
6 They pile lie upon lie
  and utterly refuse to acknowledge
    me,"
  says the LORD.

7 Therefore, this is what the LORD
    of Heaven's Armies says:
"See, I will melt them down in
    a crucible
  and test them like metal.
What else can I do with my people?*
8  For their tongues shoot lies like
    poisoned arrows.

They speak friendly words to their
    neighbors
  while scheming in their heart to
    kill them.
9 Should I not punish them for this?"
  says the LORD.
"Should I not avenge myself against
    such a nation?"

10 I will weep for the mountains
  and wail for the wilderness
    pastures.
For they are desolate and empty of
    life;
  the lowing of cattle is heard no
    more;
  the birds and wild animals have
    all fled.

11 "I will make Jerusalem into a heap
    of ruins," says the LORD.
  "It will be a place haunted by
    jackals.
The towns of Judah will be ghost
    towns,
  with no one living in them."

12 Who is wise enough to understand all this? Who has been instructed by the LORD and can explain it to others? Why has the land been so ruined that no one dares to travel through it?

¹³The LORD replies, "This has happened because my people have abandoned my instructions; they have refused to obey what I said. ¹⁴Instead, they have stubbornly followed their own desires and worshiped the images of Baal, as their ancestors taught them. ¹⁵So now, this is what the LORD of Heaven's Armies, the God of Israel, says: Look! I will feed them with bitterness and give them poison to drink. ¹⁶I will scatter them around the world, in places they and their ancestors never heard of, and even there I will chase them with the sword until I have destroyed them completely."

¹⁷This is what the LORD of Heaven's
    Armies says:
"Consider all this, and call for the
        mourners.
    Send for the women who mourn
        at funerals.
¹⁸Quick! Begin your weeping!
    Let the tears flow from your eyes.
¹⁹Hear the people of Jerusalem* crying
        in despair,
    'We are ruined! We are completely
        humiliated!
We must leave our land,
    because our homes have been torn
        down.'"

²⁰Listen, you women, to the words of
        the LORD;
    open your ears to what he has to say.
Teach your daughters to wail;
    teach one another how to lament.
²¹For death has crept in through our
        windows

and has entered our mansions.
    It has killed off the flower of our
        youth:
    Children no longer play in the
        streets,
    and young men no longer gather in
        the squares.

²²This is what the LORD says:
"Bodies will be scattered across the
        fields like clumps of manure,
    like bundles of grain after the
        harvest.
    No one will be left to bury them."

²³This is what the LORD says:
"Don't let the wise boast in their
        wisdom,
    or the powerful boast in their power,
    or the rich boast in their riches.
²⁴But those who wish to boast
    should boast in this alone·
that they truly know me and
    understand that I am the LORD
    who demonstrates unfailing love
    and who brings justice and
        righteousness to the earth,
and that I delight in these things.
    I, the LORD, have spoken!

²⁵"A time is coming," says the LORD, "when I will punish all those who are circumcised in body but not in spirit—²⁶the Egyptians, Edomites, Ammonites, Moabites, the people who live in the desert in remote places,* and yes, even the people of Judah. And like all these pagan nations, the people of Israel also have uncircumcised hearts."

9:7 Hebrew *with the daughter of my people?* Greek version reads *with the evil daughter of my people?*
9:19 Hebrew *Zion.*   9:26 Or *in the desert and clip the corners of their hair.*

NOTES

9:3 [2] *My people bend their tongues like bows.* Holladay (1986:300), followed by Lundbom (1999:542), interprets the bow, rather than the tongue, as falsehood. The Heb. has no simile; it lit. reads, "they bend their tongue, their bow is falsehood" (*sheqer* [TH8267, ZH9214]). It is only in 9:8 that lies, like arrows, are released.

*They refuse to stand up for the truth.* The word *gabar* [TH1396, ZH1504] (prevail, be mighty) supports a translation that continues the war image of 9:3a, "They do battle in the land not for truth (*'emunah* [TH530, ZH575]) but for falsehood" (*sheqer* [TH8267, ZH9214]).

**9:4 [3]** *For brother takes advantage of brother.* The pun on '*aqob* and *ya'qob* [TH6121A/6815, ZH3290/3620] (cf. "cheat/Jacob") is felicitously rendered by Lundbom (1999:539): "and every brother is a Gypping-Jacob" (cf. Gen 27–29).

**9:5 [4]** *They all fool and defraud each other.* The contexts of other occurrences of *talal* [TH2048A, ZH9438] (hiphil, "deceive," "mock") provide illustrations: Laban with Jacob (Gen 31:7); Delilah with Samson (Judg 16:10-15); and an individual with God (Job 13:9).

**9:8 [7]** *while scheming in their heart to kill them.* This is perhaps more dramatic than the Heb., "inwardly he sets a trap for him."

**9:13 [12]** *my people have abandoned my instructions.* Lit., "my *torah* [TH8451, ZH9368] (instruction), which I set before them."

**9:17 [16]** *the women who mourn at funerals.* Lit., the "skilled ones" (feminine). Ancient societies had professional mourners on call as prompters to facilitate the grieving process (cf. Esth 4:1-3; Ezek 27:32).

**9:21 [20]** *It has killed off the flower of our youth.* The NLT has added this line to explain what follows.

**9:23 [22]** *Don't let the wise boast in their wisdom.* Wisdom, power, and riches, representative of royal history, are contrasted with another triad in 9:24 [23], "unfailing love" (*khesedh* [TH2617, ZH2876]), "justice" (*mishpat* [TH4941, ZH5477]), and "righteousness" (*tsedhaqah* [TH6666, ZH7407]). The second triad is illustrative of Mosaic-covenantal history, according to Brueggemann (1992a:285), who notes that the three terms in the first triad occur together nowhere else.

**9:26 [25]** *the people of Israel also have uncircumcised hearts.* For this image of unyielding stubbornness, see 4:4; Deut 10:16; Ps 51:17; Ezek 44:7. "This is as strong a repudiation of empty ritual and formalism as one will find in the OT" (Craigie et al. 1991:154). For the view that the nations listed (other than Judah) practiced an incomplete or partial circumcision, see Steiner (1999:497-505).

COMMENTARY

The rhythm of the three topics—sin, siege, and sorrow, familiar from the preceding chapter—is repeated (see commentary on 8:4). The foremost sin is lying (9:3-9), the siege is by one of several destructive forces (9:11-15), and the sorrow involves professional mourners (9:10, 17-22). An instructive oracle about Yahweh's priorities is added, a critical part of which is "knowing Yahweh" (*yada'* [TH3045, ZH3359]). This idea shows up several times in the larger Hebrew unit (e.g., 8:7, 12b; 9:3b, 6b, 12; 10:23-24a, 25a) and is a lens through which to view the entire book (see "Major Themes and Theological Concerns" in the Introduction). Knowing Yahweh (9:23 [22]) is also a key theme by which this chapter can be analyzed.

First, while the Hebrew word for "know," like the English term, includes the idea of possessing information, it is also marked by a dimension of familiarity-through-experience. So, for example, despite his stay with the priest Eli, Samuel is said not to know the Lord (1 Sam 3:7). That is, Samuel was not yet experientially familiar with the ways of God.

Second, God places high priority on persons who know him experientially as Yahweh (LORD). The clause of self-identification ("I am the LORD") is from the theophanic appearance of the LORD (e.g., Gen 28:13; cf. Exod 3:13-15). The name Yahweh, as explained to Moses, means "present to act in salvation" (Exod 6:2-8), and it was the covenant name by which Israel knew God. To experience God is to experience him in his delivering power.

Third, experience of Yahweh will be associated with three things that Yahweh delights in: unfailing love, justice, and righteousness. "Unfailing love" translates the Hebrew word *khesed* [TH2617, ZH2876], which denotes a disposition by someone of means to voluntarily help someone in need or trouble (cf. Ps 136:10-14). "Justice" goes beyond fairness; it represents putting things right and maintaining relationships that are honorable according to God's behavioral prescriptions. "Righteousness" is a commitment to doing what is right. To discover Yahweh is to discover him in his habitat. Ancient deities were gods of fertility, the weather, and war; Yahweh is distinguished by quite different passions.

A rival triad to these three core values is wisdom, wealth, and power. It is folly to pursue these to the exclusion of Yahweh. One wonders whether Jeremiah was thinking of King Jehoiakim, who took pride in his wealth and took pains to display it (22:13-14), or nations like Moab (48:18, 32-33) or Babylon (50:29; 51:13). Were the scribal elite "the wise," and did prophets revel in their power? Today we offer accolades to scholars, particularly in the sciences. We glory in corporate military strength and celebrate athletic prowess. We follow the fortunes of the rich, sports stars, entertainers, and entrepreneurs. Scripture is not negative about riches, power, or wisdom, except when these usurp the place that God should have.

Wisdom literature speaks of misplaced trust in riches (cf. Ps 49:7; Prov 11:28; 23:5; 27:24), as did Jesus (Luke 12:15-21). Paul refers to the full triad of wealth, power, and wisdom (1 Cor 1:26-31; 2 Cor 10:17; cf. Phil 3:3-11). "Jeremiah's critique of wisdom, power, and wealth as false sources of identity that violate the covenant are re-imaged by Paul as a critique of wisdom, power, and wealth that impede God's saving acts in Jesus Christ" (O'Day 1990:267).

Fourth, in this unit Jeremiah twice associates failure to know God with the social practice of falsehood and deceit (9:3b, 6). Much of the unit targets lying and deception generally (9:2b, 3-6, 8; cf. 8:8, 10-12; Lev 19:11). "The very bases of society, trust and truth, have been corrupted" (Craigie et al. 1991:144). In connecting the two factors—lying and failure to know God (cf. 9:3b with 9:3c, 6)—the unit calls attention to both halves of the Ten Commandments, in the ninth commandment about false witness and the first commandment about "no other god." A commitment to Yahweh as the only true God is a commitment to truth. Many societies are plagued by forms of corruption and deceit, both in business and at high levels of government. For example, the movie industry in America, while it rates many of its products as unfit for children, nevertheless deliberately targets its advertising to children.

Fifth, failure to experience God is a recipe for disaster. For Jeremiah, the sequence is firmly established: with sin comes disaster. If the people ask, "What is the reason for this disaster?" the answer is that they have followed their own desires (9:14), and they do not boast of knowing God (9:24). The disaster announced earlier (e.g., 8:14-16) is sketched in general terms: mountains are empty of life (9:10), Jerusalem is a heap of ruins (9:11), the land is devastated (9:12), the citizenry is dispersed abroad (9:16), and death is at hand (9:21-22; cf. "sword" 9:15).

Sixth, experiencing Yahweh means feeling pained by what pains God. Tears of sorrow come near the end of the unit (9:17-22; cf. 8:18–9:2a). In an earlier scene, the tears were those of the prophet (9:1). Then professional mourners took over prompting the people's expression of grief (9:17). Now, the people break into grief over their loss of property and their humiliation (9:19). Pain has become a way of life. Mothers will have no reason to teach daughters the skills of homemaking, for the experience of death will be the norm. African church leaders who struggle with deaths because of HIV/AIDS (4,900 Africans a day in 2000; see Morgan 2000) ask themselves whether they have become too busy with death.

What begins in Jeremiah as carelessness regarding the truth ends in ruin and bitter grief. Destiny depends upon knowing Yahweh.

◆     ## 3. A study in contrasts: idols and Yahweh (10:1-25)

Hear the word that the LORD speaks to you, O Israel! ²This is what the LORD says:

"Do not act like the other nations,
     who try to read their future in the stars.
Do not be afraid of their predictions,
     even though other nations are terrified by them.
³Their ways are futile and foolish.
     They cut down a tree, and a craftsman carves an idol.
⁴They decorate it with gold and silver
     and then fasten it securely with hammer and nails
     so it won't fall over.
⁵Their gods are like
     helpless scarecrows in a cucumber field!
They cannot speak,
     and they need to be carried because they cannot walk.
Do not be afraid of such gods,
     for they can neither harm you nor do you any good."

⁶LORD, there is no one like you!
     For you are great, and your name is full of power.
⁷Who would not fear you, O King of nations?
     That title belongs to you alone!

Among all the wise people of the earth
     and in all the kingdoms of the world,
     there is no one like you.

⁸People who worship idols are stupid
     and foolish.
The things they worship are made
     of wood!
⁹They bring beaten sheets of silver
     from Tarshish
     and gold from Uphaz,
     and they give these materials to skillful craftsmen
     who make their idols.
Then they dress these gods in royal
     blue and purple robes
     made by expert tailors.
¹⁰But the LORD is the only true God.
     He is the living God and the everlasting King!
The whole earth trembles at his anger.
     The nations cannot stand up to his wrath.

¹¹Say this to those who worship other gods: "Your so-called gods, who did not make the heavens and earth, will vanish from the earth and from under the heavens."*

¹²But God made the earth by his power,
     and he preserves it by his wisdom.

With his own understanding
he stretched out the heavens.
¹³When he speaks in the thunder,
the heavens roar with rain.
He causes the clouds to rise over the
earth.
He sends the lightning with the rain
and releases the wind from his
storehouses.
¹⁴The whole human race is foolish and
has no knowledge!
The craftsmen are disgraced by the
idols they make,
for their carefully shaped works are
a fraud.
These idols have no breath or power.
¹⁵Idols are worthless; they are ridiculous
lies!
On the day of reckoning they will
all be destroyed.
¹⁶But the God of Israel* is no idol!
He is the Creator of everything that
exists,
including Israel, his own special
possession.
The LORD of Heaven's Armies is his
name!

¹⁷Pack your bags and prepare to leave;
the siege is about to begin.
¹⁸For this is what the LORD says:
"Suddenly, I will fling out
all you who live in this land.
I will pour great troubles upon you,
and at last you will feel my anger."

¹⁹My wound is severe,
and my grief is great.

My sickness is incurable,
but I must bear it.
²⁰My home is gone,
and no one is left to help me
rebuild it.
My children have been taken away,
and I will never see them again.
²¹The shepherds of my people have lost
their senses.
They no longer seek wisdom from
the LORD.
Therefore, they fail completely,
and their flocks are scattered.
²²Listen! Hear the terrifying roar of
great armies
as they roll down from the north.
The towns of Judah will be destroyed
and become a haunt for jackals.

²³I know, LORD, that our lives are not
our own.
We are not able to plan our own
course.
²⁴So correct me, LORD, but please be
gentle.
Do not correct me in anger, for
I would die.
²⁵Pour out your wrath on the nations
that refuse to acknowledge you—
on the peoples that do not call upon
your name.
For they have devoured your people
Israel*;
they have devoured and consumed
them,
making the land a desolate
wilderness.

10:11 The original text of this verse is in Aramaic. 10:16 Hebrew *the Portion of Jacob.* See note on 5:20.
10:25 Hebrew *devoured Jacob.* See note on 5:20.

NOTES

**10:2 *Do not act like the other nations.*** Lit., "Do not learn the way of the nations" (cf. Rom 12:1-2). Babylon, the place of exile, was known for astrology and its interpretation of eclipses, comets, etc.

**10:3 *Their ways are futile and foolish.*** The Heb. term *hebel* [TH1892, ZH2039] (empty, void) describes their activities as inconsequential (cf. 2:5; 10:15). The product of the artisan's work is not even dignified by the name "idol" but is merely called a "work," a "thing" (*ma'aseh* [TH4639, ZH5126]). This happens also in 10:9 (twice); see Clendenen (1987).

**10:5** *Their gods are like helpless scarecrows.* Most scholars read the *hapax legomenon*, *tomer* [TH8560A, ZH9473] as "scarecrow," but several versions (Vulgate, Syriac, and Targum) read "palm tree" (*tamar* [TH8558, ZH9469], cf. KJV, ASV, NKJV).

**10:7** *Who would not fear you?* To fear (*yare'* [TH3372, ZH3707], awe, reverence) God differs from *khathath* [TH2865, ZH3169] (terrify, dismay; 10:2). The first is constructive, the second debilitating.

*That title belongs to you alone!* A forceful translation of the *hapax legomenon*, *ya'ah* [TH2969, ZH3278] (be fitting). Cf. "For that is your due" (NRSV).

**10:8** *People who worship idols are stupid and foolish.* To be "stupid" (*ba'ar* [TH1197B, ZH1279]) is to be like cattle (cf. 10:21; this Heb. verb is in the niphal, "lost their senses").

**10:9** *silver from Tarshish and gold from Uphaz.* Tarshish is in southern Spain (cf. other exports, Ezek 27:12); Uphaz is unidentified (cf. Dan 10:5, NRSV).

**10:11** The original text of this verse is in Aramaic (see NLT mg), the trade language of the Babylonians. The Aramaic of this verse, expanded in the Targum as a letter by Jeremiah to the exiles, is best explained as giving a programmed answer to invitations by the locals to engage in idol worship (Lundbom 1999:594-595).

**10:12** *But God made the earth.* The opening participle *'oseh* [TH6213, ZH6913] (the one making) suggests that what follows is hymnic. Jeremiah 10:12-16 is repeated in 51:15-19.

**10:14** *their carefully shaped works are a fraud.* Here, the words for "idol" are *pesel* [TH6459, ZH7181] and *nesek* [TH5262A, ZH5822]. The idol is likely a sculpted piece of wood or stone (*pesel*) overlaid (*nasak* [TH5258, ZH5818]) with precious metal (cf. similar vocabulary in Judg 17:4). The resulting product is *sheqer* [TH8267, ZH9214] (false).

**10:15** *they are ridiculous lies!* Since the word *ta'tu'im* [TH8595, ZH9511] signifies "errors," an alternate translation might be, "they are a bag of blunders."

**10:18** *at last you will feel my anger.* The Heb. is problematic, since "they will find" (*yimtsa'u* [TH4672, ZH5162]) appears without an object. Cf. "so that they may find me" (Syriac), "that they may find it so" (KJV), or "so that they may be captured" (NIV, following the LXX).

**10:19** *My sickness is incurable.* The speaker is Jeremiah (so Lundbom [1999:603-604] who, like others, ascribes 10:20 to Jerusalem), though some propose that Jeremiah is speaking for Judah collectively. Between the two parts of 10:19, perhaps to emphasize grim determination, the Heb. has the clause, omitted by the NLT, "But *I* said."

**10:23** *our lives are not our own.* This is a possible translation of the Heb., which lit. reads, "a man's ways do not belong to him" (cf. "that the way of human beings is not under their control," NRSV). The second line lit. reads, "It is not for a man walking to establish his steps" (cf. Prov 16:9; 20:24).

**10:24** *for I would die.* A better rendering is "lest you reduce me to nothing" (NIV); see Ps 6:1.

## COMMENTARY

The structure of this chapter is sustained, as in the previous two sections, with an exposé of sin (10:1-16), an announcement of judgment through siege (10:17-18, 22), and a cry of pain and sorrow (10:19-21; see commentary on 8:4; 9:3). A personal prayer (10:23-25) concludes the larger unit, which begins in 8:4. The initial poem about sinful practices (10:1-16) alternates between sarcastic mockery of idols (and idol-making) and doxologies to Yahweh (see Craigie et al. 1991:158, leaning on the work of M. Margaliot; cf. Clendenen 1987): (1) the weakness of idols (10:2-5) vs.

the power of God (10:6-7); (2) dead idols (10:8-9) vs. the living Lord (10:10); (3) non-creating idols (10:11) vs. the creator God (10:12-13); and (4) foolish worshipers of idols (10:14-15) vs. the wise worshipers of the Lord (10:16).

The comparisons between idols and the Lord are stark, even absurd, and range beyond those stated in the outline (cf. Isa 44:9-17). The contrasts are achieved by "strophes whose topic entities alternate between Yahweh and the pagan gods" (Clendenen 1987:402). The idols are artisans' products, whether plain or ornate (10:3, 4, 9). God is a category of one, without peer (10:6-7). The idols are immobile and ineffectual (10:5b); God is highly active, bringing clouds and sending lightning (10:13). The idols are nameless, and need not be feared (10:5b), whereas God's name, "The LORD of Heaven's Armies" (10:16), is feared by nature and by nations (10:10). The idols are fragile, easily toppled, and of no account (10:4b), whereas the whole earth trembles before the Lord (10:10b). The idols of wood are frauds that represent a distorted reality (10:14). The Lord is the true God (10:10).

The critique of idolatry could have been made against the backdrop of covenant and commandment. Israel was not to have any other god besides Yahweh and was not to make images (Exod 20:3-4). Yet Jeremiah invokes human reason, not the covenant. So ludicrous, even absurd, is the comparison between idols and God, and so obvious is the folly of making gods in one's own image, that persons so engaged are "foolish," "stupid," and "without knowledge." On the basis of reasoned analysis, alternatives to God, however ingenious, are foolish. Persuading others to go God's way includes encouraging them to think through their assumptions and weigh the evidence. If the temptation in Jeremiah's time was to worship the gods of Babylon, then "in our day the comparable temptation may be the gods of militarism, of nationalism, of naturalism, of consumerism, of technology" (Brueggemann 1998:102). "All human beings have their hearts set somewhere, hold something sacred, worship at some shrine. We are spontaneously idolatrous—where, by 'idolatry,' I mean the worship of some creature, the setting of the heart on some particular thing (usually oneself)" (Lash 1986:21-22).

In idolatrous practices, humans attempt to manipulate deities in order to control destinies. But God is King, fully in control (10:6-10), and thus outside the manipulations of those who would control him. As Creator, God, and not the storm deity Baal, controls the clouds, lightning, and winds (10:13). He also created Israel (10:16), and his sovereignty is trumpeted in his name, "The Lord of Heaven's Armies" (10:6). Any attempt by an individual or a society to be totally autonomous is as absurd as giving one's devotion to an idol.

The announcement of the siege was accompanied by instructions to seek safety (10:17-18, 22). There is no hint that citizens were to resist the enemy. Attempts to deny the inevitable cycles of sin, disaster, and pain are folly. Jeremiah blamed the leaders (shepherds) who were responsible for the evil and its terrible consequences (10:21).

Jeremiah grieved, as did Jerusalem (10:19-21). God's messengers are inevitably moved on behalf of others, even when the punishment is deserved. When shortsightedness precipitates public ruin, one reaction is anger, but sadness is not far behind. The punishment is the more painful because it could have been prevented. It is not easy to come to terms with the evil inherent in others, especially in persons who hold positions of responsibility and authority. The attitude of those who are not in power and helpless to bring about change becomes one of resignation: "My sickness is incurable, but I must bear it."

Jeremiah's final prayer (10:23-25), which gathers up the themes of sin and siege from the foregoing chapters, is in two parts: an acknowledgment of human finitude (10:23) and a request for himself and for the nations (10:24-25). His personal request, with its admission and plea, models a possible response for Judah. Even the prophet/preacher is not exempt from evil. The prayer is fitting for all: God be merciful to me, a sinner (10:24). However, where one might expect a Christian plea for the enemies, there is instead a cry for God to pour out his wrath on them (10:25). Like the imprecatory Psalms (e.g., Pss 109, 137), this cry must be understood as voicing the feelings of an exasperated believer. The language of vengeance is filled with strong emotion. Still, here as elsewhere, Jeremiah refused to take vengeance into his hands, believing that vengeance belongs to God (Deut 32:35). Finally, Jeremiah burned in righteous anger against the nations because of their ruthlessness and their declared independence from God. They refused to submit to God's governance (10:7; cf. Ps 79:6-7 and its echoes in 79:17-25).

## ◆ IV. Stories about Wrestling with Both People and God (11:1–20:18)
### A. Preaching to People and Protesting before God (11:1–12:17)
#### 1. Covenant talk (11:1-17)

The LORD gave another message to Jeremiah. He said, ²"Remind the people of Judah and Jerusalem about the terms of my covenant with them. ³Say to them, 'This is what the LORD, the God of Israel, says: Cursed is anyone who does not obey the terms of my covenant! ⁴For I said to your ancestors when I brought them out of the iron-smelting furnace of Egypt, "If you obey me and do whatever I command you, then you will be my people, and I will be your God." ⁵I said this so I could keep my promise to your ancestors to give you a land flowing with milk and honey—the land you live in today.'"

Then I replied, "Amen, LORD! May it be so."

⁶Then the LORD said, "Broadcast this message in the streets of Jerusalem. Go from town to town throughout the land and say, 'Remember the ancient covenant, and do everything it requires. ⁷For I solemnly warned your ancestors when I brought them out of Egypt, "Obey me!" I have repeated this warning over and over to this day, ⁸but your ancestors did not listen or even pay attention. Instead, they stubbornly followed their own evil desires. And because they refused to obey, I brought upon them all the curses described in this covenant.'"

⁹Again the LORD spoke to me and said, "I have discovered a conspiracy against me among the people of Judah and Jerusalem. ¹⁰They have returned to the sins of their forefathers. They have refused to listen to me and are worshiping other gods. Israel and Judah have both broken the covenant I made with their ancestors. ¹¹Therefore, this is what the LORD says: I am going to

bring calamity upon them, and they will not escape. Though they beg for mercy, I will not listen to their cries. ¹²Then the people of Judah and Jerusalem will pray to their idols and burn incense before them. But the idols will not save them when disaster strikes! ¹³Look now, people of Judah; you have as many gods as you have towns. You have as many altars of shame—altars for burning incense to your god Baal—as there are streets in Jerusalem.

¹⁴"Pray no more for these people, Jeremiah. Do not weep or pray for them, for I will not listen to them when they cry out to me in distress.

¹⁵"What right do my beloved people have to come to my Temple,

when they have done so many immoral things?
Can their vows and sacrifices prevent their destruction?
They actually rejoice in doing evil!
¹⁶I, the LORD, once called them a thriving olive tree,
beautiful to see and full of good fruit.
But now I have sent the fury of their enemies
to burn them with fire,
leaving them charred and broken.

¹⁷"I, the LORD of Heaven's Armies, who planted this olive tree, have ordered it destroyed. For the people of Israel and Judah have done evil, arousing my anger by burning incense to Baal."

## NOTES

**11:2 *terms of my covenant with them.*** "This covenant" may refer to the Mosaic covenant (cf. 11:4, 6, 7) or to Josiah's covenant renewal (2 Kgs 23:3). Since the language is expansive and repetitious, echoing Deuteronomy (cf. Jer 11:3/Deut 27:26; Jer 11:4/Deut 4:20; "oath" in Jer 11:5/Deut 7:8; productive land, Jer 11:5/Deut 6:3; covenant, Jer 11:8-9/Deut 4:13), scholars label such passages as deuteronomistic.

**11:3 *Cursed is anyone who does not obey.*** To be cursed (*'arur* [TH779, ZH826]) is to be placed in a state of "anti-blessing" (so Cain, Gen 4:11; Canaan, Gen 9:25; cf. Lev 26; Deut 27–28). The term *shama'* [TH8085, ZH9048] (obey, listen) occurs eight times in 11:1-17 (11:2, 3, 4, 6, 7, 8, 11, 14).

**11:4 *iron-smelting furnace.*** Lit., "iron furnace." For furnace imagery, see Deut 4:20; 1 Kgs 8:51. Iron was already known in the third millennium BC (cf. Gen 4:22).

**11:5 *a land flowing with milk and honey.*** This idiom for agricultural abundance was a way of speaking of "God's country" since in ancient Near Eastern myths, milk and honey were the preferred foods of the gods (or alternatively, their gift). J. P. J. Olivier (NIDOTTE 2:135-137) proposes that milk and honey (made of date and grape syrup, presupposing gardens) refer to two ways of living in the land—as pastoral herdsmen or as settled farmers.

**11:7 *repeated this warning over and over to this day.*** Lit., "to rise early and testify." The idiom is about persistence, repeated activity, or even eagerness (cf. 7:25; 25:4; 29:19; 35:15).

**11:8 *stubbornly followed their own evil desires.*** The word *sheriruth* [TH8307, ZH9244] (stubbornness) occurs ten times in the OT, eight of these in Jeremiah and always in combination with "heart," better rendered as "will" (so NRSV, cf. 3:17; 7:24; 9:13; 11:8; 13:10; 16:12; 18:12; 23:17).

**11:9 *conspiracy.*** This was probably a revolt against Yahweh due to Baal worship, a possible spin-off of which was the political conspiracy of King Zedekiah against Nebuchadnezzar (Jer 27).

**11:10 *broken the covenant.*** To break (*parar* [TH6565, ZH7296]) is to invalidate, nullify, and render inoperable. Most occurrences of *parar* are in the hiphil or causative stem (e.g., a husband breaking (*parar*) his wife's vow; Num 30:8-15 [9-16]).

**11:13** *altars of shame.* The word "shame" (*bosheth* [TH1322A, ZH1425]) is a pejorative surrogate for Baal (cf. Ishbosheth, "man of shame" for Eshbaal "man of Baal"; cf. 2 Sam 2:8-10 with 1 Chr 8:33; 9:39; also Mephibosheth, 2 Sam 4:4; 9:6-13 with Meribbaal, 1 Chr 8:34; 9:40).

**11:15** *immoral things.* The verse has several difficulties, such as the sentence gaps that occur when one speaks in exasperation. More lit., it might read, "she had done" (without specifying an object; NLT supplies "immoral things"), and "Will numerous [supply "sacrifices"] avert [destruction]?" Some English translations (cf. NLT) follow the LXX, which for the word "numerous" (*harabim* [TH7227, ZH8041]) reads "vows" (*hanedarim* [TH5088, ZH5624]).

**11:16** *once called them a thriving olive tree.* The "once" is supplied in the translation to prepare for the contrast. As for "them," most of 11:15-17 is written in second person, in direct address to the audience. For olive imagery, see Hos 14:6; Ps 52:8 [10].

**11:17** *the people . . . have done evil.* The wordplay is caught in the more literal rendering, "The Lord of hosts has threatened evil (*ra'ah* [TH7451B, ZH8288]) on account of [their] evil (*ra'ah*)."

### COMMENTARY

The subject is the covenant. The Hebrew word *berith* [TH1285, ZH1382] (covenant) occurs five times in this chapter (11:2, 3, 6, 8, 10), more than in any other chapter in Jeremiah except for Jeremiah 34 (also 5 times). A covenant is a formal arrangement between two parties that cements mutual loyalty. The bond and solidarity that are the objectives of covenant are clearly stated here. That bond is emphasized in the covenant formula, "You will be my people, and I will be your God" (11:4; 24:7; 30:22), which brackets the entire Bible (Exod 6:7; Rev 21:3). Some Bible readers understand covenant primarily in terms of promise. Promise is not absent, of course, since loyalty is a basic requirement, but additional promises, such as land (see 11:5), should perhaps be seen as secondary to solidarity.

Hebrew covenants, by and large, follow a pattern known to us from Middle Eastern political treaties of the second millennium BC. They contain stipulations and curses for violating those covenant requirements (cf. Lev 26:14-39; 27:14-26; Deut 28:15-68). Examples of curses or punishments resulting from disobedience might be God's "selling" Israel into enemy hands in the time of the judges (Judg 2:14; 3:8), or the destruction of the northern kingdom (722 BC).

**Curses.** The curse that opens the announcement section (11:3) is an inescapable calamity (11:11), later defined metaphorically as burning the branches of the olive tree (Israel), leaving them charred, broken (11:16), and ultimately destroyed (11:17). The threat of the curse both begins and ends the message (11:3, 17). The curse is not capricious, but arises from the Lord's great displeasure with his people (11:17). The reason for his anger is the people's disloyalty to the covenant. It was not a single action that precipitated this curse threat, but pervasive disloyalty and evil behavior.

**Obedience.** The passage details three scenarios, each focused on obedience or the lack of it. The first scene (11:3-5) relates to the people's Exodus from Egypt and the making of the covenant (cf. Exod 19:5, where obedience is listed as a condition). The second scene (11:6-8) alludes to subsequent history, from the time of the

Exodus to Jeremiah's day (note "today" in 11:5). Again, God emphasizes obedience (11:7). The third scene (11:9-13) is set at the time of writing and is introduced with a new message (11:9). That generation, like earlier ones, was disobedient. The worship of idols constituted a breach of loyalty in the current generation (11:10), an act totally contrary to single-minded loyalty to God (cf. the covenant demand for exclusive devotion to God, Exod 20:3). The covenant, which was to cement the bond between Israel and her God, was broken, and the curses for breaking the covenant would go into effect.

**Covenants, Not Contracts.**   The terms of a contract, as well as their infringements, are easily tallied and action is summarily taken. A covenant is different because there is something elastic about the interpretation of loyalty. At what point is a party to the relationship to be characterized as disloyal? When severely stretched, an elastic band will snap; so also there comes a time, not really definable but nevertheless definite, when it is clear that the partner's commitment has drained away. God is not engaged in hard-nosed calculation, as in a contract, but has extended enormous forbearance. God reviewed the situation, noting the brazenness of a people who trafficked in the Temple with hearts that were really committed to Baal (11:15-17). When God determined that the disloyalty had become a fixed disposition, the curses had to go into effect. It was over! The covenant was off! God even forbade the prophet to pray lest the verdict be altered (11:14).

## ◆    2. An endangered prophet (11:18-23)

18Then the LORD told me about the plots my enemies were making against me. 19I was like a lamb being led to the slaughter. I had no idea that they were planning to kill me! "Let's destroy this man and all his words," they said. "Let's cut him down, so his name will be forgotten forever."

20O LORD of Heaven's Armies,
   you make righteous judgments,
      and you examine the deepest
         thoughts and secrets.
   Let me see your vengeance against
      them,

for I have committed my cause
   to you.

21This is what the LORD says about the men of Anathoth who wanted me dead. They had said, "We will kill you if you do not stop prophesying in the LORD's name." 22So this is what the LORD of Heaven's Armies says about them: "I will punish them! Their young men will die in battle, and their boys and girls will starve to death. 23Not one of these plotters from Anathoth will survive, for I will bring disaster upon them when their time of punishment comes."

NOTES

**11:18 the LORD told me.** No hint is given of the way in which God disclosed (hiphil of *yada'* [TH3045, ZH3359], "made known") the townspeople's plot to Jeremiah.

**11:19 like a lamb being led to the slaughter.** Cf. Isa 53:7 which, except for its use of "sheep" (*seh* [TH7716, ZH8445]), contains the same key words. The Heb. text emphasizes the trusting and unsuspecting nature of the lamb (cf. Ps 44:11 [12], 22 [23]).

**11:20 O LORD of Heaven's Armies.** Jeremiah's prayer to the Lord of hosts (*tseva'oth* [TH6635, ZH7372], armies) is an appeal to the commander-in-chief. The phrase puts this personal matter into the context of a broadly historical, if not cosmic, perspective (cf. 11:22). *Let me see your vengeance against them.* Cf. Jeremiah's other "confessions" or laments (cf. 15:15; 20:12). God's vengeance (*neqamah* [TH5360, ZH5935]) is not associated with cruelty, arbitrariness, or a get-even mentality, but with righteousness (*tsedeq* [TH6664, ZH7406], cf. 11:20a), vindication, and salvation (cf. Isa 63:1). In biblical terms, vengeance has a positive connotation and has to do "with lawfulness, justice, and salvation" (NIDOTTE 3:154). See commentary on 20:7 (cf. Diamond 1987:21-35; 149-157).

C O M M E N T A R Y

From the broad national concerns of the previous panel (11:1-17), the focus in the next two panels is on the personal life of the prophet (11:18-23; 12:1-17). Both scenes show the prophet's vulnerability, whether to outside intrigues or inner uncertainties. In each, there is an indication of Jeremiah's coping mechanisms and "God's further word." This panel (11:18-23) is the first in a series of confessions by the prophet that are a hallmark of the book (cf. 12:1-6; 15:10-21; 17:14-18; 18:18-23; 20:7-18; cf. commentary on 20:7). In these, as in the lament psalms, the complaint is identified (11:18-19), there is prayer (11:20), and God's intervention is reported or celebrated (11:21-23, cf. Ps 13). Laments were preserved, we may conjecture, not only in the interests of personal biography but because they resonated with the anxieties of the larger community.

**The Plot (11:18-19).** Jeremiah's disturbing message brought opposition (cf. the temple sermon, 7:1-15; 26:7-11). The community, which reacted with intense malice, may well have included Jeremiah's family, for Jeremiah complained at one point that he was isolated and without support (15:17). The anti-Jeremiah feelings were not limited to verbal abuse. There were plans to kill and so to silence him. The scene foreshadows later events when Jeremiah is put in prison to face an inevitable, slow death (38:6). King Jehoiakim would try to eradicate any memory of Jeremiah by slicing and burning his scroll (36:20-26). Jesus and many of God's servants since have been physically threatened and maltreated. Jeremiah escaped death; others have not.

**Jeremiah's Response (11:20).** Jeremiah's response shows the degree to which he was in dialogue with God about his ministry and his life. First, he did not take matters into his own hands or scheme to pay back the evil conspirators. Wisely, he committed the case to God, who promised, "Vengeance is mine; I will repay" (Deut 32:35). However, Jeremiah's prayer against his opponents may seem less than Christian. After all, Jesus taught his followers that they should love their enemies (Matt 5:44). However, the ability to love is made possible in part by setting aside (or rather, turning over to God) the issues of justice pertaining to one's personal situation.

Second (though first in the reporting order), the prophet coped with this ugly attack against him by asserting that God is Lord of Heaven's Armies (11:20). Jeremiah did not lose his spiritual balance over this disconcerting report. Instead, the perspective he embraced was that God, as commander-in-chief of all the world, fully

*370*

knew this threat. Furthermore, he knew that God is fully just and would discrimi-
nate between motives and intentions, his own and those of his persecutors. This
conviction about God's competent jurisdiction in human affairs grounded his own
restraint in taking either defensive or offensive action.

**God's Announcement (11:21-23).** God dealt with these conspirators according to
the principle that the punishment should fit the crime. Did they seek the death of
God's servant? They, in turn, would meet untimely deaths, and as so often happens,
the ripple effect of their evil would touch their descendants. The impression from
this report is that God is not slow to act. He enacts justice for his own, just as he
promised (cf. 1:17-19).

◆     ## 3. Audience with the Almighty (12:1-17)

LORD, you always give me justice
    when I bring a case before you.
So let me bring you this complaint:
Why are the wicked so prosperous?
    Why are evil people so happy?
² You have planted them,
    and they have taken root and
    prospered.
Your name is on their lips,
    but you are far from their hearts.
³ But as for me, LORD, you know my
    heart.
You see me and test my thoughts.
Drag these people away like sheep to
    be butchered!
Set them aside to be slaughtered!

⁴ How long must this land mourn?
    Even the grass in the fields has
    withered.
The wild animals and birds have
    disappeared
because of the evil in the land.
For the people have said,
    "The LORD doesn't see what's ahead
    for us!"

⁵ "If racing against mere men makes
    you tired,
how will you race against horses?
If you stumble and fall on open
    ground,
what will you do in the thickets near
    the Jordan?

⁶ Even your brothers, members of your
    own family,
have turned against you.
They plot and raise complaints
    against you.
Do not trust them,
    no matter how pleasantly they
    speak.

⁷ "I have abandoned my people, my
    special possession.
I have surrendered my dearest ones
    to their enemies.
⁸ My chosen people have roared at me
    like a lion of the forest,
so I have treated them with
    contempt.
⁹ My chosen people act like speckled
    vultures,*
but they themselves are surrounded
    by vultures.
Bring on the wild animals to pick
    their corpses clean!

¹⁰ "Many rulers have ravaged my
    vineyard,
trampling down the vines
and turning all its beauty into a
    barren wilderness.
¹¹ They have made it an empty
    wasteland;
I hear its mournful cry.
The whole land is desolate,
    and no one even cares.

<sup>12</sup>On all the bare hilltops,
  destroying armies can be seen.
The sword of the LORD devours people
  from one end of the nation to the
  other.
No one will escape!
<sup>13</sup>My people have planted wheat
  but are harvesting thorns.
They have worn themselves out,
  but it has done them no good.
They will harvest a crop of shame
  because of the fierce anger of the
  LORD."

<sup>14</sup>Now this is what the LORD says: "I will uproot from their land all the evil nations reaching out for the possession I gave my people Israel. And I will uproot Judah from among them. <sup>15</sup>But afterward I will return and have compassion on all of them. I will bring them home to their own lands again, each nation to its own possession. <sup>16</sup>And if these nations truly learn the ways of my people, and if they learn to swear by my name, saying, 'As surely as the LORD lives' (just as they taught my people to swear by the name of Baal), then they will be given a place among my people. <sup>17</sup>But any nation who refuses to obey me will be uprooted and destroyed. I, the LORD, have spoken!"

12:9 Or *speckled hyenas.*

## NOTES

**12:1** Several words and concepts in this lament recall the previous lament: "justice" (*tsaddiq* [TH6662, ZH7404]; cf. "just," *tsedeq* [TH6664, ZH7406], 11:20), "case" (same root as "cause," 11:20, *rib* [TH7378, ZH8189]), and "sheep led to slaughter" (*tibkhah* [TH2878, ZH3186], 12:3; 11:19). Other comparisons could be made about (1) an ordered/disordered world, (2) God's response to evil, and (3) Jeremiah's posture before God.

*Why are evil people so happy?* The "evil" people are "perpetrators of treachery" (the verb *bagad* [TH898, ZH953] and its cognate). "Happy" renders *tsalakh* [TH6743A, ZH7503] (to be at ease).

**12:2** *you are far from their hearts.* The parallelism in 12:2b denotes two spatial terms ("near" and "far") and two body organs ("lips" and "hearts"—lit., "kidneys," figurative for the source of emotions). For hypocrisy, see 9:5-7 [4-6].

**12:4** *The wild animals and birds have disappeared.* For the link between moral behavior and the health of the environment, see Hos 4:1-3. An ethos of evil-doing results in the casting off of constraints; wildlife is then unconsciously exterminated.

**12:5** *thickets near the Jordan.* The KJV renders "swelling of the Jordan," no doubt on the supposition that the word *ga'on* [TH1347, ZH1454] (height) refers to waves (Job 38:11), but in the context of land travel, *ga'on* refers to the dense, high vegetation along the river, at one time a wildlife habitat.

**12:8** *My chosen people.* The special status of this people is captured in several terms: *nakhalah* [TH5159, ZH5709] (an allotted possession, cf. 12:7, 9); *yediduth* [TH3033, ZH3342] (an endearing term, "beloved," or "dearest," 12:7); *bethi* [TH1004, ZH1074] ("my house," temple, land, or people, 12:7). The term *nakhalah* has family overtones; it is property allotted in a kinship setting and sometimes refers to inheritance. The people (12:7) and the land (12:14) are God's heritage (*nakhalah*).

*I have treated them with contempt.* Lit., "on account of this I hated her" (cf. Hos 9:15). God's love for Israel is affirmed elsewhere in Jeremiah (cf. 31:3). The paradox may be eased by noting the Heb. way of stating comparisons. Thus Mal 1:2-3 is to be understood, "In comparison to my love, my revised attitude is like hatred."

**12:11** *no one even cares.* The Heb. expression is idiomatic: "there is not anyone who has put [it] upon [his] heart."

**12:12 *No one will escape!*** The Heb. reads, "there is no well-being (*shalom* [TH7965, ZH8934]) to any flesh."

**12:13 *worn themselves out.*** Some have proposed a repointing of the verb to mean "sifted" (*nakhalu*) rather than "worked hard," "be exhausted" (*nekhlu* [TH2470, ZH2703]). For details, see Craigie et al. 1991:183. A wordplay with *nakhalah* [TH5159, ZH5709] (inheritance) may be intended (Holladay 1986:388).

***it has done them no good.*** The issue of benefit, "to gain or profit" (*ya'al* [TH3276, ZH3603]) occurs elsewhere (see the Heb. of 2:8, 11; 7:8; 16:19; 23:32).

**12:14 *I will uproot Judah from among them.*** The term "uproot" (*nathash* [TH5428, ZH6004], which generally has negative connotations (cf. 1:10), may here be positively understood as deliverance. God will pluck her out of the grasp of the nations.

**12:15 *I will bring them home to their own lands again.*** For the promise of Israel's return to its land, see 24:6; 31:10-12. In later oracles, only certain enemy nations are specifically promised return to the homeland, assuming that the expression *shub shebuth* [TH7622, ZH8654] ("bring about the restoration"; cf. 30:3) includes resettlement on the land (for Moab, see 48:47; for Ammon, see 49:6; for Elam, see 49:39). Others, such as Hazor, are to remain desolate (49:33).

**12:16 *As surely as the LORD lives.*** To swear by Yahweh's name is to give him recognition and honor (for its use as an element of repentance, see 4:2).

**12:17 *any nation who refuses to obey me will be uprooted and destroyed.*** The evil ones, who Jeremiah claimed were planted by Yahweh (12:2), were not exempt from divine uprooting in the negative sense.


## COMMENTARY

The trigger for the prophet's reflection on life may be the plot mentioned in Jeremiah 11:18-23 (cf. 12:6). The question of theodicy (judgments God makes) is also raised elsewhere (cf. Job, Ps 73; Hab 1:1-17). This dialogue contains the speeches of both Jeremiah (12:1-4) and God (12:5-17) on the topic of life's injustices. Some see God's reply as ending in 12:6, others in 12:13. Despite the shift to prose in 12:14, the subject matter of dealing with evil continues in 12:14-17.

**The Problem Posed (12:1-4).** Jeremiah's complaint begins with a three-word creedal confession, "You, Yahweh [are] righteous" (cf. 11:20; Ps 89:14). Righteousness entails a standard, often conceptualized as a set of rules. However, the standard has less to do with abstract morality than with right relationships, which, while guided by rules, go beyond conformity to them. So, for example, in interceding for Sodom, Abraham casts himself upon something other than a code of laws when he asks, "Should not the Judge of all the earth do what is right?" (Gen 18:25). Similarly, Judah's remark about Tamar, "She is more in the right than I am" (Gen 38:26), transcends the mechanics of a code in identifying the right action in the context of their relationship. Although righteousness is about appropriate behavior within a relationship, the basic elements of rightness or justice as rewards for good behavior and punishment for evil behavior are not thereby set aside. God, Jeremiah claimed, does not maintain moral order in human society. He does not punish the wicked, such as hypocrites who say one thing and do another, but allows them to prosper. Their evil actions even ruin the environment. Still God remains silent. In exasperation, Jeremiah called on God to take these culprits to the slaughter house, "Let me see your vengeance against them" (11:20). Was Jeremiah here calling for God to get on with doing what was right (cf. commentary on 20:7)?

**Dimensions of the Solution (12:5-17).**   God's reply skirts any direct answer. It is God's prerogative to define what is right, as well as to give or to withhold an answer (cf. Job). As though a seasoned answer to the perplexity would not really benefit the questioner, God offered counsel on coping with life's inequities.

The gist of the first response is gentle chiding. Jeremiah 12:5 could read, "If you stumble on flat ground, how will you do when jousting in Jordan's jungles? If the little things in life get you down, what will you do when you come upon really tough times?" There seems to be little empathy for the questioner and his dilemma and there is no reassuring answer (as in 1:17-19). In fact, Jeremiah had already given the answer: God is righteous. If a believer stumbles at the least apparent in-consistency between what is believed about God and what is experienced in life (as though there were no answer), what will one do when these examples multiply? The issue is the robustness of a faith that says, "You, God, are righteous."

God's further reply is counsel for Jeremiah's next steps. Be wary of others, no mat-ter how smooth their talk. Live life with a suspicious edge since wickedness is a real factor. How one negotiates life, given this reality, is what counts. By implication, trust can rest without reservation only in a righteous God, not in people.

Yet, there was a bigger problem at hand: God was turning in anger on his own people. God had announced an "unelection": he was abandoning the people he had chosen (12:7). Here is an intellectual and emotional problem of giant propor-tions. How could God's abandonment be squared with assertions of God's faithful-ness, with statements such as, "He (Yahweh) will not abandon his own special possession" (Ps 94:14)? It is the question Jesus asks, "My God, my God! Why have you forsaken me?" (Mark 15:34). One can perhaps understand God's withdrawal from a sinful people, but is there even a glimmer of an explanation for God's with-drawal from his Son? Isaiah offers some help: "For a brief moment I abandoned you, but with great compassion I will take you back" (Isa 54:7, NIV).

Jeremiah must have felt the perplexity of the matter, especially when God's affec-tionate feeling for his people was expressed in phrases such as "my special posses-sion," "my dearest ones" (12:7), "my chosen people" (12:8, 9). At the same time, God expressed feelings of disgust, even hate (12:8). This special people had roared its defiance against God, their benefactor, so God had allowed the invaders to rav-age the land of his chosen ones. Here is displayed the anguish of a righteous God who in love and in anger must render a verdict. Jeremiah was permitted a glimpse into God's heart.

The conversation, now about compassion (12:14-17), nevertheless deals with theodicy and God's intolerance of evil persons and nations that appear to prosper (cf. 12:1). These evil nations want the territory that God allotted to Israel. In the end, God will not stand idly by, but will uproot and destroy them (12:14). The answer concerning evil on a large scale is the same as God's answer to the attack on Jeremiah's person—retribution (cf. 11:22). Yet punishment is not the last word even for evil nations, because a righteous God is also compassionate and takes the initiative in reconciliation. It is not because of their merit that these nations are returned to their land, but because of God's graciousness. God will not allow evil to go unpunished, but Jeremiah, like us, must learn that righteousness incorporates compassion.

◆   ## B. A Ruined Loincloth, Smashed Wine Jars, and Awful Pride (13:1-27)
### 1. A sermon in street theater style (13:1-11)

This is what the LORD said to me: "Go and buy a linen loincloth and put it on, but do not wash it." ²So I bought the loincloth as the LORD directed me, and I put it on.

³Then the LORD gave me another message: ⁴"Take the linen loincloth you are wearing, and go to the Euphrates River.* Hide it there in a hole in the rocks." ⁵So I went and hid it by the Euphrates as the LORD had instructed me.

⁶A long time afterward the LORD said to me, "Go back to the Euphrates and get the loincloth I told you to hide there." ⁷So I went to the Euphrates and dug it out of the hole where I had hidden it. But now it was rotting and falling apart. The loincloth was good for nothing.

⁸Then I received this message from the LORD: ⁹"This is what the LORD says: This shows how I will rot away the pride of Judah and Jerusalem. ¹⁰These wicked people refuse to listen to me. They stubbornly follow their own desires and worship other gods. Therefore, they will become like this loincloth—good for nothing! ¹¹As a loincloth clings to a man's waist, so I created Judah and Israel to cling to me, says the LORD. They were to be my people, my pride, my glory—an honor to my name. But they would not listen to me.

13:4 Hebrew *Perath;* also in 13:5, 6, 7.

### NOTES

13:1 *buy a linen loincloth.* Since the *'ezor* [TH232, ZH258] (loincloth) is described as hugging the hips (13:11), it is not a slender fastening belt, but something like an outer garment. An undergarment would hardly be noticed by the public for whom the action was to be a sign (cf. Friebel 1999:99-115, who has the rendering "waist-sash").

13:4 *go to the Euphrates River.* The distance to this major river in Mesopotamia was 350 miles; such a trip is not likely (Friebel 1999:106-107). Some propose the place as Parah (similar in sound to Heb. *perath* [TH6578, ZH7310], "Euphrates") within the country not far from Anathoth, or even that the name is symbolic since the Babylonians, instruments of Judah's destruction, lived along the Euphrates river.

13:9 *I will rot away the pride of Judah and Jerusalem.* The Heb. text uses the word "pride" (*ga'on* [TH1347, ZH1454]) twice, emphasizing the great pride of Jerusalem, possibly because of its worship show-piece, the temple built by Solomon.

13:10 *They stubbornly follow their own desires.* The phrase "stubborn of their heart" (*sheriruth libbam* [TH8307, ZH9244]) is a trademark phrase in the book (see note on 11:8), occurring elsewhere only in Deut 29:19 [18] and Ps 81:12 [13].

### COMMENTARY

This is the first of several sign-acts or symbolic actions by the prophet, intended to catch people's attention and to reinforce his message (cf. 19:1-2; 27:1-28; 32:1-15; cf.

Ezekiel's use of sign acts in Ezek 4–5; 12; 37; see Friebel 1999). The literary genre of symbolic action is here followed closely, with instruction, report of compliance, and explanation. The explanation turns on three terms, "cling," "useless," and "ruin."

**Cling.** The word "cling" (*dabaq* [TH1692, ZH1815]) is used here in the sense of loyalty or devotion ("remained faithful" in 2 Kgs 18:6 is the same Heb. word). Jeremiah's wearing the garment is mentioned three times in the sign-act section. The explanation is that Israel, as a showpiece community, should exhibit the divinely-revealed way of living, testify to the greatness of the one true God, and in so doing, augment God's reputation, glory, and honor (cf. Exod 19:5-6; Isa 43:8-11; Rev 4:11).

**Useless.** A second key term is "useless," "good for nothing" (same Heb. expression). The garment was ruined through long exposure to water, soil, and probably insects. Israel, pictured as a decorative but practical garment, will also become useless because of her refusal to listen (contrast Jeremiah's compliance), her corroded (stubborn) heart, which preferred idols to Yahweh, and her pride and arrogance. Each of these factors detracted from the pleasure that God might take in his people. It is an account of human actions spoiling God's intentions, of a people coming short of the glory of God (Rom 3:23).

**Ruin.** The third key term, employed both in the story of the garment and in its explanation, is the word "ruin" (niphal of *shakhath* [TH7843, ZH8845], "be destroyed," "brought to ruin"), rendered as "mildewed" and "rotting" (13:7). God resists the proud (13:15; Prov 8:13); he has zero tolerance for idolatry (Exod 20:3) and prefers obedience over sacrifice (1 Sam 15:22). Pride precipitates God's punishment (cf. Moab, Jer 48:29-35). The symbolic action, which stresses God's intention for intimacy with his people, serves also as a wake-up call for Israel to change her ways or face ruin.

◆    ## 2. A proverb: smashed wine jars (13:12-14)

¹²"So tell them, 'This is what the LORD, the God of Israel, says: May all your jars be filled with wine.' And they will reply, 'Of course! Jars are made to be filled with wine!'

¹³"Then tell them, 'No, this is what the LORD means: I will fill everyone in this land with drunkenness—from the king sitting on David's throne to the priests and the prophets, right down to the common people of Jerusalem. ¹⁴I will smash them against each other, even parents against children, says the LORD. I will not let my pity or mercy or compassion keep me from destroying them.'"

### NOTES

**13:12 *May all your jars be filled with wine.*** The word *nebel* [TH5035, ZH5574] (wineskin) is taken by lexicographers to mean both "jar," which would fit the idea of smashing (13:14), and "wineskin," which accentuates the humor of persons filled with wine.

**13:13 *I will fill everyone . . . with drunkenness.*** God's "filling" everyone may obliquely refer to the cup of wrath (25:15-17; Hab 2:15-16).

COMMENTARY

Jeremiah, it seems, turns a proverb on its head. Ezekiel also did so (cf. the negative nuance of "vine" for Israel, Ezek 15:1-8). Full wineskins are evidence of a bounteous harvest of grapes and of a generally healthy economy. All is well; no shortages exist, even of luxury items. As an earlier political promise in America of "a car in every garage" evoked images of security within an economy that permitted luxuries, so did the saying about full wineskins for Judah. But the prophet overturns this popular banter. The wineskin is reinterpreted as many inebriated human bodies filled with wine. These drunken, out-of-control persons wreak havoc and destruction. God orchestrates this debacle of self-destruction and madness (cf. the covenant curse, Deut 28:28). He is firmly determined to bring about such confusion, and he will not be dissuaded. And yet, strangely, in the following verses, the people are urged to change their behavior so that God might change.

The initial arrogant response to the statement about filling their wineskins took this anticipated prosperity for granted. In effect, the hearers retorted, "We are entitled to such prosperity, and we will take the credit for the good times." Such is the language of independent and prideful people, who in their self-sufficiency think they can engineer their own future. But they were mistaken. The common saying was soon to take on an unexpected meaning. Sometimes obvious conclusions, when placed beneath God's scrutiny, are wrong conclusions.

◆　　3. Pride and punishment (13:15-27)

15 Listen and pay attention!
　　Do not be arrogant, for the LORD has
　　　spoken.
16 Give glory to the LORD your God
　　before it is too late.
　　Acknowledge him before he brings
　　　darkness upon you,
　　causing you to stumble and fall on
　　　the darkening mountains.
　　For then, when you look for light,
　　　you will find only terrible darkness
　　　and gloom.
17 And if you still refuse to listen,
　　I will weep alone because of your
　　　pride.
　　My eyes will overflow with tears,
　　　because the LORD's flock will be led
　　　away into exile.

18 Say to the king and his mother,
　　"Come down from your thrones
　　　and sit in the dust,
　　for your glorious crowns

will soon be snatched from your
　heads."
19 The towns of the Negev will close their
　　gates,
　　and no one will be able to open
　　　them.
　　The people of Judah will be taken
　　　away as captives.
　　All will be carried into exile.

20 Open up your eyes and see
　　the armies marching down from the
　　　north!
　　Where is your flock—
　　　your beautiful flock—
　　　that he gave you to care for?
21 What will you say when the LORD takes
　　　the allies you have cultivated
　　　and appoints them as your rulers?
　　Pangs of anguish will grip you,
　　　like those of a woman in labor!
22 You may ask yourself,
　　　"Why is all this happening to me?"

It is because of your many sins!
That is why you have been stripped
    and raped by invading armies.
²³ Can an Ethiopian* change the color of
        his skin?
    Can a leopard take away its spots?
    Neither can you start doing good,
        for you have always done evil.

²⁴ "I will scatter you like chaff
    that is blown away by the desert
        winds.
²⁵ This is your allotment,

the portion I have assigned to you,"
    says the LORD,
"for you have forgotten me,
    putting your trust in false gods.
²⁶ I myself will strip you
    and expose you to shame.
²⁷ I have seen your adultery and lust,
    and your disgusting idol worship
        out in the fields and on
        the hills.
What sorrow awaits you, Jerusalem!
How long before you are pure?"

13:23 Hebrew *a Cushite.*

## NOTES

**13:18** *your glorious crowns will soon be snatched.* The verb *yarad* [TH3381, ZH3718] (go down) and other verbs in 13:18-19 are best construed as prophetic perfects—i.e., future actions regarded as having already taken place. Read historically, however, the king in question could be Jehoiachin, who ruled for three months (598–597 BC); the queen mother would be Josiah's widow (cf. 2 Kgs 24:8-12).

**13:20** *see the armies marching down from the north!* The verb form indicates that the addressee is feminine; it may refer to Zion (so LXX; cf. "Jerusalem" in 13:27). The foe from the north has already been mentioned in 1:13-15.

**13:22** *you have been stripped and raped.* The feminine imagery (perhaps alluding to Zion) continues (lit., "your skirts are removed; they violate your heels"). Heels here represent the body. The expression is reminiscent of the English "from head to toe."

**13:25** *putting your trust in false gods.* The term *sheqer* [TH8267, ZH9214] (deception), which here is used of "false gods," is pervasive in Jeremiah (thirty-four out of 115 times in the OT).

**13:26** *expose you to shame.* The Heb., continuing the feminine imagery, is less delicate: "I will pull up your skirts over your face and your indecency will be seen."

**13:27** *your disgusting idol worship.* The rendering is interpretive. Jeremiah continues to use sexual language, following Hosea, who depicted idolatry as sexual promiscuity (lit., "your plans for harlotry, prostitution, your abominations").

## COMMENTARY

The subject of pride runs like a red thread through the three sections of this chapter. Each section contains an ominous note of judgment against pride and its related evils. Pride is merely mentioned in the first segment (13:1-11), it is documented in the arrogant response in the second section (13:12-14), and it becomes the topic of a prophetic discourse in the third section (13:15-27).

**Discourse on Pride.** Pride is announced as the topic in the initial warning (13:15). The antidote to pride is forthright: "Give glory to the LORD." The admonition is thus linked to the sign-act that showed that God's goal for Israel was to enhance his glory (13:11). The motivation given is that time is running out (13:16b), and things are about to change for the worse. Prideful behavior centers on self, vaunts achievements, and ignores God. The admonition gains credibility from the prophet's genuine concern. So serious, ugly, and fraught with bad consequences is Judah's pride that unless things change, Jeremiah will give himself over to isolation and weeping. It is burdensome for a concerned person to identify an evil, whether in society or in an individual, which if unchecked will lead to grave consequences. Jeremiah was no stranger to tears, because his concern for his people's waywardness was profound and intense (4:19-20; 8:18-19; 9:1). If Jeremiah is the final speaker (it is God who speaks in 13:24-27a), his agony is obviously acute. "How long will it be before you are pure?" (13:27b).

The admonition to humility is made concrete in the prophet's address to royalty, calling them to humble themselves before they are humiliated (13:18; cf. Prov 8:13; 16:5, 18). But the problem of Israel's pride was major, as though it were part of their DNA. A dark-skinned person cannot change his or her skin; an animal has permanent distinguishing features, and Israel (like humankind in general) is an evildoer by definition (13:23). Pride is illustrated elsewhere by the king of Babylon (Isa 14:4-19), Judah's King Uzziah (2 Chr 26:16), and Nebuchadnezzar (Dan 4:37). The prohibition against human pride is echoed in the New Testament (Jas 4:6, 16; cf. Rom 1:30). Sir Thomas More, author of *Utopia* (1516), wrote: "Pride is the infernal serpent that steals into the hearts of men, thwarting and holding them back from choosing the better way of life."

**Punishment for Pride.** The topic of God's judgment on evil, like the subject of pride, is first touched upon lightly in the sign-act (13:8); then announced forthrightly in connection with the proverb (13:14) and finally crescendoes to shrillness (13:24-26).

The judgment would take several forms. Physically, the land would come under foreign rule (13:19). The invading armies would come from the north (cf. 1:13-15); these are eventually identified as Babylon (20:4). For Judah, the result would be exile (the darkness of 13:16), announced starkly and without hedging (13:19; cf. 52:28-30). Two metaphors about exile follow. The first is the scattering of chaff, familiar to every Israelite from the winnowing of grain on the threshing floors at harvest (13:24). The second metaphor of a woman, likely a prostitute, is more telling. Her skirts will be lifted high to expose her indecency and shame. If the physical punishment is that of being mastered by others, the emotional punishment is that of being subjected to shame. In the ancient Israelite society, which scholars increasingly depict as an honor-shame society, such shameful treatment was especially abhorrent.

These calamities are cause-driven. The question of "why?" is posed and answered: "It is because of your many sins" (13:22). Pride is the focus of this chapter, but other spin-off sins are also listed, especially adultery and promiscuity, which can be understood either physically, or metaphorically and spiritually as idolatry, or as both (13:27). When persons proceed independently of God, they eventually become their own gods. As their accountability vanishes, they throw off moral restraints, take large moral license, and follow their desires (cf. 13:10).

◆   **C. Crises, Regional and Personal (14:1–15:21)**
   **1. A regional drought crisis (14:1–15:9)**

This message came to Jeremiah from the LORD, explaining why he was holding back the rain:

² "Judah wilts;
   commerce at the city gates grinds to
      a halt.
All the people sit on the ground in
      mourning,
   and a great cry rises from
      Jerusalem.
³ The nobles send servants to get water,
   but all the wells are dry.
The servants return with empty
      pitchers,
   confused and desperate,
   covering their heads in grief.
⁴ The ground is parched
   and cracked for lack of rain.
The farmers are deeply troubled;
   they, too, cover their heads.
⁵ Even the doe abandons her newborn
      fawn
   because there is no grass in the
      field.
⁶ The wild donkeys stand on the bare
      hills
   panting like thirsty jackals.
They strain their eyes looking for
      grass,
   but there is none to be found."

⁷ The people say, "Our wickedness has
      caught up with us, LORD,
   but help us for the sake of your own
      reputation.
We have turned away from you
   and sinned against you again and
      again.
⁸ O Hope of Israel, our Savior in times of
      trouble,
   why are you like a stranger to us?
Why are you like a traveler passing
      through the land,
   stopping only for the night?
⁹ Are you also confused?
   Is our champion helpless to save us?

You are right here among us,
      LORD.
We are known as your people.
   Please don't abandon us now!"

¹⁰ So this is what the LORD says to his
      people:
"You love to wander far from me
   and do not restrain yourselves.
Therefore, I will no longer accept you
      as my people.
Now I will remember all your
      wickedness
   and will punish you for your
      sins."

¹¹ Then the LORD said to me, "Do not pray for these people anymore. ¹²When they fast, I will pay no attention. When they present their burnt offerings and grain offerings to me, I will not accept them. Instead, I will devour them with war, famine, and disease."

¹³ Then I said, "O Sovereign LORD, their prophets are telling them, 'All is well—no war or famine will come. The LORD will surely send you peace.'"

¹⁴ Then the LORD said, "These prophets are telling lies in my name. I did not send them or tell them to speak. I did not give them any messages. They prophesy of visions and revelations they have never seen or heard. They speak foolishness made up in their own lying hearts. ¹⁵Therefore, this is what the LORD says: I will punish these lying prophets, for they have spoken in my name even though I never sent them. They say that no war or famine will come, but they themselves will die by war and famine! ¹⁶As for the people to whom they prophesy—their bodies will be thrown out into the streets of Jerusalem, victims of famine and war. There will be no one left to bury them. Husbands, wives, sons, and daughters—all will be gone. For I will pour out their own wickedness on them. ¹⁷Now, Jeremiah, say this to them:

"Night and day my eyes overflow with
tears.
I cannot stop weeping,
for my virgin daughter—my precious
people—
has been struck down
and lies mortally wounded.
¹⁸ If I go out into the fields,
I see the bodies of people
slaughtered by the enemy.
If I walk the city streets,
I see people who have died of
starvation.
The prophets and priests continue
with their work,
but they don't know what they're
doing."

¹⁹ LORD, have you completely rejected
Judah?
Do you really hate Jerusalem?*
Why have you wounded us past all
hope of healing?
We hoped for peace, but no peace
came.
We hoped for a time of healing, but
found only terror.
²⁰ LORD, we confess our wickedness
and that of our ancestors, too.
We all have sinned against you.
²¹ For the sake of your reputation, LORD,
do not abandon us.
Do not disgrace your own glorious
throne.
Please remember us,
and do not break your covenant
with us.

²² Can any of the worthless foreign gods
send us rain?
Does it fall from the sky by itself?
No, you are the one, O LORD our God!
Only you can do such things.
So we will wait for you to help us.

## CHAPTER 15

Then the LORD said to me, "Even if Moses
and Samuel stood before me pleading for
these people, I wouldn't help them. Away
with them! Get them out of my sight!

²And if they say to you, 'But where can we
go?' tell them, 'This is what the LORD says:

"'Those who are destined for death, to
death;
those who are destined for war, to
war;
those who are destined for famine, to
famine;
those who are destined for captivity,
to captivity.'

³"I will send four kinds of destroyers
against them," says the LORD. "I will send
the sword to kill, the dogs to drag away,
the vultures to devour, and the wild animals to finish up what is left. ⁴Because of
the wicked things Manasseh son of Hezekiah, king of Judah, did in Jerusalem, I will
make my people an object of horror to all
the kingdoms of the earth.

⁵"Who will feel sorry for you,
Jerusalem?
Who will weep for you?
Who will even bother to ask how
you are?
⁶ You have abandoned me
and turned your back on me,"
says the LORD.
"Therefore, I will raise my fist to
destroy you.
I am tired of always giving you
another chance.
⁷ I will winnow you like grain at the
gates of your cities
and take away the children you
hold dear.
I will destroy my own people,
because they refuse to change their
evil ways.
⁸ There will be more widows
than the grains of sand on the
seashore.
At noontime I will bring a destroyer
against the mothers of young men.
I will cause anguish and terror
to come upon them suddenly.
⁹ The mother of seven grows faint and
gasps for breath;

| her sun has gone down while it is still day. She sits childless now, disgraced and humiliated. | And I will hand over those who are left to be killed by the enemy. I, the LORD, have spoken!" |

14:19 Hebrew *Zion?*

## NOTES

**14:4 *The farmers are deeply troubled*.** These farmers (*'ikkarim* [TH406, ZH438]) were not independent landowners, but, judging by the Akkadian cognate, more like hired hands (Holladay 1986:431). The drought affected all layers of society, from nobles to hired hands. The word *bosh* [TH954, ZH1017] has to do with shame, disappointment, and humiliation, and only obliquely with anxiety or fear. Holladay (2001) has proposed the date of Nov/Dec 601 BC for the public response to the crisis.

**14:7 *Our wickedness has caught up with us*.** The word "wickedness" translates two Heb. words: *'awon* [TH5771, ZH6411] (perversity), a frequent word for evil in the OT, and *meshubah* [TH4878, ZH5412] ("turning," here "apostasy"; cf. the Heb. of 2:19; 3:6, 8, 11, 12, 22; 5:6; 8:5; found elsewhere only three times, Prov 1:32, Hos 11:7, 14:5 [4]).

**14:10 *I will no longer accept you as my people*.** As often occurs, Jeremiah's radical statement echoes Hosea (cf. Hos 1:9). For similar language about remembering Israel's wrongdoing, see Hos 8:13.

**14:14 *They prophesy of visions and revelations they have never seen or heard*.** The Heb. text has a threefold description: deceptive (*sheqer* [TH8267, ZH9214]) visions, worthless divinations (*qesem* [TH7081, ZH7877]), and fabrications (*tarmith* [TH8649C, ZH9567]) of their hearts. For God's view of false prophets, see 23:9-32; 28–29.

**14:17 *Now, Jeremiah, say this to them*.** Some plausibly suggest that this sentence concludes the foregoing (14:14-16), which allows for the possibility that Jeremiah, and not God, is the speaker in what follows (14:17, 18).

**14:18 *they don't know what they're doing*.** The Heb. is cryptic: "they do not know." Other options for completing the idea are "they do not know what God is doing," or "they do not know what time it is."

**14:19 *Do you really hate Jerusalem?*** The translation handles an idiom, "the soul goes up," by conveying a sense of loathing or revulsion (cf. 12:8 for an unambiguous statement about God's hatred).

**15:4 *the wicked things Manasseh . . . did*.** The actions of Judah's King Manasseh (687–642 BC) are described in 2 Kgs 21:1-8 (cf. 2 Chr 33:1-9). Divine punishment continues to the third or fourth generation (Exod 34:7); here the time span was about sixty years.

**15:6 *I am tired of always giving you another chance*.** If God relents (niphal of *nakham* [TH5162, ZH5714]), this change of stance will amount to offering another chance (18:8, 10; Amos 7:3,6; Jonah 4:2).

## COMMENTARY

The extended section (14:1–15:9) depicts the disaster of drought and famine and reports the response of the people, the prophet, and God. A recurring issue is the connection between natural disasters or calamities and the wrongdoing of the people. The first complaint is about the drought (14:2-6); the concluding divine response is about battle, and in between (14:11-16), both drought and battle are mentioned (cf. Holladay 1986:422). The parallel structure, broadly in the form of a lament, includes complaint (14:2-6 and 14:17-18), prayer (14:7-9 and 14:19-22), and divine response (14:10-12 [13-16] and 15:1-9). The comments that follow are organized according to this schema.

**Depicting the Disaster (14:1-6, 17-18).**  The drought is described in terms of its effects on people (e.g., servants, 14:3), the land (14:4), and animals. Wildlife such as deer and donkeys face starvation and extinction (14:6-7). For a description of a grasshopper plague as a natural disaster, see Joel 1:5-12. For a prose account of famine (Jeremiah's description is in poetry), see 2 Kings 6:25-29.

This commentary assumes, contrary to the NLT, that the emotional reaction in the second complaint (14:17-18) was by Jeremiah rather than God (see note on 14:17). To be sure, Jeremiah mirrored the concern of God's heart for his people, but the on-the-ground report is more appropriate to Jeremiah than to God (14:18). The observations about prophets and priests also seem to be made by a colleague. To see human beings destroyed, whether in natural disaster or war, brings a sensitive person to grief. How much more so when those perishing are cherished—"my precious people"—and the reason for the disaster was easily preventable. God's servants, even when their message is one of judgment, remain tenderhearted.

**Prayers by People and Prophet (14:7-9, 19-22).**  Does sin cause calamity? The answer is *Yes.* The underlying assumption throughout the text is that there is a close connection between sin and disaster. God specifies that the evil of disloyalty brings punishment (14:10), which may take the form of famine, war, or disease (14:12; for famine as a consequence of evildoing, see the story of Elijah and Ahab in 1 Kgs 18:17-18). Still, not every famine or drought is the result of human sinfulness (such as the famine in Abraham's time, Gen 12:10). The connection between sin and famine is not unlike that between smoking and cancer. Smoking causes cancer, but not all cancer is the result of using tobacco. So while the Bible is clear that sin precipitates calamity such as drought, it is not proper theology to assert the reverse, that drought (crop failures) or calamities are always or necessarily to be traced to human evildoing.

Israel, though culpable, also knew the appropriate arguments to advance when praying. First, the people acknowledged their evil (an initial stage in the repentance process) and verbalized a confession (cf. 3:22b-25). Second, they appealed to God's reputation because God's own honor was at stake (cf. Pss 25:11; 106:8; 143:11; Ezek 20:9, 14, 22; 36:20-23). Third, Israel was identified as God's people (14:9), so both Israel and God would be disgraced by misfortune. Fourth, Israel rather crudely cast a question about God's abilities by posing the problem of the drought as a challenge for God to solve. Fifth, Israel appealed to their feelings of abandonment. "Why are you like a stranger to us?" (14:8). This attempt to arouse God's pity for a helpless victim was reinforced with a final cry, "Please don't abandon us now."

The scene of those perishing, whether by drought or war, prompts the prophet to pray (14:19-22), even though God had prohibited him from doing so (14:11). The prohibition made the point that God would not respond to prayers for deliverance, a point proved in God's answer to Jeremiah (15:1). Some of the elements in this prayer—confession of sin (14:20), appeal to God's reputation (14:21a) and to his pity for a weak people (14:21b)—are similar to the people's prayer (14:7-9). What is new is the appeal to the covenant, indirectly (14:19a) and then directly (14:21c). Jeremiah expressed more pointedly than the people that God was the only one who could help. God, not Canaanite idols marketing fertility, was the deity capable of changing the weather and the situation (14:22). When Elijah prayed, rain came (1 Kgs 18:41-45). Not so when Jeremiah prayed.

**Interjection: An Alternative Message (14:13-16).** Lying prophets took a competing view of the drought. Their confident message about true peace (*shelom 'emeth* [TH7965/571, ZH8934/622]) was given in the Lord's name (14:13). The lying prophets did not consider that God might send natural disasters (earthquakes, hurricanes, floods, and drought), as his deliberate response to wrongdoing. Since detractors from God's message are ubiquitous, listeners and readers then and now need to discern where the truth lies.

**God's Stance (14:10-12, 14-16; 15:1-9).** The expected sequel to such a lament is a salvation oracle, but the people receive only confirmation of the Lord's intent to punish them. God's response can be summarized: First, the people's acknowledgment of guilt, if not accompanied by a change of ways, was insufficient (14:10; cf. 4:1-2). Admitting guilt, even if sincerely (and in this instance there remains some doubt), did not automatically guarantee a reversal of circumstances (cf. 3:24-25; 4:1-2). Second, God's decision would not necessarily be overturned by the people's prayer (14:10; 15:1), nor could he be bribed though offerings (14:12). God functions as a person, not as a dispensing machine. Even intercessors such as Moses (Exod 32:11-14, 30-34) and Samuel (1 Sam 7:7-11; cf. 12:9-23; Ps 99:6) would not reverse God's decision at that point (15:1). Third, God's decision in this instance stood firm (14:12, 16), and it was not an arbitrary decision, for the covenant terms included drought as a possible punishment for covenant breaking (Deut 28:23-24). "Sword, famine, and plague" are a frequent triad (21:7; 24:10; 27:8; 32:24). Fourth, any contrary interpretations such as those given by the lying prophets were to be ignored because they were not divinely authorized (14:14-16). Fifth, patience has its limits; opportunities for change, as illustrated in the flood story, are not limitless (15:6).

For those who think of God as dispensing goodies and warm fuzzies, the portrait of a God with clenched fists (15:6) is disconcerting. The appeal in Jeremiah's prayer for God to remember his people (14:21) had an ironic twist following the assertion that God would remember the people's sins (14:10). With ample justification, God announced calamity (14:10; 15:7). God would not be dissuaded from his course of action even by prayer. The account urges the revision of a stereotypical view of God as perpetually benign.

◆     2. Personal ministry crisis (15:10-21)

¹⁰Then I said,

"What sorrow is mine, my mother.
    Oh, that I had died at birth!
    I am hated everywhere I go.
I am neither a lender who threatens to
        foreclose
    nor a borrower who refuses to pay—
    yet they all curse me."

¹¹The LORD replied,

"I will take care of you, Jeremiah.
    Your enemies will ask you to plead
        on their behalf
    in times of trouble and distress.
¹²Can a man break a bar of iron from
        the north,
    or a bar of bronze?
¹³At no cost to them,
    I will hand over your wealth and
        treasures
    as plunder to your enemies,
        for sin runs rampant in your land.
¹⁴I will tell your enemies to take you
        as captives to a foreign land.
For my anger blazes like a fire
    that will burn forever.*"

¹⁵Then I said,

"LORD, you know what's happening to
        me.
    Please step in and help me. Punish
        my persecutors!
Please give me time; don't let me die
        young.
    It's for your sake that I am
        suffering.
¹⁶When I discovered your words, I
        devoured them.

They are my joy and my heart's
        delight,
    for I bear your name,
    O LORD God of Heaven's Armies.
¹⁷I never joined the people in their
        merry feasts.
    I sat alone because your hand was
        on me.
    I was filled with indignation at their
        sins.
¹⁸Why then does my suffering
        continue?
    Why is my wound so incurable?
Your help seems as uncertain as a
        seasonal brook,
    like a spring that has gone dry."

¹⁹This is how the LORD responds:

"If you return to me, I will
        restore you
    so you can continue to serve me.
If you speak good words rather than
        worthless ones,
    you will be my spokesman.
You must influence them;
    do not let them influence you!
²⁰They will fight against you like an
        attacking army,
    but I will make you as secure as
        a fortified wall of bronze.
They will not conquer you,
    for I am with you to protect and
        rescue you.
    I, the LORD, have spoken!
²¹Yes, I will certainly keep you safe from
        these wicked men.
    I will rescue you from their cruel
        hands."

15:14 As in some Hebrew manuscripts (see also 17:4); most Hebrew manuscripts read *will burn against you.*

NOTES

**15:10** *Oh, that I had died at birth!* Lit., "Woe is me, my mother that you bore me." Cf. God's intentions for Jeremiah prior to his birth (1:5).

**15:11** *I will take care of you.* Both announcements in the verse are introduced with words from an oath formula (*'im-lo'*), heightening the certainty of what is said. The verse is difficult. Translations vary, depending on whether a key word, *sherithi*, is derived from *sharah* [TH8281, ZH9223] ("to deliver," so NLT; cf. "surely I have intervened in your life for good,"

NRSV) or from *sha'ar* [TH7604, ZH8636] ("to remain," cf. "It shall be well with thy remnant," KJV) or even from a root for "to serve" (*sharath* [TH8334, ZH9250]; cf. "I have served you," JB, NAB; see Huey 1993:160).

**15:12** *Can a man break a bar of iron from the north?* The Heb. syntax allows for another meaning: "can bronze and iron break northern iron?" (cf. NRSV). The interpretation is that an alloy of metals (Judah and her allies) will hardly be enough to break choice iron from the north—i.e., the enemy from the north, Babylon. Alternatively, Jeremiah's intercession will not be sufficient to forestall the coming invasion.

**15:14** *my anger blazes like a fire.* Cf. Deut 32:22. The addition of "forever" in some translations derives from a few manuscripts and from 17:4, which is almost identical in meaning.

**15:15** *don't let me die young.* The Heb. wording is sarcastic, lit., "Do not, given your great tolerance (*le'erek 'appeka* [TH750/639, ZH678/800]; lit., "length of nose") let them take me away." The sense is that it takes God a long time to become angry; in idiomatic English we would say, "God has a long fuse." Jeremiah, remonstrating with God, suggests that by the time God gets around to taking action it will be too late.

**15:16** *When I discovered your words.* This may refer to the discovery of the book of the law in the Temple and the consequent reform orchestrated by King Josiah (622 BC; 2 Kgs 22:13; 23:2).

**15:18** *Your help seems as uncertain as a seasonal brook.* The prophet is very confrontational: "you are to me as a falsified (*'akzab* [TH391, ZH423], "lying") brook, one that is untrustworthy (root *'aman* [TH539, ZH586], from which derives English "Amen").

**15:19** *If you return to me, I will restore you.* The Heb. has no word meaning only "return." The same root (*shub* [TH7725, ZH8740], "turn") functions for "return" and "restore" and occurs two more times in the verse as "influence" (15:19e-f). Although the word *shub* means "repent" in many contexts (here implied by the NLT's addition of "to me") and is usually so interpreted, that meaning is unlikely here. Nowhere else are Jeremiah's laments met with a divine rebuke. Jeremiah's assertions were not sinful, though they were unbecoming and disqualified him from continuing as a prophet. To paraphrase: "If you turn away from this way of acting, and/or turn to your [prophetic] task, that is, change your attitude and your tune, then I will reinstate you."

**15:20** *I am with you to protect and rescue you.* This promise echoes God's word to Moses (Exod 3:12; cf. Isa 41:10).

## COMMENTARY

The first lament here (15:10-14) departs from the pattern of conventional lament by omitting any prayer or statement of confidence after the complaint (Ps 13 is a good example of the typical pattern). After an indication of God's response, this lament is immediately followed by another (15:15-21; cf. the commentary on lament at 20:7-13, 14-18).

The focus of the complaint (15:10) is the hatred of others toward Jeremiah, a concern voiced again in 20:10 and illustrated by the death plot against him by his home community (11:19). Jeremiah engages in self-vindication. Conflict between lender and borrower can be expected in money transactions, but his is a different vocation. The continual harassment has made him so despondent that he wishes that his mother had not brought him to birth. Here and elsewhere (cf. 20:7-11),

Jeremiah shares his feelings freely. Of all the prophets, Jeremiah told the most about his inner life, thus making himself vulnerable.

God's response (15:11-14) includes an assurance (15:11); it also capitalizes on the occasion to emphasize the reality of the impending doom (15:12-14). In proverbial style, God compared Israel to an inferior tool, inadequate for dealing effectively with the foe from the north (see note on 15:12). Even allowing for the poetic license of overstatement (in Jeremiah's wish for non-existence and in God's word about fire), the point of God's severe irritation with wrongdoing should not be missed. The lamenting prophet was not forgotten; rather, he was reassured (15:11).

Owning and verbalizing one's feelings should not be censored. There are cultural rules of propriety in such matters, but God did not rebuke the prophet, even when his emotional explosions were raw and, by some peoples' perceptions, inappropriate. God did urge that these feelings be put in perspective, for though God reassures, he does not pamper. God challenged his emotionally confused spokesperson to stick with his assignment and with the message he had been given.

Although some regard 15:15-21 as continuing the dialogue between God and Jeremiah from 15:10-14, the second lament has its own agenda and integrity and is best treated separately. The initial "then" of 15:15 (NLT) is missing in the Hebrew text. The passage begins without a conjunction of any kind, but with an explosive, "You, you know."

Jeremiah's complaint was wide-ranging (cf. 20:7-13). People had been opposing and mistreating him (cf. 11:19). He was totally fed up with the never-ending hassles that others inflicted on him. Jeremiah spoke the language of vengeance, but as elsewhere, he turned the matter of retribution over to God (11:20, 12:3; 20:12; especially 18:18-23; Deut 32:35). Like Jonah, who felt that God's forbearance and longsuffering would preclude swift divine action, Jeremiah prayed that God's reluctance to act not make Jeremiah the victim of his persecutors (cf. Exod 37:6; Num 14:18; Ps 86:15; Jonah 4:2).

The complaint changed to introspection (15:16). Jeremiah was exuberant when the word of God sustained him (cf. Ps 119:11; Ezek 2:8-3:3) or when there were flashes of public response (see notes on 15:16). He had moments of exhilaration when he considered that his life and work were under the banner of Almighty God. The flip side of these emotional highs were his feelings of isolation, ostracization, and frustration.

Most serious was Jeremiah's perplexity about God's ways with him (15:18). He experienced this God who called him, and whom he proclaimed as "the fountain of living water" (2:13), as a dry streambed. Jeremiah found the God who described himself as faithful (9:24 [23]) to be unreliable. In his despondency, he could be compared to Elijah (1 Kgs 19:1-18) and to many others who have known the "dark night of the soul." The God who presents himself as the solution is experienced instead as the problem.

The divine response (15:19-22) was direct and compassionate. God admonished but did not scold Jeremiah. God invited him to change, for the prophet had some sorting out to do. Not all that he had spoken was "worthy" or would withstand close scrutiny. The prophet had overstated his case, a common failing among those who are despondent.

God counseled him on how to deal with his persecutors (15:19). He must not take his cue from others, for public opinion was not the compass by which to navigate. God's reply, however, was weighted in the direction of Jeremiah's last-mentioned problem: God. Basically, God asserted that he would come through for the prophet (cf. 1:18-19). God had addressed all three of Jeremiah's concerns: harassment by others (15:15, 19), his own personal frustration (15:16-17, 19), and God's apparent neglect (15:18, 20-22).

The lament illustrates what is meant by a "personal relationship." Such a relationship is two-way. It involves speaking and listening . . . about expectations, for example. A relationship between two persons holds the potential for intimacy, and also for confrontation. It is dynamic rather than static, for it does not short-circuit difficulties that arise within the relationship. It calls for honesty, which may precipitate hurt but which can end in understanding and confidence. Both parties function in freedom. The lament belongs to the prophet, but its incorporation into the canon opens the possibility of its appropriateness for the people, as well. Could this lament voice the feelings of a people in exile? "As Jeremiah can address God abrasively, so can Israel in exile. As Jeremiah is pressed to more serious obedience by Yahweh, so is Israel in exile. As Jeremiah receives a promise of God's solidarity in trouble, so does Israel in exile" (Brueggemann 1998:150).

◆    ## D. Something Is Desperately Wrong! (16:1-21)

The LORD gave me another message. He said, [2]"Do not get married or have children in this place. [3]For this is what the LORD says about the children born here in this city and about their mothers and fathers: [4]They will die from terrible diseases. No one will mourn for them or bury them, and they will lie scattered on the ground like manure. They will die from war and famine, and their bodies will be food for the vultures and wild animals."

[5]This is what the LORD says: "Do not go to funerals to mourn and show sympathy for these people, for I have removed my protection and peace from them. I have taken away my unfailing love and my mercy. [6]Both the great and the lowly will die in this land. No one will bury them or mourn for them. Their friends will not cut themselves in sorrow or shave their heads in sadness. [7]No one will offer a meal to comfort those who mourn at the dead— not even at the death of a mother or father. No one will send a cup of wine to console them.

[8]"And do not go to their feasts and parties. Do not eat and drink with them at all. [9]For this is what the LORD of Heaven's Armies, the God of Israel, says: In your own lifetime, before your very eyes, I will put an end to the happy singing and laughter in this land. The joyful voices of bridegrooms and brides will no longer be heard.

[10]"When you tell the people all these things, they will ask, 'Why has the LORD decreed such terrible things against us? What have we done to deserve such treatment? What is our sin against the LORD our God?'

11"Then you will give them the LORD's reply: 'It is because your ancestors were unfaithful to me. They worshiped other gods and served them. They abandoned me and did not obey my word. 12And you are even worse than your ancestors! You stubbornly follow your own evil desires and refuse to listen to me. 13So I will throw you out of this land and send you into a foreign land where you and your ancestors have never been. There you can worship idols day and night—and I will grant you no favors!'

14"But the time is coming," says the LORD, "when people who are taking an oath will no longer say, 'As surely as the LORD lives, who rescued the people of Israel from the land of Egypt.' 15Instead, they will say, 'As surely as the LORD lives, who brought the people of Israel back to their own land from the land of the north and from all the countries to which he had exiled them.' For I will bring them back to this land that I gave their ancestors.

16"But now I am sending for many fishermen who will catch them," says the LORD.

"I am sending for hunters who will hunt them down in the mountains, hills, and caves. 17I am watching them closely, and I see every sin. They cannot hope to hide from me. 18I will double their punishment for all their sins, because they have defiled my land with lifeless images of their detestable gods and have filled my territory with their evil deeds."

19LORD, you are my strength and
  fortress,
  my refuge in the day of trouble!
Nations from around the world
  will come to you and say,
"Our ancestors left us a foolish
  heritage,
  for they worshiped worthless
  idols.
20Can people make their own gods?
  These are not real gods at all!"

21The LORD says,
"Now I will show them my power;
  now I will show them my might.
At last they will know and understand
  that I am the LORD.

## NOTES

**16:3** *in this city.* Lit., "in this place." The Heb. ends the verse with "in this land," which best identifies the meaning of "this place" as "land" rather than "city" (cf. 16:9).

**16:5** *funerals.* The *beth marzeakh* [TH4798, ZH5301] (presumably "house of mourning," hence, "funerals") is mentioned elsewhere only in Amos 6:7, where it denotes revelry. The *marzeakh* was an elaborate institution of eating and drinking appropriate to the wealthy (so, similarly, in eight of the nine texts from Ugarit, cf. NIDOTTE 2:1102 and Barstad [1997] who proposes "banquet house"). Alternatively, one may think of rituals similar to a wake.

*I have removed my protection and peace.* The Heb. is colorful, though ominous: "I have gathered up my peace (*shalom* [TH7965, ZH8934]) from among this people."

**16:9** *happy singing and laughter.* Joviality, happy singing (*sason* [TH8342, ZH8607]), and laughter (*simkhah* [TH8057, ZH8525], "joy") are associated with catastrophe by their absence. By contrast, their presence denotes restoration (31:13).

**16:11** *your ancestors were unfaithful.* The same word, *'azab* [TH5800, ZH6440] (to forsake, to abandon) is used twice in the verse, rendered once as "unfaithful" and once as "abandoned." Israel was frequently accused of dismissing God from their lives (1:16; 2:13; 9:13; 19:4). For a similar question-and-answer format, see 5:19 (cf. 9:12b-16; 22:8-9; Deut 29:21-27).

**16:15** *the land of the north.* This refers to Babylon (see 20:4).

**16:18** *I will double their punishment.* Double punishment is announced also in 17:8 ("double destruction"; cf. Isa 40:2, but with different vocabulary). In Jeremiah, *mishneh* [TH4932, ZH5467] (twice as much) may mean "equivalent" (M. Tsevat, noted in Craigie et al. 1991:218;

cf. Huey 1993:170 citing M.G. Kline). The two-fold punishment might alternatively mean repeated punishments or be connected to the two agents, fishermen and hunters.

**16:19 *they worshiped worthless idols.*** "Idols" are no doubt intended; however, without specifying "idols," the Heb. uses language of *hevel* [TH1892, ZH2039] (vaporous, void, empty), *sheqer* [TH8267, ZH9214] (deceitful, lying), and *mo'il* (negative *'en* [TH369, ZH401] with the participle of *ya'al* [TH3276, ZH3603], to be profitable).

COMMENTARY

The ominous note of coming disaster precipitated by the people's wrongdoing is found in every section of this chapter, whether the genre is a divine prohibition (16:1-9), a disputation (16:10-13), a salvation oracle (16:14-15), a judgment oracle (16:16-17) or a prayer (16:19-21).

**Prohibitions (16:1-9).**    Each of the three prohibitions bears on the prophet's lifestyle: don't marry, don't have children, don't socialize. Jeremiah's single status was to be a sign-act just as Hosea's marriage was to convey a message (Hos 1; 3; cf. Ezek 24:15-18). Not having children was a major disgrace in a culture that frowned on barrenness.

With each of these three prohibitions comes a mini-sermon about Israel's dismal prospects because of her evil. War, famine, and accompanying diseases, common agents of punishment according to the covenant curses (Deut 28:22, 26), will leave exposed corpses everywhere as food for bird and beast. Since the population will be decimated, there will not be enough interest or energy to bury the dead (16:3-4). Even the closest relatives will not be mourned, and being unburied and unmourned were major disgraces (cf. 8:1-3; 22:18-19). The third prohibition, with its juxtaposition of weddings and funerals, is jarring (16:8). The three prohibitions touch three landmarks in a human life: birth (16:2), marriage (16:2, 9), and death (16:4, 6-7).

**Disputations (16:10-18).**    Israel's questions may seem to seek information, but they are essentially acts of self-vindication that indirectly accuse God of injustice (16:10). The query, "What is our sin?" is a telltale mark of spiritual obtuseness. Israel's acts of idolatry were so habitual that they failed to see what was wrong with them. The Lord's answer pointed them to the ways that they had (1) deserted the Lord (see note on 16:11), (2) disregarded God's law, and (3) descended to idolatry, becoming absorbed by entities other than God. God was emphatic in saying that the decree for their exile would in no way be mitigated (16:13).

The two oracles that follow are best understood as continuing the argumentative mode. The salvation oracle about the return from exile (16:14-16) seems odd after such harsh words as "I will throw [hurl] you out of this land" (16:13). The salvation oracle partially qualifies the finality of decreed punishment (16:13) and it is perhaps to be related to Israel's first question, "Why has the Lord decreed such terrible things?" (16:10). The answer is that beyond judgment, there is hope. The exile becomes a giant detour, after which the promise to the ancestors can be reinstated (16:15). For the assertion that the return from exile will be greater than the Exodus from Egypt, see 23:7, which is virtually a duplicate statement in a context where it more easily fits.

The second oracle (16:16-18) introduces an image about unnamed fishermen (Egyptians?) and hunters (Babylonians), both of whom work to flush out the prey that have withdrawn to safety. Some, however, propose that the unnamed "them" (16:16) are the plundering nations against whom judgment is brought (cf. proximity of 16:19). If so, then a common pattern is observed: restoration of Judah (16:14-15), the judgment of nations (16:16-18), and the conversion of nations (16:19-21; Bracke 2000a:144).

**Prayer with Imagination (16:19-21).**   Statements such as those found in Jeremiah's prayer, "Nations will come . . . and say . . ." (cf. Isa 2:2-4; Mal 1:11) represent what Brueggemann (1986) calls "hopeful imagination," and what therapists call "creative visualization"—a focus on changes for the good. The prophets have the capacity to envision an alternate future from that to which Israel seems doomed. The prayer is a gigantic stretch. Not only will Israel admit the futility of God-substitutes (idols) in the future, but nations from every quarter will admit the barrenness of their traditions. The prophet dared to hope for a global transformation. In this he was justified, and so are we, for God announces a show of his force and power (16:21; Bracke 2000a). Indeed, Jeremiah's prediction of nations renouncing their idolatrous ways, while already partially fulfilled as a result of missionary activity, awaits complete fulfillment. The final word, "they will know . . . that I am the LORD," anticipates the use of this phrase in the book of Ezekiel (seventy-eight times), reiterating a similar imaginative word about a worldwide transformation (e.g., Ezek 36:38).

The passage prompts further theological reflection along two lines. First, the stubbornness of Israel's heart (16:12) was like the hardness of Pharaoh's heart. Just as it was difficult for God to penetrate the Egyptians' defenses, so it was difficult for God to convince a defensive Israel that he was serious about his intended action. Before the threats to Pharaoh and Israel were actualized, however, ample warning and ample incentives were offered. Both incidents elicit astonishment about (1) the armor-plated insensitivity that can develop through prolonged resistance to God's message, and (2) the varied ways that God employs to penetrate the self-justifying shield.

The second reflection is about God's persistence and the variety of tactics he uses to get a hearing. In Pharaoh's case, God brought on plagues, signs that reinforced his words. For Israel, God initiated sign-acts, such as the lifestyle of his prophet, to emphasize his threats. The "don'ts" that God issued to Jeremiah are disconcerting, but listeners are left in no doubt as to the divine verdict: the wages of sin is destruction.

◆     ## E. Sin Runs Rampant (17:1-27)
### 1. Metaphor-Making (17:1-11)

"The sin of Judah
   is inscribed with an iron chisel—
engraved with a diamond point on
    their stony hearts
   and on the corners of their altars.

[2] Even their children go to worship
   at their pagan altars and Asherah
    poles,
   beneath every green tree
   and on every high hill.

³So I will hand over my holy mountain—
  along with all your wealth and
    treasures
  and your pagan shrines—
as plunder to your enemies,
  for sin runs rampant in your land.
⁴The wonderful possession I have
    reserved for you
  will slip from your hands.
I will tell your enemies to take you
  as captives to a foreign land.
For my anger blazes like a fire
  that will burn forever."

⁵This is what the LORD says:
"Cursed are those who put their trust
    in mere humans,
  who rely on human strength
  and turn their hearts away from
    the LORD.
⁶They are like stunted shrubs in the
    desert,
  with no hope for the future.
They will live in the barren wilderness,
  in an uninhabited salty land.

⁷"But blessed are those who trust in
    the LORD
  and have made the LORD their hope
    and confidence.

⁸They are like trees planted along
    a riverbank,
  with roots that reach deep into
    the water.
Such trees are not bothered by the
    heat
  or worried by long months of
    drought.
Their leaves stay green,
  and they never stop producing
    fruit.

⁹"The human heart is the most
    deceitful of all things,
  and desperately wicked.
  Who really knows how bad it is?
¹⁰But I, the LORD, search all hearts
  and examine secret motives.
I give all people their due rewards,
  according to what their actions
    deserve."

¹¹Like a partridge that hatches eggs
    she has not laid,
  so are those who get their wealth
    by unjust means.
At midlife they will lose their riches;
  in the end, they will become poor
    old fools.

NOTES

**17:2 *Asherah poles.*** These wooden cult objects depicted the female goddess Asherah, a deity worshiped from Mesopotamia to Asia Minor. In Ugaritic mythology, she was the consort of the high god, El. Josiah's reform eradicated Asherah worship in Jerusalem (2 Kgs 23:4-10).

**17:9 *desperately wicked.*** The word *'anush* [TH605A, ZH631] signifies desperation; in the context of illness, it means "beyond cure." Jeremiah uses the term five times (7:16; 15:18; 17:9; 30:12, 15). Cf. this comparison of sin to chronic illness with the comparison to permanent engraving in 17:1.

**17:11 *who get their wealth by unjust means.*** Jehoiakim's means of building his palace illustrates this wisdom-oriented proverb (Jer 22:13-19).

COMMENTARY

This chapter returns repeatedly to the subject of sin, through metaphors and by means of a case study. The threat of judgment, while less dominant than in Jeremiah 13–16, is nevertheless made in all three sections. The forms of judgment mentioned are exile or life in the desert wasteland (17:4, 6), death (17:13), and economic collapse (17:27).

**Metaphors.** The first of several metaphors comes from the stone-cutter's trade (17:1-4). Sin's endemic nature is emphasized by the image of a hard-pointed chisel permanently etching the people's fundamental contrariness in stone. The new covenant will be designed to undo this condition (31:33; cf. Prov 7:3). This perversity is recorded at the altars for future generations.

The second metaphor is agricultural (17:5-8). The stunted shrub on salty flats is a picture of one who trusts solely in human resources, including his own. The key trait is autonomy. By contrast, the person whose support system is initially and primarily the Lord is a flourishing tree perpetually producing fruit. The key trait is dependence on God. To trust in God is to rely on, lean on, and place one's confidence in God (cf. Ps 62:8 [9]; Isa 7:4-9). The background agenda for the comparison may be Judah's overtures for military help from Egypt, against which Jeremiah protested (2:18). An Egyptian wisdom writing puts it this way:

> The "heated man" [an Egyptian way of referring to an angry, and hence, uncontrolled person] is like a tree growing in the open. But the truly silent man holds himself apart.
> He is like a tree growing in a garden.
> It flourishes and doubles its yield;
> It (stands) before its lord.
> Its fruit is sweet; its shade is pleasant;
> And its end is reached in the garden. (ANET 422)

Prophets also make comparisons between humans and trees (Ezek 17:1-10; 22-24; Dan 4:9-27). The details of Jeremiah's comparison can be highlighted. One person, who trusts himself, is like a stunted shrub; he lives in the desert, salty flats, he is unproductive, and he wilts in hard times. Another person, who trusts God, is rooted in him. This person is a leafy tree, drawing nourishment from a riverbank; he is productive and withstands hard times.

The third metaphor is anatomical. In Hebrew thought, the physical heart represents the person, or more specifically, the will. The human heart is altogether diseased and something about the human person is grossly flawed. It is incorrect to say that people are basically good. There is a bent toward sin, as Luther explained, and the situation is chronic. Furthermore, the patient is incapable of proper diagnosis. "Who really knows how bad it is?" Only God, the heart and kidney specialist (kidneys represent feelings and motives, cf. 12:3), fully knows the answer.

The fourth metaphor about evil is drawn from wildlife (17:11). It was believed that partridges preempted the nests of others, and that the hatched brood would then turn on their "mothers." Just as birds appropriate to themselves what does not belong to them, so the greedy person acquires what is not rightfully his. He will lose his ill-gotten gain (Luke 12:13-21; cf. Prov 23:4-5).

**Sin.** Sin is an unpleasant subject but an ever-present reality. Jeremiah did not flinch from expounding on it, taking pains to emphasize its pervasiveness, its manifestations, and its consequences. Sin is deep-seated, characterized chiefly by the human propensity to turn from God (17:5, 13) and to proceed autonomously (17:5) without regard for God. Judah's sin was in substituting Asherah, the craze of Israel's surrounding cultures (17:2), for God. The problem is detailed in the book of Judges, which according to a recent commentary has for its theme the "Canaanization of Israelite society during the period of settlement" (Block 1999:58). Then, as in Jeremiah's time, people's lives circled around God-substitutes (Judg 6:25-28). Jesus often addressed the subject of money, which often takes the place of God in people's lives (Luke 6:24).

Sin is subtle and insidious. Like cancer, it progresses in seriousness without easy detection. The heart is devious and people are self-deceived; they deceive others and often overreach themselves. In Israel, sin's reach extended, among other things, to desecrating the Sabbath. In time, the Sabbath was taken less and less seriously; more and more liberties were taken in their non-observance of the day, and eventually the day was trivialized to the point of desecration. The erosion of commitments is often slow and gradual, which is all the more reason to be alert to sin's deceptiveness.

◆        2. A spiritual oasis (17:12-18)

<sup>12</sup> But we worship at your throne—
  eternal, high, and glorious!
<sup>13</sup> O LORD, the hope of Israel,
  all who turn away from you will be
    disgraced.
They will be buried in the dust of the
    earth,
  for they have abandoned the LORD,
    the fountain of living water.
<sup>14</sup> O LORD, if you heal me, I will be truly
    healed;
  if you save me, I will be truly saved.
  My praises are for you alone!
<sup>15</sup> People scoff at me and say,
  "What is this 'message from the LORD'
    you talk about?

  Why don't your predictions come
    true?"

<sup>16</sup> LORD, I have not abandoned my job
    as a shepherd for your people.
  I have not urged you to send disaster.
    You have heard everything I've said.
<sup>17</sup> LORD, don't terrorize me!
  You alone are my hope in the day of
    disaster.
<sup>18</sup> Bring shame and dismay on all who
    persecute me,
  but don't let me experience shame
    and dismay.
  Bring a day of terror on them.
    Yes, bring double destruction upon
    them!

NOTES

**17:12 we worship at your throne.** The NLT supplies "we worship." The Heb. is an exclamation, "O glorious throne!" The word *kabod* [TH3519, ZH3883] (glorious) "encompasses a monarch's total power, wealth, splendor, magnificence, and glory" (Metzer 1991, as quoted in *Old Testament Abstracts* 15 [1992] no. 1576).

**17:13 buried in the dust of the earth.** The Heb. phrase is cryptic, lit., "written in the ground." It suggests impermanence (cf. the permanence of their sin, 17:1), burial, or even being consigned to death or the underworld as Dahood (1959) suggests from the Ugaritic.

**17:16 I have not urged you to send disaster.** "Disaster" translates *yom 'anush* [TH605A, ZH631] ("day of despair"; cf. 17:9; "Nor have I desired the fatal day," NRSV).

COMMENTARY

The God-oriented material in this panel is in two parts, a mini-meditation on worship (17:12-13) and a prophet's lament (17:14-18). The transition to worship and God's throne (17:12-13) from a proverbial saying about wealth is abrupt (see note on 17:12; cf. Isa 6:1). Jeremiah is unique in addressing God as the "Hope of Israel" (cf. 14:8; 50:7); the epithet correlates well with the description of God as the "fountain of living waters" (17:12; cf. 2:13). Contrasts (as in 17:5-8) continue in 17:12-13: heaven/earth, glorious/inglorious, secure/shamed, hoping in God/turning from him. The trajectory set in 17:5-8 ends in 17:12-13. The one trusting God rises to see God's throne. The self-trusting man spirals down into the dust of the netherworld.

The lament (17:14-18) incorporates most of the features of the conventional lament but not in the usual order of complaint, prayer, statement of confidence, and praise. The complaint is about the humiliating finger-pointing by the naysayers who take Jeremiah's message lightly (cf. 15:15; 20:7, 10). Jeremiah's request for God to deal punitively with his troublemakers is familiar from other laments (17:18; cf. 11:20; 12:3; 15:15; see comments at 18:18-23 and 20:7-13). The typical statement of confidence is modified here to include self-vindication (17:14). The prophet claims to have been faithful in his assignment of proclamation (17:16c) and nurture (17:16a).

◆     ## 3. Measuring obedience (17:19-27)

¹⁹This is what the LORD said to me: "Go and stand in the gates of Jerusalem, first in the gate where the king goes in and out, and then in each of the other gates. ²⁰Say to all the people, 'Listen to this message from the LORD, you kings of Judah and all you people of Judah and everyone living in Jerusalem. ²¹This is what the LORD says: Listen to my warning! Stop carrying on your trade at Jerusalem's gates on the Sabbath day. ²²Do not do your work on the Sabbath, but make it a holy day. I gave this command to your ancestors, ²³but they did not listen or obey. They stubbornly refused to pay attention or accept my discipline.

²⁴"'But if you obey me, says the LORD, and do not carry on your trade at the gates or work on the Sabbath day, and if you keep it holy, ²⁵then kings and their officials will go in and out of these gates for ever. There will always be a descendant of David sitting on the throne here in Jerusalem. Kings and their officials will always ride in and out among the people of Judah in chariots and on horses, and this city will remain forever. ²⁶And from all around Jerusalem, from the towns of Judah and Benjamin, from the western foothills* and the hill country and the Negev, the people will come with their burnt offerings and sacrifices. They will bring their grain offerings, frankincense, and thanksgiving offerings to the LORD's Temple.

²⁷"'But if you do not listen to me and refuse to keep the Sabbath holy, and if on the Sabbath day you bring loads of merchandise through the gates of Jerusalem just as on other days, then I will set fire to these gates. The fire will spread to the palaces, and no one will be able to put out the roaring flames.'"

17:26 Hebrew *the Shephelah.*

## NOTES

**17:19** *the gate where the king goes in and out.* In the Heb. text, this gate is called "the People's Gate." Cf. Jeremiah's sermon at the Temple gate (7:2).

**17:21** *Listen to my warning!* The Heb. idiom is "Guard (*shamar* [TH8104, ZH9068]) your soul" (*nepesh* [TH5315, ZH5883], "life"); it conveys great seriousness (cf. Deut 4:9, 15).

**17:24** *if you keep it holy.* For instructions, see Deut 5:12-14; debate continues about Jeremiah's use of that passage (e.g., Gladson 2000). For various views on present day application, see Carson (1982), Swartley (1983), and Blomberg (1991).

## COMMENTARY

This section has two prominent themes, Jeremiah's castigation of Israel's non-observance of the Sabbath and directives for making amends.

**Non-observance of the Sabbath.** The charge that Judah had not listened or obeyed is not new; it is found more than thirty times in Jeremiah (see chs 7, 11, 26, 35, 42). In this sermon, the charge is verified with a focus on one sign of infidelity, Judah's practices on the Sabbath. The venues for the sermons are the city gates, where the practices Jeremiah confronted were going on. Jeremiah was not unlike a protester at an abortion clinic. The prohibition concerning the Sabbath was, "Do not do your work" (17:22; cf. Exod 20:10). The positive command was, "make it a holy day" (17:22; Deut 5:12). By desecrating the day, the people were vitiating its value as a sign of their covenant with God (Ezek 20:20). The benefits of observing the command about the Sabbath were stable government and vigorous spirituality (17:24-26). By contrast, disregard of the Sabbath prompted God's confiscation of the traded merchandise, an action broadly comparable to Jesus' overturning the tables of the money changers in the Temple (John 2:13-16).

**A Barometer of Obedience.** Obedience to God entails a disposition, an attitude, but the proof of obedience comes down to specific actions. Jeremiah was not alone in selecting Sabbath-keeping as a barometer for obedience (cf. Neh 13:15-22; Amos 8:5; Isa 58:13). The Pharisees well understood the importance of the Sabbath, but their fixation on the mechanics of what was allowed and disallowed became a perversion that Jesus confronted (Matt 12:1-8). Jesus did not overturn the command for observing the Sabbath; rather, he clarified what it entailed.

Christians differ in their opinions as to whether or not, and to what extent, the instructions about a holy day are binding (see note on 17:24). Some segments of the church in the past have been fastidious about substituting Sunday—the Lord's Day—for the Sabbath. By contrast, the libertarian attitudes of some toward the observance of the Sabbath/Sunday fly in the face of Jesus' assertion that the law still holds (Matt 5:17-20). The question may be hard to answer, but it needs to be asked. Has secularization corrupted the so-called Christian West in regard to observance of the Lord's Day? If so, in what way? If observance of the Lord's Day is not a legitimate measure of obedience for the believer, then what might be properly proposed in its place? The message that consequences, and even eternal destinies, are in some way connected to obedience is one on which Jesus (Matt 7:24-27) and the apostles (1 Pet 3:19-20) agree.

◆ F. Pottery-Making and Pottery-Smashing (18:1–20:6)
 1. Shaping pottery and shaping disaster (18:1-23)

The LORD gave another message to Jeremiah. He said, 2"Go down to the potter's shop, and I will speak to you there." 3So I did as he told me and found the potter working at his wheel. 4But the jar he was making did not turn out as he had hoped, so he crushed it into a lump of clay again and started over.

5Then the LORD gave me this message: 6"O Israel, can I not do to you as this potter has done to his clay? As the clay is in the potter's hand, so are you in my hand. 7If I announce that a certain nation or kingdom is to be uprooted, torn down, and destroyed, 8but then that nation renounces its evil ways, I will not destroy it as I had planned. 9And if I announce that I will plant and build up a certain nation or kingdom, 10but then that nation turns to evil and refuses to obey me, I will not bless it as I said I would.

11"Therefore, Jeremiah, go and warn all Judah and Jerusalem. Say to them, 'This is what the LORD says: I am planning disaster for you instead of good. So turn from your evil ways, each of you, and do what is right.'"

12But the people replied, "Don't waste your breath. We will continue to live as we want to, stubbornly following our own evil desires."

13So this is what the LORD says:

"Has anyone ever heard of such a thing,
 even among the pagan nations?
My virgin daughter Israel
 has done something terrible!
14Does the snow ever disappear from the
 mountaintops of Lebanon?
Do the cold streams flowing from
 those distant mountains ever
 run dry?

15But my people are not so reliable,
 for they have deserted me;
they burn incense to worthless
 idols.
They have stumbled off the ancient
 highways
and walk in muddy paths.
16Therefore, their land will become
 desolate,
a monument to their stupidity.
All who pass by will be astonished
 and will shake their heads in
 amazement.
17I will scatter my people before their
 enemies
as the east wind scatters dust.
And in all their trouble I will turn my
 back on them
and refuse to notice their distress."

18Then the people said, "Come on, let's plot a way to stop Jeremiah. We have plenty of priests and wise men and prophets. We don't need him to teach the word and give us advice and prophecies. Let's spread rumors about him and ignore what he says."

19LORD, hear me and help me!
 Listen to what my enemies are
 saying.
20Should they repay evil for good?
 They have dug a pit to kill me,
 though I pleaded for them
 and tried to protect them from your
 anger.
21So let their children starve!
 Let them die by the sword!
Let their wives become childless
 widows.
 Let their old men die in a plague,
 and let their young men be killed
 in battle!

²² Let screaming be heard from their
       homes
   as warriors come suddenly upon
       them.
   For they have dug a pit for me
       and have hidden traps along my path.

²³ LORD, you know all about their
       murderous plots against me.
   Don't forgive their crimes and blot
       out their sins.
   Let them die before you.
   Deal with them in your anger.

## N O T E S

**18:3 *[I] found the potter working at his wheel.*** Ancient pottery making was done on two wheels (the Heb. form is dual) joined by a vertical axle, or with the top disk socketed into the lower disk. The lower wheel was spun with the feet, turning the upper wheel on which the clay was formed. For a helpful description of the craft in the context of this chapter, see King (1993:163-174).

**18:4 *so he crushed it.*** The Heb. is less graphic: "he turned to make another item." The word *keli* [TH3627, ZH3998] is generic for items, articles, or gear. For other uses of the potter and clay image, see Isa 29:16; 45:9; 64:8; Rom 9:21.

**18:8 *I will not destroy it as I had planned.*** The NLT reading skirts a critical phrase: "I will change my mind" (niphal of *nakham* [TH5162, ZH5714]). *nakham* is usually translated "repent," or, when used of God, "relent" (26:3). For the same verb applied to God elsewhere, see the Heb. of Jer 26:13, 19; 1 Sam 15:11; and Amos 7:3, 6. For use of this passage in support of the "open view" of God, that is, that "the future is not exhaustively fixed," and that God's knowledge of it is thus not total, see Boyd (2000:75-81, "Jeremiah 18 and the Flexible Potter").

**18:11 *I am planning disaster.*** The Heb. includes "and planning (*khosheb* [TH2803, ZH3108]) plans (*makhashabah* [TH4284, ZH4742]) against you" (for the same verb and noun cognates, see 18:18). The same word *ra'ah* [TH7451B, ZH8288] is employed twice, once to mean "disaster" and once to mean "evil."

***do what is right.*** This is more expansive in the Heb.: "do good with regard to your ways and deeds."

**18:12 *Don't waste your breath.*** The expression renders a single word, *no'ash* [TH2976, ZH3286], found also in 2:25, which is compared in one lexicon to the crass interjection, "To hell with it!" (Holladay 1971:126). The expression is about inability to change a hopeless situation.

***stubbornly following.*** See note on 11:8.

**18:13 *has done something terrible!*** The term *sha'arurith* [TH8186B, ZH9137] (horrible) is found elsewhere (5:30; 23:14) to indicate something extremely shocking and unnatural.

**18:14 *Does the snow ever disappear?*** By using the root *'azab* [TH5800, ZH6440] (forsake, leave) for "disappear," the Heb. recalls frequent accusations of Israel's forsaking (*'azab*) God (cf. note on 16:11).

**18:15 *walk in muddy paths.*** For other uses of *nethibah* [TH5410A, ZH5986] (path) in negative contexts, see Prov 7:25; Isa 59:8.

**18:16 *a monument to their stupidity.*** A translation closer to the Heb. would be "an ugly monument."

**18:18 *We have plenty of priests and wise men and prophets.*** The Heb. tightly associates each office with a function: instruction (*torah* [TH8451, ZH9368]) from the priests, wisdom sayings (*'etsah* [TH6098, ZH6783]) from the wise, and a word (*dabar* [TH1697, ZH1821]) from the prophet.

**18:20 *They have dug a pit to kill me.*** The complaint about antagonists digging a pit is reminiscent of the Psalms (57:6 [7]; 119:85).

COMMENTARY

In each of these two chapters (18 and 19), a story of clay jars launches God's message about freedom and disaster. Jeremiah first observes a potter at work. Then he stages a demonstration before religious leaders. Both incidents are sign-acts, with an interpretation following the action (cf. 13:1-7). The symmetry of the two chapters (and beyond) can be outlined:

| Symbolic Action | Pottery making (18:1-10) | Pottery smashing (19:1-13) |
|---|---|---|
| Public Message | "I am planning disaster" (18:11-17) | "I will bring disaster" (19:14-15) |
| Audience Response | "Let's . . . stop him" (18:18) | "[They] arrested him" (20:2) |
| Lament | A personal complaint (18:19-23) | Despair and a death wish (20:7-18) |

**Shaping Pottery (18:1-10).**   The potter's shop provides a place for a message about God's freedom. The potter's product was flawed, so without consulting anyone, he changed his mind and began again.

From this commonplace industry, the prophet is instructed about a principle of divine activity. God has the same freedom as does the potter (18:6-10). It is his choice whether to continue with a current plan or to abort it in favor of another course of action. Just as the potter changed his mind, so God is at liberty to change his (see note on 18:8). The potter still had the goal of fashioning a vessel, and we infer that God's goal of fashioning a people to his praise and a glory also remains (13:11).

The divine freedom in dealing with people is not arbitrary or capricious, but is governed by certain principles, as illustrated by two hypothetical situations about God's action (18:7-10). In the first illustration, God had decreed a judgment of total destruction against Nineveh. When its rulers and citizens repented, God overturned his verdict (Jonah 3:10). An opposite situation is documented in Judges. God decreed good for a people, but that people turned from God, so God withheld the good and sent evil instead (Judg 2:11-15). The answer to the charge that such changes in God's course of action make him undependable is that God is fully consistent. The operating principle is that people's responses are decisive to their destinies. God establishes "relationships of integrity" wherein the words and actions of all parties "really count" (Fretheim 1987).

**Shaping Disaster (18:11-17).**   No longer was the discussion hypothetical. The first of the two illustrations applied to Judah, doomed to destruction—a victim, so to speak, of God's decree. Yet the announcement of God's plan against Judah was at once followed by an appeal, "So turn from your evil ways." The message from the potter's shop is not only that God is free to change, but that people are also free to change. In this respect, the analogy of pottery-making does not hold.

The assertion that God is sovereign in executing his plans is usually seen as contradictory to the concept of human freedom. How can both be true? Rationally this may not compute. Intellectual reasoning cannot really resolve the tension between these two assertions. That is why the Old Testament does not give us a philosophical essay on human freedom and divine sovereignty, but an intelligible illustration from everyday concerns. The Bible asserts that God is fully in charge. It is equally insistent that humans have a choice, that they are accountable and not mysteriously predestined to a fate. An analogy from chess may help. The experienced player plans his or her moves and can execute them. The playing partner nevertheless remains free to make choices (cf. Carson 1981).

If the paradox of divine freedom and human responsibility is disconcerting, even more unsettling is the reality that humans will consciously choose evil, thereby inviting their own doom and destruction. In full knowledge of the options, and with an attitude of defiance, Judah decided to follow its wicked desires (see note on 18:12).

What follows are some divine musings on this incredible human decision to sin (18:13-16). Such a decision is irrational; even pagans would do better. It is contrary to nature, in which one can at least find some stability. Snows do not leave the uppermost mountain peaks for they belong there, but Judah has quite unnaturally left her place with Yahweh. She then followed the low paths rather than the high road of God's righteousness (18:15).

In keeping with the potter's action and the principle that the people's compliance is factored into God's course of action, the destruction of Judah—to the utter amazement of onlookers—is imaginatively depicted (18:16). Its people will be scattered, and God will not help them (18:17; cf. 16:13).

**A Personal Complaint before the Lord (18:18-23).** This lament, like some other laments, was triggered by the bad treatment Jeremiah received at the hands of his opponents (cf. 11:18-23; 15:15; 20:10; cf. commentary at 20:7). The opponents insisted that they had access to other leaders and so did not need him. They could, therefore, ignore his message while tormenting him with rumors. Disdain is sometimes more difficult to deal with than specific points of contention.

As in other laments, reasons were advanced as to why God should intervene, among which was Jeremiah's own fidelity (18:20; cf. 17:16). More than the others, this complaint contains vengeful sentiments (18:21-23). For some interpreters, these are not problematic because they are consequences that God had prescribed for determined disobedience and had asked Jeremiah to proclaim (6:11-12; Holladay 1986:528, 533). If, however, these were Jeremiah's own thoughts, several considerations should guide our interpretation. First, the prophet did, per instruction, put the matter of retribution in God's hands and did not take upon himself the prerogative of settling the score (Deut 32:35). Second, there is in most cultures a language of exasperation (e.g., among friends and family members, "Ohhh! I'm gonna' kill you!"), which is hardly to be interpreted literally. If Jeremiah's outcry was unbecoming, it was at least understandable. Third, his humanity is given expression. He was upset and vented his emotion in verbal exclamations, giving free reign to imagining the worst of evils for his opponents (cf. Pss 40:15 [16]; 58:6-11 [7-12]; 137:8-9).

Perhaps an argument could be made that such verbal bad wishes were cathartic. The believer is not warranted, however, in emulating the prophet. Even biblical heroes have their shortcomings. The Bible points to other and better ways of dealing with opponents. Teachers of wisdom advise that one should refrain from retaliation (Prov 15:1). Jesus taught us to love our enemies (Matt 5:44) and himself prayed for them (Luke 23:34). Paul encouraged kindness as a way of returning good for evil, even though such behavior might be very unsettling (Rom 12:20).

◆     ## 2. Smashing pottery and smashing structures (19:1–20:6)

This is what the LORD said to me: "Go and buy a clay jar. Then ask some of the leaders of the people and of the priests to follow you. ²Go out through the Gate of Broken Pots to the garbage dump in the valley of Ben-Hinnom, and give them this message. ³Say to them, 'Listen to this message from the LORD, you kings of Judah and citizens of Jerusalem! This is what the LORD of Heaven's Armies, the God of Israel, says: I will bring a terrible disaster on this place, and the ears of those who hear about it will ring!

⁴"'For Israel has forsaken me and turned this valley into a place of wickedness. The people burn incense to foreign gods—idols never before acknowledged by this generation, by their ancestors, or by the kings of Judah. And they have filled this place with the blood of innocent children. ⁵They have built pagan shrines to Baal, and there they burn their sons as sacrifices to Baal. I have never commanded such a horrible deed; it never even crossed my mind to command such a thing! ⁶So beware, for the time is coming, says the LORD, when this garbage dump will no longer be called Topheth or the valley of Ben-Hinnom, but the Valley of Slaughter.

⁷"'For I will upset the careful plans of Judah and Jerusalem. I will allow the people to be slaughtered by invading armies, and I will leave their dead bodies as food for the vultures and wild animals. ⁸I

will reduce Jerusalem to ruins, making it a monument to their stupidity. All who pass by will be astonished and will gasp at the destruction they see there. ⁹I will see to it that your enemies lay siege to the city until all the food is gone. Then those trapped inside will eat their own sons and daughters and friends. They will be driven to utter despair.'

¹⁰"As these men watch you, Jeremiah, smash the jar you brought. ¹¹Then say to them, 'This is what the LORD of Heaven's Armies says: As this jar lies shattered, so I will shatter the people of Judah and Jerusalem beyond all hope of repair. They will bury the bodies here in Topheth, the garbage dump, until there is no more room for them. ¹²This is what I will do to this place and its people, says the LORD. I will cause this city to become defiled like Topheth. ¹³Yes, all the houses in Jerusalem, including the palace of Judah's kings, will become like Topheth—all the houses where you burned incense on the rooftops to your star gods, and where liquid offerings were poured out to your idols.'"

¹⁴Then Jeremiah returned from Topheth, the garbage dump where he had delivered this message, and he stopped in front of the Temple of the LORD. He said to the people there, ¹⁵"This is what the LORD of Heaven's Armies, the God of Israel, says: 'I will bring disaster upon this city and its surrounding towns as I promised,

because you have stubbornly refused to listen to me.'"

## CHAPTER 20

Now Pashhur son of Immer, the priest in charge of the Temple of the LORD, heard what Jeremiah was prophesying. ²So he arrested Jeremiah the prophet and had him whipped and put in stocks at the Benjamin Gate of the LORD's Temple.

³The next day, when Pashhur finally released him, Jeremiah said, "Pashhur, the LORD has changed your name. From now on you are to be called 'The Man Who Lives in Terror.'* ⁴For this is what the LORD says:

'I will send terror upon you and all your friends, and you will watch as they are slaughtered by the swords of the enemy. I will hand the people of Judah over to the king of Babylon. He will take them captive to Babylon or run them through with the sword. ⁵And I will let your enemies plunder Jerusalem. All the famed treasures of the city—the precious jewels and gold and silver of your kings—will be carried off to Babylon. ⁶As for you, Pashhur, you and all your household will go as captives to Babylon. There you will die and be buried, you and all your friends to whom you prophesied that everything would be all right.'"

20:3 Hebrew *Magor-missabib*, which means "surrounded by terror"; also in 20:10.

### NOTES

**19:1 *Go and buy a clay jar.*** The jug (*baqbuq* [TH1228, ZH1318]), a narrow-necked, often ring-burnished decanter, is known from archaeological sites. See King (1993:170-73) for details and a sketch. For Jeremiah's other purchases, also used as sign-acts, see 13:1; 32:6-25.

**19:2 *the Gate of Broken Pots.*** Often identified with the Dung Gate (Neh 2:13), this gate led to the waste disposal area of pottery shards and possibly garbage.

***Valley of Ben-Hinnom.*** The valley runs west and south of the Temple Mount. Gehenna (Heb. *ge'* [TH1516, ZH1628], "valley of" *hinnom* [TH2011, ZH2183]) was a site for burning refuse in NT times.

**19:4 *the blood of innocent children.*** Lit., "the blood of innocent," which elsewhere and possibly here refers to miscarriage of justice wherein persons were punished who were innocent of a crime (see 22:17; cf. 2 Kgs 21:16).

**19:5 *there they burn their sons as sacrifices to Baal.*** Baal was the youthful god in the Canaanite pantheon associated with fertility (Hos 2:8ff). Child sacrifice was forbidden (Lev 20:2-5) but was introduced by Ahaz and Manasseh (2 Kgs 16:3; 21:3-7). Josiah abolished it (2 Kgs 23:10).

**19:6 *Topheth.*** The word is onomatopoeic and means "spit" (Num 12:14; Job 17:6; NIDOTTE 4:327-328). Some see it as a cognate from Aramaic and Arabic denoting a firepit. Jer 19:6-7 echoes Jer 7:32-33.

**19:7 *I will upset the careful plans.*** Lit., "I will empty the counsel of Judah." Lundbom (1999:840) captures the word play (*baqaq* [TH1238, ZH1327], "to empty, make void" [decimate] and *baqbuq* [TH1228, ZH1318], "decanter" [19:1, 10]) with "I will decimate the council of Judah." For covenant curses here invoked, see Deut 28:25-26, 37, 53-54.

**19:8 *I will reduce Jerusalem to ruins, making it a monument to their stupidity.*** A more word-for-word rendering from the Heb. would be, "And I will make this city a horror, a thing to be hissed at" (NRSV).

**19:13 *where you burned incense on the rooftops.*** In 1992, excavators at Ashkelon found incense burners that had been used on the roofs of houses (King 1993:xxv).

**19:15 *you have stubbornly refused.*** Lit., "you have stiffened your neck." For this idiom, see 7:26; 17:23.

**20:2 So he arrested Jeremiah.** Hoffmeier (1998:317-318) draws some parallels between Pashhur barring Jeremiah's preaching and Amaziah persecuting Amos (Amos 7:7-17).

**20:3 The Man Who Lives in Terror.** By this act of naming, Jeremiah took charge, challenging Pashhur's power over him. The same name (*magor-missabib* [TH4036, ZH4474], "terror surrounds") is given to Jeremiah by his opponents (20:10). Holladay (1986:544) proposes that Pashhur, from the Aramaic *push* (be fruitful), meant "fruitful all around." Cf. his fate (20:6).

### COMMENTARY

The chapter about smashing a jar complements the one about making a jar (Jer 18); both are symbolic acts with a message of coming disaster (cf. 19:3, 11, 15 with 18:11). Jeremiah's public messages, two in the valley and one at the temple, conform broadly to the judgment form of oracles with the two parts, sometimes inverted, of accusation and announcement. The arrest by Pashhur (20:1-6) parallels the negative response of the people (18:18).

**Pre Pottery-Smashing Speech (19:1-9).** The announced disaster is of unusual magnitude (19:3), accounting for a name change from "Topheth," a mildly pejorative name (see note on 19:6) to "Valley of Slaughter." This speech about carnage and cannibalism is made memorable by "rhetorical overkill" (Brueggemann 1998:176; cf. 2 Kgs 6:26-29; Lam 2:20-21; 4:10).

The dire disaster results from a drastic disregard of the first commandment, "Do not worship any other gods besides me" (Exod 20:3). Israel had imported a foreign religion, and its deities embodied values different from Yahweh's. These perverted values were reflected in Israel's twisted justice system and in her cultic practices of child sacrifice (19:4b-5). Notions that child sacrifice would impress a deity toward a favorable response are light years away from God's values (cf. Mic 6:7). Other deities abetted bribery and emphasized the power pyramid. As a result, the guilty, playing their cards of wealth and influence, were exonerated while innocent people were condemned to die. Adopting other religions resulted in social and moral decay and in spiritual degeneracy. Violating the first commandment subverts the creator-creature relationship, undercuts the covenant, and wreaks havoc with all of the other commandments.

**Post Pottery-Smashing Speech (19:10-13).** The unusual act of a prophet's lifting his newly purchased decanter over his head and forcefully smashing it upon the rocks (which are plentiful in the valley), must have startled his audience (19:10). The message is appropriate to the action; all civil and religious structures would be smashed, and like the proverbial Humpty-Dumpty, would never be put together again (19:11). The valley where these assembled civic and religious leaders were standing would become a cemetery.

The message focuses on defilement, a factor of great significance for Israel (Lev 21:1; Num 5:2-3). Throughout, there was "defilement from the corpses, defilement from the pagan cult practices, and defilement from the garbage dump" (Craigie et al. 1991:262). To hear an entire city and its population pronounced "defiled," "contaminated," and "unfit" must have strained the sensibilities of the hearers, even though the evidence of the Baal altars was before them. The worship of the "hosts of heaven" (NLT, "star gods," 19:13; cf. 8:2; 32:29) was an affront to God, who is "Yahweh of hosts" (NLT, "LORD of Heaven's Armies," 19:3, 15), and was one more instance of failure to observe the first commandment.

**Temple-Gate Speech (19:14-15).**    For a follow-up speech, the prophet chose the sacred venue of the Temple (cf. 7:1). The previous two speeches are summarized in an inverted judgment oracle in which an announcement of disaster is followed by an accusation of spiritual stubbornness (see 7:26; 17:23). The accusation penetrates beyond actions of injustice and child sacrifice to an underlying root attitude of stubbornness. Thus, in the literary construction of the chapter, the announcement "I will bring disaster" brackets the speeches like bookends (19:3, 15). Prophetic announcements of judgment are not out-of-the-blue predictions but are grounded in human behavior.

**Jeremiah Arrested (20:1-6).**    Jeremiah's opponents are no longer anonymous but have names. Pashhur, the chief of the temple guard, incarcerated Jeremiah for one night after he was flogged. Attempts were made on Jeremiah's life (11:19; 26:11) and he would experience other imprisonments (37:15-16; 38:6).

Oracles of judgment to individuals are relatively infrequent (but cf. 28:16). The announcement of catastrophic exile and death dominates this oracle (the customary accusation is obvious but unspoken). Pashhur's family and those who sided with him were not exempt (20:6). In the extended section of announcements of destruction (13:1-19:15), the invaders remained unnamed. Now, for the first time they too have names; they are the Babylonians, whose plundering action (rather than human destruction) is elaborated (cf. 20:4-5).

Although the prophet addressed the public generally, as at the Temple (19:14), his target audience included civic leaders and often kings (19:3) that he also confronted directly (e.g., Zedekiah, 34:1-7). Jeremiah was not alone in challenging government (cf. Nathan, 2 Sam 12:1-14; John the Baptist, Matt 14:1-4; Jesus, Luke 13:32). Other prophets challenged the business community (Mic 3:1, 9). Leaders espoused values and set directions along lines of justice or injustice (Pss 72; 82). The spiritual condition of a community reflects the quality of its leaders. Pastors may not fully fit the role of prophet, but a question for every age is who speaks for God to government, civic, and business leaders.

◆    ## G. Jeremiah's Complaint before God (20:7-18)

7 O LORD, you misled me,
   and I allowed myself to be misled.
You are stronger than I am,
   and you overpowered me.
Now I am mocked every day;
   everyone laughs at me.

8 When I speak, the words burst out.
   "Violence and destruction!" I shout.
So these messages from the LORD
   have made me a household joke.
9 But if I say I'll never mention the LORD
   or speak in his name,

his word burns in my heart like a fire.
It's like a fire in my bones!
I am worn out trying to hold it in!
I can't do it!
10 I have heard the many rumors about
me.
They call me "The Man Who Lives
in Terror."
They threaten, "If you say anything,
we will report it."
Even my old friends are watching me,
waiting for a fatal slip.
"He will trap himself," they say,
"and then we will get our revenge
on him."

11 But the LORD stands beside me like
a great warrior.
Before him my persecutors will
stumble.
They cannot defeat me.
They will fail and be thoroughly
humiliated.
Their dishonor will never be
forgotten.
12 O LORD of Heaven's Armies,
you test those who are righteous,
and you examine the deepest
thoughts and secrets.

Let me see your vengeance against
them,
for I have committed my cause to
you.
13 Sing to the LORD!
Praise the LORD!
For though I was poor and needy,
he rescued me from my oppressors.

14 Yet I curse the day I was born!
May no one celebrate the day
of my birth.
15 I curse the messenger who told
my father,
"Good news—you have a son!"
16 Let him be destroyed like the cities
of old
that the LORD overthrew without
mercy.
Terrify him all day long with battle
shouts,
17     because he did not kill me
at birth.
Oh, that I had died in my mother's
womb,
that her body had been my grave!
18 Why was I ever born?
My entire life has been filled
with trouble, sorrow, and shame.

NOTES

**20:7** *you misled me.* This is a charge with strident overtones. The word "misled" (piel of *patah* [TH6601, ZH7331], "deceive," "persuade") occurs elsewhere with the sense of enticement by trickery (1 Kgs 22:20-21, Prov 16:29) and seduction (Exod 22:16-17; Judg 14:15).

**20:8** *Violence and destruction!* This was a desperate cry of violence (*khamas* [TH2555, ZH2805]) equivalent to "Emergency! Help!" but the prophet was thought to be crying "Wolf!" (cf. 17:15).

**20:10** *The Man Who Lives in Terror.* Lit., "terror surrounds" (cf. 20:3; also 6:25).

*Even my old friends.* The Heb. is *'enosh shelomi* [TH582/7965, ZH632/8934] (men of my peace), an ironic description, given their objectives.

**20:11** *They cannot defeat me.* Four times the verb *yakol* [TH3201, ZH3523] (hold on to, conquer) is used to indicate that power is the critical issue (20:7, 9, 10, 11). In 20:9, the NLT translates *yakol* as "holding it in"; in 20:10, *yakol* is not specifically translated but is incorporated in "then we will get our revenge on him."

**20:13** *Sing to the LORD!* The sudden change of mood from gloom to praise, from exasperation to song, which is characteristic of laments, has been variously explained. (1) A priest gave an oracle in response to the lament (cf. 1 Sam 1:17). (2) The petitioner anticipated a future resolution and broke out in praise. (3) The ugly circumstance was resolved because God intervened. (4) The poem summarized an event now some time in the past.

**20:14** *Yet I curse the day I was born!* The NLT follows the usual interpretation that the prophet invoked a curse, an evil word. The verb form *'arur* [TH779, ZH826] is passive. Instead, scholars propose that Jeremiah was simply stating a fact. The day of his birth, and the messenger, too, were cursed, since Jeremiah's life was so filled with agony (so Holladay 1986:561). "Jeremiah fully identifies with Judah and shares the destiny of Judah: curse and, eventually, exile (cf. 15:13-14)" (Bracke 2000a:166).

**20:16** *like the cities of old.* The overthrow of Sodom and Gomorrah (Gen 19:24-28) is a paradigm of God's judgment on wickedness (Deut 29:23; Isa 13:19; Jer 23:14; 49:18; 50:40; Ezek 16:49; Amos 4:11; Rom 9:29).

*Terrify him all day long with battle shouts.* Lit., "may he hear cries in the morning and shouts at noontime."

**20:17** *that her body had been my grave!* The more literal sense is of a womb forever pregnant—Jeremiah's permanent resting place.


COMMENTARY

This lament (20:7-13) closely follows the classic lament form (cf. Ps 13): address (20:7a), complaint (20:7-10), statement of confidence (20:11), petition (20:12), and witness of praise (20:13). The curse poem (20:14-18), along with the lament, is to be read as an exasperated finale in response to the repeated predictions of coming destruction and not only as a response to the overnight imprisonment (20:1-6). For the symmetry of Jeremiah 18 and 19–20, see the commentary on 18:1.

**Lament of Desperation (20:7-13).** In this section, Jeremiah complains about God, his opponents, and his interior life. He presents himself, as depressed persons often do, as a victim (20:7). He is caught in the middle and is clearly on the horns of a dilemma, damned if he speaks and damned if he doesn't speak (cf. Amos 3:8; 1 Cor 9:16). While the three reasons for complaint are the same as those in 15:15-18, the intensity is greater here. The petition is unsettling when read in light of the New Testament and Christ's instructions to pray for one's enemies (see comments on 18:18-23).

This final emotional expression of feelings within a series of laments (11:18-23; 12:1-13; 15:10-14, 15-21; 17:14-18; 18:18-23) calls for reflection at several levels, irrespective of whether an individual or a community is in view. First, these laments are a reality check. Prophets, for all their spirituality, were not always on an even keel emotionally. The laments affirm the vagaries of human emotions. Christians are not exempt from low times when life is not sunny or exciting. Indeed, the final view of the prophet's interior life is of a man most unhappy, unfulfilled and lacking the energy or enthusiasm to go on (20:14-18).

Second, the laments repeatedly point to other people as the source of life's difficulties. Jeremiah was forever harassed by others' interfering in his life. Jeremiah's laments are on a trajectory that includes Psalm 22, Isaiah 53, and Jesus' passion (Boers 1999:86-102).

Third, life with God is hardly tension-free, and God, the partner, can be the source of the frustration. Why, Jeremiah wanted to know, does a righteous God not deal summarily with the wicked (12:1-4; cf. 15:15)? Jeremiah considered God to be manipulative (20:7), and sometimes God seemed withdrawn and uninvolved. To Jeremiah, God was like a deceitful brook, erratic, or not there at all (15:18). When God seemed to be the problem, there was no one higher than God to whom appeal might be made.

Fourth, a life that is intimate with God allows for complete honesty. Jeremiah's challenge to God appears blunt, impolite, and disrespectful. There is, after all, little point in hiding one's negative feelings, even about God, since God knows all. The laments, for all the trouble they describe, are nevertheless refreshing glimpses into the life of an individual fully at home with God and on speaking terms with him, even when the relationship between the two is strained and momentarily murky.

Fifth, God neither ignores such outbursts nor scolds those who make them. While not every recorded lament is followed by a recorded divine response, the recorded responses are of a God who is sympathetic to the prophet's frustration, yet who will not pamper him. Rather, God would lead him beyond the stalemate. God disclosed his own pathos in answering Jeremiah on the question of his righteousness (12:5-13). More significant, however, are the reassurances that God will always be present and that the ministry will not be fruitless in the end (15:20-21).

**A Death Wish (20:14-18).** This unit, distinct from the foregoing in form and content, consists of a double curse (20:14-17a) and a death wish (20:17b-18; cf. 15:10; Job 3:2-10). For Jeremiah, a birthday was not a time of celebration but of loathing. He called down a curse on the day of his birth, though not on God or his parents (the latter was prohibited; Exod 21:17; see note on 20:14). The double curse on the messenger is for the messenger to experience a diminution of life. A curse is the very opposite of blessing, for it invokes a wish for the deity to bring evil instead of good, enfeeblement instead of empowerment, poverty instead of prosperity, brokenness instead of wholeness, and death instead of life.

Strictly speaking, the final outcry was not so much a death wish as it was a desire to have never existed at all. His life, and more particularly his vocation of service, should never have happened. The final question, "Why was I ever born?" is addressed to no one in particular. In the Hebrew, it is followed by infinitives, "to see toil and sorrow and have days filled with shame." The question about the meaning of human existence becomes acute when life is oppressive and filled with setbacks. Philosophers, poets, peasants, and theologians have asked the question. Lundbom (1999:874), quoting Shakespeare's Hamlet, notes a universal application here: "The time is out of joint. O cursed spite/That ever I was born to set it right."

The question is acute for God's ministers, individuals, or groups, not only because labor seems pointless, but because the experience of futility contradicts a theology of promise and power. No divine answer follows this desperate complaint, perhaps because the answer cannot be put succinctly. Or possibly the answer about vocation and meaning has already been given (1:4-10).

◆ V. Disputations with Kings and Prophets (21:1–29:32)
   A. Critiquing Kings (21:1–23:8)
      1. King Zedekiah, the lightweight (21:1-10)

The LORD spoke through Jeremiah when King Zedekiah sent Pashhur son of Malkijah and Zephaniah son of Maaseiah, the priest, to speak with him. They begged Jeremiah, 2"Please speak to the LORD for us and ask him to help us. King Nebuchadnezzar* of Babylon is attacking Judah. Perhaps the LORD will be gracious and do a mighty miracle as he has done in the past. Perhaps he will force Nebuchadnezzar to withdraw his armies."

3Jeremiah replied, "Go back to King Zedekiah and tell him, 4'This is what the LORD, the God of Israel, says: I will make your weapons useless against the king of Babylon and the Babylonians* who are outside your walls attacking you. In fact, I will bring your enemies right into the heart of this city. 5I myself will fight against you with a strong hand and a powerful arm, for I am very angry. You have made me furious! 6I will send a terrible plague upon this city, and both people and animals will die. 7And after all that, says the LORD, I will hand over King Zedekiah, his staff, and everyone else in the city who survives the disease, war, and famine. I will hand them over to King Nebuchadnezzar of Babylon and to their other enemies. He will slaughter them and show them no mercy, pity, or compassion.'

8"Tell all the people, 'This is what the LORD says: Take your choice of life or death! 9Everyone who stays in Jerusalem will die from war, famine, or disease, but those who go out and surrender to the Babylonians will live. Their reward will be life! 10For I have decided to bring disaster and not good upon this city, says the LORD. It will be handed over to the king of Babylon, and he will reduce it to ashes.'

21:2 Hebrew *Nebuchadrezzar*, a variant spelling of Nebuchadnezzar; also in 21:7.   21:4 Or *Chaldeans;* also in 21:9.

NOTES

21:1 *King Zedekiah sent Pashhur.* This is the first of several meetings of the king and Jeremiah (37:3-10, 17-21; 38:14-18). Pashhur, possibly a royal advisor (not the one who arrested Jeremiah, 20:1), will later call for Jeremiah's death (38:1-6). Though a priest is present, a prophet still serves as intermediary (cf. 42:1-22; cf. Isa 37:4).

21:2 *King Nebuchadnezzar . . . is attacking.* This probably occurred in 589/588 BC. The Babylonian ruler (605–562 BC) is first mentioned by name here, by a variant of the name Nebuchadrezzar. Both forms occur in Jeremiah for a total of thirty-seven times (cf. Dan 1–4).

*mighty miracle.* This was deliverance from the Assyrians (see 2 Kgs 19:1-35; cf. 2 Kgs 7:1-7; 2 Chr 20; Ps 86:10).

21:4 *I will make your weapons useless against the king of Babylon and the Babylonians.* "Make useless" renders *sabab* [TH5437, ZH6015] (hiphil, "to encircle," "change direction"). A similar phrase, "turning the weapons" (with the deity as subject), is known from a thir-teenth century Hittite king's treaty and a seventh-century Babylonian treaty (cf. Judg 7:22). The Old Babylonian Empire was known as "the Chaldeans" (*kasdim* [TH3778, ZH4169]).

21:5 *a powerful arm.* Lit., "with outstretched hand and arm of strength," a combination associated with the divine warfare (Exod 6:6; Deut 5:15; cf. Josh 23:10; Isa 30:32).

21:9 *go out and surrender to the Babylonians.* Jeremiah's counsel (cf. 27:1-15), easily construed as a traitorous act, understandably got him into trouble (cf. 11:19; 37:13).

## COMMENTARY

This chapter begins a largely narrative section dominated by many named kings and prophets. These officials, kings such as Jehoahaz, Jehoiakim, Jehoiachin, and Zedekiah, can be historically dated, but the chapters are not chronologically arranged. Zedekiah (598–587 BC) is the last of Judah's kings, but the delegation's visit to Jeremiah is placed early in the story, possibly because Babylon's invasion, now a reality, was programmatic and colored everything else. The earlier dire threats now touched down like a hurricane as Judah came under siege (21:2).

Zedekiah followed precedent in asking a prophet for prayer (cf. Isa 37:4). It is not known whether Jeremiah honored the delegation's request (cf. 14:11). The hope for a miracle was empty. God is not infinitely patient and the city would be ravaged by numerous agents of death. God had turned against his people, a divine stance altogether opposite from the "I am for you" promised to the exiles (Isa 40:1-11; cf. Gideon, Judg 6:12). When God's unlimited power is channeled on behalf of his own, the question is rhetorical, "If God is for us, who can ever be against us?" (Rom 8:31). When God resists instead of assisting a nation, ruin is inevitable (Ezek 35:3), even for Israel (cf. 23:30; Isa 63:10). God's fierce anger (21:5) is as much a reality as his compassion (cf. 2 Thess 1:6-8; see comments on 25:15-38).

"Take your choice of life or death." For the residents of Jerusalem beset by siege, the recommended escape route—surrender to the Babylonians—must have seemed odd. What they assessed as the way of death was actually the way of life. God's kingdom in the world is an "upside down" kingdom. Jeremiah followed his own advice and survived (40:1-6; 42:7-22). Beyond the existential moment of choice in 588 BC, the challenge to choose well can be applied to life as a whole, as in the words of Moses, "Today I am giving you a choice between prosperity and disaster, between life and death" (Deut 30:15, 19; cf. Josh 24:15, 1 Kgs 18:21). Jesus also clearly set out the alternatives and urged his listeners to choose life (Matt 7:13-14).

◆  ## 2. Basics for good government (21:11–22:9)

11"Say to the royal family of Judah, 'Listen to this message from the LORD! 12This is what the LORD says to the dynasty of David:

"'Give justice each morning to the people you judge!
Help those who have been robbed;
rescue them from their oppressors.
Otherwise, my anger will burn like an unquenchable fire
because of all your sins.
13I will personally fight against the people in Jerusalem,
that mighty fortress—

the people who boast, "No one can touch us here.
No one can break in here."
14And I myself will punish you for your sinfulness,
says the LORD.
I will light a fire in your forests
that will burn up everything around you.'"

## CHAPTER 22

This is what the LORD said to me: "Go over and speak directly to the king of Judah. Say to him, 2'Listen to this message from the LORD, you king of Judah, sitting on

David's throne. Let your attendants and your people listen, too. ³This is what the LORD says: Be fair-minded and just. Do what is right! Help those who have been robbed; rescue them from their oppressors. Quit your evil deeds! Do not mistreat foreigners, orphans, and widows. Stop murdering the innocent! ⁴If you obey me, there will always be a descendant of David sitting on the throne here in Jerusalem. The king will ride through the palace gates in chariots and on horses, with his parade of attendants and subjects. ⁵But if you refuse to pay attention to this warning, I swear by my own name, says the LORD, that this palace will become a pile of rubble.'"

⁶Now this is what the LORD says concerning Judah's royal palace:

"I love you as much as fruitful Gilead
    and the green forests of Lebanon.
But I will turn you into a desert,
    with no one living within your
    walls.
⁷I will call for wreckers,
    who will bring out their tools to
    dismantle you.
They will tear out all your fine cedar
    beams
    and throw them on the fire.

⁸"People from many nations will pass by the ruins of this city and say to one another, 'Why did the LORD destroy such a great city?' ⁹And the answer will be, 'Because they violated their covenant with the LORD their God by worshiping other gods.'"

## NOTES

**21:12 *Give justice each morning.*** The Heb. word *mishpat* [TH4941, ZH5477] (justice) derives from the root *shapat* [TH8199, ZH9149] (to decide). The term is not limited to the law courts but is used pervasively to describe honorable, God-prescribed actions in domestic, social, and religious arenas.

**21:13 *that mighty fortress.*** Lit., "the rock on the plain." Jerusalem has valleys on three sides. Judah's kings, such as Hezekiah, fortified the city, taking advantage of its location (2 Kgs 20:20).

**21:14 *fire in your forests.*** This is not referring to wooded forests but probably to the Temple and palace, which because of their cedar pillars and beams had the name Palace of the Forest of Lebanon (1 Kgs 7:2; 10:21).

**22:3 *Do not mistreat foreigners, orphans, and widows.*** Mosaic instructions insisted that such persons, all of them vulnerable with respect to work, social acceptance, and legal access, be cared for (Exod 22:21 [20]; Lev 19:33). Jeremiah prohibited violence and any oppression of others, which included the economic exploitation of reducing someone to slavery (Deut 23:15-16).

**22:5 *I swear by my own name.*** Cf. Isa 45:23; Jer 49:13.

**22:6 *I love you as much as fruitful Gilead.*** Gilead, east of Galilee, was wooded in ancient times. Lebanon's forests supplied lumber for Solomon's Temple and palace (1 Kgs 5:7-12).

**22:8 *Why did the LORD destroy such a great city?*** Similar questions with a rhetorical flourish are also posed elsewhere (5:18-19; 16:10-11; cf. 9:12-13).

**22:9 *Because they violated their covenant.*** Lit., "they forsook the covenant."

***worshiping other gods.*** This violates the first commandment and therefore the loyalty and devotion that the commandment is intended to safeguard.

COMMENTARY

The two panels, 21:11-14 and 22:1-9, have parallel material (with some variations) and a similar structure:

|  | Jeremiah 21:11-14 | Jeremiah 22:1-9 |
|---|---|---|
| Address to Government | to "the dynasty of David" | to "the king of Judah" |
| Basic Demand | "Give justice to the people" | "Be fair-minded and just" |
| Exposition | Help . . . rescue . . . do right | Help . . . rescue . . . quit evil deeds |
| Motivation | [If not . . .] "I will fight against this city" | "If you obey . . . always a Davidic King." |
| Addendum | Fire destroys a palace | Fire destroys a "favored" palace |

In both panels, the addressee is the royal court, specifically the king. The subject is God's expectation from civil leaders—the practice of justice (21:12; 22:3). God offers incentives, both negative and positive, for compliance.

**Justice, a Priority.** Justice has a high priority in God's hierarchy of values. His throne is built on justice and righteousness (Ps 89:14). He declares without ambiguity, "I, the LORD, love justice" (Isa 61:8), and the importance given to justice distinguishes Yahweh's court (Ps 82:1-7). God requires that his people practice justice (Mic 6:6-8; cf. Isa 5:7), a requirement emphasized in Jeremiah's sermon to the people (7:5) and now urged upon government (cf. Isa 9:7). God will himself judge kings according to their exercise of justice (22:15-16).

Justice is commonly interpreted as fair treatment (22:3), by which is meant rewarding the law-abiding and punishing criminals. The biblical concept of justice (*mishpat* [TH4941, ZH5477]) entails much more. Often the general call to do justice is explicated at once, as here, with details. For governments, the implementation of justice has not to do chiefly with prosecuting the criminal; the focus is far more on the victim. Justice has to do with extending a helping hand to the disadvantaged. Justice means becoming a champion for those who are oppressed (21:12; cf. Ps 82:4). In the Old Testament, justice is tied to compassion. The just person is described as one "who does not rob the poor but instead gives food to the hungry and provides clothes for people in need" (Ezek 18:5). The just king treats the poor fairly; his task is to "defend the poor, to rescue the children of the needy" (Ps 72:1-4, 12-14). Retributive justice ensures that the criminal is appropriately punished. Restorative justice pays attention to the victim of a crime, ensuring that as much as possible the victim recovers his or her losses, and that harmonious rather than hostile attitudes prevail.

**Motivation for Being Just.** While doing justice is rewarding in itself, God reinforced his demand that the king practice justice with both the proverbial carrot and the big stick. The incentive to govern with justice is the good that God will send. For Judah, this meant a Davidic king. The vision of the king riding in splendor on parade presumed a peaceful time when royalty and subjects could indulge in such celebrations without fear (22:4; cf. 17:25). The big stick was the threat of disaster should Judah's kings fail to practice justice. Then God himself would besiege the city (21:13), calling in "wreckers" (foreign armies, 22:7); the palace would be so thoroughly burned (see note on 21:14) that its cedar beams could not be salvaged (22:7) and no one would live there any more (22:6).

## 3. A parade of royal failures (22:10-30)

¹⁰ Do not weep for the dead king or
  mourn his loss.
Instead, weep for the captive king
  being led away!
For he will never return to see his
  native land again.

¹¹ For this is what the LORD says about Jehoahaz,* who succeeded his father, King Josiah, and was taken away as a captive: "He will never return. ¹²He will die in a distant land and will never again see his own country."

¹³ And the LORD says, "What sorrow
  awaits Jehoiakim,*
who builds his palace with forced
  labor.*
He builds injustice into its walls,
  for he makes his neighbors work for
  nothing.
He does not pay them for their
  labor.
¹⁴ He says, 'I will build a magnificent
  palace
with huge rooms and many
  windows.
I will panel it throughout with
  fragrant cedar
and paint it a lovely red.'
¹⁵ But a beautiful cedar palace does not
  make a great king!
Your father, Josiah, also had plenty
  to eat and drink.
But he was just and right in all his
  dealings.
That is why God blessed him.

¹⁶ He gave justice and help to the poor
  and needy,
and everything went well for him.
Isn't that what it means to know me?"
  says the LORD.
¹⁷ "But you! You have eyes only for greed
  and dishonesty!
You murder the innocent,
oppress the poor, and reign
  ruthlessly."

¹⁸ Therefore, this is what the LORD says about Jehoiakim, son of King Josiah:

"The people will not mourn for him,
  crying to one another,
  'Alas, my brother! Alas, my sister!'
His subjects will not mourn for him,
  crying,
  'Alas, our master is dead! Alas, his
  splendor is gone!'
¹⁹ He will be buried like a dead
  donkey—
dragged out of Jerusalem and
  dumped outside the gates!
²⁰ Weep for your allies in Lebanon.
  Shout for them in Bashan.
Search for them in the regions east of
  the river.*
See, they are all destroyed.
  Not one is left to help you.
²¹ I warned you when you were
  prosperous,
but you replied, 'Don't bother me.'
You have been that way since
  childhood—
you simply will not obey me!

²² And now the wind will blow away your allies.
All your friends will be taken away as captives.
Surely then you will see your wickedness and be ashamed.
²³ It may be nice to live in a beautiful palace
paneled with wood from the cedars of Lebanon,
but soon you will groan with pangs of anguish—
anguish like that of a woman in labor.

²⁴ "As surely as I live," says the LORD, "I will abandon you, Jehoiachin* son of Jehoiakim, king of Judah. Even if you were the signet ring on my right hand, I would pull you off. ²⁵ I will hand you over to those who seek to kill you, those you so desperately fear—to King Nebuchadnezzar* of Babylon and the mighty Babylonian* army. ²⁶ I will expel you and your mother from this land, and you will die in a foreign country, not in your native land. ²⁷ You will never again return to the land you yearn for.

²⁸ "Why is this man Jehoiachin like a discarded, broken jar?
Why are he and his children to be exiled to a foreign land?
²⁹ O earth, earth, earth!
Listen to this message from the LORD!
³⁰ This is what the LORD says:
'Let the record show that this man Jehoiachin was childless.
He is a failure,
for none of his children will succeed him on the throne of David
to rule over Judah.'

22:11 Hebrew *Shallum,* another name for Jehoahaz.   22:13a The brother and successor of the exiled Jehoahaz. See 22:18.   22:13b Hebrew *by unrighteousness.*   22:20 Or *in Abarim.*   22:24 Hebrew *Coniah,* a variant spelling of Jehoiachin; also 22:28.   22:25a Hebrew *Nebuchadrezzar,* a variant spelling of Nebuchadnezzar. 22:25b Or *Chaldean.*

## NOTES

**22:10 *Do not weep for the dead king.*** Josiah (640–609 BC) initiated reform (622 BC) but died tragically at age forty at the Megiddo pass, where his army tried to cut off the Egyptians en route to fighting at the Euphrates (2 Kgs 23:29).

***captive king.*** This was Jehoahaz, Josiah's son, who reigned for only three months in 609 BC. The Egyptians took him first to Riblah, then to Egypt, where he died (2 Kgs 23:31-34).

**22:13 *What sorrow awaits Jehoiakim.*** This king, who reigned from 609–598 BC, was also Josiah's son. He was arrogant, pretentious, unjust, contemptible, and ungodly (cf. his irreverent treatment of Jeremiah's scroll, 36:20-26).

**22:15 *he was just and right in all his dealings.*** Josiah's "justice and righteousness" (*mishpat* [TH4941, ZH5477] and *tsedaqah* [TH6666, ZH7407]) are contrasted with Jehoiakim's lack of the same (see the NLT note on 22:13).

**22:17 *You murder the innocent.*** This was precisely forbidden, along with violence, in the divine mandate for royalty (22:3).

**22:18 *our master is dead!*** A follow-up phrase is left untranslated: "Alas, his majesty!"

**22:20 *Weep for your allies.*** The feminine singular addressee is likely Jerusalem (22:21-23). The allies, called "lovers" (singular form *me'aheb* [TH157C, ZH170], cf. Ezek 23:5-6), were Lebanon in the north, Bashan in the northeast, and Abarim (where Mount Nebo was located) in the southeast.

**22:22 *the wind will blow away your allies.*** The Heb. is picturesque, lit. saying, "the wind is shepherding the shepherds" (a common designation for leaders, cf. 23:1).

**22:23 *It may be nice to live in a beautiful palace.*** The addressee remains feminine. Jerusalem, sporting foreign imports from Lebanon, fits this image.

**22:24 *I will abandon you, Jehoiachin.*** This king, at age eighteen, ruled for three months, from December 598 to March 597 BC (2 Kgs 24:8-17; 2 Chr 36:9-10), a date established from the Babylonian Chronicle that narrates Nebuchadnezzar's campaigns.

***signet ring.*** This highly cherished ring represented vested authority (Esth 8:8; Hag 2:23).

**22:30 *Jehoiachin was childless.*** This king had seven sons (1 Chr 3:17-19), but since none would take the throne (22:30b), he was without dynastic succession. Zerubbabel, a grandson, was a leader, but not a king (Hag 2:23).

### COMMENTARY

Three of the last four kings of Judah (who ruled between 609 and 597 BC) are listed in order and indicted. The first and the last mentioned, Jehoahaz and Jehoiachin, each ruled for only three months and were both destined for death in foreign countries (Egypt and Babylon). Jeremiah dashed any hopes people might pin on Jehoiachin, who was taken by Nebuchadnezzar to Babylon in 597 BC (cf. 28:4). An undignified death was predicted for the major offender, Jehoiakim.

**Justice and Injustice.** A central idea in the judgment speech against Jehoiakim (accusation, 22:13-17; announcement, 22:18-19) is the miscarriage of justice. Kings are to dispense justice. The theme is continued from the double mandate directed to kings earlier (21:11-14; 22:1-9). In the roster of Judah's kings, Jehoiakim's record is particularly flat and problematic. His greed drove him to violence. He took advantage of the poor, an action against which God had expressly warned (22:3; cf. 22:17). He used forced labor, refusing to pay the requisite wages.

If wages matter to the worker, they clearly matter to God, for God is a careful accountant. Kings (and corporations), for all their power, cannot escape accountability. How much injustice is built into garments and other products manufactured in non-Western countries due to the exploitation of cheap labor abroad? Fair compensation is important irrespective of the job. An earlier appeal, "Take your choice between death and life" (21:8), against the background of Jehoiakim's story becomes "Take your choice between luxury and assisting others."

**Justice and Experiencing God.** The practice of justice is tantamount to knowing God (22:16), a daring and far-reaching claim. Josiah, Jehoiakim's father, practiced justice, knew God, and enjoyed God's blessings. The son was greedy and unjust, made riches his goal, and lost everything. The son who wanted to be a "somebody" ended up a "nobody," without a burial or a positive legacy. The prophet did not deny Josiah the perks that come with public office, but political power was to be harnessed in the interests of the needy, not in the enhancement of one's favorites. Those who help disaster and drought victims, refugees, and groups in need near and far put themselves in a position to experience God, for God is experienced through social action as well as through the reading of Scripture, prayer, and worship. Isaiah would say much the same (Isa 58:6-7) and so would Jesus (Matt 25:31-46), but it is James who makes charity a hallmark of true religion (Jas 1:27).

**The Price of Injustice.** The inserted oracle, presumably addressed to the capital city Jerusalem, contains a blanket charge that "she" (perhaps the people or their leaders) did not listen from the outset (22:20-23; cf. 2:2). For the capital city and the royal court, the two essential qualities were justice and obedience. The fate of the remaining two kings—Jehoahaz and Jehoiachin—would be death far from home. More shocking still, the Davidic dynasty, an institution for 350 years, would come to an end with Jehoiachin. Disregard for justice broke the covenant intended to be "forever" (2 Sam 7:16).

The immediate consequence for the capital city was the loss of its allies (22:20). Such an announcement would sting, since Judah was jockeying for help from the Egyptians, especially during Zedekiah's reign. God did not renege on his insistence on obedience and justice. If God's administration of justice meant tearing off the signet ring, he would do so. Similarly, though God had delighted in Jerusalem, he would proceed to destroy it (22:6-7) because of sin, but not without pathos and disappointment over the punishment (cf. 12:7).

◆    ## 4. Presenting a future king (23:1-8)

"What sorrow awaits the leaders of my people—the shepherds of my sheep—for they have destroyed and scattered the very ones they were expected to care for," says the LORD.

²Therefore, this is what the LORD, the God of Israel, says to these shepherds: "Instead of caring for my flock and leading them to safety, you have deserted them and driven them to destruction. Now I will pour out judgment on you for the evil you have done to them. ³But I will gather together the remnant of my flock from the countries where I have driven them. I will bring them back to their own sheepfold, and they will be fruitful and increase in number. ⁴Then I will appoint responsible shepherds who will care for them, and they will never be afraid again. Not a single one will be lost or missing. I, the LORD have spoken!

⁵"For the time is coming," says the LORD,

"when I will raise up a righteous descendant*
from King David's line.
He will be a King who rules with wisdom.
He will do what is just and right throughout the land.
⁶And this will be his name:
'The LORD Is Our Righteousness.'*
In that day Judah will be saved,
and Israel will live in safety.

⁷"In that day," says the LORD, "when people are taking an oath, they will no longer say, 'As surely as the LORD lives, who rescued the people of Israel from the land of Egypt.' ⁸Instead, they will say, 'As surely as the LORD lives, who brought the people of Israel back to their own land from the land of the north and from all the countries to which he had exiled them.' Then they will live in their own land."

23:5 Hebrew *a righteous branch.*   23:6 Hebrew *Yahweh Tsidqenu.*

NOTES

23:1 *What sorrow awaits.* The oracle lit. begins with "Woe" (*hoy* [TH1945, ZH2098], "alas"), a cry appropriate to a funeral (so also 22:13).

*shepherds.* This is a common designation for leaders in the ancient world (cf. Ezek 34:1-16).

**23:2 *Now I will pour out judgment.*** The phrase renders the participle *paqad* [TH6485, ZH7212] (visit, attend to), which, when God is the subject, can signify either a wholesome outcome of salvation or a negative action of punishment. A wordplay emphasizes that the punishment fits the crime. The leaders have not "attended to" (*paqad*, "cared for") the sheep; now God will "attend to" (*paqad*) them by pouring out judgment. Another word play turns on the Heb. homonyms "shepherd" and "evil": *ro'eh* [TH7462A, ZH8286] (shepherds), from the root *ra'ah* [TH7462, ZH8286]; and *ro'a* [TH7455, ZH8278] (evil) from the root *ra'a'* [TH7489, ZH8317].

**23:5 *I will raise up a righteous descendant.*** The term *tsemakh* [TH6780, ZH7542] ("branch," hence "descendant"—see NLT mg) evokes the image of a family tree (cf. "scion," a designation for a person in the royal line of succession). A Phoenician inscription uses the language of a "righteous branch" for a legitimate scion (Holladay 1986:618). For "Branch" as a technical designation for the "Coming One," the Messiah, see Zech 3:8; 6:12; cf. Jer 33:15 and Van Groningen (1990:704).

**23:6 *The LORD Is Our Righteousness.*** Because the name *Yahweh tsidqenu* [TH3068/6664, ZH3378/7406] (Yahweh our righteousness) differs only slightly from King Zedekiah's name (*tsidqiyyahu* [TH6667A, ZH7409], "righteous is Yahweh") some (e.g., Bright 1965:143) propose that the oracle was given early in Zedekiah's reign when "dynastic hopes were attached to that king." Others (e.g., Holladay 1986:617) date the oracle toward the end of Zedekiah's reign as a repudiation of him, for though he carried the name, he did not embody righteousness. As the material is now ordered, allusions to Zedekiah in 21:1 and 23:6 form a set of bookends. The promise of 23:7-8 addresses Zedekiah's request for a miracle (21:2).

**23:8 *back to their own land from the land of the north.*** See the comment on the virtually identical oracle in 16:14-15.

### COMMENTARY

The series of short oracles (23:2-4, 5-6, 7-8) continues with the topics of leadership and exile from the prior oracles against kings (22:10–23:2).

Exile was precipitated by bad leadership. "Mismanaged royal power is the single cause of the Exile" (Brueggemann 1998:206). The contrast in leadership is between the irresponsible kings of Israel, under whose stewardship the nation had been fractured, and the coming ideal leader who would bring unity by gathering them back. Because the derelict kings had failed in their stewardship of caring for those under their charge, the people, like sheep, were scattered and exposed to destruction (cf. Mark 6:34). Ezekiel spoke of bad and good shepherds (Ezek 34:2-4; 11-16), as did Jesus (John 10:1-18) and Peter (1 Pet 5:1-4).

Beyond the Exile, God would take the initiative, as he did at the Exodus, to reverse a bad situation. Jeremiah will return to the themes of re-gathering (30:3; 31:9-10), resettlement (32:42), repopulation (33:10-11), prosperity (33:6-9), new leadership (33:14-17), and security (31:23, 35-37). So striking will be the undoing of the Exile that the Exodus will pale by comparison (23:7-8). God spoke a word of hope, a promise of transformation, into a chaotic, unraveling society.

The word of promise is about a righteous leader. At the conclusion of the roll call of Judah's kings, the poet returns to the subject of righteousness (cf. 21:12; 22:3). God himself models righteous governance, defined as including compassionate treatment of the disadvantaged and ensuring conditions for their productivity and increase (22:3-4). Leaders and their deputies must do the same.

Jeremiah made only a limited number of messianic announcements (30:8-9; 30:21; 33:15-16). Having announced the coming of the ideal king, the prophet tapped into a tradition of royal ideology that was already well established, as seen in the Psalms (cf. psalms of enthronement, 2; 110; and royalty, 21; 45; 72). The prophet Isaiah fleshed out the portrait of a ruler (11:1-9, with which this oracle can profitably be compared). The "Coming One" will be both root (Isa 11:1) and branch, a clue that he is more than human, even divine. Isaiah mentions a Branch that will be beautiful and glorious (Isa 4:2), which the rabbis understood as a reference to the "Messiah of the Lord." Although the New Testament does not use the word "Branch" for Jesus, Christians have properly identified this language about the royal lineage of David as pointing to Jesus Christ, King David's greater Son. Jesus Christ is that righteous Branch (see 1 Cor 1:30), that Servant who will be preoccupied with justice (Isa 42:1-4). No post-exilic leader fully qualifies to bear that name, "The Lord Is Our Righteousness," but the heaven-sent God-man, Jesus, qualifies fully. Hope for a righteous future leader centers finally on Jesus.

◆   **B. Sparring with Prophets (23:9-40)**

⁹My heart is broken because of the
    false prophets,
and my bones tremble.
I stagger like a drunkard,
    like someone overcome by wine,
because of the holy words
    the LORD has spoken against them.
¹⁰For the land is full of adultery,
    and it lies under a curse.
The land itself is in mourning—
    its wilderness pastures are dried up.
For they all do evil
    and abuse what power they have.

¹¹"Even the priests and prophets
    are ungodly, wicked men.
I have seen their despicable acts
    right here in my own Temple,"
    says the LORD.
¹²"Therefore, the paths they take
    will become slippery.
They will be chased through the dark,
    and there they will fall.
For I will bring disaster upon them
    at the time fixed for their
      punishment.
I, the LORD, have spoken!

"I saw that the prophets of Samaria
    were terribly evil,
for they prophesied in the name
    of Baal
and led my people of Israel into sin.
¹⁴But now I see that the prophets of
    Jerusalem are even worse!
They commit adultery and love
    dishonesty.
They encourage those who are doing
    evil
so that no one turns away from
    their sins.
These prophets are as wicked
    as the people of Sodom and
      Gomorrah once were."

¹⁵Therefore, this is what the LORD of Heaven's Armies says concerning the prophets:

"I will feed them with bitterness
    and give them poison to drink.
For it is because of Jerusalem's
    prophets
    that wickedness has filled this land."

¹⁶This is what the LORD of Heaven's Armies says to his people:

13

"Do not listen to these prophets when
    they prophesy to you,
    filling you with futile hopes.
They are making up everything they
    say.
They do not speak for the LORD!
<sup>17</sup>They keep saying to those who despise
    my word,
    'Don't worry! The LORD says you will
    have peace!'
And to those who stubbornly follow
    their own desires,
    they say, 'No harm will come your
    way!'
<sup>18</sup>"Have any of these prophets been in
    the LORD's presence
    to hear what he is really saying?
Has even one of them cared enough
    to listen?
<sup>19</sup>Look! The LORD's anger bursts out like
    a storm,
    a whirlwind that swirls down on the
    heads of the wicked.
<sup>20</sup>The anger of the LORD will not
    diminish
    until it has finished all he has
    planned.
In the days to come
    you will understand all this very
    clearly.

<sup>21</sup>"I have not sent these prophets,
    yet they run around claiming to
    speak for me.
I have given them no message,
    yet they go on prophesying.
<sup>22</sup>If they had stood before me and
    listened to me,
    they would have spoken my words,
    and they would have turned my people
    from their evil ways and deeds.
<sup>23</sup>Am I a God who is only close at hand?"
    says the LORD.
"No, I am far away at the same time.
<sup>24</sup>Can anyone hide from me in a secret
    place?
    Am I not everywhere in all the
    heavens and earth?"
    says the LORD.

<sup>25</sup>"I have heard these prophets say, 'Listen to the dream I had from God last night.' And then they proceed to tell lies in my name. <sup>26</sup>How long will this go on? If they are prophets, they are prophets of deceit, inventing everything they say. <sup>27</sup>By telling these false dreams, they are trying to get my people to forget me, just as their ancestors did by worshiping the idols of Baal.

<sup>28</sup>"Let these false prophets tell their
    dreams,
    but let my true messengers
    faithfully proclaim my every word.
There is a difference between straw
    and grain!
<sup>29</sup>Does not my word burn like fire?"
    says the LORD.
"Is it not like a mighty hammer
    that smashes a rock to pieces?

<sup>30</sup>"Therefore," says the LORD, "I am against these prophets who steal messages from each other and claim they are from me. <sup>31</sup>I am against these smooth-tongued prophets who say, 'This prophecy is from the LORD!' <sup>32</sup>I am against these false prophets. Their imaginary dreams are flagrant lies that lead my people into sin. I did not send or appoint them, and they have no message at all for my people. I, the LORD have spoken!

<sup>33</sup>"Suppose one of the people or one of the prophets or priests asks you, 'What prophecy has the LORD burdened you with now?' You must reply, 'You are the burden!* The LORD says he will abandon you!'

<sup>34</sup>"If any prophet, priest, or anyone else says, 'I have a prophecy from the LORD,' I will punish that person along with his entire family. <sup>35</sup>You should keep asking each other, 'What is the LORD's answer?' or 'What is the LORD saying?' <sup>36</sup>But stop using this phrase, 'prophecy from the LORD.' For people are using it to give authority to their own ideas, turning upside down the words of our God, the living God, the LORD of Heaven's Armies.

<sup>37</sup>"This is what you should say to the

prophets: 'What is the LORD's answer?' or 'What is the LORD saying?' [38]But suppose they respond, 'This is a prophecy from the LORD!' Then you should say, 'This is what the LORD says: Because you have used this phrase, "prophecy from the LORD," even though I warned you not to use it, [39]I will forget you completely. I will expel you from my presence, along with this city that I gave to you and your ancestors. [40]And I will make you an object of ridicule, and your name will be infamous throughout the ages.' "

23:33 As in Greek version and Latin Vulgate; Hebrew reads *What burden?*

## NOTES

23:9 *because of the false prophets.* "False" is supplied by the NLT. The prophets are described as such in the text but not explicitly labeled (so also in chs 28–29). It was incumbent on the audience to determine which speakers were false.

23:10 *the land is full of adultery.* The term *na'aph* [TH5003, ZH5537] (commit adultery) was used by Jeremiah, as also by Hosea, to stand for infidelity toward God (Jer 3:8-9; 9:2 [1]; Hos 2:2) as well as to one's spouse (Jer 5:7; 7:9; Hos 3:1; 4:2), and perhaps sometimes to both (Hos 4:13-14; 7:4). Judging by what follows (23:14; 29:23), sexual immorality may be in view here.

*The land itself is in mourning.* Moral abuse leads to environmental disaster (cf. Hos 4:1-3).

23:13 *the prophets of Samaria were terribly evil.* The description of their evil (*tiplah* [TH8604, ZH9524], from *tapel* [TH8602A/B, ZH9522], "tasteless," "unseemly") is best understood as "morally or religiously offensive" (W. McKane, quoted in NIDOTTE 4:323; cf. "repulsive thing," NIV; "disgusting thing," NRSV). Historically speaking, by the time of Jeremiah, their destruction had already come at the hands of the Assyrians when Samaria was taken (722 BC).

23:14 *the prophets of Jerusalem are even worse!* More serious than *tiplah* [TH8604, ZH9524] ("offensive," 23:13) is *sha'arurah* [TH8186A, ZH9136] (horrid). These prophets are described as *sheqer* [TH8267, ZH9214] (deceitful, lying), which, beyond being dishonest, represents a way of being that is counterfeit, inauthentic, and lacking in integrity (the word reappears in 23:25, 26, 32).

*Sodom and Gomorrah.* These cities are synonymous with the worst kind of evil (20:16; 49:18; Isa 1:9; Ezek 16:49-50).

23:18 *in the LORD's presence.* With the use of *sod* [TH5475, ZH6051] (council), the Heb. depicts a royal briefing chamber. This is the place for hearing and seeing what God is planning (cf. 23:22; 1 Kgs 22:19-23).

23:19 *The LORD's anger bursts out like a storm.* The saying about the unleashing of God's anger underlines how strongly God feels about the matter; here, it concerns the evil influence of corrupt religious functionaries (23:19-20; cf. 30:23-24).

23:23 *Am I a God who is only close at hand? . . . No, I am far away at the same time.* God asserts his omnipresence as a response to the widespread mindset that certain matters were beyond God's notice (cf. Jer 12:4; Ps 139:7-12).

23:28 *Let these false prophets . . . let my true messengers.* The adjectives "false" and "true" are not in the original. The question for audiences in Judah was, "Who is the true prophet?"

23:29 *Does not my word burn like fire?* The answer for Jeremiah is "yes" (20:9). Both fire and hammer are agents in the refining process. Cf. 4:12 where God's word is a blast of wind.

**23:32** *they have no message at all.* As elsewhere in the book, the issue of "profit" (hiphil, *ya'al* [TH3276, ZH3603]) is raised mostly with regard to idols and false prophets (see the Heb. of 2:8, 11; 7:8; 12:13; 16:19). To paraphrase, "they do absolutely no good."

**23:33** *You are the burden.* The sarcastic word play is on "burden" (*massa'* [TH4853/4853A, ZH5362/5363]), which can mean "load" or "prophetic oracle." The spin on the word continues in 23:34, 36, 38, where it is translated "prophecy."

COMMENTARY

If the key issues for kings are justice and righteousness (22:10–23:6), the key issues for prophets are authenticity and integrity. This section alternates between poetry and prose, and while it can be variously segmented, it is in two parts if judged by content over form: 23:9-20 and 23:21-40. Each opens with a fundamental accusation against unnamed prophets, some of which will be identified later (chs 28–29). Each ends with a threat of punishment. Other comparisons between the two sections can be made, among which are the following.

|                    | Inauthentic Persons (23:9-20)                              | Inauthentic Messages (23:21-40)                                                  |
| ------------------ | --------------------------------------------------------- | -------------------------------------------------------------------------------- |
| Characterization   | "they all do evil" (23:10b)                               | "I gave them no message, yet they prophesy" (23:21b)                             |
| Elaboration        | lead Israel into sin (23:13b)                             | tell lies in Yahweh's name (23:25)                                               |
|                    | commit adultery (23:14a)                                  | steal messages from others (23:30)                                               |
| Divine Counsel     | To the people: "Do not listen to these prophets" (23:16)  | To the prophets: "Stop using this phrase, 'prophecy from the Lord'" (23:35)      |
| Divine Reaction    | "The LORD's anger bursts out like a storm" (23:19)        | "I will forget you completely" (23:39)                                           |

**Inauthentic Prophets.** First, as persons, the false prophets were without integrity, a point that is highlighted by repetition of the word *sheqer* [TH8267, ZH9214] (deceitfulness, lying; see note on 23:14) and by the sweeping assertion that priests and prophets are "ungodly, wicked men" (23:11). Documentation follows. They performed despicable acts in God's Temple (23:11; cf. Ezek 8:6-18). The prophets, whose calling it was to turn people from their evil ways (23:22; cf. Lam 2:14), instead led people into sin through fascination with the Baal cult (23:13). They lent the support of their office to persons of questionable ethics and so became partners in corruption (23:14). They were unfaithful to their spouses by committing adultery and they lived a lie (23:14). Their morals were those of Sodom and Gomorrah. They betrayed their mandate, which was to redirect people from their evil ways to God. They were untrustworthy.

In an earlier century, Micah singled out prophets for blame, especially for their mistakenly-timed message and their bribery (Mic 3:5, 11). Micaiah ben Imlah, in an earlier century still, identified the Achilles' heel of the court prophets; they spoke what would please the listeners, King Ahab and King Jehoshaphat (1 Kgs 22:5-6, 11-12). Isaiah caricatured the priests for their drunkenness and meaningless drivel (Isa 28:7-10). Malachi offered strident critiques of the priests (e.g., Mal 1:6-14). John the Baptist took on his religious colleagues with the epithet, "You brood of snakes" (Matt 3:7), as did Jesus (Matt 23:1-36).

The biblical premise is that religious leaders are to be models of integrity. Samuel could assert that his life was blameless (1 Sam 12:3). Paul declared that he was a man with a clean conscience toward all (Acts 24:16), and he insisted that leaders be persons of character and of clean conscience (1 Tim 3:9). What they portrayed on the outside should correspond to their inner reality. God's vehement outburst of anger against the pseudoprophets gives evidence of the premium he places on integrity (23:19-20). He is a God of holiness, a God totally true to himself. God is authentic; he makes no attempt to deceive. Those who represent him are to mirror that integrity. Duplicity, through shading the truth or misrepresenting themselves or their beliefs, is not tolerated in ministers of the gospel.

Hypocrisy is a dangerous snare for religious personnel. The despicable acts in the Temple of which Jeremiah spoke were illustrated by Jesus in the story of the arrogant Pharisee's self-righteous prayer (Luke 18:9-14). In the spirit of Jeremiah, Jesus confronted the Sadducees and Pharisees with their saying one thing and doing another, their casuistry, their hypocrisy, and their intent to keep up good appearances so they would be well thought of (Matt 23:3, 16-22, 23-24).

Church history is marred by the records of religious leaders who have been exposed for their lack of integrity. Under pressure they have compromised their message. Interested in securing the good will of others, they have aligned themselves with persons of unwholesome influence. Some have misused the power that comes with their position and have misappropriated funds. Others have taken sexual liberties, including committing adultery.

**Unauthorized Messages.** Equally problematic is the charge that the prophets' messages were not divinely authorized (23:21-40). Jeremiah charged that the prophets invented their own messages but presented them in God's name. As prophets, it was their calling to listen to God. The divine council into which they were invited both to see and to hear God's word (see note on 23:22) is depicted as an earthly king's council at which leaders gather to plan strategy, and where they give an account (cf. Job 1-2). The proceedings of such a council are pictured in Psalm 82 (cf. the prophet Micaiah, 1 Kgs 22:19-23). False prophets, however, found the source of their messages in their own dreams. They plagiarized the word of others and deliberately turned their listeners' attention away from God (23:27). While professing to be God's prophets, they marched to a different drummer, Baal.

They were culpable because they trivialized the word of God (23:36). They pretended that their message was the "burden" given them by God. In caustic tones, Jeremiah made a pun on the word "burden": they don't have a burden (message), rather, they are a burden (a load that should be dumped; 23:33). It is not a light thing to speak in the Lord's name. It is irresponsible and reprehensible for persons to glibly claim that they are speaking in God's name when they are unauthorized.

God's stance on the matter is unambiguous. He is against such perpetrators of deceit (23:32). He will expel them and give them a legacy of ignominy (23:40). The judgment is severe. The true prophet, however, does not gloat when judgment comes on pseudoprophets. Jeremiah was broken over the situation (23:9). Like Jeremiah, Jesus was emotionally moved by the spiritual havoc brought on by bogus religious leaders (Matt 7:15; 23:16) and he deeply yearned to have it otherwise (Matt 23:37). True prophets listen to God. They expose sin and preach judgment, not vindictively but with tears.

Pseudo-prophets do not present themselves as false prophets. Instead, then as now, they pose as persons who have an inside track on what God is saying. While dreams may be revelatory (Gen 20:3; 28:12; 1 Kgs 3:5; Dan 2:28), other subjective elements such as desires, ambitions, and misplaced optimism too easily distort a prophecy. The gullible and the spiritually immature often take an unhealthy interest in the newest revelations about identifying anti-Christ figures, interpreting current events, supposedly in the light of Scripture, or discovering secret codes. Pandering to the curious is less demanding than standing in the council of the Almighty. Messages can readily be tailored to the prejudices of listeners so that truth is mixed with error, and neither messenger nor audience is able to tell the difference between chaff and wheat.

◆   ## C. Two Baskets of Figs and a Cup of Wine (24:1–25:38)
### 1. Figs: some good, some rotten (24:1-10)

After King Nebuchadnezzar* of Babylon exiled Jehoiachin* son of Jehoiakim, king of Judah, to Babylon along with the officials of Judah and all the craftsmen and artisans, the LORD gave me this vision. I saw two baskets of figs placed in front of the LORD's Temple in Jerusalem. ²One basket was filled with fresh, ripe figs, while the other was filled with bad figs that were too rotten to eat.

³Then the LORD said to me, "What do you see, Jeremiah?"

I replied, "Figs, some very good and some very bad, too rotten to eat."

⁴Then the LORD gave me this message: ⁵"This is what the LORD, the God of Israel, says: The good figs represent the exiles I sent from Judah to the land of the Babylonians.* ⁶I will watch over and care for

them, and I will bring them back here again. I will build them up and not tear them down. I will plant them and not uproot them. ⁷I will give them hearts that recognize me as the LORD. They will be my people, and I will be their God, for they will return to me wholeheartedly.

⁸"But the bad figs," the LORD said, "represent King Zedekiah of Judah, his officials, all the people left in Jerusalem, and those who live in Egypt. I will treat them like bad figs, too rotten to eat. ⁹I will make them an object of horror and a symbol of evil to every nation on earth. They will be disgraced and mocked, taunted and cursed, wherever I scatter them. ¹⁰And I will send war, famine, and disease until they have vanished from the land of Israel, which I gave to them and their ancestors."

24:1a Hebrew *Nebuchadrezzar*, a variant spelling of Nebuchadnezzar. 24:1b Hebrew *Jeconiah*, a variant spelling of Jehoiachin. 24:5 Or *Chaldeans*.

## NOTES

**24:1** *Nebuchadnezzar of Babylon exiled Jehoiachin.* For Jehoiachin, see 22:24. People hoped for his return (28:2-4). Evil-merodach (52:31), a Babylonian ruler, accorded Jehoiachin a measure of freedom in Babylon.

*two baskets of figs.* Their place before the Temple suggests that these were offerings of firstfruits, perhaps made in June (Deut 16:9-12; 26:2-11). The location prepares the listener (and reader) for a divine word.

**24:3** *What do you see?* The question fixes attention and invites interaction (cf. 1:11, 13; Amos 7:8; 8:2, also about a fruit basket).

**24:5** *The good figs represent the exiles.* The adjective "good" (*tob* [TH2896, ZH3202]) is not descriptive of the character of the exiles but of their destiny, as shown in the Heb.: "I will regard (hiphil, *nakhar* [TH5234, ZH5795]), recognize them for good" (*letobah* [TH2896D, ZH3208]). Cf. Walton (1989).

**24:6** *I will watch over and care for them.* A more literal rendering, "And I will set my eyes upon them for good" (NRSV), conveys more determination than does the pastoral nuance of the NLT.

*I will build them up.* The vocabulary of building, planting, tearing down, and uprooting echoes Jeremiah's call (1:10; cf. 31:27-28), except that God is now the agent.

**24:7** *hearts that recognize me as the* LORD. The more literal phrase, "a heart to know me," recalls Hosea (2:20; 6:3, 6) and the recurring emphasis in Jeremiah about knowing Yahweh (cf. 9:23-24 [22-23]; 22:16; cf. Ezek 6:7, 10). Jeremiah spoke of the heart more than any other prophet (e.g., 4:4, 14; 17:1-2).

**24:8** *those who live in Egypt.* Perhaps they accompanied Jehoahaz (609 BC, 2 Kgs 23:34). Escapees to Egypt prior to the siege were joined after the siege in 587 BC by some survivors (42:1–43:7).

## COMMENTARY

The extended series of oracles focuses, in turn, on kings (21:1–23:6), prophets (23:9-40), and people (24:1-10), with attention to the destinies of each. Both the vision of the baskets and its interpretation underline that one set of figs was very choice and the other very spoiled. The obvious conclusion would have been that those carried off to exile by Nebuchadnezzar were to blame; they were bad figs. God's future, it could then be reasoned, lay with those like Zedekiah and other survivors who remained in the city (cf. their argument, Ezek 33:24; cf. Ezek 11:14-21). But the obvious conclusion can be the wrong conclusion. Instead, those who remained were the ones that were doomed.

God's surprising word is that the future lies instead with those in exile. He will take up with a remnant, but it will be the exiled remnant rather than the remnant that remained in the land. God offered no reason other than his own initiative, though one might infer that the discipline of the exile would result in a God-fearing people.

Two additional divinely established intentions will be realized through the return of the exiles. First, his people will know him in the sense of experiencing him in depth (see note on 24:7). For that to happen, God addressed the root problem that occasioned the Exile in the first place, namely, a stubborn heart (3:17; 5:23; 11:8). He promises that he will give them a heart transplant (31:34; 32:39; Deut 30:6; Ezek

36:26-27). Their wills will be changed so that they will seek after God. A second, equally important objective enunciated long ago will also be realized: "I will be their God, and they will be my people" (Exod 6:7; cf. Jer 7:23; 11:4; 30:22; 31:1, 33; 32:38). God's objectives will yet be achieved despite the setbacks, the detours, and the exiles.

This modus operandi of choosing the least likely as candidates to fulfill his purpose is God's rule rather than an exception. God chose the younger, Jacob, rather than the culturally appropriate Esau (Mal 1:2-3) and young Joseph rather than his brothers (Gen 37–41). For Israel's first king, God chose someone from the least of the families of the least of the tribes (1 Sam 9:21). Samuel's choice of a king from among the sons of Jesse's family may have seemed obvious to him and to Jesse, but both were mistaken (1 Sam 16:1-13). Jesus overturned many an obvious conclusion (e.g., Luke 13:1-3; John 4:21), and God's ways frequently run counter to human ways (1 Cor 1:26-27). Obvious conclusions may be wrong conclusions.

◆     ## 2. A conclusive oracle of judgment (25:1-14)

This message for all the people of Judah came to Jeremiah from the LORD during the fourth year of Jehoiakim's reign over Judah.* This was the year when King Nebuchadnezzar* of Babylon began his reign.

²Jeremiah the prophet said to all the people in Judah and Jerusalem, ³"For the past twenty-three years—from the thirteenth year of the reign of Josiah son of Amon,* king of Judah, until now—the LORD has been giving me his messages. I have faithfully passed them on to you, but you have not listened.

⁴"Again and again the LORD has sent you his servants, the prophets, but you have not listened or even paid attention. ⁵Each time the message was this: 'Turn from the evil road you are traveling and from the evil things you are doing. Only then will I let you live in this land that the LORD gave to you and your ancestors forever. ⁶Do not provoke my anger by worshiping idols you made with your own hands. Then I will not harm you.'

⁷"But you would not listen to me," says the LORD. "You made me furious by worshiping idols you made with your own hands, bringing on yourselves all the disasters you now suffer. ⁸And now the LORD of Heaven's Armies says: Because

you have not listened to me, ⁹I will gather together all the armies of the north under King Nebuchadnezzar of Babylon, whom I have appointed as my deputy. I will bring them all against this land and its people and against the surrounding nations. I will completely destroy* you and make you an object of horror and contempt and a ruin forever. ¹⁰I will take away your happy singing and laughter. The joyful voices of bridegrooms and brides will no longer be heard. Your millstones will fall silent, and the lights in your homes will go out. ¹¹This entire land will become a desolate wasteland. Israel and her neighboring lands will serve the king of Babylon for seventy years.

¹²"Then, after the seventy years of captivity are over, I will punish the king of Babylon and his people for their sins," says the LORD. "I will make the country of the Babylonians* a wasteland forever. ¹³I will bring upon them all the terrors I have promised in this book—all the penalties announced by Jeremiah against the nations. ¹⁴Many nations and great kings will enslave the Babylonians, just as they enslaved my people. I will punish them in proportion to the suffering they cause my people."

25:1a The fourth year of Jehoiakim's reign and the accession year of Nebuchadnezzar's reign was 605 BC.
25:1b Hebrew *Nebuchadrezzar*, a variant spelling of Nebuchadnezzar; also in 25:9.   25:3 The thirteenth year of
Josiah's reign was 627 BC.   25:9 The Hebrew term used here refers to the complete consecration of things
or people to the LORD, either by destroying them or by giving them as an offering.   25:12 Or *Chaldeans.*

## NOTES

**25:1** *This message for all the people.* This continues a series targeting kings (21:1–23:8),
prophets (23:9-40), the general population (24:1–25:14), and the nations (25:15-38). The
interest in "theological staging" overrides chronology (this message is given in 605 BC; ch
24 is post-597 BC). For a new reading of the chapter, see Hill (1999).

**25:4** *Again and again.* The Heb. idiom, lit., "to rise early (hiphil, *shakam* [TH7925, ZH8899]
and to send" (*shalakh* [TH7971, ZH8938]) conveys repeated, persistent, and even eager action
(cf. 7:13, 25; 26:6; 29:19; 35:15).

**25:5** *Only then will I let you live in this land.* The gift of land is forever, but enjoyment
of it is conditional on obedient listening (cf. 7:3).

**25:6** *Do not provoke my anger.* The Heb. term in the hiphil *ka'as* [TH3707, ZH4087] (cause
to anger) in Jeremiah refers exclusively to God's reaction to idols (8:19; 25:6-7; 32:30, 32;
44:3) and to devotion to specific deities such as the "Queen of Heaven" (7:18-19), gods of
the land of Egypt (44:8), and Baal (11:17; 32:29), all of which blatantly disregards the first
and second commandments (Exod 20:3).

**25:9** *whom [Nebuchadnezzar] I have appointed as my deputy.* For "my deputy," the Heb.
reads "my servant" (*'abdi* [TH5650, ZH6269]), daringly used here of a Gentile (cf. Cyrus, the
anointed, Isa 44:28; 45:1; Assyria, Isa 10:5; and "his servants the prophets," 25:4).

**25:12** *after the seventy years of captivity are over.* The seventy years of Babylonian rule
(the Heb. does not use the word "captivity") over "other nations" (Israel included, 25:11),
when taken lit. are best calculated from 609/605 BC when Babylon became a primary force
in the region, to 539/535 BC when the Persians conquered Babylon. Another proposal suggest that it was from 586 BC (the destruction of the Temple) to 516 BC (the rebuilding of
the Temple). Taken more figuratively, seventy years represents one person's lifetime, or a
long time (cf. Ps 90:10). See P. J. Scalise's excursus in Keown et al. 1995:73-75; cf. Winkle
(1987), and Applegate (1997).

**25:13** *all the terrors I have promised in this book.* Some scholars (e.g., John Bright) think
that "this book" (chs 1–25 and chs 46–51) was the scroll burned by Jehoiakim (36:27).
The LXX, omitting 25:14, places chs 46–51 after 25:13. The effect of the MT is to end the
first book with a comment on the fate of the Babylonians (25:14) and to similarly end the
second book (chs 50–51; cf. Isa 47:6).

**25:14** *in proportion to the suffering they cause my people.* The NLT makes specific what
the Heb. leaves general: "their work and the deeds of their hands" (the latter expression
earlier refers to idol-making, 25:7).

## COMMENTARY

This section has the feel of a conclusion since it summarizes what has happened in
the previous twenty-four chapters. Simply put, the message from God is for Israel to
repent. Failure to do so will incite God's wrath.

The word for repent (*shub* [TH7725, ZH8740]) speaks of turning around. A person or
nation headed in one direction turns around to head in the opposite direction. The
term is at home in secular language about walking, and "walking" and "way" came
to be used of life patterns, ways of being in the world. The Hebrew understanding of

repentance envisions a person that changes course on a journey; it differs from the Greek word *metanoia* [TG3341, ZG3567] (change of mind), which, according to etymology, envisions an intellectual thought process. For twenty-three years Jeremiah had urged Israel, who repeatedly headed away from God toward the worship of homemade idols, to make an about-face. He had told them to leave the idols and turn wholeheartedly toward God. His opening chapters are laced with calls to *shub* [TH7725, ZH8740] ("turn," e.g., 3:12, 22). His Temple sermon is a call to changed ways of acting and thinking (7:3-5). His message is not novel but is aligned with those of his predecessors, especially Hosea, to whom Jeremiah is most indebted (Hos 6:1-4; 10:12; 14:1-3).

The summons to repentance is a summons of grace. It is for Israel's good, to forestall God's judgment. The motivation for Israel to make this spiritual move towards God is that only then can they continue life in the God-given land (25:5; cf. 7:3, 7). Aside from this appeal to their physical self-interest is the theological reality of God's anger, mentioned twice here and often elsewhere (25:6, 7; cf. 4:4; 30:23-24). It is God whom they have provoked, and he is not to be trifled with. Still, the appeals were and have been ignored for decades, even centuries.

Behavior, according to modern conventional wisdom, is a function of consequences. Changed behavior is more likely when the consequences of actions are clearly grasped. From the first, Jeremiah laid out the consequences, should Israel continue in its sinful ways (4:13-18). Now reality had set in. The agent of punishment would be Nebuchadnezzar, who in the very year the oracle was given (605 BC), succeeded his father Nabopolassar as king of Babylon. Even the extent of the exile—seventy years—is specified (see note on 25:12). The principle of sin being punished is universally applicable—to Israel the covenant people and also to Babylon (25:12-14).

◆   ### 3. The wine cup of wrath served to the nations (25:15-38)

15This is what the LORD, the God of Israel, said to me: "Take from my hand this cup filled to the brim with my anger, and make all the nations to whom I send you drink from it. 16When they drink from it, they will stagger, crazed by the warfare I will send against them."

17So I took the cup of anger from the LORD and made all the nations drink from it—every nation to which the LORD sent me. 18I went to Jerusalem and the other towns of Judah, and their kings and officials drank from the cup. From that day until this, they have been a desolate ruin, an object of horror, contempt, and cursing. 19I gave the cup to Pharaoh, king of Egypt, his attendants, his officials, and all his people, 20along with all the foreigners living in that land. I also gave it to all the kings of the land of Uz and the kings of the Philistine cities of Ashkelon, Gaza, Ekron, and what remains of Ashdod. 21Then I gave the cup to the nations of Edom, Moab, and Ammon, 22and the kings of Tyre and Sidon, and the kings of the regions across the sea. 23I gave it to Dedan, Tema, and Buz, and to the people who live in distant places.* 24I gave it to the kings of Arabia, the kings of the nomadic tribes of the desert, 25and to the kings of Zimri, Elam, and Media. 26And I gave it to the kings of the northern countries, far and

near, one after the other—all the kingdoms of the world. And finally, the king of
Babylon* himself drank from the cup of
the LORD's anger.

²⁷Then the LORD said to me, "Now tell
them, 'This is what the LORD of Heaven's
Armies, the God of Israel, says: Drink from
this cup of my anger. Get drunk and
vomit; fall to rise no more, for I am sending terrible wars against you.' ²⁸And if
they refuse to accept the cup, tell them,
'The LORD of Heaven's Armies says: You
have no choice but to drink from it. ²⁹I
have begun to punish Jerusalem, the city
that bears my name. Now should I let you
go unpunished? No, you will not escape
disaster. I will call for war against all the
nations of the earth. I, the LORD of Heav-
en's Armies, have spoken!'

³⁰"Now prophesy all these things, and
say to them,

"'The LORD will roar against his own
land
from his holy dwelling in heaven.
He will shout like those who tread
grapes;
he will shout against everyone
on earth.
³¹His cry of judgment will reach the
ends of the earth,
for the LORD will bring his case
against all the nations.
He will judge all the people of the
earth,
slaughtering the wicked with the
sword.
I, the LORD, have spoken!'"

³²This is what the LORD of Heaven's
Armies says:
"Look! Disaster will fall upon nation
after nation!
A great whirlwind of fury is rising
from the most distant corners of the
earth!"

³³In that day those the LORD has slaughtered will fill the earth from one end to the
other. No one will mourn for them or gather up their bodies to bury them. They will
be scattered on the ground like manure.

³⁴Weep and moan, you evil shepherds!
Roll in the dust, you leaders of the
flock!
The time of your slaughter has
arrived;
you will fall and shatter like
a fragile vase.
³⁵You will find no place to hide;
there will be no way to escape.
³⁶Listen to the frantic cries of the
shepherds.
The leaders of the flock are wailing
in despair,
for the LORD is ruining their
pastures.
³⁷Peaceful meadows will be turned into
a wasteland
by the LORD's fierce anger.
³⁸He has left his den like a strong lion
seeking its prey,
and their land will be made
desolate
by the sword of the enemy
and the LORD's fierce anger.

25:23 Or who clip the corners of their hair.   25:26 Hebrew of Sheshach, a code name for Babylon.

NOTES

**25:15 take from my hand this cup . . . and make all the nations . . . drink from it.** The
"cup of the wine of wrath" is a figure of speech most elaborated by Jeremiah, though found
elsewhere (51:6-8; Lam 4:21; Ezek 23:31-33; cf. Isa 51:17-23; Nah 3:11). The figure of
speech has been traced to the trial cup (Num 5:11-31), though some think Jeremiah originated it. A full cup signifies the filled-up measure of God's fury against evil (Ps 75:8 [9]).
Just as wine stupefies, so the sword will stupefy (25:16, 27). The assignment to carry the cup
physically to a nation's headquarters is rhetorical; probably the prophet did not visit these
nations, though some (e.g., Huey 1993:228) regard this as a sign-act and imagine Jeremiah
seeking out merchants representing these nations in Jerusalem (cf. 27:3).

**25:20 Uz.** Uz is possibly located south of Damascus. Others place it between Edom and northern Arabia (cf. Job 1:1).

**Ashkelon, Gaza, Ekron, . . . Ashdod.** These were four of the five Philistine city-states (with Gath) southwest of Jerusalem (Josh 13:4).

**25:21 Edom.** This country lay south of the Dead Sea.

**Moab.** This country was east of the Dead Sea.

**25:23 Dedan.** Dedan was both a city and a people in northwest Arabia; it was linked with a caravan route (Isa 21:13).

**Tema.** This may have been an oasis in the Arabian desert, a district possibly inhabited by the descendants of Ishmael (Gen 25:15).

**Buz.** This was a desert tribe.

**25:25 Zimri.** This place is unknown.

**Elam.** This is the area east of the Tigris and north of the Persian Gulf.

**Media.** It was located north of Elam, beyond the Zagros mountains toward the Caspian Sea.

**25:26 the king of Babylon.** The word for Babylon, Sheshach, is a cryptogram for Babel derived by numbering the Heb. alphabet beginning with its last letter, and then substituting the corresponding letters for B-B-L. This method of coding is known as *athbash* (see notes on 51:1 and 51:41).

**25:27 I am sending terrible wars.** The stupefying effect of the "sword" ("war," NLT) is comparable to the stupor brought on by intoxication (cf. 25:29, 31).

**25:34 evil shepherds.** In royalty-related terms, they are ironically addressed as "lords" (*'addire* [TH117A, ZH129]; see 25:34-36).

**Roll in the dust.** The Ugaritic cognate of *palash* [TH6428, ZH7147] ("roll," found four times in the OT, always hithpael) signifies wallowing in the dust, as in the story of Baal and Mot, "when at the death of Baal the 'dust of wallowing' is scattered on the head of El" (NIDOTTE 3:630). This behavior was part of a mourning ritual.

**25:38 by the sword of the enemy.** Most translations follow the Greek, Targum, and other Heb. MSS by reading "sword," as found in the comparable phrasings of 46:16; 50:16. The MT, rather than reading "sword" (*khereb* [TH2719, ZH2995]), reads "anger" (*kharon* [TH2740, ZH3019]), as in the last line, and so reinforces the wrath motif. Brueggemann's (1998:227) comment that "This text [25:30-38] is not really a statement of punishment but of Yahweh's sovereignty (cf. 25:30-31)" is too one-sided.

## COMMENTARY

The final section in the series, which began in 21:1, culminates in oracle(s) against the nations (see note on 25:1). The section is in two parts, or panels, each of which begins with a directive (25:15, 30). Each treats the subject of God's anger (25:15-29, 30-38). In the first panel, mostly in prose, the centerpiece is the symbol of a wine cup; in the second, the metaphor is of a lion's roar. Together, they lead to several observations about God's anger.

First, God's anger is directed against all nations but it is first administered to Judah because judgment, as Peter explained, begins with the household of God (1 Pet 4:17; cf. Jer 21:1-10). Those who will imbibe the cup of God's anger include the smaller nations and people groups, beginning with those to the south of Judah and continuing in a circle up the Mediterranean coast to Tyre and Sidon. The circle extends to include the nearby nations surrounding Israel, such as Edom and Moab, but then opens wider to include distant nations such as Elam and Media. The final recipient to drink the cup is Babylon, which like Egypt, the first of the other nations to drink the cup, is a superpower. So from west (Egypt) to east (Babylon), all nations were included. Small and large, near and far, "elect" or not, all nations without exception became objects of God's wrath (25:26, 29; cf. Rev 14:10). The poetry with the lion as metaphor continues the emphasis that the reach of God's anger is to the last nation. There is no escape (25:30-35).

Second, God's wrath is intense. He is not a little angry. As strong drink intoxicates the imbiber, so God's anger expressed through the destructive striking of the sword will make people drunk to the point of vomiting (cf. Isa 51:17-23). The second oracle, which both begins and ends with a reference to the lion (25:30, 38), especially to his roar, emphasizes the vehemence of God's anger. Jeremiah may have been drawing from Amos, whose book begins with a description of a divine roar, mentions desolate pastures, and lists God's terror against neighboring nations (Amos 1:2). Like a threatening hurricane, the "great whirlwind of fury" approaches (25:32). The effect of God's severe and drastic action of judgment is to totally frustrate the "mighty" leaders whose flocks and properties (pastures) have been completely destroyed (25:36). Because of God's anger, even peaceful meadows will be overturned (25:37). Other prophets designate the same drastic action as the Day of the Lord, best explained as the Day of the Big Audit (Joel, Zephaniah). Even the vocabulary for wrath, *khemah* [TH2534, ZH2779] in the opening line and *kharon* [TH2740, ZH3019] ("burning," used only of God) in the closing line, conveys intensity.

Third, while much is said here about the extent and effects of God's anger, there is only a hint as to the reason for it. Judah, the first recipient, was characterized in the preceding section as the people who made God "furious by worshiping idols" (25:7). Loyalty, the basic plank of the covenant, had been shattered, and God was angry. Divine anger is not, as with humans, an emotion of hostility gone out of control but "the legitimate rage of a suzerain against a disobedient vassal" (ABD 6:990), a point made in the covenant curses (Lev 26:14-39; Deut 28:15-68). God then extended his anger beyond his covenant people to all nations (25:30, 31), because even apart from direct revelation, as Amos explained, they were guilty before God for unholy, specifically inhumane actions (Amos 1:3-2:3). The bridge between the oracles specifies that Babylon was guilty of oppression (25:14).

Indeed, from the whole of the Old Testament it is clear that the motivation for God's wrath is rebellion (acting against God's will) on the one hand and oppression (excessive cruelty) on the other. These two acts of rebellion are contrary to the two great commandments to "love your God with all your heart" and "love your neighbor as yourself." As Martin Luther reportedly said, "God's wrath wasn't poured out on sinners, but on unbelievers" (quoted by Ives 1990, sermon on Jer 4:5–6:30; for a comprehensive chart of the vocabulary for "wrath" and all Old Testament references to divine wrath [387 verses], including this two-fold classification, see Baloian 1992:189-210).

Fourth, God's anger is dominant, but it is not the predominant characterization of God. Though other prophets, when speaking of the Day of the Big Audit, had room for salvation, there seems here to be no such option, except that the dismantling of Babylon spelled hope for Israel. However, this oracle must be interpreted in the light of Jeremiah's other oracles, in which there is salvation for the nations (12:14-16), and in the light of Ezekiel's assertion that God does not desire the death of the wicked (Ezek 33:11). God will not "remain angry forever" (Ps 103:9) and his destructive anger is an aspect of his holiness. God's restorative work of redemption expresses his love. The opposite of love is not anger but apathy. Indeed, so intensely does God love that which is just that anger against what is sinful is the predictable reflex of that passion.

God's wrath is purposeful, not to avenge personal insult, but as an expression of his justice in order to bring about justice in the world. God's anger is tied to "legal justification and legal genres" (Baloian 1992:71, 77-98), and is directed against the oppression that humans inflict on each other. As such, God's anger is the flip-side of his love and his desire for the well-being of persons. "He [God] is passionately concerned about the lives of human beings and whether justice takes place among them" (NIDOTTE 4:381). God's anger, whereby injustices are righted, is an illustration of God's caring for persons, and a blessing in that it offers hope for those who have been violated. More generally, it guarantees a dependable ordering of the world in which right will eventually triumph over wrong.

God's anger targets those who refuse him. Baloian (1992:177-78) concludes that God's anger against idolatry is because in idolatry humans deny an essential element of their humanity, namely that they are dependent on their Creator. Such denial readily results in the seductive illusion that they are not derived from God but are independent and autonomous. God's wrath is wholesome in that it has the potential of arresting humans from this harmful illusion. His wrath must be interpreted as working for the good of persons, and so is another aspect of his love, however negative in appearance.

That God's ultimate purpose is love rather than destruction through wrath is illustrated in the fact that the cup of God's wrath (cf. Mark 14:36) has been replaced by the "cup of blessing" (1 Cor 10:16) for those who believe. "There is a massive 'cup of reeling,' commensurate with massive human sin. . . . But there is, however, a second cup (Matt 26:27; Mark 14:23) which is a cup of healing" (Brueggemann 1998:228).

◆  ## D. Deciding about Prophetic Voices (26:1–29:32)
### 1. A controversial sermon (26:1-24)

This message came to Jeremiah from the LORD early in the reign of Jehoiakim son of Josiah,* king of Judah. ²"This is what the LORD says: Stand in the courtyard in front of the Temple of the LORD, and make an announcement to the people who have come there to worship from all over Judah. Give them my entire message; include every word. ³Perhaps they will listen and turn from their evil ways. Then I will change my mind about the disaster I am ready to pour out on them because of their sins.

⁴"Say to them, 'This is what the LORD says: If you will not listen to me and obey my word I have given you, ⁵and if you will not listen to my servants, the prophets—for I sent them again and again to warn you, but you would not listen to them—⁶then I will destroy this Temple as I destroyed Shiloh, the place where the Tabernacle was located. And I will make Jerusalem an object of cursing in every nation on earth.'"

⁷The priests, the prophets, and all the people listened to Jeremiah as he spoke in front of the LORD's Temple. ⁸But when Jeremiah had finished his message, saying everything the LORD had told him to say, the priests and prophets and all the people at the Temple mobbed him. "Kill him!" they shouted. ⁹"What right do you have to prophesy in the LORD's name that this Temple will be destroyed like Shiloh? What do you mean, saying that Jerusalem will be destroyed and left with no inhabitants?" And all the people threatened him as he stood in front of the Temple.

¹⁰When the officials of Judah heard what was happening, they rushed over from the palace and sat down at the New Gate of the Temple to hold court. ¹¹The priests and prophets presented their accusations to the officials and the people. "This man should die!" they said. "You have heard with your own ears what a traitor he is, for he has prophesied against this city."

¹²Then Jeremiah spoke to the officials and the people in his own defense. "The LORD sent me to prophesy against this Temple and this city," he said. "The LORD gave me every word that I have spoken. ¹³But if you stop your sinning and begin to obey the LORD your God, he will change his mind about this disaster that he has announced against you. ¹⁴As for me, I am in your hands—do with me as you think best. ¹⁵But if you kill me, rest assured that you will be killing an innocent man! The responsibility for such a deed will lie on you, on this city, and on every person living in it. For it is absolutely true that the LORD sent me to speak every word you have heard."

¹⁶Then the officials and the people said to the priests and prophets, "This man does not deserve the death sentence, for he has spoken to us in the name of the LORD our God."

¹⁷Then some of the wise old men stood and spoke to all the people assembled there. ¹⁸They said, "Remember when Micah of Moresheth prophesied during the reign of King Hezekiah of Judah. He told the people of Judah,

'This is what the LORD of Heaven's
    Armies says:
Mount Zion will be plowed like an
    open field;
Jerusalem will be reduced to ruins!
A thicket will grow on the heights
    where the Temple now stands.'*

¹⁹But did King Hezekiah and the people kill him for saying this? No, they turned from their sins and worshiped the LORD. They begged him for mercy. Then the LORD changed his mind about the terrible disaster he had pronounced against them. So we are about to do ourselves great harm."

²⁰At this time Uriah son of Shemaiah from Kiriath-jearim was also prophesying for the LORD. And he predicted the same terrible disaster against the city and nation as Jeremiah did. ²¹When King Jehoiakim and the army officers and officials heard what he was saying, the king sent someone to kill him. But Uriah heard about the plan and escaped in fear to Egypt. ²²Then King Jehoiakim sent Elnathan son of Acbor to Egypt along with several other men to capture Uriah. ²³They took him prisoner and brought him back to King Jehoiakim. The king then killed Uriah with a sword and had him buried in an unmarked grave.

²⁴Nevertheless, Ahikam son of Shaphan stood up for Jeremiah and persuaded the court not to turn him over to the mob to be killed.

26:1 The first year of Jehoiakim's reign was 608 BC.   26:18 Mic 3:12.

NOTES

**26:2 Stand . . . in front of the Temple.** This instruction, along with the chapter's content, strongly suggests that this is another version of Jeremiah's Temple sermon (7:1-15 and commentary).

**26:3 Then I will change my mind.** See note on 18:8.

**26:5 I sent them again and again.** See note on 25:4. The prophet Uriah was one of the many prophets God sent (26:20-23).

**26:6 as I destroyed Shiloh.** See 7:12, notes.

**26:10 the New Gate.** The location of this gate is not certain. Jotham built an Upper Gate (2 Kgs 15:35; cf. Jer 36:10). Commerce and judicial matters were transacted in gate areas (Ruth 4:1-12; 2 Sam 15:2).

**26:13 if you stop your sinning.** The Heb. is cast positively in the imperative, lit., "make good your words and your deeds" (cf. the Heb. text of 7:3 for the identical expression). This counsel is in accord with the principle enunciated in 18:8 (cf. 26:3).

**26:14 I am in your hands.** Jeremiah's submissive behavior compares to that of the suffering servant with whom Jeremiah has sometimes been identified (Isa 53:7).

**26:17 Micah of Moresheth prophesied.** Moresheth was a village thirty-five miles southwest of Jerusalem in the vicinity of Gath. Micah's prophesy went unfulfilled at the time because Hezekiah (715–687 BC) repented (2 Kgs 18:3-8).

**26:19 they turned from their sins and worshiped the LORD.** In this way, the NLT explains the more cryptic Heb., usually rendered, "he [they] feared (*yare'* [TH3372, ZH3707]) Yahweh."

**changed his mind.** See 26:3, 18:8.

**26:20 Uriah son of Shemaiah.** His story, told here but not in the historical books, highlights the courage of Jeremiah and documents Jehoiakim's hardness of heart, especially in contrast to Hezekiah, who repented when the same message was given (2 Kgs 18:3ff).

**26:22 Jehoiakim sent Elnathan.** King Jehoiakim (609–597 BC) was self-serving (22:13-19) and altogether irreverent (36:20-26). Elnathan seems to have been sympathetic to Jeremiah's concerns (36:12, 15).

**26:23 had him buried in an unmarked grave.** Lit., "he sent his corpse to the common people's grave." Jehoiakim, the perpetrator of this undignified burial, would himself suffer even greater indignities. He was not buried at all but was disposed of on the refuse heap (22:19; 36:30).

**26:24 Ahikam son of Shaphan.** Shaphan, a royal scribe, was sympathetic to Josiah's reforms (2 Kgs 22:3-14; other of his sons appear in a favorable light; Elasah, 29:3; Gemariah, 36:12, 25) as does his grandson Gedaliah (39:14; 40:5-41:3). For a detailed examination of Jeremiah and the several generations of the Shaphan family, see Seidel (1997).

COMMENTARY

This chapter begins a section detailing the opposition that Jeremiah endured, mostly from the religious establishment in Jerusalem and from religious leaders already in exile in Babylon (chs 26–29). Behind the narratives about the prophet are the larger issues of interpreting history and of deciding between true and false prophets. This chapter tells of three prophets with the same message and of the varying responses to it. The commentary is here confined to the prophetic vocation.

Preaching can be dangerous. Jeremiah's message was confrontational and even threatening. It certainly was judgmental, directed as it was to a religiously active crowd (26:2). Jeremiah predicted destruction for Solomon's Temple, in which the people took great pride. For a preacher to call a distinctive belief into question or to subvert a value held dear by the audience is to court hostility. The audience, incited by religious officials who would face job loss and much more if Jeremiah's words were to come true, attempted to silence this subversive messenger.

Faithfulness in proclaiming the truth of God's message may be costly to the point of death. John the Baptist paid for his message with his life (Matt 14:1-12). Jesus, like Jeremiah, was accused of undermining the status of the Temple (Matt 26:57-68). Stephen, an early martyr, angered his audience when, in retelling Israel's story, he took an alternative view of the Temple (Acts 7:47-50). Martyrs for the Christian faith have been numerous from the first centuries of the Christian era to the present. The "enemies" may be religionists from within the broadly Christian institution as at the time of the Reformation, or opposition may come from entrenched religious interests such as Hinduism or Islam. Messengers who are outspoken against evil especially become the targets of evil schemes (as with Martin Luther King, Jr.).

Still, deliverance comes to some, and that through the strangest means. In this instance, credit for sparing Jeremiah (on whom the religious leaders and the mob had pronounced a death sentence) goes to three different kinds of people. First, palace officials intervened, adjudicating the validity of the accusations (26:10, 16). Good government that is committed to justice should deal objectively with inflamatory situations. Second, a certain individual in a highly placed position championed the helpless Jeremiah (26:24; cf. Ebed-melech, a court official, and his crucial role in sparing the prophet, 38:7-13). Political leaders can use their influence for good. Third, a group of elders invoked history to calm a crowd and helped them to reconsider their course of action (26:17). Jeremiah was helpless and clearly at the mercy of his assailants, but by divine providence, other people were agents of his deliverance.

Deliverance does not come to all—Uriah was martyred for his faithfulness. All three prophets mentioned in this chapter—Jeremiah, Micah, and Uriah—proclaimed a similar message that identified evil and announced God's coming judgment on evildoers. Micah's message was heard and acted upon, so sometimes a ministry is fulfilled. Jeremiah and Uriah were disregarded. Jeremiah was nearly lynched. Uriah escaped, but was extradited from Egypt and killed (26:20-23).

Jeremiah and Uriah, with one spared and the other killed, have their counterparts among the New Testament preachers, Peter and James. Peter, a pillar of the church, miraculously escaped with his life during the persecution, but James, his preaching colleague, was killed (Acts 12:1-12). The ways of Providence are not readily deciphered. God chooses to extend the lives of some while allowing the lives of others to be cut short. One can hardly invoke a standard of merit, as though James were less deserving or valuable than Peter; both were mainstays of the early church. Both Jeremiah and Uriah were faithful in delivering the message.

Uriah's attempted escape cannot be charged against him (cf. Elijah who also fled,

1 Kgs 19:3). Under surveillance and with orders given for his arrest, Jeremiah also went into hiding (36:19, about which it is said, "But the LORD had hidden them," 36:26). Faithfulness, Christians believe, will ultimately be rewarded.

The vocation of Christian ministry is not without conundrums. Rationally considered, it is odd that persons who would be helped by a preacher's message should not only disregard the message but be intent on stifling it. The messenger risks his life for the well-being of his audience, but the audience does not see the hope; instead, it seizes on the accusation and with anger and defiance turns on the messenger. The message was ominous—city and Temple would be destroyed. But hope was there too, and God would relent if the people would repent. Through selective listening, however, the people heard only a part of the message without grasping that repentance opened into God's salvation. The people's choices were self-destructive. This strange behavior validates Jeremiah's diagnosis: "The human heart is most deceitful and desperately wicked" (17:9).

◆     ## 2. Persuading public officials and people (27:1-22)

This message came to Jeremiah from the LORD early in the reign of Zedekiah* son of Josiah, king of Judah.

²This is what the LORD said to me: "Make a yoke, and fasten it on your neck with leather thongs. ³Then send messages to the kings of Edom, Moab, Ammon, Tyre, and Sidon through their ambassadors who have come to see King Zedekiah in Jerusalem. ⁴Give them this message for their masters: 'This is what the LORD of Heaven's Armies, the God of Israel, says: ⁵With my great strength and powerful arm I made the earth and all its people and every animal. I can give these things of mine to anyone I choose. ⁶Now I will give your countries to King Nebuchadnezzar of Babylon, who is my servant. I have put everything, even the wild animals, under his control. ⁷All the nations will serve him, his son, and his grandson until his time is up. Then many nations and great kings will conquer and rule over Babylon. ⁸So you must submit to Babylon's king and serve him; put your neck under Babylon's yoke! I will punish any nation that refuses to be his slave, says the LORD. I will send war, famine, and disease upon that nation until Babylon has conquered it.

⁹" 'Do not listen to your false prophets, fortune-tellers, interpreters of dreams, mediums, and sorcerers who say, "The king of Babylon will not conquer you." ¹⁰They are all liars, and their lies will lead to your being driven out of your land. I will drive you out and send you far away to die. ¹¹But the people of any nation that submits to the king of Babylon will be allowed to stay in their own country to farm the land as usual. I, the LORD, have spoken!' "

¹²Then I repeated this same message to King Zedekiah of Judah. "If you want to live, submit to the yoke of the king of Babylon and his people. ¹³Why do you insist on dying—you and your people? Why should you choose war, famine, and disease, which the LORD will bring against every nation that refuses to submit to Babylon's king? ¹⁴Do not listen to the false prophets who keep telling you, 'The king of Babylon will not conquer you.' They are liars. ¹⁵This is what the LORD says: 'I have not sent these prophets! They are telling you lies in my name, so I will drive you from this land. You will all die—you and all these prophets, too.' "

¹⁶Then I spoke to the priests and the people and said, "This is what the LORD

says: 'Do not listen to your prophets who claim that soon the gold articles taken from my Temple will be returned from Babylon. It is all a lie! ¹⁷Do not listen to them. Surrender to the king of Babylon, and you will live. Why should this whole city be destroyed? ¹⁸If they really are prophets and speak the LORD's messages, let them pray to the LORD of Heaven's Armies. Let them pray that the articles remaining in the LORD's Temple and in the king's palace and in the palaces of Jerusalem will not be carried away to Babylon!'

¹⁹"For the LORD of Heaven's Armies has spoken about the pillars in front of the Temple, the great bronze basin called the Sea, the water carts, and all the other ceremonial articles. ²⁰King Nebuchadnezzar of Babylon left them here when he exiled Jehoiachin* son of Jehoiakim, king of Judah, to Babylon, along with all the other nobles of Judah and Jerusalem. ²¹Yes, this is what the LORD of Heaven's Armies, the God of Israel, says about the precious things still in the Temple and in the palace of Judah's king: ²²'They will all be carried away to Babylon and will stay there until I send for them,' says the LORD. 'Then I will bring them back to Jerusalem again.'"

27:1 As in some Hebrew manuscripts and Syriac version (see also 27:3, 12); most Hebrew manuscripts read *Jehoiakim.* 27:20 Hebrew *Jeconiah,* a variant spelling of Jehoiachin.

NOTES

27:1 *Zedekiah.* This is the reading of some Heb. MSS and the Syriac; other Heb. MSS read "Jehoiakim" (see NLT mg). Scholarly consensus opts for "Zedekiah" (cf. 27:3, 12, 20; 28:1). Cf. the excursus in Friebel (1999:136-139).

27:2 *Make a yoke.* See the detailed instructions in other sign-acts (e.g., the purchase of the loin cloth and the pot, 13:1; 19:1). The yoke was a crossbar placed over the neck of an animal with thongs (or vertical pieces of iron or wood) holding in place a second crossbar under the neck that made a collar. For discussion of this sign-act see Friebel (1999:136-154).

27:3 *send messages to the kings.* It is generally held that a summit meeting of foreign envoys was held in Jerusalem in 594 BC, perhaps at Egypt's instigation, to deal with (plot a rebellion against?) Babylon. Since 27:2 has the plural form *mototh* [TH4133, ZH4574] (yoke bars), and the MT is lit., "send them," Friebel (1999:142-143) urges that the indefinite pronoun "them" be understood as "yokes" (contrast the NLT, "messages") and that Jeremiah sent a yoke home with each of the visiting diplomatic messengers. Jeremiah engaged in a political demonstration (cf. Matt 21:1-17). For the claim that Jesus likewise engaged the political powers, see Yoder (1972).

27:4 *the LORD of Heaven's Armies.* The "hosts" (*tseba'oth* [TH6638, ZH7377], "armies") over which God is commander-in-chief include Israel's armies (1 Sam 17:45), heavenly beings (1 Kgs 22:19), and cosmic entities such as planets and stars (see the Heb. of Gen 2:1; Ps 33:6).

27:6 *King Nebuchadnezzar of Babylon, who is my servant.* See note on 25:9 (cf. 43:10).

27:7 *his son, and his grandson.* This expression may refer to two generations. Historically, Evil-Merodach, Nebuchadnezzar's son, ruled Babylon for two years. He was followed, not by his son, but by Neriglissar, Nebuchadnezzar's son-in-law. After a nine-month reign by Neriglissar's son, Labasi-Marduk, Nabonidus became the ruler. His son Belshazzar was king when Cyrus the Persian took Babylon in 539 BC.

27:8 *So you must submit to Babylon's king.* The imperative is not explicit, but it is implied by the description of consequences for unsubmissive nations.

27:9 *Do not listen to your false prophets.* The word "false" is interpretive, though it can be justified from 27:10. The law forbade giving a hearing to mediums, sorcerers, and the like (Deut 18:9-13; Exod 22:18; cf. the practice of Nebuchadnezzar, Ezek 21:21).

**27:14 They are liars.** Forms of the word "deceive" (*shaqar* [TH8266, ZH9213], "lie," "be false," "pretend") occur in this chapter (27:10, 14, 15, 16) and elsewhere, predominantly in connection with prophets and their message (23:14, 32; 28:15; 29:9, 21, 23, 31).

**27:16 soon the gold articles . . . will be returned from Babylon.** One issue between true and false prophets had to do with the timing of the return. Jeremiah spoke of a long exile of seventy years (25:12); Hananiah predicted two years (28:3).

**27:18 let them pray.** The irony of this advice is in the literal phrase "let them come near to Yahweh," who did not send them, and in the epithet, "LORD of Heaven's Armies" whose majestic decree would be contrary to their request (27:19). For a prophet who intercedes, cf. Amos 7:1-6.

**27:19 great bronze basin called the Sea.** For the free-standing, twenty-seven foot bronze pillars, Jakin and Boaz, see 1 Kgs 7:15-22; for the bronze basin in the courtyard, see 1 Kgs 7:23-26; for the ornate water carts, possibly used for the washing of sacrificial animals, see 1 Kgs 7:27-39. At the first siege, the Babylonians took much treasure from the Temple, but apparently not everything (2 Kgs 24:8-17). The "Sea" was traditionally associated with chaos. Contained in a "basin," chaos was under control. However, destruction of these temple items would signify a return to chaos.

## COMMENTARY

The three chapters of Jeremiah 27–29 share the theme of authentic and inauthentic prophets (Jer 23:9-40). Jeremiah warned against unauthorized prophets (Jer 27), then confronted one, Hananiah (Jer 28); in correspondence with the exiles, he exposed several others (Jer 29). Jeremiah's message, gainsaid by others, was that the Babylonian advance would result in an extended exile and that the best political strategy was for Judah (and other nations) to submit to Babylon, God's agent of punishment.

Jeremiah's preaching about sin, repentance, and judgment took a turn, and the prophet engaged in a public policy debate. The setting for this debate was the aftermath of Babylon's sweep into the region to capture the elite of the city, including King Jehoiachin, and to remove them and some Temple utensils to Babylon (598–597 BC). Suddenly, faced with the common threat of quarrelsome neighboring nations, they were ready to collaborate. Foreign envoys met in Jerusalem to discern the best public policy. Jeremiah, not unlike modern protesters, entered the debate with a proposal (demand) for voluntary submission to Nebuchadnezzar. His message was reinforced by the awkward ox yoke he carried on his shoulders. Advocating surrender to the enemy was tantamount to treason (cf. 37:13).

Jeremiah was forthright, even aggressive, and he certainly took a public position. This man wearing an ox yoke was not easily dismissed. Moreover, at God's command he made certain that the message about submission was conveyed by envoys to the kings of nations bordering Israel to the east (Edom, Moab, and Ammon) and to neighbors to the northwest beyond the Babylonian-controlled corridor (Tyre and Sidon). Passing the cup of wrath to the nations was probably a symbolic or visionary gesture (25:15); this message-sending was probably implemented.

Public officials in neighboring countries were faced with the claim of an Israelite prophet who spoke in the name of God (27:5), who was universal in his jurisdiction but belonged especially to Israel (27:4). This God, identified as creator of all and as sovereign in implementing his decisions, was not partisan to Israel, but to Babylon! God was on Nebuchadnezzar's side! For people touting the powers of their national deities, this message about God's aligning himself with the huge Babylonian Empire against smaller nations must have seemed radical if not absurd. Judah's king, to whom the identical message about surrender was given, could not be blamed if he questioned Jeremiah's theology.

Jeremiah's minority position meant that he had to take on challengers who predicted that Nebuchadnezzar would not conquer the area (27:9). His persuasive tactics, apart from wearing the ox yoke and insisting that his message was from Yahweh (27:4 11, 15, 16, 19), included warnings for kings at home and elsewhere lest they listen to other voices (27:9, 16). Jeremiah not only branded the other voices as liars, but stated that the effect of following them would be exile and death (27:10, 14). He articulated the alternatives: they could stay and die, or they could submit and live (27:13). The stakes were high.

Other prophets, such as Nathan and Elijah, had confronted kings with rebuke (2 Sam 12:1-14; 1 Kgs 21:17-19). Moses pled in Pharaoh's court for permission for his people to leave (Exod 5:1). In rare instances a prophet also took the prerogative to address the state on matters of diplomacy, as Isaiah did with Ahaz (Isa 7:3-9). "Prophetic faith does not live in a religious vacuum, but must take sides on the public issues of the day" (Brueggemann 1998:43).

Can the same be said for the church? Is there a precedent here that offers believers a warrant for protesting problematic governmental decisions and/or practices (e.g., governments siding with dictators, declarations of war, legislation supporting race prejudice, abortion)? The argument for Christians not to be politically involved on the grounds that Israel was a theocracy and that modern states are not may carry some weight, but the conclusion that Christian leaders are thereby absolved from addressing the state is invalid. Jeremiah addressed his country and foreign governments as well. At the least, Jeremiah's action stirs the debate about the nature of Christian leaders' responsibility to government.

◆     ## 3. Conflicting prophetic voices (28:1-17)

One day in late summer* of that same year—the fourth year of the reign of Zedekiah, king of Judah—Hananiah son of Azzur, a prophet from Gibeon, addressed me publicly in the Temple while all the priests and people listened. He said, ²"This is what the LORD of Heaven's Armies, the God of Israel, says: 'I will remove the yoke of the king of Babylon from your necks. ³Within two years I will bring back all the Temple treasures that King Nebuchad-nezzar carried off to Babylon. ⁴And I will bring back Jehoiachin* son of Jehoiakim, king of Judah, and all the other captives that were taken to Babylon. I will surely break the yoke that the king of Babylon has put on your necks. I, the LORD, have spoken!'"

⁵Jeremiah responded to Hananiah as they stood in front of all the priests and people at the Temple. ⁶He said, "Amen! May your prophecies come true! I hope

the LORD does everything you say. I hope he does bring back from Babylon the treasures of this Temple and all the captives. ⁷But listen now to the solemn words I speak to you in the presence of all these people. ⁸The ancient prophets who preceded you and me spoke against many nations, always warning of war, disaster, and disease. ⁹So a prophet who predicts peace must show he is right. Only when his predictions come true can we know that he is really from the LORD."

¹⁰Then Hananiah the prophet took the yoke off Jeremiah's neck and broke it in pieces. ¹¹And Hananiah said again to the crowd that had gathered, "This is what the LORD says: 'Just as this yoke has been broken, within two years I will break the yoke of oppression from all the nations now subject to King Nebuchadnezzar of Babylon.' " With that, Jeremiah left the Temple area.

¹²Soon after this confrontation with Hananiah, the LORD gave this message to Jeremiah: ¹³"Go and tell Hananiah, 'This is what the LORD says: You have broken a wooden yoke, but you have replaced it with a yoke of iron. ¹⁴The LORD of Heaven's Armies, the God of Israel, says: I have put a yoke of iron on the necks of all these nations, forcing them into slavery under King Nebuchadnezzar of Babylon. I have put everything, even the wild animals, under his control.' "

¹⁵Then Jeremiah the prophet said to Hananiah, "Listen, Hananiah! The LORD has not sent you, but the people believe your lies. ¹⁶Therefore, this is what the LORD says: 'You must die. Your life will end this very year because you have rebelled against the LORD.' "

¹⁷Two months later* the prophet Hananiah died.

28:1 Hebrew *In the fifth month*, of the ancient Hebrew lunar calendar. The fifth month in the fourth year of Zedekiah's reign occurred within the months of August and September 593 BC. Also see note on 1:3.
28:4 Hebrew *Jeconiah*, a variant spelling of Jehoiachin. 28:17 Hebrew *In the seventh month of that same year.* See 28:1 and the note there.

## NOTES

**28:1** *Hananiah son of Azzur, a prophet from Gibeon.* Nothing more is known about Hananiah (whose name means "Yahweh is gracious") than is told here about his parentage, home town, vocation, message, and death. He is called "the prophet" (*hannabi'* [TH5030, ZH5566]) each time his name is mentioned in the Heb. text except at 28:11, 13, 15.

*Gibeon.* This city was six miles northwest of Jerusalem. It was one of the priests' cities (Josh 21:17); it was also where the sun stood still (Josh 9:1-26).

**28:3** *Within two years I will bring back all the Temple treasures.* These had been taken by Nebuchadnezzar in the siege of 598-597 BC (2 Kgs 24:10-17). Jeremiah had prophesied their eventual return (27:22), for Babylon's rule would extend to seventy years (25:12-14). The controversy was about timing. Concerning the return of the vessels, see Ezra 1:7-11.

**28:6** *Amen! May your prophecies come true!* This conciliatory response (though some read it as sarcastic), representing Jeremiah's own feelings, contrasts sharply with his later oracle given in the Lord's name (28:15; cf. his "Amen" in 11:5). See the discussion in Overholt (1970:37-45).

**28:8** *warning of war, disaster, and disease.* There are other examples of prophets issuing such warnings: Isaiah (3:13-15), Hosea (4:6), and Amos (2:4). In the words of Abraham Heschel (1962:106), a prophet "is a person who knows what time it is."

**28:9** *must show he is right.* The NLT adds this phrase to catch the gist of the reply. The verse lit. ends, "when the prophecy happens it will be known that Yahweh sent him in truth" (cf. Deut 18:20-22). Peter Fry tells of conflicting messages by shamans (intermediaries between people and gods) among the Zezuru people of southern Rhodesia. A certain shaman named Wild Man claimed to be the medium for the spirit Chaminuka. Another shaman, Muchatera, who also claimed to be the spokesperson for Chaminuka, challenged Wild Man to make rain as a test of his legitimacy. Wild Man mounted a rock, waved his arms, and rain clouds appeared. Followers of Wild Man forced Muchatera to leave in disgrace (cited in Long 1981:36-37).

**28:14 *even the wild animals.*** This added touch underscores Yahweh's determined decision to give Nebuchadnezzar full control (cf. 27:6).

**28:16 *You must die.*** The Heb. employs a wordplay between the accusation, "The Lord has not sent (*shalakh* [TH7971, ZH8938], qal stem) you" (28:15), and the prediction of disaster, "I am going to send (*shalakh*, piel stem) you off the face of the earth" (28:16, NRSV).

COMMENTARY

The issue of unauthorized prophets, introduced in chapter 27 (cf. 23:9-40), now becomes concrete with the name of one pseudoprophet and a specific issue, the future of the exiled king, Jehoiachin, and the confiscated Temple items. The mention of the ox yoke links chapters 27 and 28. Jeremiah spoke of an extended exile while Hananiah, his professional colleague, predicted a temporary hiatus. It was one man's word against another's. Who was to be believed and why?

Both Jeremiah and Hananiah were regarded as prophets. Each prophet spoke in the name of the LORD of Heaven's Armies (28:2, 14), and both engaged in symbolic action. Jeremiah wore the ox yoke and brought the message that God had given Nebuchadnezzar wide latitude in bringing other nations to serve him (27:6; 28:14). Hananiah broke the wooden ox yoke as a sign-act that God would break the Babylonian Empire in pieces. The crucial point of dissimilarity was in the message—Jeremiah spoke a dark word, Hananiah a hopeful word. The obligation to decide rested upon the audience. By what criteria was that (or any) audience to decide between the authentic word from God and the bogus message? Counsel is available.

First, true prophets do not speak a word of peace to ungodly and immoral situations. A true prophet who discerns evil also knows that it is in the very nature of evil to spawn evil consequences. A message about dire consequences could be derived by perceptive human diagnosis quite apart from divine revelation.

Second, prophetic precedent dictates that the word for an evildoing people is judgment, not salvation. An optimistic message for a God-deserting people runs against the grain of past paradigms. However, even tradition requires interpretation. Hananiah could have invoked precedent for his position and perhaps did, as God had averted an Assyrian conquest in the time of Hezekiah (Isa 37:33-36). Moreover, Hananiah's understanding of God's faithfulness to his people probably tilted him toward a soft message. Jeremiah had heard from God (23:18). At issue was faithfulness to a God of righteousness and his sovereign decisions about the course of Judah's history, given her spiritual waywardness.

A third test of prophetic authenticity is whether or not the prophecy is actualized (Deut 18:21-22), although even the fulfillment of a prophecy is not absolute proof (Deut 13:1-3). On the grounds of fulfillment, people had reason to prefer Jeremiah over Hananiah because what Jeremiah had announced about the coming foe from the north had already happened, quite apart from his prediction that Hananiah would die within a year.

A fourth test of true prophecy examines the moral character of the prophet. The actions of bogus prophets belie their claims. Jeremiah pointed to immorality and adultery as a telltale sign of false prophets (23:14; 29:21-23). A minister's lifestyle is one gauge, among others, of authenticity.

Fifth, the report of a divine call from God to be a prophet is reason, when added to others, to give credence to a prophet's message (Isa 6:1-8; Jer 1:4-10; Ezek 2:1-10; Amos 7:14-15).

In short, false prophets, at least in this instance, were characterized by their reassuring words (cf. Zedekiah and the 400 court prophets, 1 Kgs 22:11-12), speaking what people desired to hear. Their message was predictable. By contrast, God's true prophets did not pander to itching ears but were confrontational. Their lives were exemplary, and their predictions came true.

Jesus warned of smooth-tongued but illegitimate prophets (Matt 7:15-16). Paul frequently sounded the note of warning: be discerning about false teachers and prophets (Gal 3:1; Col 2:8; 1 Tim 6:3-5; 2 Tim 3:13). John spoke of anti-Christs (1 John 4:1-3). In third-world churches, perhaps more than in America, church leaders alert their congregations to questionable teachers and false cults. The church needs guidelines for distinguishing between orthodox beliefs and cults, between the true gospel and its deviations.

◆     ## 4. Counseling exiles (29:1-32)

Jeremiah wrote a letter from Jerusalem to the elders, priests, prophets, and all the people who had been exiled to Babylon by King Nebuchadnezzar. ²This was after King Jehoiachin,* the queen mother, the court officials, the other officials of Judah, and all the craftsmen and artisans had been deported from Jerusalem. ³He sent the letter with Elasah son of Shaphan and Gemariah son of Hilkiah when they went to Babylon as King Zedekiah's ambassadors to Nebuchadnezzar. This is what Jeremiah's letter said:

⁴This is what the LORD of Heaven's Armies, the God of Israel, says to all the captives he has exiled to Babylon from Jerusalem: ⁵"Build homes, and plan to stay. Plant gardens, and eat the food they produce. ⁶Marry and have children. Then find spouses for them so that you may have many grandchildren. Multiply! Do not dwindle away! ⁷And work for the peace and prosperity of the city where I sent you into exile. Pray to the LORD for it, for its welfare will determine your welfare."

⁸This is what the LORD of Heaven's Armies, the God of Israel, says: "Do not let your prophets and fortune-tellers who are with you in the land of Babylon trick you. Do not listen to their dreams, ⁹because they are telling you lies in my name. I have not sent them," says the LORD.

¹⁰This is what the LORD says: "You will be in Babylon for seventy years. But then I will come and do for you all the good things I have promised, and I will bring you home again. ¹¹For I

know the plans I have for you," says the LORD. "They are plans for good and not for disaster, to give you a future and a hope. ¹²In those days when you pray, I will listen. ¹³If you look for me wholeheartedly, you will find me. ¹⁴I will be found by you," says the LORD. "I will end your captivity and restore your fortunes. I will gather you out of the nations where I sent you and will bring you home again to your own land."

¹⁵You claim that the LORD has raised up prophets for you in Babylon. ¹⁶But this is what the LORD says about the king who sits on David's throne and all those still living here in Jerusalem—your relatives who were not exiled to Babylon. ¹⁷This is what the LORD of Heaven's Armies says: "I will send war, famine, and disease upon them and make them like bad figs, too rotten to eat. ¹⁸Yes, I will pursue them with war, famine, and disease, and I will scatter them around the world. In every nation where I send them, I will make them an object of damnation, horror, contempt, and mockery. ¹⁹For they refuse to listen to me, though I have spoken to them repeatedly through the prophets I sent. And you who are in exile have not listened either," says the LORD.

²⁰Therefore, listen to this message from the LORD, all you captives there in Babylon. ²¹This is what the LORD of Heaven's Armies, the God of Israel, says about your prophets—Ahab son of Kolaiah and Zedekiah son of Maaseiah—who are telling you lies in my name: "I will turn them over to Nebuchadnezzar* for execution before your eyes. ²²Their terrible fate will become proverbial, so that the Judean exiles will curse someone by saying, 'May the LORD make you like Zedekiah

and Ahab, whom the king of Babylon burned alive!' ²³For these men have done terrible things among my people. They have committed adultery with their neighbors' wives and have lied in my name, saying things I did not command. I am a witness to this. I, the LORD, have spoken."

²⁴The LORD sent this message to Shemaiah the Nehelamite in Babylon: ²⁵"This is what the LORD of Heaven's Armies, the God of Israel, says: You wrote a letter on your own authority to Zephaniah son of Maaseiah, the priest, and you sent copies to the other priests and people in Jerusalem. You wrote to Zephaniah,

²⁶"The LORD has appointed you to replace Jehoiada as the priest in charge of the house of the LORD. You are responsible to put into stocks and neck irons any crazy man who claims to be a prophet. ²⁷So why have you done nothing to stop Jeremiah from Anathoth, who pretends to be a prophet among you? ²⁸Jeremiah sent a letter here to Babylon, predicting that our captivity will be a long one. He said, 'Build homes, and plan to stay. Plant gardens, and eat the food they produce.'"

²⁹But when Zephaniah the priest received Shemaiah's letter, he took it to Jeremiah and read it to him. ³⁰Then the LORD gave this message to Jeremiah: ³¹"Send an open letter to all the exiles in Babylon. Tell them, 'This is what the LORD says concerning Shemaiah the Nehelamite: Since he has prophesied to you when I did not send him and has tricked you into believing his lies, ³²I will punish him and his family. None of his descendants will see the good things I will do for my people, for he has incited you to rebel against me. I, the LORD, have spoken!'"

**29:2** Hebrew *Jeconiah,* a variant spelling of Jehoiachin. **29:21** Hebrew *Nebuchadrezzar,* a variant spelling of Nebuchadnezzar.

## NOTES

**29:1 *Jeremiah wrote a letter.*** For other writings of Jeremiah, see 30:2; 36:2-4; for royal letters, cf. Dan 6:25-27; Esth 1:21-22; for apostolic letters, cf. Romans, 1 Peter, Revelation.

**29:2 *after King Jehoiachin . . . had been deported.*** His three-month reign ended in March, 597 BC. Cf. Jeremiah's oracle about him (22:24-30).

***queen mother.*** This was the wife of King Josiah, who had been killed at Megiddo in 609 BC. The letter, most think, may have been sent in 594 BC, when Nebuchadnezzar faced troubles near home and those exiled were in a mood to stage a rebellion.

**29:3 *He sent the letter with Elasah . . . and Gemariah.*** Shaphan's family, apparently in the upper social strata, was one of the few sympathetic to Jeremiah (cf. 36:10-12; 39:14; 40:5 and Seidel 1997). Elasah was a brother to Ahikam (26:24). The royal envoy probably professed Judah's loyalty and/or paid Israel's tribute to the Babylonian overlord.

**29:6 *Marry and have children.*** Jeremiah, who was asked to remain celibate (16:2), counsels marriage and large families, since theirs will be an extended exile, a point disputed by the false prophets.

**29:7 *peace.*** The Heb. *shalom* [TH7965, ZH8934] (peace) speaks of total well-being. The counsel anticipates Jesus' words about loving one's enemies (Matt 5:44; cf. Rom 12:21; 1 Pet 2:21-23). Self-interest, as opposed to selfishness, is a legitimate motivation (cf. Matt 6:20). For self-interest as a tactic for nonviolent social resistance, see D. Smith (1989).

**29:9 *they are telling you lies.*** Some of these lies pertained to a short exile (cf. 28:3; 29:10), a prediction that fueled notions of rebelling against Babylon.

**29:10 *You will be in Babylon for seventy years.*** The Heb. text speaks of seventy years to be filled for Babylon (i.e, of Babylon's supremacy), a period not strictly coextensive with Israel's exile (see note on 25:12).

**29:12 *In those days when you pray.*** The Heb. is verbose: "Then when you call upon me and come and pray to me" (NRSV). The Heb. leaves the time period open; "in those days" is interpretive.

**29:14 *I will end your captivity and restore your fortunes.*** The Heb. phrase, *shub shebuth* [TH7725/7622, ZH8740/8654] (turn/turning) was earlier etymologically rendered as "bring back from captivity" (cf. NIV) as *shebuth* was thought to be derived from *shabah* [TH7617, ZH8647] (take captive). Currently, however, a consensus is emerging that *shebuth* is derived from *shub* and the phrase is to be rendered lit. as "turn the turning," or better, "bring about the restoration (of fortunes)." God is always the subject (cf. Job 42:10; Hos 6:11; the Heb. of Jer 32:44; 49:6; Amos 9:14). This understanding of "turn the turning" broadens the promise beyond the end of captivity to include spiritual restoration (cf. 30:3). The NLT has incorporated both understandings.

**29:16 *the king who sits on David's throne.*** This was Zedekiah, Judah's last king. The LXX omits 29:16-20. The connection between 29:15 and 29:16 rests in the prophets' optimism in Babylon about Jerusalem's permanency and their own short period of exile.

**29:17 *like bad figs.*** For Jerusalem pictured as rotten figs, see the symbolic action of Jer 24:1-3, 8-10; cf. 27:3-15.

**29:18 *I will make them an object of damnation.*** This was in accordance with the covenant curses (Deut 28:37).

**29:21 *Ahab . . . and Zedekiah.*** Nothing more is known of these prophets than is given here. They were regarded as prophets raised up by the Lord despite their duplicity and immorality (29:15, 23). The descriptor *sheqer* [TH8267, ZH9214] (falsehood) is applied to Hananiah (28:15), Ahab and Zedekiah (29:23), and Shemaiah (29:31). For an elaborate discussion of *sheqer*, see Overholt (1970:86-104).

**29:23 these men have done terrible things.** The Heb. *nebalah* [TH5039, ZH5576] speaks "of a sexual crime that breaks the peace of a family or community" (Keown et al. 1995:78; cf. Gen 34:7; Deut 22:21; Judg 19:23-24; 20:6, 10; 2 Sam 13:12).

**29:25 You wrote . . . to Zephaniah.** Zephaniah, next in rank to the high priest, is mentioned in 21:1; 37:3 (cf. 2 Kgs 25:18). The elite, exiled to Babylon, continued to rule from a new power base, despite their demotion. The story that began in 29:24 continues in 29:30; the intervening verses provide the background.

## COMMENTARY

This chapter contains Jeremiah's letter to the exiles, in which he gives general counsel to the exiles and their leaders (note the address, 29:1, 4, 20, 31), with a postscript to one man, Shemaiah (29:24-32). The letter and the postscript (or possibly a second letter) continue the theme of inauthentic prophets, mostly on the concrete question of the length of exile.

Communication by letter has a long history and is not likely to be fully replaced by modern electronics. While letters vary in purpose, Jeremiah's letter, like the New Testament letters (epistles), offers instruction and warning. Shemaiah's letter had a different purpose, to agitate people against Jeremiah and other "crazy men" (29:26) and especially to exert his leadership, although from a distant power base, by ousting the presiding Jerusalem priest and appointing another priest—one presumably more in sympathy with the notions held by the exiles (29:26).

Jeremiah's letter is in two parts, containing counsel for the exiles to settle down in exile (29:4-14) and admonitions against falling for the message of false prophets (29:15-23). What entitled Jeremiah, in Jerusalem, to meddle with the beliefs and way of life of the exiles, 700 miles distant? The obvious answer is that the Lord had instructed him to do so. Jeremiah's responsibility did not end once the ax of punishment had fallen. He not only maintained contact but shared God's message and sought their spiritual and physical welfare. A true leader's heart aches for wayward people and seeks them out even after earlier counsel has been ignored. Perhaps the underlying reason for making contact with the exiles was to head off any notion of staging a rebellion against their captors. Caring leaders cannot rest when others are misled (cf. Paul's letter to the Galatians).

**Counsel.**   Jeremiah's counsel was for families to take root by building homes and having children (29:4-9). People sometimes decide, in the face of what they consider to be an ominous future, not to have children. There are situations, as in the period of persecution in the early church, in which domestic relationships are determined largely by circumstances (1 Cor 7:25-31). Christian discernment is needed to know the pertinent theology and to know the times.

If this longer exile of seventy years of which Jeremiah spoke was interpreted as coming from an overly punitive God, Jeremiah was quick to set the record straight. God would bring good to his people (29:10, 11). This is a verbal overture to the theme for the Book of Comfort that follows (Jer 30–33; cf. especially 33:9). From the account of God's creation, in which God pronounced that what he had made was good (i.e., met his purpose), to the story of Joseph (Gen 50:20), to the deliverance of the oppressed at the Exodus, to the abundance of the land of settlement, the uniform message was that God's plans were for good (cf. Pss 85:12; 103:5; 119:68). A firm hold on this conviction carries people through difficult times of exile and spiritual deserts. The claim that God desires to give his people a future and a hope (29:11) is more basic than words about God's anger. For Israel, that specifically meant eventual release from their status as captives, their return to the land, and the restoration of their fortunes (29:14; cf. 24:6-7; Ezra 1:2-4).

Such extravagant goodness, while not totally dependent on the spiritual condition of a people, is nevertheless not detached from it. This prospect of God's goodness outpoured is linked with a wholehearted search for God (29:13). It is astonishing that God promises to respond to a people's prayer when those very people have rejected him. Those who seek will find (cf. Deut 4:29-31; Isa 55:6-7; Matt 7:7-8). The promise accords with God's plan (Prov 19:21; Isa 46:10).

**Admonitions.** The remainder of the letter takes up the agenda of lying prophets (29:15-32) in three stages: (1) a generalized word about non-commissioned prophets (29:15-19); (2) a diatribe about two specific prophets, Ahab and Zedekiah (29:20-23); and (3) a scathing rebuke to Shemaiah, a leader in some capacity and a propagator of lies (29:24-32).

The generalized word to prophets addresses an unidentified message that Jerusalem was only temporarily in trouble but would soon snap back into prominence. The leadership in exile would not accept the hard news that this was no blip on the screen but a long-term condition of trouble. Psychologists today would describe this approach as denial. Jeremiah, rather than simply decrying their statements, offered a pronouncement about those remaining in Jerusalem. The obvious conclusion, that God's future lay with those in Jerusalem, was the wrong conclusion (cf. Jer 24). The form of this judgment speech is irregular in that the announcement (29:17-18) precedes the accusation (29:19).

Two men, both prophets, are named and singled out as guilty of lying (29:21), adultery (29:23; cf. 23:14), and speaking under false pretenses (29:23b). Here, the stereotypical components of the judgment speech—accusation and announcement—take on an expanded configuration of accusation (29:21a), announcement (29:21b-22), and accusation (29:23). In the instance of Shemaiah, after the background for the oracle was explained (29:23-28), the more usual form of the judgment speech was observed in accusation (e.g., of deception, 29:31b) followed by announcement (29:32).

**Confrontation.** The theme of inauthentic prophets was sounded in 23:9-40 and was negatively illustrated by the contrasting actions of the authentic prophets Jeremiah, Micah, and Uriah (26:12-23). It was described in the confrontation of the two kinds of prophets, Jeremiah and Hananiah (28:1-17), and concretized in the persons of Ahab and Zedekiah. Shemaiah embodied the politics of religious power. Deception, deluding others, and even self-delusion all come into sharp focus here, more or less paralled in the New Testament by the Pharisees and by Ananias and Sapphira (Acts 5; for comments on testing prophetic voices, see commentary on Jer 28).

One should not miss the fundamental difference in theology between the true and the false prophets. Jeremiah, Uriah, and Micah understood God as a free agent who was committed to his covenant. This God was free and sovereign in chastising his people, as signaled by the repeated epithet, "LORD of Heaven's Armies" (29:4, 8, 17, 21), and in the twofold expression, "I the LORD have spoken" (29:23, 32). Ahab, Zedekiah, and Shemaiah understood God as not only committed but virtually shackled to a promise to safeguard Jerusalem. For them, God was predictable, for they understood God's passion as prospering his people regardless of what they did. False prophets misread God.

◆ VI. The Book of Consolation (30:1–33:26)
   A. Recovering What Was Lost and More! (30:1–31:1)

The LORD gave another message to Jeremiah. He said, [2]"This is what the LORD, the God of Israel, says: Write down for the record everything I have said to you, Jeremiah. [3]For the time is coming when I will restore the fortunes of my people of Israel and Judah. I will bring them home to this land that I gave to their ancestors, and they will possess it again. I, the LORD, have spoken!"

[4]This is the message the LORD gave concerning Israel and Judah. [5]This is what the LORD says:

"I hear cries of fear;
   there is terror and no peace.
[6]Now let me ask you a question:
   Do men give birth to babies?
Then why do they stand there, ashen-faced,
   hands pressed against their sides
   like a woman in labor?
[7]In all history there has never been
   such a time of terror.
It will be a time of trouble for my
   people Israel.*
Yet in the end they will be saved!
[8]For in that day,"
   says the LORD of Heaven's Armies,
"I will break the yoke from their necks
   and snap their chains.
Foreigners will no longer be their
   masters.
[9]   For my people will serve the LORD
   their God

and their king descended from David—
   the king I will raise up for them.

[10]"So do not be afraid, Jacob, my
   servant;
   do not be dismayed, Israel,"
says the LORD.
"For I will bring you home again from
   distant lands,
   and your children will return from
   their exile.
Israel will return to a life of peace and
   quiet,
   and no one will terrorize them.
[11]For I am with you and will save you,"
   says the LORD.
"I will completely destroy the nations
   where I have scattered you,
but I will not completely destroy you.
I will discipline you, but with justice;
   I cannot let you go unpunished."

[12]This is what the LORD says:
"Your injury is incurable—
   a terrible wound.
[13]There is no one to help you
   or to bind up your injury.
No medicine can heal you.
[14]All your lovers—your allies—have left
   you
   and do not care about you anymore.
I have wounded you cruelly,
   as though I were your enemy.
For your sins are many,
   and your guilt is great.

15 Why do you protest your punishment—
  this wound that has no cure?
I have had to punish you
  because your sins are many
  and your guilt is great.

16 "But all who devour you will be
    devoured,
  and all your enemies will be sent
    into exile.
All who plunder you will be plundered,
  and all who attack you will be
    attacked.
17 I will give you back your health
  and heal your wounds," says the
    LORD.
"For you are called an outcast—
  'Jerusalem* for whom no one
  cares.'"

18 This is what the LORD says:
"When I bring Israel home again from
    captivity
  and restore their fortunes,
Jerusalem will be rebuilt on its ruins,
  and the palace reconstructed as
    before.
19 There will be joy and songs of
    thanksgiving,
  and I will multiply my people, not
    diminish them;
I will honor them, not despise them.

20 Their children will prosper as they
    did long ago.
I will establish them as a nation before
    me,
  and I will punish anyone who hurts
    them.
21 They will have their own ruler again,
  and he will come from their own
    people.
I will invite him to approach me," says
    the LORD,
  "for who would dare to come unless
    invited?
22 You will be my people,
  and I will be your God."

23 Look! The LORD's anger bursts out like
    a storm,
  a driving wind that swirls down on
    the heads of the wicked.
24 The fierce anger of the LORD will not
    diminish
  until it has finished all he has
    planned.
In the days to come
  you will understand all this.

## CHAPTER 31

"In that day," says the LORD, "I will be the
God of all the families of Israel, and they
will be my people.

30:7 Hebrew *Jacob;* also in 30:10b, 18. See note on 5:20.   30:17 Hebrew *Zion.*

NOTES

30:2 *Write down for the record.* The resulting "book" extends through ch 31, but the label "Book of Comfort" includes Jer 30–33. Isaiah was asked to write (8:1), as was Habakkuk (Hab 2:2; cf. Jer 29:1; 36:4).

30:3 *I will restore the fortunes of my people.* See commentary notes for meaning at 29:14. Here, this general promise about a restoration (spiritual and socio-political for Israel and Judah) is followed by the specific statement, *I will bring them home.* The two themes of restoration/rehabilitation and return (to the land) are laced throughout the Book of Comfort.

30:5 *I hear cries of fear.* The MT and LXX read "We" instead of "I." The Lord is quoting the people, a point not gainsaid by 30:6, where Heb. has a plural imperative, "Ask now," instead of first person. See also Keown et al. 1995:90-91.

30:7 *It will be a time of trouble.* The verb can equally well be translated in the present tense. It has been interpreted as referring to the fall of Jerusalem (586 BC), the overthrow of Babylon (539 BC), an end-time period, the Great Tribulation, or as a paradigm for times of great stress.

**30:8 *I will break the yoke.*** The yoke is Babylon's rule. Cf. the sign-act of Jer 27:2-11.

**30:9 *their king descended from David.*** Huey (1993:261-68), leaning on G. van Groningen, cites other messianic passages: 3:14-17; 23:1-8; 31:31-40; and 33:14-26.

**30:10 *So do not be afraid.*** The "word of consolation" characterizes the "assurance" type of salvation oracle (cf. Isa 43:1, 5 and the duplicate Jer 46:27-28). Other components of this genre are a word of address (here "Jacob my servant"), and motivations for the assurance, such as announcements (cf. 30:10b-c) and promise of the divine presence (30:11a).

**30:11 *For I am with you.*** This divine assistance formula occurs often (Gen 28:15, Exod 3:12; Josh 1:9, Jer 1:19; Matt 28:19-20).

***I cannot let you go unpunished.*** Lit., "I will not hold you innocent."

**30:12 *Your injury is incurable.*** The metaphor of illness (and medicine) for Israel's problems is found already in Hosea (Hos 6:1; 7:1; cf. Mic 1:9; Nah 3:19; Jer 8:11, 15, 21-22).

**30:13 *There is no one to help you.*** The use of *din* [TH1777, ZH1906] (govern, administer justice, restore order) does not interrupt the metaphor of healing, but extends the sense of injury to include more than the physical.

**30:16 *But all who devour you.*** The word "but," rendered for *laken* [TH3651C, ZH4338] (therefore), usually introduces the punishment section of a judgment speech. Its sequel here is surprising, though Brueggemann (1992b:300) lists eight similar instances in which hope is introduced by *laken* and follows a denunciation (Isa 30:18; Jer 15:19; 16:14; Ezek 36:2-7, 13-15; 37:11-12; Hos 2:16; Mic 5:2).

**30:17 *I will . . . heal your wounds.*** For Yahweh as healer, see Ps 103:3 (cf. Brown 1995:191-95).

***Jerusalem for whom no one cares.*** It has been suggested (in a doctoral seminar by Prof. W. H. Brownlee) that for *tsiyon* [TH6726, ZH7482] ("Zion," here "Jerusalem") one might read *tso'n* [TH6629, ZH7366] (flock), a change from the metaphor of health to one of sheep. The suggestion arises based on the LXX translation that appears to come from the Heb. word *tsayid* ("prey") instead of *tsiyon*, which seems to suggest that there was some irregularity in the text. In Heb. orthography a confusion between the two consonants in question is not unlikely. Moreover, a new subunit seems to begin with 30:17b. The resultant reading is attractive: "Indeed, 'driven off,' they designate you, 'She is a flock none seeks.'" The nations' taunts now galvanize Yahweh to act (cf. Ezek 36:22-32).

**30:18 *When I . . . restore their fortunes.*** The NLT catches the gist of the promise (cf. 30:3). The Heb. includes showing compassion (*rakham* [TH7355, ZH8163]) to dwellings, a point amplified in 30:18b (cf. 31:20 for the same verb deriving from *rekhem* [TH7358, ZH8167], womb).

**30:21 *who would dare to come unless invited?*** This is a felicitous rendering of the Heb., "who is this [with] a pledge of his heart to draw near me." The leader has royal and priestly functions.

**30:23 *The LORD's anger bursts out like a storm.*** Jer 30:23-24, which also appears at 23:19-20, shows how serious God is about the matter and guarantees the foregoing promises (for God's anger, see 25:15-38).

## COMMENTARY

The next chapters (Jer 30–33) dramatically shift the tone from the foregoing sin-and-judgment chapters to one of hope, with the basic message that God will act to bring good things to his covenant people. The Lord will return the exiles home to their land and restore a close bond between himself and Israel. These two themes alternate in the Book of Comfort (chs 30–33; notes, 30:3).

The two themes amplify the term "salvation." Comment about this is facilitated through attention to various identifiable genres, such as "pronouncement of salvation" (30:5-9), "assurance of salvation" (30:10-11), and "announcement of salvation" (30:12-17a, 17b-22). The final verses (30:23-24) provide an "oath of salvation." (An "announcement of salvation" comes ordinarily in response to a lament and is consoling in tone. A "pronouncement of salvation" has about it a tone of dispute and of rebuke as though there was need to convince. Cf. Martens 1986:295).

The portrayal of salvation is one feature of the pronouncement of salvation (30:5-9). Another feature is the argumentative tone, represented here in the question by an onlooker (the Lord?) who asks why the soldiers are immobilized. The fear and the terror refer to war. This "time of trouble" was thought by Jewish rabbis to describe pre-messianic days (see note on 30:7). This time is like the "day of the Lord," a day monopolized by the Lord Yahweh that will bring destruction to some and salvation to others (Isa 2:12-21; Joel 1:15; Amos 5:18).

The God who breaks the stranglehold of the enemy (Assyria, Babylonia) is none other than the commander-in-chief of the hosts of heaven and of nations (30:8). Both divine initiative and unlimited power are brought to bear on the community's predicament by snapping their chains and raising up a leader. As at the Exodus, such deliverance made possible a change of masters. Now the Lord, not some foreign power, would be the Master. Salvation is release from trouble, difficulty, oppression, and panic—all that restricts, confines, and makes for non-peace and anxiety. Salvation issues in freedom and hope and, notably, in a new life under a new Master.

God assures his people of salvation (30:10-11) by addressing the emotional condition of the oppressed, as well as the promise of a changed situation. Characteristic of the assurance of salvation is the word of consolation: "Fear not" (cf. Isa 43:1, 5). In this oracle, two motivations for allaying fear are specified, a specific intervention (the homecoming from the exile, 30:10) and God's promise of his presence (see note on 30:11). Again, as in the "pronouncement of salvation," the realities of the difficulty are not glossed over. God will not let Israel go unpunished (30:11). Salvation, contrary to the word of false prophets, comes "beyond the judgment," but the fear has been removed (cf. 30:5). Salvation means having "peace and quiet" with the inner turmoil allayed. Moreover, the people have been saved to serve. Salvation entails change in both the circumstances and the person.

The announcement of salvation (30:12-17a) begins with an allusion to a lament (here, the incurable bruise, 30:12, explained as resulting from the punishment for their many sins, 30:14-15a), continues with a clarification of the Lord's stance (30:15b), and concludes with a promise of what the Lord will do (30:17a) and what the consequences of his intervention will be (30:16). For oracles of this genre, see Isa 41:17ff; Jer 31:2-6. The wound, pronounced incurable (30:15), will paradoxically be healed by an Almighty, caring God. The themes in these verses are wound/ healing, allies/enemies, and sins/punishment. "For the Old Testament as a whole the idea of salvation retains a full political and physical embodiment" (Clements 1988:183). Salvation means healing by the God who can do the impossible. Persons and communities at the ends of their ropes (with no healer and no allies) experience God as healer and ally.

A second announcement of salvation (30:17b-22) characteristically refers to a problematic situation (Israel is an outcast, isolated, if not disoriented; see note on 30:17). The Lord's stance is incorporated in his promise that they will return from captivity and their fortunes will be restored (30:18a). The sequel to this intervention will be a reconstituted community (30:18b), in which the mood will be optimistic and joyful, with a government of home rule (30:19-21) of which God will be an integral part (30:21b). Sometimes, as here, the goal of God's action is stated: "You will be my people, and I will be your God" (30:22). Salvation is intended to produce a godly community in which God is properly revered and worshiped. The divine design for a bonded community over which God presides is reinforced by an oath-like poem (30:23-24) and by the double statement about personhood that brackets it (30:22 and 31:1). Salvation is a divine transformation from captivity to freedom, from sorrow to joy, from chaos to order, and from isolation and alienation to acceptance and community.

To summarize with an eye to the New Testament, salvation is a transformative act of God that entails at least some of the following: release from that which constricts (exile, in Jeremiah; sin, in the NT), an undoing of captivity (Babylonian, in Jeremiah; slavery to sin, John 8:32), a change of situation or circumstance (externally in Jeremiah; internally in the NT; cf. Rom 8), an altered emotional condition (from fear and anxiety to peace and joy, from isolation to community, from alienation from God to fellowship with him). From both testaments, it is clear that God intends good things for his covenant people. High on the list of these good things is deliverance.

◆  ## B. Promises of Unrestrained Goodness (31:2-22)

²This is what the LORD says:

"Those who survive the coming destruction
will find blessings even in the barren land,
for I will give rest to the people of Israel."

³Long ago the LORD said to Israel:
"I have loved you, my people, with an everlasting love.
With unfailing love I have drawn you to myself.

⁴I will rebuild you, my virgin Israel.
You will again be happy
and dance merrily with your tambourines.
⁵Again you will plant your vineyards on the mountains of Samaria
and eat from your own gardens there.
⁶The day will come when watchmen will shout
from the hill country of Ephraim,
'Come, let us go up to Jerusalem*
to worship the LORD our God.'"

⁷Now this is what the LORD says:
"Sing with joy for Israel.*
Shout for the greatest of nations!
Shout out with praise and joy:
'Save your people, O LORD,
the remnant of Israel!'
⁸For I will bring them from the north
and from the distant corners of the
earth.
I will not forget the blind and lame,
the expectant mothers and women
in labor.
A great company will return!
⁹Tears of joy will stream down their
faces,
and I will lead them home with
great care.
They will walk beside quiet streams
and on smooth paths where they
will not stumble.
For I am Israel's father,
and Ephraim is my oldest child.

¹⁰"Listen to this message from the LORD,
you nations of the world;
proclaim it in distant coastlands:
The LORD, who scattered his people,
will gather them and watch over
them
as a shepherd does his flock.
¹¹For the LORD has redeemed Israel
from those too strong for them.
¹²They will come home and sing songs of
joy on the heights of Jerusalem.
They will be radiant because of the
LORD's good gifts—
the abundant crops of grain, new
wine, and olive oil,
and the healthy flocks and herds.
Their life will be like a watered garden,
and all their sorrows will be gone.
¹³The young women will dance for joy,
and the men—old and young—will
join in the celebration.
I will turn their mourning into joy.
I will comfort them and exchange
their sorrow for rejoicing.
¹⁴The priests will enjoy abundance,

and my people will feast on my good
gifts.
I, the LORD, have spoken!"

¹⁵This is what the LORD says:

"A cry is heard in Ramah—
deep anguish and bitter weeping.
Rachel weeps for her children,
refusing to be comforted—
for her children are gone."

¹⁶But now this is what the LORD says:
"Do not weep any longer,
for I will reward you," says the LORD.
"Your children will come back to you
from the distant land of the enemy.
¹⁷There is hope for your future," says
the LORD.
"Your children will come again to
their own land.
¹⁸I have heard Israel* saying,
'You disciplined me severely,
like a calf that needs training for
the yoke.
Turn me again to you and restore me,
for you alone are the LORD my God.
¹⁹I turned away from God,
but then I was sorry.
I kicked myself for my stupidity!
I was thoroughly ashamed of all
I did in my younger days.'

²⁰"Is not Israel still my son,
my darling child?" says the LORD.
"I often have to punish him,
but I still love him.
That's why I long for him
and surely will have mercy on him.
²¹Set up road signs;
put up guideposts.
Mark well the path
by which you came.
Come back again, my virgin Israel;
return to your towns here.
²²How long will you wander,
my wayward daughter?
For the LORD will cause something new
to happen—
Israel will embrace her God.*"

31:6 Hebrew *Zion;* also in 31:12.   31:7 Hebrew *Jacob;* also in 31:11. See note on 5:20.   31:18 Hebrew *Ephraim,*
referring to the northern kingdom of Israel; also in 31:20.   31:22 Hebrew *a woman will court a suitor.*

## NOTES

**31:2 *coming destruction.*** The NLT translates this as a future (the verb is regarded as prophetic perfect). Alternatively—and grammatically quite as possible if not preferable—is a straightforward past perfect tense: "those who survived the destruction (lit. "sword, "*khereb* [TH2719, ZH2995]) found blessings." The historic event in view could be the Egyptian pursuit at the Exodus (Exod 14) and/or the sword of the Amalekites (Exod 17:8-13; cf. van der Wal 1996).

**31:3 *Long ago the LORD said to Israel.*** The Heb. *rakhoq* [TH7350A, ZH8158] (distant) can be either spatial ("from afar," 31:10) or temporal (long ago). For "said," the Heb. has "appeared" (niphal of *ra'ah* [TH7200, ZH8011]). For assertions of God's love, cf. Deut 7:8.

***everlasting love.*** This translates *khesed* [TH2617, ZH2876] (faithfulness in action), a term that occurs 245 times in the OT (cf. Exod 34:6; Ps 136).

**31:5 *eat from your own gardens there.*** The first fruits of new plantings (e.g., the total crop in the fourth year) were dedicated to the Lord (Lev 19:23-25). The promise implies both agricultural productivity and political security.

**31:6 *from the hill country of Ephraim.*** The Ephraim tribe belonged to northern Israel. In Jeremiah, as in Hosea (5:3-14), Ephraim was a surrogate name for Israel. It speaks of reunification and the restoration of pre-exilic worship.

**31:8 *from the north.*** This announcement may have in view the northern tribes deported by Assyria to the river Habor (2 Kgs 15:29; 17:6). Or, since trade routes from Babylon led into Israel from the north, the Judean exiles in Babylon may be intended. Promises of return from exile are frequent in Jeremiah (e.g., 24:6; 30:3; 32:41; cf. Isa 14:1; Ezek 36:22).

***from the distant corners of the earth.*** The NLT omits "I will gather them" before this phrase, which is parallel to "I will bring them" (cf. the repetition of "gather" in 31:10). The reference to "gather" not only reinforces the promise of bringing the exiles back but calls to mind the Lord's earlier dispersion of a people. In an action suggesting reconciliation, that dispersion will now be undone.

**31:9 *Tears of joy.*** The Heb., "they will come with weeping," leaves unspecified whether the tears are of joy or regret.

***with great care.*** This expression, from *takhanunim* [TH8469, ZH9384], is more understandable if the Israelites are weeping in regret.

**31:11 *For the LORD has redeemed Israel.*** The one word "redeemed" translates the two words *padah* [TH6299, ZH7009] (ransom) and *ga'al* [TH1350, ZH1457] (redeem, buy back), which are sometimes parallel (e.g., Hos 13:14). The first is the broader term used in commercial law (Exod 21:8), as well as in cult legislation (Num 18:15-16). With God as subject, the verb recalls the redemption from Egypt (Mic 6:4). The second has no cognate in other languages and is limited in its technical usage mostly to Israelite family law (e.g., Lev 25:25; 27:31).

**31:12 *all their sorrows will be gone.*** The infinitive *da'abah* [TH1669, ZH1790] signifies languishing as much as sorrow. Israel will no longer be debilitated.

**31:15 *A cry is heard in Ramah.*** Ramah, five miles north of Jerusalem, is the site of Rachel's burial (1 Sam 10:2ff) and was also the depot from which exiles were deported (40:1). Rachel, Jacob's second wife and the mother of Joseph and Benjamin (and so the grandmother of Joseph's sons Ephraim and Manasseh), is here depicted as the mother of Israel.

**31:16 *I will reward you.*** Lit., "there is a reward for your work." The NLT specifies Yahweh as the agent and omits "work."

**31:18** *saying.* More graphically, Israel is "moaning" (hitpolel of *nud* [TH5110, ZH5653], "sway back and forth," "bemoan one's fate").

*Turn me again to you.* This is a word play on *shub* [TH7725, ZH8740] (turn), which can refer to a physical turn-around (return) but is also a common term for repentance (i.e., relational restoration). The NLT, by adding "to you," eliminates the ambiguity. The possible meaning "return to my homeland" should not be disregarded, however, since that is the issue in 31:17, where *shub* is used.

**31:19** *I kicked myself for my stupidity!* Lit., "I slapped my thighs; I was ashamed." Striking the thighs was a sign of sorrow (Ezek 21:12).

**31:20** *That's why I long for him.* Lit., "my inward parts [seen as the locus of emotions] are warm" (cf. 1 Kgs 3:16-28).

*mercy.* The term so translated comes from the same root as *rekhem* [TH7358, ZH8167] (womb). Trible (1978:44) translates, "I will truly show motherly-compassion upon him."

**31:21** *Come back again.* The Heb. word is *shub* [TH7725, ZH8740] (turn). Cf. the repetition in the next line and the note on 31:18.

**31:22** *the LORD will cause something new to happen.* Anderson (1978) posits that the new thing the land (*'erets* [TH776, ZH824]) will experience is the return of a lost son, Ephraim, so that the sense of the following saying is that Mother Israel, bereft of children (cf. 31:15), will again have children to embrace. For Israel to embrace God as her *geber* [TH1397, ZH1505] (valiant warrior) would be new. This new act prepares for the new covenant in 31:31.

*Israel will embrace her God.* This enigmatic statement (cf. NLT mg, "a woman will court a suitor") is interpreted by some as a proverb, by Jerome (4th century AD) as Mary's virginal conception of Jesus (cf. *bara'* [TH1254, ZH1343], "create," 31:22a), or symbolically as women with soldierly prowess (cf. RSV). Some see it as a role reversal in which a woman takes the initiative in sexual matters (Holladay 1989:195), or as the military strength associated with the male giving way to qualities of compassion associated with the female (Brown-Gutoff 1991). Others interpret it as a virgin Israel returning to God (Keown et al. 1995:123). Trible (1978:49) holds that the enigmatic statement refers to the poem itself, since 31:15-17 and 21-22, both about females, surround 31:18-20, which is about Ephraim.

## COMMENTARY

Chapters 30 and 31 deal with the twin topics of Israel's physical return to the land and her spiritual restoration to right relationship with God. One key to each of these announcements is God's ultimate goal, "I will be their God, and they shall be my people" (30:22; 31:1, 33). Another key, especially in this chapter, which is mostly about the spiritual intimacy of God with his people, is the opening assertion, "I have loved you with an everlasting love." Addressed to survivors, this word about God's love and goodness is spoken into a bleak situation (31:2). God's passionate affection for Israel can be a lens through which to view the series of announcements in 31:2-20.

The enduring quality of love is transparent in God's earlier record of delivering Israel (31:2), but especially in a series of three announcements, each beginning with *'od* [TH5750, ZH6388] ("again," 31:4-5) to match the three "I" sentences of 31:3-4a. The "again" provides a flashback to Israel's earlier devotion to Yahweh (2:2), her prosperity in the land (2:7; cf. Deut 8:1-14), and the worshipers' joyful required pilgrimage (Deut 16:9-17). The chaos introduced by the Exile was not God's intended last word. The "again" moves beyond the past punishments of drought, sword, and exile and addresses several matters: (1) the enterprise of building a people (31:4a); (2) enthusiasm and exuberance (31:4b; cf. silencing of joy, 7:34; 16:9); (3) physical prosperity and security; and (4) devoted worship (31:6, without the word "again"). Divine love does not give up on Israel, despite failures.

The energy of divine love is sketched in the second scene (31:7-9). God will bring his saving power to bear on the exiles (cf. 31:7). Reminiscent of a slave people brought out of Egypt, the announcement is about "smooth paths" (cf. forty years of wilderness wandering). Deported Israel is in view, whether the peoples of the northern kingdom taken by the Assyrians (730–722 BC) or Judah/Benjamin exiled by the Babylonians (586 BC). As a compassionate God, he attends to those who are weak, vulnerable, or in difficulty, such as the blind, lame, and pregnant (31:8; cf. Isa 35:4-7). Though God is sometimes metaphorically characterized as having maternal qualities (Isa 49:15 ; Jer 31:20), the designation of God as father (31:9; cf. 3:19; Deut 32:6; Matt 6:9) points to strength, energy, and firmness, as well as to caring and the disposition of an inheritance.

The extravagance of divine love is noted in scene three (31:10-14). Divine vigilance over a people is supplemented with a cornucopia of good gifts. Freedom is the first of these, for Israel had been released from its captors (31:11). God lavished his people with bountiful material goods, abundant crops, a rich life compared to a watered garden (cf. Deut 28:1-14), and exuberant celebrations. Divine love prepared a feast of good things for his people's homecoming.

In an emotional scene (31:15-22), the eagerness of maternal love is featured for a people in difficult times. The pain that comes with loss is neither ignored nor denied. Mother Rachel grieves at the disappearance of her progeny into exile (31:15). Deeply moved in his unceasing and caressing love, God envisions an alternative future, one not unlike a resurrection (31:17; cf. 29:11). However, love does not shrink from a results-oriented discipline (Heb 12:7-11). In Jesus' parable, the father awaits the return of the prodigal son (Luke 15:20); so here God eagerly awaits the return of a wayward daughter (31:22a). Though Israel had earlier divorced herself from her Savior, in the final vignette, as in a romantic movie, Israel is locked in an embrace with her God (31:22). God remains the God of newness (31:22; cf. Isa 43:19).

Israel had reason, then, to take definite initial steps on the way to a brighter future by setting up geographical road signs, interpreted symbolically as Torah signposts. Seen less as a serial list of announcements than as a portrayal of divine love in action, 31:2-22 becomes a helpful backdrop to Paul's more conceptual depiction in 1 Corinthians. God's actions with Israel describe how love, in addition to its extravagance, energy, and eagerness, "never loses faith, is always hopeful, and endures through every circumstance" (1 Cor 13:7).

◆     ## C. Promises of Newness (31:23-40)

23This is what the LORD of Heaven's Armies, the God of Israel, says: "When I bring them back from captivity, the people of Judah and its towns will again say, 'The LORD bless you, O righteous home, O holy mountain!' 24Townspeople and farmers and shepherds alike will live together in peace and happiness. 25For I have given rest to the weary and joy to the sorrowing."

26At this, I woke up and looked around. My sleep had been very sweet.

27"The day is coming," says the LORD, "when I will greatly increase the human population and the number of animals here in Israel and Judah. 28In the past I deliberately uprooted and tore down this nation. I overthrew it, destroyed it, and brought disaster upon it. But in the future I will just as deliberately plant it and build it up. I, the LORD, have spoken!

29"The people will no longer quote this proverb:

'The parents have eaten sour grapes,
    but their children's mouths pucker
        at the taste.'

30All people will die for their own sins—those who eat the sour grapes will be the ones whose mouths will pucker.

31"The day is coming," says the LORD, "when I will make a new covenant with the people of Israel and Judah. 32This covenant will not be like the one I made with their ancestors when I took them by the hand and brought them out of the land of Egypt. They broke that covenant, though I loved them as a husband loves his wife," says the LORD.

33"But this is the new covenant I will make with the people of Israel on that day," says the LORD. "I will put my instructions deep within them, and I will write them on their hearts. I will be their God, and they will be my people. 34And they will not need to teach their neighbors, nor will they need to teach their relatives, saying, 'You should know the LORD.' For everyone, from the least to the greatest, will know me already," says the LORD. "And I will forgive their wickedness, and I will never again remember their sins."

35It is the LORD who provides the sun to
        light the day
    and the moon and stars to light the
        night,
    and who stirs the sea into roaring
        waves.
His name is the LORD of Heaven's
        Armies,
    and this is what he says:
36"I am as likely to reject my people
        Israel
    as I am to abolish the laws of
        nature!"
37This is what the LORD says:
    "Just as the heavens cannot be
        measured
    and the foundations of the earth
        cannot be explored,
    so I will not consider casting them
        away
    for the evil they have done.
    I, the LORD, have spoken!

38"The day is coming," says the LORD, "when all Jerusalem will be rebuilt for me, from the Tower of Hananel to the Corner Gate. 39A measuring line will be stretched out over the hill of Gareb and across to Goah. 40And the entire area—including the graveyard and ash dump in the valley, and all the fields out to the Kidron Valley on the east as far as the Horse Gate—will be holy to the LORD. The city will never again be captured or destroyed."

NOTES

**31:23 *When I bring them back from captivity.*** A better reading is, "when I restore their fortunes" (cf. 30:3). Judah is now the specific subject. Restoration of worship (cf. 31:6) is an important topic here, as in passages dealing with Israel generally.

**31:25** *joy to the sorrowing.* Lit., "I will fill the languishing."

**31:26** *I woke up and looked around.* This emphasizes the envisioned future (so unlike their present). For dream visions, see Dan 2:28; 10:9; Zech 4:1.

**31:28** *plant it and build it up.* "The terms [build, plant] bespeak a full resumption of all of life" (Brueggemann 1998:290).

**31:29** *The parents have eaten sour grapes.* The proverb addresses what is considered an unfair state of affairs; children suffer for the sins of their ancestors (cf. Ezek 18:2-4).

**31:32** *They broke that covenant.* For a broken political covenant, see 1 Kgs 15:19; for a broken religious covenant, see Deut 31:16, 20; Jer 11:10.

*as a husband loves his wife.* A gratuitous rendering. Ownership and bondedness, more than love, are nuanced in the Heb. *ba'al* [TH1166, ZH1249] (to possess, to own, to rule over). Cf. P. J. Scalise's careful and extensive treatment (Keown et al. 1995:124-129).

**31:36** *I am as likely to reject my people Israel.* The conditional form, "If these ordinances [of moon and stars in 31:35] are removed, then the seed of Israel will cease from being a people before me" has a more mellow tone than the NLT.

**31:38** *from the tower of Hananel to the Corner Gate.* The tower in northeast Jerusalem is situated between the sheep gate and the fish gate (Neh 3:1; Zech 14:10). The Corner Gate at the northwest corner was added by Uzziah (783–742 BC; see 2 Chr 26:9).

**31:39** *over the hill of Gareb and across to Goah.* The locations of Gareb and Goah are unknown. For measurements in restoration contexts, see Ezek 40:3-35; 42:15-20. "Measurement precedes building" (Neh 3:11; Job 38:5; Keown et al. 1995:138).

**31:40** *Kidron Valley . . . Horse Gate.* The Kidron Brook just east of the Temple mount was where Josiah destroyed pagan idols and altars (2 Kgs 23:4). The Horse Gate was at the southeast end of the Temple area (Neh 3:28).

### COMMENTARY

The earlier parts of the Book of Comfort have exuberantly portrayed the restoration of the exiles to the land and their spiritual restoration to God. As often happens, after the excitement of great promises come realistic questions. This section can be understood as addressing some nagging questions concerning repopulation and the cycles of sin.

**Who Is the Audience?**     The headline for the Book of Comfort mentions both Israel and Judah (30:3). Israel, known by the name of the major tribe, Ephraim, is largely in view in 31:2-21 (cf. 31:6, 9, 18, 20, and Samaria and Ramah, cities within Ephraim, 31:5, 15). A brief oracle is then directed specifically to Judah (31:23-25), after which Judah and Israel are again addressed together (31:27-37). The final verses about Jerusalem appear to be a postscript (31:38-40). With their interest in Jerusalem, these verses function as an inclusio for this section, which began by telling about Judah's cities generally (31:24; "towns" in the NLT).

**What Will the Promised New Situation Be Like?**     The section addressed to Judah resumes the theme of the Book of Comfort about restored fortunes (see note on 31:23). Zion speaks of restored worship (cf. 31:6; Ps 126). Diverse people with diverse interests will coexist peaceably (31:24). These include farmers and shepherds that clashed because of competing aspirations for the same land. Reassuring promises of community solidarity and joy, idyllic as a dream, promised earlier to Israel (cf. 31:10, 12-13), are now promised to Judah (31:25). Jeremiah 31:26 is a transition between an imagined time of the fully good life and additional divine messages that address concerns prompted by the realism of the current situation.

**How Can These Things Be?**  The section of 31:27-34 addresses questions raised by this portrayal of a perfect future. One question is whether Israel will be able to re-inhabit and prosper in their land, now depopulated by foreign invaders and ruined for agriculture. God's answer is affirmative (31:27). Returning to the language of Jeremiah's call, which spoke first of uprooting and destroying and then of building and planting (1:10), God affirms that his last word is not of destruction but of constructive action. The first resulted in disaster. The second will result in prosperity and the good life.

**Can the Crime-punishment Cycle Be Broken?**  This is an implicit question. Even if a new start is made, in the light of Exodus 34:7, will the people not be at the mercy of their parents' failures (31:29)? The answer does not negate the principle that the consequences of sin affect future generations, but it affirms that future generations are not necessarily victimized by the wrongdoings of their ancestors. Since every sinner suffers for his or her own sins, a new beginning is not doomed from the start. The critical factors are the obedience and spiritual devotion of those making the new beginnings.

This question about sin's cycle receives a second answer, the justly famous word about the new covenant (31:31-34). A covenant seeks bonding and solidarity. It is a formal arrangement that entails obligations and the loyalty of both parties. A covenant is not the same as a contract. The enforcement of a contract turns on performance. In a covenant, performance is also a factor, but the loyalty factor is more critical, and loyalty does not readily yield to measurement. Loyalty can be intense or it can be indecisive. Like elastic, its stretching capacity is large but limited. When the devotion or loyalty of a covenant partner clearly "snaps," the bond is broken (cf. comments on 11:10). The faithful partner is now detached, however deeply that partner longs for intimacy in the relationship. A broken covenant, however, does not preclude a fresh start, a new covenant—as explained in Hebrews 8:7, where the quotation of Jeremiah 31:31-34 (Heb 8:8-12) is the longest quotation of the Old Testament in the New Testament.

**How Is This "New" Covenant New?**  The new covenant is new in three ways. First, in the new covenant, formerly external directives would be internalized. To be sure, directives in the Sinaitic covenant touched on internal matters, such as coveting. But these instructions were nevertheless external in the sense that they came from an outside source (e.g., Moses). Specific instructions can never cover all situations that arise in a relationship of mutuality between two persons or parties, so now in the new covenant the locus for directives or the control center for the peoples' lives would be governed by a God-given desire to do what is right, and they would be empowered by a God-given ability to respond in loyalty. Ezekiel described the same phenomenon as a heart transplant, in which the heart of stone (resistance) would be replaced by a heart of flesh manifested by a pliant, receptive attitude (Ezek 36:26; cf. Ps 40:8). Israel was promised a change. Christians relate to this promise through the coming of the Holy Spirit, who indwells believers and who both prompts toward the good and empowers persons to accomplish it.

Second, the newness of the new covenant consisted in a democratizing of the knowledge of God. In the old covenant, the priests served as mediators between God and the Israelites. Part of this mediating work was to offer instruction (Mal 2:7). For Jewish hearers, this promise meant the elimination of elitism and the promise of divine immediacy. The sixteenth-century reformers in Europe captured this feature in the phrase, "the priesthood of all believers."

Third, the new covenant addressed the issue of forgiveness, in which the newness consists in its permanence. Under the Sinai covenant, forgiveness was clearly a reality for the people (Lev 4:26, 31; 5:10; Ps 32:1), but in God's overarching economy of justice, forgiveness was ultimately secured through the death of Jesus, the God-man (Acts 13:38-39). Even so, for the exiles, this message of God's forgiveness at his initiative was the basis for any kind of renewal. In forgiveness, the offended party does not hold the offender hostage.

**Is There a Guarantee?**  The new covenant came on the heels of a collapsed covenant and had new emphases. It was like the old in that its goals of solidarity and intimacy remained unchanged, as expressed in the formula "I will be their God, and they will be my people" (31:33; cf. Lev 24:7; 26:12; Jer 24 and comments). The poetic section answers a third implied question as to what kind of guarantee stood behind this promise of a glorious future (31:35-37). The short answer is that God, the cosmic commander-in-chief (31:35), guaranteed it. Jeremiah 31:35-37 is a "powerful and innovative argument used as assurance for the amazing, transformational affirmation of Jer 31:31-34" (Huffmon 1999:182). For the ultimate survival of God's people, this affirmative answer could not be clearer. Some interpret this oracle more literally (as well as the final word of the postscript) to mean that God's salvation for Israel is linked—even to this day—to their possession of the physical land of Israel. Others understand it as a pastoral word, grounded in the created order, about the certainty of God's fulfilling his purposes, whatever they may be.

The postscript about the rebuilding of Jerusalem answers another question: where is one to begin? The answer is that God will take the initiative in his own time ("the day is coming," v. 38) and that the promises do not exclude the physical structures of the city. God will undo the havoc wrought by the people's sins.

◆   ## D. A Real Estate Transaction with a Message (32:1-15)

The following message came to Jeremiah from the LORD in the tenth year of the reign of Zedekiah,* king of Judah. This was also the eighteenth year of the reign of King Nebuchadnezzar.* ²Jerusalem was then under siege from the Babylonian army, and Jeremiah was imprisoned in the courtyard of the guard in the royal palace.

³King Zedekiah had put him there, asking why he kept giving this prophecy: "This is what the LORD says: 'I am about to hand this city over to the king of Babylon, and he will take it. ⁴King Zedekiah will be captured by the Babylonians* and taken to meet the king of Babylon face to face. ⁵He will take Zedekiah to Babylon, and I will deal with him there,' says the LORD. 'If you fight against the Babylonians, you will never succeed.'"

⁶At that time the LORD sent me a message. He said, ⁷"Your cousin Hanamel son of Shallum will come and say to you, 'Buy my field at Anathoth. By law you have the right to buy it before it is offered to anyone else.'"

⁸Then, just as the LORD had said he would, my cousin Hanamel came and visited me in the prison. He said, "Please buy my field at Anathoth in the land of Benjamin. By law you have the right to buy it before it is offered to anyone else, so buy it for yourself." Then I knew that the message I had heard was from the LORD.

⁹So I bought the field at Anathoth, paying Hanamel seventeen pieces* of silver for it. ¹⁰I signed and sealed the deed of purchase before witnesses, weighed out the silver, and paid him. ¹¹Then I took the sealed deed and an unsealed copy of the deed, which contained the terms and conditions of the purchase, ¹²and I handed them to Baruch son of Neriah and grandson of Mahseiah. I did all this in the presence of my cousin Hanamel, the witnesses who had signed the deed, and all the men of Judah who were there in the courtyard of the guardhouse.

¹³Then I said to Baruch as they all listened, ¹⁴"This is what the LORD of Heaven's Armies, the God of Israel, says: 'Take both this sealed deed and the unsealed copy, and put them into a pottery jar to preserve them for a long time.' ¹⁵For this is what the LORD of Heaven's Armies, the God of Israel, says: 'Someday people will again own property here in this land and will buy and sell houses and vineyards and fields.'"

32:1a The tenth year of Zedekiah's reign and the eighteenth year of Nebuchadnezzar's reign was 587 BC.
32:1b Hebrew *Nebuchadrezzar*, a variant spelling of Nebuchadnezzar; also in 32:28.   32:4 Or *Chaldeans*; also in 32:5, 24, 25, 28, 29, 43.   32:9 Hebrew *17 shekels*, about 7 ounces or 194 grams in weight.

NOTES

**32:3** *he [Nebuchadnezzar] will take it.* For earlier prophecies about Babylon's invasion, see 27:6-8. For the siege, see Jer 39.

**32:4** *face to face.* The Heb. includes, perhaps for emphasis, "his [Zedekiah's] eyes will see his [Nebuchadnezzar's] eyes." This is what happened (52:9-11).

**32:7** *Anathoth.* The prophet's hometown lay two miles from Jerusalem.

*you have the right to buy it.* Guidelines for property transactions between relatives are specified in Lev 25:25-28 and illustrated in Ruth 4:1-12.

**32:10** *paid him.* The Heb. mentions scales used for weighing the silver; coins came later. Standard weights of stone, often inscribed or carved for recognition, were used on a balance scale with two pans (cf. Deut 25:13; Prov 16:11; Mic 6:11). For real estate purchases, see Gen 23:16; 2 Sam 24:24.

**32:11** *the sealed deed and an unsealed copy.* The unsealed copy, open for public inspection, was attached to the tied and sealed papyrus copy, on the outside of which were the names of the witnesses and sometimes the scribe (see details by P.J. Scalise in Keown et al. 1995:154). See the discussion in Friebel (1999:315-329).

**32:12** *I handed them to Baruch.* Baruch, mentioned here for the first time (cf. 43:3, 6; chs 36 and 45), had a brother, Seraiah, who was also enlisted by Jeremiah for scribal duties dealing with the future of Babylon (51:59-64).

COMMENTARY

Historians are interested in this account for the details it gives about ancient business practices. Literary analysts see Jeremiah 32–33 as a prose parallel to the poetry of Jeremiah 30–31 (cf. Judg 4–5), or they compare the rhetorical parallelism of Jeremiah 32 and 33 (Ho 1999:172-80). To Jeremiah's hearers, however, Jeremiah's purchase of land was a sign-act. Some sign-acts were ominous (the belt, 13:1-11; pottery smashing, 19:1-13; yoke bars, 27–28). Others were challenges to reform (pottery-making, 18:1-11). This sign-act inspired hope. Present-day believers who read this story as God's word to them are challenged to rethink their experience of God and to take risks.

In this section, God is pictured as an investment counselor who is concerned with business affairs. This incident supplements other stories of property purchases (e.g., the lengthy description of Abraham's purchase of a burial plot from the Philistines, Gen 23:1-20; David's purchase of an altar site, 2 Sam 24:18-25; Ahab's appropriation of Naboth's vineyard, 1 Kgs 21:1-16; and Jehoiakim's venture into palace-building, Jer 22:13-17) and directives about business transactions found in the wisdom literature (e.g., Prov 16:11; 20:10, 16, 23). God is not a remote person that confines himself to spiritual matters but is close at hand in all the details of our lives. God's span of concerns includes home ownership, and here he intervenes in an individual's life to give directions about a material purchase.

God is a teacher who communicates both orally and visually. The oral message about a hope-filled future is made concrete in this transaction involving monies and records. In this instance, a people weak in faith and hope are nurtured by what they see with their eyes. God has gone public with his promises and has offered guidance through signs (cf. Gideon's fleece, Judg 6:36-40; Paul, Acts 16:6-10). God attends to left-brained persons, who thrive on a well-reasoned discourse, and to right-brained individuals, who are more at home with images. God is the great communicator.

God is also the agent of change. Already, the Book of Consolation has told about the new things God would do (31:22, 31-34). God will not allow the negative experience of the Exile to be the final word. Instead, the dark experience of God's discipline will yield to the dawning of a new day. Like Job, who lost his possessions but eventually had them restored, the exiles removed from their land would again enjoy the satisfactions of property ownership.

When viewed existentially from the standpoint of human experience, the story has much to say about risk-taking. From the standpoint of rational calculation, Jeremiah's purchase was ill advised. Jeremiah had preached that the Babylonians would invade the country. Since at that very moment the Babylonian army was besieging the city, a purchase would be a losing proposition (32:2, 25). Humanly speaking there could be no more than the tiniest sliver of hope for recovering this investment; it was a risk no one would take. What reason, then, was there for Jeremiah, in prison with an uncertain future, to make any kind of purchase? Furthermore, a questionable purchase such as this might render Jeremiah ludicrous in the eyes of the people he was seeking to persuade. But taking risks is not a mistake when God so directs. Once the reason for the land purchase, namely the promise of the people's return to the land, is given, the circumstance was somewhat altered, though the call for faith remained. The future can include the unimaginable because God is part of that future. G. K. Chesterton is quoted as saying, "As long as matters are really hopeful, hope is mere flattery or platitude. It is only when everything is hopeless that hope begins to be a strength at all. Like all the Christians' virtues, it is as unreasonable as it is indispensable" (quoted by Ives [1998], sermon on Jer 32).

◆  ### E. Nothing is Too Hard for God (32:16-44)

16Then after I had given the papers to Baruch, I prayed to the LORD:

17"O Sovereign LORD! You made the heavens and earth by your strong hand and powerful arm. Nothing is too hard for you! 18You show unfailing love to thousands, but you also bring the consequences of one generation's sin upon the next. You are the great and powerful God, the LORD of Heaven's Armies. 19You have all wisdom and do great and mighty miracles. You see the conduct of all people, and you give them what they deserve. 20You performed miraculous signs and wonders in the land of Egypt—things still remembered to this day! And you have continued to do great miracles in Israel and all around the world. You have made your name famous to this day.

21"You brought Israel out of Egypt with mighty signs and wonders, with a strong hand and powerful arm, and with overwhelming terror. 22You gave the people of Israel this land that you had promised their ancestors long before—a land flowing with milk and honey. 23Our ancestors came and conquered it and lived in it, but they refused to obey you or follow your word. They have not done anything you commanded. That is why you have sent this terrible disaster upon them.

24"See how the siege ramps have been built against the city walls! Through war, famine, and disease, the city will be handed over to the Babylonians, who will conquer it. Everything has happened just as you said. 25And yet, O Sovereign LORD, you have told me to buy the field—paying good money for it before these witnesses—even though the city will soon be handed over to the Babylonians."

26Then this message came to Jeremiah from the LORD: 27"I am the LORD, the God of all the peoples of the world. Is anything too hard for me? 28Therefore, this is what the LORD says: I will hand this city over to the Babylonians and to Nebuchadnezzar, king of Babylon, and he will capture it. 29The Babylonians outside the walls will come in and set fire to the city. They will burn down all these houses where the people provoked my anger by burning incense to Baal on the rooftops and by pouring out liquid offerings to other gods. 30Israel and Judah have done nothing but wrong since their earliest days. They have infuriated me with all their evil deeds," says the LORD. 31"From the time this city was built until now, it has done nothing but anger me, so I am determined to get rid of it.

32"The sins of Israel and Judah—the sins of the people of Jerusalem, the kings, the officials, the priests, and the prophets—have stirred up my anger. 33My people have turned their backs on me and have refused to return. Even though I diligently taught them, they would not receive instruction or obey. ³⁴They have set up their abominable idols right in my own Temple, defiling it. ³⁵They have built pagan shrines to Baal in the valley of Ben-Hinnom, and there they sacrifice their sons and daughters to Molech. I have never commanded such a horrible deed; it never even crossed my mind to command such a thing. What an incredible evil, causing Judah to sin so greatly!

³⁶"Now I want to say something more about this city. You have been saying, 'It will fall to the king of Babylon through war, famine, and disease.' But this is what the LORD, the God of Israel, says: ³⁷I will certainly bring my people back again from all the countries where I will scatter them in my fury. I will bring them back to this very city and let them live in peace and safety. ³⁸They will be my people, and I will be their God. ³⁹And I will give them one heart and one purpose: to worship me forever, for their own good and for the good of all their descendants. ⁴⁰And I will make an everlasting covenant with them: I will never stop doing good for them. I will put a desire in their hearts to worship me, and they will never leave me. ⁴¹I will find joy doing good for them and will faithfully and wholeheartedly replant them in this land.

⁴²"This is what the LORD says: Just as I have brought all these calamities on them, so I will do all the good I have promised them. ⁴³Fields will again be bought and sold in this land about which you now say, 'It has been ravaged by the Babylonians, a desolate land where people and animals have all disappeared.' ⁴⁴Yes, fields will once again be bought and sold—deeds signed and sealed and witnessed—in the land of Benjamin and here in Jerusalem, in the towns of Judah and in the hill country, in the foothills of Judah* and in the Negev, too. For someday I will restore prosperity to them. I, the LORD, have spoken!"

**32:44** Hebrew *the Shephelah.*

## NOTES

**32:16-44** The prayer and response are outlined here as adapted from Ho (1999:68).
I. Jeremiah's Prayer (32:16-25)
    A. Narrative Introduction (32:16)
    B. Hymnic Description of Yahweh (32:17-23)
        1. "Nothing is too hard for you!" (32:17)
        2. Liturgical credo (32:18-19)
        3. Historical credo (32:20-23)
    C. The Present Plight of Jerusalem (32:24)
    D. Perplexity about Restoration (32:25)
II. Yahweh's Answer (32:26-44)
    A. Narrative Introduction (32:26)
    B. Self-Description of Yahweh: "Is anything too hard for me?" (32:27)
    C. The Impending Fate of Jerusalem (32:28-35)
    D. Promise of Restoration (32:36-44)

**32:18** *You show unfailing love to thousands.* The statement about *khesed* [TH2617, ZH2876] (faithfulness in action; cf. Ps 136) is drawn from Exod 34:6.

**32:20** *signs and wonders.* Signs (*'othoth* [TH226, ZH253]) are events which, while important in themselves, point to another reality. Wonders (*mopethim* [TH4159, ZH4603]) are extraordinary events such as miracles, as in the Exodus (cf. Pss 78:43; 105:27).

**32:21** *overwhelming terror.* The word *mora'* [TH4172, ZH4616] (terror, respect, worship, NIDOTTE 2:527-533), when referring to "signs and wonders," has the meaning of "awesome" (Deut 4:34; 26:8; 34:12). The LXX apparently translates *mar'eh* [TH4758, ZH5260] (appearance, spectacle). For more detail, see Shead (1998).

**32:22** *a land flowing with milk and honey.* This suggests an abundance of cattle herds and horticulture, especially if "honey" refers to "a sort of molasses made from grapes" (Keown et al. 1995:156). The phrase is found about fifteen times in the Pentateuch (e.g., Exod 13:5; Lev 20:24, Num 14:8; Deut 6:3).

**32:24** *war, famine, and disease.* This is a frequent triad of agents of God's punishment (24:10; 29:17-18; 32:36; 38:2; 42:22; 44:13; cf.14:12; 16:4; 44:12).

**32:27** *Is anything too hard for me?* The root *pala'* [TH6381, ZH7098] (difficult, extraordinary) is often connected in hymnic literature with the Exodus (Mic 7:15), wonders on the wilderness journey (Ps 78:12ff), the crossing of the Jordan (Josh 3:5), and salvific acts for individuals (e.g., Pss 71:17; 107:15, 21, 24). God is extolled as the doer of wonders (Pss 72:18; 86:10; 98:1; 136:4).

**32:29** *the people provoked my anger.* Concerning God's anger, see comments on 25:15-38.

*by burning incense to Baal.* This storm god, associated with rain and fertility, was the principal Canaanite deity whose father was the high god El. For Israel's fascination with Baal subsequent to the endorsement of the Baal cult by Ahab, see 1 Kgs 16:31; Jer 2:8, 7:9; 23:27 (cf. 1 Kgs 18:18-40; Hos 2:5-13; NIDOTTE 4:422-428).

**32:30** *all their evil deeds.* The "works of their hands" (the literal reading) would include their making bull calf idols early in the Israelite experience (Exod 32:1-6; cf. Jer 10:3-9); Temple objects for the Baals, especially by Ahaz (2 Chr 24:7; 28:2); altars to Baal by Manasseh (2 Kgs 21:3-6; 2 Chr 33:3); and foul play generally (Amos 8:4-6).

**32:32** *sins of Israel and Judah.* Jeremiah amply documents the sins of the people (7:9-10, cf. Ezek 20:1-26), kings (22:13-17), priests (2:8; 5:31; 6:13), and prophets (23:9-40).

**32:35** *valley of Ben-Hinnom.* See comments on 7:30–8:3; 19:5.

*Molech.* This may have been an underworld deity (see Scalise in Keown et al. 1995:158 summarizing the research of J. Day).

**32:37** *scatter them in my fury.* "Fury" handles three Heb. terms. *'aph* [TH639, ZH678] (anger), *khema'* [TH2534A, ZH2771] (wrath), and *qetsep* [TH7110, ZH7912] (rage, fury, indignation). See comments on 25:15-38.

**32:39** *I will give them one heart.* Cf. the LXX, "another heart"; Syriac, "new" heart (cf. 31:33; Ezek 36:26).

**32:44** *I will restore prosperity.* This employs the vocabulary of 30:3 (*shub shebuth* ["turn/turning," TH7725/7622, ZH8740/8654], restore fortunes) and so forms an inclusio. See the note on 29:14.

COMMENTARY

The prayer (32:16-25) and its answer from Yahweh (32:26-44) are in literary symmetry (see note on 32:17). Both begin with the twin themes of creation and God's ability to do the extraordinary (32:17, 27), continue with Israel's total failure to obey and the resultant siege (32:23-24; cf. siege and disobedience, 32:28-30), and conclude with mention of a land purchase (32:25, 44). Both the prayer and the reply contain variations on the theme, "Nothing is too hard for you!" (32:17, 27; cf. Gen 18:14, Luke 1:37; 18:27).

**Divine and Human Perspectives.** Jeremiah's prayer was "faith seeking understanding" and it illustrates Evagrius's dictum: "If you are a theologian, you will pray truly, and if you pray truly, you are a theologian" (quoted in Moberly 2000:39). Jeremiah's opening confession about God's unlimited ability has the effect of putting the dilemma of his ridiculously-timed land purchase in perspective. He was reassured when he realized that this real estate transaction was connected with the command of the Creator of all. If his nagging inward question was about God's ability to come through for him, Israel's confession about God as Creator offered an immediate answer. God was equal to the problem.

Similarly, other persons of faith in desperate straits have fixed their gaze on God by reciting the creed, much as storm-tossed sailors are oriented by the beacon from an on-shore lighthouse. When in deep trouble, Hezekiah recalled God's creative word (Isa 37:16). The Lord's apostles, threatened by a hostile council, prayed, "O Sovereign Lord, Creator of heaven and earth, the sea, and everything in them" (Acts 4:24). Such recognition diminishes the size of the problem in the face of "the great and powerful God, the LORD of Heaven's Armies" (32:18).

God's extraordinary ability has been demonstrated in redemptive history, as well as in creation. The Israelite creed about God as creator bears on Jeremiah's situation. So does the memory of God's power as displayed in collective past experiences, most notably in Egypt, but also elsewhere in the world (32:20-21). One may surmise that Jeremiah was thinking of Jericho (Josh 6), of Hezekiah's deliverance from the Assyrians (Isa 36–37), or of the contest at Mount Carmel (1 Kgs 18). Similarly, a Christian facing a troubling situation, whether personal, within the church, or in the larger society, recalls God's "signs and wonders" (Acts 2:22), most memorably in Christ's resurrection.

**Divine Justice.** "Is anything too hard for me?" asks God, as if testing Jeremiah's grasp of his own assertion (32:27). God's own answer points to his strange move against his own people by bringing on a foreign invader (32:28-29). Is this action hard for God? Of course it is. His goodness had been lavishly poured out on his people, while their evils, including those of their leaders, had been thrown in God's face. Was it a light thing to be turning on a people whose salvation and well-being God had worked so mightily to secure? Lest anyone conclude that God's patience was infinite, God made it clear that his anger was aroused by evil. There was a reason for his fierce action; God is not capricious. He loved his people, but he was passionately committed to justice and righteousness. In the interests of righteousness, God will do what may be perceived as impossible, to turn with passionate emotion against his own people to destroy their homes and deport them (32:31). The greatness of God's power was reassuring when it was deployed on Israel's behalf but devastating when directed against her—a conclusion understood by Jeremiah (32:24) and underscored in the Lord's reply (32:28-29).

**Divine Power and Transformation.** "Is anything too hard for me?" The question played into an abrupt announcement of restoration that would follow the judgment (32:36-44). "The paradox of banishment followed by gathering . . . is an example of the paradoxical confession in 32:18, which is a short form of Exod 34:6-7" (Keown et al. 1995:162-163). Could God return his people who would be taken captive and exiled? Yes! The judgment inflicted by the Babylonians, God's agent, was not the last word (32:43). The word beyond the deserved judgment was restoration, wholeness, and a totally undeserved abundant life. God's extraordinary power made for transformation—as from death by crucifixion to resurrection in glory.

The scenario for the future is of material well-being earthed in family togetherness; life in peace and safety (32:37); and economic vitality (32:43-44). The restoration does not begin with but extends to a spiritual restoration: a united people under God (32:38), a worshiping community (32:39-40). God made it clear that his unlimited power is not used for destruction but for constructive action. Nor would God bestow good on this once-stubborn people grudgingly. It is his delight to do good (32:41), a theme already forcefully sounded in the Book of Consolation (30:18-21; 31:3-6, 10-14, 27ff). So also the New Testament Christian community knows that God's mighty power is deployed in making the abundant life possible (John 10:10), and that it has been "blessed with every spiritual blessing" (Eph 1:3). As if echoing the refrain, "Is anything too hard for God?" Paul continues: "I pray that you will begin to understand the incredible greatness of his power for us who believe him" (Eph 1:19).

◆    F. Fortunes Reversed—Guaranteed! (33:1-26)

While Jeremiah was still confined in the courtyard of the guard, the LORD gave him this second message: ²"This is what the LORD says—the LORD who made the earth, who formed and established it, whose name is the LORD: ³Ask me and I will tell you remarkable secrets you do not know about things to come. ⁴For this is what the LORD, the God of Israel, says: You have torn down the houses of this city and even the king's palace to get materials to strengthen the walls against the siege ramps and swords of the enemy. ⁵You expect to fight the Babylonians,* but the men of this city are already as good as dead, for I have determined to destroy them in my terrible anger. I have abandoned them because of all their wickedness.

⁶"Nevertheless, the time will come when I will heal Jerusalem's wounds and give it prosperity and true peace. ⁷I will restore the fortunes of Judah and Israel and rebuild their towns. ⁸I will cleanse them of their sins against me and forgive all their sins of rebellion. ⁹Then this city will bring me joy, glory, and honor before all the nations of the earth! The people of the world will see all the good I do for my people, and they will tremble with awe at the peace and prosperity I provide for them.

¹⁰"This is what the LORD says: You have said, 'This is a desolate land where people and animals have all disappeared.' Yet in the empty streets of Jerusalem and Judah's other towns, there will be heard once more ¹¹the sounds of joy and laughter. The joyful voices of bridegrooms and brides will be heard again, along with the joyous songs of people bringing thanksgiving offerings to the LORD. They will sing,

'Give thanks to the LORD of Heaven's
    Armies,
    for the LORD is good.
    His faithful love endures forever!'

For I will restore the prosperity of this land to what it was in the past, says the LORD.

¹²"This is what the LORD of Heaven's Armies says: This land—though it is now desolate and has no people and animals—will once more have pastures where shepherds can lead their flocks. ¹³Once again shepherds will count their flocks in the towns of the hill country, the foothills of Judah,* the Negev, the land of Benjamin, the vicinity of Jerusalem, and all the towns of Judah. I, the LORD, have spoken!

¹⁴"The day will come, says the LORD, when I will do for Israel and Judah all the good things I have promised them.

¹⁵"In those days and at that time
    I will raise up a righteous
        descendant* from King David's
        line.
    He will do what is just and right
        throughout the land.
¹⁶In that day Judah will be saved,
    and Jerusalem will live in safety.
    And this will be its name:
    'The LORD Is Our Righteousness.'*

¹⁷For this is what the LORD says: David will have a descendant sitting on the throne of Israel forever. ¹⁸And there will always be Levitical priests to offer burnt offerings and grain offerings and sacrifices to me."

¹⁹Then this message came to Jeremiah from the LORD: ²⁰"This is what the LORD says: If you can break my covenant with the day and the night so that one does not follow the other, ²¹only then will my covenant with my servant David be broken. Only then will he no longer have a descendant to reign on his throne. The same is true for my covenant with the Levitical priests who minister before me. ²²And as the stars of the sky cannot be counted and the sand on the seashore cannot be measured, so I will multiply the descendants of my servant David and the Levites who minister before me."

²³The LORD gave another message to Jeremiah. He said, ²⁴"Have you noticed what people are saying?—'The LORD chose Judah and Israel and then abandoned them!' They are sneering and saying that Israel is not worthy to be counted as a nation. ²⁵But this is what the LORD says: I would no more reject my people than I would change my laws that govern night and day, earth and sky. ²⁶I will never abandon the descendants of Jacob or David, my servant, or change the plan that David's descendants will rule the descendants of Abraham, Isaac, and Jacob. Instead, I will restore them to their land and have mercy on them."

33:5 Or *Chaldeans.*  33:13 Hebrew *the Shephelah.*  33:15 Hebrew *a righteous branch.*  33:16 Hebrew *Yahweh Tsidqenu.*

## NOTES

**33:2 *The LORD who made the earth.*** Lit., "The LORD, the one making her (it)" (cf. KJV). The accusative "her" may well refer to "earth" (so LXX) but could also refer to Jerusalem (cities are feminine in Hebrew), past events (i.e., history), or the future. Cf. 33:3ff, which speaks more to human history than to creation.

**33:3 *I will tell you remarkable secrets.*** The root idea of *batsur* [TH1219C, ZH1290] (secrets) is "inaccessible"; it also describes fortifications (2 Kgs 18:13; cf. "mighty things," KJV; "unsearchable things," NIV). The NLT telescopes the Heb. "I will answer and I will declare" into "I will tell." The "secrets" are disclosed in 33:6-26.

**33:5 *the men of this city are already as good as dead.*** The Heb. is vivid; the Babylonians are coming to fill them (the valleys or the torn-down houses, 33:4) with corpses.

**33:7 *rebuild their towns.*** The Heb. leaves the object of "build" unspecified (lit., "as formerly," cf. the NIV). The rebuilding is probably generic, as is the "restoration of fortunes"; cf. 29:14; 30:3).

**33:8 I will . . . forgive all their sins.** God is always the subject of the verb *salakh* [TH5545, ZH6142] ("forgive"; cf. 1 Kgs 8:34; Jer 31:34). The verse employs three of the dominant roots for "sin": *khata'* [TH2398, ZH2627] (miss the goal or way); *'awon* [TH5771, ZH6411] (be perverse), and *pasha'* [TH6586, ZH7321] (make a breach, rebel).

**33:12 shepherds can lead their flocks.** The "shepherds" could refer metaphorically to civil rulers or to leaders generally (23:1-4; Ezek 34:1-6).

**33:15 I will raise up a righteous descendant.** The verb *tsamakh* [TH6779, ZH7541] (piel, "make sprout") recalls the noun *tsemakh* [TH6780, ZH7542] (branch), a metaphor for the coming Messiah (23:5; Zech 3:8; 6:12; and almost certainly Isa 4:2, which some, however, take to refer to land).

**just and right.** The "Branch" (see NLT mg) will do what is just (*mishpat* [TH4941, ZH5477]) and right (*tsedaqah* [TH6666, ZH7407]), words that are often coupled (Ps 89:14; Isa 5:7; Amos 5:24). A duplicate oracle is found in 23:5-6, except that a king rather than a city bears the name of righteousness.

**33:18 offer burnt offerings and grain offerings and sacrifices.** The first two were largely for expressing thanksgiving (Lev 1-2). Sacrifices addressed sins and forgiveness (Lev 4-5).

**33:21 my covenant with my servant David.** See 2 Sam 7:8-16.

**covenant with the Levitical priests.** See Exod 32:27-29; Num 25:10-13; Neh 13:29.

## COMMENTARY

The two promise oracles (33:1-22; 23-26) that round out the expanded Book of Comfort both deal with the now-familiar promises of restoration. Both also emphasize the guarantee attached to them. Listeners to this good news were apparently too stunned to accept the extraordinary announcement that God would do "all the good things I [God] have promised them" (33:14). That statement is a bridging comment on either side of which, according to content, lie two kinds of announcements, the first dealing with resettlement in the land (33:1-13) and the second with the permanency of leaders (33:15-26). For each, the guarantee is God's creative work (33:1, 25), and within each is a summary statement about God (33:11, 16).

Guarantees matter, sometimes because the promise-maker is of dubious character, and sometimes because what is promised seems preposterous. Jeremiah's listeners had little reason to doubt the reliability of the promise-maker, for the threat that God had made through the prophet about the siege was now reality (cf. 32:1-2). The promise was about a situation turned upside down for the better. People understandably found it hard to embrace such a promise when all indicators pointed otherwise. The reality of the present moment was not denied; in fact, it was identified as desperate (33:4-5). To counter the Babylonian siege, the city's people had gone all out, even dismantling their homes to add to the fortifications, or alternatively destroying those near the city walls lest they add to the combustibles. There existed, however, a reality more endangering than an enemy siege. God had withdrawn his protection (33:4; Deut 31:17). In that situation, any promise of good things to come had better carry a weighty warranty.

The warranty for resettlement in the land was the name of Yahweh (33:2). It was the product of his creative and superintending power, whether of the cosmos or of world history (notes, 33:2). The argument is like that of Jeremiah 32, for what was at issue was both God's power and his benevolence. The promises pointed to his benevolent work, which can be summarized as God's wide-ranging restoration (33:7). The details recall Jeremiah 30-31. Ho (1999:180-184) includes in the rhetorical parallelism between Jeremiah 32-33 and Jeremiah 30-31 motifs such as Yahweh as sovereign creator and variations on covenant language; he sees in both segments a flow from judgment to salvation. Some specific correspondences between Jeremiah 33 and 30-31 follow:

1. Healing Jerusalem's wounds, the gashes in the people's psyches as well as in the city's physical structure (33:6; cf. 30:17).
2. Cleansing people from their sins through forgiveness (33:8). The sins of people and leaders (itemized in 7:17-26; 25:3-7; 32:31-35) had precipitated the catastrophe of the Babylonian invasion as a just consequence of their action. But that left the fractured relationship between God and the people unattended. God would now take the initiative in extending forgiveness (cf. Ps 103:3; Mic 7:18; cf. Jer 31:34). To forgive is to remove the offense as the negative factor that destroys cordial relationships.
3. Lavishing on the city all that bespeaks good, so much so that the city, now trampled in defeat by a foreign nation, would blossom to the surprise and awe of the nations (33:9; cf. 31:10).
4. Repopulating a depopulated city (33:10). The mention of animals is in keeping with God's awareness of and care for all his creatures (31:27; cf. Ps 104:17-23; Jonah 4:11).
5. Returning a city to social conviviality (e.g., joys of weddings earlier eliminated 7:34; 16:9; 25:10; 33:10-11a; cf. 31:12-16). God is not negative about parties and socializing.
6. Reinstituting worship (33:11b; cf. 31:6-7).
7. Revitalizing the economy (33:12-13; cf. 31:27-28). God is interested in people's livelihood.

Taken in context, this list comprises the "remarkable secrets" to be disclosed (cf. 33:3). So radical and so comprehensive is the list of transformations that a guarantee is warranted, lest these announcements appear to be merely rhetorical. The guarantee is rooted in creation itself. The doctrine of creation is therefore not only an item of belief as in a creed, but becomes functional in prayer (32:17), in addressing the future (33:6-22), and in obedience. William Carey's sermon, "Expect great things from God; attempt great things for God," based on Jeremiah 33:3, birthed the modern missionary movement.

The second half (33:15-26) shifts from general concern about the city's future to the issues of future leadership and God's covenants. There is concern for the city's well-being, prosperity, and peace. In the section about leadership, the centering realities are God's righteousness (33:16) and fidelity (33:20, 26). The future king from David's line will be devoted to what is just and righteous—to setting things right and to the interior commitment to adhere to what is right. Leaders are obligated to do both, as outlined in an earlier standard for monarchs (22:3; Ps 72:1-2). As world cities today have reputations (cf. New York, Tokyo), so the idealized Jerusalem would have a reputation. It would be known for its chief personality, Yahweh, and for its practice of righteousness (33:16).

The righteousness that characterizes Yahweh consists of fidelity in covenant keeping (33:20-26). Righteousness cannot be divorced from integrity. Both the covenant made to David (2 Sam 7:8-16) and the covenant made to the Levites (Num 25:10-13) were secured by a guarantee consisting of the creative order (33:20, 25). The stability of night following day was invoked as the reason for the continuation of both the Davidic and the priestly lines. It is little wonder that the Qumran community, tapping into the messianic announcement with its mention of the sprouting of the Branch (see note on 33:15), anticipated two Messiahs, a kingly Messiah and a priestly Messiah. They were right to the extent that Jesus the Messiah is both king and priest (Ps 110:4; Heb 7:23-28).

What was said about God's covenant fidelity with an individual (David) and with a group (the Levites) was also true for an entire people, Judah and Israel (33:24-25). God was totally committed to his people (33:26). For that reason, though his discipline may lead some to negative conclusions about God, the truth remains that God is not vacillating, but firm and steady. He accommodates himself to the human weakness of disbelief and spells out guarantees!

## ◆ VII. Rushing Headlong to Destruction (34–39)
### A. The Making and Breaking of a Pact (34:1-22)

King Nebuchadnezzar of Babylon came with all the armies from the kingdoms he ruled, and he fought against Jerusalem and the towns of Judah. At that time this message came to Jeremiah from the LORD: 2"Go to King Zedekiah of Judah, and tell him, 'This is what the LORD, the God of Israel, says: I am about to hand this city over to the king of Babylon, and he will burn it down. 3You will not escape his grasp but will be captured and taken to meet the king of Babylon face to face. Then you will be exiled to Babylon.

4" 'But listen to this promise from the LORD, O Zedekiah, king of Judah. This is what the LORD says: You will not be killed in war 5but will die peacefully. People will burn incense in your memory, just as they did for your ancestors, the kings who preceded you. They will mourn for you, crying, "Alas, our master is dead!" This I have decreed, says the LORD.'"

6So Jeremiah the prophet delivered the message to King Zedekiah of Judah. 7At this time the Babylonian army was besieging Jerusalem, Lachish, and Azekah—the only fortified cities of Judah not yet captured.

8This message came to Jeremiah from the LORD after King Zedekiah made a covenant with the people, proclaiming freedom for the slaves. 9He had ordered all the people to free their Hebrew slaves—both men and women. No one was to keep a fellow Judean in bondage. 10The officials and all the people had obeyed the king's command, 11but later they changed their minds. They took back the men and women they had freed, forcing them to be slaves again.

¹²So the LORD gave them this message through Jeremiah: ¹³"This is what the LORD, the God of Israel, says: I made a covenant with your ancestors long ago when I rescued them from their slavery in Egypt. ¹⁴I told them that every Hebrew slave must be freed after serving six years. But your ancestors paid no attention to me. ¹⁵Recently you repented and did what was right, following my command. You freed your slaves and made a solemn covenant with me in the Temple that bears my name. ¹⁶But now you have shrugged off your oath and defiled my name by taking back the men and women you had freed, forcing them to be slaves once again.

¹⁷"Therefore, this is what the LORD says: Since you have not obeyed me by setting your countrymen free, I will set you free to be destroyed by war, disease, and famine. You will be an object of horror to all the nations of the earth. ¹⁸Because you have broken the terms of our covenant, I will cut you apart just as you cut apart the calf when you walked between its halves to solemnize your vows. ¹⁹Yes, I will cut you apart, whether you are officials of Judah or Jerusalem, court officials, priests, or common people—for you have broken your oath. ²⁰I will give you to your enemies, and they will kill you. Your bodies will be food for the vultures and wild animals.

²¹"I will hand over King Zedekiah of Judah and his officials to the army of the king of Babylon. And although Babylon's king has left Jerusalem for a while, ²²I will call the Babylonian armies back again. They will fight against this city and will capture it and burn it down. I will see to it that all the towns of Judah are destroyed, with no one living there."

## NOTES

**34:1 *King Nebuchadnezzar . . . fought against Jerusalem.*** Nebuchadnezzar (605–562 BC) earlier subjugated Judah (597 BC) and installed King Zedekiah (2 Kgs 24:10-17), who as a disloyal vassal broke covenant (2 Kgs 24:20; Ezek 17:12-16). The Babylonians laid another siege against Jerusalem in 588 BC.

**34:3 *you will be exiled to Babylon.*** Zedekiah had heard a similar message earlier (21:1-10). Cf. 38:17-24, which forms an inclusio with 34:1-7. For a comparison between 34:1-7 and 32:1-5, see Ho (1999:189-194).

**34:5 *[you] will die peacefully.*** This might be in contrast to death in war, or a conditional promise (so Brueggemann 1998:324; cf. Jer 34:4). For his fate, see 39:5-7; 52:11; 2 Kgs 25:4-7.

**34:7 *Lachish, and Azekah.*** Lachish lay twenty-three miles southwest of Jerusalem. Identified as Tell ed-Duweir, it was excavated by James Starkey in 1932–38, and its city-gate complex in 1973 by David Ussishkin. Among the twenty-one ostraca (pottery shards inscribed in black ink) were messages from Hoshaiah, stationed some distance from Lachish, to Yaosh, military commander at Lachish. Part of Lachish Letter IV reads, "we are watching for the [fire] signals of Lachish, according to all the signs which my lord hath given, for we cannot see Azekah." Probably Azekah, eleven miles northeast of Lachish, had already been captured (King 1993:79-84; ANET 321-322).

**34:8 *proclaiming freedom for the slaves.*** Mosaic law called for owners to free their indebted slaves in the seventh year (Deut 15:12-18; cf. Exod 21:1-11). The action may have coincided with a jubilee year (Lev 25:39-46). Anbar (1999) notes a similar release of slaves in a letter from Mari (c. 1765 BC).

**34:10 *obeyed the king's command.*** The Heb. is repetitious. The restating of the command from 34:9 is omitted by the NLT, as is also the phrase "[they] entered into covenant" (cf. NIV; 2 Chr 15:12). For an exhibit of the narrative parallelism of Jer 34 and 35 and the importance of "obey" (*shama'* [TH8085, ZH9048]), see Martens (1987:37-43).

**34:14** *be freed after serving six years.* The NIV and NRSV add, as does the Heb., "every seven years each of you must set free . . ." The slave became legally free at the end of seven years.

**34:17** *I will set you free.* The word play is ironic. God will now free up (*qara' deror,* "call freedom") for destruction those who were to "call freedom" to slaves.

*object of horror.* This connotes an element of fear or shock (cf. Deut 28:25; for the three other occurrences of *zawa'ah* [TH2113, ZH2317] in Jeremiah, see 15:4; 24:9; 29:18).

**34:18** *just as you cut apart the calf.* The ceremony, known also from elsewhere in the ancient Near East, is described in Gen 15:7-21. Halves of an animal or pairs of animals were set across from one another to make an aisle. In walking the aisle, covenant partners committed themselves to observing the terms on pain of forfeiting their lives as had the animals. For other means of ratifying a covenant, see Exod 24:6-8; Num 18:19; 1 Sam 18:1-4.

**34:21** *although Babylon's king has left Jerusalem.* With news of the Egyptians coming to Israel's aid, King Nebuchadnezzar temporarily halted his campaign to deal with Egypt (37:5, 11).

## COMMENTARY

Beginning with Jeremiah 34, five chapters treat themes of disobedience and obedience (Jer 34–35) and royal arrogance and vacillation (Jer 36–38). The two chapters about obedience paint King Zedekiah as opportunistic; for him, obedience was not a high-priority commitment. Circumstance rather than principle determined his course of action. The following chapter about the Recabites depicts a very different group; they would not be dissuaded from following their principles under any circumstances. At the center of Jeremiah 34 is the brief story of keeping or not keeping the covenant (34:8-11, retold in 34:12-16), framed by considerations of the immediate situation (34:1-7) and by a theological assessment (34:17-22).

The historical situation in which King Zedekiah functioned was life-threatening (34:1, 7). Nebuchadnezzar, at whose pleasure he served as puppet king, had tired of this subordinate who courted allies such as Egypt in a move to gain independence. The Babylonian emperor's strategy was to lay siege against Zedekiah and, by defeating him, to gain full control of the land of Israel. In this episode, dated 588 BC, the king had come down the coastal route from the north and taken all the important guard towns except for Lachish and Azekah, both southwest of Jerusalem (see note on 34:7). He intended to subdue all the areas around Jerusalem before marching on the city, not only to eliminate blindsiding attacks from opponents, but so that his full energies could be given to the siege of Jerusalem. Zedekiah faced the battle of his life.

The personal circumstance involved a word from Yahweh through Jeremiah so that Zedekiah would know the outcome, which would be devastating for the city but tolerable for him personally (34:2-5). Zedekiah's leadership was ineffective; he had not been able to stand up to the pro-Egyptian voices. God seemed to take his weakness into account when deciding his fate, for it was less humiliating than that experienced by Jehoiakim, Zedekiah's predecessor (22:18-19). The circumstance of the threatening siege and the prophetic announcement about city and king should have had a sobering effect on the king, enabling him to make right choices.

Instead, Zedekiah's decisions were an example of situational ethics. He would look after his own interests, and the situation would dictate his actions. Initially, he complied with Mosaic legislation and decreed the release of the slaves. His reasons are not stated, but almost certainly Zedekiah, faced with an army too big for him to repulse, sought God's favor. In the crisis, Zedekiah became pious. The story of his choice is framed by the word "burn" (34:2, 22). Perhaps freed slaves would help in the war effort, and with food and water becoming scarce, slave owners would no longer take responsibility for slaves (for assessments of conjectural motivations, see P. Scalise in Keown et al. 1995:187). Obedience to divine law was pragmatically beneficial and easy because it fit into his personal game plan.

Then the threat eased. The siege was not going to intensify, after all; instead, King Nebuchadnezzar was drawn away to deal with an emergency created as the approaching Egyptians under Pharaoh Hophra came to assist Israel. One could have argued (erroneously, as it turned out) that Nebuchadnezzar would be deflected permanently from his purpose. With the threat gone, Zedekiah rescinded his action, broke his promise, and recaptured the freed slaves. This vignette about the king speaks volumes about the spiritual condition of the country and gives divine justification for the harsh judgment that follows.

God did not act situationally but according to his covenant when he appraised Zedekiah's flip-flop action (34:17-22). The real context for the decision was not the danger of the moment but the large span of God's covenant-making activity. Zedekiah's actions were not to be measured by expediency but by God's example. A covenant entails loyalty and commitment, as illustrated by the ritual procedure in making a covenant (see note on 34:18). When a covenant with God is broken, evil consequences follow (as spelled out in detail in Deut 26-28; Lev 26:14-39).

The same principle holds when a covenant between humans is broken. God monitors and enforces covenants. Zedekiah's political maneuverings came under God's examining eye, as did the well-being of slaves as a part of God's passion for justice. Zedekiah operated within a situational ethic and a mindset of power politics. More decisive than politics managed by force is "theo-politics," a God-oriented politics that is ordered by loyalty and truth-speaking. Zedekiah's trivializing of a commitment—his maltreatment of slaves—brought death to his people (34:20), captivity to his commanders (34:21), and a fiery destruction to his cities (34:22). God takes the breaking of an oath with utter seriousness (34:19). Loyalty matters to God, and he comes to the aid of the abused.

◆    ## B. Testing for Obedience (35:1-19)

This is the message the LORD gave Jeremiah when Jehoiakim son of Josiah was king of Judah: ²"Go to the settlement where the families of the Recabites live, and invite them to the LORD's Temple. Take them into one of the inner rooms, and offer them some wine."

³So I went to see Jaazaniah son of Jeremiah and grandson of Habazziniah and all his brothers and sons—representing all

the Recabite families. ⁴I took them to the Temple, and we went into the room assigned to the sons of Hanan son of Igdaliah, a man of God. This room was located next to the one used by the Temple officials, directly above the room of Maaseiah son of Shallum, the Temple gatekeeper.

⁵I set cups and jugs of wine before them and invited them to have a drink, ⁶but they refused. "No," they said, "we don't drink wine, because our ancestor Jehonadab* son of Recab gave us this command: 'You and your descendants must never drink wine. ⁷And do not build houses or plant crops or vineyards, but always live in tents. If you follow these commands, you will live long, good lives in the land.' ⁸So we have obeyed him in all these things. We have never had a drink of wine to this day, nor have our wives, our sons, or our daughters. ⁹We haven't built houses or owned vineyards or farms or planted crops. ¹⁰We have lived in tents and have fully obeyed all the commands of Jehonadab, our ancestor. ¹¹But when King Nebuchadnezzar* of Babylon attacked this country, we were afraid of the Babylonian and Syrian* armies. So we decided to move to Jerusalem. That is why we are here."

¹²Then the LORD gave this message to Jeremiah: ¹³"This is what the LORD of Heaven's Armies, the God of Israel, says:

Go and say to the people in Judah and Jerusalem, 'Come and learn a lesson about how to obey me. ¹⁴The Recabites do not drink wine to this day because their ancestor Jehonadab told them not to. But I have spoken to you again and again, and you refuse to obey me. ¹⁵Time after time I sent you prophets, who told you, "Turn from your wicked ways, and start doing things right. Stop worshiping other gods so that you might live in peace here in the land I have given to you and your ancestors." But you would not listen to me or obey me. ¹⁶The descendants of Jehonadab son of Recab have obeyed their ancestor completely, but you have refused to listen to me.'

¹⁷"Therefore, this is what the LORD God of Heaven's Armies, the God of Israel, says: 'Because you refuse to listen or answer when I call, I will send upon Judah and Jerusalem all the disasters I have threatened.'"

¹⁸Then Jeremiah turned to the Recabites and said, "This is what the LORD of Heaven's Armies, the God of Israel, says: 'You have obeyed your ancestor Jehonadab in every respect, following all his instructions.' ¹⁹Therefore, this is what the LORD of Heaven's Armies, the God of Israel, says: 'Jehonadab son of Recab will always have descendants who serve me.'"

35:6 Hebrew *Jonadab*, a variant spelling of Jehonadab; also in 35:10, 14, 16, 18, 19. See 2 Kgs 10:15.
35:11a Hebrew *Nebuchadrezzar*, a variant spelling of Nebuchadnezzar.   35:11b Or *Chaldean and Aramean*.

NOTES

35:1 *Jehoiakim son of Josiah was king.* Jehoiakim ruled from 609–598 BC. Chapter 35 does not chronologically follow ch 34, which dates from King Zedekiah (597–586 BC); the organization is according to theme.

35:2 *the families of the Recabites.* This semi-nomadic group of Kenite descent (Judg 1:16; 4:11; 1 Chr 2:55) had temporarily settled in Jerusalem as a haven during the war, possibly during the Babylonian invasion of 598–597 BC (cf. 35:6, 10).

35:3 *Jaazaniah son of Jeremiah.* This is not Jeremiah the prophet, who remained unmarried (16:2).

*representing.* While not in the text, this addition makes the most sense of the Heb. "all the house of the Recabites." Alternately, some understand the "house of the Recabites" as a building.

35:4 *the Temple.* Solomon's Temple had three stories of rooms adjoining both long walls, where priestly garments and sacrificial utensils were stored. Some rooms were used by cult functionaries, and some may have been living quarters for priests. Of the names mentioned, nothing more is known. Is this Maaseiah the father of Zephaniah (21:1; 29:25)?

*man of God.* See Deut 33:1 (Moses), 1 Sam 9:6 (Samuel), 1 Chr 8:14 (David), 2 Kgs 1:9 (Elijah), and 2 Kgs 4:7 (Elisha).

**35:6 Jehonadab.** By aligning himself with Jehu (842–815 BC) in the purge of the house of Omri, Jehonadab showed a fanatical political zeal (2 Kgs 10:15-31); in the same spirit, he imposed dietary and lifestyle regulations, possibly in keeping with an earlier desert Israelite ideal (2:1-3). For some fresh proposals regarding the identity of the Recabites (e.g., guild of artisans) and of Jehonadab (householder with servants), see Keown et al. 1995:195-196.

**35:7 plant crops or vineyards.** The Heb. adds, "or own them" (cf. NIV). Cf. their compliance, 35:9.

**35:11 Syrian armies.** The campaign of 597 BC was clearly under Nebuchadnezzar's command, but like the later campaign of 588 BC, it included soldiers from conquered lands (34:1) such as Syria (lit., "Aram"; the LXX has "Assyrian," the Syriac, "Edom").

**35:13 learn a lesson.** This is an apt rendering of "receive instruction" (*laqakh musar* [TH4148, ZH4592]; cf. 17:23; 32:33).

**35:14 you refuse to obey me.** The key word "obey" (*shama'* [TH8085, ZH9048], listen, obey) occurs also in the Heb. at 14b (cf. 35:8, 10, 13, 15, 16, 17, 18). Overall, *shama'* occurs 184 times in 179 verses in Jeremiah. For God's persistence, see 7:25; 25:4; 26:5; 29:19.

**35:19 Jehonadab . . . will always have descendants.** For other personal oracles of salvation, see 45:5b (Baruch) and 39:15-17 (Ebed-melech).

COMMENTARY

From a large-scale scene involving royal politics (Jer 34), the book moves to the story of a family (Jer 35), not because one story follows the other in history but because both stories drive home a similar point. The theme is captured in the invitation, "Come and learn a lesson about how to obey me" (35:13b). The additional twist on the theme of obedience in this family story has to do with testing.

The test has to do with whether or not certain families will comply with ancient instructions not to drink wine. The story is not a lesson on abstinence from alcohol; no judgment is passed on the rightness or wrongness of drinking wine or of owning vineyards. For whatever reason, an ancestor had established a family rule that he and his descendants should not drink wine. Then, as now, foods allowed or disallowed were frequently used as identity markers. At that time, Hebrews were forbidden to eat pork. In modern times, observant Hindus abstain from beef. A Buddhist in Los Angeles sued Taco Bell for mistakenly serving him a taco with meat. His one bite brought on such guilt that he went to a temple in London to get cleansing. Religiously important food is noted in both testaments (cf. Dan 1:8-16; Matt 23:23-26; 1 Cor 8:1-13).

The test as to whether the clan members would adhere to the ancient instructions consisted of several inducements to compromise. The invitation to drink wine came from a source of authority, God's spokesperson, Jeremiah. The invitation was given in the precincts of the Temple, which added another authoritative element to the invitation. The sparkling wine was before them in bowls; cups were furnished. It would have been easy to rationalize that an exception to the rule was warranted in this instance. The test can be compared to Adam and Eve's fruit test (Gen 3). A test of obedience was also administered to King Saul more than once (1 Sam 13:8-14; 15:17-23).

A test may be distinguished from a temptation. The test in itself is neutral; it establishes whether or not a certain course of action will be taken, and presents options without prejudicing the result. A temptation is an enticement to do evil. A test can be given by God (or, as here, his deputy; cf. Gen 22:1; Prov 17:3; Jer 12:3), but God does not tempt anyone (Jas 1:13). Temptation is from Satan and capitalizes on human weakness. Scholars have debated whether or not testing is possible without temptation.

The test of the Recabites' obedience should be read alongside the story of King Zedekiah's action (Jer 34), for both stories are about obedience (they are compared in Martens 1987:37-43; cf. Ho 1999:186-200). The irony of the conclusion cannot be missed. The so-called simple folk obeyed despite a preponderance of reasons to disobey. The king, who should have been a model for the people, brazenly disobeyed. The two stories reinforce a basic principle. Obedience leads to an experience of the good, while disobedience paves the way to disaster. The Recabites obeyed despite a shaky rationale for their beliefs, and they were given a word of promise that their lineage would endure. The contrast between the Recabites and Israel is stark; the nomadic families obeyed fully, while Israel was flagrantly disobedient (35:15). The consequences of the coming disaster (35:17) had already been elaborated in Jeremiah 34 (cf. 34:17b-22). The two chapters illustrate the priority God places on obedience. In the words of another prophet, Samuel, "Obedience is far better than sacrifice" (1 Sam 15:22).

◆     ## C. Despising the Written Word of God (36:1-32)

During the fourth year that Jehoiakim son of Josiah was king in Judah,* the LORD gave this message to Jeremiah: ²"Get a scroll, and write down all my messages against Israel, Judah, and the other nations. Begin with the first message back in the days of Josiah, and write down every message, right up to the present time. ³Perhaps the people of Judah will repent when they hear again all the terrible things I have planned for them. Then I will be able to forgive their sins and wrongdoings."

⁴So Jeremiah sent for Baruch son of Neriah, and as Jeremiah dictated all the prophecies that the LORD had given him, Baruch wrote them on a scroll. ⁵Then Jeremiah said to Baruch, "I am a prisoner here and unable to go to the Temple. ⁶So you go to the Temple on the next day of fasting, and read the messages from the LORD that I have had you write on this scroll. Read them so the people who are there from all over Judah will hear them. ⁷Perhaps even yet they will turn from their evil ways and ask the LORD's forgiveness before it is too late. For the LORD has threatened them with his terrible anger."

⁸Baruch did as Jeremiah told him and read these messages from the LORD to the people at the Temple. ⁹He did this on a day of sacred fasting held in late autumn,* during the fifth year of the reign of Jehoiakim son of Josiah. People from

all over Judah had come to Jerusalem to attend the services at the Temple on that day. ¹⁰Baruch read Jeremiah's words on the scroll to all the people. He stood in front of the Temple room of Gemariah, son of Shaphan the secretary. This room was just off the upper courtyard of the Temple, near the New Gate entrance.

¹¹When Micaiah son of Gemariah and grandson of Shaphan heard the messages from the LORD, ¹²he went down to the secretary's room in the palace where the administrative officials were meeting. Elishama the secretary was there, along with Delaiah son of Shemaiah, Elnathan son of Acbor, Gemariah son of Shaphan, Zedekiah son of Hananiah, and all the other officials. ¹³When Micaiah told them about the messages Baruch was reading to the people, ¹⁴the officials sent Jehudi son of Nethaniah, grandson of Shelemiah and great-grandson of Cushi, to ask Baruch to come and read the messages to them, too. So Baruch took the scroll and went to them. ¹⁵"Sit down and read the scroll to us," the officials said, and Baruch did as they requested.

¹⁶When they heard all the messages, they looked at one another in alarm. "We must tell the king what we have heard," they said to Baruch. ¹⁷"But first, tell us how you got these messages. Did they come directly from Jeremiah?"

¹⁸So Baruch explained, "Jeremiah dictated them, and I wrote them down in ink, word for word, on this scroll."

¹⁹"You and Jeremiah should both hide," the officials told Baruch. "Don't tell anyone where you are!" ²⁰Then the officials left the scroll for safekeeping in the room of Elishama the secretary and went to tell the king what had happened.

²¹The king sent Jehudi to get the scroll. Jehudi brought it from Elishama's room and read it to the king as all his officials stood by. ²²It was late autumn, and the king was in a winterized part of the palace, sitting in front of a fire to keep warm. ²³Each time Jehudi finished reading three or four columns, the king took a knife and cut off that section of the scroll. He then threw it into the fire, section by section, until the whole scroll was burned up. ²⁴Neither the king nor his attendants showed any signs of fear or repentance at what they heard. ²⁵Even when Elnathan, Delaiah, and Gemariah begged the king not to burn the scroll, he wouldn't listen.

²⁶Then the king commanded his son Jerahmeel, Seraiah son of Azriel, and Shelemiah son of Abdeel to arrest Baruch and Jeremiah. But the LORD had hidden them.

²⁷After the king had burned the scroll on which Baruch had written Jeremiah's words, the LORD gave Jeremiah another message. He said, ²⁸"Get another scroll, and write everything again just as you did on the scroll King Jehoiakim burned. ²⁹Then say to the king, 'This is what the LORD says: You burned the scroll because it said the king of Babylon would destroy this land and empty it of people and animals. ³⁰Now this is what the LORD says about King Jehoiakim of Judah: He will have no heirs to sit on the throne of David. His dead body will be thrown out to lie unburied—exposed to the heat of the day and the frost of the night. ³¹I will punish him and his family and his attendants for their sins. I will pour out on them and on all the people of Jerusalem and Judah all the disasters I promised, for they would not listen to my warnings.'"

³²So Jeremiah took another scroll and dictated again to his secretary, Baruch. He wrote everything that had been on the scroll King Jehoiakim had burned in the fire. Only this time he added much more!

36:1 The fourth year of Jehoiakim's reign was 605 BC.  36:9 Hebrew *in the ninth month,* of the ancient Hebrew lunar calendar (also in 36:22). The ninth month in the fifth year of Jehoiakim's reign occurred within the months of November and December 604 BC. Also see note on 1:3.

## NOTES

**36:1** *the fourth year.* In the year 605 BC, the Babylonians defeated the Egyptians at Carchemish. Nebuchadnezzar succeeded his father Nabopolassar as ruler.

**36:2** *Get a scroll.* The scroll was likely made of sewn parchment sheets (leather would not burn readily). Some scrolls measured thirty feet by ten inches. For prophets who wrote, see Isa 8:16; Jer 30:2; Hab 2:2.

*Josiah.* This king (640–609 BC) is noted for the reformation of 622 BC (2 Kgs 22). Jeremiah's evaluation of the reform is not given, nor is it known which parts of the current book date from that era.

**36:4** *Baruch.* The name Baruch (meaning "blessed") and his occupation appear on a bulla (baked clay piece) dating from the period (King 1993:95). His brother Seraiah was Zedekiah's staff officer (51:59).

**36:5** *I am a prisoner here.* The NLT over-translates here (cf. Jeremiah's going into hiding, 36:19). Jeremiah was restrained from moving freely in public, perhaps because of his sermon (Jer 26:1-19), but he was imprisoned only under Zedekiah (37:14).

**36:7** *terrible anger.* Lit., "great anger and wrath"; see 25:15-38.

**36:9** *a day of sacred fasting.* Some prescribed fasts were annual (e.g., the Day of Atonement in early autumn; Lev 16:29, 31; Num 29:7). Four other fasts were observed after the Exile, each to mark disasters in Jewish history, according to the Talmud. Occasional fasts were called to implore God for help (Deut 9:9; 2 Sam 12:16-23; Ezra 8:21-23; cf. Zech 7:5). The emergency (nine months after the command to write a scroll) may be that of Nebuchadnezzar's first southern military sweep in 604 BC and his sack of Ashkelon.

**36:10** *Shaphan.* Shaphan was the king's scribe to whom the discovery of the book of the law was reported (2 Kgs 22:3). Gemariah, one of his three sons (cf. 2 Chr 24:20; Jer 29:3), protested Jehoiakim's burning of the scroll (36:10-12, 25). A clay tablet from that period found in 1982 reads, "belonging to Gemariah, son of Shaphan the scribe" (King 1993:93-95).

*New Gate.* See commentary on 26:10-11.

**36:12** *Elishama . . . Delaiah . . . Elnathan . . . Zedekiah.* For Elishama, possibly of royal descent, see 41:1 (cf. 2 Kgs 25:25). Elnathan was sent to extradite Uriah (26:22). His father Acbor, with Shaphan, Gemariah's father, was involved in finding the scroll in Josiah's time (2 Kgs 22:12). Nothing is known of Delaiah and Zedekiah.

**36:29** *the king of Babylon would destroy this land.* This announcement can be found in 6:1-8 and may have been part of the original scroll.

**36:30** *His dead body will be thrown out.* This was a great disgrace (cf. 8:1-2). For a similar announcement to Jehoiakim, see 22:19.

**36:32** *he added much more!* Lit., "he added many similar words." A likely suggestion is that the first scroll contained material now in 1:4–25:13 (note the ending of 25:13), but not all of it. The three readings of the scroll in one day suggest a shorter scroll.

## COMMENTARY

Once again the prophet and the monarch faced off, but not in person (cf. the many parallels between this account and Jeremiah 37–38, where king and prophet do meet in person; see commentary at Jer 38). Jeremiah's written message was brought before King Jehoiakim. The story could be explored according to its episodes: (1) God's command to Jeremiah (36:1-3); (2) Jeremiah's contract with Baruch (36:4-

7); (3) the first reading at the Temple (36:8-10); (4) the second reading in the secretary's room (36:11-20); (5) the third reading before King Jehoiakim (36:21-26); and (6) the rewriting of the scroll (36:27-32). For the purposes of this discussion, however, I will consider the story in three broad movements, (1) the scroll prepared and read; (2) the scroll destroyed; and (3) the scroll rewritten, with a particular focus on the divinely written word and the people's response to it. Bracke (2000b:57, 59) notes that "word" and "words" occur sixteen times in thirty-two verses, and that there is a shift from "all the people" (36:6, 9, 10) to "all the officials" (36:12).

**The Scroll Is Read (36:1-20).** Who was the listening audience? Perhaps Jehoiakim was the intended audience. This king was ill-disposed to the prophet who exposed his wrong-doings (22:13-19). But Jeremiah, though he addressed individual political and religious rulers (e.g., 28:5), was intent on turning the entire people toward God (cf. 7:1-15). His letter was not written for a single person or a particular group but for all of Israel and Judah, and in keeping with his commission, for other nations as well (36:2; cf. 1:10; chs 46–51). God clearly held his chosen people accountable, but other nations were also in his purview and needed to account for themselves. Jeremiah's parish was the world.

Jeremiah's work was banned and he was forced to go underground. His written book, at least in part, was an oblique illustration of the principle that good things can come out of adversity. Some of Paul's Epistles were written from prison, and readers of Jeremiah are similarly able to benefit from the circumstances of his persecution.

The scroll had a double function. Since it was the written form of all the messages that Jeremiah had given orally, the scroll became a record of God's spoken word and of God's self-disclosure. In it, we learn of God's expectations, his justice, and his solicitude. The scroll's message was also to bring salvation to the people. "The scroll is not designed to give information, nor even to make an argument, but it is to authorize, energize, and evoke a transformed life that will avoid and deter the coming evil" (Brueggemann 1998:346). The people were called to change, to repent, and so to be saved (36:3, 7). Israel's "sins and wrongdoings" (36:3), which are detailed elsewhere (2:11-13; 7:9; 9:3-6; 16:11-12), had always been at issue. God takes no pleasure in punishment (Ezek 33:11), but his righteousness cannot be compromised. His anger against evil is the natural consequence of his righteous dealing with sin (36:7). The good news is that God will forgive, and no longer hold the sinners hostage. The one condition is that to be forgiven, sinners must humble themselves and repent. In this instance, the written word was intended to move a sinful people to repentance.

The first readings of the scroll registered a remarkable impact. Both the time of reading (a fast day appropriate for repentance; cf. Isa 58:5-7) and the place of reading (the Temple) underscored the seriousness of the message. The reaction of the general public is not reported. Micaiah, quite possibly a younger person, became a key figure in relaying the message to administrative officials (36:11-15), who forwarded the news to the king. Reading the scroll induced a sense of terror (36:16) in the administrative officials, which led to further inquiry on their part (36:17). They became concerned for the preservation of the book and its author (36:19-20) and also wanted to pass the message along (36:20b). Much of Israel's evil was systemic, which meant that those in power held the keys to needed change.

**The Scroll Is Destroyed (36:21-26).** The king's action of systematically destroying the written scroll was reprehensible. Josiah tore his clothes in penitence upon hearing the reading of the discovered scroll (2 Kgs 22:11), but Jehoiakim, upon listening to God's word, remained unmoved. His action was the more brazen when compared to the receptivity of his subordinates. They sensed the rightness of the message and were afraid. This king had no fear (*pakhad* [TH6342, ZH7064] 36:24; the identical word is used in 36:16). He ignored the urgings of his officials (36:25) and would not even listen to those closest to him. Jehoiakim displayed the arrogance that goes with a pretension of total autonomy. He acted as though he were not accountable to anyone.

Civility alone would dictate that he raise some questions or satisfy himself on a point as did his subordinates (36:17). His body language spoke louder than words his utter disregard for Yahweh. Should there be any doubt about his depravity, he proceeded to order the arrest of the messengers (cf. his cruelty to Uriah, 26:20-23). By his non-listening, he sealed his doom and that of the nation. Tyrants through the ages have had the mistaken idea that by silencing the messengers of God's judgment, they were putting themselves out of harm's way. In the end, the king personified a trait that Jeremiah had repeatedly identified in the people generally: he refused to listen (cf. 35:14).

**The Scroll Is Rewritten (36:27-32).** Evil persons cannot silence or thwart God's message. Arrogant kings cannot stifle God's word. God makes a way for his message to be heard against all odds. The scroll was rewritten and the ominous note of judgment was not removed but rather was intensified. Sinners must know that their deliberate rejection of God's offer of repentance carried a tragic consequence (cf. 36:3, 7). Jehoiakim was robbed of a legacy and of a personal future, and he would die in disgrace (36:30; cf. 22:18-19). In addition to the judgment on the intransigent wicked, the consequences would be felt by their children (36:31). Leaders that failed to comply with God's ways bore the additional responsibility of burdening their followers with repeated disasters. The eternal laws of a righteous God would not be controverted, certainly not by a king with pretensions to immunity from those laws. The rewritten scroll stated even more clearly than the first that rebellion pays tragic dividends.

Jeremiah's persistence in confronting the king is a telling illustration of the role of prophets in confronting governmental powers. Elijah stood up to Ahab, Nathan to David, and John the Baptist to King Herod. None of these left written documents. Jeremiah confronted the royal powers in person, and when denied access, he still found ways to transmit God's message.

God's persistence in addressing a people who so often spurned him carries a strong message of grace. God did not withdraw even when Jehoiakim defiantly burned the scroll. God's word—both of judgment and of grace—cannot be eradicated.

### ◆ D. A King Inquires of a Prophet (37:1-21)

Zedekiah son of Josiah succeeded Jehoiachin* son of Jehoiakim as the king of Judah. He was appointed by King Nebuchadnezzar* of Babylon. ²But neither King Zedekiah nor his attendants nor the people who were left in the land listened to what the LORD said through Jeremiah.

³Nevertheless, King Zedekiah sent Jehucal son of Shelemiah, and Zephaniah the priest, son of Maaseiah, to ask Jeremiah, "Please pray to the LORD our God for us." ⁴Jeremiah had not yet been imprisoned, so he could come and go among the people as he pleased.

⁵At this time the army of Pharaoh Hophra* of Egypt appeared at the southern border of Judah. When the Babylonian* army heard about it, they withdrew from their siege of Jerusalem.

⁶Then the LORD gave this message to Jeremiah: ⁷"This is what the LORD, the God of Israel, says: The king of Judah sent you to ask me what is going to happen. Tell him, 'Pharaoh's army is about to return to Egypt, though he came here to help you. ⁸Then the Babylonians* will come back and capture this city and burn it to the ground.'

⁹"This is what the LORD says: Do not fool yourselves into thinking that the Babylonians are gone for good. They aren't! ¹⁰Even if you were to destroy the entire Babylonian army, leaving only a handful of wounded survivors, they would still stagger from their tents and burn this city to the ground!"

¹¹When the Babylonian army left Jerusalem because of Pharaoh's approaching army, ¹²Jeremiah started to leave the city on his way to the territory of Benjamin, to claim his share of the property among his relatives there.* ¹³But as he was walking through the Benjamin Gate, a sentry arrested him and said, "You are defecting to the Babylonians!" The sentry making the arrest was Irijah son of Shelemiah, grandson of Hananiah.

¹⁴"That's not true!" Jeremiah protested. "I had no intention of doing any such thing." But Irijah wouldn't listen, and he took Jeremiah before the officials. ¹⁵They were furious with Jeremiah and had him flogged and imprisoned in the house of Jonathan the secretary. Jonathan's house had been converted into a prison. ¹⁶Jeremiah was put into a dungeon cell, where he remained for many days.

¹⁷Later King Zedekiah secretly requested that Jeremiah come to the palace, where the king asked him, "Do you have any messages from the LORD?"

"Yes, I do!" said Jeremiah. "You will be defeated by the king of Babylon."

¹⁸Then Jeremiah asked the king, "What crime have I committed? What have I done against you, your attendants, or the people that I should be imprisoned like this? ¹⁹Where are your prophets now who told you the king of Babylon would not attack you or this land? ²⁰Listen, my lord the king, I beg you. Don't send me back to the dungeon in the house of Jonathan the secretary, for I will die there."

²¹So King Zedekiah commanded that Jeremiah not be returned to the dungeon. Instead, he was imprisoned in the courtyard of the guard in the royal palace. The king also commanded that Jeremiah be given a loaf of fresh bread every day as long as there was any left in the city. So Jeremiah was put in the palace prison.

37:1a Hebrew *Coniah,* a variant spelling of Jehoiachin.  37:1b Hebrew *Nebuchadrezzar,* a variant spelling of Nebuchadnezzar.  37:5a Hebrew *army of Pharaoh;* see 44:30.  37:5b Or *Chaldean;* also in 37:10, 11.  37:8 Or *Chaldeans;* also in 37:9, 13.  37:12 Hebrew *to separate from there in the midst of the people.*

## NOTES

**37:1** *Zedekiah . . . succeeded Jehoiachin.* Jehoiachin, son of Jehoiakim, ruled for only three months, from December 598 to March 597 BC. Nebuchadnezzar removed him to Babylon and appointed Zedekiah, Jehoiakim's brother (i.e., Jehoiachin's uncle), as a puppet king (2 Kgs 24:17).

**37:2** *the people who were left in the land.* These were the people who remained after the removal of craftsmen and other elite in 597 BC (29:2). For various understandings of 'am ha'arets (people of the land), whether people of the country, a disparaging term, landowners, or people in general, see the bibliography in Huey (1993:328n42).

**37:3** *Jehucal . . . and Zephaniah.* The priest Zephaniah had been part of an earlier delegation (21:1-7) and is mentioned in 29:25, 29; 52:24. Jehucal (a variant of Jucal) was not well disposed toward the prophet (38:1, 4).

**37:5** *Pharaoh Hophra.* Hophra (589–570 BC) was known to the Greeks as Apries. Judah's King Zedekiah had courted Egypt as an ally (37:7) to help him against the Babylonians to whom he was legally subject. Jeremiah had counseled against such an alliance and urged submission to Babylon (21:8-10).

**37:7** *to ask me what is going to happen.* The NLT supplies a direct object for "ask." The "episodic parallelism" between Zedekiah's inquiry of Jeremiah (Jer 37–38) and Hezekiah's inquiry of Isaiah (2 Kgs 18–19) has been explored by Ho (1999:215-218).

**37:12** *his share of the property among his relatives.* This is not the property sold by Hanamel (Jer 32) when Jeremiah was incarcerated. Here he is free. Chronologically, Jer 37 precedes Jer 32 (see Huey 1993:328-29).

**37:14** *Irijah wouldn't listen.* Nothing more is known about him. His mindset was that of his colleagues (37:2).

**37:16** *dungeon cell.* This is the first of several imprisonments (cf. "courtyard of the guard," 37:21; "cistern," 38:6; and "courtyard of the guard," 38:13. For his eventual release, see 39:14).

**37:18** *What crime have I committed?* According to Irijah, the "crime committed" (khata' [TH2398, ZH2627], "sin") was treason (37:13; 38:4). Some Judeans had defected to Babylon (38:19; 52:15).

## COMMENTARY

Chapters 37 and 38 interweave the stories of King Zedekiah and the prophet Jeremiah prior to the final siege. While the stories include some minor characters (Zephaniah, Jucal, Irijah), the cast consists of three major characters, the king, God and the prophet. King Zedekiah is depicted as vacillating and pretentiously pious. The prophet was misunderstood, harassed, and even imprisoned. God spoke a consistent message about Babylon's prevailing in the upcoming conflict.

**King Zedekiah.**    Zedekiah, a vassal of Nebuchadnezzar of Babylon, was expected to show loyalty to his foreign overlord. But King Zedekiah, apparently pressured by his advisors, sought military help from Egypt in a bid for political independence. The narrative fast-forwards to Nebuchadnezzar's reprisal in what would be the final siege of Jerusalem, beginning in 588 BC. It appeared for a moment that Zedekiah's political move would gain him reprieve, for Pharaoh Hophra of Egypt marshaled an army and was en route to Jerusalem to help the embattled Judean king. To combat the advancing Egyptian army, King Nebuchadnezzar temporarily abandoned his siege on Jerusalem in the summer of 588 BC. For whatever reason, the Egyptians turned back, and Israel's hoped-for help from Egypt never materialized.

For most of his reign, the king had been torn between two courses of action. One proposal was for him to turn to Egypt for military help. Another, urged by Jeremiah, was to make his peace with Nebuchadnezzar and submit to Babylon. The narrator characterizes him and his officials as not listening to the Lord (37:2). "'Listening' is to acknowledge that Yahweh and the torah tradition provide the dominant clues to life and to power" (Brueggemann 1998:354). Although King Zedekiah chose the Egyptian option, he wanted to keep his other options open. As he had done earlier, so now he sent a delegation inviting Jeremiah to pray to God for him (37:3; cf. 21:1-2).

Zedekiah suddenly turned pious, a move typical of him (cf. his release of slaves during this time [34:8-9] and his later secret inquiry about a message from the Lord, [37:17]). Zedekiah kept his piety secret because he wanted to avoid public association with the prophet (cf. Nicodemus, John 3:1), but he was not wholly unsympathetic to Jeremiah because he responded favorably to Jeremiah's request for better quarters and commanded that he be provided with food (37:20-21).

In the end, the portrait is of a man who knew in his heart what was right but was not sufficiently strong in standing up to contrary pressures. Jeremiah's argument was hard to refute since his message about the Babylonian attack had become a reality (37:19). Zedekiah was vacillating and non-listening (37:2), as was Judah. "A tragic sameness [non-listening] seems to afflict Judah from one generation to another" (Keown et al. 1995:218).

**God.** In this story, God shows himself to be communicative, consistent, and caring. For Zedekiah, he had the straightforward message that the Babylonians would see to his downfall and that of the city of Jerusalem (37:7-10, 17b). The message was not new, and Zedekiah had heard it before (21:3-7). Nor was the message ambiguous. Just as he had been informed earlier that resistance would be useless, so now in graphic terms Zedekiah learned that God's judging word was unalterable— even a handful of wounded Babylonian soldiers would be sufficient to execute God's decree and to burn the city to the ground. God was consistent in his message. As Jeremiah had learned at the potter's shed, God's decree of judgment stood unless there were a change of heart (18:6-8). Clearly there was no change of heart on the part of the king, the leaders, or the people (37:2).

God was also patient and longsuffering, and, despite the king's pretentious piety, God answered him not once but twice (37:7-10, 17). Clearly, God gave Zedekiah ample opportunity to change his course of action. God's generosity in responding repeatedly to the vacillating king left the king without excuse. This forbearance vindicated God when the judgment finally fell.

**Jeremiah.** The prophet is portrayed as the faithful and courageous proclaimer of the divine message, despite inconvenience and hardship. He was misunderstood and misjudged by the sentry Irijah and by the officials (and quite possibly by the people generally) as a treasonous deserter to the Babylonians (37:13-16; cf. 38:4). Jeremiah's message, which called for submission to the Babylonians, could easily be interpreted as treasonous. The irony was that a people that very much wanted safety and well-being turned in anger against the messenger who promised them these things.

It is not uncommon for God's messengers to be misunderstood—Jesus faced the same dilemma. Jeremiah was a prophet of enormous courage who stood his ground, even when it meant imprisonment. Like Jesus, Jeremiah was interrogated by the authorities and flogged, even though he was innocent (37:15). Persons who are harassed or persecuted can and perhaps should appeal to reason or seek protection under the law (37:18-19; cf. Paul's action, Acts 22:25-27). Jeremiah pressed his case with King Zedekiah by noting that his word about the Babylonian advance and siege had come true, whereas the soothing words of the competing prophets had proven to be false (37:19). He appealed to the humanitarian instincts of the king by requesting that he be given better treatment (37:20). Jeremiah was misunderstood, but he did not retreat into inactivity.

## ◆ E. A Divine Ultimatum (38:1-28)

Now Shephatiah son of Mattan, Gedaliah son of Pashhur, Jehucal* son of Shelemiah, and Pashhur son of Malkijah heard what Jeremiah had been telling the people. He had been saying, 2"This is what the LORD says: 'Everyone who stays in Jerusalem will die from war, famine, or disease, but those who surrender to the Babylonians* will live. Their reward will be life. They will live!' 3The LORD also says: 'The city of Jerusalem will certainly be handed over to the army of the king of Babylon, who will capture it.'"

4So these officials went to the king and said, "Sir, this man must die! That kind of talk will undermine the morale of the few fighting men we have left, as well as that of all the people. This man is a traitor!"

5King Zedekiah agreed. "All right," he said. "Do as you like. I can't stop you."

6So the officials took Jeremiah from his cell and lowered him by ropes into an empty cistern in the prison yard. It belonged to Malkijah, a member of the royal family. There was no water in the cistern, but there was a thick layer of mud at the bottom, and Jeremiah sank down into it.

7But Ebed-melech the Ethiopian,* an important court official, heard that Jeremiah was in the cistern. At that time the king was holding court at the Benjamin Gate, 8so Ebed-melech rushed from the palace to speak with him. 9"My lord the king," he said, "these men have done a very evil thing in putting Jeremiah the prophet into the cistern. He will soon die of hunger, for almost all the bread in the city is gone."

10So the king told Ebed-melech, "Take thirty of my men with you, and pull Jeremiah out of the cistern before he dies."

11So Ebed-melech took the men with him and went to a room in the palace beneath the treasury, where he found some old rags and discarded clothing. He carried these to the cistern and lowered them to Jeremiah on a rope. 12Ebed-melech called down to Jeremiah, "Put these rags under your armpits to protect you from the ropes." Then when Jeremiah was ready, 13they pulled him out. So Jeremiah was returned to the courtyard of the guard—the palace prison—where he remained.

14One day King Zedekiah sent for Jeremiah and had him brought to the third entrance of the LORD's Temple. "I want to ask you something," the king said. "And don't try to hide the truth."

¹⁵Jeremiah said, "If I tell you the truth, you will kill me. And if I give you advice, you won't listen to me anyway."

¹⁶So King Zedekiah secretly promised him, "As surely as the LORD our Creator lives, I will not kill you or hand you over to the men who want you dead."

¹⁷Then Jeremiah said to Zedekiah, "This is what the LORD God of Heaven's Armies, the God of Israel, says: 'If you surrender to the Babylonian officers, you and your family will live, and the city will not be burned down. ¹⁸But if you refuse to surrender, you will not escape! This city will be handed over to the Babylonians, and they will burn it to the ground.'"

¹⁹"But I am afraid to surrender," the king said, "for the Babylonians may hand me over to the Judeans who have defected to them. And who knows what they will do to me!"

²⁰Jeremiah replied, "You won't be handed over to them if you choose to obey the LORD. Your life will be spared, and all will go well for you. ²¹But if you refuse to surrender, this is what the LORD has revealed to me: ²²All the women left in your palace will be brought out and given to the officers of the Babylonian army. Then the women will taunt you, saying,

'What fine friends you have!
   They have betrayed and misled you.
When your feet sank in the mud,
   they left you to your fate!'

²³All your wives and children will be led out to the Babylonians, and you will not escape. You will be seized by the king of Babylon, and this city will be burned down."

²⁴Then Zedekiah said to Jeremiah, "Don't tell anyone you told me this, or you will die! ²⁵My officials may hear that I spoke to you, and they may say, 'Tell us what you and the king were talking about. If you don't tell us, we will kill you.' ²⁶If this happens, just tell them you begged me not to send you back to Jonathan's dungeon, for fear you would die there."

²⁷Sure enough, it wasn't long before the king's officials came to Jeremiah and asked him why the king had called for him. But Jeremiah followed the king's instructions, and they left without finding out the truth. No one had overheard the conversation between Jeremiah and the king. ²⁸And Jeremiah remained a prisoner in the courtyard of the guard until the day Jerusalem was captured.

38:1 Hebrew *Jucal,* a variant spelling of Jehucal; see 37:3.   38:2 Or *Chaldeans;* also in 38:18, 19, 23.   38:7 Hebrew *the Cushite.*

## NOTES

**38:1** *Shephatiah . . . Gedaliah . . . Jehucal . . . and Pashhur.* Jehucal and Pashhur had been on previous royal delegations sent to interview Jeremiah (21:1; 37:3). For a list of tensions within this and the previous chapter and for a proposed solution of two "voices" within a paratactic arrangement, see Callaway 1999.

**38:2** *war, famine, or disease.* This is a familiar triad of God's agents of judgment (e.g., 14:12; 21:7, 9; 24:10; 27:8). A threefold promise of life follows.

**38:4** *This man is a traitor!* The NLT collapses into the single word, traitor, a longer Heb. description, lit., "this man is not seeking the welfare of this people but instead [their] harm."

**38:5** *I can't stop you.* The LXX, with the reading, "The king was unable to do anything against them," makes this the narrator's comment. The king's speech then ends with, "Do as you like." Cf. Holladay 1989:266.

**38:7 Ebed-melech . . . an important court official.** The word *saris* [TH5631, ZH6247] means "eunuch" but seems to have come more generally to mean "official" (cf. 29:2). Ebed-melech ("servant of the king") came from the Upper Nile region in Africa.

**38:10 thirty of my men.** Other MSS read "three men" (cf. NRSV).

**38:16 As surely as the LORD our Creator lives.** Zedekiah took an oath, lit., "By the life of the Lord who made us as persons."

**38:20 if you choose to obey the LORD.** The Heb. uses the imperative, "Please obey."

**38:22 All the women left in your palace will be brought out.** Cf. the victor Absalom taking his defeated father's harem (2 Sam 16:21-22).

**When your feet sank in the mud.** This was Jeremiah's plight in the cistern into which Zedekiah allowed him to be cast (38:4-6). One receives in kind what one does to others.

COMMENTARY

The saga of Jeremiah's confrontation with Zedekiah and his government continues from chapter 37. The account in chapters 37-38 has parallels with chapter 36. Jehoiakim tried to silence the divine word by burning the written message (Jer 36). Zedekiah's court officials wanted to silence the messenger, the bearer of the divine word (Jer 37-38).

At center stage in chapter 38 is the message about the certainty of the coming catastrophe should Zedekiah fail to heed the Lord's directive (cf. 38:1-3, 21-23). This message drew a mixed, polarized response. The four court officials committed to a pro-Egyptian foreign policy were negative, hostile, and destructive (38:1-6). Ebed-melech, a foreigner, sided with the prophet by rescuing him (38:7-13). King Zedekiah waffled (38:14-28). Jeremiah, the messenger, did not flinch.

**The Patriotic Option (38:1-6).** The message of surrender was hard to accept. Jeremiah's message was not conducive to building military morale or self-respect (38:4). Strong patriots mostly wanted to go it alone. These court officials wanted to be allied with Egypt rather than with Yahweh. They may have reasoned that Yahweh was unconditionally committed to them (cf. the theology of "presence" embraced by the people; 7:4). Moreover, realistic politics virtually dictated strategic alliances (e.g., with Egypt) against an oncoming foe. When these patriots sought the death of the messenger Jeremiah, they had their reasons. The basis for argument was supposedly their self-interest, but they were in error precisely on this point. If Jeremiah's message were true, their self-interest in securing their safety would be met precisely by heeding the divine message. They chose the course frequently adopted by those who prefer not to face the truth, and sought to eliminate the messenger of unacceptable tidings (cf. the Pharisees and Jesus).

**The "Trust God" Option (38:7-13).** Jeremiah's message, while largely unheeded, was nevertheless heard and accepted by a few, such as Ebed-melech (cf. Baruch and Shaphan's family, Jer 45; 36:11). Granted the stance of the officials, Ebed-melech took a large risk in interceding for the prophet before the king. The care and tenderness with which he drew the prophet from the cistern is its own commentary on his embrace of the prophet and his message. Because he trusted God, God brought him to safety (39:18). Presumably, among those who took Jeremiah seriously there were those who defected and turned themselves over to the Babylonians (38:19).

Jeremiah, the harassed prophet and messenger, found deliverance from unexpected quarters (cf. 26:10-19). God had his agents for punishment, such as the Babylonians. He also had his agents of salvation, such as Ebed-melech. God's intervention may be direct, as at the Exodus, but more often his work of deliverance comes through other persons. In this instance, it came through highly-placed government officials (cf. Joseph, Esther). Still, the cost of faithfulness to his mandate was major. (1) Jeremiah was incarcerated in the dungeon of Jonathan's house (37:15-16). (2) He served time in the detention quarters of the guardhouse (37:21). (3) He was cast into the partly dry cistern belonging to the king's son (38:6). (4) He was returned to the guard house (38:13) before being released by the Babylonians to stay with Gedaliah (39:14).

**The Waffling Option (38:14-28).** The most striking—and tragic—figure in the narrative is King Zedekiah. Though a king, he was weak-willed and indecisive. He capitulated to the requests of his officials regarding Jeremiah. Rather than ruling, he was being ruled.

The king also lacked the resolve to obey the divine word. The ultimatum—surrender and live, or refuse and suffer the negative consequences for himself and the city—could not have been clearer. This message about surrender to the Babylonians cut across the conventional human wisdom that in times of threat insists upon escalating military preparations, strategy, and mobilization. Jeremiah's message moved against any notion of human self-sufficiency. The message called for a humble acceptance of the divine terms, but Zedekiah feared the pro-Egyptian faction in his government. He also feared that surrender to the Babylonians might mean his countrymen would give him a beating. Defeated kings often faced torture and then death (1 Sam 15:33). Jeremiah's assurances that surrender to the Babylonians would mean that his life would be spared were insufficient to change his mind (38:20). Failure to heed Jeremiah meant death by war, famine, and disease for his people (38:2, 18, 21-23). Zedekiah's behavior raises the perplexing question—why do people disobey God when so many good reasons exist for them to obey? Zedekiah was not totally disinclined to go God's way, but his failure to decide ultimately defined his decision: he remained a committed waffler.

**A Non-compromising Prophet (38:14-28).** The pressure for Jeremiah to compromise his message in the one-on-one meeting with the king was no doubt intensified by the prospect that a reassuring message would put him in the good graces of the king and likely issue in his freedom. Nevertheless, the prophet gave no other message than the one God had given him from the beginning: "The city will be handed over to the Babylonians" (38:18; for similar wording cf. 34:2; 38:3). Jeremiah's action following the interview may raise a question about his courage or about his truth-telling. The king intended to spare Jeremiah's life and give him a way out should the officials ask him about the interview. Jeremiah's answer to those inquiring was to repeat the king's instruction. Did his action endorse a view that one can shade the truth when a life (Jeremiah's own and/or the king's) was at stake? Was this an instance of a moral dilemma in which it was best to choose the lesser of two evils? Or is one to conclude that for all his moral strength the prophet was human and failed in truth-telling? Jeremiah's courage throughout means that he should be given the benefit of the doubt in this ethical dilemma. Things are not always black and white.

> The torture and suffering of Jeremiah—a passion story of its own—invites comparison with that great passion story of Jesus Christ in the New Testament. Both Jesus and Jeremiah made Jerusalem a teaching center. Both were perceived as preaching against the Temple. Each was opposed by religious leaders. Both Jeremiah and Jesus carried their messages before political magistrates. Both were tortured. While sympathetic to God's spokesman, Pilate, like Zedekiah, was caught between the innocent prisoner and the pressure of officials. A striking contrast is that while in Jeremiah's story the guilty were put to death and the innocent were vindicated, in the story of Jesus the innocent one was put to death so that the guilty might be vindicated (justified) (adapted from Martens 1986:230-231).

◆   F. Jerusalem Falls (39:1-18)

In January* of the ninth year of King Zedekiah's reign, King Nebuchadnezzar* came with his army to besiege Jerusalem. ²Two and a half years later, on July 18* in the eleventh year of Zedekiah's reign, the Babylonians broke through the wall, and the city fell. ³All the officers of the Babylonian army came in and sat in triumph at the Middle Gate: Nergal-sharezer of Samgar, and Nebo-sarsekim,* a chief officer, and Nergal-sharezer, the king's adviser, and all the other officers.

⁴When King Zedekiah and all the soldiers saw that the Babylonians had broken into the city, they fled. They waited for nightfall and then slipped through the gate between the two walls behind the king's garden and headed toward the Jordan Valley.*

⁵But the Babylonian* troops chased the king and caught him on the plains of Jericho. They took him to King Nebuchadnezzar of Babylon, who was at Riblah in the land of Hamath. There the king of Babylon pronounced judgment upon Zedekiah. ⁶He made Zedekiah watch as they slaughtered his sons and all the nobles of Judah. ⁷Then they gouged out Zedekiah's eyes, bound him in bronze chains, and led him away to Babylon.

⁸Meanwhile, the Babylonians burned Jerusalem, including the palace, and tore down the walls of the city. ⁹Then Nebuzaradan, the captain of the guard, sent to Babylon the rest of the people who remained in the city as well as those who had defected to him. ¹⁰But Nebuzaradan left a few of the poorest people in Judah, and he assigned them vineyards and fields to care for.

¹¹King Nebuchadnezzar had told Nebuzaradan, the captain of the guard, to find Jeremiah. ¹²"See that he isn't hurt," he said. "Look after him well, and give him anything he wants." ¹³So Nebuzaradan, the captain of the guard; Nebushazban, a chief officer; Nergal-sharezer, the king's adviser; and the other officers of Babylon's king ¹⁴sent messengers to bring Jeremiah out of the prison. They put him under the care of Gedaliah son of Ahikam and grandson of Shaphan, who took him

back to his home. So Jeremiah stayed in Judah among his own people.

¹⁵The LORD had given the following message to Jeremiah while he was still in prison: ¹⁶"Say to Ebed-melech the Ethiopian,* 'This is what the LORD of Heaven's Armies, the God of Israel, says: I will do to this city everything I have threatened. I will send disaster, not prosperity. You will see its destruction, ¹⁷but I will rescue you from those you fear so much. ¹⁸Because you trusted me, I will give you your life as a reward. I will rescue you and keep you safe. I, the LORD, have spoken!'"

39:1a Hebrew *in the tenth month*, of the ancient Hebrew lunar calendar. A number of events in Jeremiah can be cross-checked with dates in surviving Babylonian records and related accurately to our modern calendar. This event occurred on January 15, 588 BC.; see 52:4a and the note there.    39:1b Hebrew *Nebuchadrezzar*, a variant spelling of Nebuchadnezzar; also in 39:11.    39:2 Hebrew *On the ninth day of the fourth month*. This day was July 18, 586 BC.; also see note on 39:1a.    39:3 Or *Nergal-sharezer, Samgar-nebo, Sarsekim*.    39:4 Hebrew *the Arabah*.    39:5 Or *Chaldean;* similarly in 39:8.    39:16 Hebrew *the Cushite*.

NOTES

**39:1** *Nebuchadnezzar came with his army to besiege Jerusalem.* The provocation was Zedekiah's rebellion (2 Kgs 25:1). An earlier siege in December 598–March 597 BC resulted in the deportation of King Jehoiachin and the elite (2 Kgs 24:10-17; 2 Chr 36:8-10; Jer 29:1-2).

**39:3** *Samgar.* This is a district in Babylon.

*Nergal-sharezer, the king's adviser.* It is likely that he later succeeded to the Babylonian throne (560 BC). The list in this verse may designate names of persons only (cf. KJV), or mostly (so NLT), or it may include titles and places.

**39:5** *Riblah.* This town, about 200 miles north of Jerusalem on the Orontes River, was campaign headquarters as it had been earlier for Pharaoh Neco II (2 Kgs 23:31-35).

**39:8** *the Babylonians burned Jerusalem.* This is attested in excavations by archaeologists Naham Avigad (1970) and Yigal Shiloh (1978). Avigad found bronze arrowheads of the so-called "Scythian type" (with triangular fins and a hollow socket) at the base of a north wall defense tower. Shiloh uncovered burnt remains of wooden furnishings and ceiling beams in the southeastern hill area (King 1993:72-76).

*including the palace.* The Heb. specifies both the palace (*beth hammelek* [TH4428, ZH4889]) and the "house of the people" (*beth ha'am* [TH5971A, ZH6639]), possibly the people's meeting place (so King [1993:78] who follows B. Mazar), rather than "houses" (NIV, NRSV, but cf. 52:13).

**39:9** *sent to Babylon the rest of the people who remained in the city.* The Heb. distinguishes three groups, two of which are not readily identified: a remnant, the defectors, and the ones who remained, possibly artisans (cf. 52:15).

**39:12** *Look after him well.* Nebuchadnezzar knew of Jeremiah, possibly through intelligence given by defectors. Or perhaps the king simply gave a general order favorable to all Babylonian sympathizers.

**39:13** *Nebuzaradan . . . Nebushazban . . . Nergal-sharezer.* This delegation was unusually ostentatious (cf. 39:3).

*Gedaliah.* First mentioned here, he would later be a significant administrator (cf. Jer 40–41).

**39:18** *and keep you safe.* Lit., "you will not fall by the sword."

COMMENTARY

The denouement of the story, which has been so long in building, comes in this chapter. The city was taken and burned (39:1-3, 8; cf. 2 Kgs 25:1-21; Jer 52:3-27).

The king was captured and his sons killed (39:4-7). Some people were spared, and some were sent off (39:9-10). Good news came to two individuals, Jeremiah (39:11-14) and Ebed-melech (39:15-18). The chapter is dominated by a matter-of-fact narrative without interpretation. It ends with two quotations, one from Nebuchadnezzar and one from Yahweh. Especially when read in the larger context, this story gives witness to God's patience and trustworthiness. The chapter layout also highlights a contrast in the matter of trust.

**God's Patience.** God is mentioned only in the final three verses in connection with Ebed-melech, a non-Israelite, but the reader knows that God is the determining factor in the military story about the fall of Jerusalem (39:1-10). If there is a surprise, it is that the disaster has been so long in coming. God's patience is large but not infinite (Exod 34:6-7). Jeremiah had been preaching for more than two decades (25:3-6; cf. 35:15). God waited 120 years in Noah's time before sending the flood (Gen 6:3).

Prior to each of these strategic nodes in Israel's national history—Israel's fall to the Assyrians (722 BC), Jerusalem's conquest by the Babylonians (587 BC), and the destruction of Jerusalem by the Romans (AD 70)—God raised up prophets, Amos and Hosea for the northern kingdom, and Jeremiah, Ezekiel, Habakkuk, and Zephaniah for the southern kingdom. For Second Temple Judaism, there were John the Baptist and Jesus.

Judgment came, but not before God had waited for a long, long time.

**God's Trustworthiness.** The narrative is sparse in military details of the siege. When read in the larger context, it must be understood as reporting events that fulfilled God's threatening word. Jeremiah repeatedly warned that God's agent, the foe from the north (later identified as Nebuchadnezzar the Babylonian), would bring disaster to the city. He would sit in the gates of Jerusalem (1:15; cf. 39:3) and sack the city (6:6; 21:10; 32:24; 33:4-5; 34:2, 22; 37:8-10; 38:17-18), and so it happened (39:1-10). King Zedekiah was given the option of submitting to Babylon and remaining alive, or of resisting and dying (38:17-23). He resisted, and as announced, his fate was brutal (39:4-10; cf. 52:11). The prophet Jeremiah was reassured that God would hedge him about and keep him safe (1:19; 15:20-21). This happened, not through a miraculous intervention, but by the decisions of some highly placed governing officials, chiefly Nebuchadnezzar, king of Babylon, and his subordinate, Nebuzaradan (39:11-14). God may perform a miracle to protect his own (e.g., Daniel), but often he fulfills his purpose through unwitting individuals. Either way, God is a promise-keeper. The promise to Ebed-melech was no doubt given earlier (Holladay 1989:268 relocates the promise after 38:27) but is perhaps placed here to drive home the point that though many officials lost their lives (39:6), this one man Ebed-melech was spared, as promised (39:15-18).

**Trust in God.** The promise to Ebed-melech, may be placed here rather than with the story of his heroism in rescuing Jeremiah (38:7-13) for the purpose of contrast (so Keown et al. 1995:229, following W. Rudolph). Ebed-melech's trust in God

(39:18) was concretely expressed in his request that the king have Jeremiah brought out of the pit and in his own efforts to bring about his release. This act of trust contrasts with the actions of King Zedekiah, who seemed to acknowledge the correctness of Jeremiah's message about submitting to Babylon but failed to act on it. The irony, then, is that an anointed Israelite king was condemned to pain and death because of his failure to trust God, whereas a Gentile from Ethiopia risked his life because he trusted God, and lived through the disaster. God rewards those who seek him in faith (Heb 11:6).

## ◆ VIII. After Catastrophe (40:1–45:5)
## A. Toward Normalcy (40:1–12)

The LORD gave a message to Jeremiah after Nebuzaradan, the captain of the guard, had released him at Ramah. He had found Jeremiah bound in chains among all the other captives of Jerusalem and Judah who were being sent to exile in Babylon.

²The captain of the guard called for Jeremiah and said, "The LORD your God has brought this disaster on this land, ³just as he said he would. For these people have sinned against the LORD and disobeyed him. That is why it happened. ⁴But I am going to take off your chains and let you go. If you want to come with me to Babylon, you are welcome. I will see that you are well cared for. But if you don't want to come, you may stay here. The whole land is before you—go wherever you like. ⁵If you decide to stay, then return to Gedaliah son of Ahikam and grandson of Shaphan. He has been appointed governor of Judah by the king of Babylon. Stay there with the people he rules. But it's up to you; go wherever you like."

Then Nebuzaradan, the captain of the guard, gave Jeremiah some food and money and let him go. ⁶So Jeremiah returned to Gedaliah son of Ahikam at Mizpah, and he lived in Judah with the few who were still left in the land.

⁷The leaders of the Judean guerrilla bands in the countryside heard that the king of Babylon had appointed Gedaliah son of Ahikam as governor over the poor people who were left behind in Judah—the men, women, and children who hadn't been exiled to Babylon. ⁸So they went to see Gedaliah at Mizpah. These included: Ishmael son of Nethaniah, Johanan and Jonathan sons of Kareah, Seraiah son of Tanhumeth, the sons of Ephai the Netophathite, Jezaniah son of the Maacathite, and all their men.

⁹Gedaliah vowed to them that the Babylonians* meant them no harm. "Don't be afraid to serve them. Live in the land and serve the king of Babylon, and all will go well for you," he promised. ¹⁰"As for me, I will stay at Mizpah to represent you before the Babylonians who come to meet with us. Settle in the towns you have taken, and live off the land. Harvest the grapes and summer fruits and olives, and store them away."

¹¹When the Judeans in Moab, Ammon, Edom, and the other nearby countries heard that the king of Babylon had left a few people in Judah and that Gedaliah was the governor, ¹²they began to return to Judah from the places to which they had fled. They stopped at Mizpah to meet with Gedaliah and then went into the Judean countryside to gather a great harvest of grapes and other crops.

40:9 Or *Chaldeans;* also in 40:10.

NOTES

**40:1 *The LORD gave a message to Jeremiah.*** The message is unspecified unless it is the quote from Nebuzaradan (40:2-5a). Others posit editorial lapses.

***Ramah.*** Meaning "height," this hometown of Samuel (1 Sam 2:11; cf. Jer 31:15) lay in the territory of Benjamin a few miles north of Jerusalem. The site is still disputed, but it is possibly Er-Ram or Ramallah.

**40:3 *these people have sinned.*** Nebuzaradan uses the second person plural, "you [people] have sinned" (*khata'them* [TH2398, ZH2627]).

**40:6 *Gedaliah.*** Quite possibly, this is the one referred to on an inscribed stamp seal found at Lachish by James Starkey in 1935, "belonging to *gedhalyahu* [TH1436A, ZH1546], the one over the house" (i.e., royal administrator).

***Mizpah.*** This city was eight miles north of Jerusalem and was likely within miles of Ramah to the west (see 40:1; cf. 1 Sam 7:5-12; 10:17). It was possibly Tel en-Nasbeh.

**40:7 *The leaders of the Judean guerrilla bands.*** Lit., "princes (*sarim* [TH8269, ZH8569]) of the armies" (*khayalim* [TH2428, ZH2657]). Cf. 2 Kgs 25:23-24.

**40:8 *Ishmael.*** Ishmael assassinated Gedaliah (Jer 41). A clay bulla with script from that period reads, "Belonging to Ishmael son of the king." G. Barkay, after detailed study, is convinced that the reference is to Ishmael son of Nethaniah, a member of the royal family (King 1993:99).

***Johanan.*** He later led a group to Egypt (Jer 42).

***Netophathite.*** Netophah was a village near Bethlehem.

**40:9 *Gedaliah vowed to them.*** He swore by means of an oath (niphal of *shaba'* [TH7650, ZH8678], swore).

**40:11 *Moab, Ammon, Edom.*** Moab and Ammon, regions east of the Jordan, and Edom, south of the Dead Sea, were countries to which Judean refugees fled.

COMMENTARY

After Judah fell to the Babylonians, there was a brief return to normalcy. The narrative interweaves the story of the prophet Jeremiah (40:1-6) with the fortunes of the larger political order within Judean society (40:7-12).

At this point, Jeremiah was no longer a prisoner. Ironically, his own people had held him hostage, but a foreign, pagan government had released him to freedom (40:1-6). Nebuzaradan, the official charged by Nebuchadnezzar with post-conquest military and political operations, was given specific instructions to treat Jeremiah favorably. Jeremiah chose to remain in solidarity with his people and so stayed with Gedaliah, which enhanced Gedaliah's prestige and proved that Jeremiah was not a traitor to his people. This second account of the Babylonian handling of the situation (cf. 39:11-14) is best considered as amplifying what transpired before Jeremiah settled in Mizpah. In the confusion following his release from the court prison, Jeremiah may have been mistakenly thrown in with the group bound for exile. Thus freed a second time, his freedom vindicated his message that surrender to the Babylonians would be favorable.

Further vindication for the prophet came in a speech by a Babylonian army officer, Nebuzaradan, who acknowledged that the disaster that had come to Judah had come through the sovereign administration of Yahweh (40:2). As a devotee of the

Babylonian religion, he might have credited his own deity Marduk or his own army. Only God could have given this outsider to the faith such an insight about the source of the disaster, as the opening line of the chapter indicates. Both Nebuzaradan and Jeremiah attributed the disaster to the sin of the people, specifically to their disobedience (40:3; cf. 35:17). It was a Gentile who gave a true interpretation of what had transpired in this critical event in salvation history; a parallel might be the Roman centurion's assertion at Jesus' crucifixion that Jesus was God's Son (Matt 27:54; Mark 15:39). Both army officers became bearers of divine revelation. For such acknowledgments by other non-Israelites, see Genesis 41:38 (Pharaoh) and Daniel 4:34-37 (Nebuchadnezzar).

This section also tells us that the Judean region was given political stability (40:7-12). In a shrewd move, Nebuchadnezzar set Gedaliah, a Judean, to govern the citizens that were too unimportant to be exiled. This man's family had supported Jeremiah. Shaphan, Gedaliah's grandfather, was a key figure in the discovery of the law scroll that touched off Josiah's reforms (2 Kgs 22:12). Ahikam, his father, had spoken on behalf of the prophet at the time of his arrest (Jer 26:4). The people on the right side of the debate were being rewarded, or so it seemed.

Gedaliah essentially repeated Jeremiah's political line: "Serve the king of Babylon, and all will go well" (40:9; cf. 27:12). Gedaliah challenged the remaining troops to leave the military, become civilians, and contribute to the economy. It seems, as some scholars have argued, that Nebuchadnezzar's chief strategy was to remove King Zedekiah. To be sure, Nebuchadnezzar was interested in gaining political control, but he was not on a rampage to devastate the country. Proof of that assertion is that the returning Judeans were able to harvest an abundant crop by the end of summer (assuming a date of October 588 BC), a point emphasized twice (40:10, 12). The country, it seems, was returning to normal.

◆   ## B. Terrorism at Mizpah (40:13–41:18)

¹³Soon after this, Johanan son of Kareah and the other guerrilla leaders came to Gedaliah at Mizpah. ¹⁴They said to him, "Did you know that Baalis, king of Ammon, has sent Ishmael son of Nethaniah to assassinate you?" But Gedaliah refused to believe them.

¹⁵Later Johanan had a private conference with Gedaliah and volunteered to kill Ishmael secretly. "Why should we let him come and murder you?" Johanan asked. "What will happen then to the Judeans who have returned? Why should the few of us who are still left be scattered and lost?"

¹⁶But Gedaliah said to Johanan, "I forbid you to do any such thing, for you are lying about Ishmael."

## CHAPTER 41

But in midautumn,* Ishmael son of Nethaniah and grandson of Elishama, who was a member of the royal family and had been one of the king's high officials, went to Mizpah with ten men to meet Gedaliah. While they were eating together, ²Ishmael and his ten men suddenly jumped up, drew their swords, and killed Gedaliah, whom the king of Babylon had appointed governor. ³Ishmael also killed all the Judeans and the Babylonian* soldiers who were with Gedaliah at Mizpah.

⁴The next day, before anyone had heard about Gedaliah's murder, ⁵eighty men arrived from Shechem, Shiloh, and Samaria to worship at the Temple of the LORD. They had shaved off their beards, torn their clothes, and cut themselves, and had brought along grain offerings and frankincense. ⁶Ishmael left Mizpah to meet them, weeping as he went. When he reached them, he said, "Oh, come and see what has happened to Gedaliah!"

⁷But as soon as they were all inside the town, Ishmael and his men killed all but ten of them and threw their bodies into a cistern. ⁸The other ten had talked Ishmael into letting them go by promising to bring him their stores of wheat, barley, olive oil, and honey that they had hidden away. ⁹The cistern where Ishmael dumped the bodies of the men he murdered was the large one dug by King Asa when he fortified Mizpah to protect himself against King Baasha of Israel. Ishmael son of Nethaniah filled it with corpses.

¹⁰Then Ishmael made captives of the king's daughters and the other people who had been left under Gedaliah's care in Mizpah by Nebuzaradan, the captain of the guard. Taking them with him, he started back toward the land of Ammon.

¹¹But when Johanan son of Kareah and the other guerrilla leaders heard about Ishmael's crimes, ¹²they took all their men and set out to stop him. They caught up with him at the large pool near Gibeon. ¹³The people Ishmael had captured shouted for joy when they saw Johanan and the other guerrilla leaders. ¹⁴And all the captives from Mizpah escaped and began to help Johanan. ¹⁵Meanwhile, Ishmael and eight of his men escaped from Johanan into the land of Ammon.

¹⁶Then Johanan son of Kareah and the other guerrilla leaders took all the people they had rescued in Gibeon—the soldiers, women, children, and court officials* whom Ishmael had captured after he killed Gedaliah. ¹⁷They took them all to the village of Geruth-kimham near Bethlehem, where they prepared to leave for Egypt. ¹⁸They were afraid of what the Babylonians* would do when they heard that Ishmael had killed Gedaliah, the governor appointed by the Babylonian king.

41:1 Hebrew *in the seventh month*, of the ancient Hebrew lunar calendar. This month occurred within the months of October and November 586 BC; also see note on 39:1a.  41:3 Or *Chaldean.*  41:16 Or *eunuchs.*  41:18 Or *Chaldeans.*

## NOTES

40:14 *Baalis, king of Ammon.* The Ammonites, with Judah, were part of a coalition against Babylon in 594 BC (27:2-3). Jeremiah charged Ammon with aggression (49:1-6). Baalis is otherwise unknown (but cf. Becking 1993).

40:15 *volunteered to kill Ishmael.* The NLT summarizes Johanan's direct speech, "Please let me go and strike Ishmael son of Nethaniah and no one will know it."

41:1 *in midautumn.* Quite possibly, as the NLT assumes, this was the same year that Jerusalem fell, making Gedaliah's tenure short, some three to four months. Others suggest a time much later, to which Nebuchadnezzar's raid of 582 BC was the Babylonian response (cf. Jer 52:30).

41:5 *Shechem, Shiloh, and Samaria.* All these places are north of Jerusalem (Shiloh, eighteen miles; Samaria, forty-two miles) in the previous territory of the Northern Kingdom.

*cut themselves.* This was a cultural rite of mourning (Lev 19:27-28; 21:5; Deut 14:1), in this case, probably for the fall of the city and the Temple.

41:6 *come and see what has happened to Gedaliah!* The Heb. is cryptic: "Come to Gedaliah."

**41:8** *The other ten had talked Ishmael into letting them go.* The Heb. reports direct speech: "Do not kill us, for we have wheat, barley . . . hidden in the fields." Provisions may have been stored back home or buried nearby.

**41:9** *The cistern where Ishmael dumped the bodies.* King Asa (911–870 BC) of the Southern Kingdom braced himself against Baasha's attack from the Northern Kingdom by fortifying Mizpah and securing a water supply (1 Kgs 15:22).

**41:10** *king's daughters.* Their fortunes are detailed in 38:22; 41:16; 43:6. As members of the royal family, they were a symbol of legitimacy (cf. 2 Sam 16:15ff).

**41:12** *at the large pool near Gibeon.* Gibeon was three miles south-southwest of Mizpah. Excavators found a pit thirty-three feet deep with steps cut into the rock. At the bottom was a tunnel, and steps led to the water chamber.

**41:17** *the village of Geruth-kimham.* The name means "lodging place of Kimham," possibly named for the son of Barzillai, King David's friend (2 Sam 19:31-40).

## COMMENTARY

The terrorist activity that struck the remnant community trying to build a life in Mizpah after the destruction of Jerusalem involved three main characters: Gedaliah, the inexperienced governor (40:13-16); Ishmael, the ruthless assassin (41:1-10); and Johanan, the enterprising deliverer (41:11-18). Each of the incidents invites commentary on separate issues.

**Gedaliah.** Gedaliah, the Babylon-appointed governor in Mizpah, was warned by Johanan of a plot against his life (40:13-16). Ishmael, one of the Judean military commanders who with Johanan had accepted Gedaliah's assurances, had joined those remaining in the land. Ishmael had the ear of Baalis, the Ammonite King, who may have feared the nearby Babylonians. He schemed to undermine any Babylonian-imposed government.

Gedaliah refused either to be warned or to take appropriate action for his own protection (40:13-16). His refusal raises a question about his trusting or not trusting his colleagues. Was he too good-natured? In his eagerness to build group unity, was he too naive? Administrators who have a phobia that others are out to destroy them become ineffective. However, those who will not investigate suspicious behavior also stand to lose. Certainly, there are times when it is incumbent on a leader to listen to voices of warning. Gedaliah, for reasons of inexperience and naivete rather than spiritual obstinacy, nevertheless joined a sequence of three persons in the story who refused to listen. The other two were Zedekiah (37:2) and Johanan (43:4; Keown et al. 1995:240-41).

**Ishmael.** Ishmael was the ex-military officer who showed himself capable of a most dastardly act, assassinating his leader, Gedaliah, while dining with him (41:1-10). Ishmael, a strong nationalist, likely saw matters in black and white terms and could not tolerate a situation in which a Judean like Gedaliah would be hand-in-glove with Babylon, Judah's unambiguous enemy. The motives for his vile acts are not given. He may have been a disgruntled member of the royal family who had been snubbed. He may simply have been an unprincipled mercenary. Ishmael

feigned friendship, like Judas the betrayer or like Brutus, the assassin-friend of Jul-
ius Caesar (so Huey 1993:352). He was scheming and brutal, killing not only the
innocent and trusting Gedaliah but seventy devoted persons on their way to worship, an inexplicable action. The tragedy was memorialized by a fast (Zech 7:5;
8:19) and the narrative graphically depicts the subsequent breakdown of the social
order (cf. Judg 19–21). Sociologically, terrorist activity may be explained as characteristic of a society in transition; theologically, terrorism and brutality are but further ugly expressions of sinful human nature.

Ishmael's dastardly action and the death of the innocent raise the question of
God's justice. That a rebellious nation should be punished by conquest can be justified (Jer 39). But that Gedaliah should be struck down while functioning in accord
with God's directive to submit to the Babylonians calls into question God's promise
that things would go well for those who obeyed. That unarmed men, grieving for
the fate of their country on their way to prayer and worship, should be cut down by
a man on a terrorist rampage poses the question, "Why does God allow the innocent to die?" The answers are not in this text, in which God is not mentioned, nor is
it ever fully given in Scripture. Is it possible that acts of terrorism, like those depicted
here and experienced in our own times, are simply the consequence of God's decision to grant to humans the power of choice? How is one to live with the tensions
raised between assertions of faith and tragic events in human experience? Can one
live with the unanswered questions and still live in faith? Any answer must take account of Jesus Christ, who was innocent without question, who fully obeyed God,
and yet who endured brutality and violence.

**Johanan.**    Johanan was the deliverer (41:11-18) who would not let evil prevail. He
mustered the forces, pursued the villain, and reclaimed those captured. Like Abraham pursuing the kings who had captured Lot (Gen 14), Johanan succeeded. One
interpretation might be that God uses good-hearted people to stop evil persons in
their tracks. Yet his action raises the question as to whether there are ever occasions
when individuals are entitled to take the law into their own hands. If acts of violence are almost always followed by further acts of violence, how can violence be a
solution? Does the comment about the fear of the Chaldeans (41:18) indicate that
Johanan's solution, momentarily seen as laudatory, was nonetheless flawed?

Viewed politically rather than theologically, the three men represent the three
options available prior to Jerusalem's fall: submit to the Babylonians (like Jeremiah), resist the enemy, or get help from Egypt. "Gedaliah is a Babylonian ac-
commodator, Ishmael is a fierce actor for resistance and independence, and
Johanan now opts for Egypt" (Brueggemann 1998:385).

◆    ## C. Decision about Leaving for Egypt (42:1–43:7)

Then all the guerrilla leaders, including
Johanan son of Kareah and Jezaniah* son
of Hoshaiah, and all the people, from the
least to the greatest, approached [2]Jere-
miah the prophet. They said, "Please pray
to the LORD your God for us. As you can

see, we are only a tiny remnant compared to what we were before. ³Pray that the LORD your God will show us what to do and where to go."

⁴"All right," Jeremiah replied. "I will pray to the LORD your God, as you have asked, and I will tell you everything he says. I will hide nothing from you."

⁵Then they said to Jeremiah, "May the LORD your God be a faithful witness against us if we refuse to obey whatever he tells us to do! ⁶Whether we like it or not, we will obey the LORD our God to whom we are sending you with our plea. For if we obey him, everything will turn out well for us."

⁷Ten days later the LORD gave his reply to Jeremiah. ⁸So he called for Johanan son of Kareah and the other guerrilla leaders, and for all the people, from the least to the greatest. ⁹He said to them, "You sent me to the LORD, the God of Israel, with your request, and this is his reply: ¹⁰'Stay here in this land. If you do, I will build you up and not tear you down; I will plant you and not uproot you. For I am sorry about all the punishment I have had to bring upon you. ¹¹Do not fear the king of Babylon anymore,' says the LORD. 'For I am with you and will save you and rescue you from his power. ¹²I will be merciful to you by making him kind, so he will let you stay here in your land.'

¹³"But if you refuse to obey the LORD your God, and if you say, 'We will not stay here; ¹⁴instead, we will go to Egypt where we will be free from war, the call to arms, and hunger,' ¹⁵then hear the LORD's message to the remnant of Judah. This is what the LORD of Heaven's Armies, the God of Israel, says: 'If you are determined to go to Egypt and live there, ¹⁶the very war and famine you fear will catch up to you, and you will die there. ¹⁷That is the fate awaiting every one of you who insists on going to live in Egypt. Yes, you will die from war, famine, and disease. None of you will escape the disaster I will bring upon you there.'

¹⁸"This is what the LORD of Heaven's Armies, the God of Israel, says: 'Just as my anger and fury have been poured out on the people of Jerusalem, so they will be poured out on you when you enter Egypt. You will be an object of damnation, horror, cursing, and mockery. And you will never see your homeland again.'

¹⁹"Listen, you remnant of Judah. The LORD has told you: 'Do not go to Egypt!' Don't forget this warning I have given you today. ²⁰For you were not being honest when you sent me to pray to the LORD your God for you. You said, 'Just tell us what the LORD our God says, and we will do it!' ²¹And today I have told you exactly what he said, but you will not obey the LORD your God any better now than you have in the past. ²²So you can be sure that you will die from war, famine, and disease in Egypt, where you insist on going."

## CHAPTER 43

When Jeremiah had finished giving this message from the LORD their God to all the people, ²Azariah son of Hoshaiah and Johanan son of Kareah and all the other proud men said to Jeremiah, "You lie! The LORD our God hasn't forbidden us to go to Egypt! ³Baruch son of Neriah has convinced you to say this, because he wants us to stay here and be killed by the Babylonians* or be carried off into exile."

⁴So Johanan and the other guerrilla leaders and all the people refused to obey the LORD's command to stay in Judah. ⁵Johanan and the other leaders took with them all the people who had returned from the nearby countries to which they had fled. ⁶In the crowd were men, women, and children, the king's daughters, and all those whom Nebuzaradan, the captain of the guard, had left with Gedaliah. The prophet Jeremiah and Baruch were also included. ⁷The people refused to obey the voice of the LORD and went to Egypt, going as far as the city of Tahpanhes.

42:1 Greek version reads *Azariah;* compare 43:2.   43:3 Or *Chaldeans.*

## NOTES

**42:1 *Jezaniah son of Hoshaiah.*** The LXX gives the father's name as Maasaiou (Maaseiah) here and in 43:2, suggesting that Azariah (43:2) was another name for Jezaniah or that the two were brothers.

**42:2 *Please pray to the LORD your God for us.*** The "please" condenses an expansive but respectful request, more lit., "May our petition fall before you" (i.e., meet with your favor). Zedekiah made a similar request (21:2; 37:3) and was also committed to non-listening (37:2; cf. 42:21). He met with disaster, as did the remnant (Keown et al. 1995:248-249).

**42:6 *everything will turn out well for us.*** The petitioners are repeating to Jeremiah the theology they had heard from him (cf. 26:3; Deut 28:2).

**42:10 *I will build you up . . . I will plant you.*** The language echoes details from Jeremiah's call (1:10; cf. 24:6-10; 31:28).

***I am sorry.*** This could also mean "I relent" or "I regret" (see NIV; cf. 18:8, 10; 26:3; Gen 6:6).

**42:11 *I am with you.*** This "divine assistance formula" is also found elsewhere in Jeremiah (e.g., 1:19; Heb. of 15:20; 30:11; 46:28; cf. Gen 28:20; Isa 43:5; Matt 28:20).

**42:12 *he will let you stay here in your land.*** The NLT follows the Syriac and LXX here in repointing the MT *heshib* (hiphil of *shub* [TH7725, ZH8740], "turn," "restore"; cf. NIV, NRSV) as a form derived from *yashab* [TH3427, ZH3782] (stay).

**42:14 *the call to arms.*** Lit., "the sound of the *shophar* [TH7782, ZH8795]." This trumpet-like instrument was used at festivals and in times of war for alerts and rallies.

**42:18 *my anger and fury.*** God's anger and fury were frequent threats prior to Jerusalem's destruction.

***an object of damnation, horror, cursing, and mockery.*** See 19:8; 43:12; Lam 1:15-16.

**42:19 *Don't forget this warning.*** Lit., "Know with certainty [an infinitive absolute combined with a verb in the imperfect is emphatic] that I have testified against you." "Testified" (hiphil of *'udh* [TH5749A, ZH6387]) has the same root as "witness" (*'edh* [TH5707, ZH6332], 42:5).

**42:20 *you were not being honest.*** Lit., "You were wandering in your souls." The meaning of this idiom is similar to the English "You did not level with me."

**42:22 *you can be sure.*** The verbal construction emphasizing certainty is identical to that of 42:19 (the NLT has, "Don't forget . . .").

**43:2 *You lie!*** The people hurl an accusation often on Jeremiah's lips (8:8; 9:4; 14:14; 23:25-26; 28:15). They claim that God had not said, "Do not go to Egypt to settle there." They quote the first part of the Lord's speech of 42:19 precisely except that they substitute *lo'* [TH3808, ZH4202] (permanent prohibition) for *'al* [TH408, ZH440] (circumstantial prohibition).

**43:3 *Baruch son of Neriah has convinced you.*** The term *suth* [TH5496, ZH6077] has connotations of "allure" and "incite," which are stronger than "convince." For a proposal that Baruch is a "character in the text" and a "key to the canonizing process" of the book, see Brueggemann (1994:405-420).

**43:7 *Tahpanhes.*** This Egyptian border fortress is in the East Delta region of the Nile.

## COMMENTARY

This segment of the narrative describes a decision-making process by leaders. It consists of an appeal by the remnant for Jeremiah to pray for guidance (42:1-6), a report of Yahweh's answer (42:7-18), Jeremiah's personal exhortation (42:19-22), the remnant's verbal response (43:1-3), and a report of the remnant's departure to Egypt (43:4-7).

**Praying for Guidance (42:1-6).**   Johanan and his impromptu militia, together with those recaptured from Ishmael, were encamped near Bethlehem and headed towards Egypt (41:17). The group, along with the two guerrilla leaders, Johanan and Jezaniah, paused to reconsider their decision. Because of uncertainty, or perhaps because of divided opinions in the camp, they agreed to ask for divine guidance. Usually priests gave answers, sometimes with the use of the Urim and Thummim, especially to questions that could be answered by "yes" or "no." But after the initial exile of the elite, priests may have been in short supply, so the prophet was asked. In times of extremity, people will turn to religious leaders in the belief that the prayers of professionals, pastors or priests, will more likely be heard (cf. 2 Kgs 4:22).

The narrative about their request is structured by a note of setting (42:1), followed by a dialogue of all the people with Jeremiah who abruptly entered the story (42:2-6). Jeremiah was last mentioned in 38:28. The second speech of all the people to Jeremiah affirms that they will follow divine direction irrespective of the nature of that decision. They echoed the responses of their predecessors (Exod 24:3, 7; Josh 24:21, 24; 1 Sam 7:4, 6, 8; 12:19; so Brueggemann 1998:388). On the surface, this was laudable, for they basically signed the contract and allowed another, Yahweh, to fill in the blanks. They mouthed the theology often repeated by Jeremiah, who insisted that obedience would result in everything going well. Had the hymn been around, one gets the sense they'd have been singing, "Trust and obey, for there's no other way."

Jeremiah, formerly forbidden to pray, was in a new situation (cf. 7:16; 11:14; for prophetic intercession, see Amos 7:2, 5). Some might explain the delay in his receiving an answer to demonic interference (Dan 10:13). However, the ten day waiting period may better be interpreted as making the point that God, while open to his people's prayer, reserves his freedom. God is not to be summoned on demand, like a cosmic bellhop (cf. 28:11-12). This incident contradicts the opinion that God does not respond to prayer unless there is full willingness to comply with God's will. In mercy, God responded to those requesting direction even when the petitioners were ill-disposed to obey.

God's guidance, given in the name of the Chief Commander of Armies, was for the people to remain within the country. It was as though the prophet stretched himself to his full height when reporting the directive, together with its promises and threats. The promises included (1) assurances that they would become firmly established (42:10a); (2) a change of divine posture toward them (42:10b); (3) the familiar "divine assistance formula" of presence (42:11); and (4) an assurance that they would be safe from any untoward actions by the Babylonians (42:11b-12). The second promise was the most surprising and puzzling in the light of God's frequent angry threats and his so-called unchangeability. God's answer showed that his anger in destroying the city was not the anger of vengeance but a sorrowful anger. When the people displayed a malleable attitude, God at once reversed his position (cf. 18:7-10). God's immutability does not mean that God is stoical or impassive, meeting situations without feeling. God is capable of passion and emotion, but he is still consistent and can still be fully trusted.

The threat portion of the reply began with a warning about faulty, though understandable, reasoning on the part of the people (42:13-18). It seemed plausible to them that Egypt could offer what a war-devastated country could not: peace and sustenance (42:13). They could not know except through this God-given word that their prospects would be the totally negative experience of war and famine, which was exactly what they wanted to avoid (42:16-17). Dire predictions frequently elicit the response, "O, it won't happen to me" (cf. Amos 9:1-4). Twice, the divine word averred that there would be no exceptions (42:17, 18).

**Giving Unsolicited Reinforcement (42:19-22).** Although Jeremiah briefly quoted God directly, "Do not go to Egypt," the subsequent statements of exhortation were his own. The accusation that the people would not listen seems premature since their decision was reported in 43:1-7. Is one to envision Jeremiah as reading their body language while he reported to them? Was he sure, given all the earlier resistance to his messages, that this remnant group was cut from the same cloth as the earlier Jerusalem citizenry? Or had he been given a private revelation from God about the insincerity of the petitioners? We do not know, but his premonition, if that is what it is, was correct.

**Responding to Divine Guidance (43:1-3).** The adjective "proud" already prepares us for an action contrary to divine counsel. Proud persons are likely to trust their own conclusions and intuitions. The remnant repudiated this word of guidance that cut against the grain of their desires, and they accused Jeremiah of outright deception, saying "You lie" (43:2). To add insult to injury, they intimated that Jeremiah was a weak-willed person subject to the beck and call of his scribe, whom they put down as having sinister designs. How could they think of Jeremiah as weak when, though in the minority, he had spoken with courage? Besides, he had been vindicated. Nothing that is scripturally recorded about Baruch gives credence to their suspicion about this man. Evasion and rationalization as justification for disobedience have a long history, beginning with the first parents.

**Deciding for Egypt (43:4-7).** The fear of remaining in the land must have been very great, or the persuasive techniques of these erstwhile army generals considerable. In any case, the crowd acquiesced and decided to go to Egypt, contrary to the word from God. The story shows that if there were people not deported to exile in Babylon, it was not because they were God-fearing. The decision for the remnant to go to Egypt is a further commentary on human perversity.

The scene is also a commentary on the pastoral heart of the prophet. He would not forsake his people, but went with them despite his own counsel not to go. Perhaps his action was intended to mirror God's persistence in befriending even disobedient listeners. If so, his action was a model for God's ministers in being both confrontational and pastoral.

◆   **D. Courting Disaster Again! (43:8–44:30)**

⁸Then at Tahpanhes, the LORD gave another message to Jeremiah. He said, ⁹"While the people of Judah are watching, take some large rocks and bury them under the pavement stones at the entrance of Pharaoh's palace here in Tahpanhes. ¹⁰Then say to the people of Judah, 'This is what the LORD of Heaven's Armies, the God of Israel, says: I will certainly bring my servant Nebuchadnezzar,* king of Babylon, here to Egypt. I will set his throne over these stones that I have hidden. He will spread his royal canopy over them. ¹¹And when he comes, he will destroy the land of Egypt. He will bring death to those destined for death, captivity to those destined for captivity, and war to those destined for war. ¹²He will set fire to the temples of Egypt's gods; he will burn the temples and carry the idols away as plunder. He will pick clean the land of Egypt as a shepherd picks fleas from his cloak. And he himself will leave unharmed. ¹³He will break down the sacred pillars standing in the temple of the sun* in Egypt, and he will burn down the temples of Egypt's gods.'"

## CHAPTER 44

This is the message Jeremiah received concerning the Judeans living in northern Egypt in the cities of Migdol, Tahpanhes, and Memphis,* and in southern Egypt* as well: ²"This is what the LORD of Heaven's Armies, the God of Israel, says: You saw the calamity I brought on Jerusalem and all the towns of Judah. They now lie deserted and in ruins. ³They provoked my anger with all their wickedness. They burned incense and worshiped other gods—gods that neither they nor you nor any of your ancestors had ever even known.

⁴"Again and again I sent my servants, the prophets, to plead with them, 'Don't do these horrible things that I hate so much.' ⁵But my people would not listen or turn back from their wicked ways. They kept on burning incense to these gods.

⁶And so my fury boiled over and fell like fire on the towns of Judah and into the streets of Jerusalem, and they are still a desolate ruin today.

⁷"And now the LORD God of Heaven's Armies, the God of Israel, asks you: Why are you destroying yourselves? For not one of you will survive—not a man, woman, or child among you who has come here from Judah, not even the babies in your arms. ⁸Why provoke my anger by burning incense to the idols you have made here in Egypt? You will only destroy yourselves and make yourselves an object of cursing and mockery for all the nations of the earth. ⁹Have you forgotten the sins of your ancestors, the sins of the kings and queens of Judah, and the sins you and your wives committed in Judah and Jerusalem? ¹⁰To this very hour you have shown no remorse or reverence. No one has chosen to follow my word and the decrees I gave to you and your ancestors before you.

¹¹"Therefore, this is what the LORD of Heaven's Armies, the God of Israel, says: I am determined to destroy every one of you! ¹²I will take this remnant of Judah—those who were determined to come here and live in Egypt—and I will consume them. They will fall here in Egypt, killed by war and famine. All will die, from the least to the greatest. They will be an object of damnation, horror, cursing, and mockery. ¹³I will punish them in Egypt just as I punished them in Jerusalem, by war, famine, and disease. ¹⁴Of that remnant who fled to Egypt, hoping someday to return to Judah, there will be no survivors. Even though they long to return home, only a handful will do so."

¹⁵Then all the women present and all the men who knew that their wives had burned incense to idols—a great crowd of all the Judeans living in northern Egypt and southern Egypt*—answered Jeremiah, ¹⁶"We will not listen to your messages from the LORD! ¹⁷We will do whatever we

want. We will burn incense and pour out liquid offerings to the Queen of Heaven just as much as we like—just as we, and our ancestors, and our kings and officials have always done in the towns of Judah and in the streets of Jerusalem. For in those days we had plenty to eat, and we were well off and had no troubles! ¹⁸But ever since we quit burning incense to the Queen of Heaven and stopped worshiping her with liquid offerings, we have been in great trouble and have been dying from war and famine."

¹⁹"Besides," the women added, "do you suppose that we were burning incense and pouring out liquid offerings to the Queen of Heaven, and making cakes marked with her image, without our husbands knowing it and helping us? Of course not!"

²⁰Then Jeremiah said to all of them, men and women alike, who had given him that answer, ²¹"Do you think the LORD did not know that you and your ancestors, your kings and officials, and all the people were burning incense to idols in the towns of Judah and in the streets of Jerusalem? ²²It was because the LORD could no longer bear all the disgusting things you were doing that he made your land an object of cursing—a desolate ruin without inhabitants—as it is today. ²³All these terrible things happened to you because you have burned incense to idols and sinned against the LORD. You have refused to obey him and have not followed his instructions, his decrees, and his laws."

²⁴Then Jeremiah said to them all, including the women, "Listen to this message from the LORD, all you citizens of Judah who live in Egypt. ²⁵This is what the LORD of Heaven's Armies, the God of Israel, says: 'You and your wives have said, "We will keep our promises to burn incense and pour out liquid offerings to the Queen of Heaven," and you have proved by your actions that you meant it. So go ahead and carry out your promises and vows to her!'

²⁶"But listen to this message from the LORD, all you Judeans now living in Egypt: 'I have sworn by my great name,' says the LORD, 'that my name will no longer be spoken by any of the Judeans in the land of Egypt. None of you may invoke my name or use this oath: "As surely as the Sovereign LORD lives." ²⁷For I will watch over you to bring you disaster and not good. Everyone from Judah who is now living in Egypt will suffer war and famine until all of you are dead. ²⁸Only a small number will escape death and return to Judah from Egypt. Then all those who came to Egypt will find out whose words are true—mine or theirs!

²⁹"'And this is the proof I give you,' says the LORD, 'that all I have threatened will happen to you and that I will punish you here.' ³⁰This is what the LORD says: 'I will turn Pharaoh Hophra, king of Egypt, over to his enemies who want to kill him, just as I turned King Zedekiah of Judah over to King Nebuchadnezzar* of Babylon.'"

43:10 Hebrew *Nebuchadrezzar,* a variant spelling of Nebuchadnezzar.  43:13 Or *in Heliopolis.*  44:1a Hebrew *Noph.*  44:1b Hebrew *in Pathros.*  44:15 Hebrew *in Egypt, in Pathros.*  44:30 Hebrew *Nebuchadrezzar,* a variant spelling of Nebuchadnezzar.

NOTES

43:9 *the entrance of Pharaoh's palace.* This was probably a royal or government house used for a state visit to this border town. For a discussion of terminology and rhetoric, see Friebel (1999:351-362).

43:12 *he will burn.* The NLT and others appropriately follow the LXX, Syriac, and Vulgate by reading "he will burn" instead of the MT's "I will burn."

*the idols.* The NLT interprets the indefinite "them" as idols; other versions, as Temple structures (cf. NIV, NRSV).

**44:1** *Migdol, Tahpanhes, and Memphis.* These were towns in the Nile delta region of Lower Egypt. Migdol, meaning "tower" (possibly Tell el-Her), is twenty-five miles east-northeast of Tahpanhes (cf. 46:14; Ezek 29:10; 30:6). Memphis, thirteen miles south of modern Cairo, was the capital during the Old Kingdom and the site of the first stepped pyramid, Saqqara (cf. Ezek 29:8-16; 30:13-19).

*southern Egypt.* Lit., "Pathros," some 300 miles distant from the delta region. A Jewish colony in Upper Egypt at Elephantine, an island in the Nile, is known (from archaeology) to have existed from the fifth century BC.

**44:4** *Don't do these horrible things.* Horrible things (*to'ebah* [TH8441, ZH9359]) are abominable, offensive, and repugnant (cf. 44:12; cf. the Heb. of 7:10; 32:35; 42:18). Concerning *to'ebah*, NIDOTTE says, "Pagan worship practices, deceit and insubordination within the covenant nation, and superficial worship of Yahweh constitute three major realms of abhorrent activities" (4:315). Cf. the Heb. of Deut 18:9; 25:16; 32:16.

**44:6** *my fury boiled over.* Two words, *khemah* [TH2534A, ZH2771] (wrath) and *'ap* [TH639, ZH678] (anger), can be read as referring to a single reality, "fierce anger" (NIV) or "fury" (NLT). Cf. 7:20; 42:18; comments on 25:15-38.

**44:7** *Why are you destroying yourselves?* The Heb., "cut (hiphil, *karath* [TH3772, ZH4162]) yourselves off," denotes separation (excommunication) from the community or even from God (cf. 44:26).

**44:10** *you have shown no remorse.* The root *daka'* [TH1792, ZH1917] (remorse) denotes "smashing" or "crushing," as a moth is crushed under foot (cf. Job 4:19). Spiritually, it can indicate contrition, humility, or remorse (cf. Pss 34:18 [19]; 51:17 [19]).

**44:11** *I am determined.* Lit., "I set my face"; so also 44:12.

**44:17** *Queen of Heaven.* In the Bible, this name appears only in Jeremiah (cf. 7:18; 44:17-25). It is commonly accepted as a title for a Mesopotamian goddess, Ishtar, or the Canaanite goddess Ashtoreth (Gr. Astarte). It has recently been thought to be the name of a syncretistic deity (ABD 5:586-587). The rare word *meleketh* [TH4446, ZH4906], rather than "queen," could signify "heavenly handiwork," namely stars (IBD 3:1308). See G. L. Keown's excursus, with bibliography (Keown et al. 1995:266-268).

**44:21** *Do you think the LORD did not know?* At issue is remembrance (Heb. verb *zakar* [TH2142, ZH2349], remember) and divine reflection (lit., "go up in his heart [mind]") more than omniscience.

**44:22** *all the disgusting things.* The phrase collapses two clauses in the original, "the evil of your deeds" and "the horrible things you were doing."

**44:27** *I will watch over you.* The expression with *shoqed* [TH8245, ZH9193] (watch) recalls the wordplay of 1:11-12 (see notes).

### COMMENTARY

Little is told of how the exiles fared in Babylon. Instead, the book expands on the spiritual condition of the group that chose to go to Egypt. The report, in two parts, reintroduces Jeremiah. First, Jeremiah engaged in symbolic action to describe Nebuchadnezzar's foray into Egypt (43:8-13). Second, Jeremiah disputed with the exiles about worship in several interchanges (44:1-30). The section begins and ends with a pronouncement on Egypt, its temples (43:8-13), and its king (44:30).

**Symbolic Action (43:8-13).**   The prophet's putting large rocks at the entrance to an Egyptian government building was the last of his sign-acts (also called "nonverbal acts" or "street theater" by some). With each such action had come an appropriate message (cf. 13:9-11; 19:1-13; 27:1–28:16). With the visual aid of rocks placed as "concealed marker stones" (Friebel 1999:357) in a pavement area, Jeremiah told about a foreign conqueror's throne with a canopy to be placed at that very spot. The local citizenry would be reduced through the death-dealing measures of exile and military combat (43:11).

The concluding simile about a shepherd picking fleas off of his cloak conveys the way in which Nebuchadnezzar would go after the last holdout of resistance, or perhaps better, the last of the irritating idol centers. Jeremiah insisted that national maneuvers and victories played into God's purposes. A pagan king, like a dutiful servant, could fulfill God's purposes (25:9; 27:6; cf. Cyrus, Isa 44:28). God's sovereignty extended beyond monarchs to the so-called gods (43:13).

Historically, Nebuchadnezzar did enter Egypt in his thirty-seventh year (568/7 BC), more as a punitive action than as a large-scale takeover of the country. The details remain sketchy.

**Historical Overview (44:2-6).** The prophet's word to the people, later vigorously disputed, began with a review of recent history (44:1-6). Most vivid in the people's memory was the sacking of Jerusalem (44:2). The prophet's historical review focused on the reason for the disaster. Specifically, the list of their past sins could be reduced to one item, the breach of the first commandment given in the Decalogue (Exod 20:3; cf. Deut 6:5). Judeans had burned incense (the term is also broadly used for sacrifice, Lev. 1:9; 3:11; 1 Sam 2:16) to foreign deities, which was altogether contrary to the first commandment (44:3, 5). The chiastic pattern (so also Brueggemann 1998:405) turns on the "extra exertion" of sending prophets as a way to forestall Israel's continuing evil (7:25; 25:4; 26:5).

The chiastic structure of 44.2-6b is as follows.

A. present calamity 44:2
   B. divine anger 44:3a
      C. wickedness of worship of other gods 44:3b
         D. divine pleas through the prophets 44:4a
      C'. wickedness, burning incense 44:5
   B'. divine anger 44:6a
A'. present calamity 44:6b

**A Judgment Oracle (44:7-15).** Jeremiah's oracle follows the pattern of the classic judgment speech in which an accusation (44:7-10) became the ground for an announcement (44:11-14). The form had overtones of the law court. The accusation is cast largely in questions: (1) Why continue on a course that is self-destructive (44:7)? (2) Why incite God's anger through idolatry (44:8)? (3) Where was the historical memory of sin's consequences (44:9; e.g., God's punishment of the Northern Kingdom by Assyria)? The problem at its base was deliberate inattention to God with no readiness to acknowledge sin (cf. the publican, Luke 18:13). Divine anger was a factor here, as in the historical review (44:3, 6; see discussion on 25:15-38).

As was often the case, the announcement portion of the judgment speech begins with "therefore." The speech harps on the hearers' location in Egypt (four times), for they were there in direct disobedience to God (43:4; cf. the last-mentioned accusation, 44:10b). God's decision to punish, even to the point of the virtual extinction of the community, was commensurate with the pervasive nature of the evil committed. It can be set down as a principle that God will set his face against those who set their face against him. "Jeremiah 44 represents perhaps the strongest word of denunciation in the entire prophetic tradition" (Keown et al. 1995:267).

**Disputation and Self-Justification.** A threat that should have promoted repentance resulted (alas, true to form) in a protest of self-justification in which feminine voices were strangely dominant. The note about these women calls into question the view that the ancient world was an exclusively male world. The blatantly defiant "We will not listen" echoes their earlier Jerusalem counterparts (6:17; 18:12). "They condemned themselves as recalcitrant as well as apostate" (Ho 1999:258). As often happens in justification of wrongdoing, the argument concluded with a version of "others don't see our act as a problem" (44:19). The people's lengthy rebuttal shows (1) the entrenched nature of their waywardness, (2) their polar-opposite position to Jeremiah, (3) their determination not to change their evil ways, (4) the wholesale sellout to non-Yahwist views and practices, and (5) the reason why Israel's future was not with them (cf. Jer 24). The vociferous responses documented precisely the accusations Jeremiah had made (44:10b).

The popular reasoning was worlds apart from Jeremiah's reasoning. Jeremiah had just explained that their troubles came as a result of their evil idol worship (44:3-5). The popular view was that their troubles came because they had halted their idolatrous worship (44:18). The disaster was there for all to see, but the reason for that disaster was in contention because of competing worldviews. Both Jeremiah and the people reasoned from effect to cause. The people reasoned pragmatically that before Josiah's reform when they honored the Queen of Heaven, things had gone well for them. Jeremiah argued from the perspective that God deals righteously with his world. There was not a humanly-designed, foolproof way of knowing whose view was correct. However, that Jeremiah's words came true and that the faith community has recognized his book as canonical validates Jeremiah's conclusions. Interpretations of experience remain highly determined by one's worldview.

**Jeremiah's Rebuttal (44:20-30).** With good debating form, Jeremiah reiterated the earlier points of God's disgust and anger (44:22; cf. 44:3, 6, 8); the double sin of substituting other gods for Yahweh and of disregarding/disobeying Yahweh (44:23; cf. 44:5); the desolation already in evidence (44:22b; cf. 44:2, 6); the fate of destruction bordering on extermination (44:27; cf. 44:7); and the relatively few who would ever return to Judah (44:28; cf. 44:14). To these he added three formerly unmentioned factors. First, God had withdrawn the opportunity for his people to swear by his name (44:26). Some have suggested that the people had made vows to the Queen of Heaven by invoking Yahweh's name. By placing this limitation on his people, God had essentially cut himself off from access and was no longer within their reach. Second, the scattering of returnees to Judah would be proof that the disasters in Egypt were those brought on by God (44:29). Third, Pharaoh would suffer the same fate as Judah's king Zedekiah—that is, he would be given into the hand of his enemies (44:30; cf. 39:5-7). This happened in 566 BC. Pharaoh Hophra (also known as Apries) of the twenty-sixth dynasty was executed three years after being deposed in favor of Amasis, one of his generals (ABD 3:286).

So straightforward and so often repeated were the words of threat that the hearers could not possibly plead ignorance about the consequences of their actions. It remains something of a surprise that God so painstakingly laid out the principles by which he was operating. Even the brazen defiance of his audience did not silence his message.

◆    ### E. A Message for Baruch (45:1-5)

The prophet Jeremiah gave a message to Baruch son of Neriah in the fourth year of the reign of Jehoiakim son of Josiah,* after Baruch had written down everything Jeremiah had dictated to him. He said, ²"This is what the LORD, the God of Israel, says to you, Baruch: ³You have said, 'I am overwhelmed with trouble! Haven't I had enough pain already? And now the LORD has added more! I am worn out from sighing and can find no rest.'

⁴"Baruch, this is what the LORD says: 'I will destroy this nation that I built. I will uproot what I planted. ⁵Are you seeking great things for yourself? Don't do it! I will bring great disaster upon all these people; but I will give you your life as a reward wherever you go. I, the LORD, have spoken!' "

45:1 The fourth year of Jehoiakim's reign was 605 BC.

### NOTES

**45:1 *Baruch*.** Jeremiah's scribe, mentioned in Jeremiah 36. Chapter 45 does not fit chronologically, but it brings closure to the so-called "Baruch document" (Jer 36–45) and even to the larger Jeremiah section, Jer 1–45.

**45:3 *Haven't I had enough pain already?*** This is a good example of a dynamic equivalent translation that captures the pathos of the Heb. expression *'oy-na' li* [TH188, ZH208], usually rendered, "Woe is me" (cf. NIV, NRSV, and the Heb. of 4:31; 10:19; 15:10).

**45:4 *I will destroy this nation*.** The Heb. syntax stresses the extent to which dismantling and uprooting will take place by ending with an accusative clause "[even] the whole land [nation]," matched by "all flesh [people]" (Heb. of 45:5), and so anticipates the succeeding chapters (Brueggemann 1998:416).

### COMMENTARY

Personal messages from God to individuals, apart from Jeremiah, are relatively few. Several are recipients of words of judgment: Pashhur (20:3-6); Hananiah (28:15-16); Ahab and Zedekiah (29:21-23); Shemaiah (29:24-28); and individual kings (e.g., Zedekiah, 38:17-23). The word to Baruch can be compared to the one given to Ebed-melech, Jeremiah's deliverer (39:15-18), since both are words of salvation and illustrate the New Testament assertion about God's reward policy (Heb 6:10).

The oracle is a response to Baruch's lament (cf. Jeremiah's laments, e.g. 15:15-22; 20:7-13 and comments). Was Baruch already as misunderstood in 605 BC as he was later (43:2-3)? Was he rejected and ridiculed like Jeremiah, or like him, was he burdened by the severity of God's message? Was he simply exhausted? We are not told, but we are reassured that God had heard the lament.

For Baruch, unlike Ebed-melech, there was a word of rebuke. "Pared of unessentials, God's loaded question to the complaining disciple was merely this: 'What is your hurt, O man, compared to mine?' " (Blank, quoted in Ho 1999:268n10). Baruch was a scribe, a professional of some status in the ancient world. Would Baruch's personal ambition have interfered with the task at hand? This is possible. God's counsel to the scribe was intended to prevent ministerial derailment. God discerns human motives. Ambitions are not in themselves evil, but they need scrutiny and chastening lest they detract from the divine calling. Sanctified ambition requires that personal ambitions be subservient to God's program.

This chapter ends the long section of God's threats to Israel, which affect the nation as a whole as well as individuals, some godly even if not perfect, like Baruch.

## ◆ IX. Oracles About the Nations (46:1–51:64)
### A. Egypt: Terrorized at Every Turn (46:1-28)

The following messages were given to Jeremiah the prophet from the LORD concerning foreign nations.

2This message concerning Egypt was given in the fourth year of the reign of Jehoiakim son of Josiah, the king of Judah, on the occasion of the battle of Carchemish* when Pharaoh Neco, king of Egypt, and his army were defeated beside the Euphrates River by King Nebuchadnezzar* of Babylon.

3"Prepare your shields,
    and advance into battle!
4Harness the horses,
    and mount the stallions.
Take your positions.
    Put on your helmets.
Sharpen your spears,
    and prepare your armor.
5But what do I see?
    The Egyptian army flees in terror.
The bravest of its fighting men run
    without a backward glance.
They are terrorized at every turn,"
    says the LORD.

6"The swiftest runners cannot flee;
    the mightiest warriors cannot
        escape.
By the Euphrates River to the north,
    they stumble and fall.

7"Who is this, rising like the Nile
        at floodtime,
    overflowing all the land?
8It is the Egyptian army,
    overflowing all the land,
boasting that it will cover the earth
        like a flood,
    destroying cities and their people.
9Charge, you horses and chariots;
    attack, you mighty warriors of
        Egypt!
Come, all you allies from Ethiopia,
        Libya, and Lydia*
    who are skilled with the shield and
        bow!
10For this is the day of the Lord, the
        LORD of Heaven's Armies,
    a day of vengeance on his enemies.
The sword will devour until it is
        satisfied,

yes, until it is drunk with your
blood!
The Lord, the LORD of Heaven's Armies,
will receive a sacrifice today
in the north country beside the
Euphrates River.

¹¹ "Go up to Gilead to get medicine,
O virgin daughter of Egypt!
But your many treatments
will bring you no healing.
¹² The nations have heard of your shame.
The earth is filled with your cries of
despair.
Your mightiest warriors will run into
each other
and fall down together."

¹³ Then the LORD gave the prophet Jeremiah this message about King Nebuchadnezzar's plans to attack Egypt.

¹⁴ "Shout it out in Egypt!
Publish it in the cities of Migdol,
Memphis,* and Tahpanhes!
Mobilize for battle,
for the sword will devour everyone
around you.
¹⁵ Why have your warriors fallen?
They cannot stand, for the LORD has
knocked them down.
¹⁶ They stumble and fall over each other
and say among themselves,
'Come, let's go back to our people,
to the land of our birth.
Let's get away from the sword of
the enemy!'
¹⁷ There they will say,
'Pharaoh, the king of Egypt, is
a loudmouth
who missed his opportunity!'
¹⁸ "As surely as I live," says the King,
whose name is the LORD of Heaven's
Armies,
"one is coming against Egypt
who is as tall as Mount Tabor,
or as Mount Carmel by the sea!
¹⁹ Pack up! Get ready to leave for exile,
you citizens of Egypt!
The city of Memphis will be destroyed,
without a single inhabitant.

²⁰ Egypt is as sleek as a beautiful young
cow,
but a horsefly from the north is on
its way!
²¹ Egypt's mercenaries have become like
fattened calves.
They, too, will turn and run,
for it is a day of great disaster for Egypt,
a time of great punishment.
²² Egypt flees, silent as a serpent gliding
away.
The invading army marches in;
they come against her with axes like
woodsmen.
²³ They will cut down her people like
trees," says the LORD,
"for they are more numerous than
locusts.
²⁴ Egypt will be humiliated;
she will be handed over to people
from the north."

²⁵ The LORD of Heaven's Armies, the God
of Israel, says: "I will punish Amon, the
god of Thebes,* and all the other gods of
Egypt. I will punish its rulers and Pharaoh, too, and all who trust in him. ²⁶ I will
hand them over to those who want them
killed—to King Nebuchadnezzar of Babylon and his army. But afterward the land
will recover from the ravages of war. I,
the LORD, have spoken!

²⁷ "But do not be afraid, Jacob, my
servant;
do not be dismayed, Israel.
For I will bring you home again from
distant lands,
and your children will return from
their exile.
Israel* will return to a life of peace
and quiet,
and no one will terrorize them.
²⁸ Do not be afraid, Jacob, my servant,
for I am with you," says the LORD.
"I will completely destroy the nations
to which I have exiled you,
but I will not completely destroy you.
I will discipline you, but with justice;
I cannot let you go unpunished."

**46:2a** This event occurred in 605 BC, during the fourth year of Jehoiakim's reign (according to the calendar system in which the new year begins in the spring). **46:2b** Hebrew *Nebuchadrezzar*, a variant spelling of Nebuchadnezzar; also in 46:13, 26. **46:9** Hebrew *from Cush, Put, and Lud*. **46:14** Hebrew *Noph*; also in 46:19. **46:25** Hebrew *of No*. **46:27** Hebrew *Jacob*. See note on 5:20.

## NOTES

**46:1** *concerning foreign nations.* In view of the content, the word *'al* [TH5921, ZH6584], though it can mean "against" (cf. KJV), is better rendered as "concerning," or "about." The LXX places the section (46:1ff) after 25:13 and alters the sequence of the nine oracles (cf. Watts 1992). For similar oracles elsewhere, see Isa 13–23; Ezek 25–32; Amos 1–2; Obadiah; Nahum.

**46:2** *the battle of Carchemish.* The two superpowers, Egypt under **Pharaoh Neco** (610–594 BC) and westward-advancing Babylon under Nabopolassar, clashed at Carchemish, sixty miles northeast of Aleppo, in 605 BC. Nabopolassar died in 605 (though not in the battle), and his son **Nebuchadnezzar** succeeded him.

**46:3** *Prepare your shields.* The Heb. differentiates two types of shields, *magen* [TH4043, ZH4482] (a small shield held in the left hand) and *tsinnah* [TH6793A, ZH7558] (a large shield covering the whole body (1 Kgs 10:16-17). For military orders and procedures, see 6:1-6.

**46:5** *They are terrorized at every turn.* The war-related expression *magor missabib* ("terror on every side"; see notes at 6:25; 49:29) was applied by Jeremiah to Pashhur (20:3) and by others to Jeremiah (20:10).

**46:7** *rising like the Nile at floodtime.* This is a simile for the surging, expansive Egyptian power (cf. 46:11, 20, 21, 22, 23 for other metaphors and similes).

**46:9** *Ethiopia, Libya, and Lydia.* Soldiers from these places could be mercenaries or allies (46:16). Ethiopia lay south of Egypt in the region of the Upper Nile; Libya was a territory west of Egypt. Lydia (Lud), possibly an African people connected with Egypt (Ezek 30:5) or inhabitants of a territory in west-central Asia Minor, was an ally of Tyre (Ezek 27:10; see ABD 4:397; cf. Acts 2:9-10).

**46:10** *a day of vengeance.* The root *naqam* [TH5358, ZH5933], it has been argued, has more to do with vindication than with vengeance (Mendenhall 1973:69-104).

**46:11** *Go up to Gilead to get medicine.* This is ironic advice, as Egypt had control over this prized trade route area between 609–605 BC. For medicine, cf. 8:22.

**46:13** *Nebuchadnezzar's plans to attack Egypt.* The attack could be in 601 BC (indecisive), 588 BC, or 568/7 BC. For a full discussion of proposed dates and scholars' positions, see Keown et al. (1995:287-88).

**46:14** *Migdol, Memphis and Tahpanhes.* See notes at 44:1 and King (1993:30-32).

**46:15** *Why have your warriors fallen?* Some take *'abbir* [TH47, ZH52] (warrior, mighty one, bull) to refer to an Egyptian god, a suggestion more credible if the verb in niphal, *niskhap* [TH5502, ZH6085] (swept away), is divided into two, *nas* [TH5127, ZH5674] (fleeing) and *khap* to read "Why did *Haph Apis* (worshiped in the form of a bull) flee?" (cf. NRSV). So understood, the Egyptian deities are the first to fall.

**46:17** *Pharaoh, the king of Egypt, is a loudmouth.* This is a felicitous rendering of *sha'on* [TH7588A, ZH8623] (din, clash, uproar). Other translations propose what may be a word play on the king's name, Hophra: "King Bombast" (NEB), and "Braggart" (NRSV).

**46:18** *Mount Tabor.* At 1,843 feet, this mountain dominates the Plain of Jezreel.

*Carmel.* This mountain ridge (maximum height of 1,742 feet) is in the vicinity of modern Haifa, impressive for its topography and memorable for the Elijah story (1 Kgs 18–19).

**46:21** *a day of great disaster for Egypt.* The NLT takes the indefinite "their" ('*edam* [TH343, ZH369], their disaster), to be "Egypt," but the antecedent could be "mercenaries."

**46:23** *They will cut down her people like trees.* The Heb. does not refer to people but to a dense (niphal of *lo' khaqar* [TH2713, ZH2983], unsearchable) forest. In this context, that could mean people or actual trees (used in war as battering rams), or, metaphorically, the Temple and palace buildings (cf. 21:14; 22:7).

**46:25** *Amon, the god of Thebes.* Thebes, some 300 miles upstream from Cairo and known also as Karnak and Luxor, was the capital of Upper Egypt during the New Kingdom (1552–1070 BC). Amun (a version of Amon, also Amon-Re) was the state god, "king of the gods."

*all who trust in him.* This could include the pro-Egyptian party in Jerusalem, especially if the date was 601 BC (cf. 46:13).

**46:26** *the land will recover.* Cf. Isa 19:25; Ezek 29:13-16. For other nations given a message of hope, see 48:47; 49:6; 49:39 (cf. Pentecost; Acts 2:10).

**46:27** *Jacob, my servant.* An almost identical oracle is found at 30:10-11 (cf. Isa 41:8-13).

C O M M E N T A R Y

The story about Judah has ended, and Jeremiah has become the prophet to the nations (cf. 1:10). The effect of putting these oracles after Israel's story (contrast other prophets) suggests an apocalyptic view of the nations. Such a view is usually trans-historical and depicts the nations as God's enemies. The book essentially ends (apart from the appendix, Jer 52) on a universal note. "The Lord God has no native country" (Ives 2000).

The first two oracles are about Egypt (46:2-26) and Philistia (47:1-7), both nations situated to the southwest of Judah, and a brief oracle about Israel is sandwiched in between (46:27-28). The oracle about Egypt is in two parts, one of which is dated to 605 BC and is about Egypt's defeat in a battle far from Egypt (46:2-12). The second (46:13-26) is about distress at home within the country. Military language predominates in both.

**Egypt's Defeat at Carchemish (46:2-12).** The second oracle mentions Nebuchadnezzar (46:26), and the first one is (quite indirectly) about him also (cf. 46:2). Egypt was at war, and God was the antagonist. Politically, the battle at Carchemish shifted the balance of power to Babylon. For Jeremiah, what occurred was a "theological happening" (Brueggemann 1998:428), construed by Jeremiah as *Theopolitik*—a political perspective that factors in the sovereignty of God (Huwyler 1996).

The battle with Egypt is depicted as the "day of the Lord." The technical expression *yom yhwh* (day of the Lord) is not used, but the phrase, "That day belongs to the Lord ('*adonay* [TH136, ZH151]) Yahweh" (46:10) is certainly a reference to God's awesome intervention. On this "day" God comes on the world scene in striking fashion, both to judge and to save. It is a day of darkness (Joel 2:2; Amos 5:18), of ruin and devastation (Zeph 1:15), but for some a day of abundance and plenty (Joel 2:23-26). In that day, a day fully monopolized by Yahweh, nations will appear before the universal magistrate in the valley of decision (Joel 3:12, 14 [4:12, 14]) and God will be vindicated (see note on 46:10). The visual enemy may be Nebuchadnezzar (cf. mention of Euphrates in 46:10), but the focus is on how God, "The LORD of

Heaven's Armies," will deal with Egypt (46:11). This superpower, Egypt, will have to deal with God.

Egypt was altogether helpless in the face of the enemy (God). Military massiveness would not be enough (46:8). Egypt might have the swiftest of soldiers, but in the retreat of battle, their speed would not be enough to save them (46:6). Egypt may have had many allies, but their skills would not be sufficient (46:9). Even should Egypt have access to the traditional "balm of Gilead," it would not be enough to bring healing to the casualties (46:11). The contest would end in defeat, a point that punctuates the poem (46:5, 6, 10, 12). Even a superpower like Egypt was no match for God—her helplessness was everywhere apparent.

**Egypt's Distress at Home (46:13-26).** It is one thing to lose a battle abroad. It is quite another to be conquered on home turf. The conqueror, the one who "is coming," was Nebuchadnezzar (46:18, 26), but the real aggressor was the "LORD of Heaven's Armies" (46:10, 15). As before, Egypt was summoned to do its best (46:14; cf. 46:3-4). Again, as before, the Egyptian force was defeated (46:15-16, 21-26). The tone of mockery and sarcasm is partly in the metaphors and similes. "Egypt is as sleek as a beautiful young cow" (46:20). Her mercenaries were "like fattened calves" (46:21). Egypt retreated "silent as a serpent," which is ironic because the serpent was a royal emblem (46:22). Egypt was defeated. The sarcasm is most poignant in the quote by the mercenaries about Pharaoh; he was the big mouth with ample talk and minimum action who did not have the sense to seize an opportunity when it was before him (46:17).

The reason for Egypt's troubles was, in part, an inept leader. Another reason, alluded to almost obliquely, was her overbearing demeanor or perhaps ambition (46:7-8) and her pagan deities such as Amon (46:25). The oracle is not about reasons, however. The oracle is about painting a worldview in which God directs the course of history, so that even superpowers, or especially superpowers, will have their day in court (or better, their day of battle) with the Almighty.

The text of 46:27-28, while it holds up a picture of restoration for Israel, makes the point that God is "for" his people in a distinctive way. See comments on this duplicate text at 30:10-11.

◆  ## B. Philistia: Ripe for Destruction (47:1-7)

This is the LORD's message to the prophet Jeremiah concerning the Philistines of Gaza, before it was captured by the Egyptian army. ²This is what the LORD says:

"A flood is coming from the north
  to overflow the land.
It will destroy the land and everything
  in it—

cities and people alike.
People will scream in terror,
  and everyone in the land will wail.
³ Hear the clatter of stallions' hooves
  and the rumble of wheels as the
    chariots rush by.
Terrified fathers run madly,
  without a backward glance at their
    helpless children.

⁴"The time has come for the Philistines
     to be destroyed,
along with their allies from Tyre
     and Sidon.
Yes, the LORD is destroying the
     remnant of the Philistines,
those colonists from the island
     of Crete.*
⁵Gaza will be humiliated, its head
     shaved bald;
Ashkelon will lie silent.
You remnant from the Mediterranean
     coast,*

how long will you lament and
     mourn?

⁶"Now, O sword of the LORD,
     when will you be at rest again?
Go back into your sheath;
     rest and be still.

⁷"But how can it be still
     when the LORD has sent it on
     a mission?
For the city of Ashkelon
     and the people living along the sea
     must be destroyed."

47:4 Hebrew *from Caphtor.*   47:5 Hebrew *the plain.*

## NOTES

**47:1 *the Philistines of Gaza.*** The Philistines came from Crete (also called Caphtor) and other Mediterranean islands in the 12th–11th centuries BC (Deut 2:23; Amos 9:7). Gaza, on the north–south trade route near the Mediterranean coast, was the southernmost of the five principal Philistine cities (cf. Ekron, Askelon, Ashdod, Gath, Josh 13:3; cf. King 1993:32-34). Historical details about Egypt's attack on Gaza are sparse; for scholars' proposals with a preference for 601 BC, see Keown et al. 1995:300.

**47:2 *A flood is coming from the north.*** The enemy from the north, eventually identified as Babylon, is a frequent theme in the book (1:14; 4:6; 6:22; 25:9).

**47:3 *their helpless children.*** The expression, "limpness of hands" (*ripyon yadayim* [TH7510, ZH8342]) is better understood as describing the fathers than the children (cf. the Heb. of 6:24; 50:43).

**47:4 *their allies from Tyre and Sidon.*** The Phoenicians in Tyre and Sidon, two of their prominent cities on the Mediterranean coast north of the Philistines, were also seafaring people and possibly commercial allies.

***Crete.*** This is Caphtor (see NLT mg; cf. 47:1).

**47:5 *its head shaved bald.*** This was a practice in times of mourning (16:16; 41:5; 48:37). Alternatively, this could be understood as the city shorn of its occupants.

***Askelon.*** This principal Philistine city was on the Mediterranean, ten miles north of Gaza (cf. 47:1), under Egyptian control in 630 BC and attacked by Nebuchadnezzar in 604 BC for resisting him (according to the Babylonian Chronicle).

## COMMENTARY

The Philistines, immediately adjacent to Israel on the west, were often entangled with Israel (Josh 10:40-42; Judg 16:21-31 [Samson]; 2 Sam 8:1 [David]; for other oracles about them, see Isa 14:29-31; Ezek 25:15-17; Amos 1:6-8; Zeph 2:4-7).

The cryptic message was that the Philistines were facing extermination, a virtual genocide (47:2, 4, 7). Metaphors sketch the devastation; a destructive power (enemy) is compared to a flood (47:2; cf. Isa 8:7-6) and a sword, addressed (by the Philistines [?]) as though it were a person (47:6). Mostly, however, the destruction is poetically captured in the effects of the army attack. There are abandoned children (47:3), a silent ghost town (47:5), and a humiliated people (47:5).

This chapter about the destruction of cities can be compared to the destruction of Sodom and Gomorrah (Gen 18–19), the announced destruction of Nineveh (Jonah), and the burning of Jerusalem (21:10). For all these (but not for Philistia), a reason for destruction is supplied. Still, the pattern of the overthrow of cities leaves little doubt that evil of some kind is the reason for the large-scale destruction. Cities, then and now, often represent the economic, political, and religious heart of a people. Good may be concentrated there, but so may evil.

God, clearly the behind-the-scenes actor, appears as a violent God. The Bible's fuller word about God is that while he punishes to the third and fourth generation, he is gracious to a thousand generations of those who trust him (Exod 34:6-7). The proportions say much about God. The Philistine oracle belongs to that smaller proportion of the description. Nevertheless, the fierceness of God's destructive power should not be underestimated.

## ◆ C. Moab: Doomed and Weeping (48:1-47)

This message was given concerning Moab. This is what the LORD of Heaven's Armies, the God of Israel, says:

"What sorrow awaits the city of Nebo;
it will soon lie in ruins.
The city of Kiriathaim will be humiliated and captured;
the fortress will be humiliated and broken down.
2 No one will ever brag about Moab again,
for in Heshbon there is a plot to destroy her.
'Come,' they say, 'we will cut her off from being a nation.'
The town of Madmen,* too, will be silenced;
the sword will follow you there.
3 Listen to the cries from Horonaim,
cries of devastation and great destruction.
4 All Moab is destroyed.
Her little ones will cry out.*
5 Her refugees weep bitterly,
climbing the slope to Luhith.
They cry out in terror,
descending the slope to Horonaim.
6 Flee for your lives!
Hide* in the wilderness!

7 Because you have trusted in your wealth and skill,
you will be taken captive.
Your god Chemosh, with his priests and officials,
will be hauled off to distant lands!
8 "All the towns will be destroyed,
and no one will escape—
either on the plateaus or in the valleys,
for the LORD has spoken.
9 Oh, that Moab had wings
so she could fly away,*
for her towns will be left empty,
with no one living in them.
10 Cursed are those who refuse to do the LORD's work,
who hold back their swords from shedding blood!

11 "From his earliest history, Moab has lived in peace,
never going into exile.
He is like wine that has been allowed to settle.
He has not been poured from flask to flask,
and he is now fragrant and smooth.
12 But the time is coming soon," says the LORD,

"when I will send men to pour him
    from his jar.
They will pour him out,
    then shatter the jar!
¹³ At last Moab will be ashamed of his
    idol Chemosh,
    as the people of Israel were
        ashamed of their gold calf at
        Bethel.*

¹⁴ "You used to boast, 'We are heroes,
    mighty men of war.'
¹⁵ But now Moab and his towns will be
    destroyed.
    His most promising youth are
        doomed to slaughter,"
    says the King, whose name is the
        LORD of Heaven's Armies.
¹⁶ "Destruction is coming fast for Moab;
    calamity threatens ominously.
¹⁷ You friends of Moab,
    weep for him and cry!
    See how the strong scepter is broken,
        how the beautiful staff is shattered!

¹⁸ "Come down from your glory
    and sit in the dust, you people of
        Dibon,
    for those who destroy Moab will
        shatter Dibon, too.
    They will tear down all your towers.
¹⁹ You people of Aroer,
    stand beside the road and watch.
    Shout to those who flee from Moab,
        'What has happened there?'

²⁰ "And the reply comes back,
    'Moab lies in ruins, disgraced;
        weep and wail!
    Tell it by the banks of the Arnon River:
        Moab has been destroyed!'
²¹ Judgment has been poured out on the
        towns of the plateau—
    on Holon and Jahaz* and Mephaath,
²² on Dibon and Nebo and Beth-
        diblathaim,
²³     on Kiriathaim and Beth-gamul and
        Beth-meon,
²⁴ on Kerioth and Bozrah—
    all the towns of Moab, far and near.

²⁵ "The strength of Moab has ended.
    His arm has been broken," says the
        LORD.
²⁶ "Let him stagger and fall like
    a drunkard,
    for he has rebelled against the LORD.
    Moab will wallow in his own vomit,
        ridiculed by all.
²⁷ Did you not ridicule the people of
        Israel?
    Were they caught in the company
        of thieves
    that you should despise them as
        you do?

²⁸ "You people of Moab,
    flee from your towns and live in the
        caves.
    Hide like doves that nest
        in the clefts of the rocks.
²⁹ We have all heard of the pride of Moab,
    for his pride is very great.
    We know of his lofty pride,
        his arrogance, and his haughty
        heart.
³⁰ I know about his insolence,"
    says the LORD,
    "but his boasts are empty—
        as empty as his deeds.
³¹ So now I wail for Moab;
    yes, I will mourn for Moab.
    My heart is broken for the men of
        Kir-hareseth.*

³² "You people of Sibmah, rich in
        vineyards,
    I will weep for you even more than
        I did for Jazer.
    Your spreading vines once reached as
        far as the Dead Sea,*
    but the destroyer has stripped you
        bare!
    He has harvested your grapes and
        summer fruits.
³³ Joy and gladness are gone from
        fruitful Moab.
    The presses yield no wine.
    No one treads the grapes with shouts
        of joy.
    There is shouting, yes, but not of joy.

³⁴"Instead, their awful cries of terror can be heard from Heshbon clear across to Elealeh and Jahaz; from Zoar all the way to Horonaim and Eglath-shelishiyah. Even the waters of Nimrim are dried up now.

³⁵"I will put an end to Moab," says the LORD, "for the people offer sacrifices at the pagan shrines and burn incense to their false gods. ³⁶My heart moans like a flute for Moab and Kir-hareseth, for all their wealth has disappeared. ³⁷The people shave their heads and beards in mourning. They slash their hands and put on clothes made of burlap. ³⁸There is crying and sorrow in every Moabite home and on every street. For I have smashed Moab like an old, unwanted jar. ³⁹How it is shattered! Hear the wailing! See the shame of Moab! It has become an object of ridicule, an example of ruin to all its neighbors."

⁴⁰This is what the LORD says:

"Look! The enemy swoops down like an
    eagle,
    spreading his wings over Moab.
⁴¹ Its cities will fall,
    and its strongholds will be seized.
Even the mightiest warriors will be in
    anguish
    like a woman in labor.

⁴² Moab will no longer be a nation,
    for it has boasted against the LORD.

⁴³ "Terror and traps and snares will be
    your lot,
    O Moab," says the LORD.
⁴⁴ "Those who flee in terror will fall into
    a trap,
    and those who escape the trap will
    step into a snare.
I will see to it that you do not get away,
    for the time of your judgment has
    come,"
    says the LORD.
⁴⁵ "The people flee as far as Heshbon
    but are unable to go on.
For a fire comes from Heshbon,
    King Sihon's ancient home,
to devour the entire land
    with all its rebellious people.

⁴⁶ "O Moab, they weep for you!
    The people of the god Chemosh are
    destroyed!
Your sons and your daughters
    have been taken away as captives.
⁴⁷ But I will restore the fortunes of Moab
    in days to come.
    I, the LORD, have spoken!"

This is the end of Jeremiah's prophecy concerning Moab.

48:2 *Madmen* sounds like the Hebrew word for "silence"; it should not be confused with the English word *madmen.*   48:4 Greek version reads *Her cries are heard as far away as Zoar.*   48:6 Or *Hide like a wild donkey;* or *Hide like a juniper shrub;* or *Be like* [the town of] *Aroer.* The meaning of the Hebrew is uncertain.   48:9 Or *Put salt on Moab, / for she will be laid waste.*   48:13 Hebrew *ashamed when they trusted in Bethel.*   48:21 Hebrew *Jahzah,* a variant spelling of Jahaz.   48:31 Hebrew *Kir-heres,* a variant spelling of Kir-hareseth; also in 48:36.   48:32 Hebrew *the sea of Jazer.*

## NOTES

**48:1** *Moab.* This region, peopled by descendants of Lot (Gen 19:37), is east of the Dead Sea. It has rugged hills and valleys and a plateau at 3,000 feet above sea level.

*Nebo.* A city two miles southeast of Mount Nebo.

*Kiriathaim.* Lit., "two towns." For the other towns mentioned, see King (1993:34-38), who draws on the work of J. Andrew Dearman.

**48:2** *Heshbon.* At one time the capital of Sihon of the Amorites (Num 21:21-30), this city in northern Moab was occupied, according to excavations (begun in 1968), from the Iron Age (1200 BC) until AD 400.

**48:5** *Luhith.* Its identity is uncertain; perhaps it was situated at a higher elevation in the south and connected by a road to Horonaim at the bottom of a descent at the southwest corner of the Dead Sea.

**48:6 *Hide in the wilderness.*** The Heb. reads, "You will be like Aroer"; the LXX reads, "you will be like a wild ass." A better rendering, assuming an Arabic cognate for *'aro'er* [TH6176A, ZH6875], is "like a sand grouse in the wilderness" (NEB).

**48:7 *your wealth and skill.*** Or, "deeds" (*ma'asim* [TH4639, ZH5126]) and "treasure-houses" (*'otseroth* [TH214, ZH238]).

***Chemosh.*** This Moabite god (Num 21:29) is mentioned on the inscribed Moabite Stone discovered in 1868 at Dibon. The inscription, left by King Mesha of Moab, tells of a victory over Israel at the time of Ahab. The Moabite king then honored the god Chemosh by building a high place in gratitude.

**48:8 *All the towns will be destroyed.*** The destroyer (participle of *shadad* [TH7703, ZH8720], lay waste) is left unnamed but is almost certainly a military army, like Babylon, which overran the region around 598 BC and again in 582 BC.

**48:9 *Oh, that Moab had wings.*** Some advocate "salt" (from the Ugaritic) for the problem word *tsits* [TH6731A, ZH7490] (petal, flower, wing?) and so translate, "Give a salt field for Moab" (cf. Judg 9:45; Holladay 1989:341).

**48:10 *who refuse to do the LORD's work.*** Lit., "doing the Lord's work [i.e., destroying Moab] deceitfully" (*remiyah* [TH7423, ZH8244]) perhaps in the sense of sluggishness (cf. NRSV).

**48:13 *his idol Chemosh . . . gold calf at Bethel.*** The NLT inserts "idol" and "gold calf," which are not present in the Heb. Jeroboam set up golden calves at Bethel (1 Kgs 12:28-29; cf. Amos 5:5; 7:10-17). But Bethel, a god worshiped in Syria, was apparently also known and worshipped in Israel. The Heb., with its formulation "because of Bethel" suggests either a deity by that name (in parallelism with Chemosh) or the incident at Bethel.

**48:17 *See how the strong scepter is broken.*** This line and the next one quote what the "friends" who know Moab's fame will say.

**48:18 *Dibon.*** Mentioned in the Moabite Stone inscription. It was three miles north of the Arnon River and thirteen miles east of the Dead Sea.

**48:19 *Aroer.*** This fortress on the north bank of the Arnon guarded the King's Highway.

***stand . . . shout.*** These words are imperatives in the Heb.

**48:20 *And the reply comes back.*** This is inserted in the NLT for clarification. The Arnon River, which often marked Moab's northern border, empties into the Dead Sea opposite En-gedi, in Judah (Judg 11:18-19).

**48:21 *towns of the plateau.*** See King (1993:34-38) for conjectural identifications. Israel fought Sihon, king of the Amorites at Jahzah (Jahaz; Num 21:23-26).

**48:22 *Beth-diblathaim.*** This may have been one of Israel's stopping places on the way to Canaan (Num 33:46-47).

**48:24 *Kerioth.*** Kerioth is mentioned on the Moabite Stone inscription. It was located northwest of Dibon.

***Bozrah.*** This was not the Edomite city (49:13) but may be the same as Bezer, eight miles northeast of Madaba.

**48:26 *he has rebelled against the LORD.*** Lit., "he has made [himself] great" (hiphil of *gadal* [TH1431, ZH1540]). An identical construction appears in 48:42.

**48:27 *that you should despise them as you do?*** The Heb. is idiomatic and graphic: "that whenever you have words about her, you should shake [your head in disdain]?" (hitpolel of *nud* [TH5110, ZH5653], "wander," "move back and forth").

**48:31 *My heart is broken.*** The NLT uses an English idiom for the Heb., "I will cry for all of them . . . it will moan" (*hagah* [TH1897, ZH2047]).

*Kir-hareseth.* The name, or variations of it, occurs in Isa 16:7 and 2 Kgs 3:25. It was an ancient Moabite capital and is generally identified with Kerak (Holladay 1989:361). It is situated 3,110 feet above sea level and the remains of a famous Crusader fort are still there.

**48:32 *Sibmah.*** This area in the region of Heshbon (cf. Isa 16:8-11) was famous for its wines.

*Jazer.* This town was eight miles west of Rabbah (modern Amman).

**48:34 *Elealeh.*** This city is thought to be two miles northeast of Heshbon.

*Zoar.* This was one of the "five cities of the plain," located south of the Dead Sea in the Sodom-Gomorrah region (Gen 19:24-30).

*Nimrim.* This was a wadi, possibly ten miles south of the Dead Sea.

**48:35 *I will put an end to Moab.*** Strictly speaking, this meant an end to those sacrificing at pagan shrines.

**48:43 *Terror and traps and snares.*** There is assonance in the Heb.: *pakhad* [TH6343, ZH7065] (terror), *pakhath* [TH6354, ZH7074] (pit), and *pakh* [TH6341, ZH7062] (trap).

**48:44 *I will see to it that you do not get away.*** This line is not found in the Heb.

**48:47 *I will restore the fortunes of Moab.*** For the expression as applied to Israel, see 29:14; 30:3 (cf. 46:28; 49:6, 39).

*end of Jeremiah's prophecy.* More lit., "Thus far the decision/judgment (*mishpat* [TH4941, ZH5477]) on Moab."

COMMENTARY

The prophet's scanner, which first brought into view the southern peoples of Egypt and the Philistines (Jer 46–47), now turns eastward to several of Israel's neighbors. Moab, Ammon, and Edom were southeast of the Jordan (48:1–49:22), and Damascus and Kedar were northeast of Judah (49:23-33). A possible purpose for these oracles may have been to emphasize that the doom of these enemy nations would spell deliverance for Judah and Israel. Another reason, especially clear from the oracle about Moab, was to warn against certain evils. Portions of this oracle are almost identical to Isaiah 15–16. Ezekiel also prophesied about Moab (25:8-11; cf. Num 21:29-30).

The Moab oracle has been variously analyzed for its structure. By taking account of the repeated call for weeping and wailing, the material can be segmented as follows: a nation doomed (48:1-16); doom deserved (48:17-30); a huge tragedy (48:31-35); no escape (48:36-45); and not forever (48:46-47). Several other themes—the reason for the calamity, its extent, the pathos it entailed, and its inevitability—appear in most segments. The commentary develops these themes in five sections.

**Utter Sadness at the Nation's Doom (48:1-16).** The initial word, "weep," is a translation of a Hebrew exclamation customarily used at funerals and tragedies. It sets the tone for the entire oracle and also concludes it (48:46). The poem is laced with expressions of grief and sorrow. The pathos engendered by the devastation centers in the first segment on listening to the cries of little ones (48:4) and refugees (48:5), as well as on witnessing the slaughter of the most promising youth (48:15). Moab's pathos is felt in the wishful desire for wings by which she might escape the disaster (48:9) and in the agony of knowing that this cannot happen. God 's intent for destruction was fixed, and his appointed executioners would be cursed if they became slack in carrying out their task (48:10).

Tears flow as onlookers remember the history of Moab (48:17). Wine is best when the sediment settles over a long time, but if left too long, it becomes syrupy. Moab had become stale over time and would have "tilters" coming to empty her. The lengthy period of stability would come to a sad end. Sorrow increasingly dominates the poem (48:17, 20, 31, 32, 36, 39, 46). Even God mourns (assuming he is the speaker, 48:39; cf. 8:18–9:2). This interpretation runs counter to the view of some, who see the exhortations to weep as tongue-in-cheek expressions of vengeance.

There may be occasions for people to gloat over the misery that befalls others, but here and elsewhere God's judgment elicits sorrow. It is sad to see persons or nations who have fared well come under God's judgment because of fatal flaws. Jeremiah's heart broke as he announced the fall of Jerusalem (8:18). Jesus knew that the rebuilt city under Herod would in the future come under the sword of the Romans, and he agonized over it (Matt 23:37). Those who are called to preach the judgment of God on wickedness dare not do so out of vindictiveness, but must speak with a real sense of the hurt and pain involved in their message.

**Doom Deserved (48:17-30).** To feel the pain brought on by tragedy is not to be numb to reality. There were reasons for Moab's destruction. Those reasons, concentrated in the second segment, had to do with pride. "Come down from your glory" (48:18). These people had become arrogant, and their pride was "very great" (48:29; cf. Isa 16:6). This nation exalted itself, was consumed with its own importance, and boasted of its achievements and its status. God hates pride and has no tolerance for arrogance (Prov 6:17); such attitudes lead to autonomy and soon eclipse any sense of needing God. Pride can lead to disparagement of others, so it is not surprising that Moab had been ridiculing Israel (48:27). Pride was also the sin that brought Babylon down (50:31).

Pride and arrogance are expressed in different ways, but their common denominator is inordinate preoccupation with self that results in self-centered behavior. The proud are altogether self-absorbed and self-sufficient (Ezek 28:2-5, 12-17; Luke 18:11-12), whereas humility brings a believer under God's rule. In humility and brokenness, persons come to faith in Christ; in humility they continue their lives of sanctification, and with humility they serve God and others.

Pride was not Moab's only failing. Other stanzas point to the evil of pagan shrines and the worship of other gods (48:35). The worship of Chemosh as a rival god to Yahweh was totally unacceptable (48:13). Moab trusted in its own resources, its wealth, and its skill (48:7). The image of wine settled in its flask, while pointing to stability, may also negatively indicate a stale or complacent smugness (48:11). These shortcomings, serious in themselves, should perhaps be understood as subsidiary to the major evil, excessive pride and arrogance.

**Large Scale Calamity (48:31-35).** The tragedy of Moab affected the whole country and its entire population. Sibmah boasted of its vineyards, as a California city might boast of being the raisin capital of the world (48:32). The "sea" of 48:32, while commonly regarded as the Dead Sea, could possibly be the Mediterranean or conceivably the Red Sea/Aqaba Gulf and so point to international trade. Commerce, not to mention local harvests and local safety, were hugely affected by this large disaster. Cries of terror were heard from one end of the country to the other (48:34). Alas, "even the waters of Nimrim are dried up" (48:34). This segment ends, as do most of the others, with a succinct statement calling attention to the wholesale disaster: "I will put an end to Moab" (48:35; cf. 48:16, 26, 38, 45).

All segments have the same refrain about major destruction. The theme is elaborated by the listing of the many towns, all to be leveled (48:1, 2, 3, 15, 18, 19, 21-24, 32, 34, 45). It is hammered home by the mention of various age groups: children (48:4), youth (48:15), and mighty warriors (48:41). The theme of total destruction is also highlighted through metaphors of men pouring out old wine and shattering the jar (48:12), the disposal of an unwanted bottle (48:38), a strong arm broken (48:25), or an eagle or vulture swooping over the whole land (48:40). There was no hiding place (48:28).

**Inescapable Calamity (48:36-45).** The final stanza, while repeating other themes —weeping (48:36-38), wide-scale devastation (48:41), and the sin of rebellion (48:45)—insists that no one will get away (48:44). People may try to flee, but they will not be able to circumvent the harsh reality (48:45). It was time for God to attend to this people in judgment (48:44), and a fateful day for proud persons (Isa 2:10-19; cf. Rev 6:15-16). The tendency to think "I will be exempt" is also addressed elsewhere (cf. Ps 139:7-12; Amos 9:1-4).

**Recovery (48:46 47).** Moab's pride brought on their disaster, but no motivation is offered for Moab's eventual restoration. That reason is hidden within God, unless one were to infer that God's sorrow for Moab (48:36) would move him to work for her restoration. Perhaps, given God's nature, no reason was necessary. The judgments were anchored in legal considerations, so that identified crimes became the grounds for judgment. It was not legal procedure, however, that looked beyond judgment to salvation, but rather a magnanimous and gracious God.

◆    ## D. Ammon and Edom: Sounds of Battle Cries (49:1-22)

This message was given concerning the Ammonites. This is what the LORD says:

> "Are there no descendants of Israel
>     to inherit the land of Gad?
> Why are you, who worship Molech,*
>     living in its towns?
> ²In the days to come," says the LORD,
>     "I will sound the battle cry against
>     your city of Rabbah.

It will become a desolate heap of ruins,
    and the neighboring towns will be burned.
Then Israel will take back the land
    you took from her," says the LORD.

> ³"Cry out, O Heshbon,
>     for the town of Ai is destroyed.
> Weep, O people of Rabbah!
>     Put on your clothes of mourning.

Weep and wail, hiding in the hedges,
for your god Molech, with his
priests and officials,
will be hauled off to distant lands.
⁴You are proud of your fertile valleys,
but they will soon be ruined.
You trusted in your wealth,
you rebellious daughter,
and thought no one could ever harm
you.
⁵But look! I will bring terror upon you,"
says the Lord, the LORD of Heaven's
Armies.
"Your neighbors will chase you from
your land,
and no one will help your exiles as
they flee.
⁶But I will restore the fortunes of the
Ammonites
in days to come.
I, the LORD, have spoken."

⁷This message was given concerning
Edom. This is what the LORD of Heaven's
Armies says:

"Is there no wisdom in Teman?
Is no one left to give wise counsel?
⁸Turn and flee!
Hide in deep caves, you people of
Dedan!
For when I bring disaster on Edom,*
I will punish you, too!
⁹Those who harvest grapes
always leave a few for the poor.
If thieves came at night,
they would not take everything.
¹⁰But I will strip bare the land of Edom,
and there will be no place left to
hide.
Its children, its brothers, and its
neighbors
will all be destroyed,
and Edom itself will be no more.
¹¹But I will protect the orphans who
remain among you.
Your widows, too, can depend on me
for help."

¹²And this is what the LORD says: "If the
innocent must suffer, how much more

must you! You will not go unpunished!
You must drink this cup of judgment!
¹³For I have sworn by my own name," says
the LORD, "that Bozrah will become an object of horror and a heap of ruins; it will
be mocked and cursed. All its towns and
villages will be desolate forever."

¹⁴I have heard a message from the LORD
that an ambassador was sent to the
nations to say,
"Form a coalition against Edom,
and prepare for battle!"

¹⁵The LORD says to Edom,
"I will cut you down to size among the
nations.
You will be despised by all.
¹⁶You have been deceived
by the fear you inspire in others
and by your own pride.
You live in a rock fortress
and control the mountain heights.
But even if you make your nest among
the peaks with the eagles,
I will bring you crashing down,"
says the LORD.

¹⁷"Edom will be an object of horror.
All who pass by will be appalled
and will gasp at the destruction
they see there.
¹⁸It will be like the destruction of Sodom
and Gomorrah
and their neighboring towns," says
the LORD.
"No one will live there;
no one will inhabit it.
¹⁹I will come like a lion from the
thickets of the Jordan,
leaping on the sheep in the pasture.
I will chase Edom from its land,
and I will appoint the leader of my
choice.
For who is like me, and who can
challenge me?
What ruler can oppose my will?"

²⁰Listen to the LORD's plans against
Edom
and the people of Teman.

| | |
|---|---|
| Even the little children will be<br>dragged off like sheep,<br>and their homes will be<br>destroyed.<br>²¹ The earth will shake with the noise<br>of Edom's fall,<br>and its cry of despair will be heard<br>all the way to the Red Sea.* | ²² Look! The enemy swoops down like<br>an eagle,<br>spreading his wings over<br>Bozrah.<br>Even the mightiest warriors will be<br>in anguish<br>like a woman in labor. |

**49:1** Hebrew *Malcam,* a variant spelling of Molech; also in 49:3.   **49:8** Hebrew *Esau;* also in 49:10.
**49:21** Hebrew *sea of reeds.*

NOTES

**49:1 *Ammonites.*** These were descendants of Lot (Gen 19:38). Ammon lay east of the Dead Sea and north of Moab between the Arnon and the Jabbok rivers. Its people were often in conflict with Israel and Judah (Judg 10–11, 1 Sam 11, 2 Sam 10).

***Gad.*** This tribe of Israel occupied Ammonite territory.

***Molech.*** Or, Milcom (LXX; MT, *malkam* [TH4428, ZH4889], "their king"). This Ammonite deity, associated with child sacrifice, was sometimes worshiped in Israel (1 Kgs 11:7, 33).

**49:2 *Rabbah.*** This capital of the Ammonites (modern Amman) lay twenty-five miles east of the Jordan. For archaeology there, see King (1993:39).

***Israel will take back the land.*** Ammon repossessed Gad after Tiglath-pileser III raided Israel in 733 BC.

**49:3 *Cry out, O Heshbon.*** Heshbon, near the Moab border, only belonged to Moab during certain periods (48:45).

***Ai.*** The name means "ruin"; it is a different town than the one mentioned in Josh 8:1.

***hiding in the hedges.*** If for *baggederoth* [TH1448, ZH1556] (by walls) one reads *bigdudoth* [TH1418, ZH1523] ("with gashes," cf. Heb. of 48:37) then the reading, better suited to the context, becomes "scourge yourself with whips" (so NRSV), an act associated with mourning.

**49:4 *no one could ever harm you.*** The Heb. uses a direct quote, "Who will come against me?"

**49:6 *I will restore the fortunes.*** For the idiom as applied to Israel, see 30:3; for other nations, see 48:47; 49:39.

**49:7 *Edom.*** Edom, peopled by descendants of Esau (Gen 36:1-19; cf. Jer 49:8), stretched 100 miles south of the Dead Sea to the Gulf of Aqaba.

***Teman.*** This was an Edomite town. Teman may be an alternate name for Edom.

***Is no one left to give wise counsel?*** The NLT collapses two parallel sentences that use *'etsah* [TH6098, ZH6783] (counsel) and *bin* [TH995, ZH1067] (discernment).

**49:8 *Dedan.*** This was an oasis on a trade route in northwest Saudi Arabia. Some clans from there may have settled in Edom.

**49:11 *I will protect the orphans.*** Some suggest a change of speaker to an ally of Edom (Holladay 1989:376).

**49:13 *Bozrah will become an object of horror.*** Bozrah, a chief city twenty-one miles south of the Dead Sea, was once a large fortified town (nineteen acres), but lies in ruins today. It was excavated in 1971–1976 (King 1993:48-49).

**49:16 *You live in a rock fortress.*** This possibly refers to Petra, the red-rock fortress with houses and temples cut into its cliffs. It was accessible through a narrow gorge and to all appearances was impregnable.

**49:17 *will gasp at the destruction.*** This is a felicitous rendering. The Heb. *sharaq* [TH8319, ZH9239] (hiss, whistle) can also refer to the sound of inhaling, as in a gasp. "Destruction" is more lit. "the striking."

**49:19 *leaping on the sheep in the pasture.*** "Sheep" is an NLT insertion. The last phrase, more lit., is "richness or well-watered pasture."

### COMMENTARY

Three countries—all Israel's neighbors—lay to Israel's east and south. Of these, Moab is given the longest judgment oracle (48:1-47). The word against Ammon is the shortest (49:1-6; cf. Ezek 25:1-7; Amos 1:13-15; Zeph 2:8-11). The message to Edom, while partly specific to the region, employs stereotypical language (49:7-22; cf. Isa 21:11-12; 34:5-15; Ezek 25:12-14; 35:1-15; Obad 1-21). The two oracles against Ammon and Edom have common components, questions (49:1, 7b), advice/counsel (49:3, 8a), first-person announcements of Yahweh's actions (49:2a, 5-6, 8b, 10, 11, 13, 15a, 19), accusations (49:4, 16), and consequences of God's action (49:2b, 5b, 17-18, 20-22). Attention to the stereotyped vocabulary helps in isolating the more novel dimensions within these oracles.

**Judgment on Ammon (49:1-6).** Molech, Ammon's deity, would be taken into captivity along with its attendants, just as Chemosh and its ministers would be removed (48:7). As in other oracles, God would move against the offending nation's capital (here Rabbah) by means of war (49:2). Also as in other oracles, though with different rhetoric, the call was for people to weep over the devastation (49:3; cf. 48:37-38). As with Moab and other countries, destruction would not be the last word. Ammon would recover (cf. 48:31-32; 49:39).

Ammon was rebuked for her aggression (49:1-2; cf. Amos 1:13-15) and specifically for seizing land that belonged to others, a reason for many a war. Ammon trusted in her wealth. She thought she was beyond the reach of harm but was badly mistaken. She was indicted for an attitude of complacency and self-sufficiency (49:4b). Ammon became just one more example of a people who preferred another god (Molech) over Yahweh and who organized life around wealth and self-serving interests. Generic as it was, her problem became a forceful warning to any nation taking its wealth for granted and in danger of becoming a "rebellious daughter."

**Judgment on Edom (49:7-22).** Many descriptions of the severity of Edom's destruction were composed of stock phrases and images representing such events (cf. 49:9-10 with Obad 5-6; 49:14-16 with Obad 1-4). Armies were summoned to battle (49:14; cf. 46:3-6, 9; 49:2; 50:14, 16; 51:3, 11, 16). Judgment was likened to a wild animal pouncing on the unsuspecting (49:19). God was pictured as a lion coming from the forest (4:7; 5:6; 50:44-46) or like an eagle (or vulture) swooping down to destroy (49:22; cf. 48:40). Drinking a cup of judgment was also a common notion (25:15-38; 49:12). God would demolish the city, leaving it ruined and without an inhabitant (49:10, 13; cf. 44:22). Soldiers trying to fend off the disaster would be as terrified and disconcerted as a woman giving birth (48:41; 49:22; 50:43; Isa 26:17; Mic 4:9). To describe the devastation, since not much new could be said, the prophet resorted to standard vocabulary, virtual cliches, and the classic illustration of Sodom and Gomorrah (49:18; Gen 14:2, 8; 19:24-25; Deut 29:23; Isa 13:9). While such vocabulary can become familiar to the point of having little impact, it can also conjure up standard images that leave no doubt as to what is being communicated.

Much the same can be said about preaching. The words are ones the congregation has heard before. Certain common phrases are familiar to the point of emptiness. And yet, repeated statements about the fate of God-resisters or the reality of salvation do carry a punch. Now, as in ancient times, not everything is determined by words, usual or unusual, but by the authoritative voice of the One speaking, the One who has "sworn by [his] own name" (49:13), as the LORD of Heaven's Armies (49:7).

Peculiar to this oracle of judgment is the opening question about wisdom, for which Teman, a city or district in Edom, was renowned (Obad 8). True wisdom (defined elsewhere as the fear of the Lord) was absent. The truly wise would know better than to be proud (49:16; cf. comments on 48:29-30; cf. 50:29, 31-32; Ezek 28:2, 5, 17; Prov 16:5). This oracle is country-specific—Edom was unique in its natural mountain fortifications (49:16), but its favored position became its undoing. God would judge the resulting pride and self-sufficiency by cutting this nation down to size (49:15) and casting it to the ground (49:16). Those who boast, the wise know, boast not in status but in understanding and knowing Yahweh, who delights in practicing justice (9:23-24 [22-23]). As part of his justice, he will come to the aid of children and widows (49:11). In wrath, he still remembers mercy.

◆ ### E. Damascus, Kedar, Hazor, and Elam: Trouble from All Directions (49:23-39)

²³This message was given concerning Damascus. This is what the LORD says:

"The towns of Hamath and Arpad are struck with fear,
    for they have heard the news of their destruction.
Their hearts are troubled
    like a wild sea in a raging storm.
²⁴Damascus has become feeble,
    and all her people turn to flee.
Fear, anguish, and pain have gripped her
    as they grip a woman in labor.
²⁵That famous city, a city of joy,
    will be forsaken!

²⁶Her young men will fall in the streets and die.
    Her soldiers will all be killed,"
    says the LORD of Heaven's Armies.
²⁷"And I will set fire to the walls of Damascus
    that will burn up the palaces of Ben-hadad."

²⁸This message was given concerning Kedar and the kingdoms of Hazor, which were attacked by King Nebuchadnezzar* of Babylon. This is what the LORD says:

"Advance against Kedar!
    Destroy the warriors from the East!
²⁹Their flocks and tents will be captured,

and their household goods and
camels will be taken away.
Everywhere shouts of panic will be
heard:
'We are terrorized at every turn!'
³⁰Run for your lives," says the LORD.
"Hide yourselves in deep caves, you
people of Hazor,
for King Nebuchadnezzar of Babylon
has plotted against you
and is preparing to destroy you.

³¹"Go up and attack that complacent
nation,"
says the LORD.
"Its people live alone in the desert
without walls or gates.
³²Their camels and other livestock will
all be yours.
I will scatter to the winds these
people
who live in remote places.*
I will bring calamity upon them
from every direction," says the LORD.
³³"Hazor will be inhabited by jackals,
and it will be desolate forever.
No one will live there;
no one will inhabit it."

³⁴This message concerning Elam came
to the prophet Jeremiah from the LORD at

the beginning of the reign of King Zedekiah of Judah. ³⁵This is what the LORD of
Heaven's Armies says:

"I will destroy the archers of Elam—
the best of their forces.
³⁶I will bring enemies from all
directions,
and I will scatter the people of Elam
to the four winds.
They will be exiled to countries
around the world.
³⁷I myself will go with Elam's enemies to
shatter it.
In my fierce anger, I will bring great
disaster
upon the people of Elam," says the
LORD.
"Their enemies will chase them with
the sword
until I have destroyed them
completely.
³⁸I will set my throne in Elam," says the
LORD,
"and I will destroy its king and
officials.
³⁹But I will restore the fortunes of
Elam
in days to come.
I, the LORD, have spoken!"

49:28 Hebrew *Nebuchadrezzar*, a variant spelling of Nebuchadnezzar; also in 49:30.   49:32 Or *who clip the corners of their hair.*

NOTES

**49:23 *Damascus.*** Damascus was the capital of Syria. It is one of the world's oldest cities.

***Hamath.*** Also in Syria, on the Orontes River between Damascus and Aleppo to the north, Hamath was once an independent kingdom but later was occupied in turn by Israel, Assyria, Egypt, and Babylon.

***Arpad.*** Arpad lay twenty miles northwest of Aleppo. It is always mentioned together with Hamath in the Bible.

**49:27 *Ben-hadad.*** Lit., "son of Hadad," this was the throne name of a Syrian ninth- and eighth-century dynasty king (1 Kgs 15:18; 20:1-34). Hadad (Thunderer) was the Aramaean name for the Canaanite storm god, Baal.

**49:28 *Kedar.*** This influential nomadic tribe was descended from Ishmael; its people settled in the Syrian-Arabian desert (Gen 25:13; Isa 21:16; Jer 2:10). Their tents were made of black goat hair (cf. *qadar* [TH6937, ZH7722] "be dark").

***Hazor.*** This is an unknown site, if a site at all (but cf. 49:32); it is not the Hazor in Israel. The Heb. term *khatser* [TH2691, ZH2958] can mean "courts" or "settlements" (cf. Holladay

1989:382-383), that is, "kingdoms of settled folk," not nomads (cf. *khatserim*, "unwalled settlements" Isa 42:11).

**49:29 We are terrorized at every turn!** The cryptic *magor missabib* [TH4032, ZH4471] (terror surrounds) occurs in 6:25 and 46:5; it is a name applied to Pashhur (20:3) and Jeremiah (20:7).

**49:32 people who live in remote places.** The designation "those with shaven temples" is perhaps pejorative. Israel was not to follow this pagan practice (Lev 19:27; cf. Jer 9:25-26 [24-25]).

**49:34 Elam.** This territory was 200 miles east of Babylon beyond the Tigris, with Susa as its capital. Elam was absorbed by the Persians in the sixth century and is now southwest Iran. Its people are known as skilled archers (Isa 22:6) from bas reliefs found in Nineveh.

**49:37 Their enemies will chase them with the sword.** Lit., "I will send a sword after them."

**49:38 I will set my throne in Elam.** This is a divine coup d'etat. For the image, see 1:15; 43:10.

**49:39 I will restore the fortunes.** This is an idiom. See comment on 29:14; see also a similar message to Moab (48:47) and Ammon (49:6).

COMMENTARY

In the series of oracles about the nations, God's searchlight now swings to the regions northeast of Israel and Judah. Damascus, Kedar, and Hazor were regions not too distant from Israel, but Elam was very remote. Some Judeans may have thought that Elam would curb, if not overthrow, Babylon. Jeremiah, a prophet to the nations (1:10), squelched such notions. Jeremiah's full roster of nations was bracketed by two superpowers, Egypt (Jer 46) and Babylon (Jer 50-51). Next to each, inside the bracket, was placed a smaller nation, Philistia (Jer 47) and Elam (Jer 49:34-39). Neither large nations nor small lay beyond God's judgment.

**Damascus and the LORD of Hosts (49:23-27).** Though the oracle against Damascus is the briefest of the oracles against the nations, an ominous refrain sounds: "the LORD of Heaven's Armies" (49:26). The expression punctuates the oracles against the nations (more than twenty times—e.g., 46:10; 48:15) and it occurs frequently in messages of judgment against Israel (19:11; 25:8). Whereas most messages carry the signature formula, "says the LORD" (49:30) or "This is what the LORD says" (49:1), in some, the heavy-sounding cadence of *yhwh tseba'oth* [TH3068/6635, ZH3378/ 7372], the LORD of Heaven's armies, is added. Its effect is to emphasize the gravity of the announcement, for now the full weight of the cosmic commander's authority enforces the announcement. A further effect is to relativize all pretensions to power, whether by small or by formidable nations. Human systems of politics and economics are destabilized before the One who has the armies of heaven at his command. Little wonder that people seem feeble (49:24). This heavyweight title further meant that there was something inexorable about the announcements with their determinative "I will" (49:27). In two oracles, it is said that trouble will come from all directions so as to overwhelm the defenders (49:32, 36), but few things add to the gravity of the situation like the title, "The LORD of Heaven's Armies."

**Kedar and Hazor Panic (49:28-33).**  Nomads scattered in the desert relied for their security on their isolation and their mobility (49:31). They did not need to protect any specific territory. Nonetheless, God commandeered Nebuchadnezzar to make an assault on these unsuspecting desert peoples. The result was terror (49:29), the loss of their household goods, camels, and cattle (49:29-32), and ultimately, dispersion (49:32). The Babylonian Chronicle, which recounts Nebuchadnezzar's raid in 599/8 BC, notes that "scouring the desert, they [the raiding companies] took much plunder from many Arabs, their possessions, animals, and goods." The panic was greater because of the nomads' mistaken notion that they had nothing to fear. They realized that they were helpless, for disaster approached them from every direction.

**God's Fierce Anger against Elam (49:34-39).**  God ominously stated that he would destroy Elam's chief strength, the skill of its archers (49:35). It is quite clear that their disintegration is unalterable when God announces, "I myself will go with Elam's enemies" (cf. the frequency of "I will"). When the LORD of Heaven's Armies takes the enemy's side, the outcome is inevitable. Once God is arrayed against a nation or a power, there are no chances for victory. "Ammon depended on Molech and its riches (49:3-4). Edom depended on wisdom and its inaccessible location (49:7, 16). Damascus depended on its fame (49:25). Kedar depended on its remoteness (49:31) and Elam on its bow but all of them failed" (Huey 1993:407).

In different ways, then, each of the oracles makes clear that the coming judgment is inexorable. The final audit was inevitable for individuals and nations. It is appointed for humans to die and then they will be judged (Heb 9:27). In the Day of the Big Audit, nations will also appear before the Almighty for punishment or reward (Matt 25:31-46).

## ◆  F. Babylon Will Fall (50:1-46)

The LORD gave Jeremiah the prophet this message concerning Babylon and the land of the Babylonians.* ²This is what the LORD says:

"Tell the whole world,
  and keep nothing back.
Raise a signal flag
  to tell everyone that Babylon will
    fall!
Her images and idols* will be
    shattered.
  Her gods Bel and Marduk will be
    utterly disgraced.
³For a nation will attack her from the
    north
  and bring such destruction that no
    one will live there again.

Everything will be gone;
  both people and animals will flee.

⁴"In those coming days,"
  says the LORD,
"the people of Israel will return home
  together with the people of Judah.
They will come weeping
  and seeking the LORD their God.
⁵They will ask the way to Jerusalem*
  and will start back home again.
They will bind themselves to the LORD
  with an eternal covenant that will
    never be forgotten.

⁶"My people have been lost sheep.
  Their shepherds have led them
    astray

and turned them loose in the
   mountains.
They have lost their way
   and can't remember how to get back
     to the sheepfold.
⁷All who found them devoured them.
   Their enemies said,
'We did nothing wrong in attacking
   them,
   for they sinned against the LORD,
their true place of rest,
   and the hope of their ancestors.'

⁸"But now, flee from Babylon!
   Leave the land of the Babylonians.
Like male goats at the head of the
   flock,
   lead my people home again.
⁹For I am raising up an army
   of great nations from the north.
They will join forces to attack Babylon,
   and she will be captured.
The enemies' arrows will go straight
   to the mark;
   they will not miss!
¹⁰Babylonia* will be looted
   until the attackers are glutted with
     loot.
   I, the LORD, have spoken!

¹¹"You rejoice and are glad,
   you who plundered my chosen
     people.
You frisk about like a calf in a meadow
   and neigh like a stallion.
¹²But your homeland* will be
   overwhelmed
   with shame and disgrace.
You will become the least of nations—
   a wilderness, a dry and desolate
     land.
¹³Because of the LORD's anger,
   Babylon will become a deserted
     wasteland.
All who pass by will be horrified
   and will gasp at the destruction
     they see there.
¹⁴"Yes, prepare to attack Babylon,
   all you surrounding nations.

Let your archers shoot at her; spare no
   arrows.
For she has sinned against the LORD.
¹⁵Shout war cries against her from every
   side.
Look! She surrenders!
   Her walls have fallen.
It is the LORD's vengeance,
   so take vengeance on her.
   Do to her as she has done to others!
¹⁶Take from Babylon all those who plant
   crops;
   send all the harvesters away.
Because of the sword of the enemy,
   everyone will run away and rush
     back to their own lands.

¹⁷"The Israelites are like sheep
   that have been scattered by lions.
First the king of Assyria ate them up.
   Then King Nebuchadnezzar* of
     Babylon cracked their bones."
¹⁸Therefore, this is what the LORD of
   Heaven's Armies,
   the God of Israel, says:
"Now I will punish the king of Babylon
   and his land,
   just as I punished the king of Assyria.
¹⁹And I will bring Israel home again to
   its own land,
   to feed in the fields of Carmel and
     Bashan,
and to be satisfied once more
   in the hill country of Ephraim and
     Gilead.
²⁰In those days," says the LORD,
   "no sin will be found in Israel or
     in Judah,
   for I will forgive the remnant
     I preserve.

²¹"Go up, my warriors, against the land
   of Merathaim
   and against the people of Pekod.
Pursue, kill, and completely destroy*
   them,
   as I have commanded you," says the
     LORD.
²²"Let the battle cry be heard in the
   land,

a shout of great destruction.
²³ Babylon, the mightiest hammer in all
the earth,
lies broken and shattered.
Babylon is desolate among the
nations!
²⁴ Listen, Babylon, for I have set a trap
for you.
You are caught, for you have fought
against the LORD.
²⁵ The LORD has opened his armory
and brought out weapons to vent
his fury.
The terror that falls upon the
Babylonians
will be the work of the Sovereign
LORD of Heaven's Armies.
²⁶ Yes, come against her from distant
lands.
Break open her granaries.
Crush her walls and houses into heaps
of rubble.
Destroy her completely, and leave
nothing!
²⁷ Destroy even her young bulls—
it will be terrible for them, too!
Slaughter them all!
For Babylon's day of reckoning has
come.
²⁸ Listen to the people who have escaped
from Babylon,
as they tell in Jerusalem
how the LORD our God has taken
vengeance
against those who destroyed his
Temple.

²⁹ "Send out a call for archers to come
to Babylon.
Surround the city so none can escape.
Do to her as she has done to others,
for she has defied the LORD, the
Holy One of Israel.
³⁰ Her young men will fall in the streets
and die.
Her soldiers will all be killed,"
says the LORD.

³¹ "See, I am your enemy, you arrogant
people,"

says the Lord, the LORD of Heaven's
Armies.
"Your day of reckoning has arrived—
the day when I will punish you.
³² O land of arrogance, you will stumble
and fall,
and no one will raise you up.
For I will light a fire in the cities of
Babylon
that will burn up everything around
them."

³³ This is what the LORD of Heaven's
Armies says:
"The people of Israel and Judah have
been wronged.
Their captors hold them and refuse
to let them go.
³⁴ But the one who redeems them is
strong.
His name is the LORD of Heaven's
Armies.
He will defend them
and give them rest again in Israel.
But for the people of Babylon
there will be no rest!

³⁵ "The sword of destruction will strike
the Babylonians,"
says the LORD.
"It will strike the people of Babylon—
her officials and wise men, too.
³⁶ The sword will strike her wise
counselors,
and they will become fools.
The sword will strike her mightiest
warriors,
and panic will seize them.
³⁷ The sword will strike her horses and
chariots
and her allies from other lands,
and they will all become like
women.
The sword will strike her treasures,
and they all will be plundered.
³⁸ The sword will even strike her water
supply,
causing it to dry up.
And why? Because the whole land is
filled with idols,

and the people are madly in love
with them.

39 "Soon Babylon will be inhabited by
desert animals and hyenas.
It will be a home for owls.
Never again will people live there;
it will lie desolate forever.

40 I will destroy it as I* destroyed Sodom
and Gomorrah
and their neighboring towns," says
the LORD.
"No one will live there;
no one will inhabit it.

41 "Look! A great army is coming from
the north.
A great nation and many kings
are rising against you from far-off
lands.

42 They are armed with bows and spears.
They are cruel and show no mercy.
As they ride forward on horses,
they sound like a roaring sea.
They are coming in battle formation,
planning to destroy you, Babylon.

43 The king of Babylon has heard reports
about the enemy,
and he is weak with fright.
Pangs of anguish have gripped him,
like those of a woman in labor.

44 "I will come like a lion from the
thickets of the Jordan,
leaping on the sheep in the pasture.
I will chase Babylon from its land,
and I will appoint the leader of my
choice.
For who is like me, and who can
challenge me?
What ruler can oppose my will?"

45 Listen to the LORD's plans against
Babylon
and the land of the Babylonians.
Even the little children will be dragged
off like sheep,
and their homes will be destroyed.

46 The earth will shake with the shout,
"Babylon has been taken!"
and its cry of despair will be heard
around the world.

50:1 Or *Chaldeans;* also in 50:8, 25, 35, 45.  50:2 The Hebrew term (literally *round things*) probably alludes to dung.  50:5 Hebrew *Zion;* also in 50:28.  50:10 Or *Chaldea.*  50:12 Hebrew *your mother.*  50:17 Hebrew *Nebuchadrezzar,* a variant spelling of Nebuchadnezzar.  50:21 The Hebrew term used here refers to the complete consecration of things or people to the LORD, either by destroying them or by giving them as an offering.  50:40 Hebrew *as God.*

## NOTES

**50:1 *Babylon.*** The city, situated on the southern Euphrates River fifty-four miles south of modern Baghdad (Iraq), gave its name to the powerful empire under Hammurabi (1793–1750 BC). The neo-Babylonian empire (626–539 BC) became a superpower by defeating Egypt in the west at Carchemish (605 BC), overrunning Palestine and Transjordan. Chaldea was earlier a synonym for the city named Babylon (cf. Isa 23:13). It came to stand for the whole country of Babylon after Nabopolassar, a governor of the southern region, Chaldea, came to the Babylonian throne in 626 BC.

**50:2 *idols.*** Lit., "dung pellets" (see NLT mg), as is often seen in Ezekiel (see MT of 23:49).

***Bel and Marduk.*** "Bel" was essentially a title, "lord," or "master." It was associated with Enlil, a deity of the Sumerians. Later, in the second millennium, the title was transferred to the Babylonian god Marduk who, as chief god, was held to be the creator of the universe. He was known as Bel Marduk, or sometimes just as Bel (ABD 1:652).

**50:3 *a nation will attack.*** The Heb. uses the "past" tense for the verb (so also in 50:2b), a grammatical oddity called "prophetic perfect" or "perfect of certainty," as though what was envisioned had already transpired.

**50:5 *eternal covenant.*** The expression occurs sixteen times in the OT (e.g., Gen 9:16; Exod 31:16; Jer 31:31-34; 32:40).

**50:7 *their true place of rest.*** Lit., "habitation (*neweh* [TH5116A, ZH5659], "sheepfold pen," "home") of righteousness" (*tsedeq* [TH6664, ZH7406]). "True" is possibly a reference to the Temple.

**50:12 *your homeland.*** The NLT thus collapses two designations, "your mother" and "the one who bore you," into one.

**50:15 *She surrenders!*** Lit., "she gives her hand." Babylon fell to Cyrus the Persian in 539 BC, but "without a battle," according to an extra-biblical record. Language about walls falling is conventional for defeat. For the notion that "to give the hand" means to make or break a covenant, see Keown et al. (1995:366).

**50:17 *king of Assyria.*** Israel, in the north, became subject to the Assyrian Shalmaneser V (2 Kgs 17:1-6). Samaria was captured by his successor, Sargon II, in 722 BC (2 Kgs 17:1-6).

**50:19 *Carmel and Bashan . . . Ephraim and Gilead.*** Carmel is a mountain range near the Mediterranean near modern Haifa; Ephraim is the central rolling hills region. Both Bashan (a high grazing plateau east of Galilee) and Gilead further south are east of the Jordan. The reference is thus to all of Palestine.

**50:20 *no sin will be found.*** The NLT conflates two parallel Heb. lines, each using a different word for "sin": *khatto'th* [TH2403A, ZH2633] (failure to hit the mark) and *'awon* [TH5771, ZH6411] (perversity).

**50:21 *Merathaim.*** Merathaim is likely a wordplay on a region in southern Babylon near the mouth of the Tigris and Euphrates Rivers, a district in the vicinity of the "bitter river" (cf. the Akkadian *nar marratu*). The Heb. root *marah* [TH4784, ZH5286] means "to be rebellious"; thus the dual form *merathayim* [TH4850, ZH5361] suggests "double rebellion" and possibly "double bitterness," with a play on the root *mar* [TH4751, ZH5253] (bitter).

***Pekod.*** The name "Pekod" (root *paqad* [TH6485, ZH7212], "punishment") is a wordplay on *puqudu*, the name of an Aramaean tribe east of the lower Tigris. The same nickname is used of this tribe in Ezek 23:23. The prophet, by working off the Akkadian names for places in Babylon and by similar sounding Heb. words, makes a memorable point.

**50:24 *You are caught.*** A better reading is, "You are caught unawares."

***fought.*** This could also be rendered "contend" or "meddle" (*garah* [TH1624, ZH1741]).

**50:29 *Do to her as she has done to others.*** A parallel line, not represented by the NLT, reads, "Repay (piel of *shalem* [TH7999, ZH8966]) her for her deeds."

**50:34 *He will defend them.*** The Heb. depicts the intensity of the defense, which is more legal than military: "he will surely litigate (*rib* [TH7378, ZH8189]) their litigation."

**50:36 *wise counselors.*** The Heb. word *bad* [TH907A, ZH967] is more accurately "diviner"; Babylon was known for mantic practices.

**50:40 *No one will live there.*** The same is said of Edom and Hazor (49:18, 33b; cf. Isa 13:19-22).

**50:43 *weak with fright.*** Lit., "his hands droop [go limp]," an idiom for being disheartened. For similar language, see 6:22-24.

**50:44-45** Nearly identical with 49:19-21; see comments there.

## COMMENTARY

Two lengthy chapters about Babylon conclude the series of oracles about Israel's neighboring nations (cf. 121 verses for Babylon; 110 verses for the other eight nations). The series is bracketed by an oracle against Egypt, the superpower in the west (Jer 46), and Babylon, the superpower in the east (Jer 50–51).

The theme is Babylon's destruction and Israel's consequent restoration, and the mood is especially aggressive. It was Babylon that subjugated Judah, burned their capital city, and destroyed their Temple. Babylon was God's agent in delivering the judgment that God had threatened against Judah. But Babylon was not without evils of its own, such as overreaching her mandate. However, the chapter gives more details of her destruction than about her evils.

The verses of 50:2-3 are programmatic for the chapter if not for the entire oracle. Different scenes tumble into view: (1) Babylon will be attacked; (2) Babylon will fall; (3) Babylon's destruction will be total; (4) Babylon's demise will be world news; and (5) Babylon's demise will spell hope for Israel (implied).

The subsequent segments, of varying lengths, each take one of these scenes as a theme. The chapter both opens and closes with the charge for all the world to take notice (50:2, 46). The chapter could be outlined by giving attention to (1) Babylon, (2) the invading foe, and (3) Israel; or according to movements (50:4-20; 21-32; 33-46) with variations on a rhetorical pattern of three "ground-elements" (1) situation, (2) intervention, and (3) outcome (Aitken 1984). Bellis (1995) delineates six individual poems for the two chapters (50–51) and elsewhere (Bellis 1999) elaborates on the three in Jeremiah 50 as dealing with God's forgiveness of his people (50:2-20), the rebellion and punishment of Babylon (50:21-32), and Israel's complaint against Babylon (50:33-38).

**Hope for Israel and Judah (50:4-8).** No sooner was it announced that mighty Babylon would crumble to the dust, than the implication was quickly drawn: Babylon's defeat would mean that those she held captive, including the Judeans captured by Nebuchadnezzar and exiled to Babylon, would be free to return home (50:4-5). Such a return would also include the Israelites, for the demise of Babylon would mean the breakup of the entire empire, including the territories around the Habor River—to which persons from the northern kingdom of Israel had been deported (2 Kgs 17:5-6).

As often occurs, the physical return to the homeland was linked with the spiritual return of the people to Yahweh and the covenant (50:5b). The arrangement had been spelled out: (1) the Lord had given Israel the land (3:18); (2) continued possession of the land was conditional on the people's loyalty to Yahweh (7:5-7); (3) disloyalty to God would bring eventual punishment in the loss of the land (7:14-15); and (4) physical restoration to the land and spiritual restoration to God were linked. For Jeremiah, the restoration to God was a pre-condition for return (31:15-22). Ezekiel spoke as though the return to the land would come first, after which the people would be restored to the Lord (Ezek 20:40-44). In either case, the covenant between God and Israel had to do with both the physical land and a spiritual relationship.

The causal connection between ethical behavior and land possession was never lost sight of. The blame for the Exile was placed initially on the behavior of the leaders (50:6-7). The political rulers as well as the religious leaders had the responsibility of nurturing Israel in the way of righteousness. Their failure was not only documented (prophets, 23:9-40; kings, 22:9-30) by Jeremiah, but also by the eighth-century prophets (Mic 3:1-11) and later by Ezekiel (Ezek 34:1-16). Even so, the people could not be absolved of blame. In the words of their attackers, "they [Is-rael] sinned against the Lord" (50:7; cf. 40:3 Nebuzaradan). Their sin, already hor-rendous, was even more outrageous because they spurned the faith of their ancestors. They shortchanged themselves since they did not reach for God, who was available to them as their security and their resting place (50:7b).

**Babylon To Be Attacked (50:9-10).** God raised up an enemy from the north to bring Israel down (4:27, 6:8; 9:11). Similarly, a northern power would descend upon Babylon. Since that power, Persia, came from the east, "north" is to be under-stood as symbolic for something ominous. Of course, "north" can also mean a di-rection on the compass. Historically, Cyrus, whose rule incorporated the former Median empire, would take the city of Babylon after several battles and enter as vic-tor in October, 539 BC. If a nation stronger than Babylon now overpowered the ex-isting superpower, it was an act of divine sovereignty: "I the LORD have spoken!" (50:10). As in the conquest of Judah, so here the prophets emphasized that God was behind the maneuvers of political powers. Historians may offer economic or political reasons for the fall of an empire, but the prophets insist that behind such causes the more ultimate cause is God.

**Babylon Will Fall (50:11-16).** The prophet-poet relished the contrast between the once carefree nation that had the total run of the world stage—even as animals have free run of the farm pasture (50:11)—and the devastated land it had become. At one time, her unquestioned superiority among the nations gave her a sense of exu-berance (50:11). In the new situation of her defeat, matters would be vastly differ-ent. Instead of self-satisfaction, there would be disgrace and shame (50:12). Instead of being the number-one nation, she would be a nation of no account (50:12b). In-stead of lush meadows (50:11), there would be dry desolation—with no planters and no harvesters (50:12, 16). Instead of being gazed upon with admiration, there would be gasps of incredulity at her demise (50:13).

More is to be noted than that a city had fallen, although Babylon's surrender and the collapse of her walls were notable enough. The destruction of this world-class city was to be understood as God's having moved against her in anger (50:13a). Such anger was not an uncontrolled emotional flare-up, like human anger. Rather, it was God's strong negative emotion against one who had sinned against the Lord. God does not take vengeance as one who seeks to get even, but to vindicate himself (50:15; cf. 50:28). He will be in the clear, with an uncompromised standard. Brueg-gemann (1998:469) explains that God's vengeance, which consists in the reestab-lishment of God's rule, "is the abrasive factor in sovereign rule and order." Politically speaking, an economic and political center had fallen. Theologically, the fall of that commercial center was a display of God's righteousness.

**Reprieve for Judah (50:17-20).** Israel was still pictured as sheep, as it was earlier when the problem was with its shepherds or leaders (50:6). Now, however, the

secondary causes of her problem were paraded, namely, the lion-like foreign destroyers, Assyria and Babylon. The first was responsible for Israel's defeat; the second, for Judah's. God would now deal with these predatory nations. Jeremiah drew
on a tradition of nations depicted as wild animals. This unflattering depiction is
continued in Daniel's vision (Dan 8) and in the New Testament (Rev 13).

The good news was that God would take decisive action against these powers. His
own people would be free to return to the fertile fields of Carmel and Bashan
(50:19). Had the exiles lived in deprivation? They would now experience abundance. God's intent was for his people's well-being (32:40-42). The material aspect
of prosperity is interwoven with the spiritual reality of forgiveness (50:20; cf. Mic
7:18). If forgiveness means that the other party is no longer held hostage, then the
good news for Judah is not only that they would be physically free from Babylon,
but that God would no longer hold them hostage.

**Attack Once More (50:21-30).**   The poem might end here, but now another round
begins. In case there should still be pockets of military hold-outs, the commander
in chief ordered another all-out attack (50:21). Babylon, a cipher for evil, would be
completely eliminated. Distant countries were invited to trample this city (50:26).
Storehouses of grain were breached and every structure was reduced to rubble. Living things, both animal and human, were exterminated (50:27, 29a, 30).

Here too, as in almost every stanza, the interpretation returns to the spiritual reality. Babylon had "defied the LORD, the Holy One of Israel" (50:29). Nations as well
as individuals must know their place with the Almighty. Persons or nations who
snub their noses at God will incur God's wrath.

**Babylon, Fallen for Good (50:31-32).**   The poem describes this city as so beaten
down that she would not rise again (50:32). Whatever was left after all the havoc
had been carried out would be burned (50:32b). But the emphasis of the stanza is
upon the reason for this unhappy ending. Babylon was arrogant (50:31a, 32a).
Were it justified to speak of a sin that was the mother of all sin, pride and arrogance
would be strong candidates. The spirit of self-sufficiency, autonomy, and independence is associated with pride. These qualities, while not evil in certain contexts, become fatal flaws when persons or societies then jettison God from their lives.
Babylon's demise was one more illustration of the dictum that God deals decisively
with hubris. If Babylon represented the archetypal chaotic power that challenged
God (cf. Hill 1999a), then her fall signaled God's victory over all that was anti-God.

**God, both Destroyer and Redeemer (50:33-34).**   God addressed a situation in
which the punishment of Babylon meant the redemption of Israel and Judah (for
God as Redeemer, see Isa 43:1; 44:24; 54:5). The oracle against Babylon, like the oracles against all these nations, carried the simple but profound message that God
would set matters right. Something would be done about evil in the world. "A sense
of purpose strongly animates these prophecies" (Clements 1988:261). The LORD of
Heaven's Armies was sufficiently strong to deal with the greatest evil empire. The
flip side of that reality is that God is sufficiently strong to rescue those who have

been wronged. At the end of the day, some will enjoy the rest that God provides (50:34), but for the wicked there will never be rest (Isa 57:21).

**The Death Blow to Babylon (50:35-40).** The "sword song" in this chapter has its counterpart in the "song of the battle ax" (51:20-23). Both are weapons of destruction. In a graphic way, the prophet-poet listed the candidates for death in the big city, and as usual, the leaders took the hit (50:35-36a). The death-dealing sword put all security measures, here represented by warriors, horses, chariots, and the military generally, out of commission. (50:37). Destruction came to the things prized (treasures, 50:37) and finally to items essential for survival, such as water (50:38). With the depletion of their sources of livelihood, the possibility of life was soon gone altogether. The emptiness, where once there was fullness, was epitomized by the reference to Sodom and Gomorrah, the classic case of God's judgment on sin (50:40). Babylon fell to Cyrus the Persian in 539 BC.

As in other stanzas, more is at issue than the fall of a government or an empire. Idolatry, another form of pride in which humans determine their own objects of worship, was the sin of choice, which provoked divine action. The first commandment not to displace God was applicable to all, not only to Israel. God's action against Babylon asserted his supremacy over this people and over the gods (idols) they worshiped, such as Bel and Marduk (50:2).

**Pummeled Again (50:41-44).** Still another war alert! One wave of invaders after another rolled in. These invaders were more numerous and more vicious than the others had been. The king was totally debilitated. Throughout the poem, the descriptions of attackers alternate with the description of the city being sacked, giving the reader the impression of a repeated pummeling. This was no small-time operation.

It was a big-time operation because God masterminded the whole affair, and he would not be opposed. He could not be effectively challenged because there is no one like him. The theme of God's incomparability is frequent in the Psalms (e.g., 35:10; 89:8; 113:5), but here the context is of deconstruction. If God is the great creator, he is also the great demolisher.

**News flash (50:45-46).** Enough talk of army advances, of the loss of life and of everything reduced to rubble. The crescendo rises to a climax with the announcement, "Babylon has been taken."

◆   **G. Babylon's Fall Guaranteed (51:1-64)**

This is what the LORD says:
"I will stir up a destroyer against
    Babylon
and the people of Babylonia.*
² Foreigners will come and winnow her,
    blowing her away as chaff.

They will come from every side
    to rise against her in her day of
    trouble.
³ Don't let the archers put on their
    armor
    or draw their bows.

Don't spare even her best soldiers!
Let her army be completely
destroyed.*
⁴They will fall dead in the land of the
Babylonians,*
slashed to death in her streets.
⁵For the LORD of Heaven's Armies
has not abandoned Israel and Judah.
He is still their God,
even though their land was filled
with sin
against the Holy One of Israel."

⁶Flee from Babylon! Save yourselves!
Don't get trapped in her
punishment!
It is the LORD's time for vengeance;
he will repay her in full.
⁷Babylon has been a gold cup in the
LORD's hands,
a cup that made the whole earth
drunk.
The nations drank Babylon's wine,
and it drove them all mad.
⁸But suddenly Babylon, too, has fallen.
Weep for her.
Give her medicine.
Perhaps she can yet be healed.
⁹We would have helped her if
we could,
but nothing can save her now.
Let her go; abandon her.
Return now to your own land.
For her punishment reaches to the
heavens;
it is so great it cannot be measured.
¹⁰The LORD has vindicated us.
Come, let us announce in Jerusalem*
everything the LORD our God has
done.

¹¹Sharpen the arrows!
Lift up the shields!*
For the LORD has inspired the kings
of the Medes
to march against Babylon and
destroy her.
This is his vengeance against those
who desecrated his Temple.
¹²Raise the battle flag against Babylon!

Reinforce the guard and station the
watchmen.
Prepare an ambush,
for the LORD will fulfill all his plans
against Babylon.
¹³You are a city by a great river,
a great center of commerce,
but your end has come.
The thread of your life is cut.
¹⁴The LORD of Heaven's Armies has taken
this vow
and has sworn to it by his own
name:
"Your cities will be filled with enemies,
like fields swarming with locusts,
and they will shout in triumph over
you."

¹⁵The LORD made the earth by his power,
and he preserves it by his wisdom.
With his own understanding
he stretched out the heavens.
¹⁶When he speaks in the thunder,
the heavens are filled with water.
He causes the clouds to rise over the
earth.
He sends the lightning with the rain
and releases the wind from his
storehouses.

¹⁷The whole human race is foolish and
has no knowledge!
The craftsmen are disgraced by the
idols they make,
for their carefully shaped works are
a fraud.
These idols have no breath or power.
¹⁸Idols are worthless; they are ridiculous
lies!
On the day of reckoning they will
all be destroyed.
¹⁹But the God of Israel* is no idol!
He is the Creator of everything that
exists,
including his people, his own special
possession.
The LORD of Heaven's Armies is his
name!

²⁰"You* are my battle-ax and sword,"
says the LORD.

"With you I will shatter nations
and destroy many kingdoms.
21 With you I will shatter armies—
destroying the horse and rider,
the chariot and charioteer.
22 With you I will shatter men and
women,
old people and children,
young men and maidens.
23 With you I will shatter shepherds and
flocks,
farmers and oxen,
captains and officers.

24 "I will repay Babylon
and the people of Babylonia*
for all the wrong they have done
to my people in Jerusalem," says the
LORD.

25 "Look, O mighty mountain, destroyer
of the earth!
I am your enemy," says the LORD.
"I will raise my fist against you,
to knock you down from the
heights.
When I am finished,
you will be nothing but a heap of
burnt rubble.
26 You will be desolate forever.
Even your stones will never again be
used for building.
You will be completely wiped out,"
says the LORD.

27 Raise a signal flag to the nations.
Sound the battle cry!
Mobilize them all against Babylon.
Prepare them to fight against her!
Bring out the armies of Ararat, Minni,
and Ashkenaz.
Appoint a commander,
and bring a multitude of horses like
swarming locusts!
28 Bring against her the armies of the
nations—
led by the kings of the Medes
and all their captains and officers.

29 The earth trembles and writhes in
pain,

for everything the LORD has planned
against Babylon stands
unchanged.
Babylon will be left desolate without a
single inhabitant.
30 Her mightiest warriors no longer
fight.
They stay in their barracks, their
courage gone.
They have become like women.
The invaders have burned the houses
and broken down the city gates.
31 The news is passed from one runner to
the next
as the messengers hurry to tell the
king
that his city has been captured.
32 All the escape routes are blocked.
The marshes have been set aflame,
and the army is in a panic.

33 This is what the LORD of Heaven's
Armies,
the God of Israel, says:
"Babylon is like wheat on a threshing
floor,
about to be trampled.
In just a little while
her harvest will begin."

34 "King Nebuchadnezzar* of Babylon has
eaten and crushed us
and drained us of strength.
He has swallowed us like a great
monster
and filled his belly with our riches.
He has thrown us out of our own
country.
35 Make Babylon suffer as she made us
suffer,"
say the people of Zion.
"Make the people of Babylonia pay for
spilling our blood,"
says Jerusalem.

36 This is what the LORD says to Jerusalem:

"I will be your lawyer to plead your
case,
and I will avenge you.

I will dry up her river,
as well as her springs,
<sup>37</sup> and Babylon will become a heap of
ruins,
haunted by jackals.
She will be an object of horror and
contempt,
a place where no one lives.
<sup>38</sup> Her people will roar together like
strong lions.
They will growl like lion cubs.
<sup>39</sup> And while they lie inflamed with all
their wine,
I will prepare a different kind of
feast for them.
I will make them drink until they fall
asleep,
and they will never wake up again,"
says the LORD.
<sup>40</sup> "I will bring them down
like lambs to the slaughter,
like rams and goats to be sacrificed.

<sup>41</sup> "How Babylon* is fallen—
great Babylon, praised throughout
the earth!
Now she has become an object of horror
among the nations.
<sup>42</sup> The sea has risen over Babylon;
she is covered by its crashing waves.
<sup>43</sup> Her cities now lie in ruins;
she is a dry wasteland
where no one lives or even passes by.
<sup>44</sup> And I will punish Bel, the god of
Babylon,
and make him vomit up all he has
eaten.
The nations will no longer come and
worship him.
The wall of Babylon has fallen!

<sup>45</sup> "Come out, my people, flee from
Babylon.
Save yourselves! Run from the
LORD's fierce anger.
<sup>46</sup> But do not panic; don't be afraid
when you hear the first rumor of
approaching forces.
For rumors will keep coming year by
year.

Violence will erupt in the land
as the leaders fight against each
other.
<sup>47</sup> For the time is surely coming
when I will punish this great city
and all her idols.
Her whole land will be disgraced,
and her dead will lie in the streets.
<sup>48</sup> Then the heavens and earth will
rejoice,
for out of the north will come
destroying armies
against Babylon," says the LORD.
<sup>49</sup> "Just as Babylon killed the people of
Israel
and others throughout the world,
so must her people be killed.
<sup>50</sup> Get out, all you who have escaped the
sword!
Do not stand and watch—flee while
you can!
Remember the LORD, though you are
in a far-off land,
and think about your home in
Jerusalem."

<sup>51</sup> "We are ashamed," the people say.
"We are insulted and disgraced
because the LORD's Temple
has been defiled by foreigners."

<sup>52</sup> "Yes," says the LORD, "but the time
is coming
when I will destroy Babylon's idols.
The groans of her wounded people
will be heard throughout the land.
<sup>53</sup> Though Babylon reaches as high as the
heavens
and makes her fortifications
incredibly strong,
I will still send enemies to plunder her.
I, the LORD, have spoken!

<sup>54</sup> "Listen! Hear the cry of Babylon,
the sound of great destruction from
the land of the Babylonians.
<sup>55</sup> For the LORD is destroying Babylon.
He will silence her loud voice.
Waves of enemies pound against her;
the noise of battle rings through the
city.

⁵⁶Destroying armies come against
  Babylon.
Her mighty men are captured,
  and their weapons break in their
  hands.
For the LORD is a God who gives just
  punishment;
he always repays in full.
⁵⁷I will make her officials and wise men
  drunk,
  along with her captains, officers,
  and warriors.
They will fall asleep
  and never wake up again!"
says the King, whose name is
  the LORD of Heaven's Armies.

⁵⁸This is what the LORD of Heaven's
  Armies says:
"The thick walls of Babylon will be
  leveled to the ground,
  and her massive gates will be burned.
The builders from many lands have
  worked in vain,

for their work will be destroyed by
  fire!"
⁵⁹The prophet Jeremiah gave this message to Seraiah son of Neriah and grandson of Mahseiah, a staff officer, when
Seraiah went to Babylon with King Zedekiah of Judah. This was during the fourth
year of Zedekiah's reign.* ⁶⁰Jeremiah had
recorded on a scroll all the terrible disasters that would soon come upon Babylon—
all the words written here. ⁶¹He said to
Seraiah, "When you get to Babylon, read
aloud everything on this scroll. ⁶²Then say,
'LORD, you have said that you will destroy
Babylon so that neither people nor animals
will remain here. She will lie empty and
abandoned forever.' ⁶³When you have finished reading the scroll, tie it to a stone
and throw it into the Euphrates River.
⁶⁴Then say, 'In this same way Babylon and
her people will sink, never again to rise,
because of the disasters I will bring upon
her.'"
  This is the end of Jeremiah's messages.

51:1 Hebrew *of Leb-kamai,* a code name for Babylonia.   51:3 The Hebrew term used here refers to the
complete consecration of things or people to the LORD, either by destroying them or by giving them as an
offering.   51:4 Or *Chaldeans;* also in 51:54.   51:10 Hebrew *Zion;* also in 51:24.   51:11 Greek version reads
*Fill up the quivers.*   51:19 Hebrew *the Portion of Jacob.* See note on 5:20.   51:20 Possibly Cyrus, whom God
used to conquer Babylon. Compare Isa 44:28; 45:1.   51:24 Or *Chaldea;* also in 51:35.   51:34 Hebrew
*Nebuchadrezzar,* a variant spelling of Nebuchadnezzar.   51:41 Hebrew *Sheshach,* a code name for Babylon.
51:59 The fourth year of Zedekiah's reign was 593 BC.

## NOTES

**51:1** *I will stir up a destroyer.* This refers to the Medes, among others (51:11).

*Babylonia.* Lit., *"leb kamai,"* a code name for Babylon (see NLT mg) that means "heart of
those who arise against me." It is derived from applying a technique called *athbash* to a
name for the Babylonians (*khasdim* [TH3778A, ZH4169], "Chaldeans"). In *athbash,* the last letter of the Heb. alphabet is substituted for the first, the second last letter for the second, and
so on (as in substituting "a" for "z" and "b" for "y"; cf. 51:41), making *athbash* a simple
cryptogram. The informed could understand this language, but the uninitiated would be
nonplussed.

**51:2** *Foreigners.* Some Greek versions and the Vulgate read "winnowers" instead of "foreigners" (cf. Judah being winnowed, 4:11; 13:24; 18:17).

*blowing her away as chaff.* If the etymology suggested in BDB is accepted, the literal
expression, "empty her land," may not continue the winnowing image but instead introduce a new image of emptying (*baqaq*) a bottle (cf. the verb *baqaq* [TH1238, ZH1327], "make
gurgling sound" and the noun *baqbuq* [TH1228, ZH1318], "pitcher" or "canister").

**51:5** *the LORD . . . has not abandoned Israel.* The word for abandoned is "widowed"
(*'alman* [TH488, ZH527]). Cf. the image of God's bride in 2:1-3.

*He is still their God.* This is added in the NLT to convey the Heb. nuance.

**51:9** *it is so great it cannot be measured.* Lit., "It [her punishment] is lifted to the clouds."

**51:11** *kings of the Medes.* Media, an ancient kingdom with its capital in Ecbatana, was located in what is now northwestern Iran. Media was subjugated by Cyrus in 550 BC.

*march against Babylon.* This somewhat obscures the idea that this was Yahweh's plan (*mezimmah* [TH4209, ZH4659]).

**51:13** *The thread of your life is cut.* This metaphor for death comes from weaving, where the woven fabric is cut from the loom once it reaches the desired length.

**51:15** *The LORD made the earth.* The "Creator Poem" (51:15-19), with variations, is from 10:12-16.

**51:17** *their carefully shaped works are a fraud.* Fraud (*sheqer* [TH8267, ZH9214]) is a trademark word in Jeremiah; it occurs in thirty-four verses (e.g., 9:2; 27:14, 15, 16).

**51:19** *his own special possession.* Lit., "the tribe of his inheritance" (*nakhalah* [TH5159, ZH5709]).

**51:20** *You are my battle-ax and sword.* The "song of the war club" (cf. NRSV) complements the "sword song" (50:35-38). Cf. Assyria as God's instrument in an earlier century (Isa 10:5). The shatterer ("you") is usually taken to be Cyrus (see NLT mg), but some suggest it is the prophet Jeremiah. Holladay (1989:405-407) thinks that the war club is Israel.

**51:24** *I will repay Babylon.* The NLT omits the Heb. phrase "before your eyes," or "in your sight," which grammatically modifies "all the wrong they have done" (cf. NIV).

**51:25** *mighty mountain.* This perhaps refers figuratively to an imposing nation. Babylon was located on a plain. Alternatively, the reference may be to a man-made mountain/temple/tower, a ziggurat.

**51:27** *Ararat, Minni, and Ashkenaz.* Ararat is ancient Urartu, or modern eastern Turkey; Minni or "Mannai" were hill folk whose territory lay southeast of Lake Urmia. The Ashkenaz people lived east of Lake Urmia and during one period were known as Scythians.

**51:28** *Medes.* This people populated areas east of the Tigris and north of Babylon.

**51:31** *his city has been captured.* The Heb. is more emphatic: "his city is taken from end to end" (NRSV).

**51:32** *All the escape routes are blocked.* Lit., "the river fords are seized." Reeds in marshes would be burned so that fugitives could not hide there.

**51:33** *Babylon is like wheat on a threshing floor.* The NLT supplies "wheat," but the harvest had not begun; a better rendering is, "Babylon is like a prepared threshing floor."

**51:34** *drained us of strength.* The Heb. is more colorful: "he has set us as an emptied vessel." The last line continues the serpent-monster theme: "he has spewed me [us] out." Some Heb. versions have the collective singular, "me"; others the plural, "us."

**51:39** *I will make them drink.* The Heb. follows with "exult" (*'alaz* [TH5937, ZH6600]), then "fall asleep" (*yashen* [TH3462, ZH3822]).

**51:41** *How Babylon is fallen.* The code name Sheshach is derived via *athbash* (cf. 51:1; MT of 25:26). The name is formed by representing the Heb. letters *bet, bet, lamed* (*babel,* "Babylon") by corresponding consonants from the opposite end of the Heb. alphabet, yielding *shin, shin, kaf* ("Sheshak").

**51:56** *God who gives just punishment.* This is better nuanced as, "He is a God of retribution."

**51:58** *The thick walls of Babylon will be leveled.* When the Persians conquered Babylon, they did so peaceably. Poetic language is figurative.

*their work will be destroyed by fire!* See Hab 2:13.

**51:59** *Seraiah son of Neriah.* Seraiah was Baruch's brother (32:12), an officer responsible for bivouac arrangements when the party stopped to camp. In the excavations at Jerusalem, a seal stamp with the words "belonging to Seraiah [son of] Neriah" has been found (Keown et al. 1995:373). As vassal, King Zedekiah may have been summoned to Babylon to give an accounting, possibly in view of a consultation by nations hostile to Babylon (27:2-3).

**51:63** *throw it into the Euphrates River.* For other symbolic actions, see 13:1-11; 18:1-12; 19:1-13; 28:1-16; 32:1-15; and the discussion in Friebel (1999:154-169).

### COMMENTARY

Babylon would most certainly fall. That shrill message, already heard in Jeremiah 50, becomes even more shrill in Jeremiah 51. One way of viewing the chapter is to follow Aitken (1984) in seeing three movements in chapter 51 that supplement three movements in chapter 50, the six being framed by 50:2-3 and 51:54-58. Each of the three movements (51:1-33, 34-44, 45-53) has five or six sub-units that carry rhetorical themes related to a pattern of situation, intervention, and outcome (see commentary on ch 50 above). The first movement both begins and ends with the threshing floor motif (51:1, 33).

Another way to read Jeremiah 51 is as a series of five concentric spirals that each culminate with the climactic moment, the fall of the empire. A given arm of the spiral may begin with a battle scene or a hymn of God's power but soon comes around once more to the shared centerpoint—Babylon's fall. The spirals elaborate on military preparedness, scenes of battle, the flights of fugitives, or the resulting city rubble, but they always return to the theme of Babylon's collapse. This commentary will approach the chapter from this perspective, taking as the five spirals verses 1-10, 11-14, 15-26, 27-41, and 42-58. The final symbolic action of a stone sinking into the Euphrates underscores the announcement of Babylon's demise (51:59-64).

**Destruction by Foreigners (51:1-10).** The demise of the Babylonian Empire is credited to a major invader, a wolfish devastator. The first spiral moves quickly to the battle scene (51:3-4) and before long, to the outcome: "Babylon too has fallen." (51:8). This refrain, at first stated rather matter of factly, is taken up repeatedly and with increasing vehemence in the statements of the larger poem, "your end has come" (51:13-14); "you will be completely wiped out" (51:26); "How Babylon is fallen" (51:41); "the walls of Babylon will be leveled" (51:58); and "Babylon and her people will sink" (51:64).

That destruction will come at the hands of an agent stronger than Babylon that will overpower Babylon's soldiers (51:4, 30), breach the walls and city gates (51:30), reduce all to rubble (51:25), and block all escape routes (51:32). Military talk of archers and armor (51:3), arrows and shields (51:11), battle-ax and sword (51:20) is dominant. The Medes will be the lead destroyer (51:11, 28), but others, such as the armies of Ararat, Minni, and Ashkenaz that once resisted Media but were conquered, will join forces against Babylon (51:27).

Babylon's fall will free the exiles for their return to Judah, so a sub-theme within the oracle is encouragement for the exiles to leave Babylon (51:6, 50). That which is destructive for one party can be the salvation of another. The bad news for Babylon becomes good news for Judah.

**God Takes Vengeance (51:11-14).** The poet insists throughout that there is more to the fall of Babylon than one power or coalition of nations subjugating another. Behind these nations moves the Lord, who has inspired the Medes to march against Babylon. "This is his vengeance" (51:11). In various ways, the prophet calls attention to the Cause behind all other named causes. He explains that what transpired on the political front with ancient powers was according to God's plan (51:12, 29). Nothing on the world scene happens by chance or accident. The prophet punctuates the entire poem, including this segment, with the loaded title, "The LORD of Heaven's Armies" (51:14; cf. 51:5, 58) or its expanded version, "The LORD of Heaven's Armies, the God of Israel, for that is his name" (51:19, 33, 57). If the name already stood for power to deliver (such is the meaning of Yahweh), the designation "Creator" compounds the power factor (51:19). Creation theology is in the service of redemption. The citation of God the Creator countered any pretense to power by idols (51:15-19) and assured Israel that God was well up to the challenge represented by the power politics of Babylon. Behind *Realpolitik* is "Theopolitik" (see commentary at 46:2-12). When this God, commander of armies and Creator of all that exists, takes up a cause such as vindicating his name, there is no doubt about the outcome. Confession of God as Creator changes the perspective on any difficult situation, for problems diminish when placed against the power of God, the Creator.

The theme of God's vengeance surfaces again in 51:35. Emotions were raw. The cry was for Babylon to be hurt even as she had hurt others. Such sentiments can hardly become a model for dealing with others who inflict harm, unless the prayer-wish is addressed to God and is thus in keeping with the dictum, "Vengeance is mine, I will repay, says the Lord" (Deut 32:35). It is not for God's people to redress the wrongs of the world with violence. That is properly and safely left with God. That prayer for retribution would be answered quickly, for God announced that he would be the lawyer and would deal punitively with Babylon (51:36-37).

**God Is a Full Match for the Adversaries (51:15-26).** The next rung of this spiral ascent begins as though unrelated to the topic of Babylon's future. The hymn of praise to the Creator extols God's power and wisdom (51:15-16). God is clearly a God who acts, by making a world, filling the heavens with waters, and releasing wind from his storehouses. Making this confession is not only theoretical but impinges on a society's culture.

Babylon's culture was one of idols, but these appear empty and laughable, as do all humanly engineered god-substitutes, in the presence of the towering Creator God (51:17-18). Idols who have no power (51:17b) are no competition to a God who has all power (51:15). The God who is an adversary to idols is also an adversary to those who destroy the earth, even if they view themselves as a mighty force (51:25).

The phrase, "destroy the earth" is generic; it is legitimate to read into it a reference to those who wreak havoc on peaceful towns and villages, as well as those who tear up a stabilized natural environment. All adversaries, whether idols or political powers, faced the same fate—they were destroyed (51:18), knocked from their heights to be "nothing but a heap of burnt rubble" (51:25). Relatively little is said in Jeremiah 50 about God's power; but this is a major consideration in Jeremiah 51. The failure to confess God as Creator had everything to do with the dreadful evils of Babylon, as it does with the evils of modern times.

While God is fully in control and may intervene directly, he more often remains a step removed. Babylon would be fully shattered by God, yet not by himself personally but through his instrument, here described as the Lord's "battle-ax and sword" (51:20). The "you" of 51:20 is singular rather than plural. Perhaps, as the NLT's footnote suggests, this refers to Cyrus the Persian, the general who took Babylon in 539 BC. But the singular "you" may also be applied in a collective sense to a specific nation (e.g., the Medes) or to any nation in general. The "song of the war club" (51:20-23) not only makes a point about total destruction but paints a picture of a God so large that even huge nations are nothing more than hand tools accomplishing his purposes.

**A Perpetual Sleep (51:27-41).** Like the other spirals, this one comes around (though less quickly) to Babylon's fall, "great Babylon, praised throughout the earth!" (51:41). Prominent in this segment is God's "ultimate solution." In different ways, the poet conveys that this was a once-for-all punishment. The damage was so vast that Babylon would be uninhabitable, "a place where no one lives" (51:29, 37) or even passes by (51:43). It will be a place of rubble (51:37), totally in ruins (51:43). Beyond these bald assertions, the prophet employs the image of drunkenness. Earlier in the poem, it was Babylon that made others drunk to the point of madness (51:7). In this segment, God prepares the feast and makes Babylon drink to the point of sleep—never to wake up again (51:39; cf. 51:57). Babylon had been demolished for good! Those who had become victims or had been violated craved the assurance that such a misdeed would never again be perpetrated upon them. God provided that assurance, partly through the "I will" statements (51:36, 39, 40). The evil empire would be silenced forever.

Readers are rightly disturbed by the repeated theme of Babylon's punishment, her fall, and her never rising again. It seems like overkill, but the reason for the repeated point of the spirals is not hard to find. All oracles about the nations, and perhaps most of all the oracle against Babylon, make the argument that God will deal decisively with the perpetrators of evil. Persons can rest in the certainty that God is unquestionably in charge. Evil actions yield a harvest of destruction. God may be patient, but like a harvester he will swing into action in due time, and then Babylon will be trampled (51:33). Evil will not have the last word, especially in its systemic forms of arrogance and oppression. Wrongs will be righted. Nations will reap what they sow, and if they sow suffering, as Babylon did, then they will be made to suffer (51:35). Has blood been spilled? Nations will pay for their atrocities with blood (51:35b). God will not stand idly by.

The New Testament echoes this message on a cosmic scale. Sin, like Babylon, is a force of large proportions. The cross dealt a death blow to sin, but the resurrection did so even more decisively, so that Paul could ask, "O Death, where is your victory?" (1 Cor 15:55). God will be victorious over evil, within history and within the cosmos. In the end, evil will never again raise so much as a finger. Herein lies hope for those who live righteously, as well as for those who seek release from the power of evil.

**Punishment for a Reason (51:42-58).** In the longer oracle, the rationale for punishment is muted but not altogether absent. In the final segment, which once again concludes with a picture of a proud city leveled and burned, the prophet-poet disclosed what had brought on this tragedy. The culprit was the Babylonian god Bel, for he had usurped the place that Yahweh demanded in worship (51:44). A concomitant evil was the worship of idols (51:52), a point made earlier in comparing the lifelessness and powerlessness of the idols with the high energy and power of Yahweh (51:17). Nations outside the covenant and apart from prophetic revelation were nevertheless held accountable to God, apparently because such elemental matters of religion are instinctively known. One reason for Babylon's demise was to eradicate the worship given to false gods (51:47).

Another justification for destroying this empire was its arrogance, a point made more forcefully in the previous chapter (50:31-32), but noted here obliquely. "Though Babylon reaches as high as the heavens" (51:53) recalls the archetypal sin of Babel (Gen 11:1-9), a sin of pride ("let us make a name for ourselves") and of overreaching. God runs interference with arrogant peoples. Incredibly strong fortifications could not ensure that Babylon would have its way (51:53).

An arrogant people who were preoccupied with their own importance not only dismissed those of lesser standing but readily mistreated them, even eliminating them when they stood in the way of their selfish pursuits. Babylon mistreated and wantonly killed the people of Israel (51:49). The *lex talionis* (law of recompense) applies to nations as well as to individuals (Exod 21:24-25). Here, God in judgment operated on the "eye for an eye" principle. Was Babylon ruthless, disregarding the sanctity of life? Her punishment would be ruthless treatment by others (51:49). God was aware of the disrespect with which arrogant people treated others. Proud Babylon treated Judah's Temple as trivial, though even common decency demanded better (51:51). Justifying her aggrandizement by the gift of her god Bel, Babylon grasped territory and resources that were not hers. King Nebuchadnezzar swallowed up little Judah (51:34), but God would disgorge him (51:44). Dominant world powers may gobble up smaller territories as big fish swallow small defenseless ones, but not without penalty. Such action was evil and deserved God's intervention and punishment.

Babylon, the representative of all things evil, and especially of evil nations, surfaces in the book of Revelation as a symbol of Rome (Rev 17:5-18; 18:10, 21). There too she will be cast down from her high perch. The cry "Fallen! Fallen is Babylon the Great" in Revelation (18:2) echoes Jeremiah (50:46; 51:8, 41). Subsequent history bears out the principles underlying the oracle against Babylon. The ancient Roman Empire and the communist Soviet empire of the twentieth century met the same judgment. No people are immune from the consequences of disregarding God, living arrogantly, or violating human rights through mistreatment of others.

**A Sinking Stone, A Sinking Empire (51:59-64).** A prose account dated to the time before Jerusalem's fall at the hands of the Babylonians is placed as an addendum to the poetic oracle. Even before Babylon's attack on Jerusalem, the prophet envisioned a later time when the invader would receive its due. A written document was the medium of the message at one level (cf. 30:2; 36:20). The oral proclamation, perhaps spoken to an audience of exiles, perhaps to no audience at all (51:61), or perhaps to God and the people (Friebel 1999:158-159), summarizes well the multiple stanzas that have had as their theme the annihilation of Babylon (51:62). Baruch was pro-Babylonian, and at Jeremiah's dictation (36:4), he wrote about Babylon's subjugation of Judah. Seraiah, Baruch's brother, was anti-Babylonian and at Jeremiah's dictation wrote of the northerners subjugating Babylon. "Together the two brothers present the whole claim of the book of Jeremiah that the Lord reigns over the nations—over Judah to be sure, but also over mighty Babylon" (Bracke 2000b:167).

The symbolic action of tossing the stone with the scroll tied to it into the Euphrates can be compared to the symbolic action of the paving stones in Egypt (43:8-13). Both actions point to the fate of the dominating world empires, Babylon and Egypt. The sinking scroll reinforces the oral message with a visual image of the Babylonian Empire sinking out of sight. The threat from that quarter will not appear again. The final scene is that of a mighty empire sinking into oblivion; the last sound is the gurgling of the waters (see note on 51:2).

# ◆ X. Historical Documentation (52:1-34)

Zedekiah was twenty-one years old when he became king, and he reigned in Jerusalem eleven years. His mother was Hamutal, the daughter of Jeremiah from Libnah. ²But Zedekiah did what was evil in the LORD's sight, just as Jehoiakim had done. ³These things happened because of the LORD's anger against the people of Jerusalem and Judah, until he finally banished them from his presence and sent them into exile.

Zedekiah rebelled against the king of Babylon. ⁴So on January 15,* during the ninth year of Zedekiah's reign, King Nebuchadnezzar* of Babylon led his entire army against Jerusalem. They surrounded the city and built siege ramps against its walls. ⁵Jerusalem was kept under siege until the eleventh year of King Zedekiah's reign.

⁶By July 18 in the eleventh year of Zedekiah's reign,* the famine in the city had become very severe, and the last of the food was entirely gone. ⁷Then a section of the city wall was broken down, and all the soldiers fled. Since the city was

surrounded by the Babylonians,* they waited for nightfall. Then they slipped through the gate between the two walls behind the king's garden and headed toward the Jordan Valley.*

⁸But the Babylonian troops chased King Zedekiah and caught him on the plains of Jericho, for his men had all deserted him and scattered. ⁹They took him to the king of Babylon at Riblah in the land of Hamath. There the king of Babylon pronounced judgment upon Zedekiah. ¹⁰He made Zedekiah watch as they slaughtered his sons and all the other officials of Judah. ¹¹Then they gouged out Zedekiah's eyes, bound him in bronze chains, and led him away to Babylon. Zedekiah remained there in prison until the day of his death.

¹²On August 17 of that year,* which was the nineteenth year of King Nebuchadnezzar's reign, Nebuzaradan, the captain of the guard and an official of the Babylonian king, arrived in Jerusalem. ¹³He burned down the Temple of the LORD, the royal palace, and all the houses of Jerusalem. He destroyed all the important buildings* in the city. ¹⁴Then he supervised the entire Babylonian* army as they tore down the walls of Jerusalem on every side. ¹⁵Nebuzaradan, the captain of the guard, then took as exiles some of the poorest of the people, the rest of the people who remained in the city, the defectors who had declared their allegiance to the king of Babylon, and the rest of the craftsmen. ¹⁶But Nebuzaradan allowed some of the poorest people to stay behind in Judah to care for the vineyards and fields.

¹⁷The Babylonians broke up the bronze pillars in front of the LORD's Temple, the bronze water carts, and the great bronze basin called the Sea, and they carried all the bronze away to Babylon. ¹⁸They also took all the ash buckets, shovels, lamp snuffers, basins, dishes, and all the other bronze articles used for making sacrifices at the Temple. ¹⁹Nebuzaradan, the captain of the guard, also took the small bowls, incense burners, basins, pots, lampstands, dishes, bowls used for liquid offerings, and all the other articles made of pure gold or silver.

²⁰The weight of the bronze from the two pillars, the Sea with the twelve bronze oxen beneath it, and the water carts was too great to be measured. These things had been made for the LORD's Temple in the days of King Solomon. ²¹Each of the pillars was 27 feet tall and 18 feet in circumference.* They were hollow, with walls 3 inches thick.* ²²The bronze capital on top of each pillar was 7½ feet* high and was decorated with a network of bronze pomegranates all the way around. ²³There were 96 pomegranates on the sides, and a total of 100 on the network around the top.

²⁴Nebuzaradan, the captain of the guard, took with him as prisoners Seraiah the high priest, Zephaniah the priest of the second rank, and the three chief gatekeepers. ²⁵And from among the people still hiding in the city, he took an officer who had been in charge of the Judean army; seven of the king's personal advisers; the army commander's chief secretary, who was in charge of recruitment; and sixty other citizens. ²⁶Nebuzaradan, the captain of the guard, took them all to the king of Babylon at Riblah. ²⁷And there at Riblah, in the land of Hamath, the king of Babylon had them all put to death. So the people of Judah were sent into exile from their land.

²⁸The number of captives taken to Babylon in the seventh year of Nebuchadnezzar's reign* was 3,023. ²⁹Then in Nebuchadnezzar's eighteenth year* he took 832 more. ³⁰In Nebuchadnezzar's twenty-third year* he sent Nebuzaradan, the captain of the guard, who took 745 more—a total of 4,600 captives in all.

³¹In the thirty-seventh year of the exile of King Jehoiachin of Judah, Evil-merodach ascended to the Babylonian throne. He was kind to* Jehoiachin and released him from prison on March 31 of that year.* ³²He spoke kindly to Jehoiachin and

gave him a higher place than all the other exiled kings in Babylon. ³³He supplied Jehoiachin with new clothes to replace his prison garb and allowed him to dine in the king's presence for the rest of his life. ³⁴So the Babylonian king gave him a regular food allowance as long as he lived. This continued until the day of his death.

52:4a Hebrew *on the tenth day of the tenth month,* of the ancient Hebrew lunar calendar. A number of events in Jeremiah can be cross-checked with dates in surviving Babylonian records and related accurately to our modern calendar. This day was January 15, 588 BC.    52:4b Hebrew *Nebuchadrezzar,* a variant spelling of Nebuchadnezzar; also in 52:12, 28, 29, 30.    52:6 Hebrew *By the ninth day of the fourth month* [in the eleventh year of Zedekiah's reign]. This day was July 18, 586 BC.; also see note on 52:4a.    52:7a Or *the Chaldeans;* similarly in 52:8, 17.    52:7b Hebrew *the Arabah.*    52:12 Hebrew *On the tenth day of the fifth month,* of the ancient Hebrew lunar calendar. This day was August 17, 586 BC.; also see note on 52:4a.    52:13 Or *destroyed the houses of all the important people.*    52:14 Or *Chaldean.*    52:21a Hebrew *18 cubits* [8.1 meters] *tall and 12 cubits* [5.4 meters] *in circumference.*    52:21b Hebrew *4 fingers thick* [8 centimeters].    52:22 Hebrew *5 cubits* [2.3 meters].    52:28 This exile in the seventh year of Nebuchadnezzar's reign occurred in 597 BC. 52:29 This exile in the eighteenth year of Nebuchadnezzar's reign occurred in 586 BC.    52:30 This exile in the twenty-third year of Nebuchadnezzar's reign occurred in 581 BC.    52:31a Hebrew *He raised the head of.* 52:31b Hebrew *on the twenty-fifth day of the twelfth month,* of the ancient lunar Hebrew calendar. This day was March 31, 561 BC.; also see note on 52:4a.

## N O T E S

**52:1-34** The same material with some variations is found in 2 Kgs 24:18–25:30.

**52:1 *Zedekiah.*** He was appointed as vassal king by Nebuchadnezzar in 597 BC, after King Jehoiachin, who reigned for only three months, was taken into exile.

***Hamutal.*** She was also the mother of Jehoahaz, who reigned for three months in 609 BC (cf. 2 Kgs 23:31; 24:18, with different spelling).

**52:2 *Jehoiakim.*** Jehoiakim (609–598 BC) was father to King Jehoiachin (598/7 BC) and brother to Zedekiah (597–586 BC). For a sampling of Jehoiakim's evil, see 22:13-19; 36:20-31.

**52:3 *Zedekiah rebelled against the king of Babylon.*** Zedekiah failed to pay tribute as a vassal of Babylon. He also aligned Judah with Egypt (Ezek 17:13-18).

**52:6 *the food was entirely gone.*** For famine conditions in times of siege, see Lam 2:12; 4:4, 9-10.

**52:7 *between the two walls.*** Major fortifications had both an outer and an inner wall, usually less than ten feet apart. Kathleen Kenyon's excavations in Jerusalem exposed sections of two walls, one of which was built in the seventh century. "The double wall may refer to the wall built by Hezekiah to protect the Siloam pool" (King 1993:79). The "gate between the two walls" was in the southeast section. Babylon's forces breached the northern wall. For more details of Zedekiah's escape, see 39:1-10; 2 Kgs 25:4-6; Ezek 12:12-14.

**52:9 *Riblah.*** The headquarters of King Nebuchadnezzar north of Palestine was situated at the trade crossroads between Egypt and Mesopotamia on the Orontes River in Syria.

**52:12 *Nebuzaradan.*** He was introduced earlier in the story (see 39:11). The date of his entry, noted here as the tenth day of the month, is given in 2 Kgs 25:8 as the seventh day of the month, though other MSS read "ninth day." It may be that the two passages, 2 Kgs 25 and Jer 52 derive from an archival source.

**52:17 *the bronze pillars.*** These twenty-seven foot high, freestanding wooden pillars with bronze casings were called Jakin and Boaz when Solomon had them built (1 Kgs 7:13-22).

***bronze water carts.*** See 1 Kgs 7:27-37. This oversized bronze basin had a capacity of 11,000 gallons. It was fifteen feet in diameter and was supported by a base of twelve bronze oxen; it stood in the court before the Temple (1 Kgs 7:23-25).

**52:21 *They were hollow.*** The three-inch thick bronze cylinder was slipped over a wooden post to make a "bronze" pillar.

**52:22 *decorated with a network of bronze pomegranates.*** "Network" (*sebakah* [TH7639, ZH8422]) is usually translated "lattice-work" (cf. NRSV). Pomegranates are a fruit that symbolized fertility.

**52:24 *Seraiah the high priest.*** Seraiah was the grandson of Hilkiah, who was priest at the time of Josiah's reform. He was the grandfather of the high priest Joshua who served after the Exile (1 Chr 6:13-15).

**52:28 *The number of captives . . . was 3,023.*** The higher number of 18,000 in 1 Kgs 24:14-16 probably included women and children. For a profile of the exiles, see Jer 29:1-2.

**52:30 *In Nebuchadnezzar's twenty-third year.*** The removal of persons into exile in 561 BC is traditionally explained as Babylon's reprisal for the assassination of Gedaliah (ch 41).

**52:31 *Evil-merodach.*** He was also known as Amel-Marduk ("man of Marduk"). Succeeding Nebuchadnezzar, he ruled "lawlessly and wantonly" (so Josephus) for only two years (562–560 BC). Evil-merodach was killed in a plot engineered by his brother-in-law, Neriglissar, who then became king (ABD 2:679). The Heb. idiom for Jehoiachin's "release" is that "he [Evil-Merodach] lifted his [Jehoiachin's] head" (cf. MT of Gen 40:13). Jeremiah promised a restored Davidic ruler (23:5-6; 30:8-9, 21; 33:14-17).

**52:34 *a regular food allowance.*** Archaeologists have found tablets from the sixth century at the Babylonian Ishtar gate that mention the rations for a king Ya'ukin (= Jehoiachin) and his five sons (ANET 308b).

### COMMENTARY

This last chapter is an appendix to the book that complements the introductory first chapter. The captivity noted in 1:3 is summarized in chapter 52. Taken up with the Babylonian siege of Jerusalem, a story already told (Jer 39), the chapter does not easily fit, especially after "This is the end of Jeremiah's message" in the previous chapter (51:64). Neither the prophet Jeremiah nor any of his words appear in the chapter. Still, topics treated throughout the book do surface: leaders, wrongdoing, Jerusalem, Babylon, the Lord's anger, exile. Editors must have added this chapter from 2 Kings 24–25 for a reason—perhaps to show how the threats within the book came to pass. The chapter is in three parts (52:1-3, 4-27, 28-64).

**Highlighting the Background (52:1-3).** A key name, Zedekiah, a key theme, "did what was evil," a key factor, the Lord's anger, and a key consequence, exile, ring the changes on the last eleven years of Judah's existence as an independent nation.

Throughout the book, Jeremiah had critiqued political and religious leadership (e.g., Jer 22–23). Like his brother, Zedekiah did evil (e.g., 34:7-16). The slide toward evildoing is seldom easily halted. At some point, a single action triggers an entire nasty sequence. Such was Zedekiah's story. He broke his treaty and rebelled against his overlord. With that action, he sank the ship of state and much besides. Leaders are legitimately charged with greater accountability because they carry greater responsibility (cf. Jas 3:1). Like Jeremiah, Jesus' harshest words were against the people's leaders (Matt 23).

However, common people were not absolved from accountability, even if they lacked positive role models. The "LORD's anger" (52:3) is an oft-repeated note in the book (e.g., 15:14; 25:15-38 and comments; 33:5). Political and daily life were not lived apart from the watchful eye of the Almighty. Jeremiah repeatedly made it clear that God is not indifferent to evil. God will deal with sin and sinners. The actors in the drama of human history are not only rulers and citizens but the unseen Lord God.

The text of 52:3 says that "these things happened because of the LORD's anger against the people of Jerusalem and Judah, until he finally banished them from his presence and sent them into exile." Given all that God had threatened through Jeremiah, this summary statement spoke volumes. God's threats are not empty or trivial. God may wait long but he does not wait forever for his people to turn. This entire chapter is a stark testimony to prophecy and its fulfillment.

**Describing the Foreground (52:4-27).** The subject, in three parts, is the Babylonian siege of Jerusalem and its aftermath. First, the narrator follows the fortunes of the people and especially their king (52:4-11). The siege reduced the unnamed masses to a famine diet (52:6). The king and his immediate officials attempted an escape, but failed. Zedekiah, the man who did evil in God's sight (52:1), suffered dearly. His last view, before he himself was blinded and led off to prison, was to see his sons put to death by the conqueror. Jeremiah had already foretold Zedekiah's end (38:18).

Second, the narrator selected the Temple, the prize jewel of Judah, to illustrate the utter devastation of the city (52:12-23). It was burned, but not before its wealth of bronze was appropriated by the enemy. Even to hear reports of such defilement by ungodly forces would shatter any remaining morale. Jeremiah had warned his listeners not to trust in the Temple, for it was no talisman (7:4). He had predicted the removal of its trappings (27:19-22), and so it happened.

Third, the narrator returns to the question of how the people, and especially the dignitaries, fared. Clearly there were advisers who counseled the king to discount Jeremiah's message about submitting to Babylon and instead urged an alliance with Egypt, an action tantamount to rebellion. The note about the awful fate of these powerful persons is a strong reminder that sin is often systemic. An entire operation, a whole "way of being," can be contrary to God. No one person but a collection of influential people charts the path that a society takes. The shapers of a cultural ethos are many, and to this day they include the political and economic pundits, analysts, and advisers, as well as the celebrities who help to set the tone and espouse the values of a society.

**The Many and the One (52:28-34).** The book of Jeremiah has championed God's values. It ends with statistics about the three groups of exiles. Names are absent, but behind the statistics of casualties, then as now, are stories of human aspirations and tragedy, of fear and hope, of lives full of promise that ended in disappointment. Still, in the dark picture of a doomed people, there is a glimmer of hope. One man was singled out for preferential treatment. Because he was from the line of David, Jehoiachin's good fortune of favorable treatment by his captor leaves the reader with a small sprig of hope as reflection on Jerusalem's fall is drawn to a close.

Indeed, this sprig of hope is suggestive of an earlier series of hope-filled promises, including the coming of a righteous king called the "Branch" (23:5), the exiles' return to their land and their Lord (24:6-7), a future of abundance (chs 30–33), and the continued presence of a just and faithful God who is sovereign over all nations (chs 46–51).

# BIBLIOGRAPHY

**Abma, R.**
1999 *Bonds of Love: Methodic Studies of Prophetic Texts with Marriage Imagery (Isaiah 50:1-3 and 54:1-10, Hosea 1-3, Jeremiah 2-3)*. Studia Semitica Neerlandica. Assen: Van Gorcum.

**Achtemeier, Elizabeth**
1984 *Preaching as Theology and Art*. Nashville: Abingdon.

**Aitken, Kenneth T.**
1984 The Oracles against Babylon in Jeremiah 50-51: Structures and Perspectives. *Tyndale Bulletin* 35:25-63.

**Anbar, Moshé**
1999 La libération des esclaves en temps de guerre: Jer 34 et ARM XXVI.363. *Zeitschrift für die Alttestamentliche Wissenschaft* 111:253-255.

**Anderson, B. W.**
1978 The Lord Has Created Something New. *Catholic Biblical Quarterly* 40:463-478.

**Applegate, John.**
1997 Jeremiah and the Seventy Years in the Hebrew Bible: Inner-Biblical reflections on the Prophet and His Prophecy. Pp. 91-110 in *Le livre de Jérémie et sa réception*. Editors, A. H. W. Curtis and T. Roemer. Leuven: Leuven University Press.

**Baloian, Bruce E.**
1992 *Anger in the Old Testament*. American University Studies VII, vol. 99. New York: Peter Lang.

**Barstad, Hans M.**
1997 Some Reflections on the Meaning of the Expression *jzrm tyb* in Jer 16:5. Pp. 17-26 in *Built on Solid Rock: Studies in Honor of Professor Ebbe Egede Knudsen*. Editor, Elie Wardini. Oslo: Novus.

**Bauer, Angela**
1999 Dressed to Be Killed: Jeremiah 4:29-31 as an Example for the Functions of Female Imagery in Jeremiah. Pp. 293-305 in *Troubling Jeremiah*. Journal for the Study of the Old Testament Supplement Series 260. Editors, A. R. Pete Diamond, Kathleen M. O'Connor, and Louis Stulman. Sheffield: Sheffield Academic Press.

**Becking, Bob**
1993 Baalis, the King of the Ammonites. An Epigraphical Note on Jeremiah 40:14. *Journal of Semitic Studies* 38:15-24.

**Bellis, Alice O.**
1995 *The Structure and Composition of Jeremiah 50:2-51:58*. Lewiston, NY: Mellen.

1999 Poetic Structure and Intertextual Logic in Jeremiah 50. Pp. 179-199 in *Troubling Jeremiah*. Journal for the Study of the Old Testament Supplement Series 260. Editors, A. R. Pete Diamond, Kathleen M. O'Connor, and Louis Stulman. Sheffield: Sheffield Academic Press.

**Berrigan, Daniel**
1999 *Jeremiah: the World, the Wound of God*. Minneapolis: Fortress.

**Block, Daniel I.**
1999 *Judges, Ruth*. The New American Commentary, vol. 6. Nashville: Broadman & Holman.

**Blomberg, Craig**
1991 The Sabbath as Fulfilled in Christ. Pp. 196-206 in *The Sabbath in Jewish and Christian Traditions*. Editor, T. Eskenazi. Denver: Denver University Press.

**Boers, Paul A.**
1999 Denouncing Lies, Modeling Truth: Lent and Easter Reflections on Jeremiah and Jesus. Pp. 86-107 in *Peace and Justice Shall Embrace*. Editors, Ted Grimsrud and Loren L. Johns. Telford, PA: Pandora.

**Boyd, Gregory A.**
2000 *God of the Possible: A Biblical Introduction to the Open View of God*. Grand Rapids: Baker.

**Bozak, Barbara A.**
1996 Heeding the Received Text: Jer 2, 20a, A Case in Point. *Biblica* 77:24-37.

**Bracke John M.**
2000a *Jeremiah 1-29*. Westminster Bible Companion. Louisville: Westminster John Knox.

2000b *Jeremiah 30–52 and Lamentations.* Westminster Bible Companion. Louisville: Westminster John Knox.

**Bright, John**

1951 The Date of the Prose Sermons of Jeremiah. *Journal of Biblical Literature* 70:15-35.

1965 *Jeremiah.* Anchor Bible. Garden City, NY: Double Day.

**Brown, M. L.**

1995 *Israel's Divine Healer.* Grand Rapids: Zondervan.

**Brown-Gutoff, Susan E.**

1991 The Voice of Rachel in Jeremiah 31: A Calling to "Something New." *Union Seminary Quarterly Review* 45:177-190.

**Brueggemann, Walter**

1986 *Hopeful Imagination: Prophetic Voices in Exile.* Philadelphia: Fortress.

1992a The Epistemological Crisis of Israel's Two Histories (Jeremiah 9:22-23). Pp. 270-295 in *Old Testament Theology. Essays on Structure, Theme, and Text.* Editor, Patrick D. Miller. Minneapolis: Fortress.

1992b The "Uncared For" Now Cared for (Jer 30:12-17): A Methodological Consideration. Pp. 296-307 in *Old Testament Theology. Essays on Structure, Theme and Text.* Editor, Patrick D. Miller. Minneapolis: Fortress.

1994 The Baruch Connection. *Journal of Biblical Literature* 113:405-420.

1998 *A Commentary on Jeremiah: Exile and Homecoming.* Grand Rapids: Eerdmans.

**Callaway, Mary C.**

1999 Black Fire on White Fire: Historical Context and Literary Subtext in Jeremiah 37–38. Pp. 171-178 in *Troubling Jeremiah.* Editors, A. R. Pete Diamond, Kathleen M. O'Connor, and Louis Stulman. Journal for the Study of the Old Testament Supplement Series 260. Sheffield: Sheffield Academic Press.

**Calvin, J.**

1990 *Sermons on Jeremiah.* Translator, Blair Reynolds. Lewiston, NY: Mellen.

**Carroll, Robert P.**

1981 *From Chaos to Covenant.* New York: Crossroad.

1986 *Jeremiah.* The Old Testament Library. Philadelphia: Westminster.

1989 *Jeremiah.* Old Testament Guides. Sheffield: Sheffield Academic Press.

**Carson, Don A.**

1981 *Divine Sovereignty and Human Responsibility: Biblical Perspectives in Tension.* Atlanta: John Knox.

1982 (editor) *From Sabbath to Lord's Day: A Biblical, Historical, and Theological Investigation.* Grand Rapids: Zondervan.

**Chisholm, Robert B.**

1991 A Theology of Jeremiah and Lamentations. Pp. 341-363 in *A Biblical Theology of the Old Testament.* Editors, R. B. Zuck, E. H. Merrill, and Darrell Bock. Chicago: Moody Press.

**Clark, Gordon R.**

1993 *The Word* Hesed *in the Hebrew Bible.* Sheffield: Sheffield Academic Press.

**Clements, R.E.**

1988 *Jeremiah.* Interpretation. Atlanta: John Knox.

**Clendenen, E. R.**

1987 Discourse Strategies in Jer 10:1-16. *Journal of Biblical Literature* 106:401-408.

**Craigie, Peter, Page H. Kelly, and Joel F. Drinkard, Jr.**

1991 *Jeremiah 1-25.* Word Biblical Commentary 26. Dallas: Word.

**Cranfield C. E. B.**

1953 St. Mark 13. *Scottish Journal of Theology* 6:189-196, 287-303.

**Cunliffe-Jones, H.**

1960 *The Book of Jeremiah: Introduction and Commentary.* The Torch Bible Commentaries. London: SCM.

**Curtis, A. H. W. and T. Roemer.**

1997 *Le livre de Jérémie et sa réception* [The Book of Jeremiah and Its Reception]. Leuven: Leuven University Press.

**Dahood, M. J.**
1959 The Value of Ugaritic for Textual Criticism. *Biblica* 40:164-166.

**Davidson, R.**
1983 *Jeremiah,* vol. 1. The Daily Study Bible. Philadelphia: Westminster.

1985 *Jeremiah,* vol. 2. The Daily Study Bible. Philadelphia: Westminster.

**Dearman, Andrew**
2002 *Jeremiah/Lamentations.* Grand Rapids: Zondervan.

**Diamond, A. R.**
1987 *The Confessions of Jeremiah in Context: Scenes of Prophetic Drama.* Journal for the Study of the
       Old Testament Supplement Series 45. Sheffield: Sheffield Academic Press.

**Dubbink, Joep**
1999 Jeremiah: Hero of Faith or Defeatist? Concerning the Place and Function of Jeremiah 20:14-18.
       *Journal for the Study of the Old Testament* 86:67-84.

**Feinberg, Charles L.**
1982 *Jeremiah: A Commentary.* Grand Rapids: Zondervan.

**Fishbane, Michael**
1985 *Biblical Interpretation in Ancient Israel.* New York: Oxford University Press.

**Fischer, Georg**
1998 Zum Text des Jeremiabuches. *Biblica* 78:305-328.

**Fretheim, Terence E.**
1987 The Repentance of God: A Study of Jeremiah 18:7-10. *Hebrew Annual Review* 11:81-92.
2002 *Jeremiah.* Macon, GA: Smith & Helwys.

**Friebel, Kelvin G.**
1999 *Jeremiah's and Ezekiel's Sign Acts.* Journal for the Study of the Old Testament Supplement Series 283.
       Sheffield: Sheffield Academic Press.

**Gladson, Jerry A.**
2000 Jeremiah 17:19-27: A Rewriting of the Sinaitic Code? *Catholic Biblical Quarterly* 62:33-40.

**Goldingay, John**
1984 *God's Prophet, God's Servant: A Study in Jeremiah and Isaiah 40–55.* Carlisle: Paternoster.

1998 *To the Usual Suspects.* Carlisle: Paternoster.

**Gordon, Robert P, editor.**
1995 *"The Place is too Small for Us": The Israelite Prophets in Recent Scholarship.* Sources for Biblical and
       Theological Study 5. Winona Lake: Eisenbrauns.

**Harrison, R. K.**
1973 *Jeremiah and Lamentations: An Introduction and Commentary.* Downers Grove: InterVarsity.

**Heschel, Abraham**
1962 *The Prophets.* Vol. 1. New York: Harper & Row.

**Hess, Richard S.**
1991 Hiphil forms of *qwr* in Jeremiah vi 7. *Vetus Testamentum* 41:347-350.

**Hill, John**
1999a *Friend or Foe? The Figure of Babylon in the Book of Jeremiah MT.* Biblical Interpretation 40. Leiden:
        Brill.

1999b The Construction of Time in Jeremiah 25 (MT). Pp. 146-160 in *Troubling Jeremiah.* Editors,
        A. R. Pete Diamond, Kathleen M. O'Connor, and Louis Stuhlman. Journal for the Study of the Old
        Testament Supplement Series 260. Sheffield: Sheffield Academic Press.

**Ho, Kit**
1999 Narrating Jeremiah: The Rhetorical Skill and Presentation Strategy in Jeremiah 26–45. PhD diss.,
       Fuller Theological Seminary.

**Hoffmeier, James K.**
1998 Once Again the "Plumb Line" Vision of Amos 7:7-9: An Interpretive Clue from Egypt? Pp. 304-319
       in *Boundaries of the Ancient Near Eastern World. A Tribute to Cyrus H. Gordon.* Editors, M. Lubetski,
       C. Gottlieb, and S. Keller. Journal for the Study of the Old Testament Supplement Series 273.
       Sheffield: Sheffield Academic Press.

Holladay, William L.

1971 *A Concise Hebrew and Aramaic Lexicon of the Old Testament.* Grand Rapids: Eerdmans.

1976 *The Architecture of Jeremiah 1–20.* Lewisburg, PA: Bucknell University Press.

1986 *Jeremiah 1.* Hermeneia. Philadelphia: Fortress.

1989 *Jeremiah 2.* Hermeneia. Minneapolis: Fortress.

1990 *Jeremiah: A Fresh Reading.* New York: Pilgrim.

2001 Plausible Circumstances for the Prophecy of Habakkuk. *Journal of Biblical Literature* 120:123-142.

House, Paul R

1998 The God Who Enforces Covenant: Jeremiah. Pp. 299-326 in *Old Testament Theology.* Downers Grove: InterVarsity.

Huey, F. B. Jr.

1993 *Jeremiah, Lamentations.* The New American Commentary, vol. 16. Nashville: Broadman & Holman.

Huffmon, Herbert B.

1999 The Impossible: God's Words of Assurance in Jer 31:35-37. Pp. 172-86 in *On the Way to Nineveh: Studies in Honor of George M. Landes.* Editors, Stephen L. Cook and S.C. Winter. Atlanta: Scholars Press.

Huwyler, Beat

1996 Politische Prophetie in der Zeit der babylonischen Bedrohung (7./6. Jh. v. Chr.). *Theologische Zeitschrift* 52:193-205.

Hyatt, J. P.

1956 *Introduction and Exegesis, Jeremiah.* Pp. 775-1142 in *Interpreter's Bible,* vol 5. Editor, G. A. Buttrick. New York: Abingdon.

Ives, Robert

1990-2000 "Sermons on Jeremiah." Sermons given at the Grantham Church, Grantham, PA.

Joclle, Ferry

1999 *Illusions et salut dans la prédication prophetique de Jérémie.* Berlin: de Gruyter.

Keown, Gerald L., Pamela J. Scalise, Thomas G. Smothers.

1995 *Jeremiah 26-52.* Word Biblical Commentary 27. Dallas: Word.

Kessler, Martin

2003 *Battle of the Gods: The God of Israel versus Marduk of Babylon: A Literary/Theological Interpretation of Jeremiah 50-51.* Assen: Van Gorcum.

2004 (Editor) *Reading the Book of Jeremiah: A Search for Coherence.* Winona Lake: Eisenbrauns.

Kidner, Derek

1987 *The Message of Jeremiah: Against Wind and Tide.* The Bible Speaks Today. Leicester: Inter-Varsity.

King, Philip J.

1993 *Jeremiah: An Archaeological Companion.* Louisville: Westminster John Knox.

Krašovec, J.

1992 The Source of Hope in the Book of Lamentations. *Vetus Testamentum* 42:223-233.

Kruger, P. A.

1996 The Psychology of Shame and Jeremiah 2:36-37. *Journal of Northwest Semitic Languages* 22:79-88.

Lash, Nicholas

1986 What Might Martyrdom Mean? Pp. 75-92 in *Theology on the Way to Emmaus.* London: SCM.

Long, Burke O.

1981 Social Dimensions of Prophetic Conflict. *Semeia* 21:31-53.

Lundbom, Jack R.

1975 *Jeremiah: A Study in Ancient Hebrew Rhetoric.* Missoula, MT: Society of Biblical Literature and Scholars Press.

1999 *Jeremiah 1-20.* Anchor Bible 21A. New York: Doubleday.

Martens, Elmer A.

1986 *Jeremiah.* Believers Church Bible Commentary. Scottdale, PA: Herald Press.

1987 Narrative Parallelism and Message in Jeremiah 34–38. Pp. 33-49 in *Early Jewish and Christian Exegesis.* Editors, Craig Evans and W. F. Stinespring. Atlanta: Scholars Press.

1996 Theology of Jeremiah. Pp. 389-392 in *The Evangelical Dictionary of Biblical Theology.*
     Grand Rapids: Baker.

1997 Jeremiah. Pp. 752-755 in *New International Dictionary of Old Testament Theology and Exegesis.*
     Vol. 4. Editor, Willem A. VanGemeren. Grand Rapids: Zondervan.

**McConville, J. G.**

1991 Jeremiah: Prophet and Book. *Tyndale Bulletin* 42:80-92.

1993 *Judgment and Promise: An Interpretation of the Book of Jeremiah.* Winona Lake: Eisenbrauns.

1997 Jeremiah: Theology of. Pp. 755-767 in *New International Dictionary of Old Testament Theology
     and Exegesis.* Vol. 4. Editor, Willem A. VanGemeren. Grand Rapids: Zondervan.

**McKane, William A.**

1980 Poison, Trial by Ordeal and the Cup of Wrath. *Vetus Testamentum* 30:474-492.

1986 *A Critical and Exegetical Commentary on Jeremiah*, vol. 1. Edinburgh: T & T Clark.

1996 *A Critical and Exegetical Commentary on Jeremiah*, vol. 2. Edinburgh: T & T Clark.

**Mendenhall, G. E.**

1973 *The Tenth Generation: The Origins of the Biblical Tradition.* Baltimore: John Hopkins University Press.

**Metzer, M.**

1991 "Thron der Herrlichkeit," Ein Beitrag zur Interpretation von Jeremia 17,12f. Pp. 237-62 in *Prophetie
     und geschichtliche Wirklichkeit im alten Israel: Festschrift für Siegfried Hermann zum 65.* Editors,
     Rüdiger Liwak and Siegfried Wagner. Stuttgart: Kohlhammer.

**Moberly, R.W. L.**

2000 *The Bible, Theology, and Faith: A Study of Abraham and Jesus.* Cambridge Studies in Christian Doctrine.
     Cambridge: Cambridge University Press.

**Morgan, Timothy C.**

2000 Have we Become Too Busy with Death? *Christianity Today*, February 7, 36-44.

**Mowinckel, S.**

1914 *Zur Komposition des Buches Jeremiah.* Kristiania: J. Dybad.

**Nicholson, E. W.**

1970 *Preaching to the Exiles: A Study of the Prose Tradition in the Book of Jeremiah.* New York:
     Schocken Books.

1973 *The Book of the Prophet Jeremiah, Chapters 1-25.* The Cambridge Bible Commentary on the
     New English Bible. Cambridge: Cambridge University Press.

1975 *The Book of the Prophet Jeremiah, Chapters 26-52.* The Cambridge Bible Commentary on the
     New English Bible. Cambridge: Cambridge University Press.

**O'Connor, Kathleen M.**

1988 The Tears of God and Divine Character in Jeremiah 2-9. Pp. 172-85 in *God in the Fray: A Tribute
     to Walter Brueggemann.* Editors, T. Linafelt and T. K. Beal. Minneapolis: Fortress.

**O'Day, Gail R.**

1990 Jeremiah 9:22-23 and 1 Corinthians 1:26-31: A Study in Intertextuality. *Journal of Biblical Literature*
     109:259-267.

**Ortlund, Raymond C.**

1996 *Whoredom: God's Unfaithful Wife in Biblical Theology.* New Studies in Biblical Theology. Grand Rapids:
     Eerdmans.

**Overholt, Thomas W.**

1970 *The Threat of Falsehood: A Study in the Theology of the Book of Jeremiah.* Naperville, IL: A. R. Allenson.

**Parke-Taylor, G. H.**

2000 *The Formation of the Book of Jeremiah: Doublets and Recurring Phrases.* SBL Monographs 51. Atlanta:
     Society of Biblical Literature.

**Perdue, Leo G.**

1999 The Book of Jeremiah in Old Testament Theology. Pp. 320-338 in *Troubling Jeremiah.* Editors, A. R.
     Pete Diamond, Kathleen M. O'Connor and Louis Stuhlman. Journal for the Study of the Old Testament
     Supplement Series 260. Sheffield: Sheffield Academic Press.

**Perdue, Leo G. and B. W. Kovacs.**

1984 *A Prophet to the Nations: Essays in Jeremiah Studies.* Winona Lake: Eisenbrauns.

1994 *The Collapse of History: Reconstructing Old Testament Theology.* Minneapolis: Fortress.

**Prévost, Jean-Pierre**
1998 *How to Read the Prophets.* New York: Continuum.

**Raitt, T. M.**
1977 *A Theology of Exile: Judgment/Deliverance in Jeremiah and Ezekiel.* Philadelphia: Fortress.

**Reimer, David J.**
1989 The "Foe" and the "North" in Jeremiah. *Zeitschrift für die Alttestamentliche Wissenschaft* 101:223-232.

**Roberts, J. J. M.**
1992 The Motif of the Weeping God in Jeremiah and Its Background in the Lament Tradition of the Ancient Near East. *Old Testament Essays* 5:361-374.

**Roshwalb, Esther H.**
1998 Build-Up and Climax in Jeremiah's Visions and Laments. Pp. 111-135 in *Boundaries in the Ancient World.* Editors, Meir Lubetski, Claire Gottlieb, and Sharon Keller. Journal for the Study of the Old Testament Supplement Series 273. Sheffield: Sheffield Academic Press.

**Seidel, Bodo**
1997 Freunde und Feinde Jeremias unter den Beamten Judas der spätvorexilischen Zeit. *Biblische Zeitschrift* 41:28-53.

**Seitz, C. R.**
1989 *Theology in Conflict: Reactions to the Exile in the Book of Jeremiah.* New York: de Gruyter.

**Shead, Andrew G.**
1998 Jeremiah 32 in Its Hebrew and Greek Recensions: The Prophet, the Text, Its Translator and His Critics. PhD thesis, University of Cambridge. (See summary in *Tyndale Bulletin* 50.2 (1999) 318-320).

**Sire, J. W.**
1975 *Jeremiah, Meet the 20th Century.* Downers Grove: InterVarsity.

**Smit, J. H.**
1998 War-related Terminology and Imagery in Jeremiah 15:10-21. *Old Testament Essays* 11:105-114.

**Smith, Daniel L.**
1989 Jeremiah as a Prophet of Nonviolent Resistance. *Journal for the Study of the Old Testament* 43:95-107.

**Smith, M. S.**
1990 *The Laments of Jeremiah and Their Contexts: A Literary and Redactional Study of Jeremiah 11-20.* Society of Biblical Literature Monographs 42. Atlanta: Scholars Press.

**Soderlund, S.**
1985 *The Greek Text of Jeremiah: A Revised Hypothesis.* Journal for the Study of the Old Testament Supplement Series 47. Sheffield: Journal for the Study of the Old Testament Press.

**Sommer, Benjamin D.**
1998 *A Prophet Reads Scripture: Allusion in Isaiah 40-66.* Stanford: Stanford University Press.

1999 New Light on the Composition of Jeremiah. *Catholic Biblical Quarterly* 61:646-666.

**Stacey, W. David**
1995 The Function of Prophetic Drama. Pp. 112-132 in *"The Place is too Small for Us": The Israelite Prophets in Recent Scholarship.* Sources for Biblical and Theological Study 5. Winona Lake: Eisenbrauns.

**Steiner, R. C.**
1999 Incomplete Circumcision in Egypt and Edom: Jeremiah (9:24-25) in Light of Josephus and Jonckheere. *Journal of Biblical Literature* 119:497-505.

**Swartley, Willard**
1983 *Slavery, Sabbath, War, and Women: Case Issues in Biblical Interpretation.* Scottdale, PA: Herald.

**Thompson, J. A.**
1980 *The Book of Jeremiah.* New International Commentary on the Old Testament. Grand Rapids: Eerdmans.

**Trible, Phyllis**
1978 *God and the Rhetoric of Sexuality.* Philadelphia: Fortress.

**Unterman, J.**
1987 *From Repentance to Redemption: Jeremiah's Thought in Transition.* Journal for the Study of the Old Testament Supplement Series 54. Sheffield: Sheffield Academic Press.

**Van Der Wal, A.**
1996 Themes from Exodus in Jeremiah 30-31. Pp. 559-66 in *Studies in the Book of Exodus.* Editor,
     M. Vervenne. Leuven: Leuven University Press.

**Van Groningen, G.**
1990 *Messianic Revelation in the Old Testament.* Grand Rapids: Baker.

**Waltke, Bruce**
1989 Aims of OT Textual Criticism. *Westminster Theological Journal* 51:93-108.

**Walton, John H.**
1989 Vision Narrative and Wordplay and Jeremiah xxiv. *Vetus Testamentum* 39:508-509.

**Watts, J. W.**
1992 Text and Redaction in Jeremiah's Oracles against the Nations. *Catholic Biblical Quarterly*
     54:432-447.

**Weippert, H.**
1973 *Die Prosareden des Jeremiabuches.* Beihefte zur Zeitschrift für die Alttestamentliche Wissenschaft
     132. Berlin: de Gruyter.

**Weiss, Herold**
1986 How can Jeremiah Compare the Migration of Birds to Knowledge of God's Justice? *Bible Review*
     2:42-45.

**Wiebe, John M.**
1987 The Form of the "Announcement of a Royal Savior" and the Interpretation of Jeremiah 23:5-7.
     *Studia Biblica et Theologica* 15:3-22.

**Winkle, Ross E.**
1987 Jeremiah's Seventy Years for Babylon: A Re-Assessment. Part I: The Scriptural Data. *Andrews
     University Seminary Studies* 25:210-214.

**Yoder, John H.**
1972 *The Politics of Jesus.* Grand Rapids: Eerdmans.

# Lamentations

ELMER A. MARTENS

# INTRODUCTION TO
# *Lamentations*

WHEN TIMES ARE HARD, whether for society, God's people, or an individual, the laments in the book of Lamentations can provide a template for processing disappointment and grief. This book gives us access into the heart of a poet who took his sorrows to God, who wrestled with this God, and who found reasons for at least some comfort.

## AUTHOR

The book of Lamentations is commonly believed to have been written by the prophet Jeremiah. The reasons for this are that (1) the introduction and title given to the book in several versions, including the Septuagint, is "The Dirges of Jeremiah"; (2) there is a long Christian tradition regarding Jeremiah as the author; and (3) there are similarities of literary expression between the books of Jeremiah and Lamentations (e.g., Jer 9:1 [8:23] and Lam 3:48 and the use of *sheber* [TH7667, ZH8691], "brokenness" and "destruction"). But an argument against Jeremiah's authorship can also be made based on style (no acrostics in Jeremiah) and content (appeal for retribution on the Babylonians, 3:64-66; cf. Huey 1993:442-443).

The book itself does not offer any direct clues about the author, and while it could have been the prophet Jeremiah, it could have just as easily been someone else. The poet of Lamentations, a skillful literary artist, was almost certainly an eyewitness to the catastrophe (1:13-15; 2:6, 9). The intense pathos in the lyrics suggests an author personally affected by the disaster. The poet was a member of the Hebrew faith community who shared the notion of divine retribution for evil with his original audience.

Some hold that not one but several poets may have been involved. For example, Westermann, when reviewing the authorial options, concludes that "the assumption of multiple authorship remains the more probable" (1994:58). But multiple authorship has been questioned on the basis of the consistent literary style found throughout the book (Marcus 1986).

## DATE AND OCCASION OF WRITING

The poems of the book focus on the agony resulting from the tragedy of Jerusalem's capture and destruction by the Babylonians. Since the descriptions are so graphic, one may assume that the poet had firsthand experience of Jerusalem's destruction, or that he knew and conversed with those who had seen it. This would mean the book was written soon after 586 BC. Recent studies, however, have focused on the use of other city-laments in the ancient Near East and propose that the lament be associated with the razing of the foundations of the old structure and the preparation to rebuild the Temple. In this view the date for the book would be 520 BC. (For a brief summary of this position and reasons why the view may not be tenable, see Dobbs-Allsopp 2002:6-12.)

The occasion for writing was the calamity that befell Jerusalem. Some had thought that this city, where the Temple stood as the symbol of God's presence, was inviolable (Jer 7:4). It had miraculously withstood past sieges (e.g., by the Assyrians, 701 BC; 2 Kgs 18:13–19:37). But now the unthinkable had happened. Jeremiah's warnings about a northern foe coming against the holy city had materialized (Jer 1:14-15). The military forces of Babylon had marched westward, defeated the Egyptians at Carchemish (605 BC), and continued southward along the Mediterranean. Hostages had been taken in 604 BC and a puppet king, Zedekiah (598–587 BC) had been put in place. That king and his counselors chose the route of insubordination. When they tried to assert Judah's independence with help from Egypt, the Babylonians laid siege against the city and took it (for more historical detail see the introduction to Jeremiah).

The city had been burned and its citizenry exiled to Babylon. An era of over 350 years' rule by Davidic kings had ended. Gone were the splendor of city, Temple, and sovereign. National independence ceased. Were God's promises also gone? Disappointment and grief had settled in. The poet voices that grief, disappointment, and confusion as he reflects on the siege, describes the hardships, cries for help, and ponders the physical and emotional pain.

## AUDIENCE

The book, or at least large parts of it, are in the genre of mourning rites well known in the ancient Near East (Pham 1999). The poems are addressed to God as a series of laments. He is presented with the details of the complaint, including the people's perplexity about his anger (2:20-22).

At another level, the book is for the benefit of the exiles and those who remained in the land after the Babylonian takeover. The book keeps the memory of that fateful event alive for coming generations. The poems provide a grief-stricken people with words for their agony.

Parts of Lamentations are reminiscent of a funeral dirge. A fast was instituted to commemorate the fall of Jerusalem in 586 BC (2 Kgs 25:8-9; Zech 7:3-5; 8:19). In later times, a fast instituted in the Babylonian month Ab commemorated the destruction of the city both in 586 BC and AD 70. There is a long tradition of reading the book on such fast days, and "it is not unreasonable to assume that it [Lamentations] was intended for this purpose from the first" (Ellison 1986:697).

## CANONICITY AND TEXTUAL HISTORY

Lamentations was not contested for inclusion into the scriptural canon, as were some other books. In the Hebrew order of the canon, the book is placed in the third

division, the "Writings." In some versions, Lamentations has preceded Daniel and
Esther. Usually, however, it is placed with the four other books—Ruth, Song of
Solomon, Ecclesiastes, and Esther—that make up the Megillot, the "Scrolls," which
are designated to be read on certain Jewish festivals. For the most part, though not
consistently, the book of Lamentations follows in a chronological order after Ecclesiastes and before Esther (ABD 4:138).

In the Septuagint's ordering of the books (followed by English versions), Lamentations comes after Jeremiah, not only because the Septuagint names Jeremiah as
the author, but because it is a fitting sequel to Jeremiah's description of the Babylonian capture of the city.

As for textual considerations, "In the book of Lamentations the MT itself seems
to be in a good state of preservation" (ABD 4:140). The Greek text, according to
some scholars, was brought into line with the Masoretic Text (MT), and thus is not
especially helpful where there are textual problems. A sizeable manuscript that has
portions of Lamentations 1, along with some fragments from other chapters, was
found among the Dead Sea Scrolls. It is known as 4QLam^a. Greater clarity on textual
transmission can be expected as these fragments are deciphered and analyzed.

## LITERARY STYLE

The book consists of five poems that correspond to the present five chapters
(though some count seven poems by segmenting Lam 3; House 1998: 485). The
central poem, a personal lament, is the longest (Lam 3). On either side of it are two
communal laments (Lam 2 and 4). The central portion of the book is bracketed by
the first and fifth chapters, each of which describes the tragic situation. Lamentations 1, which incorporates elements of the dirge, is also a communal lament, as is
Lamentations 5 (so Westermann 1994:117-119, 211, 219). As has been noted by
others, the book as a whole is in the *qinah* or lament pattern, in which three longer
poems are followed by two shorter ones.

The *qinah*, or lament rhythm, has a poetic line of three major beats followed
by another with two stresses, and so suggests a halting, sobbing movement. Both
communal and individual laments are common in the Psalms (e.g., 6; 13; 80), and
several occur in Jeremiah (e.g., 11:18–12:6; 15:15-21; 20:7-18). They are often
marked with the Hebrew word *'ekah* [TH349A, ZH377] (how), a word of dismay as in,
"How the mighty heroes have fallen!" a lament uttered by David over the death of
Saul and Jonathan (1:1; 2:1; 4:1; 2 Sam 1:19).

Laments as a literary form were known among Israel's neighbors (Ferris 1992:63-
87, 153-175). Some laments attribute the destructions of their cities to the abandonment of their patron gods. From the Mesopotamian region comes "The Lamentation
over the Destruction of Sumer and Ur" (Nana Lament; ANET 611-619). In this lament, the destruction came with an Elamite invasion, made possible because the
patron deity of the city had abandoned it. In "The Lamentation over the Destruction
of Ur" (Ningal Lament; ANET 455-463), the departure of the deity is the consequence
and not the cause of the city's calamities. In these poems, appeals are made to the

deity, also a notable feature in the book of Lamentations. A further point of comparison comes from another document, "The Curse of Agade," in which the god Inanna, after departing from the city, turns against it in battle, apparently to avenge the desecration of a shrine (ANET 646; cf. Block 1988:130-133). So also in Lamentations, God is depicted as the enemy destroying Jerusalem (2:2). The communal lament, the primary genre of the book of Lamentations, generally includes such components as accusations against God, complaints about enemies, acknowledgment of guilt, a plea for God to take heed, and a petition for reprisal against enemies. Two other customary aspects of a communal lament, retrospection and a plea for intervention, are lacking in Lamentations (Westermann 1994:118-119, 227). For a detailed discussion of the form of the communal laments, both in the ancient Near East and in the Bible, see Ferris (1992:17-61, 89-152).

The book is unique in that it consists (except for chapter 5) of acrostic poems built on the twenty-two-letter Hebrew alphabet. The four acrostic poems do not all, however, follow the same pattern. In the first two poems, only the first word of each stanza is keyed to the alphabet and each stanza is composed of three bi-cola (verse lines that may be divided into two parts that are usually parallel in some fashion). The fourth poem is like the first two except that its stanzas have two bi-cola. The third poem (Lam 3) has three bi-cola for each stanza, but each bi-cola in the stanza begins with the featured letter.

Several literary reasons for the acrostic have been advanced: (1) as an artistic device they provide a distinctive framework for an author's thoughts; (2) acrostics require an orderly form, providing some restraint to what appears to be uncontrollable grief; (3) acrostics are pleasing partly because readers anticipate the way that subsequent stanzas will be introduced; (4) acrostics facilitate memorization; and (5) acrostics convey a sense that the subject is too vast to be adequately described or comprehended in ordinary language.

Behind the alphabetic acrostics in Lamentations, one may see an ideological rationale. Jerusalem's fall was tragic beyond description. Exhausting the alphabet makes the point that the nation's trauma was so severe that language could not do justice to the topic.

Another biblical example of this use of acrostic is Psalm 119 (the longest biblical acrostic) which expounds on a topic too big for ordinary words, namely the richness of God's law. So also, because language is finally inadequate, the poet of Proverbs 31 resorts to an acrostic when praising the virtues of the capable woman. All three topics—a terrible tragedy, God's teaching, and an exceptional woman—tax their authors since each subject is really too large for words.

## MAJOR THEMES AND THEOLOGICAL CONCERNS

Various characters appear in the acrostics: the city (personified as a woman), the citizens of Jerusalem, their enemies, and God. Each poem takes account of all four characters and develops theological themes around them.

The city of Jerusalem is given a voice through the literary device of personification (Heim 1999). She is a widow deprived of companionship, luxuries, and even life's necessities. She has been emptied of her inhabitants (1:3). Those who had habitually come to this worship center came no longer (1:4). Jerusalem had lost her treasures, chief of which was the Temple (2:6). The altar was desecrated (2:7), her royal palaces were demolished (2:7), her fortified city gates had collapsed (2:9), and her walls were destroyed (2:8).

The city no longer had leaders. The king, of whose protection the people boasted, was no more (4:20). Her rulers, the princes who enjoyed the delicacies that their city and their station in life provided, were now malnourished and barely recognizable (4:7-8). The prophets became ineffective and could not get a word from God. The non-functioning priests only groaned (1:4). Women had been raped (5:11) and people killed; their bodies were in the street (2:21). The remaining citizens were starving (1:11-12; 4:4) and the city was at the mercy of its invaders (5:5).

This tragic theme of military-inflicted destruction, at home in battle accounts, was transposed into a theological key by the recognition that the force behind this disaster was Israel's God. That point is made repeatedly (1:14; 2:2-6), so that an event that from a secular viewpoint might be interpreted in economic or political terms is here interpreted theologically. The poet knew, of course, that the immediate agent of the city's grief was the Babylonian army, though Babylon is not named (1:10). But the acknowledgment that God was the distant but very real cause of the city's downfall was in keeping with Israel's traditional affirmation that God is sovereign. God's rule "continues from generation to generation" (5:19). He is the One who had earlier deployed the Assyrians against Israel (Isa 10). The ruins everywhere make visible a story about God!

The city's desolation also raised questions about sin and its consequences. Israel's God had not acted out of caprice but according to the preset demands of justice. Israel's sin had triggered God's punitive action. God's prerogative in measuring out the consequences of wrongdoing by intervening with gross destruction was not debated. Instead, it was affirmed that "The LORD is right" (1:18). Israel knew the connection between sin and punishment, a connection made necessary by God's justice and enunciated long ago (2:17; Deut 28:15-64; Jer 25:8-11). And while care must be taken not to attribute every mishap and difficulty to some wrongdoing (smoking causes cancer, but not all cancer is the result of smoking), it remains a fundamental axiom that God will inflict injury in retribution for sin. Israel knew that it had sinned (1:5, 8, 14; 4:13) and that the strike against her city was deserved (3:39).

Another character heard in the acrostics is the voice of a sufferer, an individual who speaks both for himself and for the collective population of the city (Lam 3). Here the language is not about buildings, but about skin, flesh, heart, and teeth (3:4, 13, 16). The theme is human misery. The suffering was physical, because food and water were so scarce (1:11-12; 5:4, 9-10) that mothers resorted to boiling their own children (4:10). The suffering was emotional, with tears and more tears (1:16; 2:11; 3:49). The people had no rest (5:5); they were taunted by those who conquered her (2:16), as well as by passers-by (2:15) and others who wanted nothing to do with her (4:15). Sufferers were left to their own grief, as there was no one to help (1:9, 16; 5:3). Jerusalem knew the misery of desperation and exhaustion (1:13; 3:13-20), as even God had forsaken her (5:20-21; cf. 3:5).

Pain is not unusual in human experience. Here, however, the theme of misery is transposed into the theological dimension. Israel's pain moved her to pray; she appealed to God in her distress. Many of the laments in the Psalms, after stating the complaint, break out in prayer. In Lamentations, the prayer is for God to take notice (1:11, 20; 2:20). This earnest call for help was from the depths of their experience (3:55-56). Israel desired relief from her affliction, and remarkably, the God who had afflicted her was ready to help (3:57-58). Prayer suggests hope in a good God, another theme of this book. Something about this destroyed city with its famished and vanishing population, when viewed from a perspective "under God," engendered hope. From those most severely tried came the most beautiful affirmations about God's goodness as a reason for hope: "The faithful love of the LORD never ends! . . . Great is his faithfulness. . . . The LORD is good" (3:22-25). Hope builds on belief in the reality that God does not abandon anyone forever (3:31). Exactly in the center of the book, midway through the middle acrostic, is a refrain about God's total reliability: "he also shows compassion because of the greatness of his unfailing love" (3:32; cf. Exod 34:6-7). Beyond the suffering stands a responsive and faithful God.

A third character in each acrostic is an enemy that highlights the theme of humiliation from adversaries. These enemies were the ones who raided and stripped the city (1:10; 3:46-47), inflicted injury (3:52), ceaselessly pursued fugitives (4:18), and delighted in Israel's difficulty (2:16; 3:63).

The theme about adversaries and their harmful actions is not new, but this theme is also soon given a theological cast. The victim, Israel, urged God to take vengeance on her enemies. Had God not witnessed the crimes they had perpetrated against her (3:59-63)? Her unambiguous prayer was, "Pay them back, LORD, for all the evil they have done." It is part of a language of exasperation that was also part of Israel's tradition (cf. the imprecatory Psalms, e.g., Ps 137). Based on the conviction that "Vengeance is mine; I will repay, says the LORD" (Deut 32:35), such appeals can be interpreted as expressing that God can be trusted to right what is wrong, though they sound harsh. Even speech about the enemy turns into talk about religion, and more specifically, about God.

God is the last character to be mentioned, but from first to last in every acrostic, he is listed as one to be reckoned with. The rather paradoxical theme is that of God's interventionist action in history (cf. Westermann's excursus, "Yahweh as 'Lord of History' in Lamentations," 1994:222-228). God was Israel's enemy, for he had moved against her (2:4-5). Westermann (1994:222) counts some fifty clauses that speak of God's inflicting severe hardship on his people. Yet as noted above, God was also Israel's hope and she must look to him for restoration (5:21). In this crisis of catastrophe, Israel must trust God. This trusting posture usually comes with nagging questions, as illustrated in the book's closing questions, "Or have you utterly rejected us? Are you angry with us still?"

Jerusalem's fall was tragic not only because God precipitated it but especially because he did so in anger. The theme of God's anger, wrath, and fury surfaces in each of the five poems at least once, and sometimes more often (1:12; 2:1, 22; 3:1; 4:11; 5:22). In this fiery tragedy, the city was burned just as God's fury was "poured out like fire on beautiful Jerusalem" (2:4). God's adversarial actions are graphically described in 3:2-17 as breaking bones, tearing like a bear with claws, shooting arrows, setting obstacles in the way, and stripping people of everything; they are headlined with a statement about "the rod of the LORD's anger" (3:1).

Some observations may help to situate God's anger theologically. (1) Israel's neighbors spoke of their gods as becoming angry. To speak of God's anger was to resort to anthropopathism—that is, to describe God's feelings as analogous to those of human beings. God is a person and is thus characterized by emotion and feeling. (2) Israel's tradition, from the time of Moses if not before, had spoken about God's anger in concrete language, including tangible threats against evildoers. (3) By describing what happened to her as an unleashing of God's anger, Israel could better convey the severity of her pain. (4) God's anger is prompted by the wickedness of human beings against one another and by their rebellion and pride (Baloian 1992:73, 191-210). (5) Israel understood that God's anger was not an uncontrollable petulant emotional outburst like human anger. Still, as Westermann notes (1994:224), anger is a mood and not a permanent personality trait. Whatever Israel had to say about God's anger and the hurt of being the brunt of it must be weighed against her assertion, "The LORD is right" (1:18). (6) A lot is said throughout the Bible about God's goodness, and to speak of God's anger does not invalidate claims about God's goodness. Even in this book, which is very forthright about God's anger, the affirmations about God's goodness are notable (3:22-32). God takes no pleasure in releasing his anger against wrongdoers. He "does not enjoy hurting people or causing them sorrow" (3:33). It is of the greatest importance, when discussing God's anger, to acknowledge that the biblical story, beginning with the creation and continuing with the Exodus and beyond, emphasizes God's goodness and his salvific action as a context for his anger.

This book can be read on the surface as one that portrays the ravages of war, the destructive fallout of an enemy invasion of a city, and the pain of physical and psychological suffering. At a more profound level, the poems wrestle with the consequences of sin, portray a people wounded in their consciences, and underscore that God is above, below, and around it all. People should pray to this God, for his ultimate intent is for his people's good. But this God is not to be domesticated into a harmless, now-and-again helpful pet. The historical circumstances of the destroyed Jerusalem show us the dark side of God. Like a moon that is generally experienced as giving light, God also has a dark and frigid side. Quite correctly, then, the theology of the book can be explicated around doom and hope (Gottwald 1962).

The book might also be read for hints about processing grief. Resist denial. Face and state the ugliness. Wrestle with the way that God is experienced in this difficulty. Seek consolation in the goodness of God. Give voice to your feelings and pray. For other essays on the theology of the book, see Chisholm 1991:359-363, Brown 1997, Martens 1996, Westermann 1994:221-235, and House 1998.

## OUTLINE
   I. After the Disaster (1:1-22)
     A. A City's Ruin (1:1-11a)
     B. The People's Pain (1:11b-22)
  II. God as Israel's Enemy (2:1-22)
     A. God's Angry Siege against the City (2:1-10)
     B. The Cry of an Anguished People (2:11-22)
 III. Dealing with Grief (3:1-66)
     A. Personal Afflictions (3:1-20)
     B. God is Good (3:21-39)
     C. Tears and Prayers (3:40-66)
 IV. A People's Plight (4:1-22)
     A. Then and Now (4:1-11)
     B. Problems on Every Side (4:12-22)
  V. Appeals to the Lord (5:1-22)
     A. Experiencing Hard Times (5:1-18)
     B. One Final Appeal (5:19-22)

COMMENTARY ON
# *Lamentations*

◆ **I. After the Disaster (1:1–22)**
   **A. A City's Ruin (1:1–11a)\***

Jerusalem, once so full of people,
   is now deserted.
She who was once great among the
     nations
   now sits alone like a widow.
Once the queen of all the earth,
   she is now a slave.

²She sobs through the night;
   tears stream down her cheeks.
Among all her lovers,
   there is no one left to comfort her.
All her friends have betrayed her
   and become her enemies.

³Judah has been led away into
     captivity,
   oppressed with cruel slavery.
She lives among foreign nations
   and has no place of rest.
Her enemies have chased her down,
   and she has nowhere to turn.

⁴The roads to Jerusalem\* are in
     mourning,
   for crowds no longer come to
     celebrate the festivals.
The city gates are silent,
   her priests groan,
her young women are crying—
   how bitter is her fate!

⁵Her oppressors have become her
     masters,
   and her enemies prosper,
for the LORD has punished Jerusalem
   for her many sins.

Her children have been captured
   and taken away to distant lands.

⁶All the majesty of beautiful Jerusalem\*
   has been stripped away.
Her princes are like starving deer
   searching for pasture.
They are too weak to run
   from the pursuing enemy.

⁷In the midst of her sadness and
     wandering,
   Jerusalem remembers her ancient
     splendor.
But now she has fallen to her
     enemy,
   and there is no one to help her.
Her enemy struck her down
   and laughed as she fell.

⁸Jerusalem has sinned greatly,
   so she has been tossed away like
     a filthy rag.
All who once honored her now despise
     her,
   for they have seen her stripped
     naked and humiliated.
All she can do is groan
   and hide her face.

⁹She defiled herself with immorality
   and gave no thought to her
     future.
Now she lies in the gutter
   with no one to lift her out.
"LORD, see my misery," she cries.
   "The enemy has triumphed."

<sup>10</sup>The enemy has plundered her
    completely,
    taking every precious thing she
    owns.
She has seen foreigners violate her
    sacred Temple,

the place the LORD had forbidden
    them to enter.

<sup>11</sup>Her people groan as they search
    for bread.
They have sold their treasures for
    food to stay alive.

1 Each of the first four chapters of this book is an acrostic, laid out in the order of the Hebrew alphabet. The first word of each verse begins with a successive Hebrew letter. Chapters 1, 2, and 4 have one verse for each of the 22 Hebrew letters. Chapter 3 contains 22 stanzas of three verses each. Though chapter 5 has 22 verses, it is not an acrostic. 1:4 Hebrew *Zion;* also in 1:17. 1:6 Hebrew *of the daughter of Zion.*

## NOTES

**1:1 *Jerusalem, once so full of people, is now deserted.*** The NLT has named the city. The book itself does not do so until 1:4. The book begins with *'ekah* [TH349A, ZH377], a recognized hallmark of a lament (cf. 2:1; 4:1; 2 Sam 1:19), though the word is also used in narrative and other genres (Ferris 1992:139). The poetry is in *qinah* rhythm (see Introduction). For a survey of the communal lament in the OT and the ancient Near East, see Ferris (1992) and Westermann (1994:86-98). The word *rabbath* [TH7227, ZH8041] ("abundant," "great"—in form, a remnant of an early case ending; see Waltke and O'Connor 1990:127-128) occurs in two successive cola, once modifying "city" ("so full of people") and once modifying "widow" (lit., "as a widow [once] great among the nations").

*she is now a slave.* Lit., "she exists for tribute."

**1:2 *She sobs.*** The description is made emphatic by the intensifying infinitive *bako* [TH1058, ZH1134], followed by the qal of the same root *thibkeh* [TH1058, ZH1134] (sobs bitterly).

***Among all her lovers.*** These were her friendly political allies (cf. Jer 4:30; 30:14; cf. Hos 8:9-10).

**1:3 *Judah . . . oppressed with cruel slavery.*** The Exile followed the capture of Jerusalem by the Babylonians, though they are nowhere named in this book. The number deported was 4,600 persons, at three separate times (Jer 52:28-30). A place of rest (*manoakh* [TH4494, ZH4955]) promised earlier by God (cf. 1 Kgs 8:56) could be lost as a result of their wrongdoing (Deut 28:65).

**1:4 *The roads to Jerusalem.*** The use of the word "Zion" for Jerusalem in the Heb. of this verse introduces worship-related topics. Three annual festivals brought worshipers from throughout the country: Passover and the Feast of Unleavened Bread (April/May); the Feast of Firstfruits (May/June); and the Feast of Tabernacles (October); see Deut 16. For young women participating in procession, see Ps 68:25.

**1:5 *the LORD has punished Jerusalem.*** The root *yagah* [TH3013, ZH3324] (niphal feminine participle, "crying," "grieving") used in 1:4 is repeated here in 1:5 (hiphil, *yagah*, "causing grief") with God as subject. In Lamentations, the name Yahweh (LORD) occurs thirty-two times; the title "Lord" (*adonay* [TH136, ZH151]) fourteen times. The word "God" (*'elohim* [TH430, ZH466]) does not appear in the book, but two other forms (*'el* [TH410A, ZH446] and *'elyon* [TH5945B, ZH6610]) occur three times.

**1:6 *All the majesty of beautiful Jerusalem.*** The term *hadar* [TH1926, ZH2077] (splendor, majesty) is at home in worship language (cf. extolling God's majesty, Ps 29:4); it appears also with glory (*kabod* [TH3519, ZH3883], Ps 145:5) and with holiness (*qodesh* [TH6944, ZH7731], Pss 96:9; 110:3).

***Her princes are like starving deer.*** This may allude to the king and his court, who fled the city (2 Kgs 25:4; Jer 39:4).

**1:7** *Her enemy . . . laughed.* The laughter (*sakhaq* [TH7832, ZH8471], "mocking") of the enemy was over Jerusalem's demise. An illustration of neighboring Edom's reaction is given in Ezek 35:10, 12.

**1:8** *tossed away like a filthy rag.* At issue in translation is the word *nidah* [TH5206, ZH5765], which some lexicons take as a derivation from *nud* [TH5110, ZH5653] (sway). If so, this is a gesture of the head ("so she has become a mockery," NRSV). Most, including the NLT, see it as an alternate spelling for *niddah* [TH5079, ZH5614] (menstrual flow; excretion, something detestable). The parallel cola, however, favors the meaning of "mocking" (Holladay 1971:237).

*hide her face.* This is an English equivalent for the Heb., "turn the back part."

**1:9** *She defiled herself with immorality.* The Heb. image, one of soiling (*tum'ah* [TH2932, ZH3240]) her skirts, refers to Judah's sin (cf. Jer 2:34).

*she lies in the gutter.* Her condition here has the nuance of "appalling" (*pela'im* [TH6382A, ZH7099]).

**1:10** *The enemy has plundered.* The Heb. expression compares to the colloquial English, "his grubby hands pawed over it." "Every precious thing" would include the Temple (cf. 1:7) and possibly children (1:11). Moabites and Ammonites were forbidden entry into the sanctuary (Deut 23:3; Ezek 44:7, 9).

**1:11** *their treasures.* These would have been marketable items, possibly even children to be sold into slavery.

### COMMENTARY

The first poetic acrostic (1:1-22) is in two parts. The lament is about a place, Jerusalem (1:1-11a), and a people who are hurt and distressed (1:11b-22). The first part is written in the third person, as from the viewpoint of a spectator (except for 1:9c). The second part is largely in first person (except for 1:17), interacting with the spectator. The middle verse (1:11) is a bridge that contains both third person reporting and first person exclamation.

The disaster has a personal ring to it from the start. Like a widow, Jerusalem sits forlorn, totally broken in spirit. She had lost virtually everything. The female personification is natural because in Hebrew the word "city" is feminine in gender.

**Heavy Losses.** Jerusalem had lost her status as a city of major importance (1:1). Perhaps the poet was thinking of the glory days of the Israelite empire, when David had established Jerusalem as a royal city. Solomon had made it a place of grandeur (cf. the visit of the queen of Sheba, 1 Kgs 10) when from it he presided over Israel's largest territorial expanse and extensive commercial trade. Later, King Jehoiakim (609–598 BC) built an imposing palace there (Jer 22:13-14).

The city, now widowed, had lost her allies. No one was available to comfort or help her—a point made three times, twice with the word "comfort" (*nakham* [TH5162, ZH5714], 1:2, 9) and once with the word "helper" (*'ozer* [TH5826A, ZH6468], 1:7). Worse, her political allies had turned against her (1:2). The city had lost all its leading citizens through several deportations to Babylon (1:3), and its traditional celebrations were no longer held. Roads and gates, also personified, mourned or remained silent in the absence of festal worship traffic (1:4). As a center of worship, the Temple was populated with forbidden foreigners.

The city had lost its freedom (1:5) and had become the object of mockery (1:7c) and humiliation (1:8c). Her prestige, built upon the grand structures of Temple and palace, wise leaders and princes, was gone (1:6). She who once knew station and status was now in the gutter (1:9). She had been raided and stripped (1:8) of all her valuables. All that remained was a memory of better times (1:7).

**Concentrated Evil.** The emphasis in this poetic panel is on the severity of the disaster, but the reason for that disaster receives mention twice. It was not political or military failure that brought this celebrated city to ruins, but Jerusalem's sins (1:5, 8). That sin is compared, following the NLT, to a filthy rag. The story of this city is from riches to rags.

That sin brings dire consequences is a message already pressed home with the story of Adam and Eve's fall (Gen 3). Punishment was also clearly assured for sinning cities in the story of Sodom and Gomorrah (Gen 19:1-29; cf. Tyre, Ezek 27–28). Similarly, Babylon was threatened with judgment because of her many sins (Jer 50–51, and ultimately became a symbol of evil (Rev 18:1-24).

World history is filled with battle narratives of the siege and capture of cities: Alexandria, Rome, Seoul, St. Petersburg. Just as not every personal tragedy should be interpreted as a punishment for personal sin (cf. Job), it would also be reductionist to assign collective sin as the reason for *every* city's fall. Although cities should not be universally stigmatized as dens of iniquity, it is in the cities, then and now, that evildoing is often concentrated, and this may indeed bring God's judgment. Modern, world-class cities are not infrequently associated with political corruption and with vices such as gambling (e.g., Las Vegas), the sale of sex (e.g., Bangkok), drugs and drug cartels (e.g., Bogotá), and homosexuality (e.g., San Francisco). Wrongdoing is the order of the day, and as with Jerusalem, no thought seems to be given to consequences (1:9). Sin engenders callousness and immunizes both individuals and city governments from the elementary logic of cause and effect. Jerusalem's catastrophe remains a warning.

◆ ## B. The People's Pain (1:11b-22)

"O LORD, look," she mourns,
 "and see how I am despised.

12 "Does it mean nothing to you, all you
 who pass by?
 Look around and see if there is any
 suffering like mine,
 which the LORD brought on me
 when he erupted in fierce anger.

13 "He has sent fire from heaven that
 burns in my bones.
 He has placed a trap in my path
 and turned me back.

He has left me devastated,
 racked with sickness all day long.

14 "He wove my sins into ropes
 to hitch me to a yoke of captivity.
 The Lord sapped my strength and
 turned me over to my enemies;
 I am helpless in their hands.

15 "The Lord has treated my mighty men
 with contempt.
 At his command a great army has
 come
 to crush my young warriors.

The Lord has trampled his beloved
city*
like grapes are trampled in a
winepress.

<sup>16</sup>"For all these things I weep;
tears flow down my cheeks.
No one is here to comfort me;
any who might encourage me are
far way.
My children have no future,
for the enemy has conquered us."

<sup>17</sup>Jerusalem reaches out for help,
but no one comforts her.
Regarding his people Israel,*
the LORD has said,
"Let their neighbors be their
enemies!
Let them be thrown away like a
filthy rag!"

<sup>18</sup>"The LORD is right," Jerusalem says,
"for I rebelled against him.
Listen, people everywhere;
look upon my anguish and
despair,
for my sons and daughters
have been taken captive to distant
lands.

<sup>19</sup>"I begged my allies for help,
but they betrayed me.
My priests and leaders
starved to death in the city,
even as they searched for food
to save their lives.

<sup>20</sup>"LORD, see my anguish!
My heart is broken
and my soul despairs,
for I have rebelled against you.
In the streets the sword kills,
and at home there is only death.

<sup>21</sup>"Others heard my groans,
but no one turned to comfort me.
When my enemies heard about my
troubles,
they were happy to see what you
had done.
Oh, bring the day you promised,
when they will suffer as I have
suffered.

<sup>22</sup>"Look at all their evil deeds, LORD.
Punish them,
as you have punished me
for all my sins.
My groans are many,
and I am sick at heart."

**1:15** Hebrew *the virgin daughter of Judah.*  **1:17** Hebrew *Jacob.* The names "Jacob" and "Israel" are often interchanged throughout the Old Testament, referring sometimes to the individual patriarch and sometimes to the nation.

## NOTES

**1:12 *Does it mean nothing to you?*** Lit., "not unto you" is best taken as a question. Other interpretive options are "Let it not come to you" (Talmud) or "It is nothing to you." If *lo'* [TH3808/3808A, ZH4202] expresses a wish, then "Oh that among you who pass by, you would look and see" (Huey 1993:454) is a possibility. Westermann (1994:113) holds that "the meaning of the first two words cannot be determined."

***when he erupted in fierce anger.*** The day of his fierce anger is the day of Yahweh, considered here as an event in the past. Divine anger is a dominant theme in Lamentations, as it is in Jeremiah (see comments on 2:1; Jer 25:15-38).

**1:14 *a yoke of captivity.*** The Heb. is very cryptic: forms of *'ol* [TH5923, ZH6585] (yoke) or *'al* [TH5921, ZH6584] (unto, over) occur three times in seven words. Various combinations of vowel markings (pointings) allow for meaning options. If the word *nisqad* [TH8244, ZH8567], the meaning of which is uncertain but which is usually rendered "bound," is changed slightly to *nishqad* [TH8245, ZH9193] (watchful) and the following Heb. word is repointed as the preposition *'al,* "over," the result (as in LXX, NAB, NJB) is "he kept watch over my sins" (Huey 1993:454).

**1:15 *treated my mighty men with contempt.*** God contemptibly tossed aside these men, as though they were lightweight soldiers; he allowed the Babylonian army to run roughshod over the Israelite infantry.

***winepress.*** This is an image of God's wrath (Isa 63:3; Rev 19:15). An arresting assonance is achieved using the less common word for "winepress" (*gath* [TH1660, ZH1780]) in connection with *bath* [TH1323, ZH1426] (daughter). A homonym for *bath*, which signifies a liquid measure, might well evoke association with the winepress.

**1:16 *encourage me.*** Lit., "bring restoration to my soul."

**1:17 *Jerusalem reaches out for help.*** The language is graphic; Jerusalem stretches out her hands.

***filthy rag!*** The word *niddah*, "menstrual rags" (cf. 1:8 and comments), continues the image of the city as female.

**1:18 *I rebelled against him.*** Lit., "for [against] his mouth I rebelled."

***sons and daughters.*** Lit., "virgin daughters (*bethulah* [TH1330, ZH1435], virgin) and select (*bakhur* [TH970, ZH1033]) sons."

**1:20 *see my anguish!*** The physical dimension of the pain is poignantly represented by "my stomach churns" (*khamarmaru* [TH2560/2560A, ZH2812/2813]). Note the onomatopoeic sounds (when pronounced, these Heb. syllables sound like a stomach churning). Cf. also Westermann 1994:114, "my innards smolder." The appeal for God to see (imperative of *ra'ah* [TH7200, ZH8011]) is found in both sections of the poem (cf. 1:11; cf. the call to the people, 1:18). Grammatically, the notion of rebellion is given emphasis, regarding either its duration or intensity by use of a verbal absolute.

**1:21 *Others heard my groans.*** The word "groan" (niphal of *'anakh* [TH584, ZH634]) in its various forms appears five times in the poem. In addition to the middle verse (1:11), it is found twice in each half (1:4, 8, 21, 22). Similarly, the word "comfort" (*nakham* [TH5162, ZH5714]) is found five times (1:2, 9, 16, 17, 21). For an excursus on "The Description of Misery," see Westermann (1994:121-124).

### COMMENTARY

The first section is a third-person descriptive report (1:1-11a). In the second section (1:11b-22), the victim reports the tragedy in first person. The voices are those of hurting people. Pain and anguish are the subjects, whether the poem turns to God's role in the event (1:11b-15), the absence of sympathizers and comforters (1:16-19), the current circumstances (1:20-21a), or even the closing vendetta (1:21b-22).

**God-forsaken (1:11b-15).** The sufferer recognized that the ultimate agent in the disaster was God. It is one thing to assert in confidence and joy that "God is for us." It is another matter to learn that "God is against us" in fierce anger (1:12). God's severe intervention, described as fire penetrating the bones (1:13), was a crushing blow. Israel knew, however, that God was not capricious. He did not act on whims of displeasure. Nonetheless, the fierce reality would come; sooner or later, sinners would feel the hot breath of God's indignation.

**Isolated (1:16-19).** Part of God's judgment on his people was to isolate them. Despite the victim's tears and appeals for others to take notice, there were no comforters (1:16, 21). Neighbors who might be expected to feel sorry for the hapless victim turned against her at the instigation of the Lord (1:17). Allies who might have given humanitarian aid did not do so; instead, they took delight in her misfortune (1:21). Being totally forsaken, even by God, is foreshadowed here. The common idea that people will find ample company in hell is mistaken, if by it is meant that they will have camaraderie in their misery. The misery may well be total isolation. That kind of absolute abandonment burns like fire.

**No Relief (1:16-22).** The people of Jerusalem felt anguish because there was no word from God despite their constant appeals for his attention (1:11b, 20). Their pain was compounded by the realization that their rebellion was the legitimate reason for God's silence (1:20). Rebellions against God had not turned out well, for example, in Israel's forty-year desert wandering (Num 14:33). Part of the groaning was self-reproach. They sought relief from this self-inflicted anguish by appealing to God to punish the perpetrators of the disaster. "Oh, bring the day . . . when they will suffer." To her credit, the helpless victim knew better than to take matters into her own hand—vengeance was left to God, where it belonged (Deut 32:35). There is no indication that Israel's dark thoughts against her conqueror in any way reduced her anguish.

◆ **II. God as Israel's Enemy (2:1-22)**
   **A. God's Angry Siege against the City (2:1-10)**

The Lord in his anger
   has cast a dark shadow over
      beautiful Jerusalem.*
The fairest of Israel's cities lies in
   the dust,
   thrown down from the heights
      of heaven.
In his day of great anger,
   the Lord has shown no mercy even
      to his Temple.*

2 Without mercy the Lord has
      destroyed
   every home in Israel.*
In his anger he has broken down
   the fortress walls of beautiful
      Jerusalem.*
He has brought them to the ground,
   dishonoring the kingdom and its
      rulers.

3 All the strength of Israel
   vanishes beneath his fierce anger.
The Lord has withdrawn his
      protection
   as the enemy attacks.

He consumes the whole land of Israel
   like a raging fire.

4 He bends his bow against his
      people,
   as though he were their enemy.
His strength is used against them
   to kill their finest youth.
His fury is poured out like fire
   on beautiful Jerusalem.*

5 Yes, the Lord has vanquished Israel
   like an enemy.
He has destroyed her palaces
   and demolished her fortresses.
He has brought unending sorrow
      and tears
   upon beautiful Jerusalem.

6 He has broken down his Temple
   as though it were merely a garden
      shelter.
The LORD has blotted out all memory
   of the holy festivals and Sabbath
      days.
Kings and priests fall together
   before his fierce anger.

⁷The Lord has rejected his own altar;
  he despises his own sanctuary.
He has given Jerusalem's palaces
  to her enemies.
They shout in the LORD's Temple
  as though it were a day of
  celebration.

⁸The LORD was determined
  to destroy the walls of beautiful
  Jerusalem.
He made careful plans for their
  destruction,
  then did what he had planned.
Therefore, the ramparts and walls
  have fallen down before him.

⁹Jerusalem's gates have sunk into
  the ground.
He has smashed their locks and
  bars.
Her kings and princes have been exiled
  to distant lands;
  her law has ceased to exist.
Her prophets receive
  no more visions from the LORD.

¹⁰The leaders of beautiful Jerusalem
  sit on the ground in silence.
They are clothed in burlap
  and throw dust on their heads.
The young women of Jerusalem
  hang their heads in shame.

2:1a Hebrew *the daughter of Zion;* also in 2:8, 10, 18.   2:1b Hebrew *his footstool.*   2:2a Hebrew *Jacob;* also in 2:3b. See note on 1:17.   2:2b Hebrew *the daughter of Judah;* also in 2:5.   2:4 Hebrew *on the tent of the daughter of Zion.*

NOTES

**2:1 in his anger.** Of the book's eleven occurrences of *'aph* [TH639, ZH678] (anger), five are in ch 2. In the OT, words for anger with God as the subject occur 518 times (NIDOTTE 4.380).

**beautiful Jerusalem.** The literal "daughter of Zion" (see NLT mg), with its connotations of a father-daughter relationship, sits strangely alongside God's anger (cf. 2:2). Jerusalem's fall recalls the fall of Babylon (Isa 14:12) and of Tyre (Ezek 28:17).

**Temple.** The Temple is commonly designated in the Heb. as God's footstool (Ps 132:7 NIV; Isa 60:13 NIV).

**2:3 All the strength.** The poetic image is one of "horns," symbols of strength drawn from the animal kingdom.

**2:4 finest youth.** Lit., "the delight of the eye." The youth are intended here, but the description is appropriate to God's people generally.

**2:5 demolished.** The same word (*bala'* [TH1104, ZH1180]) is found in the previous sentence (NLT, "vanquished") and in 2:2 (NLT, "destroyed").

**2:7 he despises his own sanctuary.** The root *na'ar* [TH5010, ZH5545] (abhor, spurn) occurs only in the piel form (cf. Ps 89:39 [40]). The enemy's presence within the Temple is upsetting (cf. 1:10).

**2:8 He made careful plans.** Lit., "he stretched the measuring line" like a builder. Or he might "take the measure" of the city like a military general preparing for an attack. In doing as planned, God made no effort (lit., "did not restrain his hand") to keep from "swallowing up" the population.

**2:10 young women of Jerusalem hang their heads in shame.** Mourning rites included sitting on the ground in silence (Josh 7:6; 2 Sam 13:31; Job 2:12-13), sprinkling dust or ashes on the head (2 Sam 13:19; Neh 9:1), and being clothed in sackcloth (Ps 35:13; Jonah 3:5). Wailing women were also at hand (Jer 9:20).

COMMENTARY

This poem is a description of God's laying siege to his chosen city (Ps 132:13; cf. Isa 63:10); it is strange and eerie. Even more strange is the fury, wrath, and anger with which that siege was carried out. The word "wrath" or "anger" (*'aph* [TH639, ZH678]) is found four times in this literary panel (2:1, 3, 6); other synonyms appear as well (e.g., 2:2, 4). Every chapter in Lamentations mentions God's anger.

**Vocabulary for Anger.** The usual word for anger (*'aph*) is derived from "nose," quite possibly linked to the flaring nostrils, hard breathing, or red face of an angry person. The term is used of human beings who are provoked, as Esau was by his brother Jacob (Gen 27:45, NIV), or as Moses was exasperated by Pharaoh (Exod 11:8). In an extension of anthropomorphism (God depicted in human terms), God's emotional responses (anthropopathisms) include the passion of anger. God's anger is not irrational rage but has to do with implementing his justice. The threat of God's anger breaking out against Israel's disobedience is frequently mentioned in Deuteronomy (e.g., 11:17; 13:17; 29:20). This threat provides motivation, albeit negative, for God's people to comply with his demands.

Fire (*'esh* [TH784, ZH836]) is another word readily associated with God's wrath (e.g., 2:3; Deut 32:22), which is also described as "fierce" (Jer 4:8; Lam 2:3; more lit., "heat of anger"; Lam 1:12; 4:11; cf. Isa 13:9, 13 where several synonyms for anger are grouped). Anger of this nature is illustrated in the human sphere by Potiphar's reaction upon hearing his wife accuse Joseph of attempting to seduce her (Gen 39:19). In the divine sphere, God is described as being emotionally upset and as responding with great anger when his people tested him during their wilderness journeys (Num 11:1; Ps 95:10-11). In a particularly sobering incident, God's fierce wrath broke out against Israel when Aaron made the golden calf (Exod 32:10, 11). "Yahweh does not kill in cold blood, but hot blood" (Rolf Knierim, quoted in Baloian 1992:143).

**Fallout.** The writer of Lamentations is primarily concerned with the effects of God's anger. Because of God's white-hot anger, (1) the city's fortress walls were demolished (2:2; cf. Jer 52:14); (2) the entire countryside—along with Jerusalem, its Temple, and altar—was devastated (2:3, 4, 6, 7); and (3) all the people, including kings, priests, and prophets, had been exiled or incapacitated (2:6, 9; cf. 2:14). Baloian (1992:98-99) observes that whenever God's anger is described at a specific point in time, there is almost always a description of some specific action that God will take. There are only four exceptions. Statistically, "258 [cases] out of 262 (over 98%), speak of physical consequences to Yahweh's wrath." To experience God as an enemy is ominous. To whom does one then turn for help?

**A Consistent Depiction.** Marcion, a second-century Christian thinker, reasoned that the loving God depicted in the New Testament replaced the angry God of the Old Testament. The church pronounced him a heretic. Paul clearly appropriated Old Testament language when he spoke of Christ's appearing "in flaming fire, bringing judgment on those who don't know God" (2 Thess 1:8). A scene in the heavenly places is depicted by the apostle John, often regarded as the apostle of love, in which seven angels are each given a bowl "filled with the wrath of God" (Rev 15:7), which is then emptied onto the earth (Rev 16:1, 15-17). Both testaments affirm that God is a devouring fire (Deut 4:24; Heb 12:29).

Still, mercy is a more dominant trait in God than wrath (Hos 11:9). God is slow to anger (Exod 34:6), and even when aroused, his anger continues but for a moment (Ps 30:5). Nonetheless, the Bible is so emphatic about God's anger that it cannot be explained away. The great catastrophe of Jerusalem's fall is a sober reminder that God is not to be trifled with. C. S. Lewis (1973:64) had it right in a dialogue about Aslan, the lion who is a figure for God/Christ in his *Chronicles of Narnia*. Someone asks, "Is he quite safe?" Mr. Beaver answers: "Who said anything about safe? 'Course he isn't safe. But he's good."

If little or nothing is said from modern pulpits about God's capacity for anger, it may be in an effort to avoid offense. The teaching about God's anger is easily muted, and even Christians are in danger of so downsizing God as to render him harmless, convenient, nice, and safe. In contrast, God's goodness is such that he cannot permit sin to go unpunished but must address it (both in warning and punishment) with bold and painful clarity.

## ◆ B. The Cry of an Anguished People (2:11-22)

11 I have cried until the tears no longer
    come;
  my heart is broken.
My spirit is poured out in agony
    as I see the desperate plight of
    my people.
Little children and tiny babies
    are fainting and dying in the streets.

12 They cry out to their mothers,
    "We need food and drink!"
Their lives ebb away in the streets
    like the life of a warrior wounded
    in battle.
They gasp for life
    as they collapse in their mothers'
    arms.

13 What can I say about you?
  Who has ever seen such sorrow?
O daughter of Jerusalem,
    to what can I compare your
    anguish?
O virgin daughter of Zion,
    how can I comfort you?
For your wound is as deep as the sea.
  Who can heal you?

14 Your prophets have said
    so many foolish things, false
    to the core.
They did not save you from exile
    by pointing out your sins.
Instead, they painted false pictures,
    filling you with false hope.

15 All who pass by jeer at you.
    They scoff and insult beautiful
    Jerusalem,* saying,
"Is this the city called 'Most Beautiful
    in All the World'
    and 'Joy of All the Earth'?"

16 All your enemies mock you.
    They scoff and snarl and say,
"We have destroyed her at last!
    We have long waited for this day,
    and it is finally here!"

17 But it is the LORD who did just as
    he planned.
He has fulfilled the promises
    of disaster
    he made long ago.
He has destroyed Jerusalem without
    mercy.

He has caused her enemies to gloat
over her
and has given them power over
her.

<sup>18</sup> Cry aloud* before the Lord,
O walls of beautiful Jerusalem!
Let your tears flow like a river
day and night.
Give yourselves no rest;
give your eyes no relief.

<sup>19</sup> Rise during the night and cry out.
Pour out your hearts like water
to the Lord.
Lift up your hands to him in prayer,
pleading for your children,
for in every street
they are faint with hunger.

<sup>20</sup> "O LORD, think about this!
Should you treat your own people
this way?

Should mothers eat their own
children,
those they once bounced on their
knees?
Should priests and prophets be killed
within the Lord's Temple?

<sup>21</sup> "See them lying in the streets—
young and old,
boys and girls,
killed by the swords of the
enemy.
You have killed them in your anger,
slaughtering them without mercy.

<sup>22</sup> "You have invited terrors from all
around,
as though you were calling them
to a day of feasting.
In the day of the LORD's anger,
no one has escaped or survived.
The enemy has killed all the children
whom I carried and raised."

2:15 Hebrew *the daughter of Jerusalem.*   2:18 Hebrew *Their heart cried.*

## NOTES

**2:11** *my heart is broken. My spirit is poured out.* The Heb. idioms for emotional distress are graphic: "my bowels (*me'ay* [TH4578, ZH5055]) burn (*khamarmeru* [TH2560/2560A, ZH2812/2813]); my liver (*kebedi* [TH3516, ZH3879]) is emptied out."

**2:12** *We need food.* Lit., "Where is [cereal] grain and wine?"

**2:13** *how can I comfort you?* The verse is a series of questions, a device that highlights the anguish (cf. 2:20; on comfort, cf. 1:2, 7, 9).

**2:14** *They did not save you from exile.* A variant reading (*qere*) favored by several manuscripts is "turn (root *shub* [TH7725, ZH8740]) you back from your turning" (*shebuthek* [TH7622, ZH8654]) instead of "your exile" (*shebithek* [TH7622A, ZH8669]). This striking image is apropos to the prophet's function of turning people around when they were headed in the wrong direction.

**2:15** *jeer at you.* Lit., "clap hands" in a mocking gesture. Other disparaging gestures are to "hiss" or "whistle" (*sharaq* [TH8319, ZH9239]), translated here as "scoff," or to shake (*nua'* [TH5128, ZH5675]) the head, rendered here as "insult." Jerusalem's beauty was proverbial (Ps 48:2).

**2:17** *it is the LORD who did just as he planned.* Throughout, the writer insists on God as the ultimate agent of the destruction (cf. 4:16).

*promises of disaster.* These are found in the Torah (Lev 26:14-39; Deut 28:15-68).

**2:18** *Cry aloud.* The Heb. text is grammatically incorrect and unclear. The NLT follows a proposal to read "cry" (*tsa'aq* [TH6817, ZH7590]) as an imperative, in which case the verb parallels the two successive imperatives in the subsequent poetic lines: "Let . . . flow" and "Give . . . no rest." The city has been personified from the beginning (1:1).

**2:21** *slaughtering them without mercy.* While the tragedy is attributed to the enemy in the first part of the verse, the second half of the verse immediately switches back to God as the agent: "You have killed them."

**2:22** *In the day of the LORD's anger.* The final verse, a reference to the day of the Lord, acts as an inclusio so that the subject of anger brackets the entire chapter (cf. 2:1).

## COMMENTARY

As in Lamentations 1, the poetic flow is from a predominantly third-person report in the first half of the poem to a first-person response in the last half. The first half of Lamentations 2 treats the disaster as it affects the public sector. In the second half, attention is focused on family and domestic concerns. It is an ugly picture that may be unpleasant for moderns, but a closer look at suffering can be instructive.

**Suffering.** Children, babies, and other innocent persons are most at risk in war or in times of natural catastrophe. Like the gaunt, malnourished children sometimes shown on television, the poet's depiction of human misery tugs at the reader's sympathy. The reader hears children crying, "I want food." The reader sees children fainting and lapsing into unconsciousness (2:11-12). Most gruesome of all, mothers are so famished and desperate that they resort to devouring their offspring (2:20). The streets are littered with corpses of both genders and of all ages. Emotional stressors compound the physical suffering, as spectators deride, disparage, and despise the victims of tragedy (2:15-16). They are further aggravated by isolation and especially by the knowledge that the suffering is God-inflicted (2:17, 22).

**Empathy.** Human beings tend to turn away from suffering. We would rather be deaf to cries for help. We slip into denial when images of the dead and dying intrude upon our consciousness. We do not care to know the indignities that others endure. But from among the suffering and a few other sensitive people, there come advocates and comforters for the afflicted. These, like the poet, rally people to confront the reality of suffering and encourage the lifting of hands to implore God for mercy (2:19). Some scriptures stretch our capacities for thought and reflection. Others, such as this book, enlarge our capacity for empathy.

**Prophetic Warnings.** Incorporated in this litany of anguish is an instructive piece about the function of leaders, especially prophets (2:14). It is the function of prophets to point out sin so that people might be spared its damaging consequences (cf. Jer 7:1-15). While this sin-consciousness–raising ministry is in part negative, its flip side is positive, because its purpose is to lead people into the right way. It is the roadside warning sign that, if heeded, keeps motorists from endangering themselves. Tragedies that result from failures to observe warnings are unfortunate. A greater tragedy still is the catastrophe that could have been averted had leaders not been indifferent and delinquent. Given a leader's responsibility, it is little wonder that James advises: "Not many of you should become teachers in the church, for we who teach will be judged more strictly" (Jas 3:1).

# ◆ III. Dealing with Grief (3:1-66)
## A. Personal Afflictions (3:1-20)

I am the one who has seen the afflictions
that come from the rod of the LORD's anger.
²He has led me into darkness,
shutting out all light.
³He has turned his hand against me
again and again, all day long.

⁴He has made my skin and flesh grow old.
He has broken my bones.
⁵He has besieged and surrounded me
with anguish and distress.
⁶He has buried me in a dark place,
like those long dead.

⁷He has walled me in, and I cannot escape.
He has bound me in heavy chains.
⁸And though I cry and shout,
he has shut out my prayers.
⁹He has blocked my way with a high stone wall;
he has made my road crooked.

¹⁰He has hidden like a bear or a lion,
waiting to attack me.

¹¹He has dragged me off the path and torn me in pieces,
leaving me helpless and devastated.
¹²He has drawn his bow
and made me the target for his arrows.

¹³He shot his arrows
deep into my heart.
¹⁴My own people laugh at me.
All day long they sing their mocking songs.
¹⁵He has filled me with bitterness
and given me a bitter cup of sorrow to drink.

¹⁶He has made me chew on gravel.
He has rolled me in the dust.
¹⁷Peace has been stripped away,
and I have forgotten what prosperity is.
¹⁸I cry out, "My splendor is gone!
Everything I had hoped for from the LORD is lost!"

¹⁹The thought of my suffering and homelessness
is bitter beyond words.*
²⁰I will never forget this awful time,
as I grieve over my loss.

3:19 Or is wormwood and gall.

NOTES

**3:1-66** The poem is an acrostic built on the 22 letters of the Hebrew alphabet. Three lines of poetry are devoted to each letter, and the first word in each of the three lines begins with the same letter (see introduction for further details). For the poem in a four-part arrangement featuring parallelism and contrast with hinge verses (3:21-22; 3:33-34; 3:55-56) that introduce a change from lament to hope and vice versa, see Weber (2000).

**3:1** *I am the one.* The speaker may be the city personified, or an anonymous victim of the tragedy, or possibly Jeremiah (see Ellison 1986:716, 718; cf. Lanahan 1974) or King Zedekiah (Saebo 1993). Parts of the chapter (e.g., 3:25-29) may be in the poet's voice.

*rod.* Heb. *shebet* [TH7626, ZH8657]. Cf. Job 21:9; Ps 89:32; Isa 10:5.

*the LORD's anger.* This is noted in every chapter as the source of the disaster (see commentary on Jer 2).

**3:5** *surrounded me with anguish.* The language is graphic rather than abstract: lit., "he has encircled me with a poison" (*ro'sh* [TH7219, ZH8032], "poison" or "poisonous plant"; cf. "bitterness," NRSV). Some versions (NJPS, NAB) revocalize the word to *resh* [TH7389, ZH8203] (poverty). The LXX reads "head" (derived from *ro'sh* [TH7218, ZH8031]).

**3:7 *heavy chains.*** Bronze (*nekhosheth* [TH5178, ZH5733]) is a metonymy for prison chains.

**3:11 *torn me in pieces.*** The term crucial to what is commonly treated as animal imagery, "tore" (piel of *pashakh* [TH6582, ZH7318], "leave fallow," or perhaps, "tear") occurs only here (cf. NIDOTTE 3:704).

**3:13 *deep into my heart.*** Given that the kidneys (cf. "kidney," *kilyah* [TH3629, ZH4000]), here translated "heart," were regarded as the seat of the emotions, one could render: "He completely devastated me emotionally." One Akkadian text refers to hurt feelings in the idiom of "thorns piercing the kidneys" (NIDOTTE 2:656).

**3:15** So compressed is the Heb. of this verse that the NLT uses two lines to translate four Heb. words. The two Heb. words for the last part of the sentence are lit., "He filled me with wormwood." "Wormwood" is a plant then used to give a bitter flavor to a drink.

**3:16 *He has rolled me in the dust.*** The key verb, *kapash* [TH3728, ZH4115], which occurs only here in the OT, has been translated as "cower" (NASB, NRSV), as "cover" (KJV), or as "fed" ("fed me with ashes," LXX, NEB, JB). A comparable western idiom might be, "He made me eat dirt."

**3:20 *I grieve over my loss.*** Lit., "my soul cowers [collapses]."

## COMMENTARY

This panel chronicles the series of blows that God inflicted on the sufferer. "He" is the subject of most statements. In Hebrew, the masculine pronouns "he" and "his" leave the adversary unspecified. Is Babylon the adversary? Given what has been said about God's anger (2:1, see comments), the opponent is almost certainly God. The rhythm of thought is basically "He . . . (verb) . . . me." Eventually the sufferer finds his or her own voice, saying, "I cry out" (3:18). Presumably "I" is the personification of the city Jerusalem as at the opening of the book. Alternatively, the speaker may be an anonymous individual. If the earlier descriptions used a wide-angle approach, this poem zooms in on one person caught in the tragedy. The sufferer offers a blow-by-blow description of God's strikes. The sufferer, whether an individual or the collective citizenry, is in no position to make a comeback but can only whimper.

From the first, there is an adversarial relationship between the speaker and another. Initially, God withdraws, leaving the sufferer alone in deep darkness (3:2, 6; cf. Job 12:25; Ps 82:5; contrast Ps 23:4). The sufferer feels imprisoned; perhaps the person is in a walled dungeon (cf. Jer 38:6) with no possible route of escape (3:7-9). Is he or she condemned to perpetual isolation and claustrophobia? All prayers seem to bounce back, "access denied" (3:8; Ps 88:13-14 [14-15]). There is no solace from any quarter (3:17).

At the same time, the opposition seems tangible (3:3). The divine attack results in broken bones—an expression that may be intended literally, but could also be metaphorical (3:4b). Indeed the assailant, presumably God, assaults as wild animals would (3:10-11). God, the predatory hunter, takes aim (3:12). The sufferer is emotionally torn, taunted even by those supposedly close to him (3:14). He becomes deeply bitter (3:15, 19).

Part of the troubled person's therapy is to bring feelings into verbal expression, to name the pain. In similar fashion, the Lament Psalms (e.g. Pss 13; 88) identify a troubling situation and then give voice to the speaker's complaints. Voicing one's personal experience can be cathartic and cleansing. Suppressing bitterness can eventually issue in anger, hostility, and depression. Defining the current situation can be preparatory to hope, as depicted in the subsequent panel of verses (3:21-39). The forthrightness of the hope described there matches the intensity of emotional distress depicted here.

◆    B. God is Good (3:21-39)

21 Yet I still dare to hope
    when I remember this:

22 The faithful love of the LORD never
    ends!*
    His mercies never cease.
23 Great is his faithfulness;
    his mercies begin afresh each
    morning.
24 I say to myself, "The LORD is my
    inheritance;
    therefore, I will hope in him!"

25 The LORD is good to those who depend
    on him,
    to those who search for him.
26 So it is good to wait quietly
    for salvation from the LORD.
27 And it is good for people to submit
    at an early age
    to the yoke of his discipline:

28 Let them sit alone in silence
    beneath the LORD's demands.
29 Let them lie face down in the dust,
    for there may be hope at last.
30 Let them turn the other cheek to those
    who strike them

and accept the insults of their
    enemies.

31 For no one is abandoned
    by the Lord forever.
32 Though he brings grief, he also shows
    compassion
    because of the greatness of his
    unfailing love.
33 For he does not enjoy hurting people
    or causing them sorrow.

34 If people crush underfoot
    all the prisoners of the land,
35 if they deprive others of their rights
    in defiance of the Most High,
36 if they twist justice in the courts—
    doesn't the Lord see all these
    things?

37 Who can command things to
    happen
    without the Lord's permission?
38 Does not the Most High
    send both calamity and good?
39 Then why should we, mere humans,
    complain
    when we are punished for our sins?

3:22 As in Syriac version; Hebrew reads *of the LORD keeps us from destruction.*

NOTES

3:22 *faithful love.* The word *khesed* [TH2617, ZH2876] has nuances of steadfast love (see RSV) and loving kindness (NASB). The conclusion reached by Clark (1993:267) is that *khesed* is "a beneficent action performed, in the context of a deep and enduring commitment between two persons or parties, by one who is able to render assistance to the needy party who in the circumstances is unable to help him- or herself." Here the word is in the plural.

3:23 *Great is his faithfulness.* The term *'emunah* [TH530, ZH575] (reliability, fidelity, steadiness) derives from the root *'aman* [TH539, ZH586] (have stability, stay faithful). This quality of Yahweh's character is cause for praise (Pss 33:4; 92:2 [3], cf. Ps 143:1).

**3:27** *it is good.* Each of the three verses of 3:25-27 begins with *tob* [TH2896, ZH3202] (good) in accord with the alphabetic acrostic format of the chapter, which has now reached the letter *teth.* While "yoke" (*'ol* [TH5923, ZH6585]) can refer metaphorically to "discipline," as is likely here from the context, *'ol* strictly designates the cross beams placed on the necks of animals for plowing or pulling a cart (Num 19:2). Metaphorically, *'ol* can also signify the Torah (MT of Jer 5:5, cf. NIV) in the sense of "burden," "work," or "responsibility."

**3:28** *beneath the LORD's demands.* Lit., "when he takes [it] upon him." The "it" rendered here as "demands" is unspecified in the Heb. (cf. 3:27).

**3:29** *lie them face down in the dust.* Presumably to "put one's mouth in the dust" (so lit.) is an idiom for submission, assuming that it refers to lying prostrate on the ground (Ps 72:9; Mic 7:17).

*there may be hope at last.* This is perhaps intended as a parenthetical statement (see the NRSV; see Kraŝovec [1992:231-232], who discusses this text under the heading, "The Superiority of God's Mercy").

**3:30** *Let them turn the other cheek.* For this sign of non-retaliation, see Isa 50:6; Matt 5:39; 26:67 (cf. 1 Pet 2:20-23).

**3:32** *he also shows compassion.* The verb *rakham* [TH7355, ZH8163] (have compassion on) derives from *rekhem* [TH7358, ZH8167] (womb) and so suggests a trait especially associated with women. The final word, *khesed,* is reminiscent of 3:22 (see note).

**3:34** *people.* In the MT, the subject of the verbs is left unspecified. Some (e.g., the NRSV) handle the lack of subject with the use of a passive: "when all the prisoners . . . are crushed."

**3:35** *Most High.* This designation for God (*'elyon* [TH5945B, ZH6610]) occurs only twice in Lamentations (here and in 3:38) and emphasizes the transcendence of the deity.

**3:38** *send both calamity and good.* In Israel's worldview, God was ultimately responsible for the bad (*ra'ah* [TH7451B, ZH8288], "evil," "disaster") and good (*tob* [TH2896B, ZH3205]). Cf. Job 2:10; Isa 45:7.

## COMMENTARY

Hope may spring eternal in the human breast, but not all who hope, hope in God. Nor do they all hope against odds as great as those faced by this sufferer.

**Hope and Creed.** The poet dared to hope in God in spite of the fact that it was God from whom this sufferer had received blow upon blow (3:1-19). Rather than follow the inclination to put distance between himself and such a God, this sufferer reached out to the very God who had inflicted the hurt, the God who, like a relentless hunter, had aimed to harm, even to destroy (3:10-13). The poet took this risk partly because God was all that remained. God was his portion ("inheritance" 3:24)—"Yahweh is all I have" (NJB). But there was further ground for his hope. He did not have hope because of the immediate experience, which was only negative, but because of what is affirmed in the traditional creed about God (Exod 34:6; Deut 26:3-9; Ps 73:1). One negative experience, even if enormously tragic, does not overturn the centuries-old confessional statement that God is good. On this the poet relies.

**Hope and God's Signature Actions.** The sufferer refused to focus on his present suffering and moved beyond the personal to the communal, beyond the particular to the universal, beyond immediate frustration to long-standing convictions. The confession about who God is was not wishful conjecture for times of desperation but was rooted deep in the experiences of generations past. Nor was his daring unrealistic. The sufferer knew that God, on occasion, brings grief (3:32) and even catastrophe, such as the demolition of a city and excruciating miseries to its occupants. But the hope-filled person knows that God's harsh actions, necessary because of sin (3:34-39), are not God's signature actions. To the contrary, what truly characterizes God are acts of compassion (3:32). The daring, then, is not lodged in subjective, courageous human risk-taking but in a secure grasp of who God is.

**Hope and God's Character.** God's unfailing love headlines a characterization of God that draws heavily on tradition (3:22, 31). There follow references to his mercy (3:22-23), faithfulness (3:23), goodness (3:25), and justice (3:34-39). God's unfailing love was particularly emphasized by Hosea, whose experience with his wife, Gomer, a prostitute, set the stage for an elaboration of God's undeserved love (Hos 1-3). Israel's action provided every reason for God to abandon her, but logic is not the operative principle here. Because he is a God of unfailing love, God took Israel back again (Hos 11:8-9). The same idea is featured in Jeremiah, where Ephraim (Israel) is depicted as a wayward son for whom God's heart yearned. In the end, God's decision was to have mercy on him (Jer 31:20).

God's faithfulness, trustworthiness, and constancy are also asserted in the Song of Moses (Deut 32:4) and in the Psalms, especially in the way that God honored his covenant with David (Pss 36:5; 89:24, 33-34, 49). God's goodness is celebrated in Jeremiah's Book of Comfort around the theme that God intends good things for his covenant people (Jer 32-33), an idea also found in Ezekiel (34:14) and the Psalms (100:5; 103:5; 136:1). The high value God places on justice (Ps 89:14; Isa 61:8) is illustrated in Habakkuk (2:4-20). In short, the prophetic and hymnic teaching about God's unfailing love, mercy, faithfulness, goodness, and justice have become an invaluable source of hope in difficult times.

Not infrequently, the church's cherished song, "Great is Thy Faithfulness," is sung at celebrations. But the verse on which the lyrics are based was written from a context of hardship and despair. When tragedy strikes and lives are prematurely snuffed out, those who truly believe God and are anchored on the bedrock of God's revelation about himself can still sing this song, negative circumstances notwithstanding. Hope can replace despair (Hab 3:17-18; 1 Pet 4:12-13).

◆   ## C. Tears and Prayers (3:40-66)

40 Instead, let us test and examine
      our ways.
   Let us turn back to the LORD.
41 Let us lift our hearts and hands
      to God in heaven and say,
42 "We have sinned and rebelled,
      and you have not forgiven us.

43 "You have engulfed us with your
      anger, chased us down,
   and slaughtered us without
      mercy.
44 You have hidden yourself in
      a cloud
   so our prayers cannot reach you.

⁴⁵You have discarded us as refuse and
      garbage
   among the nations.

⁴⁶"All our enemies
   have spoken out against us.
⁴⁷We are filled with fear,
   for we are trapped, devastated,
      and ruined."
⁴⁸Tears stream from my eyes
   because of the destruction of my
      people!

⁴⁹My tears flow endlessly;
   they will not stop
⁵⁰until the LORD looks down
   from heaven and sees.
⁵¹My heart is breaking
   over the fate of all the women
      of Jerusalem.

⁵²My enemies, whom I have never
      harmed,
   hunted me down like a bird.
⁵³They threw me into a pit
   and dropped stones on me.
⁵⁴The water rose over my head,
   and I cried out, "This is the end!"

⁵⁵But I called on your name, LORD,
   from deep within the pit.
⁵⁶You heard me when I cried, "Listen
   to my pleading!

Hear my cry for help!"
⁵⁷Yes, you came when I called;
   you told me, "Do not fear."

⁵⁸Lord, you are my lawyer! Plead my
      case!
   For you have redeemed my life.
⁵⁹You have seen the wrong they have
      done to me, LORD.
   Be my judge, and prove me right.
⁶⁰You have seen the vengeful plots
   my enemies have laid against me.

⁶¹LORD, you have heard the vile names
      they call me.
   You know all about the plans they
      have made.

⁶²My enemies whisper and mutter
   as they plot against me all day long.
⁶³Look at them! Whether they sit or
      stand,
   I am the object of their mocking
      songs.

⁶⁴Pay them back, LORD,
   for all the evil they have done.
⁶⁵Give them hard and stubborn hearts,
   and then let your curse fall on
      them!
⁶⁶Chase them down in your anger,
   destroying them beneath the LORD's
      heavens.

## NOTES

**3:42 *We have sinned.*** With the initial pronoun "we," in addition to the subject represented in the Heb. verb, the point is clearly made that the people owned their wrongdoing. The first person singular form, the "I" of the preceding section (e.g., 3:21, 24), has been replaced with the first person plural, "we."

**3:43 *You have engulfed us with your anger.*** God's anger remains a dominant theme (cf. 2:21; 3:66; the commentary on 2:1-22 and Jer 25:15-38).

**3:47 *We are filled with fear . . . ruined.*** For a translation that captures the alliteration, see the NRSV: "panic (*pakhad* [TH6343, ZH7065]) and pitfall (*pakhath* [TH6354, ZH7074]) have come upon us, devastation (*hashe'th* [TH7612, ZH8643]) and destruction (*hashaber* [TH7667, ZH8691])."

**3:49 *My tears flow.*** Lit., "my eye gushes."

**3:51 *My heart is breaking.*** Lit., "my eye gets hard treatment to my soul." Translators have struggled with the syntax (cf. KJV, NRSV, NIV, NASB). Two of the three lines of the acrostic that begin with the letter *ayin* begin with the word *'eni* [TH5869, ZH6524] (my eye).

**3:52 *My enemies . . . hunted me down.*** The metaphor, if it is meant to apply to the Babylonian siege of Jerusalem, applies only loosely.

**3:56 *You heard me when I cried.*** This poetic line is unusually long in Heb. The MT says lit., "Do not close your ears to the relief of me—to the cry of me."

**3:57 *Do not fear.*** The phrase, designated by biblical scholars as a "word of consolation," is part of the salvation oracle of assurance (cf. Isa 43:1, 5).

**3:58 *Plead my case!*** The Heb. *rib* [TH7379, ZH8190] is a technical word for a case in a court of law (cf. Hos 4:1).

**3:60 *You have seen the vengeful plots.*** The object of "you have seen" is twofold: their vengeance (*niqmatham* [TH5360, ZH5935]) and their plans (*makhshebotham* [TH4284, ZH4742]).

**3:61 *Lord, you have heard.*** The vocatives, "O Lord" (*yhwh* in 3:55, 59, 61, 64 and *'adonay* [TH136, ZH151] in 3:58) are not only reminders that we (as readers) are overhearing a prayer, but that the prayer is gaining in emotional intensity.

## COMMENTARY

At last, a prayer is offered acknowledging sin, after self-examination has yielded revelation. The people finally turned to God in repentance. Yet oddly enough, God did not hear or respond (3:42, 44).

"We have sinned." Sometimes only harsh experiences or the threat of punishment bring wayward people to admit their wrongdoing (cf. Saul, 1 Sam 15:24; the prodigal son, Luke 15:21). Remarkably, God offers a remedy for those so alienated: repentance, which is a complete turnabout; and confession, which is forthright in taking responsibility for the evil that has been committed. The prophets urged repentance and even prescribed the language in which confessions could be couched (Jer 3:22–4:2; Hos 14:2-3). God promises that when people turn from their sins, he will forgive them (2 Chr 7:14).

But in this instance God did not respond or forgive! It seems that inward conviction had mounted, the built-up resistance to humbling themselves had finally been overcome, and now the sinners, in something akin to victory, offered the required apology. But God was not impressed, and the expected peace of forgiveness did not follow. Indeed, God appeared to be distant, even antagonistic. The feeling of abandonment was acute (3:45). Was God testing the sincerity of their repentance? Had he become uninterested? Was he disabusing sinners of the notion that forgiveness is mechanical or easy? Were the people mindlessly resorting to traditional cliches? No clue is given. The sufferers became desperate and tearfully persisted in seeking God's favor (3:49-50), arguing that except for God's intervention, all was lost (3:54). And then comes the wonderful surprise of God's gracious reassurance: "Do not fear!"

While it is true that God forgives and that he is attuned to repentant cries, believers err if they think that the transaction of forgiveness is a matter of course and really no great thing. Moderns, who live by entitlements and hold that they have the right to whatever makes for a good life, have reason to linger with this text. Christians of an earlier generation spoke about "praying through." Some would agonize over their sin for days, sometimes for weeks, until at last they received assurance of forgiveness. In some instances, this behavior may have been pathological. Perhaps they understood, however, that while God is not stingy with his forgiveness, neither does he dispense it mechanically.

The poetic prayer continued with a plea for God to deal summarily with the unnamed "enemies" (3:58-66). They could have been national enemies, but, given the context, they were more likely personal opponents. The request is odd since it so abruptly follows the piece about forgiveness. Should those who are forgiven not be more gentle? Is this request for payback further evidence that the human heart is sick and desperately evil (Jer 17:9)? Is the prayer for vindication/revenge a traditional formula or simply an earthy touch? Life with its troubles continues after forgiveness. This is an imprecatory prayer (e.g., Ps 137; cf. Jer 11:20; 12:3; 18:21-22) and echoes similar prayers in the rest of the book (e.g., 1:21-22). Such prayers can be understood as taking seriously the divine dictum: "I will take revenge; I will pay them back" (Deut 32:35). Moreover, there is a language of heated emotion (e.g., between exasperated siblings: "You're dead meat!"), which is not meant to be taken as a literal statement of intent but only as an expression of raw emotion. Some conclude that such sentiments are non-Christian (Matt 5:38-42; 1 Pet 3:9). Even so, we can allow that there is a wholesome honesty displayed in such prayers, and in the end, vengeance is handed over to God, as the Scriptures themselves prescribe (Rom 12:19).

## ◆ IV. A People's Plight (4:1-22)
### A. Then and Now (4:1-11)

How the gold has lost its luster!
  Even the finest gold has become
  dull.
The sacred gemstones
  lie scattered in the streets!

2 See how the precious children of
  Jerusalem,*
  worth their weight in fine gold,
are now treated like pots of clay
  made by a common potter.

3 Even the jackals feed their young,
  but not my people Israel.
They ignore their children's cries,
  like ostriches in the desert.

4 The parched tongues of their little
  ones
  stick to the roofs of their mouths
  in thirst.
The children cry for bread,
  but no one has any to give them.

5 The people who once ate the richest
  foods
now beg in the streets for anything
  they can get.
Those who once wore the finest
  clothes
now search the garbage dumps for
  food.

6 The guilt* of my people
  is greater than that of Sodom,
where utter disaster struck in a
  moment
and no hand offered help.

7 Our princes once glowed with health—
  brighter than snow, whiter than
  milk.
Their faces were as ruddy as rubies,
  their appearance like fine jewels.*

8 But now their faces are blacker than
  soot.
No one recognizes them in the
  streets.
Their skin sticks to their bones;
  it is as dry and hard as wood.

⁹Those killed by the sword are better
off
than those who die of hunger.
Starving, they waste away
for lack of food from the fields.

¹⁰Tenderhearted women
have cooked their own
children.

They have eaten them
to survive the siege.

¹¹But now the anger of the LORD is
satisfied.
His fierce anger has been poured out.
He started a fire in Jerusalem*
that burned the city to its
foundations.

4:2 Hebrew *precious sons of Zion.*   4:6 Or *punishment.*   4:7 Hebrew *like lapis lazuli.*   4:11 Hebrew *in Zion.*

## NOTES

**4:1 gold has lost its luster.** This is quite possibly a reference to the effects of burning Solomon's Temple (parts were overlaid with gold, 1 Kgs 6:20-22). Gold would have blackened in a fire.

**sacred gemstones.** This expression (*'abne qodesh* [TH68/6944, ZH74/7731]) might be intended to recall priestly apparel. Israel was no longer a "kingdom of priests" (Exod 19:6). For "sacred stones" see Emerton (1967).

**4:3 They ignore their children's cries.** Lit., reading the Qere, "to be cruel like ostriches." Ostriches are mentioned elsewhere in regard to inattention to their young (Job 39:13-18).

**4:5 The people . . . beg in the streets.** Lit., "they are devastated/destitute in the streets."

**4:6 The guilt of my people.** The Heb. *'awon* [TH5771, ZH6411] (guilt) means "iniquity" but can also be a metonymy for the consequent punishment (see NLT mg). So also the synonym *khatta'th* [TH2403A, ZH2633] (sin) may here refer to the sinful act, and by metonymy (a figure of speech where one word evokes another idea associated with it) to punishment. It is of little consequence to try to decide whether the comparison of Jerusalem with Sodom is on the basis of its sin or its punishment, since these are proportionate.

**4:7 princes.** Technically, *nazir* [TH5139, ZH5687] refers to someone dedicated to God, two signs of which were that hair was not to be cut and the person was to totally abstain from wine (Num 6:2-5), but the term also denotes "prince" (Gen 49:26; Deut 33:16).

**rubies . . . jewels.** The Heb. words signify red coral and lapis lazuli, a dark blue stone.

**4:11 the anger of the LORD is satisfied.** Three words for anger occur in this verse: (1) *'aph* [TH639, ZH678] (anger); (2) *khemah* [TH2534, ZH2779] (wrath), which "conveys a stronger emotion than *'aph* when *'aph* is without modifiers" (NIDOTTE 2:171); and (3) *kharon* [TH2740, ZH3019] (fierce anger), which in the prophets "refers primarily to Yahweh's anger that comes because of Israel's disobedience to divine commands" (NIDOTTE 2:267). See the comments at 2:1 and Jer 25:15-38.

## COMMENTARY

In the grieving process, details contributing to a loss are repeatedly reviewed. The poet reiterates the losses once more, but now the focus shifts more directly to human misery.

While the poem opens with a comment about the Temple ruins—a point elaborated earlier (1:10; 2:6-7)—this mention of the Temple is apparently a literary stepping stone to another subject, God's holy people. Children were of greater worth than even the most elaborate gold-decorated structures. In desperation, mothers denied breast-feedings to infants (4:3-4), and children remained malnourished (4:4; cf. 2:12). They became—in a gruesome reference to boiling them—expendable, food for adults desperate to remain alive (4:10; cf. 2:20; 2 Kgs 6:25-29). The poet grieved over the fate of the young.

A second class of persons on whom the ravages of the eighteen-month siege took its toll were the well-to-do and those in power. Once they had been ruddy in appearance and lovely to behold (4:7). Now, barely recognizable, they were soot-dark and gaunt instead of sleek. Death by the sword (cf. 2:21) was preferable to death by starvation (4:9). Their grief was the more acute with the realization that the former good times were gone; they had been replaced with times of leanness and scarcity.

The writer compares the destruction of Jerusalem to that of Sodom (Gen 19:24-25). Sodom and Gomorrah were both destroyed through a conflagration of brimstone and are a classic instance of God punishing cities for gross and persistent evildoing (Isa 13:19; Jer 23:14; Matt 10:15). In both cases, sin was the immediate cause for the devastation. God's anger was the more distant but very real cause (4:11). In every chapter, the poet returns to the topic of God's anger (see discussion at 2:1).

◆   B. Problems on Every Side (4:12-22)

12 Not a king in all the earth—
    no one in all the world—
would have believed that an enemy
    could march through the gates of
    Jerusalem.

13 Yet it happened because of the sins
        of her prophets
    and the sins of her priests,
who defiled the city
    by shedding innocent blood.

14 They wandered blindly
        through the streets,
so defiled by blood
    that no one dared touch them.

15 "Get away!" the people shouted at
        them.
    "You're defiled! Don't touch us!"
So they fled to distant lands
    and wandered among foreign
    nations,
but none would let them stay.

16 The LORD himself has scattered them,
    and he no longer helps them.
People show no respect for the
    priests
    and no longer honor the leaders.

17 We looked in vain for our allies
    to come and save us,
but we were looking to nations
    that could not help us.

18 We couldn't go into the streets
    without danger to our lives.
Our end was near; our days were
    numbered.
    We were doomed!

19 Our enemies were swifter than eagles
        in flight.
    If we fled to the mountains, they
        found us.
If we hid in the wilderness,
    they were waiting for us there.

20 Our king—the LORD's anointed, the
        very life of our nation—
    was caught in their snares.
We had thought that his shadow
    would protect us against any nation
        on earth!

21 Are you rejoicing in the land of Uz,
    O people of Edom?
But you, too, must drink from the cup
    of the LORD's anger.

You, too, will be stripped naked in
your drunkenness.

²²O beautiful Jerusalem,* your
punishment will end;

you will soon return from exile.
But Edom, your punishment is just
beginning;
soon your many sins will be
exposed.

4:22 Hebrew *O daughter of Zion.*

### NOTES

**4:12 an enemy could march through the gates of Jerusalem.** There had been previous
attacks on Jerusalem (e.g., King Shishak of Egypt, 1 Kgs 14:25-26). The futile attempt
by the Assyrians during Hezekiah's reign had demonstrated God's protective powers
(2 Kgs 18:13–19:35), which Judah later too readily presumed would continue (Jer 7:4).

**4:13 shedding innocent blood.** Basing his views on Ezek 22:1-12, Ellison (1986:728) notes
that more is involved here than murder, viz.—"all that cut at the roots of society or that
deprived men of their land and livelihood shortened their lives and, so, was bloodshed."

**4:14 They wandered blindly.** The identity of "they" is either the prophets and priests (4:13,
16) or the citizens generally. Since people shout at them (viz., the leaders, 4:15), and since
religious leaders are specified as the subject in 4:16, it is likely that the pronoun "they"
refers to religious leaders.

**4:15 You're defiled!** The cry "defiled" (*tame'* [TH2931, ZH3238]) would normally be directed
at lepers and others who were shunned or ostracized (Lev 13:45; Deut 28:28).

**4:17 We looked in vain.** The subject changes abruptly to the first person with the word
*'odenu* [TH5750, ZH6388] ("as for us," "while we yet"); see Westermann 1994:197. The expression *tikleynah 'enenu* [TH3615, ZH3983] (lit., "our eyes were consumed") has the sense of "we
strained our eyes." The eager expectation for help is also conveyed in the second line: "we
watched" (*tsapah* [TH6822, ZH7595], piel, "to look intently").

**4:18 We couldn't go into the streets.** Lit., "they hunted down our steps."

**4:20 Our king—the LORD's anointed, the very life of our nation.** The Heb. does not specify "our king," but the mention of "the LORD's anointed" almost certainly refers to the ruling monarch. The expression, "breath of our nostrils," which the NLT renders as "the very
life of our nation," was used by the Canaanites (Amarna letters) and the Egyptians (e.g.,
Rameses II) to highlight the people's dependence on the ruling monarch (Huey 1993:483).

**We had thought that his shadow would protect us against any nation on earth!** The NLT
captures well the Heb. idiom, which is lit., "We will live in his shade among the nations."

**4:21 Uz.** See Gen 10:23; Jer 25:20.

**Edom.** It was located southeast of Israel.

**cup of the LORD's anger.** For the image of passing a cup to the nations in turn, see Jer
25:15-29; Ezek 23:31-34. The image was so common that the Heb. merely reads "cup."

**4:22 your punishment will end.** As in 4:6, the term *'awon* [TH5771, ZH6411] (guilt) does
not convey only the notion of iniquity (better: "perversity") but sometimes also its consequence or punishment. While Israel's return from exile is implied, the more literal reading
is: "he will not extend your exile."

### COMMENTARY

The second part of the acrostic poem hangs on 4:11, the verse that factors divine
anger into all this tragedy. As a pivotal verse, 4:11 serves also to clinch the first part
of the poem. If God's anger brought down negative effects on families (4:1-10), it
also threw the public square into chaos (4:12-22).

Four stanzas describe the realities of the enemy's attack (4:17-20), preceded by four stanzas that indicate the reason that all this was happening (4:13-16). The experience of the foreign invasion has its own moments of dismay and fright: (1) the absence of allies (4:17; cf. Jer 37:3-10); (2) the panic in the streets (4:18); (3) the impossibility of escape (4:19); and (4) the capture of the king (4:20). The cause of the invasion, of which all the world took note (4:13), is not ascribed to military ineptness or political incompetence. Indeed, the nations registered surprise that anyone could capture Jerusalem, no doubt with some poetic exaggeration. The reason for the enemy's success against Judah is traced to the shameful behavior of the religious leaders.

Prophets and priests, the ones chiefly at fault for the demise of the nation, were accused of wrongdoings (cf. Jer 23:11). Only a sample of their perversity is listed. They shed innocent blood (4:13). They apparently meddled in political and judicial procedures, favoring the powerful and ranging themselves against the innocent. Jeremiah explained how religious leaders were hand-in-glove with officials of dubious repute (Jer 23:11, 14). These leaders abdicated their vocation, which was to transmit their traditions and moral values (Mal 2:7). In playing favorites, they catered to the powerful and failed to defend the innocent. Prophets did not identify the shape of evil in their society (2:14). Priests strayed from their vocation of holding high standards for all. Their failure to advocate and model godly behavior set in motion an unraveling of the social fabric that led eventually to God's punishment of the entire people. So guilty were the prophets and priests that the public gave them no respect (4:16), pagan nations wanted nothing to do with them (4:15), and even God distanced himself from them (4:16).

Israel's story was also a warning to other national groups. Edom was warned that God's punishment for evil could extend well beyond Israel (4:21-22). Edom's rejoicing, perhaps because Nebuchadnezzar had allocated territories to her from southern Judah, would be short-lived (Obad 11-14). Edom's sin, which was gloating over Israel's misfortune, would not go unpunished (cf. Ezek 35:5, 10).

In modern society, political figures may well be partially to blame for a society that is disintegrating morally. Accusing fingers are commonly pointed at public figures and the media in general regarding the downward spiral of morality, described by one analyst as "slouching toward Gomorrah." But Scripture analyzes Judah's political collapse as being caused by religious leaders. If what happened to Israel is to serve Christians as an example (1 Cor 10:6), then clergy, pastors, and teachers of religion have reason for sober self-examination. Is the church itself, often in the vanguard of blame-placing, responsible for a flabby, godless society?

◆ V. Appeals to the Lord (5:1-22)
　　A. Experiencing Hard Times (5:1-18)

| | |
|---|---|
| LORD, remember what has happened to us. | ² Our inheritance has been turned over to strangers, |
| See how we have been disgraced! | our homes to foreigners. |

³We are orphaned and fatherless.
  Our mothers are widowed.
⁴We have to pay for water to drink,
  and even firewood is expensive.
⁵Those who pursue us are at our heels;
  we are exhausted but are given
  no rest.
⁶We submitted to Egypt and Assyria
  to get enough food to survive.
⁷Our ancestors sinned, but they have
  died—
  and we are suffering the
  punishment they deserved!

⁸Slaves have now become our masters;
  there is no one left to rescue us.
⁹We hunt for food at the risk of our
  lives,
  for violence rules the countryside.
¹⁰The famine has blackened our skin
  as though baked in an oven.
¹¹Our enemies rape the women in
  Jerusalem*
  and the young girls in all the towns
  of Judah.

¹²Our princes are being hanged by their
  thumbs,
  and our elders are treated with
  contempt.
¹³Young men are led away to work at
  millstones,
  and boys stagger under heavy loads
  of wood.
¹⁴The elders no longer sit in the city
  gates;
  the young men no longer dance
  and sing.
¹⁵Joy has left our hearts;
  our dancing has turned to
  mourning.
¹⁶The garlands have* fallen from our
  heads.
  Weep for us because we have
  sinned.
¹⁷Our hearts are sick and weary,
  and our eyes grow dim with
  tears.
¹⁸For Jerusalem* is empty and
  desolate,
  a place haunted by jackals.

5:11 Hebrew *in Zion.*  5:16 Or *The crown has.*  5:18 Hebrew *Mount Zion.*

NOTES

**5:1 LORD, remember.** The word "remember" (*zakar* [TH2142, ZH2349]), when addressed to God, is not about a memory lapse but is an appeal for God to bring a situation to mind with the intent of doing something about it.

**5:2 inheritance.** The Heb. *nakhalah* [TH5159, ZH5709] can also refer more generally to "posessions" (cf. Prov 20:21).

**5:5 at our heels.** Lit., "upon our neck we are pursued." The Heb. is odd. One proposal is to read *'al 'artsenu* [TH776, ZH824] (upon our land) for the MT's *'al tsawwa'renu* [TH6677, ZH7418] (upon our neck). The NRSV follows Symmachus (cf. LXX) in assuming haplography and the omission of *'ol* [TH5923, ZH6585] (yoke): "With a yoke on (*'ol 'al*) our necks we are hard driven." The NLT renders the Heb. according to the principles of dynamic equivalence.

**5:6 We submitted.** Lit., "we gave the hand to."

**Egypt.** Judah was flirting with the idea of an alliance with Egypt at the time of the Babylonian threat (Jer 2:18; 37:5, 7).

**Assyria.** Babylon had already taken over Assyria. The poet may be referring to alliances made by previous generations (Hos 5:13).

**5:10 famine has blackened our skin.** The term "blackened" (niphal of *kamar* [TH3648, ZH4023]) is considered by some to mean "hot" (e.g., RSV), by others, "black" (e.g., NRSV). Skin discoloration seems intended here.

**5:12** *princes are being hanged by their thumbs.* Lit., "their hands." For an example of impaling dead bodies in disgrace, see 2 Sam 4:12.

*our elders are treated with contempt.* Lit., "our elders are not honored."

**5:17** *our eyes grow dim with tears.* Lit., "our eyes are dark." Dull eyes are a sign of ill health, either physical or emotional.

### COMMENTARY

This entire chapter is a prayer addressed to God. Readers get to listen in on a monologue about hard times. God and the readers are informed about stressful circumstances. These likely arose from enemy occupation, in a sequel to the eighteen-month–long Babylonian siege against the city of Jerusalem. Like an orphan, the city had been cut off from the outside world (5:2-3). Procuring basic necessities such as water, firewood, and bread had become problematic, possibly because of taxation (5:4, 9). Famine had become the norm (5:10), and social and political life had been destabilized. Foreigners had taken charge (5:8). Residents were subjected to constant harassment (5:5), women to rape (5:11), and young men to forced labor (5:13). Public morale was at low tide (5:15, 17). Besides all these outward troubles, there were inward misgivings. How could it be fair that a generation should suffer for the sins of its ancestors (5:7)? Ezekiel faced the same question by the same generation and offered his own answers (Ezek 18:2-32).

**Prayer as Sharing.** Some would question the propriety of prayers such as these. What good is served, they ask, by going into such detail? If God is omniscient, does he not already know about this trouble? Why bother informing him? Such comments surely betray a misunderstanding about prayer. Prayer is more than a cry for help or the presentation of a shopping list of requests. Prayer is conversation. Prayer is talk with the divine as between two friends who enter into each other's lives precisely by the most detailed accounts of their lives. By sharing the specifics of the experience, both parties are, so to speak, brought onto the same page.

**Prayer as Persuasion.** In addition to the friendship dimension, prayer has a lawyer-like component. The petitioner argues a case before God, giving reasons why a response is warranted. A vivid presentation of the misery is offered on the assumption that God will be moved to act in mercy, especially since he is concerned about orphans (Exod 22:22; Deut 10:18; 14:29; Ps 146:9). For the petitioner to spell out the details of a situation requires of him or her both perception and honesty. For this praying community, honesty meant facing the reality that sin was a complicating factor in the circumstances (5:7).

It should not be thought that a fine-tuned description of a troubling circumstance is either boring or unnecessary. The ones who pray benefit by sorting out the nature of their problems. God is honored by such detailed petitions in that he is taken seriously as the one who responds, not as a robot, but as an intelligent and compassionate deity. So although most prayers recorded in the Bible are short, there are occasions for more extended, elaborate prayers (cf. John 17).

◆   ## B. One Final Appeal (5:19–22)

<sup>19</sup> But LORD, you remain the same
    forever!
Your throne continues from
    generation to generation.
<sup>20</sup> Why do you continue to forget us?
Why have you abandoned us for
    so long?

<sup>21</sup> Restore us, O LORD, and bring us back
    to you again!
Give us back the joys we
    once had!
<sup>22</sup> Or have you utterly rejected us?
Are you angry with us still?

### NOTES

**5:21** *and bring us back to you again!* Lit., "and we will return." Given an initial imperative and a *waw* conjunctive, the translation may also read, "that we may be restored" (see
the NRSV). The NLT translation captures the intent of the expression, but the imperative
rendering is gratuitous.

*Give us back the joys.* Lit., "make new (piel imperative of *khadash* [<sup>TH</sup>2318, <sup>ZH</sup>2542]) our days."

**5:22** *Or have you utterly rejected us?* The opening "Or" (*ki 'im* [<sup>TH</sup>3588A, <sup>ZH</sup>3955]) is translated as "but" (KJV), "or" (RSV), and "unless" (NASB, NIV, NRSV). The last is preferable.
Ellison (1986:733) observes that when Lamentations is read in the synagogue, 5:21 is
repeated following 5:22 in order not to end on such a sad note. The practice of returning
to the second to last verse as a final verse is also followed when Ecclesiastes, Isaiah, and
Malachi are read publicly.

### COMMENTARY

This part of the prayer incorporates three new elements. First, God's sovereignty is
acknowledged (5:19). Second, the request goes beyond the concerns of the physical
to concerns about relationships (5:21). Third, the prayer reflects on how God might
assess the situation (5:20, 22).

**Sovereignty.** The worship component in which God's long-standing rule is acknowledged appears to be a tacked-on feature. The press of the immediate misery
might explain why the worship component is deferred to the concluding part of the
prayer. Even so, recognition that God's throne endures forever puts the people's
dilemma in perspective. God, and not the invading enemy, is ultimately in charge.
The panic of the immediate distress is eased in the knowledge that God is cognizant
of all and that he works over the long term.

**Relationships.** The prayer for spiritual restoration (5:21) can be compared to
Habakkuk's prayer (Hab 3:2). Both are prayers for renewal, and both are in the context of perplexing realities. In Habakkuk we see how the prayer is answered. In Lamentations, as in the book of Job, there is not a word from God except for a brief
testimonial that God did break the silence (3:57).

**Reflection.** The third element of the prayer is most sobering, for now the petitioner
considers whether God has any interest in the situation at all (5:20, 22). The long silence is disconcerting (cf. Hab 1:2). Why is a response so long in coming? The
book's closing question (5:22) is perhaps the most poignant of all the depictions of
distress: God may have gone away for good (cf. Ps 22:1). It is also the most forceful
reminder that any forthcoming response will be given only because of God's grace.

# BIBLIOGRAPHY

**Albrektson, B.**
1963 *Studies in the Text and Theology of the Book of Lamentations.* Studia Theologica Lundensia 21. Lund: Gleerup.

**Baloian, Bruce E.**
1992 *Anger in the Old Testament.* American University Studies VII, vol. 99. New York: Peter Lang.

**Bergant, Dianne**
2002 The Challenge of Hermeneutics: Lamentations 1:1-11—A Test Case. *Catholic Biblical Quarterly* 64:1-16.

**Berlin, Adele**
2002 *Lamentations: A Commentary.* Old Testament Library. Louisville: Westminster John Knox.

**Block, Daniel I.**
1988 *The Gods of the Nations: Studies in Ancient Near Eastern National Theology.* Evangelical Theological Society Monograph Series. Jackson, MS: Evangelical Theological Society.

**Brown, Michael L.**
1997 Lamentations, Theology of. Pp. 884-893 in *New International Dictionary of Old Testament Theology and Exegesis.* Vol. 4. Editor, Willem A. VanGemeren. Grand Rapids: Zondervan.

**Chisholm, Robert B.**
1991 A Theology of Jeremiah and Lamentations. Pp. 341-363 in *A Biblical Theology of the Old Testament.* Editors, R. B. Zuck, E. H. Merrill, and Darrell Bock. Chicago: Moody Press.

**Clark, Gordon R.**
1993 *The Word hesed in the Hebrew Bible.* Sheffield: Sheffield Academic Press.

**Cooper, Alan**
2001 The Message of Lamentations. *Journal of the Ancient Near Eastern Society* 28:1-18.

**Dobbs-Allsop, F. W.**
1993 *Weep, O Daughter of Zion: A Study of the City-Lament Genre in the Hebrew Bible.* Biblica et Orientalia 44. Rome: Editrice Pontifico Istituto Biblico.
2002 *Lamentations.* Interpretation. Louisville: Westminster John Knox.

**Ellison, H.**
1986 *Lamentations.* Pp. 693–733 in *Expositor's Bible Commentary.* Vol. 6. Editor, Frank Gaebelein. Grand Rapids: Zondervan.

**Emerton, J. A.**
1967 The Meaning of *'avne-godesh* in Lamentations 4:1. *Zeitschrift für die Alttestamentliche Wissenschaft* 79:233-236

**Ferris, Paul W. Jr.**
1992 *The Genre of Communal Lament in the Bible and the Ancient Near East.* Society of Biblical Literature Dissertation Series 27. Atlanta: Scholars Press.

**Gottwald, N. K.**
1962 *Studies in the Book of Lamentations.* Studies in Biblical Theology 14. London: SCM.

**Gous, I. G. P.**
1993. Exiles and the Dynamic of Experiences of Loss: The Reaction of Lamentations 2 on the Loss of Land. *Old Testament Essays* 6:351-354.

**Heater, H.**
1992 Structure and Meaning in Lamentations. *Bibliotheca Sacra* 149:304-315.

**Heim, Knut M.**
1999 The Personification of Jerusalem and the Drama of Her Bereavement in Lamentations. Pp. 129-169 in *Zion, City of our God.* Editors, Richard S. Hess and Gordon J. Wenham. Grand Rapids: Eerdmans.

**Hillers, Delbert**
1992 *Lamentations: A New Translation with Introduction, Notes and Commentary.* Anchor Bible 7A. 2nd ed. New York: Doubleday.

**Holladay, W.**
1971 *A Concise Hebrew and Aramaic Lexicon of the Old Testament.* Grand Rapids: Eerdmans; Leiden: Brill.

House, Paul R.
1998 The God Who is Righteous and Faithful: Lamentations. Pp. 483-489 in *Old Testament Theology.*
      Downers Grove: InterVarsity.

Huey, F.B. Jr.
1993 *Jeremiah, Lamentations.* The New American Commentary, vol. 16. Nashville: Broadman & Holman.

Joyce, P.
1993 Lamentations and the Grief Process: A Psychological Reading. *Biblical Interpretation* 1:304-320.

Krašovec, J.
1992 The Source of Hope in the Book of Lamentations. *Vetus Testamentum* 42:223-233

Lanahan, W. F. K
1974 The Speaking Voice in the Book of Lamentations. *Journal of Biblical Literature* 93:41-49.

Lewis, C. S.
1973 *The Lion, The Witch and the Wardrobe.* The Chronicles of Narnia 1. New York: Religious Book Club.

Marcus, D.
1986 Non-Recurring Doublets in the Book of Lamentations. *Harvard Annual Review* 10:177-195.

Martens, Elmer A.
1996 Lamentations, Theology of. Pp 461-463 in *Evangelical Dictionary of Biblical Theology.* Editor,
      Walter Elwell. Grand Rapids: Baker

O'Conner, Kathleen
2001 *Lamentations.* Pp. 1011-1072 in *The New Interpreter's Bible,* vol. 6. Editor, D. L. Petersen.
      Nashville: Abingdon.

Pham, Xuan Huong Thi
1999 *Mourning in the Ancient Near East and the Hebrew Bible.* Journal for the Study of the Old Testament
      Supplement Series 302. Sheffield: Sheffield Academic Press.

Provan, Iain W.
1990 Reading Texts Against an Historical Background: The Case of Lamentations 1. *Scandinavian Journal
      of Old Testament* 4:130-143.

1991 Past, Present and Future in Lamentations iii 52-66: The Case for a Precative Perfect Re-examined.
      *Vetus Testamentum* 41:164-175.

1991 *Lamentations.* New Century Bible Commentary. Grand Rapids: Eerdmans.

Re'emi, S. Paul
1984 *Lamentations* in *God's People in Crisis: A Commentary on the Books of Amos and Lamentations.*
      International Theological Commentary. Editors, Robert Martin-Achard and S. Paul Re'emi. Grand
      Rapids: Eerdmans.

Renkema, J.
1995 The Meaning of Parallel Acrostics in Lamentations. *Vetus Testamentum* 45:379-383.
2003 Theodicy in Lamentations. Pp. 410-428 in *Theodicy in the World of the Bible,* Editors, Antti Laato and
      Johannes C. DeMoor. Leiden: Brill.

Saebø, M.
1993 Who Is 'The Man' in Lamentations 3? A Fresh Approach to the Interpretation of the Book of
      Lamentations. Pp. 294-306 in *Understanding Poets and Prophets: Essays in Honour of George Wishart
      Anderson.* Editor, A. G. Auld. Journal for the Study of the Old Testament Supplement Series 152.
      Sheffield: Sheffield Academic Press.

Watlke, B. and M. O'Connor
1990 *An Introduction to Biblical Hebrew Syntax.* Winona Lake: Eisenbrauns.

Weber, Beat
2000 Transitorische Ambiguität in Threni iii. *Vetus Testamentum* 50:111-120.

Westermann, Claus
1994 *Lamentations: Issues and Interpretation.* Translator, C.A. Muenchow. Minneapolis: Fortress.